BUSINESS
FINANCE

11E

BUSINESS FINANCE

GRAHAM PEIRSON
Monash University

ROB BROWN
University of Melbourne

STEVE EASTON
University of Newcastle

PETER HOWARD
Monash University

SEAN PINDER
University of Melbourne

The McGraw·Hill Companies

Sydney New York San Francisco Auckland
Bangkok Bogotá Caracas Hong Kong
Kuala Lumpur Lisbon London Madrid
Mexico City Milan New Delhi San Juan
Seoul Singapore Taipei Toronto

Reprinted 2012
Copyright © 2012 McGraw-Hill Australia Pty Limited
Additional owners of copyright are acknowledged in on-page credits.

Every effort has been made to trace and acknowledge copyrighted material. The authors and publishers tender their apologies should any infringement have occurred.

Reproduction and communication for educational purposes

The Australian *Copyright Act 1968* (the Act) allows a maximum of one chapter or 10% of the pages of this work, whichever is the greater, to be reproduced and/or communicated by any educational institution for its educational purposes provided that the institution (or the body that administers it) has sent a Statutory Educational notice to Copyright Agency Limited (CAL) and been granted a licence. For details of statutory educational and other copyright licences contact: Copyright Agency Limited, Level 15, 233 Castlereagh Street, Sydney NSW 2000. Telephone: (02) 9394 7600. Website: www.copyright.com.au

Reproduction and communication for other purposes

Apart from any fair dealing for the purposes of study, research, criticism or review, as permitted under the Act, no part of this publication may be reproduced, distributed or transmitted in any form or by any means, or stored in a database or retrieval system, without the written permission of McGraw-Hill Australia including, but not limited to, any network or other electronic storage.

Enquiries should be made to the publisher via www.mcgraw-hill.com.au or marked for the attention of the permissions editor at the address below.

National Library of Australia Cataloguing-in-Publication Data

Title:	Business finance / Robert Leonard Brown ... [et al.].
Edition:	11th ed.
ISBN:	9780070997592 (pbk.)
Notes:	Includes index.
	Previous ed.: 2009.
Subjects:	Business enterprises—Finance.
	Cash management.
	Corporations—Finance.
Other Authors/Contributors:	
	Brown, R. L. (Robert Leonard)
Dewey Number:	658.15

Published in Australia by
McGraw-Hill Australia Pty Limited
Level 2, 82 Waterloo Road, North Ryde, NSW 2113,
Senior publisher: Rosemary Noble
Senior development editor: Martina Edwards
Design: Em&Jon Design
Senior production editor: Yani Silvana
Permissions editor: Haidi Bernhardt
Copyeditor: Rosemary Moore
Proofreader: Susan McCreery
Indexer: Michael Ramsden
Typeset in Adobe Garamond Pro Regular 10/13 by Mukesh Technologies, India
Printed in China on 65 gsm matt art by 1010 Printing International Ltd

PUBLISHER'S FOREWORD

When this endeavour began 40 years ago, few could have foreseen the success of this publication, and few could have imagined how proud we would be to have published a resource that has guided well over 200 000 undergraduate students through their introduction to business finance. This title has become one of McGraw-Hill Australia's longest-standing and most successful textbooks. It is with the greatest pleasure that McGraw-Hill Australia now presents the eleventh edition of *Business Finance* by Graham Peirson, Rob Brown, Steve Easton, Peter Howard and Sean Pinder.

This text is an original work—not an adaptation of US material. The founding authors, Graham Peirson and Ron Bird, embarked on an ambitious undertaking: to write a meaningful introduction to the fascinating field of business finance, specifically for students in Australia and New Zealand. They succeeded, and the first edition was published in 1972. As a testament to the consistent value of the work and its ongoing relevance for generations of students and instructors, *Business Finance* continues to sell thousands of copies each year. In a market increasingly crowded with competitive texts, it is a credit to our author team that *Business Finance* continues as the market leader in its field. To our authors and the academic community who have so staunchly supported this publication we say thank you.

Quality content is clearly the key. Professor Graham Peirson and his team have worked hard, in consultation with instructors across Australia and New Zealand, to ensure that the text and its digital resource package provide recent data and up-to-date thinking in an accessible format that will engage students and instructors alike. This eleventh edition has done just that, demonstrating the authors' commitment to refining their text and ensuring that *Business Finance* not only retains a reputation for currency, but emerges once again as the standard setter.

Our focus at McGraw-Hill is wholly on providing superior content. With *Business Finance* eleventh edition we are confident we offer you the best there is.

McGraw-Hill Australia, 2011

BRIEF CONTENTS

CHAPTER 1	Introduction	2
CHAPTER 2	Consumption, investment and the capital market	12
CHAPTER 3	The time value of money: an introduction to financial mathematics	32
CHAPTER 4	Applying the time value of money to security valuation	78
CHAPTER 5	Project evaluation: principles and methods	106
CHAPTER 6	The application of project evaluation methods	132
CHAPTER 7	Risk and return	168
CHAPTER 8	The capital market	208
CHAPTER 9	Sources of finance: equity	236
CHAPTER 10	Sources of finance: debt	286
CHAPTER 11	Payout policy	334
CHAPTER 12	Principles of capital structure	378
CHAPTER 13	Capital structure decisions	418
CHAPTER 14	The cost of capital and taxation issues in project evaluation	444
CHAPTER 15	Leasing and other equipment finance	488
CHAPTER 16	Capital market efficiency	516
CHAPTER 17	Futures contracts	550
CHAPTER 18	Options and contingent claims	594
CHAPTER 19	Analysis of takeovers	640
CHAPTER 20	International financial management	684
CHAPTER 21	Management of short-term assets: inventory	738
CHAPTER 22	Management of short-term assets: liquid assets and accounts receivable	758

CONTENTS IN FULL

Publisher's foreword	v	E-student	xxx
About the authors	xxvi	E-instructor	xxxi
Acknowledgments	xxviii	Highlights of this edition	xxxii
Preface	xxix	How to use this book	xxxiv

CHAPTER 1 INTRODUCTION 2

Learning objectives 2

- 1.1 FINANCE AS AN AREA OF STUDY 3
- 1.2 FINANCIAL DECISIONS 3
- 1.3 BUSINESS STRUCTURES 4
  - 1.3.1 Sole proprietorship 4
  - 1.3.2 Partnership 4
  - 1.3.3 Company 5
- 1.4 THE COMPANY'S FINANCIAL OBJECTIVE 6
- 1.5 FUNDAMENTAL CONCEPTS IN FINANCE 6
  - 1.5.1 Value 6
  - 1.5.2 The time value of money 7
  - 1.5.3 Risk aversion 7
  - 1.5.4 Nominal and real amounts 7
  - 1.5.5 Market efficiency and asset pricing 8
  - 1.5.6 Derivative securities 8
  - 1.5.7 Arbitrage 8
  - 1.5.8 Agency relationships 9
- 1.6 OUTLINE OF THE BOOK 9

Summary 10
Key terms 10
Questions 10

CHAPTER 2 CONSUMPTION, INVESTMENT AND THE CAPITAL MARKET 12

Learning objectives 12

- 2.1 INTRODUCTION 13
- 2.2 FISHER'S SEPARATION THEOREM: A SIMPLIFIED EXAMPLE ... 13
  - 2.2.1 Introduction to the example 13
  - 2.2.2 Assumptions 13
  - 2.2.3 The shareholders' consumption opportunities and preferences 14
  - 2.2.4 Solution: introduce a capital market 14
  - 2.2.5 An analysis using rates of return 15

	2.2.6	A solution requiring borrowing	15
	2.2.7	Fisher's Separation Theorem and net present value	16
	2.2.8	Fisher's Separation Theorem: summary	16
2.3	**FISHER'S SEPARATION THEOREM: A FORMAL APPROACH**		16
	2.3.1	Assumptions	17
	2.3.2	The company	17
	2.3.3	The shareholders	18
	2.3.4	The company's decision	18
	2.3.5	Solution: introduce a capital market	19
	2.3.6	Proving there is an optimal policy	22
	2.3.7	Identifying the optimal policy	23
	2.3.8	Implications for financial decision making	25
2.4	**INVESTORS' REACTIONS TO MANAGERS' DECISIONS**		27
	2.4.1	Certainty	27
	2.4.2	The introduction of uncertainty	28

Summary ... 28
Key terms ... 29
References ... 29
Questions ... 29
Problems ... 29

CHAPTER 3 THE TIME VALUE OF MONEY: AN INTRODUCTION TO FINANCIAL MATHEMATICS   32

Learning objectives ... 32

3.1	**INTRODUCTION**		33
3.2	**FUNDAMENTAL CONCEPTS OF FINANCIAL MATHEMATICS**		33
	3.2.1	Cash flows	33
	3.2.2	Rate of return	33
	3.2.3	Interest rate	34
	3.2.4	Time value of money	34
3.3	**SIMPLE INTEREST**		35
	3.3.1	The basic idea of simple interest	35
	3.3.2	Formula development: future sum	36
	3.3.3	Formula development: present value	36
	3.3.4	Applications of simple interest	37
3.4	**COMPOUND INTEREST**		37
	3.4.1	The basic idea of compound interest	37
	3.4.2	Formula development: future sum and present value	38
	3.4.3	Nominal and effective interest rates	41
	3.4.4	Compound interest: two special cases and a generalisation	44
	3.4.5	A generalisation: geometric rates of return	48
3.5	**VALUATION OF CONTRACTS WITH MULTIPLE CASH FLOWS**		50
	3.5.1	Introduction	50
	3.5.2	Value additivity	50
	3.5.3	Formula development: valuation as at any date	52
	3.5.4	Measuring the rate of return	53

3.6	ANNUITIES		55
	3.6.1	Definition and types of annuity	55
	3.6.2	Formula development: present value of an ordinary annuity	56
	3.6.3	Formula development: present values of annuities-due, deferred annuities and ordinary perpetuities	58
	3.6.4	Future value of annuities	62
3.7	PRINCIPAL-AND-INTEREST LOAN CONTRACTS		63
	3.7.1	Basic features of the contract	63
	3.7.2	Principal and interest components	64
	3.7.3	Balance owing at any given date	65
	3.7.4	Loan term required	66
	3.7.5	Changing the interest rate	68
3.8	GENERAL ANNUITIES		69

Summary — 71
Key terms — 71
Self-test problems — 71
References — 72
Questions — 72
Problems — 72

CHAPTER 4 — APPLYING THE TIME VALUE OF MONEY TO SECURITY VALUATION — 78

Learning objectives — 78

4.1	INTRODUCTION		79
4.2	FINANCIAL ASSET VALUATION UNDER CERTAINTY		79
4.3	VALUATION OF SHARES		80
	4.3.1	Valuation of shares assuming certainty	80
	4.3.2	Valuation of shares under uncertainty	81
	4.3.3	Share valuation and the price–earnings ratio	84
4.4	VALUATION OF DEBT SECURITIES		84
4.5	INTEREST RATE RISK		86
4.6	THE TERM STRUCTURE OF INTEREST RATES		86
	4.6.1	What is the term structure?	86
	4.6.2	Term structure theories: expectations and liquidity (risk) premium	88
	4.6.3	Empirical evidence	91
	4.6.4	Inflation and the term structure	91
4.7	THE DEFAULT-RISK STRUCTURE OF INTEREST RATES		92
4.8	OTHER FACTORS AFFECTING INTEREST RATE STRUCTURES		94

Summary — 95
Key terms — 95
Self-test problems — 96
References — 96
Questions — 96
Problems — 97

APPENDIX 4.1:	DURATION AND IMMUNISATION	99
	Introduction	99
	Bond duration	99
	Duration and interest elasticity	101
	Duration and bond price changes	102
	Duration and immunisation	103

CHAPTER 5 — PROJECT EVALUATION: PRINCIPLES AND METHODS — 106

Learning objectives ... 106

5.1	INTRODUCTION	107
5.2	THE CAPITAL-EXPENDITURE PROCESS	107
5.3	METHODS OF PROJECT EVALUATION	109
	5.3.1 Discounted cash flow methods	110
5.4	THE DISCOUNTED CASH FLOW METHODS COMPARED	110
	5.4.1 Net present value	111
	5.4.2 Internal rate of return	112
	5.4.3 Choosing between the discounted cash flow methods	115
	5.4.4 Benefit–cost ratio (profitability index)	120
5.5	OTHER METHODS OF PROJECT EVALUATION	121
	5.5.1 Accounting rate of return	122
	5.5.2 Payback period	124
	5.5.3 Economic value added (EVA)	125
5.6	PROJECT EVALUATION AND REAL OPTIONS ANALYSIS	126

Summary ... 127
Key terms ... 128
Self-test problems ... 128
References ... 128
Questions ... 128
Problems ... 129

CHAPTER 6 — THE APPLICATION OF PROJECT EVALUATION METHODS — 132

Learning objectives ... 132

6.1	INTRODUCTION	133
6.2	APPLICATION OF THE NET PRESENT VALUE METHOD	133
	6.2.1 Estimation of cash flows in project evaluation	133
	6.2.2 Illustration of cash-flow information in project evaluation	136
6.3	COMPARING MUTUALLY EXCLUSIVE PROJECTS THAT HAVE DIFFERENT LIVES	138
6.4	DECIDING WHEN TO RETIRE (ABANDON) OR REPLACE A PROJECT	145
	6.4.1 Retirement decisions	145
	6.4.2 Replacement decisions	146

6.5	ANALYSING PROJECT RISK		148
	6.5.1	Sensitivity analysis	148
	6.5.2	Break-even analysis	150
	6.5.3	Simulation	152
6.6	DECISION-TREE ANALYSIS		153
6.7	QUALITATIVE FACTORS AND THE SELECTION OF PROJECTS		156
6.8	PROJECT SELECTION WITH RESOURCE CONSTRAINTS		156

Summary 159
Key terms 159
Self-test problems 159
References 160
Questions 160
Problems 161

CHAPTER 7 RISK AND RETURN 168

Learning objectives 168

7.1	INTRODUCTION		169
7.2	RETURN AND RISK		169
7.3	THE INVESTOR'S UTILITY FUNCTION		173
7.4	THE RISK OF ASSETS		175
7.5	PORTFOLIO THEORY AND DIVERSIFICATION		176
	7.5.1	Gains from diversification	179
	7.5.2	Diversification with multiple assets	181
	7.5.3	Systematic and unsystematic risk	183
	7.5.4	The risk of an individual asset	184
	7.5.5	The efficient frontier	186
7.6	THE PRICING OF RISKY ASSETS		188
	7.6.1	The capital market line	188
	7.6.2	The capital asset pricing model (CAPM) and the security market line	190
	7.6.3	Implementation of the CAPM	192
	7.6.4	Risk, return and the CAPM	195
7.7	ADDITIONAL FACTORS THAT EXPLAIN RETURNS		195
7.8	PORTFOLIO PERFORMANCE APPRAISAL		196
	7.8.1	Alternative measures of portfolio performance	197

Summary 201
Key terms 202
Self-test problems 202
References 203
Questions 204
Problems 204

CHAPTER 8 THE CAPITAL MARKET 208

Learning objectives 208

8.1	INTRODUCTION		209
	8.1.1	The flow of funds	209

		8.1.2	The capital market	210
		8.1.3	Types of financial market	210
		8.1.4	Developments in Australia's financial markets	211
		8.1.5	Business funding	212
	8.2	FINANCIAL AGENCY INSTITUTIONS		214
		8.2.1	Brokers and the stock exchange	215
		8.2.2	Investment banks and merchant banks	217
	8.3	FINANCIAL INTERMEDIARIES		221
		8.3.1	Banks	221
		8.3.2	Money market corporations	223
		8.3.3	Finance companies	223
		8.3.4	Securitisation	224
	8.4	INVESTING INSTITUTIONS		227
		8.4.1	Insurance companies and superannuation funds	227
		8.4.2	Unit trusts and investment companies	231
		8.4.3	Overseas sources and markets	232

Summary 233
Key terms 233
References 233
Questions 234

CHAPTER 9 — SOURCES OF FINANCE: EQUITY — 236

Learning objectives 236

9.1	INTRODUCTION		237
9.2	THE CHARACTERISTICS OF ORDINARY SHARES		238
	9.2.1	Fully paid and partly paid shares	238
	9.2.2	Limited liability	238
	9.2.3	No liability companies	239
	9.2.4	The rights of shareholders	239
	9.2.5	Advantages and disadvantages of equity as a source of finance	239
9.3	PRIVATE EQUITY		240
	9.3.1	What is private equity?	241
	9.3.2	Information problems and new ventures	241
	9.3.3	Sources of finance for new ventures	242
	9.3.4	Finance from business angels	242
	9.3.5	Finance from private equity funds	243
9.4	INFORMATION DISCLOSURE		244
	9.4.1	Offers of unlisted securities	245
	9.4.2	Offers of listed securities	246
	9.4.3	Offers that do not need disclosure	246
9.5	FLOATING A PUBLIC COMPANY		247
	9.5.1	Public versus private ownership	247
	9.5.2	Initial public offering of ordinary shares	248
	9.5.3	Pricing a new issue	248
	9.5.4	Underwriting and managing a new issue	250
	9.5.5	Selling a new issue	251

		9.5.6	The costs of floating a company	252
		9.5.7	Long-term performance of IPOs	256
	9.6	**SUBSEQUENT ISSUES OF ORDINARY SHARES**		**258**
		9.6.1	Rights issues	259
		9.6.2	Placements (private issues)	267
		9.6.3	Contributing shares and instalment receipts	269
		9.6.4	Share purchase plans	269
		9.6.5	Share options	270
		9.6.6	Choosing between equity raising methods	271
	9.7	**EMPLOYEE SHARE PLANS**		**274**
	9.8	**INTERNAL FUNDS**		**275**
		9.8.1	Dividend reinvestment plans	276
	9.9	**MANAGING A COMPANY'S EQUITY STRUCTURE**		**277**
		9.9.1	Bonus issues and share splits	277
		9.9.2	Share consolidations	278

Summary 279
Key terms 280
References 280
Questions 281
Problems 283

CHAPTER 10 SOURCES OF FINANCE: DEBT 286

Learning objectives 286

10.1	**INTRODUCTION**		**287**
10.2	**GENERAL CHARACTERISTICS OF DEBT**		**288**
	10.2.1	The interest cost of debt	289
	10.2.2	Effect of debt on risk	291
	10.2.3	Effect of debt on control	291
	10.2.4	Security for debt	291
10.3	**SHORT-TERM BORROWING FROM BANKS AND OTHER FINANCIAL INSTITUTIONS**		**294**
	10.3.1	Bank overdraft	294
	10.3.2	Debtor finance	295
	10.3.3	Inventory loans	297
	10.3.4	Bridging finance	297
10.4	**LONG-TERM BORROWING FROM BANKS AND OTHER FINANCIAL INSTITUTIONS**		**298**
	10.4.1	Long-term loan choices available to borrowers	298
	10.4.2	Variable-rate term loans	299
	10.4.3	Fixed-rate term loans	300
	10.4.4	Other features of term loans	300
	10.4.5	Why do borrowers use term loans?	301
10.5	**DEBT SECURITIES**		**302**
	10.5.1	Debt securities: the general principles	303
	10.5.2	Commercial paper	303
	10.5.3	Bills of exchange	305
	10.5.4	Debentures	309

		10.5.5	Unsecured notes	310
		10.5.6	Corporate bonds	310
	10.6	**PROJECT FINANCE**		314
		10.6.1	The main features of project finance	314
		10.6.2	When is project finance attractive?	315
	10.7	**INTEREST RATE SWAPS**		316
	10.8	**HYBRIDS OF DEBT AND EQUITY FINANCE**		320
		10.8.1	Convertible notes	320
		10.8.2	Preference shares	322
		10.8.3	Developments in the design of hybrid securities	324

Summary — 328
Key terms — 328
Self-test problems — 329
References — 329
Questions — 330
Problems — 331

CHAPTER 11 PAYOUT POLICY 334

Learning objectives — 334

	11.1	**INTRODUCTION**		335
		11.1.1	Dividend declaration procedures	336
		11.1.2	Types of dividend	336
		11.1.3	Legal and tax considerations	336
		11.1.4	Repurchasing shares	337
	11.2	**IS PAYOUT POLICY IMPORTANT TO SHAREHOLDERS?**		338
		11.2.1	Alternative payout policies	338
		11.2.2	Managers and payout decisions	339
		11.2.3	The irrelevance of payout policy	341
		11.2.4	The importance of full payout	343
		11.2.5	Payout policy in practice	343
	11.3	**TRANSACTION COSTS AND OTHER IMPERFECTIONS**		344
		11.3.1	Transaction costs	344
		11.3.2	Flotation costs	345
		11.3.3	Behavioural factors and dividends	345
	11.4	**DIVIDENDS AND TAXES**		345
		11.4.1	Dividends and the imputation tax system	346
		11.4.2	Imputation and capital gains tax	348
		11.4.3	Dividend policy with imputation and capital gains tax	349
		11.4.4	The market value of franking credits	351
	11.5	**INFORMATION EFFECTS AND SIGNALLING TO INVESTORS**		354
	11.6	**AGENCY COSTS AND CORPORATE GOVERNANCE**		357
	11.7	**SHARE BUYBACKS**		361
		11.7.1	Why do companies repurchase shares?	361
		11.7.2	Share repurchases in Australia	365
	11.8	**DIVIDEND REINVESTMENT PLANS AND DIVIDEND ELECTION SCHEMES**		368
	11.9	**PAYOUT POLICY AND COMPANY LIFE CYCLE**		369

Summary 371
Key terms 372
References 372
Questions 375
Problems 376

CHAPTER 12 PRINCIPLES OF CAPITAL STRUCTURE 378

Learning objectives 378

- 12.1 INTRODUCTION 379
- 12.2 THE EFFECTS OF FINANCIAL LEVERAGE 379
- 12.3 THE MODIGLIANI AND MILLER ANALYSIS (NO TAX CASE) ... 384
  - 12.3.1 Modigliani and Miller's Proposition 1 384
  - 12.3.2 Modigliani and Miller's Proposition 2 389
  - 12.3.3 Modigliani and Miller's Proposition 3 392
  - 12.3.4 Why is the MM analysis important? 392
- 12.4 THE EFFECTS OF TAXES ON CAPITAL STRUCTURE UNDER A CLASSICAL TAX SYSTEM 393
  - 12.4.1 Company income tax 393
  - 12.4.2 Company tax and personal tax 395
  - 12.4.3 Miller's analysis 397
  - 12.4.4 The scope of Miller's analysis 398
- 12.5 THE EFFECTS OF TAXES ON CAPITAL STRUCTURE UNDER AN IMPUTATION TAX SYSTEM 399
  - 12.5.1 What is an imputation tax system? 399
  - 12.5.2 The effects of tax on capital structure decisions under an imputation tax system 400
- 12.6 THE COSTS OF FINANCIAL DISTRESS 401
  - 12.6.1 Bankruptcy costs 402
  - 12.6.2 Indirect costs of financial distress 403
- 12.7 AGENCY COSTS 404
  - 12.7.1 Conflicts of interest between lenders and shareholders 404
  - 12.7.2 Conflicts of interest between shareholders and company managers 405
- 12.8 OPTIMAL CAPITAL STRUCTURE: THE STATIC TRADE-OFF THEORY 406
- 12.9 CAPITAL STRUCTURE WITH INFORMATION ASYMMETRY 407
  - 12.9.1 Pecking order theory 407
  - 12.9.2 Information asymmetry and the undervaluation of a company's assets 408
  - 12.9.3 Information asymmetry and the overvaluation of a company's assets 411
  - 12.9.4 Implications of information asymmetry for financing policy 411

Summary 412
Key terms 413
Self-test problems 413
References 413

Questions... 414
Problems... 415

CHAPTER 13   CAPITAL STRUCTURE DECISIONS   418

Learning objectives... 418

13.1 INTRODUCTION 419
13.1.1 Company financing: some initial facts... 419

13.2 EVIDENCE ON CAPITAL STRUCTURE..421
13.2.1 Evidence on taxes 421
13.2.2 Evidence on the costs of financial distress 423
13.2.3 Evidence on agency costs 425
13.2.4 Evidence on information costs and the pecking order theory 427
13.2.5 Evidence from dual issues and spin-offs 429
13.2.6 Evidence on the choice of maturity and priority of debt 430
13.2.7 Evidence from surveys 431

13.3 ASSESSING THE THEORIES OF CAPITAL STRUCTURE..........432
13.3.1 How useful is the static trade-off theory? 432
13.3.2 How useful is the pecking order theory? 434

13.4 FINANCING AS A MARKETING PROBLEM 434

13.5 DETERMINING A FINANCING STRATEGY 435
13.5.1 Business risk 436
13.5.2 Asset characteristics 436
13.5.3 Tax position 437
13.5.4 Maintaining reserve borrowing capacity ('financial slack') 437
13.5.5 Other factors 438

Summary 439
Key terms 440
References 440
Questions 441

CHAPTER 14   THE COST OF CAPITAL AND TAXATION ISSUES IN PROJECT EVALUATION   444

Learning objectives... 444

14.1 INTRODUCTION 445
14.2 RISK, RETURN AND THE COST OF CAPITAL..............................445
14.2.1 Risk independence 446
14.3 TAXES AND THE COST OF CAPITAL..446
14.4 ALTERNATIVE APPROACHES TO ESTIMATION OF THE COST OF CAPITAL 448
14.4.1 Direct use of the CAPM 448
14.4.2 The weighted average cost of capital (WACC) 449
14.5 ESTIMATION OF THE COST OF CAPITAL: AN EXTENDED EXAMPLE 451
14.5.1 The cost of debt 452

	14.5.2	The cost of preference shares	455
	14.5.3	The cost of ordinary shares	456
	14.5.4	The company's cost of capital	457
	14.5.5	Issue costs and the cost of capital	459
14.6	PROJECT AND COMPANY COST OF CAPITAL		460
	14.6.1	Calculating the cost of capital for divisions using the 'pure play' approach	461
	14.6.2	Calculating the cost of capital for divisions using the direct estimation approach	463
14.7	THE WEIGHTED AVERAGE COST OF CAPITAL AND ALTERNATIVE PROJECT EVALUATION TECHNIQUES		465
14.8	TAX ISSUES IN PROJECT EVALUATION		466
	14.8.1	Effect of taxes on net cash flows	466
	14.8.2	Illustration of cash-flow information in project evaluation with taxes	469
14.9	USING CERTAINTY EQUIVALENTS TO ALLOW FOR RISK		471

Summary — 474
Key terms — 475
Self-test problems — 475
References — 476
Questions — 476
Problems — 477

APPENDIX 14.1: THE COST OF CAPITAL UNDER ALTERNATIVE TAX SYSTEMS — 484
Introduction — 484
Deriving cost of capital formula — 484
Summary — 486

CHAPTER 15 LEASING AND OTHER EQUIPMENT FINANCE 488

Learning objectives — 488

15.1	INTRODUCTION		489
15.2	TYPES OF LEASE CONTRACTS		490
	15.2.1	Finance leases	491
	15.2.2	Operating leases	491
	15.2.3	Sale and lease-back agreements	492
	15.2.4	Leveraged leasing	492
	15.2.5	Cross-border leasing	493
15.3	ACCOUNTING AND TAXATION TREATMENT OF LEASES		494
	15.3.1	Accounting for leases	494
	15.3.2	Taxation treatment of leases	494
15.4	SETTING LEASE RENTALS		495
15.5	EVALUATION OF FINANCE LEASES		496
	15.5.1	Leasing decisions and investment decisions	498
	15.5.2	The value of leasing in competitive capital markets	499
	15.5.3	Establishing an advantage for leasing	501
	15.5.4	Taxes and the size of leasing gains	502
	15.5.5	Leasing and the imputation tax system	503
15.6	EVALUATION OF OPERATING LEASES		503

	15.7	ADVANTAGES AND DISADVANTAGES OF LEASING	505
	15.7.1	Possible advantages of leasing	505
	15.7.2	Leasing policy	508
	15.8	CHATTEL MORTGAGES AND HIRE-PURCHASE	510
	15.8.1	Equipment finance and the goods and services tax	510

Summary 511
Key terms 511
Self-test problems 512
References 512
Questions 513
Problems 513

CHAPTER 16 — CAPITAL MARKET EFFICIENCY — 516

Learning objectives 516

16.1	INTRODUCTION		517
16.2	THE EFFICIENT MARKET HYPOTHESIS		517
	16.2.1	A non-instantaneous price reaction	518
	16.2.2	A biased price reaction	518
	16.2.3	Categories of capital market efficiency	519
	16.2.4	Market efficiency and the joint test problem	519
16.3	TESTS OF RETURN PREDICTABILITY		520
	16.3.1	The relationship between past and future returns	520
	16.3.2	The presence of seasonal effects in returns	521
	16.3.3	Predicting future returns on the basis of other forecast variables	524
16.4	EVENT STUDIES		528
	16.4.1	The methodology of event studies	528
	16.4.2	Evidence: profit and dividend announcements in Australia	532
	16.4.3	Other events	534
16.5	TESTS FOR PRIVATE INFORMATION		534
16.6	MARKET EFFICIENCY AT THE MACRO LEVEL		536
16.7	BEHAVIOURAL FINANCE AND MARKET EFFICIENCY		537
16.8	IMPLICATIONS OF THE EVIDENCE WITH RESPECT TO MARKET EFFICIENCY		539
	16.8.1	Implications for investors in securities	539
	16.8.2	Implications for financial managers	541

Summary 543
Key terms 544
References 544
Questions 548

CHAPTER 17 — FUTURES CONTRACTS — 550

Learning objectives 550

17.1	INTRODUCTION	551

17.2	WHAT IS A FUTURES CONTRACT?	551
	17.2.1 Forward contracts and futures contracts	551
	17.2.2 How a futures market is organised	552
	17.2.3 Deposits, margins and the mark-to-market rule	554
	17.2.4 The present value of a futures contract	555
17.3	THE AUSTRALIAN SECURITIES EXCHANGE	555
17.4	DETERMINANTS OF FUTURES PRICES	557
17.5	FUTURES MARKET STRATEGIES: SPECULATING AND HEDGING	558
	17.5.1 Introduction	558
	17.5.2 Speculating	559
	17.5.3 Hedging	561
	17.5.4 Some reasons why hedging with futures is imperfect	562
	17.5.5 Hedging and regretting	565
	17.5.6 Selecting the number of futures contracts	565
17.6	FINANCIAL FUTURES ON THE AUSTRALIAN SECURITIES EXCHANGE: THE 90-DAY BANK-ACCEPTED BILL FUTURES CONTRACT	569
	17.6.1 A brief review of bank bills	569
	17.6.2 Specification of the bank-accepted bill futures contract	570
	17.6.3 Uses of the bank bill futures contract	571
17.7	FINANCIAL FUTURES ON THE AUSTRALIAN SECURITIES EXCHANGE: THE 10-YEAR TREASURY BOND FUTURES CONTRACT	576
	17.7.1 A brief review of bond pricing	576
	17.7.2 Specification of the 10-year bond futures contract	577
	17.7.3 Uses of the 10-year bond futures contract	578
17.8	FINANCIAL FUTURES ON THE AUSTRALIAN SECURITIES EXCHANGE: THE 30-DAY INTERBANK CASH RATE FUTURES CONTRACT	579
17.9	FINANCIAL FUTURES ON THE AUSTRALIAN SECURITIES EXCHANGE: THE SHARE PRICE INDEX S&P/ASX 200 (SPI 200) FUTURES CONTRACT	581
	17.9.1 A brief review of Australian Securities Exchange indices	581
	17.9.2 Specification of the S&P/ASX 200 futures contract	581
	17.9.3 Uses of the S&P/ASX 200 futures contract	581
17.10	VALUATION OF FINANCIAL FUTURES CONTRACTS	585
	17.10.1 Valuation of bank bill futures contracts	585
	17.10.2 Valuation of share price index futures contracts	586
17.11	FORWARD-RATE AGREEMENTS (FRAs)	587
Summary		589
Key terms		589
Self-test problems		590
References		590
Questions		590
Problems		591

CHAPTER 18 OPTIONS AND CONTINGENT CLAIMS 594

Learning objectives 594

- 18.1 INTRODUCTION 595
- 18.2 OPTIONS AND OPTION MARKETS 595
  - 18.2.1 What is an option? 595
  - 18.2.2 How options are created and traded 596
  - 18.2.3 Option contracts and futures contracts 597
  - 18.2.4 Payoff structures for calls and puts 597
  - 18.2.5 Factors affecting call option prices 600
  - 18.2.6 Some basic features of put option pricing 603
  - 18.2.7 Put–call parity 605
  - 18.2.8 The minimum value of calls and puts 608
- 18.3 BINOMIAL OPTION PRICING 610
  - 18.3.1 The basic idea: pricing a single-period call option using the binomial approach 610
  - 18.3.2 Risk neutrality as a solution method 611
  - 18.3.3 Binomial option pricing with many time periods 612
  - 18.3.4 Applying the binomial approach to other option problems 614
- 18.4 THE BLACK–SCHOLES MODEL OF CALL OPTION PRICING 615
  - 18.4.1 Assumptions 615
  - 18.4.2 The Black–Scholes equation 616
  - 18.4.3 A brief assessment of the Black–Scholes model 620
- 18.5 OPTIONS ON FOREIGN CURRENCY 621
  - 18.5.1 What is an option on foreign currency? 622
  - 18.5.2 Combinations of options on foreign currency 624
- 18.6 OPTIONS, FORWARDS AND FUTURES 625
- 18.7 OPTIONS ON FUTURES 626
  - 18.7.1 What is an option on a futures contract? 626
  - 18.7.2 Uses of options on futures 626
  - 18.7.3 Pricing options on futures 627
  - 18.7.4 Specification of the SPI 200 futures options contract 628
- 18.8 CONTINGENT CLAIMS 629
  - 18.8.1 What is a contingent claim? 629
  - 18.8.2 Rights issues 629
  - 18.8.3 Convertible bonds 629
  - 18.8.4 Valuation of levered shares and risky zero-coupon debt 630
  - 18.8.5 Valuation of levered shares and risky coupon-paying debt 630
  - 18.8.6 Project evaluation and 'real' options 631

Summary 633
Key terms 633
Self-test problems 633
References 634
Questions 635
Problems 636

CHAPTER 19   ANALYSIS OF TAKEOVERS   640

Learning objectives *640*

19.1 INTRODUCTION 641
- 19.1.1 Fluctuations in takeover activity 641
- 19.1.2 Types of takeover 643

19.2 REASONS FOR TAKEOVERS 643
- 19.2.1 Evaluation of the reasons for takeovers 644
- 19.2.2 Survey evidence of the motives for takeovers 648
- 19.2.3 The roles of takeovers 649

19.3 ECONOMIC EVALUATION OF TAKEOVERS 649
- 19.3.1 Comments on estimation of takeover gains 651
- 19.3.2 Comparing gains and costs 651
- 19.3.3 Estimating cost for a share-exchange takeover 653

19.4 ALTERNATIVE VALUATION APPROACHES 654
- 19.4.1 Valuation based on earnings 654
- 19.4.2 Valuation based on assets 655

19.5 REGULATION AND TAX EFFECTS OF TAKEOVERS 655
- 19.5.1 Off-market bids 656
- 19.5.2 Market bids 657
- 19.5.3 Disclosure requirements 657
- 19.5.4 Creeping takeover 658
- 19.5.5 Partial takeovers 658
- 19.5.6 Schemes of arrangement 658
- 19.5.7 Other controls on takeovers 659
- 19.5.8 Tax effects of takeovers 659
- 19.5.9 Break fees, takeovers and corporate governance 660

19.6 TAKEOVER DEFENCES 661
- 19.6.1 Poison pills 661
- 19.6.2 Acquisition by friendly parties 662
- 19.6.3 Disclosure of favourable information 662
- 19.6.4 Claims and appeals 662
- 19.6.5 The effects of takeover defences 663

19.7 CORPORATE RESTRUCTURING 663
- 19.7.1 Divestitures 664
- 19.7.2 Spin-offs 664
- 19.7.3 Buyouts 665

19.8 EMPIRICAL EVIDENCE ON TAKEOVERS 667
- 19.8.1 The target company 668
- 19.8.2 The acquiring company 668
- 19.8.3 Are takeovers poor investments? 670
- 19.8.4 Distinguishing between good and bad takeovers 672
- 19.8.5 The net effects of takeovers 673
- 19.8.6 The sources of gains from takeovers 674

Summary *675*
Key terms *677*
Self-test problems *677*
References *677*
Questions *679*
Problems *681*

CHAPTER 20 INTERNATIONAL FINANCIAL MANAGEMENT 684

Learning objectives 684

20.1 INTRODUCTION 685

20.2 SOME BACKGROUND STATISTICS 685

20.3 THE FOREIGN EXCHANGE MARKET 687
- 20.3.1 The spot exchange rate 687
- 20.3.2 The forward exchange rate 688
- 20.3.3 Combined spot and forward transactions 689
- 20.3.4 Calculations using foreign exchange rates 689
- 20.3.5 Triangular arbitrage and cross rates 690
- 20.3.6 Size of the foreign exchange market in Australia 691

20.4 RELATIONSHIPS BETWEEN INTEREST RATES, INFLATION RATES, SPOT EXCHANGE RATES AND FORWARD EXCHANGE RATES 692
- 20.4.1 Notation and stages of analysis 692
- 20.4.2 Interest rate parity 694
- 20.4.3 Unbiased forward rates 697
- 20.4.4 Purchasing power parity 697
- 20.4.5 Uncovered interest parity or the international Fisher effect 700

20.5 EMPIRICAL EVIDENCE ON THE BEHAVIOUR OF EXCHANGE RATES 703
- 20.5.1 Interest rate parity: evidence 703
- 20.5.2 Unbiased forward rates: evidence 703
- 20.5.3 Purchasing power parity: evidence 704
- 20.5.4 Uncovered interest parity: evidence 705
- 20.5.5 Forecasting exchange rates 705

20.6 THE MANAGEMENT OF EXCHANGE RISK 706
- 20.6.1 What is exchange risk? 706
- 20.6.2 Who faces exchange risk? 707
- 20.6.3 The hedging principle 707
- 20.6.4 Forward rate hedging 708
- 20.6.5 Hedging by borrowing or lending 709
- 20.6.6 Who should hedge exchange risk? 709
- 20.6.7 Contingent hedging 711

20.7 INTERNATIONAL DIVERSIFICATION OF INVESTMENTS 712

20.8 CURRENCY SWAPS 715

20.9 FOREIGN CURRENCY BORROWING BY AUSTRALIAN COMPANIES 718
- 20.9.1 The risk of foreign currency borrowing 719
- 20.9.2 Reasons for borrowing internationally 720
- 20.9.3 Types of borrowing transactions 722
- 20.9.4 Eurocredits 723
- 20.9.5 International debt securities 724
- 20.9.6 Syndication 727

Summary 729
Key terms 730

Self-test problems		*730*
References		*730*
Questions		*731*
Problems		*733*

CHAPTER 21 MANAGEMENT OF SHORT-TERM ASSETS: INVENTORY 738

Learning objectives … 738

- 21.1 INTRODUCTION … 739
- 21.2 THE IMPORTANCE OF SHORT-TERM FINANCIAL DECISIONS … 739
- 21.3 TYPES OF SHORT-TERM ASSET … 740
  - 21.3.1 Inventory … 740
  - 21.3.2 Liquid assets (cash and short-term investments) … 740
  - 21.3.3 Accounts receivable (debtors) … 740
- 21.4 THE NEED FOR SHORT-TERM ASSET MANAGEMENT … 740
- 21.5 SHORT-TERM ASSETS AND SHORT-TERM LIABILITIES … 741
- 21.6 OVERVIEW OF INVENTORY MANAGEMENT … 742
- 21.7 INVENTORY COSTS: RETAILING AND WHOLESALING … 742
  - 21.7.1 Acquisition costs … 742
  - 21.7.2 Carrying costs … 743
  - 21.7.3 Stockout costs … 743
- 21.8 INVENTORY COSTS: MANUFACTURING … 743
  - 21.8.1 Inventories of raw materials … 743
  - 21.8.2 Inventories of finished goods … 743
- 21.9 INVENTORY MANAGEMENT UNDER CERTAINTY … 744
  - 21.9.1 The economic order quantity (EOQ) model … 744
  - 21.9.2 Cost estimation … 747
  - 21.9.3 The EOQ model with positive lead time … 748
  - 21.9.4 The EOQ model with quantity discounts … 749
- 21.10 INVENTORY MANAGEMENT UNDER UNCERTAINTY … 750
  - 21.10.1 Specifying an acceptable probability of stockout … 752
  - 21.10.2 Specifying an acceptable expected customer service level … 752
- 21.11 INVENTORY MANAGEMENT AND THE 'JUST-IN-TIME' SYSTEM … 754

Summary … 755
Key terms … 755
Self-test problems … 755
References … 756
Questions … 756
Problems … 756

CHAPTER 22 MANAGEMENT OF SHORT-TERM ASSETS: LIQUID ASSETS AND ACCOUNTS RECEIVABLE 758

Learning objectives … 758

- 22.1 INTRODUCTION … 759

22.2		OVERVIEW OF LIQUIDITY MANAGEMENT	759
	22.2.1	What are 'liquid' assets?	759
	22.2.2	Liquidity management and treasury management	759
	22.2.3	Centralisation of liquidity management	760
	22.2.4	Motives for holding liquid assets	761
	22.2.5	Major issues in liquidity management	762
22.3		CASH BUDGETING	762
	22.3.1	Forecasting cash receipts	763
	22.3.2	Forecasting cash payments	763
22.4		THE CHOICE OF SHORT-TERM SECURITIES	765
22.5		TYPES OF SHORT-TERM INVESTMENT	766
	22.5.1	Deposits of funds with financial institutions	766
	22.5.2	Discounting of commercial bills	767
22.6		THE CORPORATE TREASURER AND LIQUIDITY MANAGEMENT	767
22.7		OVERVIEW OF ACCOUNTS RECEIVABLE MANAGEMENT	767
	22.7.1	What are accounts receivable?	768
22.8		CREDIT POLICY	769
	22.8.1	The decision to offer credit	769
	22.8.2	Selection of credit-worthy customers	770
	22.8.3	Limit of credit extended	773
	22.8.4	Credit terms	773
22.9		COLLECTION POLICY	774
22.10		EVALUATION OF ALTERNATIVE CREDIT AND COLLECTION POLICIES	775

Summary ... 779
Key terms ... 780
Self-test problems ... 780
References ... 780
Questions ... 781
Problems ... 781

APPENDIX 22.1: FINANCIAL STATEMENT ANALYSIS ... 783
Introduction ... 783
Measurement and interpretation of several financial ratios ... 783
Usefulness of financial ratio analysis ... 789
Financial ratios and short-term asset management ... 790

Appendix A ... 793
Appendix B ... 803
Glossary ... 819
Author Index ... 829
Subject Index ... 835

ABOUT THE AUTHORS

GRAHAM PEIRSON
Graham Peirson is Emeritus Professor of Accounting and Finance at Monash University (Clayton campus). He has published widely in academic and professional journals and is also co-author of *Issues in Financial Accounting*; *Accounting: An Introduction*; *Financial Accounting: An Introduction*; and *Financial Accounting Theory*. Graham is a graduate of Adelaide University, and has taught at Adelaide University; the University of California, Berkeley; the University of Illinois; the University of Florida; and the University of Washington. He has also taught short courses for a range of clients, including the Australian Competition and Consumer Commission and the National Australia Bank.

ROB BROWN
Rob Brown is Professor of Finance at the University of Melbourne. He has published many research papers in international journals, including *Economica*, the *Journal of Banking and Finance*, the *Journal of Multinational Financial Management* and the *Journal of Fixed Income*. He is a former associate editor (finance) of *Accounting and Finance*, the research journal of the Accounting and Finance Association of Australia and New Zealand. Rob has taught at the University of Sydney; Lancaster University; and Monash University and been a visiting scholar at the University of British Columbia (Canada) and the University of Manchester (UK). His current research interests are analysts' investment recommendations and the user cost of housing.

STEVE EASTON

Steve Easton is Professor of Finance at the University of Newcastle, where he previously served as Head of the Department of Accounting and Finance and Dean of the Faculty of Economics and Commerce. His research work has been accepted for publication in a wide range of journals, including the *Journal of Futures Markets*; *Economica*; and the *Journal of Banking and Finance*. Steve has taught at Adelaide University; Lancaster University; and Monash University. He has also provided short courses for a range of private and public sector organisations, including Australia Post, Macquarie Generation, State Forests of New South Wales and the Tasmanian Chamber of Commerce and Industry. His current research interests are in derivative securities and corporate governance.

PETER HOWARD

Peter Howard taught finance at Monash University (Clayton campus) for more than 25 years. Before this he worked for eight years as an engineer in the petrochemical and mining industries. He has extensive experience in project evaluation and has taught on short courses for a range of clients, including BHP Billiton and the National Australia Bank. Peter has published in academic and professional journals on lease evaluation and the effects of imputation on payout and financing decisions. He has extensive teaching experience at both postgraduate and undergraduate levels. Since retiring from Monash University he has maintained a strong interest in the finance literature and the operation of Australian financial markets.

SEAN PINDER

Sean Pinder is a Senior Lecturer in the Department of Finance at the University of Melbourne. Prior to this he held positions at Monash University and the University of Newcastle and taught at the postgraduate level at Lancaster University in England, the Melbourne Business School and the Adelaide Graduate School of Business. He has undertaken a range of consulting activities for international firms and has developed and delivered professional short courses on treasury risk management, derivatives and capital budgeting issues for major Australian and international companies. Sean has an extensive research profile, with his work appearing in leading Australian and international journals. He has received a number of prizes for his research and teaching.

ACKNOWLEDGMENTS

We have received valuable assistance from a number of people, including Philip G. Brown, Chris Deeley, Paul Docherty, Denis Pêtre and Michael Seamer.

We would like to join McGraw-Hill in thanking academic colleagues who provided their valuable time and expertise in aligning the learning resources with this edition of our book. They include:

- Hong Feng (John) Zhang, Deakin University
- Nada Kulendran, Victoria University
- Ben Marshall, Massey University (NZ)
- David Walker, La Trobe University
- Marvin Wee, University of Western Australia
- Guneratne Wickremasinghe, Victoria University
- Alfred Wong, Charles Sturt University.

We also owe a debt of thanks to the following reviewers of earlier editions who have helped us shape the text you hold today: John Ablett (University of Western Sydney), David Allen (Edith Cowan University), Vicki Baard (Macquarie University), Robert Bianchi (Griffith University), Barry Burgan (University of Adelaide), Nicholas Carline (Lancaster University, UK), Meena Chavan (Macquarie University), Andrew Child (Monash University), Scott Dobbs (University of Wollongong), Samson Ekanayake (Deakin University), Don Geyer (Charles Sturt University), Abeyratna Gunasekarage (Monash University), Neil Hartnett (University of Newcastle), Darren Henry (La Trobe University), Ben Jacobsen (James Cook University), Sian Owen (University of New South Wales), Judy Paterson (University of Canberra), Alex Proimos (Macquarie University), Boyd Scheuber (University of Southern Queensland), Chander Shekhar (University of Melbourne), Jing Shi (Australian National University), Yew Lee Tan (Victoria University), Madhu Veeraraghavan (Monash University) and David Woodliff (University of Western Australia).

In addition, we thank senior development editor Martina Edwards, senior publisher Rosemary Noble, senior production editor Yani Silvana and permissions editor Haidi Bernhardt at McGraw-Hill; and copyeditor Rosemary Moore.

Finally, and most importantly, we thank our wives—Chris, Rayna, Diane, Dawn and Debra—for their support during this project.

PREFACE

This book is designed primarily for use in a first subject in the principles and practice of business finance. Our main objectives are to introduce readers to finance theory and to the tools of financial decision making in the context of the Australian institutional environment. Nevertheless, it is also suitable for students who have completed an introductory subject on capital markets and financial institutions. It also contains sufficient material for two subjects in finance.

Readers who are familiar with the tenth edition will notice several changes that go well beyond the updating associated with every edition of this book. In particular, extensive change will be seen in Chapters 7, 9 and 16. Chapter 7 (Risk and return) has been expanded to include a more detailed discussion of models that incorporate factors other than systematic risk in explaining expected returns, and a new section has been included on alternative methods of appraising the performance of an investment portfolio. Chapter 9 (Sources of finance: equity) provides much greater detail on the various accelerated rights issue structures that have developed in the Australian market, together with recent evidence on the popularity of, and costs associated with, the main methods of raising equity capital. The greatest change will be seen in our discussion of capital market efficiency in Chapter 16, which has been completely rewritten. The chapter provides a straightforward but detailed analysis of the evidence with respect to market efficiency, with separate analysis being provided with respect to micro-efficiency and macro-efficiency. At the micro level, market efficiency concerns the extent to which the prices of securities reflect information relative to other securities within the same asset class. At the macro level, the issue is whether capital markets as a whole reflect all available information—whether, for example, the share market is correctly priced compared with a less risky asset class such as government debt.

Since the appearance of the tenth edition, the world's capital markets have experienced a period of upheaval that most commentators refer to as the 'global financial crisis'. Rather than quarantine discussion of the crisis in a single chapter or section, we have chosen to refer to the crisis at appropriate points throughout the book. To give just two examples, Chapter 8 includes a discussion of the effects of the crisis on investment banks and securitisation, as well as regulatory responses to the crisis, while Chapter 16 discusses the crisis by using the distinction between micro-efficiency and macro-efficiency.

Finally, we wish to express our special thanks to Graham Peirson. Although Graham has retired from active authorship, he made a great contribution to this edition by providing valuable comments on the draft of each chapter. Graham brings not only a deep knowledge but also an uncanny ability to detect flaws in logic and in writing style. His thoroughness has prevented many such flaws from appearing in print.

ROB BROWN STEVE EASTON
PETER HOWARD SEAN PINDER
June 2011

E-STUDENT

McGraw-Hill Connect is a web-based platform that prepares you for success and connects you to key learning resources—all in the one online space.
→ Connect offers quick access to your assignments and includes an optional upgrade to an integrated e-book.
→ Instant practice material and study questions come with specific feedback and direct links back to the e-book to help you study.
→ Access a library of online resources.

With Connect you can practise important skills at your own pace and work wherever and whenever you choose.

Students!
Getting started with Connect
To activate your Connect account, follow these three simple steps:
1. Go to the Connect course URL provided by your instructor.
2. Click on the button to register.
3. Follow the online instructions to complete registration.

Questions? Difficulty activating your account? Visit www.mcgrawhillconnect.com/support

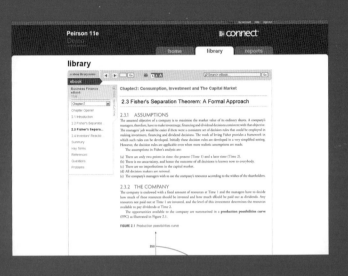

ONLINE STUDENT RESOURCES

POWERPOINT® SLIDES

PowerPoint slides summarise the key points of each chapter; these are available to both instructors and students. They can be downloaded and adapted to suit individual lectures or used as lecture notes.

STUDENT QUIZZING

Students can test their skills and knowledge with several sets of revision quizzes for each chapter.

INTERACTIVE FIN SIMS

These online simulations cover 12 focus areas in finance, offering a hands-on approach that guides students through difficult and important topics in corporate finance.

GLOSSARY

Unsure of a business finance term? The online glossary contains a quick reference to key terms and definitions.

WEBSITES

A list of useful related websites can be found inside the front cover and can also be accessed from Connect online.

E-INSTRUCTOR

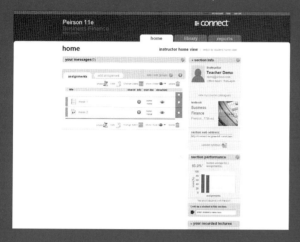

Less managing, more teaching, greater learning

McGraw-Hill's web-based assignment and assessment platform Connect offers powerful instructor tools and features to make managing assignments easier so you can spend more time teaching and less time managing. With Connect you can:

→ create and deliver assignments easily with selectable banks of questions
→ streamline lesson planning, student progress reporting and assignment grading
→ access an integrated e-book
→ take advantage of online submission and grading of student assignments
→ use the Instructor Library to access a repository of additional support materials.

For more information go to **www.mcgrawhillconnect.com** or speak to your McGraw-Hill sales consultant to arrange instructor access to Connect.

Lecturer support

A comprehensive help and support section is built into Connect including a suite of video tutorials to support instructors setting up courses, creating assignments and much more.
Visit **www.mhhe.com/support** to access FAQs and online support site for our entire digital range.

ONLINE INSTRUCTOR RESOURCES

In addition to having access to all the student resources, instructors also have password-protected access to an extensive range of further resources, including the following.

SOLUTIONS MANUAL

The solutions manual has been prepared by the authors and features comprehensive answers to the questions, and solutions to the problems, at the end of each chapter.

TEST BANK AND EZ TEST ONLINE

EZ Test is a flexible and easy-to-use testing program. It generates tests that can be exported to other course management systems (such as WebCT and Blackboard) and can be used to create hard copy tests. Questions can be selected from a number of test banks, and over a dozen question types are supported. You can scramble questions, create algorithmic questions and create multiple versions of the same test.

VIDEO AND WEB LINKS

Links to relevant videos and websites are provided for each chater to further enhance the teaching and learning experience, bringing finance to life.

CASE STUDIES WITH SOLUTIONS

A large suite of online case studies is available to give students further practice in applying their knowledge.

HIGHLIGHTS OF THIS EDITION

CHAPTER 1
- Delivers a simple, concise overview of the essential concepts of corporate finance.

CHAPTER 2
- Provides detailed coverage of Fisher's Separation Theorem and the company's objective to maximise current value.

CHAPTER 3
- Introduces simple interest, compound interest and the time value of money in one logically structured chapter.

CHAPTER 4
- Updates Australian yield curve data and Australian corporate and government ratings data.

CHAPTER 5
- Updates survey evidence of capital budgeting techniques used by Australian firms.

CHAPTER 6
- Is dedicated specifically to applying methods of project evaluation.
- Features in-depth discussion of sensitivity analysis, break-even analysis and simulations.

CHAPTER 7
- Updates estimates of the systematic risk of Australian firms.
- Updates empirical evidence concerning the market risk premium in an international and domestic context.
- Includes a detailed discussion of models that incorporate factors other than systematic risk in explaining expected returns.
- Addresses alternative methods of appraising the performance of an investment portfolio.

CHAPTER 8
- Discusses the effects of the global financial crisis on Australian financial institutions and markets, with particular emphasis on its effects on investment banks and securitisation, and regulatory responses to the crisis.

CHAPTER 9
- Provides greater detail on the various accelerated rights issue structures that have developed in the Australian market and recent evidence on the popularity of, and costs associated with, the main methods of raising equity capital.

BRIEF CONTENTS

CHAPTER 1	Introduction	2
CHAPTER 2	Consumption, investment and the capital market	12
CHAPTER 3	The time value of money: an introduction to financial mathematics	32
CHAPTER 4	Applying the time value of money to security valuation	78
CHAPTER 5	Project evaluation: principles and methods	106
CHAPTER 6	The application of project evaluation methods	132
CHAPTER 7	Risk and return	168
CHAPTER 8	The capital market	208
CHAPTER 9	Sources of finance: equity	236
CHAPTER 10	Sources of finance: debt	286
CHAPTER 11	Payout policy	334
CHAPTER 12	Principles of capital structure	378
CHAPTER 13	Capital structure decisions	418
CHAPTER 14	The cost of capital and taxation issues in project evaluation	444
CHAPTER 15	Leasing and other equipment finance	488
CHAPTER 16	Capital market efficiency	516
CHAPTER 17	Futures contracts	550
CHAPTER 18	Options and contingent claims	594
CHAPTER 19	Analysis of takeovers	640
CHAPTER 20	International financial management	684
CHAPTER 21	Management of short-term assets: inventory	738
CHAPTER 22	Management of short-term assets: liquid assets and accounts receivable	758

CHAPTER 10
- Features a new *Finance in action* piece illustrating issues associated with loan covenants.
- Discusses changes in the markets for debt securities such as debentures and corporate bonds.

CHAPTER 11
- Includes changes in the legal requirements for payment of dividends.
- Emphasises the importance of a 'full payout' policy and de-emphasises the dividend irrelevance theorem.
- Highlights recent evidence on the market value of franking credits.
- Discusses recent research on the growing importance of share buybacks and the substitution of buybacks for dividends.

CHAPTER 12
- Features a new *Finance in action* piece giving details of one company's stated policy on capital structure.
- Includes a restructured discussion of agency costs.

CHAPTER 13
- Features a new *Finance in action* piece on the benefits of the no-debt decision of a company that had previously experienced a financial collapse.
- Includes recent Australian evidence on surveys of chief financial officers.

CHAPTER 14
- Updates empirical evidence on the value of imputation tax credits in Australia.
- Features a new *Finance in action* piece dealing with the issues facing regulators in the energy industry when attempting to estimate an appropriate weighted average cost of capital for energy distributors.

CHAPTER 15
- Features a revised discussion of the advantages and disadvantages of leasing, based on recent research that suggests that in some cases leasing does conserve capital.

CHAPTER 16
- Has been completely rewritten.
- Includes discussion of micro-efficiency and macro-efficiency.
- Extensively updates empirical evidence.

CHAPTER 17
- Includes updated exchange contracts values and exchange indices throughout.
- Discusses the 30-day interbank cash rate futures contract, including updated data.

CHAPTER 18
- Includes updated examples illustrating the relationship between an option's market price and characteristics such as its term-to-expiry and exercise price.
- Features a new *Finance in action* piece describing how options written on a share price index are used to create a Volatility Index (VIX), which then provides useful information to investors about the level of uncertainty in the market.

CHAPTER 19
- Updates empirical evidence on the fluctuations in takeover activity over time.
- Includes a new section providing survey evidence of the motives of acquiring managers for takeover activity.
- Updates the discussion of the regulation of takeover activity.
- Extensively updates the empirical evidence presented on the wealth effects of alternative forms of takeovers and corporate restructuring.

CHAPTER 20
- Features extensive updating of data, including the most recent BIS triennial survey results.
- Includes two new *Finance in action* pieces, one on deviations from the Law of One Price and another on the expected effect of a depreciating Australian dollar on the tourism industry.
- Restructures the discussion of international borrowing options to clarify the choices available.
- Includes detailed data on international borrowing transactions.

CHAPTER 21
- Provides concise but thorough coverage of short-term assets, focusing on inventory, for the curious or advanced student.

CHAPTER 22
- Provides concise but thorough coverage of short-term assets, focusing on liquid assets and accounts receivable, for the curious or advanced student.

HOW TO USE THIS BOOK

Learning objectives list the information you will learn by studying the chapter. They are restated in the margins in appropriate locations and so become useful revision tools.

LEARNING OBJECTIVES
After studying this chapter you should be able to:
1. explain how a company's managers can, in principle, make financial decisions that will be supported by all shareholders
2. explain how the existence of a capital market makes this result possible
3. identify a company's optimal investment/dividend policy under conditions of certainty.

CHAPTER CONTENTS
2.1 Introduction
2.2 Fisher's Separation Theorem: a simplified example
2.3 Fisher's Separation Theorem: a formal approach
2.4 Investors' reactions to managers' decisions

5.4.3 CHOOSING BETWEEN THE DISCOUNTED CASH FLOW METHODS
Independent investments

For independent investments, both the IRR and NPV methods of investment evaluation lead to the same accept/reject decision, except for those investments where the cash flow patterns result in either multiple internal rates of return or no internal rate of return. In other words, if a project has an internal rate of return greater than the required rate of return, the project will also have a positive net present value when its cash flows are discounted at the required rate of return—that is, NPV > 0 when $r > k$, NPV < 0 when $r < k$, and NPV = 0 when $r = k$. This is always true, provided that the project's cash flows consist of one or more periods of cash outlay followed only by positive net cash flows. Such a project is referred to as a conventional project and the net present value profile of such a project is illustrated in Figure 5.2. Figure 5.2 shows that the higher the discount rate, the lower is the net present value. The intercept of the net present value profile with the horizontal axis occurs at the point where $k = r$, which is the internal rate of return because it is the discount rate at which the net present value is zero.

LEARNING OBJECTIVE 3
Explain the advantages and disadvantages of the main project evaluation methods

Chapter introductions give you an overview of the chapter's most important points and contextualise the topics to the wide area of business finance.

INTRODUCTION 3.1

Financial mathematics provides the finance specialist with some extremely useful tools with which to solve financial problems. In this chapter, we present the major tools of financial mathematics and indicate some of their important applications. You will find that a thorough understanding of these tools, and how they may be used, will be very valuable when you study later chapters. Although you will find a large number of formulae in this chapter, you will not master financial mathematics if you simply try to memorise the formulae. If you fully understand the approach and the logic that are embodied in the formulae, you will not need to memorise them.

Key terms are defined in the margins beside the term's first appearance in the text. These terms are then listed in the glossary at the end of the book.

3.2.1 CASH FLOWS
Financial mathematics concerns the analysis of **cash flows** between parties to a **financial contract**.[1] For example, when money is borrowed there is an initial flow of cash from the lender to the borrower, and subsequently one (or more) cash (re)payments from the borrower to the lender. In financial mathematics, as in finance generally, we are concerned with the cash flow consequences of a decision or a contract. How much cash will flow between the parties? When will these cash flows occur? These

cash flow
payment (cash outflow) or receipt (cash inflow) of money

xxxiv

EXAMPLE 3.4

Stars Ltd borrows $100 000 on 20 January 2012, to be repaid in a lump sum on 2 March 2012. The interest rate is 8.75 per cent per annum. Calculate the lump sum repayment.

SOLUTION

The time period involved is 42 days, consisting of 11 days in January, 29 days in February and 2 days in March; note that we do not count *both* 20 January and 2 March but we *do* count 29 February because 2012 is a leap year.

Using Equation 3.2 and the conventions explained in this section the lump sum repayment is:

$S = P(1 + rt)$

$= \$100\,000 \left[1 + (0.0875)\left(\frac{42}{365}\right)\right]$

$= \$100\,000 \times 1.010\,068\,493$

$= \$101\,006.85$

Worked examples are provided throughout the text to illustrate the practical application of the theory.

FINANCE IN ACTION

£6000 DEBT GREW TO £116 000

If you don't repay a loan, and a lot of time passes, the debt can grow to unmanageable proportions, as happened to an unfortunate borrower in Manchester in the United Kingdom.

A grandmother has been forced to put her house up for sale after she ended up owing a massive £116 000—on a £6000 loan. Esther Osei, 57, borrowed the money in 1988 to pay for her father's funeral and to buy a new cooker for her Clayton home.

But she could not meet the cost of the loan and 18 years later, the amount she owed had grown to £116 000 … Esther said: 'I borrowed the money when I was grieving for my father. I just signed the papers.'

When the lender applied to take possession of her home, Esther sought help by going to the North Manchester Law Centre. Lawyers negotiated a deal at Manchester County Court … A law centre spokesperson said Esther should never have entered into the loan agreement. 'It was a very high rate of interest.'

Finance in action is a feature containing interesting items from the business media that relate the theory to real-world practice.

SUMMARY

→ Financial managers frequently make decisions that involve the time value of money. This chapter covered the major tools of financial mathematics needed to support these decisions. These tools include calculating rates of return, present values and future values, and defining and applying interest rates, including simple interest and compound interest.

→ The definition and valuation of various streams of cash flows were considered in detail, with the present value of an ordinary annuity being used as the basis for dealing with several related

Summaries give students a checklist of the topics covered in the chapter and serve as a useful revision tool when preparing for exams.

SELF-TEST PROBLEMS

1. Andrew borrowed $6000 and repaid the loan 60 days later by a single payment of $6250. What is the implied annual simple interest rate?

2. Angela deposits $5000 today in a bank account that pays interest annually at the rate of 8 per cent. She then makes 10 more deposits of $1000 each at annual intervals.

Self-test problems at the end of selected chapters cover all the topics within the chapter for thorough exam preparation.

Solutions to self-test problems are available in Appendix B.

INTERNATIONAL ARTICLES

WWW International articles related to this topic are available on the Online Learning Centre at www.mhhe.com/au/peirson11e

REFERENCES

Crapp, H. & Marshall, J., *Money Market Maths*, Allen & Unwin, Sydney, 1986.

Knox, D.M., Zima, P. & Brown, R.L., *Mathematics of Finance*, 2nd edn, McGraw-Hill, Sydney, 1999.

Martin, P. & Burrow, M., *Applied Financial Mathematics*, Prentice-Hall, Sydney, 1991.

QUESTIONS

1. **[LO 1]** Explain the difference(s) between an interest rate and a rate of return.
2. **[LO 1]** Distinguish between simple interest and

PROBLEMS

1. **Simple interest earned [LO 1]**
   Nicholas deposits $2000 in a bank fixed deposit for 6 months at an interest rate of 13.25 per cent per annum. How much interest will he earn?

2. **Simple interest earned [LO 1]**
   If Nicholas reinvests the $2000, *plus* the interest earned (see Problem 1), for a further 6 months, again at 13.25 per cent per annum, how much interest will he earn in this second 6-month period?

3. **Implied simple interest rate [LO 1]**
   Jane borrowed $10 000 and repaid the loan 30 days later by a single payment of $10 400. What is the implied annual simple interest rate?

4. **Calculating the loan term [LO 4]**
   Mary borrowed $7250 at an annual simple interest rate of 15.50 per cent. She repaid the loan by paying a lump sum of $7394.70. What was the loan term?

Additional end-of-chapter questions and problems provide further practice and develop deeper understanding of the topics covered. They are linked back to the learning objectives for each chapter.

How to use this book 1

CHAPTER 1
INTRODUCTION

LEARNING OBJECTIVES

After studying this chapter you should be able to:

1. describe the structure of finance as an area of study
2. identify the major decisions made by financial managers and investors
3. identify the major types of business entities
4. specify the objective of the company
5. identify and explain the fundamental concepts in finance.

CHAPTER CONTENTS

1.1 Finance as an area of study
1.2 Financial decisions
1.3 Business structures
1.4 The company's financial objective
1.5 Fundamental concepts in finance
1.6 Outline of the book

FINANCE AS AN AREA OF STUDY

1.1

This book introduces the reader to the area of study known as finance. Although financial issues have been studied for centuries, it is only relatively recently—in the last 50 years or so—that finance has emerged as an area of study in its own right, with a well-established body of theory and evidence. In the chapters that follow, we will introduce you to the major issues in finance.

Finance can be described as having two main components, which are:[1]

- corporate finance
- investments.

Corporate finance takes the viewpoint of the company. The main issues involved are the choice of assets, the financing decision and the dividend decision. Imagine that a group of investors has set up a new company. The investors are the shareholders (that is, the owners) of the company. The company must decide[2] what assets it will buy and how it will fund the purchase of these assets. The company may use its own money—that is, the money contributed by the shareholders—to fund the purchase, or it may borrow the money. Or it may use both shareholders' funds and borrowed funds. When the company has been operating for a time, it may have made a profit. If so, it may decide to distribute some or all of the profit to the shareholders. Such a distribution is called a dividend. If the dividend paid is less than the profit, then some of the profit is retained within the company, and will be used to fund asset acquisitions and/or debt repayment. Corporate finance is also concerned with corporate governance issues. For example, should the Board of Directors include some 'outsiders'? Should senior managers be granted shares to encourage them to make decisions that are in the best interests of the shareholders?

Investments takes the viewpoint of the investor rather than the company. Investors are concerned about the return they will earn on an investment—the more the better. But unless investors are willing to take a risk, they cannot expect to earn a high return. All investors dream of finding an investment that produces high returns at low risk—but most will never find one. So, investors must make a trade-off between return and risk. In investments, this balancing of risk and return is a major issue. A large part of the solution is for investors to choose a diversified set of assets in which to invest. Investments is also about the pricing of securities such as shares and bonds. These securities are traded in financial markets, many of which are very active, with transactions running into the millions of dollars every day. How does the risk of a security affect the price at which it will trade in these financial markets? What factors, other than risk, might also be important? And how might the price be expected to change in the future?

> **LEARNING OBJECTIVE 1**
> Describe the structure of finance as an area of study

FINANCIAL DECISIONS

1.2

In this book we focus on financial decisions made by companies and investors. Some of these decisions are:

Corporate (or *company*) *decisions*:

- Asset management: What new assets should the company acquire? How much should it pay for these assets?
- Working capital management: How much cash should the company hold? How much inventory?
- Capital structure: How much should the company borrow?

> **LEARNING OBJECTIVE 2**
> Identify the major decisions made by financial managers and investors

---

[1] A third component, *financial markets and institutions*, overlaps to some extent with corporate finance and investments. The focus of this component is on the markets for various securities and the design of financial instruments. It also considers the financial issues faced by banks and other financial institutions.

[2] Strictly speaking, a company is just a legal structure, and hence cannot have any personal qualities, such as the ability to make decisions. Company decisions are in fact made by people such as the company's directors. However, for ease of exposition, we attribute personal qualities to companies.

- Payout policy: How much should the company pay out to its shareholders?
- Mergers and acquisitions: Should the company take over another company?

Investor decisions:

- Portfolio theory: How can an investor achieve a better trade-off between risk and return?
- Asset pricing: How much is a particular security worth? What is the relationship between long-term interest rates and short-term interest rates?

1.3 BUSINESS STRUCTURES

LEARNING OBJECTIVE 3
Identify the major types of business entities

When a business is being established, one of the first decisions that has to be made concerns the type of business structure that is to be used. In Australia, although many small businesses are sole proprietorships or partnerships, nearly all large businesses, and many thousands of small businesses, are companies. Hence, in this book, our focus is on companies. But to place the corporate (company) form in context, we first discuss the advantages and disadvantages of sole proprietorships and partnerships.

1.3.1 SOLE PROPRIETORSHIP

A **sole proprietorship** is a business owned by one person. Many small service businesses, retail stores and professional practices are operated as sole proprietorships.

sole proprietorship
business owned by one person

Advantages

The advantages of a sole proprietorship structure include:

- Control of the business rests with the owner, so it is relatively easy to make decisions and there is no scope for disagreements between owners.
- It is easy and inexpensive to form, and to dissolve.
- It is not treated as a separate entity for tax purposes. Therefore, any business profits belong to the owner and are taxed only once as part of the owner's assessable income.

Disadvantages

The disadvantages of a sole proprietorship structure include:

- It is not a separate legal entity and therefore the owner has unlimited liability for debts incurred by the business. In other words, all obligations of the business are personal obligations of the owner.
- The size of the business is limited by the wealth of the owner and by the amount that can be borrowed. It can be difficult to raise funds for expansion because lenders are usually reluctant to lend large amounts to individuals.
- Ownership of a sole proprietorship can be transferred only by selling the business to a new owner. If a sole proprietorship is not sold, then it will cease to exist when the owner retires or dies.

1.3.2 PARTNERSHIP

A **partnership** is a business owned by two or more people acting as partners. Many small service businesses, retail stores and professional practices are operated as partnerships.

partnership
business owned by two or more people acting as partners

Advantages

The advantages of a partnership structure include:

- It is easy and inexpensive to form because there are no legal requirements that need to be met. All that is necessary is an agreement, preferably in writing to avoid future disagreements, by those forming the partnership.
- A partnership can combine the wealth and talents of several individuals, and employees can be offered the prospect of becoming partners (owners) in the future.

Disadvantages

There are also important disadvantages of a partnership structure, including:

- Partnerships are not separate legal entities and the partners are therefore personally liable for obligations (including debts) entered into by the partnership.
- It can be difficult for partners to withdraw their investment because the partnership will terminate if a partner's interest in the partnership is sold or a partner dies. In either case, a new partnership will have to be formed.
- Disputes between partners or former partners can be very damaging.

1.3.3 COMPANY

A **company** is a separate legal entity formed under the *Corporations Act 2001*. The owners of a company are called *shareholders* because their ownership interests are represented by shares in the company's capital. Companies vary greatly in size. They range from large companies listed on a stock exchange with many thousands of shareholders to small family companies carrying on a relatively small-scale business. In a large company, the shareholders and the managers are usually separate groups. The shareholders elect the Board of Directors, which appoints managers to run the company on behalf of the shareholders.

company
separate legal entity formed under the *Corporations Act 2001*; shareholders are the owners of a company

Advantages

Companies have several advantages, including:

- A company is a legal entity distinct from the owners, which enables it to conduct its operations in its own name. A company can buy, own and sell property; it can sue or be sued in its own name; and it can enter into contracts with other entities. The shareholders of most companies have **limited liability**. This means that if the company fails and it is unable to pay its debts, the owners of fully paid shares are not obliged to contribute further funds to meet the company's debts. However, if shares are partly paid, then shareholders can be obliged to contribute any unpaid amount.
- A company has an indefinite life, which means that, unlike a sole proprietorship or partnership, its existence and operations are unaffected by the death or retirement of its owners.
- The *Corporations Act 2001* distinguishes between public companies, which may invite members of the public to invest in them, and proprietary companies, which have no such power. Public companies may be listed on a stock exchange, which facilitates trading in the company's shares. Ownership of shares in a listed public company can be transferred very easily without any effect on the company's operations, which are conducted by employees. Stock exchange listing also makes it relatively easy for public companies to raise capital by issuing additional shares that are sold to existing shareholders or to new investors.

limited liability
legal concept that protects shareholders whose liability to meet a company's debts is limited to any amount unpaid on the shares they hold

Disadvantages

The corporate form of ownership also has some disadvantages, which include:

- A company is more expensive to establish than a sole proprietorship or a partnership.
- A company is subject to more onerous regulation. For example, there are extensive reporting requirements, particularly for listed public companies. Capital raising by companies is also highly regulated. For example, shares and other securities can be issued only if investors are provided with information to make informed decisions about whether to invest in those securities.
- It can be difficult to motivate managers and staff who are employees of a company. In comparison, sole proprietorships and partnerships are managed by people who are also owners of the business and who will see a direct link between their efforts and the rewards they receive.
- Because a company is owned by one group (the shareholders) but may be run by a different group (the managers), there can be conflicts of interest between those who own the company and those who make decisions on their behalf. These conflicts result in 'agency costs' which are discussed further in Section 1.5.8.
- The taxation treatment of companies can be a disadvantage. Company profits are subject to income tax and shareholders may also be taxed when they receive dividends paid out of the profits. Therefore, the use of a company structure can involve double taxation. However, the extent of this problem depends on the type of taxation system imposed by the government. Under Australian tax law, many shareholders are not subject to double taxation.

Much of this book concerns listed public companies. However, most of the concepts in this book are also relevant to other forms of business entity. There will, of course, be differences in the details, depending on the entity's size and the nature of its business. In addition, many of the ideas considered in this book can be applied to not-for-profit entities including public sector entities.

1.4 THE COMPANY'S FINANCIAL OBJECTIVE

Rational solutions to investment and financing problems can only be achieved if the company's objective is clearly specified. The objective assumed in most of this book is that management seeks to maximise the market value of the company's ordinary shares. Because an alternative term for *shares* is *equity*, this objective is often expressed as the maximisation of the market value of shareholders' equity. It is consistent with the economist's assumption that companies seek to maximise economic profit. If the market value of a company's ordinary shares is maximised, then the opportunities open to the shareholders are also maximised—greater wealth implies more choices. For example, if a shareholder wishes to sell his or her shares in order to finance greater consumption, the higher the share price, the greater are his or her consumption opportunities.

LEARNING OBJECTIVE 4
Specify the objective of the company

1.5 FUNDAMENTAL CONCEPTS IN FINANCE

1.5.1 VALUE

In Section 1.4 we stated that we assume that management seeks to maximise the market value of shareholders' equity. To achieve this objective, the financial manager must understand how financial markets work. To finance a company's investments, securities, such as shares and debt securities, will need to be issued—that is, these securities will need to be sold to investors. Subsequently, investors may choose to sell their securities to other investors in financial markets. The actions of buyers and sellers in financial markets will determine the prices of the securities

LEARNING OBJECTIVE 5
Identify and explain the fundamental concepts in finance

and therefore the market value of the company. The market value, *V*, of a company may be expressed as:

$$V = D + E$$

where   *D* = the market value of the company's debt
E = the market value of the company's equity (shares)

The value that the financial markets place on a company's debt and equity securities will depend on the *risk* and *expected return* on investments in those securities. In turn, the risk and return of the securities will depend on the risk and return that the company achieves on the investments it makes in its assets. In finance, the success of an investment is judged by its ability to generate more cash than originally outlaid on the investment. This will enable the company to make interest payments to lenders and repay the amount borrowed, and to make payouts, such as dividends, to shareholders.

1.5.2   THE TIME VALUE OF MONEY

The **time value of money** principle is based on the proposition that an individual will always prefer to receive a dollar today rather than receive a dollar at any later date. Even if the individual does not want to spend the dollar today, he or she would rather receive the dollar today and then invest it, rather than receive the dollar at a later date. Therefore, a dollar is worth more (less), the sooner (later) it is to be received, all other things being equal.

This principle is discussed and applied in Chapter 3. Some further applications are considered in Chapter 4.

time value of money principle that a dollar is worth more (less), the sooner (later) it is to be received, all other things being equal

1.5.3   RISK AVERSION

In finance, it is usually assumed that investors display **risk aversion**, which means that they do not like risk. Given a choice between two investments that have the same expected return, but one has lower risk, a risk-averse investor will choose the one with the lower risk. Risk aversion does not imply that an investor will reject all risky investments. Rather, it implies that an investor will choose a risky investment only if the expected return on the investment is high enough to compensate the investor for bearing the risk. Because investors are risk averse, we expect that in the long term, the average return on high-risk investments will exceed the average return on low-risk investments—if this were not so, no-one would invest in the high-risk investments. For example, in the long term, shares produce higher returns than bank deposits because shares are riskier than bank deposits. The relationship between risk and expected return is discussed in Chapter 7.

risk aversion a dislike of risk

1.5.4   NOMINAL AND REAL AMOUNTS

The *purchasing power of money* changes as a result of price increases (inflation) and price decreases (deflation). During a period of inflation there is an increase in the general level of prices, with a consequent decrease in the purchasing power of money. In contrast, during a period of deflation there is a decrease in the general level of prices, with a consequent increase in the purchasing power of money. It is necessary, therefore, to distinguish between the *nominal* or face value of money and the *real* or inflation-adjusted value of money. For example, if the annual rate of inflation is 3 per cent, the real value of a dollar is decreasing annually by 3 per cent—that is, relative to the purchasing power of a dollar today, a dollar next year will be worth only 97 cents in real terms.[3]

---

3 This result is an approximation. With a rate of inflation of 3 per cent per annum, $1 today is equivalent to $1.03 next year and it follows that a dollar next year is worth $1/1.03 = $0.970 874 today. This issue is discussed further in Chapter 3.

Returns on investments may be measured in either nominal or real terms. In most financial markets, trading is conducted in nominal terms. Similarly, most financial contracts are written in nominal terms. For example, the interest rate agreed to in a loan must be paid whatever the future inflation rate turns out to be. Such an interest rate is called a *nominal* interest rate. An interest rate may also be expressed in *real* terms, which is equal to the nominal interest rate after taking out the effect of inflation. If the nominal rate of return on an investment exceeds the inflation rate, then the real rate of return is positive—that is, the investment will increase the investor's purchasing power.

1.5.5 MARKET EFFICIENCY AND ASSET PRICING

An *efficient financial market* is one composed of numerous well-informed individuals whose trading activities cause prices to adjust instantaneously and without bias in response to new information. Price changes are therefore caused by new information becoming available. The concept of market efficiency means that we should expect securities and other assets to be fairly priced, given their risk and expected return.

In Section 1.5.3 we explained that, because investors are risk averse, higher-risk investments will need to offer investors higher expected returns—that is, in the long term, risk and expected return will be positively related. But what are the details of this relationship? The *capital asset pricing model* (CAPM) provides one answer to this question. According to the CAPM, risk can be attributed to two sources:

(a) market-wide factors, such as changes in interest rates and foreign exchange rates—this is called *systematic risk* (also referred to as *non-diversifiable* or *market risk*)
(b) factors that are specific to a particular company, such as the possible discovery of a new mineral deposit by a mining company—this is called *unsystematic risk* (also referred to as *diversifiable* or *unique risk*).

While unsystematic risk can be largely eliminated by the investor holding a well-diversified portfolio, systematic risk cannot be eliminated.

Another model that has been developed to measure the riskiness of an investment and to establish the trade-off between risk and expected return is the *Fama–French model*. According to the CAPM and the Fama–French model, risk-averse investors can diversify their investments to eliminate unsystematic risk. Consequently, the market will only reward investors by offering a higher expected return for bearing systematic or market risk. Both models are discussed in Chapter 7. Market efficiency is considered in detail in Chapter 16.

1.5.6 DERIVATIVE SECURITIES

Derivative securities include forward contracts, futures contracts, options and swaps. In each case, the value of the derivative security depends on the value of some underlying security. For example, the value of an option to buy a share in Wesfarmers Ltd depends heavily on the market value of a Wesfarmers share. In this case, the option is the derivative, while the Wesfarmers share is the primary security, or underlying asset. Real assets, like a coal mine or an idea for a new product, may also have features that resemble derivatives. For example, the owner of a coal mine has the option to close the mine and reopen it later. Derivative securities are considered in Chapters 17 and 18.

arbitrage
simultaneous transactions in different markets that result in an immediate risk-free profit

1.5.7 ARBITRAGE

Arbitrage plays a central role in finance. If two identical assets were to trade in the same market at different prices, and if there were no transaction costs, then an arbitrage opportunity would exist. A risk-free profit could be made by traders simultaneously purchasing at the lower price and selling at the higher price. This situation could not persist because competition among traders would force up the price of the lower-priced asset and/or force down the price of the higher-priced asset until the prices of the two assets were the same.

Arbitrage therefore precludes perfect substitutes from selling at different prices in the same market. It follows that the financial prices we observe must be set by the financial markets in such a way that arbitrage is not possible. This idea is simple yet remarkably powerful. It has applications throughout finance in such diverse areas as the capital structure decision (how much should a company borrow?), payout policy, international finance, option pricing and the term structure of interest rates.

1.5.8 AGENCY RELATIONSHIPS

In Section 1.3.3 we mentioned that one of the disadvantages of the corporate structure is the possibility that managers may pursue their own objectives rather than the interests of the shareholders. For example, a company that operates in a mature industry where there are few growth opportunities may have surplus cash that cannot be invested profitably in its usual fields of operation. The company's shareholders would benefit if the surplus were paid to them as a dividend or used to buy back shares. But the managers may decide instead to use the cash to acquire another company that operates in a different industry. This investment may benefit managers by giving them greater opportunities for promotion and higher pay justified by the increase in company size. However, the acquisition may not increase shareholders' wealth. There can therefore be a conflict of interest between shareholders and managers.

Making an unprofitable takeover is only one way in which managers may pursue their own interests at the expense of the shareholders. Other examples include managers working less energetically than they could and managers directly diverting the company's resources to their own benefit, such as by acquiring expensive company cars, taking unnecessary business trips to exotic locations, and so on.

The relationship between shareholders and managers is an example of an agency relationship. In an agency relationship, one party, the *principal*, delegates decision-making authority to another party, the *agent*. In a company run by managers, the managers are the agents and the shareholders are the principals.

Shareholders are aware of the possibility that managers may pursue their own objectives and will try to limit this behaviour by *monitoring* the behaviour of managers and by instituting contracts designed to align the interests of managers and shareholders. For example, a Board of Directors that includes a significant number of non-executive directors can be effective in monitoring managers on behalf of shareholders. In addition, many companies employ *management remuneration schemes* designed to give managers an incentive to maximise shareholders' wealth. For example, these schemes often provide senior executives, particularly the chief executive, with options to purchase shares in the company at an attractive price. Finally, if agency costs are high, the company will probably be poorly run and, in consequence, its share price will be low and it may become a target for takeover. Existing managers generally fare badly when such a change of control occurs, so the desire to avoid being taken over can also limit the self-interested behaviour of managers.

Agency theory has been used to examine various corporate financial decisions including capital structure, dividend and share repurchase decisions, and leasing decisions. The application of agency theory to these decisions is discussed in Chapters 11, 12, 13 and 15.

OUTLINE OF THE BOOK 1.6

The ideas introduced in this chapter are developed in the remainder of the book.

- In Chapters 2 to 7, fundamental concepts underlying finance theory are developed.
- Chapters 8, 9 and 10 consider sources of finance for companies, and the institutional framework in which financing decisions are made.

- In Chapters 11, 12 and 13, payout decisions and financing decisions are discussed.
- Chapter 14 then considers the measurement of the cost of capital to be used in project evaluation, while Chapter 15 provides an analysis of leases.
- Chapter 16 reviews the literature on market efficiency, while Chapters 17 and 18 consider futures contracts and options respectively.
- Chapter 19 reviews the theory and evidence on takeovers.
- In Chapter 20, the application of the principles outlined earlier in the book to international financial management is explored, while Chapters 21 and 22 apply those principles to short-term asset management, including inventory, cash and accounts receivable.

Connect Plus features a case study illustrating topics covered in this chapter.
Ask your lecturer or tutor for your course's unique URL.

SUMMARY

In this chapter, we have introduced the key themes to be addressed in the book.

→ The two main components of finance are *corporate finance* and *investments*. This book focuses on financial decisions made by companies (corporate decisions), which include asset and working capital management decisions, capital structure and borrowing decisions, payout policy and merger and acquisition decisions; and financial decisions made by investors (investor decisions), including portfolio and risk decisions and asset pricing decisions.

→ The objective assumed in most of this book is that management seeks to maximise the market value of the company's ordinary shares (shareholders' equity). To do this, the financial manager must understand how financial markets work. The fundamental concepts in finance include value, the time value of money, risk aversion, nominal versus real values, market efficiency and asset pricing, derivative securities, arbitrage and agency relationships. The market value (V) of a company can be expressed as the market value of the company's debt (D) plus the market value of the company's equity (E).

KEY TERMS

arbitrage 8
company 5
limited liability 5
partnership 4
risk aversion 7
sole proprietorship 4
time value of money 7

QUESTIONS

1. [LO 2] Distinguish between investment decisions and financing decisions.
2. [LO 3] Explain the following:
   (a) a sole proprietorship
   (b) a partnership
   (c) a company.
3. [LO 3] Outline the advantages and disadvantages of a sole proprietorship.
4. [LO 3] Outline the advantages and disadvantages of a partnership.

5. **[LO 3]** What advantages does a company have over a sole proprietorship and a partnership?

6. **[LO 3]** Which types of investors have limited liability? Explain your answer.

7. **[LO 5]** Why do people usually prefer to receive $1 today instead of in a year's time?

8. **[LO 5]** Comment on this statement: *A company should borrow during times of high inflation because it can repay the loan in cheaper dollars.*

9. **[LO 5]** What is the relationship between diversifiable and non-diversifiable risk? How does this distinction affect the reward that investors receive for bearing risk?

10. **[LO 5]** What is meant by the term 'efficient market'? How does competition between traders promote efficiency?

11. **[LO 5]** What is meant by the term 'arbitrage'?

12. **[LO 5]** What is meant by the term 'agency relationships'?

CHAPTER 2
CONSUMPTION, INVESTMENT AND THE CAPITAL MARKET

LEARNING OBJECTIVES

After studying this chapter you should be able to:

1. explain how a company's managers can, in principle, make financial decisions that will be supported by all shareholders

2. explain how the existence of a capital market makes it possible for the company to make decisions acceptable to all shareholders

3. identify a company's optimal investment/dividend policy under conditions of certainty.

CHAPTER CONTENTS

2.1 Introduction

2.2 Fisher's Separation Theorem: a simplified example

2.3 Fisher's Separation Theorem: a formal approach

2.4 Investors' reactions to managers' decisions

This chapter is also featured in the complete e-book available with Connect Plus.
Ask your lecturer or tutor for your course's unique URL.

2.1 INTRODUCTION

In this chapter we present a theoretical framework, known as 'Fisher's Separation Theorem', that shows important relationships between companies, their shareholders and the capital market. We use this framework to make some observations on investment decisions, financing decisions and dividend policy. Although the framework we present is simple and rather abstract, it provides important insights into some fundamental issues in finance. To introduce the framework, we present in Section 2.2 a simplified numerical example that captures many of the main lessons of the theorem. Readers who do not wish to develop a detailed technical understanding of the theorem may wish to read only Section 2.2.

2.2 FISHER'S SEPARATION THEOREM: A SIMPLIFIED EXAMPLE[1]

2.2.1 INTRODUCTION TO THE EXAMPLE

Fisher's Separation Theorem can be traced to the work of Irving Fisher[2] and is widely regarded as laying a foundation for many fundamental results of finance theory. The theorem considers the following situation. Suppose that a company has to decide how much it should pay to its shareholders in dividends and how much it should retain for investment in the company. The more the company pays out in dividends, the less there is available for investment; the more the company invests, the less there is available to pay out as dividends. Might some shareholders want high dividends (and therefore low investment), while other shareholders want just the opposite? If so, will the company be forced to make a decision that will disappoint some of its shareholders? Fisher's answers are, yes, there may be this type of disagreement among the shareholders but, no, if there is a capital market then there is a way to please all shareholders. In this section, we outline a simplified example of Fisher's Separation Theorem that preserves much of its flavour but is based on intuition rather than a rigorous, technical approach.

> **LEARNING OBJECTIVE 1**
> Explain how a company's managers can, in principle, make financial decisions that will be supported by all shareholders

2.2.2 ASSUMPTIONS

Assume that a company is operating under conditions of certainty, that there are two time dates ('now' and 'later') and that there are two equal shareholders ('A' and 'B'). The company must decide[3] how much of its current resources it should invest and how much it should pay out as a current dividend. An investment now generates a return later, and the company then pays out all its resources as a final dividend. Shareholders can use their dividends to finance consumption. Initially, there is no capital market but at a later stage in the analysis it is assumed that transactions in a capital market are possible. The existence of the capital market enables individuals (including the shareholders A and B) to borrow and lend for one period at a fixed interest rate.

It is further assumed that the company has $800 in resources and has identified two possible investment projects called 'Project Small' and 'Project Upgrade'.

- Project Small requires an initial outlay of $500 now and will produce a cash inflow of $570 later.
- Project Upgrade requires a *further* outlay of $200 now and will produce a *further* cash inflow of $220 later.

---

1 This section is drawn from Brown (1996).
2 Fisher (1930). See also Hirshleifer (1970).
3 In fact, decisions are made by managers rather than by an inanimate 'company' but for ease of expression we frequently refer to a company making a decision. We have assumed that managers will seek to maximise the interests of the shareholders.

It is also assumed that it is impossible to invest only in Project Upgrade. Together, projects Small and Upgrade constitute 'Project Large'. Clearly, Project Large requires an outlay of $500 + $200 = $700 now and will produce a cash inflow of $570 + $220 = $790 later. If the company invests only in Project Small, it can pay a dividend of $800 − $500 = $300 now but if it invests in Project Large, it can pay a dividend of only $800 − $700 = $100 now.

This situation is summarised in Table 2.1.

TABLE 2.1 Investment/dividend opportunities facing the company

PROJECT	INVESTMENT OUTLAY NOW ($)	DIVIDEND NOW (EQUALS $800 MINUS OUTLAY) ($)	DIVIDEND LATER ($)
Small	500	300	570
Upgrade	200	n.a.[a]	220
Large	700	100	790

[a] Not applicable because Project Upgrade is not a stand-alone project.

2.2.3 THE SHAREHOLDERS' CONSUMPTION OPPORTUNITIES AND PREFERENCES

Recalling that Shareholders A and B hold equal shares, the consumption opportunities each faces are equal to half the total dividends paid by the company as shown in Table 2.1. For simplicity, it is also assumed that a dividend paid now cannot be stored in order to finance consumption later.[4] The consumption opportunities facing each shareholder are shown in Table 2.2.

TABLE 2.2 Consumption opportunities facing each shareholder

PROJECT SELECTED BY THE COMPANY	CONSUMPTION PER SHAREHOLDER NOW ($)	CONSUMPTION PER SHAREHOLDER LATER ($)
Small	150	285
Large	50	395

Suppose that Shareholder A wishes to consume $150 now, while Shareholder B wishes to consume only $50 now. Thus, Shareholder A wants a relatively high dividend now and therefore wants the company to invest in Project Small. Shareholder B, of course, is in the opposite position. Desiring only a low level of consumption now, Shareholder B wants the company to adopt a high level of investment and thus wants the company to invest in Project Large. Clearly, the company cannot make a decision that will satisfy both shareholders simultaneously and therefore it is not possible to say which investment is optimal. The company will be forced to make a decision that will be opposed by one of its two shareholders.

LEARNING OBJECTIVE 2

Explain how the existence of a capital market makes it possible for the company to make decisions acceptable to all shareholders

2.2.4 SOLUTION: INTRODUCE A CAPITAL MARKET

A solution can be found if there is a capital market in which the shareholders can borrow and lend on their personal accounts. In this example, it is assumed that the interest rate in the capital market is 12 per cent per period. It is now possible to state that there is an optimal decision that will be supported

---

4 This assumption simplifies the analysis but is not necessary. It is a simple matter to permit resources to be carried from one period to the next. In the absence of a capital market, resources can be carried forward in time at an interest rate of zero. However, any consumption opportunities opened up by allowing resources to be carried forward at an interest rate of zero will be more restricted than the opportunities that become available when a capital market is introduced and interest rates are positive.

by both shareholders. This decision is that the company should invest in Project Small and should reject the opportunity to invest in the upgrade that will convert Project Small to Project Large. In other words, allowing Shareholder B access to the capital market has caused B to change his or her support from wanting the company to invest in Project Large to wanting the company to invest in Project Small.

How do we know Shareholder B will react in this way? The answer is that the capital market allows Shareholder B to make financial arrangements that, from B's viewpoint, provide an even better outcome than is possible if the company invests in Project Large. This result can be proved as follows. When the company invests in Project Small, Shareholder B will receive a current dividend of $150. This will finance B's desired current consumption of $50, with $100 left over. This sum of $100 can be lent in the capital market for one period at an interest rate of 12 per cent, thus producing a later cash inflow to B of $100 × 1.12 = $112. This sum can then be added to the future dividend of $285. Therefore, on the later date, Shareholder B can consume resources to the value of $112 + $285 = $397. If, instead, Project Large were undertaken, Shareholder B could consume only $395 on the later date (see Table 2.2).

Therefore, provided there is a capital market, the shareholders will be unanimous and the company can make investment and dividend decisions confident that these decisions are optimal from the viewpoint of all shareholders.

2.2.5 AN ANALYSIS USING RATES OF RETURN

The analysis can be recast in terms of rates of return. The rates of return on the projects are:

$$\text{Project Small: } \frac{\$570 - 500}{\$500} = 14\%$$

$$\text{Project Upgrade: } \frac{\$220 - 200}{\$200} = 10\%$$

Comparing these rates of return with the interest rate of 12 per cent, the optimal decision is to accept Project Small (because 14 per cent exceeds 12 per cent) and to reject Project Upgrade (because 10 per cent is less than 12 per cent). In effect, the cost of investing is the opportunity cost of forgoing the capital market return of 12 per cent. For Project Small, the benefit (14 per cent) exceeds the opportunity cost (12 per cent), while for Project Upgrade the benefit (10 per cent) is lower than the opportunity cost (12 per cent).

Note also that while the *apparent* rate of return on Project Large is ($790 – $700)/$700 = 12.86 per cent, this rate of return is in fact a weighted average of the rates of return on the component projects Small and Upgrade. It is *not* valid to suggest that the company should invest in Project Large merely because 12.86 per cent exceeds 12 per cent.

2.2.6 A SOLUTION REQUIRING BORROWING

In Section 2.2.4, the interest rate (12 per cent) fell between the rates of return on Project Small (14 per cent) and Project Upgrade (10 per cent). Therefore, Project Small was accepted and, in turn, this decision required Shareholder B to lend in the capital market. If the interest rate had been lower than the rate of return on both projects—say it had been 9 per cent—then the optimal decision would have been to invest in both projects. In other words, Project Large would have been accepted. Therefore, the current dividend would have been only $50 per shareholder. While this decision would clearly have won the support of Shareholder B, who wishes to consume only $50 now, a current dividend of $50 per shareholder will be insufficient for Shareholder A to finance his or her desired current consumption of $150.

LEARNING OBJECTIVE 3

Identify a company's optimal investment/dividend policy under conditions of certainty

In this case, Shareholder A must borrow $100 from the capital market. At an interest rate of 9 per cent per period, the required repayment later is $100 × 1.09 = $109. This amount is paid out of the later dividend of $395, thus leaving Shareholder A with $395 − $109 = $286 to finance later consumption. This level exceeds the $285 of later consumption that would have been available to Shareholder A if the company had invested in only Project Small. Therefore, Shareholder A will also support the decision to invest in Project Large and there is again a unanimous decision.

2.2.7 FISHER'S SEPARATION THEOREM AND NET PRESENT VALUE

The problem facing the company's manager can also be solved by calculating a measure known as a project's 'net present value' (NPV). This measure is extremely important and is referred to in a number of later chapters. It is discussed in detail in Chapter 5. At this point we provide only a very brief introduction.

To calculate a project's net present value, we first use the project's required rate of return to convert future cash flows to their equivalent values today. We then subtract the initial outlay required. If the result is a positive number, then the project is an acceptable investment; if the result is a negative number, then the project is not acceptable. In the initial example of Project Small and Project Upgrade presented in Section 2.2.4, the interest rate in the capital market is 12 per cent. In this example, it is also the required rate of return on the project. The net present value calculations are:

$$NPV \text{ of Project Small} = \frac{\$570}{1.12} - \$500 = \$8.93 > 0$$

$$NPV \text{ of Project Upgrade} = \frac{\$220}{1.12} - \$200 = -\$3.57 < 0$$

Project Small is an acceptable investment because its NPV is positive, while Project Upgrade is not an acceptable investment because its NPV is negative. Thus, use of the NPV rule has led to the same investment decision as we discussed earlier in Section 2.2.4. Not only does an optimal decision exist, it can also be found by applying the NPV rule.

2.2.8 FISHER'S SEPARATION THEOREM: SUMMARY

LEARNING OBJECTIVE 1

Explain how a company's managers can, in principle, make financial decisions that will be supported by all shareholders

In the absence of a capital market, the shareholders disagreed on what decisions the company should make on their behalf. This problem could be 'solved' only by imposing a solution to the detriment of one of the shareholders. But if there is a capital market, the shareholders are sure to reach a unanimous decision. Thus, there is an optimal investment/dividend decision.

This resolution is possible because the existence of the capital market enables one of the shareholders to achieve a result that for him or her was indisputably better than the result that the company alone could provide, given the investment opportunities available. An optimal decision exists, and can be identified by the company's managers if they use the net present value (NPV) rule to analyse investment proposals.

2.3 FISHER'S SEPARATION THEOREM: A FORMAL APPROACH

The conclusions that we reached largely by intuition in Section 2.2 are reached in a more rigorous fashion in this section.

2.3.1 ASSUMPTIONS

The assumed objective of a company is to maximise the market value of its ordinary shares. A company's managers, therefore, have to make investment, financing and dividend decisions consistent with that objective. The managers' job would be easier if there were a consistent set of decision rules that could be employed in making investment, financing and dividend decisions. The work of Irving Fisher provides a framework in which such rules can be developed. Initially these decision rules are developed in a very simplified setting. However, the decision rules are applicable even when more realistic assumptions are made.

The assumptions in Fisher's analysis are:

(a) There are only two points in time: the present (Time 1) and a later time (Time 2).
(b) There is no uncertainty, and hence the outcome of all decisions is known now to everybody.
(c) There are no imperfections in the capital market.
(d) All decision makers are rational.
(e) The company's managers wish to use the company's resources according to the wishes of the shareholders.

2.3.2 THE COMPANY

The company is endowed with a fixed amount of resources at Time 1 and the managers have to decide how much of these resources should be invested and how much should be paid out as dividends. Any resources not paid out at Time 1 are invested, and the level of this investment determines the resources available to pay dividends at Time 2.

The opportunities available to the company are summarised in a **production possibilities curve** (PPC) as illustrated in Figure 2.1.

production possibilities curve (PPC)
curve that displays the investment opportunities and outcomes available to the company; its shape therefore determines the combinations of current dividends, investments and future dividends that a company can achieve

FIGURE 2.1 Production possibilities curve

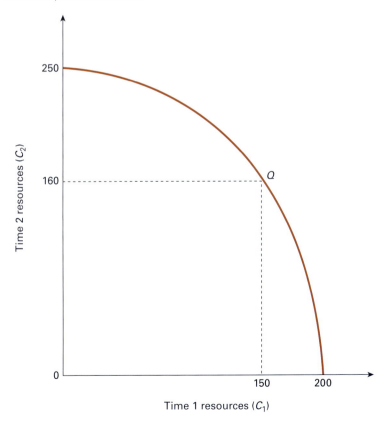

The horizontal axis measures resources available to the company at Time 1. Assume that the company has 200 units of resources available to it. It could pay this amount as a dividend at Time 1. In this case, investment would be zero and dividends at Time 2 would also be zero. The point (200, 0) represents this extreme decision. At the other extreme, the company could pay no dividend at Time 1 and invest the whole of the company's resources. This decision would result in 250 units being available for distribution as a dividend at Time 2 and is represented by the point (0, 250). Point Q is an intermediate case in which a dividend of 150 units is paid at Time 1, leaving 50 units to be invested. The PPC shows that an investment of 50 units at Time 1 can be transformed into 160 units of resources at Time 2. Therefore the dividend at Time 2 is 160 units.

2.3.3 THE SHAREHOLDERS

indifference curve
curve showing a set of combinations such that an individual derives equal utility from (and thus is indifferent between) any combinations in the set

Shareholders forgo current consumption by investing in the company at Time 1 in order to receive a return that then increases their consumption opportunities at Time 2. A person's preference for consumption at Time 1 (C_1) or at Time 2 (C_2) is represented by **indifference curves** as depicted in Figure 2.2. The term *indifference* indicates that the person derives equal utility from the bundles of C_1 and C_2 represented by all points on a single curve; for example, equal utility is derived from points X and Y in Figure 2.2. However, any point on a higher indifference curve is preferred to all points on lower curves; for example, Z is preferred to X and Y.

The slope of an indifference curve at any point shows the consumer's willingness to trade off C_1 for C_2.

It can be seen from Figure 2.2 that the indifference curves are convex; they approach the horizontal as the level of C_1 increases and approach the vertical as the level of C_2 increases. The implication is that a consumer's desire to increase consumption further at a given time decreases as the level of consumption at that time increases.

FIGURE 2.2 Indifference curves of a representative shareholder

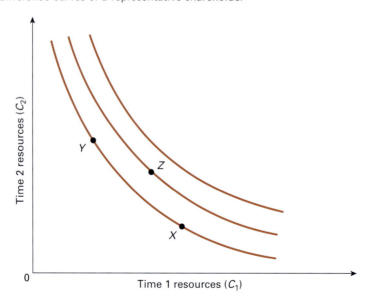

2.3.4 THE COMPANY'S DECISION

We now bring together the company and the shareholders in an attempt to identify the decision the company should make. We assume that there are two shareholders, 'A' and 'B'.

In Figure 2.3, indifference curves for Shareholder A are labelled A_1, A_2 and A_3 and indifference curves for Shareholder B are labelled B_1, B_2 and B_3. If the company chooses point A—that is, a current dividend of 90 and investment of 110, yielding a dividend of 228 at Time 2—then shareholder A's utility is maximised. However, Shareholder B's utility is not maximised at this point; it is maximised only if the company chooses point B. This requires a current dividend of 160 and investment of 40, yielding a dividend of 144 at Time 2.

FIGURE 2.3 The company with two shareholders: no capital market

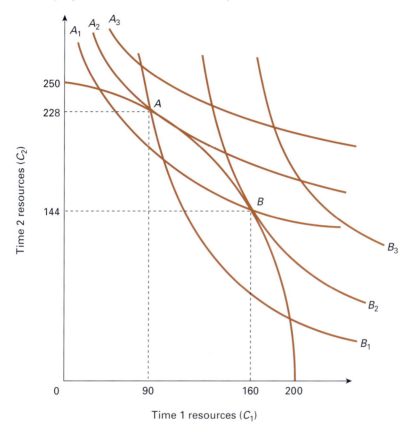

In short, the company is unable to reach a decision that will lead simultaneously to maximum utility for both shareholders. This situation poses a severe dilemma for the company because it means that the company must consider the preferences of each of its shareholders when making investment decisions. In other words, there is no simple decision rule that will satisfy all shareholders. Such a rule does exist, however, if there is a capital market.

2.3.5 SOLUTION: INTRODUCE A CAPITAL MARKET

In this simple model, the capital market can be thought of as a place where current resources may be transformed into future resources and vice versa. The rate at which these transformations may be made is in effect an interest rate. We assume that the capital market is frictionless, and therefore the interest rate for borrowers is equal to the interest rate for lenders. For example, if the interest rate is 10 per cent per period, and 100 units of current resources are placed with the capital market for one period, then $100 \times 1.1 = 110$ units of resources become available at Time 2. In effect, this is lending to the capital market. Similarly, if a person has a claim to receive 110 units of resources at Time 2, the capital market may be used to transform

LEARNING OBJECTIVE 2
Explain how the existence of a capital market makes it possible for the company to make decisions acceptable to all shareholders

this claim into 110/1.1 = 100 units of resources at Time 1. This transaction corresponds to a person borrowing 100 units at Time 1 and repaying the loan with a payment of 110 units at Time 2.

Suppose that a person has claims on resources in both periods. For example, a person may have an income of 100 units at Time 1 and an income of 165 units at Time 2. What consumption opportunities are available if the interest rate is 10 per cent per period? At one extreme, the person may choose to consume only at Time 2. In this case, consumption at Time 1 is zero and consumption at Time 2 is 165 + 100 × 1.1 = 275 units. At the other extreme, the person may choose to consume only at Time 1. In this case, consumption at Time 2 is zero and consumption at Time 1 is (165/1.1) + 100 = 250 units. Therefore, this person's claim on current resources is 250 units. In short, this person's *wealth* at Time 1 is 250 units. Figure 2.4 illustrates this case.

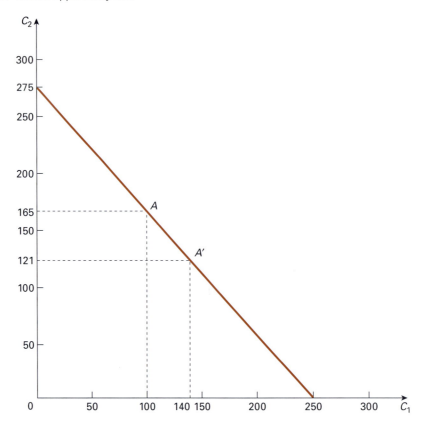

FIGURE 2.4 Market opportunity line

market opportunity line
line that shows the combinations of current and future consumption that an individual can achieve from a given wealth level, using capital market transactions

The line joining these two extreme positions is shown in Figure 2.4 and may be called a **market opportunity line** as it defines all combinations of consumption possibilities at the two Times, consistent with an initial wealth level of 250 units. If a person can reach any one point on this line, then by borrowing or lending, all other points on the line are also available to the person. For example, if a person can reach point A (100 units at Time 1 and 165 units at Time 2), then the person can also reach point A' (140 units at Time 1 and 121 units at Time 2), by borrowing 40 units today and repaying 44 units at Time 2.

The equation of a market opportunity line can be derived as follows. If a person's income at Time 1 is C_1 and at Time 2 is C_2, and the interest rate is i per period, then the person's wealth W_1 at Time 1 is:

$$W_1 = C_1 + \frac{C_2}{1+i}$$

Equivalently, this equation can be written as:

$$W_1(1 + i) = C_1(1 + i) + C_2$$

or

$$C_2 = -(1 + i)C_1 + W_1(1 + i)$$

This is a linear equation with slope $-(1 + i)$ and intercept $W_1(1 + i)$. With a current wealth level of 250 and an interest rate of 10 per cent per period the equation is:

$$C_2 = -(1 + 0.1)C_1 + 250(1.1)$$

and therefore

$$C_2 = -1.1C_1 + 275$$

To illustrate further the interpretation of market opportunity lines, suppose that the person is offered a choice of two income streams, A or B. Stream A consists of 100 units at Time 1 and 165 units at Time 2, while Stream B consists of 120 units at Time 1 and 55 units at Time 2. It has already been shown that if the interest rate is 10 per cent, Stream A corresponds to a wealth level of 250 units at Time 1 and the equation of the market opportunity line is $C_2 = -1.1C_1 + 275$. The wealth level corresponding to Stream B is $120 + 55/1.1 = 170$ units. The equation of the market opportunity line for Stream B is $C_2 = -1.1C_1 + 187$. These lines, together with the person's indifference curves, are shown in Figure 2.5.

FIGURE 2.5 Consumption opportunities offered by two wealth levels

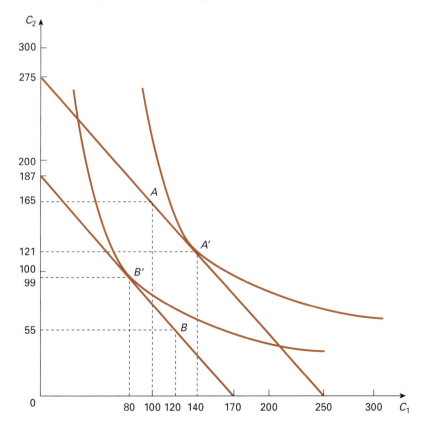

Figure 2.5 shows that this person will maximise utility by accepting income Stream A and then use a capital market transaction to convert Stream A to Stream A'. As we have seen, Stream A provides an income of 100 units at Time 1 and 165 units at Time 2, and a wealth level of 250 units. The person then enters the capital market and borrows 40 units at Time 1, achieving a consumption level of 140 units at Time 1. In return, the person's claim on Time 2 resources is reduced by 44 units (from 165 units to 121 units). The loan repayment required at Time 2 is, of course, 44 units (since $40 \times 1.1 = 44$).

Had Stream B been accepted, the optimal point would have been B', which could have been achieved by lending $120 - 80 = 40$ units at Time 1 and consuming $55 + (40)(1.1) = 99$ units at Time 2. However, point B' is on a lower indifference curve than point A' and therefore yields lower utility. To summarise: Stream A should be chosen because it corresponds to a higher wealth level, which, in turn, ensures that higher utility can be achieved, given access to a capital market.

2.3.6 PROVING THERE IS AN OPTIMAL POLICY

Fisher's Separation Theorem provides the optimal solution and involves all three elements: the company, the shareholders and the capital market.

Suppose that the company has E units of resources and is considering three investment/dividend policies, shown in Figure 2.6 as points P_1, P_2 and P.

FIGURE 2.6 Effect of company policy on shareholder wealth

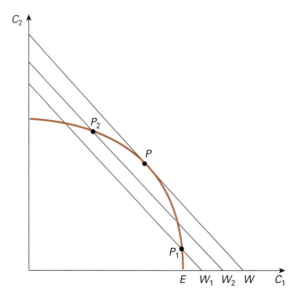

A market opportunity line with slope $-(1 + i)$ has been drawn through each of the three points. The line through P_1 shows that if policy P_1 were adopted, the shareholders' wealth would increase from E to W_1. Similarly, if policy P_2 were adopted, the shareholders' wealth would increase to W_2, and if policy P were adopted, the shareholders' wealth would be W. Because the utility of shareholders depends directly on their wealth, they will unanimously prefer policy P because the resulting wealth level W is the maximum achievable. Relative to policy P, it is clear that P_1 represents too little investment by the company, whereas P_2 represents too much investment by the company. Policy P, which occurs at the point of tangency between the PPC and the market opportunity line, is the optimal policy for the company and will receive the support of all shareholders. This result may be shown more formally by superimposing representative indifference curves for shareholders A and B on Figure 2.6. This is shown in Figure 2.7.

FIGURE 2.7 Fisher's Separation Theorem: two shareholders with access to a capital market

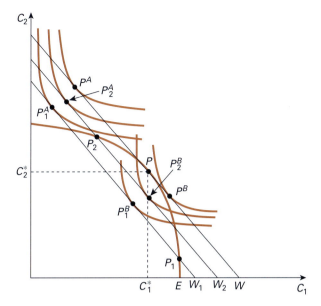

The company chooses policy P; that is, it invests $(E - C_1^*)$ and pays dividends of C_1^* at Time 1 and C_2^* at Time 2. Shareholder A enters the capital market and lends resources so that this shareholder's *personal* optimal point P^A is reached. Shareholder B borrows from the capital market in order to reach P^B, which is B's *personal* optimal point. Any policy other than P will result in lower utility for *both* shareholders. For example, if the company were to choose policy P_1, then Shareholder A's maximum utility would occur at point P_1^A, which is on a lower indifference curve than point P^A, while Shareholder B's maximum utility would occur at point P_1^B, which is on a lower indifference curve than point P^B. The same conclusion holds if the company were to choose policy P_2.

There is, therefore, just one policy P that will maximise the utility of all shareholders simultaneously. Regardless of differences in their utility functions (preferences), all shareholders will support the company's decision to choose policy P. In this sense, the company and its shareholders are *separate*. The company does *not* need to consult each shareholder before it makes its decision because it knows in advance that *all* shareholders, regardless of differences in their personal preferences, will support the choice of policy P. Since policy P does not require knowledge of any shareholder's utility function, it follows that P might be identifiable using data directly available to the company. That this is in fact the case is proved in the following section.

2.3.7 IDENTIFYING THE OPTIMAL POLICY

Suppose that a company is endowed with E units of current resources and is considering a number of *small* investment projects, each requiring an outlay of Δ units of resources. It has compiled a list of these projects, ranked from the highest rate of return to the lowest. The project with the highest rate of return will return C_2' units at Time 2. The company proposes the following decision rule: accept the project if and only if:

$$\frac{\text{Return at Time 2}}{1 + i} - \Delta > 0$$

This is illustrated in Figure 2.8.

FIGURE 2.8

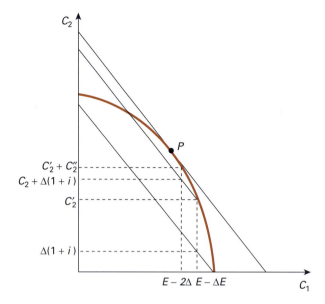

It is clear from Figure 2.8 that $C'_2 > \Delta(1+i)$ and therefore:

$$\frac{C'_2}{1+i} - \Delta > 0$$

Under the proposed rule, the project is accepted. Fisher's Separation Theorem also recommends acceptance since policy P has not yet been achieved. Now consider the second project, which also requires an outlay of Δ and which returns C''_2 at Time 2. Reading from Figure 2.8, it is found that:

$$C'_2 + C''_2 > C'_2 + \Delta(1+i)$$

and therefore

$$\frac{C''_2}{1+i} - \Delta > 0$$

Both Fisher's Separation Theorem and the decision rule recommend acceptance of this second project. Projects will continue to be accepted until policy P is reached. Beyond that point, both the theorem and the rule recommend rejection of all further projects on the list. This is shown in Figure 2.9 (see p. 25).

Reading from Figure 2.9 it is found that:

$$C''_2 + \Delta(1+i) > C''_2 + C'''_2$$

and therefore

$$\frac{C'''_2}{1+i} - \Delta < 0$$

Therefore, both the proposed rule and the theorem recommend rejection of this project.

The proposed rule and the theorem are completely consistent. All projects that are acceptable according to the theorem are also acceptable according to the rule. All projects rejected by the theorem are also rejected by the rule. Therefore, a company that always applies this rule to its investment decisions will be able to locate the optimal investment/dividend policy and will maximise the wealth of its shareholders. In turn, the shareholders can use the capital market to achieve their preferred consumption patterns and thereby maximise utility.

FIGURE 2.9

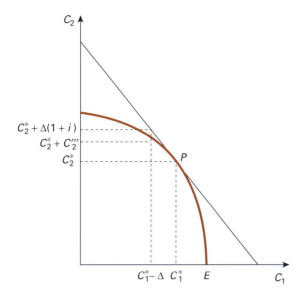

The name given to this rule is the net present value rule. The return next period is divided by the factor $(1 + i)$ to convert the future return into a present value. The investment outlay is then subtracted from the present value to give the net present value (NPV). If the NPV is positive, the project will increase the wealth of the shareholders and should therefore be accepted. If the NPV is negative, the project will decrease the wealth of the shareholders and should therefore be rejected. The NPV rule is frequently used in practice and is considered further in Chapter 5.

2.3.8 IMPLICATIONS FOR FINANCIAL DECISION MAKING

A number of implications for investment, financing and dividend decisions can be drawn from Fisher's analysis. These implications will hold where there are perfect markets for both capital and information. However, Fisher's analysis is unaffected by the introduction of uncertainty, provided it is assumed that all participants have the same expectations.[5] Further, although the presentation of Fisher's analysis has been confined to a case involving only two periods, its implications are unaffected by extension to the multiperiod case.[6]

The investment decision

Fisher's Separation Theorem means that a company can make investment decisions in the interests of every shareholder, regardless of differences between shareholders' preferences—that is, a company can make an investment decision with which every shareholder will agree. Moreover, there is a rule that will identify that decision: a company should invest up to the point where the net present value of the marginal unit of investment is zero. In this simple model, an equivalent rule is to invest up to the point where the rate of return on the marginal unit of investment equals the market interest rate. These two rules and other commonly implemented investment evaluation techniques are considered in Chapter 5 in the context of certainty. This discussion is extended in Chapter 6 to investment evaluation where there is uncertainty.

---

5 Fama and Miller (1972, pp. 301–4).
6 ibid., pp. 64–7.

The financing decision

In Fisher's analysis there is a single market interest rate. In effect, there is no distinction between debt and equity securities, and the cost to the company of acquiring funds is independent of the type of security issued. It follows that the value of the company and the wealth of its shareholders are independent of the company's capital structure. As a result, the financing decision can be described as 'irrelevant'. When the financing decision is discussed in Chapter 12 this result is confirmed in a less restrictive framework.

The dividend decision

In Fisher's analysis, all resources not invested at Time 1 are distributed to shareholders as dividends, and all returns at Time 2 are also distributed as dividends—that is, it is assumed that the company does not borrow or lend in the capital market, although its shareholders may do so. Suppose, however, that the company is permitted to borrow or lend in the capital market. In that case, the company has greater choice in its dividend policy, while maintaining the same level of investment. For example, the company could pay a higher dividend at Time 1 and borrow the resources needed to maintain investment at the optimal level given by the point of tangency between the PPC and the market opportunity line. This is illustrated in Figure 2.10.

FIGURE 2.10

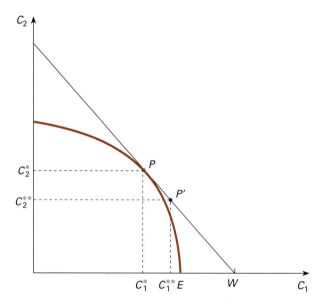

Compared with the basic Fisher analysis (Fig. 2.7), the company in Figure 2.10 pays a larger dividend at Time 1 ($C_1^{**} > C_1^*$) and a smaller dividend at Time 2 ($C_2^{**} < C_2^*$). To maintain the company's investment level at $E - C_1^*$, the company borrows $C_1^{**} - C_1^*$ from the capital market. At Time 2 the company's gross return is C_2^* but the loan repayment reduces the net return at Time 2 to C_2^{**}. In short, the company's investment decision is unchanged but its dividend decision is different. The important point to note is that the new policy P' lies on the same market opportunity line as the original 'Fisher policy' P and therefore the wealth of shareholders is unchanged. The ability of shareholders to maximise their utility is also unchanged. As explained previously, if any one point on a market opportunity line is attainable, then, by borrowing or lending, all other points on the line are also attainable. From the shareholders' point of view, therefore, point P' is no better or worse than point P.

In summary, provided that the company does not alter its investment decision, the dividend decision does not affect shareholders' wealth. In this sense dividend policy is irrelevant. This proposition is discussed further in Chapter 11.

INVESTORS' REACTIONS TO MANAGERS' DECISIONS

2.4

The link between decisions made by a company's managers and the resultant actions by investors is illustrated in Figure 2.11.

FIGURE 2.11

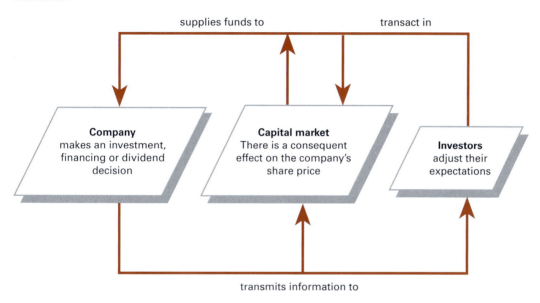

A company's managers may, on behalf of the company, make an investment decision, a financing decision or a dividend decision. Information about this decision is transmitted to investors. On the basis of this information, investors may adjust their expectations of future returns from an investment in the company, and revise their valuation of the company's shares. Investors will then compare the current market price of the company's shares with their revised valuation and either buy or sell shares in the company. Investors' actions in the share market will determine the new market price of the company's shares.

2.4.1 CERTAINTY

Pursuing a goal of maximising the market value of a company's shares is easy when there are no market imperfections and no uncertainty. Managers know with certainty an investment's cash flows and its net present value. Therefore, they will know whether acceptance of the investment will increase the market value of the company's shares. As all investors also know the investment's net present value, there will be an immediate increase in the price of the company's shares to reflect the resulting increase in the wealth of the company. Further, managers and investors know that financing and dividend decisions are irrelevant and therefore these decisions will have no effect on the market value of the company's shares.

2.4.2 THE INTRODUCTION OF UNCERTAINTY

In practice there *is* uncertainty. What effect will the acceptance of an investment proposal have on the market value of a company's shares? As is illustrated in Figure 2.11, any change in the company's share price will depend on the reaction of investors to the decisions made by the managers. Obviously there can be no reaction unless investors obtain information about that decision. When there is uncertainty, the effect on the share price of decisions made by managers is no longer perfectly predictable. A simplification is to assume that everyone agrees about the probability distribution of the outcomes of all decisions. This means that although there is uncertainty, the exact nature of that uncertainty is agreed on by all. In this case, when investors obtain information, the share price will adjust immediately to reflect the new best estimate of the 'true' value of the company.

Sufficient conditions for this to arise are: '… a market in which (i) there are no transaction costs in trading securities, (ii) all available information is costlessly available to all market participants and (iii) all agree on the implications of current information for the current price and distribution of future prices of each security'.[7]

As these conditions are not satisfied in existing capital markets, it is fortunate that they are sufficient but *not* necessary conditions.[8] For example, managers' decisions may still have an impact on share prices even though there are transaction costs and/or there are only a limited number of investors who have access to information about these decisions.

It is true that departures from the sufficient conditions give rise to the problem that managers are unable to predict with certainty the impact that a particular decision will have on a company's share price. Fortunately there is a great deal of empirical evidence on the reaction of share prices to the release of information. This evidence is reviewed in Chapter 16. At this point we simply note that there is evidence in well-developed capital markets (such as the Australian capital market) that there are investors who react quickly to the receipt of new information, with the result that this information will be reflected in security prices. In general, therefore, managers should not depart from a course that they expect will increase the value of the company's shares.

WWW A case study illustrating topics within this chapter can be found on the Online Learning Centre that accompanies this book: www.mhhe.com/au/peirson11e

Connect Plus features a case study illustrating topics covered in this chapter.
Ask your lecturer or tutor for your course's unique URL.

SUMMARY

→ A company's shareholders are likely to be a diverse group, with different preferences regarding current and future consumption. Therefore, it might be thought that when making decisions on investments and dividends, a company's managers would find it impossible to meet the wishes of all shareholders.

→ Fisher showed that, provided there is a capital market through which shareholders can borrow and lend, a company can make decisions that will be supported by all shareholders.

---

7 Fama (1970, p. 387).
8 ibid., pp. 387–8.

→ The company should invest up to the point where the return on the marginal investment equals the interest rate in the capital market. Therefore, the optimal decisions can be identified using net present value (NPV) analysis. These decisions will maximise the wealth of the shareholders. In this sense, the company and its shareholders are 'separate'; the company's managers can make optimal decisions without having to discover the preferences of individual shareholders.

→ Although the world of business is considerably more complicated than Fisher's simple model, the central messages of his theorem remain a useful guide for company managers.

KEY TERMS

indifference curve   18   market opportunity line   20   production possibilities curve   17

REFERENCES

Brown, R.L., 'Fisher's Separation Theorem: an alternative approach', *Accounting Research Journal*, 1996, vol. 9, no. 1, pp. 78–81.

Fama, E., 'Efficient capital markets: a review of theory and empirical work', *Journal of Finance*, May 1970, pp. 383–417.

Fama, E. & Miller, M., *The Theory of Finance*, Holt, Rinehart & Winston, New York, 1972.

Fisher, I., *The Theory of Interest*, Macmillan Company, New York, 1930.

Hirshleifer, J., *Investment, Interest and Capital*, Prentice-Hall, Englewood Cliffs, New Jersey, 1970.

QUESTIONS

1. **[LO 2]** Outline the roles played by companies, shareholders and the capital market in Fisher's analysis.

2. **[LO 3]** *Fisher's Separation Theorem ties together many of the basic notions that underlie much of modern finance theory: wealth maximisation, utility maximisation and net present value.* Discuss.

3. **[LO 3]** What is Fisher's Separation Theorem? What are its major implications for financial decision making?

4. **[LO 3]** *Financial decision making is a trivial task in a world of certainty.* Discuss.

5. **[LO 3]** What are the implications for financial decision making when the interest rate on borrowing is greater than the interest rate on lending?

PROBLEMS

1. **Investment decisions: applying Fisher's Separation Theorem [LO 3]**

   A company faces a similar situation to the one described in Section 2.2. It has two equal shareholders (A and B), is operating under conditions of certainty in a two-period framework ('now' and 'later') and is considering an investment in Project Small, which can be upgraded to Project Large. Project Small requires an outlay of $11 000 today and will return $12 100 later. Project Upgrade requires an outlay of $6000 today and will return $6500 later. The company has $20 000 in resources. There is a capital market in which the interest rate for both borrowing and lending is 5 per cent per period.

   (a) Using the net present value rule, show that the company should invest in Project Large (that is, it should invest in both Project Small and Project Upgrade).

   (b) How much will the company pay each shareholder in dividends today, and how much will it pay each shareholder in dividends later?

   (c) Suppose that Shareholder A wishes to consume $4000 today. What does she do? How much will she be able to consume later? Show that this outcome is better for Shareholder A than if the company had invested only in Project Small.

   (d) Suppose instead that Shareholder A wishes to consume equal amounts now and later, and the company invests in Project Large. What does she do? Show that this action will deliver the desired outcome for Shareholder A.

2. **Investment decisions: applying Fisher's Separation Theorem [LO 3]**

   Consider exactly the same situation as in Problem 1, except that the interest rate is 9 per cent per period.

   (a) Using the net present value rule, show that the company should invest only in Project Small.
   (b) How much will the company pay each shareholder in dividends today, and how much will it pay each shareholder in dividends later?
   (c) Suppose that Shareholder A wishes to consume $4000 today. What does she do? How much will she be able to consume later?
   (d) Compare Shareholder A's consumption in Problem 1(c) with her consumption in Problem 2(c).

3. **Investment planning [LO 3]**

   Consider the following situation:
   - A company starts with $12 million in cash.
   - The interest rate is 15 per cent.
   - The optimal policy for the company is to invest $6 million in assets.
   - The net present value of this investment is $2 million.

   Answer the following questions:

   (a) In 1 year's time, how much will the company receive from the investment?
   (b) Draw, to scale, the Fisher diagram that represents this case.
   (c) What are the marginal and average rates of return on the investment?
   (d) What is the total wealth of the company's shareholders immediately after the investment plan is announced?

4. **Effect of an interest rate decrease [LO 3]**

   Resketch your diagram for Problem 3 to show the effect of an interest rate decrease on the company's investment plan. Show the net present value of the revised investment plan. Would all investors be made better off by the decrease in interest rates and the consequential revision in the investment plan? Give reasons for your answer.

5. **Effect of higher investment [LO 3]**

   Return to the diagram you have drawn for Problem 3. Suppose that the company decides to invest $7.5 million—that is, $1.5 million more than before. Redraw the market opportunity line consistent with this new level of investment. What effect has the increased level of investment had on the company's shareholders?

6. **Calculating with and without a capital market [LO 2]**

   Assume a three-date model in which a rational person has an endowment of $200 now, $100 in Year 1 and $50 in Year 2. If the person wishes to consume $40 now and $120 in Year 2, what could she consume in Year 1 if:

   (a) there is no capital market?
   (b) there is a capital market in which the interest rate is 5 per cent per year?

CHAPTER 3
THE TIME VALUE OF MONEY: AN INTRODUCTION TO FINANCIAL MATHEMATICS

LEARNING OBJECTIVES

After studying this chapter you should be able to:

1. understand and solve problems involving simple interest and compound interest, including accumulating, discounting and making comparisons using the effective interest rate
2. value, as at any date, contracts involving multiple cash flows
3. distinguish between different types of annuity and calculate their present value and future value
4. apply your knowledge of annuities to solve a range of problems, including problems involving principal-and-interest loan contracts
5. distinguish between simple and general annuities and make basic calculations involving general annuities.

CHAPTER CONTENTS

3.1 Introduction
3.2 Fundamental concepts of financial mathematics
3.3 Simple interest
3.4 Compound interest
3.5 Valuation of contracts with multiple cash flows
3.6 Annuities
3.7 Principal-and-interest loan contracts
3.8 General annuities

3.1 INTRODUCTION

Financial mathematics provides the finance specialist with some extremely useful tools with which to solve financial problems. In this chapter, we present the major tools of financial mathematics and indicate some of their important applications. You will find that a thorough understanding of these tools, and how they may be used, will be very valuable when you study later chapters. Although you will find a large number of formulae in this chapter, you will not master financial mathematics if you simply try to memorise the formulae. If you fully understand the approach and the logic that are embodied in the formulae, you will not need to memorise them.

3.2 FUNDAMENTAL CONCEPTS OF FINANCIAL MATHEMATICS

In this section, we explain four fundamental concepts used in financial mathematics: cash flows, rate of return, interest rate and time value of money.

3.2.1 CASH FLOWS

Financial mathematics concerns the analysis of **cash flows** between parties to a **financial contract**.[1] For example, when money is borrowed there is an initial flow of cash from the lender to the borrower, and subsequently one (or more) cash (re)payments from the borrower to the lender. In financial mathematics, as in finance generally, we are concerned with the cash flow consequences of a decision or a contract. How much cash will flow between the parties? When will these cash flows occur? These are the basic questions that must first be answered when analysing a financial contract using the tools of financial mathematics. We are not concerned with the possible non-cash consequences of a contract, such as effects on reported profit; nor are we concerned with effects on parties outside the contract.

cash flow payment (cash outflow) or receipt (cash inflow) of money

financial contract arrangement, agreement or investment that produces cash flows

3.2.2 RATE OF RETURN

Financial decision makers usually find it convenient to relate the cash inflows that result from a contract to the cash outflows that the contract requires. Typically, this information is presented as a **rate of return**. Where there are only two cash flows in a financial contract—one at the start of the contract and another at the end—the rate of return is usually measured by:[2]

$$r = \frac{C_1 - C_0}{C_0} \qquad [3.1]$$

where C_1 = cash inflow at Time 1
C_0 = cash outflow at Time 0
r = rate of return per period

rate of return calculation that expresses the ratio of net cash inflows to cash outflows

The value of $C_1 - C_0$ measures the dollar return to the investor. Dividing the dollar return by C_0, which is the investment outlay, measures the rate of return. Example 3.1 illustrates the calculation of a rate of return.

---

1 We use the term 'contract' broadly. For example, we include depositing money in a bank as an act carried out as part of the contract between the depositor and the bank.
2 There are other measures. For example, under some circumstances it is convenient to measure the rate of return by $\ell n(C_1/C_0)$ [natural logarithm]. This measure is discussed further in Section 3.4.4.

EXAMPLE 3.1

On 1 January 2011, Paul buys an antique clock for $20 000. On 1 January 2012, the clock is sold for $24 000. What rate of return has been achieved?

SOLUTION

Using Equation 3.1, the rate of return is:

$$r = \frac{C_1 - C_0}{C_0}$$

$$= \frac{\$24\,000 - \$20\,000}{\$20\,000}$$

$$= \frac{\$4000}{\$20\,000}$$

$$= \frac{1}{5}$$

$$= 20\% \text{ per annum}$$

Note that a rate of return is always measured over a time period. In Example 3.1 the time period is 1 year. It is meaningless to state that an investment has returned, say, 20 per cent without also specifying the time period involved.

3.2.3 INTEREST RATE

interest rate
rate of return on debt

debt
financial contract in which the receiver of the initial cash (the borrower) promises a particular cash flow, usually calculated using an interest rate, to the provider of funds (the lender)

time value of money
principle that a dollar is worth more (less), the sooner (later) it is to be received, all other things being equal

The term '**interest rate**' is an important special case of the more general term 'rate of return' and is used when the financial contract is in the form of debt. Although a precise definition of **debt** is difficult, the general principle involved is that one party (the borrower) provides a specific promise regarding the future cash flow(s) payable to the other party (the lender). Debt may be contrasted with agreements, where no particular promise is made regarding the future cash flows. For example, when Paul purchased the antique clock in Example 3.1 he was not promised any particular future cash inflow. Similarly, where an investment is made in ordinary shares, the shareholder is not promised any particular cash inflow(s) from the investment.

3.2.4 TIME VALUE OF MONEY

One of the most important principles of finance is that money has a **time value**. This principle means that a given sum of money (say, a cash flow of $100) should be valued differently, depending on *when* the cash flow is to occur.

Suppose you have the choice of receiving $100 either today or in 1 year's time. As a rational person you will choose to take the money today. Even if you do not plan to spend the money until 1 year later, you will still choose to take the money today rather than in 1 year's time because you will be able to earn interest on the money during the coming year. Because of the interest you will earn, you will have more than $100 in 1 year's time. Obviously, from your point of view this is better than receiving only $100 in 1 year's time. By choosing to take the $100 today, rather than $100 in 1 year's time, you are in effect saying that $100 received today is more valuable to you than the promise of $100 to be received in 1 year's time. To put this another way, you have implied that $100 to be received in 1 year's time is worth less than $100 today. You have recognised that money has a time value.[3]

---

[3] Other reasons for taking the money today, rather than later, are *risk* (you are not certain that the future cash flow will be paid) and *expected inflation* (you fear that in a year's time the purchasing power of $100 will be lower than it is today). While these reasons are valid, note that money has a time value, even in the absence of these reasons—that is, even if the risk is zero (you are certain that the future cash flow will be paid) and you expect that the inflation rate next year will be zero or negative (purchasing power either will not change or will increase), you will *still* take the $100 today, in preference to $100 later, simply because interest rates are positive.

An important consequence of the fact that money has a time value is that we cannot validly add cash flows that will occur on different dates. Suppose you are offered $100 today *and* a further $100 in 1 year's time. How much is this offer worth to you? At this stage we cannot answer this question, except to say that the value today is *less than* $200. The value today of the cash flow of $100 in 1 year's time is less than $100, so the total value of the two cash flows must be less than $200. In financial mathematics it is extremely important never to attempt to add cash flows that will occur on different dates.

SIMPLE INTEREST

3.3.1 THE BASIC IDEA OF SIMPLE INTEREST

Many financial contracts specify the interest rate to be paid, rather than specifying explicitly the cash payment(s) required. Suppose, for example, that you borrow $1000, and agree to repay the loan by making a lump sum payment in 1 year's time at an interest rate of 12 per cent per annum. Then:

Interest owed = 0.12 × $1000 = $120
Lump sum payment = $1000 + $120 = $1120

This example is, of course, very straightforward. Only one time period is involved—in this case it happens to be 1 year—and the interest rate is quoted on a matching (annual) basis. There is little scope for confusion in this case. But suppose the contract had specified a lump sum repayment after 2 years, but the interest rate was quoted as 12 per cent *per annum*. How do we apply an annual rate to a period that is not equal to 1 year?

To answer this question we need a rule or convention to enable us to apply an annual interest rate to a period of 2 years. There are several ways in which this can be done, one of which is **simple interest**. A distinguishing feature of simple interest is that, during the entire term of the loan, interest is computed on the original sum borrowed. For example, suppose that a loan of $100 must be repaid in a lump sum after 2 years. Simple interest is to be charged at the rate of 12 per cent per annum. Because simple interest is being used, interest in *both* years is charged on the sum of $100. The interest in each year is thus $12, so the lump sum repayment is $124. Therefore, the interest rate payable at the maturity (termination) of the loan will in fact be 2 × 12 per cent = 24 per cent. Similarly, if payment was instead due after half a year, a simple interest rate of 12 per cent per annum means that, in fact, interest will be paid at the rate of ½ × 12 per cent = 6 per cent per half-year. Example 3.2 illustrates simple interest.

3.3

LEARNING OBJECTIVE 1
Understand and solve problems involving simple interest and compound interest, including accumulating, discounting and making comparisons using the effective interest rate

simple interest
method of calculating interest in which, during the entire term of the loan, interest is computed on the original sum borrowed

EXAMPLE 3.2

Molly's Bakeries Ltd borrows $10 000 and agrees to repay the loan by a lump sum payment in 6 months' time. The interest rate is 8 per cent per annum (simple). Calculate the lump sum payment.

SOLUTION

$$\text{Interest rate per half-year} = \frac{1}{2} \times 8\%$$
$$= 4\%$$
$$\text{Interest payable} = \$10\,000 \times 0.04$$
$$= \$400$$
$$\text{Lump sum payable} = \$10\,000 + \$400$$
$$= \$10\,400$$

3.3.2 FORMULA DEVELOPMENT: FUTURE SUM

principal
amount borrowed at the outset of a loan

future sum
amount to which a present sum, such as a principal, will grow (accumulate) at a future date, through the operation of interest

Suppose an amount P—also known as the **principal**—is borrowed and will be repaid in a lump sum. The interest rate is r per period (for example, per annum) and repayment is required after t periods. Using simple interest, the interest payable is based on the original principal, so the interest owing after one period is $P \times r$. After t periods the interest payable is simply $P \times r \times t$. Therefore, the required **future sum** S, that will repay the amount borrowed, is given by:

$$S = \text{principal and interest}$$
$$= P + Prt$$

$$S = P(1 + rt) \quad\quad [3.2]$$

Example 3.3 illustrates the use of Equation 3.2 to calculate a future sum using simple interest.

EXAMPLE 3.3

(a) Use Equation 3.2 to calculate Molly's repayment of a loan of $10 000 after 6 months if simple interest is used and the interest rate is 8 per cent per annum.
(b) What would be the repayment if the lump sum repayment were instead required after 15 months?

SOLUTION

(a) $S = P(1 + rt)$
$= \$10\,000 \left[1 + 0.08 \left(\frac{6}{12}\right)\right]$
$= 10\,000 \times 1.04$
$= \$10\,400$

(b) $S = P(1 + rt)$
$= 10\,000 \left[1 + 0.08 \left(\frac{15}{12}\right)\right]$
$= \$10\,000 \times 1.10$
$= \$11\,000$

3.3.3 FORMULA DEVELOPMENT: PRESENT VALUE

present value
amount that corresponds to today's value of a promised future sum

In many practical cases, we know the future repayment S, the interest rate r and the time period t, and our problem is to find the principal P (or **present value**) that is implied. In this case we simply rearrange Equation 3.2 to find:

$$P = \frac{S}{1 + rt} \quad\quad [3.3]$$

The present value P is the sum of money that corresponds to today's value of the future sum promised. The fact that P is not equal to S follows from the fact that money has a time value. Importantly, P in Equation 3.3 can also be thought of as a price. If a prospective borrower promises to pay a sum S in t years' time, then given the interest rate r, we can calculate the price (value) of the borrower's promised future payment of S. In other words, if we view the loan from the lender's perspective, the principal represents the price (or present value) paid by the lender to secure from the borrower the promise to pay the future cash flow required by the contract. Looked at from the borrower's viewpoint, the promised future cash flow has been sold by the borrower to the lender for its present value, which is the loan principal.

3.3.4 APPLICATIONS OF SIMPLE INTEREST

There are many commercial applications of simple interest. For example, simple interest is used for Treasury notes, bills of exchange and many bank deposits. Because large sums of money are often involved, there must be clear rules or conventions used in applying simple interest. These conventions can differ between countries. Using bills of exchange as an example, the Australian conventions are:

(a) Interest rates are quoted on an annual basis.
(b) The time period *t* is calculated as the exact number of days divided by 365.
(c) In a leap year, 29 February is included in the number of days, but the year is still assumed to consist of 365 days.
(d) Calculations are made to the nearest cent.

Bills of exchange are discussed in detail in Section 10.5.3. The conventions used in Australia are illustrated in Examples 3.4 and 3.5.

EXAMPLE 3.4

Stars Ltd borrows $100 000 on 20 January 2012, to be repaid in a lump sum on 2 March 2012. The interest rate is 8.75 per cent per annum. Calculate the lump sum repayment.

SOLUTION

The time period involved is 42 days, consisting of 11 days in January, 29 days in February and 2 days in March; note that we do not count *both* 20 January and 2 March but we *do* count 29 February because 2012 is a leap year.

Using Equation 3.2 and the conventions explained in this section the lump sum repayment is:

$$S = P(1 + rt)$$
$$= \$100\,000 \left[1 + (0.0875)\left(\frac{42}{365}\right)\right]$$
$$= \$100\,000 \times 1.010\,068\,493$$
$$= \$101\,006.85$$

EXAMPLE 3.5

Moon Ltd promises to pay $500 000 in 60 days' time. For a company with Moon's credit standing the market interest rate for a loan period of 60 days is 14.4 per cent per annum. How much can Moon borrow?

SOLUTION

Using Equation 3.3 and the conventions explained in this section, Moon can borrow the sum of:

$$P = \frac{S}{1 + rt}$$
$$= \frac{\$500\,000}{1 + (0.144)\left(\frac{60}{365}\right)}$$
$$= \frac{\$500\,000}{1.023\,671\,232}$$
$$= \$488\,438.07$$

3.4 COMPOUND INTEREST

3.4.1 THE BASIC IDEA OF COMPOUND INTEREST

When interest is received by a lender, the interest can then be lent and, in due course, will earn further interest. The basic idea of **compound interest** is that interest is periodically added to the principal.

Thus interest generates further interest, which then generates still more interest, and so on. This process is illustrated in Example 3.6.

EXAMPLE 3.6

On 31 December 2010, Kee Saw deposited $100 000 in a bank account that paid interest at the rate of 5 per cent per annum. How much was in the account after 4 years?

SOLUTION

The history of Kee Saw's account is as follows:

		BALANCE
31 December 2010	Account opened	$100 000.00
31 December 2011	Interest 0.05 × $100 000.00 = $5000.00	$105 000.00
31 December 2012	Interest 0.05 × $105 000.00 = $5250.00	$110 250.00
31 December 2013	Interest 0.05 × $110 250.00 = $5512.50	$115 762.50
31 December 2014	Interest 0.05 × $115 762.50 = $5788.13	$121 550.63

As the growth in Kee Saw's account balance makes clear, with compound interest, the amount of interest each year increases. For example, in the first year the interest received was $5000.00 but in the fourth year the interest received was $5788.13. After 4 years, Kee Saw's account balance is $121 550.63 but had the account been paid interest at the fixed amount of $5000 per annum—that is, if Kee Saw had not been able to reinvest interest to earn further interest—the balance would have been only $120 000. Therefore, in 4 years, Kee Saw earned $1550.63 of 'interest on interest'.

compound interest interest calculated each period on the principal amount and on any interest earned on the investment up to that point

3.4.2 FORMULA DEVELOPMENT: FUTURE SUM AND PRESENT VALUE

Assume that a principal of P dollars is deposited—that is, lent to a bank or other financial institution—for a term of n periods, with interest paid at the rate i per period at the end of each period. Our task is to develop a formula for the future sum S that will be **accumulated** after n periods, allowing for compound interest.

After one period the interest earned is iP, so the account balance at the end of the first period is $P + iP = P(1 + i)$. In fact the balance (or accumulated sum) at the end of any given period is simply the balance at the start of that period multiplied by $(1 + i)$. During the second period interest will be earned on the amount $P(1 + i)$.

So:

$$\begin{aligned}\text{Balance at end of Period 2} &= (\text{balance at start of Period 2}) \times (1 + i)\\ &= (\text{balance at end of Period 1}) \times (1 + i)\\ &= P(1 + i) \times (1 + i)\\ &= P(1 + i)^2\end{aligned}$$

Similarly:

$$\begin{aligned}\text{Balance at end of Period 3} &= (\text{balance at start of Period 3}) \times (1 + i)\\ &= (\text{balance at end of Period 2}) \times (1 + i)\end{aligned}$$

accumulation process by which, through the operation of interest, a present sum becomes a greater sum in the future

$$= P(1 + i)^2 \times (1 + i)$$
$$= P(1 + i)^3$$

Generalising from this discussion, the sum accumulated after n periods is given by $P(1 + i)^n$, so the formula for the future sum S is:

$$S = P(1 + i)^n \qquad [3.4]$$

The corresponding formula to find the present value P of a future sum S is:

$$P = \frac{S}{(1+i)^n} \qquad [3.5]$$

where S = future sum after n periods
 P = principal (or price or present value)
 i = interest rate per period
 n = number of periods

To illustrate Equation 3.4 we use the information in Example 3.6. The value of Kee Saw's deposit after selected terms is shown in Table 3.1.

TABLE 3.1 Accumulated value (future sum) of $100 000 at 5 per cent per annum

DATE	NUMBER OF YEARS COMPLETED	CALCULATION	ACCUMULATED VALUE ($)
31 December 2011	1	$100 000 (1.05)	105 000.00
31 December 2012	2	$100 000 (1.05)^2	110 250.00
31 December 2013	3	$100 000 (1.05)^3	115 762.50
31 December 2014	4	$100 000 (1.05)^4	121 550.63
31 December 2015	5	$100 000 (1.05)^5	127 628.16
31 December 2020	10	$100 000 (1.05)^{10}	162 889.46
31 December 2030	20	$100 000 (1.05)^{20}	265 329.77
31 December 2060	50	$100 000 (1.05)^{50}	1 146 739.98

The effect of compound interest becomes more pronounced as the number of periods becomes large. For example, after 50 years, the value of Kee Saw's account is nearly $1.15 million, or more than 10 times the amount with which he opened the account.

FINANCE IN ACTION

£6000 DEBT GREW TO £116 000

If you don't repay a loan, and a lot of time passes, the debt can grow to unmanageable proportions, as happened to an unfortunate borrower in Manchester in the United Kingdom.

A grandmother has been forced to put her house up for sale after she ended up owing a massive £116 000—on a £6000 loan. Esther Osei, 57, borrowed the money in 1988 to pay for her father's funeral and to buy a new cooker for her Clayton home.

But she could not meet the cost of the loan and 18 years later, the amount she owed had grown to £116 000 ... Esther said: 'I borrowed the money when I was grieving for my father. I just signed the papers.'

When the lender applied to take possession of her home, Esther sought help by going to the North Manchester Law Centre. Lawyers negotiated a deal at Manchester County Court ... A law centre spokesperson said Esther should never have entered into the loan agreement. 'It was a very high rate of interest.'

continued →

FINANCE IN ACTION
continued

Authors' note: Equation 3.4 can be rearranged to: $i = \left(\dfrac{S}{P}\right)^{1/n} - 1$. Substituting S = £116 000, P = £6000 and n = 18 years into this equation, gives i = 17.89 per cent per annum. However, this may not have been the contract interest rate because the final debt may have included unpaid fees.

Source: '£6000 debt grew to £116 000', Jo Rostron, *Manchester Metro News*, 21 July 2006.

To illustrate Equation 3.5, which gives the present value of a future sum promised, suppose that an individual is offered the sum of $100 000 to be received after 5 years. If the relevant interest rate is 5 per cent per annum, compounded annually, the present value of this promised sum is:

$$P = \frac{S}{(1+i)^n}$$
$$= \frac{\$100\,000}{(1.05)^5}$$
$$= \frac{\$100\,000}{1.276\,281\,563}$$
$$= \$78\,352.62$$

That is, looking ahead 5 years to the receipt of this promised sum of $100 000, it is worth, in today's terms, only $78 352.62. The logic underlying this result is that if one wished to set aside money today to accumulate a sum of $100 000 in 5 years' time, the amount needed to be set aside today is $78 352.62. After 5 years, this sum will accumulate to $78 352.62 × $(1.05)^5$ = $100 000. Clearly, all other things being equal, the longer the waiting period—that is, the later the promised sum is to be received—the lower is the value today.

The process by which a future sum is converted to its equivalent present value is called **discounting**. This process is illustrated in Table 3.2, which shows the present value of $100 000 to be received at selected future dates, discounted using an interest rate of 5 per cent per annum.

discounting
process by which, through the operation of interest, a future sum is converted to its equivalent present value

TABLE 3.2 Present value of $100 000 at 5 per cent per annum

NUMBER OF YEARS TO WAIT	CALCULATION	PRESENT VALUE ($)
1	$100 000/1.05	95 238.10
2	$100 000/$(1.05)^2$	90 702.95
3	$100 000/$(1.05)^3$	86 383.76
4	$100 000/$(1.05)^4$	82 270.25
5	$100 000/$(1.05)^5$	78 352.62
10	$100 000/$(1.05)^{10}$	61 391.33
20	$100 000/$(1.05)^{20}$	37 688.95
50	$100 000/$(1.05)^{50}$	8 720.37

Again, the effect of compound interest becomes more pronounced when the number of periods is large. A promise to be paid $100 000 in 50 years' time is worth only $8720.37 in today's terms if the discount rate is 5 per cent per annum.

3.4.3 NOMINAL AND EFFECTIVE INTEREST RATES

Many financial contracts specify that a loan shall be repaid by a series of payments made on various future dates, rather than by a lump sum at the end of a single time period. For example, a so-called **interest-only loan** requires payments of interest at regular intervals followed by the repayment of the principal in a lump sum on the loan's maturity date.

In most loans, the interest rate specified is a **nominal interest rate**, which is an interest rate where interest is charged more frequently than the time period specified in the interest rate. To simplify matters, we assume that interest is charged (and therefore compounded) on the same dates as payments are required.[4] Examples of nominal interest rates are: 15 per cent per annum with quarterly payments, and 1.5 per cent per quarter with monthly payments.

Where a nominal interest rate is used in a loan contract, a convention is needed to decide how an interest rate quoted for one time period will be applied to a different time period. The convention adopted is to take a simple ratio. So, for example, '15 per cent per annum payable quarterly' means that interest will be charged each quarter at the rate of 3.75 per cent per quarter—that is, the annual rate of 15 per cent is simply scaled down to one-quarter of this rate because there are four quarters in a year. Similarly, '1.5 per cent per quarter payable monthly' means that interest will be charged each month at 0.5 per cent per month because a month is one-third of a quarter and one-third of 1.5 is 0.5.

Conversely, an **effective interest rate** is one where the frequency of charging (payment) *does* match the time period specified by the interest rate. Examples of effective interest rates are: 15 per cent per annum with annual payments and 0.5 per cent per month with monthly payments. While few financial contracts specify an effective interest rate, it is an important concept because it provides a consistent basis on which to compare interest rates. This use is illustrated later in Example 3.8.

From the lender's viewpoint it is preferable to have interest paid more frequently, all other things being equal. To illustrate this fact, suppose that a bank is willing to lend $100 000 for 1 year at 15 per cent per annum on an 'interest only' basis but has the choice of receiving either annual or quarterly interest payments. Thus, the bank faces a choice between the cash inflows shown in Table 3.3.

TABLE 3.3 Cash inflows at 15 per cent per annum

	CASH INFLOW AT TIME *t* ($)			
	AT *t* = 1 QUARTER	AT *t* = 2 QUARTERS	AT *t* = 3 QUARTERS	AT *t* = 4 QUARTERS
Annual interest	0	0	0	115 000
Quarterly interest	3750	3750	3750	103 750

If we simply add up the two streams of cash flows shown in Table 3.3 we would, of course, find that both total $115 000 but, as we explained earlier, this procedure is not valid because it involves adding cash flows that occur on different dates. Because earlier cash inflows are preferred to later cash inflows, the quarterly interest stream is worth more to the bank. It is worth more because the 'early' cash inflows of $3750 can be re-lent to earn further interest later in the year.

Exactly how much more valuable the quarterly stream will prove to be will depend on the level of interest rates during the year, but because interest rates are always positive, the bank cannot lose by accepting the quarterly payments rather than the annual payment.

An important special case can be developed by assuming that during the coming year the bank can continue to lend money at 3.75 per cent per quarter. Thus the first quarterly inflow of $3750 can be re-lent for the remaining three quarters, generating further quarterly interest payments of

---

interest-only loan loan in which the borrower is required to make regular payments to cover interest accrued but is not required to make payments to reduce the principal. On the maturity date of the loan, the principal is repaid in a lump sum

nominal interest rate quoted interest rate where interest is charged more frequently than the basis on which the interest rate is quoted. The interest rate actually used to calculate the interest charge is taken as a proportion of the quoted nominal rate. *Note:* The term 'nominal interest rate' also has another meaning (see Section 3.4.4)

effective interest rate interest rate where interest is charged at the same frequency as the interest rate is quoted

---

4 This assumption is relaxed in Section 3.8.

$0.0375 \times \$3750 = \$140.63$, together with the repayment of $\$3750$ at the end of the fourth quarter. A quarter-by-quarter analysis is shown in Figure 3.1.

As shown in Figure 3.1, taking into account the future opportunities for re-lending, the bank can secure a total cash inflow, at the end of the fourth quarter, of $\$115\,865.06$, which for the bank is clearly preferable to a cash inflow (on the same date) of only $\$115\,000$. In effect, with interest paid quarterly, the bank has earned at an annual rate of return given by:

$$\frac{\$115\,865.06 - \$100\,000}{\$100\,000}$$

$$\approx 15.865\%$$

FIGURE 3.1 Cash flows re-lent at 3.75 per cent per quarter

With only an annual interest payment, the bank would have had to specify an interest rate of 15.865 per cent per annum to equal this rate of return. Therefore, this example has established that there is a sense in which the nominal interest rate of 15 per cent per annum, which is payable quarterly, is equivalent to an effective interest rate of 15.865 per cent per annum, payable annually.

But the sum of $\$115\,865$ is simply the future sum that would result from lending $\$100\,000$ to earn compound interest at the rate of 3.75 per cent per quarter for four quarters. This is easily seen by noting that:

$$\$100\,000 \times (1.0375)^4 = \$100\,000 \times 1.158\,65 = \$115\,865$$

Generalising from this example, if a lender advances a principal of P and specifies a nominal interest rate of j per period, with interest payments required every subperiod, and there are m subperiods in every period, then the future sum at the end of one period is given by:

$$S = P\left(1 + \frac{j}{m}\right)^m$$

The effective interest rate i per period is:

$$i = \frac{S - P}{P}$$

$$= \frac{P\left(1 + \frac{j}{m}\right)^m - P}{P}$$

therefore

$$i = \left(1 + \frac{j}{m}\right)^m - 1 \qquad [3.6]$$

Equation 3.6 is the formula for calculating the effective interest rate i per period for a nominal interest rate j, compounding m times per period. The use of this formula is illustrated in Examples 3.7 and 3.8.

EXAMPLE 3.7

Calculate the effective annual interest rates corresponding to 12 per cent per annum, compounding:

(a) semi-annually
(b) quarterly
(c) monthly
(d) daily.

SOLUTION

Using Equation 3.6, the calculations are as follows:

TABLE 3.4

COMPOUNDING FREQUENCY	CALCULATION	EFFECTIVE ANNUAL INTEREST RATE (%)
(a) Semi-annually	$(1.06)^2 - 1$	12.3600
(b) Quarterly	$(1.03)^4 - 1$	12.5509
(c) Monthly	$(1.01)^{12} - 1$	12.6825
(d) Daily	$(1.000\,328\,767)^{365} - 1$	12.7475

These calculations illustrate the fact that, all other things being equal, more frequent compounding produces a higher effective interest rate.

EXAMPLE 3.8

Lake Developments Ltd wishes to borrow money and is offered its choice of the following nominal interest rates:

(a) 15.00 per cent per annum, payable annually
(b) 14.50 per cent per annum, payable semi-annually
(c) 14.00 per cent per annum, payable quarterly
(d) 13.92 per cent per annum, payable monthly.

Which of these nominal interest rates provides the lowest cost of finance in terms of the corresponding effective annual interest rate?

SOLUTION

Using Equation 3.6, the effective annual interest rates are:

(a) $i = 15$ per cent per annum
(b) $i = (1.0725)^2 - 1 = 15.026$ per cent per annum
(c) $i = (1.035)^4 - 1 = 14.752$ per cent per annum
(d) $i = (1.0116)^{12} - 1 = 14.843$ per cent per annum

Thus option (c), which is a nominal interest rate of 14.00 per cent per annum with quarterly compounding, provides the lowest effective annual interest rate.

In some problems it is necessary to find out what nominal interest rate, j, must be charged in order to achieve a target effective interest rate, i. Answering a problem of this type requires that Equation 3.6 be rearranged so that j appears on the left-hand side of the equation. This is shown below. Equation 3.6 is:

$$i = \left(1 + \frac{j}{m}\right)^m - 1$$

Adding 1 to both sides, and raising to the power $1/m$:

$$(1+i)^{1/m} = 1 + \frac{j}{m}$$

Subtracting 1 from both sides, and multiplying by m:

$$j = m\left[(1+i)^{1/m} - 1\right] \tag{3.7}$$

The use of this formula is illustrated in Example 3.9.

EXAMPLE 3.9

A financial institution raises funds from several different types of deposits but all its loans to borrowers require monthly repayments. The effective annual interest rate that it pays depositors is 7.5 per cent per annum. To cover its other costs and make a profit, the institution adds a margin of 3 per cent per annum. Therefore, its target effective interest rate is 10.5 per cent per annum. What nominal annual interest rate must it charge borrowers?

SOLUTION
Using Equation 3.7, the nominal annual interest rate is:
$j = m[(1 + i)^{1/m} - 1]$
$= 12[(1.105)^{1/12} - 1]$
$= 12 \times 0.008\,355\,155$
$= 10\%$ per annum.

The financial institution would need to charge a nominal annual interest rate of 10 per cent on the loans it makes.

3.4.4 COMPOUND INTEREST: TWO SPECIAL CASES AND A GENERALISATION

In this section we discuss real interest rates, continuous interest rates and geometric rates of return. To understand the remainder of the chapter, knowledge of these issues is *not* required, so some readers may wish to omit this section.

real interest rate
interest rate after taking out the effects of inflation

nominal interest rate
interest rate before taking out the effects of inflation. *Note*: the term 'nominal interest rate' also has another meaning (see Section 3.4.3)

Special case no. 1: the real interest rate

A **real interest rate** is an interest rate *after* taking out the effects of inflation. Hence, the word 'real' in this context is used in the same sense as it is used in phrases such as 'real GDP' and 'real wages'. An interest rate *before* taking out the effects of inflation is usually referred to as a **nominal interest rate**. The phrase 'nominal interest rate' in this context should not be confused with its use in Section 3.4.3. In that section, the phrase 'nominal interest rate' referred to an interest rate where the frequency of payment or compounding did not match the basis on which the interest rate was quoted.

Suppose that a representative basket of goods that a consumer might buy costs $500 today. If the inflation rate in the coming year is expected to be 20 per cent per annum, the price of the basket at the end of the year is expected to be $500 × 1.2 = $600. Suppose also that a lender currently has $2000 that will be lent at a nominal interest rate for 1 year. By lending this sum the lender forgoes the consumption now of four representative baskets of goods. If a *real* interest rate of 5 per cent per annum is to be achieved, then the lender requires that at the end of the year the sum generated will be sufficient to purchase 4 × 1.05 = 4.2 baskets of goods—that is, the sum required in 1 year is:

4.2 baskets × $600 per basket = $2520

Therefore, the nominal annual interest rate required is:

$$\frac{\$2520 - \$2000}{\$2000}$$

$$= 26\%$$

Generalising from this example, let:

B = the price today of a representative basket of goods
P = principal
p = expected inflation rate
i^* = required real interest rate
i = nominal interest rate

Thus the lender forgoes consumption of $\frac{P}{B}$ baskets today, to be able to consume $\frac{P}{B}(1 + i^*)$ baskets in a year's time. The expected price of one basket in a year's time is $B(1 + p)$. Therefore, the sum required in 1 year's time is $\frac{P}{B}(1 + i^*) \times B(1 + p)$. Therefore, the nominal interest rate required is:

$$i = \frac{\frac{P}{B}(1+i^*)B(1+p) - P}{P}$$

On simplifying, this gives:

$$i = (1 + i^*)(1 + p) - 1 \qquad [3.8]$$

Equation 3.8 shows the link with the idea of compounding: the nominal interest rate i is not simply the sum of the real interest rate i^* and the expected inflation rate p, but rather is in the form of the real interest rate 'compounded' by the expected inflation rate. Rearranging Equation 3.8 gives:

$$i^* = \frac{1+i}{1+p} - 1 \qquad [3.9]$$

Equation 3.9 gives the real interest rate i^* corresponding to a nominal interest rate i if the expected inflation rate is p. Expansion of Equation 3.9 gives the result:

$$i^* = i - p - pi^*$$
$$\neq i - p$$

That is, the real interest rate i^* is *not* simply the difference between the nominal interest rate i and the expected inflation rate p. However, where the rates are 'small', pi^* will also be small and the approximation $i^* \approx i - p$ will be close. The calculation of a real interest rate is illustrated in Example 3.10.

EXAMPLE 3.10

If the inflation rate is expected to be 20 per cent per annum and the nominal interest rate is 30 per cent per annum, calculate the corresponding real interest rate.

SOLUTION
Using Equation 3.9:

$$i* = \frac{1+i}{1+p} - 1$$

$$= \frac{1.30}{1.20} - 1$$

$$= 8.33\% \text{ per annum}$$

Special case no. 2: continuous interest rates

As we showed in Section 3.4.3, the more frequently compounding occurs, the higher is the effective interest rate, other things being equal. In the limiting case, compounding becomes so frequent that the time period between each interest charge approaches zero. This is known as **continuous interest** and it can be shown that continuous interest is an example of exponential growth. Using continuous interest, the future sum S is:

$$S = Pe^{jn} \qquad [3.10]$$

where S = future sum
P = principal
j = continuously compounding interest rate per period
n = number of periods
e = 2.718 281 828 46

continuous interest method of calculating interest in which interest is charged so frequently that the time period between each charge approaches zero

The calculation of a future sum using continuous interest is illustrated in Example 3.11.

EXAMPLE 3.11

If the interest rate is 12 per cent per annum, compounding continuously, how much will a principal of $100 000 be worth after 1 year? After 2 years?

SOLUTION
Using Equation 3.10, the future sum after 1 year is:

$$S = Pe^{jn}$$
$$= \$100\,000 \times e^{(0.12)(1)}$$
$$= \$100\,000 \times 1.127\,496\,852$$
$$= \$112\,749.69$$

Again using Equation 3.10, the future sum after 2 years is:

$$S = Pe^{jn}$$
$$= \$100\,000 \times e^{(0.12)(2)}$$
$$= \$100\,000 \times e^{0.24}$$
$$= \$127\,124.92$$

The effective interest rate that results from continuous compounding is found by setting n equal to 1 period and solving:

$$i = \frac{S - P}{P}$$

$$= \frac{Pe^j - P}{P}$$

$$i = e^j - 1 \qquad [3.11]$$

where i = effective interest rate per period
   j = continuously compounding interest rate per period
   e = 2.718 281 828 46

The calculation of an effective annual interest rate that is equivalent to a continuously compounding interest rate is illustrated in Example 3.12.

EXAMPLE 3.12

What is the effective annual interest rate corresponding to a nominal interest rate of 12 per cent per annum, compounding continuously?

SOLUTION

Using Equation 3.11, the effective annual interest rate i is given by:

$i = e^j - 1$
$= e^{0.12} - 1$
$= 12.749\ 69\%$ per annum

Of course, this is the interest rate implicit in Example 3.11.

Although continuous compounding is rarely used in loan contracts, it is frequently used in other contexts. In particular, academic studies of security prices often assume that returns compound continuously between the dates on which the prices are observed. Consider the security prices P_0, P_1 and P_2 observed on dates 0, 1 and 2 respectively. These dates are assumed to be equally spaced. For example, the prices may be observed at weekly intervals. Assuming that returns accrue continuously through time, we can apply Equation 3.10 to assert that in the first week:

$$P_1 = P_0 e^{r_1}$$

and in the second week:

$$P_2 = P_1 e^{r_2}$$

where r_1 is the continuously compounding weekly rate of return in the first week and r_2 is the continuously compounding weekly rate of return in the second week.

Solving for r_1 and r_2 gives:

$$r_1 = \ln(P_1/P_0)$$

and

$$r_2 = \ln(P_2/P_1)$$

where, $\ln$ means logarithm to the base e (usually referred to as the natural logarithm). More generally, we can write that the rate of return in period t is:

$$r_t = \ln(P_t/P_{t-1}) \qquad [3.12]$$

An expression of the form $\ln(P_t/P_{t-1})$ is called a **log price relative** and, when calculated this way, r_t is called a logarithmic rate of return or a continuous rate of return.

There are two reasons for choosing to measure rates of return in this way. First, the correct way to compound logarithmic rates of return is simply to add them. Thus, for example:

$$P_2 = P_1 e^{r_2}$$

But

$$P_1 = P_0 e^{r_1}$$

log price relative
natural logarithm of the ratio of successive security prices. Implicitly, it is assumed that prices have grown (or decayed) in a continuous fashion between the two dates on which the prices are observed. Also known as a *logarithmic rate of return* and a *continuous rate of return*

Substituting, we find:

$$P_2 = P_0 e^{r_1} e^{r_2}$$

That is:

$$P_2 = P_0 e^{r_1+r_2}$$

The last equation shows that, using logarithmic rates of return, the total rate of return over the two time periods is simply the sum of the rates of return in each of the two constituent periods. Thus calculations such as finding an average rate of return are simpler when using logarithmic rates of return. As discussed in Section 3.4.5, it is *not* valid to add rates of return if they are measured using the simple 'arithmetic' definition that:

$$r_t = \left(\frac{P_t - P_{t-1}}{P_{t-1}}\right)$$

The second reason for using logarithmic rates of return is a statistical one. The greatest loss an investor can suffer is when the security price falls to zero. Using the simple arithmetic definition, the rate of return associated with this event is -1—that is, the rate of return is -100 per cent. Using logarithmic rates of return, the same event will register as a rate of return of $-\infty$. Given that there is no upper limit to the rate of return that might be achieved, it follows that while arithmetic rates of return fall in the range -1 to $+\infty$, logarithmic rates of return fall in the range $-\infty$ to $+\infty$. Thus, while the statistical distribution that describes logarithmic rates of return *might* have the convenient property of symmetry, and thus *might* follow the normal distribution, arithmetic rates of return will *not* be symmetric and thus *cannot* be normally distributed.

A generalisation: geometric rates of return

geometric rate of return
average of a sequence of arithmetic rates of return, found by a process that resembles compounding

Compound interest is a special case of a **geometric rate of return**. In the case of compound interest, the interest rate is the same in each period. In the more general case of geometric rates of return, the rate of return can be different in each period. While the sum invested is still subject to the compounding process, the *rate* at which compounding occurs will differ from period to period.

Suppose that $1000 is invested for 4 years and each year the investment earns a different rate of return, as follows:

- In Year 1: 10 per cent per annum
- In Year 2: 5 per cent per annum
- In Year 3: 8 per cent per annum
- In Year 4: 15 per cent per annum.

The value of this investment therefore grows as follows:

1. After Year 1: $1000.00 × 1.10 = $1100.00
2. After Year 2: $1100.00 × 1.05 = $1155.00
3. After Year 3: $1155.00 × 1.08 = $1247.40
4. After Year 4: $1247.40 × 1.15 = $1434.51.

Of course, this result could have been found more quickly and conveniently by calculating, in one step:

$1000 × 1.10 × 1.05 × 1.08 × 1.15 = $1434.51

Writing the calculation in this way emphasises the similarity between compound interest and the more general case of geometric rates of return.

It is natural to ask: what annual compound interest rate would have produced the same result? In other words, what *single* rate of return i per year would need to be earned in *each* of the 4 years, to produce the same future sum? To answer this question we need to solve:

$$\$1000 \times 1.10 \times 1.05 \times 1.08 \times 1.15 = \$1000 (1 + i)^4$$

that is,

$$\begin{aligned} i &= [(1.10)(1.05)(1.08)(1.15)]^{1/4} - 1 \\ &= (1.43451)^{1/4} - 1 \\ &= 9.440\% \text{ per annum} \end{aligned}$$

In fact, i in this calculation is the mean (or average) geometric rate of return. It is the rate of return which, if earned in every period, and allowing for the effects of compounding, would produce the same outcome as that actually observed. In the general case, the mean geometric rate of return is:

$$i = [(1 + r_1)(1 + r_2) \ldots (1 + r_n)]^{1/n} - 1 \qquad [3.13]$$

where r_k = the rate of return in period k
$k = 1, 2, \ldots, n$
n = the number of completed periods

If the rate of return is calculated each period from security prices $P_0, P_1, \ldots, P_n$ then:

$$\begin{aligned} r_k &= \frac{P_k - P_{k-1}}{P_{k-1}} \\ &= \frac{P_k}{P_{k-1}} - 1 \end{aligned}$$

Substituting in Equation 3.13 gives:

$$\begin{aligned} i &= \left[\left(1 + \frac{P_1 - P_0}{P_0}\right)\left(1 + \frac{P_2 - P_1}{P_1}\right) \cdots \left(1 + \frac{P_n - P_{n-1}}{P_{n-1}}\right)\right]^{\frac{1}{n}} - 1 \\ &= \left[\left(\frac{P_1}{P_0}\right)\left(\frac{P_2}{P_1}\right) \cdots \left(\frac{P_n}{P_{n-1}}\right)\right]^{\frac{1}{n}} - 1 \end{aligned}$$

$$i = \left(\frac{P_n}{P_0}\right)^{\frac{1}{n}} - 1 \qquad [3.14]$$

It is important to understand that the mean rate of return is *not* $(r_1 + r_2 + \ldots + r_n)/n$—that is, it is *not* correct simply to sum the rates of return and divide by the number of periods. This fact is illustrated in Example 3.13.

EXAMPLE 3.13

An investment of $100 000 produces rates of return as follows:
In Year 1: a gain of 10 per cent
In Year 2: a loss of 5 per cent
In Year 3: a loss of 8 per cent
In Year 4: a gain of 3 per cent
Calculate the value of the investment at the end of the fourth year and calculate the mean annual rate of return.

continued →

Example 3.13 *continued*

SOLUTION

The value of the investment at the end of the fourth year is:
$100\,000 \times 1.10 \times 0.95 \times 0.92 \times 1.03 = \$99\,024.20$

Using Equation 3.14, the mean annual rate of return is:

$$i = \left(\frac{P_n}{P_0}\right)^{\frac{1}{n}} - 1$$

$$= \left(\frac{\$99\,024.20}{\$100\,000}\right)^{\frac{1}{4}} - 1$$

$$= -0.002\,448$$

$$= -0.2\,448\%$$

This small negative mean rate of return is consistent with the outcome that the final value ($99 024.20) is less than the sum invested ($100 000)—that is, the investment has produced a loss after 4 years. Note that the *incorrect* calculation of the mean as:

$$\frac{10\% - 5\% - 8\% + 3\%}{4}$$

$$= 0\%$$

clearly gives a nonsensical answer because in this example the mean rate of return must be negative.[5]

3.5 VALUATION OF CONTRACTS WITH MULTIPLE CASH FLOWS

3.5.1 INTRODUCTION

LEARNING OBJECTIVE 2
Value, as at any date, contracts involving multiple cash flows

Many loan contracts stipulate that more than one cash flow is required to repay the loan. For example, a housing loan may require monthly repayments over a period of 20 years—a total of 240 repayments. In this section we consider the valuation of contracts that involve multiple cash flows. We do not assume that the amount or timing of the cash flows follows any particular pattern. Some important special cases involving equal amounts at equally spaced time intervals are considered in Section 3.6.

3.5.2 VALUE ADDITIVITY

While it is *not* valid to add cash flows that occur at *different* times, it *is* valid to add cash flows that occur at the *same* time. Therefore, if a contract requires cash payments to be made on, say, 1 April and 1 May, we should not simply add these cash flows.

However, if we first value the 1 April cash flow *as if* it were to occur on 1 May, we could then add the two cash flows, since one is actually a May cash flow and the other has, so to speak, been converted to the *equivalent* of a May cash flow. Alternatively, we could first value the 1 May cash flow *as if* it were to occur on 1 April; summation of these two cash flows then provides the total value of the two cash flows as at 1 April. For that matter we could choose any date at all, value the two cash flows as if they were to occur on that date, and thus produce a valuation as at that date.

---

[5] Note that we are discussing here the correct measurement of *past* returns. We are not discussing the forecasting of *future* returns.

To implement this approach we need to decide how we can value, as at any given date, a cash flow that occurs on some earlier or later date. For example, we need to decide how a 1 April cash flow can be valued as at 1 May. The answer is provided by the interest rate. Using our knowledge of compound interest we can use Equation 3.4 to carry forward in time ('accumulate') the value of any cash flow, provided we know the interest rate to use. Similarly, we can use Equation 3.5 to carry backward in time ('discount') the value of any cash flow if we know the interest rate to use. The process of valuation as at any given date is illustrated in Example 3.14.

EXAMPLE 3.14

On 1 February 2011 you sign a contract that entitles you to receive two future cash flows, as follows:

On 1 February 2013: $10 000
On 1 August 2014: $6000

Assuming that the relevant interest rate is 5 per cent per annum (effective), value this contract as at:

(a) 1 February 2011
(b) 1 February 2013 and
(c) 1 August 2014.

The following time line shows the timing of the cash flows in this problem.

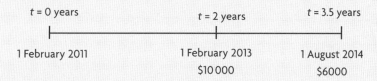

SOLUTION

(a) Valuation as at 1 February 2011

Both cash flows must be discounted to 1 February 2011. This requires that the $10 000 to be received on 1 February 2013 be discounted for 2 years and the $6000 to be received on 1 August 2014 be discounted for 3.5 years. The equation we need to use in each case is Equation 3.5. The valuation as at 1 February 2011 is:

$$V_a = \frac{\$10\,000}{(1.05)^2} + \frac{\$6000}{(1.05)^{3.5}}$$
$$= \$9070.2948 + \$5058.1151$$
$$= \$14\,128.41$$

Because this valuation is made as at the start of the contract, V_a is called the **present value of the contract**.

(b) Valuation as at 1 February 2013

The cash flow of $6000 on 1 August 2014 must be discounted for 1.5 years to calculate an equivalent amount as at 1 February 2013. Therefore, the valuation as at 1 February 2013 is:

$$V_b = \$10\,000 + \frac{\$6000}{(1.05)^{1.5}}$$
$$= \$10\,000 + \$5576.57$$
$$= \$15\,576.57$$

present value of a contract
the value today that is equivalent to the stream of cash flows promised in a financial contract

continued →

Example 3.14 *continued*

(c) Valuation as at 1 August 2014

The cash flow of $10 000 on 1 February 2013 must be accumulated for 1.5 years to calculate an equivalent amount as at 1 August 2014. The equation we need to use is Equation 3.4. Therefore, the valuation as at 1 August 2014 is:

$$V_c = \$10\,000(1.05)^{1.5} + \$6000$$
$$= \$10\,759.30 + \$6000$$
$$= \$16\,759.30$$

Because 1 August 2014 is the date of the final cash flow of the contract, V_c is called the **terminal value of the contract**.

terminal value of a contract
the value, as at the date of the final cash flow promised in a financial contract, that is equivalent to the stream of promised cash flows

In Example 3.14, the three valuations V_a, V_b and V_c are all valuations of the same financial contract. They differ because the date of valuation differs. There should, therefore, be logical connections between the three valuations. For example, the contract's present value (V_a, the valuation as at 1 February 2011) should be the same as taking the contract's terminal value (V_c, the valuation as at 1 August 2014) and discounting for 3.5 years. In fact, the mathematics underlying the valuation process guarantees this result, as the following calculation confirms:

$$\frac{V_c}{(1.05)^{3.5}}$$
$$= \frac{\$16\,759.30}{(1.05)^{3.5}}$$
$$= \$14\,128.41$$
$$= V_a$$

In effect, the valuation process consists of using compound interest to discount and accumulate cash flows to calculate value equivalents at a common date. The valuation as at that date is then found simply by adding the value equivalents for that date.

3.5.3 FORMULA DEVELOPMENT: VALUATION AS AT ANY DATE

Where a cash flow of C dollars occurs on a date t, the value of that cash flow as at a valuation date t^* is given by:

$$V_{t^*} = C_t(1+i)^{t^*-t} \qquad [3.15]$$

If date t^* occurs after date t, then t^* is greater than t and, in Equation 3.15, the power $(t^* - t)$ is positive, and the equation correctly indicates that an accumulation of C_t is required. Conversely, if date t^* occurs before date t, then t^* is less than t and, in Equation 3.15, the power $(t^* - t)$ is negative, and the equation correctly indicates that a discounting of C_t is required.

Where there is more than one cash flow to be valued, the total value of the contract is the sum of the values of each cash flow. The calculation of a contract's value at various dates is illustrated in Example 3.15.

EXAMPLE 3.15

Confirm that Equation 3.15 is correct by using it to recalculate the valuations made in Example 3.14. In each case, i = 5 per cent per annum, C_2 = $10 000 and $C_{3.5}$ = $6000. The valuation date t^*, however, differs in each case.

SOLUTION

(a) Valuation as at 1 February 2011

In this case, t^* = 0. Using Equation 3.15:

$$V_0 = \$10\,000(1.05)^{0-2} + \$6000(1.05)^{0-3.5}$$
$$= \$10\,000(1.05)^{-2} + \$6000(1.05)^{-3.5}$$
$$= \frac{\$10\,000}{(1.05)^2} + \frac{\$6000}{(1.05)^{3.5}}$$
$$= \$9070.2948 + \$5058.1151$$
$$= \$14\,128.41$$
$$= V_a \text{ as calculated in Example 3.14}$$

(b) Valuation as at 1 February 2013

In this case, $t^* = 2$. Using Equation 3.15:

$$V_2 = \$10\,000(1.05)^{2-2} + \$6000(1.05)^{2-3.5}$$
$$= \$10\,000(1.05)^0 + \$6000(1.05)^{-1.5}$$
$$= \$10\,000 + \frac{\$6000}{(1.05)^{1.5}}$$
$$= \$10\,000 + \$5576.57$$
$$= \$15\,576.57$$
$$= V_b \text{ as calculated in Example 3.14}$$

(c) Valuation as at 1 August 2014

In this case, $t^* = 3.5$. Using Equation 3.15:

$$V_{3.5} = \$10\,000(1.05)^{3.5-2} + \$6000(1.05)^{3.5-3.5}$$
$$= \$10\,000(1.05)^{1.5} + \$6000(1.05)^0$$
$$= (\$10\,000 \times 1.075\,929\,83) + \$6000$$
$$= \$16\,759.30$$
$$= V_c \text{ as calculated in Example 3.14}$$

3.5.4 MEASURING THE RATE OF RETURN

When there are multiple cash flows in an investment, there are also multiple time periods. Inevitably the question arises: For a given set of cash flows extending over two or more time periods, how can we measure the rate of return *per period*? There are a number of different answers to this question, but the answer most frequently offered is to employ a measure known as the internal rate of return. In this section we outline this method. It is discussed in greater detail in Section 5.4.2.

First, however, we review the measurement of the rate of return over a *single* period. Consider a one-period investment that costs $1000 and promises a cash inflow of $1120 a year later. Such an investment would usually be described simply as a 1-year loan of $1000 at an interest rate of 12 per cent per annum. We would infer that the interest rate is 12 per cent per annum by observing that the interest component of the cash flow after 1 year is $120, so the interest rate is $120/$1000 = 12 per cent. This is, of course, the result given by the simple definition of 'rate of return' in Equation 3.1. Equally, we could have said that the rate of return is the value of r that solves the following equation:

$$\frac{\$1120}{1+r} - \$1000 = 0$$

The calculation $\$1120/(1 + r)$ is the present value of $1120 using a discount rate of r. On solving this equation we would, of course, find that $r = 0.12$, or 12 per cent.

The advantage of thinking about the rate of return in this way is that we can readily see how to extend this approach to the case of many cash flows and time periods. Consider the following investment. An initial investment of $1000 is made and, as before, a cash flow of $1120 is to be received after 1 year but, in addition, a further cash flow of $25 is to be received 2 years after making the initial investment. In tabular form, the cash flows of this investment are:

TABLE 3.5

YEAR	CASH FLOW ($)
0	− 1000
1	+ 1120
2	+ 25

Obviously this investment promises a rate of return of more than 12 per cent per annum, since the first cash inflow alone is sufficient to produce a rate of return of 12 per cent per annum. As an investor, however, we would prefer the $25 inflow to have been promised for Year 1 rather than Year 2. Had this occurred, the cash inflow after 1 year would be $1145, representing a rate of return of 14.5 per cent per annum. Putting these observations together, the investment's annual rate of return must be more than 12 per cent, but less than 14.5 per cent.

The internal rate of return measure proposes that the rate of return in this case is the value of r that satisfies the following equation:

$$\frac{\$1120}{1+r} + \frac{\$25}{(1+r)^2} - \$1000 = 0$$

The term $\$25/(1+r)^2$ can be thought of as the present value of $25, discounted for 2 years at the rate r per annum. Solving this equation, we find $r = 14.19$ per cent per annum.[6] We can confirm this result by noting that:

$$\frac{\$1120}{1.1419} + \frac{\$25}{(1.1419)^2} - \$1000$$
$$= \$980.821\,438 + \$19.172\,725 - \$1000$$
$$= -\$0.005\,836$$
$$\approx 0$$

The figure of 14.19 per cent falls within the range of 12 per cent to 14.5 per cent, as suggested earlier by our intuitive reasoning.

Where there are n cash inflows C_t (where $t = 1, \ldots, n$), following an initial cash outflow of C_0, the internal rate of return is that value (or values) of r that solves the equation:[7]

$$\frac{C_1}{1+r} + \frac{C_2}{(1+r)^2} + \ldots + \frac{C_n}{(1+r)^n} - C_0 = 0$$

---

[6] In this particular case, r can be found by solving the resulting quadratic equation. In more general cases, numerical methods are usually required.

[7] If the cash flows are produced by a bond, it is conventional to call the internal rate of return the bond's *yield-to-maturity* (or 'yield' for short). For further discussion, see Sections 4.4 and 4.7. The Microsoft Excel® function IRR uses numerical methods to calculate the internal rate of return for a given initial outlay and set of cash flows.

or

$$\sum_{t=1}^{n} \frac{C_t}{(1+r)^t} - C_0 = 0 \qquad [3.16]$$

ANNUITIES 3.6

3.6.1 DEFINITION AND TYPES OF ANNUITY

In Section 3.5 we explained how to analyse contracts that require more than one cash flow to be paid. We considered a general case that can be used to deal with a wide range of contracts. There is, however, a special case that is found in a large number of financial contracts and hence requires further discussion. This is the case of the annuity.

An **annuity** is a series of cash flows, usually of equal amount, equally spaced in time. Thus, for example, $500 paid each month for a year is an annuity. Similarly, $600 per week for 12 weeks is an annuity; so is $20 000 per annum for 10 years. Annuities are involved in many personal loans and commercial loans, and in certain kinds of financial instruments such as bonds.

Initially we consider four types of annuity: ordinary annuity, annuity-due, deferred annuity and ordinary perpetuity.

> **LEARNING OBJECTIVE 3**
>
> Distinguish between different types of annuity and calculate their present value and future value

The ordinary annuity

Like all annuities, the cash flow pattern of the **ordinary annuity** consists of equal amounts, equally spaced in time. The distinguishing characteristic of the ordinary annuity is that the time period from the date of valuation to the date of the first cash flow is *equal* to the time period between each subsequent cash flow.

Diagrammatically, the cash flow pattern of the ordinary annuity, using six cash flows as an example, is:

```
0     1     2     3     4     5     6
      ─────────────────────────────────
      $C    $C    $C    $C    $C    $C
```

The annuity-due

The distinguishing feature of the **annuity-due** is that the first cash flow occurs on the valuation date—that is, *immediately*.

Diagrammatically, the cash flow pattern of the annuity-due, using six cash flows as an example, is:

```
0     1     2     3     4     5
─────────────────────────────────
$C    $C    $C    $C    $C    $C
```

The deferred annuity

The distinguishing feature of the **deferred annuity** is that the first cash flow is to occur after a time period that *exceeds* the time period between each subsequent cash flow.

Diagrammatically, the cash flow pattern of the deferred annuity, using as an example six cash flows, the first to occur after three time periods, is:

annuity
series of cash flows, usually of equal amount, equally spaced in time

ordinary annuity
annuity in which the time period from the date of valuation to the date of the first cash flow is equal to the time period between each subsequent cash flow

annuity-due
annuity in which the first cash flow is to occur 'immediately' (i.e. on the valuation date)

deferred annuity
annuity in which the first cash flow is to occur after a time period that exceeds the time period between each subsequent cash flow

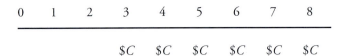

The ordinary perpetuity

ordinary perpetuity
ordinary annuity with the special feature that the cash flows are to continue forever

The **ordinary perpetuity** is an ordinary annuity with the special feature that the cash flows are to continue forever.[8]

Diagrammatically, the cash flow pattern of the ordinary perpetuity is:

```
0    1    2    3    4
     $C   $C   $C   $C  ──────────▶
```

where the arrows indicate continuing forever.

3.6.2 FORMULA DEVELOPMENT: PRESENT VALUE OF AN ORDINARY ANNUITY

The formula for the present value of an ordinary annuity is one that we will use frequently. This formula can then be adapted to apply to the other types of annuity.

The cash flow pattern of an ordinary annuity of n cash flows of C dollars each is shown below:

```
0    1    2    3        n − 1   n
     $C   $C   $C  ...   $C    $C
```

The present value P of this stream of cash flows is given by the sum of the present values of the individual cash flows:

$$P = \frac{C}{1+i} + \frac{C}{(1+i)^2} + \frac{C}{(1+i)^3} + \cdots + \frac{C}{(1+i)^{n-1}} + \frac{C}{(1+i)^n} \quad [3.17]$$

where i = the interest rate per period

Multiplying both sides of Equation 3.17 by $(1 + i)$ gives:

$$P(1+i) = C + \frac{C}{1+i} + \frac{C}{(1+i)^2} + \cdots + \frac{C}{(1+i)^{n-2}} + \frac{C}{(1+i)^{n-1}} \quad [3.18]$$

Subtracting Equation 3.17 from Equation 3.18, we find that all terms on the right-hand side cancel out, except the last term of Equation 3.17 and the first term of Equation 3.18, giving:

$$P(1+i) - P = C - \frac{C}{(1+i)^n}$$

or

$$Pi = C - \frac{C}{(1+i)^n}$$

---

8 We could, of course, also consider the categories *perpetuity-due* and *deferred perpetuity* but have not done so because the purpose at this stage is simply to introduce the idea of a perpetuity, as distinct from an annuity of finite life.

which, on rearrangement gives:

$$P = \frac{C}{i}\left[1 - \frac{1}{(1+i)^n}\right] \quad [3.19]$$

It is often convenient to consider an annuity of $1 per period—that is, we set $C = 1$ and Equation 3.19 becomes:

$$P = A(n,i) = \frac{1}{i}\left[1 - \frac{1}{(1+i)^n}\right] \quad [3.20]$$

Equation 3.20 is the formula for the present value of an ordinary annuity consisting of n cash flows, each of $1 per period. The functional notation $A(n, i)$ is simply a shorthand way of referring to this equation.[9] Values of $A(n, i)$ for different values of n and i are provided in Table 4 of Appendix A on p. 799. The valuation of ordinary annuities is illustrated in Example 3.16.

EXAMPLE 3.16

Find the present value of an ordinary annuity of $5000 per annum for 4 years if the interest rate is 8 per cent per annum by:

(a) using a calculator to discount each individual cash flow
(b) using a calculator to evaluate the formula given in Equation 3.19
(c) using the Microsoft Excel® function PV (rate, nper, pmt)
(d) using Table 4 of Appendix A to evaluate the formula given in Equation 3.20.

SOLUTION

(a) Discounting each individual cash flow:

$$P = \frac{C}{1+i} + \frac{C}{(1+i)^2} + \frac{C}{(1+i)^3} + \frac{C}{(1+i)^4}$$

$$= \frac{\$5000}{1.08} + \frac{\$5000}{(1.08)^2} + \frac{\$5000}{(1.08)^3} + \frac{\$5000}{(1.08)^4}$$

$$= \$4629.6296 + \$4286.6941 + \$3969.1612 + \$3675.1493$$

$$= \$16\,560.63$$

(b) Using Equation 3.19:

$$P = \frac{C}{i}\left[1 - \frac{1}{(1+i)^n}\right]$$

$$= \frac{\$5000}{0.08}\left[1 - \frac{1}{(1.08)^4}\right]$$

$$= \$5000 \times 3.312\,122\,684$$

$$= \$16\,560.63$$

(c) Using the Microsoft Excel® function PV (rate, nper, pmt):
The Microsoft Excel® function PV returns −1 × the present value of an ordinary annuity. The required inputs are the interest rate (as a decimal), the number of periods and the amount of each cash flow. Using a Microsoft Excel® spreadsheet, we find that −PV(0.08, 4, 5000) = $16 560.63.

continued →

---

[9] The notation $A_{\overline{n}|i}$, sometimes read as 'A angle n at rate i', is also used to indicate this equation. There is no special significance in this notation: it is simply a different convention. Mathematically, the functional notation $A(n,i)$ serves equally well.

Example 3.16 *continued*

(d) Using Table 4 of Appendix A:

$$P = C\,A(n, i)$$
$$= \$5000 \times 3.3121$$
$$= \$16\,560.50$$

Except for the relatively small rounding error when using Table 4 of Appendix A, the four answers are identical.

3.6.3 FORMULA DEVELOPMENT: PRESENT VALUES OF ANNUITIES-DUE, DEFERRED ANNUITIES AND ORDINARY PERPETUITIES

Present value of an annuity-due

The cash flow pattern of an *annuity-due* with n cash flows of C dollars each is shown below:

```
0     1     2     3           n – 2   n – 1
|-----|-----|-----|---- … ----|-------|
$C   $C   $C   $C            $C     $C
```

It is important to be aware that in an annuity-due consisting of n cash flows, there are only $(n - 1)$ time periods involved.[10]

Inspecting the annuity-due diagram, it is clear that an annuity-due of n cash flows is simply an immediate cash flow plus an ordinary annuity of $(n - 1)$ cash flows. The present value of an annuity-due is therefore:

$$P = C + \frac{C}{i}\left[1 - \frac{1}{(1+i)^{n-1}}\right] \qquad [3.21]$$

or

$$P = C[1 + A(n-1, i)] \qquad [3.22]$$

where P = present value
 C = cash flow per period
 i = interest rate per period
 n = number of cash flows

The valuation of annuities-due is illustrated in Example 3.17.

EXAMPLE 3.17

Kathy's rich uncle promises her an allowance of $10 000 per month, starting today, with a final payment to be made 6 months from today. If the interest rate is 0.5 per cent per month, what is the present value of the promised allowance?

SOLUTION

Kathy has been promised *seven* payments of $10 000 with the first being due immediately. Thus, she has been promised $10 000 today, plus an *ordinary* annuity of *six* payments. This is the logic embodied in Equation 3.21. Using this equation with n set equal to 7, gives:

---

10 This is frequently a source of confusion. For an ordinary annuity, it makes no difference whether n is defined as the number of cash flows or the number of time periods, since these are equal. For an annuity-due, we must choose whether to use n to represent the number of cash flows or the number of time periods. We have chosen to develop the formula with n representing the number of cash flows.

$$P = C + \frac{C}{i}\left[1 - \frac{1}{(1+i)^{n-1}}\right]$$

$$= \$10\,000 + \frac{\$10\,000}{0.005}\left[1 - \frac{1}{(1.005)^{7-1}}\right]$$

$$= \$10\,000 + \frac{\$10\,000}{0.005}\left[1 - \frac{1}{(1.005)^{6}}\right]$$

$$= \$10\,000 + \$58\,963.84$$

$$= \$68\,963.84$$

Present value of a deferred annuity

The cash flow pattern of a *deferred annuity* is as follows:

```
0   1   2  ...  k-1   k   k+1  ...  k+n-2   k+n-1
                     $C   $C         $C      $C
```

In this case, there are n cash flows and the first cash flow occurs on date k. To find the present value of this series of cash flows, imagine that the valuation was to be made as at date $(k-1)$ instead of date zero. Looking ahead from date $(k-1)$, the cash flow pattern is that of an ordinary annuity of n cash flows. Thus, at date $(k-1)$, the present value is given by the present value of an ordinary annuity:

$$P_{k-1} = \frac{C}{i}\left[1 - \frac{1}{(1+i)^{n}}\right] \qquad [3.23]$$

where P_{k-1} = the present value at date $(k-1)$

To shift the valuation date back from date $(k-1)$ to date zero, we simply discount the value given by Equation 3.23 for $(k-1)$ periods. Thus the required formula is:

$$P = \frac{1}{(1+i)^{k-1}} \frac{C}{i}\left[1 - \frac{1}{(1+i)^{n}}\right] \qquad [3.24]$$

or

$$P = \frac{C}{(1+i)^{k-1}} A(n,i) \qquad [3.25]$$

where C = cash flow per period
i = interest rate per period
n = number of cash flows
k = number of time periods until the first cash flow

Alternatively, the present value of a deferred annuity can be found by first imagining that cash flows are to occur on *all* $(k + n - 1)$ dates. The present value of such a stream is, of course, given by the present value of an ordinary annuity consisting of $(k + n - 1)$ cash flows. The effect of the deferral period is accounted for by subtracting the present value of the first $(k - 1)$ 'missing' cash flows, because these cash flows will not occur. That is:

$$P = \begin{bmatrix} \text{present value of an} \\ \text{ordinary annuity of} \\ (k+n-1) \text{ cash flows} \end{bmatrix} less \begin{bmatrix} \text{present value of an} \\ \text{ordinary annuity of} \\ (k-1) \text{ cash flows} \end{bmatrix}$$

That is:

$$P = \frac{C}{i}\left[1 - \frac{1}{(1+i)^{k+n-1}}\right] - \frac{C}{i}\left[1 - \frac{1}{(1+i)^{k-1}}\right]$$
$$= C[A(k+n-1, i) - A(k-1, i)] \qquad [3.26]$$

The valuation of deferred annuities is illustrated in Example 3.18.

EXAMPLE 3.18

Jason will be starting a 6-month live-in training course in 4 months' time. His father, Sam, has promised him a living allowance of $2000 per month to help support him during this time. If the simple interest rate is 9 per cent per annum, payable monthly, how much money will Sam need to set aside today to finance Jason's allowance?

SOLUTION

Sam needs to set aside the present value of the promised allowance. The allowance is an annuity of six payments, the first payment to be made 4 months from today.

Diagrammatically, the cash flows are:

```
0   1   2   3     4       5       6       7       8       9
                $2000   $2000   $2000   $2000   $2000   $2000
```

Using the logic developed in this section, we can approach this problem in two stages. First, *when viewed from the standpoint of date 3*, the cash flows form an ordinary annuity of six payments. We therefore value this stream, as at date 3, using Equation 3.19, which gives the present value of an ordinary annuity. Second, we find the value as at date zero by discounting for three periods. The calculations are shown below. Note that the interest rate is 0.09/12 = 0.75 per cent per month.

As at date 3 the value is:

$$P = \frac{C}{i}\left[1 - \frac{1}{(1+i)^n}\right]$$
$$= \frac{\$2000}{0.0075}\left[1 - \frac{1}{(1.0075)^6}\right]$$
$$= \$11\,691.195\,260$$

As at date zero, the value is thus:

$$P = \frac{\$11\,691.195\,260}{(1.0075)^3}$$
$$= \$11\,432.04$$

This is, of course, the logic embodied in Equation 3.24, as we now show. In this case, $n = 6$, $k = 4$ and $i = 0.09/12 = 0.75$ per cent per month. Using Equation 3.24:

$$P = \frac{1}{(1+i)^{k-1}} \frac{C}{i}\left[1 - \frac{1}{(1+i)^n}\right]$$
$$= \frac{1}{(1.0075)^3} \times \frac{\$2000}{0.0075}\left[1 - \frac{1}{(1.0075)^6}\right]$$
$$= \frac{1}{1.022\,669\,172} \times \$2000 \times 5.845\,597\,63$$
$$= \frac{\$11\,691.195\,260}{1.022\,669\,172}$$
$$= \$11\,432.04$$

Alternatively, using Equation 3.26, and again using $n = 6$, $k = 4$ and $i = 0.75$ per cent per month, the required sum is:

$$P = \frac{C}{i}\left[1 - \frac{1}{(1+i)^{k+n-1}}\right] - \frac{C}{i}\left[1 - \frac{1}{(1+i)^{k-1}}\right]$$

$$= \frac{\$2000}{0.0075}\left[1 - \frac{1}{(1.0075)^9}\right] - \frac{\$2000}{0.0075}\left[1 - \frac{1}{(1.0075)^3}\right]$$

$$= (\$2000 \times 8.671576423) - (\$2000 \times 2.955556237)$$

$$= \$17\,343.1529 - \$5911.1125$$

$$= \$11\,432.04$$

Present value of an ordinary perpetuity

The cash flow pattern of an *ordinary perpetuity* of C dollars per period is shown below:

```
0    1    2    3    4    5
     $C   $C   $C   $C   $C  ──────►
```

The ordinary perpetuity is an ordinary annuity where the number of cash flows n becomes indefinitely large. Therefore, to find its present value, we need to consider the formula for the present value of an ordinary annuity and allow n to become indefinitely large. Thus the problem is to value:

$$P = \lim_{n \to \infty} \frac{C}{i}\left[1 - \frac{1}{(1+i)^n}\right]$$

Because the interest rate i is positive, $(1 + i)^n$ becomes indefinitely large as n becomes indefinitely large. This means that $\frac{1}{(1+i)^n}$ becomes very small because the denominator of this fraction becomes very large. In the limit, the value of this fraction approaches zero and thus the present value of an ordinary perpetuity is:[11]

$$P = \frac{C}{i} \qquad [3.27]$$

where C = cash flow per period
       i = interest rate per period

The valuation of ordinary perpetuities is illustrated in Example 3.19.

EXAMPLE 3.19

A government security promises to pay $3 per annum forever. If the interest rate is 8 per cent per annum and a payment of $3 has just been made, how much is the security worth?

SOLUTION

Using Equation 3.27:

$$P = \frac{C}{i}$$

$$= \frac{\$3}{0.08}$$

$$= \$37.50$$

The value of the security is $37.50.

---

[11] Similarly, it is a simple matter to show that the present value of a perpetuity-due is $C + \frac{C}{i}$, and the present value of a deferred perpetuity, where the first cash flow occurs after k periods, is $\frac{1}{(1+i)^{k-1}} \times \frac{C}{i}$.

3.6.4 FUTURE VALUE OF ANNUITIES

It is frequently necessary to calculate the value of an annuity as at the date of the final cash flow. Such a calculation is required if, for example, regular savings are being made towards a target future sum.

To derive the formula for the future value of an ordinary annuity, we use a two-stage process. First, the *present* value of the annuity is calculated. Second, the *future* value is calculated by accumulating the present value for the n periods from the valuation date to the date of the final cash flow. In effect we use the compound interest formula $S = P(1 + i)^n$ where, in this case, P is given by the present value of an ordinary annuity. That is:

$$S = \frac{C}{i}\left[1 - \frac{1}{(1+i)^n}\right](1+i)^n$$

$$= \frac{C}{i}\left[(1+i)^n - 1\right] \quad [3.28]$$

If $C = \$1$, Equation 3.28 may be written as:[12]

$$S(n, i) = \frac{(1+i)^n - 1}{i} \quad [3.29]$$

Values of $S(n, i)$ for different values of n and i are given in Table 3 of Appendix A (page 797). Alternatively, the Microsoft Excel® function –FV(rate, nper, pmt) may be used. The FV function returns the value of $-1 \times$ the future value of an ordinary annuity, where 'rate' means the interest rate as a decimal, 'nper' means the number of periods and 'pmt' means the amount of each periodic cash flow. The calculation of the future value of an annuity is illustrated in Example 3.20.

EXAMPLE 3.20

Starting with his next monthly salary payment, Harold intends to save $200 each month. If the interest rate is 8.4 per cent per annum, payable monthly, how much will Harold have saved after 2 years?

SOLUTION

The monthly interest rate is 8.4/12 = 0.7 per cent. Using Equation 3.28, Harold's savings will amount to:

$$S = \frac{C}{i}\left[(1+i)^n - 1\right]$$

$$= \frac{\$200}{0.007}\left[(1.007)^{24} - 1\right]$$

$$= \$200 \times 26.034\,925\,07$$

$$= \$5206.99$$

Alternatively, using Microsoft Excel®, we find that –FV(0.007, 24 200) = $5206.99.

We could use this two-stage approach to derive formulae for the future values of annuities-due and deferred annuities. In practice, however, it is usually just as easy to apply this approach using the numbers of the particular problem. As we said at the start of this chapter, rather than learning a list of *formulae*, it is preferable to learn the *approach* and then apply this approach to the particular problem. This is illustrated in Example 3.21.

---

12 The notation $S_{\overline{n}|i}$ can also be used.

EXAMPLE 3.21

Harold's sister Janice can also save $200 per month, but whereas Harold takes 1 month to save his first $200, Janice will start by setting aside $200 immediately. With an interest rate of 0.7 per cent per month, how much will she have in 2 years' time? Reconcile this amount with the savings achieved by Harold in the previous example.

SOLUTION
This problem requires the future value of an annuity-due. We first calculate the present value, then accumulate this amount for 24 months:

Step 1

$$P = C + \frac{C}{i}\left[1 - \frac{1}{(1+i)^n}\right]$$

$$= \$200 + \frac{\$200}{0.007}\left[1 - \frac{1}{(1.007)^{24}}\right]$$

$$= \$4604.321\,714$$

Step 2

$$S = P(1+i)^n$$

$$= \$4604.321\,714(1.007)^{24}$$

$$= \$5443.43$$

Janice is thus able to save $5443.43 after 2 years, compared with Harold's savings of $5206.99. That is, Janice will save $236.44 more than Harold. Logically, this amount should equal the future value of the initial $200 Janice set aside at the start, accumulated for 24 months at 0.7 per cent per month. This is in fact the case, because $200(1.007)^{24} = \$236.44$.

PRINCIPAL-AND-INTEREST LOAN CONTRACTS 3.7

3.7.1 BASIC FEATURES OF THE CONTRACT

An important application of annuities is to loan contracts, where the principal is gradually reduced by a series of equal repayments. This type of loan is often called a **principal-and-interest loan** or a credit foncier loan. Many commercial loans, consumer loans and housing loans are in this category. The promised repayments form an annuity and the present value of the repayments is equal to the loan principal. Therefore, if the promised future repayments are made on time the debt should reduce gradually during the loan term, so that when the final promised repayment is made the debt should be extinguished. This pattern is illustrated in Example 3.22.

LEARNING OBJECTIVE 4
Apply your knowledge of annuities to solve a range of problems, including problems involving principal-and-interest loan contracts

EXAMPLE 3.22

On 31 December 2011, Pennant Ltd borrows $100 000 from ZNA Bank. Annual repayments are required over 5 years at a fixed interest rate of 11.5 per cent per annum. How much is each annual repayment? Show the year-by-year record of the loan account for the 5 years ended 31 December 2016.

SOLUTION
The annual repayments of C dollars form an ordinary annuity with a present value of $100 000. Using Equation 3.19:

$$\$100\,000 = \frac{C}{0.115}\left[1 - \frac{1}{(1.115)^5}\right]$$

$$= C \times 3.649\,877\,84$$

continued →

principal-and-interest loan

loan repaid by a sequence of equal cash flows, each of which is sufficient to cover the interest accrued since the previous payment and to reduce the current balance owing. Therefore, the debt is extinguished when the sequence of cash flows is completed. Also known as a *credit foncier loan*

Example 3.22   continued

So $C = \dfrac{\$100\,000}{3.649\,877\,847}$

$= \$27\,398.18$

The annual repayment required is $27 398.18.

Alternatively, we could use the Microsoft Excel® function PMT(rate, nper, pv). Using the spreadsheet, we find that −PMT(0.115, 5, 100 000) returns $27 398.18.

The year-by-year record of the loan account is shown in Table 3.6.

TABLE 3.6

DATE	ENTRY	BALANCE OWING
31 December 2011	Principal borrowed	$100 000.00
31 December 2012	*Add* interest 0.115 × $100 000.00 = $11 500.00	$111 500.00
	Less repayment $27 398.18	$84 101.82
31 December 2013	*Add* interest 0.115 × $84 101.82 = $9671.71	$93 773.53
	Less repayment $27 398.18	$66 375.35
31 December 2014	*Add* interest 0.115 × $66 375.35 = $7633.17	$74 008.52
	Less repayment $27 398.18	$46 610.34
31 December 2015	*Add* interest 0.115 × $46 610.34 = $5360.19	$51 970.53
	Less repayment $27 398.18	$24 572.35
31 December 2016	*Add* interest 0.115 × $24 572.35 = $2825.83	$27 398.18
	Less repayment $27 398.18	$0.00

The year-by-year record shows that annual repayments of $27 398.18 are just sufficient to repay the loan over the 5-year term.

3.7.2 PRINCIPAL AND INTEREST COMPONENTS

As shown by the loan account in Example 3.22, the required repayments are just sufficient to extinguish the debt at the required date. This is achieved by a series of repayments, each of which is sufficient to cover interest accrued since the previous repayment and to reduce the principal. As the principal decreases, so also does the interest accruing and thus, as time passes, a larger proportion of each repayment goes to reducing the principal. The principal and interest components of the repayments in Example 3.22 are shown in Table 3.7.

TABLE 3.7

YEAR ENDED 31 DECEMBER	INTEREST COMPONENT ($)	PRINCIPAL COMPONENT ($)	REPAYMENT ($)
2012	11 500.00	15 898.18	27 398.18
2013	9 671.71	17 726.47	27 398.18
2014	7 633.17	19 765.01	27 398.18
2015	5 360.19	22 037.99	27 398.18
2016	2 825.83	24 572.35	27 398.18

This pattern is more marked where the number of repayments to be made is large. This is shown in Example 3.23.

EXAMPLE 3.23

Phantom Ltd borrows $100 000 at an interest rate of 11.5 per cent per annum, repayable by equal monthly instalments over 20 years. Calculate the principal and interest components of the first and last repayments.

SOLUTION

In this example, the monthly interest rate is 0.115/12 = 0.009 583 333 and the loan term is 20 × 12 = 240 months. We use Equation 3.19 to calculate the monthly repayment:

$$\$100\,000 = \frac{C}{0.009\,583\,333}\left[1 - \frac{1}{(1.009\,583\,333)^{240}}\right]$$

$$= C \times 93.770\,840\,22$$

So
$$C = \frac{\$100\,000}{93.770\,840\,22}$$

$$= \$1066.43$$

The interest accrued during the first month of the loan is 0.009 583 333 × $100 000 = $958.33. Therefore, when the first monthly repayment of $1066.43 is made, $958.33 (or nearly 90 per cent of the repayment) is required to meet the interest accrued during the first month and only $108.10 (just over 10 per cent of the repayment) is available to reduce the principal. At the end of the loan term this pattern is reversed. Only a small amount of interest will accrue during the last month, so almost the whole of the final monthly repayment will be available to reduce the principal. The component of principal in the final repayment is $1066.43/1.009 583 333 = $1056.31; therefore, the interest component is only $10.12. One aspect of this pattern is that the balance owing decreases slowly in the early stages of repayment, but decreases rapidly as the maturity date is approached. This pattern is considered in more detail in the next section.

3.7.3 BALANCE OWING AT ANY GIVEN DATE

The balance owing at any given date is the present value of the then remaining repayments. We explained earlier how the principal is the present value of *all* promised repayments. Of course, the principal is simply the balance owing at the time the loan is made. Similarly, the balance owing at any given date is the present value of the repayments still to be made as at that date. The calculation of the balance owing on a loan is illustrated in Example 3.24.

EXAMPLE 3.24

Consider again Phantom Ltd's loan of $100 000 at an interest rate of 11.5 per cent per annum, repayable by equal monthly instalments over 20 years. As shown in Example 3.23, the required monthly repayment is $1066.43. What is the balance owing when:

(a) one-third of the loan term has expired?
(b) two-thirds of the loan term has expired?

continued →

Example 3.24 *continued*

SOLUTION

(a) The loan term is 240 months. Therefore, when one-third (or 80 months) of this term has expired, 160 monthly repayments are still to be made. The balance owing at the end of month 80 is the present value of the then remaining 160 repayments:

$$P_{80} = \frac{\$1066.43}{0.009583333}\left[1 - \frac{1}{(1.009583333)^{160}}\right]$$

$$= \$87\,087.85$$

(b) When two-thirds (or 160 months) of the loan term has expired, 80 monthly repayments still have to be made. Therefore, the balance owing at the end of month 160 is:

$$P_{160} = \frac{\$1066.43}{0.009583333}\left[1 - \frac{1}{(1.009583333)^{80}}\right]$$

$$= \$59\,394.64$$

In the previous section we explained that, in these types of loans, the balance owing reduces slowly at first and more rapidly towards the end of the loan term. This pattern is clearly evident in this example. When one-third of the loan term has expired, the balance owing is still more than $87 000 out of an original loan of $100 000. That is, the passing of one-third of the loan term has seen the principal fall by less than 13 per cent. When two-thirds of the loan term has expired, only about 40 per cent of the debt has been repaid. A more detailed presentation of this pattern is provided in Figure 3.2.

FIGURE 3.2 Balance owing as a loan is repaid

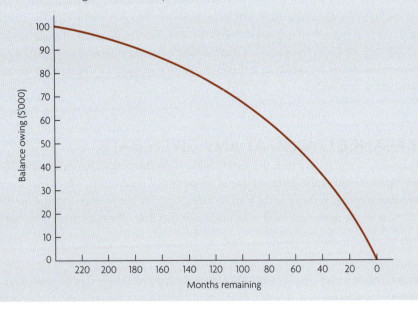

3.7.4 LOAN TERM REQUIRED

In some applications it is necessary to solve for the required loan term n given the principal, interest rate and periodic repayment. For example, in order to plan future expenditure, a borrower may wish to know when an existing loan will be repaid. Solving for the loan term requires us to rearrange Equation 3.19 so that n appears on the left-hand side:

$$P = \frac{C}{i}\left[1 - \frac{1}{(1+i)^n}\right]$$

$$\frac{1}{(1+i)^n} = 1 - \frac{Pi}{C}$$

$$(1+i)^n = \frac{C}{C - Pi}$$

and therefore:

$$n = \frac{\log[C/(C - Pi)]}{\log(1+i)} \qquad [3.30]$$

Logarithms to any base (such as base 10 or base e) will give the correct answer. The calculation of a required loan term is illustrated in Example 3.25.

EXAMPLE 3.25

One year ago, Canberra Fruit Ltd borrowed $750 000 at an interest rate of 12 per cent per annum. The loan is being repaid by monthly instalments of $16 683.34 over 5 years. As a result of making the promised repayments over the past year, the balance owing is now $633 532.48. The company can now afford repayments of $20 000 per month and the company manager wishes to know when the loan will be repaid if repayments are increased to that level. The manager also wishes to know the amount of the final repayment.

SOLUTION

Using Equation 3.30:

$$n = \frac{\log[C/(C - Pi)]}{\log(1+i)}$$

$$= \frac{\log\{\$20\,000 / [\$20\,000 - (\$633\,532.48)(0.01)]\}}{\log(1.01)}$$

$$= \frac{\log(\$20\,000 / \$13\,664.6752)}{\log(1.01)}$$

$$= \frac{\log(1.463\,627\,91)}{\log(1.01)}$$

Using 'common' logarithms (logarithms to the base 10):[13]

$$n = \frac{0.165\,430\,682}{0.004\,321\,373}$$

$$= 38.282 \text{ months}$$

The loan will be repaid after a further 39 months; for the first 38 months the repayment will be $20 000 per month, while the last (39th) repayment will be a smaller amount. The amount of the last repayment must be such that the present value of all 39 repayments equals the balance owing of $633 532.48. Using R to represent the amount of the last repayment, we therefore require that:

$$\$633\,532.48 = \frac{\$20\,000}{0.01}\left[1 - \frac{1}{(1.01)^{38}}\right] + \frac{R}{(1.01)^{39}}$$

$$\$3839.2139 = \frac{R}{(1.01)^{39}}$$

Thus:

$R = \$5659.47$

The amount of the last (39th) repayment is $5659.47.

---

[13] Use of natural logarithms (logarithms to the base e) must give the same answer. In this case the calculation is $n = 0.380\,918\,223 / 0.009\,950\,33 = 38.282$.

3.7.5 CHANGING THE INTEREST RATE

variable interest rate loan
loan where the lender can change the interest rate charged, usually in line with movements in the general level of interest rates in the economy

In some loan contracts, usually called **variable interest rate loans**, the interest rate can be changed at any time by the lender, although, in practice, changes are normally made only when there has been a change in the general level of interest rates in the economy. Such a change may be signalled or caused by the Reserve Bank of Australia changing the cash rate. In Australia, many housing loans, and many commercial loans, are in this category. Typically, the parties to the contract will at the outset agree on a notional loan term—say, 15 years for a housing loan—and the lender will then require a regular repayment that is calculated *as if* the current interest rate is fixed for 15 years. If, as is always the case, the general level of interest rates subsequently changes, the interest rate charged on the loan will then be changed. The lender will then set the new required repayment, which will be calculated *as if* the new interest rate is fixed for the remaining loan term. Alternatively, the lender may allow the borrower to continue making the same repayment and, instead, alter the loan term to reflect the new interest rate.[14] Of course, a combination of both responses is also a possibility. These choices are illustrated in Example 3.26.

EXAMPLE 3.26

Three years ago Andrew and Jane borrowed $80 000, repayable by equal monthly instalments over 15 years. At the time they borrowed the money, the interest rate was 9.6 per cent per annum calculated monthly. Following standard procedures, the lender correctly calculated the required monthly payment to be $840.21. Andrew and Jane have made all repayments on time and the balance owing is now $71 685.05. The general level of interest rates has been rising and the lender has now decided to increase the interest rate to 10.8 per cent per annum calculated monthly. What will be the new monthly repayment if the loan term is to remain unchanged? If, instead, the monthly repayment is left at $840.21, by how many months will the loan term increase?

SOLUTION

The new monthly repayment C must be set so that the present value, calculated using the *new* interest rate, of the remaining 144 repayments equals the balance outstanding of $71 685.05. The new interest rate is 10.8 per cent per annum or 0.9 per cent per month. Therefore, using Equation 3.19:

$$\$71\,685.05 = \frac{C}{0.009}\left[1 - \frac{1}{(1.009)^{144}}\right]$$

$$= 80.531\,669\,39\,C$$

$$C = \$890.15$$

The new repayment is $890.15 per month.

Alternatively, if the loan term is extended, and the monthly repayment is left at $840.21, the new loan term may be found using Equation 3.30:

$$n = \frac{\log[C/(C - P_i)]}{\log(1 + i)}$$

$$= \frac{\log\{\$840.21/[\$840.21 - (\$71\,685.05)(0.009)]\}}{\log(1.009)}$$

$$= \frac{\log(4.307\,785\,068)}{\log(1.009)}$$

$$= 162.998 \text{ months}$$

$$\approx 163 \text{ months}$$

The remaining loan term is now 163 months, which is 19 months longer than the 144 'expected' at the time of the interest rate increase.

---

14 Note, however, that if the interest rate is increased to a level where the monthly repayment is less than the monthly interest accruing (that is, $C < Pi$), then the loan term becomes infinite. In these circumstances lenders will usually require a higher monthly repayment.

GENERAL ANNUITIES

3.8

In our discussion of annuities, the frequency of compounding has coincided with the frequency of the cash flows. An annuity with this feature is called a **simple annuity**. For example, we have considered cases where interest is calculated and charged annually, and the borrower is required to make annual repayments. In practice, however, this is not always the case. Situations arise where loan repayments are required more frequently, or less frequently, than interest is charged (compounded). An annuity with this feature is called a **general annuity**.

In a general annuity, the frequency of compounding does not match the frequency of repayment. There are thus two cases to consider:

(a) *The frequency of compounding is greater than the frequency of repayment.* For example, a loan contract may specify an interest rate of 8 per cent per annum, compounding quarterly, but repayments are made annually.

(b) *The frequency of compounding is less than the frequency of repayment.* For example, a loan contract may specify an interest rate of 8 per cent per annum, compounding quarterly, but repayments are made monthly.

In both cases, to solve the problem we need first to adjust the specified interest rate to an interest rate where the compounding frequency matches the repayment frequency.[15] This adjustment is made using the concept of the effective interest rate that we discussed in Section 3.4.3. This concept was summarised in Equation 3.6, which we reproduce below:

$$i = \left(1 + \frac{j}{m}\right)^m - 1$$

where i = the effective interest rate per period
 j = the nominal interest rate, compounding m times per period

Note that in this equation the time dimension of i is for a longer period than the time dimension of j/m. For example, i might be an interest rate per annum while j/m might be an interest rate per quarter. It is convenient to restate Equation 3.6 in terms of an interest rate i_S, for the shorter time period, and an interest rate, i_L, for the longer time period. That is, Equation 3.6 is rewritten as:

$$i_L = (1 + i_S)^m - 1 \qquad [3.31]$$

where m = the number of 'short' periods in one 'long' period

The use of Equation 3.31 is illustrated in Examples 3.27 and 3.28.

LEARNING OBJECTIVE 5
Distinguish between simple and general annuities and make basic calculations involving general annuities

simple annuity
annuity in which the frequency of charging interest matches the frequency of payment

general annuity
annuity in which the frequency of charging interest does not match the frequency of payment; thus, repayments may be made either more frequently or less frequently than interest is charged

---

Use Equation 3.31 to express 8 per cent per annum, compounding quarterly, as:

(a) an effective annual interest rate
(b) an effective monthly interest rate.

SOLUTION

(a) In this case, interest is compounding quarterly and we wish to calculate an equivalent interest rate in which compounding occurs annually. Thus we are required to calculate i_L, where i_S = 0.08/4 = 0.02, and m = 4. Using Equation 3.31:

$i_L = (1 + i_S)^m - 1$
$= (1.02)^4 - 1$
$= 0.082\ 432\ 16$
$\approx 8.243\%$ per annum

EXAMPLE 3.27

continued →

---

15 Alternatively, an adjustment can be made to the repayment amount. However, when using a calculator it is generally easier to adjust the interest rate.

Example 3.27 *continued*

(b) In this case, interest is compounding quarterly and we wish to calculate an equivalent interest rate in which compounding occurs monthly. Thus we are required to calculate i_s, where $i_L = 0.08/4 = 0.02$ and $m = 3$. Using Equation 3.31:

$$i_L = (1 + i_s)^m - 1$$
$$0.02 = (1 + i_s)^3 - 1$$
$$i_s = (1.02)^{\frac{1}{3}} - 1$$
$$= 0.006\,622\,71$$
$$\approx 0.662\% \text{ per month}$$

EXAMPLE 3.28

A loan is currently being repaid by repayments of $55 000 at the end of each quarter. The interest rate is 8 per cent per annum. The borrower wishes to change to a monthly repayment schedule that will pay off the loan by the same maturity date. Calculate the amount of each monthly repayment.

SOLUTION
The repayment schedule for a typical quarter is shown in Figure 3.3.

FIGURE 3.3 Monthly and quarterly repayments

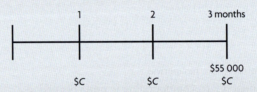

As shown in Figure 3.3, it is proposed to replace each end-of-quarter cash flow of $55 000 with three end-of-month cash flows of C dollars each. Interest is charged quarterly at a nominal rate of 8 per cent per annum—that is, the effective *quarterly* interest rate is 2 per cent per quarter. As shown in Example 3.27 (b), the equivalent effective *monthly* interest rate is 0.662 271 per cent per month. Equating the present values of the quarterly and monthly cash-flow streams gives:

$$\frac{\$55\,000}{1.02} = \frac{C}{1.006\,622\,71}\left[1 - \frac{1}{(1.006\,622\,71)^3}\right]$$

Note, however, that although we have included the calculation of $(1.006\,622\,71)^3$ in this expression, this calculation should by definition equal 1.02 (see the calculation in Example 3.27 (b) for clarification). Therefore, we need to solve:

$$\frac{\$55\,000}{1.02} = \frac{C}{0.006\,622\,71}\left[1 - \frac{1}{1.02}\right]$$

which gives $C = \$18\,212.45$.

Therefore, monthly repayments of $18 212.45 will pay the loan off at the same maturity date as quarterly repayments of $55 000. Note that 3 × $18 212.45 = $54 637.35, which is slightly less than the quarterly repayment of $55 000. This difference reflects the present-value effect of making monthly repayments earlier than the quarterly repayments they replace.

WWW

A case study illustrating topics within this chapter can be found on the Online Learning Centre that accompanies this book: www.mhhe.com/au/peirson11e

Connect Plus features a case study illustrating topics covered in this chapter. Ask your lecturer or tutor for your course's unique URL.

SUMMARY

→ Financial managers frequently make decisions that involve the time value of money. This chapter covered the major tools of financial mathematics needed to support these decisions. These tools include calculating rates of return, present values and future values, and defining and applying interest rates, including simple interest and compound interest.

→ The definition and valuation of various streams of cash flows were considered in detail, with the present value of an ordinary annuity being used as the basis for dealing with several related problems. Annuity applications, including interest-only loans and principal-and-interest loans, were also discussed.

→ A wider class of problems, in which interest is charged either more frequently or less frequently than cash flows occur, was also discussed.

→ Throughout the chapter, emphasis was placed on developing a sound understanding to support the use of the various formulae that were derived.

KEY TERMS

accumulation 38	effective interest rate 41	present value 36
annuity 55	financial contract 33	present value of a contract 51
annuity-due 55	future sum 36	principal 36
cash flow 33	general annuity 69	principal-and-interest loan 64
compound interest 38	geometric rate of return 48	rate of return 33
continuous interest 46	interest-only loan 41	real interest rate 44
debt 34	interest rate 34	simple annuity 69
deferred annuity 55	log price relative 47	simple interest 35
discounting 40	nominal interest rate 41, 44	terminal value of a contract 52
	ordinary annuity 55	time value of money 34
	ordinary perpetuity 56	variable interest rate loan 68

SELF-TEST PROBLEMS

1. Andrew borrowed $6000 and repaid the loan 60 days later by a single payment of $6250. What is the implied annual simple interest rate?

2. Angela deposits $5000 today in a bank account that pays interest annually at the rate of 8 per cent. She then makes 10 more deposits of $1000 each at annual intervals.
   (a) How much does she have when she has made the last deposit?
   (b) If Angela wished to accumulate the same sum by making a single deposit now, what amount would she need to deposit?

3. Geoff and Gail wish to borrow $75 000 to be repaid by equal monthly instalments over 25 years. The nominal annual interest rate is 9.9 per cent.

(a) What is the effective annual interest rate?

(b) What is the amount of the monthly repayment?

Solutions to self-test problems are available in Appendix B, page 803.

INTERNATIONAL ARTICLES

International articles related to this topic are available on the Online Learning Centre at **www.mhhe.com/au/peirson11e**

REFERENCES

Crapp, H. & Marshall, J., *Money Market Maths*, Allen & Unwin, Sydney, 1986.

Knox, D.M., Zima, P. & Brown, R.L., *Mathematics of Finance*, 2nd edn, McGraw-Hill, Sydney, 1999.

Martin, P. & Burrow, M., *Applied Financial Mathematics*, Prentice-Hall, Sydney, 1991.

QUESTIONS

1. **[LO 1]** Explain the difference(s) between an interest rate and a rate of return.

2. **[LO 1]** Distinguish between simple interest and compound interest.

3. **[LO 1]** *In financial mathematics, the symbol* P *can stand for 'present value', 'price' or 'principal', but all three terms really have the same meaning.* Discuss.

4. **[LO 1]** The term 'nominal interest rate' has two different meanings. Explain these two meanings, distinguishing carefully between them.

5. **[LO 1]** Rates of return should be multiplied, not added. Is this true? Why, or why not?

6. **[LO 4]** *In any variable interest rate loan, it is possible that the interest rate can be increased to a level where the loan term becomes infinite unless the periodic repayment is increased.* Explain how this can occur, and relate your answer to the characteristics of Equation 3.30.

7. **[LO 5]** Distinguish between a simple annuity and a general annuity.

PROBLEMS

1. **Simple interest earned [LO 1]**
Nicholas deposits $2000 in a bank fixed deposit for 6 months at an interest rate of 13.25 per cent per annum. How much interest will he earn?

2. **Simple interest earned [LO 1]**
If Nicholas reinvests the $2000, *plus* the interest earned (see Problem 1), for a further 6 months, again at 13.25 per cent per annum, how much interest will he earn in this second 6-month period?

3. **Implied simple interest rate [LO 1]**
Jane borrowed $10 000 and repaid the loan 30 days later by a single payment of $10 400. What is the implied annual simple interest rate?

4. **Calculating the loan term [LO 1]**
Mary borrowed $7250 at an annual simple interest rate of 15.50 per cent. She repaid the loan by paying a lump sum of $7394.70. What was the loan term?

5. **Calculating the lump sum repayment [LO 1]**
On 2 April 2011, Paradise Pencils Ltd borrows $200 000, repaying in a lump sum on 16 May 2011. The interest rate is 9.55 per cent per annum. How much is the lump sum repayment?

6. **Simple interest earned (harder) [LO 1]**
On 5 February 2011, Financial Solutions Ltd deposits $300 000 with Second Street Bank at a simple interest rate of 4.4 per cent per annum. The maturity date of the deposit is 5 May 2011. Calculate the amount of interest the deposit will earn.

7. **Present value [LO 1]**
Jupiter Mining Ltd promises to pay $500 000 in 90 days' time. Taking into account the company's credit standing, the market interest rate for a loan period of 90 days is 10.65 per cent per annum. How much can Jupiter Mining borrow?

8. **Simple and compound interest [LO 1]**
   (a) What will be the accumulated value, at the end of 10 years, of $1000 invested in a savings account that pays 8 per cent per annum? Assume that no withdrawals are made from the savings account until the end of the tenth year. What is the interest component of the accumulated value?
   (b) Assume that interest is withdrawn every year. What will be the total interest earnings at the end of the tenth year? Why does this amount differ from the interest earned in Question (a)?

9. **Compound interest earned [LO 1]**
If you invest $65 000 for 3 years at 14.7 per cent per annum (interest payable annually), how much will you have at the end of the 3 years?

10. **Compound interest earned [LO 1]**
    If you invest $87 000 at 7.35 per cent per annum (interest paid annually), how much will you have:
    (a) at the end of 3 years?
    (b) at the end of 6 years?

11. **Compound interest earned (harder) [LO 1]**
    Frank has invested $10 000 for 10 years at 12.4 per cent per annum. He has to pay tax on the interest income each year.
    (a) Calculate the value of the investment at the end of the tenth year if his tax rate is:
       (i) 45 per cent per annum
       (ii) 30 per cent per annum
       (iii) 15 per cent per annum
       (iv) zero per annum.
    (b) Rework your answer to (a)(i) if, instead of having to pay tax each year, Frank must pay in tax 45 per cent of the accumulated interest at the end of the tenth year. Which tax system is better for him? Why?

12. **Compound interest earned [LO 1]**
    Philip invests $17 200 at an interest rate of 2.5 per cent per quarter. How much is the investment worth after 2 years?

13. **Compound interest earned [LO 1]**
    Rhiannyn invests $25 000 at an interest rate of 0.6 per cent per month. How much is the investment worth after 3 years?

14. **Present value [LO 1]**
    Calculate the following present values:
    (a) $1000 payable in 5 years if the interest rate is 12 per cent per annum
    (b) $1000 payable in 10 years if the interest rate is 12 per cent per annum
    (c) $1000 payable in 5 years if the interest rate is 6 per cent per annum
    (d) $16 205 payable in 1 year if the interest rate is 1.5 per cent per month
    (e) $1 million payable in 40 years if the interest rate is 15 per cent per annum
    (f) $1 million payable in 100 years if the interest rate is 15 per cent per annum.

15. **Compound interest [LO 1]**
    Neeta Stoves Ltd borrows $8000 repayable in a lump sum after 1 year. The interest rate agreed to is described as '15.0 per cent per annum, calculated monthly'. How much is the repayment?

16. **Implied compound interest rate [LO 1]**
    What is the annual interest rate (compound) implied by each of the following future values (FV), present values (PV) and terms (t):
    (a) FV = $92 000; PV = $82 000; t = 2 years
    (b) FV = $1 604 600; PV = $1 500 000; t = 4 years
    (c) FV = $2 000 000; PV = $1 307 600; t = 3 years
    (d) FV = $10 000 000; PV = $6 000 000; t = 6 years
    (e) FV = $10 000 000; PV = $6 000 000; t = 5.5 years

17. **Effective annual interest rate [LO 1]**
    What is the effective annual interest rate corresponding to each of the following nominal interest rates:
    (a) 18 per cent per annum, payable half-yearly
    (b) 18 per cent per annum, payable monthly
    (c) 18 per cent per annum, payable fortnightly
    (d) 18 per cent per annum, payable daily
    (e) 18 per cent per annum, payable continuously.

18. **Effective annual interest rate [LO 1]**
    What is the effective annual interest rate corresponding to each of the following nominal interest rates:
    (a) 7.5 per cent per annum, payable half-yearly
    (b) 7.5 per cent per annum, payable monthly
    (c) 7.5 per cent per annum, payable fortnightly
    (d) 7.5 per cent per annum, payable daily
    (e) 7.5 per cent per annum, payable continuously.

19. **Effective annual interest rate [LO 1]**
    Jerm Ltd buys a bank bill for $91 107 and sells it 54 days later for $93 323. What annual effective interest rate did Jerm Ltd earn?

20. **Simple interest and effective annual interest rate [LO 1]**
    Liana Ltd bought a bank bill on 7 January 2012 for $976 751 and sold it on 3 March 2012 for $987 618.
    (a) What simple interest rate did Liana Ltd earn?
    (b) What annual effective interest rate did Liana Ltd earn?

21. **Calculating the effective annual interest rate [LO 1]**
    On 16 January 2012, an investor lent a sum of money to be repaid, with interest, on 11 March 2012. The interest rate was 6.15 per cent and was quoted on a simple interest basis. What effective annual interest rate did the investor earn?

22. **Effective annual interest rate (harder) [LO 1]**

    Rock Solid Ltd sells, on credit, goods to the value of $8465.95 to University Garden Supplies Ltd. Rock Solid offers a discount of half of 1 per cent for payment within 7 days; otherwise, payment must be made on or before the thirtieth day. What is the effective annual interest rate implicit in the discount being offered? State any assumptions you make.

23. **Effective annual interest rate (harder) [LO 1]**

    Since 1 August 2010, Wing Yin's investment policy has been to lodge fixed (term) deposits at her local bank. The bank pays interest on the maturity date of a deposit and the interest rate is expressed as an annual simple interest rate. When a deposit matures, Wing Yin's policy is to re-lodge the whole sum (principal and interest) immediately for a further period. She chooses the term of each deposit according to her assessment of the interest rates available at that time. Wing Yin's decisions to date are as follows:

Date	Decision
1 August 2010	8-month deposit at 9.15 per cent per annum
1 April 2011	6-month deposit at 8.45 per cent per annum
1 October 2011	10-month deposit at 8.16 per cent per annum

    Calculate, as at 1 August 2012, the effective annual interest rate Wing Yin has earned since she began this policy. (Assume that all months are of equal length.) Briefly explain each step.

24. **Nominal interest rate [LO 1]**

    A retail chain operates its own credit provision system for customers. Company policy is to set a nominal annual interest rate, and to charge interest monthly. To cover its costs and make a return on capital, the company has a target effective interest rate of 19.5 per cent per annum. What nominal annual interest rate should it set?

25. **Nominal interest rate [LO 1]**

    If the real interest rate is 10 per cent per annum, and the expected inflation rate is 25 per cent per annum, what should be the nominal interest rate?

26. **Nominal interest rate (harder) [LO 1]**

    George is intending to lend money to his nephew to help him set up a new business. The loan will be made now, and is to be repaid in a lump sum after 3 years. George wishes to earn a real interest rate of 3.5 per cent per annum. He expects the inflation rate in the coming year to be 10 per cent but believes that it will fall steadily thereafter to 6 per cent in the following year and to 4 per cent in the third year. What annual interest rate should George set on the loan?

27. **Nominal interest rate (harder) [LO 1]**

    Grose Paterson Bank Ltd is intending to lend money to a client. The loan is to be repaid in a lump sum after 7 years. The bank's required real rate of return is 3 per cent per annum. The bank expects the inflation rate in the coming year to be 8 per cent per annum, falling to 5 per cent per annum the following year, and 4 per cent per annum thereafter. What annual interest rate should the bank set?

28. **Real annual rate of return [LO 1]**

    In Xanadu, the consumer price index (CPI) stood at 147.6 on 1 January 2007. On that date, SBF Ltd invested $50 000 for 4 years at an interest rate of 11.4 per cent per annum (compound). On 1 January 2011 the CPI stood at 193.8. What real annual rate of return has SBF earned?

29. **Log price relative [LO 1]**

    An investor purchases 1000 shares at $5.50 per share on 31 May 2011. Over the next 6 months the investor notes down the price of the share at the end of each month. The result is shown below:

End of June	$5.85
End of July	$6.12
End of August	$5.75
End of September	$5.75
End of October	$6.44
End of November	$6.60

    There were no dividends paid in this period. Calculate, for each month, the log price relative, using natural (base e) logarithms. What does the sum of the log price relatives represent? Compare this sum to $\ell n(\$6.60/\$5.50)$. Explain.

30. **Average annual rate of return [LO 1]**

    Matthew bought an apartment for $364 000. After 4 years he estimates that its value has changed as follows:

In Year 1: an increase of 7 per cent
In Year 2: an increase of 27 per cent
In Year 3: a decrease of 5 per cent
In Year 4: an increase of 11 per cent
How much is it worth now? What is the average annual rate of return?

31. **Present value [LO 1]**
    What is the present value (at 7 per cent per annum) of a contract that provides for the following three payments to be made:
    After 6 months: $7601
    After 2.5 years: $9900
    After 7 years: $18 522

32. **Present and future values [LO 1]**
    A company is entitled to receive a cash inflow of $8000 in 2 years' time and a further cash inflow of $14 000 in 5 years' time. If the interest rate is 8.5 per cent per annum, how much is this stream of cash inflows worth:
    (a) today
    (b) in 5 years' time.

33. **Internal rate of return [LO 1]**
    An investment costs $50 000 and generates cash inflows of $40 000 after 1 year and $30 000 after 2 years. Show that the internal rate of return on this investment is approximately 27.2 per cent per annum.

34. **Calculating principal and interest repayments [LO 4]**
    Luke borrows $800 000 from a bank to set up a medical practice. He agrees to pay a fixed interest rate of 10.2 per cent per annum (calculated monthly) and to repay by equal monthly instalments over 10 years. Calculate the monthly repayment. By how much does Luke's *first* repayment reduce the principal? If the loan is paid off as planned, by how much will the *last* repayment reduce the principal?

35. **Calculating principal outstanding [LO 4]**
    After making 21 monthly repayments, Luke (see Problem 34) inherits a large sum of money and decides to repay the (remaining) loan. When he arrives at the bank to make the twenty-second repayment he asks for the payout figure. How much should it be?

36. **Calculating the loan term [LO 4]**
    John decides that he desperately needs a new Italian suit priced at $1999. He borrows the money and agrees to pay $71.07 each month at an interest rate of 16.8 per cent per annum, payable monthly. For how long will he be making repayments?

37. **Annual rate of return [LO 4]**
    What is the approximate annual rate of return on an investment with an initial cash outlay of $10 000 and net cash inflows of $2770 per year for 5 years?

38. **Monthly interest, nominal interest rate and effective annual interest rate [LO 4]**
    Warren Cameron buys a boat for $30 000, paying $5000 deposit. The remainder is borrowed from the Goodfriend Loan Co. to be repaid by 15 monthly payments of $2027.50 each. What is the monthly interest rate being charged? What is the nominal annual interest rate? What is the effective annual interest rate?

39. **Calculating the loan term [LO 4]**
    Anne Hopewell has just borrowed $70 000 to be repaid by monthly repayments over 20 years at an interest rate of 18 per cent per annum. Based on this information, the monthly repayment is approximately $1080 but Anne intends to make higher monthly repayments. She asks you how long it will take to repay the loan if the amount she pays per month is:
    (a) $1100
    (b) $1200
    (c) $1500.

40. **Annuities [LO 3]**
    Today is Stanley's 55th birthday. He plans to retire on his 65th birthday and wants to put aside the same sum of money every birthday (starting today) up to and including his 65th birthday. He then wants to be able to withdraw $10 000 every birthday (starting with his 66th) up to and including his 85th birthday. He believes that an interest rate of 10 per cent per annum is a reasonable estimate. How much does he need to put aside each birthday?

41. **Annuities [LO 4]**
    Layla borrows $50 000, repayable in monthly instalments over 10 years. The nominal interest rate is 12 per cent per annum. What is the monthly repayment? After 3 years have passed, the lender increases the interest rate to 13.5 per cent per annum and Layla is given the choice of either increasing the monthly repayment or extending the term of the loan. What would be the new monthly repayment? What would be the new loan term?

42. **Annuities [LO 4]**
    Exactly a year ago, Stephen and Lan Kuan borrowed $150 000 from a bank, to be repaid in equal monthly

instalments over 25 years at an interest rate of 7.8 per cent per annum. Today, the bank told them that it was introducing a monthly fee of $10 but they could continue to repay the loan by making their current monthly payments. However, Stephen and Lan Kuan are worried because if they do this, the loan will take longer to repay. They have asked you to calculate how much longer it will take to repay the loan.

43. **Effective annual interest rate, repayments and loan terms [LO 4]**

    Don and Jenny wish to borrow $180 000, to be repaid over a period of 20 years by monthly instalments. The interest rate (nominal) is 7.8 per cent per annum. The first payment is due at the end of the first month.

    (a) Calculate the effective annual interest rate.
    (b) Calculate the amount of the monthly repayment if the same amount is to be repaid every month for the period of the loan.
    (c) Suppose, instead, that the lender agrees that Don and Jenny will repay $1100 per month for the first 12 months, then $1250 per month for the 12 months after that, then $X per month thereafter. Assuming that the term is to stay at 20 years, how much is $X?
    (d) Alternatively, suppose that Don and Jenny decide to repay $2500 per month from the time the money is borrowed until it is repaid. How long would it take to repay the loan? What would be the amount of the final payment?

44. **Repayments and loan terms [LO 4]**

    Peter borrowed $800 000 to refit his fishing trawler. The loan requires monthly repayments over 15 years. When he borrowed the money the interest rate was 13.5 per cent per annum, but 18 months later the bank increased the interest rate to 15.0 per cent per annum, in line with market rates. The bank tells Peter he can increase his monthly repayment (so as to pay off the loan by the originally agreed date) or he can extend the term of the loan (and keep making the same monthly repayment). Calculate:

    (a) the new monthly repayment if Peter accepts the first option
    (b) the extra period added to the loan term if Peter accepts the second option.

45. **Calculating repayments [LO 4]**

    Wahroonga Furniture Ltd (WFL) is planning a large sale of its stock of lounge suites and dining tables. As part of its marketing, WFL will offer customers loans of up to $10 000, with no repayment required during the first 6 months. The customer then makes equal monthly repayments. The total loan term (including the first 6 months) is 2 years. The effective interest rate that WFL requires on the loans is 12 per cent per annum. What monthly repayment must WFL charge on a loan of $10 000?

46. **Ordinary perpetuities [LO 3]**

    How much money would be needed to establish a permanent scholarship paying $1000 at the end of each year, if money can be invested at 8 per cent per annum?

47. **Ordinary perpetuities (harder) [LO 3]**

    Kevin Oldfellow attended Unicorn High School in the 1960s. After leaving school, Kevin established an advertising agency that proved to be highly successful. Kevin is now very wealthy and wishes to establish a fund that will provide a perpetual scholarship scheme to support students at Unicorn High. At the initiation of the scheme Kevin will award six scholarships—one each to students currently in Years 7 to 12 inclusive. These students keep these scholarships until they leave the school. In subsequent years, one scholarship will be awarded every year to a student entering the school at Year 7 and that student keeps the scholarship through to Year 12. Kevin has sought advice from the school and has been told that it costs about $6000 to keep a student at Unicorn High for 1 year.

    The current long-term nominal interest rate is 6 per cent per annum. The long-term real interest rate is estimated to be 2.5 per cent per annum. Kevin has been advised that it will cost him $636 000 to set up the scheme. However, Kevin is not convinced, arguing that, 'The current inflation rate is about 3.5 per cent per annum. If this continues then it won't be long before the real value of a scholarship will not be enough to keep a student at the school for a year. Surely this has to be factored into the calculation somehow'. Kevin has approached you for advice.

    (a) What is the logic behind the advice that a fund of $636 000 would be sufficient? Show your calculations.
    (b) Suppose that for the next 5 years the annual inflation rate continues to be 3.5 per cent and the annual interest rate continues to be 6 per cent.

What will be the real value of an annual scholarship payment after 5 years?
(c) What amount would you advise Kevin to put into the scholarship fund? Explain.
(d) Assuming that the forecasts in (b) are correct, show how the amount in the fund and the amount of each scholarship would evolve over the first 2 years.

48. **Deferred perpetuities [LO 3]**
A pine plantation returns nothing to its owner in the first 2 years. In the following 2 years, the returns are $100 000 and $150 000, respectively, and after that the return is $200 000 per year in perpetuity. All returns are in cash and occur at year end.
(a) What is the present value of the constant return stream at the beginning of the fifth year if the returns can be invested at 8 per cent per annum?
(b) What is the current present value of the whole return stream at the same required rate of return?

49. **Simple and general annuities [LO 5]**
A simple annuity of $300 per quarter is to be replaced by annual payments (the payments to be made at the end of each year). What will be the annual payments if the nominal interest rate is 6 per cent per annum?

50. **Present value of deferred perpetuities [LO 3]**
What is the present value of a perpetual cash inflow of $1000 received at the end of each year, the first inflow occurring 2 years from now, if the interest rate is 5 per cent per annum? This cash flow can be produced by investing $10 000 in a business this year and $6000 next year. What is the present value of the investment? Is it profitable?

Test yourself further with Connect Plus online! Ask your lecturer or tutor for your course's unique URL.

CHAPTER 4
APPLYING THE TIME VALUE OF MONEY TO SECURITY VALUATION

LEARNING OBJECTIVES
After studying this chapter you should be able to:

1. use the tools of financial mathematics to value debt and equity securities
2. apply the dividend growth model to value ordinary shares
3. explain the main differences between the valuation of ordinary shares based on dividends and on earnings
4. explain the nature of interest rate risk
5. understand the theories that are used to explain the term structure of interest rates
6. apply the concept of duration to immunise a bond investment.

CHAPTER CONTENTS

4.1 Introduction
4.2 Financial asset valuation under certainty
4.3 Valuation of shares
4.4 Valuation of debt securities
4.5 Interest rate risk
4.6 The term structure of interest rates
4.7 The default-risk structure of interest rates
4.8 Other factors affecting interest rate structures
Appendix 4.1 Duration and immunisation

INTRODUCTION

4.1

In Chapter 1 we discussed briefly the important concept of the time value of money. In Chapter 3 we presented some mathematical tools useful in analysing problems involving the time value of money. In particular, we showed how promised streams of future cash flows can be valued, provided that the required rate of return is known.

In this chapter we apply these tools to the valuation of debt and equity securities. Initially we assume that the security's future cash flows are known with certainty. Later in the chapter we introduce uncertainty, but only in a limited way. A more formal and detailed treatment of uncertainty is given in Chapter 6.

FINANCIAL ASSET VALUATION UNDER CERTAINTY[1]

4.2

The benefits of owning an asset are the present and future consumption opportunities attributable to it. For a financial asset, these benefits are in the form of cash. For example, an investor who holds a government bond until maturity receives cash in the form of interest payments during the bond's life and, at maturity, in the form of the payment of the face value. In the case of shares, the investor receives cash in the form of dividends and, on sale of the shares, in the form of the price obtained for the shares.

A decision to buy an asset implies a simultaneous decision to forgo current consumption. It is assumed that, at any time, investors prefer more consumption to less consumption, other things being equal. Application of this principle between two points in time implies that, other things being equal, earlier cash inflows are preferred to later cash inflows. As explained in Chapter 3, these observations may be summarised by the phrase 'money has a time value'.

To review this principle, suppose that a person is given the choice of receiving $100 now or $100 in 1 year's time. A rational person will always choose to receive the cash immediately, even if there is no desire to consume immediately. The reason, of course, is that the earlier cash flow can be invested. This will enable even greater consumption later. If the interest rate is 12 per cent per annum, the investor (consumer) in this example can invest for 1 year the immediate cash flow of $100, and at the end of the year have $112 available for consumption. Clearly $112 of consumption is preferable to $100 of consumption. In this example the cash flows were, in effect, a gift. Suppose, however, that the investor is offered the chance to *buy* the right to receive $100 in 1 year's time. What is the maximum price the investor should offer for this right? We have just seen that $100 is 'worth' $100 × 1.12 = $112 in 1 year's time. The right to receive $100 in 1 year's time is therefore worth at present:

$$P_0 = \frac{\$100}{1.12}$$
$$= \$89.29$$

The amount $89.29 is referred to as the *present value* of $100 to be received in 1 year's time if the *discount rate* is 12 per cent per annum. Therefore, the interest rate has two functions: it is the rate at which present sums can be converted to equivalent future sums, and it is also the rate at which promised future sums can be converted to equivalent present values. Therefore the value of a financial asset is *not* simply the sum of the cash that it generates in future periods. For example, a financial asset that generates returns of $100 at the end of each of the next 5 years is not worth $500 today. It is not valid to add together cash flows that occur at different times. However, adding together present values is valid because each value relates to the same time, the present.

---

[1] In this section we review some of the results explained in Chapter 3. Readers familiar with this material may safely omit this section.

Where there are many cash flows from the same asset, the present value of the asset is the sum of the present values of every future cash flow. The present value of the asset is calculated using the relevant interest rate. If the cash flows are certain to occur, as we assume here, then the relevant interest rate is the risk-free interest rate, r_f. Thus:

$$P_0 = \frac{C_1}{1+r_f} + \frac{C_2}{(1+r_f)^2} + \ldots + \frac{C_n}{(1+r_f)^n}$$

or

$$P_0 = \sum_{t=1}^{n} \frac{C_t}{(1+r_f)^t} \quad [4.1]$$

where P_0 = present value of the asset
 C_t = dollar return (cash flow) at time t
 n = term of the investment
 r_f = risk-free interest rate per time period
 $t = 1, 2, \ldots, n$

Suppose that an asset returns $100 per annum for 5 years and that an investor requires an annual interest rate of 3.6 per cent as compensation for forgoing current consumption. Substituting in Equation 4.1 we find that:

$$P_0 = \frac{\$100}{1+0.036} + \frac{\$100}{(1+0.036)^2} + \frac{\$100}{(1+0.036)^3} + \frac{\$100}{(1+0.036)^4} + \frac{\$100}{(1+0.036)^5}$$
$$= \$96.525 + \$93.171 + \$89.933 + \$86.808 + \$83.792$$
$$= \$450.229$$

Therefore, this investor would be prepared to pay $450.23 for the asset. In summary, a financial asset is valued in a world of certainty by discounting the known future cash flows at the risk-free interest rate, thus compensating investors for their preference for current consumption.

4.3 VALUATION OF SHARES

4.3.1 VALUATION OF SHARES ASSUMING CERTAINTY

If future cash flows are known with certainty, Equation 4.1 can be used to value shares.[2] The periodic cash flows from an investment in shares are called **dividends**. Unless liquidation of the company is contemplated, the dividends are assumed to continue indefinitely. Therefore, Equation 4.1 may be rewritten as:

$$P_0 = \sum_{t=1}^{\infty} \frac{D_t}{(1+r_f)^t} \quad [4.2]$$

where D_t = dividend per share in period t

The appropriate discount rate remains the risk-free interest rate, because under conditions of certainty investors require the same rate of return on all assets.

It might appear that Equation 4.2 ignores a second potential source of return from an investment in shares—that is, the capital gain from selling the shares at a price greater than the price at which they

LEARNING OBJECTIVE 1
Use the tools of financial mathematics to value debt and equity securities

dividends
periodic distributions, usually in cash, by a company to its shareholders

[2] The discussion that follows is directed towards the valuation of ordinary shares. Preference shares are another form of equity capital. The valuation of preference shares is discussed in Chapter 14 and the distinction between ordinary shares and preference shares is discussed in detail in Chapter 10.

were purchased. This impression is incorrect. Suppose that an individual purchases shares with the intention of selling them in 5 years' time. Equation 4.2 may be expanded as follows:

$$P_0 = \sum_{t=1}^{5} \frac{D_t}{(1+r_f)^t} + \frac{P_5}{(1+r_f)^5} \qquad [4.3]$$

where P_5 = share price at the end of the fifth year

The capital gain (or loss) is the difference between P_5 and P_0. The price of the shares when they are sold is the discounted value of all future dividends from Year 6:

$$P_5 = \sum_{t=6}^{\infty} \frac{D_t}{(1+r_f)^{t-5}} \qquad [4.4]$$

Substituting Equation 4.4 into Equation 4.3:

$$P_0 = \sum_{t=1}^{5} \frac{D_t}{(1+r_f)^t} + \sum_{t=6}^{\infty} \frac{D_t}{(1+r_f)^t}$$

$$= \sum_{t=1}^{\infty} \frac{D_t}{(1+r_f)^t}$$

which is Equation 4.2.

Therefore, where a company is assumed to have an infinite life, the current market price of its shares can be expressed as the present value of an infinite stream of dividends. Even in a market where investors are seeking capital gains, the valuation formula remains the same.

4.3.2 VALUATION OF SHARES UNDER UNCERTAINTY

Valuing a security under uncertainty is difficult and, in general, few (if any) people can consistently expect to reach a better valuation than that given by the current market price. This statement is discussed fully in Chapter 16. However, the statement is unhelpful if the company is not traded on a stock exchange, because there is then no current market price to observe. Moreover, to say that the best estimate of a share's 'true' value is its current market price provides no insight into the factors that give a share its value. In this section, some of the fundamental factors determining a share's value are considered.

Where there is uncertainty, investors require compensation in the form of a higher promised rate of return. Equation 4.2 becomes:

$$P_0 = \sum_{t=1}^{\infty} \frac{E(D_t)}{(1+k_e)^t} \qquad [4.5]$$

where $E(D_t)$ = expected dividend per share in period t
k_e = required rate of return on the shares

The appropriate value of k_e is determined using the concept of the opportunity cost of capital. The 'true' or economic cost of investing in a particular security is the return forgone on the next best alternative. For a risky security, this return is greater than the return on the risk-free security (r_f). In short, $k_e > r_f$. The amount by which k_e exceeds r_f is often referred to as the security's risk premium.

Further, the riskier the security being considered, the higher the risk premium will be and the higher k_e will be. Determination of exactly how much higher k_e should be requires a measurement of 'risk' and a theory linking that measure to required rates of return. These theories are developed in Chapter 7.

At this point we assume that all investors reach the same assessment of risk, and therefore apply the same opportunity cost of capital (discount rate) to the same expected dividend stream, therefore arriving at the same price for the company's shares. It may seem unrealistic to assume that everyone has the same expectations. However, at the time of making a financial decision, it may be reasonable for the company's management to assume that its assessment of the likely impact of that decision on the company's share price will prove to be correct. If this is so, then management should act *as if* it is realistic to assume that everyone has the same expectations.

The simplest assumption to make when estimating a share's value is that the company will maintain in perpetuity the current dividend per share, D_0. In this case the estimate is:[3]

$$P_0 = \frac{D_0}{k_e} \qquad [4.6]$$

The use of Equation 4.6 is shown in Example 4.1.

EXAMPLE 4.1

Rankine Ltd is currently paying a dividend of 90 cents per share. If investors expect this dividend to be maintained and require a rate of return of 15 per cent on the investment, what is the value of Rankine's shares?

SOLUTION

The value of Rankine's shares is calculated as follows:

$$P_0 = \frac{\$0.90}{0.15}$$
$$= \$6.00$$

Growth in dividends

LEARNING OBJECTIVE 2
Apply the dividend growth model to value ordinary shares

It is usually more realistic to assume that a company's dividend per share will change. For example, it may be assumed that the dividend per share will grow at a constant rate. In this case, the estimated value is:

$$P_0 = \sum_{t=1}^{\infty} \frac{D_0(1+g)^t}{(1+k_e)^t} \qquad [4.7]$$

where g = expected growth rate in dividend per share

Where k_e is greater than g and the growth in dividends is assumed to continue indefinitely, Equation 4.7 can be written as:[4]

$$P_0 = \frac{D_0(1+g)}{k_e - g} \qquad [4.8]$$

One approach to estimating g is to calculate the past growth rate in dividend per share and use this as the estimate of the expected growth rate. This is shown in Example 4.2.

---

[3] This formula treats the dividends as an ordinary perpetuity. For further details, see Section 3.6.

[4] The terms in Equation 4.7 form an infinite geometric series, with a common factor (or ratio) between each term of $\frac{1+g}{1+k_e}$. Provided that $-1 < \frac{1+g}{1+k_e} < 1$, there will be a limiting sum equal to the first term of the series, divided by (1 – the common ratio). That is:

$$P_0 = \frac{D_0(1+g)}{1+k_e} \bigg/ \left(1 - \frac{1+g}{1+k_e}\right)$$
$$= \frac{D_0(1+g)}{1+k_e} \bigg/ \frac{k_e - g}{1+k_e}$$
$$= \frac{D_0(1+g)}{k_e - g}$$

If $k_e < g$, the model breaks down. Under these circumstances: $\frac{1+g}{1+k_e} > 1$ and there is no limiting sum ($P_0 \to \infty$).

EXAMPLE 4.2

Assume that for the past 10 years the growth rate in Rankine Ltd's dividend per share has been 10 per cent per annum. Assume further that this growth rate is expected to be maintained indefinitely. The latest dividend per share was 90 cents and was paid yesterday. What is the value of Rankine's shares?

SOLUTION

Using Equation 4.8, the value of Rankine's shares is:

$$P_0 = \frac{D_0(1+g)}{k_e - g}$$

$$= \frac{\$0.90 \times 1.1}{0.15 - 0.10}$$

$$= \$19.80$$

A second approach to estimating g is to assume that the growth in dividend per share is related to the company's retained earnings and to the rate of return on those earnings. If the company retains a constant proportion b of its earnings each year and reinvests those earnings at a constant rate r, then $g = br$, and Equation 4.8 can be rewritten:

$$P_0 = \frac{D_0(1+br)}{k_e - br} \qquad [4.9]$$

The use of Equation 4.9 is shown in Example 4.3.

EXAMPLE 4.3

If Rankine Ltd retains 40 per cent of its earnings each year (b = 0.4), and these earnings are reinvested to earn a 25 per cent rate of return (r = 0.25), what is the value of Rankine's shares?

SOLUTION

The value of Rankine's shares, using Equation 4.9, is as follows:

$$P_0 = \frac{\$0.90[1 + 0.4(0.25)]}{0.15 - 0.4(0.25)}$$

$$= \$19.80$$

The assumption that the past growth rate is expected to be maintained indefinitely is unlikely to be realistic, particularly where the company has been experiencing a relatively high growth rate. We might therefore assume that the current growth rate will be maintained for several years before falling to a level expected to be sustained indefinitely. This is shown in Example 4.4.

EXAMPLE 4.4

Assume that the growth rate will remain at its current level of 10 per cent per annum (g') for only a further 3 years, and is then expected to fall to 6 per cent per annum (g) and remain at that level indefinitely. What is the share price today?

SOLUTION

This complication is easily handled by first using Equation 4.8 to estimate the value of the shares as at the end of the third year. The value of the shares today is given by the present value of this estimate, plus the

continued →

Example 4.4 *continued*

present value of the dividends to be paid in the first 3 years. The value of Rankine's shares is calculated as follows:

$$P_0 = \frac{D_0(1+g')}{(1+k_e)} + \frac{D_0(1+g')^2}{(1+k_e)^2} + \frac{D_0(1+g')^3}{(1+k_e)^3} + \frac{1}{(1+k_e)^3} \cdot \frac{D_0(1+g')^3(1+g)}{(k_e-g)}$$

$$= \frac{\$0.90(1.10)}{1.15} + \frac{\$0.90(1.10)^2}{(1.15)^2} + \frac{\$0.90(1.10)^3}{(1.15)^3} + \frac{1}{(1.15)^3} \cdot \frac{\$0.90(1.10)^3(1.06)}{(0.15-0.06)}$$

$$= \$11.75$$

Comparing the previous two examples, the reduction in the expected dividend growth rate after Year 3 has resulted in a reduction in the value of the shares from $19.80 to $11.75. This highlights the sensitivity of the share value to estimates of the future growth rate in dividend per share.

The formulae used to estimate a share value may also be used to estimate the required rate of return on a company's shares, given their current market price. This aspect is discussed further in Chapter 14.

4.3.3 SHARE VALUATION AND THE PRICE–EARNINGS RATIO

LEARNING OBJECTIVE 3
Explain the main differences between the valuation of ordinary shares based on dividends and on earnings

The ratio of a company's share price to its earnings per share—that is, its price–earnings ratio—is often used by security analysts to estimate the value of the company's shares.[5] To illustrate this method of valuation, we again use the example of Rankine Ltd, and assume that Rankine's current earnings per share is $2.25. Assume also that an analyst estimates that the appropriate price–earnings ratio for the company is 9.0. Therefore, the value of each share is estimated at $20.25—that is, $2.25 × 9.0. This estimate would then be compared with the current market price to determine whether the shares are overvalued or undervalued.

However, this leaves unanswered the question: How does an analyst estimate the appropriate price–earnings ratio? In most cases where analysts use this method of valuation, the appropriate price–earnings ratio is determined in a way that can best be described as judgemental—that is, no formal model is used but the analyst tries to take into account the factors considered to be relevant.

Two important factors are risk and growth opportunities. The riskier the analyst believes the investment to be, the lower the appropriate price–earnings ratio. To see this, imagine that an analyst is trying to value two companies that are equivalent in all respects, including their expected earnings, except that one company is riskier than the other. Because investors dislike risk, other things being equal, the company that is riskier will be less attractive to investors and will thus have a lower value. Since both companies have the same earnings, the ratio of price to earnings will be lower for the riskier company.

The other important factor is growth opportunities. If an analyst believes a company has substantial opportunities for growth, a high price–earnings ratio will be assigned. In this case the current earnings level is likely to be surpassed in the future, thereby justifying a price today that appears 'high' relative to current earnings. Other factors likely to be considered include the price–earnings ratios of companies in the same industry, and prospects for the industry and the economy as a whole.

4.4 VALUATION OF DEBT SECURITIES

As we saw in Section 4.3, the returns on an investment in shares are dividends and capital gains. In the case of an investment in debt securities (frequently called **bonds** or **debentures**), the returns are usually in the form of interest payments and the repayment of the *face value* or *principal*. As has been explained

---

[5] A discussion of the use of the price–earnings ratio to value shares is contained in most texts on investments. See, for example, Brailsford, Heaney and Bilson (2007, pp. 419–28) and Bodie, Kane and Marcus (2011, pp. 601–9).

for shares, if all securities offer certain returns, each security's opportunity cost of capital is the risk-free interest rate (or yield) r_f. Therefore, if future cash flows are known with certainty, r_f is the appropriate discount rate to apply. Equation 4.1 is rewritten for bonds as follows:

$$P_0 = \sum_{t=1}^{n} \frac{C_t}{(1+r_f)^t} + \frac{P_n}{(1+r_f)^n} \qquad [4.10]$$

where C_t = interest payment (often called 'coupon payment') at time t
P_n = face value (principal repayment) at maturity
n = number of periods to maturity
r_f = risk-free interest rate (yield)

The use of Equation 4.10 is shown in Example 4.5.

LEARNING OBJECTIVE 1
Use the tools of financial mathematics to value debt and equity securities

bonds (or debentures) debt securities issued with a medium or long term to maturity

EXAMPLE 4.5

Suppose that Rankine Ltd borrows by issuing 3-year bonds with a face value of $100, and a coupon interest rate of 10 per cent. The cash flows to a bond holder will be interest ('coupon') payments of $10 per year for 3 years, followed by payment of $100 at the end of the third year. If the required rate of return is also 10 per cent per year, what would we expect to be the value of Rankine's bonds?

SOLUTION
The value of the bonds is given by Equation 4.10:

$$P_0 = \frac{\$10}{1.1} + \frac{\$10}{(1.1)^2} + \frac{\$10}{(1.1)^3} + \frac{\$100}{(1.1)^3}$$
$$= \$9.091 + \$8.264 + \$7.513 + \$75.131$$
$$= \$100.00$$

Once a bond has been issued—that is, sold by the borrower to the lender—its promised future cash flows are fixed. Ownership of the bond entitles the owner to receive from the issuer a fixed schedule of future cash flows. If the market interest rate changes, it will affect the attractiveness of the bond to potential investors. If market interest rates decrease, the bond will become more attractive; if market interest rates increase, the bond will become less attractive. Of course, this will cause bond prices to change. A decrease (increase) in market interest rates will cause an increase (decrease) in the prices of existing bonds. This is illustrated in Example 4.6.

EXAMPLE 4.6

Suppose that immediately after Rankine's debt contract is agreed, conditions in the debt market change and the required rate of return falls to 8 per cent per annum. Rankine must still make interest payments of $10 each year, but investors now require a return of 8 per cent per annum. What is the value of Rankine's bonds now?

SOLUTION
Again applying Equation 4.10, the security is now valued more highly, as follows:

$$P_0 = \frac{\$10}{1.08} + \frac{\$10}{(1.08)^2} + \frac{\$10}{(1.08)^3} + \frac{\$100}{(1.08)^3}$$
$$= \$105.15$$

continued →

Example 4.6 *continued*

Similarly, if the required rate of return had risen from 10 per cent to 12 per cent, the price would have fallen as follows:

$$P_0 = \frac{\$10}{1.12} + \frac{\$10}{(1.12)^2} + \frac{\$10}{(1.12)^3} + \frac{\$100}{(1.12)^3}$$
$$= \$95.20$$

4.5 INTEREST RATE RISK

LEARNING OBJECTIVE 4
Explain the nature of interest rate risk

term structure of interest rates
relationship between interest rates and term to maturity for debt securities in the same risk class

default-risk structure of interest rates
relationship between default risk and interest rates

Example 4.6 shows that when interest rates change, so do bond prices. The possibility of unforeseen price changes means that a bond is risky—its future value is uncertain. Thus, even if a bond is *risk-free* in the sense that the borrower is certain to make the promised cash payments, it is *risky* in the sense that the bond holder (lender) can suffer unforeseen losses if interest rates increase.

When interest rates increase, bond prices fall. For the investor in bonds this is a capital loss, and therefore in this respect the increase in interest rates is undesirable. A benefit must be set against that loss: the interest receipts can be reinvested at the new, higher rate of interest. The opposite occurs when interest rates fall. Investors make capital gains but interest receipts can be reinvested only at the new lower rate. These effects are known as the *price effect* and the *reinvestment effect* and are always of opposite sign for a given change in market interest rate. The price effect and the reinvestment effect are both sources of *interest rate risk*. The net effect for the investor depends on the size of the interest rate change and on the period for which the bond is held. Appendix 4.1 outlines a method that an investor may use to obtain some protection against interest rate risk.

At any given time, the market-determined interest rate (or yield) on a bond will depend on the features of that bond. Two features that are usually particularly important to market participants are the term of the security and the risk of the borrower defaulting on the promised payments. The connection between term and interest rates is called the **term structure of interest rates**, while the connection between default risk and interest rates is called the **default-risk structure of interest rates**. These are now considered.

4.6 THE TERM STRUCTURE OF INTEREST RATES

4.6.1 WHAT IS THE TERM STRUCTURE?

LEARNING OBJECTIVE 5
Understand the theories that are used to explain the term structure of interest rates

To consider the effect of a bond's term on its interest rate, all other factors need to be held constant. Thus, to eliminate the effect of differences in default risk, the term structure of interest rates is usually studied by focusing on the interest rates offered by Commonwealth Government bonds since all such bonds have the same risk of default (assumed to be zero).

The least complicated measure of the term structure of interest rates is the market yield on a government bond that pays no interest during its life, but pays a fixed sum at maturity. In practice, such bonds are relatively rare. Therefore, in practice it is usual to use bond yields, which are really internal rates of return. (For further details, see Sections 3.5.4 and 5.4.2.) The pattern of yield against term is called the **yield curve**. Data for the Australian yield curve at 10 different dates are given in Table 4.1.

TABLE 4.1 Australian yield curve data

	TERM TO MATURITY				
DATE OF YIELD CURVE	**3 MONTHS**	**6 MONTHS**	**2 YEARS**	**5 YEARS**	**10 YEARS**
June 1998	4.93	4.98	5.18	5.38	5.58
June 2000	5.87	5.96	5.89	6.05	6.16
June 2002	5.21	5.32	5.44	5.78	5.99
June 2004	5.61	5.65	5.34	5.67	5.87
June 2005	5.77	5.77	5.10	5.10	5.11
June 2006	6.09	6.16	5.78	5.78	5.79
June 2007	6.58	6.66	6.45	6.40	6.26
June 2008	7.81	8.04	6.97	6.69	6.59
June 2009	3.14	3.30	3.90	5.10	5.56
June 2010	4.89	5.01	4.57	4.97	5.33

Source: Compiled from Reserve Bank of Australia data **(www.rba.gov.au)**. See tables *Interest Rates and Yields—Money Market* and *Capital Market Yields—Government Bonds*. For 1998 and 2000 yields for 3(6) months are issue yields for 13(26)-week Treasury notes. From 2002 to 2010 these yields are yields for 90(180)-day bank accepted bills. Yields for 2, 5 and 10 years are bond yields.

Yield curves can have a wide range of shapes, but they are typically either downward sloping, flat or upward sloping. These shapes are illustrated in Figure 4.1. The data in Table 4.1 show that the Australian yield curve was essentially upward sloping from 1998 to 2004, and tended to be downward sloping from 2005 to 2008. In 2009 and 2010 it was again upward sloping.

FIGURE 4.1 Alternative yield curves

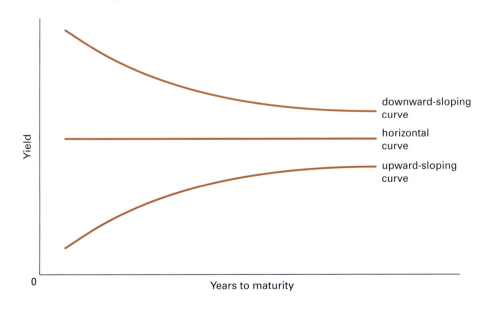

yield curve
graph of yield to maturity against bond term at a given point in time

4.6.2 TERM STRUCTURE THEORIES: EXPECTATIONS AND LIQUIDITY (RISK) PREMIUM

Obviously the term structure at any given time is no accident. Presumably, participants in the debt markets do not set the interest rate for, say, a term of 2 years without in some way considering the 1-year and 3-year interest rates. In other words, the interest rate for a particular term will be determined by the market *in the context of* interest rates for other terms. If this were not so, what would explain the smooth, regular shapes nearly always displayed by yield curves? The exact identity of the factors that explain the term structure is controversial, with different theories proposing different mechanisms. There is, however, broad agreement that expectations of the future course of interest rates are central to explaining the term structure.

The core of the **expectations theory** of the term structure is that interest rates are set such that investors can expect, on average, to achieve the same return over any future period, regardless of the term of the security in which they invest. For example, suppose that in the current term structure the interest rate for a 2-year term to maturity is 8 per cent per annum, while the interest rate for a 3-year term to maturity is 9 per cent per annum. Suppose, further, that $1000 is invested for 3 years. After 3 years, the investor will have $1000(1.09)^3 = $1295.03. Alternatively, suppose the same investor invests $1000 for 2 years. After 2 years, the investor will have $1000(1.08)^2 = $1166.40. If the investor can re-lend this sum for the third year at an interest rate of 11.028 per cent per annum, then at the end of the third year the investor will have $1166.40 × 1.110 28 = $1295.03, which is the same as the return from the 3-year investment. This is shown in Figure 4.2.

expectations theory of the term structure is that interest rates are set such that investors in bonds or other debt securities can expect, on average, to achieve the same return over any future period, regardless of the security in which they invest

FIGURE 4.2 Return from the 3-year investment

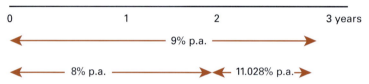

As shown in Figure 4.2, the current term structure is 8 per cent per annum for a term of 2 years and 9 per cent per annum for a term of 3 years. According to expectations theory, the factor that explains the current term structure is the market's expectation that the 1-year interest rate on the day 2 years from now will be 11.028 per cent per annum. In that case investors will earn 9 per cent per annum over the coming three years, regardless of whether they invest for three years, by:

(a) buying the 3-year bond today; or
(b) buying the 2-year bond today *and* buying a 1-year bond in 2 years' time.

Therefore, the expectation of the future interest rate determines today's term structure.

This process is extended in Figure 4.3. Suppose that today's 1-year interest rate is 6.5 per cent per annum. Then the market must expect next year's 1-year interest rate to be 9.521 per cent per annum, because $(1.08)^2 = 1.065 \times 1.09521 = 1.1664$. The economic interpretation is that the same return is expected over the next 2 years, regardless of whether an investor:

(a) buys a 1-year bond today *and* buys a further 1-year bond in 1 year's time; or
(b) buys the 2-year bond today.

FIGURE 4.3 Return from the 3-year investment (extended)

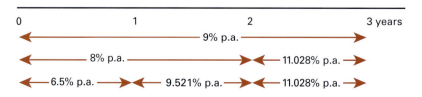

As a final illustration of the expectations mechanism, consider again the information shown in Figure 4.3 and imagine that there is an investor who intends to lend $1000 for a 2-year period. Consider the following three ways in which such an investment could be made:

(a) Buy the 2-year bond now and hold it until it matures. At the end of the 2-year period, this investment will have accumulated to $1000(1.08)^2 = $1166.40.
(b) Buy a 1-year bond now and, after 1 year, reinvest in a further 1-year bond, which is then held until maturity. At the end of the 2-year period, this investment is expected to have accumulated to $1000(1.065)(1.095\,21) = $1166.40.
(c) Buy the 3-year bond now and sell it after 2 years. At the end of the 2-year period, this investment is expected to be worth $1000(1.09)^3/1.110\,28 = $1166.40.

As these calculations show, it is expected that the outcome will be the same, regardless of the investment strategy. The market has set today's term structure in such a way that it reflects the market's expectations of the future course of interest rates.

To formalise our discussion of expectations theory, we make the following assumptions:

(a) future short-term interest rates are known with certainty
(b) there are no transaction costs.

Given these assumptions, competition in the capital market will result in a term structure that ensures that the sum to which a dollar accumulates over n years at a long-term interest rate r_n must equal the sum to which it accumulates over n years when invested at present and future short-term interest rates $i_1, i_2, \ldots, i_n$. As a consequence, an investor who wants to invest for, say, 10 years is indifferent about whether the purchase is of a 10-year government security or of a 1-year security in each of the next 10 years. Expectations theory is therefore represented by the following relationship between short-term and long-term interest rates:

$$1 + r_1 = 1 + i_1$$
$$(1 + r_2)^2 = (1 + i_1)(1 + i_2)$$
$$\vdots$$
$$(1 + r_n)^n = (1 + i_1)(1 + i_2) \ldots (1 + i_n)$$

From these relationships we can derive the appropriate formula for the long-term rate. For example, because investors must expect to receive the same capital sum by accumulating for two periods at the rate r_2, or for one period at i_1 followed by a second period at i_2, the long-term rate is equal to the geometric mean of the current one-period rate and the forward one-period rate for the next period.

Generalising this result:

$$r_1 = (1 + i_1) - 1$$
$$r_2 = \sqrt{(1 + i_1)(1 + i_2)} - 1$$
$$\vdots$$
$$r_n = \sqrt[n]{(1 + i_1)(1 + i_2) \ldots (1 + i_n)} - 1$$

Thus, in our earlier discussion, the 2-year interest rate is:

$$r_2 = \sqrt[2]{(1.065)(1.09521)} - 1$$

$$= 8\% \text{ per annum}$$

and the 3-year interest rate is:

$$r_3 = \sqrt[3]{(1.065)(1.09521)(1.11028)} - 1$$

$$= 9\% \text{ per annum}$$

The essence of expectations theory is that the term structure is determined by investors' expectations of short-term rates within the maturity of the competing long-term security.[6] Expectations theory can help to reconcile the existence of the differing shapes of the yield curve shown in Figure 4.1.

In general, an upward-sloping term structure implies that investors expect future short-term interest rates to increase.[7] In that case, investors are not prepared to invest in long-term securities unless the yield is greater than that on short-term securities, because the investors would be better off investing in short-term securities and reinvesting the proceeds at maturity.

In general, a downward-sloping term structure implies that investors expect future short-term interest rates to decrease—that is, investors are prepared to purchase long-term securities yielding less than short-term securities because they expect their return to be no larger if they adopted an investment strategy requiring continual reinvestment in short-term securities. In short, if expectations about the level of future short-term rates change, then actual long-term yields on existing securities will tend to adjust in the same direction.

A flat term structure means that investors expect future short-term interest rates to be the same as the current short-term rate. Consequently, the long-term rates will equal the short-term rates.[8]

Commentators on the expectations theory of the term structure have suggested that interest rates are not formed solely on the basis of expectations. For example, the **liquidity premium (risk premium) theory** suggests that although expectations are a foundation for the term structure, there is in addition a premium due to uncertainty about the future level of interest rates. This causes an upward bias in the yield curve because interest rate risk increases with the term to maturity of the debt security.

Our earlier discussion of interest rate risk suggested that the holder of a bond may, in the end, either benefit or lose as the result of a change in the general level of interest rates. For example, if interest rates increase, the market value of the bond will fall, but the interest receipts could be reinvested at a higher rate of return. The proponents of the liquidity premium theory concentrate on the market value effect and point out that for a given change in interest rate, the effect is greater for long-term bonds than for short-term bonds. This is illustrated in Example 4.7.

liquidity premium (risk premium) theory of the term structure is that although future interest rates are determined by investors' expectations, investors require some reward (liquidity premium) to assume the increased risk of investing long term

EXAMPLE 4.7

Assume that there is a flat yield curve where the current interest rate on all government bonds is 10 per cent per annum. The government has just issued 1-year, 2-year, 5-year and 10-year bonds, all offering an interest rate of 10 per cent, a face value of $100 and paying interest once per annum. Table 4.2 shows the market price for each of these bonds, assuming that immediately following purchase of the bonds

---

6 It is convenient to think of short-term rates as determining long-term rates, but in fact the market determines all rates simultaneously.

7 That this is not always the case may be seen from the following example. If the current term structure is: 1 year: 6 per cent; 2 years: 10 per cent; and 3 years: 11 per cent, then the 1-year interest rate, 1 year hence, is expected to be: $\frac{(1.10)^2}{1.06} - 1 = 14.15\%$ while the 1-year interest rate, 2 years hence, is expected to be: $\frac{(1.11)^3}{(1.10)^2} - 1 = 13.03\%$.

8 One of the implications of the expectations theory is that interest rates are independent of the relative supply of the bonds across the range of maturities.

at $100 there is either a parallel upward movement in the yield curve to 12 per cent per annum or a parallel downward movement in the yield curve to 8 per cent per annum.[9]

TABLE 4.2 Effect of interest rate changes on bond prices

TERM OF BOND (YEARS)	IF INTEREST RATE (REQUIRED YIELD) IS 12% ($)	CHANGE IN PRICE (%)	IF INTEREST RATE (REQUIRED YIELD) IS 8% ($)	CHANGE IN PRICE (%)
1	98.214	−1.786	101.852	+1.852
2	96.620	−3.380	103.567	+3.567
5	92.790	−7.210	107.985	+7.985
10	88.700	−11.300	113.420	+13.420

As Table 4.2 shows, the price of long-term debt is more volatile. It is true that the holders of a 10-year government bond benefit most from a fall in interest rates, but they also lose most if rates increase. In this sense, long-term bonds are 'riskier'. The liquidity premium theory suggests that investors would require a higher rate of return to compensate for this higher risk. Therefore, there is a natural tendency for the yields on long-term bonds to be greater than those on short-term bonds. Consequently, there will be a bias towards an upward-sloping yield curve. This means that compared with the yield curves that would be observed if only expectations mattered, an upward-sloping yield curve will become steeper, a downward-sloping yield curve will become less steep and a flat yield curve will become slightly upward sloping.[10]

4.6.3 EMPIRICAL EVIDENCE

The empirical evidence on the theories we have discussed presents a rather complex picture. In the US, Fama (1984), McCulloch (1987) and Richardson, Richardson and Smith (1992) found evidence supporting the existence of a premium. But Longstaff (2000) found no evidence of a premium at the very short end of the yield curve. The evidence in Australia is also mixed. In a test at the short end of the term structure (90-day interest rates, compared with 180-day interest rates), Tease (1988) found that the data quite strongly supported the expectations theory in various forms. Similarly, studies by Robinson (1998), and Young and Fowler (1990) found support for the expectations theory using 90-day and 10-year interest rates. However, studies by Alles (1995) and Heaney (1994), in both cases using more thorough statistical analyses, found little support for the expectations theory.

4.6.4 INFLATION AND THE TERM STRUCTURE

One issue yet to be considered is the relationship between the inflation rate and the term structure of interest rates. In general, we would expect lenders to require the nominal interest rate to compensate them for expected inflation.[11] Therefore, the higher the expected inflation rate, the higher will be

---

9 Market prices are calculated using Equation 4.10. A parallel movement of the yield curve occurs when yields change such that the former yield curve and the new yield curve are parallel.

10 In June 2009 the yield curve was steeply upward sloping. This yield curve is consistent with short-term interest rates having been reduced by central banks to stimulate growth in response to the global financial crisis. Higher yields for longer term securities are consistent with expectations of increasing future short-term interest rates and an increase in the risk premium.

11 See Equation 3.7 and the discussion in Section 3.4.4.

the observed nominal interest rate. As a consequence, if the inflation rate is expected to increase over time, the nominal interest rate on short-term bonds will also be expected to increase over time. According to the expectations theory we will therefore see an upward-sloping yield curve. In addition, unexpected changes in the inflation rate are also likely to have an impact on the term structure. Such unexpected changes will cause a change in the level of interest rates. As explained earlier, the possibility of such changes gives rise to interest rate risk, and the liquidity premium theory suggests that this in turn will give rise to the tendency for interest rates on long-term bonds to be higher than those on short-term bonds.

4.7 THE DEFAULT-RISK STRUCTURE OF INTEREST RATES

As explained in Section 4.3.2, the presence of uncertainty causes the opportunity cost of capital for securities to exceed the risk-free interest rate. For debt of a given term, the higher the market's assessment of the probability of default, the higher will be k_d, the required rate of return (or expected yield) on the debt. However, because debtholders rank ahead of shareholders, it is expected that the required rate of return on a company's debt will be less than the required rate of return on its shares. In short, for any given company, $r_f < k_d < k_e$.

Similarly, for debt of a given term and for a given company, the required rate of return, k_d, will be less than the yield to maturity, r, where yield to maturity is the rate of return earned by an investor *if* the company does not default. This relationship is shown in Example 4.8.

EXAMPLE 4.8

Bonds issued by the Red Vines Company mature in 1 year's time with a maturity value of $110. There is no cash flow during the year. Investors believe that there is a 90 per cent chance that the full payment of $110 will be made and a 10 per cent chance that no payment will be made. Calculate:

(a) the price of Red Vines' bonds
(b) the yield to maturity of the bonds.

SOLUTION

(a) The expected payment at the end of the year is 0.90($110) + 0.10($0) = $99. Assuming that the market requires a rate of return, k_d, of 10 per cent on these bonds, they will have a price of:

$$P_0 = \frac{\$99}{1.10}$$

$$= \$90$$

(b) The yield, r, is therefore found by solving:

$$\$90 = \frac{\$110}{1+r}$$

Therefore, yield to maturity,

$$r = \frac{\$110}{\$90} - 1$$

$$= 22.22\%$$

That is, an investor who purchases the bonds for $90 and holds them to maturity will earn a rate of return of 22.22 per cent per annum if Red Vines does not default.

Services have existed for many years that supply ratings on the 'quality' of debt securities issued by both public and private sector borrowers. There is evidence to suggest that there is a high correlation between these ratings and the probability of default and it is not surprising, therefore, that the yields are related to the quality rating.

In Australia, ratings are supplied by Fitch Ratings (www.fitchratings.com.au), Moody's Investors Service (www.moodys.com.au), and by Standard & Poor's (www.standardandpoors.com.au). Long-term debt is rated by Standard & Poor's on a 20-point scale, ranging from AAA (extremely strong capacity to pay interest and repay principal) down to C (high risk of default, or reliant on third-party arrangements to prevent default).[12] The information in Table 4.3 is indicative of the ratings supplied by Standard & Poor's.

TABLE 4.3 Australian corporate and government ratings

RATING	A$ LONG-TERM RATING		
Extremely strong capacity to pay	AAA	Australia (Commonwealth of)	New South Wales (State of)
		Australian Capital Territory (Government of)	South Australia (State of)
		Melbourne (City of)	Victoria (State of)
			Western Australia (State of)
Very strong capacity to pay	AA+	Australian Postal Corp.	Queensland (State of)
		Defence Housing Authority	Tasmania (State of)
		University of Melbourne	
	AA	Ergon Energy Corp. Ltd	University of Wollongong
	AA−	Queensland Sugar Ltd	
Strong capacity to pay	A+	BHP Billiton Ltd	SingTel Optus Pty Ltd
	A	Promina Group Ltd	Telstra Ltd
	A−	Australia Pacific Airports Corp. Ltd	General Property Trust
		Citipower Trust (The)	Stockland
		Coca-Cola Amatil Ltd	Westfield Holdings Ltd
		ETSA Utilities Finance Pty Ltd	Woolworths Ltd
Adequate capacity to pay	BBB+	Brambles Ltd	QR National Ltd
		Caltex Australia Ltd	Rio Tinto Ltd
		CSR Ltd	Santos Ltd

continued →

---

[12] Moody's rates long-term debt on a 19-point scale ranging from AAA (interest payments are protected by a large, or by an exceptionally stable, margin and principal is secure) to C (regarded as having extremely poor prospects of ever attaining any real investment standing). Both Moody's and Standard & Poor's provide ratings of short-term debt on a four-point scale.

TABLE 4.3 continued

RATING	A$ LONG-TERM RATING		
		Genesis Power Ltd	Tabcorp Holdings Ltd
		Origin Energy Ltd	Wesfarmers Ltd
		Orica Ltd	Woodside Petroleum Ltd
	BBB	Adelaide Airport Ltd	ElectraNet Ltd
		Amcor Ltd	Heritage Building Society Ltd
		Boral Ltd	Leighton Holdings Ltd
		Brisbane Airport Corp. Ltd	Mirvac Group
		Contact Energy Ltd	Qantas Airways Ltd
		Crown Ltd	United Energy Distribution Pty Ltd
	BBB–	Ansell Ltd	Envestra Ltd
		Asciano Ltd	Lend Lease Corp. Ltd
		Duet Group	Southern Cross Airports Corp. Ltd
Uncertainties or adverse conditions could lead to inadequate capacity to pay	BB+	Aristocrat Leisure Ltd	Fairfax Media Ltd
	BB	Nufarm Ltd	
	BB–	Avanti Finance Ltd	
Adverse conditions likely to impair capacity to pay	B+	Ford Motor Company of Australia Ltd	
	B	Fortescue Metals Group Ltd	
	B–	Bemax Resources Ltd	
Highly vulnerable to default	CC		

Source: Based on figures generated from www.standardandpoors.com.au.

4.8 OTHER FACTORS AFFECTING INTEREST RATE STRUCTURES

Yield differentials on securities may also result from differences in marketability—that is, the investor's ability to convert the securities into cash without a price penalty. Other things being equal, an investor will buy a security of low marketability only if the yield is greater than that on a security of high marketability. For example, a life insurance company would usually require a higher interest rate to lend mortgage funds to a company than to lend the same amount by purchasing the company's debt securities that are traded in an active market. Similarly, it is conceivable that tax effects will give rise to differences in yields on bonds.

Finally, we refer briefly to the relationship between the yield on bonds and the required rate of return on ordinary shares. In Section 4.3, we suggested that the required rate of return on ordinary shares may be expressed as the rate of discount that equates the present value of the expected future dividends with the current market price of the shares. Clearly, if dividends are expected to grow over time, the required rate of return on an investment in ordinary shares will be greater than the current dividend yield (D_0/P_0). Therefore, it is not valid to directly compare the yields on debt securities with the dividend yields on ordinary shares. Not surprisingly, the evidence suggests that the required returns on ordinary shares exceed those on debt securities.[13] This evidence is consistent with the idea that investors require a higher expected rate of return to invest in ordinary shares than to invest in, say, debentures because ordinary shareholders are exposed to greater risk. Their risk exposure is greater because ordinary shareholders are the residual claimants on the cash flows of the company. Therefore, their returns are the first to be affected by a downturn in the company's prospects and, in the event of the company being wound up, ordinary shareholders have the last claim on its assets.

Connect Plus features a case study illustrating topics covered in this chapter.
Ask your lecturer or tutor for your course's unique URL.

SUMMARY

→ Financial assets such as bonds and shares can be valued by discounting their future cash flows to present values and summing these present values. The discount rate used is the required rate of return or opportunity cost of capital.
   - If the future cash flows from an asset are certain, the required rate of return will reflect only the effect of time on the value of money.
   - If the future cash flows are uncertain, investors will also require compensation for risk and the rate will be increased by the inclusion of a risk premium.

→ The value of an ordinary share is the present value of a dividend stream that can, in principle, continue forever. The calculation of a share's value can be simplified by assuming that dividends are constant or grow at a constant rate over time. Shares can also be valued using the company's current earnings and a price–earnings ratio. The value of this ratio depends mainly on risk and expected growth in earnings.

→ Debt securities are valued based on their future interest payments and face value. For any company, the interest rate required by lenders will be less than the required rate of return on the company's ordinary shares. The prices of debt securities are sensitive to changes in interest rates and this sensitivity increases with the security's term to maturity. This is one reason why the interest rates on long-term securities are often greater than rates on short-term securities. The interest rate or yield on debt also depends on the probability that the borrower will default.

KEY TERMS

bonds (or debentures)   85
coupons   99
default-risk structure of interest rates   86
dividends   80
duration   100
expectations theory   88
immunisation   99
liquidity premium (risk premium) theory   90
term structure of interest rates   86
yield curve   87
zero-coupon bonds   99

[13] For international evidence, see Dimson, Marsh and Staunton (2003) and for Australian evidence, see Brailsford, Handley and Maheswaran (2008).

SELF-TEST PROBLEMS

1. Richards Ltd pays annual dividends on its ordinary shares. The latest dividend of 75 cents per share was paid yesterday. The dividends are expected to grow at 8 per cent per annum for the next 2 years, after which a growth rate of 4 per cent per annum will be maintained indefinitely. Estimate the value of one share if the required rate of return is 14 per cent per annum.

2. A government bond with a face value of $100 and an interest rate of 11 per cent per annum matures in 3 years' time. Interest payments occur twice each year and a payment has just been made. If the current market yield on the bond is 13 per cent per annum, what is the current price of the bond?

3. The current interest rates on government bonds are as follows:

Years to maturity	interest rate (% p.a.)
1	13.90
2	11.70
3	10.50

Assume that the term structure can be explained purely by expectations of future interest rates, and therefore there is no liquidity or risk premium. Calculate the expected 1-year rates for the next 2 years.

Solutions to self-test problems are available in Appendix B, page 803.

REFERENCES

Alles, L., 'Time varying risk premium and the predictive power of the Australian term structure of interest rates', *Accounting and Finance*, November 1995, pp. 77–96.

Bodie, Z., Kane, A. & Marcus, A.J., *Investments*, 9th edn, McGraw-Hill, New York, 2011.

Brailsford, T., Heaney, R. & Bilson, C., *Investments*, 3rd edn, Thomson, Victoria, 2007.

Brailsford, T., Handley, J.C. & Maheswaran, K., 'Re-examination of the historical equity risk premium in Australia', *Accounting and Finance*, March 2008, pp. 73–97.

Cox, J.C., Ingersoll, J.E. & Ross, S.A., 'Duration and the measurement of basis risk', *Journal of Business*, January 1979, pp. 51–61.

Dimson, E., Marsh, P.R. & Staunton, M., 'Global evidence on the equity risk premium', *Journal of Applied Corporate Finance*, Fall 2003, pp. 27–38.

Elton, E.J. & Gruber, M.J., *Modern Portfolio Theory and Investment Analysis*, 5th edn, John Wiley and Sons, New York, 1995.

Fama, E.F., 'Term premiums in bond returns', *Journal of Financial Economics*, December 1984, pp. 529–46.

Heaney, R., 'Predictive power of the term structure in Australia in the late 1980s: a note', *Accounting and Finance*, May 1994, pp. 37–46.

Longstaff, F.A., 'The term structure of very short-term rates: new evidence for the expectations hypothesis', *Journal of Financial Economics*, December 2000, pp. 397–415.

Macaulay, F., *Some Theoretical Problems Suggested by the Movements of Interest Rates, Bond Yields and Stock Prices in the US Since 1856*, National Bureau of Economic Research, New York, 1938.

McCulloch, J., 'The monotonicity of the term structure: a closer look', *Journal of Financial Economics*, March 1987, pp. 185–92.

Richardson, M., Richardson, P. & Smith, T., 'The monotonicity of the term structure: another look', *Journal of Financial Economics*, March 1992, pp. 97–105.

Robinson, E.S., 'The term structure of Australian interest rates: tests of the expectations hypothesis', *Applied Economics Letters*, July 1998, pp. 463–67.

Tease, W.J., 'The expectations theory of the term structure of interest rates in Australia', *The Economic Record*, June 1988, pp. 120–7.

Young, I. & Fowler, D., 'Some evidence on the term structure of interest rates: how to find a black cat when it's not there', *Accounting and Finance*, May 1990, pp. 21–6.

QUESTIONS

1. **[LO 1]** *Assuming certainty, the rates of return on all financial assets will be identical.* Outline why this statement is correct and indicate the factors on which this market rate of return depends.

2. **[LO 3]** *A company's share price reflects the discounted value of either its future dividends or its future earnings.* Discuss.

3. **[LO 5]** *Differences between the current yields on different bonds can be explained by their relative riskiness and different terms to maturity.* Discuss.

4. **[LO 4]** *Government bonds are not riskless.* Do you agree with this statement? Why?

5. **[LO 5]** *Although the market price of long-term bonds is much more sensitive to changes in market interest rates than the market price of short-term bonds, it is not obvious that an individual wishing to invest for a fixed period should choose to invest in a series of shorter-term bonds.* Discuss the rationale for this statement.

6. **[LO 5]** What is the term structure of interest rates? Discuss the various theories that try to explain the term structure of interest rates.

7. **[LO 5]** *Given an upward-sloping term structure, it is preferable for a company to raise debt by issuing short-term debt securities.* Discuss.

8. **[LO 5]** If the term structure is downward sloping, does this mean that liquidity preferences are not having any influence on interest rates?

9. **[LO 6]** What is 'immunisation'? (See Appendix 4.1 Introduction p. 99.) How may duration matching help? What are the problems of duration matching?

PROBLEMS

1. **Required rate of return [LO 1]**
   A 10 per cent $100 government bond that pays interest annually, and currently is 5 years from maturity, is selling for $103.29. What is the required rate of return on this bond? What is the implied real interest rate if the expected inflation rate is 5 per cent per annum?

2. **Valuation of bonds [LO 1]**
   A 12 per cent $100 government bond pays interest twice yearly and matures in 5 years' time. The current market yield on the bond is 10 per cent per annum. If an interest payment has just been made, what is the current price of the bond?

3. **Valuation of shares [LO 3]**
   The required rate of return on the shares in the companies identified in (a) to (c) below is 15 per cent per annum. Calculate the current share price in each case.

   (a) The current earnings per share of Zero Ltd are $1.50. The company does not reinvest any of its earnings, which are expected to remain constant.

   (b) Speedy Ltd's current dividend per share is 80 cents. This dividend is expected to grow at 5 per cent per annum.

   (c) Reduction Ltd's current dividend per share is 60 cents. The dividend of the company has been growing at 12 per cent per annum in recent years, a rate expected to be maintained for a further 3 years. It is then envisaged that the growth rate will decline to 5 per cent per annum and remain at that level indefinitely.

4. **Valuation of shares [LO 2]**
   Assume that today is the last day of 2011. Rednip Ltd is expected to pay annual dividends of 64 cents in 2012 (Year 1). Assume that this dividend is expected to grow at an annual rate of 10 per cent in the foreseeable future and investors require a rate of return of 20 per cent per annum.

   (a) Estimate Rednip Ltd's share price today.

   (b) What is Rednip Ltd's share price expected to be at the end of 2012?

5. **Bond prices and interest rate changes [LO 5]**
   Consider two 12 per cent $100 government bonds that differ only in that one matures in 2 years' time and the other in 5 years' time. Both bonds are currently selling for $100 and pay interest annually.

   (a) What will be the price of each bond, given an immediate fall in the required yield to 10 per cent per annum?

   (b) What will be the price of each bond, given an immediate increase in the required yield to 14 per cent per annum?

   (c) Explain the relative price movements in response to interest rate changes as evidenced by parts (a) and (b).

6. **Expectations theory of the term structure [LO 5]**
   The current interest rates on government bonds are as follows:

Years to maturity	Interest rate (% p.a.)
1	6.00
2	6.50
3	6.90
4	7.20
5	7.40

   (a) Assume that the term structure can be explained purely by expectations of future interest rates, and therefore there is no liquidity or risk premium. Calculate the expected 1-year interest rates for the next 4 years.

(b) Explain why it is not possible in this market for the interest rate on a government bond with 6 years to maturity to be 6 per cent per annum.

7. **Duration and interest rate elasticity [LO 6]**

Consider the following four bonds:

Bond	Term to maturity (years)	Coupon rate (% p.a.)
A	2	10
B	3	12
C	3	10
D	3	8

Each bond has a face value of $100 and the current market interest rate is 9 per cent per annum.

(a) Calculate the current price of each bond.
(b) Calculate the duration of each bond. (See Appendix 4.1.)
(c) Calculate what the price of each bond would be if the market interest rate increased to 11 per cent per annum.
(d) What would be the percentage capital loss on each bond?

8. **Duration and immunisation [LO 6]**

An investor is considering the purchase of a 10-year bond that pays a single annual interest payment at the rate of 10 per cent. The bond's face value is $1000 and its current price is $1134.19. Determine whether the investor can ensure a particular rate of return over a 7-year time horizon. (See Appendix 4.1 on p. 99.)

9. **Duration and immunisation [LO 6]**

If you wish to 'lock in' the current yield of 8.5 per cent per annum for 3 years, which of the following bonds should you invest in?

Bond	Term to maturity (years)	Coupon rate (% p.a.)
A	2.0	10
B	3.0	10
C	3.5	10
D	4.0	10
E	4.0	18

Each bond has a face value of $100. Assume that coupon payments are made at the end of each year.

APPENDIX 4.1 DURATION AND IMMUNISATION

INTRODUCTION

In Section 4.5 it was shown that holders of bonds are subject to interest rate risk. A change in the level of interest rates affects both the market price of an existing bond and the interest rate at which interest receipts can be reinvested. For example, an increase in interest rates means an immediate capital loss to holders of bonds because the price of their securities will fall. However, there is then the opportunity to reinvest interest receipts at the higher interest rate. The reverse applies if interest rates fall.

The possibility of changing interest rates presents difficulties for investors. Suppose, for example, that an investor wishes to have a target sum of money in 3 years' time. The challenge is to choose a bond investment that will achieve this target, regardless of interest rate changes during the 3 years. A strategy to achieve such an objective is called **immunisation**. If possible, the investor should buy a 3-year bond that makes no interest payments (known as **coupons**) during its life. Such securities are usually called **zero-coupon bonds**.[14] The investor knows with certainty the price of the bond at the end of the 3 years because the bond will then be worth exactly its face value, as it matures at that time. Since there are no coupon interest payments, the investor also has no doubts arising from uncertainty about the interest rate that will be earned on reinvested coupons. Therefore, the investor knows precisely what the investment will be worth at the end of the 3 years, and thus achievement of the target is guaranteed. The problem is that although zero-coupon bonds exist, coupon bonds are much more common. Immunisation using coupon-paying bonds is more difficult to achieve.

A technique certain to immunise an investment in coupon-paying bonds against all possible changes in interest rates has never been achieved. However, there is a technique that will immunise a bond investment in a relatively simple environment in which the yield curve is flat, but may make a parallel shift up or down.[15] This technique is based on the concept of bond duration and its origins can be traced to research undertaken by Macaulay (1938).

BOND DURATION

Macaulay realised that a bond paying a low coupon rate is in a sense a 'longer' investment than a higher coupon bond with the same term to maturity. For example, consider two 5-year bonds, both of which have a face value of $1000, pay interest annually and are currently priced to yield 10 per cent per annum. They differ, however, in that one has a coupon rate of 5 per cent per annum and the other a coupon rate of 15 per cent per annum.

The cash flows and their present values are shown in Table A4.1.

LEARNING OBJECTIVE 6
Apply the concept of duration to immunise a bond investment

immunisation
strategy designed to achieve a target sum of money at a future point in time, regardless of interest rate changes

coupons
fixed interest payments made on bonds and debentures

zero-coupon bonds
bonds that pay only one cash flow, the payment at maturity

TABLE A4.1

YEAR	5% COUPON CASH FLOW ($)	PRESENT VALUE ($)	15% COUPON CASH FLOW ($)	PRESENT VALUE ($)
1	50	45.45	150	136.36
2	50	41.32	150	123.97
3	50	37.57	150	112.70

continued →

---

14 With zero-coupon bonds, an investor receives no regular interest payments during the bond's life. A zero-coupon bond is purchased at a discount from its face value and it is either held to maturity, when the investor receives the face value, or sold before maturity at a price determined in the market.

15 For a discussion of techniques appropriate to several, more complex, environments, see Elton and Gruber (1995).

TABLE A4.1 *continued*

YEAR	5% COUPON CASH FLOW ($)	PRESENT VALUE ($)	15% COUPON CASH FLOW ($)	PRESENT VALUE ($)
4	50	34.15	150	102.45
5	50	31.05	150	93.14
	1000	620.92	1000	620.92
Total		**810.46**		**1189.54**

Therefore, the price of the 5 per cent coupon bond is $810.46 and the price of the 15 per cent coupon bond is $1189.54. For the low-coupon bond, the face value payment ($1000) represents about 77 per cent of its price (because $620.92/$810.46 ≈ 0.77). For the high-coupon bond, the face value represents only about 52 per cent of its price ($620.92/$1189.54 ≈ 0.52). Conversely, the first interest payment contributes only about 5.6 per cent to the value of the low-coupon bond ($45.45/$810.46 ≈ 0.056) but contributes nearly 11.5 per cent to the value of the high-coupon bond ($136.36/$1189.54 ≈ 0.115). It is clear that the low-coupon bond brings returns to the investor later in its life, relative to the high-coupon bond. In this sense, the low-coupon bond is 'longer'.

Macaulay proposed that this timing feature could be incorporated into a **duration** measure by weighting the number of periods that will elapse before a cash flow is received by the fraction of the bond's price that the present value of that cash flow represents. In this way the time period is weighted by the 'relative importance' of the cash flow that will occur at that time.

Table A4.2 shows the calculation of duration for the two bonds discussed above.

duration
measure of the time period of an investment in a bond or debenture that incorporates cash flows that are made prior to maturity

TABLE A4.2

TIME	5% COUPON WEIGHT	WEIGHT × TIME	15% COUPON WEIGHT	WEIGHT × TIME
1	45.45/810.46 = 0.056 08	0.056 08	136.36/1189.54 = 0.114 63	0.114 63
2	41.32/810.46 = 0.050 98	0.101 96	123.97/1189.54 = 0.104 22	0.208 44
3	37.57/810.46 = 0.046 36	0.139 08	112.70/1189.54 = 0.094 74	0.284 22
4	34.15/810.46 = 0.042 14	0.168 56	102.45/1189.54 = 0.086 13	0.344 52
5	31.05/810.46 = 0.038 31	0.191 55	93.14/1189.54 = 0.078 30	0.391 50
	620.92/810.46 = 0.766 13	3.830 65	620.92/1189.54 = 0.521 98	2.609 90
Total = duration		**4.487 88**		**3.953 21**

As suggested earlier, the duration of the low-coupon bond (4.488 years) is longer than the duration of the high-coupon bond (3.953 years). Duration and term to maturity are equal only for a zero-coupon bond. The duration of a coupon-paying bond is always less than its term to maturity.

The steps used to calculate duration D are summarised in the formula:

$$D = \sum_{t=1}^{n} \left[\frac{PV(C_t)}{P_0} \right] t \qquad [A4.1]$$

where C_t = cash flow (coupon interest or principal) at time t
$PV(C_t)$ = present value of C_t
$$= \frac{C_t}{(1+i)^t}$$

Now
P_0 = price of the bond
$$= \sum_{t=1}^{n} \frac{C_t}{(1+i)^t} + \frac{P_n}{(1+i)^n}$$

where C_t = coupon interest at time t
P_n = face value payment at maturity
i = required yield per period
n = number of periods to maturity

Equation A4.1 can be rewritten in its more usual form:

$$D = \frac{\sum_{t=1}^{n} \frac{C_t \times t}{(1+i)^t}}{\sum_{t=1}^{n} \frac{C_t}{(1+i)^t}} \qquad [A4.2]$$

Example A4.2 (see pp. 103–4) includes a duration calculation that follows Equation A4.2. First, however, we provide a brief mathematical analysis to highlight the importance of the duration measure. Readers who are not interested in this analysis can omit this section.

DURATION AND INTEREST ELASTICITY

As explained in Section 4.4, if interest rates increase (decrease), then bond prices decrease (increase). When there is a change in interest rates, all bond prices respond in the opposite direction, but they do not all respond to the same extent. In other words, different bonds have different *interest elasticities*. It is important for a bond investor to know the interest elasticity of the bond because this will be a good indicator of the interest rate risk being borne.

The notion of elasticity is prominent in economics. Perhaps the best-known example is the price elasticity of demand for a particular good. This is expressed as follows:

$$\eta = \frac{P}{Q} \frac{dQ}{dP}$$

where η = price elasticity of demand
P = price of the good
Q = quantity of the good demanded
$\frac{dQ}{dP}$ = derivative of quantity demanded with respect to price

Price elasticity indicates the response of the quantity demanded to a change in price.

What matters for a bond investor is the interest elasticity of the bond price; in other words, what matters is the response of the bond price to a change in the interest rate. The elasticity E is given by:

$$E = \frac{i}{P_0} \frac{dP_0}{di} \qquad [A4.3]$$

Writing out the formula for bond price:

$$P_0 = \frac{C_1}{1+i} + \frac{C_2}{(1+i)^2} + \ldots + \frac{C_n}{(1+i)^n} + \frac{P_n}{(1+i)^n}$$

and therefore:

$$\frac{dP_0}{di} = -\frac{C_1}{(1+i)^2} - \frac{2C_2}{(1+i)^3} - \ldots - \frac{nC_n}{(1+i)^{n+1}} - \frac{nP_n}{(1+i)^{n+1}}$$

$$= \left(\frac{-1}{1+i}\right)\left(\frac{C_1}{1+i} + \frac{2C_2}{(1+i)^2} + \ldots + \frac{nC_n}{(1+i)^n} + \frac{nP_n}{(1+i)^n}\right)$$

Substituting into Equation A4.3:

$$E = -\left(\frac{i}{P_0}\right)\left(\frac{1}{1+i}\right)\left(\frac{C_1}{1+i} + \frac{2C_2}{(1+i)^2} + \ldots + \frac{nC_n}{(1+i)^n} + \frac{nP_n}{(1+i)^n}\right)$$

or

$$E = -\left(\frac{i}{1+i}\right)D \qquad [A4.4]$$

where duration, D, is as defined in Equation A4.2.

Equation A4.4 shows that the interest elasticity of a bond's price is proportional to its duration. The longer the duration, the greater (in the sense of being more negative) is the interest elasticity. For example, if the interest rate is 10 per cent per annum and the duration is 4.5 years, the interest elasticity is:

$$E = -\left(\frac{0.10}{1.10}\right)(4.5)$$
$$= -0.409$$

If the duration is 9 years, the interest elasticity is:

$$E = -\left(\frac{0.10}{1.10}\right)(9)$$
$$= -0.818$$

DURATION AND BOND PRICE CHANGES

Given that duration is related to interest elasticity, it follows that it is possible to use duration to work out the approximate percentage price change that will occur for a given change in interest rate. Using Equations A4.3 and A4.4:

$$\frac{i}{P_0}\frac{dP_0}{di} = -\left(\frac{i}{1+i}\right)D$$

It follows that:

$$\frac{dP_0}{P_0} = -\left(\frac{1}{1+i}\right)D\,di$$

Therefore, for 'small' discrete changes in interest rates and bond prices we have the following approximation:

$$\frac{\Delta P_0}{P_0} \approx -\left(\frac{1}{1+i}\right) D \Delta i \qquad [A4.5]$$

EXAMPLE A4.1

Consider the 5-year 15 per cent coupon bond priced to yield 10 per cent per annum. As shown in Tables A4.1 and A4.2, the price of this bond is $1189.54 (per $1000 face value) and its duration is 3.953 years. What is the percentage price change if the interest rate falls to 9.5 per cent per annum?

SOLUTION

In this case the interest rate change is −0.5 per cent = −0.005. Equation A4.5 gives the approximate answer as:

$$-\left(\frac{1}{1.10}\right)(3.953)(-0.005)$$

$$= 0.017\,97$$

In other words, the result will be a capital gain of approximately 1.8 per cent. (The exact answer is close to 1.819 per cent.)

DURATION AND IMMUNISATION

Suppose that the yield curve is flat, but it may make a parallel shift up or down. If, at the time of a parallel shift, an investor is holding a bond whose duration matches the remaining investment period, the investment is immunised against the shift—that is, the investment will achieve at least the target yield, notwithstanding the yield shift. This can be seen in the following example.

EXAMPLE A4.2

Suppose that there is a flat yield curve at an interest rate of 10 per cent per annum. An investor wishes to 'lock in' this yield for a 3-year investment period. Bond A has a term of 3.4 years, a face value of $1000, a coupon rate of 7 per cent and pays interest annually. Table A4.3 shows the calculation of Bond A's duration using Equation A4.2.

$$\text{Duration} = \frac{\$2877.402}{\$958.161}$$

$$= 3.003 \text{ years}$$

TABLE A4.3 Bond A

TIME (YEARS)	CASH FLOW ($)	PRESENT VALUE OF CASH FLOW ($)	TIME × PRESENT VALUE ($)
0.4	70	67.382	26.953
1.4	70	61.256	85.758
2.4	70	55.687	133.649
3.4	1070	773.836	2631.042
Total		958.161	2877.402

According to the immunisation strategy, Bond A should provide an immunised investment because its duration matches the investment period—that is, an investment of $958.161 in Bond A will be worth at

continued →

Example A4.2 *continued*

least $958.161 \times (1.1)^3 = \$1275.312$ in 3 years' time, regardless of an interest rate shift. To demonstrate this, it is assumed that:

(a) immediately after buying Bond A, the yield curve makes a parallel shift from 10 per cent to 8 per cent, and remains at that level for the next 3 years
(b) as each coupon interest payment is received, the investor reinvests in—that is, buys more of—the same bond
(c) bonds and dollars are infinitely divisible, thereby allowing the investor to purchase or sell any fraction of Bond A.

After 0.4 years have passed, the investor receives a coupon payment of $70. The bond is now a 3-year bond. The yield curve has shifted down to 8 per cent, so the price of one bond is then:

$$\frac{\$70}{1.08} + \frac{\$70}{(1.08)^2} + \frac{\$1070}{(1.08)^3}$$

$$= \$974.229$$

Therefore, the investor can purchase the fraction 70.00/974.229 of one bond. This fraction is 0.071 852, so the investor now holds 1.071 852 bonds. After 1.4 years, the investor receives a further coupon payment of $70 per bond; therefore the cash received is $70 \times 1.071\,852 = \$75.0296$. The bond is now a 2-year bond and its price is:

$$\frac{\$70}{1.08} + \frac{\$1070}{(1.08)^2}$$

$$= \$982.167$$

The investor can now purchase a further $75.0296/982.167 = 0.076\,39$ of a bond. This type of cycle is repeated after 2.4 years and the investment in bonds is then sold after 3 years. Table A4.4 summarises the progress of the investment.

TABLE A4.4

ITEM	DATE = INVESTMENT PERIOD EXPIRED (YEARS)				
	0.0	0.4	1.4	2.4	3.0
Bond term remaining (years)	3.400 00	3.000 00	2.000 00	1.000 00	0.400 00
Coupon interest received ($)	Nil	70.000 00	75.029 60	80.377 00	Nil
Price of one bond ($)[a]	958.161 00	974.229 00	982.167 00	990.741 00	1037.563 00
Bonds purchased (no.)	1.000 00	0.071 85	0.076 39	0.081 13	Nil
No. of bonds held	1.000 00	1.071 85	1.148 24	1.229 37	1.229 37
Value of bonds held ($)	958.161 00	1044.227 00	1127.764 00	1217.987 00	1275.549 00

[a] Present value of remaining cash flows per $1000 face value. Yield used is 10 per cent per annum for the price at date zero. Yield used is 8 per cent per annum for prices calculated after date zero.

As can be seen in the bottom right-hand corner of the table, the sum received from the sale after 3 years is $1275.549. This amount exceeds the target sum after 3 years of $1275.312 and the investment has therefore achieved the target rate of return of at least 10 per cent per annum.

What if the interest rate had risen to 12 per cent (instead of falling to 8 per cent)? In that case, the progress of the investment would be as shown in Table A4.5.

TABLE A4.5

ITEM	DATE = INVESTMENT PERIOD EXPIRED (YEARS)				
	0.0	0.4	1.4	2.4	3.0
Bond term remaining (years)	3.400 00	3.000 00	2.000 00	1.000 00	0.400 00
Coupon interest received ($)	Nil	70.000 00	75.568 80	81.346 80	Nil
Price of one bond ($)[a]	958.161 00	879.908 00	915.497 00	955.357 00	1022.578 00
Bonds purchased (no.)	1.000 00	0.079 55	0.082 55	0.085 15	Nil
No. of bonds held	1.000 00	1.079 55	1.162 10	1.247 25	1.247 25
Value of bonds held ($)	958.161 00	949.905 00	1063.897 00	1191.565 00	1275.406 00

[a] Present value of remaining cash flows per $1000 face value. Yield used is 10 per cent per annum for the price at date zero. Yield used is 12 per cent per annum for prices calculated after date zero.

Again, therefore, the investment has achieved the target yield of 10 per cent per annum, notwithstanding the shift in yield after the investment was made.

Managing risk by matching Macaulay's duration to the investment horizon is an important idea but the procedure we have described has a number of limitations. In particular, it is important to investigate what happens if there is more than one yield shift during the investment period. Consider again Example A4.2 and suppose that the yield had shifted down to 8 per cent immediately after date 0.0, but then shifted up to 12 per cent just before date 3.0 (the end of the investment period). In that case, the investor will hold 1.229 37 bonds after 3 years have passed, but the price will be only $1022.578 per bond, which gives a value of 1.229 37 × $1022.578 = $1257.127. This falls short of the target of having at least $1275.312.

In principle, this problem can be solved easily. When the yield changes, so too does the duration of the bond held. When the yield shifts on the first occasion, the investor should change the bond holding so that, once again, duration matches the investment period. The investor is then immunised against the *next* yield shift. This is simple in principle but in practice there are difficulties because it implies that a rebalancing of the investment—buying and selling bonds—is needed every time the duration of the investment changes. Because duration is a function of the current yield and future coupon payments, this means that a bond transaction is needed every time the yield shifts, and every time a coupon payment is received. This can be costly and cumbersome.

Only a flat yield curve subject to parallel shifts has been considered. It may be shown that if a sloped yield curve shifts in parallel fashion the investor still matches duration and investment period, but the duration formula is slightly more complex. If a sloped yield curve shifts in some non-parallel way then the immunisation strategy will depend on the type of non-parallel shift assumed to occur. For an example, see the article by Cox, Ingersoll and Ross (1979).

CHAPTER 5
PROJECT EVALUATION: PRINCIPLES AND METHODS

LEARNING OBJECTIVES

After studying this chapter you should be able to:

1. explain the importance of each of the steps in the capital-expenditure process
2. outline the decision rules for each of the main methods of project evaluation
3. explain the advantages and disadvantages of the main project evaluation methods
4. explain why the net present value method is preferred to all other methods
5. understand the relationship between economic value added (EVA) and net present value (NPV)
6. understand the relationship between real options, managerial flexibility and firm value.

CHAPTER CONTENTS

5.1 Introduction
5.2 The capital-expenditure process
5.3 Methods of project evaluation
5.4 The discounted cash flow methods compared
5.5 Other methods of project evaluation
5.6 Project evaluation and real options analysis

INTRODUCTION

5.1

In Chapter 1 we described the primary financial functions of a financial manager as raising funds and allocating them to investment projects so as to maximise shareholders' wealth. In this chapter, we consider how such projects should be selected to ensure the maximisation of shareholders' wealth. The term *investment project* is interpreted very broadly to include any proposal to outlay cash in the expectation that future cash inflows will result. There is, therefore, a wide range of such projects. These include proposals for the replacement of plant and equipment, a new advertising campaign, research and development activities, and proposals to take over competing firms.

In this book, investment and financing decisions are discussed in the order in which they are usually considered in practice. In general, management will first examine the alternative investment projects available to it. After the acceptability of these projects has been determined, management will, if necessary, set about raising the funds to implement them. It is logical, therefore, to discuss the evaluation and selection of proposed investment projects before discussing the methods of financing them. In this chapter, we examine the principles and methods of project evaluation. In Chapter 6, the application of these principles and methods is discussed.

The evaluation and selection of investment projects is only one element of the capital-expenditure process. Before discussing the methods of project evaluation, therefore, we outline the capital-expenditure process.

THE CAPITAL-EXPENDITURE PROCESS

5.2

Capital-expenditure management involves the planning and control of expenditures incurred in the expectation of deriving future economic benefits in the form of cash inflows. Consider the following possible proposals: a manufacturer is considering building a new plant; an airline is considering the replacement of several of its aircraft; a pharmaceutical company is considering a new research and development program. Each proposal involves making current outlays in the expectation of future cash inflows and, therefore, each can be analysed as a capital-expenditure proposal. This is the case even though, for example, the costs of research and development are usually recognised for accounting purposes as expenses in the period in which they are incurred.

> **LEARNING OBJECTIVE 1**
> Explain the importance of each of the steps in the capital-expenditure process

Capital expenditures are very important for a company because frequently the amounts of money involved are large and their effects extend well into the future. After capital expenditures have been made, it is likely that their effects will continue for some time as many projects are not easily modified. If there is either no second-hand market or, at best, only a 'thin' market for capital assets, management may have to abandon a project if it proves to be unprofitable. Because of the longevity and frequent irreversibility of many investments, they are likely to commit a company to a particular technology and to have a considerable influence on the pattern of its future operating cash flows. The importance of these decisions, therefore, can extend well beyond the period in which the initial capital outlay is made.

The tasks involved in the capital expenditure process, as well as the associated outcomes from their implementation, are outlined in Table 5.1.

TABLE 5.1 Tasks and outcomes of the capital expenditure process

	TASKS	OUTCOMES
Stage 1 Generation of investment proposals	• Systematic processes are established to ensure members of the organisation may contribute ideas to enhance firm value • Incentives may be provided to reward employees who contribute ideas	• Investment proposals are forwarded to management – employees dealing in production processes will typically contribute ideas relating to eliminating operating inefficiencies – proposals by upper-level managers will mostly relate to wider issues such as product development or expansionary opportunities
Stage 2 Evaluation and selection of investment proposals	• Data about each investment proposal are collected. Data include: – a description of the proposal – the reasons for its adoption – estimates of amount and timing of cash inflows and outflows – an estimate of the time until the proposal will come into operation and the economic life of the proposal once it is adopted • All proposals are then evaluated using standard uniform procedures to ensure that assessments are conducted objectively • The economic evaluation of the projects is conducted using a variety of techniques (discussed in Section 5.3) that take into account the risk of the net cash flows that are expected to be delivered by the project	• A list of recommended projects is prepared by responsible management
Stage 3 Approval and control of capital expenditures	• A capital expenditure budget is prepared that details the estimated capital expenditure requirements on new and existing projects over the next few years: – a short-term budget is prepared that relates to a period ranging from, say, 6 months to 2 years – a longer-term budget is also prepared that provides forecasts of cash requirements over the next 2 to 5 years Processes are established to ensure that the project is properly managed and monitored. These processes typically include: – the appointment of a project manager responsible for the implementation of the project and the preparation of regular progress reports – the establishment of a realistic timetable for implementation of the project – the establishment of a separate account for each project to ensure that expenditures are readily observed	• Systematic processes are established that enable the firm to effectively manage and monitor the implementation of new projects

	TASKS	OUTCOMES
Stage 4 Post-completion audit of investment projects	• Projects are regularly re-evaluated via a *post-completion* audit to ensure that each project is meeting the expectations of the firm • The audit will identify where cash flows are significantly different from budget forecasts and possible reasons for such differences	• Initial investment decisions may be improved as those responsible for investment proposals are aware that they will be audited • Improvements in the operating performance of projects are facilitated as new information is regularly provided to managers • Unsuccessful projects are identified at the earliest possible time — leading to their abandonment and subsequent savings to the firm

METHODS OF PROJECT EVALUATION   5.3

In this section we consider the evaluation and selection of investment projects. First, we consider the net present value and the internal rate of return methods, which were explained in a one-period setting in Chapters 2 and 3. We then consider other methods that have been employed in project evaluation.

Many methods are used to evaluate and compare investment projects. The methods outlined in this section are those that surveys of business practice suggest are used most frequently. They are of two basic types:

(a) the discounted cash flow methods, such as the internal rate of return and net present value methods, which discount a project's estimated cash flows to allow for the magnitude and timing of the cash flows
(b) the non-discounted cash flow methods, such as the accounting rate of return and payback period methods.

Table 5.2 shows some of the results of a 2010 Australian survey of 76 chief financial officers who were generally employed by large listed companies. These results are broadly consistent with those of a US survey undertaken by Graham and Harvey (2001).

TABLE 5.2 Selected project evaluation methods used by the CFOs surveyed[a]

METHOD	PERCENTAGE[b]
Internal rate of return	72.06
Net present value (NPV)	70.59
Payback period	56.72
Real options analysis	26.56
Accounting rate of return	26.15
Economic value added (EVA)	15.38
Profitability index	10.94

[a] Percentages correspond to the proportion of respondents who answered that they 'always' or 'almost always' used each particular method.

[b] The aggregate percentage exceeds 100 per cent because most respondents used more than one method of project evaluation.

Source: Reprinted from Coleman, L., Maheswaran, K. & Pinder, S., 'Narratives in managers' corporate finance decisions', *Accounting and Finance*, September 2010, pp. 605–33.

independent project
one that may be accepted or rejected without affecting the acceptability of another project

In this chapter it is assumed initially that investment projects are independent. Two projects are said to be **independent** if the acceptance of one project does not preclude the acceptance of the other project. Two conditions are necessary for two or more projects to be classified as independent:

(a) It must be technically feasible to undertake one of the projects, irrespective of the decision made about the other project(s).
(b) The net cash flows from each project must be unaffected by the acceptance or rejection of the other project(s).

An example of independent investment projects is where an entity is considering whether to purchase new machinery for its factory and whether to commission a new advertising campaign. As these investments are independent, management can make an accept/reject decision on each investment without considering its relationship to other investments. Problems caused by the existence of projects that are not independent are considered in Section 5.4.3.

5.3.1 DISCOUNTED CASH FLOW METHODS

discounted cash flow (DCF) methods
those which involve the process of discounting a series of future net cash flows to their present values

It can be seen from Table 5.2 that the two most frequently employed **discounted cash flow (DCF) methods** are the net present value and internal rate of return methods.

The **net present value (NPV)** of a project is equal to the difference between the present value of its net cash flows and its initial cash outlay.[1] Assuming a cash outlay at the beginning of the project's life, and a series of net cash flows in the following periods, the net present value of the project is calculated as follows:

$$NPV = \frac{C_1}{(1+k)} + \frac{C_2}{(1+k)^2} + \ldots + \frac{C_n}{(1+k)^n} - C_0 \quad [5.1]$$

net present value (NPV)
the difference between the present value of the net cash flows from an investment discounted at the required rate of return, and the initial cash outlay on the investment

which can be written more conveniently as:

$$NPV = \sum_{t=1}^{n} \frac{C_t}{(1+k)^t} - C_0 \quad [5.2]$$

where C_0 = the initial cash outlay on the project
C_t = net cash flow generated by the project at time t
n = the life of the project
k = required rate of return

The **internal rate of return (IRR)** of a project is the rate of return that equates the present value of its net cash flows with its initial cash outlay.[2] Assuming a cash outlay at the beginning of the project's life and a series of net cash flows in the following periods, the internal rate of return is found by solving for r in the following equation:

$$C_0 = \frac{C_1}{(1+r)} + \frac{C_2}{(1+r)^2} + \ldots + \frac{C_n}{(1+r)^n} \quad [5.3]$$

internal rate of return (IRR)
the discount rate that equates the present value of an investment's net cash flows with its initial cash outlay; it is the discount rate at which the net present value is equal to zero

This can be written more conveniently as:

$$C_0 = \sum_{t=1}^{n} \frac{C_t}{(1+r)^t} \quad [5.4]$$

where C_0 = the initial cash outlay on the project
C_t = net cash flow generated by the project at time t
n = the life of the project
r = the internal rate of return

---

1 The cash flows could be discounted and/or compounded to equivalent values at any point in time. It is usual to discount the cash flows to the present; hence the use of the term *net present value*. An alternative would be to calculate a *net terminal value*. This is equal to the difference between the accumulated value of the net cash flows generated by a project, and the accumulated value of the initial cash outlay. Use of the net terminal value method gives the same decision as for the net present value method.
2 Other terms used to describe the same concept include 'the DCF return on investment', 'yield', and 'the marginal efficiency of capital'.

THE DISCOUNTED CASH FLOW METHODS COMPARED

5.4

LEARNING OBJECTIVE 2
Outline the decision rules for each of the main methods of project evaluation

The assumed objective of a company is to maximise shareholders' wealth. Consistent with this objective, projects should be accepted only if they are expected to result in an increase in shareholders' wealth. Therefore, the method of project evaluation must be consistent with maximising shareholders' wealth. Other things being equal, this will occur where a project generates more cash, rather than less cash, and generates cash sooner, rather than later. The ability of the net present value and internal rate of return methods to result in decisions that are consistent with this objective is considered in the following sections.

5.4.1 NET PRESENT VALUE

The net present value of a project is found by discounting the project's future net cash flows at the required rate of return and deducting from the resulting present value the initial cash outlay on the project. Therefore:

$$NPV = \sum_{t=1}^{n} \frac{C_t}{(1+k)^t} - C_0 \qquad [5.5]$$

Where the investment outlays occur over more than one period, C_0 in Equation 5.5 refers only to the initial cash outlay. All subsequent outlays are included in the calculation of the net cash flows of future periods. Of course, this may result in subsequent negative net cash flows in addition to the initial cash outlay.

Management should select projects with a positive net present value and reject projects with a negative net present value. The amount of any positive net present value represents the immediate increase in the company's wealth that will result from accepting the project—that is, a positive net present value means that the project's benefits are greater than its cost, with the result that its implementation will increase shareholders' wealth. Conversely, projects that have a negative net present value would reduce shareholders' wealth.

The magnitude of a project's net present value depends on the project's cash flows and the rate used to discount those cash flows. It follows that the estimation of a project's future cash flows is an important step in project evaluation. This involves deciding what cash flow data are relevant for project evaluation and then estimating those data. While both aspects are important, the mechanics of estimation, which is the job of engineers, market research analysts and others, is beyond the scope of this book. We focus on the first aspect—that is, the principles involved in defining and measuring project cash flows.

There are essentially two approaches to measuring a project's net cash flows. The most popular method is to forecast the expected net profit from the project and adjust it for non-cash flow items, such as depreciation. The second method, and the approach used in this book, is to estimate net cash flows directly. The cash inflows will comprise receipts from the sale of goods and services, receipts from the sale of physical assets, and other cash flows. Cash outflows include expenditures on materials, labour, indirect expenses for manufacturing, selling and administration, inventory and taxes. While the measurement of a project's net cash flows may seem to be straightforward, there are some aspects that warrant further consideration. These are discussed in Chapter 6.

In addition to estimating a project's future cash flows, it is also necessary to estimate the life of the project and determine the required rate of return to be used in discounting the cash flows. The correct discount rate to apply is the opportunity cost of capital.[3] This is the rate of return required on the next

---

[3] Estimation of the required rate of return, or discount rate, is discussed in Chapter 14. It is sufficient at this stage to point out that the required rate of return is simply the rate of return that a project must generate in order to justify raising funds to undertake it. Where there is perfect certainty about the outcome of an investment, the risk-free rate, such as the current yield on government securities of the same maturity as the investment, is the appropriate discount rate. However, where there is uncertainty about the outcome of the investment, a risk-adjusted required rate of return must be used. Throughout the remainder of the book we will use the term *required rate of return* to indicate the discount rate used in discounted cash flow calculations.

best—that is, forgone—alternative investment. If the net cash flows have been estimated on an after-tax basis, then, to be consistent, the appropriate required rate of return is the after-tax rate. The measurement of the required rate of return is considered in Chapter 14.

Example 5.1 illustrates the application of the net present value method.

EXAMPLE 5.1

Bruce Barry is considering an investment of $900 000 in a project that will return net cash flows of $509 000, $450 000 and $400 000 at the end of Years 1, 2 and 3, respectively. Assuming a required rate of return of 10 per cent per annum, what is the net present value of the project?

SOLUTION

The net present value may be calculated as shown in Table 5.3.

TABLE 5.3 Calculating a project's net present value (NPV)

YEAR	NET CASH FLOWS ($)	DISCOUNT FACTOR AT 10%	PRESENT VALUE ($)
0	(900 000)[a]		(900 000)
1	509 000	0.909 09	462 727[b]
2	450 000	0.826 45	371 901[b]
3	400 000	0.751 31	300 526[b]
NPV ($)			235 154

[a] The amount in brackets represents the initial cash outlay.
[b] The sum of $462 727 + $371 901 + $300 526 = $1 135 154 is the maximum amount the company would be prepared to pay for the project if the required rate of return is 10 per cent per annum.

At a discount rate of 10 per cent per annum, the project has a positive NPV of $235 154 and is therefore acceptable.

This method is consistent with the company's objective of maximising shareholders' wealth. If a company implements a project that has a positive net present value, the company will be more valuable than before it undertook the project, and therefore, other things being equal, the total market value of the company's shares should increase *immediately* by the same amount as the net present value of the new project. In other words, the company is undertaking a project that has a net present value in excess of that necessary to leave its share price unchanged. This was shown formally in Chapter 2 using Fisher's Separation Theorem.

In summary, the decision rule for the net present value method is as follows:

> *Accept a project if its net present value is positive when the project's net cash flows are discounted at the required rate of return.*

5.4.2 INTERNAL RATE OF RETURN

The internal rate of return for a project is the rate of return that equates the present value of the project's net cash flows with its initial cash outlay. This means that Equation 5.4 can be rewritten as follows:

$$\sum_{t=1}^{n} \frac{C_t}{(1+r)^t} - C_0 = 0 \quad [5.6]$$

From Equation 5.6, the internal rate of return is the discount rate that results in a zero net present value. However, the internal rate of return is not only the discount rate that causes the net present value of the project's cash flows to be zero. It also represents:

> … the highest rate of interest an investor could afford to pay, without losing money, if all the funds to finance the investment were borrowed, and the loan (principal and accrued interest) was repaid by using the cash proceeds from the investment as they were earned.[4]

---

4 See Bierman and Smidt (1993).

Even if the investment outlays occur in more than one period, C_0 in Equation 5.6 refers only to the initial cash outlay. Any subsequent investment outlays are subtracted from the cash flows of future periods, which suggests that some of the net cash flows in Equation 5.6 may be negative. The effect on the internal rate of return of negative net cash flows in subsequent periods is discussed later in this section.

If, as is usual in practice, the project's net cash flows in each period are not equal, the internal rate of return can be found only by trial and error—that is, by varying the discount rate until the present value of the cash flows is equal to the investment outlay. If this process shows that the present value of the net cash flows is greater than the initial cash outlay, then some higher discount rate should make them equal, and vice versa.

After the internal rate of return has been measured, the acceptability of an investment project is determined by comparing the internal rate of return r with the required rate of return k. Any project with $r > k$ should be accepted and any project with $r < k$ should be rejected.

Example 5.2 illustrates the application of the internal rate of return method.

EXAMPLE 5.2

If we take the cash flows of Example 5.1, the project's internal rate of return may be calculated using Equation 5.3 as follows:

$$C_0 = \frac{C_1}{(1+r)} + \frac{C_2}{(1+r)^2} + \frac{C_3}{(1+r)^3}$$

Thus:

$$\$900\,000 = \frac{\$509\,000}{(1+r)} + \frac{\$450\,000}{(1+r)^2} + \frac{\$400\,000}{(1+r)^3}$$

By trial and error, $r = 25$ per cent.[5] If the required rate of return is, say, 15 per cent, the project's internal rate of return of 25 per cent exceeds the required rate of return and the project is acceptable.

The use of this method, therefore, appears to be consistent with the company's objective of maximising shareholders' wealth. If the required rate of return is the minimum return that investors demand on investments then, other things being equal, accepting a project with an internal rate of return greater than the required rate should result in an increase in the price of the company's shares.

Multiple and indeterminate internal rates of return

In Example 5.2 the investment's cash flows consisted of an initial cash outlay, followed by a series of positive net cash flows. In such cases a unique positive internal rate of return will usually exist.

In certain circumstances, however, it is possible for the present value of the future net cash flows to be equal to the initial cash outlay at more than one discount rate—that is, a project may have more than one internal rate of return. A *necessary* condition for multiple internal rates of return is that one or more of the net cash flows in the later years of a project's life must be negative. The presence of negative net cash flows in the later years of a project's life is not a *sufficient* condition for multiple internal rates of return. In many cases, negative cash flows in the later years of a project's life are consistent with there being only one internal rate of return.[6]

---

[5] In practice, a financial calculator may be used to calculate the internal rate of return and eliminate the time-consuming computations involved in the trial-and-error process. Alternatively, the 'IRR' function in Microsoft Excel® might also be used.

[6] Descartes's rule of signs states that there can be as many positive roots for $1 + r$ as there are changes in the sign of the cash flows. Therefore, if, after the initial cash outlay, the net cash flows are always positive, there will be at most one positive root for $1 + r$, and consequently only one for r itself. However, two sign changes in the cash flow can result in two positive values for $1 + r$, so there may also be two positive values for r. For example, if the two positive values for $1 + r$ are $+1.1$ and $+1.3$, there will be two positive values for r: 10 per cent and 30 per cent. In the remainder of this section we use the term *internal rate of return* to mean *positive internal rate of return*.

While, in practice, there is little likelihood of the occurrence of multiple internal rates of return, it is important to recognise that there are circumstances where multiple internal rates do occur. Such a set of circumstances is illustrated in Example 5.3.

EXAMPLE 5.3

Consider an investment project with the cash flows shown in Table 5.4.

TABLE 5.4 Project cash flows

YEAR	CASH FLOW
0	−14 545 620
1	34 182 000
2	−20 000 000

An example of where such a cash flow pattern may occur is where a mining company is obliged, after completion of its mining operations, to restore the mine site to its original condition. If we solve for the internal rate of return of this project, then we find that its net present value is zero at both 10 per cent and 25 per cent—that is, the project has two internal rates of return. The project's net present value profile, which plots the project's net present value as a function of the required rate of return, is shown in Figure 5.1.

FIGURE 5.1 Net present value profile showing two internal rates of return

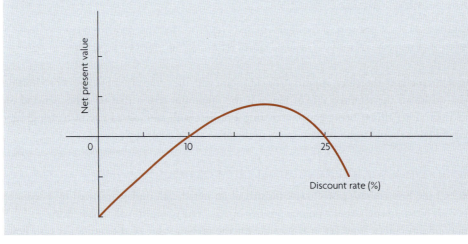

The number of internal rates of return is limited to the number of sign reversals in the cash flow stream. In this case there are two sign reversals, which is a necessary, but not sufficient, condition for two internal rates of return. Three sign reversals is a necessary condition for three rates, and so on. Hence, the number of cash flow sign reversals corresponds to the *maximum*, but not necessarily the *actual*, number of internal rates of return.

It may be argued that multiple rates are not a problem because the project may be abandoned at the beginning of the second year, thereby avoiding the subsequent negative cash flow, and also the multiple internal rate of return problem. If the project is terminable and has a positive residual value, a unique internal rate of return may be calculated. However, in some cases, abandonment of the project may not be feasible because it may involve substantial abandonment costs in the early years of operation, or there may be a legal obligation to continue the project for a number of years.

In addition to the problem of multiple internal rates of return, it is possible for an investment project to have no internal rate of return. For example, a project with the following pattern of cash flows: −$80 000, +$100 000, −$50 000, has no internal rate of return.

Projects with a cash flow stream that results in either multiple internal rates of return, or no internal rate of return, are likely to be rare in practice, but the possibility of such occurrences does exist. In what follows, it is assumed that a project's cash flow pattern results in a unique internal rate of return.

In summary, the decision rule for the internal rate of return method is:

Accept a project if it has a unique internal rate of return that is greater than the required rate of return.

5.4.3 CHOOSING BETWEEN THE DISCOUNTED CASH FLOW METHODS

Independent investments

For independent investments, both the IRR and NPV methods of investment evaluation lead to the same accept/reject decision, except for those investments where the cash flow patterns result in either multiple internal rates of return or no internal rate of return. In other words, if a project has an internal rate of return greater than the required rate of return, the project will also have a positive net present value when its cash flows are discounted at the required rate of return—that is, NPV > 0 when $r > k$, NPV < 0 when $r < k$, and NPV = 0 when $r = k$. This is always true, provided that the project's cash flows consist of one or more periods of cash outlay followed only by positive net cash flows. Such a project is referred to as a conventional project and the net present value profile of such a project is illustrated in Figure 5.2. Figure 5.2 shows that the higher the discount rate, the lower is the net present value. The intercept of the net present value profile with the horizontal axis occurs at the point where $k = r$, which is the internal rate of return because it is the discount rate at which the net present value is zero.

LEARNING OBJECTIVE 3
Explain the advantages and disadvantages of the main project evaluation methods

FIGURE 5.2 Net present value profile for a conventional project

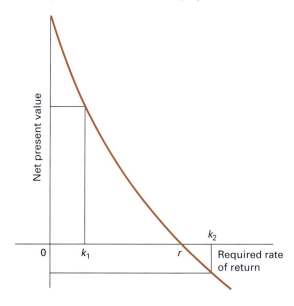

Figure 5.2 shows that at a required rate of return of k_1, the net present value is positive and $r > k_1$, while at a required rate of return of k_2 the net present value is negative and $r < k_2$. If management has to decide whether to accept or reject an independent investment project, then both the internal rate of return method and the net present value method will give results consistent with maximising shareholders' wealth.

Mutually exclusive investments

So far it has been assumed that investment projects are independent, which means that management can make an accept/reject decision about each project without considering its relationship with other projects. In this section, we allow for the fact that investment projects may be interdependent. In this case, the expected benefits from one project are affected by a decision to accept or reject another project. In the extreme case, where the expected cash flows from a project will completely disappear if another project is accepted, or it is technically impossible to undertake the proposed project if another project is accepted, the projects are said to be **mutually exclusive**. For example, if a company owns land on which it can build either a factory or a warehouse, then these two projects are mutually exclusive. If a decision is made to build the factory, the company is unable to build the warehouse. Another example of mutually exclusive projects is if different types of equipment can be used to manufacture the same product. The choice of one type of equipment automatically leads to the rejection of the other.

mutually exclusive projects
alternative investment projects, only one of which can be accepted

In the remainder of this section the discounted cash flow methods will be evaluated, assuming that investment projects are mutually exclusive. Where management has to select from mutually exclusive projects it is necessary to rank the projects in order of acceptability. This means that it is necessary to determine whether it makes any difference to project selection if projects are ranked according to their internal rates of return or their net present values.

First, we consider whether the internal rate of return or net present value methods should be used to evaluate mutually exclusive investments.

EXAMPLE 5.4

Consider the mutually exclusive investments, A and B, in Table 5.5.

TABLE 5.5

PROJECT	CASH OUTLAY ($)	NET CASH FLOW 1 YEAR AFTER THE YEAR OF OUTLAY ($)	IRR (%)	NPV @ 10% ($)
A	−1	+10	900	8.09
B	−100 000	+200 000	100	81 818.18

The internal rate of return method ranks a 900 per cent return on $1 ahead of a 100 per cent return on $100 000. At a required rate of return of 10 per cent, both investments are worth undertaking, but if a choice has to be made between the two investments, then investment B with the larger net present value is to be preferred. This is because B adds more to the company's value than A. The net present value method will ensure that the value of the company is maximised, whereas the use of the internal rate of return method will not ensure that result. It is apparent, therefore, that the internal rate of return and net present value methods can rank mutually exclusive investment projects differently. This is now explained.

Ranking mutually exclusive investments

Although both projects in Example 5.4 had the same life, the initial cash outlays were different. However, even if the initial cash outlays and the projects' lives had been the same, it is still possible that the internal rate of return and net present value methods would rank mutually exclusive investments differently. This is illustrated by Example 5.5.

EXAMPLE 5.5

Two projects, C and D, have the same initial cash outlays and the same lives but different net cash flows, as shown in Table 5.6.

TABLE 5.6

PROJECT	NET CASH FLOWS ($)		
	YEAR 0	YEAR 1	YEAR 2
C	−200 000	20 000	364 000
D	−200 000	200 000	150 000

What are the internal rates of return and net present values for projects C and D?

SOLUTION

Table 5.7 shows the internal rates of return and the net present values at a required rate of return of 10 per cent for projects C and D.

TABLE 5.7

PROJECT	INTERNAL RATE OF RETURN (%)	NET PRESENT VALUE ($)
C	40	119 008
D	50	105 785

Both projects have a positive net present value and an internal rate of return greater than the required rate of return and are therefore acceptable in their own right. In other words, if the projects are independent, both should be implemented. However, if the projects are mutually exclusive and therefore must be ranked, the two methods give different rankings. In this case using the net present value method, C is preferred to D, while using the internal rate of return method, D is preferred to C.

In Example 5.5, the difference in ranking is caused by differences in the magnitude of the net cash flows. In addition to differences in ranking caused by differences in the cash flow streams, the internal rate of return and net present value methods may give a different ranking where the investment projects have unequal lives.

It may be concluded, therefore, that:

> … any difference in the magnitude or timing of the cash flows may cause a difference in the ranking of investment projects using the internal rate of return and net present value methods.

This is illustrated in Figure 5.3, which shows the net present value profiles for two projects, E and F. Assume, as in Example 5.5, that the two projects have the same cash outlay and lives, and that the pattern of net cash flows results in the net present value profiles shown in Figure 5.3. In this case, the net present value profiles of the two projects intersect. At a discount rate of r_1, or at any other discount rate less than r_2, the net present value of E is greater than the net present value of F, while at a discount rate of r_3, or at any other discount rate greater than r_2, the net present value of F is greater than the net present value of E.[7]

---

[7] For projects such as those in Table 5.6 with the same initial cash outlay, r_2 is found by equating the present values of projects E and F as follows:

$$PV_E = \sum_{t=1}^{n} \frac{C_{Et}}{(1+r_2)^t} = \sum_{t=1}^{n} \frac{C_{Ft}}{(1+r_2)^t}$$

In this instance, r_2 = 18.89 per cent. This means that if the required rate of return is less than 18.89 per cent, the internal rate of return and net present value methods result in conflicting rankings.

FIGURE 5.3 Net present value profiles for Projects E and F

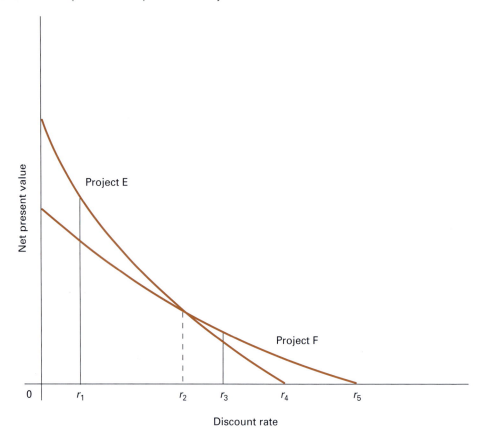

On the other hand, it has already been shown that the internal rate of return is found where the net present value is zero and, using this rule, Project F is ranked ahead of Project E because its internal rate of return, r_5, is greater than r_4, which is the internal rate of return of E.[8] In this case, the two methods can provide management with different rankings of projects E and F.

Like Example 5.5, Figure 5.3 shows that even where two mutually exclusive projects have the same initial outlays and the same lives, a difference in the projects' rankings may still occur as a result of the projects' different time patterns of net cash flows. Therefore, for mutually exclusive investment projects, the net present value method is superior to the internal rate of return method, because it always gives a wealth-maximising decision.

Even where the projects are mutually exclusive, the two methods could yield consistent rankings if the patterns of the projects' net cash flows result in net present value profiles that do not intersect. This is illustrated in Figure 5.4. In this case, the net present value of Project G at a discount rate of r_1 is greater than the net present value of Project H. This is consistent with the internal rate of return method as r_3, the internal rate of return of Project G, is greater than r_2, the internal rate of return of Project H.

---

[8] Remember that discounting of the net cash flows at the internal rate of return will result in a net present value of zero. Therefore: $0 = \sum_{t=1}^{n} \frac{C_t}{(1+r)^t} - C_0$

FIGURE 5.4 Net present value profiles for projects G and H

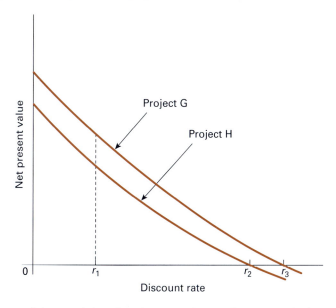

However, because of the possibility that the internal rate of return method may give an incorrect ranking of mutually exclusive investment projects, the net present value method is preferred.

The incremental internal rate of return approach to ranking mutually exclusive investments

The internal rate of return method can be adapted so that it provides a correct ranking of mutually exclusive projects. This is shown in Example 5.6.

EXAMPLE 5.6

The cash flows for two projects, I and J, are shown in Table 5.8. Are Projects I and J acceptable?

TABLE 5.8

PROJECT	CASH FLOWS ($)					
	YEAR 0	YEAR 1	YEAR 2	YEAR 3	YEAR 4	YEAR 5
I	−45 000	13 500	13 500	13 500	13 500	13 500
J	−30 000	9 150	9 150	9 150	9 150	9 150

SOLUTION

If the required rate of return is 8 per cent per annum, both projects are acceptable using either the net present value or the internal rate of return method, as shown in Table 5.9.

TABLE 5.9

PROJECT	INTERNAL RATE OF RETURN (%)	NET PRESENT VALUE ($)
I	15.2	8 902
J	15.9	6 533

If the two projects are mutually exclusive, then, using the net present value method, Project I is preferred to Project J, while using the internal rate of return method, Project J is preferred to Project I.

continued →

Example 5.6 *continued*

The incremental cash flows from choosing Project I (the project with the lower internal rate of return) rather than Project J (the project with the higher internal rate of return) are presented in Table 5.10. These cash flows may be assigned to the notional project 'I minus J'.

The internal rate of return of this notional project is 13.8 per cent. As this internal rate of return is greater than the required rate of return of 8 per cent, the notional project should be accepted. Accepting the notional project 'I minus J' is equivalent to accepting Project I in preference to Project J. This is the ranking given by the net present value method.

TABLE 5.10 Cash flows for notional project

YEAR	'I MINUS J' ($)
0	−15 000
1	4 350
2	4 350
3	4 350
4	4 350
5	4 350

LEARNING OBJECTIVE 4
Explain why the net present value method is preferred to all other methods

The possibility of conflict between the internal rate of return and net present value methods may therefore be avoided by the use of this 'incremental internal rate of return' approach. It results in a ranking of mutually exclusive projects that is consistent with the net present value method. However, the net present value method is simpler and is more obviously consistent with the objective of wealth maximisation, which is expressed in absolute dollar terms rather than in percentage terms.

5.4.4 BENEFIT–COST RATIO (PROFITABILITY INDEX)

Table 5.2 shows that a number of the surveyed chief financial officers use the profitability index method of project evaluation. In this method, instead of showing the net present value as an absolute amount, the present value of the net cash flows is divided by the initial cash outlay to give a **benefit–cost ratio** or profitability index.

benefit–cost ratio index calculated by dividing the present value of the future net cash flows by the initial cash outlay (also known as a *profitability index*)

A benefit–cost ratio for the project in Table 5.3 is calculated as follows:

$$\text{Benefit–cost ratio} = \frac{\text{present value of net cash flows}}{\text{initial cash outlay}} \quad [5.7]$$

$$= \frac{\$1\,135\,154}{\$900\,000}$$

$$= 1.26$$

LEARNING OBJECTIVE 2
Outline the decision rules for each of the main methods of project evaluation

Using the benefit–cost ratio, the decision rule is to accept projects with a benefit–cost ratio greater than 1, and to reject projects with a benefit–cost ratio less than 1. Clearly, projects with benefit–cost ratios greater than 1 will have positive net present values, and those with benefit–cost ratios less than 1 will have negative net present values. In the above example, the net present value is $235 154 and the benefit–cost ratio is 1.26. Both methods therefore indicate that the project is acceptable and, in general, both methods will give the same accept/reject decision for independent projects.

However, the benefit–cost ratio provides no information additional to that already provided by the NPV method. Thus, there is little point in using this method. In addition, the benefit–cost ratio can result in a ranking of mutually exclusive projects that differs from the ranking that would result from using the NPV method. This is shown in Example 5.7.

> **EXAMPLE 5.7**
>
> Consider the mutually exclusive investments projects in Table 5.11.
>
> **TABLE 5.11** Ranking projects using the benefit–cost ratio
>
> | | PROJECT K | PROJECT L |
> |---|---|---|
> | Present value of net cash flows ($) | 260 000 | 100 000 |
> | Initial cash outlay ($) | 180 000 | 50 000 |
> | Net present value | 80 000 | 50 000 |
> | Benefit–cost ratio = | $\frac{260\,000}{180\,000}$ | $\frac{100\,000}{50\,000}$ |
> | = | 1.44 | 2.00 |
>
> In this case, although the net present value of Project L is less than the net present value of Project K, the benefit–cost ratio of L is greater than that of K.

Therefore, if the benefit–cost ratio is used it may result in management preferring projects with lower net present values. The benefit–cost ratio must therefore be rejected as a ranking technique because it can provide incorrect rankings of mutually exclusive projects. Table 5.2 indicates that the popularity of the profitability index to managers relative to other project evaluation techniques is low. Further, survey evidence[9] suggests that the technique tends to be used by managers who face a shortage of funds available to invest in wealth-enhancing projects. Faced with such constraints, managers have to decide on the mix of acceptable projects that should be funded in order to maximise the wealth created for the firm. This process, known as *capital rationing,* is discussed in Section 6.8.

5.5 OTHER METHODS OF PROJECT EVALUATION

In Table 5.2, there were two major non-discounted cash flow methods employed by the companies surveyed. They are the accounting rate of return and the payback methods. These methods are frequently employed in conjunction with the discounted cash flow methods of project evaluation.

The accounting rate of return

There are many ways to calculate the **accounting rate of return** or return on investment. The most popular methods are those that express a project's average annual earnings as a percentage of either the initial investment or the average investment in the project. That is:

$$r_a = \frac{\text{average annual earnings}}{\text{initial investment in a project}} \times \frac{100}{1}\% \qquad [5.8]$$

$$r_a = \frac{\text{average annual earnings}}{\text{average investment in a project}} \times \frac{100}{1}\% \qquad [5.9]$$

Payback period

The **payback period** is the time it takes for an entity to recover a project's initial cash outlay. For example, the payback period of a machine that costs $300 000 and has net cash flows of $100 000 per annum is 3 years.

accounting rate of return
earnings from an investment expressed as a percentage of the investment outlay

payback period
the time it takes for the progressive accumulated net cash flows generated by an investment to equal the initial cash outlay

---
9 For surveys of capital budgeting practices, see Burns and Walker (2009).

LEARNING OBJECTIVE 2

Outline the decision rules for each of the main methods of project evaluation

Sections 5.5.1 and 5.5.2 show that the accounting rate of return and payback methods are inferior to the net present value method.

5.5.1 ACCOUNTING RATE OF RETURN

Essentially, the accounting rate of return is the earnings from a project, usually after deducting both depreciation and income tax, expressed as a percentage of the investment outlay. It is compared with a required rate of return or cut-off rate to determine the project's acceptability. If the accounting rate of return is greater than the required rate of return, the project is acceptable; if it is less than the required rate of return, the project is unacceptable.

The accounting rate of return has many variants. We will calculate only three of these. To calculate these variants of the accounting rate of return, management must first estimate:

(a) the average annual earnings to be generated by a project. This is calculated by dividing the total net profit from the project by the number of years during which the profit is expected to be received.
(b) the investment outlay on the project. This is equal to either its initial investment outlay, including additional and permanent working capital requirements, or the average capital employed in the project. The average capital employed on a project is calculated either as the average book value of the investment, or more frequently as the average of the capital invested in the project at the beginning and the end of its life.

The methods of calculating the accounting rate of return are illustrated in Example 5.8.

EXAMPLE 5.8

Assume that a company is considering an investment project that costs $10 000 000 and generates returns in Years 1, 2 and 3 as shown in Table 5.12.

TABLE 5.12 Data for calculating the accounting rate of return

ITEM	YEAR 1	YEAR 2	YEAR 3	AVERAGE
Earnings (after depreciation and income tax) ($)	2 000 000	3 000 000	4 000 000	3 000 000
Book value ($)[a]				
1 January	10 000 000	7 000 000	4 900 000	
31 December	7 000 000	4 900 000	3 430 000	
Average	8 500 000	5 950 000	4 165 000	6 205 000

[a] Assuming that depreciation is calculated at 30 per cent on the reducing balance.

Using these data, the following accounting rates of return may be calculated:

(a) Accounting rate of return based on the initial investment is:

$$\frac{\$3\,000\,000}{\$10\,000\,000} = 30\%$$

(b) Accounting rate of return based on the average book value is:

$$\frac{\$3\,000\,000}{\$6\,205\,000} = 48\%$$

(c) Accounting rate of return based on average investment as measured by the average of the capital invested at the beginning and the end of the project's life is:

$$\frac{\$3\,000\,000}{\dfrac{\$10\,000\,000 + \$3\,430\,000}{2}} = 44.68\%$$

Each variant yields a different rate of return. For example, if the rate of return is calculated by dividing average annual earnings by the *average* investment outlay, then the project's rate of return would be much higher than if it had been calculated by dividing average annual earnings by the *initial* investment outlay.

There are two fundamental problems with using the accounting rate of return, irrespective of the way it is defined. First, it is arbitrary. This is because it is based on accounting earnings rather than cash flows. As a result, factors such as the depreciation method employed and the method of valuing inventories will have a substantial bearing on the measurement of earnings and therefore on the accounting rate of return. Second, it ignores the timing of the earnings stream. Equal weight is given to the earnings in each year of the project's life. This problem is illustrated in Example 5.9.

LEARNING OBJECTIVE 3
Explain the advantages and disadvantages of the main project evaluation methods

EXAMPLE 5.9

A company is considering two projects, M and N. Both projects cost $100 000 at the beginning of the first year and have a life of 5 years. The residual value of each project at the end of the fifth year is zero. The earnings for each project are shown in Table 5.13.

TABLE 5.13

PROJECT	OUTLAY ($)	ANNUAL EARNINGS ($)					TOTAL
		YEAR 1	YEAR 2	YEAR 3	YEAR 4	YEAR 5	
M	100 000	2 500	5 000	10 000	15 000	17 500	50 000
N	100 000	17 500	15 000	10 000	5 000	2 500	50 000

The average rate of return for each project is:

$$\frac{\$50\,000/5}{\$100\,000/2} = \frac{\$10\,000}{\$50\,000} \times \frac{100\%}{1} = 20\%$$

Project M has increasing earnings while Project N has decreasing earnings. However, both result in the same total earnings, and therefore the same average annual earnings. Consequently, both projects are regarded as equally acceptable if the accounting rate of return method is used. However, the two projects are not equally acceptable because the earnings from Project N are received earlier than the earnings from Project M. Intuition would suggest, therefore, that Project N is preferable to Project M.

The accounting rate of return fails to reflect the advantages that earlier returns have over later returns. As a result, this method ranks projects with the same initial outlay, life and total earnings equally, even though the projects' patterns of earnings may be different. In addition, if projects with the same initial outlay and total earnings have different lives, the accounting rate of return method will automatically favour projects with short lives. However, there is no reason why such projects should necessarily prove to be the most profitable projects.

Because of its significant shortcomings, the accounting rate of return method should not be used to evaluate investment projects. However, as we observed earlier, in practice the accounting rate of return is often used in conjunction with the discounted cash flow methods. Because external financial analysts use earnings (profit) to assess a company's performance, management may wish to ensure that projects are acceptable according to both accounting and discounted cash flow criteria.

5.5.2 PAYBACK PERIOD

The payback period is the time it takes for the initial cash outlay on a project to be recovered from the project's net cash flows. It is calculated by summing the net cash flows from a project in successive years until the total is equal to the initial cash outlay. This is illustrated in Table 5.14.

TABLE 5.14 Calculation of payback period

YEAR	PROJECT Q		PROJECT R	
	INITIAL CASH OUTLAY ($)	NET CASH FLOW ($)	INITIAL CASH OUTLAY ($)	NET CASH FLOW ($)
0	100 000		100 000	
1		20 000		20 000
2		30 000		40 000
3		30 000		40 000
4		20 000		10 000
5		70 000		10 000
Total		170 000		120 000
Payback period		4 years		3 years

LEARNING OBJECTIVE 2

Outline the decision rules for each of the main methods of project evaluation

To decide whether a project is acceptable, its payback period is compared with some maximum acceptable payback period. A project with a payback period less than the maximum will be accepted, while a project with a payback period greater than the maximum will be rejected.

An important question is: What length of time represents the 'correct' payback period as a standard against which to measure the acceptability of a particular project? In practice a maximum payback period is set, which is inevitably arbitrary, and may be from, say, 2 to 5 years. All projects with a payback period greater than this maximum are rejected.

Calculation of the payback period takes into account only the net cash flows up to the point where they equal the investment outlay. The calculation of the payback period ignores any net cash flows after that point. As a result, the payback method of evaluation discriminates against projects with long gestation periods and large cash flows late in their lives.

The payback period is not a measure of a project's profitability. If the most profitable projects were always those that recovered the investment outlay in the shortest period of time, then current assets such as inventory and accounts receivable would yield higher returns than non-current assets, and non-current assets with short lives would yield higher returns than non-current assets with long lives. Mere recovery of the outlay on a project yields no profit at all. If there is a profit on the project it must be due to additional cash flows after the investment outlay has been recovered. Therefore, the major weakness of the payback method is its failure to take account of the magnitude and timing of all of a project's cash inflows and outflows.

Why then is payback popular as a method of investment evaluation? Many companies use payback in conjunction with other methods. One reason for its popularity is that it provides information on how long funds are likely to be committed to a project. Managers who prefer projects with short payback periods are interested in how soon the funds invested in a project will be recouped for reinvestment in other projects. Another reason is that the near-term cash flows considered in calculating the payback period are regarded as more certain than later cash flows. As a result, insistence on a short payback period is a simple but imprecise way of controlling for risk.

5.5.3 ECONOMIC VALUE ADDED (EVA)

LEARNING OBJECTIVE 5
Understand the relationship between economic value added (EVA) and net present value (NPV)

In Section 5.5.1, it was noted that the accounting rate of return method is often used in addition to the discounted cash flow methods because financial analysts generally use accounting information to assess performance year by year. To overcome the problems of measuring the accounting rate of return discussed in Section 5.5.1, the economic value added (EVA) approach to measuring performance was introduced by consulting firms in the US.[10]

Accounting profit is calculated as the difference between revenues and expenses for a reporting period. One of the costs incurred by a company that is not deducted in calculating profit is the company's required rate of return. To calculate the EVA of an investment, it is simply a matter of deducting from accounting earnings the profit required from the investment, calculated as the required rate of return multiplied by the capital invested in the project. Thus, using Example 5.8, if the required rate of return is 10 per cent, then the returns generated in Years 1, 2 and 3 would be as follows:

TABLE 5.15

	YEAR 1	YEAR 2	YEAR 3
Earnings (after depreciation and income tax) ($)	2 000	3 000	4 000
Capital charge:			
Amount invested × 10% ($)	1 000[(a)]	700	490
Economic value added (EVA)	$1 000	$2 300	$3 510

[(a)] In Year 1, the amount invested in the project is $10 000, therefore the capital charge is $10 000 × 10% = $1 000.

The EVA in Table 5.15 shows the addition to the company's wealth created by the investment. If the accounting rate of return were equal to the required rate of return, then EVA would be zero. EVA, therefore, provides management with a simple rule: invest only if the increase in earnings is sufficient to cover the required rate of return.

EVA makes the required rate of return an important element in measuring the performance of an investment. The manager of a plant can improve EVA either by increasing earnings or by reducing the capital employed. Therefore, there is an incentive for managers to identify underperforming assets and dispose of them.

Note that this approach to measuring EVA does not measure present value. However, it can be shown that the present value of a stream of future EVAs for an investment is equal to the net present value of the investment. The EVA in each period is equal to the net cash flow plus or minus the change in the value of the investment less the required rate of return. Thus:

$$EVA_t = C_t + (I_t - I_{t-1}) - kI_{t-1} \qquad [5.10]$$

where C_t = net cash flow in Year t
I_t = value of the investment at the end of Year t
I_{t-1} = value of the investment at the end of Year $t-1$
k = required rate of return

However, there are two special cases:

(a) In Year 0, $EVA_0 = C_0 + I_0$ because there is no capital charge until Year 1.
(b) At the end of the project, the investment in the project (I_t) is zero because the investment is liquidated and therefore $EVA_t = C_t - (1 + k) I_{t-1}$.

---

[10] Economic value added (EVA) is the term used by the US consulting firm Stern-Stewart. This firm has been instrumental in popularising this measure of performance.

Therefore, the present value of a stream of EVAs is:

$$EVA_0 + \frac{EVA_1}{1+k} + \frac{EVA_2}{(1+k)^2} + \ldots + \frac{EVA_{T-1}}{(1+k)^{T-1}} + \frac{EVA_T}{(1+k)^T} \quad [5.11]$$

where $EVA_0 = C_0 + I_0$
$EVA_1 = C_1 + I_1 - (1 + k) I_0$
$EVA_2 = C_2 + I_2 - (1 + k) I_1$
$EVA_{T-1} = C_{T-1} + I_{T-1} (1 + k) I_{T-2}$
$EVA_T = C_T - (1 + k) I_{T-1}$

When these values are substituted into Equation 5.11, we find that all the I terms cancel out, leaving:

$$C_0 = \frac{C_1}{1+k} + \frac{C_2}{(1+k)^2} + \ldots + \frac{C_{T-1}}{(1+k)^{T-1}} + \frac{C_T}{(1+k)^T}$$
$$= NPV$$

That is, the discounted stream of EVAs is the same as the NPV of the investment.

5.6 PROJECT EVALUATION AND REAL OPTIONS ANALYSIS

LEARNING OBJECTIVE 6
Understand the relationship between real options, managerial flexibility and firm value

Consider the following scenario: substantial oil reserves have just been discovered in Sydney Harbour and the government has called for bids for the right to extract the oil. Comprehensive geological reports estimate that there are 40 million barrels of oil that could be extracted. Owing to the unique environment in which the oil is located, and the need to ensure that any disturbance to the environment from the invasive extraction process is remedied, the present value of the expected cost of extraction is relatively high, at $80 per barrel. The long-run expected sales price of the oil is estimated to be $70 per barrel in present value terms. How much would an investor bid for the right to extract oil? Standard NPV analysis would suggest that no rational investor would bid a positive amount for the extraction right as the project has a negative NPV with each barrel of oil extracted decreasing wealth by $10.

What is wrong with this analysis? It ignores the fact that the successful bidder for the project obtains the right, but not the obligation, to commence operations. That is, the successful bidder has the *option* to extract the oil. Based upon current expectations of available technology, cost structures and revenues it is at present unprofitable to extract the oil and the option would not be immediately taken up. However, it is not difficult to think of circumstances that may result in the project having a positive NPV. For example, new technology may be developed to substantially reduce the cost of extraction or the long-run expected sales price of oil might increase. Either way, the successful bidder has purchased the right to exploit any advantageous change in circumstances.

real options
the flexibility that a manager has in choosing whether to undertake or abandon a project or change the way a project is managed

Throughout this chapter it has been implicitly assumed that the problem facing management is whether to accept or reject a project for *immediate* implementation. That is, projects have essentially been treated as 'now-or-never' prospects. In reality of course, this is rarely the case, as firms will often have some flexibility in the timing of their investment decision and the way in which the project is managed if the firm makes the decision to proceed. These 'choices' faced by management are often referred to as **real options** and problems may arise when the value of options created (or destroyed) by management decisions is not accounted for during the project evaluation stage.[11]

---

11 For an excellent and accessible discussion of the importance of incorporating real options into project evaluation see Dixit and Pindyck (1995).

Some common examples of real options include:

- Option to delay investment—this option is linked to the ability of the firm to 'wait and see' and collect more information about the project that may alter the final decision. This option is especially valuable to a firm where the level of uncertainty surrounding a project is high. When a firm finally commits to a project, it is giving up the opportunity to collect more information about the project, and hence, it is often argued, the NPV of a project must not only be positive, but be great enough to compensate the firm for the value of the flexibility it is giving up.
- Option to expand operations—when a firm first enters a market it quite often does so on unprofitable terms. That is, firms will quite willingly enter into a project that has a negative NPV. One explanation for this seemingly irrational behaviour is that by gaining a presence in the market, the firm is able to acquire valuable expansion options that would otherwise be unavailable. An example of this type of behaviour was the introduction of Virgin Blue Airlines to the Australian market. Initially the airline provided only seven daily Brisbane–Sydney return flights. However, following the collapse of Ansett Airlines (the second largest domestic carrier in Australia at the time), Virgin Blue found itself in a position where it could rapidly expand to fill the void left by Ansett.
- Option to abandon operations—once a firm makes the decision to proceed with a project, it generally retains the right to abandon operations and sell off the assets dedicated to the project at their salvage value. At the outset, of course, the firm does not expect to make use of (or exercise) this option, but it is important that it has the ability to do so if market conditions were to move significantly against the project. This does not, however, imply that the firm will abandon operations as soon as a project becomes unprofitable, since by doing so the firm gives up the ability to remain in the market were conditions to change back in the project's favour.

Once we accept the notion that managerial flexibility is valuable, identifying real options is relatively straightforward. The difficult part is to try to then value them. A discussion of the general principles underlying option pricing, as well as a more detailed discussion of real options analysis, is provided in Chapter 18.

Connect Plus features a case study illustrating topics covered in this chapter.
Ask your lecturer or tutor for your course's unique URL.

SUMMARY

→ Of the two discounted cash flow methods of investment evaluation, we recommend the net present value method because it is consistent with the objective of maximising shareholders' wealth. It is also simple to use and gives rise to fewer problems than the internal rate of return method. We have shown that where mutually exclusive projects are being considered, the internal rate of return method may result in rankings that conflict with those provided by the net present value method. In addition, we have shown that even if investment projects are independent, it is possible that a project's pattern of cash flows may give rise to multiple internal rates of return, or to no internal rate of return at all.

→ If the net present value method is adopted, the rules for making correct investment decisions are straightforward:
  – Calculate each project's net present value, using the required rate of return as the discount rate.
  – If the projects are independent, accept a project if its net present value is greater than zero, and reject it if its net present value is less than zero.
  – If the projects are mutually exclusive, accept the project with the highest net present value, provided that it is greater than zero.

→ In practice, companies often use one method of project evaluation in conjunction with other methods. For example, one of the discounted cash flow methods may be used to measure a project's profitability, but the payback period may also be used either as a check on liquidity effects, or as a means of monitoring the project's cash flows against expectations.

→ Whereas the evaluation methods considered throughout the chapter tend to treat projects as 'now-or-never' prospects, and ignore the ability of management to intervene in an ongoing project, real options analysis considers the value associated with managerial flexibility.

KEY TERMS

accounting rate of return 121	discounted cash flow (DCF) methods 110	mutually exclusive projects 116
benefit–cost ratio 120	independent project 109	net present value (NPV) 110
	internal rate of return (IRR) 110	payback period 121
		real options 126

SELF-TEST PROBLEMS

1. The management of a company is considering an investment of $180 000 in a project that will generate net cash flows of $101 800 at the end of the first year, $90 000 at the end of the second year and $80 000 at the end of the third year. Assuming a required rate of return of 10 per cent per annum, calculate the project's net present value.

2. Calculate the internal rate of return for the investment in Question 1.

3. Calculate the benefit–cost ratio for the investment in Question 1.

Solutions to self-test problems are available in Appendix B, page 803.

REFERENCES

Bierman, H. Jr & Smidt, S., *The Capital Budgeting Decision: Economic Analysis of Investment Projects*, 8th edn, Macmillan Company, New York, 1993.

Burns, R.M. & Walker, J., 'Capital budgeting surveys: The future is now', *Journal of Applied Finance*, 2009, pp. 78–90.

Coleman, L., Maheswaran, K. & Pinder, S., 'Narratives in managers' corporate finance decisions', *Accounting and Finance*, September 2010, pp. 605–33.

Dixit, A.K. & Pindyck, R.S., 'The options approach to capital investment', *Harvard Business Review*, May–June 1995, pp. 105–15.

Graham, J.R. & Harvey, C.R., 'The theory and practice of corporate finance: evidence from the field', *Journal of Financial Economics*, May–June 2001, pp. 187–243.

Walker, E.D., 'Introducing project management concepts using a jewelry store robbery', *Decision Sciences Journal of Innovative Education*, Spring 2004, pp. 65–9.

QUESTIONS

1. **[LO 1]** Outline the four steps in the capital-expenditure process.

2. **[LO 2]** What factors does the required rate of return of a project reflect?

3. **[LO 2]** Compare the internal rate of return and net present value methods of project evaluation. Do these methods always lead to comparable recommendations? If not, why not?

4. **[LO 3]** *Evidence suggests that financial managers use more than one method to evaluate investment projects.* Comment on this statement.

5. **[LO 3]** *The internal rate of return method of project evaluation is easier to use because it avoids the need to calculate a required rate of return.* Comment on this statement.

6. **[LO 4]** *Even where projects are independent, the uncritical use of the internal rate of return method can seriously mislead management.* Discuss.

7. **[LO 2]** Distinguish between independent and mutually exclusive investment projects.

8. **[LO 4]** Demonstrate, for independent investment projects, that the internal rate of return and net present value methods of evaluation yield identical decisions. Specify any assumptions you make.

9. **[LO 4]** Using the NPV profile technique, explain why the IRR and NPV rules will always result in the same accept or reject decision for independent projects.

10. **[LO 3]** What problems are associated with the use of the accounting rate of return method for the evaluation of investment proposals? Why might managers be attracted to its use?

11. **[LO 4]** The payback period method of project evaluation is biased against projects with longer developmental lives, even where they ultimately generate great value for the firm. Discuss.

12. **[LO 5]** As the present value of a stream of EVAs for an investment is the same as its net present value, why do analysts use EVA?

13. **[LO 6]** There is some evidence that when managers evaluate projects, they systematically employ discount rates that exceed the risk-adjusted required rate of return. How is this observation consistent with the notion that real options are important in project evaluation?

PROBLEMS

1. **Discount rates, IRR and NPV analysis [LO 2]**
   Assume that you are asked to analyse the following three projects:

PROJECT	YEAR 0	YEAR 1	YEAR 2	YEAR 3	YEAR 4	YEAR 5
A	−200 000	20 000	20 000	20 000	20 000	220 000
B	−200 000	527 600	52 760	52 760	52 760	52 760
C	−2 000 000	—	—	—	—	322 100

   CASH FLOW ($)

   Construct a spreadsheet, and associated graphs, that will enable you to analyse the impact of different discount rates on the NPV of a project as well as calculate the IRR for a project (an example is provided in Figure 5.1).

   (a) Rank the three projects assuming the appropriate discount rate is:
   - (i) 6 per cent per annum
   - (ii) 10 per cent per annum
   - (iii) 15 per cent per annum.

   (b) Calculate the IRR for each of the projects, then rank them.

2. **IRR and NPV analysis [LO 4]**
   Each of the following mutually exclusive investment projects involves an initial cash outlay of $240 000. The estimated net cash flows for the projects are as follows:

Year	Project A	Project B
1	140 000	20 000
2	80 000	40 000
3	60 000	60 000
4	20 000	100 000
5	20 000	180 000

   CASH FLOW ($)

   The company's required rate of return is 11 per cent. Construct a spreadsheet, and associated graphs, that will enable you to analyse the impact of different discount rates on the NPV of a project as well as calculate the IRR for a project. What is the NPV and IRR for both projects? Which project should be chosen? Why?

3. **IRR and NPV analysis for independent projects [LO 2]**
   The following investment proposals are independent. Assuming a required rate of return of 10 per cent, and using both the internal rate of return and net present value methods, which of the proposals are acceptable?

	CASH FLOW ($)		
Proposal	Year 0	Year 1	Year 2
A	–40 000	8 000	48 000
B	–40 000	42 000	—
C	–40 000	48 000	—

4. **NPV and IRR analysis for mutually exclusive projects [LO 4]**

   A company wishes to evaluate the following mutually exclusive investment proposals:

	CASH FLOW ($)					
Proposal	Year 0	Year 1	Year 2	Year 3	Year 4	Year 5
A	–97 400	34 000	34 000	34 000	34 000	34 000
B	–63 200	24 000	24 000	24 000	24 000	24 000

   (a) Calculate each proposal's net present value and internal rate of return. Assume the required rate of return is 8 per cent.

   (b) How would you explain the different rankings given by the net present value and internal rate of return methods?

5. **NPV and IRR analysis [LO 4]**

   You have been asked to evaluate the following investment proposals:

	CASH FLOW ($)		
Proposal	Year 0	Year 1	Year 2
A	100 000	–140 000	60 000
B	–12 000	24 000	–20 000

   Calculate the net present value (assuming a required rate of return of 12 per cent) and the internal rate of return for each project. Explain your results.

6. **Accounting rate of return and payback period [LO 3]**

   Using the following data, calculate:
   (a) the accounting rate of return
   (b) the payback period.

Project cost:	$40 000
Estimated project life:	5 years
Estimated residual value:	$8 000
Annual accounting profit (equal to annual net cash inflow):	$12 000

   Use the straight-line method of depreciation in your calculations.

   How would your answers to (a) and (b) differ if the estimated dollar returns were:

Year 1:	$12 000
Year 2:	$16 000
Year 3:	$24 000
Year 4:	$20 000
Year 5:	$8 000

7. **Accounting rate of return, payback period, IRR and NPV [LO 2]**

   Using the following data, calculate the:
   (a) accounting rate of return
   (b) payback period
   (c) internal rate of return
   (d) net present value.

Project cost:	$100 000
Estimated life:	5 years
Estimated residual value:	$20 000
Annual net cash flow:	$30 000
Required rate of return:	10%

   Use the straight-line method of depreciation in your calculations.

   How would your answers differ if the net cash flows were as follows?

Year 1:	$30 000
Year 2:	$40 000
Year 3:	$60 000
Year 4:	$20 000
Year 5:	$50 000

Test yourself further with Connect Plus online! Ask your lecturer or tutor for your course's unique URL.

CHAPTER 6
THE APPLICATION OF PROJECT EVALUATION METHODS

LEARNING OBJECTIVES

After studying this chapter you should be able to:

1. explain the principles used in estimating project cash flows
2. compare mutually exclusive projects that have different lives
3. determine when to retire (abandon) or replace assets
4. use sensitivity analysis and break-even analysis to analyse project risk
5. use decision-tree analysis to analyse sequential decisions
6. explain the role of qualitative factors in project selection
7. explain the effects of resource constraints on project selection.

CHAPTER CONTENTS

6.1 Introduction
6.2 Application of the net present value method
6.3 Comparing mutually exclusive projects that have different lives
6.4 Deciding when to retire (abandon) or replace a project
6.5 Analysing project risk
6.6 Decision-tree analysis
6.7 Qualitative factors and the selection of projects
6.8 Project selection with resource constraints

6.1 INTRODUCTION

In Chapter 5, methods of project evaluation were discussed and the reasons for using the net present value method of project evaluation were outlined. However, in Chapter 5 it was assumed that a project's cash flows and the discount rate applicable to those cash flows were both known. In practice, a project's cash flows and required rate of return are not known with certainty but must be estimated. In other words, practical project evaluation involves important issues concerning the estimation of cash flows and risk. These and other issues are the subject of this chapter. In particular, the matters considered in this chapter include:

- the application of the net present value method, including the estimation of cash flows
- using the net present value method to solve problems, such as comparing projects with different lives and asset-replacement decisions
- the application of techniques that allow managers to analyse the risk of projects
- the influence of qualitative factors on the selection of investment projects
- the problems associated with using the net present value method where companies are assumed to have only limited access to resources.[1]

6.2 APPLICATION OF THE NET PRESENT VALUE METHOD

Any application of the net present value method requires estimates of project cash flows. This section discusses issues that are important in defining the relevant cash flows.

6.2.1 ESTIMATION OF CASH FLOWS IN PROJECT EVALUATION

Issues that arise in defining the relevant cash flows include the:

- treatment of financing charges
- inclusion of incremental cash flows
- importance of excluding sunk costs
- treatment of allocated costs
- treatment of a project's residual value
- timing of the cash flows
- treatment of inflation.

These issues are discussed in turn.

LEARNING OBJECTIVE 1
Explain the principles used in estimating project cash flows

Financing charges

Companies should use the required rate of return to discount a project's net cash flows. The required rate of return is the return that is sufficient to compensate shareholders and debtholders for the resources committed to the project. It includes both interest paid to debtholders and returns to shareholders. Therefore, financing charges such as interest and dividends should not be included in the calculation of a project's net cash flows. The inclusion of financing charges in a project's net cash flows and in the discount rate would result in double counting.

---

1 The effects of taxes on project evaluation are discussed in Chapter 14.

Incremental cash flows

In calculating a project's net cash flows, it is the incremental net cash flows that are important. An analyst should include *all* cash flows that change if the project is undertaken. When deciding whether a particular item should be included, the analyst is interested in the answers to two questions:

(a) Is it a *cash* item?
(b) Will the amount of the item *change* if the project is undertaken?

If the answer to both questions is 'yes', then the item is an incremental cash flow. If the answer to either question is 'no', then the item is irrelevant to the analysis. For example, assume that a company is receiving $4000 per year from renting a portion of its factory, and that it is considering using that space to manufacture a product that will return net cash flows of $10 000 per year. In this case, $10 000 overstates the net cash flows from the product by an amount of $4000; the cash inflow is forgone because the portion of the factory will not be rented. The incremental net cash flow in this case is $6000 per year. The principle of including only incremental cash flows may seem simple, but it sometimes involves difficulties such as identifying sunk costs and allocated costs.

Sunk costs

Suppose that the Spilt Oil Company has spent $20 million exploring a particular area without success. Harvey Milk, the geologist who originally identified that area as potentially valuable, argues that the company should spend another $5 million to drill an additional well because: 'If we don't, the $20 million that we have already spent will be lost'. Mr Milk's argument is incorrect because the $20 million is a **sunk cost**. Sunk costs are past outlays and should be ignored in making decisions about whether to continue a project or to terminate it. In this case, the $20 million has already been spent. This figure will not change if the project is continued or abandoned. Allowing sunk costs to influence decisions can lead to 'throwing good money after bad'. Regardless of whether $2 or $20 million has already been spent, decisions on whether to continue a project should be based only on expected *future* costs and benefits.

sunk cost
cost that has already been incurred and is irrelevant to future decision making

Allocated costs

Companies often allocate costs such as rent, power, water, research and development, head office costs, travel, and other overhead costs to their divisions. Therefore, when the profitability of a project is estimated, the costs attributed to the project may include a share of these allocated costs. The analyst should remember that when a project is being evaluated, only incremental cash flows should be included. In some cases, implementing an additional project may result in significantly higher overhead costs, but in other cases any increase may be negligible. When estimating project cash flows, any allocated costs should be examined carefully to determine whether they would change if the project were to go ahead. If they would not change they should be excluded.

Residual value

When a project is terminated, it is likely that a portion of the initial capital outlay will be recovered. This is often termed the project's **residual value**. A project's residual value will be the disposal value of the project's assets, less any dismantling and removal costs associated with the termination of the project.

residual value
disposal value of a project's assets less any dismantling and removal costs associated with the project's termination

Timing of the cash flows

In some cases, financial calculations are based on the precise timing of the relevant cash flows. For example, such precision is standard practice when calculating the value of marketable debt securities such as bonds and bank bills. In these cases, both the amount and the timing of the cash flows are known. However, when an investment project is evaluated, the magnitude of the cash flows is rarely known but must be estimated, usually with some degree of error. Similarly, the timing of cash flows can rarely be estimated precisely and the simplifying assumption that net cash flows are received at the end of a period is usually adopted. This assumption reduces the complexity of the net present value calculations without causing a marked decrease in their reliability, and it is the assumption adopted in the remainder of this chapter.

Inflation and project evaluation

The Australian economy has at times experienced prolonged periods of inflation. During a period of inflation there is an increase in the general level of prices and a fall in the purchasing power of money. There are two approaches to incorporating the effects of inflation into project evaluation. Both approaches, applied consistently, will give the same net present value. Both require the analyst to estimate the future rate of inflation.

One approach involves making estimates of cash flows that are based on anticipated prices during each year of a project's life, and discounting those cash flows at the nominal required rate of return. In this case, the estimated net cash flows from a project in, say, its fourth year of operation are based on the prices expected in that fourth year. The presence of inflation therefore makes the job of estimating net cash flows more difficult, especially if prices are expected to increase at a rapid rate. The use of the *nominal* required rate of return means that the discount rate reflects the market's expectations about the rate of inflation. If it is expected that the rate of inflation will increase in the future, then market pressure should lead to an increase in the nominal required rate of return on an investment. Therefore, observed nominal rates of return have built into them expected future inflation rates. This approach is consistent, in that net cash flows based on anticipated future price levels are discounted at the nominal required rate of return, which also has built into it expected inflation rates.

The other approach involves estimating the net cash flows without adjusting them for anticipated changes in prices, and discounting those cash flows at the *real* required rate of return. In other words, the net cash flows are estimated using existing (constant) prices. To be consistent it is necessary to discount these net cash flows at the real required rate of return, which excludes expected inflation.

The following example illustrates that the two approaches, applied consistently, give the same result.

EXAMPLE 6.1

Assume that an investment of $1000 is expected to generate cash flows of $500, at constant prices, at the end of each of 3 years. Assume also that prices are expected to increase at the rate of 10 per cent per annum and that the nominal required rate of return is 15 per cent per annum. What is the project's net present value?

SOLUTION

Using the first approach, the net present value of the investment is as follows:

$$-\$1000 + \frac{\$500(1.10)}{1.15} + \frac{\$500(1.10)^2}{(1.15)^2} + \frac{\$500(1.10)^3}{(1.15)^3}$$

$$= -\$1000 = \frac{\$550}{1.15} + \frac{\$605}{1.3225} + \frac{\$665}{1.5209}$$

$$= \$373$$

Using the second approach, the net cash flow of $500 per annum at constant prices is discounted at the real required rate of return. As discussed in Sections 1.5.4 and 3.4.4, the real rate may be expressed in terms of the nominal rate as follows:

$$i^* = \frac{1+i}{1+p} - 1$$

continued →

Example 6.1 continued

where i^* = the real rate of return per annum
 i = the nominal rate of return per annum
 p = the anticipated rate of inflation per annum

Therefore:

$$i^* = \frac{1.15}{1.10} - 1$$
$$= 4.55\%$$

The net present value is then calculated as follows:

$$-\$1000 + \frac{\$500}{1.0455} + \frac{\$500}{(1.0455)^2} + \frac{\$500}{(1.0455)^3}$$

$$= -\$1000 + \frac{\$500}{1.0455} + \frac{\$500}{1.0931} + \frac{\$500}{1.1428}$$

$$= \$373$$

In subsequent examples, the first approach to incorporating the effect of inflation into project evaluation is generally adopted. Unlike the second approach, it can be readily applied where the analyst wishes to incorporate different rates of change in prices for different components of a project's cash flows. For example, the rate of change in wage rates may be forecast to be different from the rate of change in raw materials prices. In addition, the second approach requires reliable estimates of the anticipated rate of inflation, which may be difficult to obtain. Therefore, the first approach is easier to handle in practice.

6.2.2 ILLUSTRATION OF CASH-FLOW INFORMATION IN PROJECT EVALUATION

The cash flow information that should be compiled for project evaluation is illustrated in Example 6.2.

EXAMPLE 6.2

The Frank Stone Company is considering the introduction of a new product. Generally, the company's products have a life of about 5 years, after which they are deleted from the range of products that the company sells. The new product requires the purchase of new equipment costing $400 000, including freight and installation charges. The useful life of the equipment is 5 years, with an estimated residual value of $157 500 at the end of that period.

The new product will be manufactured in a factory already owned by the company. The factory originally cost $150 000 to build and has a current resale value of $350 000, which should remain fairly stable over the next 5 years. This factory is currently being rented to another company under a lease agreement that has 5 years to run and provides for an annual rental of $15 000. Under the lease agreement, the Frank Stone Company can cancel the lease by paying the lessee compensation equal to 1 year's rental payment.

It is expected that the product will involve the company in sales promotion expenditures that will amount to $50 000 during the first year the product is on the market. Additions to current assets will require $22 500 at the commencement of the project and are assumed to be fully recoverable at the end of the fifth year.

The new product is expected to generate net operating cash flows as follows:

Year 1: $200 000
Year 2: $250 000
Year 3: $325 000
Year 4: $300 000
Year 5: $150 000

It is assumed that all cash flows are received at the end of each year and the required rate of return is 10 per cent per annum. What is the net present value of adding the new product?

SOLUTION

The solution to this example is set out in Table 6.1.

TABLE 6.1 Cash flow information for adding the new product

ITEM		YEAR 0	YEAR 1	YEAR 2	YEAR 3	YEAR 4	YEAR 5
				CASH FLOWS ($'000)			
1.	Initial outlay	(400)					
2.	Sale of equipment						157.50
3.	Factory						
	The cost and the current resale value of the factory are both irrelevant						
	(a) Cancel lease	(15)					
	(b) Net cash flow forgone due to rent forgone		(15)	(15)	(15)	(15)	(15)
4.	Market research outlay		(50)				
5.	Additions to current assets	(22.50)					22.50
6.	Net cash flows from operations:						
	Year 1: $200 000		200				
	Year 2: $250 000			250			
	Year 3: $325 000				325		
	Year 4: $300 000					300	
	Year 5: $150 000						150
Total		(437.50)	135	235	310	285	315
Discount factor at 10%		1.000 00	0.909 09	0.826 45	0.751 31	0.683 01	0.620 92
Present value of net cash flows		(437.50)	122.73	194.21	232.91	194.66	195.59
Net present value		$502.60					

On the basis of this quantitative analysis the company should add the new product to its product line.

6.3 COMPARING MUTUALLY EXCLUSIVE PROJECTS THAT HAVE DIFFERENT LIVES

LEARNING OBJECTIVE 2
Compare mutually exclusive projects that have different lives

In Chapter 5 we compared mutually exclusive projects that had the same life. In practice, management will frequently have to compare mutually exclusive projects that have different economic lives. Such projects will often involve equipment that is of different quality and therefore also of different cost. Suppose that a coffee shop can buy either a Titan coffee maker with a life of 3 years or the higher quality, more expensive, Vulcan coffee maker with a life of 5 years to perform the same job. Both coffee makers generate the same cash inflows, so one way to compare them would be to calculate the present value of the cash outflows for each of them. Suppose that the present value of cash outflows is $4000 for the Titan and $5000 for the Vulcan. This does not necessarily mean that the Titan should be preferred. If the Titan is purchased, it will have to be replaced 2 years earlier than the Vulcan. The alternatives are not directly comparable because the difference in lives means that they involve different future cash flows, which have not been considered. One solution would be to assume that the Vulcan is sold after 3 years. However, the disposal value may not reflect its value in use, and it is usual to make other assumptions about what will happen at the end of the useful lives of the equipment. Consider the following two approaches:

constant chain of replacement assumption
may be used to evaluate mutually exclusive projects of unequal lives; in this case, each project is assumed to be replaced at the end of its economic life by an identical project

(a) It may be assumed that the company will reinvest in a project that is identical to that which is currently being analysed. This is known as the **constant chain of replacement assumption**.
(b) Specific assumptions may be made about the reinvestment opportunities that will become available in the future.

The second approach is the more realistic and could be implemented where the future investment opportunities are known. However, in practice this approach is difficult to implement unless managers have considerable foresight. Therefore, the first approach is often used. This approach is illustrated in Example 6.3.

EXAMPLE 6.3

Assume that a company is considering the purchase of two different pieces of equipment, A and B, that will perform the same task and generate the same cash inflows. Therefore, A and B can be compared on the basis of their cash outflows. The information in Table 6.2 relates to A and B.

TABLE 6.2 Cash outflows for equipment

EQUIPMENT	INITIAL AND OPERATING COSTS ($)			
	YEAR 0	YEAR 1	YEAR 2	YEAR 3
A (life 1 year)	15 000	6 000		
B (life 3 years)	20 000	10 000	10 000	10 000

Assuming a required rate of return of 10 per cent per annum for both pieces of equipment, calculate the present values of the costs of A and B.

SOLUTION

The present values of the costs of A and B are as follows:

$$\text{PV of costs for A} = \$15\,000 + \frac{\$6000}{1.1}$$

$$= \$20\,455$$

$$\text{PV of costs for B} = \$20\,000 + \$10\,000 \left[\frac{1 - \frac{1}{(1.1)^3}}{0.1} \right]$$

$$= \$44\,869$$

If management compares these figures, then investment in Equipment A would appear to be more desirable. However, this comparison is invalid because it ignores the fact that A and B have different lives. To make a valid comparison it is assumed that at the end of both the first and the second years Equipment A would be purchased again. If Equipment A were replaced at the end of Years 1 and 2 with the same equipment (a chain of replacement), the costs would be as shown in Table 6.3.

TABLE 6.3 Costs for chain of replacement over 3 years

	INITIAL AND OPERATING COSTS ($)			
EQUIPMENT	YEAR 0	YEAR 1	YEAR 2	YEAR 3
A	15 000	15 000	15 000	
A		6 000	6 000	6 000
Total	15 000	21 000	21 000	6 000

In this case,

$$\text{PV of costs for A} = \$15\,000 + \frac{\$21\,000}{1.1} + \frac{\$21\,000}{(1.1)^2} + \frac{\$6\,000}{(1.1)^3}$$

$$= \$55\,954$$

Based on this comparison over 3 years, the present value of the costs for A ($55 954) is greater than the present value of the costs for B ($44 869) and, therefore, B should be purchased.

In the remainder of this section it is assumed that management adopts this approach and that each project is replicated over the years. A valid comparison of two chains of replacement can be made only when both chains are of equal length. This comparison can be achieved in two ways:

(a) Suppose that Project A has a life of 6 years and Project B has a life of 9 years. If A is undertaken three times and B twice, the replacement chains will be of equal length—that is, 18 years. In this example, 18 is the lowest common multiple of 6 and 9, so this approach is usually called the *lowest common multiple method*. Although the use of this method correctly ranks mutually exclusive projects with different lives, it can be cumbersome. For example, two projects with lives of 19 and 21 years, respectively, have a lowest common multiple of 399 years and the cash flows for each of these 399 years would have to be discounted to a present value.

(b) A less complex approach, which ranks projects identically to the lowest common multiple method, is to assume that both chains continue indefinitely. In this case the 'lengths' of the chains are 'equal' in the sense that they are both infinite. This method is known as the *constant chain of replacement in perpetuity method*. If the NPV of each replacement project is N dollars and the life of each project is n years, then the constant chain of replacement is equivalent to receiving a cash inflow of N dollars at times 0, n, $2n$, $3n$, and so on, forever. Therefore, the NPV of the chain consists of N dollars at time 0 plus a perpetuity of N dollars payable at n, $2n$, $3n$, and so on. Therefore:

$$NPV = N + \frac{N}{(1+k)^n} + \frac{N}{(1+k)^{2n}} + \ldots$$

$$= N \left[1 + \frac{1}{(1+k)^n} + \frac{1}{(1+k)^{2n}} + \ldots \right]$$

$$= N \left[\frac{1}{1 - \frac{1}{(1+k)^n}} \right]$$

$$= N \left[\frac{(1+k)^n}{(1+k)^n - 1} \right]$$

The net present value of the infinite chain, NPV_∞, is therefore:

$$NPV_\infty = NPV_0 \frac{(1+k)^n}{(1+k)^n - 1} \qquad [6.1]$$

where NPV_0 = net present value of each replacement.

equivalent annual value method involves calculating the annual cash flow of an annuity that has the same life as the project and whose present value equals the net present value of the project

A variant of this method is the **equivalent annual value method**. This method involves answering the question: What amount, to be received each year for n years, is equivalent to receiving the net present value of a project whose life is n years? This amount, which is known as the *equivalent annual value* (EAV), is calculated for each project. The project with the higher EAV is preferred to the project with the lower EAV, provided that both projects have the same risk, and therefore the same required rate of return.

The stream of EAVs over n years is an ordinary annuity and therefore the net present value of the annuity is given by:

$$NPV_0 = \frac{EAV}{k} \left[1 - \frac{1}{(1+k)^n} \right]$$

or:

$$NPV_0 = EAV \left[\frac{1 - \frac{1}{(1+k)^n}}{k} \right]$$

Therefore:

$$EAV = \frac{NPV_0}{\left[\frac{1 - \frac{1}{(1+k)^n}}{k} \right]} \qquad [6.2]$$

The relationship between the constant chain of replacement and EAV methods is straightforward. Assume that a project is replicated indefinitely. The present value of an infinite stream of EAVs is:

$$PV = \frac{EAV}{k}$$

$$= \left(\frac{1}{k}\right)\frac{NPV_0}{\frac{1}{k}\left[1 - \frac{1}{(1+k)^n}\right]}$$

$$= NPV_0 \frac{1}{1 - \frac{1}{(1+k)^n}}$$

$$= NPV_0 \frac{(1+k)^n}{(1+k)^n - 1}$$

$$= NPV_\infty$$

That is, the present value of an infinite stream of EAVs is equal to the net present value of the constant chain of replacement in perpetuity. Therefore, if the net present value of the infinite chain NPV_∞ has been calculated, then the EAV can be found by multiplying NPV_∞ by the required rate of return—that is, the EAV is given by:

$$EAV = kNPV_\infty \qquad [6.3]$$

The constant chain of replacement and equivalent annual value methods are illustrated in Example 6.4.

EXAMPLE 6.4

Suppose that two assets, A and B, are mutually exclusive projects and have the characteristics shown in Table 6.4.

TABLE 6.4 Characteristics of two mutually exclusive projects

ASSET	LIFE (YRS)	INITIAL CASH OUTLAY ($)	CASH INFLOWS ($)				
			YEAR 1	YEAR 2	YEAR 3	YEAR 4	YEAR 5
A	3	10 000	10 000	23 000	25 000	—	—
B	5	30 000	12 000	15 000	25 000	30 000	30 000

It is also assumed that the required rate of return is 10 per cent per annum for both projects. Which asset should be purchased?

SOLUTION
The net present value of Asset A at time zero is:

$$NPV\,A_0 = -\$10\,000 + \frac{\$10\,000}{1.1} + \frac{\$23\,000}{(1.1)^2} + \frac{\$25\,000}{(1.1)^3}$$

$$= \$36\,882.04$$

The net present value of Asset B at time zero is:

$$NPV\,B_0 = -\$30\,000 + \frac{\$12\,000}{1.1} + \frac{\$15\,000}{(1.1)^2} + \frac{\$25\,000}{(1.1)^3} + \frac{\$30\,000}{(1.1)^4} + \frac{\$30\,000}{(1.1)^5}$$

$$= \$51\,206.70$$

continued →

Example 6.4 *continued*

Using Equation 6.1, the net present values of the infinite chains of replacement are:

$$NPV\ A_\infty = (\$36\,882.04)\frac{(1.1)^3}{(1.1)^3 - 1}$$

$$= \$148\,308.14$$

$$NPV\ B_\infty = (\$51\,206.70)\frac{(1.1)^5}{(1.1)^5 - 1}$$

$$= \$135\,081.98$$

Therefore, Asset A should be accepted, notwithstanding that its net present value (over its 3-year life) is less than the net present value of Asset B (over its 5-year life).

Using Equation 6.2, the equivalent annual value method, it is found that:

$$EAV\ A = \frac{\$36\,882.04}{\left[\dfrac{1 - \dfrac{1}{(1 + 0.10)^3}}{0.10}\right]}$$

$$= \$14\,830.81$$

$$EAV\ B = \frac{\$51\,206.70}{\left[\dfrac{1 - \dfrac{1}{(1 + 0.10)^5}}{0.10}\right]}$$

$$= \$13\,508.20$$

Therefore, Asset A should be chosen because its EAV is greater than that of Asset B. Alternatively, the equivalent annual values could have been calculated from the net present values of the infinite chains of replacement (NPV_∞) using Equation 6.3, $EAV = kNPV_\infty$ as follows:

$$EAV\ A = (0.1)(\$148\,308.14)$$

$$= \$14\,830.81$$

$$EAV\ B = (0.1)(\$135\,081.98)$$

$$= \$13\,508.20$$

These results are identical to those obtained using Equation 6.2.

In summary, the results for Asset A show that an investor would be indifferent between receiving payments of $36 882.04 every 3 years, or a single payment of $148 308.14 now, or annual payments of $14 830.81 forever. The corresponding amounts for Asset B are $51 206.70 every 5 years, $135 081.98 now, or $13 508.20 annually forever. Of these three pairs of figures, the second and third pairs adjust for the unequal lives of the assets, and both show that Asset A should be preferred.

Example 6.5 provides a more detailed illustration of the constant chain of replacement method.

EXAMPLE 6.5

Assume that Madison Company, which operates a fleet of trucks, is considering replacing them with a new model. The data in Table 6.5 are available for the old and the new trucks.

TABLE 6.5 Data for old and new trucks

ITEM	OLD TRUCKS	NEW TRUCKS
1. Net cash flows	$45 000 p.a.	$50 000 p.a.
2. Estimated life	2 years	4 years
3. Disposal value:		
(a) at present	$10 000	
(b) in 4 years' time	Nil	$10 000
4. Cost of new trucks		$60 000
5. Required rate of return (real)	10% p.a.	10% p.a.

Management is considering two proposals:
(a) Replace the old trucks now and assume that the new trucks are operated for 4 years and replaced in perpetuity.
(b) Replace the old trucks in 2 years' time and assume that the new trucks are operated for 4 years, and replaced in perpetuity.
Which of these proposals should management accept?

SOLUTION

Obviously there are other alternatives that management could consider, such as replacing the present trucks in 1 year's time or replacing the old trucks now and the new ones in 2 years' time. However, it is assumed that these possibilities have been considered and rejected by management. It is also assumed that there are no expected improvements in truck design that would make the new truck obsolete.

Proposals 1 and 2 will therefore be evaluated assuming a constant chain of replacement. The proposal with the larger net present value, provided that it is greater than zero, will be accepted, other things being equal. In the following evaluation the net present value for a single truck is calculated. If there are ten trucks in the fleet, then the net present values of the two proposals will be multiplied by 10 to find their total net present values.

(a) Replace the old trucks now, operate the new trucks for 4 years and replace them in perpetuity.
The net present value of a new truck is:

$$NPV_0 = -\$60\,000 + \$50\,000 \left[\frac{1 - \frac{1}{(1 + 0.10)^4}}{0.10} \right] + \frac{\$10\,000}{(1.1)^4}$$

$$= -\$60\,000 + \$158\,493.27 + \$6830.13$$

$$= \$105\,323.40$$

The present value of an infinite chain of these trucks is therefore:

$$NPV_\infty = (\$105\,323.40) \frac{(1.1)^4}{(1.1)^4 - 1}$$

$$= \$332\,265$$

continued →

Example 6.5 *continued*

In addition, at the start of this chain Madison Company receives a cash inflow of $10 000 from the disposal of the old truck. Therefore, the *total* net present value is:

$332 265 + $10 000 = $342 265

(b) Replace the old trucks in 2 years' time, operate the new trucks for 4 years, and replace them in perpetuity.

As in the previous calculation, NPV_∞ = $332 265. However, the first of the chain of new trucks is now purchased at Year 2 instead of at Year 0 as previously. As a result, NPV_∞ must be discounted to Year 0:

$$\frac{\$332\,265}{(1.1)^2} = \$274\,599.17$$

In addition, Madison Company obtains the net present value of operating the old trucks for the first 2 years. This is given by:

$$\frac{\$45\,000}{1.1} + \frac{\$45\,000}{(1.1)^2} = \$78\,099.17$$

The *total* net present value is therefore:

$274 599.17 + $78 099.17 = $352 698.34

The net present value of Proposal (b) is greater than the net present value of Proposal (a) and management should replace the old trucks in 2 years' time.

Chain of replacement methods and inflation

Chain of replacement methods rely on the assumption that each project will, at the end of its life, be replaced by an identical project—that is, each replacement will cost the same amount, generate the same cash flows, and last for the same time. Clearly, if there is inflation, future costs and cash flows will not be expected to remain the same in nominal terms, but they may remain the same in real terms. To ensure that inflation is treated consistently, all cash flows and the required rate of return should generally be expressed in real terms when a chain of replacement method is used.[2]

Is the chain of replacement method realistic?

A possible problem with the constant chain of replacement model is that it employs unrealistic assumptions about the replacement assets in the chain, namely that the assets and the services they provide are identical in every respect. These assumptions are unrealistic. However, the fact that the replacements may be many years in the future, and the fact that their cash flows will be discounted to a present value, reduces the impact of making such unrealistic assumptions. It may be even more unrealistic to assume that management has sufficient foresight to be able to predict such factors as the capital outlay, net cash flows, life and residual value of replacement assets. However, if such information is available, it is not a difficult matter to insert into the analysis the replacement of an existing asset with an asset of improved design.[3]

---

[2] For a discussion of this issue and presentation of a nominal version of the constant chain of replacement model, see Faff and Brailsford (1992).

[3] Brown and Davis (1998) highlight the real options that are ignored in using the constant chain of replacement model. For a discussion of real options, see Chapters 5 and 18.

The methods discussed in this section are very useful but some points should be noted. First, it is not necessary to use these methods in all cases where projects have different lives. For independent projects, the net present value method automatically allows for any such differences. The different lives 'problem' arises only for mutually exclusive projects. Second, it is particularly important, when using chain of replacement methods, to be consistent in the treatment of inflation. Third, in many cases mutually exclusive projects will involve the same benefits (cash inflows) but different costs (cash outflows). In these cases the cash inflows can be ignored and the alternatives can be compared on the basis of their cash outflows, as in Example 6.3.

6.4 DECIDING WHEN TO RETIRE (ABANDON) OR REPLACE A PROJECT

Investment projects are not always continued until the end of their estimated physical lives and, as we noted in Chapter 5, the systematic search for new investments should be complemented by a periodic review of the performance of existing projects. Such reviews may result in decisions to retire (abandon) assets or to replace existing assets.

LEARNING OBJECTIVE 3
Determine when to retire (abandon) or replace assets

In this section, a distinction is made between retirement and replacement decisions.

- *Retirement decisions* involve those situations where assets are used for some time, and then it is decided not to continue the operation in which the assets are used. Therefore, the assets are sold and not replaced.
- *Replacement decisions* involve those situations where a particular type of operation is intended to continue indefinitely—that is, a company's need for the assets is assumed to continue long after the present assets have been sold or scrapped. In this case, a company is faced with a decision about when its existing assets should be replaced.

6.4.1 RETIREMENT DECISIONS

The analysis for determining when a project should be discontinued (retired) is outlined in this section. Since the retirement of assets is just another investment decision, the net present value rule is still valid for retirement decisions. Therefore, a project should be retired if the net present value of all its future net cash flows is less than zero. Determining when an asset should be retired is illustrated in Example 6.6.

EXAMPLE 6.6

Mortlake Ltd owns an asset that is 6 years old and has an estimated remaining physical life of no more than 2 years. Table 6.6 shows the net cash flow and residual value estimates for the asset.

TABLE 6.6 Estimates of net cash flow and residual value for existing asset

END OF YEAR	NET CASH FLOW ($)	RESIDUAL VALUE ($)
6	0	12 000
7	8 000	6 000
8	5 000	0

The required rate of return is 10 per cent. When should the asset be retired?

SOLUTION
The problem is analysed by first calculating the net present value of forgoing the $12 000 current residual value to obtain a net cash flow of $8000, and a residual value of $6000 in 1 year's time. Therefore the net present value of keeping the asset for 1 more year is:

continued →

Example 6.6 *continued*

$$NPV = -\$12\,000 + \frac{(\$8000 + \$6000)}{1.1}$$

$$= -\$12\,000 + \$12\,727$$

$$= \$727$$

Since the net present value is positive, the asset should be retained for at least 1 more year. Second, management may be interested in finding out whether, given the current forecasts, the asset should be retained for the remaining 2 years of its life. If the asset is retained for a further 2 years, the company will forgo $12 000, the current residual value, and receive instead net cash flows in Years 7 and 8 of $8000 and $5000, respectively. There is no residual value at the end of Year 8. Therefore, the net present value of this alternative is:

$$NPV = -\$12\,000 + \frac{\$8000}{1.1} + \frac{\$5000}{(1.1)^2}$$

$$= -\$12\,000 + \$7273 + \$4132$$

$$= -\$595$$

Unless there is some upward revision in the estimates of cash flows for Year 8, the asset should be retired at the end of the seventh year.

6.4.2 REPLACEMENT DECISIONS

In Section 6.3 the use of the constant chain of replacement method to evaluate projects with different lives was discussed. The same approach can be used to evaluate replacement decisions. To discuss these decisions we distinguish between two cases. In the first, the decision is when to replace an existing project with an *identical* project. In the second case, the decision is when to replace an existing project with a new one, which involves *different* cash flows.

Identical replacement

In this case it is assumed that a current project will be replaced by a project identical in every respect. The capital outlay, net cash flows, physical life and residual value of both projects are the same. Example 6.7 illustrates an analysis of this type.

EXAMPLE 6.7

A machine costs $20 000 and has an estimated useful life of 5 years. The net cash flows are $12 000 in the first year, decreasing by $500 each year as a result of higher maintenance costs. Also, as the machine becomes older, its residual value will decline as shown in Table 6.7, which gives the machine's estimated residual value at the end of each year.

The required rate of return is assumed to be 10 per cent. Management wishes to know when the machine should be replaced.

TABLE 6.7 Estimated residual values for machine

YEAR	RESIDUAL VALUE ($)
1	16 000
2	14 000
3	12 000
4	6 000
5	Nil

SOLUTION

If the machine is purchased, used for only 1 year and then sold, its net present value would be as follows:

$$NPV_1 = \$20\,000 + \frac{\$12\,000}{1.1} + \frac{\$16\,000}{1.1}$$
$$= \$5455$$

If the machine is used for 2 years and then sold, the net present value would be as follows:

$$NPV_2 = -\$20\,000 + \frac{\$12\,000}{1.1} + \frac{\$11\,500}{(1.1)^2} + \frac{\$14\,000}{(1.1)^2}$$
$$= \$11\,983$$

Similarly, net present values can be calculated based on use for 3, 4 and 5 years. However, these net present values cannot be compared, because they are based on different lives. As we noted in Section 6.3, this difficulty can be overcome by assuming a constant chain of replacement. If it is assumed that the machine is replaced every year in perpetuity, the net present value will be as follows:

$$NPV_{(1,\infty)} = \$5454.55 \left[\frac{(1.1)}{(1.1)-1}\right]$$
$$= \$60\,000$$

If the machine is replaced every second year in perpetuity, the net present value will be as follows:

$$NPV_{(2,\infty)} = \$11\,983.47 \left[\frac{(1.1)^2}{(1.1)^2-1}\right]$$
$$= \$69\,048$$

The net present values, assuming the machine is replaced in perpetuity, at the end of the third, fourth and fifth years, respectively, are as follows:

$$NPV_{(3,\infty)} = \$17\,693.46 \left[\frac{(1.1)^3}{(1.1)^3-1}\right]$$
$$= \$71\,148$$

$$NPV_{(4,\infty)} = \$19\,947.41 \left[\frac{(1.1)^4}{(1.1)^4-1}\right]$$
$$= \$62\,926$$

$$NPV_{(5,\infty)} = \$22\,058.54 \left[\frac{(1.1)^5}{(1.1)^5-1}\right]$$
$$= \$58\,190$$

These results show that the machine should be replaced after 3 years. In general the decision rule is to choose the replacement frequency that maximises the project's net present value for a perpetual chain of replacement, or that maximises its equivalent annual value.

Non-identical replacement

Suppose that a machine is physically sound but technically obsolete. When the machine is replaced, its replacement will be of a new design that may have the same capacity but costs less to operate. The question is: When should the old machine be discarded in favour of the new one? The solution involves two steps. First, the optimum replacement frequency for the new machine is determined using the method illustrated in Example 6.7. Second, the equivalent annual value of the new machine at its optimum replacement frequency is compared with the net present value of continuing to operate the old machine, as shown in Example 6.6. The decision rule is that the changeover should be made when the net present value of continuing to operate the old machine for one more year is less than the equivalent annual value of the new machine.

6.5 ANALYSING PROJECT RISK

LEARNING OBJECTIVE 4
Use sensitivity analysis and break-even analysis to analyse project risk

The effect of risk on the value of a project is normally included in the evaluation by using a required rate of return that reflects the risk of the project. However, the calculated net present value is only an estimate that relies on forecasts of the project's cash flows. In practice these forecasts will, almost certainly, turn out to be incorrect, perhaps because the volume of sales turns out to be more or less than expected, the price of the product is higher or lower than expected, or operating costs differ from the forecast. Therefore, in many cases managers analysing proposed projects will need to answer questions such as:

- What are the key variables that are likely to determine whether the project is a success or a failure?
- How far can sales fall or costs increase before the project loses money?

Managers can use various techniques to answer these and other related questions. The techniques we discuss are sensitivity analysis, break-even analysis and simulation.

6.5.1 SENSITIVITY ANALYSIS

sensitivity analysis
analysis of the effect of changing one or more input variables to observe the effects on the results

A project's cash flows and required rate of return are usually specified as 'best estimates' or 'expected values' and the resulting net present value, often referred to as the *base-case net present value*, is also a best estimate or expected value. **Sensitivity analysis** involves assessing the effect of changes or errors in the estimated variables on the net present value of a project. This is achieved by calculating net present values based on alternative estimates of the variables. For instance, management may wish to know the effect on net present value if a project's net cash flows are either 20 per cent less than, or 20 per cent greater than, those estimated. Knowledge of the sensitivity of net present value to changes or errors in the variables places management in a better position to decide whether a project is too risky to accept. Also, if management knows that the net present value is sensitive to changes in particular variables, it can examine the estimates of these variables more thoroughly, or collect more data in an effort to reduce errors in forecasting.

Assuming that all variables in the analysis are uncertain, a simple example of sensitivity analysis involves the following steps:

(a) Pessimistic, optimistic and expected estimates are made for each variable.
(b) Net present value is calculated using the expected estimates for every variable except one, the value for which is, in turn, its optimistic and pessimistic estimate. This procedure is repeated until a net present value has been calculated using an optimistic and pessimistic estimate for each variable, in combination with the expected values of the other variables.
(c) The difference between the optimistic and pessimistic net present values is calculated for each variable. A small difference between the net present values suggests that the project's net present value is insensitive to changes or errors in that variable. A large difference between the net present values suggests the opposite.

For example, suppose that in a project involving the use of a new machine, there are only five uncertain variables: sales price, variable cost, sales volume, fixed operating costs and the life of the machine. In this case, eight net present value calculations are made, using the data inputs shown in Table 6.8. The symbol O indicates the optimistic value of the variable, P indicates the pessimistic value of the variable, and E indicates the expected value of the variable.

The application of sensitivity analysis to project evaluation in a case such as that shown in Table 6.8 is illustrated in Example 6.8.

TABLE 6.8 Combinations of variable values for sensitivity analysis

ESTIMATES	(I)	(II)	(III)	(IV)	(V)	(VI)	(VII)	(VIII)	(IX)	(X)
Sales price	O	P	E	E	E	E	E	E	E	E
Variable cost	E	E	O	P	E	E	E	E	E	E
Sales volume	E	E	E	E	O	P	E	E	E	E
Fixed operating costs	E	E	E	E	E	E	O	P	E	E
Machine life	E	E	E	E	E	E	E	E	O	P

EXAMPLE 6.8

Assume that a manager is considering whether to purchase a new machine that costs $500 000. It is assumed that there are only five uncertain variables: sales price, variable cost, sales volume, fixed operating costs and the life of the new machine. The sales price is expected to be $70 per unit, the variable cost is expected to be $48 per unit, sales volume is expected to be 15 000 units per annum, with fixed operating costs of $200 000 during an expected life of 10 years. All other variables are expected to remain constant during the machine's life. The required rate of return is 10 per cent per annum.

The expected annual net cash flows are ($70 − $48) × 15 000 − $200 000 = $130 000, and the base-case net present value is:

$$\text{Base-case } NPV = -\$500\,000 + \$130\,000 \left[\frac{1 - \frac{1}{(1.1)^{10}}}{0.1} \right]$$

$$= \$298\,794$$

The information needed for the sensitivity analysis is shown in Table 6.9, which presents:

- for each uncertain variable, expected (column 1), optimistic (column 2) and pessimistic (column 3) estimates
- the net present value (column 4) when one of the uncertain variables is set at its optimistic estimate and each of the other variables is set at its expected value
- the net present value (column 5) when one of the uncertain variables is set at its pessimistic estimate and each of the other variables is set at its expected value
- in column 6, the difference between columns 4 and 5, which is frequently called the 'range of the net present value'.

Table 6.9 shows that the estimate of net present value is more sensitive to changes in sales price than to changes in the other uncertain variables. In addition, it shows that if the pessimistic estimate of either sales price or sales volume occurs, the purchase of the machine will generate a negative net present value.

continued →

Example 6.8 *continued*

TABLE 6.9 Sensitivity analysis of the purchase of a new machine, based on optimistic and pessimistic estimates of the values of each variable

VARIABLE	EXPECTED	OPTIMISTIC	PESSIMISTIC	NPV: OPTIMISTIC ESTIMATE ($)[a]	NPV: PESSIMISTIC ESTIMATE ($)[a]	RANGE OF NPV ($)
	(1)	(2)	(3)	(4)	(5)	(6)
Sales price $	70	76	63	(i) 851 805	(ii) 346 386	1 198 191
Variable cost $	48	46	50	(iii) 483 131	(iv) 114 457	368 674
Sales volume	15 000	17 000	12 500	(v) 569 155	(vi) 39 157	608 312
Fixed operating costs $	200 000	190 000	205 000	(vii) 360 239	(viii) 268 071	92 169
Life of machine (years)	10	12	9	(ix) 385 780	(x) 248 673	137 107

[a] The figures in lower case Roman numerals in these columns indicate the net present value calculation that corresponds to the input shown in Table 6.8.

Before deciding to purchase the new machine, management is therefore likely to gather more information on sales price and sales volume in an effort to minimise forecasting errors. In contrast, the value of additional data about the machine's variable costs, fixed operating costs and useful life is relatively small. The project is still acceptable, based on the pessimistic values for those variables, and therefore the company is unlikely to make a loss on the project even if these variables have been incorrectly estimated.

The use of sensitivity analysis involves some problems. One is that frequently it is difficult to specify precisely the relationship between a particular variable and net present value. If the assumed relationship is based on past outcomes, there is always the possibility that this relationship may not hold in the future. It is further complicated by relationships between the variables. For example, it is inappropriate to examine the effect on net present value of a 20 per cent reduction in sales volume without recognising that lower sales volume may also mean that the selling price is lower than expected. Allowing for these interdependencies will complicate the analysis. Another problem is that the terms 'optimistic' and 'pessimistic' are subject to interpretation, and the results may be somewhat ambiguous. For example, the marketing department's 'optimistic' sales forecasts may be so optimistic that they are virtually unachievable, while another department's 'optimistic' estimates of other variables may be more conservative.

6.5.2 BREAK-EVEN ANALYSIS

break-even analysis
analysis of the amounts by which one or more input variables may change before a project ceases to be profitable

Break-even analysis is a form of sensitivity analysis. Sensitivity analysis generally involves finding answers to 'what if' questions such as: What will be the net present value of the project if sales are 10 per cent less than expected? In break-even analysis the question is turned around, in that the manager asks: How poor can sales volume become before the project loses money? The break-even point is the sales volume at which the net present value is zero. Break-even analysis is illustrated by re-examining the information in Example 6.8.

For each of the five uncertain variables, the net present value is calculated using the expected values of the other four variables, with the values of the fifth variable being the one that results in the net present value being zero. The results for all variables are shown in Table 6.10 with the results for sales volume also being shown in Figure 6.1.

The net present value of purchasing the machine will be positive if the expected values of the other four uncertain variables are achieved and the sales price is greater than or equal to $67. Similarly, the net present value of purchasing the machine will be positive if the expected values of the other four uncertain variables are achieved and sales volume is 12 790 or more units.

EXAMPLE 6.9

TABLE 6.10 Break-even analysis of the purchase of a new machine

VARIABLE	EXPECTED	BREAK EVEN
Sales price $	70	67
Variable cost $	48	51
Sales volume	15 000	12 790
Fixed operating costs $	200 000	248 627
Life of machine (years)	10	6

FIGURE 6.1

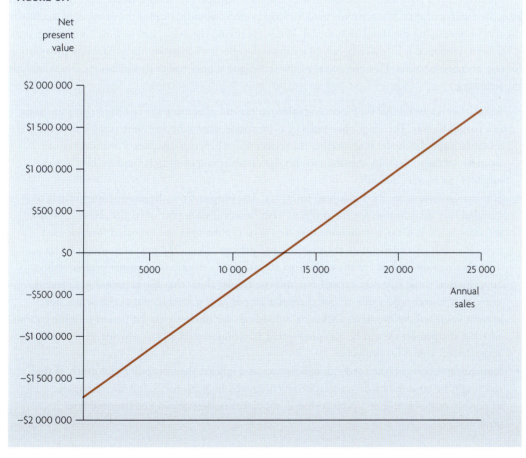

6.5.3 SIMULATION

Sensitivity analysis involves changing one variable at a time and examining the effects of the changes on the profitability of a project. On the other hand, **simulation** allows a manager to consider the effects of changing all the variables whose values are uncertain. The first step in a simulation is to identify the relevant variables and to specify the probability distribution of each variable. For example, in the case of the purchase of the new machine in Examples 6.8 and 6.9, the variables could include selling price, variable cost, sales volume, fixed operating costs and the useful life of the machine. The second step is to specify any relationships between the variables. For example, a higher sales volume may result in economies of scale in production and distribution, which should be reflected in the variable costs. The third step involves using a computer to simulate the project's cash flows. Essentially, the procedure is as follows:

(a) The computer selects values randomly from the distribution of each of the specified variables.
(b) In the first run of the simulation the computer calculates values for the project's cash flows for each year.
(c) The results of the first run are stored and a new set of values is chosen and used in the second run of the simulation, which gives further results that are also stored. This procedure is repeated at least one hundred and perhaps thousands of times.
(d) The results of all the individual runs are combined to produce a probability distribution for the project's cash flows.

Simulation is a potentially valuable tool that allows managers to analyse many aspects of the risks associated with a project. It is generally used for large projects where the size of the investment can justify the cost of developing the simulation model. While specifying the model can be time consuming, once it has been developed it is relatively easy to examine the effects of changing the probability distribution for one or more variables. However, users of the technique should realise its limitations. These include the following:

- Simulation is a technique for processing information and presenting the results of that processing in a particular way. Therefore, the results of a simulation cannot be any more reliable than the input data and the model that specifies the relationships between variables. Providing realistic estimates of the probability distributions for the variables and of the relationships between the variables can be very difficult.
- Simulation results can be difficult to interpret. The output from the simulation consists of a probability distribution for the project's cash flows for each year of its life. How should a manager use this data? The obvious first step is to use the mean or expected forecast cash flows for each year to estimate the project's net present value. The next step might be to use other possible values for the cash flows to calculate a distribution of net present values. Suppose that these steps are carried out and the results show that the expected net present value of a project is $2 million, but there is a 20 per cent probability that the actual net present value will be negative. Different individuals are likely to have different opinions about whether the project should be accepted—that is, simulation does not provide an unambiguous accept/reject signal for projects.
- Simulation focuses on the total risk of a project and ignores the possibility that much of this risk might be removed by diversification. As discussed in Section 7.5, it is the systematic or non-diversifiable risk of a project that is important in determining its required rate of return.

---

simulation

analysis of the effect of changing all of the input variables whose values are uncertain to observe the effects on the results

In summary, simulation is a potentially valuable technique for analysing the risks associated with a project, but users should be aware of its limitations.

6.6 DECISION-TREE ANALYSIS

Management is sometimes faced with the need to evaluate alternatives involving a *sequence* of decisions over time. Decision-tree analysis provides a means of evaluating such decisions. The decision-tree approach takes into account the probability of various events occurring and the effect of those events on the expected net present value of a project. Decision-tree analysis uses the concept of 'roll-back' to evaluate alternative decisions. This is illustrated in Example 6.10.[4]

LEARNING OBJECTIVE 5
Use decision-tree analysis to analyse sequential decisions

EXAMPLE 6.10

The management of a Victorian-based company is considering the proposed construction of a plant to manufacture its products in China. Initially, management is faced with the choice of constructing either a large or a small plant. If it constructs a large plant, the initial outlay will be $2 million, whereas if it constructs a small plant, the initial outlay will be $1 million. If a small plant is chosen, management will reconsider its decision after 2 years. At that time, management may, if it believes that further expansion is warranted, expand the small plant to achieve the same capacity as a large plant. The expansion will cost $1.25 million.

The company has estimated the expected net cash flows to be generated by a large plant, a small plant and an expanded plant on the basis of a two-way classification of demand: high demand and low demand. These expectations are summarised in Table 6.11.

TABLE 6.11 Expected net cash flows for different plants and levels of demand

POSSIBILITIES	EXPECTED NET CASH FLOW p.a. ($M)
Large plant, high demand	0.8000
Large plant, low demand	0.1000
Small plant, high demand	0.4000
Small plant, low demand	0.3500
Expanded plant, high demand	0.5000
Expanded plant, low demand	0.0750

Management has also estimated the probability of achieving either high demand or low demand during the project's 10-year life. It has estimated the likelihood of high demand throughout the project's life to be 0.6, the probability of achieving high demand for the first 2 years and low demand for the remaining 8 years to be 0.2, and the probability of low demand throughout the project's life to be 0.2. The probabilities and the expected net cash flows are shown in Figure 6.2 in the form of a *decision tree*.

continued →

---

[4] For a simple discussion of decision-tree analysis, see Levin, Kirkpatrick and Rubin (1992).

Example 6.10 *continued*

FIGURE 6.2

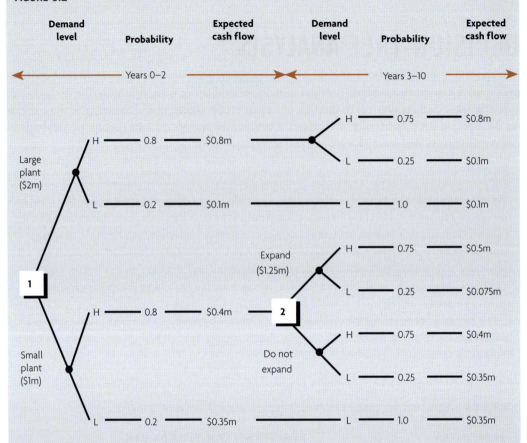

The squares in Figure 6.2 represent decision points and the small circles represent chance events that may occur during the life of the project. The base of a decision tree is the beginning, Decision point 1. Its branches begin at the first chance event. Each chance event produces two or more possible outcomes, some of which lead to other chance events and/or subsequent decision points.

The optimum sequence of decisions is determined using a *rollback* procedure, which means that the most distant decision—in this case, the decision whether to expand the small plant—is evaluated first. Each alternative is evaluated on the basis of its expected net present value. The required rate of return is assumed to be 9 per cent per annum.

Decision 2: Whether to expand the small plant
EXPAND:

$$NPV = 0.75\,(\$0.5m)\left[\frac{1-\frac{1}{(1+0.09)^8}}{0.09}\right] + 0.25\,(\$0.075m)\left[\frac{1-\frac{1}{(1+0.09)^8}}{0.09}\right] - \$1.25m$$

$$= \$929\,355$$

DO NOT EXPAND:

$$PV = 0.75(\$0.4m)\left[\frac{1-\frac{1}{(1+0.09)^8}}{0.09}\right] + 0.25(\$0.35m)\left[\frac{1-\frac{1}{(1+0.09)^8}}{0.09}\right]$$

$$= \$2\,144\,743$$

Therefore, the optimum choice is not to expand the small plant at the end of the second year. The rollback method simplifies the evaluation by eliminating the alternative of building a small plant and then expanding it after 2 years. Once management knows what it ought to do if faced with the expansion decision, it can 'roll back' to today's decision. This decision is whether to build a large plant or a small plant to be operated for 10 years.

Decision 1: Construct either a large plant or a small plant and operate for 10 years

LARGE PLANT:

$$\text{Expected } NPV = 0.8(\$0.8m)\left[\frac{1-\frac{1}{(1+0.09)^2}}{0.09}\right]$$

$$+ 0.8\left[0.75(\$0.8m)\left[\frac{1-\frac{1}{(1+0.09)^8}}{0.09}\right](1.09)^{-2}\right.$$

$$\left. + 0.25(\$0.1m)\left[\frac{1-\frac{1}{(1+0.09)^8}}{0.09}\right](1.09)^{-2}\right]$$

$$+ 0.20(\$0.1m)\left[\frac{1-\frac{1}{(1+0.09)^{10}}}{0.09}\right] - \$2m$$

$$= \$1\,583\,000 \text{ (to the nearest thousand dollars)}$$

SMALL PLANT:

$$\text{Expected } NPV = 0.8(\$0.4m)\left[\frac{1-\frac{1}{(1+0.09)^2}}{0.09}\right]$$

$$+ 0.08\left[\$2\,144\,743\,(1.09)^{-2}\right]$$

$$+ 0.2(\$0.35m)\left[\frac{1-\frac{1}{(1+0.09)^{10}}}{0.09}\right] - \$1m$$

$$= \$1\,456\,000 \text{ (to the nearest thousand dollars)}$$

In this case the expected net present value of building a large plant exceeds that of building a small plant.

This approach to evaluating a sequence of decisions relating to an investment in a risky project is operational for our simple example. It has the advantage that it forces management to consider future investment decisions when making current investment decisions. However, the complexity of decision-tree analysis is increased considerably since additional alternatives, such as allowing for a medium-sized plant and a medium level of demand, are included in the decision process.

6.7 QUALITATIVE FACTORS AND THE SELECTION OF PROJECTS

LEARNING OBJECTIVE 6
Explain the role of qualitative factors in project selection

After the quantitative analysis has been completed, management has to decide which projects to implement. While the aim is to maximise shareholders' wealth, it does not necessarily follow that project selection decisions should be guided only by the results of the quantitative analysis. Management should also consider any qualitative factors that may affect those projects.

Essentially, qualitative factors are those that management would like to include in the quantitative analysis but is unable to include because they are difficult, if not impossible, to measure in dollars. For this reason they are assessed separately, after the quantitative analysis of the alternatives has been completed.

Qualitative factors may play a vital role in project selection. For example, suppose that quantitative analysis shows that it is cheaper for a transport company to continue using some old trucks for another year rather than replacing them now. However, management may decide to replace the old trucks now because of qualitative factors such as the desire to maintain a modern image for the company and the improved satisfaction, and consequently the improved productivity, of the drivers, resulting from the comfort of the new trucks.

Some further examples of qualitative factors that may affect management's decisions about projects are:

- The introduction of labour-saving machinery may be deferred (perhaps indefinitely) because of union opposition, even though on the basis of the quantitative analysis the proposal to introduce the machinery has a net present value greater than zero.
- Two mutually exclusive investments may have net present values that are almost equal, but one requires much more management supervision, or the use of some other scarce human resource. The use of this scarce resource involves an opportunity cost that, while recognised by management, is difficult to quantify. Therefore, rather than attempting to measure the opportunity cost of using the scarce human resources, management may simply select the proposal that it believes will use fewer of those resources, other things being equal.

It is essential that such qualitative factors be considered before selecting a project. However, the recognition of qualitative factors is not a general prescription for ignoring or reducing the importance of the quantitative analysis. As all factors cannot be incorporated into the quantitative analysis, a comparison of alternative investment proposals is incomplete without an assessment of the possible effects of the qualitative factors. Indeed, the influence of qualitative factors may be sufficiently important to cause management to select proposals with lower calculated net present values.

6.8 PROJECT SELECTION WITH RESOURCE CONSTRAINTS

So far it has been assumed that management is willing and able to accept all independent investment projects that have a net present value greater than zero and, if mutually exclusive projects are being compared, those projects with the highest positive net present value. However, sometimes a company's managers believe that they are prevented from undertaking all acceptable projects because of a 'shortage' of funds. **Capital rationing** is the term used to describe such a situation. It may be classified further into internal (or 'soft') capital rationing and external (or 'hard') capital rationing.

Internal capital rationing occurs when management limits the amount that can be invested in new projects during some specified time period. There are several reasons why management may impose a limit on capital expenditure. One is that management is conservative and has a policy of financing all projects from internally generated cash because it is unwilling to borrow. Similarly, management may be unwilling to issue more shares because of possible effects on the control of the company. Alternatively, imposing capital expenditure limits can be a way of maintaining financial control. For example, in a large company, managers may attempt to expand their divisions by proposing many new projects, some of which only *appear* to be profitable because the cash flow forecasts are very optimistic. To avoid this problem, top management may delegate authority for capital expenditure decisions to divisional managers, but retain overall control by giving each division a capital expenditure limit. The aim is to force each divisional manager to decide which of the possible projects really should be adopted.

Another possibility is that it may be desirable to limit the rate at which a company expands because of the organisational difficulties inherent in hiring and training many additional staff. Management may be concerned that rapid expansion will lead to inefficiency and higher costs. To avoid these problems it may limit the number of new projects that are implemented. In this case, a capital expenditure limit is used to impose the desired restriction, but it is not *capital* that is the scarce resource. Rather, the scarce resource is management time, and the real concern is that this constraint may result in supervision problems.

External capital rationing occurs when the capital market is unwilling to supply the funds necessary to finance the projects that a company's management wishes to undertake. In this case, the company has projects that offer positive net present values but cannot raise, at a cost that management considers acceptable, the funds necessary to finance them. This situation can occur if financial intermediaries are subject to controls such as limits on the volume or growth rate of their lending. However, it is difficult to see why it should occur in deregulated financial markets. Any company that has a project expected to be profitable should be able to obtain the necessary capital, no matter how small its capital budget. For example, suppose that a small company, which plans to invest no more than, say, $50 000 in the current year, discovers an inexpensive way of extracting gold from the oceans. Raising capital to build the extraction plant should not be a problem.

Empirical evidence suggests that capital rationing is more likely to result from expenditure limits imposed by management of its own volition than from an unwillingness of the capital market to supply funds (Pike 1983). If management's decisions result in the rejection of projects with positive net present values, then management is adopting a policy inconsistent with the objective of maximising the market value of the company's shares. If capital rationing is essentially an internal 'problem', it might appear that the solution should be simple. Management should remove the constraints so that all positive net present value projects can be implemented. In some cases, this does occur. For example, in cases where capital expenditure limits are used to maintain financial control, the limits are likely to be flexible, and additional funds will be provided if a profitable investment opportunity arises unexpectedly.

However, as discussed above, capital expenditure limits may be imposed for valid reasons that do not reflect a shortage of capital. Rather, the real constraint may be a shortage of other resources such as management time. Therefore, capital rationing can be a real phenomenon and managers may need to choose the set of projects that maximises net present value, subject to a resource constraint. On the other hand, if external capital rationing exists, attempts to maximise net present value, subject to a capital expenditure limit, involve an inherent contradiction. The problem is that a project's net present value

> **LEARNING OBJECTIVE 7**
> Explain the effects of resource constraints on project selection
>
> **capital rationing**
> a condition where a firm has limited resources available for investment

is calculated using a required rate of return, but the existence of an external limit on the availability of capital implies that once the limit is reached, the required rate of return is infinite. In the following discussion, therefore, it will be assumed that capital rationing exists only because of internally imposed constraints. A manager attempting to 'maximise' the market value of the company's shares within these self-imposed constraints should calculate the net present value of each project by discounting its cash flows at the required rate of return, and then choose the combination of projects that maximises net present value.

EXAMPLE 6.11

Suppose that a company is considering the proposals listed in Table 6.12. Assume that it has a capital expenditure limit of $600 000, all projects are independent, the projects are not divisible and it is not envisaged that an expenditure limit will exist in future years.

TABLE 6.12 Ranking of projects under capital rationing

PROJECT	INITIAL CASH OUTLAY ($)	NET PRESENT VALUE ($)
A	200 000	28 000
B	200 000	20 000
C	200 000	15 000
D	200 000	35 000
E	400 000	45 000
F	400 000	22 000

Management must find the combination of projects that maximises net present value, subject to the expenditure limit of $600 000.

SOLUTION

In this example, examination of all possible outcomes shows that the largest net present value will be achieved by the combination of Projects D, A and B. This combination results in a net present value of $83 000. By comparison, the next best alternative, a combination of Projects D and E, results in a net present value of $80 000. As a result of the expenditure limit, even though Projects C, E and F have positive net present values, the company is unable to implement them this year. Without the expenditure limit, all the projects shown in Table 6.12 could have been accepted and the total net present value would have been $165 000 instead of $83 000.

In reality, ranking of investment projects where there is capital rationing is much more complex because of the large number of investment alternatives generally available to a company. To find solutions to such problems, mathematical programming models have been developed.

We now return to the earlier point that the imposition of capital rationing by management can prevent the maximisation of shareholders' wealth. Capital rationing is not in the shareholders' best interest if projects with positive net present values are rejected. In Example 6.11, Projects C, E and F, with positive net present values totalling $82 000, are rejected because of a capital constraint. Unless the company faces a real constraint, such as a shortage of personnel, or rapid expansion involves excessive risk, management should raise the funds necessary to finance these projects by reducing dividends, borrowing, issuing more shares or some combination of these actions.

Connect Plus features a case study illustrating topics covered in this chapter. Ask your lecturer or tutor for your course's unique URL.

SUMMARY

This chapter has discussed several important aspects of project evaluation, beginning with the estimation of cash flows.

→ In estimating cash flows, financing charges should be excluded, as too should allocated costs and sunk costs. Conversely, all incremental cash flows must be included. The correct treatment of inflation requires that cash flows and the required rate of return be defined in a consistent manner.

→ Projects that are mutually exclusive and have different lives can be compared using the constant chain of replacement method or by calculating the equivalent annual value of each project. These methods also provide a convenient way of analysing asset replacement decisions.

→ While the effects of risk can be incorporated in project evaluation by using a risk-adjusted discount rate, there are several methods of project analysis that can be useful in describing risk and providing managers with information about the risk of a project. The methods discussed in the chapter are sensitivity analysis, break-even analysis and simulation. Decision-tree analysis can be a useful tool for evaluating sequential decisions where probabilities can be attached to the possible outcomes.

The chapter also provided a discussion of the importance of considering qualitative factors in project evaluation, and concluded with a discussion of the effects of resource constraints on project evaluation.

KEY TERMS

break-even analysis   150
capital rationing   157
constant chain of replacement
   assumption   138
equivalent annual value method   140
residual value   134
sensitivity analysis   148
simulation   152
sunk cost   134

SELF-TEST PROBLEMS

1. The management of the TMT Company is considering purchasing a new machine and it has gathered the following data:

   (a) The cash needed to purchase the new machine is $64 000.
   (b) The residual value and annual cash operating expenses for the next 5 years are estimated to be:

Year	Residual value at end of year ($)	Annual cash operating expenses ($)
1	50 000	11 000
2	40 000	13 000
3	30 000	18 000
4	23 000	24 000
5	3 500	28 000

(c) No changes in residual values or annual cash operating expenses are expected.
(d) The required rate of return is 15 per cent per annum.
(e) The effects of company income tax may be ignored.

What is the optimum replacement policy for this machine?

2. The management of ABC Transport Ltd, which is engaged in interstate transport, is considering the replacement of its present fleet of 10 CB semi-trailers with six AZ Flexivans. A survey has revealed the following estimates of costs, and so on, *per vehicle*:

CB semi-trailers	Estimates	AZ flexivans	Estimates
Remaining life	3 years	Estimated life	5 years
Residual value:			
At the present time	$5 000	Cost	$70 000
In 3 years' time	$1 000	Annual net cash flows	$40 000
Annual net cash flows	$30 000	Residual value after 5 years' operation	$5 000

Other information is as follows:
- Net cash flows are to be regarded as received at the end of each year.
- The required rate of return is 10 per cent per annum.

Should management:
(a) retain the CB semi-trailers for 3 years and then replace them with AZ Flexivans?
(b) replace the CB semi-trailers with the AZ Flexivans now?

3. Skye Port has a Higher Education Contribution Scheme–Higher Education Loan Program (HECS–HELP) debt of $3410, which is a debt to the Australian Government. She knows that if she makes a voluntary repayment of $3100, then she will receive a 'bonus' or reduction in her debt of an additional 10 per cent or $310. Therefore, by paying $3100 she would extinguish all of her HECS–HELP debt.

If she does not pay off her HECS–HELP debt, then the amount to be repaid would be increased by the anticipated rate of inflation, which she expects to be 3 per cent for the next year. Therefore, her HECS–HELP debt in 1 year's time would be $3410(1.03) = $3512.30. She expects to have an income next year that is sufficiently high that she will have to repay the full amount of $3512.30.

Should Skye pay off her HECS–HELP debt immediately by paying $3100? When considering this decision assume that Skye has a required real rate of return of 5 per cent per annum.

Solutions to self-test problems are available in Appendix B, page 803.

REFERENCES

Brown, C. & Davis, K., 'Options in mutually exclusive projects of unequal lives', *Quarterly Review of Economics and Finance*, Special Issue 1998, pp. 569–77.

Faff, R. & Brailsford, T., 'The constant chain of replacement model and inflation', *Pacific Accounting Review*, December 1992, pp. 45–58.

Levin, R.I., Kirkpatrick, C.A. & Rubin, D.S., *Quantitative Approaches to Management*, 8th edn, McGraw-Hill, New York, 1992, pp. 231–7.

Pike, R.J., 'The capital budgeting behaviour and corporate characteristics of capital-constrained firms', *Journal of Business Finance and Accounting*, Winter 1983, pp. 663–7.

QUESTIONS

1. **[LO 1]** A property development company plans to demolish the building on a site that it already owns, and then build a convenience store. Which of the following items should be included as incremental cash flows when the project is evaluated:
   (a) the market value of the property
   (b) the cost of demolishing the old building

(c) the cost of new water and electric power connections installed 3 months ago
(d) a portion of the cost of leasing cars used by the company's executives
(e) money that has already been spent on architectural concept plans for the new building.

2. **[LO 2]** Leaving aside the effect of taxes, which of the following items should be considered in the initial outlay on a new machine for project evaluation purposes? Give reasons.
   (a) The disposal value of the old machine, which is $6000.
   (b) The $400 cost of installing the new machine.
   (c) Additional investment of $10 000 in current assets that will be required.
   (d) Costs of $3000 recently incurred in assessing the suitability of the new machine.

3. **[LO 2]** Outline two methods of solving project evaluation problems where the projects under consideration do not have common terminal dates.

4. **[LO 2]** Define the term 'mutually exclusive projects' and provide a simple example. Outline and justify the basic net present value rule applicable to them. How should this rule be modified when such projects have unequal lives?

5. **[LO 3]** How should the optimum life of a project be determined?

6. **[LO 1]** Explain the theoretical relationship between *nominal* and *real* discount rates. Outline its application to project evaluation in the context of an inflationary economy.

7. **[LO 4]** *Sensitivity analysis may be used to identify the variables that are most important for a project's success.* Discuss.

8. **[LO 4]** Outline the weaknesses of sensitivity analysis.

9. **[LO 4]** *Simulation is only useful for large-scale investment projects.* Discuss.

10. **[LO 4]** *Simulation is extremely valuable because it is useful in refining cash flow forecasts and it avoids the need to estimate a project's required rate of return.* Do you agree with these claims? Give reasons for your answer.

11. **[LO 4]** Distinguish between replacement decisions and retirement decisions.

12. **[LO 3]** Distinguish between *internal* and *external* capital rationing. Give examples of each.

13. **[LO 7]**
   (a) Outline possible reasons for the imposition by management of capital rationing. Does the imposition of internal capital rationing imply that management is failing to maximise shareholders' wealth?
   (b) If a company is subject to capital rationing, does this make any difference to project evaluation using the net present value method? Give reasons.

PROBLEMS

1. **Application of the NPV method [LO 1]**
   The furniture division of Playfurn Ltd, a profitable, diversified company, purchased a machine 5 years ago for $7500. When it was purchased the machine had an expected useful life of 15 years and an estimated value of zero at the end of its life. The machine currently has a market value of $1000. The division manager reports that he can buy a new machine for $16 000 (including installation) which, over its 10-year life, will result in an expansion of sales from $10 000 to $11 000 per annum. In addition, it is estimated that the new machine will reduce annual operating costs from $7000 to $5000. If the required rate of return is 10 per cent per annum, should Playfurn buy the new machine?

2. **Comparing mutually exclusive projects [LO 1]**
   A company must choose between two machines. Machine A costs $50 000 and the annual operating expenses are estimated to be $20 000, while Machine B costs $85 000 and has estimated annual operating expenses of $15 000. Both machines have a 10-year life and will have a zero residual value.
   (a) The company has a required rate of return of 10 per cent per annum. Which machine should it purchase?
   (b) Rework the problem for a 7 per cent required rate of return.

3. **Comparing mutually exclusive projects [LO 2]**
   A company is considering the purchase of equipment costing $125 000 that will permit it to reduce its existing labour costs by $20 000 a year for 12 years. The company estimates that it will have to spend $3000 every 2 years overhauling the equipment. The required rate of return is 10 per cent per annum. Assuming all cash flows are made at the end of each year, should the company purchase the equipment?

4. **Comparing mutually exclusive projects [LO 1]**

   The Two-Bit Mining Company has constructed a town at Big Bore, near the site of a rich mineral discovery in a remote part of Australia. The town will be abandoned when mining operations cease after an estimated 10-year period. The following estimates of investment costs, sales and operating expenses relate to a project to supply Big Bore with meat and agricultural produce over the 10-year period by developing nearby land.

   (a) Investment in land is $1 million, farm buildings $200 000 and farm equipment $400 000. The land is expected to have a realisable value of $500 000 in 10 years' time. The residual value of the buildings after 10 years is expected to be $50 000. The farm equipment has an estimated life of 10 years and a zero residual value.

   (b) Investment of $250 000 in current assets will be recovered at the termination of the venture.

   (c) Annual cash sales are estimated to be $2.48 million.

   (d) Annual cash operating costs are estimated to be $2.2 million.

   Is the project profitable, given that the required rate of return is 10 per cent per annum?

5. **Mutually exclusive projects with different lives [LO 2]**

   The management of Harbour Ferries Ltd is considering the replacement of its existing fleet of six steam ferries with three hydrofoils. The following estimates of costs, and so on, for each vessel have been calculated:

Steam ferries	Estimates	Hydrofoils	Estimates
Estimated remaining life	5 years	Cost	$500 000
Estimated scrap value:		Estimated life	10 years
Now	$50 000	Estimated scrap value:	
In 5 years' time	$10 000	In 5 years' time	$200 000
		In 10 years' time	$100 000
Annual net cash flows	$100 000	Annual net cash flows	$200 000

   Management is also aware of the development of hovercraft, which the manufacturer estimates will be available in 5 years' time. The following estimates of costs, and so on, per hovercraft have been provided by the manufacturer:

Hovercraft	Estimates
Cost	$600 000
Estimated life	15 years
Estimated disposal value:	
After 5 years' operation	$200 000
After 15 years' operation	$50 000
Annual net cash flows	$250 000

   It is considered that two of the new hovercraft will be adequate to carry the estimated number of passengers. Other information is as follows:

   - Management cannot foresee any further developments beyond the hovercraft.
   - The annual net cash flows are received at the end of each year.
   - The company's required rate of return is 10 per cent per annum.

   You are required to advise management whether it should:

   (a) replace the steam ferries with hydrofoils now, and replace the latter with hovercraft in 5 years' time

   (b) retain the steam ferries for 5 years, and then replace them with hovercraft

   (c) replace the steam ferries with hydrofoils now, and replace the latter with hovercraft in 10 years' time.

   Other alternatives are not to be considered.

6. **Replacement decision [LO 3]**

   A company is considering the installation of a new machine at a cost of $60 000 to replace a machine purchased 7 years ago for $100 000. The disposal value of the old machine is $15 000. Both machines will have similar outputs and will produce work of identical quality. The estimated yearly costs of operating each machine are as follows:

	Old machine ($)	New machine ($)
Wages	15 000	5000
Supplies, repairs, power	5000	3000
Insurance and miscellaneous	2000	3000
Total	22 000	11 000

Both machines have an estimated remaining life of 3 years, at which time both machines will have an estimated disposal value of $5000. Assume that:

(a) the required rate of return is 10 per cent per annum
(b) the operating costs of the old machine and the new machine are incurred at the end of each year.

Should the company purchase the new machine, or continue to operate the old one?

7. **Replacement decision [LO 3]**

The management of New World Airlines is considering the replacement of its present fleet of 10 piston engine planes with five turboprops. A survey has revealed the following estimates of costs, and so on, per plane:

Piston engine	Estimates	Turboprop	Estimates
Remaining life	5 years	Life	5 years
Residual value:		Cost	$3 430 000
At present time	$10 000	Annual net cash flows	$1 000 000
In 2 years' time	$5000	Residual value:	
In 5 years' time	$0	After 2 years' operation	30% of purchase price
Annual net cash flows	$100 000	After 5 years' operation	5% of purchase price

(a) Should replacement be undertaken now or in 5 years' time?

Immediately after the decision has been reached, management is informed of a superjet that will become available in 2 years' time. The estimates for the new plane are:

Superjet	Estimates
Cost	$4 500 000
Annual net cash inflows	$1 200 000
Life	5 years
Residual value after 5 years' operation	3% of purchase price

It is considered that four of the new superjets will be adequate to cover the estimated passenger load.

Other information is as follows:
- Management cannot foresee any further developments beyond the superjet.
- Annual net cash flows are assumed to be received at the end of each year.
- The required rate of return is 10 per cent per annum.

(b) Should management:
  (i) retain the piston engine planes for 5 years and replace them with superjets
  (ii) replace them immediately with turboprops, operate them for 5 years, and then replace them with superjets
  (iii) replace them now with turboprops, operate them for 2 years, and then replace them with superjets
  (iv) retain the piston engine planes for 2 years and then replace them with superjets?

Other replacement dates are not to be considered.

8. **Replacement decision [LO 3]**

A.B. Pty Ltd is currently operating a suburban taxi-truck business. It is considering the replacement of a 1.5 tonne vehicle with a 2 tonne vehicle. Details of the respective vehicles are as follows:

1.5 tonne vehicle	Estimates	2 tonne vehicle	Estimates
Remaining life	4 years	Estimated life	7 years
Residual value:		Cost	$15 000
Now	$4000	Residual value after 7 years' operation	$1000
In four years	$0		
Annual net cash flow	$6000	Net cash flow	$10 000

Other information is as follows:
- Net cash flows are to be regarded as received at the end of each year.
- The required rate of return is 10 per cent per annum. Management is considering the following alternatives:
  (a) replace the 1.5 tonne vehicle with the 2 tonne vehicle now
  (b) replace the 1.5 tonne vehicle with the 2 tonne vehicle in 4 years' time.

All other alternatives may be ignored.

Advise management as to which alternative it should adopt, and justify your analysis.

9. **Retirement decision [LO 3]**

Pulp and Paper Ltd has just planted pine trees at a cost of $12 000 per hectare on 500 hectares of land, which it purchased for $400 000. The trees are expected to grow rapidly and the company's estimates of the net future value of the cut timber are:

Time of harvest end of year	Net future value ($ per hectare)
2	17 320
3	20 000
4	22 360
5	24 495
6	26 450

The required rate of return is 10 per cent per annum and taxes can be ignored.

(a) Calculate the optimum time to harvest the crop of trees. Assume that the value of the cleared land increases at a rate of 10 per cent per annum.

(b) Estimate the net present value of the project, assuming sale of the land after the trees are harvested. Note any assumptions you make.

10. **Comparing mutually exclusive projects [LO 2]**

Hermes Pty Ltd operates a messenger/courier service. A new van is required to meet the increased demand for the company's services. The choice has been narrowed down to three vans, A, B and C, each costing $10 000. Net cash flow estimates are as follows:

Year	Net cash flow estimates ($)		
	Van A	Van B	Van C
1	$4700	$4800	$4700
2	$5000	$4000	$4800
3	$5000	$4000	$4800
4	$5800	$5200	$5500
5	0	$4200	0
Required rate of return	20%	20%	20%
NPV	$3079	$3288	$2680

By discounting each net cash flow, show that the net present value of Van A has been calculated properly. Which van should be purchased? Give reasons.

11. **Comparing mutually exclusive projects [LO 3]**

A software provider buys blank CDs at $550 per hundred and currently uses 2 million CDs per year. The manager believes that it may be cheaper to *make* the CDs rather than buy them. Direct production costs (labour, materials, fuel) are estimated at $2.50 per CD. The equipment needed would cost $3 million. The equipment should last for 15 years, provided it is overhauled every 5 years at a cost of $250 000 each time. The operation will require additional current assets of $400 000. The company's required rate of return is 12 per cent. Evaluate the proposal.

12. **Replacement decision [LO 3]**

A company is considering the replacement of an old machine with a new machine. The old machine was purchased a year ago for $12 500. Additional information relating to these machines (cash flows are in nominal terms) is as follows:

Item	Estimates	
	Old machine ($)	New machine ($)
Market value (now)	$7000	$5000
Service life (when purchased)	6 years	5 years
Residual value in 5 years' time	$0	$1000
Cash operating receipts	–	$500 p.a. in excess of old machine

The real required rate of return is 10 per cent per annum, and the anticipated inflation rate is 10 per cent per annum. Calculate the net present value of replacing the old machine with the new machine.

13. **Application of the NPV method [LO 1]**
Ozzie Nationwide Industries Ltd is a large company with interests in mining, shipbuilding, entertainment, food processing and interstate freight haulage. Its food processing division is investigating the possibility of adding mandarin-flavoured yoghurt to its current range of banana, strawberry and apple. Currently, all flavours are sold at a price of $1.50 per carton and sales are even throughout the year. Ozzie recently hired Melbourne Market Research Ltd to survey consumers to judge the likely popularity of the new flavour. The report cost $40 000 and suggested that the company should be able to sell 400 000 cartons of the new flavour next year, and 800 000 in each of the following 2 years. After that time, the fad for mandarin flavour is expected to have run its course. Ozzie's costing department has advised that the incremental cost of production is $1.20 per carton. Ozzie's sales department has advised that it is essential that all flavours in the range should be sold at the same price. Ozzie's engineers have advised that there is no spare production capacity although there is plenty of spare floor space in the factory. They have also advised that yoghurt processing machines have a production capacity of 400 000 cartons per annum and that the cost of one machine, fully installed, is $230 000. Ozzie's finance division has advised that the company's required rate of return (nominal) is estimated to be 15 per cent per annum. The machines have a life of 3 years and at that point have only a scrap value, which is estimated to be only $10 000. However, this amount usually only just covers the costs of removing the machine from the factory.

Ozzie's project analyst has recommended against proceeding with the new flavour, basing this recommendation on a net present value analysis. The net cash inflows were forecast to be $120 000 in the first year, and $240 000 in the second year and the third year. The initial outlay was $500 000. The NPV was calculated as:

$$NPV = \frac{\$120\,000}{1.15^{0.5}} + \frac{\$240\,000}{1.15^{1.5}} + \frac{\$240\,000}{1.15^{2.5}} - \$500\,000$$
$$= -\$24\,264$$

The project analyst's report contained the usual range of sensitivity analyses and supporting discussion and documentation but this calculation was the central result.

You have been asked to review the project analyst's work and report on any errors you detect. Provide reasons. Ignore tax. Note that it is not necessary to redo the analysis, or to suggest how the analysis might be extended. Your task is to identify errors.

14. **Mutually exclusive projects with different lives [LO 2]**
The Bertie Hamilton Fishing Company (BHF) purchased a trawler 6 years ago for $420 000. At the time it was purchased, the trawler had a useful life of 10 years. If BHF were to retain this boat, it is anticipated that ultrasonic detection equipment would have to be installed in the second-last year of its life at a cost of $40 000. However, the Commercial Trawler Company (CT) has recently launched a faster, computer-assisted trawler that BHF is considering as a replacement. This trawler will cost $600 000 but will need immediate refitting to suit the purchaser's specifications at an additional cost of $15 000. It has an expected useful life of 12 years.

If purchased, the new trawler is likely to increase cash operating costs by $10 per tonne of fish, which currently sell for $30 per tonne. However, future catches are likely to increase significantly by 6000 tonne in the first year, and then at a rate of

1000 tonne per annum, stabilising at 12 000 tonne from Year 7 onward. Owing to intensive usage, it is expected that towards the end of the fifth year the new trawler will require a minor engine overhaul at a cost of $30 000. Part of the purchase agreement also involves a maintenance contract with CT covering the nets and trawling apparatus, which will cost BHF $12 000, payable at the end of every fourth year.

As a competitive strategy, CT offers an optional financing package for up to 80 per cent of the invoice price on any boat. The rate of interest on this amount is 12 per cent per annum, with the first payment deferred 1 year. If the financing package is adopted, BHF must undertake to sell the trawler back to CT in 12 years' time for $50 000. BHF estimates that the current second-hand price of its present trawler is only $140 000. It is estimated that the new trawler can be sold for $100 000 at the end of its useful life.

The company's nominal required rate of return is 30 per cent.
(a) Estimate the net cash flow (NCF) at the beginning of Year 1.
(b) Estimate the NCF in Year 4.
(c) Management believes that relative to today's prices, the average inflation rate is expected to be 8 per cent per annum over the next 12 years. What is the Year 3 inflation-adjusted NCF?
(d) Estimate the appropriate discount rate to perform an NPV analysis in real terms.

15. **Sensitivity analysis [LO 4]**
Management of Ride Ltd is considering the possibility of manufacturing a new motorised golf buggy. The initial outlay for the new plant to manufacture the vehicle is $1 million. The staff of Ride Ltd have provided the following estimates for the project:

| | Estimates | | |
Item	Pessimistic	Most likely	Optimistic
Sales (units)	3 000	3 500	4 000
Selling price ($)	750	800	850
Fixed operating costs per annum ($)	100 000	90 000	80 000
Variable operating costs per annum per unit of sales ($)	25	24	23
Life of the plant (years)	4	5	6

Assuming a required rate of return of 10 per cent, conduct a sensitivity analysis. What are the major uncertainties if the project is undertaken?

16. **Break-even analysis [LO 4]**
The manager of Alsports Ltd is considering a plan to manufacture aluminium baseball bats. Equipment to manufacture the bats will cost $850 000 and is expected to have a useful life of 3 years. Fixed costs are estimated to be $80 000 per annum and the bats are expected to sell for $40 each, while variable costs will be $28 per bat. About 500 000 baseball bats are sold each year and Alsports has a required rate of return of 10 per cent. Calculate the break-even sales volume.

17. **Decision-tree analysis [LO 5]**
Pasha Bulker Ltd is considering producing a new product. It expects that the product will have a life of 10 years, by which time the market for the product will be saturated and the assets necessary to produce it will be sold. The company is uncertain as to whether the product should be manufactured on a large scale in a large plant, or on a small scale in a small plant. If the company chooses a small plant, it would consider expanding the plant after 3 years.

The company estimates that there is a 50 per cent probability that a high level of demand will be attained over the 10 years during which the product will be marketed, a 25 per cent probability that demand will be high during the first 3 years and then drop to a low level over the succeeding 7 years, and a 25 per cent probability that a low level of demand will persist over the entire 10 years.

The following table indicates the expected annual net cash flows and residual values associated with each scale of production and level of demand:

Possibilities	Annual net cash flow ($)	Residual value ($)
Large plant, high demand	500 000	500 000
Large plant, low demand	150 000	200 000
Small plant, high demand	200 000	200 000
Small plant, low demand	150 000	100 000
Expanded plant, high demand	300 000	400 000
Expanded plant, low demand	100 000	150 000

The initial cost associated with the construction of a large plant is $2 million, and that associated with a small plant is $1 million. The expected cost of expanding from a small plant to a large plant after 3 years is $1 million. The company's required rate of return of 12 per cent per annum is relevant for all alternatives.

(a) Which policy should the company pursue?
(b) Is it likely that the same discount rate will be appropriate for all alternatives? Give reasons.

Test yourself further with Connect Plus online! Ask your lecturer or tutor for your course's unique URL.

CHAPTER 7
RISK AND RETURN

LEARNING OBJECTIVES

After studying this chapter you should be able to:

1. understand how return and risk are defined and measured
2. understand the concept of risk aversion by investors
3. explain how diversification reduces risk
4. explain the concept of efficient portfolios
5. understand the importance of covariance between returns on risky assets in determining the risk of a portfolio
6. explain the distinction between systematic and unsystematic risk
7. explain why systematic risk is important to investors
8. explain the relationship between returns and risk proposed by the capital asset pricing model
9. understand the relationship between the capital asset pricing model and models that include additional factors
10. explain the development of models that include additional factors
11. distinguish between alternative methods of appraising the performance of an investment portfolio.

CHAPTER CONTENTS

7.1 Introduction
7.2 Return and risk
7.3 The investor's utility function
7.4 The risk of assets
7.5 Portfolio theory and diversification
7.6 The pricing of risky assets
7.7 Additional factors that explain returns
7.8 Portfolio performance appraisal

INTRODUCTION

7.1

A financial decision typically involves risk. For example, a company that borrows money faces the risk that interest rates may change, and a company that builds a new factory faces the risk that product sales may be lower than expected. These and many other decisions involve future cash flows that are risky. Investors generally dislike risk, but they are also unable to avoid it. The valuation formulae for shares and debt securities outlined in Chapter 4 showed that the price of a risky asset depends on its expected future cash flows, the time value of money, and risk. However, little attention was paid to the causes of risk or to how risk should be defined and measured.

To make effective financial decisions, managers need to understand what causes risk, how it should be measured and the effect of risk on the rate of return required by investors. These issues are discussed in this chapter using the framework of portfolio theory, which shows how investors can maximise the expected return on a portfolio of risky assets for a given level of risk. The relationship between risk and expected return is first described by the capital asset pricing model (CAPM), which links expected return to a single source of risk, and second, by models that include additional factors to explain returns.

To understand the material in this chapter it is necessary to understand what is meant by *return* and *risk*. Therefore, we begin by discussing these concepts.

RETURN AND RISK

7.2

The return on an investment and the risk of an investment are basic concepts in finance. Return on an investment is the financial outcome for the investor. For example, if someone invests $100 in an asset and subsequently sells that asset for $111, the *dollar return* is $11. Usually an investment's dollar return is converted to a *rate of return* by calculating the proportion or percentage represented by the dollar return. For example, a dollar return of $11 on an investment of $100 is a rate of return of $11/$100, which is 0.11, or 11 per cent. In the remainder of this chapter the word *return* is used to mean *rate of return*.

Risk is present whenever investors are not certain about the outcomes an investment will produce. Suppose, however, that investors can attach a probability to each possible dollar return that may occur. Investors can then draw up a probability distribution for the dollar returns from the investment. A *probability distribution* is a list of the possible dollar returns from the investment together with the probability of each return. For example, assume that the probability distribution in Table 7.1 is an investor's assessment of the dollar returns R_i that may be received from holding a share in a company for 1 year.

LEARNING OBJECTIVE 1
Understand how return and risk are defined and measured

TABLE 7.1

DOLLAR RETURN, R_i/($)	PROBABILITY, P_i
9	0.1
10	0.2
11	0.4
12	0.2
13	0.1

Suppose the investor wishes to summarise this distribution by calculating two measures, one to represent the size of the dollar returns and the other to represent the risk involved. The size of the dollar returns may be measured by the expected value of the distribution. The expected value $E(R)$ of the dollar returns is given by the weighted average of all the possible dollar returns, using the probabilities as weights—that is:

$$E(R) = (\$9)(0.1) + (\$10)(0.2) + (\$11)(0.4) + (\$12)(0.2) + (\$13)(0.1)$$
$$= \$11$$

In general, the expected return on an investment can be calculated as:

$$E(R) = R_1 P_1 + R_2 P_2 + \ldots + R_n P_n$$

which can be written as follows:

$$E(R) = \sum_{i=1}^{n} R_i P_i$$

The choice of a measure for risk is less obvious. In this example, risk is present because any one of five outcomes ($9, $10, $11, $12 or $13) might result from the investment. If the investor had perfect foresight, then only one possible outcome would be involved, and there would not be a probability distribution to be considered. This suggests that risk is related to the dispersion of the distribution. The more dispersed or widespread the distribution, the greater the risk involved. Statisticians have developed a number of measures to represent dispersion. These measures include the range, the mean absolute deviation and the variance. However, it is generally accepted that in most instances the **variance** (or its square root, the **standard deviation**, σ) is the most useful measure. Accordingly, this measure of dispersion is the one we will use to represent the risk of a single investment. The variance of a distribution of dollar returns is the weighted average of the square of each dollar return's deviation from the expected dollar return, again using the probabilities as the weights. For the share considered in Table 7.1, the variance is:

$$\sigma^2 = (9-11)^2(0.1) + (10-11)^2(0.2) + (11-11)^2(0.4) + (12-11)^2(0.2) + (13-11)^2(0.1)$$
$$= 1.2$$

In general the variance can be calculated as:

$$\sigma^2 = [R_1 - E(R)]^2 P_1 + [R_2 - E(R)]^2 P_2 + \ldots + [R_n - E(R)]^2 P_n$$

which can be written as follows:

$$\sigma^2 = \sum_{i=1}^{n} [R_i - E(R)]^2 P_i$$

In this case the variance is 1.2 so the standard deviation is:

$$\sigma = \sqrt{1.2}$$
$$= \$1.095$$

In these calculations we have used dollar returns rather than returns measured in the form of a rate. This is because it is generally easier to visualise dollars than rates, and because it avoids calculations with a large number of zeros following the decimal point. However, there is no difference in substance, as may be seen from reworking the example using returns in rate form. If the sum invested is $100, then a dollar return of $9, for example, is a return of 0.09 when expressed as a rate. Table 7.2 shows rates of return that correspond to the dollar returns in Table 7.1.

---

variance
measure of variability; the mean of the squared deviations from the mean or expected value

standard deviation
square root of the variance

TABLE 7.2

RETURN, R_i	PROBABILITY, P_i
0.09	0.1
0.10	0.2
0.11	0.4
0.12	0.2
0.13	0.1

Using rates, the expected return $E(R)$ is:

$$E(R) = (0.09)(0.1) + (0.10)(0.2) + (0.11)(0.4) + (0.12)(0.2) + (0.13)(0.1)$$
$$= 0.11$$
$$= 11\%$$

The variance of returns is:

$$\sigma^2 = (0.09 - 0.11)^2(0.1) + (0.10 - 0.11)^2(0.2) + (0.11 - 0.11)^2(0.4) + (0.12 - 0.11)^2(0.2)$$
$$+ (0.13 - 0.11)^2(0.1)$$
$$= 0.000\,12$$

The standard deviation of returns is therefore:

$$\sigma = \sqrt{0.000\,12}$$
$$= 0.010\,95$$
$$= 1.095\%$$

It is often assumed that an investment's distribution of returns follows a normal distribution. This is a convenient assumption because a normal distribution can be fully described by its expected value and standard deviation. Therefore, an investment's distribution of returns can be fully described by its expected return and risk. Assuming that returns follow a normal probability distribution, the table of areas under the standard normal curve (see Table 5 of Appendix A, page 801) can be used to calculate the probability that the investment will generate a return greater than or less than any specified return. For example, suppose that the returns on an investment in Company A are normally distributed, with an expected return of 13 per cent per annum and a standard deviation of 10 per cent per annum. Suppose an investor in the company wishes to calculate the probability of a loss—that is, the investor wishes to calculate the probability of a return of less than zero per cent. A return of zero per cent is 1.3 standard deviations below the expected return (because 0.13/0.10 = 1.3). Figure 7.1, overleaf, illustrates this case. The shaded area represents the probability of a loss. The table of areas under the standard normal curve (Table 5, Appendix A or the NORMSDIST function in Microsoft Excel®) indicates that the probability of a loss occurring is 0.0968 or almost 9.7 per cent.

To highlight the importance of the standard deviation of the return distribution, assume that the same investor also has the opportunity of investing in Company B with an expected return of 13 per cent and a standard deviation of 6.91 per cent. The probability distributions of the returns on investments in companies A and B are shown in Figure 7.2, overleaf.

Both investments have the same expected return but, on the basis of the dispersion of the returns, an investment in Company A (with a standard deviation of 10 per cent) is riskier than an investment in Company B (with a standard deviation of 6.91 per cent).

Suppose that the investor decides that a return of zero per cent or less is unsatisfactory. A return of zero per cent on an investment in Company B is 1.88 standard deviations below the expected return

FIGURE 7.1

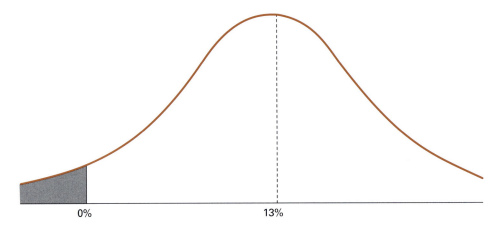

FIGURE 7.2

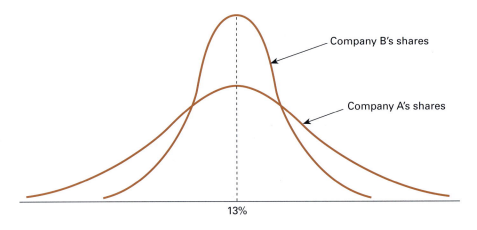

(because 0.13/0.0691 = 1.88). The probability of this occurring is 0.03. Therefore, the probability that an investment in one of these companies will generate a negative return is 3 per cent for Company B compared with 9.7 per cent for Company A. However, when the investor considers returns at the upper end of the distributions it is found that an investment in Company A offers a 9.7 per cent chance of a return in excess of 26 per cent, compared with only a 3 per cent chance for an investment in Company B. In summary the probability of both very low returns and very high returns is much greater in the case of Company A. The fact that the investor is more uncertain about the return from an investment in Company A does not mean that the investor will necessarily prefer to invest in Company B. The choice depends on the investor's attitude to risk.

Alternative attitudes to risk and the effects of risk are considered in the next section, which can safely be omitted by readers who are prepared to accept that investors are generally **risk averse**. Risk aversion does *not* mean that an investor will refuse to bear any risk at all. Rather it means that an investor regards risk as something undesirable, but which may be worth tolerating if the expected return is sufficient to compensate for the risk. Therefore, a risk-averse investor would prefer to invest in Company B because A and B offer the same expected return, but B is less risky.

risk-averse investor
one who dislikes risk

THE INVESTOR'S UTILITY FUNCTION

7.3

Consider the decision to invest in either Company A or Company B. As discussed in Section 7.2, both companies offer the same expected return, but differ in risk. A preference for investing in either Company A or Company B will depend on the investor's attitude to risk. An investor may be risk averse, **risk neutral** or **risk seeking**. A risk-averse investor attaches decreasing utility to each increment in wealth; a risk-neutral investor attaches equal utility to each increment in wealth; while a risk-seeking investor attaches increasing utility to each increment in wealth. Typical utility-to-wealth functions for each type of investor are illustrated in Figure 7.3.

LEARNING OBJECTIVE 2
Understand the concept of risk aversion by investors

FIGURE 7.3 Utility-to-wealth functions for different types of investors

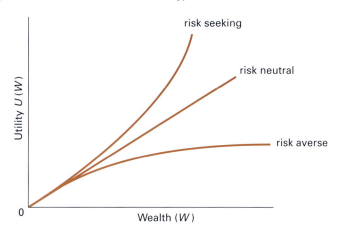

risk-neutral investor
one who neither likes nor dislikes risk

risk-seeking investor
one who prefers risk

The characteristics of a risk-averse investor warrant closer examination, as risk aversion is the standard assumption in finance theory. Assume that a risk-averse investor has wealth of $\$W^*$ and has the opportunity of participating in the following game: a fair coin is tossed and if it falls tails (probability 0.5), then $1000 is won; if it falls heads (probability 0.5), then $1000 is lost. The expected value of the game is $0 and it is, therefore, described as a 'fair game'. Would a risk-averse investor participate in such a game? If he or she participates and wins, wealth will increase to $\$(W^* + 1000)$, but if he or she loses, wealth will fall to $\$(W^* - 1000)$. The results of this game are shown in Figure 7.4, overleaf.

The investor's current level of utility is U_2. The investor's utility will increase to U_3 if he or she wins the game and will decrease to U_1 in the event of a loss. What is the expected utility if the investor decides to participate in the game? There is a 50 per cent chance that his or her utility will increase to U_3, and a 50 per cent chance that it will decrease to U_1. Therefore, the expected utility is $0.5U_1 + 0.5U_3$. As shown in Figure 7.4, the investor's expected utility with the gamble ($0.5U_1 + 0.5U_3$) is lower than the utility obtained without the gamble (U_2). As it is assumed that investors maximise their expected utility, a risk-averse investor would refuse to participate in this game. In fact, a risk-averse investor may be defined as someone who would not participate in a fair game. Similarly, it can be shown that a risk-neutral investor would be indifferent to participation, and a risk-seeking investor would be prepared to pay for the right to participate in a fair game.

Now consider the preferences of a risk-averse investor with respect to an investment in either Company A or Company B. As we have seen, the expected return from each investment is the same but the investment in A is riskier. An investment in A offers the possibility of making either higher returns or lower returns, compared with an investment in B. However, from Figure 7.2, the increased spread of returns above the expected return tends to increase expected utility. But this increase will be outweighed by the decrease in expected utility resulting from the greater spread of returns below the expected return. Therefore, the risk-averse investor's expected utility would be greater if he or she invests in B.

FIGURE 7.4

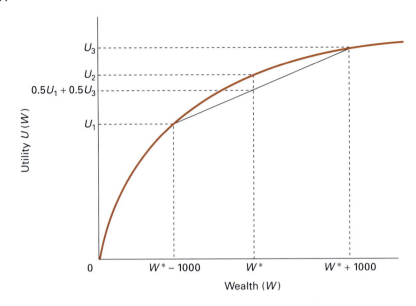

As both investments offer the same expected return, the risk-averse investor's choice implies that the increased dispersion of returns makes an investment riskier. This suggests that the standard deviation of the return distribution may be a useful measure of risk for a risk-averse investor. Similarly, it can be argued that the risk-neutral investor would be indifferent between these two investments. For any given amount to be invested, such an investor will always choose the investment that offers the higher return, irrespective of the relative risk of other investments—that is, the standard deviation is ignored. The risk-seeking investor would choose to invest in A. If a given amount is to be invested, and the investor has the choice of two investments that offer the same expected return, the risk-seeking investor will always choose the investment with the higher risk.

An investor's preferences regarding expected return and risk can be illustrated using indifference curves. For a given amount invested, an indifference curve traces out all those combinations of expected return and risk that provide a particular investor with the same level of utility. Because the level of utility is the same, the investor is indifferent between all points on the curve. A risk-averse investor has a positive attitude towards expected return and a negative attitude towards risk. By this, we mean that a risk-averse investor will prefer an investment to have a higher expected return (for a given risk level) and lower risk (for a given expected return).

Risk aversion does *not* mean that an investor will refuse to bear any risk at all. Rather it means that an investor regards risk as something undesirable, but which may be worth tolerating if the expected return is sufficient to compensate for the risk. In graphical terms, indifference curves for a risk-averse investor must be upward sloping as shown in Figure 7.5, opposite.

The risk–return coordinates for a risk-averse investor are shown in Figure 7.5 for three investments—A, B and C. It is apparent that this investor would prefer Investment B to Investment A, and would also prefer Investment B to Investment C. This investor prefers a higher expected return at any given level of risk (compare investments B and A) and a lower level of risk at any given expected return (compare investments B and C). However, this investor would be indifferent between investments A and C. The higher expected return on investment C compensates this investor exactly for the higher risk. In addition, for a given expected return the expected utility of a risk-averse investor falls at an increasing rate as the dispersion of the distribution of returns increases. As a result, the rate of increase in expected return required to compensate for every

FIGURE 7.5

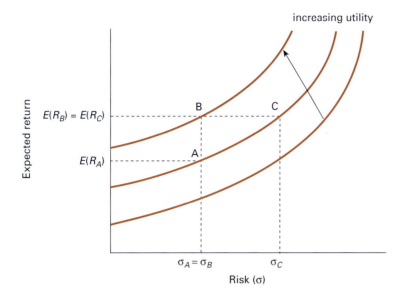

increment in the standard deviation increases faster as the risk becomes larger. Note that indifference curves for a risk-averse investor are not only upward sloping, but also convex, as shown in Figure 7.5.

So far we have concentrated on the characteristics and behaviour of a risk-averse investor. However, there are instances where individuals behave in a way contrary to risk aversion. For example, a risk-averse person will never purchase a lottery ticket, as the expected value of the gamble is less than the price of the ticket. However, many individuals whose current level of wealth is quite low relative to the lottery prize are prepared to purchase lottery tickets because, while only a small outlay is required, there is the small chance of achieving a relatively large increase in wealth. In decisions that involve larger outlays, risk aversion is much more likely. As the financial decisions considered in this book generally involve large investments and small rates of return (at least relative to winning a lottery prize), it is assumed throughout that investors behave as if they are risk averse.

THE RISK OF ASSETS   7.4

If investors' expectations of the returns from an investment can be represented by a normal probability distribution, then the standard deviation is a relevant measure of risk for a risk-averse investor. If two investments offer the same expected return, but differ in risk, then a risk-averse investor will prefer the less risky investment. Further, it has been shown that a risk-averse investor is prepared to accept higher risk for higher expected return, with the result that the required return on a particular investment increases with the investor's perception of its risk.

The standard deviation of the return from a single investment is a relevant measure of its riskiness in cases where an individual is considering the investment of all available funds in one asset. However, it is exceptional to limit investments in this way. Most people invest in a number of assets; they may invest in a house, a car, their human capital and numerous other assets. In addition, where they invest in shares, it is likely that they will hold shares in a number of companies. In other words, people typically invest their wealth in a **portfolio** of assets and will be concerned about the risk of their overall portfolio. This risk can be measured by the standard deviation of the returns on the portfolio. Therefore, when an individual asset is considered, an investor will be concerned about the risk of that asset as a *component* of a portfolio

portfolio
combined holding of more than one asset

of assets. What we need to know is how individual portfolio components (assets) contribute to the risk of the portfolio as a whole. An apparently plausible guess would be that the contribution of each asset is proportional to the asset's standard deviation. However, portfolio theory, which is discussed in the next section, shows that this guess turns out to be almost always incorrect.

7.5 PORTFOLIO THEORY AND DIVERSIFICATION

Portfolio theory was initially developed by Markowitz (1952) as a normative approach to investment choice under uncertainty.[1] Two important assumptions of portfolio theory have already been discussed. These are:

(a) The returns from investments are normally distributed. Therefore, two parameters, the expected return and the standard deviation, are sufficient to describe the distribution of returns.[2]

(b) Investors are risk averse. Therefore, investors prefer the highest expected return for a given standard deviation and the lowest standard deviation for a given expected return.

LEARNING OBJECTIVE 3
Explain how diversification reduces risk

Given these assumptions, it can be shown that it is rational for a utility-maximising investor to hold a well-diversified portfolio of investments. Suppose that an investor holds a portfolio of securities. This investor will be concerned about the expected return and risk of the portfolio. The expected return on a portfolio is a weighted average of the expected returns on the securities in the portfolio. Let $E(R_i)$ be the expected return on the ith security and $E(R_p)$ the expected return on a portfolio of securities. Then, using the notation introduced earlier:

$$E(R_p) = \sum_{i=1}^{n} w_i E(R_i) \qquad [7.1]$$

where w_i = the proportion of the total current market value of the portfolio constituted by the current market value of the ith security—that is, it is the 'weight' attached to the security
  n = the number of securities in the portfolio

Calculation of the expected return on a portfolio is illustrated in Example 7.1.

EXAMPLE 7.1

Assume that there are only two securities (1 and 2) in a portfolio and $E(R_1)$ = 0.08 and $E(R_2)$ = 0.12. Also assume that the current market value of Security 1 is 60 per cent of the total current market value of the portfolio (that is, w_1 = 0.6 and w_2 = 0.4). Then:

$E(R_p)$ = (0.6)(0.08) + (0.4)(0.12)
    = 0.096 or 9.6%

Example 7.1 illustrates the fact that the expected return on a portfolio is simply the weighted average of the expected returns on the securities in the portfolio. However, the standard deviation of the return on the portfolio (σ_p) is *not* simply a weighted average of the standard deviations of the securities in the portfolio. This is because the riskiness of a portfolio depends not only on the riskiness of the individual securities but also on the relationship between the returns on those securities. The variance of the return on a portfolio of two securities is given by:

$$\sigma_p^2 = w_1^2 \sigma_1^2 + w_2^2 \sigma_2^2 + 2w_1 w_2 \, \text{Cov}(R_1, R_2) \qquad [7.2]$$

where $\text{Cov}(R_1, R_2)$ = the covariance between the returns on securities 1 and 2

---
1 For a more extensive treatment, see Markowitz (1959).
2 Other parameters may exist if the distribution is non-normal. In this case it is assumed that investors base decisions on expected return and standard deviation and ignore other features such as skewness.

The covariance between the returns on any pair of securities is a measure of the extent to which the returns on those securities tend to move together or 'covary'. This tendency is more commonly measured using the correlation coefficient ρ, which is found by dividing the covariance between the returns on the two securities by the standard deviations of their returns. Therefore, the correlation coefficient for securities 1 and 2 is:

$$\rho_{1,2} = \frac{\text{Cov}(R_1, R_2)}{\sigma_1 \sigma_2} \qquad [7.3]$$

The correlation coefficient is essentially a scaled measure of covariance and it is a very convenient measure because it can only have values between +1 and −1. If the correlation coefficient between the returns on two securities is +1, the returns are said to be *perfectly positively correlated*. This means that if the return on security[1] is 'high' (compared with its expected level), then the return on security[2] will, unfailingly, also be 'high' (compared with *its* expected level) to precisely the same degree. If the correlation coefficient is −1, the returns are *perfectly negatively correlated*; high (low) returns on security[1] will always be paired with low (high) returns on security[2]. A correlation coefficient of zero indicates the absence of a systematic relationship between the returns on the two securities. Using Equation 7.3 to substitute for the covariance, Equation 7.2 can be expressed as:

$$\sigma_p^2 = w_1^2 \sigma_1^2 + w_2^2 \sigma_2^2 + 2w_1 w_2 \rho_{1,2} \sigma_1 \sigma_2 \qquad [7.4]$$

As may be seen from Equation 7.4, the variance of a portfolio depends on:

(a) the composition of the portfolio—that is, the proportion of the current market value of the portfolio constituted by each security
(b) the standard deviation of the returns for each security
(c) the correlation between the returns on the securities held in the portfolio.

The effect of changing the composition of a portfolio of two securities is illustrated in Example 7.2.

EXAMPLE 7.2

An investor wishes to construct a portfolio consisting of Security 1 and Security 2. The expected returns on the two securities are $E(R_1) = 8\%$ p.a. and $E(R_2) = 12\%$ p.a. and the standard deviations are $\sigma_1 = 20\%$ p.a. and $\sigma_2 = 30\%$ p.a. The correlation coefficient between their returns is $\rho_{1,2} = -0.5$. The investor is free to choose the investment proportions w_1 and w_2, subject only to the requirements that $w_1 + w_2 = 1$ and that both w_1 and w_2 are positive.[3] There is no limit to the number of portfolios that meet these requirements, since there is no limit to the number of proportions that sum to 1. Therefore, a representative selection of values is considered for w_1: 0, 0.2, 0.4, 0.6, 0.8 and 1.

Using Equation 7.1, the expected return on a two-security portfolio is:

$$E(R_p) = w_1 E(R_1) + w_2 E(R_2)$$
$$= w_1(0.08) + w_2(0.12)$$

Using Equation 7.4, the variance of the return on a two-security portfolio is:

$$\sigma_p^2 = w_1^2 \sigma_1^2 + w_2^2 \sigma_2^2 + 2w_1 w_2 \rho_{1,2} \sigma_1 \sigma_2$$
$$= w_1^2(0.20)^2 + w_2^2(0.30)^2 + 2w_1 w_2(-0.5)(0.20)(0.30)$$
$$= 0.04 w_1^2 + 0.09 w_2^2 - 0.06 w_1 w_2$$

continued →

---

3 Negative investment proportions would indicate a 'short sale', which means that the asset is first sold and later purchased. Therefore, a short-seller benefits from price decreases.

Example 7.2 continued

The standard deviation of the portfolio returns is found by taking the square root of σ. Each pair of proportions is now considered in turn:

(a) $w_1 = 0$ and $w_2 = 1$
$$E(R_p) = (0.08)(0) + (0.12)(1)$$
$$= 0.12 \text{ or } 12\% \text{ p.a.}$$
$$\sigma_p^2 = (0.04)(0)^2 + (0.09)(1)^2 - (0.06)(0)(1)$$
$$\sigma_p^2 = 0.09$$
$$\therefore \sigma_p = 0.30 \text{ or } 30\% \text{ p.a.}$$

(b) $w_1 = 0.2$ and $w_2 = 0.8$ $E(R_p) = (0.08)(0.2) + (0.12)(0.8) = 0.112$ or 11.2% p.a.
$$\sigma_p^2 = (0.04)(0.2)^2 + (0.09)(0.8)^2 - (0.06)(0.2)(0.8)$$
$$\sigma_p^2 = 0.0496$$
$$\therefore \sigma_p = 0.2227 \text{ or } 22.27\% \text{ p.a.}$$

(c) $w_1 = 0.4$ and $w_2 = 0.6$ $E(R_p) = (0.08)(0.4) + (0.12)(0.6) = 0.104$ or 10.4% p.a.
$$\sigma_p^2 = (0.04)(0.4)^2 + (0.09)(0.6)^2 - (0.06)(0.4)(0.6)$$
$$\sigma_p^2 = 0.0244$$
$$\therefore \sigma_p = 0.1562 \text{ or } 15.62\% \text{ p.a.}$$

(d) $w_1 = 0.6$ and $w_2 = 0.4$ $E(R_p) = (0.08)(0.6) + (0.12)(0.4) = 0.096$ or 9.6% p.a.
$$\sigma_p^2 = (0.04)(0.6)^2 + (0.09)(0.4)^2 - (0.06)(0.6)(0.4)$$
$$\sigma_p^2 = 0.0144$$
$$\therefore \sigma_p = 0.12 \text{ or } 12\% \text{ p.a.}$$

(e) $w_1 = 0.8$ and $w_2 = 0.2$ $E(R_p) = (0.08)(0.8) + (0.12)(0.2) = 0.088$ or 8.8% p.a.
$$\sigma_p^2 = (0.04)(0.8)^2 + (0.09)(0.2)^2 - (0.06)(0.8)(0.2)$$
$$\sigma_p^2 = 0.0196$$
$$\therefore \sigma_p = 0.14 \text{ or } 14\% \text{ p.a.}$$

(f) $w_1 = 1.0$ and $w_2 = 0$ $E(R_p) = (0.08)(1) + (0.12)(0) = 0.08$ or 8% p.a.
$$\sigma_p^2 = (0.04)(1)^2 + (0.09)(0)^2 - (0.06)(1)(0)$$
$$\sigma_p^2 = 0.04$$
$$\therefore \sigma_p = 0.20 \text{ or } 20\% \text{ p.a.}$$

These results are summarised in Table 7.3.

TABLE 7.3

	PORTFOLIO					
	(a)	(b)	(c)	(d)	(e)	(f)
Proportion in Security 1 (w_1)	0.0000	0.2000	0.4000	0.6000	0.8000	1.0000
Proportion in Security 2 (w_2)	1.0000	0.8000	0.6000	0.4000	0.2000	0.0000
Expected return E (R_p)	0.1200	0.1120	0.1040	0.0960	0.0880	0.0800
Standard deviation σ	0.3000	0.2227	0.1562	0.1200	0.1400	0.2000

Reading across Table 7.3, the investor places more wealth in the low-return Security 1 and less in the high-return Security 2. Consequently, the expected return on the portfolio declines with each step.

The behaviour of the standard deviation is more complicated. It declines over the first four portfolios, reaching a minimum value of 0.1200 when $w_1 = 0.6$, but then rises to 0.2000 at the sixth portfolio, which consists entirely of Security 1.[4] This is an important finding as it implies that some portfolios would never be held by risk-averse investors. For example, no risk-averse investor would choose Portfolio (e) because Portfolio (d) offers both a higher expected return and a lower risk than Portfolio (e). Portfolios that offer the highest expected return at a given level of risk are referred to as 'efficient' portfolios. The data in Table 7.3 are plotted in Figure 7.6.

As can be seen from Figure 7.6, portfolios (e) and (f) are not efficient.

> **LEARNING OBJECTIVE 4**
> Explain the concept of efficient portfolios

FIGURE 7.6

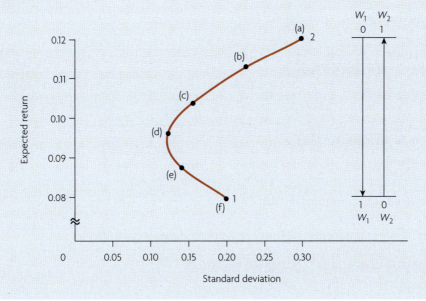

7.5.1 GAINS FROM DIVERSIFICATION

Example 7.2 shows that some portfolios enable an investor to achieve simultaneously higher expected return and lower risk; for example, compare portfolios (d) and (f) in Figure 7.6. It should be noted that Portfolio (d) consists of both securities, whereas Portfolio (f) consists of only Security 1—that is, Portfolio (d) is diversified, whereas Portfolio (f) is not. This illustrates the general principle that investors can gain from diversification.

The magnitude of the gain from diversification is closely related to the value of the correlation coefficient, $\rho_{1,2}$. To show the importance of the correlation coefficient, securities 1 and 2 are again considered. This time, however, the investment proportions are held constant at $w_1 = 0.6$ and $w_2 = 0.4$ and different values of the correlation coefficient are considered. Portfolio variance is given by:

$$\sigma_p^2 = w_1^2 \sigma_1^2 + w_2^2 \sigma_2^2 + 2w_1 w_2 \rho_{1,2} \sigma_1 \sigma_2$$
$$= (0.6)^2(0.20)^2 + (0.4)^2(0.30)^2 + 2(0.6)(0.4)\rho_{1,2}(0.20)(0.30)$$
$$= 0.0144 + 0.0144 + 0.0288\rho_{1,2}$$
$$\sigma_p = \sqrt{0.0288 + 0.0288\rho_{1,2}}$$

---

[4] The minimum value of the standard deviation actually occurs slightly beyond Portfolio (d) at proportions $w_1 = 0.6333$, and $w_2 = 0.3667$. The standard deviation for this portfolio is 0.11.92% p.a. and its expected return is 9.48% p.a.

(a) $\rho_{1,2} = +1.00$
$$\sigma_p = \sqrt{0.0288 + 0.0288\rho_{1,2}}$$
$$\sigma_p = 0.2400$$

(b) $\rho_{1,2} = +0.50$
$$\sigma_p = \sqrt{0.0288 + 0.0288\rho_{1,2}}$$
$$\sigma_p = 0.2079$$

(c) $\rho_{1,2} = 0.00$
$$\sigma_p = \sqrt{0.0288 + 0.0288\rho_{1,2}}$$
$$\sigma_p = 0.1697$$

(d) $\rho_{1,2} = -0.50$
$$\sigma_p = \sqrt{0.0288 + 0.0288\rho_{1,2}}$$
$$\sigma_p = 0.1200$$

(e) $\rho_{1,2} = -1.00$
$$\sigma_p = \sqrt{0.0288 + 0.0288\rho_{1,2}}$$
$$\sigma_p = 0$$

These results are summarised in Table 7.4.

TABLE 7.4 Effect of correlation coefficient on portfolio standard deviation

CORRELATION COEFFICIENT	STANDARD DEVIATION
$\rho_{1,2} = +1.00$	0.2400
$\rho_{1,2} = +0.50$	0.2079
$\rho_{1,2} = 0.00$	0.1697
$\rho_{1,2} = -0.50$	0.1200
$\rho_{1,2} = -1.00$	0.0000

Table 7.4 shows three important facts about portfolio construction:

(a) Combining two securities whose returns are perfectly positively correlated (that is, the correlation coefficient is +1) results only in risk averaging, and does not provide any risk reduction. In this case the portfolio standard deviation is the weighted average of the two standard deviations, which is (0.6)(0.20) + (0.4)(0.30) = 0.2400.
(b) The real advantages of diversification result from the risk reduction caused by combining securities whose returns are less than perfectly positively correlated.
(c) The degree of risk reduction increases as the correlation coefficient between the returns on the two securities decreases. The largest risk reduction available is where the returns are perfectly negatively correlated, so the two risky securities can be combined to form a portfolio that has zero risk ($\sigma_p = 0$).

By considering different investment proportions w_1 and w_2, a curve similar to that shown in Figure 7.6 can be plotted for each assumed value of the correlation coefficient. These curves are shown together in Figure 7.7.

FIGURE 7.7

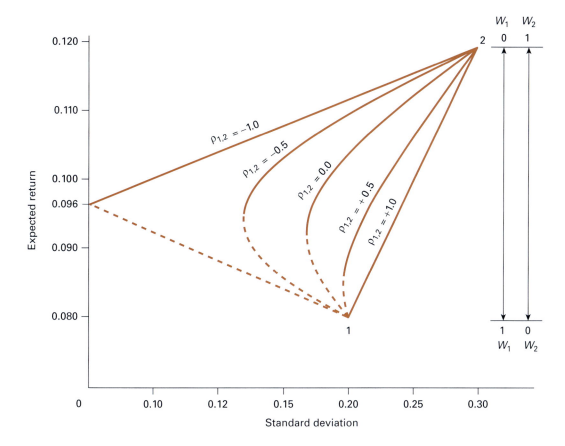

It can be seen that the lower the correlation coefficient, the higher the expected return for any given level of risk (or the lower the level of risk for any given expected return). This shows that the benefits of diversification increase as the correlation coefficient decreases, and when the correlation coefficient is −1, risk can be eliminated completely. The significance of the dotted lines in Figure 7.7 is that a risk-averse investor would never hold combinations of the two securities represented by points on the dotted lines. At any given level of correlation these combinations of the two securities are always dominated by other combinations that offer a higher expected return for the same level of risk.

7.5.2 DIVERSIFICATION WITH MULTIPLE ASSETS

While the above discussion relates to the two-security case, even stronger conclusions can be drawn for larger portfolios. To examine the relationship between the risk of a large portfolio and the riskiness of the individual assets in the portfolio, we start by considering two assets. Using Equation 7.2, the portfolio variance is:

$$\sigma_p^2 = w_1^2 \sigma_1^2 + w_2^2 \sigma_2^2 + 2w_1 w_2 \text{Cov}(R_1, R_2)$$

The variances and covariances on the right-hand side of this equation can be arranged in a matrix as follows:

	1	2
1	σ_1^2	$\text{Cov}(R_1, R_2)$
2	$\text{Cov}(R_2, R_1)$	σ_2^2

LEARNING OBJECTIVE 5

Understand the importance of covariance between returns on risky assets in determining the risk of a portfolio

With two assets the variances and covariances form a 2 × 2 matrix; three assets will result in a 3 × 3 matrix; and in general with n assets there will be an $n \times n$ matrix. Regardless of the number of assets involved, the variance–covariance matrix will always have the following properties:

(a) The matrix will contain a total of n^2 terms. Of these terms, n are the variances of the individual assets and the remaining $(n^2 - n)$ terms are the covariances between the various pairs of assets in the portfolio.
(b) The two covariance terms for each pair of assets are identical. For example, in the 2 × 2 matrix above, $Cov(R_1, R_2) = Cov(R_2, R_1)$.
(c) Since the covariance terms form identical pairs, the matrix is symmetrical about the main diagonal, which contains the n variance terms.

Remember that the significance of the variance–covariance matrix is that it can be used to calculate the portfolio variance. The portfolio variance is a weighted sum of the terms in the matrix, where the weights depend on the proportions of the various assets in the portfolio.

The first property of the matrix listed above shows that as the number of assets increases, the number of covariance terms increases much more rapidly than the number of variance terms. For a portfolio of n assets there are n variances and $(n^2 - n)$ covariances in the matrix. This suggests that as a portfolio becomes larger, the effect of the covariance terms on the risk of the portfolio will be greater than the effect of the variance terms.

To illustrate the effects of diversification and the significance of the covariance between assets, consider a portfolio of n assets. Assume that each of these assets has the same variance (σ_1^2). Also assume, initially, that the returns on these assets are independent—that is, the correlation between the returns on the assets is assumed to be zero in all cases. If we form an equally weighted portfolio of these assets, the proportion invested in each asset will be $(1/n)$. Given the assumption of zero correlation between all the asset returns, the covariance terms will all be zero, so the variance of the portfolio will depend only on the variance terms.

Since there are n variance terms and each such term is $\left(\dfrac{\sigma_1}{n}\right)^2$, the variance of the portfolio will be:

$$\sigma_p^2 = n\left(\frac{\sigma_1}{n}\right)^2 = \frac{\sigma_1^2}{n} \qquad [7.5]$$

Equation 7.5 shows that as n increases, the portfolio variance will decrease and as n becomes large, the variance of the portfolio will approach zero; that is, *if* the returns between all risky assets were independent, then it would be possible to eliminate all risk by diversification.

However, in practice, the returns between risky assets are *not* independent and the covariance between returns on most risky assets is positive. For example, the correlation coefficients between the returns on company shares are mostly in the range 0.5 to 0.7. This positive correlation reflects the fact that the returns on most risky assets are related to each other. For example, if the economy were growing strongly we would expect sales of new cars and construction of houses and other buildings to be increasing strongly. In turn, the demand for steel and other building materials would also increase. Therefore, the profits and share prices of steel and building material manufacturers should have a tendency to increase at the same time as the profits and share prices of car manufacturers and construction companies.

To reflect the relationships among the returns on individual assets, we relax the assumption that the returns between assets are independent. Instead, we now assume that the correlation between the returns on all assets in the portfolio is ρ^*. If the portfolio is again equally weighted, the portfolio variance will now be equal to the sum of the variance terms shown in Equation 7.5, plus $(n^2 - n)$

covariance terms where each such term will be $\left(\frac{1}{n}\right)^2 \rho^* \sigma_1^2$. Therefore, the variance of the portfolio will be:

$$\sigma_p^2 = \frac{\sigma_1^2}{n} + \frac{(n^2 - n)\rho^* \sigma_1^2}{n^2} \qquad [7.6]$$

$$= \frac{\sigma_1^2}{n} + \left(1 - \frac{1}{n}\right)\rho^* \sigma_1^2$$

Equation 7.6 illustrates an important result: with identical positively correlated assets, risk cannot be completely eliminated, no matter how many such assets are included in a portfolio. As n becomes large, $(1/n)$ will approach zero so the first term in Equation 7.6 will approach zero, but the second term will approach $\rho^*\sigma_1^2$; that is, the variance of the portfolio will approach $\rho^*\sigma_1^2$ which is the *covariance* between the returns on the assets in the portfolio. Thus, the positive correlation between the assets in a portfolio imposes a limit on the extent to which risk can be reduced by diversification.

In practice, the assets in a portfolio will not be identical and the correlations between the assets will differ rather than being equal as we have assumed. However, the essential results illustrated in Equation 7.6 remain the same—that is, in a diversified portfolio the variances of the individual assets will contribute little to the risk of the portfolio. Rather, the risk of a diversified portfolio will depend largely on the covariances between the returns on the assets. For example, Fama (1976, pp. 245–52) found that in an equally weighted portfolio of 50 randomly selected securities, 90 per cent of the portfolio standard deviation was due to the covariance terms.

7.5.3 SYSTEMATIC AND UNSYSTEMATIC RISK

As discussed in Section 7.5.2, if we diversify by combining risky assets in a portfolio, the risk of the portfolio returns will decrease. Diversification is most effective if the returns on the individual assets are negatively correlated, but it still works with positive correlation, provided that the correlation coefficient is less than +1. We have noted that, in practice, the correlation coefficients between the returns on company shares are mostly in the range 0.5 to 0.7. We also noted that this positive correlation reflects the fact that the returns on the shares of most companies are economically related to each other. However, the correlation is less than perfect, which reflects the fact that much of the variability in the returns on shares is due to factors that are specific to each company. For example, the price of a company's shares may change due to an exploration success, an important research discovery or a change of chief executive. Over any given period, the effects of these company-specific factors will be positive for some companies and negative for others. Therefore, when shares of different companies are combined in a portfolio, the effects of the company-specific factors will tend to offset each other, which will, of course, be reflected in reduced risk for the portfolio. In other words, part of the risk of an individual security can be eliminated by diversification and is referred to as **unsystematic risk** or **diversifiable risk**. However, no matter how much we diversify, there is always some risk that cannot be eliminated because the returns on all risky assets are related to each other. This part of the risk is referred to as **systematic risk** or **non-diversifiable risk**. These two types of risk are illustrated in Figure 7.8 on the next page.

Figure 7.8 shows that most unsystematic risk is removed by holding a portfolio of about 25 to 30 securities. In other words, the returns on a well-diversified portfolio will not be significantly affected by the events that are specific to individual companies. Rather, the returns on a well-diversified portfolio will vary due to the effects of market-wide or economy-wide factors such as changes in interest rates, changes in tax laws and variations in commodity prices. The systematic risk of a security or portfolio will depend on its sensitivity to the effects of these market-wide factors. The distinction between systematic and unsystematic risk is important when we consider the risk of individual assets in a portfolio context, which is discussed in Section 7.5.4, and the pricing of risky assets, which is discussed in Section 7.6.

LEARNING OBJECTIVE 6
Explain the distinction between systematic and unsystematic risk

unsystematic (diversifiable) risk
that component of total risk that is unique to the firm and may be eliminated by diversification

systematic (market-related or non-diversifiable) risk
that component of total risk that is due to economy-wide factors

FIGURE 7.8

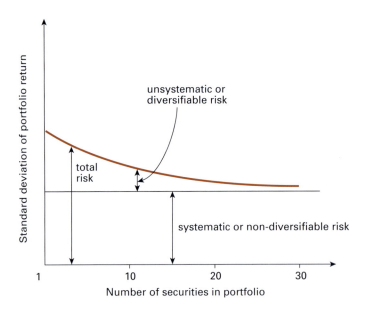

7.5.4 THE RISK OF AN INDIVIDUAL ASSET

LEARNING OBJECTIVE 7
Explain why systematic risk is important to investors

The reasoning used above can be extended to explain the factors that will determine the risk of an individual asset as a *component of a diversified portfolio*. Suppose that an investor holds a portfolio of 50 assets and is considering the addition of an extra asset to the portfolio. The investor is concerned with the effect that this extra asset will have on the standard deviation of the portfolio. The effect is determined by the portfolio proportions, the extra asset's variance and the 50 covariances between the extra asset and the assets already in the portfolio. As discussed above, the covariance terms are the dominant influence—that is, to the holder of a large portfolio the risk of an asset is largely determined by the covariance between the return on that asset and the return on the holder's existing portfolio. The variance of the return on the extra asset is of little importance. Therefore, the risk of an asset when it is held in a large portfolio is determined by the covariance between the return on the asset and the return on the portfolio. The covariance of a security i with a portfolio P is given by:

$$\text{Cov}(R_i, R_p) = \rho_{ip} \sigma_i \sigma_p \qquad [7.7]$$

The holders of large portfolios of securities can still achieve risk reduction by adding a new security to their portfolios, provided that the returns on the new security are not perfectly positively correlated with the returns on the existing portfolio. However, the incremental risk reduction due to adding a new security to a portfolio decreases as the size of the portfolio increases and, as shown in Figure 7.8, the additional benefits from diversification are very small for portfolios that include more than 30 securities (Statman 1987).

If investors are well diversified, their portfolios will be representative of the market as a whole. Therefore, the relevant measure of risk is the covariance between the return on the asset and the return on the market or $\text{Cov}(R_i, R_M)$. The covariance can then be scaled by dividing it by the variance of the return on the market that gives a convenient measure of risk, the **beta** factor, β_i, of the asset—that is, for any asset i, the beta is:

beta
measure of a security's systematic risk, describing the amount of risk contributed by the security to the market portfolio

$$\beta_i = \frac{\text{Cov}(R_i, R_M)}{\sigma_M^2}$$

Beta is a very useful measure of the risk of an asset and it will be shown in Section 7.6.2 that the capital asset pricing model proposes that the expected rates of return on risky assets are directly related to their betas.

Value Line (**www.valueline.com**) is a US website based on the Value Line Investment Survey and contains information to help determine a share's level of risk.

FINANCE IN ACTION

VALUE AT RISK (VaR)—ANOTHER WAY OF LOOKING AT RISK

Since the mid-1990s, a new measure of risk exposure has become popular. This measure was developed by the investment bank J.P. Morgan and is known as value at risk (VaR).[5] It is defined as the worst loss that is possible under normal market conditions during a given time period. It is therefore determined by what are estimated to be normal market conditions and by the time period under consideration. For a given set of market conditions, the longer the time horizon the greater is the value at risk. This measure of risk is being increasingly used by corporate treasurers, fund managers and financial institutions as a summary measure of the total risk of a portfolio.

To illustrate how value at risk is measured, suppose that $15 million is invested in shares in Gradstarts Ltd. Shares in Gradstarts have an estimated return of zero and a standard deviation of 30 per cent per annum.[6] The standard deviation on the investment of $15 million is therefore $4.5 million. Suppose also that returns follow a normal probability distribution. This means that the table of areas under the standard normal curve (see Table 5 of Appendix A page 801, or the NORMSDIST function in Microsoft Excel®) can be used to calculate the probability that the return will be greater than a specified number. Suppose also that abnormally bad market conditions are expected 5 per cent of the time. The table of areas under the standard normal curve indicates that there is a 5 per cent chance of a loss of greater than $7.4025 million per annum. This figure is equal to 1.645 multiplied by the standard deviation of $4.5 million. As shown in Figure 7.9, the value at risk of the investment in Gradstarts is therefore $7.4025 million per annum.

value at risk
worst loss possible under normal market conditions for a given time horizon

FIGURE 7.9 Value of Gradstarts Ltd

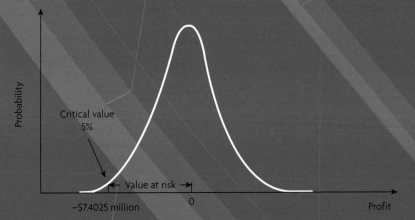

Suppose that $10 million is also invested in shares in Curzon Creative Ideas Ltd. These Curzon Creative Ideas shares have an estimated return of zero and have a standard deviation of 20 per cent per annum.

---

5 A detailed examination of value at risk is provided by Jorion (2006), while an excellent online resource for those interested in the topic is provided at www.gloriamundi.org.

6 It is usual in calculating value at risk to assume an expected return of zero. This is a reasonable assumption where the expected return is small compared with the standard deviation of the expected return.

continued ↓

FINANCE IN ACTION
continued

The standard deviation on the investment of $10 million is therefore $2 million per annum. It is again assumed that returns follow a normal probability distribution and that abnormally bad market conditions are expected 5 per cent of the time. A similar calculation to that for Gradstarts provides a value at risk of the investment in Curzon Creative Ideas of $2 million multiplied by 1.645 or $3.29 million per annum.

The benefits of diversification may be demonstrated by calculating the value at risk of a portfolio comprising a $15 million investment in Gradstarts and a $10 million investment in Curzon Creative Ideas. The weight of the investment in Gradstarts is $15 million of $25 million or 0.6 of the portfolio. The weight of the investment in Curzon Creative Ideas is 0.4. Suppose that the correlation between the returns on the shares is 0.65. Using Equation 7.4, the variance of the returns on the portfolio is:

$$\sigma_p^2 = (0.6)^2 (0.3)^2 + (0.4)^2 (0.2)^2 + 2(0.6)(0.4)(0.3)(0.2)(0.65)$$
$$= 0.05752$$

The standard deviation of portfolio returns, σ_p, is therefore 0.239 833 or 23.9833 per cent and the standard deviation on the investment is $25 million × 0.239 833 = $5.9958 million. The value at risk of the portfolio is $5.9958 multiplied by 1.645 or $9.8631 million per annum.

The total value at risk of the individual investments in Gradstarts and Curzon Creative Ideas was $7.4025 million plus $3.29 million or $10.6925 million per annum. The difference between that amount and the value at risk of the portfolio of $9.8631 million is due to the benefits of diversification. If, however, the returns on the shares of the two companies were perfectly correlated, the value at risk of the portfolio would equal the value at risk for the investment in Gradstarts plus the value at risk of the investment in Curzon Creative Ideas.

VaR is a technique that is commonly used by financial institutions to monitor their exposure to losses through adverse changes in market conditions. A pertinent example of the use of VaR is provided by the January 2004 announcement of a $360 million foreign exchange loss by the National Australia Bank. While an independent investigation by PricewaterhouseCoopers attributed most of the blame for the loss to dishonesty on the part of the currency traders involved and the lack of suitable control mechanisms in place to uncover such behaviour, the report also made some interesting comments on the bank's use of VaR. The National Australia Bank's board of directors had authorised a VaR market risk exposure limit of $80 million per day for the banking group as a whole. This limit was divided between the various divisions of the bank. The currency options desk had a VaR limit of $3.25 million per day. This limit was persistently breached over the 12-month period prior to the announcement of the $360 million loss. In relation to the implementation of a flawed VaR system the PricewaterhouseCoopers report commented that:

> … management had little confidence in the VaR numbers due to systems and data issues, and effectively ignored VaR and other limit breaches. There was no sense of urgency in resolving the VaR calculation issues which had been a problem for a period of two or more years.[7]

7.5.5 THE EFFICIENT FRONTIER

When all risky assets are considered, there is no limit to the number of portfolios that can be formed, and the expected return and standard deviation of the return can be calculated for each portfolio. The coordinates for all possible portfolios are represented by the shaded area in Figure 7.10.

Only portfolios on the curve between points A and B are relevant since all portfolios below this curve yield lower expected return and/or greater risk. The curve AB is referred to as the *efficient frontier* and it includes those portfolios that are efficient in that they offer the maximum expected return for a

---

[7] See PricewaterhouseCoopers (2004, p. 4).

FIGURE 7.10

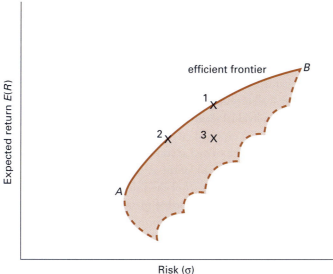

given level of risk. For example, Portfolio 1 is preferred to an internal point such as Portfolio 3 because Portfolio 1 offers a higher expected return for the same level of risk. Similarly, Portfolio 2 is preferred to Portfolio 3 because it offers the same expected return for a lower level of risk. No such 'dominance' relationship exists between efficient portfolios—that is, between portfolios whose risk–return coordinates plot on the efficient frontier.

Given risk aversion, each investor will want to hold a portfolio somewhere on the efficient frontier. Risk-averse investors will choose the portfolio that suits their preference for risk. As investors are a diverse group there is no reason to believe that they will have identical risk preferences. Each investor may therefore prefer a different point (portfolio) along the efficient frontier. For example, a conservative investor would choose a portfolio near point A while a more risk-tolerant investor would choose a portfolio near point B.

In summary, the main points established in this section are that:

(a) diversification reduces risk
(b) the effectiveness of diversification depends on the correlation or covariance between returns on the individual assets combined into a portfolio
(c) the positive correlation that exists between the returns on most risky assets imposes a limit on the degree of risk reduction that can be achieved by diversification
(d) the total risk of an asset can be divided into two parts: systematic risk that cannot be eliminated by diversification and unsystematic risk that can be eliminated by diversification
(e) the only risk that remains in a well-diversified portfolio is systematic risk
(f) for investors who diversify, the relevant measure of the risk of an individual asset is its systematic risk, which is usually measured by the beta of the asset
(g) risk-averse investors will aim to hold portfolios that are efficient in that they provide the highest expected return for a given level of risk.

The concepts discussed in this section can be extended to model the relationship between risk and expected return for individual risky assets. This extension of portfolio theory is discussed in Section 7.6 and we discuss below an alternative technique to measuring risk that focuses on the maximum dollar losses that would be expected during normal trading conditions.

7.6 THE PRICING OF RISKY ASSETS

Section 7.5 focused on investment decision making by individuals. We now shift the focus from the behaviour of individuals to the pricing of risky assets and we introduce the assumption that investors can also invest in an asset that has no default risk. The return on this risk-free asset is the risk-free interest rate, R_f. Typically, this is regarded as the interest rate on a government security, such as Treasury notes.

We continue to assume that all investors in a particular market behave according to portfolio theory, and ask: How would prices of individual securities in that market be determined? Intuitively, we would expect risky assets to provide a higher expected rate of return than the risk-free asset. In other words, the expected return on a risky asset could be viewed as consisting of the risk-free rate plus a premium for risk and this premium should be related to the risk of the asset.

However, as discussed in Section 7.5.3, part of the risk of any risky asset—unsystematic risk—can be eliminated by diversification. It seems reasonable to suggest that in a competitive market, assets should be priced so that investors are not rewarded for bearing risk that could easily be eliminated by diversification. On the other hand, some risk—systematic risk—cannot be eliminated by diversification so it is reasonable to suggest that investors will expect to be compensated for bearing that type of risk. In summary, intuition suggests that risky assets will be priced such that there is a relationship between returns and systematic risk. The remaining question is: What sort of relationship will there be between returns and systematic risk? The work of Sharpe (1964), Lintner (1965), Fama (1968) and Mossin (1969) provides an answer to this question.[8]

7.6.1 THE CAPITAL MARKET LINE

With the opportunity to borrow and lend at the risk-free rate, an investor is no longer restricted to holding a portfolio that is on the efficient frontier *AB*. Investors can now invest in combinations of risky assets and the risk-free asset in accordance with their risk preferences. This is illustrated in Figure 7.11.

FIGURE 7.11

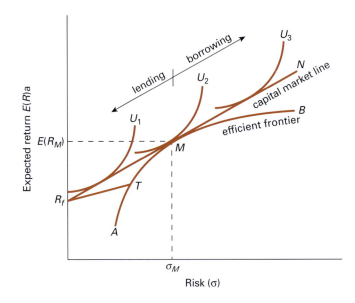

---

[8] Although we have referred to the 'pricing' of assets, much of this work deals with expected returns, rather than asset prices. However, there is a simple relationship between expected return and price in that the expected rate of return can be used to discount an asset's expected net cash flows to obtain an estimate of its current price.

The line R_fT represents portfolios that consist of an investment in a portfolio of risky assets T and an investment in the risk-free asset. Investors can achieve any combination of risk and return on the line R_fT by investing in the risk-free asset and Portfolio T. Each point on the line corresponds to different proportions of the total funds being invested in the risk-free asset and Portfolio T. However, it would not be rational for investors to hold portfolios that plot on the line R_fT, because they can achieve higher returns for any given level of risk by combining the risk-free asset with other portfolios that plot above T on the efficient frontier (AB). This approach suggests that investors will achieve the best possible return for any level of risk by holding Portfolio M rather than any other portfolio of risky assets.

The line R_fMN is tangential at the point M to the efficient frontier (AB) of portfolios of risky assets. This line represents portfolios that consist of an investment in Portfolio M and an investment in the risk-free asset. Points on the line to the left of M require a positive amount to be invested in the risk-free asset—that is, they require the investor to lend at the risk-free rate. Points on the line to the right of M require a negative amount to be invested in the risk-free asset—that is, they require the investor to borrow at the risk-free rate.

It is apparent that the line R_fMN dominates the efficient frontier AB since at any given level of risk a portfolio on the line offers an expected return at least as great as that available from the efficient frontier (curve AB). Risk-averse investors will therefore choose a portfolio on the line R_fMN—that is, some combination of the risk-free asset and Portfolio M. This is true for all risk-averse investors who conform to the assumptions of portfolio theory. The portfolios that might be chosen by three investors are shown in Figure 7.11. Having chosen to invest in Portfolio M, each investor combines this risky investment with a position in the risk-free asset. In Figure 7.11, Investor 1 will invest partly in Portfolio M and partly in the risk-free asset. Investor 2 will invest all funds in Portfolio M, while Investor 3 will borrow at the risk-free rate and invest his or her own funds, plus the borrowed funds, in Portfolio M. A fourth strategy, not shown in Figure 7.11, is to invest only in the risk-free asset. This is the least risky strategy, whereas the strategy pursued by Investor 3 is the riskiest.

If all investors in a particular market behave according to portfolio theory, *all investors hold Portfolio M as at least a part of their total portfolio*.[9] In turn, this implies that Portfolio M must consist of all risky assets. In other words, under these assumptions, a given risky asset, X, is either held by all investors as part of Portfolio M or it is not held by any investor. In the latter case, Asset X does not exist. Therefore, Portfolio M is often called the **market portfolio** because it comprises all risky assets available in the market. For example, if the total market value of all shares in Company X represents 1 per cent of the total market value of all assets, then shares in Company X will represent 1 per cent of every investor's total investment in risky assets.

The line R_fMN is called the **capital market line** because it shows all the total portfolios in which investors in the capital market might choose to invest. Since investors will choose only efficient portfolios, it follows that the market portfolio is predicted to be 'efficient' in the sense that it will provide the maximum expected return for that particular level of risk. The capital market line, therefore, shows the trade-off between expected return and risk for all efficient portfolios. The equation of the capital market line is given by:[10]

$$E(R_p) = R_f + \left(\frac{E(R_M) - R_f}{\sigma_M} \right) \sigma_p \qquad [7.8]$$

where σ_M is the standard deviation of the return on the market Portfolio M

market portfolio portfolio of all risky assets, weighted according to their market capitalisation

capital market line efficient set of all portfolios that provides the investor with the best possible investment opportunities when a risk-free asset is available. It describes the equilibrium risk–return relationship for efficient portfolios, where the expected return is a function of the risk-free interest rate, the expected market risk premium and the proportionate risk of the efficient portfolio to the risk of the market portfolio

---

9 This ignores the extreme case of investors who hold only the risk-free asset.
10 The fact that Equation 7.8 is the equation for the capital market line can be shown as follows: let Portfolio p consist of an investment in the risk-free asset and the market portfolio. The investment proportions are w_f in the risk-free asset and $w_M = 1 - w_f$ in the market portfolio. Therefore, Portfolio p is, in effect, a two-security portfolio and its expected return is given by:
$E(R_p) = w_f R_f + (1 - w_f) E(R_M)$
and the variance of its return is:
$\sigma_p^2 = w_f^2 \sigma_f^2 + (1 - w_f)^2 \sigma_M^2 + 2 w_f (1 - w_f) \rho_{fM} \sigma_f \sigma_M$

(continued)

The slope of this line is $\dfrac{E(R_M) - R_f}{\sigma_M}$, and this measures the market price of risk. It represents the additional expected return that investors would require to compensate them for incurring additional risk, as measured by the standard deviation of the portfolio.

7.6.2 THE CAPITAL ASSET PRICING MODEL (CAPM) AND THE SECURITY MARKET LINE

LEARNING OBJECTIVE 8
Explain the relationship between returns and risk proposed by the capital asset pricing model

Although the capital market line holds for efficient portfolios, it does not describe the relationship between expected return and risk for individual assets or inefficient portfolios. In equilibrium, the expected return on a risky asset (or inefficient portfolio), i, can be shown to be:[11]

$$E(R_i) = R_f + \left(\dfrac{E(R_M) - R_f}{\sigma_M^2}\right) \text{Cov}(R_i, R_M) \qquad [7.9]$$

where $E(R_i)$ = the expected return on the ith risky asset
$\text{Cov}(R_i, R_M)$ = the covariance between the returns on the ith risky asset and the market portfolio

Equation 7.9 is often called the *CAPM equation*. An equivalent version is given in Equation 7.11. The CAPM equation shows that the expected return demanded by investors on a risky asset depends on the risk-free rate of interest, the expected return on the market portfolio, the variance of the return on the market portfolio, and the *covariance* of the return on the risky asset with the return on the market portfolio.

The covariance term $\text{Cov}(R_i, R_M)$ is the only explanatory factor in the CAPM equation specific to asset i. The other explanatory factors (R_f, $E(R_M)$ and σ_M^2) are the same, regardless of which asset i is being considered. Therefore, according to the CAPM equation, if two assets have different expected returns, this is because they have different covariances with the market portfolio. In other words, the measure of risk relevant to pricing a risky asset is $\text{Cov}(R_i, R_M)$, the covariance of its returns with returns on the market portfolio, as this measures the *contribution* of the risky asset to the riskiness of an efficient portfolio. In contrast, for the efficient portfolio itself the standard deviation of the portfolio's return is the relevant measure of risk (see Figure 7.11).

As discussed in Section 7.5.4, the measure of risk for an investment in a risky asset i is often referred to as its beta factor, β_i, where:

$$\beta_i = \dfrac{\text{Cov}(R_i, R_M)}{\sigma_M^2} \qquad [7.10]$$

By definition, $\sigma_f^2 = 0$ so the variance reduces to:

$\sigma_p^2 = (1 - w_f)^2 \sigma_M^2$

Therefore:

$\sigma_p = (1 - w_f) \sigma_M$

Since the expected return and standard deviation of Portfolio p are linear functions of w_f, it follows that $R_f M$ in Figure 7.11 is a straight line. This result is not specific to portfolios consisting of the risk-free asset and Portfolio M: rather it applies to *all* portfolios that include the risk-free asset.

The equation for a straight line can be expressed as $y = mx + c$ where m is the slope of the line and c is the intercept on the y axis. Referring to Figure 7.11, it can be seen that:

$c = R_f$ and $m = \dfrac{E(R_M - R_f)}{\sigma_M}$

Therefore, the equation for the line $r_f MN$ is Equation 7.8.

11 This is a purely mathematical problem. For a derivation see Levy and Sarnat (1990) or Brailsford and Faff (1993).

Because $\text{Cov}(R_i, R_M)$ is the risk of an asset held *as part of* the market portfolio, while σ_M^2 is the risk (in terms of variance) of the market portfolio, it follows that β_i measures the risk of i relative to the risk of the market as a whole. Using beta as the measure of risk, the CAPM equation can be rewritten:

$$E(R_i) = R_f + \beta_i[E(R_M) - R_f] \qquad [7.11]$$

When graphed, Equation 7.11 is called the **security market line** and is illustrated in Figure 7.12.

security market line graphical representation of the capital asset pricing model

FIGURE 7.12 Security market line

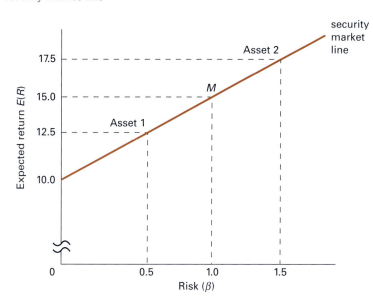

The significance of the security market line is that in equilibrium each risky asset should be priced so that it plots exactly on the line. Equation 7.11 shows that according to the capital asset pricing model, the expected return on a risky asset consists of two components: the risk-free rate of interest plus a premium for risk. The risk premium for each asset depends on the asset's beta and on the market risk premium $[E(R_M) - R_f]$. The betas of individual assets will be distributed around the beta value of the market portfolio, which is 1.[12] A risky asset with a beta value greater than 1 (that is, higher risk) will have an expected return greater than $E(R_M)$, while the expected return on a risky asset with a beta value of less than 1 (that is, lower risk) will be less than $E(R_M)$. Assuming that the risk-free rate of interest is 10 per cent and the market risk premium $[E(R_M) - R_f]$ is 5 per cent, the expected return on risky Asset 1 with a beta value of 0.5 will be 12.5 per cent. The expected return on risky Asset 2 with a beta value of 1.5 will be 17.5 per cent.

The capital asset pricing model applies to individual assets and to portfolios. The beta factor for a portfolio p is simply:

$$\beta_p = \frac{\text{Cov}(R_p, R_M)}{\sigma_M^2} \qquad [7.12]$$

where $\text{Cov}(R_p, R_M)$ = the covariance between the returns on portfolio p and the market portfolio.

---

12 Since
$$\beta_i = \frac{\text{Cov}(R_i, R_M)}{\sigma_M^2}$$
we have
$$\beta_M = \frac{\text{Cov}(R_M, R_M)}{\sigma_M^2} = \frac{\sigma_M^2}{\sigma_M^2} = 1$$

Equation 7.12 is simply Equation 7.10 rewritten in terms of a portfolio p, instead of a particular asset i. Fortunately, there is a simple relationship between a portfolio's beta (β_p) and the betas of the individual assets that make up the portfolio. This relationship is:

$$\beta_p = \sum_{i=1}^{n} w_i \beta_i \qquad [7.13]$$

where n = the number of assets in the portfolio

w_i = the proportion of the current market value of portfolio p constituted by the ith asset

Equation 7.13 states that the beta factor for a portfolio is simply a weighted average of the betas of the assets in the portfolio.[13] One useful application of Equation 7.13 is to guide investors in choosing the investment proportions w_i to achieve some target portfolio *beta*, β_p^*. An important special case is to construct such a portfolio using only the market portfolio ($\beta = 1$) and a position in the risk-free asset ($\beta = 0$). In this case, investors place a proportion w_M of their total funds in the market portfolio, and a proportion $w_f = (1 - w_M)$ in the risk-free asset. Using Equation 7.13, the target beta is given by:

$$\beta_p^* = w_f \beta_f + w_M \beta_M$$

Substituting $\beta_f = 0$ and $\beta_M = 1$ gives:

$$w_M = \beta_p^*$$
and $$w_f = 1 - \beta_p^*$$

For example, if $\beta_p^* = 0.75$, investors should invest 75 per cent of their funds in the market portfolio and lend 25 per cent of their funds at the risk-free rate. If $\beta_p^* = 1.3$, investors should borrow an amount equal to 30 per cent of their own investment funds and invest the total amount (130 per cent) in the market portfolio.

7.6.3 IMPLEMENTATION OF THE CAPM

Use of the CAPM requires estimation of the risk-free interest rate, R_f, the systematic risk of equity, β_e, and the market risk premium, $E(R_M) - R_f$. Each of these variables is discussed in turn.

The risk-free interest rate (R_f)

The assets closest to being risk free are government debt securities, so interest rates on these securities are normally used as a measure of the risk-free rate. However, as discussed in Section 4.6.1, unless the term structure of interest rates is flat, the various government securities will offer different interest rates. The appropriate risk-free rate is the current yield on a government security whose term to maturity matches the life of the proposed projects to be undertaken by the company. Since these activities undertaken by the company typically provide returns over many years, the rate on long-term securities is generally used.

---

13 Our discussion has omitted the steps between Equations 7.12 and 7.13. For the interested reader, these steps are as follows. Since:

$$R_p = \sum_{i=1}^{n} w_i R_i$$

it follows that:

$$Cov(R_p, R_M) = Cov\left(\sum_{i=1}^{n} w_i R_i, R_M\right)$$
$$= \sum_{i=1}^{n} w_i Cov(R_i, R_M)$$

Substituting in Equation 7.12:

$$\beta_i = \frac{\sum_{i=1}^{n} w_i Cov(R_i, R_M)}{\sigma_M^2}$$
$$= \sum_{i=1}^{n} w_i \beta_i$$

The share's systematic risk (β_e)

The betas of securities are usually estimated by applying regression analysis to estimate the following equation from time series data:

$$R_{it} = \alpha_i + \beta_i R_M + e_{it} \quad [7.14]$$

where α_i = a constant, specific to asset i

e_{it} = an error term

Equation 7.14 is generally called the **market model**. Its relationship to the security market line can be readily seen by rewriting Equation 7.11 as follows:

$$E(R_i) = R_f + \beta_i E(R_M) - \beta_i R_f$$
$$\therefore E(R_i) = R_f(1 - \beta_i) + \beta_i E(R_M) \quad [7.15]$$

market model
time series regression of an asset's returns

Therefore, the market model is a counterpart (or analogue) of Equation 7.15. The magnitude of the betas that result from using this model when it is applied to returns on shares is illustrated in Table 7.5, which contains a sample of betas for the shares of selected listed firms. The values are calculated using ordinary least squares (OLS) regression.

TABLE 7.5 Betas of selected Australian listed firms calculated using daily share price and index data for the period July 2007–June 2010

NAME OF FIRM	MAIN INDUSTRIAL ACTIVITY	BETA
ANZ Banking Group	Banking	1.18
Amcor	Packaging	0.62
BHP Billiton	Minerals exploration, production and processing	1.41
Qantas Airways	Airline transportation	0.96
Telstra Corporation	Telecommunication services	0.40
Toll Holdings	Transportation	0.87
Wesfarmers	Diversified operations across multiple industries	0.97
Woolworths	Food and staples retailing	0.61

The market model, as specified in Equation 7.14, is often used to obtain an estimate of ex-post systematic risk. To use the market model, it is necessary to obtain time series data on the rates of return on the share and on the market portfolio—that is, a series of observations for both R_{it} and R_{Mt} is needed. However, when using the market model, choices must be made about two factors. First, the model may be estimated over periods of different length. For example, data for the past 1, 2, 3 or more years may be used. Five years of data are commonly used, but the choice is somewhat arbitrary. Second, the returns used in the market model may be calculated over periods of different length. For example, daily, weekly, monthly, quarterly or yearly returns may be used. Again this choice is subject to a considerable degree of judgement.

From a statistical perspective, it is generally better to have more rather than fewer observations, because using more observations generally lead to greater statistical confidence. However, the greater the number of years of data that are used, the more likely it is that the firm's riskiness will have changed. This fact highlights a fundamental problem of using the market model. The market model provides a measure of how risky a firm's equity was in the past. What we are seeking to obtain is an estimate of future risk. Therefore, the choice of both the number of years of data and the length of the period over which returns are calculated involves a trade-off between the desire to have many observations and the need to have recent and consequently more relevant data.[14]

The market risk premium $[E(R_M) - R_f]$

The market portfolio specified in the CAPM consists of every risky asset in existence. Consequently, it is impossible in practice to calculate its expected rate of return and hence impossible to also calculate the market risk premium. Instead, a share market index is generally used as a substitute for the market portfolio. As the rate of return on a share market index is highly variable from year to year, it is usual to calculate the average return on the index over a relatively long period. Suppose that the average rate of return on a share market index such as the All-Ordinaries Accumulation Index over the past 10 years was 18.5 per cent per annum. If this rate were used as the estimate of $E(R_M)$ and today's risk-free rate is 8.5 per cent, the market risk premium $[E(R_M) - R_f]$ would be 10 per cent.

A problem with using this approach is that the estimate of R_f reflects the market's current expectations of the future, whereas $E(R_M)$ is an average of past returns. In other words, the two values may not match, and some unacceptable estimates may result. For example, $[E(R_M) - R_f]$ estimated in this way may be negative if the rate of inflation expected now, which should be reflected in R_f, is greater than the realised rate of inflation during the period used to estimate $E(R_M)$.

A better approach is to estimate the market risk premium directly, over a relatively long period. For example, Ibbotson and Goetzmann (2005) compare the returns on equities with the returns on bonds in the US between 1792 and 1925 and report an average difference of approximately 3.8 per cent per annum. Similarly, Dimson, Marsh and Staunton (2003) found over the 103 years from 1900 to 2002 that the long-term average premium in the US was 7.2 per cent per annum. They also examined 15 other countries over this time period, finding that the country with the lowest premium was Denmark at 3.8 per cent per annum, and the country with the highest premium was Italy at 10.3 per cent per annum. Brailsford, Handley and Maheswaran (2008) estimate that in Australia the premium on the market portfolio over the 123 years from 1883 to 2005 was approximately 6.2 per cent per annum. Using a shorter time period during which the quality of the data is higher, they estimate that the premium from 1958 to 2005 was approximately 6.3 per cent per annum.

However, estimating the market risk premium directly also has some problems. Ritter (2002) uses the example of Japan at the end of 1989 to illustrate that historical estimates can result in nonsensical numbers. He notes that estimating the market risk premium at the end of 1989 using historical data starting when the Japanese stock market reopened after World War II would have provided a market risk premium of over 10 per cent per annum. The Japanese economy was booming, corporate profits were high and average price–earnings (P–E) ratios were over 60. It was considered that the cost of equity for Japanese firms was low. However, it is not possible for the cost of equity to be low and the market risk premium to be high. Of course, it is possible for the *historical* market risk premium to be high and the *expected* market risk premium (and therefore the expected cost of equity capital) to be low.

In an important theoretical paper, Mehra and Prescott (1985) showed that a long-term risk premium such as that found in the US, Canada, the UK and Australia cannot be explained by standard models of risk and return. This finding has led to arguments that historical measures of the risk premium are subject to errors in their measurement. For example, Jorion and Goetzmann (1999) argue that estimates of the market risk premium based solely on data obtained from the US will be biased upwards simply as a result of the outperformance of the US market relative to other equity markets over the twentieth century. Others, such as Heaton and Lucas (2000), argue that increased opportunities for portfolio diversification mean that the market risk premium has fallen.

---

14 For a discussion of the issues associated with calculating systematic risk from historical data, see Brailsford, Faff and Oliver (1997).

These concerns have led to new techniques being employed to estimate the market risk premium. Fama and French (2002), among others, use the dividend growth model and conclude that the market risk premium is now of the order of 1 per cent per annum. Claus and Thomas (2001) use forecasts by security analysts and conclude that the market risk premium is approximately 3 per cent per annum. Duke University and CFO magazine have conducted a quarterly survey of chief financial officers since 1996 (see www.cfosurvey.org). The average estimated risk premium for the US over that time has been approximately 4 per cent per annum. For the third quarter of 2010, when asked how much they expect returns in the equity market in the US to exceed the returns on government bonds over the next 10 years, the average response was 3.2 per cent per annum. In summary, the disparity of estimates of the market risk premium is considerable, ranging from 1 to in excess of 6 per cent per annum.

WWW

7.6.4 RISK, RETURN AND THE CAPM

The distinction between systematic and unsystematic risk is important in explaining why the CAPM should represent the risk–return relationship for assets such as shares. This issue was discussed in Section 7.5.3 but is reiterated here because of its importance in understanding the CAPM. The returns on a firm's shares can vary for many reasons: for example, interest rates may change, or the firm may develop a new product, attract important new customers or change its chief executive. These factors can be divided into two categories: those related only to an individual firm (firm-specific factors) and those that affect all firms (market-wide factors). As the shares of different firms are combined in a portfolio, the effects of the firm-specific factors will tend to cancel each other out; this is how diversification reduces risk. However, the effects of the market-wide factors will remain, no matter how many different shares are included in the portfolio. Therefore, systematic risk reflects the influence of market-wide factors, while unsystematic risk reflects the influence of firm-specific factors.

Because unsystematic risk can be eliminated by diversification, the capital market will not reward investors for bearing this type of risk. The capital market will only reward investors for bearing risk that cannot be eliminated by diversification—that is, the risk inherent in the market portfolio. There are cases when, with hindsight, we can identify investors who have reaped large rewards from taking on unsystematic risk. These cases do not imply that the CAPM is invalid: the model simply says that such rewards cannot be *expected* in a competitive market. The reward for bearing systematic risk is a higher expected return and, according to the CAPM, there is a simple linear relationship between expected return and systematic risk as measured by beta.

7.7 ADDITIONAL FACTORS THAT EXPLAIN RETURNS

In 1977 Richard Roll published an important article that pointed out that while the CAPM has strong theoretical foundations, there is a range of difficulties that researchers face in testing it empirically. For example, in testing for a positive relationship between an asset's beta and realised returns, a researcher first needs to measure the correlation between the asset's returns and the returns on the market portfolio. The market portfolio theoretically consists of *all* assets in existence and is therefore unobservable in practice—implying that ultimately the CAPM itself is untestable.

LEARNING OBJECTIVE 9
Understand the relationship between the capital asset pricing model and models that include additional factors

Aside from the problems associated with testing for a relationship between estimates of beta and realised returns, voluminous empirical research has shown that there are other factors that also explain returns. These factors include a company's dividend yield, its price–earnings (P–R) ratio, its size (as measured by the market value of its shares), and the ratio of the book value of its equity to the market value of its equity. This last ratio is often called the company's book-to-market ratio. In a detailed study, Fama and French (1992) show that the size and book-to-market ratio were dominant and that dividend yield and the price–earnings ratio were not useful in explaining returns after allowing for these more dominant factors.

In another important paper, Fama and French (1993) tested the following three-factor model of expected returns:

$$E(R_{it}) - R_{ft} = \beta_{iM}[E(R_{Mt}) - R_{ft}] + \beta_{iS} E(SMB_t) + \beta_{iH} E(HML_t) \qquad [7.16]$$

LEARNING OBJECTIVE 10
Explain the development of models that include additional factors

In Equation 7.16, the first factor is the market risk premium, which is the basis of the CAPM discussed earlier in this chapter. The next factor, SMB, refers to the difference between the returns of a diversified portfolio of small and large firms, while HML reflects the differences between the returns of a diversified portfolio of firms with high versus low book-to-market values. β_{iM}, β_{iS} and β_{iH} are the risk parameters reflecting the sensitivity of the asset to the three sources of risk. All three factors were found to have strong explanatory power. O'Brien, Brailsford and Gaunt (2008) found that in Australia, over the period 1982 to 2006, all three factors provided strong explanatory power.

It is possible that both the size and book-to-market ratio factors might be explicable by risk. For example, Fama and French (1996) argue that smaller companies are more likely to default than larger companies. Further, they argue that this risk is likely to be systematic in that small companies as a group are more exposed to default during economic downturns. As a result, investors in small companies will require a risk premium. Similarly, Zhang (2005) argues that companies with high book-to-market ratios will on average have higher levels of physical capacity. Much of this physical capacity will represent excess capacity during economic downturns and therefore expose such companies to increased risk.

However, as discussed in detail in Chapter 16, the relationship between these additional factors and returns may not be due to risk. Further, Carhart (1997) added a fourth factor to the three described in Equation 7.16 to explain returns earned by mutual funds. In an earlier paper Jegadeesh and Titman (1993), using US data from 1963 to 1989, identified better-performing shares (the winners) and poorer-performing shares (the losers) over a period of 6 months. They then tracked the performance of the shares over the following 6 months. On average, the biggest winners outperformed the biggest losers by 10 per cent per annum. When Carhart added this momentum effect to the three-factor model, he found that it too explained returns. Unlike the size and book-to-market ratio factors, it is difficult to construct a simple risk-based explanation for this factor.

While the CAPM is clearly an incomplete explanation of the relationship between risk and returns, it is important to note that it is still widely applied. This point is perhaps best demonstrated by the Coleman, Maheswaran and Pinder (2010) survey of the financial practices adopted by senior financial managers in Australia. Financial managers employ asset pricing models to estimate the discount rate used in project evaluation techniques such as the net present value approach. Coleman, Maheswaran and Pinder reported that more than twice as many respondents used the traditional single-factor CAPM compared with models that used additional factors.

7.8 PORTFOLIO PERFORMANCE APPRAISAL

LEARNING OBJECTIVE 11
Distinguish between alternative methods of appraising the performance of an investment portfolio

A fundamental issue that faces investors is how to measure the performance of their investment portfolio. To illustrate the problem, assume that an investor observes that during the past 12 months, his or her portfolio has generated a return of 15 per cent. Is this a good, bad or indifferent result? The answer to that question depends, of course, on the *expected* return of the portfolio given the portfolio's risk. That is, in order to answer the question, we need a measure of the risk of the investor's portfolio, and then compare its performance with the performance of a benchmark portfolio of similar risk. However, even after accounting for the specific risk of the portfolio, the performance of a portfolio may differ from that of the benchmark for four reasons:

- *Asset allocation.* Investors must decide how much of their wealth should be allocated between alternative categories of assets such as corporate bonds, government bonds, domestic shares, international shares and property. This decision will ultimately affect the performance of the portfolio because in any given period a particular asset class may outperform other asset classes on a risk-adjusted basis.

- *Market timing*. In establishing and administering a portfolio, investors need to make decisions about when to buy and sell the assets held in a portfolio. For example, investors might choose to move out of domestic shares and into corporate bonds or alternatively sell the shares of companies that operate in the telecommunication industry and invest these funds in the shares of companies operating in the retail industry. Clearly, the performance of a portfolio will be affected by an investor's success in selling assets before their prices fall and buying assets before their prices rise.
- *Security selection*. Having made a decision about the desired mix of different asset classes within a portfolio, and when that desired mix should be implemented, investors must then choose between many different individual assets within each class. For example, having determined that they wish to hold half of their portfolio in domestic shares, investors must then decide which of the more than 2000 shares listed on the Australian Securities Exchange they should buy. The art of security selection requires the investors to identify those individual assets that they believe are currently underpriced by the market and hence whose values are expected to rise over the holding period. Similarly, if investors believe that any of the assets held in the portfolio are currently overpriced, they would sell these assets so as to avoid any future losses associated with a reduction in their market value.
- *Random influences*. Ultimately, investing is an uncertain activity and in any given period the performance of a portfolio may not reflect the skills of the investor who makes the investment decisions. That is, good decisions might yield poor outcomes and poor decisions might yield good outcomes in what we would label as 'bad luck' or 'good luck', respectively. Over enough time, though, we would expect the influence of good luck and bad luck to average out.

7.8.1 ALTERNATIVE MEASURES OF PORTFOLIO PERFORMANCE

We now consider four commonly used ways of measuring the performance of a portfolio. Each of these measures has a different approach to trying to determine the 'expected' performance of the benchmark portfolio in order to determine whether the portfolio has met, exceeded or failed to meet expectations.

Simple benchmark index

This is probably the most commonly used approach to appraising the performance of a portfolio and involves a simple comparison between the portfolio's return and the return on a benchmark index that has (or is assumed to have) similar risk to the portfolio being measured. For example, a well-diversified portfolio of domestic shares might be benchmarked against the S&P/ASX 200 Index, which measures the performance of the shares in the 200 largest companies listed on the Australian Securities Exchange.

The advantages associated with using this approach to performance appraisal are that it is easy to implement and to understand. The main problem with this approach is that it implies that the risk of the portfolio is identical to the risk of the benchmark index, whereas, with the exception of so-called passive funds, which are specifically established to mimic (or track) the performance of benchmark indices, this will rarely be the case.

The Sharpe ratio

The Sharpe ratio, developed by William Sharpe[15], is a measure of the excess return of the portfolio per unit of total risk and is calculated using the following formula:

$$S = \frac{\overline{r_p} - \overline{r_f}}{\sigma_p} \qquad [7.17]$$

---

15 See Sharpe (1966).

where $\bar{r}_p$ is the average return achieved on the portfolio over the time period, $\bar{r}_f$ is the average risk-free rate of return over the same time period and σ_p is the standard deviation of the returns on the portfolio over the time period and is a measure of the total risk of the portfolio. If the Sharpe ratio of the investor's portfolio exceeds the Sharpe ratio of the market portfolio, then the investor's portfolio has generated a greater excess return per unit of total risk and hence is regarded as exhibiting superior performance to the market portfolio. Conversely, if the portfolio's Sharpe ratio is less than that of the market portfolio then the portfolio has generated less excess return per unit of total risk than the market portfolio and the portfolio can be seen as having underperformed that benchmark.

The rationale behind the use of the Sharpe ratio is best demonstrated by considering the ratio's links with the risk–return trade-off described by the capital market line discussed in section 7.6.1. Consider Figure 7.13, which illustrates the risk and return profile for a superannuation fund's portfolio relative to the market portfolio.

FIGURE 7.13 The Sharpe ratio

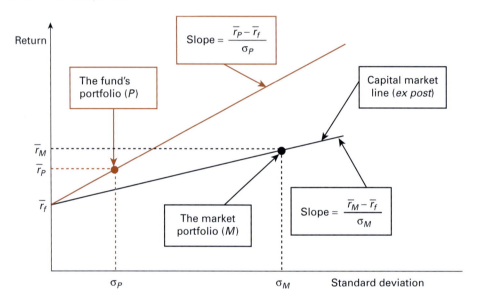

Note from Figure 7.13 that the superannuation fund's portfolio has generated a lower rate of return than the market portfolio but has also generated a lower level of total risk. That is, while $\bar{r}_p$ is less than $\bar{r}_M$, σ_p is also less than σ_M. The key point, however, is that the realised excess return *per unit of risk* is higher for the fund's portfolio compared with the market portfolio and hence the fund's portfolio is regarded as having exhibited superior performance. This is illustrated in Figure 7.13 by the fund's portfolio plotting *above* the capital market line. If the fund's portfolio had generated a lower excess return per unit of risk than the market portfolio, then it would have plotted below the capital market line and this would have implied that the portfolio had underperformed the benchmark on a total risk-adjusted basis.

Note that the Sharpe ratio assumes that in determining the risk-adjusted performance of a portfolio the appropriate measure of risk is total risk. Following on from our discussion earlier in the chapter, it is clear that total risk is an appropriate measure only when we are dealing with well-diversified portfolios rather than individual assets or undiversified portfolios.

The Treynor ratio

The Treynor ratio, named after Jack Treynor[16], is a measure that is related to the Sharpe ratio of performance measurement, in that it measures excess returns per unit of risk, but differs in that it defines risk as non-diversifiable (or systematic) risk instead of total risk. It can be calculated using the following formula:

$$T = \frac{\bar{r}_p - \bar{r}_f}{\beta_p} \qquad [7.18]$$

where σ_p^2 and $\bar{r}_f$ are the returns on the portfolio and the risk-free asset as defined earlier, and β_p is an estimate of the systematic risk of the portfolio over the period in which the returns were generated, as measured by beta and defined in Section 7.6.2. As with the Sharpe ratio, insights into the rationale behind the use of the Treynor ratio are provided by considering the link between risk and expected return—but this time, instead of considering the trade-off for efficient portfolios implied by the capital market line, we turn instead to the security market line, which applies to individual assets and inefficient portfolios. In Figure 7.14 we compare the ex-post systematic risk and excess returns of a superannuation fund relative to the market portfolio over the same period of time.

FIGURE 7.14 The Treynor ratio

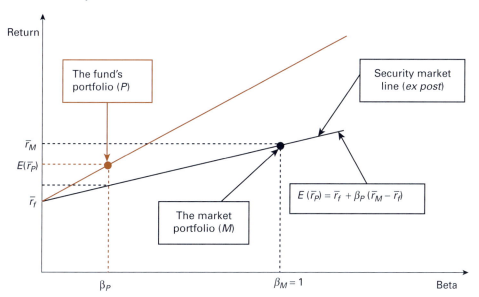

Recall that the security market line is simply the graphical representation of the CAPM. The slope of the security market line describes the extra return, in excess of the risk-free rate, that is expected for each additional unit of systematic risk (as measured by beta) and is what we have previously defined as the market risk premium $(\bar{r}_M - \bar{r}_f)$. The slope of the line that intersects the realised systematic risk and return of the fund's portfolio is in turn the Treynor ratio. Hence, the decision rule used in assessing the performance of a portfolio using this technique requires a comparison of the Treynor ratio calculated for the portfolio over a specified interval with the market risk premium generated over that same interval. Example 7.3 illustrates the three approaches to portfolio appraisal discussed above.

---

16 See Treynor (1966).

EXAMPLE 7.3

An investor holds a portfolio that consists of shares in 15 different companies and wants to assess the performance using a simple benchmark index as well as calculating the portfolio's Sharpe and Treynor ratios. She estimates the following parameters for the financial year ended 30 June 2011.

TABLE 7.6

	REALISED RETURN (% p. a.)	STANDARD DEVIATION OF RETURNS (σ) (% p.a.)	SYSTEMATIC RISK ESTIMATE (β)
Portfolio	13	30	1.2
S&P/ASX 200 share price index	11	20	1.0
Government bonds	5	0	0

Based solely on the benchmark index approach, the portfolio appears to have performed well in that it has generated an additional 2 per cent return above the proxy for the market (S&P/ASX 200). As discussed earlier, however, this assessment fails to account for differences in the risk profiles of the two portfolios.

The Sharpe ratio is estimated using Equation 7.17 for both the investor's portfolio and the ASX 200 as follows:

$$S = \frac{\bar{r}_p - \bar{r}_f}{\sigma_p}$$

$$S_{Portfolio} = \frac{13 - 5}{30} = 0.27$$

$$S_{ASX\ 200} = \frac{11 - 5}{20} = 0.30$$

As the Sharpe ratio for the portfolio is less than that of the S&P/ASX 200, the investor concludes that the portfolio has underperformed the market on a risk-adjusted basis. A possible problem with this conclusion is that, as described above, the Sharpe ratio assumes that the relevant measure of risk for the investor is total risk, as measured by the standard deviation of returns. This is not the case where, for example, the portfolio of shares represents only one component of the investor's overall set of assets.

The Treynor ratios for the portfolio and for the ASX 200 are measured as follows:

$$T = \frac{\bar{r}_p - \bar{r}_f}{\beta_p}$$

$$T_{Portfolio} = \frac{13 - 5}{1.2} = 6.67$$

$$T_{ASX\ 200} = \frac{11 - 5}{1.0} = 6$$

Note that the Treynor ratio for the S&P/ASX 200 is simply equal to the market risk premium of 6 per cent. As the Treynor ratio of the portfolio exceeds this amount the investor concludes that the portfolio has outperformed the market on a systematic risk-adjusted basis. We can reconcile this result with the seemingly contrary results provided by the Sharpe ratio by acknowledging that some of the portfolio risk that is accounted for in the Sharpe ratio may actually be diversified away once we account for the other assets in the investor's portfolio. Therefore, in this case, the Treynor ratio provides the more suitable assessment of the performance of the portfolio relative to the market generally, as it considers only that risk that cannot be eliminated by diversification.

Jensen's alpha

Jensen's alpha is a measure that was a pioneered by Michael Jensen[17] and that relies on a multi-period analysis of the performance of an investment portfolio relative to some proxy for the market generally. Recall that the CAPM suggests that the relationship between systematic risk and return is fully described by the following equation:

$$E(R_i) = R_f + \beta_i[E(R_M) - R_f]$$

The CAPM is an *ex-ante* single-period model, in the sense that it is concerned with the returns that might be *expected* over the next time period. Its conclusion is relatively simple: the return in excess of the risk-free rate that we expect any asset i to generate is determined only by the level of systematic risk reflected in the asset's β. We compute Jensen's alpha by implementing an *ex-post* multi-period regression analysis of the returns on the portfolio and the returns on the market and ask the question: Is there any evidence of systematic abnormal return performance that cannot be explained by the portfolio's systematic risk? The regression equation estimated is as follows:

$$r_{P,t} - r_{f,t} = \alpha_P + \beta_P\left[r_{M,t} - r_{f,t}\right] + e_t \qquad [7.19]$$

where $r_{P,t}$, $r_{f,t}$ and $r_{M,t}$ are the returns from the portfolio, the risk-free asset and the proxy for the market portfolio that have been observed in period t. β_P is an estimate of the portfolio's beta over the entire period in which returns were collected. α_P is an estimate of Jensen's alpha and reflects the incremental performance of the portfolio after accounting for the variation in portfolio returns that can be explained by market-wide returns.

If α_P is positive, and statistically significant, then this is an indication that the portfolio has outperformed the market, on a risk-adjusted basis, and may be interpreted as evidence of a portfolio manager's skill in managing the portfolio. Conversely, a statistically significant negative estimate of α_P might be interpreted as evidence that the portfolio manager's actions in managing the portfolio are actually destroying value!

There are many other techniques that have been developed by academics and practitioners to try to assess the performance of investment portfolios and each technique brings with it both advantages and disadvantages over the alternative approaches.[18] While much of the preceding discussion has been concerned with measuring the relative performance of a portfolio, another issue facing managers and investors is how much of the performance of a portfolio may be attributed to the different decisions made by the investment manager. Specifically, as described at the beginning of Section 7.8, an investor may be concerned with how the performance has been affected by the manager's decisions with respect to asset allocation, market timing and security selection as well as the possible interactions between each of these decisions.

Connect Plus features a case study illustrating topics covered in this chapter.
Ask your lecturer or tutor for your course's unique URL.

SUMMARY

This chapter discussed two main issues. The first, portfolio theory, concerns the approach that can be used by risk-averse investors to secure the best trade-off between risk and return. Second, the chapter dealt with the pricing of risky assets, which involves the relationship between risk and return in the market for risky assets.

---

17 See Jensen (1968 & 1969).
18 See Chapter 24 of Bodie, Kane and Marcus (2011) for an excellent review of some of these alternative techniques, and a comprehensive description of other issues faced when assessing portfolio performance.

→ The essential message of portfolio theory is that diversification reduces risk. It is also shown that the effectiveness of diversification depends on the correlation or covariance between returns on the individual assets combined into a portfolio. The gains from diversification are largest when there is negative correlation between asset returns, but they still exist when there is positive correlation between asset returns, provided that the correlation is less than perfect. In practice, the positive correlation that exists between the returns on most risky assets imposes a limit on the degree of risk reduction that can be achieved by diversification.

→ The total risk of an asset can be divided into two parts: systematic risk that *cannot* be eliminated by diversification, and unsystematic risk that *can* be eliminated by diversification. It follows that the only risk that remains in a well-diversified portfolio is systematic risk.

- The risk of a well-diversified portfolio can be measured by the standard deviation of portfolio returns. However, analysis of the factors that contribute to this standard deviation shows that, for investors who diversify, the relevant measure of risk for an individual asset is its systematic risk.

- Systematic risk depends on the covariance between the returns on the asset and returns on the market portfolio, which contains all risky assets. The systematic risk of an asset is usually measured by the asset's beta factor, which measures the risk of the asset relative to the risk of the market as a whole. Risk-averse investors will aim to hold portfolios that are efficient in that they provide the highest expected return for a given level of risk. The set of efficient portfolios forms the efficient frontier, and in a market where only risky assets are available, each investor will aim to hold a portfolio somewhere on the efficient frontier.

→ Introduction of a risk-free asset allows the analysis to be extended to model the relationship between risk and expected return for individual risky assets. The main result is the CAPM, which proposes that there is a linear relationship between the expected rate of return on an asset and its risk as measured by its beta factor.

→ Alternative asset pricing models propose that expected returns are linearly related to multiple factors rather than the single market factor proposed by the CAPM.

→ Assessment of the performance of an investment portfolio requires the specification of the 'expected' performance of a benchmark portfolio.

WWW An excellent site with a wealth of information relating to this topic is www.wsharpe.com. Professor William Sharpe's work was recognised with a Nobel Prize in 1990. Financial advisory information can also be found at www.fido.asic.gov.au.

KEY TERMS

beta 184
capital market line 189
market model 193
market portfolio 189
portfolio 175
risk-averse investor 172
risk-neutral investor 173
risk-seeking investor 173
security market line 191
standard deviation 170
systematic (market-related or non-diversifiable) risk 183
unsystematic (diversifiable) risk 183
value at risk 185
variance 170

SELF-TEST PROBLEMS

1. An investor places 30 per cent of his funds in Security X and the balance in Security Y. The expected returns on X and Y are 12 and 18 per cent, respectively. The standard deviations of returns on X and Y are 20 and 15 per cent, respectively.

   (a) Calculate the expected return on the portfolio.

   (b) Calculate the variance of returns on the portfolio assuming that the correlation between the returns on the two securities is:

   (i) +1.0 (iii) 0
   (ii) +0.7 (iv) −0.7

2. An investor holds a portfolio that comprises 20 per cent X, 30 per cent Y and 50 per cent Z. The standard deviations of returns on X, Y and Z are

22, 15 and 10 per cent, respectively, and the correlation between returns on each pair of securities is 0.6. Prepare a variance–covariance matrix for these three securities and use the matrix to calculate the variance and standard deviation of returns for the portfolio.

3. The risk-free rate of return is currently 8 per cent and the market risk premium is estimated to be 6 per cent. The expected returns and betas of four shares are as follows:

Share	Expected return (%)	Beta
Carltown	13.0	0.7
Pivot	17.6	1.6
Forresters	14.0	1.1
Brunswick	10.4	0.4

Which shares are undervalued, overvalued or correctly valued based on the CAPM?

Solutions to self-test problems are available in Appendix B, page 803.

REFERENCES

Bodie, Z., Kane, A. & Marcus, A.J., *Investments*, 9th edn, McGraw-Hill, New York, 2011.

Brailsford, T. & Faff, R., 'A derivation of the CAPM for pedagogical use', *Accounting and Finance*, May 1993, pp. 53–60.

Brailsford, T., Faff, R. & Oliver, B., *Research Design Issues in the Estimation of Beta*, McGraw-Hill, Sydney, 1997.

Brailsford, T., Handley, J. & Maheswaran, K., 'Re-examination of the historical equity premium in Australia', *Accounting and Finance*, March 2008, pp. 73–97.

Carhart, M. M., 'On persistence in mutual fund performance', *Journal of Finance*, March 1997, pp. 57–82.

Claus, J. & Thomas, J., 'Equity premia as low as three per cent? Evidence from analysts' earnings forecasts for domestic and international stock markets', *Journal of Finance*, October 2001, pp. 1629–66.

Coleman, L., Maheswaran, K. & Pinder, S., 'Narratives in managers' corporate finance decisions', *Accounting and Finance*, September 2010, pp. 605–33.

Dimson, E., Marsh, P.R. & Staunton, M., 'Global evidence on the equity risk premium', *Journal of Applied Corporate Finance*, Fall 2003, pp. 27–38.

Fama, E.F., 'Risk, return and equilibrium: some clarifying comments', *Journal of Finance*, March 1968, pp. 29–40.

——, *Foundations of Finance*, Basic Books, New York, 1976.

Fama, E.F. & French, K.R., 'The cross-section of expected stock returns', *Journal of Finance*, June 1992, pp. 427–65.

——, ——, 'Common risk factors in the returns on stocks and bonds', *Journal of Financial Economics*, February 1993, pp. 3–56.

——, ——, 'Multifactor explanations of asset pricing anomalies', *Journal of Finance*, March 1996, pp. 55–84.

——, ——, 'The equity premium', *Journal of Finance*, April 2002, pp. 637–59.

Heaton, J. & Lucas, D., 'Portfolio choice and asset prices: the importance of entrepreneurial risk', *Journal of Finance*, June 2000, pp. 1163–98.

Ibbotson, R.G. & Goetzmann, W. N., 'History and the equity risk premium', April 2005, Yale ICF Working Paper No. 05–04. http://ssrn.com/abstract=702341

Jegadeesh, N. & Titman, S., 'Returns to buying winners and selling losers: implications for market efficiency', *Journal of Finance*, 1993, pp. 65–91.

Jensen, M., 'The performance of mutual funds in the period 1945–1964', *Journal of Finance*, May 1968, pp. 389–416.

——, 'Risk, the pricing of capital assets, and the evaluation of investment portfolios', *Journal of Business*, April 1969, pp. 167–247.

Jensen, M., 'Capital markets: theory and evidence', *Bell Journal of Economics and Management Science*, Autumn 1972, pp. 357–98.

Jorion, P., *Value at Risk: The New Benchmark for Controlling Market Risk*, 3rd edn, McGraw-Hill, Chicago, 2006.

Jorion, P. & Goetzmann, W.N., 'Global stock markets in the twentieth century', *Journal of Finance*, June 1999, pp. 953–80.

Levy, H. & Sarnat, M., *Capital Investment and Financial Decisions*, 4th edn, Prentice-Hall, New Jersey, 1990, pp. 319–22.

Lintner, J., 'The valuation of risk assets and the selection of risky investments in stock portfolios and capital budgets', *Review of Economics and Statistics*, February 1965, pp. 13–37.

Markowitz, H.M., 'Portfolio selection', *Journal of Finance*, March 1952, pp. 77–91.

——, *Portfolio Selection: Efficient Diversification of Investments*, John Wiley & Sons, New York, 1959.

Mehra, R. & Prescott, E.C., 'The equity premium: a puzzle', *Journal of Monetary Economics*, March 1985, pp. 145–61.

Mossin, J., 'Security pricing and investment criteria in competitive markets', *American Economic Review*, December 1969, pp. 749–56.

O'Brien, M., Brailsford, T. & Gaunt, C., 'Size and book-to-market factors in Australia', 21st Australasian Finance and Banking Conference Paper, 2008 **http://ssrn.com/abstract=1206542**.

PricewaterhouseCoopers, *Investigation into Foreign Exchange Losses at the National Australia Bank*, Melbourne, 2004.

Ritter, J.R., 'The biggest mistakes we teach', *Journal of Financial Research,* Summer 2002, pp. 159–68.

Roll, R., 'A critique of the asset pricing theory's tests; Part 1: On the past and potential testability of the theory', *Journal of Financial Economics,* March 1977, pp. 126–76.

Sharpe, W.F., 'Capital asset prices: a theory of market equilibrium under conditions of risk', *Journal of Finance*, September 1964, pp. 425–42.

——, 'Mutual fund performance', *Journal of Business*, January 1966, pp. 119–38

Statman, M., 'How many stocks make a diversified portfolio?', *Journal of Financial and Quantitative Analysis*, September 1987, pp. 353–63.

Treynor, J.L, 'How to rate management investment funds', January 1966, *Harvard Business Review*, pp. 63–75.

Zhang, L., 'The value premium', *Journal of Finance*, February 2005, pp. 67–103.

QUESTIONS

1. **[LO 2]** Is risk aversion a reasonable assumption? What is the relevant measure of risk for a risk-averse investor?

2. **[LO 3]** What are the benefits of diversification to an investor? What is the key factor determining the extent of these benefits?

3. **[LO 5]** *Risky assets can be combined to form a riskless asset.* Discuss.

4. **[LO 5]** *Whenever an asset is added to a portfolio, the total risk of the portfolio will be reduced provided the returns of the asset and the portfolio are less than perfectly correlated.* Discuss.

5. **[LO 4]** Explain each of the following:
   (a) the efficient frontier
   (b) the capital market line
   (c) the security market line.

6. **[LO 6]** *Total risk can be decomposed into systematic and unsystematic risk*. Explain each component of risk, and how each is affected by increasing the number of securities in a portfolio.

7. **[LO 8]** *An important conclusion of the CAPM is that the relevant measure of an asset's risk is its systematic risk*. Outline the significance of this conclusion for a manager making financial decisions.

8. **[LO 8]** For investors who aim to diversify, shares with negative betas would be very useful investments, but such shares are very rare. Explain why few shares have negative betas.

9. **[LO 7]** *Diversification is certainly good for investors. Therefore investors should be prepared to pay a premium for the shares of companies that operate in several lines of business.* Explain why this statement is true or false.

10. **[LO 7]** Minco Ltd, a large mining company, provides a superannuation fund for its employees. The fund's manager says: 'We know the mining industry well, so we feel comfortable investing most of the fund in a portfolio of mining company shares'. Advise Minco's employees on whether to endorse the fund's investment policy.

11. **[LO 1]** Farmers can insure their crops against damage by hailstorms at reasonable rates. However, the same insurance companies refuse to provide flood insurance at any price. Explain why this situation exists.

12. **[LO 8]** Compare and contrast the capital asset pricing model and models that include additional factors.

13. **[LO 11]** In what situations would it be appropriate to use a simple benchmark index, such as the S&P/ASX 200 share price index, to assess the performance of a portfolio?

14. **[LO 11]** *When assessing the performance of a set of portfolios it does not really matter if you choose the Sharpe ratio or the Treynor ratio to do so as both approaches account for the risk inherent in the portfolios.* Discuss.

PROBLEMS

1. **Investment and risk [LO 2]**
   Mr Barlin is considering a 1-year investment in shares in one of the following three companies:
   Company X: expected return = 15% with a standard deviation of 15%
   Company Y: expected return = 15% with a standard deviation of 20%

Company Z: expected return = 20% with a standard deviation of 20%

Rank the investments in order of preference for each of the cases where it is assumed that Mr Barlin is:
(a) risk averse
(b) risk neutral
(c) risk seeking.
Give reasons.

2. **Variance of return [LO 5]**
An investor places 40 per cent of her funds in Company A's shares and the remainder in Company B's shares. The standard deviation of the returns on A is 20 per cent and on B is 10 per cent. Calculate the variance of return on the portfolio, assuming that the correlation between the returns on the two securities is:
(a) +1.0
(b) +0.5
(c) 0
(d) −0.5

3. **Portfolio standard deviation and diversification [LO 3]**
The standard deviations of returns on assets A and B are 8 per cent and 12 per cent, respectively. A portfolio is constructed consisting of 40 per cent in Asset A and 60 per cent in Asset B. Calculate the portfolio standard deviation if the correlation of returns between the two assets is:
(a) 1
(b) 0.4
(c) 0
(d) −1
Comment on your answers.

4. **Expected return, variance and risk [LO 3]**
You believe that there is a 50 per cent chance that the share price of Company L will decrease by 12 per cent and a 50 per cent chance that it will increase by 24 per cent. Further, there is a 40 per cent chance that the share price of Company M will decrease by 12 per cent and a 60 per cent chance that it will increase by 24 per cent. The correlation coefficient of the returns on shares in the two companies is 0.75. Calculate:
(a) the expected return, variance and standard deviation for each company's shares
(b) the covariance between their returns.

5. **Expected return, risk and diversification [LO 5]**
Harry Jones has invested one-third of his funds in Share 1 and two-thirds of his funds in Share 2. His assessment of each investment is as follows:

Item	Share 1	Share 2
Expected return (%)	15.0	21.0
Standard deviation (%)	18.0	25.0
Correlation between the returns	0.5	

(a) What are the expected return and the standard deviation of return on Harry's portfolio?
(b) Recalculate the expected return and the standard deviation where the correlation between the returns is 0 and 1.0, respectively.
(c) Is Harry better or worse off as a result of investing in two securities rather than in one security?

6. **Expected return, risk and diversification [LO 5]**
The table gives information on three risky assets: A, B and C.

Asset	Expected return	Standard deviation of return	Correlations		
			A	B	C
A	12.5	40	1.00	0.20	0.35
B	16.0	45	0.20	1.00	0.10
C	20.0	60	0.35	0.10	1.00

There is also a risk-free Asset F whose expected return is 9.9 per cent.
(a) Portfolio 1 consists of 40 per cent Asset A and 60 per cent Asset B. Calculate its expected return and standard deviation.
(b) Portfolio 2 consists of 60 per cent Asset A, 22.5 per cent Asset B and 17.5 per cent Asset C. Calculate its expected return and standard deviation. Compare your answers to (a) and comment.
(c) Portfolio 3 consists of 4.8 per cent Asset A, 75 per cent Asset B and 20.2 per cent in the risk-free asset. Calculate its expected return and standard deviation. Compare your answers to (a) and (b) and comment.
(d) Portfolio 4 is an equally weighted portfolio of the three risky assets A, B and C. Calculate its expected return and standard deviation and comment on these results.
(e) Portfolio 5 is an equally weighted portfolio of all four assets. Calculate its expected return and standard deviation and comment on these results.

7. **Expected return and systematic risk [LO 7]**
The expected return on the ith asset is given by:
$$E(R_i) = R_f + \beta_i (E(R_M) - R_f)$$

(a) What is the expected return on the ith asset where $R_f = 0.08$, $\beta_i = 1.25$ and $E(R_M) = 0.14$?
(b) What is the expected return on the market portfolio where $E(R_i) = 0.11$, $R_f = 0.08$ and $\beta_i = 0.75$?
(c) What is the systematic risk of the ith asset where $E(R_i) = 0.14$, $R_f = 0.10$ and $E(R_M) = 0.15$?

8. **Portfolio weights systematic risk and unsystematic risk [LO 8]**

The table provides data on two risky assets, A and B, the market portfolio M and the risk-free asset F.

Asset	Expected return (%)	A	B	M	F
A	10.8	324	60	48	0
B	15.6	60	289	96	0
M	14.0	48	96	80	0
F	6.0	0	0	0	0

An investor wishes to achieve an expected return of 12 per cent and is considering three ways this may be done:
(a) invest in A and B
(b) invest in B and F
(c) invest in M and F.

For each of these options, calculate the portfolio weights required and the portfolio standard deviation. Show that assets A and B are priced according to the capital asset pricing model and, in the light of this result, comment on your findings.

9. **Assessing diversification benefits [LO 7]**

You are a share analyst employed by a large multinational investment fund and have been supplied with the following information:

Asset	Expected return (%)	Standard deviation (%)
BHZ Ltd	9	8
ANB Ltd	13	48

You are also told that the correlation coefficient between the returns of the two firms is 0.8. A client currently has all of her wealth invested in BHZ shares. She wishes to diversify her portfolio by redistributing her wealth such that 30 per cent is invested in BHZ shares and 70 per cent in ANB shares.

(a) What will be the expected return of the new portfolio?
(b) What will be the standard deviation of returns for the new portfolio?

After constructing the portfolio and reporting the results to your client, she is quite upset, saying, 'I thought the whole purpose of diversification was to reduce risk? Yet you have just told me that the variability of my portfolio has actually been increased from what it was when I invested only in BHZ.'

(c) Provide a response to your client that demonstrates that the new portfolio does (not) reflect the benefits of diversification. Show all necessary calculations.

10. **Value at risk [LO 1]**

Consider a portfolio comprising a $3 million investment in Outlook Publishing and a $5 million investment in Russell Computing. Assume that the standard deviations of the returns for shares in these companies are 0.4 and 0.25 per cent per annum, respectively. Assume also that the correlation between the returns on the shares in these companies is 0.7. Assuming a 1 per cent chance of abnormally bad market conditions, calculate the value at risk of this portfolio. State any assumptions that you make in your calculations.

11. **Portfolio performance appraisal [LO 11]**

In 2011 the return on the Fort Knox Fund was 10 per cent, while the return on the market portfolio was 12 per cent and the risk-free return was 3 per cent. Comparative statistics are shown in the table below.

Statistic	Fort Knox fund	S&P/ASX 200 share price index
Standard deviation of return	15%	30%
Beta	0.75	1.00

Calculate and comment on the performance of the fund using the following three approaches:
(a) the simple benchmark index
(b) the Sharpe ratio
(c) the Treynor ratio.

CHAPTER 8
THE CAPITAL MARKET

LEARNING OBJECTIVES

After studying this chapter you should be able to:

1. understand the functions of a capital market
2. distinguish between financial agency institutions, financial intermediaries and investing institutions
3. identify and explain the role of financial agency institutions
4. identify and explain the role of financial intermediaries
5. outline the role of securitisation
6. identify and explain the role of investing institutions.

CHAPTER CONTENTS

8.1 Introduction
8.2 Financial agency institutions
8.3 Financial intermediaries
8.4 Investing institutions

8.1 INTRODUCTION

In Chapters 5 and 6 the methods used to select a company's assets were discussed. Management also has to decide how to finance those assets. This frequently involves a company raising funds by issuing financial assets. **Financial assets** are legally enforceable claims to money or future cash flows. Money in a bank account, trade creditors, debt securities and shares are different types of financial assets. The markets in which financial assets are bought and sold are commonly referred to as financial markets and include the equity (share) market, the bond market and the foreign exchange market. Companies will differ in their use of the various financial markets depending on factors such as the company's size and the scope of its operations. However, the financial markets that will be important to almost every company are those that can provide external sources of cash for company expansion. The financial markets in which companies raise long-term funds are referred to collectively as the **capital market**. In this chapter we discuss the benefits of having a capital market and the major features of the Australian capital market, paying particular attention to the characteristics of the important institutions that participate in the market.

financial assets assets such as shares, bonds and bank deposits, as distinct from real assets

capital market market in which long-term funds are raised and long-term debt and equity securities are traded

8.1.1 THE FLOW OF FUNDS

Over a given period an economic entity such as a company or a small unincorporated business will be either a 'deficit unit' or a 'surplus unit'. A deficit unit is one whose expenditure exceeds its income for a particular period, whereas a surplus unit is one whose income exceeds its expenditure for a particular period. The financing process involves a flow of funds from the surplus units to the deficit units.

If a company wishes to grow, but does not generate sufficient funds internally to finance an increase in its assets—that is, the company is a deficit unit—it will need to finance the difference by drawing on the funds held by surplus units.[1] Surplus units may be households, other businesses, governments or the overseas sector.

The flow of funds from surplus units to deficit units may be direct or indirect. A direct flow of funds may result solely from negotiation between the parties, or a financial institution may be involved as an adviser or underwriter.[2] For example, when a company issues debt securities, an investment bank may advise on and/or underwrite the issue.[3] However, the funds will flow directly from the purchasers of the debt securities to the issuing company. Direct funding is more commonly used where the borrower has a recognised credit rating and wishes to raise relatively large amounts.

Alternatively, the flow of funds may be indirect—that is, it occurs through financial intermediaries, such as banks and finance companies. In this case the deficit unit obtains funds from a **financial intermediary** that has borrowed the funds from surplus units. Intermediated funding is more commonly used where the credit risk of the deficit unit (the borrower) needs to be assessed, and where the amounts for both borrowers and lenders are relatively small. Financial intermediaries have an important role in facilitating the flow of funds from surplus units to deficit units. Collectively, financial intermediaries are a very important segment of the capital market.

financial intermediary institution that acts as a principal in accepting funds from depositors or investors and lending them to borrowers

The number of financial assets that are created in the overall financing process is an important difference between direct and indirect financing. If a company raises funds directly by issuing a bond to an investor, only one financial asset has been created. The bond is a financial asset held by the investor

---

1 Internally generated funds are discussed in Section 9.8.
2 Underwriting is discussed further in Section 8.2.2.
3 The activities of investment banks are discussed in Section 8.2.2. These institutions were generally referred to as merchant banks until the early 1990s when the US term 'investment bank' was widely adopted in Australia. In this chapter we generally use the latter term, except in cases where the historical context makes the earlier term appropriate.

and it is a liability of the issuing company. In contrast, if the investor deposits funds in a bank, which then provides a loan to a company, two financial assets are created. The bank deposit is an asset owned by the investor and it is a liability of the bank. In turn, the bank holds another financial asset because it has a claim against the company that borrowed from it.

8.1.2 THE CAPITAL MARKET

LEARNING OBJECTIVE 1
Understand the functions of a capital market

The capital market enables the suppliers of funds (the surplus units) and the users of funds (the deficit units) to negotiate the conditions on which the funds will be transferred. Equity or share markets involve an essentially permanent transfer of funds, with returns to shareholders contingent on the future profitability of the company raising the funds. Debt markets usually involve a temporary transfer of funds with predetermined promised returns to lenders. In the finance literature, equity and debt markets together form the capital market.[4]

8.1.3 TYPES OF FINANCIAL MARKET

Financial markets may be classified in several ways. For example, the distinction between debt markets and equity markets is based on the type of financial asset that is traded in the market. Similarly, markets for financial assets may be either **primary markets**, where financial assets are first sold by their originators, or **secondary markets**, where existing financial assets are traded.

primary market
market for new issues of securities where the sale proceeds go to the issuer of the securities

Primary markets are important because it is in these markets that a deficit unit, for example a company, raises new funds to finance its investments. Thus, a company may make a new share issue to finance the development of a new mine or the acquisition of another business.

A transaction in the secondary market does not raise any new funds for the issuer of the securities that are traded. All that happens is a change of ownership; the seller of the security transfers, for a price, ownership of the security to the buyer. However, secondary markets are important because they provide a way in which securities can be exchanged for cash, that is, they provide liquidity. This enables borrowers to raise long-term funds, even though individual suppliers of funds may be prepared to provide funds only for much shorter terms. In this way the existence of an active secondary market facilitates capital raising in the primary market. Without an active secondary market, many investors would not participate in primary markets because they require the flexibility to redeploy their funds. The secondary market provides this flexibility.

secondary market
market where previously issued securities are traded

exchange-traded market
market in which trading takes place by competitive bidding on an organised exchange

Another important distinction between different financial markets is based on the organisational structure of the markets. Indirect financing takes place through financial intermediaries, which raise funds by issuing financial claims against themselves and use those funds to purchase financial assets, most of which cannot be traded in a secondary market. For example, a loan provided by a bank is often retained as an asset of that bank until it has been repaid. In contrast, the financial assets created through direct financing are usually marketable securities. They may be exchange traded or they may be traded in an over-the-counter market. In an **exchange-traded market**, securities are traded through an organised exchange such as a stock exchange, where brokers carry out clients' instructions to buy or sell nominated securities. In an **over-the-counter market** there is no organised exchange and the market consists of financial institutions (dealers) who trade with clients and with each other. The Australian capital market includes financial intermediaries and markets of both these types. Exchange-traded securities include shares, options on shares and futures contracts. Debt securities, swaps and currency options are usually traded in over-the-counter markets.

over-the-counter market
there is no organised exchange and the market consists of financial institutions that are willing to trade with any counterparty

---

[4] In practice, participants in the financial markets usually refer to the direct short-term debt market—that is, where loans are for 12 months or less—as the *money market*. The term *capital market* is used to describe the direct long-term debt market.

8.1.4 DEVELOPMENTS IN AUSTRALIA'S FINANCIAL MARKETS

Some features of the financial system remain essentially constant over time while other features are subject to change, which may be gradual or, in some cases, very rapid. For example, banks have had a very important role in Australia since the first bank was established in 1817. However, the relative importance of banks has varied over time—many new banks have entered the market, a few banks have failed and several have been acquired by other banks. The factors that can trigger significant changes in the financial system include changes in regulation and technology, changes in the demand for different forms of funding and the effects of financial crises.

The evolution and expansion of the Australian financial markets in the last three decades were largely an outcome of the deregulation of those markets in the 1980s. The process of deregulation began with the establishment by the Commonwealth Government of a Committee of Inquiry into the Australian Financial System (the Campbell Committee) in 1979. In 1981 the *Final Report* of the Campbell Committee was published. It proposed the deregulation of the Australian financial markets.[5] Most of the committee's recommendations were accepted by the government.

While the Australian financial markets have been largely deregulated, this deregulation has not extended to the removal of controls that served a prudential purpose. The primary regulator of Australia's banks, insurance companies, superannuation funds, credit unions and building societies is the Australian Prudential Regulation Authority (APRA, www.apra.gov.au). APRA took over prudential supervision functions from Australia's **central bank**—the Reserve Bank of Australia (RBA, www.rba.gov.au)—on 1 July 1998.

The *Banking Act 1959* gives APRA extensive powers over almost all aspects of banking operations. Other relevant Commonwealth legislation is the *Banks (Shareholdings) Act 1972* and the *Banking Legislation Amendment Act 1989*. Arguably, the most important role fulfilled by banking regulatory authorities is ensuring that depositors' funds are adequately protected. Historically, the primary method utilised by authorities worldwide is to require banks to maintain the ratio of their equity to assets above a minimum prescribed level known as a capital adequacy requirement. From a regulator's perspective, however, a simple 'one-size-fits-all' approach to capital adequacy would be deficient in that it would not account for the differing risk profiles of the banks under its control. Consequently, the Basel Committee on Banking Supervision established a set of recommendations in 1988 known as the 1988 Capital Accord (or simply the Basel Accord). The Basel Committee was established by the Bank for International Settlements (BIS, www.bis.org), which itself can be thought of as a bank for central banks. To illustrate one simple consequence of the Basel Accord, a bank's loan to a company would be judged to be twice as risky as a first mortgage written over family-held real estate. Hence, twice as much capital would need to be maintained by the bank to protect the depositors who contributed the funds that were lent out.

Gup (2004) notes that during the period from 1980 to 1996, 133 of the 181 member countries of the International Monetary Fund experienced serious banking sector problems, including those countries that adopted the 1988 accord. Some of the deficiencies of the first set of recommendations have been addressed in a second accord, commonly referred to as Basel II, which provides a more comprehensive, and hopefully more accurate, method by which banks account for risk.[6] The Basel II framework has applied in Australia from 1 January 2008.

The adequacy of many aspects of bank regulation was called into question by the global financial crisis that began in mid-2007 when problems that originated in credit markets in the US became widespread

central bank
a bank that controls the issue of currency, acts as banker to the government and the banking system and sets the interest rate for overnight cash

---

5 In 1982 there was a change in government and the newly elected Commonwealth Government established the Martin Group to review the Campbell Committee Report. The result of this review was published in 1984 (Committee of Inquiry into the Australian Financial System, *Report of the Review Group*). Both reports supported the deregulation of the Australian financial markets. An extensive inquiry into the financial system completed in 1997 reviewed the effects of regulation and its report included recommendations for further regulatory reform (Financial System Inquiry, *Final Report*, 1997).

6 See Gup (2004) for a more comprehensive discussion of the background to the introduction of Basel II and a critical analysis of its recommendations.

throughout the developed nations. This crisis saw turmoil in many financial markets during 2008 and 2009 and the failure and near-failure of many financial institutions in the US, the UK and Europe. It also involved unprecedented actions by central banks, financial regulators and governments to restore confidence and stability in the financial system and to limit the effects of the crisis on economic activity. In December 2009, the Basel Committee released proposals to reform bank regulation. The proposed changes included tightening the definition of bank capital, higher minimum capital requirements, strengthening bank liquidity and the introduction of measures intended to discourage excessive leverage and risk taking. If accepted, these proposals, commonly referred to as Basel III, would be phased in with the new capital requirements to apply from 1 January 2013 and the liquidity rules expected to come into effect by 2018.

When the structure of the financial system is viewed in terms of the institutions that operate within it, four main developments can be identified over the post-deregulation period—that is, from 1985 to 2005 (RBA March 2006). These developments are:

- a significant increase in the importance of banks
- a decrease in the relative importance of building societies, credit unions, finance companies and money market corporations
- a significant increase in the share of assets held through managed funds, particularly superannuation funds
- rapid growth in securitisation.

These developments, which typically occurred gradually, were followed by some much more rapid changes associated with the global financial crisis. In Australia, the effects of the financial crisis were less severe than in the US, the UK and Europe but the effect on equity prices was comparable to the changes experienced in other countries: from its peak in November 2007 the Australian stock market fell by more than 50 per cent to a low in March 2009. Other effects included a further strengthening of the dominant position held by banks and a significant reversal of the previous growth in securitisation. These, and other developments, are discussed in Sections 8.2 to 8.4.

8.1.5 BUSINESS FUNDING

LEARNING OBJECTIVE 2

Distinguish between financial agency institutions, financial intermediaries and investing institutions

Sections 8.2 to 8.4 outline the major financial institutions in the Australian capital market involved in providing funds to companies. Institutions such as building societies and credit unions, whose main function is consumer lending, are not discussed.[7] The financial institutions we discuss can be divided into three broad categories: financial agency institutions, financial intermediaries and investing institutions.

A **financial agency institution** arranges or facilitates the direct transfer of funds from lenders to borrowers; typically the funds are transferred from investors to companies. Companies usually obtain the assistance of a stockbroker or investment bank when they wish to raise capital externally. For example, a broker or an investment bank may place a company's newly issued shares with institutional clients. Stockbroking firms and investment banks function as agency institutions and will receive a fee or commission for arranging a transaction. Financial agency institutions are discussed in Section 8.2.

A *financial intermediary*, such as a bank, provides funds as a principal—that is, a company that borrows from a bank has an obligation to repay the bank, but it has no obligation to the bank's depositors. Similarly, a bank acts as a principal in its relationship with depositors who have claims against the bank, rather than claims against those who have borrowed from it. In contrast to agents, whose earnings consist mostly of fees and commissions, financial intermediaries obtain a significant part of their income from an 'interest spread', which is the difference between the interest rates they charge for loans and the rates they pay to depositors. Most financial intermediaries also charge various fees.

financial agency institution arranges or facilitates the direct transfer of funds from lenders to borrowers

---
7 For a discussion of these institutions, see O'Brien (1997).

Companies with large funding requirements and high credit ratings are well placed to access funds directly. Such companies can therefore raise most or all of their funding requirements without the services of an intermediary. However, the process of intermediation offers significant benefits where there are large numbers of relatively small deposits and loans to be handled. Frequently, surplus units have relatively small amounts that they wish to lend for relatively short periods, while deficit units wish to borrow relatively large amounts for relatively long periods. Further, surplus units often desire a lower level of **default risk** than can be offered by many deficit units. By accepting deposits and repackaging the funds into loans, financial intermediaries can cater for these different preferences.

default risk
the chance that a borrower will fail to meet obligations to pay interest and principal as promised

Thus, the process of intermediation can:

- harmonise the differences in size, maturity and risk preferences between surplus units and deficit units
- generate economies of scale as a result of the specialist skills that financial intermediaries acquire in credit assessment and monitoring of the performance of borrowers
- result in the pooling of the risks associated with a portfolio of loans—that is, because intermediaries lend to borrowers in different industries and different geographical areas, they are able to diversify more effectively than most individuals and the benefits are reflected in the terms offered by intermediaries to depositors.[8]

Financial intermediaries are discussed in Section 8.3.

Investing institutions are similar to financial intermediaries in that they accept funds from the public and invest the funds in assets. However, there are important differences between them. Essentially, financial intermediaries, such as banks, accept deposits and make loans. The major roles of investing institutions—which include superannuation funds, life insurance companies and unit trusts—are to provide insurance and funds management. The funds placed with these institutions are generally not in the form of deposits and, while some of them do make loans, they also invest in shares, debt securities, infrastructure assets and property (real estate), giving them a much wider spread of assets than financial intermediaries. Another difference is that the returns provided by investing institutions usually depend directly on the performance of the assets held by them, whereas intermediaries have 'fixed' commitments to depositors that must be met even if an unexpectedly high proportion of borrowers fail to repay their loans. Investing institutions are discussed in Section 8.4.

investing institution
accepts funds from the public and invests them in assets; includes superannuation funds, life insurance companies and unit trusts

While Sections 8.2 to 8.4 discuss financial agency institutions, financial intermediaries and investing institutions, two qualifications should be noted. First, there are some entities that do not fit neatly into any one of these three categories. In particular, despite the fact that securitisation vehicles do not conform to our definition of 'financial intermediary', we discuss securitisation in Section 8.3 because it is a process widely used by financial intermediaries. Second, some of the differences between these three types of institutions have become less distinct. This has occurred in two ways. First, many investing institutions now offer products, such as housing loans, that were previously provided almost exclusively by intermediaries. Second, there has been a considerable growth in financial conglomerates that provide a wide range of financial services. For example, many banks have funds management, stockbroking and life insurance subsidiaries, while some life insurance companies have banking subsidiaries. These developments are likely to continue. However, there are still fundamental differences between financial intermediation, the life insurance business and funds management. For example, the assets and liabilities of a bank and the risks involved in banking are quite different from those of a life insurance company. Therefore, while customers see a blurring of previous distinctions, the differences between, say, banking and insurance continue to be important to those involved in managing and regulating financial institutions.

---

8 See Chapter 7 for a discussion of how diversification of a portfolio can reduce risk.

authorised deposit-taking institution
a corporation that is authorised under the *Banking Act 1959* to accept deposits from the public

Another difficulty arises from the terms used to refer to some institutions. In particular, many of the institutions originally known as 'merchant banks' are now more commonly referred to as 'investment banks'. Moreover, these terms are used despite the fact that these institutions may not be **authorised deposit-taking institutions** (ADIs) and are therefore not permitted to use the word 'bank' in their title. On the other hand, many investment banks in Australia are the local wholesale market operations of foreign banks. In summary, 'investment banking' may be carried out by a bank or by a non-bank.

The total assets of the main types of financial institutions are shown in Table 8.1, which shows that banks are the largest group of institutions in the Australian market, followed by life insurance companies and superannuation funds. The growth of banks, life insurance companies and superannuation funds, other managed funds and particularly securitisation vehicles has been relatively high in the 1990 to 2010 period, while the assets of other ADIs and registered financial corporations have generally grown more slowly. Table 8.1 also shows that for some institutions, such as life insurance companies and superannuation funds, the rate of asset growth slowed after 2007, while in other cases, including other managed funds and securitisation vehicles, the value of assets fell after 2007. Generally, these differences between pre- and post-2007 conditions reflect the effects of the global financial crisis.

TABLE 8.1 Assets of Australian financial institutions, $ billion

30 JUNE	DEPOSIT-TAKING INSTITUTIONS		REGISTERED FINANCIAL CORPORATIONS	LIFE INSURANCE COMPANIES AND SUPER FUNDS	OTHER MANAGED FUNDS	GENERAL INSURANCE COMPANIES	SECURITISATION VEHICLES	TOTAL
	BANKS (OTHER THAN RBA)	OTHER ADIS						
1990	325.8	31.4	109.0	156.6	44.7	21.7	5.7	695.0
1995	437.9	27.4	95.6	241.0	57.7	38.9	9.8	908.2
2000	731.0	34.2	134.6	451.2	152.8	61.4	65.0	1630.2
2005	1363.5	49.1	166.7	657.5	247.1	92.2	184.5	2760.7
2006	1581.1	53.6	176.3	762.7	300.3	107.6	216.5	3198.0
2007	1876.9	59.3	222.8	993.7	361.7	139.4	274.0	3927.7
2008	2324.1	64.2	251.4	962.4	338.8	133.5	239.4	4313.9
2009	2590.2	67.3	215.4	909.8	303.9	127.3	193.2	4407.3
2010	2612.5	72.8	163.3	1049.5	301.7	128.2	146.7	4480.1

Source: Table B1, Reserve Bank of Australia website, www.rba.gov.au.

Note: The figures for life insurance companies, superannuation funds and other managed funds have been consolidated by the Australian Bureau of Statistics. They should not be compared with the figures in Tables 8.6, 8.7 and 8.8, which are unconsolidated.

8.2 FINANCIAL AGENCY INSTITUTIONS

Financial agency institutions are those that facilitate direct funding but do not themselves provide the funds. These institutions operate in the primary markets to bring together surplus units and deficit units, and assist with the design of appropriate contracts. They also operate in the secondary markets. The main financial agency institutions in Australia are stockbrokers and investment banks.

8.2.1 BROKERS AND THE STOCK EXCHANGE[9]

The traditional function of the stock exchange (and of stockbrokers) is to provide facilities for the trading of shares, bonds and other securities such as convertible notes, options and preference shares. As a result, a stock exchange performs three functions. First, it mobilises savings. Because there are large numbers of investors, issues of securities can be for large sums. The presence of a stock exchange allows companies to issue debt or equity securities in relatively small units, and each surplus unit can then invest its desired amount. Second, it allocates resources. A stock exchange facilitates the allocation of resources (savings) among a large number of competing investment opportunities. Third, it allows investments to be realised through the sale of securities—that is, it provides investors with liquidity, and therefore the opportunity to adjust their portfolios. As explained earlier, the existence of a liquid secondary market encourages investment in the primary market.

LEARNING OBJECTIVE 3
Identify and explain the role of financial agency institutions

Development of the Australian Stock Exchange

In 1987 the Australian Stock Exchange Ltd (ASX, www.asx.com.au) commenced business as a national stock exchange formed by amalgamating the six independent exchanges that previously operated in the state capital cities. Until 1998, the ASX was a company limited by guarantee. However, following demutualisation in 1998, it became a company limited by shares. In 2006 the ASX merged with the SFE Corporation, the owner of the Sydney Futures Exchange, resulting in an exchange group that operated as the Australian Securities Exchange (ASX) until 1 August 2010 when it adopted the name ASX Group.

Other financial markets in Australia

In addition to the ASX Group, there are three smaller stock exchanges in Australia: the Asia Pacific Exchange, the National Stock Exchange of Australia and the Bendigo Stock Exchange.

- The Asia Pacific Exchange (formerly Australia Pacific Exchange) (APX, www.apx.com.au) evolved from markets previously operated by Austock Brokers and has three separate boards—the Property Board, the Hybrids & Debt Board and the Equity Board.
- The National Stock Exchange of Australia (NSX, www.nsxa.com.au) (which changed its name from the Stock Exchange of Newcastle in December 2006) and the Bendigo Stock Exchange are operated by NSX Limited (NSX).

These smaller or junior exchanges generally list the securities of companies that are too small to list on the ASX and their listing requirements are less demanding. For example, to list on the ASX a company must have at least 400 shareholders and a market capitalisation of at least $10 million, whereas the NSX requires only 50 shareholders and a market capitalisation of at least $500 000. In August 2010, the NSX had a total of 98 securities listed on its exchange with a total market capitalisation in excess of $2 billion. For some companies, listing on one of the junior exchanges is seen as a stepping stone to eventual listing on the ASX.

Australia also has other markets designed to meet the needs of small and medium-sized enterprises. These include the Australian Small Scale Offerings Board (www.assob.com.au) and the CAPstart Private Equity Market (www.capstart.com.au), which facilitate capital raising by small unlisted companies. Most capital raisings through these facilities are made under section 708 of the *Corporations Act 2001*, which allows small amounts of funds to be raised without a registered prospectus.

---

9 For a more detailed discussion, see Davies and Peacock (1997).

Automation of trading

In the past, the focal point of the stock exchange was the trading floor, where brokers met to buy and sell shares for their clients. The ASX Group no longer uses trading floors. Since 1990, all shares have been traded electronically through systems that enable stockbrokers to trade from terminals in their offices; clients can place orders with online brokers using the internet. Visitors to the stock exchanges can now view share prices and other information, such as local and overseas market indices, on video screens in the visitors gallery. The junior exchanges also use electronic trading and the prices of listed securities can be obtained from their websites. Table 8.2 provides some ASX market statistics for the period 1990 to 2010.

TABLE 8.2 ASX market statistics as at December, 1990–2010

YEAR	VALUE OF ALL ORDINARIES SHARE PRICE INDEX	MARKET CAPITALISATION DOMESTIC EQUITIES ($ MILLION)	NUMBER OF COMPANIES WITH EQUITIES LISTED
1990	1280	139 572	1136
1995	2203	329 647	1178
2000	3155	670 918	1406
2001	3359	732 818	1410
2002	2976	672 792	1421
2003	3306	777 100	1471
2004	4053	990 457	1583
2005	4709	1 109 596	1807
2006	5644	1 390 315	1908
2007	6421	1 478 651	2077
2008	3659	969 046	2086
2009	4883	1 403 117	2043
2010	4847	1 419 001	2072

Source: Compiled from Australian Stock Exchange Ltd, *Fact Book 2001*, 2001 and **www.asx.com.au/research/market_info/index.htm**.

The role of the stockbroker

Traditionally, the member firms of the ASX have played a leading role in the new-issues market. In the year to 30 June 2010, ASX-listed entities raised $76.5 billion in new equity capital compared with the 2008 and 2009 totals of $61.8 billion and $90 billion respectively. The 2010 total comprised $11.5 billion raised in initial public offerings by newly listed entities and $65.1 billion raised by entities that were already listed (see **www.asx.com.au/research/market_info/index.htm**). A company may maintain a continuing relationship with a stockbroking firm that advises it on the most appropriate means of raising funds and the terms of a new issue of securities. It is also usual for the same broker or an associated company to underwrite the issue, which means that the broker or associated company agrees to subscribe to any portion of the issue that is not subscribed to by other investors during a given period. In addition, a broker may undertake to sell the issue, mainly to the broker's clients and institutional investors.

The larger stockbroking firms also frequently advise companies that are considering a merger or acquisition, and may assist with negotiations if the merger or acquisition proceeds.

Many stockbroking firms have extended their services beyond those traditionally offered. Other services offered by brokers include advice on financial planning and superannuation, research and trading of derivative securities (such as options), access to stock markets outside Australia and investments in commercial bills and other money market assets.[10] Although some stockbroking firms provide these services directly, most provide them through associated investment banks.

8.2.2 INVESTMENT BANKS AND MERCHANT BANKS

Following the deregulation of the Australian financial system in the 1980s, the activities of merchant banks, which originally relied heavily on corporate lending, changed significantly. Essentially, their involvement in financial intermediation declined and they developed a greater emphasis on advisory services and securities trading and underwriting. These changes meant that their role evolved to become very similar to that of US investment banks and, since the early 1990s, this term has been widely used in Australia. For ease of exposition we refer to these organisations as 'investment banks', except where the term 'merchant bank' is appropriate in the particular context.

The role of investment banks

The term 'investment bank' has no official definition in Australia. Rather, investment banks are identified by the range of financial services that they provide. Their main activities involve wholesale banking and the financial markets. The range of activities is broad and includes financial intermediation (borrowing and lending), trading in securities, foreign exchange and derivatives, investment management, provision of corporate advisory services, underwriting and stockbroking. Thus, unlike most banks and other authorised deposit-taking institutions (ADIs), investment banks have little involvement in retail banking. Accordingly, they usually have minimal dealings with individuals except perhaps as managers of funds such as cash management trusts or as advisers to a small number of very wealthy individuals.

There is no 'typical' investment bank because many of them specialise in particular products and services. However, as a group, investment banks focus on wholesale market operations, where they deal with corporations, other financial institutions and government bodies. Their main functions can be outlined in four categories:

(a) *The wholesale banking operation* provides a service to companies that wish to deposit temporarily idle cash balances, or to borrow funds for a short to medium period.
(b) *The investment management function* involves managing the portfolios of institutional investors and an investment bank's own unit trusts. Part of this function is to direct funds to the new issues of Australian companies.
(c) *The corporate financial advisory function* involves providing advice to companies about raising additional capital, or a merger or takeover, and the provision of underwriting facilities and marketing services for new issues. The underwriter's skills, contacts and knowledge of the capital market are expected to result in a higher price than if the issuer attempted to market the securities itself. In addition, the marketing risk is assumed by the underwriter. If the issue is priced appropriately, the supply of securities will match the demand. If the issue is over-priced, the underwriter will be left holding the unsold securities.
(d) *Making a market in foreign exchange and derivative securities* involves being willing to quote both a price to buy and a price to sell in these markets—that is, this function requires the investment bank to be willing to deal on both sides of the market at all times.

---

10 Derivatives are discussed in Chapters 17 and 18, international investing in Chapter 20 and commercial bills in Chapter 10.

Regulation of investment banks

The regulatory provisions that apply to an investment bank will depend, at least in part, on its structure and the range of services that it provides. An investment bank operating in Australia will be structured either as an ADI or as a money market corporation. Those that are ADIs will be subject to the provisions of the *Banking Act 1959* and to prudential supervision by APRA (**www.apra.gov.au**). Investment banks that are structured as money market corporations are not subject to prudential supervision, but are required to register with, and provide statistical data to, APRA in accordance with the *Financial Sector (Collection of Data) Act 2001*. Their name may not include the word 'bank', but guidelines issued by APRA in January 2006 do allow corporations registered as money market corporations to use expressions such as 'merchant bank' in relation to their business. As financial corporations they are also regulated by the Australian Securities and Investments Commission (ASIC, **www.asic.gov.au**) and are subject to the same conduct and disclosure regulations as non-financial corporations.

As a provider of financial advice or as a dealer in financial markets, an investment bank must have an Australian Financial Services Licence issued by ASIC. In addition, most of those that trade in the financial markets are members of the Australian Financial Markets Association (AFMA, **www.afma.com.au**). AFMA is an industry association that represents the institutions that operate in Australia's over-the-counter financial markets. It imposes a degree of self-regulation through measures such as its code of conduct, codification of market conventions and standardisation of documentation.

Developments in Australian investment banking

The merchant banks, as they were then known, that started to operate in Australia in the 1950s were typically either associates of large stockbrokers or the local operations of foreign financial institutions. The first Australian merchant banks differed considerably from the original European merchant banks, which began as trade financiers. They also differed considerably from US investment banks, which focused on underwriting and distributing security issues for companies that needed to raise capital. The main difference was that most Australian merchant banks operated as financial intermediaries, borrowing in the money market and providing finance, mainly to corporate borrowers, either by making cash advances or by discounting bills of exchange.

The merchant banking sector grew rapidly during the 1960s and 1970s and many of the new merchant banks were owned by Australian and overseas banks. An important reason for this ownership structure was the restrictive regulations that applied to banks at the time. Banks were not permitted to pay interest on deposits accepted for periods of fewer than 30 days and one way for a bank to gain access to this part of the market was through an ownership interest in a merchant bank. This was particularly attractive to banks because merchant banks were not subject to bank regulations and their associated costs. In addition, overseas banks, which were unable to acquire banking licences, were able to gain access to the Australian market by acquiring an interest in an Australian merchant bank.

In the 1980s, merchant banks expanded their lending operations to include bill acceptance or discount facilities with terms of up to 5 years and, for large amounts, loan syndications.[11] Merchant banks were also involved, usually on an agency basis, in arranging foreign currency loans or bond issues for Australian borrowers. This was an important source of business for merchant banks with strong links overseas. In addition, most merchant banks were licensed foreign exchange dealers and were active in the rapidly evolving markets for options, futures and swaps.

---

11 For a more detailed discussion of these funding methods, see Chapter 10 for a discussion of bills of exchange and a discussion of how these instruments are used for longer-term funding.

Merchant banks fared well in the financial conditions of the 1980s and by 1988 there were more than 200 merchant banks in Australia (RBA 1988). These institutions varied from small, specialised institutions to large financial corporations providing a full range of services. Towards the end of the decade a number of factors had an adverse impact on the sector. The high level of bad debts associated with the recession of the late 1980s led to the closure of some merchant banks and initiated rationalisation in many others. This trend was further strengthened by the removal in 1988 of the regulation-driven advantages that had stimulated much of the merchant banks' earlier expansion. The removal of many of the regulatory constraints that had applied to banks eroded the merchant banks' competitiveness in the lending market. In many cases, merchant banks that were subsidiaries of banks found that their intermediation function was transferred to the parent bank, leaving them with the remaining agency function. Merchant banks that were not bank subsidiaries followed a similar strategy, since they also found that their competitive advantage lay in those areas.

Following the 1988 changes in bank regulation, both the number of merchant banks and the size of the sector's assets declined. In September 2010, 45 money market corporations were registered in Australia including ANZ Capel Court Limited, Citigroup Global Markets Australia Pty Limited, Goldman Sachs & Partners Australia Capital Markets Limited, Macquarie Acceptances Limited and Nomura Australia Limited. Most of these institutions are owned by Australian banks, foreign banks or securities firms.

While lending by money market corporations has been curtailed since deregulation, other investment banking activities have grown considerably. Since lending has become a relatively minor activity for investment banks, the value of their assets and the associated market figures shown in Table 8.3, on page 221, are not good measures of the sector's importance. Other measures, such as the value of equity capital and fees earned, are better indicators of the importance of investment banking. As noted above, investment banks that engage in securities trading and underwriting will usually be members of AFMA. In 2010, AFMA had more than 130 members and there are many investment banks that are not members of AFMA. These non-members do not trade in the financial markets and focus instead on activities such as advisory services, investment and funds management.

Investment banking can involve inherent conflicts of interest that must be managed if they cannot be avoided. These conflicts are most likely to arise in cases where the firm has a wide range of activities including stockbroking, securities trading and underwriting. In such cases, investors and regulators may be concerned that the broking analysts' recommendations on which shares to buy may be influenced by their colleagues who are seeking to attract underwriting business. The standard approach to managing such conflicts of interest is to employ internal barriers—known as 'Chinese walls'—to limit the flow of confidential client information between departments.

Concerns about the effectiveness of Chinese walls were widely publicised in the US in 2001. One outcome was that Merrill Lynch agreed to pay a fine of $US100 million because of allegations that its broking analysts issued overly optimistic reports on the shares of companies that were clients of its investment banking operation. Similarly, in Australia ASIC took civil action against Citigroup in 2006 related to trading by Citigroup in the shares of Patrick Corporation at a time when the firm was also advising Toll Holdings on a planned takeover bid for Patrick. One of the claims against Citigroup was that it did not maintain adequate arrangements for the management of conflicts between its own interests and those of its client, Toll Holdings. ASIC also claimed that Citigroup had contravened the insider trading provisions of the Corporations Act. Citigroup was successful in defending these charges but the outcome of the case highlights the importance of maintaining adequate Chinese wall arrangements. For example, the courts require that such arrangements are documented extensively, and understood and applied by employees in circumstances where conflicts of interest exist. Some investment banks avoid any exposure to inherent conflicts of interest by restricting the scope of their activities. Firms that take this approach focus on advisory services and do not engage in securities trading or underwriting.

Investment banks and the global financial crisis

The global financial crisis saw major investment banks in the US experience severe stress. Bear Stearns suffered a severe liquidity shortage in March 2008 and failure was avoided only when J. P. Morgan Chase agreed to purchase Bear Stearns in a takeover facilitated by government authorities. By the end of August 2008, the losses that had been recognised by financial institutions writing down the values of assets had accumulated to a global total of around US$500 billion. Pressure on the equity prices of financial institutions made it more difficult for banks to replenish their depleted capital bases or to raise loan funds from markets where lenders were unwilling to accept anything other than the lowest credit risks. With their higher leverage and exposures to impaired assets, investment banks experienced the greatest pressure. Of the major US investment banks, Lehman Brothers, with assets of about $639 billion, faced the most severe problems and when it was unable to raise urgently needed funding the company filed for bankruptcy protection in September 2008—the largest 'bank' failure in US history.

The failure of Lehman Brothers and the planned takeover of Merrill Lynch by the Bank of America would leave just two big investment banks: Goldman Sachs Group Inc. and Morgan Stanley. A week after Lehman Brothers failed, the US central bank, the Federal Reserve Bank, announced that, at a 9 pm meeting, its Board of Governors had approved applications delivered earlier that day by both firms to become bank holding companies—that is, firms that own or control banks. The implications of this change of status included regulation by the Federal Reserve instead of the Securities and Exchange Commission, lower financial leverage, greater reliance on deposits from retail customers rather than borrowing by issuing bonds and probably less risk taking. A report by Bloomberg began:

> *The Wall Street that shaped the financial world for two decades ended last night, when Goldman Sachs Inc. and Morgan Stanley concluded there is no future in remaining investment banks now that investors have determined the model is broken.*[12]

While the effects were less severe than in the US, the global financial crisis had significant effects on investment banks in Australia. The Sydney-based investment bank Babcock & Brown (B&B), which listed on the ASX in 2004 and had at its peak 28 offices worldwide and a market capitalisation in excess of $9 billion, became a victim of the crisis when it failed in 2009. B&B had a leading role as an adviser on structured finance including leases and securitisation, invested in real estate and infrastructure as a principal and managed several 'satellite' funds that it established. B&B relied heavily on short-term debt to finance its holdings of mostly illiquid assets, such as real estate and shareholdings in unlisted related businesses. With financial markets disrupted and concerns about the high debt levels of B&B and its satellite funds, the company was unable to refinance its debt and was placed in voluntary administration in March 2009 and then into liquidation in August 2009. The Australian subsidiaries of US and European investment banks such as Merrill Lynch and UBS reduced their workforces to offset lower revenues. As financial markets stabilised in 2009 and 2010, these and other investment banks were able to earn substantial fees by arranging and underwriting share issues for companies whose managers recognised the need to reduce their financial leverage.

---

12 See Harper and Torres (2008).

8.3 FINANCIAL INTERMEDIARIES

Financial intermediaries borrow funds on their own behalf and then lend the funds to another party. The types of financial intermediaries in the Australian capital market include banks, money market corporations, finance companies, building societies and credit unions. Recent statistics on the assets of the financial intermediaries that are important as lenders to businesses are shown in Table 8.3.

TABLE 8.3 Total assets of selected financial intermediaries ($ billion) and market shares (percentage of total)

30 JUNE	BANKS		MONEY MARKET CORPORATIONS		FINANCE COMPANIES		TOTAL
	$ BILLION	%	$ BILLION	%	$ BILLION	%	$ BILLION
1990	325.8	74.9	53.6	12.3	55.4	12.7	434.8
1995	437.9	82.1	51.2	9.6	44.4	8.3	533.5
2000	731.0	84.5	63.7	7.4	70.9	8.2	865.6
2001	807.3	83.2	81.2	8.4	82.3	8.5	970.8
2002	953.6	84.5	85.8	7.6	88.5	7.8	1127.9
2003	1069.3	85.6	99.0	7.9	80.2	6.4	1248.5
2004	1245.0	89.6	67.7	4.9	76.2	5.5	1388.9
2005	1363.5	89.1	80.1	5.2	86.5	5.7	1530.1
2006	1581.1	90.0	79.0	4.5	97.3	5.5	1757.4
2007	1876.9	89.4	106.7	5.1	116.1	5.5	2099.7
2008	2324.1	90.3	121.9	4.7	128.0	5.0	2574.1
2009	2587.3	92.3	94.5	3.4	120.1	4.3	2801.8
2010	2612.1	94.1	64.9	2.3	98.6	3.6	2775.6

Source: Table B1, Reserve Bank of Australia website, www.rba.gov.au.

LEARNING OBJECTIVE 4
Identify and explain the role of financial intermediaries

8.3.1 BANKS

A major part of banking business is borrowing from depositors and other investors and lending to a wide range of borrowers, including governments, businesses and consumers. In addition, banks are also usually involved in other financial transactions such as providing guarantees, letters of credit, bill endorsements and market-related activities such as entering into forward rate agreements, transacting in foreign currency and dealing in derivatives. The total assets of financial institutions in Australia are shown in Table 8.1, on page 214. As can be seen from Table 8.1, banks are the largest group of financial institutions in Australia. As at June 2010, their assets accounted directly for more than 58 per cent of the assets held by all financial institutions. However, this understates the overall importance of banks because many of them also have interests in other financial institutions, such as investment banks, finance companies, insurance companies, fund managers and stockbrokers. Accordingly, banks—particularly the larger ones—provide a wide range of products and financial services including funds management, insurance, underwriting, dealing in securities and stockbroking. In many cases, these activities are carried out through subsidiaries and affiliated businesses.

At the end of July 2010, 55 banks were authorised to operate in Australia. Twelve of these banks were predominantly Australian owned, nine were subsidiaries of foreign banks and 34 were branches of foreign banks. A foreign bank subsidiary is incorporated in Australia and must hold capital within Australia, whereas a foreign bank branch is essentially just a part of the parent bank that is authorised to conduct banking business within Australia. As discussed below, foreign bank branches are subject to some restrictions that do not apply to subsidiaries of foreign banks. Some foreign banks have both a branch and a subsidiary in Australia. As from 1 July 1998, the responsibility for bank supervision was transferred from the RBA to APRA. The RBA retained responsibility for monetary policy and the maintenance of financial stability, including that of the payments system—which is the cash, cheque and electronic means by which payments are effected. As a result, the current regulatory structure requires close cooperation between the RBA and APRA.

An authority from APRA is required before a bank is permitted to operate in Australia. APRA also imposes a number of other controls over banks, including minimum capital requirements and asset requirements. Banks are also required to provide APRA with extensive data on their activities and management systems. While subsidiaries of foreign banks are subject to the same requirements as locally owned banks, branches of foreign banks are not subject to minimum capital requirements in Australia. However, such branches are effectively confined to operating in the wholesale market because they are not permitted to accept initial deposits of less than $250 000 from Australian residents and non-corporate institutions. Therefore, a foreign bank that wishes to operate in the retail market must establish a subsidiary in Australia.

Due to the close relationship that developed between banks and the RBA prior to the handover of the bank supervisory role to APRA, the public has generally regarded bank deposits as being implicitly guaranteed by the RBA.[13] This has given banks an advantage in raising deposit funds. In response to the global financial crisis, the Australian Government introduced an *explicit* guarantee on deposits in banks and other ADIs that applies until October 2011.[14] (See Finance in Action.)

FINANCE IN ACTION

GOVERNMENT GUARANTEE EXTENDED ON BANK DEPOSITS

Prior to the global financial crisis, bank deposits in Australia were not guaranteed, although deposit insurance schemes were common in other countries. Faced with a crisis of confidence in late September/early October 2008, many governments increased the limit on the amount of deposits guaranteed under these schemes while others went further by providing a guarantee over all deposits, typically for a set period of around 2 years. Some governments also moved to provide a guarantee on wholesale borrowing by deposit-taking institutions. While most Australian institutions remained sound and profitable, the Australian government took similar measures so that Australian banks and other deposit-taking institutions would not be disadvantaged internationally. An article in *The Age* outlined the government's initiatives.

The Government will guarantee the $600–$700 billion deposits in Australian financial institutions in a move to shore up local confidence and protect the nation's international competitiveness. Declaring that the country is in 'the economic equivalent of a rolling national security crisis', [Prime Minister] Kevin Rudd has also announced that all borrowing by Australian banks and other deposit-taking institutions from overseas will be guaranteed. The deposit and lending guarantees are unprecedented in Australian banking history and are an immediate response to the dramatic moves by other countries to prop up their failing financial systems. ... Australian banks welcomed the Government's moves. Australian Bankers Association chief executive David Bell said Australian banks were well capitalised but were still affected by the seizure of international financial markets. 'This levels the playing field and allows Australian banks to compete equally and fairly', he said.

Source: 'Rudd's $700 billion bank guarantee', Michelle Grattan and Vanessa O'Shaughnessy, *The Age*, 13 October 2008.

---

13 The *Banking Act 1959* charges the RBA with the protection of depositors of banks subject to the Act. However, the RBA does not interpret this as an explicit guarantee of bank deposits. While the RBA no longer has responsibility for the supervision of the banks, it is the only institution that is able to provide emergency liquidity support in the event of threats to the stability of the financial markets.

14 For discussion of the guarantee measures, see Schwartz (2010).

Banks also had a unique role in the payments system in the settlement of cheques, which is conducted through exchange settlement accounts at the RBA. Until the late 1990s these accounts were held only by banks.[15] Bank assets include a range of loans, the most distinctive being the overdraft facility, which involves an arrangement whereby borrowers may draw funds, at their discretion, up to a specified limit. Banks are large lenders to the business sector and in the 6-month period ended June 2010 accounted for more than 90 per cent of commercial lending by intermediaries.[16]

The Australian banking sector is dominated by four major banks, the ANZ Banking Group (**www.anz.com.au**), the Commonwealth Bank of Australia (**www.commbank.com.au**), the National Australia Bank (**www.national.com.au**) and Westpac Banking Corporation (**www.westpac.com.au**). These banks accounted for 77 per cent of the total assets of the Australian banking sector as at December 2009 (APRA 2009b). Each has a nationwide branch network and provides a full range of banking services for individuals as well as business customers both locally and overseas. Other Australian-owned banks are smaller and many are referred to as 'regional banks' because they originally had a regional base in one state. Many of these smaller banks, including the Bendigo and Adelaide Bank, Suncorp–Metway and the Bank of Queensland, have since expanded to compete with the major banks by achieving broader coverage of the Australian market.

Historically, foreign-owned banks played only a minor role in the Australian financial system. However, in recent years they have attracted an increased share of deposits through measures such as attractive interest rates paid on internet-based savings accounts. Foreign banks have also begun to compete more aggressively in lending in Australia and at the end of 2008 they held around 16 per cent of overall Australian bank assets. By the end of 2009, their share of bank assets had declined to 13.6 per cent (APRA 2009b).

Following the collapse of Lehman Brothers in September 2008 and the failure or near-failure of many other financial institutions, there was a widespread loss of confidence in the solvency of financial institutions and the stability of the global financial system. Governments in several countries, including Australia, moved to restore confidence through measures that were in some cases unprecedented.

8.3.2 MONEY MARKET CORPORATIONS

The activities of money market corporations (MMCs) were discussed in Section 8.2.2. Table 8.3 on page 221 shows that the assets of these institutions have declined from around 10 per cent of the total assets of banks, MMCs and finance companies in the mid-1990s to around 5 per cent from 2004 to 2008, and they then fell further to only 2.3 per cent in 2010. As discussed in Section 8.2.2, the long-term decline reflects the ongoing effects of the deregulation of the Australian financial system, whereby restrictions that applied to banks were removed, allowing them to strengthen their competitive position at the expense of non-bank financial intermediaries. The more rapid decline over the 2008 to 2010 period coincides with the global financial crisis. Since MMCs are not authorised deposit-taking institutions (ADIs) their borrowings were not covered by the government guarantee announced in October 2008.

8.3.3 FINANCE COMPANIES

Initially, finance companies were primarily concerned with lending to individuals by providing instalment credit for retail sales. In 1954 this accounted for 85 per cent of finance company lending but by June 2010, lending to individuals accounted for only 23 per cent of the total assets of finance companies.[17]

---

15 The payments system has now been opened up to other financial institutions. For details of the terms on which the Reserve Bank will make exchange settlement accounts available to financial institutions, see Reserve Bank of Australia (1999).

16 This percentage is derived from the Australian Bureau of Statistics publication *Lending Finance, Australia* (cat. no. 5671.0, Table 3).

17 See Reserve Bank of Australia, Table B10, **www.rba.gov.au/statistics/tables/index.html#assets_liabilities**.

Finance companies grew rapidly during the period in which the Australian financial markets were highly regulated. They offered a wide range of financial services for companies, including instalment credit, lease financing, inventory financing, discounting of accounts receivable, mortgages and other commercial loans. Their success was due largely to the regulatory constraints on their natural competitors, the banks. In fact, each of the major banks acquired a finance company subsidiary in order to gain access to markets denied them by bank regulations.

The deregulation of the banking sector in the 1980s removed much of the competitive advantage hitherto enjoyed by finance companies. As can be seen from Table 8.3, the assets of finance companies have grown at a much lower average rate than the assets of banks over the period from 1995 to 2008 and declined in dollar terms from 2008 to 2010. Many finance companies have become specialised institutions focusing on specific areas such as motor vehicle finance or the financing of machinery and equipment. Some of the larger finance companies, such as CBFC Limited, are owned by banks—in this case, the Commonwealth Bank of Australia—which often fund particular types of loans such as those for cars and unsecured personal loans through these subsidiaries. In contrast, the National Australia Bank absorbed the operations of its finance company subsidiary (Custom Credit) into those of the parent bank. Similarly, in March 2009 the ANZ Banking Group announced that its wholly owned subsidiary, Esanda Finance Corporation, would become a division of the bank. Westpac Banking Corporation withdrew from the sector by selling its finance company (AGC) in 2002.

8.3.4 SECURITISATION[18]

LEARNING OBJECTIVE 5
Outline the role of securitisation

securitisation
the process of making assets marketable by aggregating income-producing assets in a pool and issuing new securities backed by the pool

Securitisation is the process of converting illiquid assets such as bank loans into tradeable securities. In a typical case, an originator of financial assets—such as a bank that has provided a significant number of housing loans—sells a portfolio of these loans to a specially created company or trust. This entity, generally referred to as a securitisation vehicle or special purpose vehicle (SPV), finances its purchase of the loans by issuing tradeable securities to investors using the underlying assets (the housing loans) as collateral. If these securities are long term they are generally referred to as asset-backed bonds, or if the loans involved are all mortgage loans over residential property, the securities may be referred to as residential mortgage-backed securities (RMBS). If the securities are short term—that is, their term to maturity is less than a year—they may be referred to as asset-backed commercial paper (ABCP). The end result is that securitisation allows a financial institution to fund its lending indirectly through the capital market instead of by the traditional method of gathering deposits or borrowing directly in its own name.

The securitisation market in Australia has been dominated by securitisation of residential mortgages but the range of assets that can be securitised has broadened and includes commercial mortgages, leases, trade receivables and motor vehicle loans. As shown in Table 8.1, on page 214, the assets of Australian securitisation vehicles grew from around $10 billion in June 1995 to $274 billion in June 2007 but then fell to $147 billion in June 2010. During the period of rapid growth that commenced in the 1990s, the share of residential mortgage loans funded through securitisation increased from less than 10 per cent in the late 1990s to almost 25 per cent in June 2007 (see Debelle 2009, p. 43). Current information about securitisation is provided by the Australian Securitisation Forum (ASF, www.securitisation.com.au). The assets of Australian securitisation vehicles are shown in Table 8.4.

WWW

---

18 Facts related to the Australian securitisation market mentioned in this section are mostly drawn from Reserve Bank of Australia (2004) pp. 48–56 and Debelle (2009).

TABLE 8.4 Assets of securitisation vehicles, $ million

30 JUNE	MORTGAGES	OTHER LOANS AND PLACEMENTS	ASSET-BACKED BONDS	OTHER SECURITIES	ALL OTHER ASSETS	TOTAL ASSETS
1990	4 794	845				5 734
1995	5 358	1 456	928	1 229	894	9 845
2000	41 306	7 905	8 072	2 515	5 216	65 014
2001	54 751	9 386	11 026	3 667	5 791	84 621
2002	72 809	10 548	15 016	5 848	6 242	110 463
2003	89 936	11 706	16 573	4 110	7 300	129 625
2004	125 633	9 151	15 505	3 564	8 617	162 470
2005	146 984	11 293	12 286	3 972	9 970	184 505
2006	176 288	11 162	13 738	2 946	12 327	216 461
2007	215 201	17 319	18 907	3 025	19 525	273 977
2008	179 877	19 106	20 997	2 753	16 715	239 448
2009	143 374	15 346	15 858	525	18 104	193 207
2010	116 316	11 922	9 229	435	8 835	146 737

Source: Table B19, Reserve Bank of Australia website, **www.rba.gov.au**.

There are three main differences between RMBS and non-asset-backed debt securities such as government bonds. First, the credit quality of the securities depends largely on the quality of the underlying assets and is not directly related to that of the originator of those assets. Second, almost all issues of RMBS involve some form of credit enhancement. In most cases, this is achieved by dividing the asset-backed securities into a senior tranche and one or more subordinated tranches. For example, the senior tranche might contain securities with a value equal to 95 per cent of the total value of the securities issued, with the remaining 5 per cent making up the subordinated tranche. The subordinated tranche protects the senior securities by absorbing the first round of any losses arising from defaults on the underlying assets. In this case, provided default losses do not exceed 5 per cent of the value of those assets, the senior securities can still be repaid in full. This approach usually allows the senior securities to be issued with a credit rating of AAA. However, tranching involves a repackaging of cash flows and risks, so the securities in the subordinated tranches will have lower credit ratings than they would if the securities were issued in a single tranche. In practice, other measures, such as mortgage insurance, are also employed to provide additional protection for investors. The third difference is that the principal of RMBS is amortised over the life of the security rather than being repaid as a 'bullet' payment at maturity, which is the standard procedure for most government bonds and corporate bonds.

For a loan originator, the choice between securitising its loan assets and using other sources of funds will depend on the relative costs of these alternatives. The four major banks in Australia securitise only a small proportion of their mortgage loans—prior to mid-2007 the proportion was less than 10 per cent. For these banks there is little difference between the cost of securitisation and the cost of borrowing directly in the bank's own name. Regional banks, credit unions and building societies make considerably greater use of securitisation. For example, prior to mid-2007, regional banks securitised about one-third of their housing loans. This difference is consistent with the fact that for these smaller institutions the cost of borrowing directly is noticeably higher than it is for the major banks. Finally, specialist mortgage originators that are not ADIs, who would face even higher costs if they were to borrow directly, securitise all of their loans.

As shown in Table 8.5, Australian securitisers have been active in issuing asset-backed securities in both the domestic and offshore markets, which suggests that neither market offers a systematic cost advantage. However, this does not mean that the choice between the domestic and offshore markets is unimportant, and some strong patterns can be seen. For example, most issues of RMBS by the large banks have been made offshore, while credit unions and building societies have been much more active in making domestic issues. One reason for this difference is that offshore markets can accommodate much larger security issues than the Australian domestic market. Another reason is that while large Australian institutions are well known to overseas investors, smaller Australian institutions are generally not known in offshore markets.

TABLE 8.5 Liabilities of securitisation vehicles, $ million

	ASSET-BACKED SECURITIES				
30 JUNE	ISSUED OVERSEAS	ISSUED IN AUSTRALIA		OTHER LIABILITIES	TOTAL LIABILITIES
		SHORT TERM	LONG TERM		
1990	140	636	4894		5734
1995	1401	1091	7228	125	9845
2000	20064	9869	24493	10588	65014
2001	28689	15045	30373	10514	84621
2002	33637	19798	42329	14699	110463
2003	42320	20600	51959	14746	129625
2004	61671	20324	64412	16063	162470
2005	65330	22736	79326	17113	184505
2006	72253	21277	98941	23990	216461
2007	100151	25152	122343	26331	273977
2008	68372	39555	111678	19843	239448
2009	58012	24469	98987	11739	193207
2010	35779	19024	81339	10595	146737

Source: Table B19, Reserve Bank of Australia website, **www.rba.gov.au**.

Potential investors have been attracted to asset-backed securities by their perceived high credit quality, with senior tranches almost invariably having a AAA credit rating. Despite their high credit quality, asset-backed securities appear to offer slightly higher yields than non-asset-backed bonds of similar quality. For example, over the period 2000 to 2004, issues of AAA-rated RMBS in the Australian market had an average spread of about 35 basis points above the bank bill rate. In comparison, bonds issued by the major banks, which at the time had ratings of AA−, typically had spreads of less than 20 basis points. These wider spreads probably reflect a combination of two factors. First, the duration of asset-backed bonds is uncertain because many of the underlying loans are repaid more quickly than required by the loan contract. Securitisation arrangements generally require that any additional repayments cannot be retained within the securitisation vehicle and must instead be passed on to the holders of the asset-backed bonds. Second, there is evidence that the secondary market in asset-backed securities is much less liquid than the secondary market in government bonds and corporate bonds. Secondary market liquidity may not be a major concern because asset-backed securities are mostly purchased by 'buy-and-hold' investors such as superannuation funds. Nevertheless, limited liquidity means that an investor faces the risk that a security portfolio cannot be sold quickly without having an adverse effect on the price and it is likely that investors will require compensation for this risk.

The rapid growth in securitisation up to 2007 can be attributed to two main factors. First, the demand for housing finance in Australia remained strong. Second, the composition of lenders in the mortgage market changed, with mortgage originators that securitise almost all of their loans gaining a growing share after entering the market in the 1990s (Debelle 2009, pp. 43–4). The fall in the assets of securitisation vehicles after 2007 is another outcome of the global financial crisis. At times during this crisis, markets for asset-backed securities were effectively frozen, with many sellers but no buyers, so there was little if any trading in secondary markets and issuance of new securities declined markedly and in some cases ceased altogether. With repayments on the underlying loans being applied to amortise the principal of existing securities and minimal issuance of new securities, the assets of securitisation vehicles inevitably fell. While securitisation and losses incurred on holdings of asset-backed securities were central to the global financial crisis, it has been argued that the disruption experienced in the Australian market reflects the effects of offshore factors rather than concerns about the credit quality of Australian RMBS. During 2009, conditions in the Australian market improved significantly and it is expected that securitisation will continue to be an important part of the financial system (Debelle 2009, p. 52).

8.4 INVESTING INSTITUTIONS

The main investing institutions in Australia are life insurance companies, superannuation funds, public unit trusts and general insurance companies. As noted earlier, many of these institutions are owned by banks or are parts of financial conglomerates. There is also significant overlap between the categories. In particular, management of superannuation funds is a major activity of life insurance companies, so most of the assets held by these companies are within superannuation funds.

LEARNING OBJECTIVE 6
Identify and explain the role of investing institutions

8.4.1 INSURANCE COMPANIES AND SUPERANNUATION FUNDS

As shown in Table 8.1, the total assets of general insurance companies are around $125 billion, which is less than 3 per cent of the assets of all Australian financial institutions. In Australia, around 70 per cent of their premium revenue arises from 'short tail' business. This type of business involves providing insurance cover for assets such as motor vehicles and buildings where any losses are generally incurred within 12 months of receiving the premium. Insurance companies usually match the duration of their assets with the duration of their liabilities. Thus, while general insurance companies do make some long-term investments, the majority of their assets are short term. This factor, together with their relatively small size, means that general insurance companies are not a major source of company finance. Hence, in this section we focus on life insurance companies and superannuation funds. Insurance companies and most superannuation funds are regulated by APRA, the only exception being self-managed superannuation funds (SMSFs) which are regulated by the Australian Taxation Office.

Life insurance companies and superannuation funds are major sources of company finance. These institutions raise large amounts as premiums and contributions, which are largely long-term commitments and, accordingly, such institutions tend to acquire long-term assets such as shares issued by public companies, and bonds and other forms of debt issued by governments and companies. Australia's superannuation industry has grown rapidly since the early 1990s in response to the Commonwealth Government's superannuation guarantee charge policy, which aims to promote universal superannuation coverage. Significant changes to the superannuation system announced in the Commonwealth Government's May 2006 budget further stimulated the flow of funds into superannuation. The growth of assets within the superannuation system is expected to continue, although the rate of growth will be influenced by changes in government policy and fluctuations in investment returns. Table 8.6 shows the recent growth in both the assets held by superannuation funds and the total number of funds.

TABLE 8.6 Assets and number of funds—superannuation funds

30 JUNE	ASSETS ($ BILLION)	NUMBER OF SUPERANNUATION ENTITIES CLASSIFIED BY TYPE						TOTAL
		CORPORATE	INDUSTRY	PUBLIC SECTOR	RETAIL	SMALL	POOLED SUPERANNUATION TRUSTS	
2000	484.2	3 389	155	81	293	212 538	164	216 620
2001	519.0	3 224	150	81	275	219 064	177	222 971
2002	518.1	2 484	134	76	254	235 626	179	238 753
2003	546.8	1 862	124	58	235	262 175	160	264 614
2004	643.0	1 405	106	42	232	287 982	143	289 910
2005	762.9	962	90	43	228	304 893	130	306 346
2006	917.8	555	80	45	192	323 917	123	324 912
2007	1143.2	289	74	40	172	365 992	101	366 668
2008	1139.7	226	70	40	169	389 308	90	389 903
2009	1073.3	190	67	40	166	414 707	82	415 252
2010	1225.4	168	65	39	154	432 170	79	432 675

Source: Australian Prudential Regulation Authority, **www.apra.gov.au**, *Annual Superannuation Bulletin*, June 2006, June 2007, June 2008, June 2009 and June 2010.

The large increase in total superannuation assets over the 7 years to June 2007 reflects the combined effects of positive net contribution flows—that is, contributions exceeded benefits paid—and strong investment returns on some asset classes, particularly Australian equities, after 2002. In the years immediately after 2007, net contributions remained positive but falls in the values of many financial assets, particularly equities, meant that total superannuation assets declined. The significant increase in the number of funds over the period covered by Table 8.6 is due entirely to growth in the number of small funds, most of which are SMSFs. The number of these funds is disproportionately high relative to the value of their assets. To illustrate, at 30 June 2009 SMSFs accounted for 98.8 per cent of the total number of funds but only 31 per cent of the total assets held by superannuation funds (Australian Prudential Regulation Authority 2009a).

While the number of small funds has grown strongly, Table 8.6 shows that the number of funds in other categories, particularly corporate funds, has declined dramatically in recent years. In large part, this decline reflects the effects of licensing requirements that were phased in during a transitional period that ended on 30 June 2006. The trustees of many stand-alone corporate funds chose not to seek a licence and the members and assets of these funds were transferred to other funds, particularly industry funds and retail funds. The value of assets held by superannuation funds outside life insurance companies is shown in Table 8.7. It shows that superannuation funds are large, and growing, investors in the shares of Australian companies and in units in trusts. Assets of these types typically accounted for about 45 per cent of total fund assets in the last decade compared with less than 30 per cent in 1990. These figures, in conjunction with those in Table 8.1, show that superannuation funds are potentially the largest institutional source of equity capital for Australian companies. Overseas assets made up almost 17 per cent of total assets in 2010 compared with 11.4 per cent in 1990. Similarly, cash and deposits made up 16.5 per cent of total assets in 2010 compared with 11.1 per cent in 1990. In contrast, the debt-type investments, loans and placements and short-term securities decreased from almost 15 per cent of total assets in 1990 to 6.6 per cent in 2010, while long-term government securities declined from 10.1 per cent of assets in 1990 to only 2.3 per cent in 2010. While debt-type investments have declined as a percentage of fund assets, the absolute size of their asset pool is such that superannuation funds remain a significant source of debt finance, either directly or indirectly, for businesses. For example, the investment of more than $58 billion in short-term securities at June 2010 would include bills of exchange issued by corporate borrowers. Also, the cash and deposits of $171 billion held in 2010 would consist mostly of deposits in banks, which could use these deposits to fund loans, including loans to companies.

TABLE 8.7 Assets held by superannuation funds outside life insurance companies, $ million

30 JUNE	CASH AND DEPOSITS	LOANS AND PLACEMENTS	SHORT-TERM SECURITIES	LONG-TERM GOVERNMENT SECURITIES	EQUITIES AND UNITS IN TRUSTS	LAND AND BUILDINGS	OTHER ASSETS	ASSETS OVERSEAS	TOTAL ASSETS
1990	8 986	4 234	7 703	8 191	23 052	12 668	6 760	9 226	80 820
1995	11 349	5 375	8 794	20 632	55 850	11 006	9 171	21 094	143 272
2000	24 349	16 138	19 376	19 877	142 734	17 294	21 893	68 065	329 724
2001	30 878	14 149	16 039	19 111	161 077	22 657	19 973	73 566	357 451
2002	32 618	7 061	15 582	17 463	166 061	24 338	24 100	78 575	365 800
2003	39 534	5 149	19 963	15 558	172 667	23 666	22 305	77 156	375 999
2004	49 074	4 936	25 268	16 345	232 503	26 676	25 861	101 495	482 160
2005	62 184	5 292	25 134	21 579	276 347	32 157	29 762	114 419	566 874
2006	75 848	5 378	26 903	24 883	350 476	37 259	36 218	146 411	703 377
2007	128 153	7 211	35 354	28 024	466 798	50 172	52 105	185 472	953 290
2008	132 298	7 854	39 449	24 583	438 395	58 413	55 801	180 003	936 795
2009	160 912	8 293	47 032	21 694	389 431	62 835	54 590	147 867	892 652
2010	171 097	9 992	58 284	24 263	459 256	71 953	66 785	172 969	1 034 599

Source: Table B15, Reserve Bank of Australia website, www.rba.gov.au.

WWW

Management of superannuation funds is a very important activity of life insurance companies and at the end of 2009, assets held in superannuation funds accounted for almost 90 per cent of the assets of these companies. Despite this high proportion there has been a significant decline in the share of total superannuation assets held by life insurance companies. Their share of the total superannuation pool peaked at 44 per cent in 1992 but declined to around 19 per cent by 2009 (Reserve Bank of Australia, March 2010). The assets of life insurance companies are shown in Table 8.8.

While the data in Table 8.8 will largely reflect the assets held in superannuation funds managed by life insurance companies, there are some noticeable differences between the distributions of assets in Tables 8.7 and 8.8. Compared with the superannuation funds outside life insurance companies, based on the 2010 figures, the life insurance companies have invested a higher proportion of their assets in domestic equities and trusts (70.7 per cent versus 44.4 per cent), a lower proportion in cash and deposits (4 per cent versus 16.5 per cent) and a lower proportion in overseas assets (4.7 per cent versus 16.7 per cent). Table 8.8 shows that life insurance companies are not large lenders to the corporate sector. Historically, most of their investment in debt took the form of government debt securities. However, holdings of 'Other assets', which includes debt securities issued by non-government borrowers, have tended to increase as their holdings of long-term government securities have declined. In contrast, like superannuation funds outside life insurance companies, they are significant suppliers of equity, with shares and units in trusts constituting about 71 per cent of their total assets at the end of June 2010.

TABLE 8.8 Assets held by life insurance companies—statutory funds, $ million

30 JUNE	CASH AND DEPOSITS	LOANS AND PLACEMENTS	SHORT-TERM SECURITIES	LONG-TERM GOVERNMENT SECURITIES	EQUITIES AND UNITS IN TRUSTS	LAND AND BUILDINGS	OTHER ASSETS	ASSETS OVERSEAS	TOTAL ASSETS
1990	2 685	10 693	5 358	n.a.	21 623	13 423	6 750	8 417	85 285
1995	4 913	5 809	9 929	22 106	38 073	9 487	10 987	17 217	118 523
2000	10 017	8 843	14 078	19 243	75 194	8 632	21 012	32 949	189 969
2001	9 560	7 730	11 507	15 643	98 244	9 393	18 950	30 183	201 210
2002	8 169	4 799	12 205	13 048	103 824	8 701	20 634	30 318	201 698
2003	7 735	3 633	14 428	11 034	101 349	7 952	23 866	23 091	193 108
2004	7 239	2 430	13 556	12 196	122 462	7 860	19 496	17 284	202 524
2005	6 060	2 619	12 969	9 561	148 214	n.a.	n.a.	14 101	222 754
2006	6 118	3 094	12 419	5 096	168 192	3 043	25 891	14 132	237 984
2007	6 218	2 635	11 574	4 964	196 976	3 314	25 303	12 238	263 220
2008	5 690	2 636	9 048	4 660	172 157	2 661	25 076	10 548	232 475
2009	10 051	2 524	8 187	4 121	141 877	2 533	27 049	9 363	205 704
2010	9 037	1 860	6 768	5 727	158 333	2 517	28 935	10 629	223 806

Source: Table B14, Reserve Bank of Australia website, www.rba.gov.au.

WWW

When assessing the asset distributions shown in Tables 8.7 and 8.8, two qualifications should be noted. First, the investment by superannuation funds and life insurance companies in property is considerably greater than suggested by the figures shown for 'land and buildings'. Many of these institutions invest in property by purchasing units in property trusts mainly because they prefer the liquidity that these trusts provide, particularly if the trust is listed on a stock exchange. These investments are included in the figures for 'Equities and units in trusts'. Second, the 'stock' figures shown in these tables do not necessarily provide an accurate indication of the way in which new money flowing into superannuation is invested. For example, as noted above, the tables show that equities and units in trusts make up a large and typically growing proportion of the assets of superannuation funds and life insurance companies. In the case of superannuation funds outside life insurance companies, this asset class increased from less than 30 per cent of total assets in 1990 to almost 50 per cent of total assets in 2006 and 2007 and then declined to around 44 per cent in 2009 and 2010. Thus, it might seem that the proportion of superannuation contributions directed into domestic equities peaked around 2006–07 and then declined. However, the values of the various assets held at any time will reflect past returns as well as the pattern of new investment. The returns on Australian shares were unusually high from 2002 to 2007 but negative during 2008 and 2009. Specifically, the S&P/ASX All Ordinaries share price index, which was 3163.2 at the end of June 2002, almost doubled to reach 6310.6 at the end of June 2007 and then fell to 3947.8 at the end of June 2009. Therefore, over the 2002 to 2009 period, a typical fund could exhibit an increase in the value of equities as a percentage of its total assets up to 2007, followed by a decline, even if the proportion of new contributions invested in each asset class remained constant over time.

8.4.2 UNIT TRUSTS AND INVESTMENT COMPANIES

Unit trusts are a common form of collective investment in which the funds of investors are pooled and invested by a professional management company in a wide range of investments, usually of a specific asset type. For example, there are property trusts, Australian equity trusts and international equity trusts. These and a variety of other pooled investments are classified as 'managed investment schemes'. The regulatory regime for these investments is set out in the *Managed Investments Act 1998*. It specifies that managed investment schemes are to be operated by a single 'responsible entity', which must be an Australian public company holding an appropriate Australian Financial Services Licence. Most of these responsible entities are subsidiaries of banks, investment banks or insurance companies. Investors place their money in pooled investments to obtain a spread of risk and to obtain returns from assets that are too expensive for individuals to purchase directly.

Many trusts are open-end funds, which means that new units may be created continually as investors contribute additional cash. These trusts are unlisted and investors purchase and redeem units at values, calculated daily by the fund manager, based on the value of the assets held by the trust. The trust may buy additional assets at any time and may need to sell assets at times in order to meet redemption requests from existing investors. In June 2010, public unit trusts in Australia had total assets of $256 billion and a further $35.5 billion was held by cash management trusts (Reserve Bank of Australia, Table B1, **www.rba.gov.au/statistics/tables/index.html#assets_liabilities**).[19]

A wide range of listed managed investments (LMIs) is also available. At the end of June 2010, 195 managed investments were listed on the ASX and the market capitalisation of these entities totalled $134 billion. Based on market capitalisation at that time, the largest category of LMIs is real estate investment trusts ($75 billion), followed by infrastructure funds ($35 billion) and listed investment companies and trusts ($19 billion) (Australian Securities Exchange, **www.asx.com.au/products/pdf/lmi/lmi_monthly_update_201007.pdf**).

Real estate investment trusts (REITs) allow investors to acquire an interest in a professionally managed portfolio of real estate.[20] Some REITs invest only in a particular type of real estate such as industrial (warehouses and factories), offices, hotels or retail (shopping centres, malls and cinemas). Others are more diversified and invest in two or more of these types of real estate. There are also international

---

19 Public unit trusts are investment funds open to the Australian public excluding property and trading trusts.
20 Real estate investment trusts (REITs) were traditionally referred to as property trusts, which could be listed or unlisted. The term REIT was adopted in Australia in 2008. Where such trusts are listed on the ASX, they are now referred to as A-REITs.

REITs, which are listed on the ASX but invest in specific offshore markets such as the US, Europe or Japan. A REIT listed on the ASX will have one of two structures:

- a stand-alone trust or company that provides investors only with exposure to an underlying portfolio of real estate assets; or
- a group consisting of a company and one or more related trusts. Income-producing properties will be held by the trust(s) while the company will also carry out property development and/or funds management. The group will issue **stapled securities** comprising a share in the company plus a unit in each of the trusts.

stapled securities
two or more legally separate instruments, typically an ordinary share plus units in one or more related trusts, which cannot be traded separately

In general, a trust is not taxed at the trust level provided it distributes all of its income to investors. Therefore, trust income is almost invariably distributed in full whereas a company can retain all or part of its profit to finance expansion. Therefore, a stand-alone trust is suitable for holding and managing a portfolio of assets that produce passive rental income for distribution to unit holders. The group structure is more suitable if there are operating activities such as property development, as well as ownership of income-producing assets.

Infrastructure funds invest in assets involved in the supply of essential goods and services such as railways, toll roads, airports, communication facilities, power lines and oil/gas pipelines. Most infrastructure funds involve a company/trust group that issues stapled securities. Like REITs, infrastructure funds generally receive a stable income stream and pay regular distributions to investors.

Traditionally, listed investment companies (LICs) have provided their shareholders with exposure to a diversified portfolio of investments, often consisting only of the shares of a wide range of other companies that are also listed on the ASX. Some newer LICs specialise in particular types of assets such as international shares, small companies or gold companies, or they may focus on particular geographical regions such as Europe or Asia. In contrast to unlisted managed investments, LICs are essentially closed-end, meaning that the company does not continually issue new shares or cancel shares as shareholders join and leave the company. Rather, the company's shares are traded on the ASX in the same way as all other listed shares, and the size and timing of any share issues or repurchases will be determined by the company's managers. The market price of the shares will be determined by the supply of shares offered by sellers and the demand for them from buyers. The share price will often be similar to the value of their asset backing but can be at a premium or, more often, at a discount to the asset backing.

The fact that some managed investments are structured as a trust while others use a company structure creates important taxation differences. For example, if a trust makes a profit, perhaps by selling an asset and realising a capital gain, the entire profit must be passed on to investors as a distribution and each investor will be taxed at their individual rate.[21] If a listed investment company makes the same profit, it will pay tax at the company tax rate on that profit. The after-tax profit can then be distributed to shareholders as a franked dividend.

8.4.3 OVERSEAS SOURCES AND MARKETS

The Australian capital market is part of a global market and in recent years there has been a sizeable flow of funds from overseas for investment in Australian companies. This has comprised mainly equity contributions and fixed-term lending from overseas companies, overseas portfolio investment and eurodollar loans, and other forms of fixed-term borrowing. Some Australian companies, particularly very large ones, borrow directly from overseas, but intermediaries have been very active in obtaining funds from overseas. Because they typically have high credit ratings, intermediaries such as banks are better placed to borrow overseas than many companies. The funds borrowed by the intermediary are then lent

---

21 In many cases, the distributions from REITs and infrastructure funds are partly tax deferred, which means that investors do not pay tax on the tax deferred component of the distribution until their holding in the trust or fund is sold.

to customers. Also, as discussed in Section 8.3.4, a significant proportion of the asset-backed securities issued by securitisation vehicles are purchased by offshore investors.

While sizeable funds have flowed from overseas for investment in Australian companies, Australia has also been a significant source of funds for investment in foreign companies. For example, as shown in Table 8.7, Australian superannuation funds have large investments in overseas assets and these investments have at times exceeded 20 per cent of the funds' assets. The inflow to, and outflow of capital from, Australia is consistent with investors recognising the advantages of diversification and seeking opportunities to invest in industries that may not be represented in their domestic economies.

Connect Plus features a case study illustrating topics covered in this chapter.
Ask your lecturer or tutor for your course's unique URL.

SUMMARY

→ In this chapter we discussed the capital market, which can be used by Australian companies to raise long-term funds in the form of debt and equity. The use of the capital market by companies to raise equity and long-term debt is considered in more detail in Chapters 9 and 10.

→ This chapter also outlined the main types of financial institutions that form an important part of the capital market. These include institutions that operate as agents (such as brokers), financial intermediaries (such as banks) and investors (such as insurance companies and superannuation funds). The regulation of these institutions was also discussed and the main changes that have occurred since the Australian financial system was deregulated in the 1980s were identified.

KEY TERMS

authorised deposit-taking institution 214
capital market 209
central bank 211
default risk 213
exchange-traded market 210
financial agency institution 212
financial assets 209
financial intermediary 209
investing institution 213
over-the-counter market 210
primary market 210
secondary market 210
securitisation 224
stapled securities 232

REFERENCES

Australian Bureau of Statistics, *Lending Finance, Australia*, cat. no. 5671.0, Table 3.

Australian Prudential Regulation Authority, *Annual Superannuation Bulletin*, www.apra.gov.au, Commonwealth of Australia, ACT, June 2009a.

Australian Prudential Regulation Authority, *Quarterly Bank Performance*, www.apra.gov.au, Commonwealth of Australia, ACT, December 2009b.

Bruce, R., McKern, B., Pollard, I. & Skully, M. (eds), *Handbook of Australian Corporate Finance*, 5th edn, Butterworths, Sydney, 1997.

Carew, E., *Fast Money 4*, Allen & Unwin, Sydney, 1998.

Committee of Inquiry into the Australian Financial System (J.K. Campbell, Chairman), *Final Report*, AGPS, Canberra, 1981.

Committee of Inquiry into the Australian Financial System (V. Martin, Chairman), *Report of the Review Group*, AGPS, Canberra, 1984.

Davies, P. & Peacock, D., 'The role of the stock exchange and the financial characteristics of Australian companies', in R. Bruce et al. (eds), *Handbook of Australian Corporate Finance*, 5th edn, Butterworths, Sydney, 1997, pp. 82–132.

Debelle, G., 'Whither securitisation?', Reserve Bank of Australia, *Bulletin*, December 2009, pp. 43–53.

Financial System Inquiry (S. Wallis, Chairman), *Final Report*, AGPS, Canberra, 1997.

Gup, B.E., *The New Basel Capital Accord*, Texere, New York, 2004.

Harper C. & Torres C., 'Goldman, Morgan Stanley bring down curtain on an era' (Update 5), Bloomberg, 22 September 2008. Available at **www.bloomberg.com/apps/news?pid=21070001&sid=axaX5i4871U0, 22 September 2008**.

Lewis, M.K. & Wallace, R.H. (eds), *The Australian Financial System*, Addison Wesley Longman, Melbourne, 1997.

O'Brien, K.P., 'Building societies, credit unions and friendly societies', in M.K. Lewis and R.H. Wallace (eds), *The Australian Financial System*, Addison Wesley Longman, Melbourne, 1997, pp. 162–203.

Reserve Bank of Australia, 'Asset Securitisation in Australia', *Financial Stability Review*, September 2004, pp. 48–56.

Reserve Bank of Australia, *Bulletin*, October 1988.

——, 'The Role of Exchange Settlement Accounts', *Bulletin*, March 1999, pp. 13–18.

——, 'The structure of the Australian financial system', *Financial Stability Review*, March 2006, pp. 49–61.

——, 'Developments in the financial system architecture', *Financial Stability Review*, March 2010, pp. 53–61.

Schwartz, C., 'The Australian Government Guarantee Scheme', Reserve Bank of Australia, *Bulletin*, March 2010, pp. 19–26.

Viney, C., *McGrath's Financial Institutions, Instruments and Markets*, 6th edn, McGraw-Hill, Sydney, 2009.

QUESTIONS

1. **[LO 1]** Distinguish between direct finance and intermediated finance. Discuss why some borrowers might prefer direct finance, while others might prefer intermediated finance.

2. **[LO 1]** Why is the existence of a secondary market expected to increase the demand for securities issued in the corresponding primary market?

3. **[LO 3]** Discuss the relative importance of the following institutions as providers of company finance:
   (a) stockbrokers
   (b) investment banks
   (c) banks
   (d) finance companies
   (e) superannuation funds.

4. **[LO 3]** Outline the services provided by financial institutions, such as stockbrokers and investment banks, to companies wishing to raise funds direct from the market.

5. **[LO 6]** Explain possible reasons for the rapid increase in the number of superannuation funds in existence as well as the total assets held by those funds.

6. **[LO 6]** *Institutional investors have always been major suppliers of company finance.* Discuss this statement and explain how this flow of funds occurs.

7. **[LO 1]** Distinguish between monetary policy and prudential regulation of banks. Explain how these two activities were linked in the past, but are now separate.

8. **[LO 2]** Distinguish between financial agency institutions, financial intermediaries and investing institutions. Why is there such a range of institutions in the capital market?

9. **[LO 1]** What are the main differences between an exchange-traded market and an over-the-counter market?

10. **[LO 5]** The major banks in Australia securitise only a small proportion of their mortgage loans, regional banks make greater use of this technique and specialist mortgage originators securitise most of their loans. Explain why these differences exist.

11. **[LO 3]** What distinctions can be made between the activities of large Australian banks and investment banks?

12. **[LO 3]** Investment banks can face inherent conflicts of interest. Explain how these conflicts of interest usually arise. How can they be managed?

13. **[LO 3]** During the global financial crisis, at least one Australian-based investment bank collapsed, while others, including the subsidiaries of US and European firms, continued to operate but on a somewhat smaller scale. Outline the main differences that contributed to these very different outcomes.

Test yourself further with Connect Plus online! Ask your lecturer or tutor for your course's unique URL.

CHAPTER 9
SOURCES OF FINANCE: EQUITY

LEARNING OBJECTIVES

After studying this chapter you should be able to:

1. outline the characteristics of ordinary shares
2. explain the advantages and disadvantages of equity as a source of finance
3. outline the main sources of private equity in the Australian market
4. identify the information that must be disclosed when issuing securities
5. outline the process of floating a public company
6. discuss alternative explanations for the underpricing of initial public offerings
7. outline evidence on the long-term performance of companies that are floated
8. explain how companies raise capital through rights issues, placements, share purchase plans and share options
9. outline the different types of employee share plans
10. outline the advantages of internal funds as a source of finance
11. outline the effects of bonus issues, share splits and share consolidations.

CHAPTER CONTENTS

- 9.1 Introduction
- 9.2 The characteristics of ordinary shares
- 9.3 Private equity
- 9.4 Information disclosure
- 9.5 Floating a public company
- 9.6 Subsequent issues of ordinary shares
- 9.7 Employee share plans
- 9.8 Internal funds
- 9.9 Managing a company's equity structure

9.1 INTRODUCTION

In this chapter and in Chapter 10, we discuss methods by which a company may finance its assets. In this chapter we discuss equity and Chapter 10 covers debt. Leasing is considered in Chapter 15 and foreign currency loans are considered in Chapter 20.

In this chapter, several ways of raising equity are considered. The majority of equity in Australia is raised by public companies and unit trusts with shares, units and **stapled securities** listed on a stock exchange. Important sources of equity for listed companies include initial public offerings (IPOs) of shares, 'rights' issues and share purchase plans, placements and reinvestment of dividends. Other, less significant sources of equity include share issues to employees, calls on contributing shares and exercise of company-issued options. In addition, the use of internal funds as a source of finance is discussed. Equity raised by issuing ordinary shares is an important source of finance for Australian companies. The importance of equity is illustrated by the fact that at the end of December 2010, the value of shares and other equities listed on the Australian Securities Exchange (ASX) was $1419 billion.[1] As shown in Table 9.1, equity capital of almost $170 billion was raised through the issue of shares and other securities by listed entities over the period 2008 to 2009.

stapled securities two or more legally separate instruments, typically an ordinary share plus units in one or more related trusts, which cannot be traded separately

TABLE 9.1 Listings and equity raisings by ASX-listed entities, year ended December 31 ($ billion)

TYPE OF CAPITAL RAISING	2008	2009
Primary raisings		
IPOs	2.5	7.5
Secondary raisings[a]		
Rights issues	12.8	38.3
Placements and share purchase plans	28.4	46.4
Reinvestment of dividends	15.6	11.4
Calls	0.1	0.4
Options	0.4	0.1
Others[b]	2.6	2.0
Total capital	62.5	106.1

[a] Excludes equity issued as part of a share financed merger or takeover.
[b] This category consists largely of issues to employees.
Source: Australian Securities Exchange, *Australian Cash Equity Market*, September 2010, **www.asx.com.au/professionals/pdf/australian_cash_equity_market_sept_2010.pdf**.

A much smaller but still important market is the private equity market, where finance is raised by issuing securities that are not publicly traded. Private equity includes venture capital, which refers to the financing of new ventures or 'start-up' companies. Before discussing the ways in which companies raise equity, we outline the features of the main type of equity securities they issue—that is, ordinary shares. Preference shares, which are legally equity but can also have some of the characteristics of debt, are discussed in Chapter 10.

---

[1] Australian Securities Exchange Limited. **www.asx.com.au/research/market_info/historical_equity_data.htm**. The figure quoted does not include the value of overseas-based equities listed on the ASX. There are also many private and unlisted companies, most of which are much smaller than listed companies.

9.2 THE CHARACTERISTICS OF ORDINARY SHARES

LEARNING OBJECTIVE 1
Outline the characteristics of ordinary shares

Equity is the most fundamental form of corporate finance because every company must raise some equity by issuing **ordinary shares**. An ordinary share gives the holder ownership of a proportion of the equity of the company. If a company has 100 000 issued shares and an investor holds 1000 shares, the investor has an ownership interest in 1 per cent of the net assets of the company. This does not mean that the investor can exercise ownership rights with respect to specific assets of the company. However, when dividends are paid, or if the company is taken over by another company, or is placed into liquidation, the investor has the right to receive 1 per cent of the payments made to ordinary shareholders.

If a company is profitable, its directors may decide to pay all or part of the profit to ordinary shareholders as a dividend and, as discussed in Section 4.3, the value of an ordinary share can be viewed as the present value of expected future dividends. The interest held by shareholders is a **residual claim** in the sense that shareholders will receive dividends only after a company has met its obligations to all other claimants such as suppliers, employees, lenders and governments. Similarly, if a company is placed into liquidation, ordinary shareholders have a residual claim on the proceeds from the sale of the company's assets. Because shareholders are paid last, they face greater risk than other investors in a company. To compensate for this risk, investors in ordinary shares expect a rate of return that is greater than they could obtain by lending to the company.

ordinary shares
securities that represent an ownership interest in a company and provide the owner with voting rights. Holders of ordinary shares have a residual interest in the net assets of the issuing company and are therefore exposed to greater risk than other classes of investors

residual claim
claim to profit or assets that remain after the entitlements of all other interested parties have been met

call
notice given by a company that the holders of partly paid shares must make an additional contribution of equity

9.2.1 FULLY PAID AND PARTLY PAID SHARES

When new shares are created and issued they will have a stated issue price. This price may be payable in full at the time the shares are issued or part of the issue price may be payable initially with the balance to be paid in subsequent instalments, generally known as calls. The amount and timing of each **call** may be specified initially or the company's directors may determine them later. Where only part of the issue price has been paid, shares are referred to as partly paid shares or contributing shares. Once the total issue price has been paid the shares are fully paid and the holder cannot be required to contribute any more funds to the company, although they may be given the opportunity to do so. A very similar security that has been issued to investors is called an instalment receipt. Contributing shares and instalment receipts are discussed in detail in Section 9.6.3.

9.2.2 LIMITED LIABILITY

While shareholders face greater risk than lenders, their risk is limited in that they enjoy **limited liability**. This means that a shareholder is not personally liable for the company's debts. In the case of a company limited by shares, the liability of shareholders is limited to any amount unpaid on the shares held.[2] For example, if an investor purchases shares with an issue price of $2.50 per share that are partly paid to $1.75, the investor's liability for future payments is limited to 75 cents per share. Consequently, if the company is placed into liquidation and has insufficient cash to pay its creditors, holders of its partly paid shares can be required to contribute up to 75 cents per share towards the payment of creditors. Holders of fully paid shares would not be required to make any contribution towards the payment of creditors, so the maximum amount they can lose is the amount already paid to purchase the shares.

---

[2] The advantages and disadvantages of limited liability are discussed in Lipton, Herzberg & Welsh (2010, p. 24). See also section 516 of the *Corporations Act 2001*.

9.2.3 NO LIABILITY COMPANIES

The majority of companies listed on the ASX are limited liability companies, but there are also many mining companies that are registered as no liability companies. Such companies must include the words 'No Liability' or the abbreviation 'NL' at the end of the company's name. These companies typically have partly paid shares on issue and can raise capital in stages by calling up part of the unpaid capital. No liability companies have two main features that distinguish them from other types of companies. One is that they are restricted to operating only in the mining industry. The second feature is that if the company fails, shareholders have no liability for the company's debts. Accordingly, holders of partly paid shares issued by a no liability company are not obliged to pay calls made by the company. However, shareholders who fail to pay a call forfeit their shares. No liability companies are typically involved in exploration. Therefore, this second feature allows shareholders to review their investment in a risky venture when additional funds are being raised and gives them the opportunity to abandon the investment if they believe that its prospects are unattractive.[3]

limited liability legal concept that protects shareholders whose liability to meet a company's debts is limited to any amount unpaid on the shares they hold

9.2.4 THE RIGHTS OF SHAREHOLDERS

Shareholders in a listed company have many rights, such as the right to receive an annual report, to be notified of meetings and to attend those meetings. In practice, most of these rights are of little importance and, generally, there are just three rights that are important to shareholders in listed companies:

(a) Shareholders are entitled to a proportional share of any dividend that is declared by directors.
(b) As part owners of the company, ordinary shareholders exert a degree of control over its management through the voting rights attached to their shares. These rights include the right to elect members of the Board of Directors. The Board, which is usually elected at the Annual General Meeting, has ultimate control over the operations of the company. Usually, shareholders have one vote for each share held.[4] The right of shareholders to elect the Board of Directors gives them some control over the company's operations. However, in practice, their ability to exercise control is limited because the Board of Directors is generally able to muster sufficient votes, including proxies, to ensure that its members are re-elected at the Annual General Meeting.[5]
(c) Shareholders have the right to sell their shares. This right can be exercised readily in the case of listed shares because the shares can be sold through the stock exchange.

9.2.5 ADVANTAGES AND DISADVANTAGES OF EQUITY AS A SOURCE OF FINANCE

Equity raised by issuing ordinary shares has important advantages as a source of finance:

- A company is not *required* to pay dividends to ordinary shareholders: payment of dividends is at the discretion of directors. Therefore, if a company suffers a decline in profitability or is short of cash, it can omit the payment of dividends without any serious legal consequences. In contrast, failure to pay interest on debt, or delays in paying interest, will almost certainly have serious legal consequences and can ultimately lead to a company being placed into liquidation.

LEARNING OBJECTIVE 2
Explain the advantages and disadvantages of equity as a source of finance

---

3 Arguably, another feature of no liability (NL) companies is also important. Historically, NL companies had greater flexibility than other companies to raise capital by issuing shares at a discount to their par value. When the Corporations Act was amended to abolish the par value concept from 1 July 1998, this advantage no longer existed. Subsequently, some NL companies have converted to limited liability status and the number of new NL companies listing on the ASX has declined.
4 The voting rights of a company's shareholders must be specified in its constitution. For companies listed on the ASX, the form of the voting rights is specified in Chapter 6 of the Exchange's Listing Rules.
5 As many shareholders do not attend the Annual General Meeting, the right to vote by proxy is provided. Voting by proxy involves a shareholder assigning to another person the right to vote on resolutions at the Annual General Meeting.

- Ordinary shares do not have any maturity date, which means that the issuing company has no obligation to redeem them.[6] Again, in contrast, debt *must* be repaid (or 'redeemed') when it matures.
- The higher the proportion of equity in a company's capital structure, the lower is the risk that lenders will suffer losses as a result of the borrower experiencing financial difficulty. Therefore, raising equity by issuing ordinary shares lowers the interest rate that a company will have to pay on debt.

While equity has important advantages, it also has some disadvantages.

- If a company issues more ordinary shares to raise new capital, existing shareholders will have to either outlay additional cash or suffer some dilution of their ownership and control of the company. Borrowing, on the other hand, allows funds to be raised without such dilution. Small shareholders may not be concerned if their interest in a company is diluted, provided the new shareholders pay a fair price for the shares they obtain, but investors who own a significant proportion of a company's shares may be unwilling to have their interest diluted.
- The transaction costs of raising funds by issuing shares are usually higher than the costs of borrowing a similar amount. One reason is that, as discussed in Section 9.4, a share issue by a public company often requires a prospectus. Because of the volume of information that is usually provided, a prospectus for a share issue typically runs to more than 100 pages and is costly to prepare. Also, share issues are often underwritten: this involves a fee being paid to the underwriter who guarantees to purchase any shares not taken up by investors.

In outlining the advantages and disadvantages of equity, taxation has not been mentioned because, under the Australian tax system, the overall tax burdens on debt and equity are often the same for Australian resident investors. As discussed in Section 12.5.2, the system is either neutral or biased towards equity depending on the investor's marginal tax rate. For overseas investors in Australian companies the tax burden on equity may be higher than the tax burden on debt. Therefore, in Australia, any taxation advantage or disadvantage that may arise in a particular case depends on the circumstances of the shareholder concerned and is not an inherent feature of equity as a source of finance.

9.3 PRIVATE EQUITY

LEARNING OBJECTIVE 3

Outline the main sources of private equity in the Australian market

Most of this chapter covers equity capital raising by companies whose shares are listed and traded publicly on a stock exchange. There is also a much smaller but still very important private equity market. The term 'private equity' is often used to describe two distinct types of investment. The first type is also known as 'venture capital' and refers to funding for smaller and riskier companies with potential for strong growth. For these companies, private equity can be more attractive than stock exchange listing. For example, the amount of capital required may be too small to justify the cost of a share market float. Also, the future of the venture—which at the earliest stage may be no more than an idea—may be too uncertain to attract funds from a large number of investors. The second type is the acquisition of a listed public company by a group of investors who 'privatise' the company so that it is delisted from the stock exchange. Such acquisitions usually involve a high proportion of debt finance and are commonly known as leveraged buyouts (LBOs), which are discussed in Section 19.7.3. The remainder of this section focuses on private equity funding for ventures other than LBOs.

---

6 While ordinary shares have no maturity date and can, in principle, exist in perpetuity, companies are permitted to repurchase their own shares, which leads to cancellation of those shares. Share buybacks are discussed in Chapter 11.

9.3.1 WHAT IS PRIVATE EQUITY?

The key feature of private equity is that the securities issued to investors are not publicly traded. Private equity can be raised from various sources including family members, friends and 'business angels', but the more formal private equity market involves funds being channelled to businesses by private equity fund managers. Private equity funding can be divided into four categories:[7]

(a) *start-up* financing for a business less than 30 months old where funds are required to develop the company's products
(b) *expansion* financing where additional funds are required to manufacture and sell products commercially
(c) *turnaround* financing for a company in financial difficulty
(d) *management buyout* (MBO) financing where a business is purchased by its management team with the assistance of a private equity fund.

Because private equity is not publicly traded, the market is illiquid and investors must be prepared to commit funds for the long term, with periods of 5 to 10 years being typical.

9.3.2 INFORMATION PROBLEMS AND NEW VENTURES

Entrepreneurs and investors in new ventures seeking start-up financing face three important information problems.[8]

(a) *Information gaps*: information about the value of the venture is likely to be incomplete and very uncertain.
(b) *Information asymmetry*: important information is usually distributed unevenly between the parties, which is the problem known as **information asymmetry**. In particular, the entrepreneur will almost certainly have more accurate information than outside investors about the technical or scientific merit of an idea and of the technology required to exploit the idea. On the other hand, outside investors may have more realistic information about the economic value of the idea. However, potential investors in a new venture are not concerned only with the value of the underlying idea or invention. They also need to assess the skills and commitment of the entrepreneur. Some entrepreneurs have an accurate appreciation of their own skills, ability and commitment, while others tend to be less realistic.
(c) *Information leakage*: there is the risk that others may appropriate the entrepreneur's idea. To convince prospective investors that a proposal is valuable, the entrepreneur will have to provide them with some information about the idea. Unfortunately, disclosing this information may allow someone else to exploit the opportunity.

> **information asymmetry**
> situation where all relevant information is not known by all interested parties. Typically, this involves company 'insiders' (managers) having more information about the company's prospects than 'outsiders' (shareholders and lenders)

The market for new venture finance has some unique features that have developed to minimise the effects of these information problems. The main such feature is that finance for new ventures is normally provided in stages rather than as a single lump sum. Also, the provision of finance at each stage is generally linked to the achievement of milestones, such as completion of a prototype or successful operation of a pilot plant. Achievement of these milestones or other performance benchmarks helps to reduce information asymmetry in two ways. First, it provides investors with tangible evidence about the viability of the project. Second, it also provides them with information about the skill and ability of the entrepreneur.

Providing the finance in stages is clearly sensible from the viewpoint of investors. If a project is destined to fail due to technical difficulties, lack of consumer demand or high manufacturing costs, it is better to discover these problems before all the funds needed to complete the project have been committed to it. Staged financing is also in the interest of the entrepreneur. For an entrepreneur with no track record of

---

[7] This four-category breakdown is provided by Connolly and Tan (2002).
[8] Our discussion of these information problems is based on Smith and Smith (2000, pp. 27–8).

successful ventures, it will be difficult to convince others that funds invested in a new venture will be used profitably. For the entrepreneur, raising money from outside investors in the early stages of a venture is generally expensive. In this context, 'expensive' means that the entrepreneur will have to give up a large fraction of ownership to raise a relatively small amount of capital. Achievement of each milestone reduces uncertainty and increases the value of a project. Raising finance in stages, after milestones have been achieved, therefore helps the entrepreneur to retain greater ownership than would otherwise be the case.

Finally, consider the possibility that release of information to prospective investors may lead to appropriation of the entrepreneur's idea. The entrepreneur may seek protection by asking prospective investors to sign confidentiality agreements when they are given a copy of the business plan. However, many investors refuse to sign such agreements because a leak of information from any source can result in costly legal disputes. It is more important to the entrepreneur that a potential investor is honest and can be trusted not to misuse confidential information. Therefore, private equity fund managers will try to establish and protect a reputation for honesty and integrity.

9.3.3 SOURCES OF FINANCE FOR NEW VENTURES

There are many potential sources of finance for a new venture. These sources include the entrepreneur's personal resources, private equity funds and funds raised by an **initial public offering** of shares associated with listing on a stock exchange. The suitability of these and other sources of finance varies depending on the venture's stage of development. Every venture is different and it is impossible to identify a 'life cycle' of development stages that applies to all new ventures. There are, however, some identifiable stages that will apply in many cases. Many ventures will begin with a research and development phase, which, if successful, will be followed by a start-up phase where the equipment and personnel needed for production are assembled. If the product is accepted by customers, the venture may grow, perhaps very rapidly at first, after which there will often be periods of slower growth, maturity and perhaps decline. There may be no clear demarcation point between these stages but in many cases the transition will correspond to identifiable milestones. In turn, there is often a relationship between these milestones and the availability of different sources of finance.

At the research and development stage the entrepreneur will usually rely initially on personal resources—that is savings, money that can be borrowed by mortgaging the family home and perhaps lines of credit linked to credit cards. Unless the entrepreneur is very wealthy, these resources may be exhausted before the venture is fully developed and it will usually be necessary to obtain finance from outsiders such as family members, friends, individuals known as 'business angels' and private equity funds. Outside finance raised in the early stages of a venture's development is normally in the form of equity—that is, the entrepreneur transfers a share of ownership to the new investors and the returns to these investors will depend directly on the success or otherwise of the venture.

9.3.4 FINANCE FROM BUSINESS ANGELS

Business angels are wealthy individuals prepared to invest in projects that are at an early stage of development.[9] The amounts involved typically range from tens of thousands to hundreds of thousands of dollars per investment. These investors will often provide the funds needed to develop a venture to the stage where it is possible to seek outside finance from private equity funds, banks and other financial institutions. Business angels are generally prepared to invest in a venture for 5 to 10 years. Many of them have business or technical skills and aim to add value to a new venture by providing advice and expertise as well as finance. Traditionally the market has operated informally on the basis of contacts and referrals. However, the market has recently been formalised by the development of business introduction services that seek to match investors with enterprises that need capital. Some of these services simply provide

---

initial public offering
a company's first offering of shares to the public

---

9 For a detailed discussion of this market in Australia, see Abernethy and Heidtman (1999).

information, while others maintain databases of both investors and companies and aim to actively match these parties. Services operating in Australia include Business Angels Pty Ltd (**www.businessangels.com.au**) and the Australian Small Scale Offerings Board (**www.assob.com.au**).

Some business angels will invest in perhaps one project per year while others will invest in several. Most restrict their investments to industries where they understand the technology and to projects located in their own geographical area. A typical example is 'John', a 63-year-old chartered accountant who has made 12 investments in 8 years as a full-time equity investor.[10] He points out that the expertise that business angels can provide is usually more important than the money they invest. Finding money is easy if a business is good. Angel investors look for a business with a weakness that they can help to overcome so that it becomes a good business. John looks for opportunities in industries with high growth potential. Because he does not want his money tied up for more than 5 years, he looks for a company that can benefit very quickly from reorganisation or additional expertise. Such companies are usually small and have a good idea, but lack expertise in management, marketing, manufacturing or distribution. John will invest up to $200 000, requires a seat on the Board and will spend up to half a day each week working on the company. Finally, he looks for companies that can provide high returns on his investment by development to a stage where the company can be sold to or merge with a larger company, attract the involvement of a private equity fund or list on a stock exchange.

9.3.5 FINANCE FROM PRIVATE EQUITY FUNDS

The Australian Bureau of Statistics (ABS) estimates that $17.4 billion was committed to the private equity market at 30 June 2009 of which $11.7 billion was drawn down, leaving $5.7 billion uncalled.[11] According to the ABS, at June 2009 a total of 275 private equity funds operated in Australia by 180 venture capital managers had invested in 1089 companies. Venture capital managers have two main roles: raising money from investors and selecting suitable companies in which to invest the capital. In Australia, investors include superannuation funds, which are the largest source of funds, wealthy individuals and banks. While these investors have large sums available, private equity funding is not easy to obtain. According to the ABS, the 180 managers reviewed 5670 potential new investments in 2008 and 2009, further analysis was conducted on 469 of those and only 126 were successful in attracting investment. During 2008 and 2009 these venture capital managers made new and follow-on investments totalling $1524 million and also spent an average of 3.5 days a month with the investee companies, providing them with advice and assisting in the development of their projects.

Venture capital fund managers generally invest amounts in the order of $500 000 to $20 million for periods of 3 to 7 years. They look for a business with good prospects for growth, managed by people who are capable, honest and committed to the success of the business. Private equity investments typically have a higher level of risk than most other investments. Therefore, fund managers seek a relatively high rate of return that will vary with the perceived risk. For example, provision of seed and start-up capital involves a high level of risk and investors may seek a rate of return of at least 30 to 40 per cent per annum over the life of the investment. At a later stage when production has commenced and product is being sold, provision of capital for expansion involves lower risk so that the minimum rate of return sought may be 20 to 30 per cent per annum.

To obtain private equity it is essential to have a well-documented and believable business plan. The plan should provide information on:

- the structure, activities and financial history of the business
- analysis of the investment opportunity

---

10 This example is cited by Abernethy and Heidtman (1999, pp. 137–40). The remainder of this section relies heavily on that source.
11 Australian Bureau of Statistics (2010).

- the amount of capital sought
- how the capital will be used
- financial projections
- the qualifications and experience of the management team.

As well as becoming part owners of the businesses they invest in, fund managers typically require a seat on the company's Board of Directors. This does not mean that they seek day-to-day control. Rather, private equity funds generally take a significant minority share in the company and aim to provide valuable advice on both technical and management issues. An entrepreneur may be able to obtain capital from a variety of sources, but a fund manager can also provide management input based on the experience of helping other companies overcome the problems typically encountered by new, fast-growing businesses. The investment vehicles differ considerably in size, the type of industries they invest in and the types of management support they can provide. Therefore, it is important that an entrepreneur seeking private equity should be aware of these differences and approach the financiers that are best equipped to provide the capital and support that the business is likely to need.

Most fund managers aim to achieve the majority of their return in the form of capital gain rather than dividends. Accordingly, they usually plan to dispose of the investment, typically within a period of 3 to 7 years. Disposal may take place in one of three ways:

(a) an initial public offering associated with stock exchange listing
(b) sale
(c) voluntary liquidation.

Where a sale occurs the buyer may be a larger company (a 'trade sale'), the majority owner, the management or another outside investor. While disposal of the investment can result in spectacular gains, the level of risk is high and it is to be expected that a significant proportion of the disposals that occur will involve a loss. In some cases the project will fail and the investment will be liquidated.

Private equity investment in Australia has grown rapidly since the early 1990s. Factors that have contributed to this growth include:

- growth in the volume of funds flowing into superannuation, together with increased recognition by fund managers of the role of private equity investments as part of a diversified portfolio
- government programs to encourage investment in new ventures, such as the Innovation Investment Fund program, the Early Stage Venture Capital Limited Partnerships program and the Renewable Energy Equity Fund (see **www.ausindustry.gov.au**)
- regulatory changes that allow banks to make equity investments.

9.4 INFORMATION DISCLOSURE

LEARNING OBJECTIVE 4
Identify the information that must be disclosed when issuing securities

Chapter 6D of the Corporations Act contains provisions designed to ensure that investors in public companies are protected by disclosure of information. There are particular disclosure requirements that apply to offers of securities so that investors should be able to make an informed decision on whether to purchase the securities. These requirements are generally satisfied by providing potential investors with a **disclosure document** containing information about the issuer and details of the securities offered for sale. However, there are various exemptions that mean a disclosure document is not needed for some offers of securities.

In cases where disclosure is needed, the disclosure requirements vary depending on whether the securities are already listed on the stock exchange. We now discuss the disclosure requirements for offers of securities that do not fall into any of the exempt categories.

9.4.1 OFFERS OF UNLISTED SECURITIES

Offers of unlisted securities include initial public offerings of ordinary shares and issues by listed companies of a new class of securities. In these cases, the securities do not have an observable market price and in the case of an initial public offering there may be little, if any, publicly available information about the company. Therefore, the disclosure requirements that apply to offers of unlisted securities are more stringent than those for listed securities.

The general rule is that an offer of securities to investors cannot proceed until a disclosure document has been lodged with the Australian Securities and Investments Commission (ASIC). Disclosure documents may be given to potential investors as soon as they have been lodged with ASIC. For unlisted securities, a waiting period of at least 7 days is imposed before applications by investors can be accepted. The waiting period allows the disclosure document to be examined by ASIC and other interested parties. If the document is found to be deficient, the issue of securities can be delayed until an acceptable supplementary or replacement document is provided.

The information that must be included varies with the type of disclosure document. The types most commonly used are:

- a prospectus
- a short-form prospectus
- an offer information statement.[12]

disclosure document
prospectus, profile statement or offer information statement that must be supplied to potential investors to provide information about an offer of securities

Prospectuses

A **prospectus** is the most comprehensive document and generally contains information of four main types:

(a) information about the security issue—how much capital is sought, the subscription price, how the funds will be used, any upper or lower limits on the amount that each individual can invest and any minimum subscription level that must be achieved
(b) non-financial information about the issuer—a detailed description of its business and reports from directors or experts in the industry
(c) a detailed discussion of the risks associated with the business
(d) financial information about the issuer—the most recent audited financial statements and, in many cases, financial forecasts including forecasts of profits and dividends.

prospectus
a document that, among other things, provides details of the company and the terms of the issue of securities, which must be provided to potential investors by a company seeking to issue shares or other securities

The text of all prospectuses issued in Australia since 2001 is available at: www.search.asic.gov.au/offerlist/offerlist_issuer_name.html.

A prospectus is the most expensive of the documents to prepare, print and distribute. The factors that contribute to these costs include the size of the document and the fees payable to experts whose reports are included. Moreover, deficiencies in a disclosure document can lead to people who were involved in its preparation or in the issuing of securities being liable for criminal prosecution. They may also be required to compensate investors for losses suffered as a result of a misstatement in, or an omission from, the document. However, the Corporations Act provides a 'due diligence' defence in relation to a prospectus and other disclosure documents. This is a defence against a claim of misstatement or omission if the person made all reasonable enquiries and believed on reasonable grounds that the statement was not misleading or deceptive, or that there was no omission. The preparation of a prospectus can involve extensive and costly investigations to ensure that the information provided is as accurate as possible and that the due diligence defence will be available if any deficiency is found.

---

12 These disclosure documents apply in the case of security issues by companies. If funds are being raised for a managed investment, such as a property trust, a different type of disclosure document known as a product disclosure statement (PDS) is required.

The prospectus distributed to potential investors can be in a 'short form', which means that it refers to material in documents lodged with ASIC instead of providing that material in the prospectus. A short form prospectus must inform investors that they are entitled to a free copy of the additional material on request.

Offer information statements

An offer information statement (OIS) may be used instead of a prospectus if the amount of money to be raised is relatively small. Specifically, an OIS may be used only if the amount of money to be raised by the issuer, when added to all amounts previously raised, is less than $5 million. An OIS is much less costly to prepare than a prospectus because the information to be disclosed is minimal and extensive 'due diligence' enquiries are not needed.

9.4.2 OFFERS OF LISTED SECURITIES

The disclosure requirements are less onerous for offers of securities that are already listed on a stock exchange. An example is a rights issue where new shares are offered to existing shareholders. As discussed in Section 9.6.1, a prospectus is no longer required for a rights issue, but there may be cases where such issues are accompanied by a prospectus. A listed entity is subject to continuous disclosure requirements under stock exchange listing rules backed by the Corporations Act. Any material price-sensitive information has to be disclosed to the stock exchange on a continuous basis. Therefore, much of the information that would normally have to be included in a prospectus is already publicly available, so, if a rights issue is made under a prospectus, it does not need to be as detailed as a prospectus for an issue of unlisted securities.

9.4.3 OFFERS THAT DO NOT NEED DISCLOSURE

There are various exemptions that mean a disclosure document is not needed for some offers of securities.[13] The main exemptions are outlined in Table 9.2.

TABLE 9.2 Main types of offer that do not need disclosure

OFFER TYPE	DESCRIPTION
Small-scale offerings	Personal offers that result in issues to no more than 20 investors in a rolling 12-month period, with a maximum of $2 million raised.
Rights issues	A pro-rata offer made after 28 June 2007 of additional shares to existing shareholders. The terms of the offer to each shareholder must be identical and the new shares must be of the same class as those already held.
Sophisticated investors:	The amount payable for securities must be at least:
• Large offers	$500 000, OR
• Offers to wealthy investors	the investor had a gross income over each of the previous two financial years of at least $250 000 or net assets of at least $2.5 million, OR
• Offers to experienced investors	the offer is made through a licensed securities dealer who is satisfied that the investor has sufficient previous experience in investing in securities to assess matters such as the merits of the offer and the risks involved.

[13] The circumstances where a disclosure document is not required are set out in section 708 of the Corporations Act.

OFFER TYPE	DESCRIPTION
Executive officers and associates	Offers to directors and other persons involved in the management of the issuing entity and certain of their relatives and associated entities.
Existing security holders	Offers of fully paid ordinary shares under a dividend reinvestment plan, bonus share plan or share purchase plan. Offers of debentures to existing debenture holders.

9.5 FLOATING A PUBLIC COMPANY

When a company first invites the public to subscribe for shares it is usual to refer to this as *floating* the company. An alternative term is that the company makes an initial public offering (IPO). A company making its first issue of ordinary shares to the public will usually apply for stock exchange listing, which means that shareholders in the company can sell their shares on the stock exchange.[14] To obtain listing, the directors of the company must ensure that its proposed structure complies with the requirements of the exchange. For example, the ASX has extensive listing rules that are based on several principles designed to protect the interests of listed entities, investors and the reputation of the market.

Listed entities must satisfy minimum standards of quality and size, and comply with stringent requirements on disclosure of information. For example, to achieve listing a company must usually have at least 500 shareholders, each subscribing for shares with a value of at least $2000. Entities to be listed must also satisfy either a profit test or an assets test. The requirements of the assets test include net tangible assets of at least $2 million or a market capitalisation of at least $10 million.[15]

The ASX sets these conditions in an effort to ensure that there will be an active market in the company's shares after they are listed. Companies that are unable to satisfy the requirements for listing on the ASX may opt for listing on one of the markets that have developed to meet the needs of smaller companies. These include the Bendigo Stock Exchange (www.bsx.com.au) and the National Stock Exchange of Australia (www.nsxa.com.au), both of which aim to provide a market in the shares of small and medium-sized entities with as few as 50 security holders.

LEARNING OBJECTIVE 5
Outline the process of floating a public company

WWW

9.5.1 PUBLIC VERSUS PRIVATE OWNERSHIP

A company undertaking a float may be either a new company or an existing private company. In the latter case, the company is said to be 'going public'. There are two main reasons why a private company may go public. First, listed public companies usually have better access to the capital market than private companies. As discussed in Section 9.3, private equity investors are very selective and the terms that they require may not be attractive to the owners of a company. Greater access to the capital market is most valuable to high-growth companies that require funds to implement attractive new projects. Second, a public float allows the owners of a company to cash in on the success of the business they have developed. The cash they receive by selling part of their interest in the company can be used to diversify their investment portfolio.

---

14 While stock exchange listing normally follows a public issue, a company can list without raising any capital at the time of listing provided it complies with the ASX Listing Rules. This approach is referred to as a 'compliance listing'. An alternative way to become a listed public company is by a 'back-door listing'. This involves an unlisted company taking over a company that is listed on the stock exchange.

15 These and other listing requirements apply to all companies. There are additional requirements that differ depending on whether the company's main activities involve investment, mining exploration or scientific research. They are set out in Chapter 1 of the ASX Listing Rules.

Going public also has several costs that must be considered. The most significant is usually the loss of control associated with sharing ownership of the company with many other investors. The original owners' voting power will be reduced at the time of a float and their proportional ownership may decline over time as they sell some of their shares or as the company raises capital by issuing more shares to new investors.

A public listing also involves direct costs such as stock exchange listing fees and shareholder servicing costs. In addition, listed companies incur costs associated with greater information disclosure. These costs include producing the required information and the time spent by management on investor relations. In particular, managers may need to discuss the company's plans and prospects with analysts employed by brokers and institutions because the recommendations produced by analysts can influence a company's share price and its ability to raise capital by issuing more shares. Finally, the information that a listed company is required to disclose may include details that are valuable to competitors.

9.5.2 INITIAL PUBLIC OFFERING OF ORDINARY SHARES

As shown in Table 9.3, the number of IPOs and their value can vary considerably from year to year. When a company is to 'go public', its promoters usually seek the assistance of a financial institution with expertise in arranging share issues. Typically, this has been the function of the larger stockbrokers and investment banks. Both types of institution can advise on the price of the issue, underwrite the issue and handle the sale of the shares.

TABLE 9.3 New listings on the ASX

YEAR ENDED JUNE 30	2005	2006	2007	2008	2009	2010
Number of new listings	222	227	284	236	45	93
Initial capital raised ($ billion)	14.9	23.1	19.7	11.2	1.9	11.5

Source: ASX Limited, *2010 Annual Report* and Australian Stock Exchange, *Annual Report 2006*.

9.5.3 PRICING A NEW ISSUE

Deciding on the price of a new issue is a difficult task. The issuer faces potential problems if the offer price is set too high or too low. If the price is set too high, few investors will want to subscribe and the issue may fail unless it is underwritten, in which case the underwriter will have to meet the shortfall. In turn, this outcome will have a negative effect on the market price of the shares after they are listed. If the price is set too low, the owners will suffer an opportunity loss because they would have received a higher payment if the new issue had been made at a higher price. The available evidence suggests that, on average, new issues initially trade at a price above the issue price. In this sense they are 'underpriced'. The underpricing of initial public offerings is discussed in Section 9.5.6.

The task of setting the issue price is particularly difficult when the company has just been formed, as there is no record of financial performance. Where the company has previously operated as a private company, the task is not as difficult because past profits may be a guide to future profits. The most common approach to pricing used by advisers is to use historical profits as the basis for estimating future earnings per share. The adviser will also examine the price–earnings (P/E) ratio (the market price of a share, divided by the earnings per share) of existing companies in the same or similar industries. Forecasts of future earnings per share and the information on price–earnings ratios will then be used by the adviser to suggest a possible range of issue prices for the company's shares. For example, if a company is expected to earn 30 cents per share and the price–earnings ratios of similar companies are between 9 and 14, this suggests an issue price of between $2.70 and $4.20 per share. If institutions are enthusiastic about the proposed issue, the issue price may be set close to $4.20. In contrast, if there is little interest in the issue, the issue price may be set closer to the lower end of the range. As is evident from the above description, use of this approach to set the issue price involves considerable judgement.

In the case of a fixed price offer, the price must be set before the prospectus is printed and the offer is usually open for at least 2 to 3 weeks. Consequently, the success of the offer is subject to general movements in share prices during a period of several weeks. For example, if the general level of share prices increases significantly during that period, it is likely that the fixed price will be too low. However, if share prices decrease significantly during that period, investors may regard the fixed price as being too high, and the issue will close undersubscribed.

An alternative approach when pricing a new issue is to use *book-building*—a process that involves competitive bidding by market participants, particularly institutional investors. This approach uses either *open pricing* or *constrained open pricing*. In both cases, potential investors place bids for the shares where they indicate the quantities they wish to purchase at various prices. The final price is determined at the end of the bidding process. In the case of open pricing, shares are usually allocated only to bidders who offered prices equal to or higher than the final price. Open pricing has been used in some Australian floats, but constrained open pricing is more common. In constrained open pricing, both upper and lower limits are placed on the price and all bids between those limits are considered. The prospectus will set out the criteria to be used in allocating shares to bidders. Usually, the price range can be revised during the bidding process if demand for the shares is found to be substantially greater or less than expected. Once the final price has been determined, all successful bidders pay the same price but those who made higher bids have a higher probability of receiving an allocation of shares.

Offers to institutions under a book-building process are often accompanied by an offer to the general public (a 'retail offer'), where a maximum price is specified in advance and retail investors may also be offered a price discount. For example, in the float of QR National Ltd in November 2010, there was an institutional book-build with an indicative price range of $2.50 to $3 and a retail offer, which was subject to a maximum price of $2.80 per share. Successful applicants in the retail offer paid the lower of the final price paid by institutions less a discount of 10 cents per share and the maximum retail price of $2.80.

Book-building was first used in Australia by the New South Wales Government when it sold the Government Insurance Office (GIO) in 1992. Since the GIO issue, it has been used in several large issues, including the Woolworths, Qantas and Telstra floats and in some smaller floats such as those of JB Hi-Fi (which raised $148 million in October 2003) and Kathmandu Holdings ($340 million in November 2009). The main advantage of book-building is that it allows the issuer and its advisers to obtain feedback from informed institutional investors on their assessment of the value of the shares. The information gathered from these investors can be used in setting the issue price. While this approach is expected to result in a lower level of underpricing, conducting a book-build is a costly process, so it is usually worthwhile only for larger floats. Hence, the majority of floats in Australia still involve fixed-price offers.

With a fixed-price offer, once the terms have been set, the adviser usually ensures that the proposed offer satisfies all relevant legal requirements and assists in preparing the offer document (usually a prospectus), ensures that stock exchange listing requirements are met, lodges the prospectus with ASIC and markets the shares to institutional and private investors. The costs of preparing the prospectus include legal fees, fees for the preparation of an investigating accountant's report and the cost of printing. The total costs of the advisory services, including the costs of preparing a prospectus and obtaining stock exchange listing, can vary widely and usually represent between 2 and 5 per cent of the amount raised. As discussed in Section 9.5.6, the costs can be less than 2 per cent of the amount raised for larger floats.

Conversely, for very small floats that raise $10 million or less, the costs are usually much higher than 5 per cent. If the promoters agree with the adviser's recommendations on the terms of the float, the same adviser will usually be appointed to underwrite and handle the sale of the shares.

9.5.4 UNDERWRITING AND MANAGING A NEW ISSUE

As previously indicated, with a fixed-price offer the issuer is subject to the vagaries of the market from the time when the price is set until the issue closes. In many cases the issuer will pass this risk on to an underwriter, which is typically an investment bank or a major stockbroker. If the book-building process is used, the issue is not underwritten but one or more investment banks or brokers will still be needed to receive and collate the institutional bids, advise the promoters on the issue price and manage the issue. In this case, the institutions involved are typically referred to as 'lead managers' of the issue.[16]

If the issue is underwritten, the obligations of the company and the underwriter are contained in an underwriting agreement. The underwriter contracts to purchase all shares for which applications have not been received by the closing date of the issue. In return, the underwriter charges a fee, usually based on a fixed percentage of the amount to be raised by the issue. The fee is negotiated and will reflect the underwriter's perception of the difficulty of selling the issue and this in turn will be determined by factors such as the company's stature in the market, the price of the issue and general market conditions. The underwriting agreement normally includes escape clauses that specify the circumstances in which the underwriter will be released from its obligations.[17] In some cases, the role of the institutions that manage a float may include 'price stabilisation' once the shares are listed. Price stabilisation, also known as a green shoe option after the company that first used it, requires a special dispensation from ASIC. A dispensation of this type was obtained by the investment banks that managed the November 2010 float of rail operator QR National, which was previously wholly owned by the Queensland State Government. (See Finance in Action.)

FINANCE IN ACTION

PRICE STABILISATION IN FLOAT OF RAIL OPERATOR

The QR National media release and ASX announcement about the pricing and allocation of shares in its float contained the following statement:

'Following the transfer of QR National Shares by the State to successful applicants, the State will initially retain 821,436,735 QR National Shares. This amount may increase by up to 146,400,000 QR National Shares depending on whether the Joint Lead Managers exercise an option to purchase up to 6% of QR National Shares on issue to cover any over-allocations made as part of the Offer, as described in section 2.4.3 of the Offer Document.'

The meaning of this statement was explained and discussed in articles by financial journalists. Excerpts from one such article appear below.

Read the QR National media release about today's float carefully and you realise those canny investment bankers sold 66 per cent of the shares in the company.

---

16 It is possible for a share issue to be underwritten and priced using book-building. As discussed in Section 9.6.2, this approach is often used for share placements where issuers desire certainty of funding and, given the short time involved, the underwriting risk is low and its cost may be acceptable. In the case of IPOs, vendors are generally prepared to accept the risk that the 'market clearing price' established in a book-build may be less than they expected. In such cases, the indicative price range may be lowered or the proposed share issue may be withdrawn.

17 The escape clauses in an underwriting agreement relate to factors that would seriously affect demand for shares in general, such as the outbreak of war as well as company-specific events that could reduce the value of the shares.

Why settle on 66 per cent?…

The answer takes us to the dark art of the float's joint lead managers entering the market and buying shares to support QR's price. The price support tool known as 'the greenshoe' is (very opaquely) disclosed in the prospectus … The tangled technicalities of the greenshoe specify it is an over-allocation option.

The technicalities mean the over-allocated stock can be bought back on the market by the investment banks, providing the price support.

Guess what? The over-allocation option—and therefore the price support—only kicks in after the Queensland government sells 60 per cent of the stock. And the over-allocation option is limited to 6 per cent of the total stock on issue.

Now 60 per cent plus 6 per cent explains why the offer sold a magic 66 per cent of the company. Not 61 per cent. Not 64 per cent. Right on the knocker of 66 per cent.

As in any float, it is hard to see where today's price lands …

Be certain of this: if the share price falls below the offer price, there is price support available in the form of five investment banks with about 9 per cent of the total traded shares available to buy.

If the share price is hovering above and below the offer price, read the Queensland government's victorious media releases with a degree of scepticism. The share price is more than likely being gamed.

Source: 'Greenshoe on cue may be used to keep QR National afloat', Stuart Washington, www.businessday.com/business, 22 November 2010.

WWW

The larger stockbrokers are major underwriters, primarily because they have an established clientele prepared to subscribe for the issues they underwrite. An underwriter will frequently attempt to limit its exposure to the risk of undersubscription by inviting other institutions to act as subunderwriters. These institutions may include life and general insurance companies, banks and superannuation funds. The role of the subunderwriter is to take up a proportion of any undersubscription in return for a fee, paid by the underwriter, that is based on a fixed proportion of the issue price.[18]

9.5.5 SELLING A NEW ISSUE

If a stockbroker is the underwriter or lead manager of an issue of shares it will usually act as a selling agent for the issue. By promoting an issue, a stockbroker protects its interests as underwriter and also earns brokerage fees. Depending on the size of the issue, one or more other broking firms may also be appointed as managers or co-managers to assist in publicising the issue and distributing the shares to a wide range of clients. The fees paid to these firms will usually be structured so that brokers who can distribute shares to clients have an incentive to compete against institutional bids in a book-build. To this end, the fees for brokers may be divided into a 'firm allocation fee' and a 'handling fee'. The separate handling fee encourages brokers to place bids for additional shares above their firm allocation in the expectation that the additional shares can be sold to their clients. Greater competition between institutional investors and brokers' clients (retail investors) is, of course, desirable for the issuer and the lead manager.

Where a fixed-price issue is not underwritten, a broker will still be engaged to assist in distributing the shares. Brokerage fees are negotiable and depend on factors such as the size of the issue, the status of the issuing company and the period for which the issue is to remain open. Brokerage fees are usually set between 1 and 2 per cent of the issue price.

---

18 The subunderwriting fee is usually only slightly less than the underwriting fee. For example, if the underwriting fee was 3 per cent of the issue price, the subunderwriting fee would usually be about 2.5 per cent of the issue price.

9.5.6 THE COSTS OF FLOATING A COMPANY

It was noted in Section 9.2.5 that raising capital by issuing shares can involve significant costs. In the case of company floats the costs fall into three main categories:

(a) *Stock exchange listing fees and the costs of preparing and distributing a prospectus*. These costs include legal fees, fees for the preparation of an investigating accountant's report, fees for expert reports and printing costs.
(b) *Fees paid to underwriters or lead managers and commissions paid to brokers for selling the shares*. The total of these fees and costs can vary considerably but for most floats the costs would fall in the range from 4 to 7 per cent of the funds raised.
(c) *Underpricing*. The third category of costs relates to the fact that the issue price of shares sold in an IPO is usually less than the market value of the shares once they are listed.

The costs that fall into the first two categories may be combined to form a total cost of listing. Underpricing of IPOs can be significant and is discussed after we discuss the costs of listing.

The factors that influence the costs of listing for a float include its size, the riskiness of the company and the complexity of the underlying business. The total costs will generally increase with the size of the float, but because of the fixed nature of some components of the costs, they will be larger in percentage terms when the amount of funds sought is small. For example, when the amount sought is less than $10 million, the costs can be more than 15 per cent of the amount sought. For floats that raise more than $100 million, the costs are usually from 2 to 5 per cent of the amount sought and can be even lower for larger floats. However, very large floats may be harder to sell and require a greater marketing effort. For example, if a float is so large that it is necessary to attract international investors, the average cost may be higher than for a smaller float that is sold only in the Australian market. If a company has above-average business risk, it will generally be more difficult to determine an appropriate price for the shares and more difficult to sell the shares to investors. Therefore, a mining exploration company will be more costly to float than an established industrial company with stable cash flows. Finally, if a company's operations are complex or difficult to understand, it will be more costly to carry out 'due diligence' investigations of the company, and to engage in research and marketing. For example, additional independent experts' reports may be required and additional costs may be incurred in promoting the float.

Where a float is underwritten, the underwriting fee can range from 1 to 8 per cent of the funds sought, with the average fee being about 3.7 per cent (How & Yeo 2000). Historically, the majority of Australian floats have been underwritten, but in recent years the popularity of underwriting has declined as more floats have been priced and sold using the book-building process. Where book-building is used, investment banks and brokers are still involved in the IPO. However, instead of being paid to guarantee that a certain sum will be raised, they are paid to provide a range of services, including preparation of research reports on the company, arranging seminars and analyst briefings, and managing the book-building process. Therefore, book-building involves significant costs and will not necessarily be cheaper than having a float underwritten. In practice, the use of book-building is generally confined to larger floats. For smaller floats, a fixed-price underwritten offer may be preferred, although some very small floats go to the market without an underwriter. In those cases, a broker will be involved in promoting the float on a 'best efforts' basis. In summary, the costs of listing are generally lowest for large, low-risk floats where the underlying business is easily understood by investors. For example, in the 2010 float of QR National, which raised $4.05 billion, issue costs as detailed in section 10.13.4 of the company's Offer Document amounted to $75.5 million, which is less than 1.9 per cent of the funds raised.

Underpricing of an IPO represents a real cost to the original shareholders, who are effectively selling assets to the new shareholders for less than their fair value. This difference in value is often referred to as 'money left on the table'. More precisely, money left on the table is usually defined as the return on the first day of trading, and is typically measured by the number of shares sold, multiplied by the difference between the first-day closing market price and the issue price. It has been well documented that in IPOs the amount of money left on the table is typically large. For example, Ritter and Welch found that the average first-day return for 6249 IPOs in the US between 1980 and 2001 was 18.8 per cent.[19] The underpricing phenomenon exists in every nation that has a stock market. Ritter and Welch also found that the average first-day return varied considerably over time. In the 1980s, the average first-day return was 7.4 per cent and it increased to almost 11.2 per cent during 1990–94 and 18.1 per cent during 1995–98 before jumping to 65 per cent during the 'internet bubble' period in 1999–2000 and then reverting to 14 per cent in 2001.[20]

In Australia, a study by Lee, Taylor and Walter (1996) of 266 industrial IPOs between 1976 and 1989 found an average first-day abnormal return of 11.9 per cent. Dimovski and Brooks (2003) studied 358 industrial and resource IPOs in Australia from 1994 to 1999 and found that the average first-day return was 25.6 per cent, while the median first-day return was 9.3 per cent. The IPOs they studied raised a total of $24.439 billion in capital, the total amount of money left on the table was $5.678 billion and total issue costs were $592 million. Da Silva Rosa, Velayuthen and Walter (2003) reported median underpricing of 12 per cent for their sample of 333 Australian industrial IPOs from 1991 to 1999. Gong and Shekhar (2001) studied all 11 government sector IPOs in Australia between 1989 and 1999. They found an average first-day abnormal return for retail investors of approximately 11 per cent and concluded that there is no evidence that the underpricing of these IPOs differs from that of Australian private sector IPOs or of government sector IPOs in other OECD countries.

Reasons for underpricing

Many possible explanations for the underpricing of IPOs have been proposed. One explanation is based on information asymmetry in that some investors are more informed than the issuer, perhaps about the general demand for shares in the market. It is also based on the concept that some investors are well informed about the value of the shares being offered while others are uninformed and therefore have difficulty estimating the future market price of the shares. This approach proposes that a degree of underpricing is necessary to attract these investors. Uninformed investors may apply for any IPO but informed investors will only subscribe when an issue is underpriced. Therefore, when an issue is overpriced, all the shares will be allocated to uninformed investors. Conversely, when an issue is underpriced, informed investors will 'crowd out' the uninformed, who will be allocated only a fraction of the shares.

> **LEARNING OBJECTIVE 6**
> Discuss alternative explanations for the underpricing of initial public offerings

This explanation may be illustrated with a simple example. Suppose that an uninformed investor subscribes to $10 000 worth of shares in each of two IPOs. Suppose that in one of the IPOs the investor is allocated $5000 worth of shares and the first-day return is 20 per cent, and in the second of the IPOs the investor is allocated the full $10 000 worth of shares and the first-day return is –10 per cent. The simple average first-day return from these two IPOs is 5 per cent, which, because it is positive, at first view suggests underpricing. But, from the viewpoint of the uninformed investor, the IPOs are on average fairly priced: the total first-day return is a profit of 20 per cent on $5000 plus a loss of 10 per cent on $10 000, which in total is a first-day return of 0 per cent. In summary, while IPOs involve large average initial returns, this does not necessarily mean that every investor can expect to earn abnormal returns by subscribing for company floats.

---

19 Ritter and Welch (2002). The equally-weighted average first-day return measured from the offer price to the first closing price listed by CRSP is 18.8 per cent.
20 For an analysis of possible reasons for this variation, see Loughran and Ritter (2004).

winner's curse
problem that arises in bidding because the bidder who 'wins' is likely to be the one who most overestimates the value of the assets offered for sale

Uninformed investors, therefore, face a **winner's curse**. If they get all of the shares they demand, it is because the informed investors do not want them. Faced with this situation, uninformed investors will only subscribe to IPOs if they are sufficiently underpriced, on average, to compensate for the bias in the allocation of shares (for more details, see Rock 1986). In research related to the 'winner's curse' explanation it is common to assume that larger investors are better informed than small investors. Lee, Taylor and Walter (1999) examine this issue by studying IPOs on the Stock Exchange of Singapore where detailed data on applications for and allocations of shares are routinely provided. Their results are consistent with Rock's (1986) model: larger investors are more informed in that they apply for relatively more shares in issues that are underpriced. Thus, small investors are crowded out of the most underpriced issues and receive larger proportions of the less attractive issues.

A second explanation for the underpricing of IPOs is that potential investors will attempt to judge the interest of other investors and will only subscribe for IPOs that they believe will be popular. If an investor perceives that a float is not popular with other investors, then he or she may decide not to subscribe. If the issuer sets a price that is perceived as only a little too high, there is a significant probability that the issue will be a failure, with investors deciding not to subscribe because others have also decided not to subscribe. Therefore, issuers may have an incentive to underprice an issue in order to induce some potential investors to buy. The action of these investors may then set off a cascade in which other investors are willing to subscribe. Ritter and Welch (2002) note that this explanation is supported by evidence that IPOs tend to be either undersubscribed or heavily oversubscribed, with few being moderately oversubscribed.

Using book-building to price an IPO, which is standard practice in the US, allows issuers to obtain information from informed investors. After an indicative price range has been set, the issuer and the lead manager usually go on a 'road show' to promote the company to prospective investors. The lead manager can then gauge demand for the shares as expressions of interest are received from potential investors. If demand is high, the offer price will be set at the top of the indicative price range or it may be set above that level if demand is particularly strong. However, potential investors will be unwilling to reveal their true interest in the IPO if they know that showing strong interest is likely to result in a higher offer price—unless they are offered something in return. Underpricing then becomes part of the inducement needed to get potential investors to truthfully reveal that they are willing to purchase the shares at a high price. Analysis of data on IPOs priced using book-building in the US is consistent with this argument. For example, Ritter and Welch found that over the 1980 to 2001 period, for IPOs that were priced within the indicative price range, average underpricing was 12 per cent. However, when the offer price was above the indicative price range, average underpricing was 53 per cent. The additional underpricing is regarded as compensation to induce investors to reveal their high individual demand for the shares—but as Ritter and Welch note, average underpricing of 53 per cent seems to be excessive compensation for revealing information.

Several studies have found that greater underpricing is associated with higher trading volume once the shares become listed. Accordingly, a third explanation for underpricing is that it provides benefits through greater liquidity. For example, a broker who underwrites an IPO can earn higher brokerage fees for handling trades in the post-listing market if the issue is underpriced. Liquidity can also benefit issuers, particularly if they have retained a high proportion of the company's shares. Pham, Kalev and Steen (2003) argue that greater underpricing encourages small investors to subscribe for an IPO, which results in a broader and more diffuse ownership base. Using a sample of Australian IPOs they show that these factors are significantly and positively associated with the liquidity of the shares once they are listed. Conversely, they argue that lower underpricing will give rise to a more concentrated ownership structure, which may be preferred if large shareholders obtain benefits from control or can provide valuable monitoring of the company's management.

A fourth explanation is that underpricing of IPOs is in the interests of the issuing company. One aspect of this explanation is that underpriced IPOs 'leave a good taste' with investors, raising the price at which subsequent share issues by the company can be sold.[21] A related argument is that underpricing reflects, at least in part, the cost to the issuing company of purchasing research coverage by analysts. Cliff and Denis (2004) note that in addition to pre-IPO activities related to the pricing and marketing of a share issue, investment banks provide a range of post-issue services such as market-making and analyst research coverage. They also note that issuing companies appear to place a value on securing research coverage from analysts, particularly those with strong reputations. Accordingly, issuers planning an IPO may seek out underwriters who they expect will provide research coverage by a highly rated analyst and issuers will be prepared to pay for that analyst coverage—perhaps directly by way of higher underwriting fees. However, Cliff and Denis found that underwriting fees are largely uniform and propose instead that greater underpricing serves to indirectly compensate underwriters for providing analyst coverage. For example, underwriters can benefit from underpricing by allocating shares to favoured clients who are expected to provide the underwriter with investment banking or broking business in the future.

A fifth explanation is that issuers underprice IPOs to reduce the risk of being sued by investors. While the potential legal liability of issuers may be a factor in some IPOs, particularly in the US, other countries, where litigation is much less common, experience similar levels of underpricing. Therefore, it seems unlikely that legal liability is the main factor that determines the underpricing of IPOs.

Finally, Loughran and Ritter (2002) note that issuers rarely appear to be upset about leaving substantial amounts of money on the table in IPOs. They propose a behavioural explanation for this puzzling phenomenon. Their explanation can be illustrated using a hypothetical example. Suppose that Marcus Thompson owns a large successful business and, after discussion with an investment bank, he plans to sell 60 per cent of the company in an IPO, which will be priced using a book-build. The indicative price range for the book-build is set at $4.50 to $5 per share, but, after a successful 'road show' where the investment bank records strong interest from institutions, it advises Marcus that the issue price should be increased to $6 per share. Given the good news that his company is worth at least 20 per cent more than he previously thought, Marcus accepts the advice and does not bargain for a higher issue price. When the shares are listed on the ASX, the first-day closing market price is $10. Marcus has left a large amount of money on the table but he has also discovered that the interest he retained—40 per cent of the shares—is worth twice as much as he expected. Given the pleasant surprise about his new-found wealth, Marcus may feel happy, despite the opportunity loss on the shares that he sold to other investors.

If the large initial returns on IPOs reflect rational behaviour by issuers and investors, then these returns should be related to factors such as the amount of information available to investors and the benefits that issuers may derive from underpricing. Empirical evidence supports this expectation. For example, Lee, Taylor and Walter (1996) found a strong inverse relationship between the length of the delay between prospectus registration and exchange listing and the level of underpricing. In other words, IPOs with shorter delays in listing are significantly more underpriced. This finding is consistent with the 'winner's curse' explanation in which informed investors will quickly subscribe for underpriced issues thereby ensuring that the issue will be filled in a short period. How, Izan and Monroe (1995) also found a strong relationship between delay in listing and the level of underpricing. Further, they found that underpricing is related to measures of both the quality and quantity of information available about the company. Specifically, underpricing was lower when the underwriter had a good reputation and it was also lower for companies with more information available.[22]

---

[21] For an analysis of this explanation, see Welch (1989). The explanations for underpricing of IPOs outlined above are only some of the possible explanations that have been proposed. Further explanations are discussed by Ibbotson, Sindelar and Ritter (1994) and Brau and Fawcett (2006).

[22] The underwriting fee as a percentage of the issue proceeds was used as a measure of the underwriter's reputation and the size of the company was used as a measure of the quantity of information.

Camp, Comer and How (2006) studied 49 New Zealand IPOs that listed between 1989 and 2002. They found that underpricing was significantly lower for issues that used book-building rather than a fixed-price offer. This result is consistent with the argument that book-building provides issuers with feedback from informed investors, which allows more accurate pricing of the IPO. They also found that greater underpricing is associated with higher trading volume in the post-listing market, suggesting a trade-off between the cost (underpricing) of going public and the benefit (greater liquidity) of doing so. Camp et al. also found that underpricing is positively related to the proportion of shares retained by the pre-IPO shareholders. Consistent with Loughran and Ritter's explanation, issuers who retain more shares in the company appear to be less concerned about underpricing because any loss of wealth on the shares sold in the IPO will be offset by a gain on the shares they retain.

Underpricing of IPOs is a persistent phenomenon that is yet to be fully explained. In evaluating the proposed explanations outlined previously, the question should not be: 'Which model is correct?' Rather, we should ask questions such as: 'Which model is more useful in this case?' Also, we should remember that the reasons for underpricing can change over time. For example, there is evidence that underpricing is generally lower for companies that engage higher-quality underwriters and higher-quality auditors. These parties have been viewed as providing a certification role; investors are confident that a high-quality underwriter will not overprice an IPO because doing so would harm its reputation with investors. However, the usual relationship between underpricing and underwriter quality reversed during the 1999–2000 'internet bubble'. As discussed previously, one explanation for this reversal is that the objectives of issuers changed in that they became less concerned about underpricing and were prepared to pay for research coverage by leading analysts.

9.5.7 LONG-TERM PERFORMANCE OF IPOs

LEARNING OBJECTIVE 7
Outline evidence on the long-term performance of companies that are floated

The consistent finding that IPOs are on average underpriced does not necessarily mean that issue prices are 'too low'—it is also possible that first-day market prices are 'too high'. This possibility is consistent with evidence that the positive first-day returns on IPOs are often reversed over time—that is, several studies have found that the shares of newly listed companies tend to underperform during the first few years after listing. Unfortunately, it is very difficult to accurately assess the long-run performance of companies that go public. One reason is that the market model, which was introduced in Section 7.6.3, cannot be used to estimate the betas of the securities because pre-listing return data does not exist for IPOs. Therefore, researchers have used a variety of other approaches to assess whether post-listing returns are abnormal. One approach is to compare post-listing returns on IPO companies to one or more market indices, without any adjustment for risk. Another approach is to compare the returns on the IPO companies with a control sample of other listed companies matched on the basis of one or more characteristics such as size (market capitalisation) and industry.

Ritter (1991) studied companies that went public in the US in the period 1975 to 1984.[23] He found that an investor who purchased shares in IPO companies at the closing price on the first day of public trading and then held the shares for 3 years would have earned an average total return of 34.47 per cent. For a control sample of non-IPO companies matched by size and industry, the average total return over the same period was 61.86 per cent. The underperformance by IPO companies varied significantly from year to year and across industries but it was concentrated among relatively young, growth companies, particularly those that went public in years when there was a high volume of IPOs.

seasoned equity offering
offer to sell equity securities of a class that is already traded

Loughran and Ritter (1995) found that the poor long-term performance of IPOs continued beyond 3 years and was shared by companies making subsequent equity issues—known as **seasoned equity offerings** (SEOs) in the US. Using large samples of companies that issued equity in the period 1970 to 1990, they reported average annual returns over the 5 years after the issuing of only 5 per cent for IPOs

---

23 Updated evidence on the long-term performance of US IPOs from 1970 to 2009 is available at http://bear.warrington.ufl.edu/ritter/ipodata.htm.

and 7 per cent for companies making SEOs. In contrast, investing in non-issuing companies of the same size and holding the investment for the same period would have produced an average annual return of 12 per cent for IPOs and 15 per cent for SEOs. Loughran and Ritter propose that their evidence is consistent with a market where shares are periodically overvalued and that companies take advantage of these 'windows of opportunity' by issuing equity at those times. That idea, and the related proposition that investors will respond by cutting share prices when an issue is announced, are not new. For example, Smith (1986) reported that when a US company announces an SEO, its share price falls by about 3 per cent on average. Loughran and Ritter point out that if investors are to receive the same long-term returns on issuers as on non-issuers of the same size, the fall in price when an issue is announced should be much larger. Their numbers 'imply that if the market reacted fully to the information implied by an equity issue announcement, the average announcement effect would be −33 per cent, not −3 per cent' (Loughran and Ritter 1995, p. 48). Loughran and Ritter refer to the unexplained low long-term returns following equity issues as 'the new issues puzzle'.

The significance of the new issues puzzle is controversial. Brav and Gompers (1997) show that low post-listing returns tend to be concentrated among small companies, which means that measured underperformance is much smaller when returns are value weighted rather than equally weighted. They also find that underperformance is a characteristic of small companies with low book-to-market ratios regardless of whether they are newly listed or not. In other words, Brav and Gompers find that companies that go public do not exhibit long-term underperformance when returns are measured relative to control companies matched on both size and book-to-market ratio.

Eckbo, Masulis and Norli (2000) argue that the 'new issues puzzle' identified by Loughran and Ritter can be resolved without resorting to explanations based on market underreaction to the information in announcements of security issues. Eckbo et al. analyse returns following a large sample of seasoned issues of both equity and debt from 1964 to 1995. They argue that the matched-firm technique does not provide a proper control for risk for two reasons. First, an equity issue lowers the financial leverage of the issuing company so issuers also lower their risk, and therefore their expected return, relative to the matched firms. Second, they find that share turnover increases significantly after SEOs, but turnover does not change for the matched firms. In other words, liquidity increases after SEOs so the shares of issuing companies could require lower liquidity premiums after an issue. In sum, they conclude that 'evidence of long-run underperformance produced by the matched-firm technique is an artifact of the technique itself' (Eckbo, Masulis & Norli 2000, p. 253).

Gompers and Lerner (2003) point out that most studies that report underperformance by IPOs have examined data from the time period after formation of the Nasdaq system where most US IPOs are traded. The Nasdaq is the largest electronic equity securities trading market in the US. When established in the early 1970s by the National Association of Securities Dealers, it was the world's first electronic stock market. To test whether there is a 'Nasdaq effect', they conducted an out-of-sample investigation using data on 3661 IPOs from 1935 to 1972—a period prior to the creation of Nasdaq. They found that the relative performance of an IPO sample depends critically on the method used to assess performance. One method revealed some underperformance, but this measured underperformance disappeared when the same sample was studied using other methods, including regressions based on the CAPM (see Section 7.6.2) and the Fama and French three-factor model (see Section 7.7). Gompers and Lerner conclude that the evidence for underperformance by IPOs is weak.

Mixed evidence on the long-term performance of companies that go public is not confined to the US. For Australian IPOs, long-term underperformance, relative to the market index, has been reported by Lee, Taylor and Walter (1996) over 3 years, and Dimovski and Brooks (2003) over 1 year, after listing. For their sample of 266 IPOs, Lee et al. reported a market-adjusted return of −51 per cent over 3 years. Dimovski and Brooks reported an average market-adjusted return of −4.0 per cent over 1 year for a sample of 251 IPOs from 1994 to 1998. However, the results were not uniformly negative when the sample was divided into subgroups. For example, the average market-adjusted return for 78 no liability companies was −30 per cent after 1 year but for the 173 limited liability companies the corresponding average return was +7.7 per cent. The median market-adjusted return after 1 year was negative for the sample as a whole and for every subgroup. In contrast, da Silva Rosa, Velayuthen and Walter (2003) used several benchmarks and concluded that the sample they studied did not underperform in the 2 years following listing.

In summary, the evidence on long-run performance following IPOs remains controversial. Many studies have reported underperformance by IPO companies over periods of 1 to 5 years after listing. There is evidence that companies that issue equity, whether through an IPO or a seasoned offering, tend to be poor long-term investments. However, several authors have questioned whether the 'new issues puzzle' is real and provide evidence that suggests that it may be no more than an illusion.

9.6 SUBSEQUENT ISSUES OF ORDINARY SHARES

LEARNING OBJECTIVE 8
Explain how companies raise capital through rights issues, placements, share purchase plans and share options

After a company has been floated, additional external finance will usually be required at some time to finance expansion. Management has the choice of issuing more shares and/or borrowing. If it is decided to issue more shares, there are several choices available. If the funds are to be raised from existing shareholders, the company can make a pro-rata share issue (entitlement offer) or set up a share purchase plan (SPP). A pro-rata share issue may in turn be either a traditional rights issue or an accelerated entitlement offer and in either case the offer may be renounceable or non-renounceable. If management decides to raise funds from selected investors, who may or may not be existing shareholders in the company, it must choose a placement. Share issues of these types may be carried out individually or in combination. For example, a company may raise capital through a placement and an SPP that are announced simultaneously. The regulatory regime that governs capital raisings by listed companies is outlined in Table 9.4.

TABLE 9.4 The Australian capital-raising regime for listed companies

TYPE OF CAPITAL RAISING	MAIN CHARACTERISTICS	REGULATORY REQUIREMENTS
Renounceable entitlement offer	Participation is based on each shareholder's existing interest in the company. A prospectus may be needed. Shareholders are able to sell their right to participate in the entitlement offer.	The timetable for entitlement offers is specified in the ASX Listing Rules. The disclosure requirements are set out in the Corporations Act.
Non-renounceable entitlement offer	Participation is based on each shareholder's existing interest in the company. A prospectus may be needed. Shareholders are not able to sell their right to participate in the offer. Any rights not taken up may be placed at the discretion of the company's Board of Directors.	The timetable for entitlement offers is specified in the ASX Listing Rules. The Listing Rules limit the size of the offer to a maximum of one new share for each existing share. The disclosure requirements are set out in the Corporations Act.

continued

TABLE 9.4 *continued*

TYPE OF CAPITAL RAISING	MAIN CHARACTERISTICS	REGULATORY REQUIREMENTS
Placement	Participation by investors is at the discretion of the company's Board of Directors and management. Open to 'sophisticated' or 'professional' investors. A prospectus is not required.	ASX Listing Rules restrict placements to no more than 15 per cent of issued capital over a 12-month period without approval by shareholders. The Corporations Act permits placements without a disclosure document provided a 'cleansing notice' is issued.
Share purchase plan (SPP)	Participation is open to existing shareholders. There is no requirement for a prospectus provided a cleansing notice is issued, offers are limited to $15 000 per shareholder over a 12-month period, and the shares are fully paid and issued at a discount to the average market price over the last 5 days of trading prior to the announcement of the SPP.	The SPP mechanism is stipulated in the Listing Rules. The disclosure regime has been provided by ASIC in a series of Regulatory Guides and Class Orders.

Source: ISS Governance Services, *'Equity capital raising in Australia during 2008 and 2009'*, August 2010, p. 6.

9.6.1 RIGHTS ISSUES

A rights issue—also known as an entitlement offer—is an issue of new shares to existing shareholders. Under the terms of a rights issue, shareholders receive the right to subscribe for additional shares in a fixed ratio to the number of shares already held. Provided each shareholder accepts the offer, there is no dilution of any shareholder's percentage ownership in the company.

To illustrate the elements of a rights issue: assume that an investor holds 1000 shares, which represent 1 per cent of a company's issued capital of 100 000 shares. If the company makes a rights issue that entitles each shareholder to purchase one additional share for every four shares held, the shareholder is entitled to buy an extra 250 shares, thus increasing the shareholding to 1250. In total, the company will issue 25 000 new shares. Therefore, the percentage ownership of the shareholder in the company remains unchanged at 1 per cent because 1250/125 000 = 1 per cent.

With a rights issue, shareholders buy additional shares. The company, therefore, has to set a **subscription price**. Usually, the subscription price is less than the current market price of the shares, because otherwise no-one would want to subscribe for the new shares. Given that the subscription price is below the current market price, the right to buy a new share has a value. A shareholder may have the opportunity to realise the value of the rights to the new shares by selling them to another investor—that is, the rights may be renounceable.

There is a formula, known as the *theoretical rights price*, that can be used to estimate the value of a right. To develop this formula: suppose that a company makes a 1-for-N renounceable rights issue at a subscription price of S dollars per share—that is, each shareholder obtains the right to purchase one new share for every N shares that they currently hold and will pay S dollars for each new share. All renounceable rights issues specify a date, called the **ex-rights date**. If an investor purchases shares in the company before the ex-rights date, the purchase is said to be **cum rights** and the investor *will* receive rights to purchase new shares. The rights themselves may be traded separately from the shares on or after the ex-rights date. If an investor purchases shares on or after the ex-rights date the purchase is said to be *ex-rights* and the investor *will not* receive any rights.

Assume that an investor purchases N shares just before the ex-rights date. The cost of this purchase is NM where M is the market price of a share cum rights. This investor is entitled to the right to purchase

subscription price
the price that must be paid to obtain a new share

ex-rights date
date on which a share begins trading ex-rights. After this date a share does not have attached to it the right to purchase any additional share(s) on the subscription date

cum rights
when shares are traded cum rights the buyer is entitled to participate in the forthcoming rights issue

one new share. Exactly the same investment can be achieved by entering the market just after the shares begin trading ex-rights and purchasing N shares ex-rights and also purchasing the right to one new share. This will cost $NX + R$, where X is the market price of a share ex-rights and R is the market price of the right to purchase one new share. In the absence of any new information that causes prices to change, both investment strategies should cost the same. That is:

$$NM = NX + R \quad [9.1]$$

If the subscription price is payable immediately, then the right to one new share can be immediately converted to a new share by payment of the subscription price. Therefore, when the shares begin trading ex-rights, an investor could obtain a share either by buying the right to one new share at a cost of R and then paying the subscription price of S, or by buying a share directly at a price of X. To prevent arbitrage, both investment strategies must cost the same. That is:

theoretical rights price
the expected price of one right calculated on the basis of the cum-rights share price

$$R + S = X \quad [9.2]$$

Substituting Equation 9.2 into Equation 9.1, and rearranging, gives:

$$R = \frac{N(M - S)}{N + 1} \quad [9.3]$$

theoretical ex-rights share price
the expected price of one share when shares begin to be traded ex-rights

Substituting Equation 9.3 into Equation 9.2, and rearranging, gives:

$$X = \frac{NM + S}{N + 1} \quad [9.4]$$

The prices that result from using Equations 9.3 and 9.4 are often referred to as the **theoretical rights price** and the **theoretical ex-rights share price**, respectively.

What is the effect of a rights issue on the value of an investment in shares? To answer this question, consider Example 9.1.

EXAMPLE 9.1

Athol owns 1000 shares in Raven Enterprises Ltd (REL), whose current share price (cum rights) is $2 per share. REL makes a 1-for-4 rights issue with a subscription price of $1.40 per share. Athol wishes to calculate:

(a) the value, R, of the right to buy 1 new share
(b) the ex-rights share price, X
(c) the value of his investment cum rights and ex-rights.

In this case, $N = 4$, $M = \$2.00$ and $S = \$1.40$.

SOLUTION

(a) Using Equation 9.3, the value of the right to buy 1 new share is:

$$R = \frac{N(M - S)}{N + 1}$$
$$= \frac{4(\$2.00 - \$1.40)}{4 + 1}$$
$$= 48 \text{ cents}$$

(b) Using Equation 9.4, the ex-rights share price is:

$$X = \frac{NM + S}{N + 1}$$
$$= \frac{4(\$2.00) + \$1.40}{4 + 1}$$
$$= \$1.88$$

(c) Cum rights, the investment is worth:

(1000)($2)
= $2000

Ex-rights, the investment is worth:

(1000)($1.88) + (250)($0.48)
= $2000

According to this analysis the total value of the investment is unaffected. Before the issue Athol owned 1000 shares worth $2 each—a total of $2000. After the issue he owns 1000 shares worth $1.88 each ($1880) plus 250 rights worth 48 cents each ($120), which in total is also worth $2000. Clearly, the value of the rights just offsets the decline in the value of the shares. If Athol decides to sell his rights he can expect to receive $120, which should be regarded as a partial return *of* capital as distinct from a profit or return *on* capital. Finally, suppose that instead of a 1-for-4 rights issue with a subscription price of $1.40 per share, REL makes a 1-for-2 issue with a subscription price of 70 cents per share. Clearly, both issues would raise exactly the same funds for REL and reworking the above calculations would show that the ex-rights value of Athol's investment would again be $2000.

This analysis relates to the value of an investment made at the time of the ex-rights date and it suggests three important conclusions. First, shareholders' wealth is not affected by the mere fact of a share beginning to trade on an ex-rights basis. In turn, this suggests the second conclusion that, of itself, a rights issue has no value to shareholders. This conclusion should not be a surprise. If a rights issue increased (decreased) shareholders' wealth we would expect rights issues to occur much more (less) frequently than they do. Third, it suggests that in the case of a rights issue the level of the subscription price has no effect on shareholders' wealth. If all shareholders subscribe for a rights issue, then whether a company raises, say, $2 million by issuing 1 million shares at $2 each, or 2 million shares at $1 each, should not matter to its shareholders.

However, the above analysis ignores some factors that can be important. First, the *announcement* of a rights issue may affect shareholders' wealth because the announcement can have information content. For example, US and Australian evidence suggests that, on average, the market interprets the announcement of equity capital issues, including rights issues, as 'bad' news.[24] Smith (1986) provided an explanation for the negative announcement effect: managers will try to issue equity when they believe it is overvalued. Investors are aware of managers' information advantage and will respond by reducing their estimate of the company's value when an issue is announced. The implications for financing decisions are discussed in Section 12.9.4.

Second, the terms of a rights issue such as the subscription price may affect the market reaction to an issue when it is announced. If the subscription price is set only slightly below the market price of the shares, a minor fall in the company's share price could cause the issue to fail—no rational shareholder will subscribe for the rights issue if the shares can be purchased more cheaply on the stock market. Clearly, this risk can be reduced by setting a lower subscription price, but doing so may warn investors that management is fearful of a possible fall in the company's share price. Hence, setting a lower subscription price may result in a larger fall in share price when the issue is announced.

---

24 There is evidence that the market response to the announcement of equity issues differs between countries but is consistently negative on average. Thus, in the US, Smith reports an average decline of about 3 per cent for rights issues by industrial companies (see Smith 1986), while in the UK, Marsh found a much smaller decline for such issues (see Marsh 1979). In Australia, a study of 636 rights issues by Balachandran, Faff and Theobald (2008) found an average fall in share price of 1.74 per cent when the issues were announced.

Third, the analysis assumes that the subscription price is payable on the ex-rights date, whereas, in fact, it is usually not payable until several weeks later. This gives rise to the further point that the holder of a right is permitted to purchase shares at the subscription price, but is not obliged to do so. If the share price on the subscription date is less than the subscription price, the holder of the right does not have to purchase the shares. This type of agreement is known as an **option**, but the theoretical model ignores the option-like features of a right and is therefore likely to understate the value of a right.

option
the right but not the obligation to buy or sell underlying assets at a fixed price for a specified period

The option component of a right's value is usually small in dollar terms but can be a significant proportion of the value of a right, particularly if the share price is close to the subscription price. For example, the subscription price for the rights issue by Colonial Group in 1998 was $4.50, payable no later than 13 July, and the rights were traded on the ASX from 4 June to 2 July. On 11 June, the closing price of Colonial shares was $4.53 while the rights closed at 14.5 cents. If holders of the rights were obliged to pay the subscription price and had to pay it immediately, the rights would have been worth only $4.53 – $4.50 = 3 cents. In this case, the option component of the rights' value was 11.5 cents.

Disclosure and regulation of rights issues

Historically, a company making a rights issue was required to supply shareholders with a disclosure document, usually a prospectus. The cost of preparing a disclosure document was an important factor that influenced issuers to prefer placements rather than rights issues. The requirements for rights issues have been aligned with those for placements by changes to the Corporations Act contained in the *Corporations Legislation Amendment (Simpler Regulatory System) Act 2007*. From 28 June 2007, issuers can proceed with a rights issue without a prospectus provided they:

- lodge with the ASX a notice known as a 'rights issue cleansing notice'
- send to shareholders a short document that describes the reasons for the rights issue and sets out the terms and timing of the issue.

In addition to stating that the issuer complies with certain provisions of the Corporations Act, a rights issue cleansing notice must deal with two issues. First, it must contain any 'excluded' information—that is, information that:

- has previously been withheld from investors based on one of the exceptions to disclosure contained in the listing rules[25]
- investors would reasonably require and expect to be included in a disclosure document for the purpose of assessing the financial position, performance and prospects of the issuer.

Second, the notice must provide information about any effects that the issue could have on the control of the listed entity.

If a company has disclosed all price-sensitive information related to its operations and makes a rights issue for a general purpose such as raising working capital or repaying debt, a rights issue cleansing notice would be the obvious choice. In other cases a prospectus may be preferred. For example, suppose that a company makes a rights issue to raise funds for a new project that has been under development for some time but whose existence has not been disclosed to the shareholders. In that case, a rights issue cleansing notice should contain extensive details of the new project. However, it may instead be preferable to issue a prospectus containing the same information. One factor favouring the use of a prospectus is that a cleansing notice is not defined as a disclosure document. Therefore, if a cleansing notice is found to contain errors or omissions, the 'due diligence' defence outlined in Section 9.4.1 is not available.

---

25 Rule 3.1 of the Australian Securities Exchange Listing Rules requires immediate disclosure of material information by listed entities but Rule 3.1A provides some exceptions to the continuous disclosure requirements.

As discussed in Section 9.4.2, the prospectus for a rights issue can be much less detailed than the prospectus for an issue of unlisted securities. Provided the company's shares have been listed for at least 12 months prior to the issue, the prospectus does not have to contain extensive information on the assets, liabilities, performance and prospects of the issuing company. Rather, the prospectus can focus on details of the new securities and on the effects of the new issue on the company.

The significance of rights issues

The frequency of rights issues fluctuates over time but they continue to be an important way of raising equity for Australian companies. In the 2009 calendar year, 412 companies listed on the ASX raised around $38.3 billion through rights issues. In comparison, 260 companies raised $12.8 billion through rights issues in 2008 and 315 companies raised $18.4 billion in 2007. In total, there were 987 rights issues over the 2007 to 2009 period and, on average, each issue raised around $70 million (Australian Securities Exchange, 2010, p. 27). Details of some rights issues by listed companies are shown in Table 9.5.

TABLE 9.5 Details of rights issues by listed companies

COMPANY	DATE ANNOUNCED	ISSUE RATIO	AMOUNT RAISED ($M)	ISSUE PRICE ($)	PRE-ISSUE SHARE PRICE ($)	UNDER-WRITING FEE (%)
Alumina Ltd	25/08/2008	5:19	910	3.00	3.62	2.4
Argo Investments	05/02/2007	1:8	446	7.20	8.66	n.a.[a]
Queensland Gas	04/08/2006	1:4	59.7	0.63	0.77	4.5
Rio Tinto Ltd	05/06/2009	21:40	4244	28.29	52.77	2.75
Santos Ltd	11/05/2009	2:5	3000	12.50	15.78	2.25
Wesfarmers Ltd	22/01/2009	3:7	3700	13.50	15.78	2.1

[a] Not applicable.
Source: Announcements to the ASX and company prospectuses.

Designing a successful rights issue

A rights issue that failed to raise all or most of the planned funds could be very costly for the issuing company. The costs of planning the issue and preparing a prospectus or other documentation have to be paid regardless of the outcome, and failure is likely to harm a company's reputation because it shows that existing shareholders lack confidence in the company's prospects and/or the performance of its managers. Therefore, managers will employ various measures to maximise the probability that a rights issue will be successful. An obvious measure of this type is to have the issue underwritten. Another approach might be to make the issue renounceable and to set the subscription price substantially below the current market price of the shares so there is a high probability that shareholders will either exercise their entitlement, or sell their rights to others who will subscribe for the shares. In this case, it might seem that there should be no need for the company to have the issue underwritten, but in fact the majority of rights issues in Australia are underwritten. There appear to be four main reasons for this practice. First, while the subscription price may be well below the share price at the time an issue is announced, a substantial unexpected fall in share price is always possible and could spell failure for a non-underwritten issue. Second, as discussed above, setting a low subscription price may result in a larger fall in the share price when a rights issue is announced. Therefore, managers may try to minimise the adverse effect on shareholders' wealth by setting a higher subscription price and having the issue underwritten. Third, there will always be some shareholders who have moved without notifying the company of their new address and therefore do not receive notification of an issue in time to subscribe for it. Finally, because of the high costs of complying with securities laws in countries such as the US, Australian companies usually specify that a rights issue will be made only to shareholders whose registered address is in Australia or New Zealand. ASX Listing Rule 7.7 requires that where foreign shareholders are not eligible to participate in a renounceable rights issue, they must still be advised of the issue and that the value, if any, of their entitlements should be paid to them. Therefore, one role of the underwriter is to sell any new shares that represent the entitlements of ineligible foreign shareholders. Orica Limited is an Australian-based manufacturer of chemicals and explosives with operations in about 50 countries and its shareholders include both Australian and overseas investors. In November 2005, Orica announced a fully underwritten 1-for-8 renounceable rights issue at $15 per share, substantially less than the market price of $20.55. The issue was made to all ordinary shareholders with a registered address in Australia or New Zealand and to institutional ordinary shareholders in Hong Kong, Singapore and the UK. On 19 December 2005, Orica announced a shortfall, including the entitlements of ineligible foreign shareholders, of 2.4 million shares, or approximately 7 per cent of the total. In this case, the shortfall shares were sold to institutional investors with the issue price determined by an overnight book-build conducted by the underwriters. The issue price for these shares was $20.30, which meant that Orica received $15 per share and the balance of $5.30 per share was paid to the non-subscribing shareholders and ineligible foreign shareholders.

In summary, underwriting is one way of ensuring that the issuing company will receive all the planned funds regardless of the level of subscriptions by shareholders and may be less costly than attempting to increase shareholder take-up by lowering the subscription price. The closer the subscription price on the rights issue is set to the market price of shares, the greater is the need to have the issue underwritten, and the higher the underwriting fee. The underwriting fee is usually between 1 and 3 per cent of the subscription price.

While underwriting ensures that all the planned funds will be raised, there are other measures that can be used to increase the likelihood that a rights issue will be successful. The main such measures are issuing the rights with bonus share options as a 'sweetener' and providing a **shortfall facility**. As discussed in Section 9.6.5, bonus share options are issued 'free' in a fixed proportion to the new shares taken up by existing shareholders. Balachandran, Faff and Theobald (2008) studied rights issues announced by Australian companies from 1995 to 2005 and found that almost one-third of the issues in their final sample provided bonus share options. Another measure to increase the take-up of new shares by existing shareholders is the inclusion of a shortfall facility. In its simplest form, a shortfall facility allows existing shareholders to apply for extra shares in addition to their pro-rata entitlement. In this case, any shares not subscribed for by some shareholders ('shortfall shares') will be issued to those who applied for additional shares. A shortfall facility can also allow the company to issue **shortfall shares** to other investors, including underwriters, and the company may have the right to accept oversubscriptions. For example, in February 2007 Argo Investments made a rights issue that was not underwritten and was expected to raise $441 million, but shareholders taking up their entitlements were invited to apply for additional shares and the company reserved the right to accept oversubscriptions. The end result was that the issue raised approximately $446 million.

As shown in Table 9.4, there is no upper limit on the size of a renounceable rights issue so an issue of this type can be used to raise a large amount, provided investors are prepared to subscribe for the new shares. Further, provided shareholders take up their entitlement, a rights issue will have no effect on the control of the company as there is no change in shareholders' relative voting strengths. For these reasons a rights issue may appeal to a company's board as a means of raising finance.

shortfall facility
a mechanism under which a company may issue shortfall shares to eligible shareholders or other investors

shortfall shares
new shares not subscribed for by eligible shareholders according to their entitlements under a rights issue

While many companies making rights issues specify that the issue is renounceable, sometimes a rights issue will be non-renounceable. If a company makes a non-renounceable issue, shareholders cannot sell their entitlement to take up new shares. The only choices available to them are to exercise their entitlement, either fully or partly, or to permit it to lapse.[26] If investors take the latter choices the issue will be undersubscribed. For this reason non-renounceable issues are frequently underwritten.

As noted earlier, the market interprets the announcement of equity capital issues, including rights issues, as 'bad' news. Balachandran, Faff and Theobald (2008) found an average abnormal return of −1.74 per cent over a 3-day announcement period for a sample of 636 rights issues by Australian companies from 1995 to 2005. If the terms of an issue such as whether the issue is renounceable or underwritten also convey information to investors, then the price response to issue announcements may differ between rights issues with different terms. Balachandran, Faff and Theobald found that there is no difference between the average market reaction to renounceable and non-renounceable issues but the reaction to rights issue announcements is related to the underwriting status of the issue. Almost 60 per cent of the issues in their sample were fully underwritten and the average abnormal return associated with announcement of these issues was −1.04 per cent, but for non-underwritten issues the average abnormal return was −2.23 per cent.

As discussed in Section 9.5.6, underwriters are seen as certifying the value or 'quality' of the securities being offered. When deciding whether to have an issue underwritten, issuers will consider the benefits that underwriting provides relative to the cost of the underwriter's fee. The fee will be related to the risk of undersubscription and will reflect any costs that the underwriter incurs in assessing that risk. This is likely to include the costs of investigating the current financial position and the prospects of the issuer. Thus, a decision to fully underwrite an issue will typically be associated with low risk and/or low investigation costs and is associated with a smaller negative market reaction. Where the risk and/or investigation costs are higher, issuers may choose to accept the risk of undersubscription rather than pay an underwriting fee. Not surprisingly, without an underwriter's certification, the market reaction is more negative.

Traditional and accelerated rights issues

One disadvantage of a traditional renounceable rights issue is that it is a relatively slow way of raising funds. While the ASX has revised its timetables to shorten the offer period, a traditional renounceable rights issue cannot be completed in fewer than 23 business days. A non-renounceable issue is potentially quicker since no rights trading period is required, but it is still slower than a share placement.

The traditional rights issue structure has been adapted to allow companies to raise funds more quickly. The ASX commonly grants waivers of its listing rules to allow companies to make non-traditional or 'accelerated' rights issues. These issues involve two stages: an initial accelerated offer of shares to institutions and a second offer to retail shareholders.[27] The structures used for these issues include:

---

[26] Ignoring transaction costs, the choices available to shareholders are not reduced by a non-renounceable rights issue. Shareholders can take up the rights and then realise their value by selling the shares.

[27] Amendments to the Corporations Act in 2007 introduced a new definition of 'rights' issue, which requires that the terms of such an issue must be the same for all shareholders. Since accelerated issues involve different terms for institutional and retail shareholders they do not conform to this definition and are more correctly described as entitlement offers. For ease of exposition we use the term rights issue to encompass both traditional rights issues and accelerated issues.

- Accelerated Non-Renounceable Entitlement Offer (or 'Jumbo') structure. A non-renounceable pro-rata offer is made to institutional shareholders over a period of 1 or 2 business days. The issue price may be determined by an institutional book-build or it may be fixed prior to the announcement of the issue. In the second stage, a non-renounceable pro-rata offer is made to retail shareholders at the same price as the first-stage pro-rata offer.
- Accelerated Renounceable Entitlement Offer (AREO), which differs from the 'Jumbo' structure in two ways: the offer is renounceable and the procedure involves two book-builds. In the first stage, eligible institutional shareholders may subscribe for their pro-rata entitlement to new shares at a fixed offer price. Any shares not taken up by institutional shareholders are then offered to other institutional investors through a book-build—so there is no trading of rights on the exchange and any entitlements that are renounced are sold 'off-market'. The second stage is a pro-rata entitlement offer to retail shareholders at the same fixed offer price as the institutional entitlement offer. Retail shareholders will be provided with details of the offer in a prospectus or offer booklet and will usually have about 2 weeks to decide whether to take up their entitlements. Finally, a second book-build is undertaken where any shares not taken up by retail shareholders are offered to institutional investors. If the prices established in either of the book-builds exceeds the fixed offer price, the excess is paid to the shareholders who did not take up their entitlements.
- Simultaneous Accelerated Renounceable Entitlement Offer (SAREO), which is essentially the same as the AREO structure except that any renounced entitlements are sold through a single book-build. This book-build is open only to institutional investors and is carried out after both of the entitlement offers have been completed, so it ensures that each group of investors receives the same price for any entitlements they renounce.

While accelerated rights issues can differ in significant details, all such issues have one important feature: the proceeds of the institutional component will be received very soon after the issue is launched. For a company with large institutional shareholdings, the proceeds of the institutional offer will make up the majority of the issue proceeds, so the outcome is, to a large extent, similar to making a placement. Because the time period involved is short, the risk of a significant shortfall is lower than for a traditional rights issue, so the cost of underwriting should also be lower. Importantly, the accelerated structures allow funds to be raised quickly while retail shareholders can still participate in the capital raising. Also, renounceable rights issues are regarded as the most equitable because shareholders who choose not to participate can realise some value by selling their rights. However, the accelerated structures do not necessarily ensure that all shareholders are treated fairly. First, the time allowed for completion of the institutional component can disadvantage shareholders who do not have sufficient funds available to take up their full entitlements at short notice. Second, the AREO structure with two separate book-builds means that any premium distributed to shareholders who renounce their entitlements can differ depending on whether the shareholder is an institutional or retail investor. The SAREO structure addresses the latter concern but may not provide a perfect solution because it means that institutional shareholders who 'sell' their rights have to wait for some weeks to find out what price they will receive.

ISS Governance Services (**www.issgovernance.com**) identified 78 pro-rata issues during 2008 and 2009 by entities included in the S&P/ASX 200 index as at December 2009. Twenty-one of these issues were renounceable and 57 were non-renounceable. Of the 21 renounceable issues, only four involved rights that could be traded on the ASX. The other 17 issues used an accelerated structure, where any entitlements not taken up by shareholders are sold to institutions through a book-build and any premium that results is distributed to the renouncing shareholders.

UNDERWRITER BUYS SHARES TO PROVIDE IMMEDIATE FUNDING

In some cases it is important for the issuer to receive all of the funds by a certain date and this can be achieved by extending the role of the underwriter to include the provision of short-term funding. For example, on 9 March 2007, Suncorp-Metway Ltd announced a 2-for-15 entitlement offer to raise approximately $1.17 billion from shareholders. The purpose of the issue was to partially fund the cash component of the consideration payable by Suncorp-Metway in connection with its then proposed merger with Promina Ltd. The Suncorp-Metway issue was divided into institutional and retail offers, each followed by an institutional book-build. The merger involved a Scheme of Arrangement that was subject to court approval at a hearing scheduled to take place on 12 March 2007. Once the court approved the scheme, Suncorp-Metway had an obligation to make payments to Promina shareholders, so it needed access to the issue proceeds shortly after the court hearing. This was achieved by negotiating an underwriting agreement whereby the underwriter, Citigroup Global Markets Australia, subscribed for all of the new shares that were offered for sale. The new shares were then transferred by Citigroup to shareholders who chose to take up their entitlements and to investors who acquired shares through the two book-builds. The capital raising was completed with the second book-build on 13 April 2007 but Suncorp-Metway had received the full proceeds from Citigroup on 12 March. Of course, the underwriting agreement required Suncorp-Metway to pay a daily funding fee representing interest on the funds that it effectively borrowed from the underwriter.

9.6.2 PLACEMENTS (PRIVATE ISSUES)

A **placement** of ordinary shares is one restricted to a limited number of potential investors. These issues are typically made to larger institutions such as life insurance companies and investment funds. Such organisations are major holders of Australian shares and have become the prime targets for placements because they have large sums to invest. Hence, a significant amount of capital can be raised quickly by making a placement to a small number of institutions or to a single institution. Details of some recent placements are shown in Table 9.6.

placement
an issue of securities direct to chosen investors rather than the general public

TABLE 9.6 Details of selected placements 2007–2009

COMPANY	DATE ANNOUNCED	AMOUNT RAISED ($M)	ISSUE PRICE AS % OF PRE-ANNOUNCEMENT MARKET PRICE	PRICING AND ISSUE METHOD
Fortescue Metals Group	April 2009	644.8	87.6	Issue to single investor
Macquarie Bank	May 2007	750	100.2	Book-build
National Australia Bank	July 2009	2000	91.2	Book-build
Paladin Energy	September 2009	430	93.9	Placed by investment banks
Westfield Group	February 2009	2900	86.8	Underwritten

Source: Compiled from company announcements and the *Australian Financial Review*.

In some cases the shares are purchased by another company rather than by financial institutions, often as part of the formation of a strategic alliance between two companies whose businesses are related. For example, in December 2006, Queensland Gas Company (QGC) entered into an agreement with AGL Energy under which AGL Energy purchased a 27.5 per cent ownership interest in QGC for $327 million. The two companies also entered into a 20-year gas supply agreement and AGL Energy was entitled to appoint three directors on the QGC board.

A company making a placement will usually not be required to issue a disclosure document. Placements usually involve offers of securities to sophisticated and institutional investors. As discussed in Section 9.4.3, these offers of securities do not require a disclosure document.

Many placements are underwritten, particularly where the issue is large and/or the new shares are distributed to many investors. Where an issue is not underwritten, the company making the issue generally uses the services of a broker or investment bank to assist in placing the shares with investors. The broker is not obliged to dispose of all the shares: the broker's task is best described as undertaking the placement of the shares on a 'best-efforts' basis. Underwriting fees for share placements are influenced by several factors, including the absolute size of the placement, the size, liquidity and perceived market risk of the issuing company and the reason for raising the equity. For example, a placement to fund a profitable acquisition will involve lower market risk, and lower fees, than one that is needed to recapitalise a company whose financial leverage has become excessive. The fees for arranging and/or underwriting a placement are usually not disclosed. Macquarie Capital Advisers Limited has indicated that for placements by ASX-listed companies, underwriting fees can range from around 1 per cent to 5 per cent of the gross offer proceeds.

It has become common for larger placements to institutions to be priced using the book-building process and in some cases the managers of the book-build may also underwrite the issue. For example, in November 2006, Origin Energy raised $400 million by a placement that was priced using a book-build and also underwritten by the two investment banks that conducted the book-build. Underwriting may be preferred when a company has entered into a commitment that creates a specific need for additional funds. In the case of the Origin Energy placement, the proceeds were used to partly fund the acquisition of a gas retailing business that Origin had agreed to purchase from the Queensland Government.

There has been considerable opposition from shareholders to companies making placements of shares. Some shareholders may oppose placements because they reduce the percentage of ownership and voting power of existing shareholders. Also, some shareholders may believe that they are being deprived of a possible profit from the sale of the rights. However, we have already shown that the return that shareholders receive from the sale of rights represents, in effect, a return of a portion of their investment in the company. More importantly, if the placement is made to new shareholders at a price below the current market price, there is a reduction in the value of the existing shareholders' investment.

The ASX has placed a limit of 15 per cent on the amount of capital that a company can issue privately in any 1 year without the prior approval of its shareholders.[28] However, it is not difficult to exceed this limit without violating the ASX rules. After making a placement that falls within the 15 per cent limit, a company will often have the placement ratified by shareholders. Ratification of a placement 'refreshes' the company's capacity to raise capital because it means that the placement will not be included when assessing the company's ability to make a future placement. In other words, a company may make two or more placements in a 12-month period, provided each placement increases its issued capital by less than 15 per cent and each placement is ratified by shareholders before the next placement occurs. Also, the ASX has allowed larger placements in cases where it is confident that a company's issued capital is about to be increased by another share issue. In such cases, the ASX is willing to apply the 15 per cent limit to the expanded capital base rather than to the existing issued capital. For example, a company that is

---

[28] See Rules 7.1 and 7.2 of the Australian Securities Exchange Listing Rules, which provide that, in general, only 15 per cent (formerly 10 per cent) of a company's issued share capital may be issued to non-shareholders without the prior approval of shareholders at a general meeting.

committed to making a fully underwritten 1-for-1 entitlement offer could obtain a waiver of the '15 per cent rule' that allows it to make a placement of 30 per cent of its issued capital prior to the entitlement offer (ISS Governance Services, 2010, p. 13).

Placements occur more frequently than rights issues and, on average, placements are smaller than rights issues. For example, in the period 2007 to 2009, listed Australian entities made a total of 2133 placements and 987 rights issues. As shown in Table 9.6, some placements raised more than $2 billion, but most are for much smaller amounts. The average amount raised in a placement during 2007 to 2009 was around $42 million—considerably less than the average for rights issues.

9.6.3 CONTRIBUTING SHARES AND INSTALMENT RECEIPTS

As discussed in Section 9.2, **contributing shares**, also known as partly paid shares, are shares on which only part of the issue price has been paid. The issuing company can call up the unpaid part of the issue price in one or more instalments (known as 'calls') and, in the case of a limited liability company, the holder has a legal obligation to pay these calls. Contributing shares are quite common in Australia and can be used to provide a company with a reliable source of funds. The unpaid amount is referred to as 'reserve capital' and the shares can be created by a rights issue where the issue price is to be contributed in stages at specified times. Many contributing shares are issued by mining and oil exploration companies, which make calls when additional funds are required. Contributing shares can be important in raising capital but the amounts involved are typically small in comparison to other sources of equity.[29]

> **contributing shares** shares on which only part of the issue price has been paid. Also known as *partly paid shares*

Typically, **instalment receipts** are issued when existing fully paid shares are offered to the public, with the sale price to be paid in two instalments. All three sales by the Australian Government of shares in Telstra Ltd involved instalment receipts. For example, in the case of the third Telstra share offer in November 2006, retail investors paid a first instalment of $2 with a second instalment of $1.60 payable by 29 May 2008. Partly paid shares and instalment receipts are very similar but there are some important differences between them. These differences include:

> **instalment receipt** marketable security for which only part of the issue price has been paid. The balance is payable in a final instalment on or before a specified date

- for instalment receipts, the amount and timing of all instalments are specified at the time of the original sale rather than being at the discretion of directors
- instalments are payable to the vendor of the shares rather than to the issuing company
- holders of instalment receipts are usually entitled to the same dividends as holders of fully paid shares, whereas holders of partly paid shares usually receive a partial dividend based on the proportion of the issue price that has been paid.

9.6.4 SHARE PURCHASE PLANS

Companies listed on the ASX are permitted to raise limited amounts of funds from existing shareholders through share purchase plans (SPPs). These issues do not require a prospectus provided they comply with ASIC Regulatory Guide 125, which requires that SPPs are accompanied by a cleansing notice. ASIC recognises that the costs of preparing and distributing a prospectus could be very high relative to the benefits when the risk to investors is limited because the amount that can be invested is restricted. Accordingly, the amount that a listed company can raise in this way is restricted to $15 000 per annum from each shareholder. Share purchase plans may be attractive to shareholders because the subscription price must be less than the market price prior to the announcement of the issue and there is no brokerage. As discussed in Section 9.6.6, share purchase plans are sometimes used in conjunction with an institutional placement, giving all existing shareholders the opportunity to purchase additional shares at the price paid by the institutions that took up the placement.

---

29 Contributing shares can also be issued to directors and others as part of a compensation package. This use of contributing shares is analysed by Brown and Hathaway (1991).

9.6.5 SHARE OPTIONS

An option to purchase the shares of a company gives the holder of that option the right to take up shares in the company by a specified date on predetermined terms.[30] For example, a company may issue, at no cost, 10 000 options that may be exercised by the payment of $1 per option during the next 5 years. Consequently, an investor can purchase a maximum of 10 000 shares for $1 each at any time during the next 5 years, regardless of their market price at the time. The recipient of the option therefore obtains the opportunity to benefit from an increase in the market price of the company's shares. If the company's share price increases to $1.20, then the investor can purchase 10 000 shares for $10 000, which is $2000 below their current market value.

There are three major provisions included in an option agreement:

- the exercise price of the option
- the period during which the options may be exercised
- the rights of option holders in the event of new issues of shares by the company.

In general, it is usual for the exercise price of an option to be set near the share price at the time the option is issued. The term of an option may extend for several years and, other things being equal, a long-term option is more valuable than a short-term option. In the case of company-issued options, the option holder is often prevented from exercising the option for a certain period after it has been granted. If a company makes an issue of shares during the option's life, it is possible for the value of the option to be reduced to almost zero. For example, if a company splits each of its shares into two, other things being equal, the price per share will be halved. In turn, this will result in a corresponding reduction in the possibility that the option holder will benefit from any subsequent increase in the share price. As a result, option agreements usually provide holders with the right to participate in share issues by the company during the life of the option.

Options may be issued as follows:

(a) *To employees.* The objective when making option issues is to reward employees in a way that is likely to encourage them to work towards improving the company's profitability. Such issues are typically made with an exercise price equal to the current share price, which does not expose the employee to any immediate tax obligation. If the company becomes more profitable, it is likely to command a higher share price, which, in turn, will increase the value of the option.

(b) *As a sweetener to an equity issue.* Many exploration and mining companies issue both ordinary shares and options to subscribe for additional shares. For example, an investor purchasing 1000 shares in a new issue may also receive 1000 options, each of which entitles the investor to buy one additional share at a fixed price before a specified date. Frequently these options are listed separately on the stock exchange. Therefore, an investor obtains the opportunity to make an additional gain from an increase in the company's share price. A company that issues shares accompanied by options hopes to encourage investors to participate in the issue, thereby reducing the possibility of undersubscription.

(c) *As a sweetener to a private debt issue.* On occasions, a company seeking debt finance will offer share options to the lender. The company benefits either by obtaining debt finance that it would not otherwise have received or by obtaining the funds on better terms—for example, at a lower interest rate. However, neither party to an agreement of this type can make the options conditional on the granting of the loan because this may jeopardise the tax deductibility of interest on the debt.

---

[30] An important difference between the options discussed here and the exchange-traded options discussed in Chapter 18 is that this section discusses options issued by companies whose shares can then be purchased through the exercise of the options. In contrast, an exchange-traded option is created by a contract between a buyer and a seller that does not involve the company whose shares underlie the option.

In the cases outlined above, it is evident that options are not issued primarily as a means of raising finance, although they are often issued as part of a finance package. Nevertheless, significant sums can be raised when company-issued options are exercised.

9.6.6 CHOOSING BETWEEN EQUITY RAISING METHODS

The previous sections have outlined several external methods to raise equity funds, including rights issues, placements, share purchase plans, calls on partly paid shares and the exercise of company-issued options. Most of these methods involve long-term arrangements and if a significant 'once-off' equity raising is needed, it will involve a rights issue and/or a placement of shares.

What factors influence the choice between these methods? Chan and Brown (2004) studied this question using Australian data from July 1996 to March 2001, a period in which the ASX increased the annual ceiling for 'placements without shareholder agreement' from 10 per cent to 15 per cent of ordinary share capital. They found that the ceiling imposed by the listing rules has a strong effect on company behaviour, with a significant tendency for the issue size to be chosen so that it falls just under the prescribed ceiling. As expected, 'placements without shareholder agreement' became more common after the ceiling was increased to 15 per cent and it was rare for companies to make rights issues where the amount of funds raised was less than the ceiling for placements. Where the amount of funds sought exceeded the prescribed ceiling, it was more common for companies to make a placement with shareholder agreement than to make a rights issue. In summary, their main conclusion was that companies generally prefer placements to rights issues.

Apart from the influence of any ceiling imposed by stock exchange listing rules, the main advantages of placements are speed (funds can be raised in a few days rather than weeks), certainty (a placement may be underwritten and, given that the risk of a shortfall exists for only a short period, it should not be difficult to obtain the support of an underwriter), lower transaction costs and the shares may be placed with investors considered to be 'friendly' to the existing management. Rights issues have the advantage that shareholders can preserve their ownership proportions and voting power. Thus, rights issues are seen as being more equitable to existing shareholders. A rights issue may require a prospectus and is slower than a placement, but, as noted in Section 9.6.1, for companies with mostly institutional shareholders, the majority of the funds raised by a rights issue can be received quickly if one of the accelerated offer structures is used.

The costs involved in issuing shares will consist largely of fees paid to underwriters and other advisers. Statistics including the average fees for rights issues and placements by S&P/ASX200 companies during 2008 and 2009 are shown in Table 9.7.

TABLE 9.7 Placements and rights issues by S&P/ASX200 companies during 2008 and 2009

	PLACEMENTS	NON-RENOUNCEABLE RIGHTS ISSUES	RENOUNCEABLE RIGHTS ISSUES[a]
Number of issues	140	57	21
Funds raised ($ billion)	44.84	30.95	15.18
Fees as a percentage of funds raised	1.76	2.32	2.40
Average issue size ($ million)	320.3	540.1	722.9

[a] Note that the averages for this category are influenced by an issue by Rio Tinto Ltd, which raised approximately $4.2 billion with fees of 2.75 per cent.

Source: ISS Governance Services, '*Equity capital raising in Australia during 2008 and 2009*', August 2010, pp. 11–16.

For secondary share issues by S&P/ASX 200 companies during 2008 and 2009, renounceable rights issues involved the highest average fees, followed closely by non-renounceable rights issues. For placements, the fees—at an average of 1.76 per cent of funds raised—were lower than for rights issues. The average fees for renounceable and non-renounceable rights issues were 2.40 per cent and 2.32 per cent, respectively. However, the average for renounceable issues was heavily influenced by Rio Tinto's large underwritten rights issue with fees of 2.75 per cent.

Combination issues

As noted above, where the amount of funds sought is below the ceiling for a 'placement without shareholder agreement', companies almost invariably opt for a placement rather than a rights issue. Where the amount of funds sought is above the ceiling, a rights issue may be chosen but the choice involved is not simply 'rights issue versus placement with shareholder agreement'. Rather, the company may make a placement in combination with another method of equity raising, such as a share purchase plan or a non-renounceable rights issue. Where these combination issues are used, the placement component is almost invariably just under the 15 per cent ceiling so that shareholder agreement is not required.

Another feature of combination issues is that the placement is often priced using an institutional book-build. The issue price established by the book-build is then used to determine the price of the shares for the second component of the issue. Since retail shareholders have the opportunity to participate in the capital raising at the same price as institutions, this approach addresses the concern that a placement alone discriminates against those shareholders who are not invited to participate. Combination issues involving a placement and an SPP in close proximity have become common. The ASX reported that about 100 companies made such combination issues during 2007. In 2008 the number fell to about 70 and then rose to about 200 companies during 2009.

While the placement/SPP combination may be appealing as a way of accommodating small shareholders, it has been criticised as being far less equitable to small shareholders than a rights issue. The critics make two main points. First, the limit of $15 000 per shareholder for share purchase plans means that the bulk of new shares is issued to institutions. Second, if the SPP price is set at a large discount to the market price, demand will be high and retail investors can end up with much less than their $15 000 'entitlement'. This problem arose with the issues by Origin Energy, which started with a $400 million placement to institutions in November 2006. The issue price was $7.10 per share, which represented a discount of about 2.5 per cent to the market price at the time. At the same time, Origin announced that it would raise additional funds on similar terms through an SPP early in 2007. The details announced in January 2007 included a target of $75 million for the SPP. By the closing date for applications, the market price of Origin shares had increased to about $9. Not surprisingly, many shareholders applied to purchase shares, with the result that allocations were scaled back to a maximum of 200 shares per shareholder.

Another type of combination involves three offers of shares: a placement, an institutional entitlement offer and a retail entitlement offer. For example, Alesco Corporation used this approach to raise a total of $193 million in July and August 2007. The closing price of Alesco shares on 23 July was $13.96, after which the company announced the acquisition of another business and details of an associated capital raising, including an institutional placement with the issue price to be determined by a book-build with an indicative price range of $12.10 to $12.80 per share. The capital raising also included an institutional entitlement offer and a non-renounceable underwritten 1-for-9 rights issue (retail entitlement offer). It was announced that the issue price for both of these offers would be set equal to the price set for the institutional placement. On 26 July, the company announced that the issue price had been set at the top of the book-build price range at $12.80 per share and that the institutional offers were 'strongly oversubscribed'. On 23 August, Alesco announced that its retail entitlement offer had raised approximately $61 million in addition to the amount of approximately $132 million raised from institutions in late July. The company stated that the retail offer had been 'strongly supported by existing shareholders with over 60 per cent of the rights being taken up by eligible shareholders'. The approach used by Alesco has been used by several other companies, including Asciano Group, which raised $2.35 billion in June 2009, and Graincorp, which raised about $600 million in October 2009.

While it is not very common, it is also possible to combine an issue to existing shareholders with a public offer of shares. This approach may be favoured if the company wishes to attract a wider spread of shareholders, or if the amount of funds sought is large relative to the size of the company. For example, in October 2007, Essential Petroleum Resources Ltd (EPR) (see Finance in Action), a small explorer with a market capitalisation of less than $20 million, made a 1-for-2 non-renounceable rights issue and a public offer to raise a total of $10 million.[31]

FINANCE IN ACTION

ESSENTIAL PETROLEUM MAKES RIGHTS ISSUE AND PUBLIC OFFER

Essential Petroleum hasn't exactly set the world on fire since its February 2001 listing. Friday's closing price of 5.5 cents a share tells as much. But patience with the Otway Basin oil and gas explorer, like that shown by the group's biggest shareholder, former JB Were resources guru Peter Woodford, might just deliver some big rewards in 2008. Managing director John Remfry has worked the group into a position where it will be a stock to watch next year as it sets about drilling near-term development opportunities in the onshore Otway while also chasing up the big-time potential of its offshore permits, flanking what Essential reckons could be the next major hydrocarbon province—the Discovery Bay 'High' offshore from Portland in western Victoria.

Another geological feature, the Pecten 'High' offshore from Port Campbell has already been proven as a hydrocarbon fairway. Essential reckons that back at the bigger Discovery Bay High, the potential in its permits is for more than 5 trillion cubic feet of recoverable gas and more than 2 billion barrels of recoverable oil. That's big talk from a company of Essential's size, but we'll soon know if it's hot air or not.

That's because Essential is pulling in $10 million from a $6 million rights issue (underwritten by Bell Potter and Comsec) and $4 million from a public offer at 4 cents a share. At the issue price, the group's market capitalisation will be all of $22 million.

Source: 'After a few quiet years, Essential may prove it has all the ingredients in 2008', Barry Fitzgerald, *The Age*, 29 October 2007.

---

31 In the year to 30 June 2008, EPR recorded a net loss of $10.9 million and in the following year a further loss of almost $24.8 million. In February 2010, its shareholders approved a capital restructure whereby debt obligations of $23 million were converted into equity or forgiven. Following the restructure, 51.9 per cent of the company's voting shares were held by Beach Energy Ltd, a new board was appointed and the company's name changed to Somerton Energy Ltd.

9.7 EMPLOYEE SHARE PLANS

LEARNING OBJECTIVE 9
Outline the different types of employee share plans

Table 9.1 shows that listed companies have raised significant funds through employee share plans, although the primary purpose of such plans is to motivate senior managers and other employees by giving them an ownership interest in their employer. There are several types of employee share plans that have been used in Australia, including:[32]

- *Fully paid share plans.* Employees are able to purchase new or existing shares, usually at a discount from market value. The purchases are usually funded by loans from the company that are interest-free or at a low interest rate and dividends on the shares may be used to repay the loans. Sometimes there is a provision to write off the loans if the company fails.
- *Partly paid share plans.* The shares issued to employees are initially partly paid and converted to fully paid shares by a series of calls. In this case employees can be liable for calls if the company fails before the shares are fully paid.
- *Option plans.* Under these plans employees initially purchase (or are granted) an option to buy shares at some future time at a specified price. Option plans involve a small initial outlay with potential for large capital gains if the company is successful.
- *Employee share trusts.* Employees have an interest in a trust that holds shares in the employer company. The trust is normally funded by the employer. Employees who hold units in the trust can dispose of the units only to other members of the trust.
- *Replicator plans.* Replicator plans do not involve shares in the employer company. Instead, payments are made to employees based on the achievement of certain performance criteria. For example, such a plan may involve 'phantom shares' with a price that is linked to the profitability of the company or to the performance of a division.

The popularity of the various plans varies among different types of employers. For example, in Australia the majority of employee share plans are option plans and this type of plan is particularly popular as a way of rewarding the senior executives of large listed companies. Recent changes in the taxation treatment of employee share plans may encourage more widespread use of plans of other types for general staff. The use of a trust structure can be attractive for private companies where there are restrictions on ownership of shares in the company itself. Replicator plans are popular with unlisted companies, where it is difficult to establish a market price for the shares, and can also be useful for relatively new businesses, where issuing shares would dilute the ownership and control of the founders.

In recent years, the Commonwealth Government has sought to encourage employee share ownership by providing tax concessions in cases where shares or rights to shares are given to employees or issued to them at a discount. The tax status of employee share plans has been subject to frequent change and some degree of uncertainty.

The provisions that apply to employee shares or rights to shares acquired after 28 March 1995 mean that, in general, any benefit to an employee under an employee share plan is taxable in the year in which the share or right is acquired.[33] Consequently, the difference between the market value of a share and the consideration paid to acquire it is assessable in the year of acquisition. However, where the share is a 'qualifying share' certain tax concessions are available. These concessions allow the employee to:

(a) defer inclusion of the discount in assessable income for up to 10 years provided there are restrictions on disposal of the shares; or

---
32 Characteristics of the various types of employee share plans are discussed in detail by Stradwick (1996).
33 These provisions, which are complex, are contained in Division 13A of the *Income Tax Assessment Act*.

(b) elect to have the discount included in assessable income immediately with an exemption for the first $1000 of the discount—that is, employees who acquire qualifying shares under an employee share plan can receive a benefit of up to $1000 per year with no immediate tax liability provided six conditions are met. These conditions include the following:
   (i) the shares or rights are ordinary shares in the employer company or employer holding company
   (ii) the shares are issued on a non-discriminatory basis such that at least two-thirds of the company's permanent employees are entitled to participate in the plan
   (iii) the employee does not hold more than 5 per cent of the shares in the company.

An employer who provides employee shares at a discount can be entitled to a deduction of up to $1000 per employee per year, which means that the tax effect is the same as it would have been if each employee had been paid additional wages. Fringe benefits tax does not apply to employee share plans, but shares acquired under an employee share plan are subject to capital gains tax and payroll tax can be applicable in some states.

Under the ASX Listing Rules a company must have a proposed employee share plan approved by shareholders and, in some cases, employees may have to be provided with a prospectus. Given the complexity of the taxation provisions and other regulatory requirements, the financial manager of a company that introduces an employee share plan is likely to need specialised advice.

9.8 INTERNAL FUNDS

LEARNING OBJECTIVE 10
Outline the advantages of internal funds as a source of finance

So far we have discussed external sources of equity finance. However, a company that is operating profitably will also generate funds internally. The relative importance of internal and external sources of funds may be assessed using different measures of 'internal funds'. One approach is to define internal equity finance as retained profits plus depreciation charges, where retained profit is equal to accounting profit after company tax, less dividends paid to shareholders. A problem with this approach is that a company cannot spend its accounting profit—suppliers and employees must be paid with cash. In other words, the primary source of internal funding is cash profit, which can differ significantly from accounting profit prepared on an accrual basis. Cash profit is reported by companies in their cash flow statements. The cash flow statement is a funds statement that shows the sources and uses of funds, where funds are defined as cash. A recent Reserve Bank of Australia (RBA) analysis of corporate sources and uses of funds relied on data from these statements. The approach adopted by the RBA divides sources of funds into two basic categories: internal funding and external funding. Internal funding is equal to cash profit—that is, cash received from customers and non-interest-bearing investments (e.g. dividends) less payments to suppliers, wages and salaries paid to employees and tax payments. Thus, cash profit is measured before payment of interest expense and any other financing charges and is not affected by depreciation. External funding comprises two sources: net debt and net equity, where net debt is equal to funds borrowed from intermediated (e.g. bank loans) and non-intermediated (e.g. issuing corporate bonds) sources. Finally, net equity is equal to funds raised by issuing new shares, less cash paid out to repurchase shares. Funds may be used in three ways: investment in assets, payment of dividends and payment of interest.

The use of internal funds as a source of finance has important advantages. Using internal funds does not affect the control of the company as it does not involve the company in issuing any additional shares. Therefore, using internal funds does not commit the company to increased dividend payments in the future, with the result that no additional strain is placed on the company's cash resources. A further advantage is that, unlike a new issue of shares, internal funding involves no issue costs such as brokerage, fees paid to underwriters and other advisers or costs incurred in preparing a prospectus.

Internal funds are a convenient source of finance that does not involve any explicit costs such as transaction costs, but they are not a free source of finance for a company. Internal funds generated by a company are invested by the company on its shareholders' behalf. It follows that internal funds have an opportunity cost—that is, the funds could have been invested elsewhere by shareholders. Therefore, when a company uses internal funds, shareholders will not benefit unless the company is able to invest the funds profitably. This is discussed in more detail in Chapter 14.

The relative importance of internal funds in providing a company's total financial requirements is related to the nature of a company's business and can also vary considerably over time. Over the period from 2000 to mid-2007, around two-thirds of the funding for listed non-financial Australian companies came from internal sources. Dividing the sample of companies into three groups—resource companies, real estate and infrastructure companies, and all other companies—revealed significant differences between the groups. Resource companies relied heavily on internal funds, which provided around 90 per cent of their funding compared with around 40 per cent for real estate and infrastructure companies and around 70 per cent for all other companies. From mid-2007 to mid-2009, almost all Australian companies relied more heavily on internal funding because companies' ability to raise external funds was affected by the global financial crisis (Reserve Bank of Australia, October 2009, p. 4).

9.8.1 DIVIDEND REINVESTMENT PLANS

A dividend reinvestment plan (DRP) allows shareholders the choice of using their dividends to purchase additional shares instead of receiving cash.[34] The first DRPs were introduced by Australian companies in the early 1980s. Within 10 years, most of Australia's largest companies were offering such plans and reinvestment of dividends has become a significant source of equity for listed companies, particularly larger companies. The main reason for the popularity of DRPs is related to the introduction of the dividend imputation tax system, which caused investors to demand high dividend payouts. A dividend reinvestment plan allows a company to meet the demand for a high dividend payout without straining its cash resources. Technically, investors who participate in a DRP receive the dividends and therefore obtain the tax benefits of imputation, and then reinvest the cash in additional shares. This means that dividends can be paid to investors without any cash payment by the company. Provided the shares issued under a DRP are fully paid, there is no need for a prospectus and shares issued under a DRP are exempt from the '15 per cent in 12 months' capital raising limit contained in the Listing Rules. DRPs are inflexible in that the timing of any capital raising is tied to the timing of dividend payments and may not provide a reliable source of funds because participation by shareholders is voluntary. The latter problem can be overcome, at a cost, by having a company's DRP underwritten.

The main advantage of DRPs centres on transaction costs: for many companies the costs of operating a DRP are lower than the costs involved in making rights issues and share placements to replace cash paid out as dividends. During 2007, 271 listed companies used DRPs to raise $11.9 billion. In the following year, 269 companies raised $15.6 billion and during 2009, 230 companies used DRPs to raise around $11.4 billion (Australian Securities Exchange, 2010, p. 32).

---

34 ASX statistics include dividend reinvestment as part of equity raised externally. However, we discuss DRPs in the context of internal funds because dividend reinvestment largely involves funds that companies would have retained, but for the higher dividend payouts needed to transfer tax credits to shareholders. In other words, equity 'raised' through dividend reinvestment is, in effect, internal funds that have been 'relabelled'. Dividend reinvestment plans are discussed in more detail in Chapter 11.

MANAGING A COMPANY'S EQUITY STRUCTURE

9.9

LEARNING OBJECTIVE 11
Outline the effects of bonus issues, share splits and share consolidations

In this chapter we have discussed the various sources of equity individually. In practice, the financial manager will usually have a long-term plan for management of a company's capital structure, including its equity structure. The most important aspect of such a plan involves the timing and amounts of future capital raisings based on forecasts of the company's cash flows, capital expenditures and loan repayments. As part of this process, companies' equity structures are sometimes rearranged through procedures that change the number of shares on issue without either raising capital or returning capital to shareholders. These procedures—which include bonus issues, share splits and consolidations—are now considered.

9.9.1 BONUS ISSUES AND SHARE SPLITS

A bonus issue is a 'free' issue of shares made to existing shareholders in proportion to their current investment. Bonus issues used to be common in Australia and were used as a way of increasing the dividends paid to shareholders. A bonus issue is equivalent to a rights issue with a zero subscription price. A company could make a bonus issue by using the balances of reserves, such as a share premium reserve, and/or retained earnings—that is, part of a reserve is converted to issued capital but the total of shareholders' funds remains unchanged.

Regulatory changes, including the introduction of the dividend imputation tax system and the abolition of par value for shares, removed any tax advantage associated with bonus issues. Accordingly, companies that have the capacity to pay higher dividends usually increase the rate of dividend per existing share rather than making a bonus issue and maintaining the same dividend rate.

While bonus issues have virtually disappeared from the Australian market, companies can achieve a similar result by splitting their shares. For example, a share split that doubles the number of a company's issued shares has the same effect for shareholders as a 1-for-1 bonus issue. Australian companies that have made share splits since 2002 include Toll Holdings, WHK Group, CSL Limited, Incitec Pivot and Fortescue Metals Group.

A bonus issue or share split involves no cash flow—apart from the administration costs involved— and should not have any effect on shareholders' wealth. Therefore, if a company makes, say, a 1-for-1 bonus issue, the number of shares on issue will double and the market price of each share should decrease by half, leaving unchanged the total market value of the shares held by each investor. The Australian evidence is consistent with this expectation—that is, bonus issues do not affect shareholders' wealth.[35]

Bonus issues and share splits are typically made by companies that have been performing well and that have recently experienced significant increases in share price. Also there may be an increase in the share price following the announcement by a company of a forthcoming bonus or split. This increase can occur because such an announcement may have information content. Investors are aware that, following a bonus or split, companies usually do not reduce dividends per share to the extent necessary to maintain the same total dividend payout. For example, after a 1-for-1 bonus issue, a company currently paying a dividend of 10 cents per share would need to pay a dividend of only 5 cents per share to maintain its dividend payout. However, companies will often not reduce their dividend per share to that extent. For example, the company may end up paying a dividend of, say, 7.5 cents per share after the bonus issue has been made. If the behaviour of most companies after a bonus issue follows this pattern, the market will be confident that a company making a bonus issue will probably increase its total dividend payout (Ball, Brown & Finn 1977). This, in turn, indicates the confidence of management in the company's future. Consequently, the share price may increase in response to this new information.

The dividend-based explanation for the market reaction to bonus and split announcements, which was first proposed by Fama et al. (1969), does not appear to explain fully the market reaction to such

---

[35] See Sloan (1987). This evidence contrasts with the US evidence, which has found positive abnormal returns on the ex-day for US stock dividends and share splits; see Lakonishok and Vermaelen (1986) and Grinblatt, Masulis and Titman (1984).

announcements. Asquith, Healy and Palepu (1989) studied share splits by companies that did not pay cash dividends. They found that these companies had large earnings increases before the split, but no unusual changes in earnings or initiation of dividends after the split. An important conclusion of their study was that the announcement of a split leads investors to expect that the past earnings increases are permanent.

A share split may be made by a company with a 'thin' market for its shares. Management may believe that reducing the market price per share will increase the demand for the company's shares. In September 2008, fertiliser and explosives manufacturer Incitec Pivot, which had a share price around $140, made a 20-for-1 share split. The stated purpose was to benefit shareholders by making the company's shares more affordable to retail investors. While there is evidence that both announcement and execution of share splits are associated with significant positive returns, empirical evidence that splits lead to improved liquidity and marketability is mixed. There is evidence that both the number of shareholders and the number of transactions increase after splits, but little evidence that trading volume increases. On the other hand, there is evidence that splits increase bid–ask spreads and return volatility, both of which suggest a decrease in liquidity.[36]

9.9.2 SHARE CONSOLIDATIONS

A share consolidation, or reverse split, decreases the number of shares on issue and increases the price per share. For example, if a company with 100 million issued shares makes a 1-for-10 consolidation, it will end up with 10 million issued shares. After the consolidation, the market price per share should increase by a factor of 10. Reverse splits are unusual in Australia but have become more common following the global financial crisis. For example, in September 2010, gold miner St Barbara Ltd announced that it planned a share consolidation of six existing shares for one new share. Directors noted that the company's share price of around 40 cents meant that some international institutions that were potential investors in the company were precluded from investing in companies with share prices less than US$1. Similar reasons usually given for reverse splits include raising the share price into a popular trading range, overcoming perceptions that a company is not respectable because of its low share price, and reducing shareholder servicing costs. Other companies that consolidated their securities during 2010 include Australand, Boart Longyear and GPT Group.

If these suggested reasons are correct and reverse splits provide benefits for shareholders, the market response to these events should be positive. This does not appear to be the case: several US studies report that reverse splits are associated with negative share returns. For example, Desai and Jain (1997) report an average abnormal return of –4.59 per cent in the month that reverse splits are announced. They also found that negative returns in the announcement period were followed by a drift that averaged 10.76 per cent in 1 year and 33.90 per cent in 3 years. One interpretation is that reverse splits convey a signal that management lacks confidence that there will be future share price increases resulting from improvements in earnings. There is evidence that reverse splits are followed by higher trading volume and a decrease in bid–ask spread. This finding suggests that reverse splits enhance the liquidity of a stock, which should be beneficial for investors. Taken together, the evidence suggests that 'reverse splits may be better characterised as a device that management, given its assessment of future earnings, can use to improve the liquidity of the stock' (Han 1995, p. 169).

Connect Plus features a case study illustrating topics covered in this chapter.
Ask your lecturer or tutor for your course's unique URL.

---

36 Studies that report evidence on the effects of share splits on liquidity include Ikenberry, Rankine and Stice (1996) and Muscarella and Vetsuypens (1996).

SUMMARY

→ In this chapter we considered the ways in which a company may raise equity by issuing ordinary shares. Every company must issue ordinary shares.

- Those who invest in new ventures where an entrepreneur needs finance for the development of an invention or idea include wealthy individuals and private equity funds.
- Where capital is raised by issuing securities, potential investors must generally be supplied with a disclosure document. This document, usually a prospectus, sets out information to enable investors to assess the risks involved and the value of the securities.
- Ordinary shareholders face higher risk than other investors, but are protected to some extent by limited liability. As part-owners of the company, ordinary shareholders exert a degree of control by virtue of their right to elect members of the Board of Directors. Shareholders in a listed public company may sell their shares on a stock exchange.

→ Equity has important advantages as a source of finance. Companies are not required to pay dividends or to redeem ordinary shares. Raising new equity capital lowers financial risk and lowers the interest rate that the company will have to pay when it borrows.

→ Making an initial public offering (IPO) of ordinary shares is referred to as floating a company and is usually accompanied by the listing of the shares on a stock exchange. Determining the issue price for an IPO can be difficult and in large floats it has become common to use competitive bidding by institutions to set the price. Details of the issue and the issuing company must be provided in a prospectus. Floating a company involves significant costs. Often, the largest cost is associated with the underpricing of the shares—the issue price for an IPO is usually less than the market price when trading commences.

→ After a company has been floated, additional equity can be raised in several ways, including rights issues, placements and share purchase plans.

- A rights issue (entitlement offer) is an offer to existing shareholders of new shares in a fixed ratio to the number of shares already held. A traditional rights issue is slow and involves higher costs than a placement but can be used to raise large amounts of funds. Rights issues may be renounceable or non-renounceable and can now be made without a prospectus. The funds can be received sooner than usual by adopting one of the accelerated offer structures.
- A placement is an issue of shares to brokers' clients and/or institutional investors such as life insurance companies and superannuation funds. Issue costs are lower for placements than for rights issues, but for a listed company a limit of 15 per cent is placed on the amount of capital that it can raise by placements in any year without the prior approval of shareholders. Where the amount of funds sought exceeds the 15 per cent ceiling, companies often make a placement with shareholder approval. Alternatively, a placement can be combined with a share purchase plan and/or a rights issue.
- Equity can also be raised by issuing contributing shares, options on shares and shares to employees. Employee share plans can qualify for tax concessions.

→ A major source of equity finance is internal in the sense that it results from the positive net cash flows that a successful company generates. In conjunction with higher dividend payments under the imputation tax system, many Australian companies have introduced dividend reinvestment plans that allow investors to use their cash dividends to purchase additional shares. This allows dividends to be paid and franking credits to be distributed to investors while retaining cash within the company.

KEY TERMS

- call 238
- contributing shares 269
- cum rights 259
- disclosure document 245
- ex-rights date 259
- information asymmetry 241
- initial public offering 242
- instalment receipt 269
- limited liability 239
- option 262
- ordinary shares 238
- placement 267
- prospectus 245
- residual claim 238
- seasoned equity offering 256
- shortfall facility 264
- shortfall shares 264
- stapled securities 237
- subscription price 259
- theoretical ex-rights share price 260
- theoretical rights price 260
- winner's curse 254

REFERENCES

Abernethy, M. & Heidtman, D., *Business Angels*, Allen & Unwin, St Leonards, 1999.

Asquith, P., Healy, P. & Palepu, K., 'Earnings and stock splits', *The Accounting Review*, July 1989, pp. 387–403.

Australian Bureau of Statistics, *Venture Capital and Later Stage Private Equity, Australia, 2008–09*, cat. no. 5678.0, ABS, Canberra, 2010.

Australian Securities Exchange, *Capital Raising in Australia: Experiences and Lessons from the Global Financial Crisis*, ASX Information Paper, 29 January 2010.

Balachandran, B., Faff, R. & Theobald, M., 'Rights offerings, takeup, renounceability, and underwriting status', *Journal of Financial Economics*, August 2008, pp. 328–46.

Ball R., Brown, P. & Finn, F.J., 'Share capitalisation changes, information and the Australian equity market', *Australian Journal of Management*, October 1977, pp. 105–25.

Brau, J. & Fawcett, S., 'Initial public offerings: an analysis of theory and practice', *Journal of Finance*, February 2006, pp. 399–436.

Brav, A. & Gompers, P., 'Myth or reality? The long-run underperformance of initial public offerings: evidence from venture and non-venture capital-backed companies', *Journal of Finance*, December 1997, pp. 1791–821.

Brown, R. & Hathaway, N., 'Valuing contributing shares', *Accounting and Finance*, November 1991, pp. 53–67.

Camp, G., Comer, A. & How, J., 'Incentives to underprice', *Accounting and Finance*, December 2006, pp. 537–51.

Chan, H.W. & Brown, R.L., 'Rights issues versus placements in Australia: regulation or choice?', *Company and Securities Law Journal*, 2004, pp. 299–310.

Cliff, M. & Denis, D., 'Do initial public offering firms purchase analyst coverage with underpricing?', *Journal of Finance*, December 2004, pp. 2871–901.

Connolly, E. & Tan, A., 'The private equity market in Australia', *Bulletin*, Reserve Bank of Australia, June 2002, pp. 1–5.

Da Silva Rosa, R., Velayuthen, G. & Walter, T., 'The sharemarket performance of Australian venture capital-backed and non-venture capital-backed IPOs', *Pacific-Basin Finance Journal*, April 2003, pp. 197–218.

Desai, H. & Jain, P., 'Long-run common stock returns following stock splits and reverse splits', *Journal of Business*, July 1997, pp. 409–33.

Dimovski, W. & Brooks, R., 'Financial characteristics of Australian initial public offerings from 1994 to 1999', *Applied Economics*, 2003, vol. 35, no.14, pp. 1599–607.

Eckbo, B., Masulis, R. & Norli, O., 'Seasoned public offerings: resolution of the "new issues puzzle"', *Journal of Financial Economics*, April 2000, pp. 251–91.

Fama, E., Fisher, L., Jensen M. & Roll, R., 'The adjustment of stock prices to new information', *International Economic Review*, February 1969, pp. 1–21.

Gompers, P. & Lerner, J., 'The really long-run performance of initial public offerings: the pre-Nasdaq evidence', *Journal of Finance*, August 2003, pp. 1355–92.

Gong, N. & Shekhar, C., 'Underpricing of privatised IPOs: the Australian experience', *Australian Journal of Management*, December 2001, pp. 91–106.

Grinblatt, M., Masulis, R. & Titman, S., 'The valuation effects of stock splits and stock dividends', *Journal of Financial Economics*, December 1984, pp. 461–90.

Han, K.C., 'The effects of reverse splits on the liquidity of the stock', *Journal of Financial and Quantitative Analysis*, March 1995, pp. 159–69.

Herbert, A., *Australian Private Equity & Venture Capital Guide 2010*, 17th edn, Private Equity Media, Brighton, 2010.

How, J., Izan, H. & Monroe, G., 'Differential information and the underpricing of initial public offerings: Australian evidence', *Accounting and Finance*, May 1995, pp. 87–105.

How, J., & Yeo, J., 'The pricing of underwriting services in the Australian capital market', *Pacific-Basin Finance Journal*, July 2000, pp. 347–73.

Ibbotson, R., Sindelar, J. & Ritter, J., 'The market's problems with the pricing of initial public offerings', *Journal of Applied Corporate Finance*, Spring 1994, pp. 66–74.

Ikenberry, D., Rankine, G. & Stice, E., 'What do stock splits really signal?', *Journal of Financial and Quantitative Analysis*, September 1996, pp. 357–75.

ISS Governance Services, *Equity Capital Raising in Australia during 2008 and 2009*, ISS Governance Services, August 2010.

Lakonishok, J. & Vermaelen, T., 'Tax induced trading around ex-dividend days', *Journal of Financial Economics*, 1986, pp. 287–319.

Lee, P., Taylor, S. & Walter, T., 'Australian IPO pricing in the short and long run', *Journal of Banking and Finance*, August 1996, pp. 1189–210.

Lee, P., Taylor, S. & Walter, T., 'IPO underpricing explanations: implications from investor application and allocation schedules', *Journal of Financial and Quantitative Analysis*, December 1999, pp. 425–44.

Lipton, P., Herzberg, A. & Welsh, M., *Understanding Company Law*, 15th edn, Lawbook Co., Sydney, 2010.

Loughran, T. & Ritter, J., 'The new issues puzzle', *Journal of Finance*, March 1995, pp. 23–51.

Loughran, T. & Ritter, J., 'Why don't issuers get upset about leaving money on the table in IPOs?', *Review of Financial Studies*, 2002, vol. 15, no. 2, pp. 413–43.

Loughran, T. & Ritter, J., 'Why has IPO underpricing changed over time?', *Financial Management*, Autumn 2004, pp. 5–37.

Marsh, P., 'Equity rights issues and efficiency of the UK stock market', *Journal of Finance*, September 1979, pp. 839–62.

Muscarella, C. & Vetsuypens, M., 'Stock splits: signaling or liquidity? The case of ADR "solo-splits"', *Journal of Financial Economics*, September 1996, pp. 3–26.

Pham, P., Kalev, P. & Steen, A., 'Underpricing, stock allocation, ownership structure and post-listing liquidity of newly listed firms', *Journal of Banking and Finance*, May 2003, pp. 919–47.

Reserve Bank of Australia, 'Australian corporates' sources and uses of funds', *Bulletin*, October 2009, pp. 1–12.

Ritter, J., 'The long-run performance of initial public offerings', *Journal of Finance*, March 1991, pp. 3–27.

Ritter J. & Welch, I., 'A review of IPO activity, pricing and allocations', *Journal of Finance*, August 2002, pp. 1795–828.

Rock, K., 'Why new issues are underpriced', *Journal of Financial Economics*, January–February 1986, pp. 187–212.

Sloan, R.G., 'Bonus issues, share splits and ex-day share price behaviour: Australian evidence', *Australian Journal of Management*, December 1987, pp. 277–91.

Smith, C.W. Jr, 'Raising capital: theory and evidence', *Midland Corporate Finance Journal*, Spring 1986, pp. 6–22.

Smith, R.L. & Smith, J.K., *Entrepreneurial Finance*, Wiley, New York, 2000.

Stradwick, R., *Employee Share Plans*, Pitman Publishing, Melbourne, 2nd edn, 1996.

Viney, C., *McGrath's Financial Institutions, Instruments and Markets*, 6th edn, McGraw-Hill, Sydney, 2009, Chapter 5.

Welch, I., 'Seasoned offerings, imitation costs and the underpricing of initial public offerings', *Journal of Finance*, June 1989, pp. 421–49.

QUESTIONS

1. **[LO 1]** *The interest held by ordinary shareholders is a residual claim.* Explain the meaning and significance of this statement.

2. **[LO 1]** What are the most important rights of shareholders in a company?

3. **[LO 1]** What are the main similarities between contributing shares and instalment receipts? How do they differ?

4. **[LO 2]** What are the main advantages of raising equity rather than borrowing?

5. **[LO 2]** Distinguish between limited liability and no liability companies. Why are no liability companies confined to exploration and mining companies?

6. **[LO 3]** Define private equity. What are the main features that distinguish private equity from other forms of equity finance?

7. **[LO 3]** Private equity funding for new ventures is typically provided in stages. What are the main reasons for this approach?

8. **[LO 5]** Listed public companies have the advantage of greater access to the capital market than private or unlisted companies. However, this advantage also involves significant costs. What are the main costs?

9. **[LO 5]** *A company is floated by making a public issue of ordinary shares.* Outline the procedures involved in floating a company.

10. **[LO 5]** *A company usually seeks the assistance of a financial institution before undertaking any large capital raising.* Explain why this is so. Describe fully the relevant services that a financial institution provides.

11. **[LO 5]** Outline the main advantages of using book-building for an initial public offering of shares rather than making a fixed-price offer. What are the disadvantages of book-building?

12. **[LO 5]** What are the advantages and disadvantages of having a share issue underwritten?

13. **[LO 5]** Why are underwriting fees higher for company floats than for rights issues?

14. **[LO 6]** Initial public offerings of shares are typically underpriced but vendors are rarely upset about leaving large amounts of money on the table. How is 'money left on the table' usually measured? How can the puzzling attitude of vendors be explained?

15. **[LO 6]** In discussing their research on IPOs, Camp et al. (2006) conclude that 'the choices issuers make at the offering reflect the trade-off between the costs and benefits of the IPO'. For issuers, the main cost of an IPO is represented by underpricing. What are the main benefits?

16. **[LO 8]** Although most companies permit rights to be traded on the stock exchange, a number of companies have made non-renounceable rights issues. Why would companies wish to make their rights issues non-renounceable?

17. **[LO 7]** Outline the phenomenon referred to as 'the new issues puzzle'. Why is the evidence for its existence controversial?

18. **[LO 8]** There has been resistance to companies raising funds by a private placement of shares. Describe the advantages and disadvantages to existing shareholders of a private placement.

19. **[LO 8]** MWB Ltd is a profitable company whose ordinary shares are listed on the ASX. The company has paid regular dividends to shareholders and has generally financed its growth by retaining about 50 per cent of profits. Its current 5-year plan includes investment in fixed assets on a scale that will require the raising of external equity finance during the planning period. Advise the directors on the main factors that they should consider in deciding how to raise equity. The directors are considering:
    (a) a rights issue
    (b) a series of share placements
    (c) establishing a dividend reinvestment plan.

20. **[LO 8]** *Combining a share purchase plan with a placement to institutions should satisfy shareholders who argue that as far as possible, companies should raise equity through rights issues.* Do you agree with this statement? Explain your answer.

21. **[LO 8]** *Now that rights issues can be made without a prospectus, they will become much more popular and placements may become rare.* Do you agree with this statement? Explain your answer.

22. **[LO 8]** Outline the main features of an accelerated renounceable entitlement offer. What are the main differences between such an offer and a traditional renounceable rights issue?

23. **[LO 8]** A listed company may make a public offer of shares, possibly in conjunction with a rights issue. Identify factors that may favour the use of a further public offer of shares rather than a placement or a rights issue alone.

24. **[LO 8]** *Options are often used as an incentive to various groups or individuals.* Describe how options can be used to the advantage of a company and its shareholders.

25. **[LO 10]** What are internal funds? What are their advantages as a source of equity?

26. **[LO 10]** Outline the impact of the global financial crisis on Australian companies in terms of their mix of internal versus external funding over the 2-year period from mid-2007.

27. **[LO 11]** What is a share split? Why might the directors of a company wish to split its shares?

28. **[LO 11]** What is a share consolidation? Evaluate the reasons that may be given to justify a share consolidation.

29. **[LO 11]** Explain briefly why the share price of a company may increase when the company announces a bonus issue or share split.

PROBLEMS

1. **Rights issue [LO 8]**
   Company A has 4 million shares on issue and wishes to raise $4 million by a 1-for-4 rights issue.
   (a) What is the theoretical value of 1 right if the market price of 1 share (cum rights) is $5?
   (b) What is the theoretical share price (ex-rights)?
   (c) Does an investor gain through a rights issue?

2. **Economic factors and financing policy [LO 2]**
   Choose a company and trace the major changes in its capital structure during the past 10 years. Outline the economic factors that you consider have contributed to the major changes in its financing policy during this period.

3. **Public share issue [LO 5]**
   Katz Pty Ltd is a well-established company whose directors have decided to convert to public company status, make a public share issue and list on the stock exchange. The company needs to raise $7 920 000 to expand its operations. Its prospectus forecasts a dividend of 20 cents per share in its first year as a public company and dividends are expected to grow at 6 per cent per annum indefinitely. Shareholders require a return of 14 per cent per annum and the cost of listing amounts to 12 per cent of the gross proceeds from the issue. How many shares must Katz issue?

4. **Rights issue [LO 8]**
   Crosling Ltd shares are trading at $12 each. Its directors have announced a 1-for-6 rights issue with a subscription price of $10.60 per share. What is:
   (a) the theoretical value of a right to one new share?
   (b) the theoretical ex-rights share price?

5. **Rights issue [LO 8]**
   Maxwell Ltd is a listed biotechnology company. On 5 May 2011 it announced a 1-for-3 renounceable rights issue at a subscription price of $6.20 per share with an ex-rights date of 25 May. The company also announced that funds raised by the issue would be used to establish production facilities for its new anti-malaria drug that recently passed its final clinical trials. The share price rose from $6.90 to $7.05 after those announcements. The closing price of Maxwell shares on 24 May was $7 per share.
   (a) What is a renounceable rights issue?
   (b) What is the most likely explanation for the share price rise on 5 May after the company's announcements?
   (c) What do you expect the price of the shares to be on 25 May? Show all calculations.
   (d) What is the theoretical value of a right? Show all calculations.
   (e) Explain why the share price change from 24 May to 25 May does not reflect any change in shareholders' wealth.

6. **Alternative ways of raising equity [LO 8]**
   George Banks International (GBI) Ltd has 100 million fully paid ordinary shares on issue and its shares are listed on the ASX. About 60 per cent of the shares are held by Australian financial institutions and the closing price of the shares on 15 October 2012 was $4. The company has a fully drawn $500 million bank loan facility, which is due to be rolled over or repaid on 30 November 2012. GBI Ltd is close to breaching an important covenant and its directors have resolved to raise equity to repay the loan on or before the due date. The company's last share issue occurred in 2009.
   (a) Assuming an issue price of $3.80 per share, what is the maximum amount that GBI Ltd can raise by making a share placement without shareholder approval?
   (b) Advise the directors on the feasibility of raising the required funds by a traditional renounceable or non-renounceable rights issue.
   (c) After receiving your advice, the directors are considering the combination of an institutional placement followed immediately by an accelerated entitlement offer.
      (i) Does the maximum amount that can be raised by the placement remain the same as in (a)? Why/why not?

(ii) Review your answer to (b). How will your advice change, given that an accelerated offer structure is to be used?

(d) Assume that the company proceeds with an accelerated entitlement offer. From the viewpoint of GBI's shareholders, what is the main effect of making the offer renounceable rather than non-renounceable? Will a renounceable offer necessarily ensure that all shareholders are treated equally? Why/why not?

Test yourself further with Connect Plus online! Ask your lecturer or tutor for your course's unique URL.

CHAPTER 10
SOURCES OF FINANCE: DEBT

LEARNING OBJECTIVES

After studying this chapter you should be able to:

1. identify the main forms of borrowing by Australian companies
2. explain the general characteristics of debt
3. understand the main forms of short-term bank lending and recognise when each may be suitable to a borrower's needs
4. understand debtor finance, inventory loans and bridging finance and be able to distinguish between them
5. identify and explain the features of the main types of long-term loans
6. identify and explain the features of the main types of short-term debt securities
7. understand the process of using commercial paper and bills of exchange to raise funds
8. calculate prices and yields for commercial paper and bills of exchange
9. identify and explain the features of the main types of long-term debt securities
10. identify and explain the main features of project finance
11. understand the role of interest rate swaps in managing debt
12. identify and explain the features of securities that have the characteristics of both debt and equity.

CHAPTER CONTENTS

10.1 Introduction
10.2 General characteristics of debt
10.3 Short-term borrowing from banks and other financial institutions
10.4 Long-term borrowing from banks and other financial institutions
10.5 Debt securities
10.6 Project finance
10.7 Interest rate swaps
10.8 Hybrids of debt and equity finance

10.1 INTRODUCTION

The types of debt finance used by Australian businesses can be divided into two categories based on the source of the funds. First, there are loans from banks and other financial institutions. In this case, cash that has been deposited with a financial intermediary or invested with an institution such as an insurance company is lent to a business. Thus, the flow of funds from the ultimate investors to the borrower is indirect and the process is referred to as **intermediation**. Importantly, the financial intermediary acts as a principal and the terms on which funds are advanced to the borrower may be quite different from the terms on which funds are lent to the intermediary. For example, a bank may raise short-term deposits at an interest rate of 5 per cent and provide long-term loans on which it charges interest at a rate of 8 per cent.

Second, businesses can raise funds by issuing debt **securities** such as commercial paper, bills of exchange and corporate bonds. In this case, financial institutions are usually involved in the fund raising but they act as agents rather than as principals. For example, a bank or investment bank may underwrite an issue of debt securities and distribute the securities to investors. In this case the flow of funds from the investor to the borrower is essentially direct. This method of raising debt is sometimes referred to as 'borrowing in the capital market' or 'issuing securities in open financial markets'. When this method is used in a case in which bank debt would previously have been used, the process is referred to as **disintermediation**.

The distinction between indirect and direct debt finance is important. However, for ease of exposition we refer to these two types of debt finance as 'loans' and 'debt securities', respectively. The largest providers of loans are banks, so when discussing loans we focus on bank loans. Table 10.1 shows the relative importance of debt securities and bank loans as sources of debt finance for Australian businesses.

LEARNING OBJECTIVE 1
Identify the main forms of borrowing by Australian companies

intermediation
process in which a bank or other financial institution raises funds from investors and then lends those funds to borrowers

securities
in the context of financial markets, financial assets that can be traded

disintermediation
movement of funds from accounts with deposit-taking financial intermediaries and the reinvestment of those funds in securities

TABLE 10.1 Debt securities (outstanding) issued by non-financial corporations and bank lending to business as at June 2010 ($ billion)

DEBT SECURITIES	$ BILLION
Short-term securities issued in Australia	0.8
Long-term securities issued in Australia	40.6
Securities issued offshore	114.5
Total	155.9
BANK LENDING TO BUSINESS	
Variable interest rate loans	272.1
Fixed interest rate loans	115.5
Bills outstanding	271.3
Total	658.9

Source: Tables D4 and D7, Reserve Bank of Australia website, www.rba.gov.au.

It is also common to categorise debt as either short term or long term. Short-term debt is defined as debt due for repayment within a period of 12 months. The major short-term borrowing choices available to Australian businesses include borrowing from banks and other financial institutions, which are discussed in Section 10.3, and issuing short-term debt securities such as commercial paper and bills of exchange, which are discussed in Sections 10.5.2 and 10.5.3. Long-term debt—that is, debt with a term to maturity greater than 12 months—can be raised by borrowing from banks and other financial institutions as discussed in Section 10.4. Businesses that are incorporated can also borrow long term by issuing securities such as debentures, unsecured notes and corporate bonds, which are discussed in Sections 10.5.4 to 10.5.6.

The figures in Table 10.1 show that at June 2010 bank loans totalling almost $388 billion were the largest source of debt finance for Australian businesses followed by bills outstanding of $271.3 billion. When a bill is issued, finance is provided directly by the discounter to the drawer. While the finance is direct rather than intermediated, banks are still involved in the process because a bill requires an acceptor (effectively a guarantor) and the acceptor is usually a major bank. Part of the total of $271.3 billion would comprise bills that were also discounted (bought) by banks, so at June 2010 debt finance provided by or through banks to businesses was $658.9 billion or 81 per cent of the total debt shown in Table 10.1.

In the next section, we outline the main characteristics of debt, the main effects of using debt and discuss security arrangements for debt. Next, we discuss the main types of short- and long-term debt provided by banks and other financial institutions. This is followed by discussion of the major types of debt securities used by Australian businesses, and by discussion of project finance. Interest rate swaps are also discussed because many businesses take out variable-rate loans and then enter into swaps to fix the interest rate. The chapter concludes by considering preference shares and convertible securities that are hybrids of debt and equity securities.

10.2 GENERAL CHARACTERISTICS OF DEBT

LEARNING OBJECTIVE 2
Explain the general characteristics of debt

Debt involves a contract whereby the borrower promises to pay future cash flows to the lender. Short-term debt often involves only a single cash flow payable by the borrower at the end of the contract. In the case of long-term debt, the promised cash flows usually include payments at regular intervals but the parties can negotiate arrangements that involve any set of cash flows. A debt contract will either specify the size and timing of interest payments or it will specify a set of rules that will be used to calculate those payments. For example, the contract may specify that interest will be calculated daily but charged monthly at a rate equal to the 90-day bank-bill rate plus a margin of 3 per cent per annum. The contract will also specify how the **principal** is to be repaid.

In addition to specifications about cash flows, a debt contract will usually also specify:

- whether the borrower is required to pledge assets as security for the debt
- whether ownership of the debt is transferable
- any requirements or restrictions that must be met by the borrower
- the rights of the lender if the borrower **defaults**.

principal
the amount borrowed at the outset of a loan

default
failure to perform a contractual obligation

If the borrower is required to support its promise to repay the debt with a pledge of assets, the debt is classified as *secured* debt. If the debt is *unsecured*, the borrower has an obligation to repay the loan but this obligation is not supported by any pledge of assets. Security arrangements for debt are discussed in Section 10.2.4.

If ownership of the debt is transferable, the original lender can sell the contract to another investor. If the debt is transferable it usually takes the form of securities such as commercial paper, bonds or debentures that are issued directly to investors and can then be traded in a secondary market. The ownership of all securities is transferable and some securities are traded actively in markets that are very liquid, while the markets for other securities are much less liquid. Therefore, the term 'marketable securities' is typically used to refer to securities that are easily sold and readily converted into cash. *Non-marketable* debt takes the form of loans arranged privately between two parties, where the lender is usually a bank or other financial institution.

A debt contract usually places some requirements and/or restrictions known as **covenants** on the borrower. For example, if debt is secured by a charge over assets, the borrower will be required to maintain those assets in good condition. Whether debt is secured or unsecured, the borrower may be restricted from increasing its borrowing and other liabilities beyond a specified proportion of its total assets.

The rights of the lender if the borrower defaults will depend on the nature of the default and whether the debt is secured or unsecured. Any breach by the borrower of the terms of the contract may constitute default and act as a trigger for the lender to enforce its rights under the contract. For example, the lender may have the right to increase the interest rate on the debt to a penalty rate. If the breach is of a minor or technical nature the lender may waive its right to act but if the breach is more serious, such as the failure to make a promised payment, the lender will usually enforce its rights. For example, if a borrower defaults on secured debt, the lender has the right to take possession of the assets that were pledged as security and sell them to pay off the loan.

Most types of debt have some common characteristics that we now discuss.

covenant
provision in a loan agreement to protect lenders' interests by requiring certain actions to be taken and others refrained from

10.2.1 THE INTEREST COST OF DEBT

When a company borrows, it is committed to the payment of interest and to the repayment of the principal. In Chapter 4, the default-risk structure of interest rates was discussed. It was pointed out that, given the general structure of interest rates at a point in time, the interest rate a company has to pay to borrow funds for a specified period will depend on the risk characteristics of the company. For example, at a time when the Commonwealth Government has to pay an interest rate of 8 per cent per annum to borrow funds for 5 years, a secure industrial company may have to pay 9.5 per cent, while a less secure industrial company may have to pay 12 per cent.

The interest rate applicable to debt may be fixed or variable. The interest rates on short-term and variable-rate debt are closely related to the **interbank cash rate** (or simply the *cash rate*), which is an important benchmark rate in the economy. Each bank holds an Exchange Settlement Account with the Reserve Bank of Australia (RBA), which is used to make payments between the banks. If a bank has insufficient (excess) funds in its Exchange Settlement Account, it can borrow from (lend to) other banks at an interest rate that reflects current market forces. However, the RBA has a very significant impact on the interest rates observed in the interbank market. From time to time the RBA publicly announces the target cash rate and stands ready to lend to (borrow from) banks at interest rates that are 0.25 per cent above (below) the target rate. The actual cash rate is therefore almost certain to be within ±0.25 per cent of the target rate and, in practice, the actual cash rate is rarely very different from the target cash rate. For example, during the 4-year period from September 2006 to August 2010, there were only 12 days when the cash rate deviated from the target and most of the deviations were only 0.01 percentage points.[1] The data in Table 10.2 show the cash rate. For the purposes of comparison, Table 10.2 also includes indicator lending rates on variable-rate loans made by banks to small businesses.

interbank cash rate
the interest rate on overnight loans between a bank and another bank (including the Reserve Bank of Australia)

TABLE 10.2 Selected short-term interest rates (% p.a.), 2000–10

DATE	CASH RATE[a]	INDICATOR RATES: SMALL BUSINESS[b]	
		OVERDRAFT—RESIDENTIAL SECURED	OVERDRAFT—OTHER
June 2000	6.00	8.55	9.10
June 2001	5.00	7.65	8.20

continued →

[1] Analysis by the authors of data in Reserve Bank of Australia, www.rba.gov.au, Table F1.

TABLE 10.2 *continued*

DATE	CASH RATE[a]	INDICATOR RATES: SMALL BUSINESS[b]	
		OVERDRAFT—RESIDENTIAL SECURED	OVERDRAFT—OTHER
June 2002	4.72	7.55	8.20
June 2003	4.75	7.55	8.20
June 2004	5.25	8.05	8.70
June 2005	5.50	8.30	8.95
June 2006	5.75	8.55	9.20
June 2007	6.25	9.05	9.70
June 2008	7.25	10.80	11.45
June 2009	3.00	7.90	8.80
June 2010	4.50	9.45	10.30

[a] Average of daily figures for the interbank cash rate for the month.
[b] Average indicator rates for lending by major banks to small businesses on a variable-rate basis.

Source: Tables F1, F4 and F5, Reserve Bank of Australia website, **www.rba.gov.au**.

As would be expected, the cash rate is well below the indicator rates for business lending. A significant gap is needed to cover the banks' costs and to compensate for the greater risk of lending to customers rather than to another bank.

Most long-term debt securities have a *fixed interest rate*, known as the 'coupon rate', which does not vary over the life of the security. Long-term loans can also have a fixed interest rate. Where a *variable interest rate* applies, the rate will generally consist of a base rate, or indicator lending rate, plus a margin that depends on the risk of the borrower. In some variable interest rate loans the base rate (and therefore the interest rate payable) may be changed at any time. In other variable interest rate loans, the interest rate is reviewed at fixed intervals. For example, the interest rate may be reset every quarter to reflect the general movement in interest rates since the last quarterly reset date.

Lenders rank ahead of shareholders in that dividends cannot be paid unless all accrued interest payments to lenders have been met. Further, if a company is liquidated, all obligations to lenders have priority and shareholders have only a residual claim to any cash raised from the sale of the company's assets. As a consequence, lenders are subject to less risk than are shareholders and they are therefore prepared to accept a lower expected rate of return. However, not all lenders rank equally in terms of their claims when it comes to interest and principal repayments. Some debt can be **subordinated** to other debt and, as a consequence, the holders of subordinated debt require a higher interest rate than the holders of **unsubordinated** debt. Where borrowed funds are used to generate taxable income, interest on the debt is tax deductible. However, interest income is taxable in the hands of lenders and this increases the interest rate that lenders would otherwise require. Therefore, the fact that interest is tax deductible does not necessarily give debt a cost advantage over equity finance. Under the imputation system, taxes are virtually neutral in terms of their effect on the costs of debt and equity finance. This is discussed in Chapters 12 and 13.

As noted earlier, a feature that distinguishes the various types of debt securities is their marketability. Marketability is the ease with which the holder is able to trade the security. Investors favour being able to sell securities at short notice. In other words, they favour securities that are traded actively in a liquid market. Therefore, marketable securities tend to be issued at a lower interest rate than other types of debt, provided, of course, that the other characteristics of the debt are equivalent. From the viewpoint

subordinated debt
debt that ranks below other debt in the event that a company is wound up

unsubordinated debt
debt that has not been subordinated

of the borrower, an important characteristic is the other costs associated with the borrowing. Some fees apply only to private loans, while other fees apply only to debt securities. From the borrower's viewpoint, it is the overall cost that matters.

10.2.2 EFFECT OF DEBT ON RISK

While the rate of return required by lenders is less than the rate of return that shareholders expect, increasing the amount of debt also increases the company's **financial risk**. The effects of financial risk include effects on the rate of return expected by shareholders. A company financed solely by ordinary shares is not required to pay dividends and therefore has no financial risk. Borrowing introduces financial risk, which involves two separate but related effects.

First, because the returns to lenders are 'fixed', the use of debt rather than equity has a *leverage* effect—that is, it increases the variability of returns to shareholders and increases the rate of return they expect.

Second, the more a company borrows, the greater the interest and principal repayments to which it is committed, and therefore the greater is the risk of **financial distress**. In the extreme case, where a company has insufficient cash to meet its contractual obligations, the consequences can be far reaching and may even result in the company being placed into liquidation. In such a situation, the shareholders will usually receive little or no return from the sale of the company's assets because the company's lenders have a prior claim to the proceeds. However, financial distress is costly and many of the costs fall on lenders. For example, the costs incurred by the liquidator in arranging the sale of the assets are, in effect, paid by the lenders. Therefore, lenders require a margin to compensate for the expected level of these costs and this will be reflected in higher interest rates on loans to borrowers that have a higher risk of default. Also, to limit their exposure to risk, lenders will generally impose a covenant that sets an upper limit on the financial leverage of borrowers. The effects of financial risk are discussed in more detail in Chapter 12.

financial risk
risk attributable to the use of debt as a source of finance

financial distress
situation where a company's financial obligations cannot be met, or can be met only with difficulty

10.2.3 EFFECT OF DEBT ON CONTROL

Another important feature of debt is that, provided the company meets its obligations, lenders have no control over the company's operations. Unlike shareholders, lenders have no voting rights. However, if a company fails to meet its obligations, lenders can exert, either directly or indirectly, significant influence over the operations of the company. In this case the lenders, or frequently a trustee acting on their behalf, can seek to protect their interests. This may be achieved by taking control of the security for the loan, appointing an administrator, having the company placed into receivership or having the company placed into liquidation. Therefore, while lenders usually exert no control over a company, they have a large degree of potential control, which they can exert if the company breaches a loan agreement.

10.2.4 SECURITY FOR DEBT

Lenders, particularly those providing long-term debt, generally require that the borrower enter into a loan agreement that includes various requirements designed to protect the lender against possible loss. These requirements are commonly referred to as 'security' arrangements, although strictly speaking a loan is secured only if it involves a **mortgage** or other charge over assets. The security arrangements that may be applied to debt finance used by companies include the following.

mortgage
a type of security for a loan in which specific land or other tangible property is pledged by the borrower (mortgagor) to the lender (mortgagee)

Legal ownership

Instead of providing a loan to a company to enable it to buy an asset, a bank or other financier can purchase the asset and 'lend' the asset to the company. This form of debt finance is known as leasing.

A lease is an agreement under which one party who owns an asset (the lessor) gives another (the lessee) the right to possess and use an asset for a specified period in return for rental payments. The financier has the security of legal ownership of the leased asset and can therefore repossess the asset quickly in the event of default by the lessee. Leasing is an important means of financing the use of assets by companies and is discussed in Chapter 15.

Fixed charge

A fixed charge means that the lender has a charge over a specific asset or group of assets. For example, a loan may be secured by a mortgage over land and buildings owned by the borrower. If the borrower defaults, the lender can take possession of the assets and sell them in order to recover the outstanding debt. A fixed charge restricts the ability of the borrower to deal in the asset(s). For example, an asset that has been mortgaged cannot be sold unless the mortgage is discharged prior to settlement. Borrowers may therefore prefer the flexibility inherent in a floating charge.

Floating charge

In this case, the lender has a charge over a class of assets such as inventory. This means that the borrower can deal in the inventory but must undertake to maintain the stock of inventory above a specified level. If the borrower defaults, the floating charge is said to crystallise and becomes a fixed charge over the items of inventory currently held by the borrower.

Covenants

When banks lend to small- and medium-sized businesses they generally require loans to be secured by a mortgage or other charge over assets. In the case of larger loans such as loans to listed companies, the loan may be unsecured but include various covenants to protect the lender against possible loss by imposing various restrictions on the borrower. Similarly, covenants are commonly used where borrowers issue debt securities such as bonds or debentures. Common financial covenants require the borrower to limit the size of dividend payments, to maintain a minimum ratio of profit to interest cost (known as 'interest cover') and limit total liabilities to no more than a certain percentage of total assets. Other covenants may be designed to protect investors in the event of a major asset sale or a change of control.

If a borrower breaches a covenant it is in technical default and the lender may have the right to call for immediate repayment of the loan or take other actions to limit its risk of loss. For example, the lender may waive its right to demand immediate repayment but the waiver may be conditional on the borrower taking actions such as suspending dividend payments and meeting profitability and/or cash flow targets. Thus, breaching loan covenants can effectively result in the imposition of additional covenants (see Finance in Action, on p. 293). Alternatively, if the breach is considered to be minor and the borrower has adhered to the agreed repayment schedule, the lender is likely to allow the loan to continue on the original terms.

Negative pledge

Financial institutions may be prepared to lend on an unsecured basis where the loan agreement includes a negative pledge provision. The basic principle of a negative pledge is that the borrower agrees not to do certain things. In particular, the borrower will agree not to pledge existing or future assets of the company or group to anyone else without the consent of the lender.

As well as agreeing not to borrow additional funds on a secured basis, the loan agreement usually includes other covenants that restrict the borrowing company. These covenants may include a restriction on increasing its borrowing and total external liabilities beyond a specified proportion of total tangible assets. Other covenants in the loan agreement may limit the size of dividend payments and require the borrower to maintain its interest coverage ratio above a specified level. The aim of such covenants is to provide protection for lenders, while also allowing the company to be managed in ways that maximise profits for shareholders. Borrowing on this basis initially became popular in Australia among companies that found the covenants in debenture trust deeds unduly restrictive.

FINANCE IN ACTION

COVENANT WAIVER BUYS TIME FOR NUFARM

On 15 July 2010 agricultural chemical manufacturer Nufarm Limited revealed that based on forecasts for the remainder of its financial year, which ends on 31 July, it expected to breach one of its main banking covenants. On 1 September it announced that its net debt at 31 July would be approximately $620 million (much higher than its estimate provided on 14 July of $450 million), which would cause a second covenant breach. Nufarm also confirmed that it was progressing towards securing a waiver from its bank lenders related to the covenants involved in its existing banking facilities. On 27 September Nufarm announced the outcome of the discussions with its bank lenders.

Debt-laden Nufarm has gained a short reprieve as investors brace for its crucial full-year result today.

Nufarm yesterday secured a temporary waiver on its banking covenant breaches but said it would not pay a full-year dividend. The waiver will be in place until the end of next month as it seeks a long-term solution.

Credit Suisse analyst Rohan Gallagher said this was promising but it was merely buying time. 'What is not being said is the likely prohibitive cost of receiving such a waiver and the cost involved in security over those assets,' Mr Gallagher said.

Nufarm also agreed to a short-term funding facility of $180 million to mid-December with its lenders, to meet repayments that will fall due by the end of the year. The facility is subject to satisfactory performance against 'interim milestones based on the company's own projections and objectives', as well as 'progress relating to strategy and management plans', as agreed with its lenders.

Source: Philip Wen, 'Provisional waiver for Nufarm', *The Age*, 28 September 2010.

Later press reports revealed additional details, which include the following:
- one of the company's banks registered two fixed and floating charges over Nufarm's assets on 27 September
- Nufarm would be unable to borrow any more from its existing $1.2 billion unsecured facility, which was then drawn down by $701 million
- that facility had been replaced by a $176 million secured line of credit of which $55 million was available immediately with access to the remainder subject to the provision of extra security to the lenders and to meeting confidential profitability and cash flow targets.

Limited recourse

Limited recourse debt is commonly used for project finance, which is discussed in Section 10.6.

Guarantee

A guarantee is a promise from another party to cover a debt obligation in the event of default by the borrower. Lenders may require a guarantee if a borrower does not have sufficient assets to pledge as security for a loan but other related parties are in a stronger financial position. For example, if a loan is made to a subsidiary with limited financial strength, the lender may require a guarantee from the parent company.

10.3 SHORT-TERM BORROWING FROM BANKS AND OTHER FINANCIAL INSTITUTIONS[2]

LEARNING OBJECTIVE 3

Understand the main forms of short-term bank lending and recognise when each may be suitable to a borrower's needs

Banks are the most important institutions that lend to Australian companies, but short-term funding may also be obtained from other financial institutions such as finance companies, investment banks and even (for small businesses) from credit unions. In this section we discuss the major forms of direct lending available from banks and other financial institutions. However, a major lender such as a bank will often provide a company with a funding package that includes various kinds of both short-term and long-term loans. In addition, banks may also assist those companies that borrow by issuing securities such as commercial paper and bills of exchange. This assistance may be in the form of a commercial paper underwriting facility and a bill acceptance and/or discount facility. Borrowing by issuing short-term securities is discussed in Section 10.5.

10.3.1 BANK OVERDRAFT

An overdraft permits a company to run its current (cheque) account into deficit up to an agreed limit. The **overdraft limit** specifies the amount by which the company can overdraw its account. Strictly speaking, the amount by which the company's current account is overdrawn is usually **at call**, which means that the bank can withdraw the overdraft facility at any time and require repayment of the overdrawn amount. However, banks rarely exercise this right.

The cost of a bank overdraft includes the interest cost and fees. Overdraft interest rates are negotiated between the bank and the borrower and will depend on factors such as the borrower's credit-worthiness and the purposes for which the overdraft is sought. The interest rate charged is normally on the basis of a margin above an **indicator rate** published regularly by the bank. Interest is charged only on the amount by which the borrower's account is overdrawn, not on the amount of the overdraft limit. The interest cost is calculated daily by applying the interest rate to the overdrawn balance and is then charged monthly or quarterly in arrears.

Overdraft fees will usually include an establishment fee and an account service fee to cover the bank's transaction costs. In addition a fee is charged on any unused portion of the overdraft limit. This fee reflects the costs to the bank of having to maintain liquid funds in case the borrower decides to draw extra funds. It can also be seen as a charge that reflects the value to the borrower of having the option to increase the amount borrowed.

In assessing an application for an overdraft, a bank can use the applicant company's financial statements to obtain an indication of its financial performance and financial position. In addition, an applicant will usually be required to supply a cash budget to assist the bank in assessing the applicant's ability to service an overdraft. The bank will be particularly interested in the reasons for an overdraft application and the likely effects that providing an overdraft will have on the company's future financial performance and financial position. Generally speaking, banks regard an overdraft as suitable for funding the purchase of inventory that will quickly be converted into cash, to assist a company through seasonal downturns in liquidity, to meet unexpected short-term cash flow problems and to enable short-term opportunities to be exploited.

overdraft limit
level to which a company is permitted to overdraw its account

at call
money repayable immediately, at the option of the lender

indicator rate
interest rate set and published by a lender from time to time and used as a base on which interest rates on individual loans are determined, usually by adding a margin

[2] Most banks use the internet to provide up-to-date information on their loan products. The websites of a number of Australian banks can be accessed through the Australian Financial Services Directory **www.afsd.com.au/bankdx.html**.

Some companies may be granted an overdraft without any security, but in many cases a bank will insist that an overdraft be secured. Indeed, the terms of the overdraft may depend on the security that is offered. In addition, the bank may include various covenants in the loan agreement. For example, in an effort to limit the chance of a borrower running into excessive short-term liquidity problems, the bank may impose a covenant requiring the borrower to maintain some minimum ratio of current assets to current liabilities.

After an overdraft has been granted, the borrower can draw on its current account until the overdraft limit is reached. Therefore, an overdraft provides a convenient source of funds that can be accessed simply by writing cheques and undertaking EFTPOS transactions. A borrower will generally draw on only part of the available limit so that it has ready access to cash in an emergency. The overdraft limit is reviewed by the bank at regular intervals. In general, a borrower will be able to maintain the same overdraft limit from year to year unless its financial performance or financial position has markedly deteriorated. Therefore, a profitable company can often regard a significant proportion of its overdraft as a relatively long-term source of funds, even though technically speaking the overdraft is at call.

While overdrafts are an important form of corporate borrowing, their significance has declined in recent years. Other methods of acquiring short-term finance, such as the issuing of bills of exchange and commercial paper (or promissory notes), have grown in importance.

Changes in the pricing of overdrafts relative to other bank loans have contributed to this trend. In turn, the pricing of overdraft lending has been related to a bank's costs of funding an overdraft. When a bank provides an overdraft it has to maintain contingency funds in case the borrower decides to use the full extent of the overdraft limit. Contingencies of this type are now included in calculating the capital that the Australian Prudential Regulation Authority requires a bank to maintain and banks have responded by adjusting overdraft interest rates and fees, and by encouraging customers to borrow by other means.

10.3.2 DEBTOR FINANCE

Debtor finance allows a company to raise funds by selling its accounts receivable to a provider of this form of finance, known as a **discounter** or **factor**.[3] Debtor finance is provided by most banks or bank subsidiaries and by companies specialising in this form of finance.

A typical debtor finance agreement works as follows. When an invoice is sent to a customer of the company, an account receivable is created, and the discounter advances up to 90 per cent of the invoiced amount to the company. When the customer pays the account, the money initially goes to the discounter rather than to the company. The discounter then passes the remaining 10 per cent, less a fee, to the company. A discount charge is applied to the funds drawn down by the company from the discounter. Therefore, from the company's viewpoint, debtor finance accelerates its cash inflow from accounts receivable. From the discounter's viewpoint, the account receivable provides security for the funds it has advanced to the company and it earns a return from the discount and fees it charges its client (the company).

While the agreement just described is typical, debtor finance can take many forms. Table 10.3 indicates the range of discounting agreements offered by one debtor financier operating in Australia (Oxford Funding, www.oxfordfunding.com.au). In some agreements, often known as **full service debtor finance**, the discounter takes over the responsibility of managing the client's debtors' ledger and collecting debts. In this case, the client's debtors are informed of the existence of the discounter and make payments direct to the discounter. In other agreements—such as **non-notification debtor finance**—the client (borrower) remains responsible for managing the debtors' ledger and collecting debts. When payments are received they are banked into a trust account and remitted to the discounter. Non-notification debtor finance is also known as **confidential debtor finance**. Some companies prefer full service debtor finance because it allows them to outsource much of the accounts receivable function. Other companies prefer non-notification debtor finance because it enables them to maintain closer links

---

3 We will use the term 'discounter' rather than 'factor' throughout this section.

discounter (or factor) In the context of debtor finance, a financier who provides funds by purchasing accounts receivable from a business on a continuing basis

full service debtor finance discounting agreement under which the discounter manages the company's debtors

LEARNING OBJECTIVE 4
Understand debtor finance, inventory loans and bridging finance and be able to distinguish between them

WWW

non-notification (or confidential) debtor finance discounting agreement whose existence is not disclosed to the company's debtors

partnership debtor finance
discounting agreement under which the discounter and the company share responsibility for managing the company's debtors

with their customers and also keeps their financial arrangements confidential. In still other agreements, which Oxford Funding calls **partnership debtor finance**, these responsibilities are shared between the discounter and the client.

TABLE 10.3 Debtor finance services offered by Oxford Funding[a]

	FULL SERVICE DEBTOR FINANCE	PARTNERSHIP DEBTOR FINANCE	CONFIDENTIAL DEBTOR FINANCE	DEBTOR FINANCE WITHOUT RECOURSE
Required turnover ($)[b]	>500 000	>500 000	>1 000 000	500 000[c]
Maximum %[d]	80	80	80	80
Debtors' ledger[e]	Oxford[f]	Client/Oxford	Client	Oxford
Debt collection[g]	Oxford	Client/Oxford	Client	Oxford
Disclosed?[h]	Yes	Yes	No	Yes
Invoiced account is paid to[i]	Oxford	Client	Trust account[j]	Oxford

[a]The table provides a general guide only and does not cover the full range of services. Particulars current as at 1 October 2010.
[b]The turnover (in $ p.a.) required to qualify for this form of service.
[c]Client may use the service regularly or irregularly, choosing which receivables to sell, provided that debtors are of good quality.
[d]The maximum percentage of the invoice value that will be advanced. A dollar ceiling may also apply.
[e]Who is responsible for maintaining the debtors' (i.e. accounts receivable) ledger.
[f]Oxford means Oxford Funding, which is a debtor financier.
[g]Who is responsible for debt collection.
[h]Is the contract between the client and Oxford Funding disclosed to debtors?
[i]Who receives the cash when an account receivable is paid.
[j]Payments received by the client are deposited into a trust account and remitted to Oxford Funding.
Source: Oxford Funding, **www.oxfordfunding.com.au.**

debtor finance with recourse
debtor finance agreement under which the discounter is reimbursed by the selling company if the debtor defaults

Debtor finance may also be divided into two categories: factoring and discounting. The Institute for Factors and Discounters of Australia and New Zealand (**www.factorsanddiscounters.com**) defines full service debtor finance as factoring, while other types of debtor finance are referred to as discounting. Factoring and discounting both involve the sale of accounts receivable, but under factoring the financier also manages the debtors' ledger and the collection of accounts receivable.

Most debtor finance agreements in Australia provide for **debtor finance with recourse**, which means that if an account receivable becomes a bad debt the client has to compensate the discounter for the loss. Nevertheless, to spread the risk, many discounters impose a limit on the funds they will provide against any one debtor's account. **Debtor finance without recourse** means that the account receivable is effectively sold to the discounter who thereafter bears the bad debt risk.

Debtor finance is based on a simple principle. Accounts receivable are a valuable asset of a company and, like other assets such as land and buildings, can be used to generate funds. Debtor finance is particularly well suited to smaller companies that expect to grow quickly and to companies operating in a service industry. As a company's sales increase, so does the level of accounts receivable and, in turn, so also does the flow of finance from the discounter—that is, the finance available keeps pace automatically with the company's growth. Other forms of finance, such as overdrafts, have a set limit and therefore agreements will need to be renegotiated as the company grows. Companies operating in a service industry may find debtor finance attractive because accounts receivable are often their major asset. Compared with, say, a manufacturing company that owns plant and machinery, a service company will have fewer physical assets to offer as security for a loan.

In recent years debtor finance in Australia has grown rapidly. Statistics compiled by the Institute for Factors and Discounters of Australia and New Zealand from surveying its members show that total turnover for the year to the end of March 2010 was $61.6 billion, comprising factoring of $3.3 billion and discounting of $58.3 billion. In comparison, total turnover for the year to the end of March 2005 was $32.6 billion, so turnover increased by 89 per cent over 5 years.[4] Debtor finance has been used for an increasing variety of purposes. For example, debtor finance has been used as part of a funding package to finance some management buyouts and company takeovers. It is also likely that the introduction of the goods and services tax (GST) in July 2000 increased the demand for short-term finance, and for many companies discounting is a convenient form of such funding.

For further information on debtor finance, a useful website is that of Oxford Funding (**www.oxfordfunding.com.au**). Other discounting companies include Bibby Financial Services (**www.bibby.com.au**), Business Capital Financial Group (**www.bcfg.com.au**) and Cashflow Finance Australia (**www.cashflowfinance.com.au**).

debtor finance without recourse
debtor finance agreement under which the discounter is not reimbursed by the selling company if the debtor defaults

WWW

10.3.3 INVENTORY LOANS

A company's inventory is part of its asset base and, as with accounts receivable, can be used to secure loan funds. Inventory loans are usually provided by finance companies. Inventories of most durable items may be used to secure a loan and the proceeds of the loan may be used for any purpose in the company. In the US, this type of loan is usually referred to as a **revolving credit facility**.[5] However, in Australia, the bulk of inventory loans take the form of **floor-plan** or **wholesale finance**, which is a loan designed to assist retailers to purchase the inventory that then forms the security for the loan. For example, a finance company may lend a motor vehicle retailer the funds needed to purchase an inventory of vehicles and the finance company then uses those vehicles as security for the loan.[6] The provision of floor-plan finance makes up a significant proportion of the lending by a few specialist financiers. Some of these financiers, such as Toyota Finance and BMW Financial Services, are subsidiaries of motor vehicle manufacturers or importers. The interest rate charged on inventory loans is based on the current interest rate on a specified short-term security, plus a margin, with the size of the margin varying with the size of the loan.[7] For small loans of, say, $100 000, the interest rate will generally be higher than the interest rate charged on loans exceeding $500 000.

revolving credit facility
loan for general business purposes secured against the inventory of the borrower

floor-plan (or wholesale) finance
loan, usually made by a wholesaler to a retailer, that finances an inventory of durable goods such as motor vehicles

10.3.4 BRIDGING FINANCE

Bridging finance refers to a short-term loan, often in the form of a mortgage over property, used to 'bridge' a short period of time. Often the need for this type of funding arises from the timing of a series of transactions. For example, a property investor may wish to sell one building and use the sale proceeds to buy another building but, unfortunately, the timing of the transactions is such that the payment for the second building must be made, say, a month before the sale proceeds from the first are received. A loan is required to bridge this gap of 1 month. During this period the investor will own both properties, and if necessary both may therefore be mortgaged to secure the bridging loan.

bridging finance
short-term loan, usually in the form of a mortgage, to cover a need normally arising from timing differences between two or more transactions

---

4 Institute for Factors and Discounters of Australia and New Zealand Inc., *IFD Update*, March Quarter 2010.
5 See GE Capital (1999).
6 For a detailed discussion of inventory loans, see Fitzpatrick and Hardaker (1997).
7 For example, the base rate specified may be the current yield on a 180-day bank bill. These securities are discussed in Section 10.5.3.

10.4 LONG-TERM BORROWING FROM BANKS AND OTHER FINANCIAL INSTITUTIONS

LEARNING OBJECTIVE 5
Identify and explain the features of the main types of long-term loans

As shown in Table 10.1, Australian companies obtain debt finance largely through loans rather than by issuing debt securities. Banks are the largest providers of business loans. However, investment banks, life insurance companies and other financial institutions also provide long-term loans. We illustrate the main features of long-term loans in Example 10.1.

EXAMPLE 10.1

> Atlas Global Systems Ltd (AGS) manufactures portable global positioning system (GPS) units. AGS needs to borrow $20 million to construct and install a plant that will allow it to produce a new model that is waterproof and will float. These units are expected to be popular with boat operators because none of the currently available units is designed for use in a marine environment. AGS applies to its bank for a term loan and the bank agrees to lend the company $20 million for 5 years at an interest rate of 7.5 per cent per annum with equal monthly repayments. The loan will require 60 repayments and the effective interest rate is 7.5/12 = 0.625 per cent per month. The repayments form an ordinary annuity and use of Equation 3.19 shows that each payment will be $400 759 with the first payment required 1 month after the principal of $20 million is advanced by the bank.

The loan obtained by AGS has four important features. The company has borrowed a fixed amount ($20 million), for a fixed period (5 years) at a fixed interest rate (7.5 per cent per annum) with fixed repayments ($400 759 per month) that cover both principal and interest. In practice, it is not necessary that all of these characteristics should be fixed. However, the one element common to all term loans is that they are entered into for a fixed period.

10.4.1 LONG-TERM LOAN CHOICES AVAILABLE TO BORROWERS

While the period must be fixed, the borrower can choose the length of that period within minimum and maximum limits that may be specified by the bank. Similarly, the borrower can generally exercise choices related to the amount borrowed, the interest rate and the repayment pattern. We outline the choices that are generally offered by Australian banks.

The amount borrowed

Each bank will generally specify a minimum amount for term loans but there is usually no maximum amount—the amount that may be borrowed depends on the borrower's financial position and capacity to repay the loan. As with the loan obtained by AGS, a term loan may be funded in one amount or the bank may provide the funds in separate tranches over time.

The term of the loan

Each bank will usually specify minimum and maximum terms for its long-term loans. These loans are typically available for periods of up to 10 years but longer terms are possible in some cases. For example, a bank may offer terms up to 25 years in cases where the loan is secured by a mortgage over residential property.

The interest rate

The interest rate on a term loan may be fixed or variable. Banks will typically quote fixed interest rates for periods ranging from 1 to 10 years. These rates are higher than, but related to, the yields on government bonds of the same term to maturity. If the borrower chooses a variable interest rate, it will be charged a rate that is variable at the bank's discretion. In Australia, the interest rates on variable-rate loans generally change in response to changes in the cash rate set by the RBA, but can also vary in response to other factors that cause changes in the cost and composition of banks' funds. For example, following the global financial crisis, which saw turmoil in many financial markets, particularly during 2008, the funding mix of banks operating in Australia changed. In particular, banks have increased their use of deposits and long-term debt and reduced their use of short-term debt and securitisation. Deposits and long-term debt have the advantage of being relatively stable sources of funds, but often they are also more costly than short-term debt. Therefore, between June 2007 and January 2010, the banks' overall funding costs increased relative to the cash rate and their lending rates also rose relative to the cash rate.[8]

Banks generally publish weekly advertisements containing the interest rates on their loans and these rates are also available on each bank's website. For smaller loans, such as a loan to a small business secured by a mortgage over residential property, the published rate will usually be a set rate that applies to all loans of a given type. For larger loans, banks will undertake a detailed analysis of the borrower's credit risk and will establish individual margins that are added to a published base rate.

Whether the interest rate on a loan is fixed or variable, the level of the rate will vary depending on whether the loan is secured, and may also vary depending on the type of assets that are pledged as security.

Loan repayments

Borrowers can exercise choices in terms of the pattern of repayments and the frequency of those repayments. The loan obtained by AGS involved equal monthly repayments with each repayment consisting partly of interest and partly of principal. A loan with that repayment pattern is known as a *principal-and-interest loan*, a **credit foncier loan** or an *instalment loan*. Since the principal outstanding is reduced, at first gradually and then more rapidly, over time, such a loan may also be referred to as a *reducible loan*.

credit foncier loan type of loan that involves regular repayments that include principal and interest

A related but different repayment pattern involves a fixed program of repayments covering principal only with the interest being paid separately. This repayment pattern may be described as 'principal *plus* interest' and differs from the 'principal-*and*-interest' pattern in that the payments will decline over time rather than remaining constant in each period. Alternatively, the borrower can choose to make 'interest only' payments during the loan term with a final lump sum repayment of the principal. A large final loan repayment is often known as a balloon payment. In cases where the interest rate has been fixed for a period such as a year, the bank may allow borrowers to pay interest only in advance. This may be advantageous where the borrower wishes to claim a tax deduction for interest earlier than would otherwise be the case.

As noted above, the frequency of payments can also vary with borrowers allowed to choose weekly, fortnightly, monthly, quarterly or half-yearly payments. In some cases principal repayments may be made yearly, with interest being paid more frequently. In summary, a variety of choices is available to borrowers who take out term loans but it should be noted that these choices are often linked to other choices. In particular, if the borrower chooses a variable-rate loan this usually opens up a wider variety of other choices than is the case with a fixed-rate loan. We now discuss the variable- and fixed-rate term loans offered by banks.

10.4.2 VARIABLE-RATE TERM LOANS

As discussed earlier, a term loan covers a fixed period and has three other main features—the interest rate, the amount borrowed and the repayment pattern. If the borrower chooses a variable interest rate, there

---

8 See Brown et al. (2010).

is considerable flexibility for the last two features. While the maximum amount that can be borrowed will be specified, the bank will usually allow the funds to be accessed progressively or fully drawn in a single amount.

A variable-rate loan is flexible in that it can be repaid early without penalty, and a redraw facility is often available. This allows borrowers access to any excess repayments that have been made. Also, a variable-rate loan can usually be converted to a fixed-rate loan at any time without penalty fees. Borrowers who wish to be protected against possible increases in interest rates may be offered a 'capped option', which means that the interest rate can go up, but will not exceed a specified ceiling rate for a specified term.

10.4.3 FIXED-RATE TERM LOANS

The borrower can choose to pay an agreed fixed interest rate for a period of at least 1 year. The maximum fixed-rate period usually ranges from 5 to 10 years and can therefore cover the full term of the loan or only part of the term. At the end of each fixed interest rate period, the rate may be reset for a further fixed term or the loan may continue on a variable-rate basis provided that the loan term is not exceeded. By fixing the interest rate on a loan, the borrower gives up some of the flexibility that is inherent in a variable-rate loan. Progressive draw-down is not allowed—in other words, fixed-rate term loans are funded only in one amount. However, the equivalent of progressive advances can be achieved by arranging to take out a number of separate loans, each having its own separate documentation, loan account number and fixed interest rate.

The borrower may be able to choose any of the usual repayment patterns, including interest only in advance, and the frequency of repayments can range from weekly to annually. However, the repayments, once set, cannot be changed during the fixed-rate period, but can be renegotiated at the end of the fixed-rate period. Borrowers may be allowed to make special repayments or to repay the loan in full before the end of the agreed period, but 'breaking' a fixed-rate loan in one of these ways will incur an administration fee and an early repayment adjustment.

10.4.4 OTHER FEATURES OF TERM LOANS

In addition to the interest payable on a term loan, borrowers are usually required to pay an establishment fee and periodic loan service fees.

As noted above, banks normally require that term loans are secured and this may take the form of a charge over property or other company assets, or the guarantee of an overseas bank or parent company. A loan that is secured by a mortgage over land or other property is often referred to as a mortgage loan. Mortgage finance is often used by borrowers who wish to finance their own offices, shops and factories, and by property developers who wish to undertake activities such as the construction of buildings and the subdivision of land.

The risk management measures used by banks include limits on a bank's exposure to a single borrower or group of related borrowers. Accordingly, there are often cases where a credit-worthy borrower may require more funds than a single lender is willing to provide. This problem can be overcome by obtaining a **syndicated loan**. The main feature of these loans is that a number of banks join together to provide what is in effect a term loan, with each lender having identical rights. Because each lender provides only part of the funds, the credit risk exposure is divided between the lenders. Such loans are generally unsecured and have a variable interest rate, usually based on the bank-bill rate. A lending syndicate often involves both Australian and foreign banks. For example, in 2007, Wesfarmers Limited obtained a loan of $10 billion from a syndicate of domestic and offshore banks to finance its takeover of the Coles Group (see Finance in Action, next page). The loan was originally underwritten by a group of three banks, which then arranged for at least 10 more banks to provide the majority of the funds.

syndicated loan
loan arranged by one or more lead banks, funded by a syndicate that usually includes other banks

As well as borrowing locally, Australian companies frequently borrow overseas. Reasons for borrowing overseas include diversification of funding sources and achieving exposure to one or more foreign currencies. Decisions on borrowing overseas should be based on an assessment of exchange risk as well as the interest cost. Further discussion of this avenue for obtaining funds is deferred to Chapter 20.

10.4.5 WHY DO BORROWERS USE TERM LOANS?

The interest rate on a term loan is usually higher than the yields on debt securities of the same term to maturity. This fact prompts the question: Why do businesses use term loans rather than issuing their own securities directly to investors? A partial answer to this question can be found by examining Table 10.4. Where a bank provides a credit facility of less than $2 million, variable-rate and fixed-rate loans (intermediated finance) predominate over bills (direct finance). In contrast, for facilities of $2 million and over, the value of bills is usually similar to or greater than the combined value of bank loans. The figures in Table 10.4 include both short- and long-term loans and bills, which are short-term securities that can be used to provide a longer-term source of finance, since banks will provide bill facilities for up to 10 years. However, the pattern that is evident in Table 10.4 applies to all debt regardless of its term: loans from financial intermediaries are preferred where the borrowing is small and direct finance becomes more competitive as the amount involved becomes larger.

Thus, one advantage of bank loans is that a loan can be for a relatively small amount, such as $50 000, and the transaction costs of obtaining a bank loan are also relatively low. In contrast, issuing debt securities involves transaction costs with significant fixed components, so the issue has to be large to achieve economies of scale.

FINANCE IN ACTION

WESFARMERS CAN BANK ON COLES LOAN

The biggest bank loan in Australian corporate history is largely complete, despite a credit crunch putting fear into banks. The funding will underpin Australia's largest takeover: Wesfarmers' $20 billion buy-out of Coles. The three lead arrangers of the loan, ANZ Bank, BNP Paribas and NAB, say they and 10 other banks have taken up 85 per cent of the $10 billion loan on terms drawn up before the worst of the crunch hit.

BNP Paribas would not disclose the amount of debt each lead arranger had decided to take in its own right, although market sources speculated it could be about $1 billion between them. Interest rates on the loan have not been disclosed, but Wesfarmers used a rate of 7.45 per cent in its scheme booklet to calculate its payments, or 58 basis points above the 90-day bill rate when the booklet was published.

The 10 banks' commitment to the Wesfarmers deal paints a picture of a two-speed debt market since credit fears gripped lenders in mid-August. On the one hand, there are major banks that are largely unruffled by the crisis and willing to lend to good credit risks. On the other, there are lower-quality assets that no-one is willing to lend on, and debt markets that have effectively closed. Some market commentators speculate the mortgage-backed securities market in the US may never reappear.

'What we're seeing is quite a lot of appetite for well-structured transactions', said Stephen Boyd, NAB Capital's spokesman for the deal. Mr Boyd said the syndication was on schedule, despite some views that progress had been slow since the three banks committed to the deal on July 10. 'What we have seen is, certainly, banks are more sensitive in discerning credit quality', Mr Boyd said. 'Each bank is different in how they have been impacted in this credit crunch.'

The deal now enters phase two, which includes roadshows in Sydney, Singapore and Hong Kong, as the lead banks try to place the remaining $1.5 billion in debt. Banks that have signed up are Westpac, Commonwealth, ABN Amro, Bank of Tokyo-Mitsubishi UFJ, JP Morgan Chase , Sumitomo Mitsui, WestLB, Mizuho Corporate, Sociacetace Gacenacerale and Barclays Capital.

Source: 'Wesfarmers can bank on Coles loan', Stuart Washington, *The Age*, 27 October 2007.

TABLE 10.4 Bank lending to businesses, total credit outstanding by size and by type of facility ($ million)

	UNDER $2 MILLION				$2 MILLION AND OVER			
	VARIABLE RATE	FIXED RATE	BILLS	TOTAL	VARIABLE RATE	FIXED RATE	BILLS	TOTAL
June 2001	46 815	44 286	21 245	112 346	35 621	30 459	92 652	158 732
June 2002	56 530	38 296	24 979	119 805	42 773	31 508	90 281	164 562
June 2003	62 914	37 678	28 286	128 877	58 698	24 803	86 192	169 694
June 2004	76 208	38 617	27 693	142 788	68 811	29 289	98 030	196 129
June 2005	85 941	42 166	30 324	158 431	85 749	24 026	105 854	215 628
June 2006	92 546	44 656	33 603	170 805	107 832	34 807	126 037	268 675
June 2007	96 720	50 001	40 354	187 076	133 255	46 270	158 478	338 002
June 2008	96 105	63 694	40 043	199 842	164 765	55 438	229 543	449 745
June 2009	91 157	68 572	41 381	201 111	173 287	54 542	262 098	489 927
June 2010	92 528	64 889	37 364	194 781	179 578	50 584	233 888	464 050

Source: Table D8, Reserve Bank of Australia website, **www.rba.gov.au**.

Second, a borrower can provide information about its financial position, forecast cash flows, prospects and strategic plans privately to a bank, which will use the information to assess the credit risk and price the loan. In contrast, a company that borrows by issuing debt securities has to disclose much information publicly, which may reveal valuable insights to competitors.

Third, bank loans are much more flexible than debt securities. For example, the repayment pattern on a bank loan can be tailored to suit the borrower's cash flows and, if circumstances change unexpectedly, the terms of a bank loan can often be renegotiated. In contrast, the repayment pattern and other terms of debt securities are set at the time of the issue and it is extremely difficult to make any changes to those terms later.

Fourth, debt securities may be difficult to sell to investors unless they have a rating from one of the rating agencies such as Standard & Poor's. Unless the borrower is very large it may be cheaper to deal with a bank than it is to obtain a rating. In summary, term loans have several advantages that make them attractive, particularly where smaller borrowings are involved.

10.5 DEBT SECURITIES

While loans from banks and other lenders are available to businesses of any type, larger businesses are able to borrow by creating and issuing debt securities. These securities include commercial paper, bills of exchange, debentures, notes and bonds.

10.5.1 DEBT SECURITIES: THE GENERAL PRINCIPLES

Companies can obtain short-term debt funding by issuing (selling) securities such as commercial paper and bills of exchange. The same general principles are applicable to both types of security and, in broad terms, are as follows. The securities are a promise to pay a sum of money on a future date, known as the maturity date. Provided that the promise is made by an entity of credible financial standing, such a promise is valuable and hence may be sold. In principle, the purchaser may be any entity with funds available for lending. How much the purchaser is willing to pay will depend on several factors, including the current level of interest rates. When the security is sold, the issuer receives the sale price but is, of course, committed to making the future payment promised. Thus, in effect, the security is a short-term loan where the loan principal is equal to the sale price. The purchaser, however, is not committed to holding the security for the whole period from the date of purchase until the maturity date. At any time, the purchaser may sell the security to some other party. Such a sale is known as a **secondary market transaction**. Many such transactions may be undertaken during the life of one of these securities.[9] Whoever owns the security on the maturity date will then seek payment of the sum promised. Commercial paper and bills of exchange are discussed in Sections 10.5.2 and 10.5.3, respectively.

Companies can also issue long-term securities known as debentures, notes and bonds. There can be important differences between these types of securities, but all of them are essentially the same in terms of their cash flow pattern. In common with government bonds, debentures, notes and corporate bonds are usually issued at face value. In some cases, the issue price is determined by a tender process, which can result in the issue price being greater or less than the face value. After the securities have been issued, the borrower makes regular interest payments known as **coupon payments** and then repays the face value (principal) in full at maturity. Alternatively, the security may be convertible into ordinary shares, in which case the holder has a choice. If the holder chooses not to exercise the conversion option, then the principal will be repaid. The characteristics of debentures, unsecured notes and corporate bonds are discussed in Sections 10.5.4 to 10.5.6. For details of the valuation of these securities, refer to Section 4.4 (on p. 84). Convertible notes are discussed in Section 10.8.1.

10.5.2 COMMERCIAL PAPER

Commercial paper is the term that is commonly used to refer to marketable, short-term, unsecured debt securities with the legal status of promissory notes.[10] A promissory note is simply a promise to pay a stated sum of money (such as $500 000) on a stated future date (such as a date 90 days hence). The stated sum of money is referred to as the paper's **face value**. The issuer of the paper—that is, the borrower—is the only party with an obligation to pay the face value at maturity, so commercial paper is sometimes called *one-name paper*.[11] In practice, only 'blue chip' companies—that is, large, reputable companies with a high credit rating—and government entities are able to raise funds by issuing commercial paper. Issuers of commercial paper in Australia have included Amcor, BHP Billiton, Orica and Woolworths, together with several non-bank financial institutions.

LEARNING OBJECTIVE 6
Identify and explain the features of the main types of short-term debt securities

secondary market transaction purchase or sale of an existing security

coupon payments periodic payments of interest, often at half-yearly intervals, on debt securities such as bonds and debentures

LEARNING OBJECTIVE 7
Understand the process of using commercial paper and bills of exchange to raise funds

commercial paper (or promissory note) short-term marketable debt security in which the borrower promises to pay a stated sum on a stated future date. Also known as *one-name paper*

---

9 At one time physical transactions were made but today most trades are recorded through Austraclear, which is a computerised central clearing house for promissory notes, bank bills and other money market securities. Austraclear is a subsidiary of the Australian Securities Exchange. For further details visit www.asx.com.au.

10 The term 'commercial paper' is also used as a generic term to cover short-term debt securities known by various terms, including certificates of deposit, short-term notes and transferable deposits, as well as promissory notes.

11 The term 'one-name paper' includes securities such as Treasury notes, which are issued by the government, and certificates of deposit, which are issued by banks.

face value
sum promised to be paid in the future on a debt security, such as commercial paper or a bill of exchange

discounter
in the context of marketable short-term debt securities (including commercial paper and bills of exchange), the purchaser of such a security

Commercial paper usually has short-term maturities within the range of 30 days to 180 days, although other maturities may be possible. In practice, almost all commercial paper is issued to the members of dealer panels, made up of large banks, which bid for the paper when a company announces the terms of a planned issue. The purchasers are known as **discounters** and they may hold the paper until it matures or, more usually, sell it to other investors. If an issuer subsequently finds that it does not require the funds for the full period of the loan, it can repurchase the paper by buying the securities in the secondary market at the current market price.

The amount that the seller of a security receives from the discounter depends on market forces. For example, suppose that Jindabyne Resources Ltd issues 90-day commercial paper with a face value of $500 000 and is able to sell the paper to Klondike Investments for $494 000. Jindabyne Resources will have to repay $500 000 on the maturity date, so the interest cost is $6000 on a loan of $494 000 for a term of 90 days. The simple annualised yield is ($6000/$494 000) × (365/90) ≈ 4.926 per cent per annum. In deciding to pay $494 000 for the security, Klondike Investments would, of course, have compared the yield of 4.926 per cent per annum with yields (interest rates) available at that time on similar securities. This logic, which is really just an application of simple interest, is summarised in Equation 10.1:

LEARNING OBJECTIVE 8
Calculate prices and yields for commercial paper and bills of exchange

$$P = \frac{F}{1+(r)(d/365)} \quad [10.1]$$

where F = face value (= future sum payable)
r = yield per annum on a simple interest basis
d = number of days to maturity

In practice, market participants will agree on a yield and the price will then be determined using the agreed formula. The use of simple interest to calculate the price of a security, given the yield, is illustrated in Example 10.2.

EXAMPLE 10.2

Commercial paper with a face value of $500 000 and 90 days to maturity is issued at a yield of 4.926 per cent per annum. Calculate the price of the security.

SOLUTION
Using Equation 10.1:

$$P = \frac{F}{1+(r)(d/365)}$$

$$= \frac{\$500\,000}{1+(0.049\,26)(90/365)}$$

$$= \frac{\$500\,000}{1.012\,146\,301}$$

$$= \$493\,999.73$$

Equation 10.1 also applies to commercial paper when it is traded in the secondary market. Example 10.3 provides an illustration.

EXAMPLE 10.3

Suppose that 30 days after purchasing the commercial paper (see Example 10.2), Klondike Investments decides to sell the security in the secondary market and agrees to sell it to St Andrew Bank at a yield of 5.05 per cent per annum. What price will St Andrew Bank pay?

SOLUTION

The commercial paper now has 60 days left until maturity. Using Equation 10.1, the price is:

$$P = \frac{F}{1+(r)(d/365)}$$

$$= \frac{\$500\,000}{1+(0.0505)(60/365)}$$

$$= \frac{\$500\,000}{1.008\,301\,370}$$

$$= \$495\,883.49$$

For further discussion of calculating prices and yields, see Section 3.3.4 on page 37.

Commercial paper is generally issued through a program arranged by a major bank or investment bank. The program arranger (or lead manager) will form a dealer panel, generally made up of large banks. The documents that establish the program will usually specify an upper limit on the value of the securities outstanding at any time. As existing securities mature, new securities can be created and discounted if required by the issuer. If the program is to be underwritten, an underwriting syndicate will also be formed. The dealer panel is given the first opportunity to purchase the securities. If there is a shortfall in the amount of the issue purchased by the dealer panel, the balance is bought by the underwriting syndicate. Each member of the syndicate agrees that, if required by the issuer, it will purchase securities up to a specified amount. To facilitate trading, it is usual for commercial paper issues to have a credit rating from a ratings agency (see Section 4.7, p. 92).

The size of a commercial paper program will depend on factors such as the borrower's need for funds, its credit rating and the cost of commercial paper in comparison with other sources of funds. Because of the costs involved in establishing a program, commercial paper issues are generally not viable unless the amount to be borrowed is at least $200 million. The maximum amount that a given issuer can borrow will depend on its credit rating and its reputation with investors. Thus a company with a short-term rating of A–2 might face an upper limit of $600 million to $1 billion on its commercial paper outstanding at any time. In contrast, an issuer that is rated A–1+ might be able to borrow more than $5 billion if it needed to do so.

At the end of June 2010, there was $341.6 billion in outstanding one-name paper issued by Australian borrowers. Of this amount, $239 billion was issued in Australia and $102.7 billion was issued overseas. Most of these securities were issued by banks, but $6.5 billion was issued by private companies outside the finance sector. Of this amount, only $1.4 billion was issued in Australia.[12]

10.5.3 BILLS OF EXCHANGE
The usual way bills of exchange are created and traded

LEARNING OBJECTIVE 7
Understand the process of using commercial paper and bills of exchange to raise funds

In practice, if a company does not have a credit rating from a ratings agency, it will find it very difficult to issue and sell commercial paper. For these companies an alternative is to issue a **bill of exchange**. There are many similarities between commercial paper and bills of exchange. Both are short-term debt

---

12 See Australian Bureau of Statistics (June 2010).

bill of exchange
marketable short-term debt security in which one party (the drawer) directs another party (the acceptor) to pay a stated sum on a stated future date

instruments that promise to pay a stated sum (known as the face value) on a stated future date; both can be traded in active secondary markets; and both are sold at prices that reflect the current level of interest rates. The major difference is in the number of parties to the instrument. In the case of commercial paper, only the issuer promises to pay the face value on the maturity date. In a bill of exchange there is also another party, known as the acceptor, so named because this party accepts the responsibility to pay the face value on the maturity date. Most often, this role is filled by a bank. The borrower pays a fee to the bank for this service and also agrees to reimburse the bank for paying the face value on the maturity date. Because the acceptor is a well-known institution with a high credit rating, there will be lenders willing to purchase the bill even if the borrower is not so well known. The yield on a bill will reflect the credit rating of the acceptor and bill yields are almost always lower than the yields on commercial paper of the same term to maturity.

acceptor (or drawee)
in a bill of exchange, the party agreeing to pay the holder the bill's face value on the maturity date; usually a bank or other financial institution

The parties involved in the creation of a bill of exchange are referred to as the **drawer**, the **acceptor** (or **drawee**) and the discounter. In the usual way bills of exchange are created, the drawer is the borrower and the acceptor pays the face value at maturity on behalf of the borrower. The face value is paid to whoever holds (owns) the bill on the maturity date. The role of the discounter is to provide (lend) the funds by purchasing the bill from the drawer. In principle, the discounter could be any entity with funds to lend, but in practice is usually a financial intermediary or some other financial institution. As with commercial paper, the amount paid by the discounter will depend on market forces and, in particular, on yields currently available on similar securities. By convention, simple interest is used to calculate bill prices.[13] The acceptor and discounter may be the same entity. Figure 10.1 shows the steps in the creation of a bill where the acceptor and the discounter are different entities.

FIGURE 10.1

drawer
in a bill of exchange, the party initiating the creation of the bill; usually the borrower

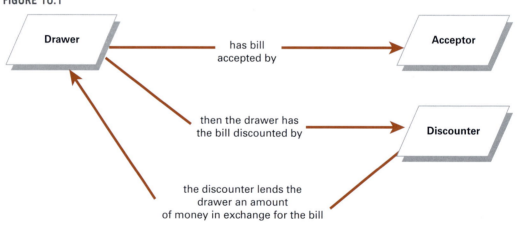

rediscounting
selling a short-term debt security in the secondary market

The discounter has the choice of either holding the bill until maturity, when payment will be received from the acceptor, or selling (**rediscounting**) the bill. However, if the bill is sold, the seller normally endorses the bill at the time of sale. **Endorsement** means that if the acceptor is unable to pay the face value on the maturity date, an endorser may be obliged to pay a subsequent holder of the bill. Consequently, when a seller endorses a bill the seller has a contingent liability until the bill matures and is paid.[14] On the bill's maturity date the acceptor pays the face value to the holder of the bill and the acceptor will require the drawer to reimburse the acceptor for this payment. In the unlikely event that the acceptor is unable to pay the face value, liability for payment falls next on the drawer. If the drawer is also unable to pay, each endorser becomes liable to pay subsequent endorsers; thus there is a 'chain of

---

13 Equation 10.1 can be used. For further details, see Section 3.3.4 on page 37.
14 For some lenders, this fact may make commercial paper, which is rarely endorsed when sold, a more attractive investment than bills of exchange.

protection' consisting of all those entities that have endorsed the bill. However, in practice it is rare for problems to arise and the acceptor pays the face value as expected. The normal process of repayment is illustrated in Figure 10.2.

FIGURE 10.2

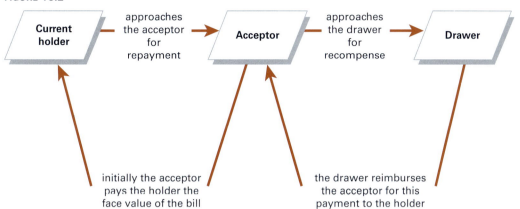

endorsement
acceptance by the seller of a bill in the secondary market of responsibility to pay the face value if there is default by the acceptor, drawer and earlier endorsers

Bank accepted bills

When a bank accepts a bill, it is obliged to repay the bill at maturity, and for this reason such a bill is usually referred to as a **bank accepted bill** or simply a **bank bill**. In principle, institutions outside the banking sector could also accept bills. Where this occurs, the bill is known as a **non-bank bill**, but in practice nearly all bills in Australia are accepted by banks.

The growth of the Australian bill market since 1990 is shown in Table 10.5.

bank bill
bill of exchange that has been accepted or endorsed by a bank

TABLE 10.5 Bills on issue ($ billion), 1990–2010

DATE	BILLS ON ISSUE
June 1990	68.3
June 1995	59.1
June 2000	76.4
June 2005	91.4
June 2006	105.1
June 2007	124.5
June 2008	141.2
June 2009	148.8
June 2010	138.5

Source: Table D2, Reserve Bank of Australia website, www.rba.gov.au.

non-bank bill
bill of exchange that has been neither accepted nor endorsed by a bank

WWW

Bill facilities

Many companies do not restrict their use of bill financing to those occasions when they require funds to meet their immediate needs, but maintain a continuing bill facility with a bank.[15] A bill facility may

---

15 A bill facility may also be offered by an investment bank or other financial institution. However, to simplify our discussion we will assume that the facility is offered by a bank.

bill discount facility
agreement in which one entity (normally a bank) undertakes to discount (buy) bills of exchange drawn by another entity (the borrower)

bill acceptance facility
agreement in which one entity (normally a bank) undertakes to accept bills of exchange drawn by another entity (the borrower)

fully drawn bill facility
bill facility in which the borrower must issue bills so that the full agreed amount is borrowed for the period of the facility

revolving credit bill facility
bill facility in which the borrower can issue bills as required, up to the agreed limit

be either a discount facility or an acceptance facility. In a **bill discount facility**, the bank undertakes to discount (buy) bills of exchange drawn by the borrower up to a specified total amount—that is, the bank promises to lend up to the specified total amount. From the bank's viewpoint, the advantage of this method of lending is that the bank holds a marketable security in the form of the bill, which it can later sell if it wishes. Thus, while the bank is committed to providing the funds initially, it is not committed to providing the funds for the full term of the bill. In a **bill acceptance facility**, the bank agrees to accept bills drawn by the borrower up to a specified total amount. The company is then able to borrow elsewhere in the capital market by selling bills. This is a relatively easy task because there is a ready market for bank bills.

Bill facilities are of two basic types.

- A **fully drawn bill facility** provides a company with a specified amount for a specified period. In this case the company has to borrow the full amount, which is provided by issuing a series of bills. New bills are issued as the existing bills mature, until the agreed period of the facility expires. The interest rate is recalculated each time a new bill is issued. For example, a 3-year facility may be covered by six 180-day bills. In some instances partial repayment may be required during the period of the loan.
- A **revolving credit bill facility** differs from a fully drawn facility in that the company is permitted to draw on the facility as the funds are required, provided that it does not borrow more than the agreed total amount. In this respect a revolving credit facility is similar to a bank overdraft.

Within these broad categories, many variations are possible. For example, some bill facilities fix in advance the interest cost to the borrower, while others provide funds at the current market rate, or at the current market rate subject to an agreed maximum rate or 'cap'. Generally, however, the term and cost conditions for bill facilities are as follows:

TERM: A company issues a bill to obtain a short-term loan. Usually the term of a bill is 30, 60, 90, 120 or 180 days. Often, however, a company will want guaranteed access to short-term funding, and will seek a bill facility for, say, 3 years.

COSTS: The cost of a bill facility has three elements. They are the fees for establishing and maintaining the facility, the interest cost and the acceptance fee. The *first element* of the costs compensates the lender for the cost incurred in establishing and administering the facility. Typically, these fees are expressed as a percentage of the amount of the facility. The *second element* of the costs is the interest cost represented by the difference between the bill's face value and the price paid by the discounter. At any given time, there is a market-determined discount rate (expressed as a yield) applicable to bills with the same term to maturity and credit-worthiness.[16] Although all bills that have been accepted and/or endorsed by a bank are normally called bank bills, there can be slight differences in yield, depending on the credit rating of the bank involved. Yields indicative of those applying to bank bills are shown in Table 10.6. The *third element* of the cost of a bill facility is the acceptance fee. This fee is the acceptor's return for taking on the risks associated with the bill facility. The main risk is that the company may default on its obligations under the facility. The margin charged by the lender depends on the amount and term of the facility and the security given by the borrower.

---

[16] Participants in the bill market, like participants in the commercial paper market, typically agree on a yield, which is then converted to a price using simple interest. For details, see Section 3.3.4 on page 37.

TABLE 10.6 Yields for 30-day, 90-day and 180-day bank accepted bills, 2001–10

DATE	30-DAY YIELD (% P.A.)	90-DAY YIELD (% P.A.)	180-DAY YIELD (% P.A.)
29 June 2001	5.06	5.02	5.04
28 June 2002	4.96	5.11	5.25
30 June 2003	4.79	4.67	4.56
30 June 2004	5.44	5.50	5.57
30 June 2005	5.62	5.66	5.69
30 June 2006	5.87	5.97	6.09
29 June 2007	6.34	6.43	6.58
30 June 2008	7.59	7.80	7.97
30 June 2009	3.16	3.20	3.30
30 June 2010	4.71	4.89	4.97

Source: Table F1, Reserve Bank of Australia website, **www.rba.gov.au**.

For a borrower, there are a number of advantages in choosing bill finance over other forms of short-term debt. The major advantage is access to funding sources that, without the credit-worthiness provided by acceptance, would not be available. Another important advantage is the variety of bill facilities available, which means that bill funding provides flexibility for the borrower. However, for a borrower with a credit rating equal or superior to that of a bank there may be few if any benefits associated with obtaining bank acceptance. Thus, for these borrowers, commercial paper may be an attractive alternative to bank bills.

10.5.4 DEBENTURES

Issuing **debentures** is a method of borrowing that is unique to companies. The *Corporations Act 2001* does not provide a precise definition of the term 'debenture', but it does require that the term 'debenture' should be used only where repayment of the money lent is secured by a charge over land or other tangible property of the borrower or guarantors.

The features of debentures include the following:

- the interest rate payable by the borrower is fixed at the time the debentures are issued
- the term to maturity is fixed and is usually in the range from 1 year to 5 years
- potential investors must be provided with a prospectus
- the security offered to debenture holders will be either a fixed charge over specific assets or a floating charge over a pool of assets
- the ownership of debentures may be transferable, so they can be listed on an exchange such as the ASX
- details such as the nature of the security for the debentures, reporting requirements, other obligations of the issuer and the rights of debenture holders must be set out in a trust deed
- a trustee must be appointed to protect the interests of debenture holders.

The importance of debentures as a source of finance for Australian companies has declined in the past decade and the number of debenture issues listed on the ASX is small. Public issues of debentures are expensive because of the costs involved in preparing a prospectus and many companies have found

LEARNING OBJECTIVE 9
Identify and explain the features of the main types of long-term debt securities

debenture
a type of fixed interest security issued by a company and secured by a charge over tangible assets

their debenture trust deed unduly restrictive. Most companies are now able to obtain fixed interest debt finance at lower cost by taking out a variable-rate bank loan and then entering into an interest rate swap. This mechanism is explained in Section 10.7.

Many debenture issues in Australia are unlisted. A survey by the Australian Securities and Investments Commission (ASIC) estimated that the total face value of debentures on issue in Australia at 31 December 2006 was $34.3 billion. A subsequent survey estimated that by 31 December 2008, the total face value of debentures on issue had declined by 51 per cent to $16.9 billion, of which $10.4 billion were unlisted. The decline in the value of debentures on issue primarily reflected decisions by investors to withdraw their money from the sector (Australian Securities and Investments Commission 2009).

10.5.5 UNSECURED NOTES

Unsecured notes are similar to debentures, but differ in that holders are usually unsecured creditors who rank below any secured creditors for repayment of debt. A related difference is that a trust deed for unsecured notes will usually include covenants that are less restrictive than those in a debenture trust deed. From the holder's point of view, therefore, unsecured notes are a riskier investment than debentures, because debenture holders have a prior claim over the company's assets in the event of the company being wound up.

To compensate for the greater risk of unsecured notes, a company usually offers a higher interest rate on unsecured notes than on debentures. In contrast to debentures, where the interest rate is fixed, the interest rate on notes is often linked to an indicator rate such as the bank-bill swap rate (BBSW). Accordingly, some issues of notes are referred to as 'floating-rate notes'. In some cases, 'unsecured notes' may be secured by a charge over shares or other intangible assets. However, such securities cannot be described as 'debentures' in a prospectus because the Corporations Act restricts the use of that term to cases where repayment is secured by a charge over tangible assets. Thus, some debt products may be described as 'unsecured notes' even though they are in fact secured. To avoid this contradiction, some issuers have instead used the term 'bond' to describe debt securities that cannot legally be labelled as debentures.

10.5.6 CORPORATE BONDS

As discussed in the previous section, the term 'bond' may be used as an alternative to 'unsecured note'. In the Australian market, the term 'corporate bond' generally refers to long-term debt securities with coupon payments every 6 months based on a defined rate of interest, issued by non-government entities in amounts of at least $500 000 per investor. Bonds issued on these terms are placed privately, mostly with institutional investors, and are usually not listed on a stock exchange. Some companies, including AMP, Primary Health Care and Tabcorp, have issued long-term debt securities designed to appeal to individual investors. For these 'retail' corporate bond issues, the minimum investment is much smaller (typically $5000), coupon payments may be made quarterly and the securities are listed on the ASX. The covenants used for corporate bonds are usually less restrictive than those in a debenture trust deed.

While Australian banks favour loans and securities with extensive covenant protection, foreign banks will consider debt with few, if any, covenants. This so called 'covenant-light' debt played an important role in the structuring of an attempt by Airline Partners Australia (APA) to acquire and privatise Qantas Airways (see Finance in Action).

FINANCE IN ACTION

APA USES CASH TO REDUCE RISKS IN QANTAS BID

APA, a consortium that included Macquarie Bank and Texas Pacific, offered to pay $13.5 billion for Qantas, financed by about $10 billion of debt and the rest equity. Given that Qantas had net debt of $4.8 billion, its debt would be more than doubled, increasing the expected returns, and risks, for equity holders. The level of debt in leveraged buyout transactions is typically assessed by calculating the ratio of the value of debt to earnings before interest, tax, depreciation and amortisation (EBITDA). The following excerpt outlines an innovative approach used to structure the financing of the proposed Qantas privatisation.

Recent leveraged buyout transactions in Australia have been struck at a debt-to-EBITDA multiple of 7.5 times. Of that, about 6 multiple points is senior debt and the balance subordinated.

Given Qantas has a more volatile earnings profile, leverage in this privatisation is not as high at 6.4 times EBITDA. Applying that typical LBO structure would have resulted in a senior debt level of 5.2 times and the rest subordinated.

The problem is that senior debt comes with myriad covenants that, if breached, can result in the lenders seeking remedial action, even foreclosing. A typical covenant would be that EBITDA-to-interest cover could not fall below a specified level.

If a hiccup occurs the owners can quickly find themselves in a nasty situation. But this is the airline industry and there are always temporary shocks. It's not like the business is in danger of going broke.

So essentially Macquarie had enlisted five banks to try and fit a square peg into a round hole. Morgan Stanley, which was not invited to tender for the debt package, had a strong relationship with Texas Pacific and could see the problem. So it knocked on the door to present an alternative structure—the one ultimately adopted.

Of the $10 billion in debt, half would be in the form of tradeable bonds backed by aircraft leases. The balance is a layer of fixed and floating-rate notes, denominated in different currencies, and finally, subordinated debt. The beauty is that there are no covenants on the bonds, known as enhanced equipment trust certificates. The only requirement is to meet the $900 million in annual interest payments. That's it. It's a far simpler and more suitable financing structure than senior debt.

To ensure interest payments can always be met, APA will keep $2 billion in cash as a buffer. It also has a $950 million credit line 'revolver', which again is free of those annoying covenants.

Rick Schifter of Texas Pacific was so appreciative of the work Morgan Stanley in New York did that he shipped them two cases of Barossa Valley E&E Black Pepper Shiraz 2001. At $70 a pop it's a smoky and dusty, but by all accounts wonderful, drop.

Source: 'Two cases of shiraz for innovative debt structuring', Brett Clegg, *Australian Financial Review*, 15 December 2006.

Statistics on the value of long-term non-government debt securities issued by Australian borrowers are shown in Table 10.7. Panel A shows the securities issued in the Australian domestic market while Panel B covers securities issued in the capital markets of other countries. The issuers of these securities are divided into three categories:

(a) banks, finance companies and other financial institutions
(b) 'non-financial corporations' consisting of industrial and mining companies
(c) issuers of asset-backed securities.

Asset-backed securities are marketable debt securities issued by specialised entities associated with financial institutions, and these securities are backed by non-marketable financial assets such as mortgage

TABLE 10.7 Long-term non-government debt securities outstanding ($ billion)

A Long-term non-government debt securities issued in Australia by Australian borrowers

DATE	BANKS AND OTHER FINANCIAL CORPORATIONS	NON-FINANCIAL CORPORATIONS	ASSET-BACKED	TOTAL
June 2001	23.7	22.8	30.4	76.9
June 2002	26.7	27.5	42.3	96.5
June 2003	28.2	31.8	52.0	111.9
June 2004	34.7	33.2	64.4	132.3
June 2005	48.0	38.8	79.3	166.2
June 2006	64.0	42.3	98.9	205.3
June 2007	78.2	48.3	122.3	248.8
June 2008	99.4	45.4	111.7	256.5
June 2009	134.7	41.4	99.0	275.2
June 2010	171.6	40.6	81.3	293.6

B Long-term non-government debt securities issued offshore by Australian borrowers

DATE	BANKS AND OTHER FINANCIAL CORPORATIONS	NON-FINANCIAL CORPORATIONS	ASSET-BACKED	TOTAL
June 2001	82.5	36.8	28.7	148.0
June 2002	93.0	41.4	33.6	168.1
June 2003	119.4	53.4	42.3	215.1
June 2004	153.1	58.2	61.7	272.9
June 2005	183.5	74.2	65.3	323.0
June 2006	206.3	77.2	72.3	355.7
June 2007	225.3	87.6	100.2	413.1
June 2008	262.8	90.4	68.4	421.5
June 2009	295.9	104.8	58.0	458.7
June 2010	355.9	114.5	35.8	506.2

Source: Table D4, Reserve Bank of Australia website, www.rba.gov.au.

loans and credit card receivables. In the Australian market, most of these issues have been backed by residential mortgages. When asset-backed securities are combined with those issued by banks and other financial corporations, it is clear that most of the corporate bonds issued by Australian borrowers are issued by financial institutions.

The Australian corporate bond market has grown rapidly since 1995 when the value of long-term non-government bonds on issue was about $20 billion. As shown in Table 10.7, the market reached $166 billion during 2005 and $294 billion in June 2010, but as noted above most of the 'corporate' bonds are issued by banks and other financial institutions rather than by non-financial companies. In May 2010, ASIC issued Regulatory Guide 213 *Facilitating debt raising* to encourage the development of the corporate bond market by simplifying the disclosure requirements for 'vanilla' **bonds** to be listed on the ASX and issued to retail investors. Bonds may be described as 'vanilla' if they do not have any unusual or complex terms or conditions. In this case, ASIC defined them as unsubordinated, non-convertible bonds denominated in Australian dollars with a fixed term of 10 years or less and the principal repayable at maturity, issued at the same price to all investors and paying interest on specified dates at either a fixed rate or a floating rate comprising a market indicator rate plus a fixed margin. To facilitate liquidity in the secondary market, an issue must be for at least $50 million but this limit will be reviewed after 2 years.

Provided it meets certain conditions related to disclosure and governance, a listed entity may issue bonds using a 'vanilla bonds prospectus', which is similar to a transaction-specific prospectus. A transaction-specific prospectus does not need to contain all the information that s.710 of the Corporations Act requires in a full prospectus. Rather, it focuses on the terms of the securities being offered for sale and the effect of the offer on the issuing entity. An entity that is entitled to use a vanilla bonds prospectus may issue bonds under a two-part prospectus. A two-part vanilla bonds prospectus consists of a base prospectus, valid for 2 years, which can be used for a number of offers where each offer is accompanied by a second-part prospectus that contains details of that specific offer of bonds.

The first issue of bonds under the simplified disclosure regime was by Primary Health Care Ltd, whose activities include the operation of medical centres and provision of pathology services. On 24 August 2010, the company announced that it had lodged a prospectus to raise approximately $125 million by issuing bonds with a face value of $100 each with a minimum investment of $5000. Interest is payable quarterly at a floating rate based on the 90-day bank bill swap rate, plus a margin of 4 per cent, until the bonds mature on 28 September 2015. The offer opened on 1 September 2010 and was scheduled to close on 24 September 2010. On 27 September the company announced that the offer was complete and had raised $150 million from institutional investors plus $2.3 million from the offers to shareholders, brokers' clients and the public. In summary, the issue was 'successful' but only 1.5 per cent of the bonds was issued to retail investors. Of course, investors may become more familiar with corporate bonds, and the proportion of the Primary Health Care bonds held by retail investors may increase through secondary trading. However, the initial results support the argument that development of an active retail corporate bond market in Australia may require additional measures to lower the costs of issuing bonds and distributing them to investors.

The volume of bonds issued offshore by Australian borrowers is considerably larger than the volume issued onshore and, as shown in Table 10.7, the largest Australian issuers of bonds in offshore markets are financial institutions, of which banks are the largest borrowers. Moreover, the value of financial corporations' bonds on issue in offshore markets is typically at least double the value of their domestic bonds. Issues by non-financial corporations have also grown significantly but are generally less than one-quarter of the total. Issues of asset-backed securities grew rapidly until 2007 but have since declined considerably, reflecting the effects of the global financial crisis on the popularity of securitisation.

Some indication of the reasons for issuing bonds offshore rather than domestically can be obtained by examining the characteristics of issues made by Australian borrowers in the two markets. The main reason appears to be that offshore markets, particularly the US market, have greater capacity to absorb securities of lower credit quality.[17] For both the financial and the non-financial sectors, the credit ratings of Australian domestic bond issues are higher, on average, than those of offshore issues. Issuing bonds in a variety of offshore markets also provides a larger and more diversified funding base, which can be advantageous if markets differ in terms of the costs and availability of funds. Financial intermediaries such as banks are known to prefer a diversified funding base.

bonds
debt securities, issued with a medium or long term to maturity by borrowers such as governments, state authorities and corporations in return for cash from investors

---

17 For a more detailed discussion of this topic see Battellino (2002). Facts and statistics in the next two paragraphs are also drawn from Reserve Bank of Australia (August 2006). See also Black et al. (2010).

foreign bond
bond issued outside the borrower's country and denominated in the currency of the country in which it is issued

Eurobond
medium- to long-term international bearer security sold in countries other than the country of the currency in which the bond is denominated

Other reasons that have been suggested for issuing offshore include differences in term to maturity, amounts borrowed and currency of denomination. However, these do not appear to be major factors. For a sample of domestic and offshore bond issues by Australian banks from 2001 to 2006, the maturities of both types ranged from 3 to 5 years. Larger issues are possible in offshore markets, but in practice domestic and offshore issues tend to be similar in size. For the 2001 to 2006 sample, the average size of a domestic issue by Australian banks was $304 million while the average offshore issue was $356 million.

Most offshore issues are denominated in foreign currency, primarily US dollars with significant issues in euro and yen, but issuers almost invariably hedge against foreign currency risk mainly by swapping the foreign currency back into Australian dollars. Therefore, gaining access to a broader range of investors may be important but exposure to different currencies does not appear to be a motivating factor. Comparisons of the interest cost of domestic bond issues and offshore issues, after allowing for the cost of hedging, show that there is no systematic cost difference between the domestic and offshore markets. Bonds issued by an Australian borrower in a foreign country and denominated in the currency of that country are known as **foreign bonds**. Bonds denominated in US dollars and issued in the US domestic market by offshore borrowers and bonds denominated in yen and issued in Japan by offshore borrowers are both examples of foreign bonds.

Australian companies can also raise funds offshore by issuing Australian dollar **Eurobonds**. Eurobonds are medium- to long-term securities sold in countries other than the country of the currency in which the bond is denominated. An Australian dollar Eurobond is a debt security denominated in Australian dollars but issued outside Australia with a view to attracting non-Australian investors. Further discussion of this avenue for obtaining long-term funds is deferred to Chapter 20.

10.6 PROJECT FINANCE

Project finance is a technique that is commonly used to raise funds for major mining and natural resource projects, infrastructure such as power stations, pipelines and toll roads, tourist resorts and other property developments.[18] It can also be used to fund the acquisition of assets that will be used in large industrial operations. Project finance has been defined as:

> A method of raising long-term debt financing for major projects through 'financial engineering', based on lending against the cash flow generated by the project alone; it depends on a detailed evaluation of a project's construction, operating and revenue risks, and their allocation between investors, lenders and other parties through contractual and other arrangements. (Yescombe 2002, p. 1)

LEARNING OBJECTIVE 10
Identify and explain the main features of project finance

This definition shows that an important feature of project finance loans is that the lenders rely essentially on the cash flows of a single project as the source of the loan repayments. As a result, the financial risk for the originators of the project who provide equity finance is limited. The projects involved are usually large and the loans required can exceed $1 billion. For example, Transurban's City Link toll road project in Melbourne cost $1.7 billion, of which $1.25 billion was provided by lenders. With such large projects it is usual for a syndicate of lenders to provide funds so the credit risk is spread between them.

10.6.1 THE MAIN FEATURES OF PROJECT FINANCE

Each project is unique and there is no such thing as 'standard' project finance, but several features that are common to many project finance transactions can be identified. These include:

- The project is established as a special purpose legal entity whose sole business activity is the project. This entity is the legal owner of the project assets and is the borrower in all project finance loans.

---

18 This section relies heavily on Yescombe (2002), Chapter 2.

- The special purpose entity is usually a company but in some cases a partnership, unit trust or unincorporated joint venture may be used. For simplicity we will refer to this entity as the 'project company'.
- Project finance is usually raised to undertake a new project rather than a business that is already established.
- A high proportion of debt finance is used. In typical cases debt may provide 70 to 90 per cent of the cost of the project. The project sponsors who own equity in the project company provide the balance of the funds.
- The lenders' decision on whether to provide funds is based on the expected cash flows and assets of the project rather than on the assets and financial positions of the project sponsors.
- The debt finance is provided on a limited-recourse basis. This means that the project sponsors provide only limited guarantees in relation to the project debt. Typically, these guarantees allow lenders to claim against the sponsors only until the project is completed. Once the project is completed and operational, the lenders rely entirely on the project's cash flows and assets.
- The main security for lenders is in the form of intangible assets, such as the project company's contracts or rights to natural resources. If the project company's tangible assets have to be sold following default on the debt finance, their market value is likely to be much lower than the outstanding debt.
- Project finance loans are generally for much longer terms than normal corporate loans. However, the life of a project is finite so the loans must be repaid by the end of that life. In contrast, lenders that provide corporate loans are concerned to see that the company has the capacity to pay interest on the loan but will assume that the company's debt is likely to be rolled over when it matures.

10.6.2 WHEN IS PROJECT FINANCE ATTRACTIVE?

In addition to the usual features of project finance outlined above, the assessment and management of risk is a vital part of any project finance transaction. As well as being confident that the project is technically sound, lenders must be confident that the project can be completed within the budgeted capital cost and that its operation will generate sufficient cash flows to service their debt. It follows that lenders need to evaluate carefully the terms of any project contracts that may affect its construction and operating costs. They also need to ensure that, wherever possible, project risks are controlled by allocating them to parties other than the project company. For example, if the project involves construction and operation of a power station, the lenders may require that a government authority guarantees to purchase all of the output.

The process of evaluating risks and negotiating suitable contracts can be slow, complex and costly, so the margin that lenders charge over their cost of funds can be considerably higher than for normal corporate loans. Therefore, any suggestion that project finance loans are 'cheap debt' is false. Despite the higher cost of debt, project finance can be viable in cases where the operating cash flows are relatively predictable so the low risk of the project allows a high proportion of debt to be used. High financial leverage can gear the rate of return on equity to an attractive level, while the limited recourse nature of project debt enables the risk exposure of equity investors to be minimised. It is common for the original debt to be refinanced when the project reaches completion and many of the original risks have been resolved. In some cases, refinancing prior to completion can achieve significant savings in interest costs (see Finance in Action, overleaf).

FINANCE IN ACTION

REFINANCING OF CONNECTEAST'S DEBT FACILITIES

ConnectEast Group is expected to announce a refinancing of its $2.1 billion debt facilities today amid speculation that the group, owner of the Eastlink toll road, is up to a year ahead of schedule on the construction timetable.

The deal has improved the terms of the group's financing on the project in south-east Melbourne. Interest on debt during the construction phase is set to fall by 40 basis points to 110 basis points.[a] It will remain at this level for the first two years of operations once the road has opened. It had been set to increase to 165 basis points during this period.

This is set to save 1.3 cents a unit each year, which will be available to support distributions. This amount represents 20 per cent of the 6.5 cents in distributions paid by the group for the year to June 30. The refinancing is the first of its kind on a greenfields toll road project in Australia and involved a consortium of seven banks.

[a] In this article, the interest on debt is expressed as a margin over a benchmark rate such as the bank-bill swap rate.

Source: 'ConnectEast may refinance debt facilities', Henry Byrne, *Australian Financial Review*, 21 December 2006, p. 36.

In summary, project finance does not allow projects that should be rejected as uneconomic to become viable through 'financial magic'. However, through the use of measures such as joint ventures to spread risk and careful contracting to allocate risks to parties who are best placed to bear them, major projects that would be difficult for any single company to implement can often go ahead.

10.7 INTEREST RATE SWAPS

LEARNING OBJECTIVE 11
Understand the role of interest rate swaps in managing debt

An interest rate swap is an agreement that enables a floating-rate borrower to convert the loan to a fixed-rate loan. This mechanism has become the most common way in which Australian companies raise long-term debt at a fixed interest rate.[19] A swap is an arrangement between two or more parties to exchange a set of cash flows over a specified period of time. No exchange of principal is involved—only interest payments are exchanged—but these payments relate to a notional principal amount. The parties that agree to the swap are known as counterparties. The first interest rate swap occurred in the early 1980s, and since then the volume of interest rate swaps has grown rapidly. Figures prepared for the Australian Financial Markets Association indicate that the turnover of interest rate swaps and cross-currency swaps in the Australian market in 2009–10 was $5923 billion, of which $4646 billion, or 78 per cent, was interest rate swaps (Australian Financial Markets Association 2010, **www.afma.com.au**).

In a fixed-for-floating interest rate swap, Counterparty A makes a series of payments to Counterparty B that are based on the future course of interest rates. For example, each quarter for the next four quarters, A may pay B an amount calculated according to that quarter's 90-day bank-bill rate. Thus, each quarter, a different interest rate will be used to calculate this payment. In return, B agrees to pay A an amount each quarter that is calculated on the basis of a fixed interest rate agreed to today. Thus, each quarter the same interest rate will be used to calculate this payment. The amounts payable will depend on the notional principal involved (say, $10 million) and, in practice, instead of A paying B and B paying A, only the net amount is paid each quarter. Note that no exchange of principal is involved; only interest flows are exchanged. These features are illustrated in Example 10.4.

---

19 For a more detailed discussion of swap markets, see Montague (1997) or Hunt and Terry (2008, Chapter 13).

EXAMPLE 10.4

On 1 April 2012, counterparties A and B enter into an interest rate swap. The notional principal is $10 million and cash flows are to occur quarterly, in arrears, for 1 year. Counterparty A agrees to pay B floating-rate payments based on the bank-bill rate. Counterparty B agrees to pay A fixed-rate payments at 9 per cent per annum. A year later the agreement has ended and A's financial manager calls for a report on the cash flows that were made in the swap. On 1 April 2012, when the swap was entered into, the bank-bill rate was 7.60 per cent per annum. Subsequently, on the following dates it was:

1 July 2012	8.70 per cent
1 October 2012	9.35 per cent
1 January 2013	9.25 per cent.

The report could take the form shown in Table 10.8.

TABLE 10.8 Company A: report on interest rate swap

DATE	DAYS IN PERIOD ENDED	BANK-BILL RATE (% P.A.)	FLOATING-RATE SWAP PAYMENT (A PAYS B)	FIXED-RATE SWAP PAYMENT (B PAYS A)	SWAP PAYMENT MADE
1 April 2012	—	7.60	—	—	—
1 July 2012	91	8.70	(0.076)(91/365)($10m) = $189 479.45	(0.09)(91/365)($10m) = $224 383.56	$34 904.11 (B paid A)
1 October 2012	92	9.35	(0.0870)(92/365)($10m) = $219 287.67	(0.09)(92/365)($10m) = $226 849.32	$7 561.65 (B paid A)
1 January 2013	92	9.25	(0.0935)(92/365)($10m) = $235 671.24	(0.09)(92/365)($10m) = $226 849.32	$8 821.92 (A paid B)
1 April 2013	90	—	(0.0925)(90/365)($10m) = $228 082.19	(0.09)(90/365)($10m) = $221 917.81	$6 164.38 (A paid B)

As shown in Table 10.8, each quarter a swap payment was made with interest calculated in arrears. When the bank-bill rate exceeded the fixed rate of 9 per cent, A paid B; when the bank-bill rate was less than 9 per cent, B paid A.

While Example 10.4 sets out the mechanics of an interest rate swap, it does not make clear the motivations for such transactions. Australian companies have largely used interest rate swaps to exchange floating interest rate obligations for long-term fixed interest rate obligations. This typically involves the company first borrowing from a bank on a floating interest rate basis. For example, it may negotiate a continuing bill facility with a bank where the bank agrees to provide the company with a loan (say, $1 million) over a specified period (say, 5 years) with interest payments calculated at a floating rate (say, 2 per cent above the bank-bill rate).

Suppose that the company really wants a $1 million 5-year loan at a *fixed interest rate*, similar to that which it could obtain by issuing debentures. To achieve this it enters into an interest rate swap under which it receives floating-rate cash flows (thus offsetting its floating-rate payments to the bank) and pays fixed-rate cash flows. Fortunately, there are investment banks willing to be counterparties in such swap arrangements, hence indirectly providing Australian companies with the fixed-rate borrowings that many of them require.

This is perhaps the most attractive feature of the swaps market to many companies. It enables them to borrow fixed-rate funds that otherwise would not be available and/or would be available only at higher interest rates. The main reason for this is that many companies are assessed by institutional lenders as being too risky to lend to on a long-term fixed interest rate basis. However, the banks are willing to lend to them at a floating interest rate. It is an easy process to swap this floating rate for a fixed rate as the other party to the swap is taking on very limited risk exposure. The potential cost savings associated with using swap arrangements are illustrated in Example 10.5.

EXAMPLE 10.5

Assume that the floating-rate and fixed-rate borrowing costs in Table 10.9 apply to a company with a BBB credit rating and a commercial bank with a AA credit rating.

TABLE 10.9 Interest rates for Example 10.5

	INTEREST RATE	
	FLOATING RATE (%)[a]	**FIXED RATE (%)**
Company (BBB)	Bank-bill rate + 1.0	10
Bank (AA)	Bank-bill rate + 0.5	8
Difference in rates	0.5	2

[a] The floating rates are based on the yield on bank bills, plus a margin.

Compared with the company, the bank faces lower interest rates for both fixed-rate and floating-rate borrowings. However, the bank has a relatively greater advantage in the fixed-rate market than in the floating-rate market: its borrowings are 2 per cent cheaper in the fixed-rate market, but only 0.5 per cent cheaper in the floating-rate market. Despite the fact that the bank has an absolute cost advantage in both markets, both the bank and the company can gain if they enter into an interest-rate swap agreement.[20] Under this agreement, the bank will borrow funds at a fixed interest rate of 8 per cent, while the company will borrow funds at a floating interest rate, which is 1 per cent above the bank-bill rate. Under the swap agreement the bank makes floating-rate payments to the company, while the company makes fixed-rate payments to the bank. These 'swap payments' can be set at levels that produce a net saving of interest costs for both parties.

A possible explanation for how and why this is possible is given below. Suppose that the company paid the bank at a fixed rate of 8 per cent, and the bank paid the company at a floating rate of the bank-bill rate plus 1 per cent. This is equivalent to a straight swap of debt and the net costs are a fixed rate of 8 per cent for the company and a variable rate of the bank-bill rate plus 1 per cent for the bank. This would save the company 2 per cent (since its 'direct' fixed rate is 10 per cent) but would cost the bank 0.5 per cent (since its 'direct' floating rate is the bank-bill rate plus 0.5 per cent). The total savings available are therefore 2 per cent minus 0.5 per cent = 1.5 per cent.

Of course the bank would not agree to these swap payments but the calculations show that a total saving of 1.5 per cent is achievable. The only thing wrong with the straight swap is that the division of this saving between the two parties is unequal; in fact, it is so unequal that the bank would lose. To make the swap attractive to both parties requires that more of the total saving available flows to the bank. This can be achieved by requiring the company to make higher swap payments to the bank and/or requiring the bank to make lower swap payments to the company. Adopting the first solution, suppose that the company's swap payments to the bank are set at 9.2 per cent. The resulting costs and savings are shown in Table 10.10.

---

20 Note that in the same way that banks do not generally 'link together' particular borrowers and depositors, they do not necessarily link together particular swap partners.

TABLE 10.10 Interest rate swaps and borrowing costs

	BORROWING INTEREST RATE	+	INTEREST RATE SWAP PAYMENTS	−	INTEREST RATE SWAP RECEIPT	=	NET BORROWING COST	COST SAVING
Company	Bank bill + 1%	+	9.2%	−	Bank bill +1%	=	9.2%	0.8%
Bank	8%	+	Bank bill +1%	−	9.2%	=	Bank bill −0.2%	0.7%
Total saving								1.5%

The swap results in a saving of 0.8 per cent for the company because had it borrowed 'directly' at a fixed rate of interest it would have had to pay 10 per cent. The bank borrows from the public at a fixed rate of interest of 8 per cent, while it has to make payments to the company at a rate that is 1 per cent above the ruling bank-bill rate, but it receives 9.2 per cent from the company. The interest rate swap therefore reduces the bank's borrowing costs to 0.2 per cent below the yield on bank bills, which is a saving of 0.7 per cent compared with the 'direct' floating-rate borrowing. Therefore, as a result of the swap transaction, the 1.5 per cent cost saving is divided fairly evenly between the two parties.[21]

The explanation for the interest rate swap given in Example 10.5 is based on the argument that each party to the swap has a comparative advantage in the market in which it borrows—that is, by borrowing in the market in which each has a comparative advantage and by swapping their interest payments, both of the parties achieve a lower cost of borrowing than could be achieved without the swap. This could arise if the fixed- and floating-rate debt markets were segmented, which could occur if the lenders in the two markets were different groups of individuals and institutions (Viney 2009, pp. 726–27). However, while the comparative advantage explanation is appealing, it is unlikely that such cost-saving opportunities could be sustained over successive swap transactions. This is because arbitrage would be expected to eliminate any such cost-saving opportunities. There are other explanations for the availability of these cost-saving opportunities, including the idea that swaps enable companies to engage in tax and regulatory arbitrage.[22]

The form of swap arrangement described above is a simple arrangement. Variations include providing an option to reverse the swap where a specified event occurs, such as where the bank-bill rate rises above a certain level. Another form of interest rate swap involves a cross-currency transaction. For example, a company may swap an Australian dollar loan for a US dollar loan. Of course, this will involve a currency risk but it is possible to obtain cover for the currency risk, which may still make it cheaper to borrow using a cross-currency swap. A discussion of how a currency exposure might be hedged is contained in Chapter 20.

In contrast to the market for debentures, the swap market offers a high level of liquidity. As a result, a swap counterparty can, in effect, reverse its commitment, simply by entering into a further swap. Often the new counterparty takes over the obligations of the existing counterparty. A highly liquid swap market benefits both borrowers and lenders. For example, a borrower can use swaps to try to keep its interest costs down by paying on a floating-rate basis when interest rates fall, and on a fixed-rate basis when interest rates rise.

---

21 This example makes clear a possible motivation for swaps. However, note that, in practice, swaps are now standardised in format so that the variable rate flow is always based on the bill rate, while the fixed rate is determined by market forces.
22 The explanations for the growth in interest rate swaps are considered in more detail in Smithson (1998).

A further advantage of having a swaps market relates to credit assessment. Before a bank makes a floating-rate loan, it assesses the credit-worthiness of the borrower. On the basis of this assessment it may advance the loan principal to the borrower. If, subsequently, the borrower enters into an interest rate swap, the swap counterparty in effect converts this to a fixed-rate loan. However, the principal of the loan is undisturbed: only the interest-rate basis has changed. In effect, where the equivalent of a fixed-rate loan is created via an interest rate swap, its 'fixed-rate' feature is provided by the swap counterparty but the 'loan' itself stays with the original floating-rate lender. Typically the original lender is a bank. Thus, interest rate swaps allow the important task of credit assessment to remain largely in the hands of the banks, which are usually seen as having more experience and better access to information than many other potential lenders.

10.8 HYBRIDS OF DEBT AND EQUITY FINANCE

In this section we consider securities that have characteristics common to both debt and equity and are therefore regarded as hybrids of debt and equity. Australia has an active market in hybrid securities. At the end of June 2010, hybrids listed on the ASX had a market capitalisation of almost $16 billion (Australian Financial Markets Association 2010). Some hybrids are complex but most are based on a convertible note or on a preference share. Because convertible notes are simpler, they are discussed first, followed by preference shares. The section concludes with a discussion of developments in the design of hybrids.

LEARNING OBJECTIVE 12
Identify and explain the features of securities that have the characteristics of both debt and equity

10.8.1 CONVERTIBLE NOTES

A convertible note is usually unsecured debt that is issued for a fixed term at a fixed rate of interest, with the additional feature that the holder has the right to convert the note to an ordinary share at certain specified dates.

In effect, the purchaser of a convertible note acquires a fixed interest security plus an option to purchase ordinary shares in the company at a specified price. As a result, note holders gain from an increase in the company's share price. Assume that a company issues 10-year, 8 per cent, convertible notes with a face value of $10 that at maturity can be converted to shares at a conversion ratio of one to one. The note holder will convert if the price of the company's shares at the note's maturity is above $10. For example, if the share price is $11, the holder will make a gain of $1 per note by converting, rather than allowing the notes to be redeemed. It is usual for convertible note holders to be able to participate in new issues, such as rights issues and bonus issues, in the same ratio as if the notes had already been converted. It is also usual for the holders to be given the opportunity by the issuer to convert the notes into shares immediately, if there is a takeover offer for the issuing company.

Investors accept lower interest rates on convertible notes than they do on unsecured notes because the option inherent in convertible notes is valuable. The conversion price can be set at an amount that is greater than the current market price of the company's shares because the option to convert will have a value, provided that there is some chance that the share price may eventually exceed the conversion price.

Convertible notes typically have terms of up to 10 years, which make them attractive to issuers requiring long-term, fixed-rate debt finance. Because the convertible notes are unsecured they can be issued by companies whose existing assets are pledged as security for other loans. As a long-term security, convertible notes are a natural investment for life insurance companies and superannuation funds, which have long-term liabilities.

Convertible notes can be issued to existing shareholders or by a placement to institutions. Placements of convertible notes by listed companies are restricted under ASX listing rule 7.1, the '15 per cent rule', which provides that issues of 'equity securities' without shareholder approval are restricted to no more than 15 per cent of a company's issued ordinary shares in any 12-month period. Since convertible notes are convertible into ordinary shares, they are defined as equity securities by the ASX. In September 2010, a total of 20 issues of convertible notes were listed on the ASX.

Some Australian companies have issued convertible notes on offshore markets, in which case they may be described as 'convertible bonds'. The convertible note framework allows scope for innovative security design, and some issues by Australian companies have been undated and/or subordinated. Undated notes can usually be converted to ordinary shares at any time during a specified period, which may be several years. If a holder does not exercise the right of conversion by the final date, the notes become irredeemable or 'perpetual' debt. Therefore, such notes will generally be treated as equity for the purpose of calculating balance sheet ratios used in loan agreements, but can be designed so that they will be treated as debt for tax purposes.

Why do companies issue convertible notes?

Convertible notes may appear to be 'cheap' debt—the interest rates on convertible debt securities are lower than for straight debt, while they also allow companies to issue shares 'at a premium' over the current price. For example, a company that could borrow at an interest rate of 8 per cent may issue 5-year convertible notes with a coupon rate of 6 per cent and a face value of $10 that are convertible into ordinary shares on a 1-for-1 basis when its share price is $9. A moment's reflection should show that there must be something wrong with this suggested explanation. If convertible notes really offer 'cheap finance', they should be much more popular than they are. In a competitive market, convertible notes should be issued on terms that are fair for both investors and issuers. In fact, of course, the interest rate on a convertible debt will be lower than on otherwise equivalent debt because it also provides an option to convert the security into shares. This option is valuable; its value is reflected in the lenders requiring a lower interest rate than they would on ordinary debt.

There is evidence from the US that the price of a company's ordinary shares falls, on average, by about 2 per cent when an issue of convertible notes is announced.[23] However, for companies with certain characteristics the price response is less negative and in some cases positive. An explanation that is consistent with the evidence is that convertible notes can be suitable for companies with high growth potential that are likely to find both conventional debt and equity financing very costly. Suppose that a young company is developing products that rely on new technology. The company has high growth potential but its net operating cash flows are currently negative and its assets are mostly intangible. Under those conditions, raising new debt finance is not attractive. If the company is able to borrow, debt will be costly due to the company's high-risk, short track record and limited debt capacity. Its management may also be reluctant to raise funds by issuing more ordinary shares because they may be concerned that the current share price does not accurately reflect the company's growth prospects.

For a company in that situation, issuing convertible notes may be more attractive than issuing either straight debt or ordinary shares. One advantage of convertible notes is that the lower interest rate reduces the issuer's cash payments to lenders and so reduces the probability of getting into financial difficulty. In turn, this means that raising finance by issuing convertible notes can reduce the probability that levered companies will be forced to forgo valuable investment opportunities.[24] Research by Jen, Choi and Lee (1997) supports this argument. Their study found that the market reacts

---

23 Jen, Choi and Lee (1997) report that the average market announcement response is approximately −2 per cent based on several studies published between 1984 and 1992.

24 A second explanation for the use of convertible securities is related to the conflicts of interest between lenders and shareholders discussed in Section 12.7.1. Borrowing more and taking on riskier projects can transfer wealth from lenders to shareholders. If the debt held by lenders is convertible, this conflict should be minimised because lenders can exercise the conversion option and become shareholders.

more favourably to announcements of convertible issues by companies with high capital expenditures and high market-to-book ratios—that is, high-growth companies—but with low credit ratings and high financial leverage.

10.8.2 PREFERENCE SHARES

A **preference share** is a security that gives the holders preference over ordinary shareholders with respect to the payment of dividends, and usually with respect to capital repayment in the event of the company's liquidation. As a result, dividends cannot be paid to ordinary shareholders until preference dividends have been paid. In many instances the dividend is fixed for the life of the preference share. The dividends on preference shares may be franked or the terms of the issue may specify that all dividends will be unfranked. The franking of dividends is discussed in Chapter 11. With respect to capital repayment, the preference shareholders may be entitled to full repayment of the amount subscribed before any payment is made to ordinary shareholders, but they will rank after lenders and other creditors.

Both the Corporations Act and the Australian Securities Exchange's Listing Rules require that the rights of preference shareholders be stated fully in the company's Constitution. Therefore, a company that issues preference shares must abide by the provisions specified in its Constitution with respect to those shares. Preference shares may have various characteristics, including the following:

Cumulative or non-cumulative

A company that issues cumulative preference shares is required to pay any accumulated preference dividends before a distribution may be made to ordinary shareholders. For example, if a company that has issued 1 million 10 per cent preference shares at an issue price of $1 fails to pay preference dividends for 2 years, it has accumulated an obligation to pay $200 000 in preference dividends. Non-cumulative preference shares do not oblige the company to pay any past accumulation of unpaid preference dividends.

Redeemable or irredeemable

Unless they are specifically referred to as 'redeemable', 'converting' or 'convertible', preference shares are irredeemable, which means that, like ordinary shares, they are intended to be perpetual and have no maturity date. **Redeemable preference shares** are issued with a specified maturity (redemption) date and are therefore similar to debt. The amount that is repayable on the redemption date will be specified when the shares are issued and is not necessarily equal to the amount originally subscribed by investors.

Converting, convertible or exchangeable

A **converting preference share** automatically converts to ordinary shares at some specified time in the future. A **convertible preference share** can be converted to ordinary shares at the option of the holder. An **exchangeable preference share** is similar to a convertible preference share but differs in that it can be 'converted to' (exchanged for) a security issued by a subsidiary or affiliate of the original issuer.

Participating or non-participating

If the company grants preference shareholders the right to participate in the distribution of profit available to ordinary shareholders, preference shareholders may be entitled to a return in excess of the stated preference dividend rate. For example, a company may issue participating preference shares, which allow the holders to share in any profit earned in excess of a certain amount. As a result, preference

---

preference shares
shares that rank before ordinary shares for the payment of dividends and in the event of liquidation of the issuing company. They often provide an entitlement to a fixed dividend

redeemable preference share
a preference share that can be repurchased by the issuing company on a specified maturity date

converting preference share
a preference share that will automatically convert into an ordinary share on a specified date unless it is redeemed by the issuer prior to that date

convertible preference share
a preference share that may be converted at the option of the holder into an ordinary share

exchangeable preference share
a preference share that may be exchanged for a security issued by a subsidiary or affiliate of the issuer

shareholders can obtain a dividend in excess of the preference dividend rate if the company has a very profitable year. A non-participating preference shareholder is not entitled to a dividend in excess of the stated dividend rate.

Voting or non-voting

Holders of preference shares usually have voting rights but these rights are restricted compared with those of ordinary shareholders. For example, they would be able to vote at any meetings of preference shareholders but not at general meetings of shareholders, unless payments of preference dividends are in arrears or there is a proposal to wind up the company.

Classification as debt or equity

As noted earlier, preference shares are often regarded as hybrids of debt and equity. However, for tax and accounting purposes it is usually necessary to classify each financial instrument as either debt or equity. Traditionally, the classification of individual financial instruments as either debt or equity has been based on their legal form. However, new tests for defining the borderline between debt and equity for tax purposes were introduced in the *New Business Tax System (Debt and Equity) Act 2001*. The new rules classify an interest in a company as equity or debt according to the economic substance of the rights and obligations of the parties to a financing arrangement, rather than its legal form.

Essentially, an interest in a company that provides 'contingent returns'—that is, where the returns depend on the economic performance of the company—will generally be treated as equity for tax purposes, whereas an interest that provides 'non-contingent returns' will generally be treated as debt, provided that the value of the returns is at least equal to the issue price. Under these rules, preference shares may be either debt or equity depending on their individual characteristics. For example, preference shares that are redeemable at the issue price will be classified as debt, whereas perpetual non-cumulative preference shares will be classified as equity because the issuer is not required to repay the capital invested and payment of dividends is contingent on the solvency of the issuer. Similarly, converting preference shares will generally be considered equity before conversion but if the contingent component of the returns is negligible they may be considered as debt. If a particular preference share is classified as debt, the 'dividends' paid to holders will be treated in the same way as interest payments for tax purposes. Therefore, the payments will be deductible for the issuer and fully taxable for the investor. Conversely, if the share is classified as equity, the dividends will, like dividends on ordinary shares, be non-deductible but can be franked, in which case they will provide tax credits that can be used by resident shareholders.

Why do companies issue preference shares?

When the properties of preference shares are compared with those of ordinary shares and debt, three advantages can be identified.[25] First, like debt, preference shares can be non-voting, so issuing preference shares allows a company to raise capital without affecting the control of ordinary shareholders. Second, unlike lenders, preference shareholders cannot force a company into liquidation, so the advantage is that issuing preference shares does not cause the same increase in the risk of corporate failure that would occur with greater borrowing. Third, preference shares are much easier to value than ordinary shares because they usually pay a fixed dividend and interest rates on debt are readily observable. Thus, new investors who are not well informed about a company's financial situation and its prospects may be prepared to buy preference shares even though they would be reluctant to buy ordinary shares issued by the same company.

---

25 The three advantages of preference shares outlined here are discussed in more detail in Baskin and Miranti (1997). In addition to these advantages, the tax treatment of preference shares can also be a significant factor.

10.8.3 DEVELOPMENTS IN THE DESIGN OF HYBRID SECURITIES

Given the range of possible characteristics, preference shares provide considerable scope for innovative security design. Traditionally, most preference share issues were cumulative, irredeemable and non-participating and usually paid a fixed dividend. However, factors such as changes in taxation rules and the classification of preference shares as debt or equity have influenced the development of different types of shares. One innovation was the development of converting preference shares, which became popular during the 1990s.

Converting preference shares

Converting securities automatically change from one form of security to another at a particular date. For example, some companies have issued converting preference shares, which change automatically from a preference share to an ordinary share.

A converting preference share offers a promised dividend prior to a specified conversion date, at which time the preference shares automatically convert to ordinary shares in the company.[26] Since the conversion to ordinary shares is automatic, these converting shares differ from convertible shares, where the holder can exercise a choice. The conversion date for such shares is typically 5 to 10 years from the date of issue, with the issuer often having the option to enforce early conversion. The number of ordinary shares received by the holder of each converting preference share is known as the **conversion ratio**, which may be fixed at the time the shares are issued. For example, each preference share may convert into one ordinary share. Alternatively, the conversion ratio may be expressed in terms of the price of the ordinary shares at the time of the conversion. This conversion mechanism ensures that the holder receives at least a minimum number of ordinary shares at the date of conversion. This minimum number of ordinary shares is usually set so that the value of the ordinary shares received is at least equal to the issue price of the hybrid. The effect of arranging the conversion in this way is shown in Example 10.6.

conversion ratio
relationship that determines how many ordinary shares will be received in exchange for each convertible or converting security when the conversion occurs

EXAMPLE 10.6

In October 2011, ABC Ltd issued converting preference shares with a face value of $20, which convert to ordinary shares on 30 October 2016. At the date of the issue, the market price of ABC ordinary shares was $7.50. The terms of the issue provide that the conversion ratio will be determined by dividing $20 by:

(a) an amount equal to the price of ABC's ordinary shares on 30 October 2016, less 10 per cent; or
(b) $20, whichever yields the greater number of shares.

What is the conversion ratio and the value of the ordinary shares received in exchange for each converting preference share, if the ordinary share price on 30 October 2016 is:

(i) $8.23?
(ii) $17.78?
(iii) $22.22?
(iv) $25?

SOLUTION

(i) The amount specified in (a) above is equal to $8.23 × 0.9 = $7.407, so the conversion ratio will be:
$$\frac{\$20}{\$7.407} = 2.7$$
The value of the ordinary shares received is 2.7 × $8.23 = $22.22.

(ii) The amount specified in (a) above is equal to $17.78 × 0.9 = $16, so the conversion ratio will be
$$\frac{\$20}{\$16} = 1.25$$
The value of the ordinary shares received is 1.25 × $17.78 = $22.22.

---

[26] For a detailed discussion of converting preference shares and factors motivating their use, see Davis (1996).

(iii) The amount specified in (a) above is equal to $22.22 × 0.9 = $20. In this case, both (a) and (b) give the same result—a conversion ratio of 1. Therefore, the value of the ordinary shares received is again $22.22.

(iv) Since the ordinary share price is greater than $22.22, (b) will give a higher conversion ratio, which will again be equal to 1. Therefore, the value of the ordinary shares received is $25.

In summary, the results show that for *any* ordinary share price up to $22.22, each preference share will convert to ordinary shares *worth* $22.22. Given the ordinary share price at the time of the issue ($7.50), this is by far the most likely outcome.

Alternatively, if the ordinary share price is greater than $22.22, each preference share will convert to one ordinary share worth, perhaps, $25. Therefore, the holder of each preference share is assured of receiving ordinary shares, worth *at least* $22.22 at the time of conversion. While it is possible that the shares received will be worth *more than* $22.22, the probability of this outcome is very low.

While converting preference shares are legally equity, Example 10.6 shows that they are financially very similar to debt. Investors receive a fixed dividend during the life of the security and the conversion terms provide the same type of capital protection as a bond.

During the 1990s, several Australian companies issued converting preference shares of the type illustrated in Example 10.6. Of course, those shares disappeared as they reached their conversion dates and later issues of preference shares have generally been of different types such as *reset preference shares* and then *step-up preference shares*. Before discussing these types of preference shares, it should be noted that the term 'converting preference share' (CPS) is also used to refer to hybrid securities where eventual conversion to ordinary shares is not mandatory but is the most likely of several possible outcomes. Securities of this type have been issued by banks and are designed to qualify for inclusion in the bank's Tier 1 capital. These hybrids may be legally a preference share or they may be structured as a stapled security. For example, in August 2009, the Commonwealth Bank of Australia (CBA) announced a $900 million issue of Perpetual Exchangeable Resaleable Listed Securities (PERLS V), which are stapled securities comprising an unsecured note and a preference share with a face value of $200 each. While the securities are technically perpetual it is expected that they will be exchanged on 31 October 2014 by one of three possible methods. First, the CBA may arrange a resale of the securities where the purchaser will acquire all PERLS V at the face value of $200 each. Second, if a resale does not occur, PERLS V will convert into ordinary CBA shares worth approximately $202.02, provided the conversion conditions are satisfied. The main such condition is that the market price of CBA ordinary shares at the conversion date must be equal to at least 56 per cent of the market price at the issue date. If a conversion condition is not satisfied on that date, then conversion may take place on the next distribution payment date on which the conversion conditions are satisfied. Finally, if resale and conversion have not occurred, the CBA may elect to repurchase all PERLS V at face value. Other banks to issue CPS that are similar to PERLS V include the ANZ Banking Group, the Bank of Queensland and Westpac Banking Corporation.

Reset preference shares

Several companies, including banks and other financial institutions, have issued **reset preference shares** that were, at the time, classified as equity. Reset preference shares have no fixed repayment date and an initial dividend entitlement that may be a fixed rate or it may be specified as a margin over a benchmark rate such as the 90-day bank bill swap rate. The initial dividend applies for a specified period, typically 5 years. At the end of that period, the shares are usually re-marketed, with possible outcomes generally including redemption, conversion to ordinary shares or the setting of a new dividend rate. In summary, reset preference shares provide issuers with a debt-like, essentially fixed, cost source of funds, for several years. If they are

reset preference share
a preference share where the dividend rate can be varied at specified intervals

not redeemed or converted to ordinary shares at the reset date, the reset mechanism should ensure that the subsequent dividend rate is in line with current interest rates.

Under International Financial Reporting Standards (IFRS) that were adopted in Australia in 2005, reset preference shares that had been classified as equity were reclassified as debt. This change was followed by an increase in the popularity of perpetual step-up preference shares, which, under IFRS, can be classified as equity in a company's statement of financial position.

Step-up preference shares

> **step-up preference share**
> a preference share where the dividend rate is reset at a higher rate on a specified date unless the securities have been re-marketed, redeemed or converted

The name used to identify issues of **step-up preference shares** (SPS) will differ between issuers, but most issues have essentially the same main features. SPS have no fixed repayment date and pay distributions based on a floating rate, usually set at a margin over a benchmark interest rate until a specified step-up date. When that date is reached, the issuer has the right to choose between two or more alternatives. These can include:

- re-marketing the securities to establish a new margin and to adjust certain other terms of the securities
- redeeming the securities at face value
- converting the securities into ordinary shares.

Following the step-up date, if the securities have not been successfully re-marketed, redeemed or converted, the distribution will be automatically increased (stepped up) to a higher margin. SPS rank before ordinary shares, but after creditors and other preference shares for the payment of distributions and for payments in a winding up of the issuer.

In February 2006, chemicals and mining services company Orica Ltd announced that it planned to raise $500 million by an issue of SPS. The issue was regarded as innovative, being the first hybrid issue in Australia to be assigned an 'intermediate equity' content by ratings agency Standard & Poor's. When designing a hybrid security, the issuer and its advisers need to determine its characteristics to achieve the desired accounting and tax treatment, satisfy the needs of investors and, if the security is to be rated, meet the requirements of the ratings agencies. The Orica SPS issue shows that these multiple aims can result in a security that is quite complex. The features of the Orica SPS are detailed in a 30-page appendix in the prospectus but the main ones are:

> **stapled securities**
> two or more legally separate instruments, typically an ordinary share plus units in one or more related trusts, which cannot be traded separately

- **stapled securities** with a face value of $100, comprising a fully paid preference share and a fully paid unsecured note
- distributions are discretionary, unfranked, semi-annual, floating rate and non-cumulative
- the distribution rate is equal to the 180-day bank bill swap rate (BBSW) plus a margin determined by a book-build
- no fixed repayment date
- following 30 November 2011, if Orica has not reset the margin through a successful re-marketing process, repurchased or converted the SPS, Orica will increase the margin by 2.25 per cent
- the SPS have an investment grade credit rating of BBB– from Standard & Poor's
- an additional 1 per cent will be added to the distribution rate during any period that the credit rating falls below BBB–.

Despite criticisms from some analysts that these terms exposed investors to considerable risks, the issue was oversubscribed and the book-build resulted in an initial margin of 1.35 per cent. SPS have become the most common type of hybrid security in the Australian market and investors usually expect that they will be redeemed at the step-up date, particularly if the issuer is an entity that is likely to raise funds in this way again and wishes to maintain a favourable reputation. If the cost of raising funds is unexpectedly high, the issuer may choose to pay the stepped-up rate rather than redeeming its SPS. In that case, the issuer is not locked in to paying the higher rate in perpetuity because it can redeem the shares on any future distribution date.

Hybrid securities and credit ratings[27]

Issuers of hybrid securities are usually interested in how the securities will be treated by credit ratings agencies. Financial ratios are important in the ratings process and measures such as interest cover, leverage and cash flow-to-debt can vary depending on how a hybrid security is treated. Standard & Poor's groups hybrids into three categories depending on whether the security's equity content is assessed as minimal, intermediate or high. Hybrids categorised as having minimal equity content are treated as debt in ratio calculations, while those with a high equity content are treated as equity in these calculations. For hybrids in the intermediate equity category, half of each period's distribution is treated as a dividend and half as interest. Similarly, half of the outstanding principal is allocated to equity and half to debt.[28]

In assessing the equity content of a hybrid security that is convertible into ordinary shares, Standard & Poor's considers two factors:

- how predictable is the conversion
- how soon will it occur.

The likelihood of conversion to equity will vary with the type of security and its features, including covenants. Consider a security that can be redeemed for cash or converted into ordinary shares of equivalent value at the option of the issuer. No equity credit would be given for this security because the rating analyst would be concerned that the security is unlikely to result in a permanent increase in the company's equity. This is because managers are rarely satisfied that the market price of their company's shares is adequate, so they are more likely to choose redemption rather than conversion. Even if the conversion to shares is mandatory, managers who are unwilling to issue shares at the market price could simply implement a share buy-back for the same number of shares.

The outcome can be influenced by covenants such as one that calls for automatic conversion to shares when a trigger event occurs—such as a rating downgrade. Inclusion of this covenant is an equity feature because it ensures that debt will be eliminated at a time when the company might find the debt difficult to service. Ratings agencies give the most favourable treatment to securities where conversion to equity is mandatory at a fixed time and at a fixed price. In these cases, conversion is certain and the issue price of the ordinary shares is effectively locked in at the time the hybrid is issued. Therefore, there is no opportunity for managers to reconsider the decision regardless of any change in the share price.

The basic issue for the ratings agencies is whether issuing a hybrid security has improved the issuer's credit quality and expanded its debt capacity. In making this assessment they focus on the economic impact of the hybrid issue, not on its classification for other purposes. Accordingly, it is possible that a hybrid that is classed as debt for tax, accounting or regulatory purposes may be viewed as equity for rating purposes, and vice versa.

---

27 This discussion relies heavily on 'Equity credit: What is it and how do you get it?', Standard & Poor's, *2006 Corporate Criteria Book*, pp. 74–84, www.corporatecriteria.standardandpoors.com.

28 This treatment of 'intermediate equity' hybrids is detailed in Standard & Poor's, *Australian Corporate Ratios Explained*, 13 June 2006, www.standardandpoors.com.

Connect Plus features a case study illustrating topics covered in this chapter.
Ask your lecturer or tutor for your course's unique URL.

SUMMARY

In this chapter, we considered the sources of debt finance. There are many types of debt, including loans, which are non-marketable, and debt securities, which are marketable, but all types involve a temporary transfer of funds which must be repaid by the borrower.

→ Banks and other financial institutions offer several kinds of loans. Banks offer overdrafts, which are a flexible form of finance in which the borrower obtains, and is charged interest on, only the level of debt funding that is required from time to time. Other, more specialised forms of finance include debtor finance, which uses a company's accounts receivable as a basis for short-term funding, and inventory loans and bridging finance. Banks, finance companies and other non-bank financial institutions are often involved in offering these forms of finance. Debt with a term to maturity of more than 12 months is classified as long term. Loans from banks and other financial intermediaries are the most important types of long-term debt finance for Australian companies. Banks provide variable-rate loans and fixed-rate term loans.

→ A company can raise funds by issuing debt securities. Commercial paper and bills of exchange are short-term marketable securities. Both types of security promise the payment of a fixed sum on a stated future date and are sold on a simple interest basis. In the case of commercial paper, the promise is made only by the borrower, while in a bill of exchange there is also an acceptor, who in the usual case repays the debt on behalf of the borrower. Both types of security can be traded in secondary markets. In these markets, it is conventional for participants to sell commercial paper without endorsement but to sell bills of exchange with endorsement. Commercial paper is usually issued under a program that may be underwritten, and a bill of exchange may be issued as part of an ongoing arrangement known as a bill facility.

→ Companies can also issue long-term debt securities, including debentures, unsecured notes and corporate bonds. Public issues of these securities are a relatively minor source of finance in the Australian market, and companies that require long-term fixed-rate debt often issue securities in offshore markets. Long-term fixed-rate debt can also be obtained by taking out a variable-rate bank loan and then entering into interest rate swaps.

→ Project finance is important in the Australian market and it allows large natural resource and infrastructure projects to be financed with a high proportion of debt.

→ Australian companies also issue hybrid securities such as convertible notes, convertible preference shares and converting preference shares. The main feature of these securities is that they are convertible into ordinary shares in the future. Other hybrid securities such as step-up preference shares are also important in the Australian market.

KEY TERMS

acceptor (or drawee)   306
at call   294
bank bill   307
bill acceptance facility   308
bill discount facility   308
bill of exchange   305
bond   313
bridging finance   297
commercial paper (or promissory note)   303
conversion ratio   324
convertible preference share   322
converting preference share   322
coupon payments   303
covenant   289
credit foncier loan   299
debenture   309
debtor finance with recourse   296
debtor finance without recourse   296
default   288
discounter   304
discounter (or factor)   295
disintermediation   287
drawer   306
endorsement   307
Eurobond   314
exchangeable preference share   322
face value   304
financial distress   291
financial risk   291
floor-plan (or wholesale) finance   297
foreign bond   314
full service debtor finance   295
fully drawn bill facility   308
indicator rate   294

interbank cash rate 289	preference shares 322	securities 287
intermediation 287	principal 288	stapled securities 326
mortgage 291	redeemable preference share 322	step-up preference share 326
non-bank bill 307	rediscounting 307	subordinated debt 290
non-notification (or confidential) debtor finance 295	reset preference share 325	syndicated loan 300
	revolving credit bill facility 308	unsubordinated debt 290
overdraft limit 294	revolving credit facility 297	
partnership debtor finance 296	secondary market transaction 303	

SELF-TEST PROBLEMS

1. What is the price of a 180-day bill of exchange, with a face value of $500 000, if the yield is 6.50 per cent per annum?

2. If the purchaser in the previous problem sells the bill 60 days later, at which time it is priced to yield 6.30 per cent per annum, what effective annual interest rate has been earned?

Solutions to self-test problems are available in Appendix B, page 803.

REFERENCES

Australian Bureau of Statistics, *Australian National Accounts, Financial Accounts*, cat. no. 5232.0, Table 27, June quarter 2010.

Australian Financial Markets Association, *2010 Australian Financial Markets Report*, AFMA, Sydney, 2010.

Australian Securities and Investments Commission, *Debentures: Second Review of Disclosure to Investors*, ASIC Report 173, October 2009.

Baskin, J.B. & Miranti, P.J., *A History of Corporate Finance*, Cambridge University Press, 1997, pp. 151–7.

Battellino, R., 'Why do so many Australian borrowers issue bonds offshore?', *Reserve Bank of Australia Bulletin*, December 2002, pp. 19–24.

Black, S., Brassil, A. & Hack, M., 'Recent trends in Australian banks' bond issuance', Reserve Bank of Australia, *Bulletin*, March 2010, pp. 27–33.

Brown, A., Davies, M., Fabbro, D. & Hanrick, T., 'Recent developments in banks' funding costs and lending rates', *Reserve Bank of Australia Bulletin*, March 2010, pp. 35–44.

Bruce, R., McKern, B., Pollard, I. & Skully, M. (eds), *Handbook of Australian Corporate Finance*, 5th edn, Butterworths, Sydney, 1997, Chapters 9, 13 and 14.

Carew, E., *Fast Money 4*, Allen & Unwin, Sydney, 1998.

Davis, K., 'Converting preference shares: an Australian capital structure innovation', *Accounting and Finance*, November 1996, pp. 213–28.

Fitzpatrick, P. & Hardaker, R., 'Finance company finance', in R. Bruce, B. McKern, I. Pollard & M. Skully (eds), *Handbook of Australian Corporate Finance*, 5th edn, Butterworths, Sydney, 1997.

GE Capital, *Guide to Asset Based Lending*, 1999, GE Capital Commercial Finance, Stamford, **www.securitization.net/pdf/asset_guide.pdf**. WWW

Hunt, B. & Terry, C., *Financial Institutions and Markets*, 5th edn, Thomson Learning, Melbourne, 2008.

Institute for Factors and Discounters of Australia and New Zealand Inc., *IFD Update*, March 2010, **www.factorsanddiscounters.com**. WWW

Jen, F.C., Choi, D. & Lee, S., 'Some new evidence on why companies use convertible bonds', *Journal of Applied Corporate Finance*, Spring 1997, pp. 44–53.

Montague, B., 'Swaps', in R. Bruce & D. Morrison (eds), *Handbook of Australian Corporate Finance*, 5th edn, Butterworths, Sydney, 1997, Chapter 13.

Reserve Bank of Australia, Tables D2, D4, D7, D8, F1, F4 and F5, September 2010, **www.rba.gov.au**. WWW

——, 'The global financial environment', *Financial Stability Review*, September 2010, pp. 3–14.

——, 'Central bank market operations', *Bulletin*, September 2007, pp. 19–26.

——, 'Australian banks' global bond funding', *Bulletin*, August 2006, pp. 1–6.

——, 'Australian financial markets', *Bulletin*, June 2002, pp. 6–21.

Smithson, C.W., *Managing Financial Risk*, 3rd edn, McGraw-Hill, New York, 1998.

Standard & Poor's, *2006 Corporate Criteria Book*, **www.corporatecriteria.standardandpoors.com**.

———, *Hybrid Capital Handbook: September 2008 edn*, **www.corporatecriteria.standardandpoors.com**.

Viney, C., *McGrath's Financial Institutions, Instruments and Markets*, 6th edn, McGraw-Hill, Sydney, 2009.

Yescombe, E.R., *Principles of Project Finance*, Academic Press, San Diego, 2002.

QUESTIONS

1. [LO 2] *A debt contract will always include specifications about cash flows.* Outline the forms that these specifications may take. Identify the nature of other specifications usually included in a debt contract.

2. [LO 2] Distinguish between:
   (a) secured debt and unsecured debt
   (b) subordinated debt and unsubordinated debt
   (c) indirect and direct debt finance.

3. [LO 2] The financial risk associated with borrowing involves two separate effects. Outline these effects.

4. [LO 2] *Lenders usually have no control over a company's operations but they have considerable potential control.* Explain.

5. [LO 2] The forms of security available to commercial lenders include fixed charge, floating charge and negative pledge. What are the main similarities between these three forms of security? What are the main differences between them?

6. [LO 3] Discuss the factors that affect the terms of a bank overdraft negotiated by a borrower.

7. [LO 3] *A bank overdraft provides a company with a flexible source of funds.* Discuss the significance of this flexibility for the financial manager and the difficulties it may cause for the bank.

8. [LO 4] Distinguish between 'with recourse debtor finance' and 'without recourse debtor finance'.

9. [LO 4] Identify the basic feature that is common to all the types of debtor finance shown at **www.oxfordfunding.com.au**.
   (a) Critically evaluate the advantages of debtor finance that are shown at the above website.
   (b) Use information available at the Oxford Funding website to compare debtor finance with an overdraft.

10. [LO 3] *Only small companies ever need bridging finance.* Do you think this statement is likely to be true or untrue? Why?

11. [LO 3] Describe the major types of bank lending other than bank overdraft.

12. [LO 3, 5] (a) Select one of the four major Australian banks (ANZ, CBA, NAB or Westpac) and, from the bank's website, identify the types of business loans offered by the bank. Record the current interest rates on these business loans and on overdrafts offered by the same bank. Explain the differences between these rates.

    (b) In January 2008, Federal Treasurer Wayne Swan criticised a decision by the ANZ bank to lift interest rates on variable-rate mortgages by 0.2 per cent. The Treasurer said: 'We believe the rise is excessive, and over and above anything that could be justified by the increase in costs flowing to those organisations from the fallout from the US sub-prime [mortgage] crisis'. What aspects of the rate increase announced by the ANZ bank were unusual? Evaluate the reasons put forward by the ANZ to justify the rate increase.

13. [LO 5] What are the terms of the typical mortgage agreement?

14. [LO 5] *Variable-rate term loans have much greater flexibility than fixed-rate term loans.* Explain.

15. [LO 5] *Bank loans provide much greater flexibility than borrowing by issuing debt securities.* Discuss.

16. [LO 5] Define a mortgage loan. What are the similarities between a debenture and a mortgage loan? How do they differ?

17. [LO 7] Describe the main features of commercial paper. Why do issues of commercial paper generally involve large-scale borrowing?

18. [LO 7] How does commercial paper differ from a bill of exchange?

19. [LO 7] From the viewpoint of a potential purchaser, what are the advantages and disadvantages of a bank bill compared with commercial paper?

20. [LO 7] What are the advantages of issuing commercial paper rather than bills of exchange?

21. [LO 7] Describe the usual roles of the drawer, acceptor and discounter of a bill of exchange.

22. [LO 8] Ingrid deposits $40 000 with a fund that invests mainly in bank bills and commercial paper.

The next day the Reserve Bank of Australia announces an increase in the cash rate. Three days later Ingrid withdraws her deposit and is stunned to find that she has lost money. 'Interest rates have gone up! How can I have lost money?' Enlighten her.

23. **[LO 7]** Distinguish between a 'fully drawn bill facility' and a 'revolving credit bill facility'.

24. **[LO 9]** Discuss the term 'security' as it relates to the difference between debentures and unsecured notes.

25. **[LO 9]** What are the functions of the trustee and the trust deed to a debenture issue?

26. **[LO 9]** Corporate bonds and debentures have many similarities. What are these similarities? What are the main differences between them?

27. **[LO 9]** *Debt securities secured by a charge over intangible assets may be described as notes or bonds but not as debentures.* Explain.

28. **[LO 9]** Many commentators have suggested that it would be desirable to encourage the growth of the corporate bond market in Australia. Outline the regulatory changes introduced by ASIC during 2010 to reduce the cost of issuing corporate bonds. Identify other measures that might stimulate further development of the corporate bond market.

29. **[LO 10]** Outline the main features of project finance. What distinguishes project finance from other types of long-term finance? Explain why 'completion' is of critical importance to the project sponsors and the lenders of funds to the project.

30. **[LO 11]** Explain why interest rate swaps are popular with corporate borrowers and also many traditional lenders.

31. **[LO 12]** It has been suggested that preference shares offer advantages over ordinary shares and bonds in three areas: (a) the control of the original shareholders; (b) the ability of relatively uninformed investors to value the securities; and (c) the bankruptcy risk of the company (Baskin & Miranti 1997, pp. 151–7).

    Consider each of these three areas in turn and compare the issue of new preference shares with the alternatives of issuing new ordinary shares or issuing new bonds.

32. **[LO 12]** *Most companies regard preference shares as a form of long-term debt.* What causes them to hold such a view? How does this affect their use of preference shares to raise funds?

33. **[LO 12]** *There is evidence that the price of a company's ordinary shares typically falls when an issue of convertible notes is announced.* Discuss this statement. Does it follow that issuing convertible notes is never in the best interests of shareholders?

34. **[LO 12]** Hybrid securities may be classified as either debt or equity for tax purposes. What is the main criterion for this classification?

35. **[LO 12]** Identify the main differences between a reset preference share and a step-up preference share. Why have reset preference shares been largely replaced by step-up preference shares in Australia?

36. **[LO 12]** In October 2007, Sydney Properties Ltd, which has assets valued at more than $5 billion, raised $200 million by issuing step-up preference shares (SPS) that pay quarterly distributions at a floating rate equal to the 90-day bank bill swap rate plus a margin of 2 per cent per annum for a period of 5 years. The SPS have a face value of $100 each and their current price on the ASX is $95. The step-up date is 30 November 2012 and if the shares are not redeemed on that date the interest margin will increase to 4.5 per cent per annum. What factors should the directors of Sydney Properties take into account when considering whether to redeem the SPS on the step-up date?

PROBLEMS

1. **Calculating price of commercial paper [LO 8]**
   Calculate the price of commercial paper with a face value of $1 million and 180 days to maturity if the yield is 8.9 per cent per annum.

2. **Calculating yield on bill of exchange [LO 8]**
   To raise $485 000, a company draws up a bill of exchange with a face value of $500 000, payable in 180 days. What is the implicit simple annual interest rate (yield) on the bill? What is the implicit effective annual interest rate on the bill?

3. **Calculating bill prices [LO 8]**
   Calculate the bill prices needed to complete the table overleaf. Assume in every case that the face value is $1 million.

TERM	YIELD = 5.1% p.a.	YIELD = 5.2% p.a.	YIELD = 5.3% p.a.
30 days			
90 days			
180 days			

What patterns are there in the table?

4. **Bank bill prices and returns [LO 8]**
   On 8 March 2012, JDF Investments Ltd purchased a bank bill maturing on 7 May 2012 at an annual yield of 6.95 per cent per annum. The bill had a face value of $1 million. On 23 March 2012, JDF sold the bill at a yield of 6.80 per cent per annum. Calculate:
   (a) the purchase price paid by JDF
   (b) the sale price received by JDF
   (c) the dollar return earned by JDF
   (d) the simple annual interest rate earned by JDF
   (e) the effective annual interest rate earned by JDF.

5. **Bank bill prices and returns [LO 8]**
   An investor buys a 90-day bank bill priced at a yield of 12.55 per cent per annum and sells it a week later priced at a yield of 13.60 per cent per annum. What effective annual interest rate has the investor earned? Explain your result.

6. **Bank bill prices and returns [LO 8]**
   An investor bought a 90-day bank bill priced at a yield of 7.45 per cent per annum. Three weeks later the market yield on the bill had fallen slightly to 7.35 per cent per annum. The RBA then unexpectedly announced that it had reduced the target cash rate by 0.5 per cent per annum. As a result, short-term interest rates and bill yields rapidly adjusted downwards and the bill's yield fell to 7.05 per cent per annum. The investor then sold the bill. Calculate the effective annual interest rate the investor earned. What effective annual interest rate would the investor have earned if the RBA had not announced a new target cash rate?

7. **Fixed-rate term loans [LO 5]**
   Sealex Ltd has a fixed-rate term loan of $2 million at an interest rate of 8.75 per cent per annum. The company has earnings before interest and tax (EBIT) of $1.4 million per annum. A covenant in the term loan agreement specifies that EBIT must be at least 3.5 times greater than the total interest paid on the company's debt. The directors of Sealex are planning to raise additional debt by borrowing at a variable rate, initially 7.5 per cent per annum. What is the maximum amount that Sealex can borrow on these terms?

8. **Calculating annual repayments and interest rates [LO 5]**
   Cominco Ltd needs to borrow approximately $2 million to finance the purchase of a gem-sorting machine for its diamond mine. Its financial manager is considering the following alternatives:
   (i) Cominco's bank will lend $2 million, repayable in four annual payments at an interest rate of 8.5 per cent per annum.
   (ii) The equipment supplier has offered to finance the gem sorter with an initial payment of $500 000, followed by annual instalments of $460 000 at the end of each of the next 4 years.
   (iii) A finance broker can arrange a $2 million loan repayable in a lump-sum payment of $2 761 513 in 4 years' time. The broker will charge an up-front fee of 1 per cent of the loan principal.
   (a) What are the annual repayments on the bank loan?
   (b) What is the interest rate (ignoring the up-front fee) on the finance broker's loan?
   (c) Which of the three alternatives provides the lowest cost finance?

9. **Converting preference shares [LO 12]**
   XYZ Ltd converting preference shares have a face value of $15 and are due to convert to ordinary shares on 31 July 20X1. Each converting preference share will convert to a number of ordinary shares that is determined by dividing $15 by:
   (i) an amount equal to the price of XYZ ordinary shares on 31 July 20X1, less 5 per cent; or
   (ii) $15,
   whichever yields the greater number of ordinary shares. How many ordinary shares will be received by the holder of one converting preference share if the price of XYZ ordinary shares is:
   (a) $5?
   (b) $7.50?
   (c) $10?
   (d) $15?
   (e) $20?

10. **Analysis of conversion terms [LO 12]**
    Using the information in Problem 9, calculate the value of the ordinary shares that will be received on conversion of each converting preference share in cases (a) to (e). Based on your results, suggest an alternative name that describes the nature of converting preference shares.

Test yourself further with Connect Plus online! Ask your lecturer or tutor for your course's unique URL.

PAYOUT POLICY

LEARNING OBJECTIVES

After studying this chapter you should be able to:

1. explain why cash payments to shareholders are important and understand some institutional features of dividends and share buybacks

2. outline the argument that payout policy is irrelevant to shareholders' wealth in a perfect capital market with no taxes

3. define the full payout policy and explain why it is important that companies follow this policy

4. explain how transaction costs, flotation costs and behavioural factors may affect payout policy

5. outline the imputation tax system and explain the effects of imputation and capital gains tax on returns to investors

6. understand the argument that payout decisions may have a role in providing signals to investors

7. explain the ways in which agency costs can be related to payout decisions

8. understand the nature of share buybacks, dividend reinvestment plans and dividend election schemes

9. explain how payout policy may change as a company moves through its life cycle.

CHAPTER CONTENTS

11.1 Introduction
11.2 Is payout policy important to shareholders?
11.3 Transaction costs and other imperfections
11.4 Dividends and taxes
11.5 Information effects and signalling to investors
11.6 Agency costs and corporate governance
11.7 Share buybacks
11.8 Dividend reinvestment plans and dividend election schemes
11.9 Payout policy and company life cycle

11.1 INTRODUCTION

Many companies have never distributed any cash to shareholders, while others typically distribute cash at least twice each year. Companies that distribute cash to their shareholders do so in two main ways: by the payment of dividends and by repurchasing shares.[1] Payout policy involves two fundamental questions. First, a companys' directors must decide how much cash, if any, to pay to shareholders. Second, they must determine the form of the payments—that is, should the payment be made as a dividend or through a share buyback? Alternatively, should the company pay dividends *and* repurchase shares?[2]

As discussed in Chapter 4, financial assets such as shares are valuable only because of the benefits they provide in the form of cash payouts. It is true that some companies have operated successfully for many years without paying a dividend, while simultaneously their shareholders have experienced significant capital gains. The prime example of such a company is Microsoft, which was founded in 1975, went public in 1986 and did not pay its first dividend until 2003. From 1986 to 2003, Microsoft grew rapidly and its cash flows were retained to finance that growth. Microsoft's first dividend was modest—8 cents per share, followed by a dividend of 16 cents per share in 2004, when it also announced plans to return up to $75 billion to investors through dividends and share repurchases, including $32 billion paid as a special dividend of $3 per share. Presumably, investors were willing to hold the company's shares during the period 1986 to 2003 because they expected that eventually the company's growth would slow and it would start to return cash to investors through dividends and/or share repurchases. 'At the most basic level, investors supply capital to businesses only because they (or the people to whom they might sell their securities) have a reasonable expectation of eventually receiving payouts in one form or another' (De Angelo & De Angelo 2007, p. 12).

Decisions on a company's payout policy should be consistent with the overall objective of maximising shareholders' wealth. However, payout decisions can involve several factors and the optimal policy may be far from obvious. For example, consider a profitable copper mining company that has paid the same dividend each year for the last 5 years. Suppose that this year, the company's operating cash flow and profit doubles because of a large increase in the price of copper. What payout decision will be best for shareholders? Should the extra cash be paid out, and if so, should the company simply pay a larger dividend or should it repurchase shares? Should the company retain the extra cash and use it to expand its exploration program? Should the extra cash be used first to repay debt with the dividend being increased only if surplus cash remains after all existing loans have been repaid? These are only some of the possibilities that may exist. This example shows that payout decisions are often related to other financial decisions. While, in practice, payout decisions should not be made in isolation, for the purpose of analysing payout policy we need to isolate it from other financial decisions by holding constant both investment decisions and other financing decisions.

In addition to determining the level and form of payout, managers also need to consider issues such as the effects of changing dividends and whether to adopt a dividend reinvestment plan. In Australia, companies that pay dividends usually make two dividend payments each year, so decisions on payouts need to be made frequently and a company's payout policy may need to be reviewed regularly. In this chapter we analyse payout policy and discuss the relevant empirical research. But first we describe briefly some institutional features of dividends and share repurchases.

> **LEARNING OBJECTIVE 1**
> Explain why cash payments to shareholders are important and understand some institutional features of dividends and share buybacks

---

1 See s. 6(1) of the *Income Tax Assessment Act 1936* for a definition of what constitutes a dividend under the Act.
2 Officially, the term share buyback is used in Australia while the term share (or stock) repurchase is more common in the US. In this chapter, the terms buyback and repurchase are used interchangeably.

ex-dividend date
date on which a share begins trading ex-dividend. A share purchased ex-dividend does not include a right to the forthcoming dividend payment

cum dividend period
period during which the purchaser of a share is qualified to receive a previously announced dividend. The cum dividend period ends on the ex-dividend date

11.1.1 DIVIDEND DECLARATION PROCEDURES

Provided that the legal requirements and the exchange's listing requirements are met, a company's dividend decisions are at the discretion of its directors. In Australia, companies generally pay an *interim dividend* after the end of the first half of the financial year and a *final dividend* after the company's Annual General Meeting. A company's Board of Directors, when announcing a dividend, will specify a date, known as the 'record date', on which the company's 'books' will close for the purpose of determining who is currently a shareholder, and hence entitled to receive the dividend. For shares listed on the Australian Securities Exchange (ASX), the rules of the exchange specify an **ex-dividend date**, which is four business days before the record date.[3] Investors who purchase shares before the ex-dividend date buy the shares **cum dividend** and are entitled to receive the dividend. Those who purchase shares on or after the ex-dividend date are not entitled to receive the dividend.

11.1.2 TYPES OF DIVIDEND

Dividends are normally paid in cash, but many Australian companies have adopted dividend reinvestment plans that give shareholders the option of using all or part of their dividend to purchase additional shares in the company. These plans are discussed in Section 11.8. Dividends are sometimes given a designation such as 'special' to indicate that shareholders should not expect them to be repeated.

11.1.3 LEGAL AND TAX CONSIDERATIONS

Historically, the *Corporations Act 2001* specified that a company's dividend may be paid only out of profits, and must not be paid out of capital.[4] The purpose of this restriction was to protect creditors by maintaining a company's capital. Under amendments to the Corporations Act, which came into effect on 28 June 2010, the profits test was replaced by new requirements that prohibit a company from paying a dividend unless:

- the company's assets exceed its liabilities immediately before the dividend is declared and the excess is sufficient for the payment of the dividend
- the payment of the dividend is fair and reasonable to the company's shareholders as a whole
- the payment of the dividend does not materially prejudice the company's ability to pay its creditors.

imputation tax system
system under which investors in shares can use tax credits associated with franked dividends to offset their personal income tax. The system eliminates the double taxation inherent in the classical tax system

franked dividend
dividend paid out of Australian company profits on which company income tax has been paid and which carries a franking credit

The new requirements are intended to focus on the solvency of the company and mean that a company may be able to pay a dividend in the absence of accounting profits. For example, a company with surplus cash may have recorded a net loss (in accounting terms) due to large non-cash expenses such as impairment losses on property, plant and equipment. It could now pay a dividend provided the three requirements are met. Payments to shareholders may also be restricted by covenants in loan agreements. If a company has additional classes of shares such as preference shares, then any priority rights to dividends must be observed. If a share buyback causes a company to become insolvent, the directors may be personally liable for insolvent trading and the company's liquidator may seek a court order that the buyback transactions are void and the proceeds can be recovered from shareholders who sold.

The **imputation tax system** allows companies to pay dividends that carry credits for income tax paid by the company. Such dividends are known as **franked dividends** and the tax credits can be used by resident shareholders to reduce their income tax. It is important to note that, generally, the tax credits associated with franked dividends arise only from payment of Australian company tax. New Zealand also operates an imputation tax system and in 2003 the Australian and New Zealand imputation systems were

---

[3] Many Australian companies choose a Friday as the record date, which means that the ex-dividend date will be the previous Monday. From the start of trading on the ex-dividend date to the close of trading on the record date there are in fact 5 days of trading. The trading period between the ex-dividend and record dates has been as long as 7 business days. It was reduced to 5 days following full adoption of electronic settlement and transfer procedures.

[4] See s. 254T, *Corporations Act 2001*.

extended to include companies resident in the other country. Companies that operate in both Australia and New Zealand ('trans-Tasman companies') are now able to distribute both Australian and New Zealand tax credits to all shareholders. However, tax credits originating in each country can be claimed only by residents of that country. The operation of the trans-Tasman imputation rules is illustrated in Section 11.4.1.

When a dividend is declared, the company must state the extent to which the dividend is franked. When a dividend is paid, the company is required to provide each shareholder with a dividend statement. This statement shows the amount of the dividend and the date of payment, the amount of any franked and unfranked parts of the dividend and, if the dividend is fully or partially franked, the amount of the **franking credit**. Where dividends are paid to non-residents, the company may be required to deduct **withholding tax**, in which case the amount of any withholding tax deducted must also be shown.

The imputation system requires a franking account to be maintained by each company. If a company earns a pre-tax profit of $100 and pays company income tax of $30, the credit to its franking account will be $30. When a franked dividend is paid, the franking account must be debited and the debit is equal to the franking credits attached to the dividend. Franked dividends received by resident companies are handled in the same way as dividends received by individuals and superannuation funds. Partnerships and trusts are not taxable entities and are therefore unable to use franking credits. However, any franking credits received by a partnership or trust can be passed on to the partners or beneficiaries who can use them if they are Australian residents.

franking credit
credit for Australian company tax paid, which, when distributed to shareholders, can be offset against their tax liability

withholding tax
the tax deducted by a company from the dividend payable to a non-resident shareholder

11.1.4 REPURCHASING SHARES

While payment of dividends is the most common way of paying cash to shareholders, some countries allow companies to pay out cash by repurchasing or 'buying back' their own shares. The law may require that repurchased shares are cancelled or it may allow the company to retain them as **treasury stock**.

In Australia, s. 259A of the Corporations Act generally precludes a company from purchasing its own shares. However, exceptions to this general prohibition were introduced in 1989 and revised in 1995 to simplify the procedures. Buybacks have since become routine for many companies. Five different types of buybacks are specified in the legislation. Each type involves different legal formalities, but in general companies are able to repurchase up to 10 per cent of their ordinary shares in a 12-month period. This is often referred to as the 10/12 limit. In each case, once the transfer of ownership has been processed the shares must be cancelled.

treasury stock
US term for a company's own shares that have been repurchased and held rather than cancelled

Further details of the different types of share buyback are as follows:

(a) *Equal access buybacks.* Offers are made to all ordinary shareholders to purchase the same percentage of the shares that they hold.[5] The proposed buyback must be approved by shareholders passing an ordinary resolution only if it exceeds the 10/12 limit.

(b) *Selective buybacks.* In this case offers are made to only some of the shareholders in a company. Because some shareholders could be disadvantaged, the procedural requirements are more stringent than for other types of buyback. A selective buyback must be approved by shareholders either unanimously or by a special resolution in which the selling shareholders and their associates are unable to vote.

(c) *On-market buybacks.* A listed company is able to buy back its shares in the ordinary course of trading on the stock exchange. The Australian Securities and Investments Commission (ASIC) and the ASX must be notified of the proposed buyback, but shareholder approval via an ordinary resolution is required only if the 10/12 limit is exceeded.

(d) *Employee share scheme buybacks.* A company may buy back shares held by or for employees who initially acquired the shares through an employee share scheme. The procedural requirements are the same as for on-market buybacks.

---

5 Off-market share buybacks take place under the equal access provisions. Section 257B of the Corporations Act states that the company must offer to purchase the same percentage of the shares held by each shareholder. In practice, ASIC allows companies to invite shareholders to tender some or all of their shares.

(e) *Minimum holding buybacks.* A listed company may buy back parcels of shares that are smaller than a specified minimum. No resolution is needed and the only legal requirement is that ASIC must be notified of the cancellation of the shares.

Importantly, the tax treatment depends on whether the buyback takes place on- or off-market. In the case of an off-market buyback, the transaction can be structured so that part of the payment received by a shareholder is treated as a dividend for tax purposes. Any such dividend can be franked. An on-market buyback cannot include a dividend component and the whole amount paid to the shareholder is treated as proceeds from the sale of the shares. Accordingly, on-market buybacks are subject only to the capital gains tax provisions—that is, the tax treatment is the same as if the shares were sold to a third party.

There is another difference between regular dividends and share buybacks that can be important. A regular dividend affects taxes for all shareholders, but a share buyback will affect taxes only for shareholders who decide to sell and, at least for on-market buybacks, only if the investor realises a capital gain. These differences mean that a share buyback can have tax advantages for shareholders.

On-market buybacks are more common in Australia than off-market buybacks but, on average, the latter are larger so the total amount of capital returned to shareholders over time by each method is similar. For example, during the 1996 to 2003 period, listed companies paid out a total of $10.5 billion in 350 on-market share buybacks. Over the same period, $12.1 billion was paid out via 45 off-market buybacks (Brown 2007). During the 2007 calendar year, Australian listed companies returned about $12 billion to shareholders by repurchasing shares. In 2008 and 2009, when companies and financial markets were affected by the global financial crisis, share repurchases declined to $4.6 billion and $2.1 billion, respectively (ASX 2010b, p. 3).

The remainder of the chapter consists of eight main sections. First, we analyse the primary question: Is payout policy important to shareholders? Second, we discuss the effects of transaction costs, flotation costs and behavioural factors. Third, we discuss the effects of taxes, including both the taxation of dividends and the taxation of capital gains. Fourth, we discuss information effects and signalling as reasons for the relevance of payout policy. Fifth, we discuss the role of agency costs as a factor that influences payout decisions. Sixth, we discuss share repurchases as a way of distributing cash to shareholders. Seventh, we discuss dividend reinvestment plans and dividend election schemes. Finally, we examine how a company's payout policy may evolve as the company moves through its life cycle.

11.2 IS PAYOUT POLICY IMPORTANT TO SHAREHOLDERS?

Before discussing reasons why payout policy may or may not be important to shareholders, we outline some of the payout policies a company's directors might adopt.

LEARNING OBJECTIVE 2
Outline the argument that payout policy is irrelevant to shareholders' wealth in a perfect capital market with no taxes

11.2.1 ALTERNATIVE PAYOUT POLICIES

Payout policy involves two fundamental questions. One is *whether* to pay any cash to shareholders and the other is the *form* of the payment. In many cases a payment may be inappropriate—perhaps because the company has attractive investment opportunities and shareholders are expected to receive a greater benefit if the company's cash is used to take up these opportunities instead of paying it out now. If cash is to be paid out, the directors must decide whether it will be paid as a dividend, or whether the company will repurchase some of its shares or whether it will both pay a dividend and repurchase shares. We now outline three payout policies that might be adopted. For ease of expression they are referred to as 'dividend' policies, but, in practice, the cash paid out could be wholly or partly in the form of a share buyback. Also, since these policies have a long history in many countries we continue to describe them by referring to dividends being paid from a company's profits.

Residual dividend policy

One possibility is simply to treat dividends as a residual. A company that adopts this policy would pay out as dividends any profits that, in the opinion of management, cannot be profitably invested. Alternatively, if the company's investment needs are greater than its profit, then no dividend would be paid and extra finance would be raised externally. This policy can result in dividends fluctuating significantly from year to year.

Stable (or progressive) dividend policy

A more popular policy is the stable dividend policy. Under this policy, management sets a target **dividend-payout ratio**—that is, a target proportion of annual profit to be paid out as dividends. This target is such that dividends are related to the long-run difference between expected profits and expected investment needs. The amount of each dividend is changed only when this long-run difference changes. For example, the dividend per share will be increased if there is an increase in profit that is regarded as sustainable, but it will not be changed in response to fluctuations in profit that are believed to be only temporary. Similarly, if profit falls, the dividend per share will be maintained unless the outlook for profits is so poor that the current dividend level is considered to be unsustainable. The aims of a stable dividend policy are to reduce uncertainty for shareholders while providing them with a reliable income. Many companies that follow a policy of this type refer to it as a 'progressive' dividend policy.

> **dividend-payout ratio**
> percentage of profit paid out to shareholders as dividends

There are two consequences of a stable or **progressive dividend policy**. First, changes in dividends tend to lag behind changes in profits, and dividends are much less variable than profits. Second, the dividend-payout ratio may fluctuate dramatically. For example, if profit is unexpectedly high in a particular year, the dividend-payout ratio will fall.

> **progressive dividend policy**
> directors aim to steadily increase or at least maintain the dividend at each payment

Constant payout policy

If management is concerned to avoid fluctuations in payout ratio, then it could adopt a *constant payout policy*, whereby the dividend-payout ratio remains essentially the same each year.

11.2.2 MANAGERS AND PAYOUT DECISIONS

There is abundant empirical evidence that managers regard payout decisions as significant. In an important early study, Lintner (1956) interviewed the managers of 28 US companies and found that in most cases dividends were an 'active decision variable', and were seldom regarded purely as a residual or influenced significantly by financing requirements. He also found that most managers were reluctant to make changes in dividends that are likely to have to be reversed in the near future. In a much larger study, Brav, Graham, Harvey and Michaely (2005) surveyed 384 financial executives of US companies and interviewed another 23 to find the factors that drive dividend and repurchase decisions.

Their findings, some of which are consistent with those of Lintner, include:[6]

(a) Maintaining the current level of dividend per share is a high priority and is of similar importance to investment decisions. Managers have a strong desire to avoid dividend cuts. External funds would be raised to finance planned investments before the dividend would be cut.

---

6 Brav et al. found that Lintner's key finding that dividend policy is conservative still holds. That is, managers of companies that pay dividends are reluctant to cut them and non-payers are reluctant to initiate them because, once they do, they feel they will be locked in to maintaining dividend payments. Brav et al. identified two important differences relative to Lintner. First, managers target the dividend payout ratio less than they used to and give more prominence to the current level of dividend payments. Second, share repurchases have become an important form of payout and are favoured by managers because of their flexibility relative to dividends.

(b) Apart from the importance of maintaining the level of dividend per share, payout policy is of secondary concern. Managers see little reward for increasing dividends and will consider doing so only after investment and liquidity needs are met.
(c) Dividends are 'sticky', inflexible and 'smoothed' over time relative to profits. Many companies that pay dividends would prefer that they did not. If they could 'start all over again' they would pay lower dividends and place greater emphasis on share repurchases.
(d) In contrast to dividends, share repurchases are very flexible with no need for smoothing. Repurchase decisions are made after investment decisions—that is, repurchases are made using the residual cash flow after investment spending.

In some cases companies adopt a stated dividend policy. For example, the large resources companies BHP Billiton and Rio Tinto have both announced that they have adopted a progressive dividend policy. However, shareholders should be aware that when a company adopts such a policy, its directors are stating their intentions rather than providing a guarantee that dividends will never fall (see Finance in Action). In other cases, a company may not explicitly state a dividend policy but investors may be able to infer that it is following a particular policy by observing its payout record.

The findings outlined above also show that there are significant differences between the factors that determine dividends and those that influence decisions to repurchase shares. In summary, there is evidence that managers treat some aspects of payout decisions as being very important. In contrast, a well-known analysis by Miller and Modigliani (MM) (1961) proved that under certain restrictive assumptions, dividend policy has no effect on shareholders' wealth.

FINANCE IN ACTION

DIVIDEND POLICY PROVIDES NO GUARANTEE FOR SHAREHOLDERS

Several companies have adopted a progressive dividend policy whereby it is intended that the dividend payout will increase in line with profits but not fall during economic downturns. Shareholders should be aware that this does not necessarily mean that the dividend income they receive will never decline. For example, in 2009 some companies reduced their dividends significantly with the intention that they would be able to resume a progressive dividend policy from the 'rebased level'. In other cases, shareholders have suffered from the effects of exchange rate changes, as the following excerpts from an article by Barry FitzGerald explains.

BHP Billiton stands alone among the global miners in being able to increase its dividend payment despite the damage being done to its December half profit from the now waning impact of the global financial crisis.

But Australian shareholders will not be at the front of the line thanking the company for its generosity.

While the interim dividend has been increased 2.4 per cent from 41 US cents to 42 US cents, it has gone backwards in Australian dollar terms by more than 25 per cent due to the impact of the strong Australian dollar …

There were no apologies from BHP today for the haircut local shareholders will be taking on their dividends. It extolled the virtue of the group's 'progressive' dividend policy, another way of saying its intent is that dividends will always go onwards and upwards, albeit in the group's 'functional' currency— the battered US dollar.

Source: 'BHP's haircut for local investors', Barry FitzGerald, 10 February 2010, www.smh.com.au/business/bhps-haircut-for-local-investors-20100210-nr1y.html.

WWW

11.2.3 THE IRRELEVANCE OF PAYOUT POLICY

The proposition that a company's dividend policy has no effect on shareholders' wealth was advanced by MM (1961).[7] Their analysis demonstrated the irrelevance of dividend policy under the following assumptions:

(a) The company has a given investment plan, and has determined how much of the assets to be acquired will be financed by borrowing.
(b) There is a perfectly competitive capital market, with no taxes, transaction costs, flotation costs or information costs.
(c) Investors are rational so they always prefer more wealth to less and are equally satisfied with a given increase in wealth, regardless of whether it is in the form of cash paid out or an increase in the value of the shares they hold.

To define dividend policy, suppose that a company is to increase its dividend payment. With the investment plan and the borrowing decision fixed, the extra funds used to pay the higher dividend can be replaced from only one source: a new share issue. Alternatively, suppose that the dividend is to be reduced. In this case, there is only one way that the surplus cash can be used—that is, to repurchase some shares. Therefore, in the MM framework, *dividend policy* involves a trade-off between higher or lower dividends and issuing or repurchasing ordinary shares. Using this approach, MM proved that dividend policy is irrelevant to shareholders' wealth. Example 11.1 illustrates the approach that MM used to prove that dividend policy is irrelevant.

EXAMPLE 11.1

The ABC Company has 10 000 shares on issue, with a market price of $11 each. Its statement of financial position ('balance sheet') in market values is shown in Table 11.1.

Table 11.1 ABC Company market value statement of financial position ($)

Cash	15 000	Debt	5 000
Non-current assets	100 000	Equity	110 000
Total assets	115 000	Value of company	115 000

The $15 000 cash has been reserved for an investment opportunity that has not yet been taken up. Suppose that management decides instead to use the cash to pay a dividend of $15 000, and then issues more shares to new shareholders to replace the cash and proceed with the new investment. What is the effect of these transactions on the value of the existing shares and shareholders' wealth?

SOLUTION

After the dividend and the share issue, the company still has the same assets, so that its value should still be $115 000. The new shares should be worth the amount paid for them, $15 000, so that the value of the original shares is:

Value of original shares = value of company − value of debt − value of new shares

= $115 000 − $5 000 − $15 000

= $95 000

The original shareholders have suffered a capital loss of $15 000, exactly offsetting the dividend of $15 000, which is now cash in their hands. By having the ABC Company pay a dividend, its original

continued →

---

7 MM (1961) only considered dividends and their article does not mention share repurchases, probably because they were rare at the time. The MM analysis could be extended to include share repurchases and to show that, under their assumptions, the form in which cash is paid out has no effect on shareholders' wealth.

> **Example 11.1** *continued*
>
> shareholders have converted part of their stake in the company into cash of $15 000. Since the stake transferred to the new shareholders is also worth $15 000, the net change in the wealth of the original shareholders is zero.
>
> Paying a dividend and then issuing new shares to replace the cash paid out involves a transfer of ownership between the 'old' and 'new' shareholders. Provided the terms of this transfer are fair, neither party gains nor loses—that is, the new shareholders receive shares that are worth the price paid for them and, for each dollar they receive in dividends, the old shareholders give up future dividends with a present value of $1, which reduces the value of their shares by $1.

Essentially, MM's argument is that the value of a company depends only on its investments. The net cash that can be paid out to investors is a residual: the difference between profits and investment. This net payout consists of cash paid out in dividends and share repurchases, less any cash raised by issuing shares. It follows that a company can adjust its payouts to any chosen level by making a corresponding adjustment to the number of shares on issue. In a perfect capital market where the company's investments remain the same, these adjustments will have no effect on the net payout of cash and no effect on company value. As shown in Example 11.1, paying out additional cash—$15 000 in that case—and then raising $15 000 by issuing additional shares is simply recycling cash and cannot affect shareholders' wealth.

Now suppose that the ABC Company pays the $15 000 dividend and does not replace the cash by issuing more shares. In this case, paying the dividend is effectively a partial liquidation of the company because its assets have been reduced by $15 000 and the value of its equity must fall to $110 000 − $15 000 = $95 000. The shareholders now have $15 000 cash in hand and have incurred a capital loss on their shares of $15 000. As a check, we can calculate their wealth, which is $15 000 + $95 000 = $110 000: exactly the same as it was prior to the dividend. Alternatively, suppose that the company does not pay any dividend, but the shareholders want to raise $15 000 in cash. The shareholders can do this by selling part of their holding to other investors—which is often referred to as creating a 'homemade dividend'. After these transactions, the original shareholders will again have cash of $15 000 and the value of their remaining shares must be equal to $110 000 − $15 000 = $95 000. Clearly, the wealth of the original shareholders is still $110 000. We can conclude that the partial liquidation of a company (by paying a dividend) cannot increase shareholders' wealth because, in the absence of taxes and transaction costs, shareholders can achieve the same result by liquidating part of their holding.

Since the 1960s, most discussions of payout policy have been based on the MM dividend irrelevance theorem. For example, empirical research has typically been based on the idea that if dividend policy is important in practice, the reasons for its importance must relate to factors that MM's assumptions excluded from their analysis. Accordingly, the large body of research on dividend policy has mainly examined whether the policies that companies adopt, and share price responses to dividend announcements, can be explained by market imperfections such as taxes, agency costs and the role that dividends may play in conveying information to investors. More than 40 years after the MM irrelevance theorem was published, De Angelo and De Angelo (2006) argued that it is inadequate as a starting point for understanding payout policy. De Angelo and De Angelo (DD) do not claim that the MM analysis is wrong; they accept that it is 'correct', given the underlying assumptions. However, DD point out that the MM analysis relies on an unstated but implicit assumption that, in their view, means that MM's irrelevance theorem is itself irrelevant. DD argue that the concept of 'full payout' is a more logical starting point for discussion of payout policy. The full payout policy that DD advocate means that the full present value of a company's *free cash flow* should be paid out to shareholders. Free cash flows are defined as cash flows in excess of those required to fund all available projects that have positive net present values. Their argument is explained in the next section.

11.2.4 THE IMPORTANCE OF FULL PAYOUT

To explain DD's criticisms of MM, we use a simplified version of a numerical example provided by DD (2006). Suppose that an all-equity company undertakes a project with a net present value (NPV) of $10. The project generates free cash flow of $1 per year in perpetuity and the required rate of return is 10 per cent. The MM proof implicitly assumes that a company will distribute all of its free cash flow in every period. In this case, the company must distribute at least $1 per year. MM show that the company can distribute *more* than $1 per year by issuing more shares and distributing the proceeds to shareholders. For example, if the company's managers wish to pay a dividend of $1.10 in a given year, the company sells shares worth 10 cents to new shareholders and pays a dividend of $1.10 to the old shareholders. DD point out that by issuing new shares and paying a higher dividend, the company is effectively carrying out financial intermediation. In reality, cash of 10 cents was transferred from new to old shareholders with the company only touching the cash for an instant. Accordingly, DD argue that the cash actually paid from the company's resources remains $1, so, in substance, its payout policy has not changed.

> **LEARNING OBJECTIVE 3**
> Define the full payout policy and explain why it is important that companies follow this policy

MM's assumptions constrain a company to paying out all of its free cash flow each year and this is an optimal payout policy. Clearly, it is also true that paying higher dividends, financed by issuing more shares, cannot increase company value or shareholders' wealth. Hence, what MM *did* prove is that changing payout policy cannot add to the value created by a company's investment policy. However, DD argue that the MM approach does not prove that payout policy is irrelevant because company value *can* be changed if companies retain part of their free cash flow. To continue the numerical example, suppose that the company's mangers decide to permanently distribute only 99 cents per year. The 1 cent that is retained is invested in zero-NPV projects so the company still has investments with an NPV of $10, but the reduced payout means that the value of its shares is only $9.90. In contrast to the outcomes envisaged by MM, the value lost through the suboptimal payout policy cannot be restored by investors selling some of their shares or borrowing against them to manufacture 'homemade' dividends. Given the distributions of 99 cents per year, the market will value the shares at $9.90 and that is the price at which investors can sell or borrow against their shares. Thus, DD distinguish between 'investment value' and 'distribution value'. Investment value is defined as the present value of the free cash flow *to the company* generated by its investments. Distribution value is the present value of the cash flow paid out *to shareholders*. These two values can be equal—but they will be equal only if the company's payout policy is optimal. Distribution value cannot be *more* than investment value but it will be *less* than investment value if free cash flow is retained.

In contrast to MM, DD conclude that both investment policy and payout policy are important. Their approach emphasises the importance of a **full payout policy**. In summary, DD argue that managers have two important jobs. First, they are responsible for selecting good investment projects that generate profits and provide the capacity for cash to be paid out to investors. Second, they should 'ensure that over the life of the enterprise, investors receive a distribution stream with the greatest possible present value. And so managers should think full payout and not irrelevance when setting payout policy' (2007, p. 12).

full payout policy
distribution of the full present value of a company's free cash flow to shareholders

11.2.5 PAYOUT POLICY IN PRACTICE

We have discussed two models of payout policy, both of which assume there is a perfect capital market with no taxes. First, the MM dividend irrelevance theorem suggests that any payout policy will do. Second, DD argue that MM relied on the implicit assumption that all of a company's free cash flow is paid out and point out that this is a critical requirement of optimal payout policies. If part of a company's free cash flow is never paid out, company value will be reduced, so DD support a full payout policy. In the context of a perfect or 'frictionless' market, full payout means that the present value of free cash flow should be paid out over the life of the enterprise. However, the model does not say anything about the timing of payouts—timing is irrelevant, provided the total payout is optimised. Similarly, neither the MM analysis nor the full payout model says anything about the form of the payout—shareholders are equally happy with a dollar of dividends or a dollar paid out to repurchase shares. Regardless of which of these models is used as a starting point, if we aim to develop a model that managers can use, then it is necessary to consider the effects of the imperfections or 'frictions' that may encourage or discourage the payout of cash. We must also consider factors that may influence the preferred form of payouts. Lease et al. (2000) divide the factors that may be important into two groups: the 'big three imperfections'—taxation, information asymmetry, and signalling and agency costs and the 'little three frictions'—transaction costs, flotation costs, and behavioural considerations. Because discussion of the latter factors raises some issues that are important in assessing the possible effects of imperfections, they are considered first in Section 11.3. Taxes, information asymmetry, and signalling agency costs are discussed in Sections 11.4 to 11.6.

11.3 TRANSACTION COSTS AND OTHER IMPERFECTIONS

11.3.1 TRANSACTION COSTS

LEARNING OBJECTIVE 4
Explain how transaction costs, flotation costs and behavioural factors may affect payout policy

If trading in shares does not involve any transaction costs, shareholders have the opportunity to effectively develop their own payout policy without incurring any costs. For example, if an investor received a dividend that was not needed, the cash could be used to buy more shares in the company. Conversely, if additional cash was needed, a shareholder could sell some shares to create a 'homemade' dividend. Thus, shareholders can create their preferred cash flow stream that is independent of the payouts made by the company. As De Angelo, De Angelo and Skinner (2009) point out, provided the company eventually distributes full value to investors, all shareholders 'will view each such dividend policy as equally valuable, regardless of the degree of heterogeneity in their preferences for immediate versus future payouts' (p. 203).

dividend clientele
group of investors who choose to invest in companies that have dividend policies that meet their particular requirements

In practice, shareholders who buy or sell shares to create a preferred cash flow stream will incur transaction costs such as brokerage fees, so investors who require income may prefer to hold shares that pay regular dividends. This is an example of **dividend clienteles**, which may develop when there are different classes of investors with different preferences for current income—that is, a company will tend to attract a clientele of investors who are suited by its dividend policy. Companies that do not pay dividends or pay only low or residual dividends would attract investors with adequate income from other sources. Such investors would reinvest any dividends they receive, but can avoid the transaction costs of doing so by investing in companies that retain most or all of their profits. Conversely, companies that routinely pay high dividends would attract investors such as retirees, who require income from their share portfolio to meet consumption needs. Thus, a stable dividend policy may reduce or eliminate the transaction costs that some shareholders would incur if the company followed a residual dividend policy.

However, this does not necessarily mean that the stable policy will increase the market value of the company's shares. If transaction costs are the only imperfection that exists in a market, companies may compete to pay dividends to the clientele of investors who wish to minimise transaction costs. This competition among companies could result in an equilibrium, where the supply of dividends is equal to investors' demand for cash payouts. As MM noted, if such an equilibrium exists and the needs of all investor clienteles are met, then one clientele is as good as another. In other words, there will be no incentive for one more company to adopt a dividend policy designed to suit the needs of a particular dividend clientele.

11.3.2 FLOTATION COSTS

If a company pays dividends and its retained profits are insufficient to meet its investment needs, then one solution is to raise funds externally. Alternatively, the company could increase the funds that are available internally by reducing or even eliminating its dividend. Under the MM assumption of no flotation costs, shareholders would be indifferent between these alternatives. In practice, a company that raises funds externally will incur flotation costs, which can be substantial. For example, if a company needs $1 million and flotation costs are 5 per cent, the company will need to issue shares with a value of $1 000 000/0.95 = $1 052 632 to raise a net $1 million. Existing shareholders may incur an additional cost if shares are issued to new shareholders when a company's management has confidential information that indicates that the company's shares are undervalued.[8] The existence of flotation costs provides an incentive to preserve shareholders' wealth by restricting dividends. Therefore, the best outcome for shareholders may be a *residual dividend policy*, where the company pays dividends only to the extent that it has profits which it cannot profitably invest.

11.3.3 BEHAVIOURAL FACTORS AND DIVIDENDS

Arguably, investors are not always rational and behavioural factors may result in dividends being valued more highly than cash generated by selling shares. One argument is that if investors sell shares to fund consumption they may sell more shares than necessary and 'overconsume'—at least initially. In other words, investors may lack self-control and may benefit from a source of external discipline. If investors adjust their consumption based on the dividends they receive, a company's dividend policy can provide that discipline by acting as a substitute for the self-control that investors lack when selling shares. In other words, dividends are a rationed source of cash that investors feel they can spend without needing to draw on their capital. Another argument is that investors who sell shares to generate cash just before the share market rises will regret their decision to sell, and this problem can be avoided if companies pay generous dividends.

There is evidence that investors are not always rational—but does an 'irrational' preference for dividends affect share prices? Given that there are many listed companies with a wide range of dividend policies, it should not be difficult to construct diversified portfolios that provide almost any dividend yield that an investor desires. Therefore, it is unlikely that investors will be prepared to pay a premium for the shares of an individual company that adopts a particular dividend policy. In summary, behavioural factors, like transaction costs, may mean that the total supply of dividends from the corporate sector is important to investors, but this does not mean that any individual company can affect its share price by adopting a particular dividend policy.

11.4 DIVIDENDS AND TAXES

Taxes can either favour or penalise the payment of dividends, depending on whether the tax burden on profits distributed as dividends is greater or less than the tax burden on capital gains arising from retained profits. Under the **classical tax system**, which applied in Australia until 30 June 1987, dividends were taxed in the hands of an investor at the investor's marginal tax rate, whereas capital gains were either tax-free or taxed at lower rates than dividends. The classical tax system is still used

---

8 The effects of this type of information asymmetry, which were analysed by Myers and Majluf (1984), are discussed in Section 12.9.2.

classical tax system
tax system that operates in the US and which operated in Australia until 30 June 1987; under this system company profits, and dividends paid from those profits, are taxed separately—that is, profit paid as a dividend is effectively taxed twice

LEARNING OBJECTIVE 5
Outline the imputation tax system and explain the effects of imputation and capital gains tax on returns to investors

in some countries, including the US.[9] Since dividends were paid from profits that were subject to company income tax, the classical tax system involved double taxation of company profits. Therefore, from a purely tax viewpoint, many investors were disadvantaged if they received a dividend and would have preferred that companies retain profits, thus allowing investors to realise returns as tax-advantaged capital gains. Despite the apparent tax disadvantage of paying dividends, many Australian companies did pay out a significant percentage of their profits as dividends. Of course, there may be a simple explanation: factors other than taxes affect payout decisions and, with share repurchases prohibited until 1989, payment of dividends was the only way of transferring cash from companies to their shareholders. However, in the US, where share repurchases were legal and taxes favoured repurchases relative to dividends, the amount of cash paid out as dividends exceeded the value of share repurchases each year until 1999. The additional tax burden on dividends suggested that the values of US companies would probably increase if cash was paid out by repurchasing shares instead of paying dividends. This observation caused Black (1976) to conclude that the dividend policies of US companies were a puzzle.

11.4.1 DIVIDENDS AND THE IMPUTATION TAX SYSTEM

The *imputation tax system* that was introduced in July 1987 has important effects on the taxation of dividends paid to investors in Australian companies. The basic intention of the imputation system is to eliminate the double taxation of company profits, which is inherent in the classical tax system previously used in Australia. This intention is achieved by giving resident shareholders a credit for the Australian income tax paid by a company on its taxable income. The overall effect is that the profit of a company distributed as dividends is effectively taxed only at the investor level, but the tax is collected primarily at the company level.

The imputation system operates as follows:

(a) Company income tax is assessed at the company income tax rate t_c. Therefore, at the current company income tax rate of 30 cents in the dollar, $100 of company profit will result in $30 being paid in company tax. It is critical to understand that this amount of $30 is therefore *both* profit earned by the company *and* company tax paid. The imputation system recognises this dual nature by adding $30 to the shareholder's income and *also* giving shareholders credit for $30 of tax paid.

(b) Dividends paid out of a company's after-tax profit are referred to as *franked dividends*. In this case, the maximum franked dividend that could be paid is $70. Each dollar of franked dividend carries a *franking credit* equal to $t_c/(1 - t_c)$. Therefore, a franked dividend of $70 will carry a franking credit of $70 × 0.30/(1 − 0.30) = $30. Shareholders who receive a franked dividend of $70 will include in their taxable income both the dividend received ($70) and the franking credit ($30). The shareholders' taxable income is thus $100.

(c) Shareholders are then taxed at their marginal tax rate but are then allowed a tax credit in recognition of the company tax paid. If, for example, the shareholder's personal tax rate is 45 cents in the dollar, then their tax liability is 0.45 × $100 = $45, less the tax credit of $30, so the *net* personal tax is $15. Therefore, the total tax on the $100 company profit is $45, of which $30 was collected from the company and $15 from the shareholder.

The effects of the imputation system on different types of resident shareholders who receive a franked dividend paid from a company profit of $100 are shown in Table 11.2.

---

[9] The classical tax system is still used in the US and much of the empirical research on dividend policy is based on US data, so it is important to have an understanding of the classical tax system.

TABLE 11.2 Effects of dividend imputation on resident shareholders

SHAREHOLDER	SUPERANNUATION FUND	MEDIUM-INCOME INDIVIDUAL	HIGH-INCOME INDIVIDUAL
Marginal tax rate (%)	15	30	45
Company profit ($)	100	100	100
less Company tax ($)	30	30	30
Franked dividend ($)	70	70	70
Net shareholder tax ($)	−15[a]	0	15
After-tax return ($)	85	70	55

[a] Excess franking credits are refunded (that is, paid in cash to the shareholder by the tax authorities).

Table 11.2 shows two important features of the imputation system. First, a company's after-tax profit paid out as franked dividends is effectively taxed only at the shareholders' 'personal' tax rate. To pay a franked dividend of $70 requires pre-tax company profit of $100 and if this amount were simply taxed at the shareholders' marginal tax rate, the after-tax returns would be the same as those shown in the final row of Table 11.2. Second, the after-tax return from franked dividends does *not* depend on the company income tax rate, and company income tax can be regarded as a *withholding tax* against the personal tax liabilities of shareholders. In other words, under imputation, payment of company income tax is effectively a pre-payment of personal tax.

Under the imputation system, it is only by payment of franked dividends that credits for company tax paid can be transferred to investors, who can then use the credits to offset their personal tax liabilities—that is, shareholders are unable to use tax credits until franked dividends are paid. Therefore, in an imputation system, the after-tax return to shareholders depends heavily on the company's dividend policy.

As discussed in Section 11.1.3, companies with operations in both Australia and New Zealand may elect to distribute Australian franking credits and New Zealand imputation credits to all shareholders. Such distributions have been allowed since 1 October 2003 and their effects are illustrated in Example 11.2.

EXAMPLE 11.2

All Black Ltd is owned 70 per cent by New Zealand residents and 30 per cent by Australian residents. The company has operations in Australia where it pays A$100 000 of company tax. It also pays company tax of NZ$200 000. The resultant Australian franking credits and New Zealand imputation credits are fully distributed and both are attached to the same dividends. What are the tax credits that can be claimed by the Australian and New Zealand resident shareholders? How much of the tax credits cannot be utilised?

SOLUTION

The Australian and New Zealand tax credits are distributed to all shareholders in proportion to their shareholdings in All Black Ltd. However, the tax credits from each country can be claimed only by residents of that country. Therefore, Australian resident shareholders will receive A$30 000 in franking credits (30 per cent of the total Australian company tax of A$100 000) and the remaining A$70 000 will be distributed to New Zealand resident shareholders who are unable to use them. Similarly, New Zealand resident shareholders will receive imputation credits of NZ$140 000 (70 per cent of the total New Zealand company tax of NZ$200 000) and the remaining NZ$60 000 will be distributed to Australian resident shareholders who are unable to use them.

11.4.2 IMPUTATION AND CAPITAL GAINS TAX

So far we have focused on the taxation of dividends, but, in practice, a significant proportion of the returns to shareholders are in the form of capital gains. Example 11.1 showed that payment of dividends reduces the value of shares and it follows that payment of dividends reduces the potential for shareholders to incur capital gains tax. If companies retain profits, the prices of their shares are likely to rise relative to those of companies that distribute profits, giving rise to capital gains tax liabilities for shareholders if and when the shares are sold.[10]

In Australia, capital gains tax applies only to gains on assets acquired on or after 20 September 1985, and is payable only when gains have been realised. The calculation of capital gains tax can differ depending on whether the asset was purchased before or after 21 September 1999. However, provided that the asset has been held for at least 12 months, the maximum rate of capital gains tax for an individual will be half the marginal tax rate on the individual's 'ordinary' income. In the case of superannuation funds, the maximum rate of capital gains tax on long-term gains is 10 per cent compared with their normal income tax rate of 15 per cent. The time value of money means that the present value of any capital gains tax payable is lower, the longer that realisation of gains is delayed. Also, investors are able to choose the time at which assets are sold and may therefore be able to realise gains at times when their marginal tax rate is low. In summary, effective rates of capital gains tax are likely to be low for many investors. However, where a capital gain arises from retention of profits that have been taxed, any capital gains tax that is payable will be *in addition* to the tax already paid by the company. In other words, retention of profits can involve double taxation: company income tax plus capital gains tax.

Future capital gains tax can be reduced by the payment of dividends, regardless of whether the dividend is franked or unfranked. Unfranked dividends are taxed as ordinary income in the hands of investors and carry no tax credits—in other words, the classical system of taxation continues to apply to unfranked dividends. Given that the effective rate of capital gains tax is likely to be less than an investor's marginal income tax rate, most investors are likely to prefer capital gains rather than unfranked dividends. As discussed in the next section, many investors will also have a tax-based preference for franked dividends rather than capital gains arising from retention of taxed profits.

The effects of taxation on dividends and capital gains for the main classes of investors in the Australian market are summarised in Table 11.3. Note that in relation to capital gains, the table shows details only of capital gains tax applicable at the investor level—that is, tax in addition to any company tax paid on retained profits that underlie the capital gains.

TABLE 11.3 Taxation of dividends and capital gains

	RESIDENT INDIVIDUALS	COMPANIES	SUPERANNUATION FUNDS	NON-RESIDENTS
Dividends	Dividend imputation effective from 1 July 1987. Franking credits can be offset against income tax on the shareholders' income (including capital gains), but not against the Medicare levy. Excess franking credits are refunded from 1 July 2000.	Franked dividends received by a resident company are handled using the same gross-up and credit approach that applies to resident individuals and superannuation funds. Thus, franking credits received reduce the amount of company tax payable.	Introduction of a 15% tax on earnings from 1 July 1988. Dividend imputation effective from that date. Excess franking credits are refunded from 1 July 2000.	Withholding tax on dividends, applied from 1 July 1960. From 1 July 1987, franked dividends exempt from withholding tax. Unfranked dividends are subject to a 30% withholding tax or 15% if covered by a double taxation treaty.

10 Remember that share prices drop on the ex-dividend date. The significance of this drop in price is discussed in Section 11.4.4.

	RESIDENT INDIVIDUALS	COMPANIES	SUPERANNUATION FUNDS	NON-RESIDENTS
Capital gains	Assets acquired after 19 September 1985 are subject to capital gains tax. If the asset is held for more than 1 year, it applies to the real component only until September 1999. On or after 21 September 1999, the amount of any capital gain realised on an asset held for at least 12 months may be discounted by 50%.	Same as for resident individuals until 20 September 1999. From 21 September 1999, the capital gain is included in the company's taxable income. Discounting of gains does not apply to companies.	All assets disposed of after 1 July 1988 subject to capital gains tax at the rate of 15%. If the asset is held for more than 1 year, it applies to the real component only until 20 September 1999. For capital gains realised on or after 21 September 1999 on assets held for at least 12 months, a discount of $33\frac{1}{3}$% is allowed.	Australian-related assets acquired after 19 September 1985 are subject to capital gains tax. Indexation for inflation applies to September 1999. For gains realised on or after 21 September 1999 discounting may apply. Exempt from Australian capital gains tax on shares in resident companies if the investor owns less than 10% of the company's shares.

Source: This table is based on T. Callen, S. Morling & J. Pleban, 'Dividends and taxation: a preliminary investigation', *Research Discussion Paper 9211*, Economic Research Department, Reserve Bank of Australia, p. 9, and updated based on *Master Tax Guide* 2004, CCH Australia Ltd, Sydney.

11.4.3 DIVIDEND POLICY WITH IMPUTATION AND CAPITAL GAINS TAX

In Section 11.4.1 we showed that company profits paid out as franked dividends are effectively taxed once at the shareholder's marginal tax rate. For example, company profit distributed as franked dividends to an investor on the top marginal rate will be taxed at 45 per cent. For each $1 of company taxable income, company tax of 30 cents will be payable, leaving 70 cents that can be paid out as a franked dividend. An Australian resident receiving that dividend will be taxed on an income of $1 (the dividend plus the franking credit of 30 cents) and can claim the franking credit. With a marginal tax rate of 45 per cent, the net tax payable by the investor will be 15 cents and the dividend income after all taxes will be $0.70 − $0.15 = $0.55.

The alternative to payment of dividends is retention of profits, which, as discussed in Section 11.4.2, can involve double taxation: income tax paid by the company plus capital gains tax paid by the shareholder. Now suppose that the after-tax income of 70 cents is instead retained by the company and the retained funds result in a capital gain of 70 cents when the shares are sold. If the date of the sale is less than 1 year after the shares were purchased, the capital gain of 70 cents will be taxed at 45 per cent, resulting in capital gains tax of $0.70 × 0.45 = $0.315. Therefore, the shareholder's after-tax income will be $0.70 − $0.315 = $0.385. Since this is much less than $0.55, it is clear that the Australian tax system provides a strong incentive for companies to pay the maximum possible in franked dividends. If the date of the sale is more than 1 year after the shares were purchased, the taxable capital gain will be 50 per cent of 70 cents or 35 cents, so the capital gains tax will be $0.35 × 0.45 = $0.1575. In this case the net receipts will be $0.70 − $0.1575 = $0.5425, which is still less, albeit only slightly so, than the income from profit distributed as a franked dividend. However, as discussed in Section 11.4.2, effective rates of capital gains tax can be lower than the rate we have used in this calculation. Thus, while the imputation system favours distribution of profits, the fact that long-term capital gains are taxed at lower rates than ordinary income reduces the incentive for distribution and for some investors the effective rate of capital gains tax may be so low that they would prefer retention of profits. Overall, the combination of the imputation system and capital gains tax means that investors could differ in their preferences for dividend income versus capital gains: shareholders with low (high) marginal tax rates will tend to prefer companies that pay dividends (retain profits).

Many Australian companies have significant operations offshore. Profits that are earned and taxed outside Australia cannot be paid to investors as franked dividends. Any dividends from these profits will be unfranked and therefore subject to tax at the shareholders' marginal income tax rate. In general, shareholders can be divided into three categories based on their tax position:

(a) Shareholders who are taxed at the same rate on ordinary income and capital gains. Investors in this category will be indifferent between payment of unfranked dividends and retention of profits.
(b) Shareholders who are taxed at a lower rate on capital gains than on ordinary income. Investors in this category will prefer retention of profits rather than payment of unfranked dividends.
(c) Shareholders who are taxed at a higher rate on capital gains than on ordinary income. Any investors in this category would prefer all profits to be distributed.

Under the Australian tax system, share traders who sell shares after holding them for less than 12 months would fall into the first category. Investors who hold shares for more than 12 months are in the second category. It is unlikely that any investors would fall into the third category. Therefore, many investors will have a tax-based preference for retention of profits rather than unfranked dividends, some will be indifferent between these alternatives and none should prefer payment of unfranked dividends.

Pattenden and Twite (2008) examined the dividend policies of a sample of Australian companies over the period 1982 to 1997 to assess the effects of the introduction of the imputation tax system in 1987. They found significant changes in both the magnitude and form of dividends, which supports the argument that taxes have an important role in determining payout policies. Their study is broad in that they examined the distribution of tax credits across all types of dividend payments. Accordingly, they measured gross dividend payouts defined as the sum of all cash dividends, scrip dividends, bonus shares issued in lieu of dividends and share repurchases. Investor demand for distribution of franking credits was expected to boost dividend payouts after the introduction of the imputation system, but corporate funding needs may well prompt additional share issues to offset the additional payouts. Therefore, Pattenden and Twite also examined net dividend payouts defined as gross dividend payouts net of cash raised by issuing shares through dividend reinvestment plans, rights issues, public issues and placements. In addition, they examined cases where companies began to pay dividends for the first time—known as dividend initiations—and also tested for changes in the volatility of payouts.

Consistent with investor demand for distribution of franking credits, Pattenden and Twite found that the introduction of the imputation tax system resulted in a higher frequency of dividend initiations, increases in gross and net dividend payout, greater use of dividend reinvestment plans and that the volatility of the gross dividend payout increased. They also found that the effects of the change in tax system differed across companies. For example, after the introduction of the imputation system, gross dividend payouts were higher for companies with a high effective Australian company tax rate and companies with a greater capacity to frank dividends were more likely to initiate dividends.

In summary, the imputation system creates an incentive to distribute profits as dividends—but only to the extent that the dividends can be franked. Where a company has profits that could be distributed as unfranked dividends, many investors will prefer that these profits be retained.

11.4.4 THE MARKET VALUE OF FRANKING CREDITS

The argument that investors will prefer franking credits to be distributed rather than retained assumes that these tax credits are valuable to investors. There is strong evidence to support this assumption. Much of this evidence has been obtained by observing rates of return on shares on the ex-dividend day and by observing the **dividend drop-off ratio**, which is the ratio of the decline in the share price on the ex-dividend day to the dividend per share. The basis for this approach is straightforward. Suppose that shares in XYZ Ltd will begin trading on an ex-dividend basis tomorrow. What effect should this have on the share price? Investors who buy XYZ shares tomorrow are paying for an interest in the company's future net cash flows. Investors who bought XYZ shares today were buying essentially the same interest in future net cash flows, *plus* the dividend. Therefore, the drop-off in share price between today and tomorrow should reflect the value to investors of the dividend. If the dividend is franked, then the drop-off in share price should reflect the combined value of the cash dividend and the associated franking credit. Example 11.3 illustrates the effect of franking credits on the ex-dividend drop-off.

dividend drop-off ratio
ratio of the decline in the share price on the ex-dividend day to the dividend per share

EXAMPLE 11.3

Norfolk Ltd shares have a closing price of $10.85 on 9 November 2012. On the next day they will begin trading on an ex-dividend basis. The dividend is 40 cents per share, fully franked at the company tax rate of 30 per cent. What is the expected ex-dividend share price?

SOLUTION
Investors who buy Norfolk shares on 10 November are paying for an interest in the company's future net cash flows. Investors who bought the shares on 9 November were buying essentially the same interest in future net cash flows, *plus* the dividend. Since the dividend is fully franked, it carries a tax credit that is equal to (dividend × t_c)/(1 − t_c) = ($0.40 × 0.30)/0.70 = 17.14 cents. Therefore, if expectations of Norfolk's future cash flows remain unchanged, and if both the dividend and the tax credit are fully valued by investors, the ex-dividend drop-off should be 40 cents + 17.14 cents = 57.14 cents, giving an expected ex-dividend share price of approximately $10.28.[11]

As shown in Example 11.3, the ex-dividend drop-off for franked dividends can be larger than the dividend because of the value of franking credits. There is clear evidence to support this claim in cases where companies pay large special dividends that are franked. In such cases, the share price fall on the ex-dividend date is typically more than the amount of the cash dividend. For example, in 1995 Energy Resources of Australia Ltd (ERA) paid a special dividend of $2.50 per share. The dividend was franked and carried a franking credit of $1.56 per share.[12] The ex-dividend date was 29 June 1995. The closing price of ERA shares on 28 June was $6.86 and on 29 June the closing price was $3.10. Thus, based on daily closing prices, the ex-dividend drop-off was $3.76, which is considerably more than the cash dividend of $2.50 and somewhat less than $4.06, which is the sum of the cash dividend plus the franking credit.

Several Australian studies of large samples of companies also provide evidence that franking credits are valuable. Bellamy (1994, p. 282) found that for each year in the period 1987–88 to 1991–92, the mean drop-off ratio for franked dividends exceeded that for unfranked dividends. For the whole period, the mean drop-off ratio for franked dividends was 0.89 compared with 0.66 for unfranked dividends. Brown and Clarke (1993) and Hathaway and Officer (2004) both studied the drop-off ratio and found

---
11 This result assumes that the tax rate on the grossed-up dividend is the same as the tax rate on capital gains.
12 At that time the company tax rate was 36 cents in the dollar, so a fully franked dividend of $2.50 would carry a tax credit of approximately $1.41. The larger tax credit for ERA's dividend reflects the fact that some of its tax credits were based on the company tax rate of 39 cents in the dollar, which applied previously. Other companies that paid similar special fully franked dividends include Joe White Maltings Ltd and George Weston Foods Ltd. The case of ERA's special dividend is discussed by McDonald and Collibee (1996).

that the market places a positive value on franking credits, but each study encountered difficulties in quantifying that value. For example, when their sample was restricted to large companies, Hathaway and Officer estimated that the value of franking credits was between 49 and 52 per cent of their face value. However, the results for small- and medium-sized companies were erratic and unreliable—a problem that they attributed to the fact that the shares of many small companies do not always trade over the ex-dividend date period. A related problem is that in many cases the dividends (and the associated franking credits) on ordinary shares are small relative to the share price and those prices can be quite volatile, which makes it difficult to accurately quantify the effect of shares beginning to trade ex-dividend. In other words, with relatively small dividends and high price volatility, the 'signal-to-noise ratio' is low in studies of this type. Feuerherdt, Gray and Hall (2010) address this problem by focusing on hybrid securities—preference shares—which have high dividend yields and prices that are relatively insensitive to market movements so the signal-to-noise ratio is much higher than for ordinary shares. During the period they studied, the company tax rate was 30 cents in the dollar, so a fully franked $1 dividend carried a franking credit of 43 cents.[13] Feuerherdt, Gray and Hall found that for all the securities they examined, the package of a $1 dividend and the associated franking credit had a value of $1. Hence, if cash dividends are fully valued by investors, they find that franking credits do not affect share prices—which is consistent with security prices being set by non-resident investors who place no value on franking credits.

Another problem in research of this type is that the cum dividend and ex-dividend prices are not simultaneous. The ex-dividend drop-off is typically measured from the close of trading on the last day of cum dividend trading to the close of trading on the following day. Over a 24-hour period the share price may change significantly due to overall market movements or the arrival of company or industry information. Therefore, ex-dividend drop-off ratios typically exhibit extreme variation. Walker and Partington (1999) overcame this problem by analysing data from 1 January 1995 to 1 March 1997, a period when the ASX allowed trading in cum dividend shares after the official ex-dividend date. By observing essentially simultaneous trades in cum dividend and ex-dividend shares they were able to observe an 'instantaneous drop-off ratio'. For a sample of 1015 trades covering 93 ex-dividend events they found that the average instantaneous drop-off ratio for fully franked dividends is 1.23. Therefore they concluded that a dollar of franked dividends is worth significantly more than $1.

Cannavan, Finn and Gray (2004) also identify problems inherent in using the dividend drop-off approach to estimate the value of franking credits. One problem is that efforts to separate the values of cash dividends and the tax credits attached to them rely on the implicit assumption that the value of dividends is independent of the degree of franking. If there are 'imputation clienteles' where resident investors are attracted to companies paying fully franked dividends, this assumption may not be valid. Another problem is that dividend drop-off studies typically assume that the value of tax credits remains the same over the sample period and is constant across companies in the sample.

Cannavan, Finn and Gray avoid these problems by inferring the value of tax credits from the relative prices of individual share futures contracts and the prices of the underlying shares. One advantage of this approach is that a larger number of observations can be used because it is not necessary to restrict the data to observations around the ex-dividend date. Another advantage is that the value of tax credits can be estimated separately for different types of shares. For example, tax-paying resident investors will value all tax credits highly, but non-residents will value tax credits only if they can in some way transfer tax credits to residents. Some schemes have been developed for making such transfers, but they can involve significant transaction costs, and the use of such schemes may be worthwhile only for high-yielding shares with fully franked dividends. Hence, if the marginal investors in Australian shares are non-residents, then the market value of tax credits may be related to the dividend yield.

---

13 The franking credit is 43 cents because $1/(1 − 0.3) − $1 = $1.43 − $1 = 43 cents.

In an effort to restrict transfers of tax credits between investors, the tax laws were amended in 1997 with the introduction of a holding period rule, which provides that an investor can use a franking credit only if the shares in the company are held at risk for at least 45 days around the date of dividend entitlement. Cannavan, Finn and Gray found that prior to the 45-day rule, franking credits were valued at up to 50 per cent of face value for high-yielding companies. After the introduction of the 45-day rule, they found no evidence of franking credits having any value. These results are consistent with share prices in the Australian market being set by non-resident investors who were able to extract some value from franking credits distributed by large high-yielding companies prior to the introduction of the 45-day rule. After the introduction of the rule, franking credits appear to be worthless in the hands of non-resident investors.

Beggs and Skeels (2006) examined the effects of dividend imputation on the ex-dividend share price drop from its inception to mid-2004. They addressed two more issues that complicate the use of dividend drop-off ratios to estimate the value of franking credits. First, the market value of a dollar of cash dividend may not be equal to the market value of a dollar of franking credit. Second, the values of both cash dividends and franking credits could change over time and any such changes may be related to amendments to the tax regime such as the introduction of the 45-day rule in 1997 and the refunding of excess franking credits from 1 July 2000. Beggs and Skeels found that gross drop-off ratios—that is, the ex-dividend price drop divided by the cash dividend plus the franking credit—were significantly less than 1 over the whole period studied. When their model was extended to provide separate estimates of the cash drop-off ratio and the franking credit drop-off ratio for each financial year, they found that the cash drop-off ratio was generally close to one but the estimated value was significantly less than one in five of the 18 years. In the case of the franking credit drop-off ratio, its value was not significantly different from zero for much of the period, which suggests that marginal investors placed no value on franking credits. Importantly, Beggs and Skeels found that the value of franking credits was positive in the 2001 to 2004 period. This finding suggests that the introduction of refunds for excess franking credits from 2000 caused a significant increase in the value of franking credits to marginal investors.

As discussed in Chapter 14, the findings outlined above have important implications for the debate on the effects of imputation on the cost of capital for Australian companies. However, it is important to note that the factor used to reflect the value of franking credits when estimating the cost of capital under the imputation tax system will not necessarily be the same as the value of a dollar of franking credits as discussed in this section. The studies discussed here provide estimates of the value of a dollar of franking credits, *given* that those credits have been distributed. In contrast, as discussed in Section 14.5.4 the effective company tax rate used in estimating the cost of capital also depends on the extent to which franking credits are used to reduce personal taxes.[14] This depends on a company's payout policy and on the ability of shareholders to utilise franking credits. While a full imputation tax system has the potential to 'eliminate company tax', Handley and Maheswaran (2008) analysed Australian Taxation Office data and found that, on average, only 67 per cent of the franking credits distributed by Australian companies were used to reduce personal taxes over the period 1990 to 2000. The average utilisation rate increased to 81 per cent over 2001 to 2004.

Under New Zealand's imputation tax system, imputation credits are normally attached to cash dividends but can also be distributed via taxable stock dividends (bonus issues). Thus, there are taxable stock dividends with imputation credits attached and non-taxable stock dividends that do not carry imputation credits. This provides another setting for examining whether investors value imputation credits.

Imputation credits cannot be used until they are distributed to shareholders. However, the value of any such credits being stored by a company should be reflected in its share price. This argument implies that shareholders can realise the value of undistributed imputation credits at any time by simply selling

---

14 This point is emphasised by Hathaway and Officer (2004), pp. 6–7.

their shares. Anderson, Cahan and Rose (2001) argue that taxable stock dividends distributed by New Zealand companies have two advantages. First, shareholders can realise the tax benefits of imputation credits without selling their shares. Second, the present value of the tax benefits is greater, the sooner they are distributed to investors. Therefore, if imputation credits are valuable to investors, the share price should increase when a company announces a taxable stock dividend. Moreover, the size of this increase should exceed the size of the reaction to the announcement of a non-taxable stock dividend. Consistent with this expectation, Anderson, Cahan and Rose found that taxable stock dividends were associated with average abnormal returns of 4.39 per cent over a 2-day announcement period, compared with 2.96 per cent for non-taxable stock dividends.

11.5 INFORMATION EFFECTS AND SIGNALLING TO INVESTORS

LEARNING OBJECTIVE 6
Understand the argument that payout decisions may have a role in providing signals to investors

There is empirical evidence that share price changes around the time of the announcement of dividend changes and share repurchases are positively related to the change in payout. For example, it is clear that announcements of large increases in dividends are often followed immediately by increases in share prices, and that reductions in dividends can result in decreases in share prices.[15] Miller and Modigliani (1961, pp. 415–21) claimed that these facts do not invalidate their dividend irrelevance theorem. They maintained that it is not the dividend payments *per se* that determine the value of a company, but the present and future cash flows from the company's investments. Managers will usually have better information about a company's prospects than outside shareholders and if this information affects their decisions about current dividend payments, then changes in dividends will convey management's 'inside' information about future cash flows to the market. Thus, the announcement of a change in dividends provides the *occasion* for a change in share price, but the change in dividends is not itself the *cause* of the price change. In summary, Miller and Modigliani's response was that the information effect of dividends can be consistent with their irrelevance theorem.

De Angelo and De Angelo dispute this approach and argue that the market's response to payout announcements can be explained without invoking the idea that the market is really responding to information about future earnings. They argue that payout policy does matter—that is, that the share market places a value on dividends—because investors value securities only for the payouts they are expected to provide (2006, p. 309). Therefore, it is logical that higher (lower) share prices follow the announcement of higher (lower) payouts.

If dividend announcements do convey information, it is possible that management deliberately uses dividend policy to *signal* information to investors.[16] This argument relies on the existence of information asymmetry, whereby management has valuable inside information about the company. For example, management may be very confident about the success of a new product it has launched. Could management not simply release a media statement telling everyone the good news? Yes it could—but would it be believed? A company might release such a statement even if it were not true. How can management release information in a manner that will be believed? Dividends may provide a credible signal about a company's 'quality' because the payment of dividends is evidence that the company generates sufficient cash to be able to pay dividends, and also provides information on management's expectations as to the company's future profitability. Other companies, with less favourable prospects, that attempt to imitate higher quality companies by increasing their payout cannot do so without increasing the risk of being forced to cut their dividend in the future.

---

15 Studies that formally document these effects include Healy and Palepu (1988) and Balachandran and Faff (2004).
16 Signalling models are discussed by Miller (1987).

As noted earlier, there is clear evidence that changes in dividends appear to convey new information about company value. Several US studies report that dividend increases (decreases) are associated with positive (negative) share price changes. For example, Grullon, Michaely and Swaminathan (2002) studied a large sample of dividend changes of at least 12.5 per cent over the period 1967 to 1993. They found that the average abnormal return over a 3-day announcement period was 1.34 per cent (median 0.95 per cent) for dividend increases and –3.71 per cent (median –2.05 per cent) for dividend decreases. Not surprisingly, dividend initiations (omissions) are associated with positive (negative) price changes that are larger than those that accompany dividend increases and decreases. Michaely, Thaler and Womack (1995) found average abnormal returns over a 3-day announcement period of 3.4 per cent for dividend initiations and –7.0 per cent for omissions. Using Australian data from 1996 to 1999, Balachandran and Faff (2004) found that announcements of special dividends were associated with mean (median) abnormal returns of 5.44 per cent (4.15 per cent) over a 3-day period.

Many studies focus on the relationship between current dividends and future earnings. In an early study, Watts (1973) tested whether current dividends can be used to predict earnings in the following year. He found that the relationship between dividends and future earnings was positive but weak. Watts concluded that: '… in general, if there is any information in dividends it is very small'. Healy and Palepu (1988) studied the profit performance of companies that initiated dividends and companies that omitted dividends. For their sample of companies that initiated dividends, earnings had increased rapidly prior to the dividend and continued to increase for the next 2 years. For companies that omitted dividends, earnings decreased in the year of omission but then increased significantly in subsequent years—which is the opposite of the prediction made by signalling models.

Benartzi, Michaely and Thaler (1997) found that there is a strong correlation between increases in dividends and recent increases in profit—that is, when dividends are increased, profits have already increased. However, they found little evidence that increases in dividends are followed by further increases in profit. In the 2 years following dividend increases, they found that profit changes are essentially unrelated to the dividend changes. In the case of dividend decreases they found that profits tend to *increase* over the next 2 years. Hence, their findings support the perverse result reported by Healy and Palepu.

De Angelo, De Angelo and Skinner (1996) examined the dividend decisions made by managers of 145 companies whose profit declined after at least 9 consecutive years of growth in profits. The dividend decision in Year 0, the year that the record of sustained profit growth was broken, could convey valuable information to outsiders to help them assess whether the downturn was likely to be transient or persistent. The managers of 99 of the 145 companies increased dividends in Year 0, but De Angelo, De Angelo and Skinner found no evidence that these dividend increases were associated with favourable profit surprises in the future. Also, the subsequent profit performance of the companies that increased dividends was no better than that of the companies that did not change their dividends. Essentially, the study found virtually no support for the notion that dividend decisions provide reliable signals about future profit.

The findings of Grullon, Michaely and Swaminathan (2002) confirm the results from earlier studies. They examined the profitability (measured by return on assets) of companies 3 years before and 3 years after a change in dividends of at least 12.5 per cent. They found that dividend-increasing companies move from a period of increasing return on assets before the dividend increase to a period of declining return on assets after the increase. Moreover, companies that increased their dividends the most experienced the greatest decline in profitability. Dividend decreases follow a period of declining return on assets, but after the dividend decrease, company profitability tends to recover rather than decline further.

After reviewing the large body of empirical evidence on the information signalling argument, Allen and Michaely (2003) conclude that: 'The overall accumulated evidence does not support the assertion that dividend changes convey information about future profit'. They also conclude that if company managers do use dividends to signal, 'the signal is not about future growth in earnings or cash flows'.

While there is agreement that the traditional view that managers use dividends to signal their expectations of future profits is not supported by empirical evidence, several authors have suggested that payout policy may still provide useful information to investors. For example, Allen, Bernardo and Welch (2000) argue that paying dividends is an effective way of attracting institutions as shareholders. Institutions such as pension funds are either largely or fully exempt from taxes and therefore may be happy to invest in dividend-paying shares. Also, because of their scale, institutions have a greater incentive than individuals to become well informed about a company's activities and to monitor its performance. Therefore, paying dividends increases the likelihood that a company's true quality will be detected by investors. It follows that companies that are successful and well managed have an incentive to pay dividends, even if this increases taxes for some investors—as is the case for most individual investors under the classical tax system. Allen, Bernardo and Welch argue that having institutions as shareholders makes it likely that a company will remain well managed so the resultant benefit to all shareholders can offset the tax disadvantage of dividends for taxable investors. Companies that are less successful or poorly managed have no incentive to imitate the better companies because they will prefer that their shareholders remain uninformed and inactive.

Grullon, Michaely and Swaminathan (GMS) (2002) take a different approach. They reason that if the information conveyed by dividend changes is not about future profitability, then it may relate to changes in risk and, therefore, discount rates. As noted earlier, they studied a large sample of dividend changes of at least 12.5 per cent announced by US companies between 1967 and 1993. GMS found that companies that increase (decrease) dividends experience a significant decrease (increase) in systematic risk. Companies that increase dividends also experience a significant decline in return on assets and increases in their payout ratio tend to be permanent.

GMS propose what they refer to as the 'maturity hypothesis'. As companies make the transition from a higher growth phase in their life cycle to a lower growth (mature) phase, their investment opportunities decline, which shows up in a declining rate of reinvestment, declining return on investment and declining risk. The declining reinvestment rate gives rise to excess cash, which should be paid out to investors. This maturation process is likely to be a lengthy one, but GMS argue that larger cash payouts may be important signs of this lengthy process. Why would the market react positively to higher cash payouts if they are associated with companies making the transition from a growth phase to a mature stage with lower return on assets and lower growth prospects? GMS found that the decline in risk experienced by dividend-increasing companies results in an economically significant decline in their cost of capital. They also 'show that this decline in the cost of capital can account for the positive price reaction to the dividend-increase announcement, even when the dividend change conveys information about a decline in the company's growth prospects' (2002, p. 421).

Skinner and Soltes (2011) test whether payout policy provides information about the 'quality' of a company's reported earnings.[17] They find that the relationship between current earnings and future earnings is stronger for companies that pay dividends than for those that do not. In other words, the reported earnings of dividend-paying companies are more persistent than those of other companies and they find that it is dividends *per se* that matter rather than the magnitude of those dividends. Given that share repurchases are another important way of paying out cash, Skinner and Soltes also test whether repurchase activity is informative about earnings quality. They find that it is, but repurchases provide a less credible signal than dividends—which is to be expected, since dividends represent a stronger commitment to continue to distribute cash to shareholders.

---

17 There is no single definition of 'earnings quality' but the concept may be illustrated by noting that a high-quality reported earnings number is one that accurately reflects a company's operating performance and is a useful measure for assessing the value of the company. Skinner and Soltes use the persistence of earnings to measure earnings quality.

As noted earlier, Brav, Graham, Harvey and Michaely (2005) surveyed and interviewed financial executives to determine the factors that are important in making payout decisions. They find that managers agree that both dividends and repurchases can convey information to investors. However, their responses to more detailed questions reveal little support for the signalling theories we have discussed. In particular, it is rare that managers view either type of payout as a tool that can be used to reveal private information or to signal a company's quality relative to competitors. Similarly, managers believe that dividends and repurchases are equally attractive to most institutional investors. Consequently, even companies that wish to attract institutions as shareholders do not consciously use payout policy as an important tool to convince institutions to hold their shares. Managers do, however, see a connection between risk reduction and dividend increases. Many hold views that are consistent with the 'maturity hypothesis' proposed by GMS—that is, companies typically increase dividends when they become more mature and less risky.

The next section discusses the role of dividends in reducing agency costs. The signalling and agency cost arguments are related, but the way they are viewed differs depending on the underlying model that is adopted. If the Miller and Modigliani (MM) dividend irrelevance theorem is used as the starting point, the signalling argument says that dividend changes *convey* news. Alternatively, the De Angelo and De Angelo (DD) full payout model holds that dividends are important, so it has no need to invoke the information and signalling concepts to explain why share prices react to dividend-related announcements. In the case of agency costs, there is no difference between the MM and DD approaches: in both cases the agency cost argument says that dividends *are* good news.

AGENCY COSTS AND CORPORATE GOVERNANCE 11.6

We saw in Chapter 1 that, given the separation of ownership and control of companies, there can be conflicts of interest between shareholders and managers resulting in agency costs. Shareholders are aware that these costs exist and may therefore impose restrictions on managers and give them incentives to make financing and investment decisions that are expected to increase shareholders' wealth. Various authors have argued that paying higher dividends can reduce agency costs, but there is no single or generally agreed model of how dividends achieve this outcome. Different authors have suggested different mechanisms.

LEARNING OBJECTIVE 7

Explain the ways in which agency costs can be related to payout decisions

One approach is based on the fact that higher dividends will force a company to raise capital externally more frequently than would otherwise be the case (Easterbrook 1984). Capital raising is accompanied by the provision of information to investors, underwriters and other capital market agents, particularly potential new investors. As a result, investors will have the opportunity to scrutinise the company closely at a relatively low cost. The capital raising process provides an efficient mechanism for contributors of new capital to monitor the performance of the managers. Existing shareholders also benefit from this process because managers who are subject to regular monitoring are more likely to act in shareholders' interests than managers subject to less scrutiny.

Another approach focuses on the agency costs that are likely to arise when a company generates *free cash flows*, which are defined as cash flows in excess of those required to fund all available projects that have positive NPVs. Managers have incentives to achieve growth because it is likely that the larger the company, the greater will be their power and remuneration. Therefore, managers of companies with free cash flows are likely to retain cash and invest it in new projects, even if the projects have negative NPVs. This problem is known as overinvestment. It follows that shareholders' wealth will be increased if managers commit themselves to paying out this cash as dividends rather than retaining it within the company (Jensen 1986).[18] This argument provides another possible explanation for the positive market response to announcements of dividend increases: investors welcome the higher payout mainly because they believe that managers cannot be relied upon to invest retained funds profitably.

This argument should be particularly strong for cash-rich companies in mature industries with few growth opportunities. Lang and Litzenberger (1989) tested this hypothesis using a measure known as Tobin's Q, which is the ratio of the market value of a company's assets to the estimated replacement cost of those assets. If a company is successful (unsuccessful) in identifying investments with positive NPVs, its Q ratio should be greater (less) than one. For announcements of dividend increases, Lang and Litzenberger found that low Q companies had larger share price increases than high Q companies. They interpreted this finding as being consistent with the free cash flow hypothesis. However, this interpretation was questioned by Denis, Denis and Sarin (1994) and Yoon and Starks (1995), who found that after controlling for the effects of dividend yield and change in dividend yield, the market reaction to announcements of dividend changes was not related to a company's Q ratio.

Lie (2000) undertook a direct examination of the relationship between excess cash and payout policy in the context of special dividends, increases in regular dividends and share repurchases. He found that in all three cases, companies making these payouts had higher cash holdings prior to the payout than others in the same industry. Lie also found that the market reaction to the announcement of special dividends and share repurchases was positively related to the level of cash relative to industry norms. Moreover, this relationship was stronger for companies with poor investment opportunities as indicated by their having a Q ratio of less than one. Lie concluded that shareholders' wealth could be enhanced by distributing cash and thereby restricting potential overinvestment by managers. As discussed in the previous section, the findings of Grullon, Michaely and Swaminathan (2002) are also consistent with the free cash flow hypothesis.

In summary, evidence on the significance of the free cash flow hypothesis is mixed, but most of it is consistent with the argument that higher payouts can add value by reducing the potential for management to overinvest. Similarly, it is not hard to find cases where investors welcome increased payouts because the higher payout indicates that management has changed its priorities. The response to an announcement by the Chairman of Telstra Corporation in June 2004 is a good example (see Finance in Action, on p. 360).[19]

La Porta, Lopez-De-Silanes, Shleifer and Vishny (2000) outline and test two agency models of dividends using legal protection of shareholders as a proxy for agency problems between corporate insiders and outsiders. The 'outcome model' proposes that dividends are paid because effective legal protection allows outside shareholders to pressure corporate insiders to pay out cash, thus limiting the extent to which insiders can use company profits to benefit themselves.[20]

Alternatively, dividends may be seen as a substitute for legal protection of shareholders. This view is based on the need for companies to approach the capital markets to raise funds externally, at least occasionally. The 'substitute model' proposes that insiders, who are interested in raising equity in the future, pay dividends to establish a reputation for favourable treatment of outside shareholders. A good reputation will be of greatest value in countries where legal protection of minority shareholders is weak and such shareholders have little to rely on apart from a company's reputation.

La Porta, Lopez-De-Silanes, Shleifer and Vishny tested these models using a sample of more than 4000 companies from 33 countries with different legal systems and different legal protection of

---

18 Jensen argues that the use of debt finance will be particularly effective in reducing these agency costs because severe penalties are associated with failure to meet obligations to lenders. Commitments to pay regular dividends may have a similar, but less pronounced, effect because of the well-known reluctance of managers to reduce dividends.

19 The example outlined here is discussed more fully by Easton and Howard (2005).

20 This argument does not rely on outside shareholders having any specific right to dividends. Rather, the argument is that shareholders who have the more general rights to vote for directors and to resist oppression and wealth expropriation will be able to extract dividends from companies. For example, shareholders may vote for directors who offer better dividend policies or may sue companies that use resources in ways that benefit only the insiders.

shareholders. Investor protection is generally stronger in common law countries such as the US, UK and Australia than it is in civil law countries such as France, Spain and Japan. The outcome model has two testable predictions. First, if dividends are an outcome of an effective system of legal protection for investors, then dividends should be higher in countries where that protection is better. Second, for companies in these countries it predicts a relationship between investment opportunities and dividends. High-growth companies should make lower payouts than low-growth companies because shareholders who feel well protected will accept low payouts from companies with good investment opportunities. The alternative substitute model makes only one prediction: dividend payouts should be higher in countries where legal protection of investors is weak.

La Porta, Lopez-De-Silanes, Shleifer and Vishny found consistent support for the outcome model. Companies operating in countries where legal protection of investors is better pay higher dividends. This result is consistent with the outcome model and is the reverse of the substitute model's prediction. Also, in countries where investors are well protected, there is a relationship between dividends and growth. Companies that are growing more rapidly, as measured by growth in sales, pay lower dividends than slow-growth companies. This finding is consistent with the view that investors who are well protected legally are prepared to wait for dividends provided that a company has good investment opportunities.

Correia Da Silva, Goergen and Renneboog (2004) propose that dividend policy may be influenced by corporate governance regimes that, like investor protection, differ between countries. They define a corporate governance regime as 'the amalgam of mechanisms which ensure that the agent (the management of a corporation) runs the company for the benefit of one or multiple principals (shareholders, creditors, suppliers, clients, employees and other parties with whom the company conducts its business)' (p. 156).

Corporate governance regimes may be market based or blockholder based. The market-based regime applies in countries such as the UK, the US and Australia and is characterised by diffuse ownership of listed companies, the one-share-one-vote rule, an active market for corporate control and strong shareholder and creditor rights. In contrast, the blockholder system that is common in Europe involves the presence of large blockholders, complex ownership structures such as cross-ownership between companies, frequent violations of the one-share-one-vote rule and weak legal protection of shareholders. Correia Da Silva, Goergen and Renneboog suggest that dividend policy may have different roles under these two regimes. For example, the greater concentration of control that is inherent in the blockholder system may mean that there is less pressure on managers to commit to paying high dividends as a way of avoiding overinvestment. Also, dividends may be less important as a signal when control is more concentrated.

As well as involving differences in the concentration of control, the two regimes differ in terms of the nature of control. In market-based countries, most shares are held by financial institutions but the holding of each institution in a given company is usually small. In European countries the main shareholder categories are families or individuals, corporations and, in the case of Germany, banks. Banks are an important source of finance for German companies and often hold significant voting stakes as well as being the main provider of debt finance. Thus, the separation of ownership and control that is the source of many agency problems under the market-based regime is not an issue for many German companies.

Correia Da Silva, Goergen and Renneboog examined the dividend policies of German companies and compared their findings with those from the existing body of empirical research, most of which has been conducted on companies operating under the market-based system. They found several differences between the dividend practices of German companies compared with UK and US companies. First, German companies pay out a lower proportion of their cash flows. Second, while the dividends per share of UK and US companies are relatively smooth over time with frequent small adjustments, the dividends per share of German companies exhibit less frequent but larger changes. In particular, German companies frequently reduce or omit dividends if they incur a loss, but quickly revert to the payout prior to the reduction or omission once profitability is restored. These findings contrast with Lintner's prediction that managers will only make dividend changes that they believe will not have to be reversed in the short run. In other words, the blockholder regime of corporate governance appears to provide companies with greater flexibility in terms of their dividend policies. Another important result is that bank ownership of the voting equity of German companies is associated with a lower level of dividends and a greater propensity to omit the dividend when profit falls. Thus, direct control by a bank can be seen as reducing agency costs.

In summary, the legal protection of investors that was stressed by La Porta, Lopez-De-Silanes, Shleifer and Vishny may not be the most important factor that explains differences in dividend policy between countries. Other differences between corporate governance regimes, such as the concentration and nature of control, are also important and the evidence from Correia Da Silva, Goergen and Renneboog's study is consistent with the view that control is a substitute for dividends as a mechanism for monitoring management and reducing agency costs.

FINANCE IN ACTION

AGENCY COSTS AT TELSTRA

The market reaction to the announcement in June 2004 of a new capital management strategy for Telstra Corporation provides an excellent illustration of the role that payout policy can play in alleviating investors' concerns about the use of free cash flows.

Telstra, Australia's largest telecommunications company, had been strongly criticised in previous years over its strategy of growth by acquisition. This strategy—regarded by critics as poorly executed—led to investments in Asia and technology-related investments that resulted in write-downs of more than $2 billion. A failed attempt to merge its directories business with media company John Fairfax Holdings also attracted criticism, split the Telstra board and contributed to the resignation in April 2004 of former chairman, Bob Mansfield. The Fairfax plan had been put forward by Mansfield together with [then] Telstra CEO, Dr Ziggy Switkowski.

On 21 June 2004, the new chairman of Telstra released a statement on capital management which included the following:

> The Telstra Board of Directors has undertaken with management its review of the Company's strategy as part of the annual budget and planning process. The operating strategy of Telstra has been reaffirmed and new capital settings have been established.
>
> The Company expects future cash flows from operations to remain robust.
>
> Accordingly, the Board has adopted the following capital management policies from the 2004–05 year:
>
> - The Board's policy will be to declare ordinary dividends of around 80 per cent of normal profits after tax.
> - The Board expects to return $1.5 billion to shareholders each year for the next three years through special dividends and/or share buybacks, subject to maintaining the Board's target balance sheet ratios.
> - The Board notes that after appropriate capital expenditures and the proposed capital returns to shareholders, the company will have sufficient balance sheet capacity to support <u>well targeted acquisitions of moderate scale and which satisfy strict financial criteria</u> [emphasis added].

Analysts noted that the higher cash payout would result in higher financial leverage and the announcement sparked a credit downgrade by rating agencies such as Standard & Poor's. Telstra shares jumped by 4.6 per cent in response to the announcement to a nine-month high of $5.02. Peter Morgan, director of fund manager 452 Capital, said: 'This is a step in the right direction. If they have excess capital, they should be returning it to shareholders. What the market has been concerned about is that their acquisitions so far have been disappointing'. Other commentators pointed to the significance of the Board's commitment to an 80 per cent payout ratio in comparison to the previous commitment to distribute at least 60 per cent of profits.

Source: www.telstra.com.au/abouttelstra/investor/docs/tls235_capitalmanagement.pdf.

11.7 SHARE BUYBACKS

Most cash paid out to the shareholders of Australian companies is distributed as dividends. As discussed in Section 11.1.4, changes to the Corporations Act in 1989 and 1995 mean that companies can also pay cash to shareholders by repurchasing shares. This method of distributing cash has grown rapidly since 1995. In the 1995 financial year, share repurchases by listed companies totalled $770 million (Renton 2000, p. 38) and, as noted in Section 11.1.4, the total peaked at about $12 billion in the 12 months to December 2007 before declining significantly during the global financial crisis. Rapid growth in share repurchases during the 1990s appears to be a global phenomenon. Many other countries that previously prohibited share repurchases, such as Germany and Japan, also introduced provisions that allow companies to repurchase shares. Share repurchases also grew dramatically in countries like the US, Canada and the UK where repurchases had long been permitted. For example, between 1985 and 1996, the value of open-market repurchase programs announced by US industrial companies increased by 750 per cent from $15.4 billion to $113 billion, while aggregate dividends increased by a factor of just over two during the same period (Jagannathan, Stephens & Weisbach 2000, p. 356). In 1999, for the first time in history, and again in 2000, US industrial companies distributed more cash to investors through share repurchases than through cash dividends (Grullon & Michaely 2004, p. 651).

> **LEARNING OBJECTIVE 8**
> Be familiar with the nature of share buybacks, dividend reinvestment plans and dividend election schemes

11.7.1 WHY DO COMPANIES REPURCHASE SHARES?

If there are no taxes or other imperfections, repurchasing shares is effectively the same as paying a cash dividend. Accordingly, many of the factors that may explain why companies repurchase shares are the same as those that may explain why they pay dividends. For example, if the agency costs of free cash flow can be reduced by paying dividends, they can also be reduced by repurchasing shares. In terms of a company's assets and operations, the end result of taking surplus cash out of the company should be the same, regardless of the method used to pay out the cash. Indeed, Grullon and Michaely (2004) report that their analysis 'indicates strong similarities between companies that increase dividends and those that use open-market share repurchases' (p. 653). In both cases, profitability does not increase and risk and the cost of capital decline. They conclude that these and other similarities suggest that 'similar factors motivate companies to repurchase shares in the open market and to increase dividends' (p. 654). However, the method of payment can matter. For example, suppose that managers are more reluctant to cut dividends than they are to cancel share repurchase programs. It follows that dividends may be better in controlling agency costs because they represent a stronger commitment to continue paying out cash. Similarly, dividends and share repurchases may both be used as signals of a manager's expectations but the information conveyed to investors may be different. In particular, an increase in dividends is likely to signal a more permanent increase in cash flows than a one-off share repurchase.

In this section we discuss several factors that may influence the decision to return cash to shareholders by repurchasing shares and review empirical evidence on the effects of share repurchases.

Improved performance measures

Company announcements of share buybacks and reports in the financial press often mention that the buyback is expected to have a favourable effect on performance measures, particularly earnings per share (EPS) and net assets per share. Focusing on the effects on EPS may reflect an assumption that the market will react mechanically to increases in EPS by increasing the share price. This 'EPS-based' rationale for buybacks raises two main issues.

First, to repurchase shares a company must use cash that could have been invested elsewhere. Therefore, unless the buyback is financed by borrowing, the company will have fewer assets after the buyback. If the assets were being used efficiently, earnings will also be lower so EPS will increase only if the decrease in earnings is less, in percentage terms, than the decrease in the number of shares on issue. If the company has surplus cash that it cannot invest profitably, then using the cash to repurchase shares should certainly increase EPS. However, the real source of any gain to investors is the more efficient use of resources, not some magical reaction to the higher EPS.

Second, a share buyback reduces the company's equity and increases its financial leverage, particularly if the buyback is financed by borrowing. Higher leverage means higher risk for shareholders and this will tend to reduce the share price and hence lower the price–earnings (P/E) ratio. In summary, if the only reason for a share buyback is that it is expected to increase EPS, the probability that the share price will increase is low.

Signalling and undervaluation

As discussed in Section 11.5, managers are likely to have better information about a company's true value than outside investors and may use changes in dividends to convey information to investors. Arguably, share repurchases may serve a similar purpose. In the case of share repurchases, there are two versions of the signalling hypothesis. The first version is that the announcement of a share repurchase could provide *new* information: managers expect that earnings and cash flows will be higher in the future. The second version is that managers may use repurchases to indicate that they disagree with the market's valuation of the company based on *existing* public information. Several studies, including Comment and Jarrell (1991), find negative abnormal returns in the months prior to the announcement of open-market repurchase programs. This finding suggests that managers make repurchase announcements at times when they believe that the shares are undervalued.

Early studies, such as Bartov (1991), found support for the first version of the signalling hypothesis in that there is some evidence of earnings growth following repurchases. However, the findings of a more recent and comprehensive study (Grullon & Michaely 2004) are inconsistent with the hypothesis that repurchases signal good news about future earnings. This study found a significant decline in operating profit as a percentage of total assets over the 3 years following the announcement of a repurchase program. It also found that analysts revise their forecasts of earnings per share downwards after these announcements are made.

Managers who believe that their company's shares are undervalued could try to signal that belief by increasing dividends or repurchasing shares. Any share price increase following an increase in dividends accrues proportionately to all current shareholders. In contrast, if the share price appreciates following a repurchase, then insiders and any other shareholders who do not sell will benefit disproportionately. This difference suggests that perceived undervaluation may lead managers to favour repurchases rather than dividend increases.

To examine the undervaluation version of the signalling hypothesis, Ikenberry, Lakonishok and Vermaelen (1995) analysed share returns for a period of 4 years following repurchase announcements by more than 1200 US companies. For the whole sample they found excess returns of more than 12 per cent over the 4-year period. Excess returns were measured relative to a benchmark portfolio formed on the basis of company size and book-to-market ratio. This overall result is consistent with the possibility that companies are undervalued, on average, at the time repurchases are announced. Ikenberry, Lakonishok and Vermaelen also found that excess returns over the 4-year period were strongly related to the book-to-market ratio. For companies with the lowest book-to-market ratio ('glamour' stocks), the average excess return was slightly negative, while for those with the highest book-to-market ratio ('value' stocks), the average excess return was extremely high. The sample contained companies with a wide range of book-to-market ratios and was not significantly biased towards value stocks.

In summary, the results suggest that some groups of companies are fairly priced at the time of repurchase announcements, but in other cases managers do appear to be indicating that their company is undervalued.

Resource allocation and agency costs

The share market plays an important role in allocating capital between competing investment opportunities. Profitable companies with good investment opportunities should experience increases in share price that make it easier to raise capital. Conversely, if a company has run out of positive NPV investments, then any surplus capital should be returned to shareholders, who are then free to invest it elsewhere. If share repurchases are part of this process of resource allocation in the capital market, then repurchases should be associated with reduced investment opportunities.

The empirical evidence is consistent with this suggestion. US companies that repurchase shares via tender offers do, on average, have smaller asset bases after the repurchase transactions. Similarly, US companies subsequently make lower capital expenditures after open market repurchases (Nohel & Tarhan 1998). Grullon and Michaely (2004) found that any changes in profitability in the years after share repurchase are negative rather than positive. Like Nohel and Tarhan, they found that companies that repurchase their shares subsequently decrease their investments. Grullon and Michaely conclude that repurchase announcements are viewed positively by investors because they are related to a reduction in the agency costs of free cash flow.

In summary, there is evidence that share repurchases are important in allowing capital to be released from declining sectors of the economy and reallocated to sectors where the investment opportunities are better.

Financial flexibility

Jagannathan, Stephens and Weisbach (2000) propose that the choice between dividends and repurchases is influenced by financial flexibility. As suggested by Lintner, managers prefer to increase dividends regularly and try to avoid decreasing them. Therefore, dividends are effectively an ongoing commitment, whereas repurchases do not implicitly commit the company to future payouts. In other words, repurchases preserve financial flexibility relative to dividends. Jagannathan, Stephens and Weisbach test the hypothesis that repurchases are used to distribute cash flows that are likely to be temporary, while dividends are used to distribute 'permanent' cash flows. The results of their tests support this hypothesis. For example, they found that companies with higher operating cash flows are more likely to increase dividends, while companies with higher non-operating cash flows are more likely to increase repurchases. Guay and Harford (2000) address the same issue using a different methodology and reach the same conclusion: the 'permanence' of an increase in cash flows is an important factor that influences the choice between paying out the extra cash by increasing dividends and making a share repurchase.

Employee share options

Another factor that can influence the choice between dividends and repurchases is the existence of employee share options. Employees, particularly senior managers, may receive part of their remuneration in the form of call options on the company's shares. The existence of these options is likely to favour repurchases relative to dividends because dividends and share repurchases have different effects on the prices of options on shares. As discussed in Section 18.2.5, the value of a call option is negatively related to future dividends on the underlying share because the price of a share is expected to fall on each ex-dividend date. In contrast, repurchasing shares at the market price should not affect the share price or the value of call options held by managers. Fenn and Liang (2001) examined this issue and found that option holdings by management are strongly related to the composition of payouts. Management share options induce a substitution of repurchases for dividends.

Dividend substitution

The dividend substitution hypothesis proposes that share repurchases and payment of dividends are simply alternative ways of distributing company profits to shareholders. For example, if a company reports higher earnings and maintains the same dividend but also announces a share repurchase, then the repurchase may be seen as a substitute for dividends. One important difference between share repurchases and dividends involves the tax treatment of investors' income. Under most tax systems (including Australia's), long-term capital gains are taxed less heavily than ordinary income. Even if the marginal tax rates applicable to capital gains and dividends are the same, investors are likely to prefer capital gains because they are able to defer the realisation of gains and the payment of taxes. Therefore, the rapid growth of share repurchases may reflect, at least in part, a tax-driven substitution of repurchases for dividends. Fama and French (2001) reported that the proportion of US companies paying cash dividends has fallen relentlessly since 1978 and that by 1999 only 20.8 per cent of publicly traded non-financial non-utility companies paid dividends. Their analysis suggests that the decision to pay dividends is influenced by three characteristics:

(a) profitability
(b) investment opportunities
(c) size.

Companies that are larger and more profitable are more likely to pay dividends, while dividends are less likely for companies with more investment opportunities. The decline in the proportion of companies that pay dividends is due in part to the listing of very large numbers of small 'growth' companies that make large investment outlays and have yet to pay any dividends. However, after controlling for company characteristics, Fama and French (2001) also found a significant decline in the likelihood that a company pays dividends. In other words, the perceived benefits of paying dividends appear to have declined over time, leading to an increase in the relative popularity of share repurchase. They found that most repurchases are made by companies that also pay dividends and conclude that: 'the large share repurchases of 1993–98 are mostly due to an increase in the desired payout ratios of dividend payers, which they are reluctant to satisfy with cash dividends' (p. 39).

Grullon and Michaely (2002) reported several findings which indicate that US companies have gradually substituted share repurchases for dividends. The dividend-payout ratios of US companies declined in the 1980s and 1990s but the total payout ratio did not decline over that period. Also, companies that initiated cash payouts favoured repurchases over dividends. The proportion of companies initiating distributions through repurchases rather than dividends increased from 27 per cent in 1973 to 81 per cent in 1998. They also found that, since the mid-1980s, established dividend-paying companies rely more on share repurchases than dividends to increase their cash payouts. Finally, they found evidence that investors view repurchases as a substitute for dividends. In particular, they found that the market reaction to dividend decreases—which is generally negative—is not significantly different from zero if the company has repurchased shares in the recent past.

Skinner (2008) also finds strong evidence that since share repurchases first became significant in the US in the early 1980s they have increasingly been substituted for dividends. For example, in the case of companies that pay annual dividends and make regular repurchases, the relationship between earnings and dividends becomes weaker from 1980 to 2005, but repurchases adjust quickly to changes in earnings, which is consistent with the greater flexibility of repurchases. Companies in this category have generally been paying dividends for many years (or decades) and Skinner argues that they continue to do so because of their history—given the well-known reluctance to cut dividends, these companies are essentially forced to continue paying them. In the case of companies with no significant dividend history which make repurchases either regularly or occasionally, Skinner again finds that earnings are increasingly important in explaining repurchases over the period of his study. He argues that newer companies without a dividend history are unlikely to initiate dividends once they are in a position to commence payouts and that dividends may eventually disappear in the US.

11.7.2 SHARE REPURCHASES IN AUSTRALIA

As in the US and other countries, the factors discussed in the previous section may be important in motivating the management of an Australian company to repurchase some of its shares. In addition, as noted in Section 11.1.4, in Australia an off-market share buyback can be structured to include a franked dividend and this feature can have significant tax advantages for resident investors, particularly those with a low marginal tax rate such as superannuation funds (see Finance in Action).

FINANCE IN ACTION

WOOLWORTHS' 2010 OFF-MARKET SHARE BUYBACK

The share buyback completed in October 2010 by Woolworths Ltd (WOW) is typical of the off-market buybacks conducted by several large Australian companies. Two important features of such buybacks are that the buyback price includes a significant fully franked dividend component as well as a capital component, and that the buyback price is determined by a tender process.

In August 2010, Woolworths announced that it intended to buy back up to $700 million worth of shares. Shareholders who chose to participate in the buyback were invited to select a tender discount from seven discounts of 8 per cent to 14 per cent inclusive to the Market Price—which was defined as the volume weighted average price of WOW shares traded on the ASX over the five trading days up to and including the closing date for tenders (8 October). The closing price of WOW shares on 25 August 2010 (the last trading day before details of the buyback were announced) was $26.90. All shares bought through the buyback were bought at the same price, the buyback price, which was determined through the tender process. Tenders were accepted only if the shareholder's tender discount was equal to or greater than the buyback discount. Shareholders could also choose to make a 'Final Price Tender', in which case they would receive the buyback price but there was no assurance that successful tenders would be accepted in full because the company had the right to apply a scale back if the number of shares tendered exceeded the number it was prepared to buy. Therefore, the success of each tender depended on the shareholder's tender discount, the size and discount of tenders lodged by other shareholders, and the total number of tenders the company accepted. In summary, shareholders who decided to tender their shares faced uncertainty about the number of their shares that might be bought back and about the price they would receive.

The buyback price had two components: a capital component of $3.08 and a fully franked dividend component, which made up the balance of the price. The capital gains tax consequences of participating in the buyback are complicated by the fact that the Australian Taxation Office determines a 'tax value' for the shares. In the case of the WOW buyback, the tax value was determined by adjusting the pre-announcement

continued ↓

FINANCE IN ACTION
continued

average price of $26.36 to reflect any change in the S&P/ASX 200 Index between 26 August and 8 October. In its advice to shareholders, Woolworths assumed that the tax value would be $27. For capital gains tax purposes, Australian resident individual and superannuation entity shareholders would be deemed to have disposed of each share for the capital proceeds of $3.08 plus any amount by which the tax value exceeded the buyback price.

The estimated effects of participating in the buyback for resident individuals are shown in Table 11.4. The calculations assume a buyback price of $23.22, so the fully franked dividend component is $20.14 with franking credits of $8.63, giving assessable income of $28.77 per share.

TABLE 11.4 Estimated effects of WOW buyback for resident individuals

Marginal tax rate (i)	16.5%	31.5%	38.5%	46.5%
Dividend component				
Dividend (ii)	$20.14	$20.14	$20.14	$20.14
Franking credit (iii)	$8.63	$8.63	$8.63	$8.63
Assessable income (ii) + (iii) = (iv)	$28.77	$28.77	$28.77	$28.77
Tax on assessable income (i) × (iv) = (v)	($4.75)	($9.06)	($11.08)	($13.38)
Proceeds net of tax (iv) − (v)	**$24.02**	**$19.71**	**$17.69**	**$15.39**
Capital component—proceeds net of tax[a]	$3.75	$4.36	$4.65	$4.97
Total after-tax proceeds	**$27.77**	**$24.07**	**$22.34**	**$20.36**

(a) The proceeds net of tax are equal to the capital component of the buyback price ($3.08) plus tax savings ranging from 67 cents to $1.89. Details of the capital gains tax calculations are not shown since the amounts are small and the capital gains tax consequences of participating in the buyback depend on the shareholder's cost base (assumed to be $15), the length of time the shares are held and the shareholders' ability to utilise capital losses to offset capital gains derived from other assets.

Source: Woolworths Limited, *Off-Market Buy-Back Booklet*, September 2010, p. 25.

Table 11.4 shows that the value of the buyback was greater the lower the shareholder's marginal tax rate. Moreover, for shareholders on low marginal tax rates, the total after-tax proceeds could be greater than the buyback price—assumed to be $23.22. This comes about because, for these shareholders, the franking credit attached to the dividend component is greater than the personal tax on the dividend. It is clear that shareholders with low marginal tax rates would determine pricing of the buyback. Since the market price of the shares was about $27, high tax rate investors who wished to sell WOW shares were better off selling on market rather than through the buyback.

On 11 October 2010, WOW announced that the buyback price was $25.62, reflecting a buyback discount of 14 per cent. The buyback price consisted of a capital component of $3.08 and a fully franked dividend of $22.54 per share. The tax value of the shares bought back was $28.54 ($2.92 more than the buyback price) so for capital gains tax purposes the deemed disposal price of each share was $3.08 + $2.92 = $6. Woolworths returned $704 million to shareholders through the buyback and successful tenders were scaled back by 88.2 per cent.

Research on share buybacks in Australia has focused on two issues: the motivations for buybacks and the market response when a buyback is announced. In both cases there are good reasons to expect that the results may differ between buybacks of different types. For example, managers might use an on-market buyback to signal their belief that a company is undervalued. In the case of off-market buybacks, the consideration for the repurchased shares is often less than the current market price so a buyback of that type is unlikely to be effective as a way of signalling undervaluation. A study of the stated motivations for 67 buybacks over the period 1990 to 1995 found that the motivations differed depending on the type of buyback. The main motivations for on-market buybacks were to signal management's perception of the true value of the company and to improve financial performance. Selective buybacks were used mainly to remove specific shareholders from the share register, while equal access (off-market) buybacks were viewed primarily as an alternative to dividends (Mitchell & Robinson 1999). Brown and Norman (2010) identified the largest 75 Australian industrial companies in 1997 and found that from 1997 to 2007, 36 of these companies made 23 off-market and 86 on-market share buybacks. The off-market buybacks were typically larger than the on-market buybacks. The average transaction size was $742.9 million (9.5 per cent of the company's shares) for off-market buybacks and $219.6 million (3.3 per cent of the company's shares) for on-market buybacks. In addition to being favoured for larger buybacks, Brown and Norman found that an off-market buyback is more likely to be chosen when a company has accumulated excess franking credits and when a company is generating larger free cash flows. They conclude that the incentive to distribute accumulated franking credits 'is a major motivation for undertaking an off-market buyback in Australia' (p. 780). Moreover, their results support the view that franking credits are valuable to participating shareholders because they are willing to sell their shares at less than the market price to obtain the franking credits that are usually distributed through an off-market buyback. Finally, Brown and Norman found that the market-to-book ratio is significantly lower for companies making on-market buybacks, which suggests that they are favoured as a way of signalling undervaluation. This result is consistent with the findings of Mitchell and Dharmawan (2007), whose comprehensive study of on-market buybacks concluded that under the transparent buyback regime in Australia, signalling of undervaluation is one of the strongest incentives for on-market buybacks.

Otchere and Ross (2002) note that ASX Listing Rules require that companies undertaking on-market buybacks must give a reason for the transaction. They studied 132 Australian on-market buybacks announced between January 1991 and July 1999 where the stated reason was 'undervaluation' of the company's shares. These announcements were associated with abnormal returns averaging in excess of 4 per cent while industry rivals recorded smaller but still significant abnormal returns. Thus, it appears that these announcements conveyed value-relevant information that was not just company-specific but related to the industry as a whole. Balachandran and Faff (2004) found that during the period 1996 to 1999, announcements of on-market buybacks were associated with mean abnormal returns of 2.72 per cent over a 3-day period.

Brown (2007) studied off-market share buybacks between January 1996 and December 2003 and found that abnormal returns on the announcement date were small but significant, averaging around 1.2 per cent. She argues that signalling is unlikely to explain the positive market reaction which she suggests is more likely to be a response to the distribution of franking credits. Brown also documents a 'dramatic' increase in trading volume on the announcement date and finds that trading volumes remain elevated, on average, over the next 3 days. This temporary increase in trading volume is attributed to demand for the shares from superannuation funds and other low-tax rate investors who value the franking credits that are often distributed through off-market buybacks.[21]

---

21 Twenty of the 28 buybacks in Brown's sample included a dividend component. The sample size is limited because share buybacks were rare in Australia until the laws governing them were liberalised in December 1995, and the study period finishes in December 2003 prior to the January 2004 changes in the calculation of the capital gains tax liability for shareholders participating in equal access share buybacks.

11.8 DIVIDEND REINVESTMENT PLANS AND DIVIDEND ELECTION SCHEMES

As discussed in Section 11.4.3, most resident investors will prefer that Australian companies distribute franking credits by paying the maximum possible franked dividends. However, simply maximising the payout of franked dividends is unlikely to be an optimal dividend policy, because companies that pay substantially increased dividends may be in danger of running short of cash to finance new investments. This problem has been addressed through dividend reinvestment plans. These plans and dividend election schemes are discussed in this section.

Dividend reinvestment plans (DRPs) were introduced by some Australian companies in the early 1980s. They offer shareholders the option of using all or part of their dividends to buy additional shares. While shareholders have always had this option, DRPs enable shareholders to purchase additional shares without incurring brokerage. In addition, the shares can sometimes be obtained at a discount. The discount may be from 1.5 to 10 per cent of the current market price, depending on the company, with 2.5 per cent being a typical choice. However, many companies offer no discount at all. Where a discount applies, it benefits shareholders taking up the new shares at the expense of those who do not. As a result, there is an incentive for shareholders to join dividend reinvestment plans that offer discounts.

The incentive to increase payouts under the imputation system has undoubtedly contributed to the popularity of DRPs. In 2009, 230 listed companies used DRPs to raise about $11.4 billion (ASX 2010a, p. 32). Clearly, a company that responds to the demand for franked dividends by increasing its payout may run short of cash. Management could respond by making additional rights issues or share placements to replace the extra cash paid out as dividends. However, as discussed in Section 9.6, these measures can be slow and involve significant transaction costs. The adoption of a DRP can be a more attractive and less costly solution. A DRP does not require a prospectus or other disclosure document provided the shares issued are fully paid. Where a shareholder chooses to reinvest a franked dividend, the company pays out no cash, but franking credits are still transferred to the shareholder.

The evidence suggests that DRPs are well received by shareholders. Examination of daily share returns has shown that, prior to imputation, there was little market reaction when a company announced that it was introducing a DRP. However, after the introduction of imputation, such announcements were associated with a significant positive market response, particularly in the period after 1 July 1988, when imputation was extended to superannuation funds and other institutional investors (Chan, McColough & Skully 1993).

Several companies have found that dividend reinvestment has been so popular with investors that the company has accumulated surplus cash that it is unable to invest profitably. If this occurs, a possible response is to make dividend reinvestment less attractive by reducing or eliminating the discount at which shares are offered under the DRP. Also, some companies have imposed limits on participation in DRPs. For example, each shareholder may be allowed to participate in the DRP for a maximum of 10 000 shares. Another response is to suspend the company's DRP until its investment opportunities improve, but suspension of a DRP may not be popular with shareholders. In May 1996, Lend Lease Corporation announced an innovative solution, which allowed shareholders to reinvest their dividends while avoiding the possibility of the company accumulating surplus cash. The solution was simple: after each dividend Lend Lease would buy back shares at the market price so that the net number of issued shares remains unchanged. Other large companies have since adopted the same approach.

DRPs are the most popular of the various dividend-related plans in the Australian market. Some companies also operate a **dividend election scheme**, which offers shareholders the option of receiving their dividends in one or more of a number of forms. The popularity of dividend election schemes

---

dividend reinvestment plan (DRP)
arrangement made by a company that gives shareholders an option of reinvesting all or part of their dividends in additional shares in the company, usually at a small discount from market price

dividend election scheme (DES)
arrangement made by a company that gives shareholders the option of receiving their dividends in one or more of a number of forms

increased considerably following the introduction of the imputation system, although subsequent legislative changes have reduced their tax effectiveness. As well as fully franked dividends, the options could include unfranked dividends (at a higher rate than the franked dividends), dividends paid by an overseas subsidiary, or bonus shares issued in lieu of dividends. These schemes were designed to make a company's shares attractive to different classes of shareholders and to enable franking credits to be 'streamed' to those shareholders who could use them most effectively. For example, fully franked dividends appeal to superannuation funds and resident individuals in low personal income tax brackets. Higher unfranked dividends appeal to non-residents who cannot use franking credits. Bonus shares issued instead of a dividend are not treated as a dividend for tax purposes and cannot carry franking credits. But for capital gains tax purposes, they are deemed to be acquired at the same time as the original holding. Further, if the original holding was purchased before the introduction of capital gains tax on 20 September 1985, they are not subject to capital gains tax and the bonus shares inherit their tax-free status. Bonus shares may also be attractive to overseas and resident investors who do not pay Australian income tax and are therefore unable to use franking credits.

The use of dividend election schemes to 'stream' franking credits to particular classes of investors has now been restricted.[22] Despite the restrictions, some companies have retained their dividend election scheme, but typically the choice of dividend substitutes is now confined to bonus shares and dividends paid by an overseas subsidiary. These choices are offered through separate plans, typically called *bonus share plans* and *overseas dividend plans*. Overseas dividend plans can be attractive to non-resident shareholders in Australian companies with overseas subsidiaries. For example, shareholders who reside in the UK might elect to receive dividends paid by a UK subsidiary of an Australian company instead of dividends from the Australian parent company. The dividends could then carry a tax credit that the shareholders can use to offset their tax liabilities in the UK.

PAYOUT POLICY AND COMPANY LIFE CYCLE   11.9

In this section we draw on the theories and empirical evidence discussed earlier in the chapter to outline a model that will help financial managers to develop payout policies for individual companies. Given that payout decisions can be influenced by many factors, including a company's investment opportunities, taxes, information effects, signalling, agency costs and transaction costs, it is unrealistic to expect that any single model can provide a complete explanation of payout policy. However, if a model is to be useful it should be able to explain important empirical findings, including the following:[23]

LEARNING OBJECTIVE 9
Explain how payout policy may change as a company moves through its life cycle

(a) Aggregate payouts (dividends plus share repurchases) are massive and have increased steadily in real terms over the years.
(b) Dividends tend to be paid by mature companies whose retained earnings far exceed their contributed equity, and not by early-stage companies, which are largely financed by capital infusions.
(c) Companies pay dividends on an ongoing basis and avoid accumulating large cash balances.
(d) Individuals in high tax brackets receive large amounts in cash dividends and pay substantial amounts of taxes on these dividends.

---

22 The schemes are still allowed, but their tax effectiveness has generally been eliminated. From 1 July 1990, a company must debit its franking account if an unfranked or partly franked dividend is paid to a shareholder as a substitute for a franked dividend. Similarly, the franking account must be debited if tax-exempt bonus shares are issued as a substitute for a franked dividend.

23 These are not the only empirical observations on payout policies that may be regarded as important. Items (d) and (e) on our list have been selected from a total of six observations presented by Allen and Michaely (2003). The other five items are from a further 10 presented by De Angelo and De Angelo (2007).

(e) The market reacts positively to announcements of repurchase and dividend increases, and negatively to announcements of dividend decreases.
(f) Unexpected dividend changes are of little help in forecasting future earnings surprises.
(g) Once they initiate regular dividends, managers are reluctant to cut or omit them.

De Angelo and De Angelo (DD) (2007) argue that their full payout approach is a more promising foundation for a model of payout policy than the Miller and Modigliani (MM) dividend irrelevance theorem. For example, authors who adopt the MM theorem find it puzzling (see Black 1976) that dividends are as common and large as they are in countries such as the US where the classical tax system typically means that dividends are taxed more heavily than capital gains. Attempts to explain the empirical findings using information asymmetry and signalling have met with limited success. As noted in Section 11.5, changes in dividends are of little if any help in forecasting future earnings. Moreover, signalling theory predicts that a company will pay dividends when outside investors find it particularly difficult to assess the company's prospects. This suggests that young, small companies with good growth prospects that are not fully recognised by investors would find signalling valuable. However, few such companies pay dividends. In fact, dividends are mostly paid by large, profitable, mature companies that have less information asymmetry than smaller 'growth' companies.

DD argue that a theory of payout policy should be based on the principle that shares have value only for the payouts delivered to their holders. Therefore, the cash flows generated by a company's assets must be converted into cash distributions to make shareholders as well off as possible. While an optimal payout policy will deliver the full value of a company's free cash flow to shareholders, the full payout model is silent on the timing of the payments. DD suggest that the time profile of a company's payouts will depend on a trade-off between the advantages of internal capital, such as savings in flotation costs, and the disadvantages of retaining cash. In their view, the main disadvantage of retention is the agency problems that can develop with free cash flow. Further, the balance between the advantages of internal capital and the disadvantages of retaining cash will change as the investment opportunities available to the company change. In other words, the full payout approach leads naturally to a life-cycle theory of payout policy.

DD were not the first to suggest a life-cycle theory of payout policy. Clearly, the life-cycle approach is consistent with the concept, discussed in Section 11.5, that cash payouts will typically increase as a company matures and its investment opportunities shrink. Similarly, Lease et al. (2000) pointed out that a company's payout policy may need to change as it moves through its life cycle. For example, when a new business with good growth prospects is started, capital requirements will generally be large and access to the capital markets will be restricted because outsiders know little about the company. Therefore, payment of dividends is usually not practical at this stage. Subsequently, the company may experience rapid growth and begin to raise more external funds by borrowing and by making share issues. Despite large investment needs, the company may start to pay modest dividends to establish a track record of payouts and to increase its appeal to institutional investors, some of which may be restricted to investing only in dividend-paying shares. When the company reaches maturity, positive NPV projects are harder to find, the ownership of the founders will have been diluted by successive capital raisings and agency problems are likely to arise. At this stage companies generate ample amounts of cash, which should be paid out through dividends and share buybacks unless it can be invested profitably by the company. For companies in mature stages of the life cycle, payouts to shareholders become more important because the agency costs of free cash flow would be large if they allowed large amounts of cash to accumulate within the company.

Tests carried out by De Angelo, De Angelo and Stulz (DDS) (2006) supported a life-cycle theory of dividends, which, as they note, is essentially a theory of how the trade-off between the benefits and costs of retention evolves as a company moves through its life cycle. While the benefits of retention (such as saving flotation costs and reducing personal taxes) are well accepted in the literature as being large enough to influence payout decisions, there is less agreement about the significance of factors that are supposed to motivate the managers of mature companies to distribute cash. This difference has probably arisen because factors such as the agency costs of free cash flow are much harder to measure than the costs of issuing securities and the effects on share prices of new issue announcements. To provide some, admittedly indirect, evidence on the economic magnitude of the effects of excess retention, DDS selected the 25 largest, long-standing dividend-paying industrial companies in the US as at 2002, and projected how their financial structures would appear at that time if these companies had not paid any dividends over the period 1950 to 2002, while keeping their investment outlays unchanged.

Collectively, at the end of 2002, the 25 companies held cash of $157 billion and had a long-term debt of $639 billion. Measured in 2002 dollars, these companies paid an estimated $1.6 trillion in dividends over the period 1950 to 2002. If that cash had instead been retained, the cash holdings of these companies in 2002 would have totalled almost $1.8 trillion and the median company's cash holding would have equalled 51 per cent of total assets. Alternatively, these companies could have repaid all their long-term debt *and* increased their cash balances by about $1 trillion. DDS concluded that: 'Most likely, the payouts we observe reflect direct or indirect pressure to pay out cash from stockholders concerned that managers might use the ample discretion provided by enormous cash balances and trivial debt obligations to make self-serving decisions that hurt stockholders' (2006, p. 252). Most of the 25 companies that DDS examined are mature companies in stable industries and their behaviour seems consistent with the life-cycle theory in which companies pay dividends when the costs of retaining free cash flow (mainly agency costs) exceed the benefits of retention. However, DDS point out that the large payouts typically made by mature companies with ample cash flows can also be explained without invoking the agency costs of free cash flow as an important factor. An alternative explanation is that the managers of these 25 companies may have paid substantial dividends 'simply because they wished to maximise stockholder wealth, and they recognised that shares have value only to the extent that stockholders eventually receive distributions from the firm' (2006, p. 252).

Connect Plus features a case study illustrating topics covered in this chapter.
Ask your lecturer or tutor for your course's unique URL.

SUMMARY

In this chapter we have discussed dividend and share repurchase decisions with an emphasis on the central issue of the effects of payout decisions on the wealth of shareholders.

→ When dividend policy is defined as the trade-off between:
  – retaining profit, and
  – paying dividends and making share issues to replace the cash paid out,

  it can be shown that dividend policy does not affect shareholders' wealth in a perfect capital market with no taxes. This approach emphasises the importance of investment decisions in determining company value and shareholders' wealth.

→ The 'dividend irrelevance' theorem has been challenged as a basis for understanding payout decisions and the alternative 'full payout' approach is based on the principle that shares have value only for the payouts delivered to shareholders.

→ This approach maintains that as well as making the right investment decisions, managers should ensure that the full present value of a company's free cash flows is paid out to shareholders.
→ Taxes, agency costs and information effects are the main imperfections that may cause a relationship to exist between payout policy and shareholders' wealth.
→ While the payment of dividends is the most common way of distributing cash to shareholders, companies can also distribute cash by repurchasing shares.
  – A dividend will have tax effects for virtually all shareholders, but a share buyback will affect taxes paid by only the shareholders who sell. In many countries share repurchases grew more rapidly than dividends during the 1990s and this trend has also occurred in Australia since 1995.
  – Dividend decisions are important under the imputation tax system because franking credits, which are valuable to Australian resident taxpayers, can be distributed to shareholders only by payment of franked dividends. Many listed companies have increased their dividend payouts substantially, while others have initiated dividends since imputation was introduced. However, maximising the payout of franked dividends could leave the company short of cash and may not suit all shareholders. These problems are addressed by dividend reinvestment plans and dividend election schemes, respectively.
  – Share repurchases are more flexible than dividends, because once a company initiates dividend payments, investors expect the payments to be maintained and, preferably, increased over time.
→ A change in tax policy that favours capital gains relative to dividends occurred in Australia in 1999. Following this change, most resident investors will prefer that dividends paid by Australian companies are franked. Where a company has profits that can be distributed only as unfranked dividends, many investors are likely to prefer that these profits are retained rather than distributed.
→ There is evidence that dividends and share repurchases have a valuable role in reducing agency costs. In particular, the results of recent studies support the argument that distributing free cash flows to shareholders increases their wealth by reducing the potential for managers to overinvest.
→ Announcements of share repurchases and changes in dividends can have significant effects on share prices. While there is no doubt that changes in payouts often convey information to the market, the traditional argument that such changes act as signals of future cash flows is not supported by the evidence. Rather, higher payouts are associated with lower cash flows, shrinking investment opportunities and lower risk. The characteristics of companies that repurchase shares are similar to those of companies that increase dividends.
→ The full payout approach leads to a life-cycle theory of payout policy, which proposes that payouts will be determined by a trade-off between the benefits and costs of retaining cash. This trade-off will evolve as a company moves through its life cycle.

KEY TERMS

classical tax system 346
cum dividend period 336
dividend clientele 344
dividend drop-off ratio 351
dividend election scheme (DES) 368
dividend reinvestment plan (DRP) 368
dividend-payout ratio 339
ex-dividend date 336
franked dividend 336
franking credit 337
full payout policy 343
imputation tax system 336
progressive dividend policy 339
treasury stock 337
withholding tax 337

REFERENCES

Allen, F., Bernardo, A. & Welch, I., 'A theory of dividends based on tax clienteles', *Journal of Finance*, December 2000, pp. 2499–536.

——, & Michaely, R., 'Payout policy', in G. Constantinides, M. Harris & R. Stulz (eds), *Handbook of the Economics of Finance*, Elsevier North Holland, Amsterdam, 2003.

Anderson, H., Cahan, S. & Rose, L., 'Stock dividend announcement effects in an imputation tax environment',

Journal of Business Finance and Accounting, June–July 2001, pp. 653–69.

Australian Securities Exchange, *Capital Raising in Australia: Experiences and Lessons from the Global Financial Crisis*, ASX Information Paper, 29 January 2010a.

Australian Securities Exchange, *Australian Cash Equity Market September 2010*, ASX, Sydney, 2010b, **www.asx.com.au/professionals/pdf/australian_cash_equity_market_sept_2010.pdf**.

Balachandran, B. & Faff, R., 'Special dividends, bonus issues and on-market buybacks: signalling in an imputation environment', *Finance Letters*, 2004, pp. 23–6.

Bartov, E., 'Open-market stock repurchases as signals for earnings and risk changes', *Journal of Accounting and Economics*, September 1991, pp. 275–94.

Beggs, D. & Skeels, C., 'Market arbitrage of cash dividends and franking credits', *The Economic Record*, September 2006, pp. 239–52.

Bellamy, D., 'Evidence of imputation clienteles in the Australian equity market', *Asia Pacific Journal of Management*, October 1994, pp. 275–87.

Benartzi, S., Michaely, R. & Thaler, R., 'Do changes in dividends signal the future or the past?', *Journal of Finance*, July 1997, pp. 1007–34.

Black, F., 'The dividend puzzle', *Journal of Portfolio Management*, Winter 1976, pp. 5–8.

Brav, A., Graham, J., Harvey, C. & Michaely, R., 'Payout policy in the 21st century', *Journal of Financial Economics*, September 2005, pp. 483–527.

Brown, C., 'The announcement effects of off-market share repurchases in Australia', *Australian Journal of Management*, December 2007, pp.369–85.

——, & Norman, D., 'Management choice of buyback method: Australian evidence', *Accounting and Finance*, December 2010, pp. 767–82.

Brown, P. & Clarke, A., 'The ex-dividend day behaviour of Australian share prices before and after dividend imputation', *Australian Journal of Management*, June 1993, pp. 1–40.

Cannavan, D., Finn, F. & Gray, S., 'The value of imputation tax credits in Australia', *Journal of Financial Economics*, April 2004, pp. 167–97.

Chan, K., McColough, D. & Skully, M., 'Australian tax changes and dividend reinvestment announcement effects: a pre- and post-imputation study', *Australian Journal of Management*, June 1993, pp. 41–62.

Comment, R. & Jarrell, G., 'The relative signalling power of Dutch-auction and fixed-price self-tender offers and open-market share repurchases', *Journal of Finance*, September 1991, pp. 1243–71.

Correia Da Silva, L., Goergen, M. & Renneboog, L., *Dividend Policy and Corporate Governance*, Oxford University Press, Oxford, 2004.

De Angelo, H. & De Angelo, L., 'The irrelevance of the MM dividend irrelevance theorem', *Journal of Financial Economics*, February 2006, pp. 293–315.

——, ——, 'Payout policy pedagogy: what matters and why', *European Financial Management*, January 2007, pp. 11–27.

——, ——, & Skinner, D., 'Reversal of fortune, dividend signaling and the disappearance of sustained earnings growth', *Journal of Financial Economics*, March 1996, pp. 341–71.

——, ——, & ——, 'Corporate payout policy', *Foundations and Trends in Finance*, 2009, vol. 3, issue 2–3, pp. 95–287.

——, ——, & Stulz, R., 'Dividend policy and the earned/contributed capital mix: a test of the life-cycle theory', *Journal of Financial Economics*, August 2006, pp. 227–54.

Denis, D., Denis, D. & Sarin, A., 'The information content of dividend changes: cash flow signaling, overinvestment and dividend clienteles', *Journal of Financial and Quantitative Analysis*, December 1994, pp. 567–87.

Easterbrook, F., 'Two agency-cost explanations of dividends', *American Economic Review*, September 1984, pp. 650–9.

Easton, S. & Howard, P., 'Agency costs at Telstra: a case study', *Australian Economic Review*, 2005, vol. 38, no. 2, pp. 229–32.

Fama, E. & French, K., 'Disappearing dividends: changing firm characteristics or lower propensity to pay?' *Journal of Financial Economics*, April 2001, pp. 3–43.

Fenn, G. & Liang, N., 'Corporate payout policy and managerial stock incentives', *Journal of Financial Economics*, April 2001, pp. 45–72.

Feuerherdt, C., Gray, S. & Hall, J., 'The value of imputation tax credits on Australian hybrid securities', *International Review of Finance*, September 2010, pp. 365–401.

Grullon, G. & Michaely, R., 'Dividends, share repurchases and the substitution hypothesis', *Journal of Finance*, August 2002, pp. 1649–84.

——, ——, 'The information content of share repurchase programs', *Journal of Finance*, April 2004, pp. 651–80.

Grullon, G., Michaely, R. & Swaminathan, B., 'Are dividend changes a sign of firm maturity?', *Journal of Business*, July 2002, pp. 387–424.

Guay, W. & Harford, J., 'The cash-flow performance and information content of dividend increases versus repurchases', *Journal of Financial Economics*, September 2000, pp. 385–415.

Handley, J. & Maheswaran, K., 'A measure of the efficacy of the Australian imputation tax system', *The Economic Record*, March 2008, pp. 82–94.

Hathaway, N. & Officer, R., 'The value of imputation tax credits: 2004 update', Capital Research Pty Ltd, Melbourne, November 2004, www.capitalresearch.com.au.

Healy, P. & Palepu, K., 'Earnings information conveyed by dividend initiations and omissions', *Journal of Financial Economics*, September 1988, pp. 149–75.

Ikenberry, D., Lakonishok, J. & Vermaelen, T., 'Market underreaction to open market share repurchases', *Journal of Financial Economics*, October–November 1995, pp. 181–208.

Jagannathan, M., Stephens, C. & Weisbach, M., 'Financial flexibility and the choice between dividends and stock repurchases', *Journal of Financial Economics*, September 2000, pp. 355–84.

Jensen, M., 'Agency costs of free cash flow, corporate finance and takeovers', *American Economic Review*, May 1986, pp. 323–9.

La Porta, R., Lopez-De-Silanes, F., Shleifer, A. & Vishny, R., 'Agency problems and dividend policies around the world', *Journal of Finance*, February 2000, pp. 1–33.

Lang, L. & Litzenberger, R., 'Dividend announcements: cash flow signaling vs. free cash flow hypothesis', *Journal of Financial Economics*, 1989, pp. 181–92.

Lease, R., John, K., Kalay, A., Loewenstein, U. & Sarig, O., *Dividend Policy: Its Impact on Firm Value*, Harvard Business School Press, Boston, 2000.

Lie, E., 'Excess funds and agency problems: an empirical study of incremental cash disbursements', *Review of Financial Studies*, Spring 2000, pp. 219–48.

Lintner, J., 'Distribution of incomes of corporations among dividends, retained earnings and taxes', *American Economic Review*, May 1956, pp. 97–113.

McDonald, R.J. & Collibee, P., 'Giving credit where it's due: unlocking value from franking credits', *JASSA*, July–September 1996, pp. 12–17.

Marsh, T. & Merton, R., 'Dividend behavior for the aggregate stock market', *Journal of Business*, January 1987, pp. 1–40.

Michaely, R., Thaler, R. & Womack, K., 'Price reactions to dividend initiations and omissions: overreaction or drift?', *Journal of Finance*, June 1995, pp. 573–608.

Miller, M., 'The informational content of dividends', in J. Bossons, R. Dornbusch & S. Fischer (eds), *Macroeconomics: Essays in Honor of Franco Modigliani*, MIT Press, Boston, 1987, pp. 37–58.

Miller, M. & Modigliani, F., 'Dividend policy, growth and the valuation of shares', *Journal of Business*, October 1961, pp. 411–33.

Mitchell, J.D. & Dharmawan, G.V., 'Incentives for on-market buy-backs: evidence from a transparent buy-back regime', *Journal of Corporate Finance*, March 2007, pp. 146–69.

——, & Robinson, P., 'Motivations of Australian listed companies effecting share buy-backs', *ABACUS*, February 1999, pp. 91–119.

Myers, S. & Majluf, N., 'Corporate financing and investment decisions when firms have information that investors do not have', *Journal of Financial Economics*, June 1984, pp. 187–221.

Nohel, T. & Tarhan, V., 'Share repurchases and firm performance: new evidence on the agency costs of free cash flow', *Journal of Financial Economics*, August 1998, pp. 187–222.

Otchere, I. & Ross, M., 'Do share buy-back announcements convey firm-specific or industry-wide information? A test of the undervaluation hypothesis', *International Review of Financial Analysis*, 2002, pp. 511–31.

Pattenden, K. & Twite, G., 'Taxes and dividend policy under alternative tax regimes', *Journal of Corporate Finance*, February 2008, pp. 1–16.

Renton, N. (ed.), *Australian Dividend Handbook and Contact Directory*, 2000–2001 edn, Information Australia, Melbourne.

Skinner, D., 'The evolving relation between earnings, dividends and stock repurchases', *Journal of Financial Economics*, March 2008, pp. 582–609.

——, & Soltes, E., 'What do dividends tell us about earnings quality?', *Review of Accounting Studies*, March 2011, pp. 1–28.

Walker, S. & Partington, G., 'The value of dividends: evidence from cum-dividend trading in the ex-dividend period', *Accounting and Finance*, November 1999, pp. 275–96.

Watts, R., 'The information content of dividends', *Journal of Business*, April 1973, pp. 191–211.

Woolworths Limited, *Off-Market Buy-Back Booklet*, Woolworths Limited, NSW, September 2010, p. 25.

Yoon, P. & Starks, L., 'Signaling, investment opportunities and dividend announcements', *Review of Financial Studies*, Winter 1995, pp. 995–1018.

QUESTIONS

1. **[LO 1]** Define the following terms:
   (a) ex-dividend date
   (b) franked dividend
   (c) dividend reinvestment plan
   (d) dividend drop-off ratio
   (e) overseas dividend plan
   (f) franking account
   (g) free cash flow
   (h) full payout policy
   (i) progressive dividend policy.

2. **[LO 1, 2, 5]** Are the following statements true or false?
   (a) A company can pay a dividend only if it is currently earning profits.
   (b) In Australia, dividends and capital gains are taxed at the same rate for individual investors.
   (c) The residual dividend policy is used by most companies.
   (d) The imputation system involves personal tax being collected at the company level.
   (e) To Australian resident investors, a dollar of franked dividends is worth more than a dollar of unfranked dividends.
   (f) According to the Miller and Modigliani dividend irrelevance theorem, an unmanaged (residual) dividend policy is no better or worse than a carefully designed, managed policy.

3. **[LO 3]** It has been argued that company managers should adopt a 'full payout policy'. Why is the adoption of this policy considered to be so important?

4. **[LO 7]** The payment of dividends is said to have a role in reducing agency costs. Outline the ways in which the payment of dividends can limit the extent of agency problems.

5. **[LO 5]** *Dividends are taxed at a lower rate than capital gains. This suggests that companies should have high dividend-payout ratios.* Discuss this statement, giving special attention to its appropriateness in the Australian tax environment.

6. **[LO 4]** What reasons are there to suppose that there is a dividend–clientele effect? Does the empirical evidence support the existence of such an effect? If such an effect exists, does this mean that a company can influence its market value by changing its dividend policy? Why/why not?

7. **[LO 4, 6]** Some companies have investment opportunities well in excess of the earnings available to finance them but they still insist on paying dividends. Why?

8. **[LO 4, 6]** There is evidence to suggest that dividends have a more stable pattern than earnings. What reasons can you suggest for management adopting a policy of paying a stable dividend in the face of fluctuating earnings?

9. **[LO 4, 6]** *When dividends are taxed more heavily than capital gains and there are transaction costs, a company that pays dividends and subsequently makes a rights issue is behaving illogically.* Discuss this statement.

10. **[LO 4, 6]** Usually the Board of Directors increases dividend per share only slowly in response to rising profits, and is even more reluctant to decrease dividend per share than to increase it. Give reasons for this behaviour pattern. Is this behaviour more likely to be observed under an imputation tax system than under a classical tax system? Why/why not?

11. **[LO 5]** *Under the imputation tax system, there is an optimal dividend policy for all Australian companies: always pay the maximum possible franked dividend, given the balance in the franking account.* Discuss this statement.

12. **[LO 8]** *The imputation system encourages payment of high dividends. Companies that do so may be left short of cash.* Comment on this statement.

13. **[LO 5, 6]** Explain how the following circumstances could affect a company's dividend policy:
    (a) The company issues cumulative preference shares carrying an entitlement to fully franked dividends.
    (b) The company receives a large unexpected fully franked dividend from another company.

(c) Owing to continued losses, retained profits have been reduced to almost zero.
(d) A large US investor recently acquired 40 per cent of the company's shares.
(e) The exploration division of the company has confirmed that several ore deposits are economically viable and ready for development into mines.

14. [LO 3] *Dividends and share repurchases must be important because investors will value a share only for the cash payouts it is expected to provide.* Do you agree? Explain your answer.

15. [LO 4, 5] Explain the likely effects on dividend-payout ratios of each of the following:
    (a) The imputation tax system is modified to allow investors only partial (50 per cent) credit for company tax paid.
    (b) Personal income (but not capital gains) tax rates are increased.
    (c) Capital gains tax is abolished.
    (d) Interest rates increase substantially.
    (e) Company profitability increases.
    (f) Prospectus requirements are tightened, increasing the costs of share issues.

16. [LO 6] *Allen and Michaely (2003) conclude that if company managers do use dividends to signal, 'the signal is not about future growth in earnings or cash flows'.* Outline evidence that supports this conclusion. If Allen and Michaely are correct, how can the usual market responses to announcements of changes in dividends be explained?

17. [LO 6] The 'maturity hypothesis' has been proposed as an explanation for the nature of the information conveyed by dividend changes. Outline the key aspects of this hypothesis.

18. [LO 7] *Dividends and control may be substitute mechanisms for monitoring management.* Explain.

19. [LO 7, 9] *The nature of the investment opportunities available to a company is likely to have an important influence on dividend decisions.* Discuss.

20. [LO 9] *A company's payout policy can be expected to change over time as the company moves through its life cycle.* Explain the life-cycle theory of payout policy.

21. [LO 3] Distinguish between 'investment value' and 'distribution value'. Why is the distribution value concept important?

22. [LO 2, 4, 6, 7] In an article titled 'BP should resist slashing dividend' (*Wall Street Journal*, 9 June 2010), Liam Denning noted that UK-based oil company BP was under pressure to reduce or omit dividends on its ordinary shares as a result of a major oil spill from one of its exploration wells in the Gulf of Mexico. Subsequently, BP announced that it would omit some of its quarterly dividend payments. Carefully examine why the reduction in, or omission of, BP's dividends may harm its shareholders.

PROBLEMS

1. **Dividend payment policy [LO 4]**
   The Dromana Dredging Company has asked your advice on its dividend policy. There has been only a small change in earnings and dividends over the years and the company's share price has also been relatively stable during the same period. It has been suggested that the company should expand its activities from dredging into providing services for offshore oil exploration companies. To undertake the proposed expansion activity the company intends to make a rights issue. As the expansion is expected to average approximately 25 per cent return on investment each year, it is not expected that there will be any difficulty in convincing shareholders to take up their rights. Below are data on earnings, dividends and share prices for the years 2009–12 and the expected figures for 2013.

   Dromana Dredging Company: data for 2009–12 and expected figures for 2013 ($)

	2009	2010	2011	2012	2013
Earnings per share	0.40	0.42	0.44	0.43	0.44
Cash available per share	0.60	0.67	0.67	0.66	0.66
Dividend per share	0.20	0.20	0.22	0.22	?
Average market price of ordinary shares	4.00	4.10	4.40	4.35	4.40

   Make a recommendation on the dividend payment for 2013. Give reasons.

2. **Analysing dividend policy [LO 1]**

   As noted in Section 11.2.2, investors may attempt to infer a company's dividend policy by observing its profits, dividends and payout ratio over time. Data collected from the annual reports of the listed company Cabcharge Australia Limited are shown in the following table.

Year to 30 June	Profit after tax ($M)	Dividend per share (cents)	Dividend payout ratio (%)
2002	16.1	10.0	68.9
2003	20.3	12.0	66.8
2004	23.1	13.75	66.7
2005	27.8	17.0	68.7
2006	38.0	23.0	67.9
2007	51.8	30.0	68.0
2008	59.0	34.0	68.5
2009	61.4	34.0	66.7
2010	57.6	34.0	71.0

   (a) Based on the dividend payout ratio data for the period 2002 to 2009, how would you describe Cabcharge's dividend policy?

   (b) When the figures for 2010 are included, how might your inferences about the company's dividend policy change? Give reasons.

3. **Dividend payment policy [LO 4, 5, 6]**

   The Wrex Manufacturing Company has a history of rapid growth, with a rate of return on assets of about 20 per cent per annum. For the past 5 years its dividend-payout ratio has been approximately 60 per cent. A high payout has been justified on the grounds that the company is operated in the shareholders' interests and dividends paid by the company have a beneficial effect on the company's share price. What factors would you take into consideration when deciding on the appropriate dividend policy for the company? Is the current dividend policy justified?

4. **Information effects of dividends [LO 6]**

   Examine the daily share price behaviour of any company in the 4-week period before and after its most recent change in cash dividends. What conclusions can you draw from the movements in the share price?

5. **Ex-dividend share price drop [LO 5]**

   Dribnor Ltd has announced a fully franked dividend of $1 per share. The company tax rate is 30 per cent. By how much should the share price fall on the ex-dividend date if:
   (a) franking credits are of no value?
   (b) franking credits are fully valued?

6. **Share buybacks and earnings per share [LO 8]**

   Share buybacks are sometimes motivated by the desire to increase earnings per share. Falcon Ltd recorded an operating profit of $2 million in the last financial year. It has 4 million shares on issue and the market price of the shares is $5 each. Falcon announces that it will repurchase 10 per cent of each shareholder's shares at $5 per share.
   (a) Calculate Falcon's price–earnings ratio before the buyback.
   (b) An observer comments as follows: 'Falcon's buyback should boost its earnings per share from 50 cents to 55 cents, so with the price–earnings ratio remaining the same, the share price should increase'.
      (i) If the observer's argument is correct, what will Falcon's share price be after the buyback?
      (ii) Critically evaluate the observer's argument.

CHAPTER 12
PRINCIPLES OF CAPITAL STRUCTURE

LEARNING OBJECTIVES

After studying this chapter you should be able to:

1. explain the effects of financial leverage and distinguish between business risk and financial risk
2. understand the 'capital structure irrelevance' theory of Modigliani and Miller
3. explain how tax may influence capital structure decisions
4. explain how the costs of financial distress may influence capital structure decisions
5. explain how agency costs may influence capital structure decisions
6. understand the concept of an optimal capital structure based on a trade-off between the benefits and costs of using debt
7. explain the 'pecking order' theory of capital structure.

CHAPTER CONTENTS

12.1 Introduction

12.2 The effects of financial leverage

12.3 The Modigliani and Miller analysis (no tax case)

12.4 The effects of taxes on capital structure under a classical tax system

12.5 The effects of taxes on capital structure under an imputation tax system

12.6 The costs of financial distress

12.7 Agency costs

12.8 Optimal capital structure: the static trade-off theory

12.9 Capital structure with information asymmetry

12.1 INTRODUCTION

In Chapters 9 and 10 we outlined the sources of funds that may be used to finance a company's operations. The mix of sources of funds used by a company is called its capital structure. The two basic sources are debt[1] and equity, so that, in practice, a company's **capital structure** typically refers to the mix of debt and equity that it uses to finance its activities. Two major questions are considered in this chapter. The first is: How does a company's capital structure affect its risk? The second is: How does a company's capital structure affect its market value?

capital structure
mix of debt and equity finance used by a company

The fundamental source of a company's value is the stream of net cash flows generated by its assets. This stream is usually referred to as the company's 'net operating cash flows' or 'earnings before interest and tax' (EBIT).[2] The capital structure adopted by a company divides this stream between different classes of investors. If a company is financed entirely by equity and there is no company tax, then all of this stream is available to provide income to shareholders. If a company also borrows funds, the lenders have first claim on the net operating cash flows and shareholders are entitled to the riskier, residual cash flows that remain after the lenders have been paid. Therefore, if a company has a given set of assets, then asking whether there is an **optimal capital structure** for the company amounts to asking whether the value of the stream of net operating cash flows depends on how it is divided between payments to lenders and shareholders.

optimal capital structure
the capital structure that maximises a company's value

Does the value of a company's stream of net operating cash flows depend on how this stream is divided between lenders and shareholders? This question sounds simple, but the answer can be either simple or complex, depending on the approach used to find the answer. The Modigliani and Miller analysis of capital structure (without tax), which we discuss in this chapter, provides a simple answer—no. But this answer is reached under a set of restrictive assumptions. When these assumptions are relaxed, the answer is not as simple—capital structure decisions may be influenced by several factors, including taxes, the costs of financial distress, agency costs and information asymmetries.

Capital structure involves many issues, and, as a result, our discussion of it is divided into two chapters. In this chapter we discuss the principles of capital structure. In Chapter 13 we discuss empirical evidence on the validity of those principles and the main factors that managers should consider in making capital structure decisions.

12.2 THE EFFECTS OF FINANCIAL LEVERAGE

All companies are subject to **business risk**. When the management of a company decides to enter a particular line of business, it knows that there are risks involved. For example, new competitors may emerge, technology may change in unexpected ways, new government regulations may be introduced or consumers' tastes may change. These and other factors contribute to a company's business risk, which will be reflected in changes in the company's net operating cash flows.

LEARNING OBJECTIVE 1
Explain the effects of financial leverage and distinguish between business risk and financial risk

---

1. For ease of exposition, we use the term 'debt' to refer to all forms of finance that produce a rate of return that is fixed, or varies in accordance with specified rules. Hence, 'debt' includes interest-bearing loans, marketable fixed and variable interest rate securities, lease finance and some types of preference shares.
2. Company net operating cash flows are also often referred to as 'net operating income', but in general we reserve the term 'income' for cash flows to investors. In the examples in this chapter, before-tax net operating cash flows are assumed to remain constant in perpetuity. This assumption implies that the company keeps the same assets in place at all times. Therefore, the before-tax net operating cash flows must be net of the investment required each year to replace assets that deteriorate through use or obsolescence. Deducting this investment is the same, in principle, as deducting depreciation to determine the 'earnings' or 'profit' that can be distributed while maintaining capital intact. Therefore, we use the terms 'net operating cash flows' and 'earnings before interest and tax' interchangeably.

business risk variability of future net cash flows attributed to the nature of the company's operations. It is the risk shareholders face if the company has no debt

financial leverage (or **gearing**) the effect of company debt on the returns earned by shareholders. Financial leverage is measured by ratios such as the debt–equity ratio and the ratio of debt to total assets

If a company is financed entirely by shares—that is, it has no debt—then business risk is the sole cause of variations in the return to shareholders. But if a company is financed partly by debt, the shareholders are exposed to a second source of risk called financial risk. This type of risk results from the fact that the payments promised to lenders must be made, even if the company suffers a serious decline in its net operating cash flows.[3] Therefore, the more debt the company has, the greater is the financial risk faced by its shareholders.

Why, then, do companies borrow, if borrowing involves extra risk? The reason is that by borrowing, a company may be able to increase the rate of return earned by its shareholders. This effect is known as **financial leverage**, or **gearing**. If the rate of return on a company's assets is greater than the interest rate on its debt, borrowing will increase the rate of return to shareholders. But if the rate of return on a company's assets is less than the interest rate on its debt, borrowing will decrease the rate of return to shareholders. Thus borrowing increases the variability in the rate of return earned by shareholders—that is, financial leverage exposes shareholders to financial risk. A high proportion of debt means that a small percentage change in the return on a company's assets will generate a large percentage change in the profit available to shareholders. Most directors of companies are well aware of the relationship between borrowing and returns—for example, a particularly clear statement appeared in the 2009 annual report of Cabcharge Australia Ltd (see Finance in Action).

FINANCE IN ACTION

CAPITAL MANAGEMENT AT CABCHARGE AUSTRALIA LTD

Many company annual reports provide statements about the company's approach to capital management—that is, to issues such as the company's debt–equity ratio. The 2009 annual report of Cabcharge Australia Ltd included the following statements of Board policy (p. 56):

The Board's policy is to maintain a strong capital base so as to maintain investor, creditor and market confidence and to sustain future development of the business. The Board of Directors monitors the return on capital, which the Group defines as net operating income divided by total shareholders' equity. The Board of Directors also monitors the level of dividends to ordinary shareholders.

The Board seeks to maintain a balance between the higher returns that might be possible with higher levels of borrowings and the advantages and security afforded by a sound capital position. The Group's target is to achieve a return exceeding its cost of capital; during the year ended 30 June 2009 the return was 44.4% (2008: 42.7%). In comparison, the weighted average interest expense on interest-bearing borrowings (excluding liabilities with imputed interest) was 6.1% (2008: 7.1%).

Source: Cabcharge Australia Ltd, *Annual Report 2009*, p. 56.

Table 12.1 presents two measures of leverage that we have calculated from publicly available data for 14 listed Australian companies. The numerator of each measure is the book value of net debt defined as interest-bearing liabilities (or borrowings) less cash and assets very similar to cash. Ideally, we would have used market values rather than book values but corporate debt is often in the form of loans that

---

3 If a company is unable to meet its obligations to lenders, they can take control of the company, and this action may result in its liquidation.

TABLE 12.1 Leverage ratios of Australian listed companies, June 2009

COMPANY	DEBT/(DEBT + MVE) %[a]	DEBT/BOOK VALUE OF ASSETS %
Amcor	31.3	38.6
BHP Billiton	7.1	5.6
Bluescope Steel	8.5	14.1
Cabcharge Australia	18.8	11.2
David Jones	7.8	3.7
Fairfax Media	24.2	39.1
Foster's Group	32.7	21.6
Hills Industries	18.6	32.4
Orica	14.9	12.3
Qantas	9.4	29.3
Telstra	39.9	27.4
UXC	12.7	36.4
Wattyl	16.6	44.9
Wesfarmers	10.3	13.3

[a] MVE = market value of equity.

Source: Compiled from company annual reports and end-of-year share prices on the ASX.

are not traded, so we were unable to calculate the market value of debt. The denominator of the first ratio is the book value of debt plus the market value of the company's shares (also known as its equity). Because the market value of equity reflects the company's expected future cash flows, this ratio should be a good indicator of a company's ability to meet its interest payments in the *future*. The denominator of the second ratio is the book value of the company's assets. This ratio is usually not a particularly good measure of a company's ability to meet either current or future interest payments. Rather, it reflects the extent to which a company has used debt in the *past* to finance the acquisition of new assets.

Table 12.1 shows that leverage varies significantly between companies. Differences in leverage can be related to industry membership and asset type. For example, Cabcharge, which is a service company, relies much less on debt finance than Amcor, a packaging manufacturer, and Foster's Group, a brewer and winemaker. In this chapter and in Chapter 13 we discuss the factors that may explain why some companies rely more heavily on debt finance than others.

To illustrate the calculation and interpretation of debt–equity ratios, suppose Woodlands Ltd has equity of $10 million, debt of $8 million and assets of $18 million. Its capital structure can be summarised by its debt–equity ratio, which is 0.8. Suppose that Woodlands then borrows $5 million to buy a new factory. It still has equity of $10 million, but its debt is now $13 million and its assets have grown to $21 million. Its debt–equity ratio is now 1.3. Note that Woodlands has simultaneously changed both its debt–equity ratio and its assets—that is, it has simultaneously changed both its capital structure and its investment policy. While many companies frequently make such simultaneous decisions, when we examine the effects of a change in capital structure we need to hold everything else constant. Naturally, 'everything else' includes the company's investment policy. This outcome could be achieved by a company borrowing money to fund the repurchase of some of its shares. We use this approach in Example 12.1, which illustrates the effects of leverage on shareholders.

EXAMPLE 12.1

Dribnor Ltd is currently unlevered—that is, it has not borrowed—and has an issued capital of 1 million shares that have a market price of $2 each. Dribnor's expected earnings before interest are $300 000 per annum and the market value of its assets is $2 million. There are no taxes and all earnings available to ordinary shareholders are paid out as dividends. Ron Peacock, who is Dribnor's financial manager, is considering whether the company should borrow $1 million at an interest rate of 12 per cent per annum, and use the borrowed money to repurchase 500 000 shares at their market price of $2 each. If this proposal is implemented, Dribnor's capital structure will be different—it will have some debt—but its assets and earnings before interest will be the same. While Dribnor's expected earnings before interest are $300 000 per annum, it is not certain that these earnings will be achieved, and Ron wishes to analyse the effects if earnings increase to $400 000 per annum or decrease to $200 000 per annum. Ron also wishes to analyse the effect if earnings are $240 000 per annum, because, in that event, the rate of return on assets would be 12 per cent per annum, which is the same as the interest rate on debt.

SOLUTION

The results of the financial manager's calculations are shown in Table 12.2.

TABLE 12.2 Effect of leverage on returns to Dribnor shareholders

Earnings before interest ($)	200 000	240 000	300 000	400 000
Rate of return on assets (%)	10	12	15	20
Existing capital structure (100% equity)				
Number of shares (million)	1.0	1.0	1.0	1.0
Earnings per share (cents)	20	24	30	40
Rate of return on equity (%)[a]	10	12	15	20
Proposed capital structure (50% equity, 50% debt)				
Number of shares (million)	0.5	0.5	0.5	0.5
Interest on debt ($)	120 000	120 000	120 000	120 000
Earnings available to ordinary shareholders ($)	80 000	120 000	180 000	280 000
Earnings per share (cents)	16	24	36	56
Rate of return on equity (%)[a]	8	12	18	28

[a] Rate of return on equity = Earnings per share (cents)/Market price per share. The market price per share is $2.

Example 12.1 illustrates two important effects of financial leverage. First, it shows that when a company borrows, the *expected rate of return on equity is increased*. If the expected earnings before interest of $300 000 per annum are maintained, the proposed capital structure results in an increase in the expected rate of return on equity from 15 per cent to 18 per cent per annum. There is a corresponding change in expected earnings per share (EPS), which increases from 30 cents to 36 cents. Second, when a company borrows, the *variability of returns to shareholders is increased*. If earnings before interest are $400 000 per annum, the proposed structure *increases* the rate of return on equity from 20 per cent to 28 per cent per annum, but if earnings before interest are only $200 000 per annum, the proposed structure *decreases* the rate of return on equity from

FIGURE 12.1 The effect of leverage on returns

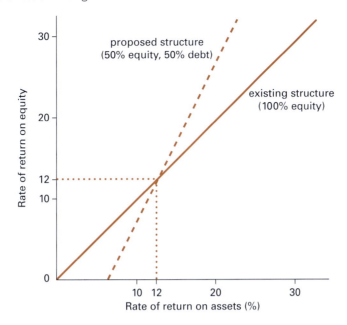

10 per cent to 8 per cent per annum. The effects of the alternative capital structures on the returns to shareholders are shown in Figure 12.1.

With the existing all-equity capital structure, the rate of return on equity is, by definition, always equal to the rate of return on Dribnor's assets. Under the proposed structure, this remains true only when the rate of return on Dribnor's assets is equal to the interest rate paid on its debt, which is 12 per cent. If the rate of return on assets is greater than 12 per cent, the levered structure results in a higher rate of return on equity than the all-equity structure. If the rate of return on assets is less than 12 per cent, the levered structure results in a lower rate of return on equity. In other words, from the viewpoint of the shareholders, leverage applies in both directions: it turns a good year into an even better one but it turns a bad year into an even worse one. The effect of leverage in creating financial risk is shown clearly by the different slopes of the two lines in Figure 12.1.

In summary, the choice of capital structure for Dribnor involves a trade-off between risk and expected return. Clearly, any valid analysis of this choice must consider *both* factors: the financial manager should not determine a target debt–equity ratio based only on the expected level of EPS or the rate of return on equity. Provided that the expected rate of return on assets is greater than the interest rate on debt, increasing the debt–equity ratio will *always* increase both expected EPS and the expected rate of return on equity. But these expected benefits come at the price of increased financial risk.

We have shown that financial leverage increases both expected return and risk for shareholders. However, we have not yet considered the most important question: Is the increase in expected return enough to compensate shareholders for the increase in risk? If it is just enough to compensate (but no more), then the value of the company will be unchanged by leverage. But if it more (less) than compensates, then the value of the company will be higher (lower). A rigorous analysis of this question by Modigliani and Miller (1958) showed that, in a perfect capital market with no taxes, the higher expected return is just enough to compensate for the higher risk—no more and no less. Therefore, the value of the company is neither increased nor decreased by leverage; capital structure is thus irrelevant to company value. Their analysis is considered in the next section.

12.3 THE MODIGLIANI AND MILLER ANALYSIS (NO TAX CASE)

12.3.1 MODIGLIANI AND MILLER'S PROPOSITION 1

LEARNING OBJECTIVE 2
Understand the 'capital structure irrelevance' theory of Modigliani and Miller

Modigliani and Miller (MM) (1958) analysed the effect of capital structure on company value based on a set of restrictive assumptions. The most important assumptions are:

(a) Securities issued by companies are traded in a **perfect capital market**; this is a frictionless market in which there are no transaction costs and no barriers to the free flow of information.
(b) There are no taxes.
(c) Companies and individuals can borrow at the same interest rate.
(d) There are no costs associated with the liquidation or reorganisation of a company in financial difficulty.
(e) Companies have a fixed investment policy so that investment decisions are not affected by financing decisions.

perfect capital market
frictionless capital market in which there are no transaction costs and no barriers to the free flow of information

Given these assumptions, MM proved that the value of a company is independent of its capital structure. They concluded that if a company has a given investment policy, then changing its ratio of debt to equity will change the way in which its net operating cash flows are divided between lenders and shareholders, but will not change the total value of the cash flows. Therefore, the value of the company will not change. This is their now-famous Proposition 1.

Clearly, in most cases, these assumptions are not realistic. For example, MM's assumptions exclude taxes and default risk. But this does not mean that their analysis is useless. One of the great virtues of MM's analysis is that by implication it points the way forward. If capital structure does in fact matter at least a little—as most people believe—then it must matter for reasons that MM excluded from their analysis. We discuss this issue further in Section 12.3.4.

Proposition 1 can be proved in many different ways. The proof provided by MM is based on the idea that investors can create *homemade leverage* as an alternative to corporate leverage. Suppose that we could observe two companies, U and L, which are equivalent, except that U has no debt while L has debt—that is, U is unlevered, while L is levered. Suppose, contrary to Proposition 1, that the market value of L (which we denote V_L) exceeds the market value of U (which we denote V_U). Then a shareholder in L should sell his shares in L and, by borrowing money, will be able to structure an investment in U that produces:

1. a higher return at the same risk
2. the same return at a lower risk
3. the same return at the same risk for a lower investment outlay.

That is, if $V_L > V_U$ then all three of these strategies are available to a shareholder in L.

This is illustrated in Example 12.2.

EXAMPLE 12.2

Suppose we observe two companies, U and L, which are equivalent except for their capital structure. Both companies produce net operating cash flows (*NCF*) of $11 000 a year. The market value of the levered company, L, is V_L = $105 000, comprised of debt, D_L, whose market value is $25 000 and equity, E_L, whose market value is $80 000. The market value of the unlevered company, U, is V_U = $100 000, which by definition is comprised only of equity (that is, E_U = $100 000). The interest rate for both companies (and all investors) is 4 per cent per annum. Consider an investor who owns 1 per cent of the shares in L. The market value of his shareholding is 0.01 × $80 000 = $800.

(a) What is the investor's return and risk?
(b) How could the investor achieve:
   (i) a higher return at the same risk?
   (ii) the same return at a lower risk?
   (iii) the same return at the same risk and also have money left over?

SOLUTION

(a) The investor's return is:

$$\begin{aligned}
\text{Return} &= 0.01 \times \text{net income of L} \\
&= 0.01 \times (NCF - \text{interest expense}) \\
&= 0.01 \times (\$11\,000 - 0.04 \times \$25\,000) \\
&= 0.01 \times \$10\,000 \\
&= \$100
\end{aligned}$$

The investor's risk is measured by L's debt–equity ratio:

$$\begin{aligned}
\text{Risk} &= \text{L's debt–equity ratio} \\
&= \frac{\$25\,000}{\$80\,000} \\
&= 0.3125
\end{aligned}$$

(b) Recognising that, according to MM, the shares in L are overvalued because $V_L > V_U$, the investor first sells his shares in L for $800.

   (i) Achieving a higher return at the same risk.

   The investor borrows $250 at 4 per cent and invests the whole sum ($800 + $250 = $1050) in shares of company U. Because the total market value of all shares in U is $100 000, he must now own 1.05 per cent of the shares of U. Hence, the return on this shareholding is 1.05 per cent of the net operating cash flows of U.

   The return on this investment is:

$$\begin{aligned}
\text{Return} &= \text{return on shares} - \text{interest on debt} \\
&= 0.0105 \times \$11\,000 - 0.04 \times \$250 \\
&= \$115.50 - \$10.00 \\
&= \$105.50 \\
&> \$100
\end{aligned}$$

   The risk of this investment is:

$$\begin{aligned}
\text{Risk} &= \text{investor's debt–equity ratio} \\
&= \frac{\$250}{\$800} \\
&= 0.3125
\end{aligned}$$

   Thus, the investor has achieved a higher return ($105.50) at the same risk (0.3125).

   (ii) Achieving the same return at a lower risk.

   The investor borrows $171.43 at 4 per cent and invests the whole sum ($800 + $171.43 = $971.43) in shares of company U. Therefore he owns 0.971 43 per cent of the shares of U.

continued →

Example 12.2 *continued*

The return on this investment is:

Return = return on shares − interest on debt
= 0.0097143 × $11 000 − 0.04 × $171.43
= $106.86 − $6.86
= $100

The risk of this investment is:

Risk = investor's debt−equity ratio
$$= \frac{\$171.43}{\$800}$$
= 0.2143
< 0.3125

Thus, the investor has achieved the same return ($100) at a lower risk (0.2143).

(iii) Achieving the same return at the same risk and also having money left over.

The investor retains $41.71 of the $800, leaving $758.29, then borrows $236.97 and invests the whole sum ($758.29 + $236.97 = $995.26) in shares of company U. Therefore he owns 0.995 26 per cent of the shares of U.

The return on this investment is:

Return = return on shares − interest on debt
= 0.0099526 × $11 000 − 0.04 × $236.97
= $109.48 − $9.48
= $100

The risk of this investment is:

Risk = investor's debt−equity ratio
$$= \frac{\$236.97}{\$758.29}$$
= 0.3125

Thus, the investor has achieved the same return ($100) at the same risk (0.3125), and the investor also has some money ($41.71) to spend or to invest elsewhere.

For a risk-averse investor all of these strategies produce a better outcome than if he continued to hold the shares in company L.

It can be proved algebraically that the results in Example 12.2 hold in all cases where the value of the levered company is greater than the value of the unlevered company. As an example, we provide the algebraic proof for achieving a higher return at the same risk.

Notation

E_L = market value of the equity (shares) of company L
D_L = market value of the debt of company L
V_L = market value of company L ≡ $E_L + D_L$
E_U = market value of the equity of company U
V_U = market value of company U ≡ E_U
r = interest rate on debt

NCF = net operating cash flow (the same for both companies)
p = the percentage of the shares of company L that the investor owns

The value of the shares held by the investor in L = $p \times E_L$. The return on these shares is the proportion, p, of the net income of company L. That is,

Return = $p(NCF - rD_L)$

The risk is measured by the debt–equity ratio of company L, which is $\dfrac{D_L}{E_L}$.

The investor borrows an amount, A, such that his personal debt–equity ratio equals the debt–equity ratio of company L. That is, A is chosen such that:

$$\frac{A}{pE_L} = \frac{D_L}{E_L}$$

Therefore $A = p \times D_L$.

The amount to be invested in U shares is therefore:

$$pE_L + pD_L = p(E_L + D_L) = pV_L$$

Therefore, the proportion of U shares on issue owned by the investor is $\dfrac{pV_L}{V_U}$

Thus the return on this investment is:

New return = return on shares – interest on debt

$$= \frac{pV_L}{V_U} \times NCF - r \times pD_L$$

Hence, the difference between the new return and the previous return is:

Difference in return = new return – previous return

$$= \left[\frac{pV_L}{V_U} \times NCF - prD_L\right] - p(NCF - rD_L)$$

$$= p \times NCF \times \left(\frac{V_L}{V_U} - 1\right)$$

> 0 if $V_L > V_U$

Investor's debt–equity ratio = $\dfrac{A}{pE_L} = \dfrac{pD_L}{pE_L} = \dfrac{D_L}{E_L}$

Therefore, the investor has achieved a higher return at the same risk.

Example 12.2 shows that if the value of the levered company exceeds the value of the unlevered company, an investor in the levered company should sell her shares and instead borrow money and invest in the shares of the unlevered company. This action will be profitable for as long as the value of the levered company remains greater than the value of the unlevered company. If enough investors undertake similar transactions, there will be downward pressure on the price of L shares (because there are many sellers) and upward pressure on the price of U shares (because there are many buyers). Equilibrium will be restored when security prices have adjusted to the point where the market values of the two companies are equal.

What happens if the opposite of Example 12.2 arises—that is, if the value of the levered company is *less* than the value of the unlevered company? In that case, an investor in U shares should sell these shares and buy shares in L. Of course, this action will increase the investor's risk because L has borrowed whereas U has not. However, this risk can be offset by the investor also lending money. In effect, the investor can undo the effect of corporate leverage.

The central mechanism in MM's proof is the substitutability between corporate debt and personal debt. If a levered company is overvalued, an investor in that company's shares can replicate his risk and return by investing instead in the shares of an unlevered company and adjusting the debt–equity ratio by borrowing *personally*. Hence, leverage does not add value to a levered company because, by borrowing, the levered company is not doing anything that its shareholders cannot do for themselves. Therefore, there is no reason for investors to pay a premium for the shares of levered companies. Similarly, if an unlevered company is overvalued, an investor in that company's shares can replicate his risk and return by investing instead in the shares of a levered company and adjusting his debt–equity ratio (to zero) by lending *personally*. Leverage neither adds to, nor subtracts from, the value of a company.

Proposition 1 is a *law of conservation of value*. A company is a collection of assets that generate a stream of net operating cash flows, which are then divided between different suppliers of finance. Proposition 1 says that the value of a set of assets remains the same, regardless of how the net operating cash flows generated by the assets are divided between different classes of investors. If this law is breached then investors can earn immediate profits with no risk. The process of taking advantage of such an opportunity is called **arbitrage**, which should ensure that perfect substitutes will not sell at different prices in the same market at the same time. In the context of the MM analysis, two companies with the same assets, but different capital structures, are perfect substitutes. If their market values are not the same, investors will enter the market to take advantage of the arbitrage opportunity and, in doing so, will force the values of the two companies to be the same.

It is sometimes argued that the arbitrage process employed by MM is unrealistic because company leverage and personal leverage are not perfect substitutes. For example, individual borrowers often pay higher interest rates and higher transaction costs than companies. Although true, this observation has little substance as a criticism because the particular arbitrage procedure used by MM is not the only way to prove their proposition. Another way, which uses a different arbitrage procedure, is shown in Example 12.3.

arbitrage
simultaneous transactions in different markets that result in an immediate risk-free profit

EXAMPLE 12.3

This example again compares Company L and Company U using the information provided in Example 12.2. Recall that both companies have net operating cash flows of $11 000 a year. Company U has no debt and the market value of its equity is $100 000. Company L has borrowed $25 000 at an interest rate of 4 per cent per annum and the market value of its equity is $80 000. Hence, contrary to MM, the market value of L, which is $80 000 + $25 000 = $105 000, exceeds the market value of U, which is $100 000. If an investor owns 1 per cent of L—that is, 1 per cent of its shares *and* 1 per cent of its debt—what is the market value of the investment and what is the annual return on the investment?

SOLUTION

The market value of this investment is:

Equity: 1% x $80 000 = $ 800
Debt: 1% x $25 000 = $ 250
Total market value: $1050

The annual return produced by this investment is:

Equity: 1% x ($11 000 − 0.04 x $25 000) = $100
Debt: 0.04 x $250   = $10
Total annual return: $110

The investor can arbitrage this situation by first selling his portfolio of the debt and equity of company L for its market value of $1050. The investor then retains $50, and invests the remaining $1000 in U's shares. This shareholding represents 1 per cent of the equity of company U and hence entitles the investor to

> 1 per cent of the net operating cash flows generated by company U—that is, the annual return on this investment is 0.01 × $11 000 = $110. Therefore, the investor's return is $110—the same as before—but the investor also has $50 left over to consume or to invest elsewhere.
>
> Clearly, the difference between the values of the two companies could not persist and the actions of investors selling L's securities and buying U's shares would quickly establish an equilibrium in which their values would be exactly the same.

In summary, MM's Proposition 1 states that a change in the company's capital structure simply changes the way in which the net operating cash flows generated by the assets are divided between shareholders and lenders. Regardless of how they are divided, their total size remains the same. Therefore, the value of the company's assets remains the same. Because the company's securities represent claims against those assets, the total market value of the securities also remains the same. To illustrate this with an everyday analogy, we cannot change the size of a cake simply by slicing it up in a different way!

12.3.2 MODIGLIANI AND MILLER'S PROPOSITION 2

Proposition 1 focuses on dollar values—in particular, it states that the dollar value of a company is independent of the company's capital structure. Proposition 2 focuses on a company's cost of capital, which is the required rate of return on the company's securities. Proposition 2 states that a company's weighted average cost of capital is independent of the company's capital structure. In short, Proposition 2 is like retelling the story of Proposition 1 but in a different language.

If a company's net operating cash flows are constant in perpetuity, then the expected rate of return on the company's assets, k_0, is simply the expected net operating cash flows per annum divided by the market value of the company V. That is:

$$k_0 = \frac{\text{annual net operating cash flows}}{V} \quad [12.1]$$

Consider an investor who owns all of a company's shares and has also provided all of its debt finance. As discussed in Chapter 7, the expected rate of return on a portfolio is a weighted average of the expected rates of return on the assets in the portfolio. Therefore, in this case, the investor's expected rate of return is a weighted average of the rates of return on the company's equity and the company's debt, where the weights are the proportions of equity and debt in the company's capital structure. Because this investor has provided all of the company's equity capital and all of its debt capital, this investor is entitled to all of the net operating cash flows generated by the company's assets. Hence, the investor's expected rate of return is equal to k_0. Therefore, the expected rate of return on the company's assets is:

$$k_0 = k_e \left(\frac{E}{V}\right) + k_d \left(\frac{D}{V}\right) \quad [12.2]$$

where

k_0 = expected rate of return on assets (or weighted average cost of capital)
k_e = expected rate of return on equity (or cost of equity capital)
k_d = expected rate of return on debt (or cost of debt capital)
E = the market value of the company's equity capital
D = the market value of the company's debt capital
$V \equiv E + D$ = the total market value of the company

The alternative terms used to describe the variables k_e and k_d may need to be explained. Investors will purchase a security only if the expected rate of return on the security is at least equal to the minimum rate of return that the investor requires or demands. The rates of return received by investors must be provided by the issuers of securities, and, from the issuer's viewpoint, the rate of return required by investors is effectively a cost—typically referred to as a cost of capital. Similarly, the expected rate of return on a portfolio of all the securities issued by a company, as calculated in Equation 12.2, is often referred to as the weighted average cost of capital. The weighted average cost of capital is typically used as the discount rate when estimating the net present value (NPV) of projects that are of the same risk as the company's existing assets. The weighted average cost of capital is discussed in detail in Chapter 14.

Equation 12.2 can be rearranged to show how the cost of equity capital, k_e, is affected by the use of debt finance. This gives:

$$k_e = k_0 + (k_0 - k_d)\left(\frac{D}{E}\right) \qquad [12.3]$$

Equation 12.3 is MM's Proposition 2, which shows that for a levered company the cost of equity capital consists of two components. The first component is k_0. If a company had no debt ($D = 0$), then Equation 12.3 tells us that for this company, $k_e = k_0$. That is, k_0 is equal to the rate of return required by shareholders on a company that has no debt. If a company has no debt, it has no financial risk, but it will have business risk. So, in Equation 12.2, k_0 can be interpreted as the rate of return required because of the company's business risk. The second component is an increment for financial risk and is proportional to the company's debt–equity ratio, $\frac{D}{E}$, and also depends on the difference between k_0 and k_d—which must be positive.

default risk
the chance that a borrower will fail to meet obligations to pay interest and principal as promised

If a company can always borrow with no **default risk**, the cost of debt, k_d, will remain constant as the company's debt–equity ratio increases, and the relationship between the cost of equity capital and the debt–equity ratio will be linear. Proposition 2 for the case of default-free debt is shown in Figure 12.2.

Propositions 1 and 2 may appear contradictory. Proposition 1 says that shareholders will be indifferent to borrowing by a company. But Proposition 2 says that borrowing by a company increases a shareholder's expected rate of return. Why would a shareholder be indifferent to getting a higher expected rate of return? The answer is that because of the financial risk associated with borrowing, the shareholders' *required* rate of return also increases exactly in line with the increase in their *expected* rate of return. The extra expected rate of return is just enough—no more and no less—to compensate for the extra financial risk. Therefore, borrowing by a company has no effect on its shareholders' wealth.

How can the weighted average cost stay the same when the cost of one component (equity) has risen and the cost of the other component (debt) has stayed the same? Why doesn't the average increase? The answer is that when a company changes its capital structure, the securities market reacts by also changing the market value of the company's debt and the market value of the company's equity. Therefore, the weights, which are market-value weights, also change. Here is a hypothetical numerical example where the company's debt is default-free and the interest rate is always 4.5 per cent. The company is considering three alternative capital structures.

FIGURE 12.2 Modigliani and Miller's Proposition 2 with default-free debt

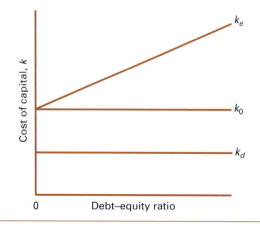

Low leverage (80 per cent equity and 20 per cent debt)

The cost of equity capital (k_e) is 11.125 per cent.

So $k_0 = 0.8 \times 11.125\% + 0.2 \times 4.5\% = 9.8\%$

Medium leverage (60 per cent equity and 40 per cent debt)

The cost of equity capital (k_e) is 13.33 per cent.

So $k_0 = 0.6 \times 13.33\% + 0.4 \times 4.5\% = 9.8\%$

High leverage (20 per cent equity and 80 per cent debt)

The cost of equity capital (k_e) is 31 per cent.

So $k_0 = 0.2 \times 31\% + 0.8 \times 4.5\% = 9.8\%$

In each case, the cost of debt remains at 4.5 per cent but the cost of equity increases as more debt is issued. As required, the weights always sum to 1, but the weighted average remains at 9.8 per cent.

This outcome is *not* the result of assuming default-free debt. In practice, there is always some risk that a corporate borrower will default. For many large companies this risk is very small but it is never zero. Therefore, as a company borrows more, it will have to pay higher rates of interest. But this does not mean that the weighted average cost of capital must increase as borrowing increases. Here is a simple numerical example of what could happen:

Low leverage (80 per cent equity and 20 per cent debt)

The cost of equity capital (k_e) is 11.1 per cent.

The cost of debt capital (k_d) is 4.6 per cent.

So $k_0 = 0.8 \times 11.1\% + 0.2 \times 4.6\% = 9.8\%$

Medium leverage (60 per cent equity and 40 per cent debt)

The cost of equity capital (k_e) is 13 per cent.

The cost of debt capital (k_d) is 5 per cent.

So $k_0 = 0.6 \times 13\% + 0.4 \times 5\% = 9.8\%$

High leverage (20 per cent equity and 80 per cent debt)

The cost equity captial (k_e) is 25 per cent.

The cost of debt capital (k_d) is 6 per cent.

So $k_0 = 0.2 \times 25\% + 0.8 \times 6\% = 9.8\%$

In each case, the cost of debt *and* the cost of equity increase as more debt is issued. As required, the weights always sum to 1, but the weighted average remains at 9.8 per cent.

While Proposition 1 is a law of conservation of *value*, Proposition 2 is a law of conservation of *risk*. Assume that a company is able to borrow with no risk of default. When the company borrows, it transfers a risk-free cash flow stream to lenders. The business risk associated with the company's assets, and therefore with its net cash flows, remains the same regardless of its capital structure. Under the assumption of risk-free debt, this risk will affect only shareholders. While changing the capital structure does not change the *total* risk to which shareholders are exposed, it concentrates that risk on a smaller amount of equity capital. Therefore, borrowing increases the risk *per dollar* of equity. Because shareholders are assumed to be risk averse, they respond by requiring a higher rate of return. But perfect capital markets do not provide something for nothing: the increased expected rate of return is just enough—no more and no less—to compensate for the extra risk.

Because lenders rank ahead of shareholders in the division of net operating cash flows, the required rate of return on a company's debt is always less than the required rate of return on its equity. This has led some people to believe that debt is 'cheaper' than equity from the viewpoint of the company as a whole. Proposition 2 highlights the error in this belief. Example 12.4 provides an illustration.

EXAMPLE 12.4

Consider again Example 12.1, in which Dribnor Ltd is financed solely by equity and its shareholders require a rate of return of 15 per cent per annum. This rate reflects the risk of Dribnor's assets. Dribnor can borrow at an interest rate of 12 per cent per annum. Suppose that Dribnor borrows $1 million and uses these funds to repurchase shares. What will happen to Dribnor's cost of equity capital? What will happen to its weighted average cost of capital?

SOLUTION

We can answer the first question using Proposition 2 as shown in Equation 12.3:

$$k_e = k_0 + (k_0 - k_d)\left(\frac{D}{E}\right)$$
$$= 0.15 + (0.15 - 0.12)\left(\frac{1}{1}\right)$$
$$= 0.18 \text{ or } 18\% \text{ per annum}$$

Dribnor's weighted average cost of capital can be calculated using Equation 12.2:

$$k_0 = k_e\left(\frac{E}{V}\right) + k_d\left(\frac{D}{V}\right)$$
$$= 0.18 \times 0.5 + 0.12 \times 0.5$$
$$= 0.15 \text{ or } 15\% \text{ per annum}$$

The introduction of debt finance has not changed Dribnor's weighted average cost of capital of 15 per cent, despite the fact that the interest rate on debt is only 12 per cent. The reason is that the borrowing causes the cost of equity capital to increase to a level that exactly offsets the effect of the apparently cheaper debt. In other words, the interest cost of debt is only its *explicit* cost. The financial risk created by borrowing increases the cost of equity capital, and this increase is an *implicit* cost associated with the debt.

12.3.3 MODIGLIANI AND MILLER'S PROPOSITION 3

MM's Proposition 3 states that the appropriate discount rate for a particular investment proposal is independent of how the proposal is to be financed. The appropriate discount rate depends on the features of the investment proposal—in particular, its riskiness. Whether the investing company obtains the funds by borrowing, or by issuing shares, or both, has no effect on the appropriate discount rate. This implication is consistent with the irrelevance of the financing decision as stated in Proposition 1.

Taken together, the MM propositions maintain that in a perfect capital market with no taxes, it is only the investment decision that is important in the pursuit of wealth maximisation. The financing decision is of no consequence. Therefore, investment decisions can be completely separated from financing decisions.

12.3.4 WHY IS THE MM ANALYSIS IMPORTANT?

We have given considerable space to an explanation of the MM analysis. This should not be taken to imply that we regard the MM analysis as providing a complete description of the effects of financing decisions. Clearly, it cannot do so because important factors such as taxes have so far been ignored. So why is the MM analysis so important? There are two reasons. The first reason is that it helps us to ask the right questions about financing decisions. In particular, as Miller (1988) later observed, 'showing what *doesn't* matter can also show, by implication, what *does*'.[4] By making the assumptions they did, MM excluded from their analysis a number of factors that could be important. These factors include company taxes, personal taxes and default (and the associated costs of liquidating a bankrupt company). By implication, if capital structure does in fact matter, then taxes and default risk could be good places to look for the reasons why it matters. The second reason, which is related to the first, is that an understanding of the MM propositions helps to distinguish between logical and illogical reasons for particular financing decisions. For example, it may be suggested that companies should use at least some debt finance because debt is 'cheaper' than equity. Using the MM analysis, we can state that if this reason is based on the observation that interest rates are lower than required rates of return on equity, then that reason is illogical. But a logical reason *might* be that there is a tax advantage to using debt rather than equity.

The basic MM analysis that we have presented envisages only two sources of finance: debt and equity. In practice, there are many other sources of finance, including preference shares, leases and hire-purchase agreements. Furthermore, debt may be short term or long term, it can be denominated in different currencies such as US dollars, euro or yen and some types of debt and preference shares can be convertible into ordinary shares. But the fundamental MM message is that any combination of finance sources is as good as any other. No matter how many sources of finance are used, the resulting capital structure is just another way of dividing the net operating cash flows between the people who have contributed the capital that sustains the company's operations.

We now turn to a discussion of some of the factors that MM omitted from their basic analysis.

THE EFFECTS OF TAXES ON CAPITAL STRUCTURE UNDER A CLASSICAL TAX SYSTEM 12.4

MM excluded company tax and personal tax from their basic analysis. However, they were well aware that company tax might be an important factor and extended their analysis to include company tax. There are two main types of company tax systems. Under the *classical tax system*, which applies in the US, and to foreign companies operating in Australia, companies and their shareholders are taxed independently. That is, for tax purposes, a company is an entity distinct from the shareholders who own it. Under an *imputation tax system*, which is used in many countries, including Australia, Canada and New Zealand, the taxation of companies and shareholders is integrated. We begin by considering the effects of company tax under the classical tax system. The effects of personal taxes are discussed in Sections 12.4.2 to 12.4.4. The effects of taxes under an imputation tax system are discussed in Section 12.5.

> **LEARNING OBJECTIVE 3**
>
> Explain how tax may influence capital structure decisions

12.4.1 COMPANY INCOME TAX

MM extended their original no-tax analysis to incorporate the effect of company income tax under the classical system.[5] Company profit is taxed after allowing a deduction for interest on debt, which means that borrowing causes a significant reduction in company tax and a corresponding increase in the after-tax net

---

[4] In other words, if financing decisions are important, the reasons for their importance must be related to the factors that MM excluded through their assumptions. However, it does not necessarily follow that all such factors will cause a departure from MM's conclusions. As Myers (2003, p. 221) commented, perhaps Miller should have said 'what *may* matter'.

[5] The original Modigliani and Miller (1958) article included the effect of tax savings on interest, but valued the savings incorrectly. The error was rectified in Modigliani and Miller (1963).

cash flows to investors. The tax savings associated with debt are shown in Example 12.5, which is based on the same data as Example 12.1.

EXAMPLE 12.5

Dribnor Ltd is subject to company income tax at the rate of 30 cents in the dollar and interest on debt is tax deductible. What is the effect of borrowing $1 million at 12 per cent per annum on the after-tax net cash flows to investors?

SOLUTION

The two capital structures proposed for Dribnor Ltd are compared in Table 12.3, assuming that earnings before interest and tax are $300 000 per annum.

Table 12.3 shows that by borrowing $1 million, Dribnor increases its after-tax cash flow by $36 000 per annum. This increase is equal to the annual tax savings on interest, which is calculated by multiplying the annual interest payment, I, by the company income tax rate, t_c. That is:

Annual tax savings on interest = $t_c \times I$
= 0.30 × $120 000
= $36 000 per annum

TABLE 12.3 The effects of borrowing and company tax on cash flows

CAPITAL STRUCTURE	100% EQUITY	EQUITY AND DEBT OF $1 MILLION
Earnings before interest and tax ($)	300 000	300 000
Interest on debt ($)	—	120 000
Taxable income ($)	300 000	180 000
Company income tax ($) (tax rate, t_c = 0.30)	90 000	54 000
After-tax company income ($)	210 000	126 000
After-tax cash flow available to investors (shareholders and lenders) ($)[a]	210 000	246 000
Increase in after-tax cash flow available to investors ($)	—	36 000

[a] Earnings before interest and tax less company income tax

What is the effect of these tax savings on the value of the company? Since the annual after-tax cash flow increases by an amount equal to the annual tax savings on interest, it follows that the market value of a levered company, V_L, must be equal to the value of an equivalent unlevered company, V_U, plus the present value (PV) of the tax savings on interest. That is:

$$V_L = V_U + (PV \text{ of tax saving on interest}) \qquad [12.4]$$

What is the appropriate risk-adjusted discount rate to apply to the tax savings? Assuming that the tax savings are just as risky as the interest payments on debt, the appropriate discount rate is simply the cost of debt, k_d.

If the annual interest payment remains constant in perpetuity, Equation 12.4 becomes:

$$V_L = V_U + \frac{t_c I}{k_d} \qquad [12.5]$$

In this case the annual interest payment, I, is equal to the cost of debt, k_d, multiplied by the value of debt, D. Making these substitutions, Equation 12.5 can be rewritten as follows:

$$V_L = V_U + \frac{t_c k_d D}{k_d} \qquad [12.6]$$
$$= V_U + t_c D$$

Equations 12.4 to 12.6 express MM's Proposition 1, modified to incorporate the effects of company tax. Note that if there is no company tax, then $t_c = 0$, and Equation 12.6 becomes $V_L = V_U$, which is MM's no-tax result. Equation 12.6 implies that a levered company is always worth more than an equivalent unlevered company. Moreover, the more it borrows, the greater is its debt, D, and the more its value increases. If the company tax rate is 30 per cent, then, according to Equation 12.6, company value increases by 30 cents for every dollar of debt in a company's capital structure.

In Section 12.3.1 we summarised Proposition 1 in the no-tax case using the analogy of slicing a cake: slicing a cake in a different way does not change the size of the cake. Introducing company tax is analogous to cutting the cake into three slices instead of two—there is now a slice for the government as well as slices for the shareholders and lenders. Saving company tax by borrowing is equivalent to increasing the size of the shareholders' slice by reducing the size of the government's slice.

The main implication of Proposition 1 with company tax is clear but extreme: a company should borrow so much that its company tax bill is reduced to zero. In practice, very few companies use such extremely high levels of debt. This fact indicates that while debt must have some advantages, there must also be other factors that offset the company tax advantages of debt. One important factor that can do so is income tax payable by individuals, which we refer to as *personal taxes*.[6]

12.4.2 COMPANY TAX AND PERSONAL TAX

In practice, the company tax system and the personal tax system interact in complex ways. Although we cannot provide a complete analysis here, we can capture the main features by considering a simplified case. This case is presented in Example 12.6.

EXAMPLE 12.6

In 2009–10, Nowra Ltd had earnings before interest and tax of $250 000 and its interest expense was $100 000. All its lenders and shareholders are individuals. The company operates under a classical tax system. All companies are taxed at the rate of 30 per cent on company income, while all individuals are taxed at the rate of 40 per cent on interest income and 25 per cent on income from shares. How much tax does the government collect?

SOLUTION
Table 12.4 sets out the calculations.

TABLE 12.4 Taxes collected from Nowra Ltd, its lenders and shareholders

INCOME AND EXPENSES	AMOUNT ($)	TAX PAID ($)	TYPE OF TAX AND TAX RATE
Earnings before interest and tax (EBIT)	250 000	—	—
less Interest	100 000	40 000	Personal tax (40%)
Earnings after interest, before tax	150 000	—	—
less Company tax	45 000	45 000	Company tax (30%)
Earnings available to shareholders	105 000	26 250	Personal tax (25%)
Total tax collected		111 250	

As shown in Table 12.4, the government collects tax of $111 250, of which $45 000 is company tax and $66 250 is personal tax.

---

[6] The term 'personal taxes' is widely used in the finance literature to refer to taxes paid at the investor level. Such taxes include the income tax paid by superannuation funds as well as that paid by individual investors, but to be consistent with the literature we will use the term personal taxes.

Consider $100 of Nowra's earnings before interest and tax. If this $100 is paid to one of the lenders as interest, then the government collects $40 in tax from the lender, and the lender keeps $60. If this $100 is not paid to a lender, then it forms part of earnings after interest and will be subject to company tax. The government will collect $30 in company tax, leaving $70 to be passed on to a shareholder. But the shareholder must pay 25 per cent of the $70 in personal tax, which is 0.25 × $70 = $17.50. The shareholder therefore receives $70 − $17.50 = $52.50. This is summarised in Table 12.5. The table also shows the general case in which the company tax rate is t_c, the personal tax rate on interest income is t_p and the personal tax rate on income from shares is t_s.

TABLE 12.5 Effect of taxes on the income of lenders and shareholders

SOURCE OF FINANCE	LENDERS		SHAREHOLDERS	
	NOWRA LTD	GENERAL CASE	NOWRA LTD	GENERAL CASE
Earnings before interest and tax (EBIT) ($)	100	100	100	100
Company tax ($)	Nil	0	30	100 × t_c
Earnings after company tax ($)	100	100	70	100(1 − t_c)
Personal tax ($)	40	100 × t_p	17.50	100(1 − t_c) × t_s
Net income after all taxes ($)	60	100(1 − t_p)	52.50	100(1 − t_c)(1 − t_s)

t_c is the company income tax rate.
t_p is the personal tax rate on interest income.
t_s is the personal tax rate on income from shares.

Therefore, as shown in the bottom line of Table 12.5, the preferred source of finance depends on a comparison between $(1 − t_p)$ and $(1 − t_c)(1 − t_s)$. With personal taxes and company tax, the effect of debt on company value becomes:

$$V_L = V_U + \left[1 - \frac{(1-t_c)(1-t_s)}{(1-t_p)}\right]D \qquad [12.7]$$

where D = the market value of debt

Equation 12.7 can be used to consider two special cases.

Special case No. 1: Suppose that the personal tax rate on interest income is equal to the personal tax rate on income from shares—that is, $t_p = t_s$. In this case, Equation 12.7 simplifies to: $V_L = V_U + t_c D$, which is MM's result when they include company tax in their analysis (Equation 12.6). In other words, personal taxes do not affect the company tax savings associated with debt, provided that the personal tax rates on income from debt and equity are the same.

Special case No. 2: Suppose that $(1 − t_p)$ is equal to $(1 − t_c)(1 − t_s)$, which means that the overall tax burdens on debt and equity are the same. In this case, Equation 12.7 simplifies to: $V_L = V_U$—that is, the effects of company tax and personal taxes offset each other exactly, so changing a company's capital structure will not affect its value. This result is the same as MM's no-tax case.

How likely are these special cases to arise in practice? In most classical tax systems Special case No. 1 is unlikely to arise because capital gains are often taxed at a lower rate than ordinary income. Typically, interest income is regarded as ordinary income and hence is taxed at the full personal tax rate, t_p. Income from shares will usually consist partly of dividends, which are taxed at the full rate, and partly of capital gains, which are taxed at a lower rate. So the overall tax rate on shareholders' income, t_s, is less than the full rate, t_p. But Special case No. 2—or something very similar—is quite likely to arise. Suppose that the company tax rate, t_c, is 0.30 and an investor has a personal tax rate of 0.45 on interest and dividends but the tax rate on capital gains is 0.10.[7] Also assume that dividends make up one-third of the return to equity while capital gains make up two-thirds. For this investor, t_p = 0.45 and t_s = 0.45 × 1/3 + 0.1 × 2/3 = 0.217. The after-tax return from debt will be $100(1 − 0.45) = $55 and from equity it will be $100(1 − 0.3)(1 − 0.217) = $54.81. These returns are almost identical, which suggests that it is possible for the effect of personal taxes to offset the effect of company tax, provided that the personal tax rate on equity returns is significantly lower than the personal tax rate on interest. This outcome is possible if capital gains are tax-free or are taxed at a lower rate than ordinary income—a situation that frequently arises in practice.

One complication that we have not considered is the fact that personal tax rates differ between investors. The effects of taxes and their implications for capital structure decisions when different investors have different personal tax rates were analysed formally by Miller (1977). This analysis is presented in the next section.

12.4.3 MILLER'S ANALYSIS

To outline Miller's analysis of the effects of debt and taxes under the classical tax system, we assume that all the income received by shareholders is in the form of unrealised capital gains, so the personal tax rate on shareholders' income, t_s, is zero. Suppose that all companies were financed entirely by equity. That situation cannot persist because there would be a strong incentive for companies to reduce company tax by borrowing. This means that some investors will have to switch from holding shares to holding debt. Tax-exempt investors should readily move from holding shares to holding debt because they would pay no tax in either case. The initial impact of the change from all-equity financing would be to reduce total taxes, because company tax is being reduced without any increase in personal tax. When tax-exempt investors have been satisfied, companies that wish to borrow will have to persuade taxable investors to purchase debt. The interest rate offered to potential lenders must therefore increase, in order to attract investors with higher and higher marginal personal income tax rates, t_p.

Companies can afford to persuade investors to switch from holding shares to holding debt, provided that the company tax saved by issuing the additional debt is greater than the personal tax payable by the lender (remember that t_s = 0). Companies should be able to do this if the investor's marginal tax rate is less than the company tax rate. But it should not be tax effective for investors on marginal tax rates greater than the company tax rate to become lenders: the personal tax paid on interest would be greater than the company tax saved. Therefore, the 'migration' of investors should stop when, for the marginal investor, t_p equals t_c. If the tax rate of the marginal investor is lower than the company tax rate, then there would be an incentive for companies to reduce overall taxes by increased borrowing. However, companies cannot afford to pay interest rates that are high enough to attract investors whose tax rate is higher than the company tax rate. The logical result is an equilibrium in which there is no incentive for companies to borrow either more or less.

Miller's analysis has several implications. These include:

- There is an optimal debt–equity ratio *for the corporate sector as a whole*, and this optimal debt–equity ratio will depend on the company income tax rate and on the funds available to investors who are subject to different tax rates.
- The securities issued by different companies will appeal to different types of investors. For example, tax-exempt investors should invest only in debt securities, while investors subject to marginal personal income tax rates greater than the company income tax rate should invest only in shares. Therefore, companies with different capital structures will attract different investor clienteles, but,

---

7 A capital gains tax rate of 10 per cent may seem low. For example, in Australia, capital gains are frequently taxed at half the rate on ordinary income, which in this example would be 22.5 per cent. However, capital gains tax is usually not payable until the shares are sold, which may not occur until many years after the shares were bought. Because of the time value of money, this deferral of tax payable benefits the taxpayer and may well imply that the effective capital gains tax rate is as low as 10 per cent.

according to Miller (1977), 'one clientele is as good as the other'. Consequently, in equilibrium there is no optimal debt–equity ratio *for an individual company*.
- The shareholders of levered companies end up receiving no benefit from the company tax savings on debt because the saving is passed on to lenders in the form of a higher interest rate on debt— that is, companies are effectively required to compensate the lenders for the additional personal tax payable on interest income. The compensation is paid in the form of an interest rate that is higher than it would be if personal income taxes did not exist.

Miller's analysis is valuable in explaining empirical observations such as the fact that the average debt–equity ratio of US companies did not increase substantially from the 1920s to the 1970s, despite an almost five-fold increase in the company income tax rate during that period. Miller's explanation is that personal income tax rates increased in a similar manner, thereby offsetting what would otherwise have been a strong incentive for companies to issue more debt.

12.4.4 THE SCOPE OF MILLER'S ANALYSIS

Miller proposed that the effects of personal and company taxes can exactly offset each other, implying that an *individual* company's value is independent of its capital structure, even though there is an optimal debt–equity ratio for the corporate sector *as a whole*. His analysis is important in highlighting the need to consider personal tax as well as company tax when analysing the effects of borrowing on company value. However, Miller's analysis relied on some simplifying assumptions.

An important assumption is that the effective company income tax rate is the same for all companies. Suppose that the tax rate for all companies equals the statutory rate, which is, say, 30 per cent. A profitable company that has borrowed will save 30 cents of company tax for every dollar of interest paid. However, not all companies make profits all the time. If a company makes a loss, the amount of the loss is carried forward as a deduction against later years' taxable income. Therefore, for a loss-making company, the present value of the tax savings on an additional dollar of interest will be less than 30 cents.

Moreover, as De Angelo and Masulis (1980) have pointed out, borrowing is not the only way for companies to save tax. For example, depreciation on many assets can be claimed as a tax deduction, and the larger a company's deductions for depreciation and other non-debt items, the smaller is any advantage associated with saving company tax by borrowing. In other words, non-debt tax deductions are a substitute for interest as a tax deduction.

With uncertain future interest tax savings and non-debt tax deductions, debt may be more valuable for some companies than it is for others. The companies whose shareholders will benefit most from corporate borrowing will be those best able to use the tax deductions generated by the interest paid on debt.[8] In other words, borrowing by a company can add value if the company tax saved by borrowing is greater than the additional personal tax paid; this is most likely for companies with profits that are large and stable. Conversely, for companies with low profits and particularly those with accumulated losses being carried forward, borrowing can reduce company value and shareholders' wealth because borrowing increases the personal tax payable on interest received and hence increases total taxes.

It should also be noted that in discussing the limitations of Miller's analysis we have not yet allowed for the fact that interest may not be the only cost incurred when a company borrows. Other costs include the costs of financial distress and agency costs. Miller recognised that in principle these costs are relevant to capital structure decisions. However, he argued that in practice they are too small to have a significant effect on company value. We discuss these costs in Sections 12.6 and 12.7. In summary, his analysis is important in that it shows that the effects of personal and corporate taxes tend to be offsetting, and can be exactly offsetting if the personal tax rate on interest income is significantly greater than the personal tax rate on income from shares.

---

8 For US evidence that the marginal effective tax rate differs between companies and is related to financial leverage, see Graham (1996).

THE EFFECTS OF TAXES ON CAPITAL STRUCTURE UNDER AN IMPUTATION TAX SYSTEM

12.5

12.5.1 WHAT IS AN IMPUTATION TAX SYSTEM?

In Chapter 11 we provided a detailed discussion of the imputation tax system that operates in Australia. In this section we therefore provide only a brief summary. Since 1987, Australian-owned companies operating in Australia have been taxed under an imputation system. The hallmark of an imputation system is that company taxes and personal taxes are integrated. Look again at Table 12.4, which sets out the amount of tax collected from Nowra Ltd under a classical tax system. Note that, although the highest tax rate in this example is 40 per cent, Nowra's earnings before interest and tax (EBIT) of $250 000 has generated tax collections of $111 250—equivalent to a tax rate of 44.5 per cent. This high implied tax rate arises because the classical system taxes company income in the hands of the company and then taxes it again when that income is passed on to the company's shareholders as a dividend. Critics of the classical system describe this outcome as 'double taxation'. An imputation system is designed to eliminate this feature of the classical tax system. Its operation is illustrated in Example 12.7.

LEARNING OBJECTIVE 3
Explain how tax may influence capital structure decisions

EXAMPLE 12.7

In 2010–11, as in the previous year, Nowra Ltd had earnings before interest and tax (EBIT) of $250 000 and its interest expense was $100 000. All its lenders and shareholders are individuals resident in Australia. The company now operates under an imputation system. In this tax system, all companies are taxed at the rate of 30 per cent on company income, while all individuals are taxed at the rate of 40 per cent on interest income and 40 per cent on dividends. Nowra's dividend policy is to pay out all its after-tax income in dividends. How much tax does the government collect?

SOLUTION

Table 12.6 sets out the calculations.

TABLE 12.6 Taxes collected from Nowra Ltd, its lenders and shareholders

INCOME AND EXPENSES	AMOUNT ($)	TAX PAID ($)	TYPE OF TAX AND TAX RATE
Earnings before interest and tax (EBIT)	250 000		
less Interest	100 000	40 000	Personal tax (40%)
Earnings after interest, before tax	150 000		
less Company tax	45 000	45 000	Company tax (30%)
Earnings available to shareholders	105 000		
Franked dividend	105 000		
plus Franking credit[1]	45 000		
Shareholders' taxable income	150 000		
Shareholders' gross tax liability (at 40%)	60 000		
less Franking credit	45 000		
Shareholders' net tax payable	15 000	15 000	Personal tax
Total tax collected		100 000	

[1] For the calculation of the franking credit see overleaf:

continued →

Example 12.7 *continued*

$$\text{franking credit} = \frac{t_c}{1-t_c} \times \text{franked dividend}$$

$$= \frac{0.30}{0.70} \times \$105\,000$$

$$= \$45\,000$$

Given Nowra's dividend policy, the government has collected tax of $100 000 from Nowra's earnings of $250 000—equivalent to a tax rate of 40 per cent. This tax rate is, of course, equal to the personal tax rate levied on interest and dividend income. The imputation system is intended to produce this outcome.

12.5.2 THE EFFECTS OF TAX ON CAPITAL STRUCTURE DECISIONS UNDER AN IMPUTATION TAX SYSTEM

To compare the effects of taxes on debt and equity under an imputation tax system, consider a dollar of EBIT and think of the company's capital structure as determining whether this dollar is paid out as interest to lenders or used to provide a return to shareholders. The return to shareholders could be in the form of either dividends or capital gains, depending on whether profit is distributed or retained by the company. As discussed in Chapter 11, if Australian company tax has been paid, then most resident shareholders will benefit if profits are distributed as franked dividends rather than retained. The after-tax returns to lenders and shareholders from a dollar of EBIT used to pay interest or franked dividends are shown in Table 12.7.

TABLE 12.7 After-tax returns to investors under an imputation tax system

	LENDERS	SHAREHOLDERS
EBIT ($)	1	1
Company income tax ($)	0	t_c
Income after company tax ($)	1	$(1 - t_c)$ (franked dividend)
Franking credit ($)	0	t_c
Investors' taxable income ($)	1	$1 - t_c + t_c = 1$ (grossed-up dividend)
Net personal tax ($)	t_p	$(t_p - t_c)$ (gross personal tax less tax credit)
Income after all taxes ($)	$(1 - t_p)$	$(1 - t_c) - (t_p - t_c) = (1 - t_p)$

If the dollar of EBIT is used to pay interest to lenders, then company tax is zero because interest paid is tax deductible for the company. Interest received is taxable in the hands of lenders at the personal tax rate, t_p, so that the lender's net income after all taxes is $\$(1 - t_p)$. Alternatively, if the dollar of EBIT is used to provide a return to shareholders, then the company will have to pay tax of $\$t_c$ which leaves after-tax profit of $\$(1 - t_c)$. This profit can be used to pay a franked dividend of $\$(1 - t_c)$ carrying a franking credit of $\$t_c$. The shareholder will then be taxed on the grossed-up dividend ($1), which means that, after allowing for the franking credit, net personal tax will be $\$(t_p - t_c)$. Finally, the shareholder's income after all taxes will be the cash dividend, $\$(1 - t_c)$, less net personal tax, $\$(t_p - t_c)$—that is, the shareholder's after-tax income is $\$(1 - t_c) - \$(t_p - t_c) = \$(1 - t_p)$. While the calculation of shareholders' after-tax income under imputation may seem complex, the end result is simple: income distributed as franked dividends to resident shareholders is effectively taxed only once, at the shareholders' personal tax rate. As shown in Table 12.6, interest paid to lenders is also taxed only once at the lenders' personal tax rate. Thus, the important result is that, for any given investor, the overall tax burden is the same for both debt and equity. In other words, in this case the imputation tax system is neutral between debt and equity.

If neutrality is achieved, we are back to MM's Proposition 1 in the original no-tax case: the choice of capital structure does not affect a company's value. In showing that the imputation tax system can be neutral we have assumed that all profits are distributed as franked dividends. Other results may be possible if profits are retained.

In Australia in 2010–11 the income tax rate payable by companies was 30 per cent. All companies face the same rate—it does not vary with company income. However, the income tax rate payable by individuals depends on the individual's taxable income. Thus different individuals pay different income tax rates. In 2010–11 the top marginal tax rate for personal income, excluding the Medicare levy, was 45 per cent. Consider an investor on this rate. This investor's after-tax return from a dollar of EBIT paid out as interest will be $(1 − 0.45) = 0.55. Alternatively, if this investor receives a capital gain of $1, the tax law provides that only half this amount (50 cents) is subject to tax if the gain is realised after a period of more than 12 months. Effectively, the income tax rate is halved; in this case, the rate would be t_g = 22.5 per cent. If the same investor holds shares in a company that retains all profits and provides returns only as capital gains, then the after-tax return will be $(1 − t_c)(1 − t_g) = (1 − 0.30)(1 − 0.225) = 0.5425$. The after-tax return from equity (0.5425) is only slightly lower than the after-tax return from debt (0.55). However, this analysis understates the attractiveness of the investment in equity. While it is true that this investor will pay a tax rate of 22.5 per cent on a capital gain, *this tax does not have to be paid until the shares are sold*. Therefore, if the investor keeps the shares for, say, 10 years before selling them, the payment of the capital gains tax is deferred for 10 years. Taking into account the time value of money, this is equivalent to a reduction in the capital gains tax rate. In this case, an investment in shares is more attractive than an investment in debt. The implication is that for this investor, the tax system is not neutral, but the bias favours equity rather than debt as a source of company finance. To state this in another way, for a company to borrow from investors in the top tax bracket, the interest rate needed to attract such investors would have to be so high that company value would be reduced.

In summary, the Australian imputation tax system does not favour the use of debt finance by companies. The system is either neutral or biased towards equity, depending on the investor's marginal tax rate. Therefore, we arrive at essentially the same conclusion as Miller: borrowing will not add value because the interest rate paid will reflect personal tax rates on interest that are equal to or higher than the overall tax rates on equity returns. While this conclusion is essentially the same as Miller's, the reason is different. Miller's argument relied on market equilibrium, whereas in the case of the Australian tax system it is the structure of the system that ensures that it is either neutral or biased towards equity.

The designers of the imputation tax system had as one of their main objectives the removal of any tax-related bias towards the use of debt finance by companies. Our analysis indicates that this objective should be achieved in the case of companies that are wholly owned by Australian resident investors. However, taxes can still be an important influence on financing decisions for many companies. For example, overseas investors in Australian companies are outside the imputation tax system and are effectively still taxed under the classical system. Consequently, debt may have tax advantages for Australian companies with a large overseas ownership.

THE COSTS OF FINANCIAL DISTRESS 12.6

The costs of financial distress may also cause a company's value to depend on its capital structure. We first outline the nature of financial distress. The effects of direct bankruptcy costs are then discussed in Section 12.6.1. Indirect costs of financial distress are discussed in Section 12.6.2.

> **LEARNING OBJECTIVE 4**
>
> Explain how the costs of financial distress may influence capital structure decisions

A company is said to be in a state of **financial distress** when it has difficulty meeting its commitments to lenders. In serious cases, financial distress may lead to the liquidation of the company. Alternatively, an administrator or receiver-manager may be appointed by the lenders—this may lead either to eventual liquidation or to control reverting to shareholders if the company trades out of its difficulties. In less serious cases of financial distress, a company may trade out of its difficulties without resorting to formal measures such as receivership. In other, even less serious cases, a company may meet all its commitments but the mere *possibility* of financial difficulties can change people's behaviour. For example, suppliers may demand cash on delivery if the customer is rumoured to be facing financial difficulties. Therefore, we can distinguish between costs associated with a formal transfer of control to lenders, that is, **bankruptcy costs**, and indirect costs of financial distress, which can affect companies whose problems are less serious.[9]

financial distress
situation where a company's financial obligations cannot be met, or can be met only with difficulty

bankruptcy costs
direct and indirect costs associated with financial difficulty that leads to control of a company being transferred to lenders

12.6.1 BANKRUPTCY COSTS

In Section 12.2 we explained that any borrowing by a company creates financial risk for shareholders. This is true even if the debt–equity ratio is so low that there is no risk of default. MM's analysis shows that financial risk increases the cost of equity capital but has no effect on the weighted average cost of capital or on a company's market value.

Increasing a company's debt–equity ratio increases financial risk and also increases a separate but related risk: the risk that the company will default on its debt. When there is some probability of default, debt is described as 'risky'. MM's Proposition 1 holds even if debt is risky: a company's market value is not affected by its debt–equity ratio. This conclusion also relies on the assumption that, while default is possible, there are no costs associated with default—that is, bankruptcy costs are assumed to be zero.[10]

In practice, there are both direct and indirect costs associated with bankruptcy and these costs will affect companies that issue risky debt. The direct costs are out-of-pocket costs associated with receivership or liquidation and consist mainly of fees paid to parties such as lawyers, accountants and liquidators. Indirect costs relate to factors such as the effects of lost sales, reduced operating efficiency and the cost of managerial time devoted to attempts to avert failure.

The effect of bankruptcy costs on company value is easily seen in the case of direct bankruptcy costs. When a company issues risky debt there is some probability that the company will subsequently default, in which case direct bankruptcy costs will be incurred. Therefore, by issuing risky debt, a company gives outsiders (lawyers, accountants, liquidators, and so on) a potential claim against its assets, which must decrease the value of the company to its shareholders and/or its lenders. Where debt finance offers both benefits (such as tax savings) and the possibility of bankruptcy costs, the value of a company can be written as follows:

Value of a company
= value of an equivalent all-equity financed company
+ present value of the benefits of debt
− present value of expected bankruptcy costs

The present value of expected bankruptcy costs will be positively related to both the probability of bankruptcy and the present value of costs incurred if bankruptcy does occur.

---

[9] Strictly speaking, the term 'bankruptcy' in Australia applies only to the insolvency of individuals. When a company fails to meet its financial obligations, its creditors have a number of options, such as seeking the appointment of a receiver, a receiver-manager or a liquidator. We use the term 'bankruptcy' to describe the status of such companies because of its widespread use in the finance literature.

[10] The assumption of no costs associated with default does not mean that there are no losses incurred by investors. Typically, both lenders and shareholders will incur losses because the value of the company's assets has declined. This decline causes the company to default but if there are no costs associated with default, the total, albeit reduced, value of the assets is available for distribution to investors. Therefore, investors do not suffer additional losses as a result of default.

The probability of bankruptcy will depend on the company's business risk and on its financial leverage, but at any given level of business risk, the higher the company's leverage, the higher will be the probability of bankruptcy. Therefore, the present value of expected bankruptcy costs will increase as a company's debt–equity ratio increases. Hence, on this view, the decision to borrow involves a trade-off between the advantage of tax savings and the disadvantage of expected bankruptcy costs.

Bankruptcy costs would not concern shareholders if they were borne entirely by other parties such as lenders. When a company is liquidated, it is rare for shareholders to receive any return. In other words, the company's equity is usually worthless and any proceeds from the sale of assets will be distributed to lenders. The costs incurred in administering the liquidation, therefore, reduce the pool of funds available for distribution to lenders. However, before they lend money, potential lenders should realise that they will suffer in the event of liquidation and respond by demanding a higher interest rate on their loans. Consequently, while lenders will bear *realised* liquidation costs, the *expected* costs are likely to be borne by shareholders. Therefore, expected liquidation costs decrease both company value and shareholders' wealth. In addition to the fairly obvious direct costs of financial distress, there are also other less obvious indirect costs. Some sources of these indirect costs are discussed in the next section.

12.6.2 INDIRECT COSTS OF FINANCIAL DISTRESS

As noted above, the indirect costs of financial distress relate to factors such as the effects of lost sales, reduced operating efficiency and the cost of managerial time devoted to attempts to avert failure. The basic problem is that the threat of corporate bankruptcy provides incentives for managers and other stakeholders such as customers, suppliers and employees to behave in ways that can disrupt a company's operating activities and thus decrease its value. For example, if a company is experiencing financial difficulties, managers are likely to pay less attention to issues such as product quality and employee safety.

Clearly, if product quality falls and this fall is easily noticed by customers, sales and revenue will be lost. If product quality is important, but difficult to assess, the mere perception that a company's product quality is likely to suffer because of financial difficulties can deter customers. For example, travellers are likely to be wary of financially insecure airlines because of fears that safety may be impaired by inadequate maintenance. Therefore, it can be important for companies to maintain an image of low risk. Restricting the level of debt is one way of restricting a company's overall risk.

Titman (1984) points out that shareholders and lenders are not the only parties who can suffer if a company liquidates or withdraws voluntarily from a particular line of business. Titman argues that expected future costs imposed on parties such as employees and customers will affect shareholders' wealth. For example, suppose that a machinery manufacturer is considered likely to liquidate. Customers will expect problems in obtaining spare parts and service, so the price they are prepared to pay for the company's products will fall. Sales, profits and share price would be greater if the company could assure customers and other stakeholders that it is very unlikely to liquidate. Titman suggests that the choice of capital structure can, in effect, help to provide this assurance. By borrowing less, a company decreases the probability of liquidation and hence improves the terms on which it trades with customers and other parties. Conversely, for companies that borrow, the adverse effect on the company's current terms of trade is part of the cost of borrowing.

Titman's model has the testable implication that companies such as car manufacturers and computer manufacturers, whose liquidation would impose large costs on customers and other associates, will adopt capital structures that feature relatively low levels of debt. Empirical evidence on this issue is presented in Chapter 13. In addition to its adverse effects on sales, a company's risk of financial distress can also increase its operating costs and its financing costs. For example, a greater risk of financial distress will mean that it is harder to attract and retain skilled employees. Similarly, it can impair a company's ability to borrow and to obtain trade credit.

12.7 AGENCY COSTS

LEARNING OBJECTIVE 5
Explain how agency costs may influence capital structure decisions

Companies enter into contractual or agency relationships with various parties, including managers, shareholders, lenders, customers and suppliers. These relationships involve agency costs, which arise from the potential for conflicts of interest between the parties. In this section, we discuss the major ways in which agency costs can affect financing decisions. The relevant costs include those associated with conflicts of interest between lenders and shareholders, and the incentive effects of debt. Equity finance also has agency costs because there can be conflicts of interest between shareholders and managers.

12.7.1 CONFLICTS OF INTEREST BETWEEN LENDERS AND SHAREHOLDERS

When a company borrows, lenders may fear that management will make decisions that will transfer wealth from lenders to shareholders. This conflict of interest is one type of agency problem. The following examples illustrate the potential for such conflicts of interest (Myers 1977; Smith & Warner 1979).

- *Claim dilution.* A company may issue new debt that ranks equally with, or has a higher ranking than, its existing debt. If the proceeds from the issue are used to pay dividends, the total assets of the company are maintained and the only change is in the company's debt–equity ratio. However, the holders of the old debt now have a less secure claim on the company's assets and therefore their investment has become riskier. Accordingly, the market value of their loans decreases. Unless the value of the company also decreases because of the new debt, wealth is transferred from the holders of the old debt to shareholders.
- *Dividend payout.* If a company significantly increases its dividend payout, it decreases the company's assets and increases the riskiness of its debt. Again, this results in a wealth transfer from lenders to shareholders. Further, the incentives for management to increase a company's dividends become greater when the company is facing financial distress. In this case, the dividend payout provides a means for the shareholders to receive returns that otherwise are likely to go to the lenders on liquidation of the company.
- *Asset substitution.* When a company borrows, its incentive to undertake risky investments increases, especially if the market value of its shares is very low. In fact, this incentive can be so strong that a company may undertake a high-risk investment even if the investment has a negative net present value. The reason is that if the investment proves successful, most of the benefits will flow to shareholders, but if the investment fails, most of the costs will be borne by lenders. Therefore, at the time the investment is undertaken, the total value of the company will decrease (because the investment has a negative net present value), but the value of the shares will increase and the value of the debt will fall. Again there is a transfer of wealth from lenders to shareholders.
- *Underinvestment.* A company may reject proposed low-risk investments that have a positive net present value. If a company's debt is very risky, it may not be in the interest of shareholders to contribute additional capital to finance profitable new investments. While undertaking the investments would increase company value, shareholders can still lose because the risk of the debt will fall and its value will increase. The amount of this increase can be greater than the net present value of the investments.

Lenders should realise that their wealth may be eroded by managers' decisions made in the best interests of the company's shareholders. Lenders would be expected to attempt to protect themselves against such behaviour by managers. The more the company borrows, the greater is the need to seek such protection. One response by lenders is to require a higher interest rate on debt than would otherwise be the case, in order to compensate them for the losses they may suffer. This imposes costs on the company that will be borne largely by shareholders.

Lenders may also protect themselves by requiring covenants to be included in loan agreements. Examples of covenants are restrictions on issuing additional debt, particularly debt that has a higher ranking; restrictions on the disposal of assets; a limitation on the payment of dividends; limitations on the types of investments the company can undertake; and requirements that the company maintain specific financial ratios.[11] The fact that these types of covenants have been in existence for many years suggests that lenders are well aware of their need for protection.

Covenants affect the value of the company and shareholders' wealth in two ways:

(a) Monitoring will be required to ensure that the covenants are not breached.
(b) There may be opportunity costs in cases where the restrictive covenants prevent managers from implementing value-maximising decisions. For example, covenants designed to prevent the company undertaking high-risk projects with negative net present values may also result in some profitable, high-risk projects being forgone.

12.7.2 CONFLICTS OF INTEREST BETWEEN SHAREHOLDERS AND COMPANY MANAGERS

The agency costs discussed in Section 12.7.1 relate only to debt but there can also be agency costs associated with equity. These costs arise when a company's shares are owned by 'outside' investors rather than by 'insiders' such as top-level managers. To see this, consider a company owned entirely by an entrepreneur who also manages its operations. In this case, there are no agency costs of equity because one person both owns and controls the company. Many companies are clearly too large to be structured in this way and equity capital is provided by shareholders who have little or no involvement in the company's operations. Instead, managers are employed to control the day-to-day operations of the company. With this separation of ownership and control there can be conflicts of interest between shareholders and managers. For example, managers are unlikely to be as motivated as an entrepreneur to work hard, strive for maximum efficiency and search actively for profitable investment opportunities.

The agency costs of equity can be reduced by measures that align the objectives of managers with those of shareholders. These measures include employee share ownership schemes and the inclusion of options on the company's shares as part of the remuneration of top-level managers. If these measures are effective, this prompts the question: Would it be efficient to eliminate the costs associated with the separation of ownership and control by having a company's equity capital provided *only* by its managers? The answer is generally no, for two main reasons. First, while the owner-manager structure (rather than the employee-manager structure) is preferred for many small businesses, there are few individuals who have the combination of wealth and skills to both own and manage a very large company. Second, while having an owner-manager has advantages in terms of agency costs, it has disadvantages in terms of risk bearing. As discussed in Chapter 7, investors can reduce risk by diversification and it is easy for them to diversify by combining the shares of many companies in a portfolio. Diversification can eliminate firm-specific or unsystematic risk, and investors will require compensation only for bearing systematic risk that cannot be removed by diversification. In other words, the existence of a stock market allows companies to raise equity capital on terms that reflect the benefits of diversification. But where a company's manager is also one of its shareholders, the manager is unlikely to reap the full benefits of

---

11 Smith and Warner (1979). In addition, the law may limit the behaviour of managers. For example, under Australian law, a company can pay a dividend only if three conditions are met. These are: (i) the company's assets must exceed its liabilities immediately before the dividend is declared and the excess must be sufficient to pay the dividend; (ii) it must be fair and reasonable to the shareholders; and (iii) it must not materially prejudice the company's ability to pay its creditors.

diversification. As an employee, the manager's wealth is linked to some extent to the fortunes of the company. For example, managers generally develop skills and knowledge that are firm-specific—that is, they have skills and knowledge that are valuable in their current employment, but are of less value elsewhere. Therefore, managers would require a higher rate of return on their investment than 'outside' investors. In other words, managers would 'charge' more for bearing risk than outside investors, who can diversify. Consequently, the owner-manager structure is not efficient from the viewpoint of risk bearing.

Jensen (1986) outlines an important application of agency theory to capital structure decisions. This application is based on the concept of '**free cash flow**', which Jensen defines as the cash flow in excess of that required to fund all projects that have positive net present values. Consider, for example, a highly profitable company in a declining industry. Because the company is profitable, it will generate positive net operating cash flows, but because the industry is declining, it will have few new investment projects that have a positive net present value. Hence, it has large free cash flows. Managers have considerable discretion in deciding how to use free cash flows and Jensen argues that managers will be tempted to use free cash flows in ways that benefit them rather than the shareholders. For example, managers may invest in new projects or takeovers that increase their command over resources, even though these investments have negative net present values. Similarly, having free cash flows may allow managers to avoid making hard decisions, such as retrenching surplus employees and adapting to rapidly changing technology. The upshot is that the company becomes less efficient and the interests of shareholders are damaged.

One way to reduce the agency costs of free cash flows is through the payment of dividends or by buying back shares. Jensen argues that shareholders' wealth should be increased if managers commit to paying out this cash as dividends or to buying back shares rather than retaining the cash within the company. However, promises to continue to pay high dividends or to buy back shares are weak because shareholders cannot enforce them. But if a company borrows, it is obliged to make agreed payments of interest and repayments of principal to the lender. Thus, debt has a 'control effect' whereby managers are forced to pay out cash because the penalties for default are severe. Jensen argues that the control effect of debt will be important in companies that generate large net operating cash flows but have low growth prospects. Such companies can be expected to have higher financial leverage than others. He acknowledges that high leverage can be dangerous but also believes that it can add value in cases where companies generate large free cash flows.

free cash flow
cash flow in excess of that required to fund all projects that have positive net present values

12.8 OPTIMAL CAPITAL STRUCTURE: THE STATIC TRADE-OFF THEORY

LEARNING OBJECTIVE 6
Understand the concept of an optimal capital structure based on a trade-off between the benefits and costs of using debt

Debt offers a company advantages, which include the tax deductibility of interest, but also disadvantages, which include increased costs of financial distress. Therefore, there is the possibility of a trade-off between the advantages and the disadvantages of debt, leading to an optimal capital structure.[12] If an all-equity company decides to issue a small amount of debt, it is likely that the probability of financial distress will be increased only negligibly. Under a classical tax system, the resulting tax savings are therefore likely to outweigh the very small increase in expected costs of financial distress. Consequently, the value of the company will increase. However, as the proportion of debt is further increased, the probability of financial distress also increases and hence the expected costs of financial distress also increase. At some point, the higher costs will equal the higher tax savings. The optimal debt–equity ratio has been reached. If the debt–equity ratio is increased still further, the value of the company starts to decrease. This is illustrated in Figure 12.3.

12 Several authors have discussed optimal capital structure theories of this type. See, for example, Kraus and Litzenberger (1973) and Scott (1976).

FIGURE 12.3 The static trade-off theory of capital structure

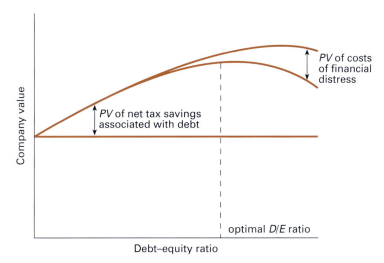

The **static trade-off theory** outlined here has been a popular way of reconciling observed capital structures with the MM analysis (with company income tax). There are several reasons for suggesting that the static trade-off theory provides an over-simplified view of the relationship between capital structure and company value. These include the following:

- Miller has argued that when both corporate and personal taxes are considered, the net effect of taxes on company value can be zero.
- The imputation tax system has the potential to be neutral between debt and equity as sources of company finance. In cases where it is not neutral, the system is biased towards equity, not debt.
- There is evidence that the direct costs of bankruptcy are small relative to company value (Warner 1977; Pham & Chow 1987, Weiss 1990; Andrade & Kaplan 1998).[13]
- Companies used debt finance long before the introduction of income taxes, which suggests that there must be non-tax advantages of debt. The main such advantage probably involves agency costs. As discussed in Section 12.7.2, debt can be valuable in reducing the agency costs of equity.

While the static trade-off theory has significant limitations, its central message may still be valid: there are both advantages and disadvantages of debt, which can give rise to an optimal capital structure consisting of a combination of different types of finance. Therefore, despite its limitations, the static trade-off theory is useful in that it can help managers to focus on some of the factors that can be important in financing decisions.

static trade-off theory
theory that proposes that companies have an optimal capital structure based on a trade-off between the benefits and costs of using debt

CAPITAL STRUCTURE WITH INFORMATION ASYMMETRY

12.9

LEARNING OBJECTIVE 7
Explain the 'pecking order' theory of capital structure

12.9.1 PECKING ORDER THEORY

Donaldson (1961) carried out an extensive survey to find out how the capital structures of US companies were actually established. His main findings can be summarised as follows:

---

13 Warner estimated that the direct bankruptcy incurred by a sample of 'failed' US railroad companies averaged only 5.3 per cent of the market value of their assets. This figure falls to 1 per cent if company value is measured 7 years before bankruptcy. Weiss estimates that direct costs for large financially distressed firms are on average 2.8% of the book value of assets. Pham and Chow reported direct bankruptcy costs averaging 3.6 per cent of company value at the date of bankruptcy for a sample of Australian companies. When the probability of failure is also taken into account, it appears that expected direct bankruptcy costs would be very small.

(a) Managers prefer to use internal finance rather than raise funds externally by borrowing or issuing shares.
(b) Dividend–payout ratios are set based on companies' expected future cash flows and expected investment opportunities. The aim is to ensure that there are sufficient internal funds to meet a company's capital expenditure needs under 'normal' conditions, but managers are also reluctant to make sudden changes in dividends—that is, dividend policy is 'sticky'.
(c) With sticky dividend policy and unexpected changes in both cash flows and investment opportunities, a company may or may not be able to finance all of its capital expenditure internally. In periods when the funds available internally are greater than the company's investment needs, it may pay off debt, invest in marketable securities or increase dividends. Conversely, if the funds available internally are insufficient to meet the company's investment needs, it may run down its cash, sell marketable securities and, if further funds are needed, raise funds externally.
(d) If external funds are needed, borrowing is preferred. A new issue of ordinary shares is a last resort.

pecking order theory
theory that proposes that companies follow a hierarchy of financing sources in which internal funds are preferred and, if external funds are needed, borrowing is preferred to issuing riskier securities

In summary, Donaldson observed that companies tend to follow a hierarchy or **pecking order** of financing sources. The pecking order is:

(a) internal finance
(b) external funds raised by borrowing
(c) external funds raised by issuing hybrid securities, such as convertible notes and preference shares
(d) external funds raised by issuing ordinary shares.

Donaldson's pecking order roughly corresponds to the transaction costs of raising new capital. For example, internal finance usually imposes lower transaction costs than external finance. Therefore, the pecking order could perhaps be explained by a desire to minimise the transaction costs of raising finance. According to Myers (1984), information asymmetry provides another explanation.

12.9.2 INFORMATION ASYMMETRY AND THE UNDERVALUATION OF A COMPANY'S ASSETS

Information asymmetry exists when company managers have more information about their companies' asset values and prospects than outside investors. If management has information that the share market does not have, then management should have a more accurate idea than the share market of the company's 'true value'. Sometimes management may know that the company is worth more than its market value, while at other times management may know that the company is worth less than its market value. In this section we consider the case where management knows that the share market has undervalued a company's assets.

Suppose that Alpha Books Ltd has on issue 100 000 ordinary shares with a market price of $4.50 each, but management knows that the 'true' value of the company's assets is greater than the share market believes—the 'true' value of a share is $5. In the long term, perhaps when more information is publicly available, the share market will also value the shares at $5 each. But in the short term, there is information asymmetry between the managers and the share market. Suppose further that Alpha Books also has an investment opportunity that requires an outlay of $200 000, which will have to be financed externally, and which has an NPV of $17 000. The existence of this investment opportunity is not known to outsiders and is not reflected in the current share price. Hence, there is a second information asymmetry between the managers and the share market. But when the market is informed of the new investment, the share price will respond positively to this information. Should Alpha Books make the new investment? If so, should the investment be made before or after the share market learns the true value of the company's existing assets? And should the investment be financed by issuing new shares or by issuing new debt? To answer these questions, we consider the four scenarios shown in Table 12.8.

TABLE 12.8 Alternative information and financing scenarios for Alpha Books Ltd

TIME THAT THE INVESTMENT ANNOUNCEMENT IS MADE	FINANCING METHOD	
	NEW SHARE ISSUE	NEW DEBT ISSUE
Before the share market learns the true value of the existing assets	Scenario 1	Scenario 3
After the share market learns the true value of the existing assets	Scenario 2	Scenario 4

We now analyse each of these scenarios. For ease of expression we use 'short term' to mean the period before the share market learns the true value of the existing assets. We use 'long term' to mean the period after the share market learns the true value of the existing assets.

Scenario 1: Investment announcement made before the market learns the true value of the existing assets; new shares are issued

Initially, the share price is $4.50, so the number of new shares to be issued is $200 000/$4.50 = 44 444. After the new investment is announced, and the new shares are issued, the share price in the short term will be:

$$P_S = \frac{\$450\,000 + \$200\,000 + \$17\,000}{144\,444} = \$4.62$$

Had the new investment not been made, the share price would have remained at $4.50, so in the short term the shareholders gain 12 cents per share.

In the long term the share market learns the true value of the existing assets and the share price will be:

$$P_L = \frac{\$500\,000 + \$200\,000 + \$17\,000}{144\,444} = \$4.96$$

Had the new investment not been made, the share price would have been $5.00, so in the long term the shareholders lose 4 cents per share.

Therefore, the 'new' shareholders—those who bought the new shares at $4.50 each—will gain both in the short term and the long term, because both $4.62 and $4.96 exceed $4.50. The 'old' shareholders are better off in the short term (because $4.62 exceeds $4.50), but in the long term would be better off without the new investment and the new share issue (because $4.96 is less than $5.00).

Scenario 2: Investment announcement made after the market learns the true value of the existing assets; new shares are issued

In the short term the share price remains at $4.50. In the long term, the share market learns the true value of the existing assets and the share price increases from $4.50 to $5.00. Therefore, the number of new shares to be issued is $200 000/$5.00 = 40 000. After the new investment is announced, and the new shares are issued, the share price will be:

$$P_L = \frac{\$500\,000 + \$200\,000 + \$17\,000}{140\,000} = \$5.12$$

In this scenario, both the new shareholders and the old shareholders gain in the long term by 12 cents per share.

Scenario 3: Investment announcement made before the market learns the true value of the existing assets; new debt is issued

If the company borrows to finance the project, all the benefit of the positive NPV will go to the current shareholders. After the new investment is announced, and the new debt is issued, the share price will be:

$$P_S = \frac{\$450\,000 + \$17\,000}{100\,000} = \$4.67$$

In the short term the shareholders gain by 17 cents per share. In the long term the share market learns the true value of the existing assets, and the share price will be:

$$P_L = \frac{\$500\,000 + \$17\,000}{100\,000} = \$5.17$$

Had the new investment not been made, the share price would have been $5.00, so in the long term the shareholders gain by 17 cents per share.

Scenario 4: Investment announcement made after the market learns the true value of the existing assets; new debt is issued

In the short term, the share price remains at $4.50. In the long term the share market learns the true value of the existing assets and the share price increases from $4.50 to $5.00. After the new investment is announced, and the new debt is issued, the share price will be:

$$P_L = \frac{\$500\,000 + \$17\,000}{100\,000} = \$5.17$$

In this scenario the shareholders gain in the long term by 17 cents per share.

In summary, *without the new investment*, the short-term outcome is a share price of $4.50 while the long-term outcome is a share price of $5.00. *With the new investment*, the short-term and long-term outcomes are those shown in Table 12.9.

TABLE 12.9 Share price outcomes of alternative information and financing scenarios for Alpha Books Ltd

	FINANCING METHOD	
TIME THAT THE INVESTMENT ANNOUNCEMENT IS MADE	**NEW SHARE ISSUE**	**NEW DEBT ISSUE**
Before the share market learns the true value of the existing assets	Scenario 1	Scenario 3
	Share price in the short term: $4.62	Share price in the short term: $4.67
	Share price in the long term: $4.96	Share price in the long term: $5.17
After the share market learns the true value of the existing assets	Scenario 2	Scenario 4
	Share price in the short term: $4.50	Share price in the short term: $4.50
	Share price in the long term: $5.12	Share price in the long term: $5.17

Comparing the four scenarios, the clear winner is Scenario 3, in which the new investment project should be accepted immediately, and should be financed by debt. Scenario 3 produces the highest share price in the short term ($4.67) and the equal highest share price in the long term ($5.17). The worst outcome in the long term is clearly Scenario 1, in which the new investment is undertaken immediately and is financed by shares. In this example, Scenario 1 is so bad that in the long term the shareholders lose as a result of undertaking an investment with a positive NPV.

12.9.3 INFORMATION ASYMMETRY AND THE OVERVALUATION OF A COMPANY'S ASSETS

Now consider a different situation. The current share price of Alpha Books is $4.50 and there is no new investment opportunity. Management has information that implies that the share price should be only $3.50. In the short term the share market does not have this information but will learn of it in the long term. Management decides to issue 50 000 new shares while the market price is still $4.50 and use the cash raised ($225 000) to repay debt. In the short term, this changes the capital structure but not the value of the company. In the long term, when the share market learns the true value of the company's assets, the share price will be:

$$P_L = \frac{\$350\,000 + \$225\,000}{150\,000} = \$3.83$$

While this price is less than the previous price of $4.50, it is *more* than $3.50, which the share price would have been had the new share issue not been made. Having new shareholders pay more than the shares are worth cushions the impact of the bad news on the old shareholders.

12.9.4 IMPLICATIONS OF INFORMATION ASYMMETRY FOR FINANCING POLICY

Information asymmetry can cause the share market to undervalue or to overvalue a company. If a company's managers believe that its shares are undervalued, they will prefer to borrow. If they believe that the shares are overvalued, they will prefer to issue new shares. However, while outside investors are not as well informed as managers, they understand managers' motives. Therefore, the share market may see the announcement of a new share issue as evidence that the company's managers know bad news that is not yet known to outsiders. Consequently, the share price will decrease when a new share issue is announced. This possibility provides another reason why new share issues rank very low in the pecking order.

The main implication for company managers is that there are advantages in restricting financial leverage so that a company will be able to borrow at short notice if a profitable investment opportunity arises. To see this, suppose that a company is so highly levered that any unexpected need for funds can be met only by issuing shares. The announcement of a share issue will cause the company's share price to fall, unless the managers succeed in convincing investors that they are not concealing adverse information. But failing to make an issue will mean that a profitable investment opportunity must be forgone. This choice between two unattractive alternatives can be avoided by maintaining 'reserve borrowing capacity' or 'financial slack'. In turn, this can be achieved by restricting debt to a moderate level, holding marketable securities that can be sold to provide cash and/or arranging lines of credit with unused borrowing limits.

An important difference between the pecking order theory and the static trade-off theory is that the pecking order theory does not rely on the concept of a target debt–equity ratio.[14] Instead, a company's observed capital structure will simply reflect its history in terms of capital requirements. For example, suppose that a company enjoys exceptional profitability, which results in a substantial increase in its

---
14 Note that internal equity and external equity are at opposite ends of the pecking order.

share price. Therefore, in market value terms, the company's debt–equity ratio will have decreased. According to the static trade-off theory, if a company's optimal capital structure has not changed, then the company's next capital raising should be debt, to move back towards the target debt–equity ratio. However, the pecking order theory suggests otherwise. Indeed, because of the company's exceptional profitability, it may not need to raise external funds at all. Therefore, profitable companies will tend to have low debt–equity ratios because of the availability of internal funds. Less profitable companies in the same industry will have higher debt–equity ratios because they generate fewer funds internally and because debt is first on the pecking order of external sources of funds.

Connect Plus features a case study illustrating topics covered in this chapter.
Ask your lecturer or tutor for your course's unique URL.

SUMMARY

→ Financial leverage increases the expected rate of return to shareholders, but also increases the risk of their returns. These effects are offsetting, and in a perfect capital market with no taxes, changing a company's capital structure does not change company value or shareholders' wealth. Under these conditions, capital structure is irrelevant because changing it simply changes the way in which the stream of net operating cash flows is divided between different classes of investors. In a perfect capital market, dividing this cash flow stream is costless and cannot change its total value.

→ When the perfect capital market assumptions are relaxed, several factors could make capital structure important. These factors include company income tax, personal income tax, the costs of financial distress, agency costs and information asymmetry.
  – When there are income taxes, debt finance can increase company value if the company tax saved by borrowing is greater than the extra personal tax paid. While this is possible for at least some companies under the classical tax system, the imputation tax system is designed to remove any tax advantages of debt.

→ Debt issued by companies is risky in that there is some probability of default, which can lead to receivership or liquidation. These outcomes involve direct bankruptcy costs, largely in the form of fees paid to insolvency specialists. Therefore, any company that borrows is giving outsiders a potential claim against its assets, which reduces the value of the company to investors. Direct bankruptcy costs appear to be small as a proportion of company value, but financial distress can also involve various indirect costs.

→ Agency costs may also influence capital structure decisions. These costs arise because there may be conflicts of interest between lenders and shareholders and because there may also be conflicts of interest between shareholders and company managers. The latter case may be particularly severe where a company has a large free cash flow. Jensen suggests that, in these cases, debt may be a useful way to control the behaviour of managers.
  – The static trade-off theory suggests that debt should be expanded until the point where the advantages of more debt just equal the disadvantages of more debt. This point is the optimal capital structure.
  – The pecking order theory proposes that, in raising finance, managers follow a 'pecking order' in which internal funds are preferred, followed by debt, hybrid securities and then, as a last resort, a new issue of ordinary shares. Information asymmetries between management and investors may help to explain the pecking order. According to the pecking order approach, a company's debt–equity ratio will vary over time, depending on its needs for external finance.

KEY TERMS

arbitrage 388	capital structure 379	free cash flow 406
bankruptcy costs 402	default risk 390	optimal capital structure 379
business risk 380	financial distress 402	pecking order theory 408
	financial leverage (or gearing) 380	perfect capital market 384
		static trade-off theory 407

SELF-TEST PROBLEMS

1. Barry Todd, an entrepreneur, is planning to establish an inland fish farm. The total cost of the necessary earth moving, construction of ponds and installation of pumps is estimated to be $1 million. Three possible financing plans are being considered. These are as follows:

   (a) equity of $1 million
   (b) equity of $750 000 and a bank loan of $250 000
   (c) equity of $250 000 and a bank loan of $750 000.

   The interest rate on the loans will be 10 per cent per annum. Barry is uncertain about the returns from fish farming and wishes to analyse the effects of the alternative financing plans on the rate of return on his investment.

   Prepare a table showing the rate of return on Barry's investment for each financing plan if the annual net operating cash flows generated by the fish farm are $0, $100 000 and $200 000. The effects of taxes may be ignored. Comment on the results.

2. Emu Farms Ltd has assets with a market value of $1.5 million. Its capital structure consists of equity, plus a loan of $500 000 at an interest rate of 8 per cent per annum. The company's cost of equity has been estimated at 21.5 per cent and its manager is considering a proposal to borrow a further $250 000, which would be used to buy back shares. The interest rate on the new loan is also 8 per cent per annum.

   (a) Use MM's Proposition 2 to calculate the effect of the increase in leverage on the cost of equity.
   (b) Calculate the company's weighted average cost of capital before and after the increase in leverage.

3. Cosmic Press Ltd is all-equity financed and is expected to generate net operating cash flows of $600 000 per annum. The company income tax rate is 30 per cent. Cosmic's shareholders expect a 15 per cent rate of return (after company tax).

   (a) What is Cosmic's value?
   (b) If the company borrows $1 million at an interest rate of 10 per cent:
      (i) what is Cosmic's after-tax operating cash flow?
      (ii) what is Cosmic's value according to MM's Proposition 1 (with company tax)?

Solutions to self-test problems are available in Appendix B, page 803.

REFERENCES

Andrade, G. & Kaplan, S., 'How costly is financial (not economic) distress? Evidence from highly leveraged transactions that became distressed', *Journal of Finance*, October 1998, pp. 1443–93.

De Angelo, H. & Masulis, R., 'Optimal capital structure under corporate and personal taxation', *Journal of Financial Economics*, March 1980, pp. 3–29.

Donaldson, G., *Corporate Debt Capacity*, Graduate School of Business Administration, Harvard University, Boston, 1961.

Graham, J., 'Debt and the marginal tax rate', *Journal of Financial Economics*, May 1996, pp. 41–73.

Jensen, M., 'Agency costs of free cash flow, corporate finance and takeovers', *American Economic Review*, May 1986, pp. 323–9.

Kraus, A. & Litzenberger, R., 'A state-preference model of optimal financial leverage', *Journal of Finance*, September 1973, pp. 911–22.

Miller, M., 'Debt and taxes', *Journal of Finance*, May 1977, pp. 261–75.

———, 'The Modigliani–Miller propositions after thirty years', *Journal of Economic Perspectives*, Fall 1988, pp. 99–120.

Modigliani, F. & Miller, M., 'The cost of capital, corporation finance and the theory of investment', *American Economic Review*, June 1958, pp. 261–97.

——, ——, 'Corporate income taxes and the cost of capital: a correction', *American Economic Review*, June 1963, pp. 433–43.

Myers, S., 'Determinants of corporate borrowing', *Journal of Financial Economics*, November 1977, pp. 147–75.

——, 'The capital structure puzzle', *Journal of Finance*, July 1984, pp. 575–92.

——, 'Financing of corporations', in G. Constantinides, M. Harris & R. Stulz (eds), *Handbook of the Economics of Finance*, Elsevier North Holland, Amsterdam, 2003.

Myers, S. & Majluf, N., 'Corporate financing and investment decisions when firms have information that investors do not have', *Journal of Financial Economics*, June 1984, pp. 187–221.

Pham, T. & Chow, D., 'Some estimates of direct and indirect bankruptcy costs in Australia: September 1978–May 1983', *Australian Journal of Management*, June 1987, pp. 75–95.

Scott, J., 'A theory of optimal capital structure', *Bell Journal of Economics*, Spring 1976, pp. 33–54.

Smith, C. & Warner, J., 'On financial contracting: an analysis of bond covenants', *Journal of Financial Economics*, June 1979, pp. 117–61.

Titman, S., 'The effect of capital structure on a firm's liquidation decision', *Journal of Financial Economics*, March 1984, pp. 137–51.

Warner, J., 'Bankruptcy costs: some evidence', *Journal of Finance*, May 1977, pp. 337–47.

Weiss, L., 'Bankruptcy resolution: direct costs and violation of priority of claims', *Journal of Financial Economics*, October 1990, pp. 285–314.

QUESTIONS

1. **[LO 1]** What are the potential advantages and disadvantages to a company's shareholders if the company increases the proportion of debt in its capital structure?
2. **[LO 1]** Distinguish between business risk, financial risk and default risk.
3. **[LO 2]**
   (a) Outline the Modigliani and Miller valuation propositions. Specify the assumptions on which their propositions are based.
   (b) *Modigliani and Miller's Propositions 1 and 2 are contradictory. Shareholders cannot be indifferent to the use of debt when it increases the expected rate of return on their investment.* Comment on this statement.
4. **[LO 2]** *Alternative proofs of the MM propositions show that it is not necessary to assume the operation of arbitrage involving personal borrowing for the propositions to hold.* Discuss this statement.
5. **[LO 3]** Outline Miller's argument that the tax advantages of debt are reduced or completely offset once personal taxes are included in the analysis. How appropriate is Miller's analysis, given the Australian tax system?
6. **[LO 3]** Miller's analysis assumes that a company can fully utilise the tax deductions generated by interest payments on debt. Is this assumption likely to be true for all companies? Give reasons.
7. **[LO 3]** *An investor will wish to invest in a company because of its capital structure.* Discuss this statement.
8. **[LO 4]** Outline the significance of bankruptcy costs in the capital structure debate.
9. **[LO 5]** *Management, when pursuing the objective of maximising the value of the company to its shareholders, may make decisions that are not in its lenders' best interest.* Explain why this statement may be true, and give examples of decisions that may lead to a transfer of wealth from lenders to shareholders.
10. **[LO 5]** What are agency costs? Of what significance are they in capital structure decisions?
11. **[LO 3, 4]** Comment on the following statements:
    (a) *The Australian imputation tax system is neutral in the sense that there is no bias towards the use of either debt or equity.*
    (b) *Costs of financial distress will be borne entirely by lenders.*
    (c) *Evidence such as that provided by Warner, Weiss, and Pham and Chow indicates that the costs of financial distress are too small to have any effect on capital structure decisions.*
12. **[LO 6]** Critically evaluate the following statements:

(a) *It is obvious that companies should use as much debt as possible. It is cheaper than equity and the interest is tax deductible as well.*

(b) *The probability of financial distress should be negligible for companies with a low proportion of debt. Therefore, a low proportion of debt should not have any noticeable effect on the cost of equity.*

PROBLEMS

1. **Effect of leverage [LO 1]**

   An entrepreneur is planning to establish a company with $50 million in assets and is investigating three possible capital structures for the company: (i) no debt; (ii) 20 per cent debt; and (iii) 50 per cent debt. The interest rate on the debt is 10 per cent per annum. The entrepreneur believes that the annual earnings before interest and tax will be $2.5 million in a poor year, $5 million in an average year and $10 million in a good year.

   (a) Complete the table below.
   (b) Plot the results for the three capital structures together on the one diagram, with return on assets (RoA) on the horizontal axis and return on equity (RoE) on the vertical axis. Comment.

2. **Debt–equity ratio and arbitrage [LO 3]**

   Lancelot Ltd and Universal Ltd operate under the conditions assumed by Modigliani and Miller in their analysis without tax. The two companies are identical except for their capital structures. Both companies have annual net operating cash flows of $500 000. The market value of Lancelot's debt is $2 million. The interest rate is 9 per cent per annum. Lancelot has 3.2 million shares on issue; their current market price is 59 cents per share. Universal has no debt. It has 1.5 million shares on issue; their current market price is $2.45 per share. Harold owns 200 000 shares in Lancelot.

   (a) What is the market value of Harold's investment? What is the current return on his investment? What is the risk of his investment, as measured by the debt–equity ratio?
   (b) Show Harold that each of the following three strategies is an arbitrage:
      (i) Sell the 200 000 shares in Lancelot. Borrow $125 000 and invest the whole proceeds in Universal shares.
      (ii) Sell the 200 000 shares in Lancelot. Borrow $85 672 and invest the whole proceeds in Universal shares.
      (iii) Sell the 200 000 shares in Lancelot. Spend $9798. Borrow $114 619, add this to the remaining cash, and invest the whole proceeds in Universal shares.

3. **Debt–equity ratio and arbitrage (harder) [LO 3]**

   Levity Ltd and Unicorn Ltd operate under the conditions assumed by Modigliani and Miller in their

	Capital structure (i)			Capital structure (ii)			Capital structure (iii)		
Assets									
Debt/Assets									
Debt ($)									
Equity ($)									
EBIT ($)	$2.5m	$5.0m	$10.0m	$2.5m	$5.0m	$10.0m	$2.5m	$5.0m	$10.0m
Interest ($)									
Net income ($)									
RoA (%)[a]									
RoE (%)[b]									

[a] RoA (Return on Assets) = EBIT/Assets (where EBIT means earnings before interest and tax).
[b] RoE (Return on Equity) = Net income/Equity.

analysis without tax. The two companies are identical except for their capital structures. Both companies have annual net operating cash flows of $10 million. The market value of Levity's debt is $30 million. The interest rate is 7.5 per cent per annum. Levity has 1.25 million shares on issue; their current market price is $20.48 per share. Unicorn has no debt. It has 40 million shares on issue; their current market price is $1.30 per share. Jessica owns 10 000 shares in Levity.

(a) What is the market value of Jessica's investment? What is the current return on her investment? What is the risk of her investment, as measured by the debt–equity ratio?

(b) Show Jessica that each of the following strategies is an arbitrage:
  (i) To achieve a higher return at the same risk, first sell the 10 000 shares in Levity, then borrow $240 000 and invest the whole proceeds in Unicorn shares.
  (ii) To achieve the same return at a lower risk, first sell the 10 000 shares in Levity, then borrow $192 787 and invest the whole proceeds in Unicorn shares.

(c) What would Jessica need to do to achieve an investment in Unicorn that has the same return and risk as her current investment but also leaves cash left over to spend?

4. **Increasing income by arbitrage [LO 3]**
Quarrion Books Ltd and Cockatiel Books Ltd are identical in every respect except that Quarrion has no debt while Cockatiel has a $2 million loan at an interest rate of 8 per cent. The valuation of the two companies is as follows:

	Item	Quarrion Books	Cockatiel Books
	Earnings before interest ($)	700 000	700 000
less	Interest on loan ($)	—	160 000
equals	Income available to ordinary shareholders ($)	700 000	540 000
divided by	Cost of equity (k_e)	0.14	0.16
equals	Market value of equity ($)	5 000 000	3 375 000
plus	Market value of debt ($)	—	2 000 000
equals	Total market value ($)	5 000 000	5 375 000

Jane owns $10 000 worth of Cockatiel shares. Show the process and the amount by which Jane could increase her income by the use of arbitrage.

5. **Increasing income without increasing risk [LO 3]**
The following information relates to two companies with the same business risk.

Item	Parramatta Pet Food	Penrith Pet Food
Earnings before interest ($)	10 000	10 000
Market value of debt ($)	50 000	—
k_d (%)	4	—
k_e (%)	12	10
Market value of equity ($)	66 666	100 000
Total market value ($)	116 666	100 000

According to Modigliani and Miller, the total market value of the two companies should be the same, irrespective of the methods used to finance their investments.

Suppose you hold 1 per cent of the shares in Parramatta Pet Food. Show the process and the amount by which you could increase your income without increasing your risk.

6. **Effect of company tax [LO 3]**
The following information relates to Ceel Ltd, assuming two different capital structures. The valuation in the table opposite assumes that there is no company tax and no personal tax.

	Item	Financed by	
		All equity	Equity and 10% loan
	Earnings before interest ($)	600 000	600 000
less	Interest on loan ($)	—	150 000
equals	Earnings available to ordinary shareholders ($)	600 000	450 000
divided by	Cost of equity (k_e)	0.15	0.18
equals	Market value of equity ($)	4 000 000	2 500 000
plus	Market value of loan ($)	—	1 500 000
equals	Total market value of company ($)	4 000 000	4 000 000

The government then introduces company tax at the rate of 30 cents in the dollar. Assuming that there are still no personal taxes, calculate the total market value of the company for both capital structures. Comment on your findings.

7. **Arbitrage leading to lower investment outlay [LO 2]**
Rockmelon Pty Ltd and Cantaloupe Pty Ltd are two identical companies with expected earnings before interest and taxes of $1.5 million per annum. The only difference between the two companies is that Rockmelon has issued debt securities to finance the identical activities that Cantaloupe has financed with equity securities alone. Details of the two companies are as follows:

Item	Rockmelon Pty Ltd	Cantaloupe Pty Ltd
Market value of equity ($)	6 000 000	8 000 000
Market value of debt ($)	4 000 000	—
Number of shares issued	6 000 000	5 000 000
Cost of debt (k_d)	0.08	—

Chee Weng owns 600 000 shares in Rockmelon Pty Ltd.

(a) What is the current market value of Chee Weng's shares, and what is his income from Rockmelon Pty Ltd?
(b) Show how Chee Weng can obtain an identical income with a lower net outlay.

8. **Effect of leverage [LO 1]**
   (a) Calculate the rate of return available to shareholders for a company financing $1 million of assets with the following three arrangements:
      (i) all equity
      (ii) 50 per cent equity, and 50 per cent debt at an interest rate of 12 per cent per annum
      (iii) 25 per cent equity, and 75 per cent debt at an interest rate of 12 per cent per annum.

   The assets are expected to generate earnings before interest of $150 000 per annum in perpetuity.
   (b) Interpret your answer, and explain what effect a change in the perpetual earnings stream might have on the rate of return available to shareholders.

9. **Information asymmetry and capital structure [LO 7]**
Sophie Pharmaceuticals Ltd has 9.6 million ordinary shares on issue. The current market price is $12.50 per share. However, the company manager knows that the results of some recent drug tests have been remarkably encouraging, so that the 'true' value of the shares is $13. Unfortunately, because of confidential patent issues, Sophie Pharmaceuticals cannot yet announce these test results. In addition, Sophie Pharmaceuticals has a property investment opportunity that requires an outlay of $15 million and has a net present value of $2.5 million. At present, Sophie Pharmaceuticals has little spare cash or marketable assets, so if this investment is to be made it will need to be financed from external sources. The existence of this opportunity is not known to outsiders and is not reflected in the current share price. Should Sophie Pharmaceuticals make the new investment? If so, should the investment be made before or after the share market learns the true value of the company's existing assets? Should the investment be financed by issuing new shares or by issuing new debt?

Test yourself further with Connect Plus online! Ask your lecturer or tutor for your course's unique URL.

CAPITAL STRUCTURE DECISIONS

LEARNING OBJECTIVES

After studying this chapter you should be able to:

1. outline empirical evidence from recent studies of capital structure
2. assess the implications of the evidence for the static trade-off and pecking order theories
3. explain how financing can be viewed as a marketing problem
4. outline the main factors that financial managers should consider when determining a company's financing strategy.

CHAPTER CONTENTS

- **13.1** Introduction
- **13.2** Evidence on capital structure
- **13.3** Assessing the theories of capital structure
- **13.4** Financing as a marketing problem
- **13.5** Determining a financing strategy

13.1 INTRODUCTION

In Chapter 12 we outlined theories of capital structure, beginning with the Modigliani and Miller (MM) analysis in the absence of taxes. This analysis implies that in a perfect capital market, *all* capital structure decisions are unimportant. While that conclusion is valid under their assumptions, one positive message from the MM analysis is that if capital structure is in fact important, then the reasons for its importance must relate to factors that MM excluded by their assumptions. These factors include taxes, the costs of financial distress, agency costs and differences in the information available to managers and investors.

These other factors have provided the foundation for alternative theories of capital structure. The *static trade-off theory*, outlined in Section 12.8, proposes that there is an optimal capital structure that maximises the value of a company. Companies will borrow until the advantages of additional debt are exactly equal to the disadvantages of additional debt. The advantages of additional debt include the tax savings that may be made because interest paid is tax deductible. The disadvantages of additional debt include the expected costs of financial distress that will arise if the company is unable to pay the interest that it owes. In Section 12.7.2 we outlined Jensen's analysis of the agency costs of free cash flows. We noted that profitable companies in mature industries are likely to generate large free cash flows and managers may invest these cash flows in ways that benefit them rather than the shareholders. Jensen pointed out that debt can provide a solution to this overinvestment problem because it forces managers to pay out cash. In Section 12.9, we outlined the *pecking order theory*, which is based on the effects of financing decisions under information asymmetry. It suggests that capital structures are determined largely by companies' past needs for external finance. In contrast to the static trade-off theory, the pecking order theory is dynamic in that it attempts to explain financing decisions over time.

In this chapter we review empirical evidence on capital structure and we develop recommendations for financial managers. The reader who examines the available evidence in search of support for 'the one correct' theory of capital structure will inevitably be disappointed. There is no universal theory of capital structure. Rather, each of the theories highlights different aspects of the choice between debt and equity. The static trade-off theory emphasises taxes and financial distress; the pecking order theory emphasises differences in information. It is also important to realise that, while capital structure theories usually focus on the relatively simple generic issue of debt-versus-equity, in practice, capital structure decisions may involve many different types of debt, including long-term debt, short-term debt, fixed-rate debt, floating-rate debt, bank debt and marketable debt. In addition, financial managers may also need to consider hybrid securities such as the various forms of preference shares.

13.1.1 COMPANY FINANCING: SOME INITIAL FACTS

US evidence provided by Wright (2004) suggests that, for the non-financial corporate sector as a whole, the ratio of debt to equity stayed within a narrow range during the twentieth century. Wright reports that the ratio of total liabilities to total market value typically fell within the range 50% ± 10%. This is a remarkable finding given that the twentieth century saw huge changes in the size, structure and activities of the corporate sector. Evidence compiled by Frank and Goyal (2008) indicates that, across the non-financial corporate sector as a whole, capital expenditure is approximately equal to the volume of internal funds generated—that is, the evidence suggests that most of the investment by non-financial companies is generally financed from internal cash flows. However, there is wide variation between companies. Debt is used more heavily at both ends of the size spectrum, with large listed companies and private firms showing a bias towards debt. But for small listed companies debt issues are fairly minor and equity is the favoured method. As Frank and Goyal note, it is worth remembering that much of the research published on capital structure is limited to listed companies.

Another pervasive finding is that financial leverage differs across industries. For example, in the US, industries with consistently high leverage include paper, steel and airlines, while those with low leverage include pharmaceuticals and electronics (Harris & Raviv 1991). In fact, some companies effectively have *negative* debt–equity ratios because their holdings of cash and marketable securities are greater than their debt so they are net lenders. Myers (2001, pp. 82–3) notes that large net lenders in the US at that time included the major pharmaceutical companies, Ford Motor Company and Microsoft. In Australia, pharmaceutical and biotechnology company CSL is a net lender: at the end of the 2008–09 financial year it held $2528 million in cash and cash equivalents and had only $718 million in interest-bearing debt. At the same date, the online travel service company Wotif.com Holdings held $102 million in cash and cash equivalents and had only $251 000 in interest-bearing debt. Similarly, the budget department store Harris Scarfe pursues a no-debt policy (see Finance in Action).

FINANCE IN ACTION

PURSUING A NO-DEBT POLICY

Some companies choose to keep debt at extremely low levels. One reason that some companies choose this policy is to signal to other parties—such as its suppliers—that the company is financially sound and hence is safe to do business with. The department store Harris Scarfe is a case in point, as a story in the *Australian Financial Review* **explains.**

The private equity owners of budget department store chain Harris Scarfe said a decision to run the company without any debt had been a godsend as the global credit crunch spilt over into worsening economic conditions. Momentum Private Equity bought Harris Scarfe in April last year, with department store operator Myer taking a 20 per cent stake as part of the $80 million deal. Like other retailers, Harris Scarfe is now facing tougher conditions as the broader retail sector slows down under the weight of rising interest rates and high petrol prices. The managing director of Momentum's corporate division, Kevin Jacobson, said Harris Scarfe was deliberately structured to be ungeared, which had turned out to be fortuitous as the world battled the credit crunch …

Momentum was taking a 'build and hold' strategy with Harris Scarfe, and the decision to have the business ungeared initially had been a big plus in its relationships with suppliers to the retailer. The retailer has now been trading successfully for almost seven years after a financial collapse in early 2001.

Source: 'Harris Scarfe counts blessings of no-debt policy', Simon Evans, *Australian Financial Review*, 11 March 2008.

Leverage is generally low for 'growth' companies and for companies with significant intangible assets. In addition, high business risk tends to be associated with low financial leverage. International studies by Rajan and Zingales (1995) and Wald (1999) find that differences in leverage between major industrial countries are moderate. They also find that the correlations between debt–asset ratios and factors such as the tangibility of assets and profitability are similar across countries. Financial leverage is also associated with the intensity of competition in an industry. In a study of US manufacturing companies, MacKay and Phillips (2005) report that financial leverage is higher in industries where a few large companies dominate than in more competitive industries.

If, as MM's Proposition 1 suggests, capital structure is irrelevant, we would not expect to see any empirical patterns in capital structure. Hence, these empirical observations suggest that capital structure decisions are regarded as important. The next section outlines the results of empirical research on factors that may influence capital structure decisions.

13.2 EVIDENCE ON CAPITAL STRUCTURE

As noted earlier, the main theories of capital structure attempt to explain different aspects of the choice between debt and equity, and each theory emphasises different factors. Accordingly, our discussion of the evidence is divided into subsections that outline evidence on taxes, costs of financial distress, agency costs and information costs.

LEARNING OBJECTIVE 1
Outline empirical evidence from recent studies of capital structure

13.2.1 EVIDENCE ON TAXES

As discussed in Chapter 12, the effects of taxes on capital structure decisions involve personal tax as well as company tax, and the effects of these tend to be offsetting—that is, while the tax deductibility of interest on debt reduces company tax, interest income is taxed more heavily than dividends and capital gains. As discussed in Section 12.4.3, lenders will effectively require companies that borrow to pay the extra tax for them by paying a higher interest rate on debt relative to the returns to shareholders. In other words, the argument is that companies will bear the full effects of the taxes generated by their operations, regardless of whether the tax is paid directly by the company or indirectly through higher interest rates required by lenders.

While the effects of company tax and personal tax tend to be offsetting, a company's tax position can still have important effects. For example, suppose that a company is profitable but its taxable income is negative, either because it has large tax deductions for depreciation on assets that were purchased recently or because it has tax losses carried forward from previous years. For this company, borrowing is likely to have a tax disadvantage because lenders will have to pay personal tax on the interest, but there will be no immediate reduction in company tax—the interest deductions will add to the tax losses being carried forward. Therefore, in making financing decisions, managers can be expected to view **non-debt tax shields (NDTS)**, such as depreciation deductions or tax losses carried forward, as substitutes for interest deductions. To reflect tax effects, many studies of capital structure include measures of NDTS as an explanatory variable with the expectation that NDTS will be negatively related to leverage.

non-debt tax shields (NDTS)
tax deductions for items such as depreciation on assets and tax losses carried forward

The evidence on this issue is mixed. Studies that test for a relationship between leverage and NDTS typically find that the effect is insignificant or that the NDTS variable has a positive coefficient—the opposite of the theoretical prediction. The findings of these studies are difficult to interpret because a company with large depreciation deductions is likely to have mainly tangible assets. Companies with mainly tangible assets will find it less costly to borrow because tangible assets can be pledged as security for debt. Similarly, a company that has tax losses being carried forward may be in financial distress. For a company in distress, the market value of equity will usually fall, causing leverage to increase. In summary, NDTS may not be an adequate proxy for a company's tax position. Rather than indicating that the tax benefits of debt are low, high NDTS may indicate high tangible assets or financial distress.

In the pre-1990 literature, evidence of any significant relationship between leverage and taxes is sparse. As MacKie-Mason (1990) notes, this is somewhat surprising because 'nearly everyone believes' that taxes must be important in financing decisions. He suggests that taxes are important, but had failed to show up in most previous studies because they were designed to test for average rather than marginal effects. To see this point, consider the argument that the incentive to save tax by borrowing is less when a company has non-debt tax shields. The underlying logic is that higher non-debt tax shields will lower a company's *expected* marginal tax rate, thus reducing the expected tax savings on additional debt. While this logic is sound, non-debt tax shields will lower a company's *actual* marginal tax rate only if they are large enough to reduce its taxable income to zero—a condition known as 'tax exhaustion'.

MacKie-Mason argues that in most cases, non-debt tax shields will cause only a small change in the probability of tax exhaustion and a similarly small change in a company's expected marginal tax rate. Therefore, differences in expected marginal tax rates among companies will be small and difficult to measure. Another problem is that previous studies have typically measured the leverage of companies using accounting ratios, which reflect the cumulative results of many separate financing decisions made over several years. To overcome these problems it is necessary to examine individual financing decisions on a marginal basis for companies that are at, or near, the point of tax exhaustion. Using this approach, MacKie-Mason finds strong evidence that taxes do influence financing decisions.

The results of MacKie-Mason are supported by those of Graham (1996), who examined the incremental use of debt by more than 10 000 US companies for the years 1980 to 1992. When allowance is made for the effects of operating losses and investment tax credits, he finds that the marginal tax rate varies considerably across companies and that high tax-rate companies borrow more heavily than those with low tax rates.

In a later study, Graham (2000) makes a detailed estimate of the effects of taxes on company value. By examining the interest rate spread between taxable corporate bonds and tax-free municipal bonds he estimates the personal tax rate of marginal investors in corporate debt. The estimated rate varies with changes in statutory tax rates and is approximately 30 per cent from 1993 to 1994, the last year covered by the study. Graham also estimates that the average tax rate on equity income is about 12 per cent. This effective rate is much lower than the marginal income tax rate of 30 per cent because of the benefits associated with deferring the realisation of capital gains. What do these tax rates imply in terms of the net tax effects of borrowing under the US classical tax system with a company tax rate of 35 per cent?

Assume that Company X borrows $1 million at an interest rate of 10 per cent and uses the funds to repurchase shares worth $1 million. Company X will pay an extra $100 000 in interest each year and reduce its company tax bill by $35 000 per year. The marginal lender will pay an extra $30 000 per year income tax. Equity income will fall by $65 000 per year—equal to the extra interest of $100 000 less the company tax saving of $35 000. Therefore, taxes paid by investors on equity income will fall by $65 000 × 0.12 = $7800 per year. The net tax saving is $35 000 − ($30 000 − $7800) = $12 800 per year. In this case the extra tax paid by investors reduces the net tax saving to less than 40 per cent of the company interest tax saving. Despite this large reduction, the net tax saving is still significant and should be very valuable. Graham estimated that in 1994, the net tax benefits of debt added 3.5 per cent to the value of a typical US company. Over the whole of the 1980 to 1994 period covered by his study, Graham estimated that on average the tax benefit of debt added 9.7 per cent to company value (or 4.3 per cent, net of personal taxes).

The studies referred to above were all based on companies subject to the classical tax system. Many countries, including Australia, Canada and New Zealand, have switched to the imputation tax system. As discussed in Section 12.5.2, the imputation tax system is designed to remove any tax-related bias towards the use of debt finance by companies. At least three studies provide evidence that supports this expectation. Schulman et al. (1996) examine the effects of imputation on corporate leverage in New Zealand and Canada. New Zealand introduced a full imputation tax system in 1988. Canada introduced partial imputation in 1972 and simultaneously introduced a capital gains tax on the sale of shares. These two changes have opposing effects: the introduction of imputation should reduce leverage while a capital gains tax increases taxes on equity and favours the use of debt finance. Accordingly, the sample of Canadian companies was divided into four portfolios:

(a) companies that experienced a net operating loss during the study period (NOL sample)
(b) a high-dividend low-growth sample
(c) a low-dividend high-growth sample
(d) a fourth portfolio that contained all other companies.

The authors expected that the introduction of imputation would have little effect on the leverage of companies in the NOL sample because those companies have a low marginal tax rate. Similarly, the tax changes should provide little benefit for low-dividend companies that deliver returns to investors mainly as capital gains. Conversely, companies in the 'high-dividend' sample should experience a significant reduction in leverage. The results for Canadian companies were consistent with these expectations. After the tax changes, the average debt–equity ratio fell significantly for companies in the 'high-dividend' and 'all others' portfolios but did not change significantly for the 'NOL' and 'high-growth' portfolios. In the case of New Zealand, there was a highly significant reduction in the average debt–equity ratio of sample companies.

Richardson and Lanis (2001) examined the influence of income taxes on the use of debt by Australian companies under the imputation system. They used data for 1997 to study a sample of 269 large, listed, non-financial companies. Their main finding was that, under imputation, the tax advantage of debt is neutralised. In addition, they found that companies that do not pay dividends prefer internal equity to debt. Richardson and Lanis also found a significant tax substitution effect—other things being equal, companies that have high non-debt tax shields use less debt.

Pattenden (2006) studied 67 Australian companies that were listed on the Australian Securities Exchange continuously from 1982 to 1993. Thus, every company existed both before and after the introduction of the imputation system in 1987. Pattenden tested the apparent effect of the marginal tax rate on capital structure under the classical system (1982 to 1986) and under the imputation system (1989 to 1993). The result was very clear: taxes were very important under the classical system but were of considerably less importance under the imputation system. An extension of the post-imputation time period to 1998 saw the importance of the tax rate decline even further.

In summary, the evidence from these studies supports theoretical arguments that the imputation system removes the tax advantage of debt and results in lower corporate financial leverage than is typical under the classical system.

13.2.2 EVIDENCE ON THE COSTS OF FINANCIAL DISTRESS

The trade-off theory proposes that each company has an optimal capital structure based on a trade-off between the benefits of debt on the one hand and the adverse effects of financial distress costs on the other. Costs of financial distress refer to the costs of liquidating or restructuring a company that has failed, and also to the agency costs that can arise when there is doubt about a company's ability to meet its obligations to lenders. The discussion in this section is confined to evidence on costs directly associated with financial distress. The agency costs associated with high levels of debt together with other agency costs of debt are discussed in the next section.

While few would dispute the argument that the costs associated with financial distress can reduce company value, there is some dispute about whether these costs are large enough to have an economically significant effect. First, there is evidence that suggests that the direct costs are too small to have a significant effect on company value. For example, Warner (1977) estimated that the direct ('out-of-pocket') expenses incurred in the administration of the bankruptcy process for 'failed' US railroad companies averaged only 5.3 per cent of the market value of their assets at the date of bankruptcy. This figure falls to 1 per cent if company value is measured 7 years before bankruptcy. Weiss (1990) investigated a sample of bankrupt listed US companies and found that the direct costs of bankruptcy averaged 3.1 per cent of the sum of the book value of debt and the market value of equity measured at the end of the fiscal year prior to filing for bankruptcy. This percentage falls to 2.8 per cent if direct costs are measured as a proportion of the book value of total assets. Similarly, Pham and Chow (1987) reported direct costs averaging 3.6 per cent of company value at the date of failure for a sample of Australian companies. The figures quoted in this paragraph refer to the *actual* costs incurred by failed companies. For a company that is not in financial distress, the *expected* costs would be far smaller because the actual costs have to be multiplied by the probability of failure. For most companies, it seems that expected direct costs of financial distress would be minuscule.

While expected direct costs of financial distress appear to be very small, companies considered likely to fail may incur significant indirect costs. For example, sales may be lost because customers change to more reliable suppliers, and efficiency is likely to suffer because management's efforts are directed towards attempts to avert failure. There is empirical evidence indicating that the indirect costs can be a significant proportion of a company's value. Altman (1984) has estimated *both* direct and indirect costs of financial distress for a sample of 26 bankrupt US companies. He found that in many cases the aggregate costs exceeded 20 per cent of the value of the company just before bankruptcy. Using a revised version of Altman's methodology, Pham and Chow (1987) found that, for a sample of 14 failed Australian companies, aggregate costs of financial distress averaged 22.4 per cent of company value just before failure. These estimates are much greater than the reported levels of direct costs.

Further support for the significance of the indirect costs of financial distress was provided by Opler and Titman (1994), who examined the performance of companies during industry downturns. They found that highly levered companies lost substantial market share to their more conservatively financed competitors during these periods of economic distress. Opler and Titman also found that the companies that suffered the most were highly levered companies that engaged in research and development. This finding is consistent with Titman's theory that companies with specialised or unique products are particularly vulnerable to financial distress. Evidence consistent with Titman's theory that low levels of corporate debt will be preferred in cases where liquidation would impose high costs on customers and other stakeholders was also provided by Titman and Wessels (1988).

More recent evidence on the costs of financial distress is provided by Andrade and Kaplan (1998), who studied highly levered companies that encountered financial distress. They point out that it is difficult to measure the costs of financial distress. The source of this difficulty is 'an inability to distinguish whether poor performance by a company in financial distress is caused by the financial distress itself or is caused by the same factors that pushed the company into financial distress in the first place' (Andrade & Kaplan 1998, p. 1444). Suppose that a particular industry suffers a significant unexpected fall in sales. All companies in the industry will experience lower profits (economic distress), but those that are highly levered will be most likely to also experience difficulty in meeting repayments to lenders (financial distress). Therefore, the large indirect costs of financial distress found by authors such as Altman are likely to reflect the effects of economic distress as well as those of financial distress.

All the companies studied by Andrade and Kaplan have operating margins that are positive, and typically exceed the industry median, in the years they are distressed. Therefore, the sample companies appear to be largely financially distressed, not economically distressed. For the whole sample they estimate that the net costs of financial distress are between 10 and 20 per cent of company value. As they are unable to completely eliminate economic distress or the effects of economic shocks, Andrade and Kaplan regard their estimates as upper bounds on the costs of financial distress for the sample companies. They also divide their sample into two subsamples based on whether companies suffered an adverse economic shock, such as a severe downturn in industry sales. The costs of financial distress are found to be negligible for the subsample that did not experience an economic shock. It is possible that the results obtained by Andrade and Kaplan are influenced by a selection bias—it may be that companies with low costs of financial distress are more likely to become highly leveraged. If that is the case, their estimates may understate the costs of financial distress for a typical company. On the other hand, the probability of financial distress is very small for most public companies. Therefore, even if the actual costs of financial distress are as high as 20 per cent of company value, the expected costs of financial distress should be modest for most public companies.

In summary, the direct costs of financial distress are small relative to company value. The indirect costs appear to be considerably larger than the direct costs but are very difficult to distinguish from the costs of economic distress. Unless the probability of financial distress is high, the expected costs of financial distress appear to be modest.

13.2.3 EVIDENCE ON AGENCY COSTS

As we explained in Section 12.7.1, there may be conflicts of interest between shareholders and lenders, which can lead to several problems, including the problem that the company may *underinvest*. If a company's value consists largely of investment opportunities and the company is highly levered (and hence at greater risk of experiencing financial distress), the underinvestment problem is likely to be severe. We also explained in Section 12.7.2 that because managers' interests may diverge from shareholders' interests, managers may *overinvest* on the company's behalf; the primary motive for making such investments is to benefit the managers rather than the shareholders. In this section we consider empirical evidence relevant to underinvestment and overinvestment.

Debt and underinvestment

To illustrate the underinvestment problem, suppose that Zenacom Pty Ltd, a high-growth technology company with a new product ready to manufacture, persuades its bank to finance the necessary plant and equipment with a high percentage of debt.[1] Also suppose that sales of the product grow more slowly than anticipated and management now faces a choice between two unattractive alternatives. If it is to keep up the loan repayments it will have to cut the research and development (R&D) budget, but its R&D activities are expected to generate much of the company's growth. If it maintains the R&D budget, there is a high probability of defaulting on the bank loan.

What Zenacom really needs in this case is an injection of new equity. However, attracting new shareholders is likely to be difficult. Because of Zenacom's financial situation, much of the value created (or preserved) by injecting additional equity will serve largely to support the lender's position. To induce new shareholders to invest, either the bank will have to write down its loan substantially—which it would be reluctant to do—or the new equity will come at a very high price, in the form of excessive dilution of ownership. Management will probably decide that the best alternative is to cut the R&D budget—in which case its financing decision has caused Zenacom to pass up valuable investment opportunities.

As the Zenacom example illustrates, a company whose value consists mostly of intangible investment opportunities is likely to find that debt is very costly for two reasons. First, the lack of tangible assets to serve as security will mean that debt is both expensive and difficult to obtain. Second, if such a company does borrow, there are likely to be further costs in the form of investments forgone if it gets into financial difficulty. The clear implication is that 'growth' companies should restrict their financial leverage.

While the underinvestment problem can be severe for growth companies, it should not be significant for mature companies with few profitable investment opportunities. The value of such companies comes mostly from assets in place that can be used as security for debt. In summary, mature companies with a high proportion of assets in place are expected to have higher leverage than growth companies. This difference should be reflected in a negative relationship between leverage and investment opportunities.

Debt and overinvestment

In some cases, the use of high leverage can add value because of the beneficial effects of debt in controlling the inclination of managers to overinvest. Suppose that Mammoth Ltd generates large, stable cash flows

---

1 For a more detailed discussion of this example and topic, see Barclay, Smith and Watts (1995, pp. 8–9).

from its operations in a mature industry where there are few profitable new investments. Nevertheless, its managers may continue to invest in the same industry, making expensive attempts to gain market share, or they may attempt to achieve growth by acquiring companies in other industries. These diversifying acquisitions are likely to destroy value for Mammoth's shareholders, who can diversify their own portfolios by purchasing the shares of companies in other industries without paying any premium for control. As noted earlier, Jensen's (1986) free cash flow theory is applicable to companies like Mammoth and it suggests that for such companies a high proportion of debt may be beneficial. Increasing leverage is an effective way of forcing managers to pay out cash because of the contractual obligations to make payments to lenders.

In summary, debt finance can be beneficial for mature companies with few investment opportunities by curbing managers' inclination to overinvest. The necessity of servicing debt should mean that managers will be more critical in evaluating capital expenditure proposals. The role of debt in reducing overinvestment is an additional factor that suggests that leverage will be negatively related to the extent of a company's investment opportunities.

In empirical studies the extent of a company's investment opportunities is typically measured using the ratio of the market value of assets to the book value of assets, which is usually referred to as the market-to-book ratio. By definition, a 'growth' company is expected to have extensive investment opportunities in the future. The value of these opportunities should be reflected in its share price, but not in its statement of financial position (or 'balance sheet'). Assets appearing on a balance sheet are 'assets in place', not dreams of the future. Therefore, the larger are a company's investment opportunities relative to its assets in place, the higher its market-to-book ratio is expected to be. In contrast, mature companies with few investment opportunities and a relatively high value of assets in place are predicted to have low market-to-book ratios.

Barclay, Smith and Watts (BSW) (1995, pp. 4–19) assessed the importance of investment opportunities when they studied a sample of more than 6700 US industrial companies over the period 1963 to 1993. Leverage was calculated as the ratio of the book value of debt to the market value of the company (debt plus equity). The authors expected leverage to be determined largely by the extent of a company's investment opportunities, which was measured using the ratio of market value to book value. The results provided strong support for the importance of investment opportunities as a determinant of leverage. As expected, companies with high market-to-book ratios had significantly lower leverage than those with low market-to-book ratios. The relationship between leverage and the market-to-book ratio was highly significant in a statistical sense and was also 'economically' significant. Economic significance refers to the size of the change in leverage ratio associated with changes in market-to-book ratios. BSW found that moving from the bottom tenth percentile of corporate market-to-book ratios to the ninetieth percentile corresponded to a fall in the predicted leverage ratio of 14.3 percentage points—a large fraction of the average ratio of 25 per cent.

BSW interpreted their results as showing that the extent of a company's investment opportunities appears to be the most important systematic determinant of its leverage ratio. Their explanation for this finding is that for companies whose value consists largely of intangible investment opportunities, the underinvestment problem associated with a high proportion of debt finance makes high leverage potentially very costly. On the other hand, for mature companies with limited investment opportunities, high leverage has benefits in controlling the problem associated with free cash flow. As discussed above, free cash flow tempts managers to overinvest in mature businesses or make diversifying acquisitions that may not be in the interests of shareholders.

BSW acknowledged that their results are also consistent with an explanation that includes taxes. Low-growth companies, with low costs of financial distress and potentially large benefits from using debt because of its role in controlling overinvestment, are also likely to have greater use for interest-tax deductions than high-growth companies. However, the results of their tests do not support the argument that taxes have an important effect on corporate leverage decisions. Consequently, BSW's preferred explanation for their results does not include the effect of taxes.

BSW also pointed out that their main findings are fundamentally inconsistent with the predictions made by the pecking order theory. It would 'suggest that companies with few investment opportunities and substantial free cash flow will have low debt ratios—and that high-growth firms with lower operating cash flows will have high debt ratios'. BSW (1995, p. 12) predicted, and found, results that are the exact opposite of those suggested by the pecking order theory. On the other hand, there is evidence from other studies that provides support for the pecking order theory. In particular, one finding to emerge clearly from all relevant studies is that leverage is negatively related to profitability. As noted earlier, this finding is the opposite of the static trade-off theory's prediction, and instead supports the pecking order theory—that is, companies with high profitability may use less debt than other companies, simply because they have less need to raise funds externally and because debt is first on the pecking order of external fund sources.

Evidence of a relationship between leverage and investment opportunities has been found in several countries. Rajan and Zingales (1995) used 1987 to 1991 data to examine the capital structures of public companies in seven countries: the US, Japan, Germany, France, Italy, the UK and Canada. For each country, they found that leverage was positively related to the tangibility of assets (measured by the ratio of fixed assets to total assets) and negatively related to the market-to-book ratio.

As we discussed in Section 12.7.2, Jensen (1986) pointed out that a high level of debt forces companies to pay interest, and hence prevents managers from wasting free cash flow on poor investments or organisational inefficiencies. The most prominent example of this role of debt can be found in leveraged buyouts. Indeed, as we discuss in Chapter 19, their primary role is to provide a solution to the free cash flow problem. While the role of debt in restricting the use of free cash flow may be very important for large 'cash cow' companies, it is probably of limited relevance in most other circumstances. It appears that listed companies do not generally overinvest because announcements of capital investments are associated with small but significant share price increases. Further, if increased leverage generally adds value by disciplining managers, then debt issues should be associated with share price increases. However, there is no evidence of such price increases, even for issues of high-risk debt, where the pressure on managers to pay out cash is high (Shyam-Sunder 1991).

13.2.4 EVIDENCE ON INFORMATION COSTS AND THE PECKING ORDER THEORY

The pecking order theory outlined in Section 12.9 is based on information asymmetry, which occurs when managers know more than outside investors about the value of their company. When there are such information differences—which in practice is often the case—the company may incur large 'information costs' if it issues (that is, sells) new shares to outside investors. Potential buyers of new shares will be aware that they are at an information disadvantage compared with the company's managers. They are therefore likely to take the sensible precaution of assuming that the managers must have some information that leads them to believe that the shares are overvalued: why else would they be willing to sell new shares to outsiders? Therefore, potential investors will demand a price discount on the shares they are offered. Of course, the managers are also aware that this will occur—even if in fact they don't believe that the shares are overvalued. Therefore, managers will generally sell new shares to outside investors only as a last resort. Myers (1984) suggests that, intuitively, issuing risky debt would rank between using internally generated funds and issuing new shares. This conclusion is the cornerstone of the pecking order theory: managers' first choice is to use internal funds, followed by borrowing and lastly by issuing new shares. The pecking order theory is consistent with the observation that internally generated cash is the largest single source of finance for companies and debt is the larger of the external sources. Of course, the fact that these observations are consistent with the pecking order theory does not prove that the theory is correct—there may be other explanations for the data. The evidence we discuss concerns share price responses to announcements of security issues and the relationship between profitability and leverage.

Share price response to new financing

An important prediction of the pecking order theory is that the announcement of a new share issue will cause the company's share price to fall. When debt or hybrid security issues are announced, the fall in share price should be smaller. The empirical studies reviewed by Smith (1986) report findings that are consistent with these predictions. Various proposed explanations were investigated, but the only consistent result was that the price response was related to the type of security issued. However, it seems likely that the market response should also depend on the company's growth prospects. For example, Jensen (1986) argued that free cash flow is likely to be invested unprofitably, or wasted by allowing inefficiencies to develop. When a company announces that it intends to raise new funds, the market will assess the company's ability to invest the funds profitably. If the company is mature, with few investment opportunities, the market is likely to perceive that the new funds will create excess cash, so the company's share price will fall. On the other hand, if the company is growing rapidly, it is more likely that the new funds will be invested in positive net present value (NPV) projects, so its share price is likely to rise.

The effect of investment opportunities on the share price response to new security issues was studied by Pilotte (1992). He found that for share issues, the average share price response was negative, but the average price fall was much larger for mature companies than for growth companies. For issues of debt, the share prices of mature companies fell significantly, but for growth companies, there was no significant price change. Therefore, Pilotte's results show that the share price response to new financing depends on the company's investment opportunities and is not related only to the type of security being issued.

Leverage and the pecking order theory

The pecking order theory does not have any role for an optimal capital structure or a target debt–equity ratio. According to the theory there are two forms of equity—internal equity and external equity—and they are at opposite ends of the pecking order. The theory implies that a company's leverage will depend on the difference between its operating cash flow and its investment needs over time. Therefore, the pecking order theory predicts that, other things being equal, a company's leverage will be negatively related to its profitability. Consider two companies that operate in the same industry and are similar except for their efficiency and, hence, their profitability. Suppose that the two companies invest at similar rates to keep up with the average growth of the industry. The less profitable company will have larger needs for external finance and will end up with higher leverage because debt is first on the pecking order of external sources of finance.

Consistent with the pecking order theory, several studies of capital structure find that leverage is negatively related to profitability. For example, studies by Bradley, Jarrell and Kim (1984), Titman and Wessels (1988), Rajan and Zingales (1995), Wald (1999), Graham (2000) and Graham and Harvey (2001) all report this finding, which holds over different time periods and in different countries.

Testing the pecking order and the static trade-off theories

Suppose that each company has a target debt ratio as proposed by the static trade-off theory. In practice, of course, a company's actual debt ratio will vary over time due to factors such as unexpected changes in operating cash flows and changes in the market value of its shares. To test the static trade-off theory empirically, it is often assumed that actual debt ratios will be described by a 'target-adjustment' model where companies have a leverage target and make gradual adjustments towards it. In contrast, the pecking order theory assumes that there is no target debt ratio and states that a company's debt ratio will vary over time depending on the company's cumulative needs for external finance.

Shyam-Sunder and Myers (1999) examined a panel of 157 companies from 1971 to 1989 and tested the time-series predictions of both models. They found that it is difficult to distinguish between the models. For example, in one test they assumed that each company followed the pecking order exactly. The researchers then calculated the corresponding annual debt ratios. They found that a target-adjustment model fitted this simulated data just as well as it fitted the actual data. In other words, the statistical tests indicated that the static trade-off theory was consistent with debt ratios generated by the pecking order theory. This finding suggests that tests of the static trade-off theory have low statistical power. Shyam-Sunder and Myers concluded that the pecking order theory provided the best explanation of the financing behaviour of the companies in their sample.

Fama and French (2002) examined both the pecking order and the static trade-off theories by testing whether the predictions of these two models were consistent with the dividend and financing behaviour of a large sample of US companies from 1965 to 1999. In their tests, both models had considerable success but also recorded some notable failures. Specifically, as in previous studies, the static trade-off theory is unable to explain the strong negative relationship between profitability and leverage. On the other hand, in the case of small growth companies, those with the lowest leverage rely most heavily on equity issues. Since these low-leverage companies appear to have the capacity to issue low-risk debt, this finding is not consistent with the pecking order theory. Frank and Goyal (2003) also found weaknesses in the pecking order theory when they tested it on a large sample of publicly traded US companies from 1971 to 1998. Small companies do not follow the pecking order, which works best for large companies in the earlier years. However, even for larger companies, support for the pecking order theory declines over time.

In summary, support for the pecking order theory is mixed and the strongest evidence in its favour is probably the negative relationship between leverage and profitability that consistently emerges from studies on broad samples of companies. However, several authors have noted that this relationship could also arise in other ways. Suppose that companies have target leverage ratios. When a company earns profits, debt is often repaid so leverage can fall automatically. There may be an incentive to borrow more in order to capture the tax benefits of leverage. However, if companies face fixed costs in raising debt finance and buying back shares, adjustments towards the leverage target may take place only periodically rather than frequently. More generally, suppose that every company has a target debt–equity ratio. Between 'refinancing points', such as when new securities are issued, many companies will not have achieved their target. How can a researcher decide when a company is off-target because it has no target and when a company has a target but has not been able to achieve it?[2]

To overcome this problem some recent studies have used narrow samples of companies selected so that time series effects such as the 'automatic' repayment of debt do not distort the observed leverage. These studies are discussed in the next section.

13.2.5 EVIDENCE FROM DUAL ISSUES AND SPIN-OFFS

Hovakimian, Hovakimian and Tehranian (HHT) (2004) studied 'dual issues'—that is, cases where companies raise both debt and equity in the same financial year. They reported that dual issues are typically large and therefore have the potential to make substantial changes in a company's capital structure. In the case of dual issues, the post-issue structure should reflect each company's leverage target

---

[2] A simulation study has suggested that in these circumstances cross-sectional statistical tests can be very misleading. If companies in fact trade off the costs and benefits of leverage but change their debt–equity ratio only infrequently, then a cross-section test could show a negative relation between expected profitability and leverage even though the 'true' relationship is known to be positive at refinancing points. See Strebulaev (2007).

without any distortions induced by accumulated profits or losses. Hence, dual issues provide a setting that should make it easier to determine whether corporate financing behaviour is better explained by the static trade-off or pecking order theories.

The static trade-off theory predicts that high-growth companies will have low leverage targets while low-growth companies will have high leverage targets. HHT found results consistent with this prediction: companies with a high market-to-book ratio (indicating high growth prospects) have a low target debt ratio. However, there is an alternative explanation for this finding: perhaps companies tend to make equity issues when their market-to-book ratio is high. Baker and Wurgler (2002) proposed that managers will prefer to issue equity when they believe that the company's shares are overvalued, which will tend to be at times when the market-to-book ratio will also be higher than usual. Moreover, they contend that observed capital structures reflect the cumulative outcome of these attempts by managers to time the equity market. HHT did find some evidence of market timing in that recent increases in share price increase the probability of an equity issue.

HHT also examined the effects of profitability and found that there is no relationship between profitability and leverage after a dual issue. Thus, their results imply that the usual negative relationship between profitability and observed leverage is due to the cumulative effects of profits and losses. An important conclusion of the study is that the evidence 'supports the hypothesis that firms have target capital structures' (p. 539).

Historical effects can also be avoided by examining the capital structure of companies that emerge from corporate spin-offs—that is, transactions in which a subsidiary is separated from its parent company and each becomes a separate listed entity. In comparison to studies of broad samples, this setting should make it easier to detect relationships between leverage and company characteristics because the leverage ratios of the 'new' companies can be chosen deliberately. Mehrotra, Mikkelson and Partch (2003) studied a sample of 98 spin-offs from 1979 to 1997.[3] They tested whether the *difference* in leverage of the two companies that emerge from a spin-off is explained by differences in:

- profitability
- variability of industry operating income
- the nature of assets
- tax status.

They found that higher leverage is related to *higher* profitability, lower variability of industry operating income and a greater proportion of tangible assets. They also found no evidence of a relationship between leverage and tax status. Thus, in this setting, the relationship between leverage and profitability is the *opposite* of the pervasive negative relationship that is regarded as providing strong evidence against the static trade-off theory. Except for the lack of support for a corporate tax effect, Mehrotra, Mikkelson and Partch's results are consistent with the static trade-off theory.

13.2.6 EVIDENCE ON THE CHOICE OF MATURITY AND PRIORITY OF DEBT

So far we have discussed the effects of capital structure largely in terms of financial leverage, which implicitly assumes that all debt is the same. In practice, the debt used by companies can vary considerably in terms of features such as maturity, covenant restrictions, priority, security and whether the debt is in the form of marketable securities or non-marketable loans. Therefore, as well as deciding *how much* debt to use, the financial manager has to make decisions about *what type(s)* of debt to use

---

[3] Dittmar (2004) also studied capital structure in corporate spin-offs. Since her results are consistent with those of Mehrotra, Mikkelson and Partch, we discuss only one of the studies.

and whether debt should be secured or unsecured, short term or long term, and so on. Barclay and Smith (1996) suggest that one factor that may be important in making such decisions is flexibility: private bank loans are relatively easy to renegotiate if circumstances change, whereas once marketable debt securities have been issued it is much more difficult to vary the rights of the holders. Flexibility is likely to be more important to growth companies than it is to others, because they are more likely to get into financial difficulty than mature companies. Therefore, growth companies that borrow are likely to prefer private debt.

Barclay and Smith investigated the significance of two features of debt—maturity and priority—by examining 6000 US companies over the period 1981 to 1993. They pointed out that it may be difficult to assess the individual effects of some features of debt because many of them are related. For example, bank loans are typically shorter term, cheaper to arrange and contain tighter covenant restrictions than publicly issued corporate bonds. Consistent with the findings of Barclay, Smith and Watts (1995), they argued that, because of the higher risk that growth companies pose for lenders, such companies will find it prohibitively expensive to obtain long-term debt. Consequently, these companies are likely to use shorter-term, private debt, which, by its nature, provides greater financing flexibility than long-term debt. Similarly, the managers of growth companies might prefer to issue debt that is unsecured or subordinated in order to retain financing flexibility. However, Barclay and Smith argued that prospective lenders will require very high interest rates on such risky debt, so growth companies are likely to be forced to issue higher priority secured debt instead.

The results of their analysis were consistent with these arguments. Companies with high ratios of market value to book value ('growth' companies) tend to use debt of shorter maturity and higher priority than mature companies. Barclay and Smith found little evidence that maturity and priority choices were determined by taxes or signalling effects.

13.2.7 EVIDENCE FROM SURVEYS

An alternative approach to empirical testing is to ask chief financial officers (CFOs) what factors they consider when they make capital structure decisions. This approach has the virtue of being direct and simple but has two weaknesses. First, the survey respondents may be unrepresentative of the population of CFOs. Second, what a CFO believes, says and does may be three different things. Nevertheless, well-conducted surveys provide a timely reality check.

The results of an important survey of 392 US CFOs were published in Graham and Harvey (2001). The survey was repeated by Brouwen, de Jong and Koedijk (2006) in a study of 313 CFOs from France, Germany, The Netherlands and the UK and repeated again by Coleman, Maheswaran and Pinder (2010) in a survey of 76 Australian CFOs. All three studies used the same questions on capital structure. Unfortunately, the response rates were only 9 per cent in the US and just 5 per cent in Europe and Australia. Survey respondents were provided with 14 factors that might explain their capital structure decisions and were asked to rank the importance of each factor on a five-point scale. Table 13.1 (overleaf) lists the top five factors in each country.

The results of the studies are remarkably similar. Of the 14 factors, the most important was clearly the desire to maintain financial flexibility: this factor ranked second in Australia and first in the other five countries. At first sight, this response appears to support the pecking order theory, but on further questioning it did not appear that the motivation for this desire was information asymmetry or growth options, as implied by the theory. Of the 13 other factors, only six appeared in the top five responses across the countries, suggesting that a similar set of factors is considered important in all countries. One of these is the tax advantage of debt. There was some support for the static trade-off theory, with CFOs reporting that company tax was of moderate importance, while the importance accorded to earnings volatility and the company's credit rating is consistent with a desire to avoid financial distress.

TABLE 13.1 Top five responses of CFOs to the question: What factors affect how you choose the appropriate amount of debt for your firm?

RANK	AUSTRALIA	FRANCE	GERMANY	NETHERLANDS	UK	USA
1	Volatility	Flexibility	Flexibility	Flexibility	Flexibility	Flexibility
2	Flexibility	Customers	Credit rating	Volatility	Volatility	Credit rating
3	Credit rating	Credit rating	Volatility	Tax advantage	Tax advantage	Volatility
4	Transaction costs	Tax advantage	Transaction costs	Credit rating	Transaction costs	Tax advantage
5	Tax advantage	Volatility	Tax advantage	Bankruptcy costs	Customers	Transaction costs

Sources: Australia: Coleman, Maheswaran and Pinder (2010); France, Germany, Netherlands and UK: Brounen, de Jong and Koedijk (2006); US: Graham and Harvey (2001).

The full statement of each factor was:

Volatility	The volatility of our earnings and cash flows
Flexibility	Financial flexibility (restrict debt so we have enough internal funds available to pursue new projects when they come along)
Credit rating	Our credit rating (as assigned by ratings agencies)
Transaction costs	The transaction costs and fees for issuing debt
Tax advantage	The tax advantage of interest deductibility
Customers	We limit debt so our customers/suppliers are not worried about our firm going out of business
Bankruptcy costs	The potential costs of bankruptcy, near-bankruptcy or financial distress

This similarity in responses is perhaps surprising given that company tax rates in Europe are considerably higher than in the US. Curiously, German CFOs were the least concerned about company tax despite Germany having the highest tax rate. The importance of company tax ranked lowest in Australia, which is consistent with Australia's use of a pure form of imputation. None of the surveys found much evidence that CFOs considered that asset substitution, asymmetric information, free cash flows or personal tax were important factors.

13.3 ASSESSING THE THEORIES OF CAPITAL STRUCTURE

LEARNING OBJECTIVE 2
Assess the implications of the evidence for the static trade-off and pecking order theories

In Section 13.2 we reviewed empirical evidence on the effects of several factors that may influence capital structure decisions: taxes, costs of financial distress, agency costs and information costs. In this section we discuss the implications of that evidence for the two main contenders to explain capital structure: the static trade-off theory and the pecking order theory.

13.3.1 HOW USEFUL IS THE STATIC TRADE-OFF THEORY?

The static trade-off theory emphasises the effects of taxes and also recognises that costs of financial distress act as a deterrent to high financial leverage. It proposes that companies should borrow until the marginal tax advantage of additional debt is exactly offset by the increase in the present value of the expected costs of financial distress. The static trade-off theory is consistent with much of the evidence presented earlier. For example, it is consistent with the fact that companies with tangible assets borrow more than those with riskier, intangible assets in the form of valuable investment opportunities. Similarly, it is consistent with the fact that companies with less volatile cash flows (low business risk) borrow more than those with higher business risk.

While the static trade-off theory is consistent with some observations, Myers argues that 'the trade-off theory is in immediate trouble on the tax front' (2001, p. 89). Essentially Myers' argument is that the static trade-off theory does not do a good job of explaining capital structure decisions because there are cases where corporate leverage is much lower than the theory suggests it should be. For example, many large profitable companies such as Microsoft and the major pharmaceutical companies have operated for years with low debt ratios. These companies have high credit ratings and could achieve significant interest tax savings by increasing their debt ratios without the probability of financial distress becoming more than remote. Graham (2000) found that conservative use of debt finance was typical of US companies. About half the companies in his sample paid company tax at the full statutory rate. Graham noted that the average company in this subsample could have doubled its interest payments and almost certainly doubled its interest tax savings. How would such an increase in leverage affect company value? Graham estimated that on average these companies could have added 7.5 per cent to company value by increasing leverage to take advantage of the net tax benefits of debt. Graham's study did not ignore the fact that increasing leverage will increase the likelihood of financial distress. His estimates suggest that for most companies the expected costs of financial distress are simply too small to offset the net tax benefits of debt.

Historically, the static trade-off theory has been criticised because it appears to be inconsistent with the evidence that profitability is negatively related to financial leverage. For example, as Myers points out, 'if managers can exploit valuable interest tax shields as the trade-off theory predicts, we should observe exactly the opposite relationship. High profitability means that the firm has more taxable income to shield, and that the firm can service more debt without risking financial distress' (2003, p. 231). This criticism was certainly valid based on the evidence available at the time, but the more recent evidence outlined in Section 13.2.5 indicates that profitability is positively related to target leverage.

While critical of the static trade-off theory, Myers points out that there are many examples of *tactical* financing decisions that are tax-driven. For example, finance leases are largely tax-driven. As discussed in Chapter 16, when the lessor's effective tax rate is higher than the lessee's tax rate, a lease can provide an overall tax advantage that arises from deferring the payment of tax. There are formal studies that demonstrate that taxes have a material effect on financing decisions. For example, MacKie-Mason (1990) found that companies with low marginal tax rates are more likely to issue equity than companies that are paying tax at the full statutory rate. Similarly, Graham (1996) found that changes in long-term debt are positively related to the company's effective marginal tax rate. Both of these studies show that taxes affect financing decisions and their results are consistent with the static trade-off theory. However, these studies do not show that taxes give rise to a net benefit that increases company value.

Similar results would be expected under the imputation system, which is designed to ensure that corporate debt does not have a net tax advantage. For example, if a company operating under imputation is not in a tax-paying position, but needs to raise finance, it should be better for it to issue equity rather than debt. In comparison to issuing equity, borrowing would involve an immediate increase in taxes for investors with no immediate tax saving at the company level. Therefore, studies that show that taxes affect *marginal* financing decisions only show that taxes are important at the *tactical* level. They do not show that the present value of interest tax savings is positive and influences the choice of company debt ratios. In other words, while it is clear that taxes affect financing *tactics*, it is much more difficult to find evidence that taxes have a predictable effect on financing *strategy*. Indeed, Fama and French (1998), who conducted an extensive statistical investigation of relationships between company value, dividends and debt, were unable to find any evidence that debt has net tax benefits.

The static trade-off theory can explain many of the differences in capital structure that exist between companies in different industries. In particular, it can explain why leverage is generally low when business risk is high and when most of a company's assets are intangible. It can also explain the fact that the companies that become private in leveraged buyouts (discussed in Chapter 19) are typically mature companies with stable cash flows and tangible assets but few opportunities for growth.

While the static trade-off theory has commonsense appeal and can explain some aspects of capital structure, there are some facts that it struggles to explain. First, the static trade-off theory cannot explain why companies are generally conservative in using debt finance. Second, it is difficult to explain why financial leverage is similar, on average, across many countries despite differences in their tax systems. If corporate borrowing has a significant tax advantage, as proposed by the static trade-off theory, then leverage should be higher in the US with its classical tax system than in other countries with imputation tax systems. Third, there is the inconvenient historical fact that companies used debt long before companies were required to pay income tax. Something caused them to use debt and it certainly wasn't tax.

13.3.2 HOW USEFUL IS THE PECKING ORDER THEORY?

The pecking order theory, which we discussed in Section 12.9, can explain why internal finance is so popular and why debt is generally the first choice when external finance is needed. But, as is the case with the static trade-off theory, there are some observations that are difficult for the pecking order theory to explain. Frank and Goyal (2003) found that some companies make extensive use of external financing. Barclay, Smith and Watts (1995) found that leverage is typically low in high-technology industries where there are large growth opportunities and large needs for external finance. They noted that their finding was the exact opposite of what the pecking order theory predicts. However, their finding may not be difficult to explain. High-technology, high-growth companies typically have mostly intangible assets and would therefore find debt very expensive. Further, heavy borrowing by such companies should expose them to the underinvestment problem. In other words, the empirical finding can be explained more easily by considering costs of financial distress and agency costs rather than relying on the pecking order theory.

Is this criticism of the pecking order theory a fair one? Perhaps not. The pecking order theory does not say that debt is *always* the best source of external finance. It does say that companies should raise external equity only when they have exhausted their debt capacity. For high-technology, high-growth companies, debt capacity may well be very low.

13.4 FINANCING AS A MARKETING PROBLEM

LEARNING OBJECTIVE 3

Explain how financing can be viewed as a marketing problem

Companies raise external finance by borrowing, issuing preference shares and issuing ordinary shares. The differences between these three methods are significant in terms of risk, required rate of return, tax treatment, voting rights attached (if any) and priority for repayment in the event of liquidation. Less obvious perhaps are the differences that can exist within these categories, particularly debt. For example, companies can borrow in different currencies, for different periods of time, and the interest rate may be fixed or variable. In addition, the repayment terms can differ, in that the principal may be repayable in instalments or in a lump sum. Also, the priority of the lender's claim can differ and some debt is convertible to ordinary shares. The reason for outlining all these differences is to show that in choosing a capital structure, a company is essentially choosing a particular package of financial services that it supplies to investors—that is, in raising different forms of finance, a company provides financial assets that offer investors different combinations of risk, return, liquidity and voting power. Further, the return can consist of different proportions of capital gains, compared with ordinary income, which in turn will have taxation consequences for the investor.

Shapiro (1998) points out that to a person skilled in marketing, the reason for these different combinations is obvious.[4] Different securities coexist for the same reason that different makes and models of cars coexist: individuals have different tastes, preferences and levels of wealth. The sales of a given model of car will depend on the demand for the package of features it offers, the cost of manufacturing that package, and the competition from suppliers of similar vehicles. Similarly, the capital structure decisions of companies will be influenced by the demand for different financial services, the costs of providing each package of financial services, and the level of competition from financial institutions that provide similar services.

The marketing approach suggests another way in which Modigliani and Miller's Proposition 1 can be violated. Cars and other products will sell at a higher price if they are well designed and have characteristics tailored to the preferences of potential buyers. The same principle can be applied to security issues. If a company's financial manager can design a security that appeals to a particular clientele of investors, such that these investors are prepared to pay a higher price for it, the company can raise funds at a lower cost than would otherwise be the case—that is, the required rate of return on the security is less than the market's required rate of return on other securities of the same risk. In other words, the marketing approach focuses on the *disequilibrium* that can exist when there is some mismatch between the demands of investors and the available supply of securities.

In a competitive market, a disequilibrium of this type will generally be short lived but can certainly occur. For example, a heightened fear of inflation could increase the demand for indexed bonds. When the unsatisfied demand for a particular type of security becomes evident, innovative financial managers will move to exploit the opportunity, and the supply of suitable securities is likely to increase substantially. Therefore, while there are rewards for financial innovation, the benefits are likely to go mainly to the companies whose financial managers are the genuine innovators. As the supply of new securities increases, the price investors are prepared to pay for them will decrease, and therefore the required rate of return will increase. Once the clientele's needs have been met, there are no further opportunities to sell more securities at a premium.

DETERMINING A FINANCING STRATEGY

13.5

The evidence discussed in this chapter shows that financing decisions are important and can be influenced by many factors. There is no single model or theory that can be used to specify the best financing strategy for any particular company. Such a strategy might include a long-term leverage target, but in most cases such a target is unlikely to be adhered to precisely. Even where a target is chosen, it may be only one part of an overall strategy. For example, suppose a company has decided to raise new funds by borrowing. There are then many more decisions to be made. Should the company borrow from banks or should it issue marketable debt securities direct to lenders? What should be the term of the loan? Should the interest rate be fixed or variable? Are there opportunities to add value by adding some new features to the security? Clearly, there are no simple solutions that will always be the best, but by drawing on both theory and evidence, it is possible to specify some general principles and guidelines that can be used by financial managers to determine a company's financing strategy.

> **LEARNING OBJECTIVE 4**
>
> Outline the main factors that financial managers should consider when determining a company's financing strategy

An important principle is that it is usually harder to add value by making good financing decisions than by making good investment decisions. While a company may be able to find investment projects with positive net present values, the highly competitive nature of financial markets means that it is much more difficult to make financing decisions that have positive net present values. For example, as discussed in Section 13.4, any marketing advantage associated with issuing a security that is in high demand will generally be short lived. Investment decisions are important because the primary source of a company's value is the cash flows generated by its assets. By comparison, the financing decision is less important. Even so,

---

[4] Shapiro is not the only one to emphasise that the financing decision can be viewed as a marketing problem. See Brealey, Myers and Allen (2008, pp. 486–7).

the financing decision determines more than how the company's cash flows are divided between different classes of investors—there is evidence that financing decisions can also have important effects on investment decisions. However, given the primacy of investment decisions, it seems sensible to suggest that a company's financing strategy should be designed to complement and support its investment strategy. In particular, factors such as business risk and asset type, which are discussed below, can have important effects.

A second important principle is that while it is not easy to add value by making good financing decisions, it is certainly possible to reduce value by making poor financing decisions. For example, a high proportion of debt can reduce shareholders' wealth because the expected bankruptcy costs become significant.

We now turn to some of the more important factors to be taken into account when making capital structure decisions.

13.5.1 BUSINESS RISK

In Section 12.6 we pointed out that a company's expected bankruptcy costs reduce its market value. The expected bankruptcy costs are positively related to the present value of bankruptcy costs and the probability of bankruptcy occurring. The probability of bankruptcy depends partly on the company's ability to meet its fixed financial commitments. By issuing debt, the company increases these financial commitments, and hence also increases its probability of bankruptcy.

In order to gauge the bankruptcy cost implications of issuing (more) debt, a financial manager has to consider the variability of the company's future net cash flows. The greater the variability, the greater is the probability that, at some future time, the company will be unable to meet its financial commitments. The variability of the net cash flows from a company's assets is typically taken as a measure of its business risk. Therefore, the greater a company's business risk, the less the company can borrow before its probability of bankruptcy is increased. As a result, the optimal capital structure for a company will be affected by its business risk. Therefore, some similarities may be expected between the capital structures of companies in the same industry, and the leverage used by similar companies may be a useful guide for the financial manager.

13.5.2 ASSET CHARACTERISTICS

Most companies have both tangible assets and intangible assets. Also, some assets, referred to as 'general purpose assets', can easily be redeployed to alternative uses, while other assets, referred to as 'company-specific assets', are worth much more in their current use than in any alternative uses. For example, a motor vehicle is a general-purpose asset, while a specialised item of equipment may be company-specific. Many company-specific assets are also intangible. These asset characteristics are important in determining how much a company can borrow. This is the case because a lender's risk is lower if the company's value is largely attributable to assets that can be sold with low transaction costs and little or no loss of value.

Tangible assets are usually easier to sell than intangible assets; indeed, many intangible assets cannot be sold separately from the business as a whole. This suggests that companies with a high proportion of tangible assets would be able to borrow more than companies that have a high proportion of intangible assets. For example, companies in many service industries, such as advertising agencies and consulting companies, have a high proportion of intangible assets and are largely financed by equity capital. Similarly, general purpose assets can support more debt than company-specific assets. Lenders recognise that company-specific assets will lose much of their value if the borrower defaults and is liquidated. In other words, expected bankruptcy costs will be high and this will be reflected in the interest rate charged.

A related argument is that the agency costs of debt are high for companies with a high proportion of intangible assets. For example, if a company relies heavily on research and development (R&D) activities, problems such as asset substitution will be difficult for lenders to detect. Therefore, borrowing would involve high monitoring costs that would also be passed on to borrowers in the form of higher interest rates. Rather than incur the higher interest cost, such companies will tend to rely on equity capital and hence will operate on relatively low debt–equity ratios.

13.5.3 TAX POSITION

The effects of taxes on financing decisions will depend to a large extent on the nature of the country's tax system. However, under any tax system it should not be assumed that debt has a tax advantage just because interest is tax deductible. Such an assumption is unwarranted because it ignores personal taxes. As discussed in Section 12.4.3, Miller has shown that, under the classical system, the effects of corporate and personal taxes can offset each other exactly. If there is, in practice, any net tax advantage of corporate borrowing under the classical system, this advantage is likely to go only to companies with high and stable earnings. For companies that are unable to make immediate use of interest deductions (because, for example, they have tax losses being carried forward), borrowing will increase personal taxes, but there will be no immediate reduction in company tax. Therefore, in this case, borrowing is likely to have a net tax disadvantage.

Under a full imputation tax system, company income tax is, as discussed in Section 11.4.1, effectively a withholding tax and can be recovered by resident shareholders. If all company tax paid is effectively recovered by shareholders through receipt of franked dividends, any advantage from reducing company tax would be due only to differences in the timing of tax payments. However, in practice, many Australian companies have both resident and non-resident shareholders. While Australian residents can use franking credits, non-residents cannot use them and are therefore effectively still taxed under the classical system. In other words, if a company pays franked dividends and some of its shares are held by non-residents, some tax credits will be 'wasted'. One way to reduce this waste is to issue a further class of shares that allows a higher proportion of the tax credits to be transferred to resident investors. Some companies have achieved this by issuing converting preference shares, which typically carry an entitlement to fully franked dividends at a fixed rate. If these shares are issued to ordinary shareholders via a renounceable rights issue, non-resident shareholders can sell their rights to residents. The price residents are prepared to pay for the rights will reflect the value, to them, of the tax credits. Therefore, reduction of the wastage of tax credits means that all shareholders are able to benefit, either directly or indirectly.

As discussed in Section 12.5.2, the imputation tax system has the potential to be neutral between debt and equity, but, in its Australian version, it tends to be biased towards equity. Thus the conclusion is that, under the imputation system, simply changing a company's debt–equity *ratio* is unlikely to have any significant tax-based effect on company value. However, the above discussion shows that changing the *type* of equity securities that a company issues can have important tax effects.

13.5.4 MAINTAINING RESERVE BORROWING CAPACITY ('FINANCIAL SLACK')

As discussed in Section 12.9, when there is information asymmetry between managers and investors, the announcement of a new share issue is likely to cause the company's share price to fall. Therefore, if a company needs to issue new shares to finance a new project, the overall effect can be a reduction in shareholders' wealth, even though the project has a positive net present value. This problem does not occur if the project can be financed internally or financed by borrowing. In other words, information asymmetry can effectively force companies to follow a financing pecking order in which internal funds are the first choice and external equity is the last choice.

The problem of being forced to choose between forgoing a positive NPV project and seeing the share price fall because of a share issue can be overcome by maintaining reserve borrowing capacity or 'financial slack'. In this way additional finance can always be raised at short notice to take advantage of profitable investments. Clearly, the value of maintaining reserve borrowing capacity will be greatest for companies that operate in industries where there are significant investment opportunities.

A survey of financial managers by Allen (1991) found that the majority of Australian companies have a policy of maintaining a substantial 'cushion' of reserve borrowing capacity, typically in the form of unused credit facilities established with banks and other financial intermediaries. Allen (2000) investigated the extent to which a sample of listed Australian, British and Japanese companies maintained spare borrowing capacity. He reported that 60 per cent of Australian, 90 per cent of British and 32 per cent of the Japanese respondents to his survey maintained spare borrowing capacity.

While financial slack is valuable for some companies, it is not valuable for all companies. Suppose that a company is currently very profitable but operates in an industry with few investment opportunities. If this company has a low debt–equity ratio, it will have considerable financial slack. However, it will also have a large free cash flow, so there is a danger that its managers may squander resources on takeovers or diversification projects that benefit them but harm the shareholders. In other words, as discussed in Section 12.7.2, the agency costs of equity can be large when a company has large free cash flow. One solution to this problem is to increase debt.

13.5.5 OTHER FACTORS

In discussing the effects of business risk we referred to the variability of cash flows as a measure of risk. A company's cash flows can vary for many reasons, and financial managers should not assume that business risk will be identical for all companies in a given industry. To illustrate some of the many risk factors that can influence financing decisions, we consider political risk and inflation risk.

Political risk

Many multinational companies have operations in countries that can be politically unstable. There is the risk that a sudden change of government may be followed by expropriation of foreign-owned assets. In addition, it is typically much more difficult to take dividends out of such countries than it is to move investment capital into them. Multinational companies will therefore structure the financing of foreign operations and projects to minimise the impact of political risk. For example, they may invest as little of their own funds as possible and raise most of the finance within the foreign country.

Inflation risk

Financial managers should consider the effects of inflation when deciding whether to borrow at fixed or floating interest rates. If the rate of inflation increases, nominal interest rates will increase, with the result that floating-rate borrowers will incur higher loan repayments. This may not be a significant problem if net operating cash flows also increase in line with inflation. For example, companies that provide services are generally able to increase their prices in line with inflation, or they may have contracts with their customers that provide for regular price reviews in accordance with a general price level index, such as the consumer price index. On the other hand, capital-intensive industries are likely to suffer reductions in real cash flows under inflationary conditions. One reason for this is that the cost of replacing productive assets as they wear out will increase, but for tax purposes companies can only claim depreciation based on the historical cost of their assets. For a company in this situation, borrowing at a fixed interest rate may be preferred because borrowing at a floating interest rate will tend to increase the variability of its net cash flows.

Connect Plus features a case study illustrating topics covered in this chapter.
Ask your lecturer or tutor for your course's unique URL.

SUMMARY

→ Empirical evidence indicates that corporate financial leverage has noticeable patterns, including similarities within industries and differences between industries that tend to persist over time. Across the US non-financial corporate sector as a whole, the ratio of debt to equity stayed within a narrow range during the twentieth century. The principles discussed in Chapter 12 suggest that capital structure decisions may be important because of the effects of factors such as taxes, asset type, costs of financial distress and the extent of a company's investment opportunities.

→ Many studies focus on differences between companies and try to explain their observed leverage in terms of variables chosen as empirical proxies for these and other factors. The results of these studies suggest that capital structures are chosen systematically and that financial leverage is positively related to the proportion of assets that are tangible and negatively related to earnings volatility, non-debt tax shields and profitability.

- One factor that appears to be of particular importance is investment opportunities: leverage is negatively related to investment opportunities as measured by the ratio of market value to book value. Companies with high ratios of market value to book value ('growth companies') also tend to use debt of shorter maturity and higher priority than mature companies. The relationship between leverage and a company's tax position is relatively weak, but examination of financing decisions on a marginal basis shows that taxes do influence these decisions.

→ Tests of the pecking order theory find evidence that is consistent with the financing pecking order being caused by information asymmetry between managers and investors. There is also evidence that, consistent with the pecking order theory, announcement of an external capital raising, particularly a share issue, causes a company's share price to fall.

→ Evidence from companies that make 'dual issues' of debt and equity and from capital structures of corporate spin-offs is consistent with the predictions of the static trade-off theory. In particular, these studies provide evidence that financial leverage is positively related to profitability.

→ Evidence from surveys of CFOs gives some support to the static trade-off theory, with both tax benefits and financial distress receiving attention from CFOs. Other theories received less support.

→ Company financing can be viewed as essentially a marketing problem. This approach uses the fact that different investors have different tastes, preferences and levels of wealth to explain the coexistence of securities that differ in terms of characteristics such as risk, return, tax treatment and voting rights.

- If the supply of each type of security exactly matches the demand for it, then a market equilibrium would exist in which there would be no incentive for a company to change its capital structure.

- However, if there is disequilibrium such that there is a clientele of investors whose needs are not satisfied by the range of securities available, then the Modigliani and Miller propositions can be violated.

- To exploit such a disequilibrium, a financial manager needs to design a security that meets the requirements of the unsatisfied clientele of investors. In other words, there can be rewards for financial innovation, but because capital markets are highly competitive, any such disequilibrium is likely to be short lived and the rewards are likely to go only to the companies whose financial managers are the real innovators, rather than to those who merely imitate the leaders.

→ Because a company's value depends primarily on the cash flows generated by its assets, a company's financing strategy should be designed to complement and support its investment strategy. In applying this principle the financial manager may need to consider many factors, the main ones being the company's business risk, the nature of its assets, its tax position and the need for reserve borrowing capacity.

KEY TERMS

non-debt tax shields 421

REFERENCES

Allen, D.E., 'The determinants of the capital structure of listed Australian companies: the financial manager's perspective', *Australian Journal of Management*, December 1991, pp. 103–27.

——, 'Spare debt capacity: company practices in Australia, Britain and Japan', *Australian Journal of Management*, December 2000, pp. 299–326.

Altman, E., 'A further empirical investigation of the bankruptcy cost question', *Journal of Finance*, September 1984, pp. 1067–89.

Andrade, G. & Kaplan, S., 'How costly is financial (not economic) distress? Evidence from highly leveraged transactions that became distressed', *Journal of Finance*, October 1998, pp. 1443–93.

Baker, M. & Wurgler, J., 'Market timing and capital structure', *Journal of Finance*, February 2002, pp. 1–32.

Barclay, M. & Smith, C., 'On financial architecture: leverage, maturity and priority', *Journal of Applied Corporate Finance*, Winter 1996, pp. 4–17.

——, ——, & Watts, R., 'The determinants of corporate leverage and dividend policies', *Journal of Applied Corporate Finance*, Winter 1995, pp. 4–19.

Bradley, M., Jarrell, G. & Kim, E., 'On the existence of an optimal capital structure: theory and evidence', *Journal of Finance*, July 1984, pp. 857–78.

Brealey, R. Myers, S. & Allen, F., *Principles of Corporate Finance*, 9th edn, McGraw-Hill, New York, 2008.

Brounen, D., de Jong, A. & Koedijk, K., 'Capital structure policies in Europe: survey evidence', *Journal of Banking and Finance*, May 2006, pp. 1409–42.

Coleman, L., Maheswaran, K. & Pinder, S., 'Narratives in managers' corporate finance decisions', *Accounting and Finance*, September 2010, pp. 605–34.

Dittmar, A., 'Capital structure in corporate spin-offs', *Journal of Business*, January 2004, pp. 9–43.

Fama, E. & French, K., 'Taxes, financing decisions and firm value', *Journal of Finance*, June 1998, pp. 819–43.

——, ——, 'Testing trade-off and pecking order predictions about dividends and debt', *Review of Financial Studies*, Spring 2002, pp. 1–33.

Frank, M. & Goyal, V., 'Testing the pecking order theory of capital structure', *Journal of Financial Economics*, February 2003, pp. 217–48.

——, ——, 'Trade-off and pecking order theories of debt', in B.E. Eckbo (ed.), *Handbook of Corporate Finance: Empirical Corporate Finance*, vol. 2, Elsevier North Holland, Amsterdam, 2008, pp. 135–202.

Graham, J., 'Debt and the marginal tax rate', *Journal of Financial Economics*, May 1996, pp. 41–73.

——, 'How big are the tax benefits of debt?', *Journal of Finance*, October 2000, pp. 1901–41.

——, & Harvey, C., 'The theory and practice of corporate finance: evidence from the field', *Journal of Financial Economics*, May 2001, pp. 187–243.

Harris, M. & Raviv, A., 'The theory of capital structure', *Journal of Finance*, March 1991, pp. 297–355.

Hovakimian, A., Hovakimian, G. & Tehranian, H., 'Determinants of target capital structure: the case of dual debt and equity issues', *Journal of Financial Economics*, March 2004, pp. 517–40.

Jensen, M., 'Agency costs of free cash flow, corporate finance and takeovers', *American Economic Review*, May 1986, pp. 323–9.

MacKay, P. & Phillips, G.M., 'How does industry affect firm financial structure?', *Review of Financial Studies*, Winter 2005, pp. 1433–66.

MacKie-Mason, J., 'Do taxes affect corporate financing decisions?', *Journal of Finance*, December 1990, pp. 1471–93.

Mehrotra, V., Mikkelson, W. & Partch, M., 'The design of financial policies in corporate spin-offs', *Review of Financial Studies*, Winter 2003, pp. 1359–88.

Myers, S., 'The capital structure puzzle', *Journal of Finance*, July 1984, pp. 575–92.

——, 'Capital structure', *Journal of Economic Perspectives*, Spring 2001, pp. 81–102.

——, 'Financing of corporations', in G. Constantinides, M. Harris & R. Stulz (eds), *Handbook of the Economics of Finance*, Elsevier North Holland, Amsterdam, 2003, pp. 215–53.

Opler, T. & Titman, S., 'Financial distress and corporate performance', *Journal of Finance*, July 1994, pp. 1015–40.

Pattenden, K., 'Capital structure decisions under classical and imputation tax systems: a natural test for tax effects in Australia', *Australian Journal of Management*, June 2006, pp. 67–92.

Pham, T. & Chow, D., 'Some estimates of direct and indirect bankruptcy costs in Australia: September 1978– May 1983', *Australian Journal of Management*, June 1987, pp. 75–95.

Pilotte, E., 'Growth opportunities and the stock price response to new financing', *Journal of Business*, July 1992, pp. 371–94.

Rajan, R. & Zingales, L., 'What do we know about capital structure? Some evidence from international data', *Journal of Finance*, December 1995, pp. 1421–60.

Richardson, G. & Lanis, R., 'The influence of income taxes on the use of debt held by publicly listed Australian corporations', *Australian Tax Forum*, 2001, pp. 3–32.

Schulman, C., Thomas, D., Sellers, K. & Kennedy, D., 'Effects of tax integration and capital gains tax on corporate leverage', *National Tax Journal*, March 1996, pp. 31–54.

Shapiro, A.C., 'Guidelines for long-term corporate financing strategy', in J. Stern and D. Chew (eds), *The Revolution in Corporate Finance*, Basil Blackwell, Oxford, 3rd edn 1998, pp. 174–87.

Shyam-Sunder, L., 'The stock price effect of risky versus safe debt', *Journal of Financial and Quantitative Analysis*, December 1991, pp. 549–58.

——, & Myers, S., 'Testing static trade-off against pecking order models of capital structure', *Journal of Financial Economics*, February 1999, pp. 219–44.

Smith, C.W. Jr, 'Raising capital: theory and evidence', *Midland Corporate Finance Journal*, Spring 1986, pp. 6–22.

Strebulaev, I., 'Do tests of capital structure theory mean what they say?', *Journal of Finance*, August 2007, pp. 1747–86.

Titman, S. & Wessels, R., 'The determinants of capital structure choice', *Journal of Finance*, March 1988, pp. 1–19.

Wald, J., 'How firm characteristics affect capital structure: an international comparison', *Journal of Financial Research*, Summer 1999, pp. 161–87.

Warner, J., 'Bankruptcy costs: some evidence', *Journal of Finance*, May 1977, pp. 337–47.

Weiss, L., 'Bankruptcy resolution: direct costs and violation of priority of claims', *Journal of Financial Economics*, October 1990, pp. 285–314.

Wright, S., 'Measures of stock market value and returns for the US nonfinancial corporate sector, 1900–2002', *Review of Income and Wealth*, December 2004, pp. 561–84.

QUESTIONS

1. **[LO 1]** Outline the characteristics you would expect a company to have if it had:
   (a) a very low debt–equity ratio
   (b) a very high debt–equity ratio.

2. **[LO 1]** *Empirical evidence suggests that management takes account of market conditions and recent security prices when determining whether to make a debt or an equity issue.* Discuss the relevance of these factors for management's decision.

3. **[LO 1]** Would you necessarily expect companies in the same industry to have similar debt–equity ratios? Give reasons for your answer.

4. **[LO 1]** Suppose that the government substantially reduced the company tax rate in a classical tax system.
   (a) What would the Modigliani and Miller (with company tax) approach suggest about the effect of this change on the capital structures of companies?
   (b) What would Miller's model predict about the effect on:
     (i) the quantity of debt for the corporate sector as a whole?
     (ii) the capital structures of individual companies?

5. **[LO 1]** The costs of financial distress are likely to be high for some types of companies, and low for others. Outline the types of companies for which these costs are likely to be:
   (a) high
   (b) low.

6. **[LO 2]** *The empirical observation that there is a negative relationship between profitability and leverage is embarrassing for the static trade-off theory of capital structure.* Do you agree? How reliable is the evidence that the relationship between profitability and leverage is negative rather than positive?

7. **[LO 1]** *A sample of companies that make 'dual issues' of debt and equity provides a better setting than a broad sample of companies for testing whether companies have capital structure targets.* Explain why you agree or disagree with this statement.

8. **[LO 1]** *The empirical studies of capital structure decisions are attempts to infer from the data the decision-making processes of company managers. Such attempts are heroic because they face numerous problems of statistical design and interpretation. Surely there is a much simpler approach: why not just ask company managers what factors they consider when they make capital structure decisions?* Discuss.

9. **[LO 2] (a)** The static trade-off theory of capital structure can explain some of the debt–equity ratio differences *between* industries, but cannot explain such differences between companies *within* a given industry. Explain why this statement is correct or incorrect.
   (b) Briefly outline another theory that can explain differences in capital structures between companies in the same industry.

10. **[LO 1]** Study the capital structures of a bank, a finance company, a retailer and a manufacturer. Are there discernible differences in the capital structures of the companies chosen? Give reasons for any differences you find.

11. **[LO 1]** Choose a company and trace the major changes in its capital structure over the past 10 years. Outline the economic factors you consider have contributed to the major changes in its financing policy during this period.

12. **[LO 1]** 'The problem is how to motivate managers to disgorge the cash rather than investing it below the cost of capital or wasting it on organisational inefficiencies' (Jensen 1986, p. 323). Explain how debt finance can provide a solution to this problem.

13. **[LO 1]** The Modigliani and Miller (MM) analysis of capital structure assumes that the company's net operating cash flows are given. Capital structure is irrelevant under the MM assumptions because, in a perfect capital market with no taxes, the value of this cash flow stream is unaffected by capital structure decisions. One reason why capital structure decisions may be important in practice is that cash flows are *not* independent of these decisions. Explain how this could occur for:
    (a) a company that generates large free cash flow
    (b) a company that is highly levered.

14. **[LO 4]** An executive of a mining company explains that it has a policy of maintaining a portfolio of projects at various stages of development. In this way the need for external finance is minimised because the cash flow generated by operating mines can be used to finance the development of new ones. Also the company's net cash flows can be smoothed by adjusting production plans to suit the timing of new projects. For example, if there are delays in bringing a new mine into production, the life of an old mine might be extended by mining low-grade ore that would not normally be considered economic. Critically evaluate the company's strategy from the viewpoint of shareholders.

15. **[LO 4]** The chief executive of Planets Ltd, a young company that has just been set up, says: 'We decided to borrow most of the funds needed to establish our operations because high leverage would signal to the markets that we were confident and fully committed to making this business succeed.' Evaluate this strategy, assuming that Planets produces:
    (a) voice-activated software systems
    (b) household detergents.

16. **[LO 4]** In April 1997, Telstra, then a telecommunications company wholly owned by the Australian Government, announced a capital restructuring ahead of its proposed partial privatisation through a share market float during the second half of 1997. The capital restructuring involved payment of a special dividend of $3 billion to the government and the borrowing of $3 billion by Telstra. Its finance director reportedly said that 'the restructuring would lower the average cost of capital and enable greater financial flexibility'. Similarly, one journalist noted that 'debt financing is cheaper than equity raising'. His article also stated that 'debt interest payments are also tax deductible, while dividends are not'. Critically evaluate these comments on the effects of, and reasons for, the restructuring.

17. **[LO 4]** The capital restructuring of Telstra outlined in Question 16 prompted rating agencies to downgrade Telstra's debt. For example, Standard & Poor's lowered Telstra's rating from AAA to AA+. The restructuring was the subject of many comments

by financial journalists, economists and financial analysts, some of whom differed widely in their predictions about its effects. The comments included:

(a) A spokesman for the Australian Telecommunications Users Group predicted increased charges to phone users. Conversely, another commentator stated that 'most importantly, it does not mean higher charges to "get the money back"'. He added that future telephony charges would depend on a mix of Telstra's monopoly power versus the effectiveness of competition and that, 'provided the regulators do their job half-well, the Telstra balance sheet is irrelevant'.

(b) Some critics noted that the rating downgrade would increase Telstra's borrowing costs, while others suggested that despite the reduction of $3 billion in net assets it was likely that Telstra would fall in value by something less than $3 billion and might not lose any value at all. The latter argument is supported by the comment that the payment did not put any financial pressure on Telstra and 'might concentrate minds on how it spends its huge cash flow'. Similarly, a broking analyst commented that 'by their nature, more highly geared companies exercise tighter cost disciplines'.

Critically evaluate the arguments outlined in (a) and (b).

Test yourself further with Connect Plus online! Ask your lecturer or tutor for your course's unique URL.

THE COST OF CAPITAL AND TAXATION ISSUES IN PROJECT EVALUATION

LEARNING OBJECTIVES

After studying this chapter you should be able to:

1. understand the concept of the cost of capital
2. understand the effect of risk on the cost of capital
3. understand how the cost of capital can be measured under the imputation tax system
4. understand why the cost of capital for a company is expressed as a weighted average of the costs of all of the company's sources of capital
5. estimate the cost of each source of capital and combine these costs into a weighted average cost of capital for a company
6. explain how to treat issue costs in project evaluation
7. understand the distinction between the cost of capital for a project and a company's weighted average cost of capital
8. estimate the cost of capital for a division of a diversified company
9. understand the advantages and disadvantages of using the weighted average cost of capital in project evaluation
10. understand the effects of taxes on project cash flows
11. understand the application of the certainty-equivalent method of incorporating risk into project evaluation.

CHAPTER CONTENTS

14.1 Introduction
14.2 Risk, return and the cost of capital
14.3 Taxes and the cost of capital
14.4 Alternative approaches to estimation of the cost of capital
14.5 Estimation of the cost of capital: an extended example
14.6 Project and company cost of capital
14.7 The weighted average cost of capital and alternative project evaluation techniques
14.8 Tax issues in project evaluation
14.9 Using certainty equivalents to allow for risk
Appendix 14.1 The cost of capital under alternative tax systems

This chapter is also featured in the complete e-book available with Connect Plus. Ask your lecturer or tutor for your course's unique URL.

14.1 INTRODUCTION

As we noted in Chapter 5, when a project is evaluated using the net present value (NPV) method, it is necessary to have information on the project's forecast *net cash flows* and its *required rate of return*. Under the NPV method, the forecast net cash flows are discounted at the project's required rate of return and the project should be undertaken if it has a positive NPV. In this case, the decision to undertake the new project should increase shareholders' wealth, because it is expected to generate net cash flows that are sufficient to compensate the suppliers of capital for the resources committed to the project.

The rate of return required by the suppliers of capital is also known as the 'cost of capital'. It is an **opportunity cost** because capital suppliers will require that a project should produce a rate of return at least as great as the rate of return they could obtain on other investments of similar risk. In turn, this rate of return is usually thought of as consisting of two components: the risk-free rate of return to compensate for the time value of money, plus a premium to compensate for risk.

The cost of capital is a crucially important input to the investment decision. Often the decision to accept or reject a proposed project can change if the estimated cost of capital is changed by as little as a few percentage points. There are, however, different definitions of the cost of capital that can be adopted. The **consistency principle** requires that the definition of the cash flows in the numerator of an NPV calculation must match the definition of the discount rate in the denominator of the calculation. For example, inflation must be treated consistently in the cash flows and the cost of capital. Therefore, if the cash flows are nominal—that is, are based on prices expected in future years—then the discount rate must also be expressed in nominal (rather than real) terms. Similarly, taxes must be treated consistently in the cash flows and the cost of capital. In this chapter we consider the definition, estimation and use of the cost of capital.

In practice, risky projects are usually evaluated by using a cost of capital that reflects the risk of the project. In this chapter we also consider the certainty-equivalent approach. This approach incorporates risk into the analysis by adjusting the cash flows rather than the discount rate.

LEARNING OBJECTIVE 1
Understand the concept of the cost of capital

opportunity cost highest price or rate of return that would be provided by an alternative course of action. The *opportunity cost of capital* is the rate of return that could be earned on another investment with the same risk

14.2 RISK, RETURN AND THE COST OF CAPITAL

In Chapter 7 we discussed the relationship between risk and return for risky assets such as shares. In that discussion we used the terms 'expected return' and 'required return' to refer to the returns demanded by investors. The returns received by investors in securities must be provided by the issuers of those securities and, from the issuer's viewpoint, the return demanded by investors is effectively a cost—typically referred to as the cost of capital. Therefore, the terms 'cost of capital' and 'required return' could be used interchangeably, and, in assessing the **cost of capital** for any project, we focus on the return required by investors to compensate them for providing capital.

Suppose that a company has two new projects available: one is risk-free and the other is risky. How should the company's financial manager assess the cost of capital for each of these projects? Essentially, the financial manager should ask: What rate of return would our *shareholders* require from these projects? Clearly, a decision to undertake the risk-free project will increase shareholders' wealth only if the project's expected rate of return is at least as great as the rate that investors can earn on other risk-free investments, such as government debt securities. In other words, the cost of capital for the risk-free project is the risk-free rate in the securities market. The cost of capital for the risky project will be higher than the risk-free rate and will depend on the rate of return that investors require from other investments of similar risk. In summary, the cost of capital for a project depends on the risk of the project.

The relationship between risk and return is discussed in Chapter 7 and one of the main conclusions is that the relevant measure of risk for any asset is its systematic or non-diversifiable risk, because investors

LEARNING OBJECTIVE 2
Understand the effect of risk on the cost of capital

consistency principle in applying the NPV model, the net cash flows in the numerator should be defined and measured in a way that is consistent with the definition of the discount rate

cost of capital
minimum rate of return needed to compensate suppliers of capital for committing resources to an investment

will not be compensated for bearing risk that can be eliminated by diversification—that is, they will not be compensated for unsystematic or diversifiable risk. Consistent with this conclusion, the capital asset pricing model (CAPM) states that the required return on an investment depends on the investment's systematic risk. Hence, according to the CAPM, the relevant measure of risk for a project is the *systematic risk of the project*, measured by its beta.

14.2.1 RISK INDEPENDENCE

If the cost of capital for a project depends on the risk of the project then it does *not* depend on the characteristics of the company considering the project. The decision rule is to accept all projects whose net present values are positive when the expected cash flows are discounted at the project-specific discount rate. Thus, the value of a project depends on what the project is, not who the investor is.

Further, projects can be evaluated as if their risk is independent of the risk of all other projects undertaken by the company. This principle of risk independence can be explained by considering company diversification. It is explained in Chapter 7 that a rational risk-averse investor will hold a well-diversified portfolio and that the risk of an asset in a large portfolio depends on the covariance of the returns on the individual asset with the returns on the portfolio. It could be argued that companies should also diversify. If so, then companies would take into account the correlation between returns on the proposed project and returns on their existing projects.

Fortunately this argument is incorrect, because investors can diversify for themselves simply by investing in the shares of many different companies. Therefore, diversification by a company does not provide any investment opportunity that is not already available to investors.[1] Consequently, each project should be evaluated using the cost of capital appropriate for that project. This depends on the risk of the particular project. Risk independence comes about because of the effectiveness of the capital market in providing opportunities for investors to diversify.

14.3 TAXES AND THE COST OF CAPITAL

LEARNING OBJECTIVE 3
Understand how the cost of capital can be measured under the imputation tax system

As mentioned in Section 14.1, taxes must be treated consistently in the net cash flows and in the cost of capital. Projects are normally evaluated on an after-company-tax basis—that is, after-company-tax cash flows are discounted using an after-company-tax required rate of return. While this principle sounds simple, it can be difficult to apply because there is more than one way to define 'after-company-tax' cash flows. Particular care is needed under the imputation tax system because, as discussed in Chapter 11, some or all of the tax collected from a company is, in effect, personal tax, not 'true' company tax. Officer (1994) discussed several alternative ways of defining net cash flows and the cost of capital under imputation. One way to define after-tax cash flows is that they are equal to the before-tax cash flows multiplied by $(1 - t_e)$, where t_e is the *effective* company income tax rate. The effective company tax rate is $t_e = t_c(1 - \gamma)$, where t_c is the statutory company tax rate and γ represents the proportion of the tax collected from a company that is paid out to shareholders and recovered through tax credits associated with franked dividends. Note that if γ is equal to 1, then the effective company tax rate is zero, while if γ is equal to zero, then the effective company tax rate is the same as the statutory rate. The corresponding definition of the cost of capital is discussed in Section 14.4.2.

Officer also showed that, under the imputation tax system, adjustments may be needed where observed market rates of return are used to estimate the cost of equity. Conventionally, the cost of equity, k_e, is

---

1 Interestingly, in the context of companies acquiring other companies, Mukherjee, Kiymaz and Baker (2004) report that diversification is the second-most popular reason for acquisitions cited by a sample of chief financial officers of acquiring companies. This popularity exists despite shareholders being able to diversify their portfolios to match their risk appetite and, in many cases, being able do so more cheaply than the acquiring company, which is forced to pay a control premium. This point is discussed in greater depth in Section 19.2.2.

defined and measured on an after-company-tax, but before-personal-tax, basis. Under the classical tax system this approach is straightforward, because observed market rates of return on equity are also after company tax, but before personal tax. However, under the imputation system, part of the return to equity consists of tax credits. Because these tax credits are not included in conventional rate-of-return measures, adjustments are required to obtain true after-company-tax rates of return.

The adjustment of the dividend yield component of the return to equity to reflect the inclusion of tax credits is illustrated in Example 14.1.

EXAMPLE 14.1

The shares of PXT Ltd have a market price of $4 and an annual dividend of 17.5 cents per share, fully franked at the company tax rate of 30 per cent. Calculate:

(a) the dividend yield on the shares of PXT that would be reported in the financial press
(b) the dividend yield after company tax, but before personal tax
(c) the dividend yield after company tax and after personal tax, for shareholders with personal tax rates of:
  (i) 30 per cent
  (ii) 45 per cent.

SOLUTION

(a) Dividend yields reported in the financial press are based on cash dividends excluding any imputation tax franking credits. The reported dividend yield on the shares is:

$$\frac{\$0.175}{\$4.00} = 0.04375 \text{ or } 4.375\%$$

(b) The dividend yield after company tax, but before personal tax, is based on the cash dividend of $0.175 per share, plus the imputation tax franking credit, which represents personal tax already paid. As discussed in Section 11.4.1, the imputation tax franking credit is:

$$\frac{D_t \times t_c}{1 - t_c}$$

$$= \frac{\$0.175 \times 0.30}{0.70}$$

$$= \$0.075$$

The dollar return to shareholders after company tax is $0.175 + $0.075 = $0.250, so the dividend yield after company tax is $\frac{\$0.250}{\$4.00} = 0.0625$ or 6.25 %.

(c) The shareholders' personal tax will be calculated as follows:

Taxable dividend income = dividend + imputation franking credit
$$= \$0.175 + \$0.075$$
$$= \$0.250$$

Gross personal tax = $\$0.250 \times t_p$
Net personal tax = $\$0.250 \times t_p - \$0.075$

(i) When $t_p = 0.30$

Net personal tax = $\$0.250 \times 0.30 - \$0.075 = 0$

In this case, the dividend yield after all taxes is $\frac{\$0.175}{\$4.00}$ = 4.375 %, which is exactly equal to the reported dividend yield.

continued →

> **Example 14.1** *continued*
>
> (ii) When $t_p = 0.45$
>
> Net personal tax = $\$0.250 \times 0.45 - \$0.075$
> = $\$0.0375$
>
> The dividend after all taxes is $\$(0.175 - 0.0375) = \$0.1375$ and the corresponding dividend yield is $\dfrac{\$0.1375}{\$4.00} = 0.034\,375$ or 3.4375%.
>
> As a check, this yield can be converted to a before-personal tax yield, which is $\dfrac{3.4375\%}{(1-0.45)} = 6.25\%$: exactly the same as the answer to part (b).

Example 14.1 shows that where dividends are franked, observed rates of return on shares need to be adjusted to obtain after-company-tax rates of return. The adjustment is simple: add back the value of imputation tax franking credits that represent personal tax that has already been paid. The value of these tax credits can be expressed as a rate of return, τ, by dividing the tax credits by the share price. It follows that a similar adjustment is needed when the CAPM is used to estimate the cost of capital. Therefore, the CAPM would become:

$$k_e = R_f + \beta e[E(R_M + \tau) - R_f]$$

franking premium
that part of the return on shares or a share market index that is due to tax credits associated with franked dividends

Adding τ, which can be called a **franking premium**, adjusts the observed return on the market portfolio to an after-company-tax rate of return. The value of τ will depend on the average dividend yield on the shares in the market portfolio and the extent to which the dividends are franked. Suppose a share market index represents the market portfolio, the average dividend yield on shares in the index is 3 per cent and dividends are 80 per cent franked at a company tax rate of 30 per cent. In this case, the tax credits received on an investment of $100 would be:

$$\frac{\$3 \times 0.8 \times 0.30}{(1-0.30)} = \$1.0286$$

Therefore, the franking premium, τ, is approximately 1 per cent.

14.4 ALTERNATIVE APPROACHES TO ESTIMATION OF THE COST OF CAPITAL

It is important to recognise that the cost of capital reflects rates of return that investors expect to receive in the future. Because investors' expectations cannot be observed, it is usually not possible to measure the cost of capital precisely. It must be *estimated* and the preferred approach will be influenced by the availability of data and the importance of the investments that will be evaluated using the estimated cost of capital. The following sections discuss two approaches: the direct use of the CAPM and the use of the weighted average cost of capital (WACC).

14.4.1 DIRECT USE OF THE CAPM

According to the CAPM, which is discussed in Section 7.6.2, the cost of capital, k_j, for project j is:

$$k_j = R_f + \beta_j[E(R_M) - R_f] \qquad [14.1]$$

Therefore, to use the CAPM directly, it is necessary to estimate the risk-free interest rate, R_f, the expected rate of return on the market portfolio, $E(R_M)$ and the project's systematic risk, β_j. Estimation of R_f and

$E(R_M)$ is discussed in Section 14.5.3, but for now we focus on the problem of estimating the systematic risk or beta of a project.

Techniques for estimating the betas of securities, such as shares, using numbers derived from share market data, are explained in Section 7.6. The necessary data are readily available if the securities concerned are traded actively on a stock exchange. Proposed investment projects are, of course, not traded on a stock exchange, or on any other market, and therefore the data required to estimate project betas directly are not available. This problem could easily be overcome if all of a company's projects had the same beta, and if the company were financed solely by equity. Shareholders would bear all the risk associated with the company's net cash flows. As these cash flows are generated by the company's projects (or assets) the beta of the company's assets would be equal to the beta of its shares.

In practice, the vast majority of companies use debt finance as well as equity. This increases the beta of equity because shareholders of levered companies face financial risk as well as business risk. In the absence of taxes, the beta of a company's assets would be equal to the weighted average of the betas of its equity and its debt. While equity betas are routinely estimated using data on share market returns, this is not the case for debt. In Australia, most corporate debt is either not listed on a stock exchange or, at best, traded irregularly, and it is therefore very difficult to estimate the beta of debt. Moreover, in practice, the relationship between security betas and asset betas can be more complicated than it is in the no-tax case.

In summary, the direct use of the CAPM to estimate the cost of capital involves two main problems. First, there is the problem of the limited availability of data to estimate betas of debt. Second, care is needed to ensure that tax and leverage effects are handled correctly. These problems mean that the direct use of the CAPM is generally not feasible. However, this does not mean that the model should be disregarded. The CAPM can be very useful in estimating some components of the weighted average cost of capital.

14.4.2 THE WEIGHTED AVERAGE COST OF CAPITAL (WACC)

In Section 14.2, we emphasise the principle that the cost of capital is project-specific. In other words, evaluation of a proposed project should be based on the project's cost of capital. However, it can be very difficult to measure a project's cost of capital. This is because when a company raises capital, there is generally no direct link between the returns to the suppliers of the company's capital and the returns on individual projects. For example, suppose that a company borrows, using an existing asset as security, to provide the cash for a new project. The interest rate on the debt is *not* a valid measure of the new project's cost of capital. The reason is simple: the interest rate on the debt depends on the risk of the company and its existing assets, and does not depend solely on the risk of the new project. The situation is similar if a company makes a share issue to raise the cash needed for a new project. Shareholders are exposed to the risk of the whole company. Therefore, the cost of equity will depend on the average risk of all the company's assets and on its financial leverage, not just on the characteristics of the new project. In summary, the rates of return to the suppliers of a company's capital do not necessarily reflect the cost of capital that is applicable to any individual project, even if the new capital is raised at the time the project is implemented.

However, there is an important special case that often provides a practical solution to these problems. Suppose that a company's assets are all of similar risk and that the risk of the proposed project is the same as the risk of the company's existing assets. This should be the case if the project is simply an expansion of the company's existing operations. Since there is no change in risk, the cost of capital for the company as a whole should also be a valid measure of the cost of capital for the new project.

The *company cost of capital* is defined as the discount rate that equates the present value of a company's expected future cash flows to the company's value. To make this definition useful it is necessary to define both 'cash flows' and 'value'. The *value* of a company is the market value of its equity plus the market value of its debt. However, this definition of value can be combined with several definitions of *cash flow*,

LEARNING OBJECTIVE 4

Understand why the cost of capital for a company is expressed as a weighted average of the costs of all of the company's sources of capital

weighted average cost of capital (WACC)

the cost of capital determined by the weighted average cost of all sources of finance

leading to different versions of the cost of capital. For example, cash flows can be measured before tax or after tax. We use after-tax cash flows, defined as being equal to the before-tax cash flows multiplied by $(1 - t_e)$, where t_e is the *effective* company income tax rate. The effective company income tax rate is $t_c(1 - \gamma)$, where t_c is the statutory company income tax rate and γ is the proportion of the tax collected from the company that is claimed as a credit by shareholders. For example, if the before-tax cash flow is $1 million, the company income tax rate is 30 cents in the dollar, and 60 per cent of the tax collected from the company is claimed as a credit by shareholders, then the effective company tax rate is $0.30(1 - 0.6) = 0.12$ and the after-company-tax cash flow is $1\,000\,000 \times (1 - 0.12) = \$880\,000$.

When net cash flows are defined in this way, a company's **weighted average cost of capital (WACC)** can be found as follows. Consider a company that has financed its assets using both debt and equity finance. The company's cost of capital is the minimum rate of return that it needs to earn on its assets in order to meet the cost of debt finance and provide the rate of return that shareholders require. To simplify matters, assume that the company's net operating cash flows remain constant in perpetuity. In this case, the annual interest cost of the company's debt is:

Interest rate (after tax) × market value of debt
$$= k_d(1 - t_e) \times D$$

where k_d = lenders' required rate of return—that is, the cost of debt
t_e = the effective company income tax rate
D = the market value of the company's debt

If t_c = 30 cents in the dollar and γ = 0.60, then t_e = 0.12. Then if k_d = 10 per cent per annum and D = $10 million, the annual interest cost of the company's debt is:

$0.1 \times (1 - 0.12) \times \$10\,000\,000$
$= \$880\,000$

Similarly, the minimum net cash flow required by shareholders is:

Required rate of return on equity × market value of equity
$$= k_e \times E$$

where k_e = shareholders' required rate of return—that is, the cost of equity
E = the market value of the company's equity

For example, if k_e = 20 per cent per annum and E = $10 million, the minimum cash flow required by shareholders is $2 million per year.

To meet these required rates of return, the company's minimum annual net operating cash flows must be:

$$k_e E + k_d(1 - t_e)D$$

Since we assume that cash flows are constant in perpetuity, the company's cost of capital k' is simply the annual net operating cash flow divided by the total market value of the company—that is:

$$k' = \frac{\text{annual net operating cash flow}}{\text{total market value of company}}$$

$$= \frac{k_e E + k_d(1 - t_e)D}{E + D}$$

$$= k_e \left[\frac{E}{E + D}\right] + k_d(1 - t_e)\left[\frac{D}{E + D}\right]$$

$$= k_e \left[\frac{E}{V}\right] + k_d(1 - t_e)\left[\frac{D}{V}\right] \qquad [14.2]$$

where $V = E + D$

= the total market value of the company

For example, if k_d = 10 per cent per annum, t_c = 30 cents in the dollar, γ = 0.60, D = $10 million, k_e = 20 per cent per annum and E = $10 million, the company's cost of capital k' is:

$$k' = (0.2)\left[\frac{10}{20}\right] + (0.10)(1 - 0.12)\left[\frac{10}{20}\right]$$

$$= 0.10 + 0.044$$

$$= 0.144 \text{ or } 14.4\% \text{ per annum}$$

Equation 14.2 shows that a company's cost of capital can be expressed as a weighted average of the costs of its equity and debt. Our derivation of Equation 14.2 shows that the concept underlying the WACC formula is that, to be acceptable, a new project should generate net cash flows that are sufficient to meet the after-tax cost of debt used to finance the project, as well as provide at least the required rate of return on the equity used to finance the project.

Equation 14.2, which we use for the valuation of companies and projects under the imputation tax system, is also derived in Appendix 14.1, where it appears as Equation A14.7. The valuation approach we adopt, which involves using an effective company tax rate in the calculation of the cash flows and the weighted average cost of capital, is consistent with the method derived by Monkhouse (1996).[2]

ESTIMATION OF THE COST OF CAPITAL: AN EXTENDED EXAMPLE

14.5

Equation 14.2 shows that a company's after-tax cost of capital is equal to the weighted average of the costs of debt and equity, where the cost of each individual source of capital is weighted according to its proportion in the company's capital structure. While the WACC has been explained assuming that there are only two classes of capital, namely equity and debt, in reality a company may issue different classes of shares, as well as different classes of debt. These additional classes of capital can be handled by extending Equation 14.2 to include all sources of finance used by the company. Consequently, estimation of the WACC requires the estimation of each variable in Equation 14.2 if only one class of debt and equity is employed, or an extended version of it if more than one class of debt and equity is employed.

To estimate the cost of capital it is necessary to estimate the cost of each source of finance and the proportion of each source of finance in the company's capital structure. Since we are estimating a cost of capital based on investors' expectations of future returns, it is important to use current market rates and current market values, rather than historical rates and book values.

Fixed-interest debt may be used as an example to explain why current market rates, rather than historical rates, must be used in estimating the cost of capital. Suppose that a company has a loan with a fixed interest rate of 10 per cent per annum, but the current market rate on similar loans is 15 per cent per annum. When estimating the company's cost of capital, the current market rate of 15 per cent should be used. This may appear to ignore the fact that the company is paying only 10 per cent on its existing loan. Surely there must be some advantage in paying only 10 per cent instead of 15 per cent? There *is* an advantage, but the company's shareholders have already received the benefit of the old, lower interest rate, and the current share price will take this into account. Investments to be made now must be attractive in comparison with the current cost of capital, and the old interest rate is irrelevant.

LEARNING OBJECTIVE 5

Estimate the cost of each source of capital and combine these costs into a weighted average cost of capital for a company

---

2 Monkhouse showed that the approach he derived is applicable to non-uniform cash flow streams of finite duration.

In the next four sections, we discuss estimation of the individual components of the WACC. Each component is illustrated using the information on Tasman Industries Ltd (TIL). The discussion concludes in Section 14.5.4 with an estimate of the company's WACC as at 30 June 2012, using the components calculated in the previous three sections. The sources of finance used by TIL are shown in Table 14.1.

TABLE 14.1 Tasman Industries Ltd: selected balance sheet data as at 30 June 2012

SOURCES OF FINANCE	BOOK VALUE ($M)
Commercial bills	20.000
Bank overdraft	7.368
Bonds	10.000
Preference shares, 8%	2.000
Ordinary shares: issued and paid up, 12 500 000 at 50 cents	6.250

TIL's financial manager also has the following information:

(a) The commercial bills have a current interest rate (yield) of 6.08 per cent per annum. The existing bills mature on 31 August 2012 but will be replaced by a further issue at that date.
(b) The interest rate on the bank overdraft is 9.5 per cent per annum, calculated daily and charged to TIL's account twice per year.
(c) There are 100 bonds, each with a face value of $100 000 and a coupon interest rate of 10 per cent per annum, payable on 30 June and 31 December each year. The bonds will be redeemed at their face value on 30 June 2015. On 30 June 2012 the market value of each bond was $102 474.18.
(d) The preference shares are irredeemable, have a face value of $2 and pay a dividend rate of 8 per cent per annum. Dividends are payable on 30 June and 31 December each year.[3] On 30 June 2012, the market price of each preference share was $1.50.
(e) TIL pays dividends on its ordinary shares once per year on 30 June. The latest dividend was 17.5 cents, fully franked. On 30 June 2012, the market price of each ordinary share was $4.20.
(f) The company income tax rate is 30 per cent.

14.5.1 THE COST OF DEBT

Companies can raise debt from a variety of sources. There are short-term and long-term sources of debt and debt may be marketable or non-marketable. The overall cost of debt for a company is a weighted average of the costs of its individual sources of debt. This weighted average cost will not be accurate if the individual costs are expressed inconsistently. For example, it would be inconsistent to average nominal interest rates that are based on different repayment frequencies. To ensure consistency, all costs of debt for TIL will be expressed as effective annual rates.

The after-tax cost of debt is found by multiplying the before-tax cost by $(1 - t_e)$, where t_e is the effective company income tax rate. For example, if the before-tax cost of debt is 10 per cent per annum, the company income tax is 30 cents in the dollar, and the proportion of tax collected from the company that is claimed by shareholders is 0.60, then the effective company tax rate is $30(1 - 0.6) = 12$ cents in the dollar and the after-tax cost of debt is $10(1 - 0.12) = 8.80$ per cent per annum. This calculation assumes that the company is operating profitably and that there is no time lag in the payment of company

---

[3] It is assumed for simplicity in this example that coupon interest payments are made on 30 June and 31 December, and that preference dividends are also payable on 30 June and 31 December.

income tax. The calculation is the same for each item of debt and is reflected in Equation 14.2. Therefore, in this example the annual interest rates applicable to the individual sources of debt finance will be stated as before-tax rates and the conversion to an after-tax cost of debt will be made in the final WACC calculation.

For convenience, debt may be classified as shown in Table 14.2.

TABLE 14.2 Types of debt

	SHORT-TERM DEBT	**LONG-TERM DEBT**
Marketable	Commercial paper	Bonds
	Commercial bills	Debentures
		Unsecured notes
		Floating-rate notes
Non-marketable	Accounts payable	Mortgage loans
	Bank overdraft	Finance leases
	Money market loans	Term loans

Cost of short-term debt

Short-term debt securities, such as commercial bills and commercial paper, are marketable, and current interest rates are quoted in the financial press.[4] From these quotations the current effective annual interest rate on marketable debt can be calculated. In the case of TIL's commercial bills, the quoted interest rate is 6.08 per cent per annum. The market conventions are to quote nominal annual rates and to use simple interest for short-term securities. In calculating the effective annual interest rate on the bills, the first step is to convert the nominal rate of 6.08 per cent per annum to the effective rate i for the 62 days from 30 June to 31 August. Therefore:

$$i = 6.08 \times \frac{62}{365}$$
$$= 1.032\,767\%$$

The second step is to convert this rate to an annual rate as follows:

$$(1+i)^{\frac{365}{62}} - 1$$
$$= (1.010\,327\,67)^{5.8871} - 1$$
$$= 0.062\,355$$

Therefore, the rate applicable to bills issued by TIL is approximately 6.24 per cent per annum before tax.

To calculate the WACC it is also necessary to know the market value of debt, which can be found using the nominal interest rate. Therefore, for a commercial bill or commercial paper:

$$P = \frac{F}{\left[1 + \frac{jt}{365}\right]} \qquad [14.3]$$

---

[4] Details of these securities are provided in Chapter 10.

where P = current market price of the security
F = face value of the security
j = nominal interest rate per annum
t = the number of days from the date of price calculation to the maturity date

For TIL's commercial bills, the market value at 30 June 2012 is:

$$p = \frac{\$20\,000\,000}{\left[1 + 0.0608 \times \frac{62}{365}\right]}$$

$= \$19\,795\,558$

The cost of non-marketable interest-bearing debt, such as a bank overdraft, will be its current interest rate, converted if necessary to an effective annual rate. The interest rate on TIL's overdraft is 9.5 per cent per annum or 4.75 per cent per half-year. Therefore, the effective annual rate is:

$(1.0475)^2 - 1$

$= 0.097\,256$

That is, the rate applicable to the bank overdraft is approximately 9.73 per cent per annum before tax. Other forms of non-marketable short-term debt such as taxes payable, wages payable and accounts payable, which do not have an explicit interest cost, should be excluded. The reason is *not* that these forms of debt are 'free'; rather, their costs are accounted for in other ways. For example, the cost of trade credit (the difference between the price of goods purchased with cash on delivery and the price when purchased on credit) has already been deducted in calculating the cash flows. Therefore, accounts payable do not have to be serviced out of those cash flows; to include accounts payable as a source of finance would be inconsistent.

Cost of long-term debt

Some forms of long-term debt, such as debentures, unsecured notes and corporate bonds, are marketable. We use the term 'bonds' to refer to these long-term debt securities. Given a current market price, P, the effective interest rate on a company's bonds is equal to the discount rate that equates the market price of the bond with the discounted value of the cash flows promised under the terms of the bond. Most bonds pay interest twice a year, and the price of such a bond on a coupon payment date is given by:

$$P = \left\{\frac{R}{i}\left[1 - \frac{1}{(1+i)^n}\right] + \frac{C}{(1+i)^n}\right\} \qquad [14.4]$$

where P = current market price of the bonds
i = the effective interest rate per half-year
R = interest payments = $\frac{Fj}{2}$, where F = face value of the bonds, and j = nominal interest rate per annum
C = redemption price of the bonds
n = number of future interest payments

Equation 14.4 can be used to calculate the effective interest rate per half-year and it is then a simple matter to calculate the annual rate.

The logic of Equation 14.4 can be explained using the bonds issued by TIL as an example. On 30 June 2012, a TIL bond was sold for $102\,474.18$. The terms of the bond were as follows: face value, F, is $100\,000$; nominal interest rate, j, is 10 per cent per annum payable on 30 June and 31 December each year; redemption price, C, is $100\,000$; and maturity date is 30 June 2015. Therefore, each interest payment, R, is equal to ($100\,000$)($0.10/2$) = $5000. There are six interest payments to be made, the first on 31 December 2012, then two in each of the years 2013 and 2014 and the last on 30 June 2015.[5] The redemption price is a lump sum payable in exactly 6 half-years' time. At a yield (or required rate of return) of i per half-year, the value of the bond calculated as at 30 June 2012 is given by:

(Present value of the interest payments) + (present value of the lump sum)

$$= \frac{\$5000}{i}\left[1-\frac{1}{(1+i)^6}\right] + \frac{\$100\,000}{(1+i)^6}$$

Therefore:

$$\$102\,474.18 = \left\{\frac{\$5000}{i}\left[1-\frac{1}{(1+i)^6}\right] + \frac{\$100\,000}{(1+i)^6}\right\}$$

As noted in Section 4.2, equations of this type cannot be solved directly for i but the required value for i can be found by other methods. In this case, i equals 0.0452. This is shown as follows:

$$\left\{\frac{\$5000}{0.0452}\left[1-\frac{1}{(1.0452)^6}\right] + \frac{\$100\,000}{(1.0452)^6}\right\}$$
$$= \left\{(\$5000)(5.154\,546) + \frac{\$100\,000}{1.303\,756}\right\}$$
$$= \{\$25\,772.73 + \$76\,701.45\}$$
$$= \$102\,474.18$$

The required rate of return on this bond is therefore 4.52 per cent per half-year. Converting this rate to an effective annual rate gives a rate equal to:

$$(1.0452)^2 - 1 = 0.092\,443$$

Therefore, the rate applicable to TIL's bonds is approximately 9.24 per cent per annum before tax.

Where a fixed-interest debt contract, such as a mortgage, is not marketable, the current cost of the debt cannot be measured in the way described for bonds. The best measure of the current cost in this case is an estimate of the interest rate that the company would now have to pay to raise mortgage funds on conditions that match those of the existing mortgage.

14.5.2 THE COST OF PREFERENCE SHARES

Preference shares have attributes of both debt and equity. As explained in Section 10.8.3, it is usual for irredeemable preference shares to be cumulative and non-participating. Such preference shares pay a fixed dividend per share, D_p, at regular time intervals. Although the payment of a preference dividend is at the discretion of the Board of Directors, it is unusual to omit payment. As a result, preference dividends form a perpetuity, and for a share that pays dividends twice a year, the share price on a preference dividend payment date is given by:

$$P = \left[\frac{D_p}{i}\right] \quad [14.5]$$

where P = current market price of preference shares
i = effective yield per half-year
D_p = half-yearly preference dividend per share

---

[5] These six payments comprise an ordinary annuity. See Section 3.6.2 for an explanation of the valuation of an ordinary annuity.

For TIL's preference shares the market price was $1.50 on 30 June 2012 and the next dividend of 8 cents per share is due on 31 December. Therefore:

$$\$1.50 = \left[\frac{\$0.08}{i}\right]$$

In this case, $i = 0.05333$, so the effective annual cost of the preference shares, k_p, is:

$$k_p = (1.05333)^2 - 1$$
$$= 0.109511$$

Therefore, the rate applicable to TIL's preference shares is approximately 10.95 per cent per annum after company tax.

If the preference shares are redeemable on a predetermined date, the calculation of the cost of preference shares is the same as the calculation of the effective interest rate on debt. However, preference dividends are generally a distribution of profit rather than a tax-deductible expense. Thus, certain preference shares may carry franked dividends, and their cost can be calculated using the procedures outlined for ordinary shares.

14.5.3 THE COST OF ORDINARY SHARES

In contrast to debt, ordinary shares issued by a company do not involve a contractual obligation to provide any specific return. Therefore, it is necessary to estimate the rate of return that investors expect the shares to provide in the future. One approach is to focus on the company's expected future dividend stream and estimate the discount rate implied by the current share price. This approach was discussed in Section 4.3.2 and is summarised in Equation 14.6:

$$P_0 = \sum_{t=1}^{\infty} \frac{E(D_t)}{(1+k_e)^t} \qquad [14.6]$$

where P_0 = current share price
$E(D_t)$ = expected dividend per share to be paid at time t
k_e = required rate of return—that is, the cost of ordinary shares

The current share price will be known and, given an estimate of expected future dividends, an estimate of the cost of ordinary shares can be derived. In estimating a company's future dividend stream it is usual to make simplifying assumptions. For example, if it is assumed that the dividend per share will grow at a constant rate, g, indefinitely, then as shown in Section 4.3.2, Equation 14.6 becomes:

$$P_0 = \frac{D_0(1+g)}{k_e - g} \qquad [14.7]$$

where D_0 = the current period's dividend per share

The model expressed by Equation 14.7 is usually referred to as the **dividend growth model**. To find k_e, Equation 14.7 may be rewritten as:

$$k_e = \frac{D_0(1+g)}{P_0} + g$$

dividend growth model
model expressing the value of a share as the sum of the present values of future dividends where the dividends are assumed to grow at a constant rate

TIL's share price at 30 June 2012 was $4.20 and the latest annual dividend was 17.5 cents per share, fully franked. Since the dividend is fully franked, the 17.5 cent dividend carries a tax franking credit of $\$0.175 \times \left[\frac{t_c}{1-t_c}\right]$. With a company tax rate of 30 per cent, this tax franking credit is $\$0.175 \times \frac{0.30}{0.70} = \$0.075$.

This tax franking credit represents personal tax that has been paid by TIL on behalf of its shareholders and must be added to the cash dividend to give the after-company-tax dividend D_0^*. Therefore, D_0^* is $0.175 + $0.075 = $0.250. If the dividend growth rate is estimated to be 8 per cent per annum, then TIL's cost of equity can be calculated as follows:

$$k_e = \frac{D_0^*(1+g)}{P_0} + g$$

$$= \frac{\$0.250(1.08)}{\$4.20} + 0.08$$

$$= 0.1443$$

Therefore, the after-company-tax cost of equity applicable to TIL's ordinary shares is 14.43 per cent.

It was shown in Section 4.3.2 that estimates of current share price based on the dividend growth model are extremely sensitive to estimates of the future growth rate in dividend per share. The same problem arises when the model is used to estimate the cost of equity. Therefore, while the model is theoretically correct given its assumptions, the practical problems involved in its application mean that the CAPM may be preferred. The CAPM describes the equilibrium relationship between systematic risk (beta) and expected returns on risky assets, and can therefore be used to estimate the cost of equity. The implementation of the CAPM is discussed in Section 7.6.3 and requires estimation of the risk-free interest rate, R_f, the expected rate of return on the market portfolio, $E(R_M)$, and the systematic risk of equity, β_e.

After estimates of the three variables have been prepared, the cost of equity can be calculated using Equation 14.1. As noted in Section 14.3, if the expected return on the market, $E(R_M)$, is based on rates of return observed under the imputation system, the observed rates should be adjusted by adding back a franking premium, τ. This adjustment is needed to express the return on the market on an after-company-tax basis. Over the period since the introduction of the imputation tax system in Australia in 1987 until 2005, Brailsford, Handley and Maheswaran (2008) estimate the franking premium to be of the order of 0.5 per cent per annum. Therefore, Equation 14.1 becomes:

$$k_e = R_f + \beta_e \left[E(R_M + \tau) - R_f \right]$$

If TIL's financial manager has the following estimates:

R_f = 5% or 0.05
$E(R_M)$ = 10% or 0.10
τ = 0.5% or 0.005
β_e = 1.2

then: k_e = 0.05 + 1.2(0.10 + 0.005 − 0.05)
 = 0.116 or 11.6%

14.5.4 THE COMPANY'S COST OF CAPITAL

After the explicit cost of each source of funds has been calculated, they should be checked for consistency. For example, the estimated cost of ordinary shares should exceed the estimated cost of preference shares, which in turn should exceed the estimated cost of debt. The company's cost of capital may then be calculated by applying the appropriate weights to the cost of each source of funds. The appropriate weights are the proportion that each source represents of the total sources used to finance proposed projects. If the company's capital structure is expected to change, the weights should be the proportions of debt and equity in the target capital structure. However, unless there is reason to believe that implementing new projects will alter the company's optimal capital structure, its current capital structure can be used to calculate the weights. The weights should be calculated using market values.

Debt

Recall that TIL has three classes of debt comprising commercial bills, bonds and bank overdraft.

(a) The market value at 30 June 2012 of TIL's commercial bills was calculated previously to be $19 795 558.
(b) Each TIL bond had a market value of $102 474.18, so with 100 bonds on issue, their total market value will be $10 247 418.
(c) Bank overdrafts carry a variable interest rate, which is adjusted in accordance with fluctuations in market rates. Therefore, the market value of a bank overdraft will always equal its book value, which, in this case, is $7 368 000. The data for TIL's debt are summarised in Table 14.3.

TABLE 14.3 Calculation of the weighted average cost of debt for TIL

TYPE OF DEBT	MARKET VALUE ($)	PROPORTION	COST (%)	WEIGHTED COST
Commercial bills	19 795 558	0.529 14	6.24	3.301 82
Bank overdraft	7 368 000	0.196 95	9.73	1.916 30
Bonds	10 247 418	0.273 91	9.24	2.530 97
	37 410 976			7.749 09

The average cost of debt for TIL is approximately 7.75 per cent before tax.

Equity

TIL also has two classes of equity comprising preference shares and ordinary shares.

(a) The $2 preference shares issued by TIL have a book value of $2 million, so it is clear that there are 1 million shares outstanding. Since the share price at 30 June 2012 was $1.50, the total market value is $1 500 000.
(b) There were 12 500 000 ordinary shares issued by TIL and the share price was $4.20, giving a market value of $52 500 000. The data for TIL's equity are summarised in Table 14.4.

TABLE 14.4 Calculation of the weighted average cost of equity for TIL

TYPE OF EQUITY	MARKET VALUE ($)	PROPORTION	COST (%)	WEIGHTED COST
Preference shares	1 500 000	0.0278	10.95	0.304 41
Ordinary shares	52 500 000	0.9722	11.60	11.277 52
	54 000 000			11.581 93

The average cost of equity for TIL is approximately 11.58 per cent.

These weighted average costs of debt and equity can then be combined to form a weighted average cost of capital for TIL using Equation 14.2. The total value of the company is equal to the market value of debt plus the market value of equity, which for TIL is $37 410 976 + $54 000 000 = $91 410 976.

If Equation 14.2 is used, then the effective company tax rate, t_e, must also be estimated, and this means that the proportion of the tax collected from the company that is claimed as tax credits by shareholders, γ, must be estimated. As explained in Section 11.4.4, the value of γ depends on the company's dividend policy and on the tax class(es) of its shareholders. Even if a company adopts a policy of paying the maximum possible franked dividends, it will be difficult to determine the appropriate value of γ in cases where some of the company's shares are held by resident taxpayers (for whom theoretically γ equals 1) and other shares are held by tax exempt or non-resident investors (for whom theoretically γ equals 0).

The value of γ should reflect the value of tax credits to the marginal (as distinct from average) shareholder. As Officer (1994, p. 4) points out, if there is a market for tax credits, the market price could be used to estimate the value of γ for the marginal investor. However, any market in tax credits is hidden, so the 'market price' of tax credits is usually estimated through dividend drop-off ratios. As discussed in Section 11.4.4, these estimates are unfortunately subject to a large degree of error. While Hathaway and Officer (2004) and Walker and Partington (1999) both provide positive estimates for γ, Cannavan, Finn and Gray (2004) find that γ may be zero. Beggs and Skeels (2006) report evidence consistent with a zero value for γ prior to the year 2000, when changes in the tax system allowed for the refund of unused franking credits—and a positive value for γ subsequent to this legislative change. For TIL we will assume that γ equals 0.60, which means that with a statutory company tax rate of 30 cents in the dollar, the effective company tax rate, t_e, is 0.12.

Using Equation 14.2, the weighted average cost of capital for TIL is:

$$k' = k_e \left[\frac{E}{V}\right] + k_d (1 - t_e) \left[\frac{D}{V}\right]$$

$$= 0.1158 \left[\frac{\$54\,000\,000}{\$91\,410\,976}\right] + 0.0775(1 - 0.12)\left[\frac{\$37\,410\,976}{\$91\,410\,976}\right]$$

$$= 0.096\,319$$

or approximately 9.6 per cent after effective company tax.

> **issue costs**
> costs of raising new capital by issuing securities, including underwriting fees and legal, accounting and printing expenses incurred in preparing a prospectus or other offer documents. Also known as *flotation costs*

14.5.5 ISSUE COSTS AND THE COST OF CAPITAL

So far we have discussed the cost of capital without recognising that if a company undertakes a new project, it may incur **issue costs** involved in raising new capital. These costs include underwriters' fees as well as legal and administration costs.

When evaluating a project, such costs should not be included in the cost of capital. As we emphasised in Section 14.2, the cost of capital is an opportunity cost that depends on the risk of the project in which the capital is invested. It does not depend on the source of the funds. However, issue costs will be incurred if a project is undertaken and cannot be ignored. They must therefore be included in the cash flows associated with the project. The incorporation of issue costs into project evaluation is illustrated in Example 14.2.

> **LEARNING OBJECTIVE 6**
> Explain how to treat issue costs in project evaluation

EXAMPLE 14.2

TIL is evaluating a project that will require an initial investment of $10 million and will generate an annual after-tax cash flow of $2 million in perpetuity. The net present value of this project, ignoring issue costs, is:

$$NPV = -\$10\,000\,000 + \frac{\$2\,000\,000}{0.096}$$

$$= \$10\,833\,333$$

What is the net present value of the project, after allowing for issue costs if issue costs for equity, f_e, are 8 per cent and issue costs for debt, f_d, are 2 per cent?

SOLUTION

Using the market value weights of TIL's outstanding securities, the weighted average issue cost, f_a, will be:

$$f_a = f_e \left[\frac{E}{V}\right] + f_d \left(\frac{D}{V}\right)$$

$$= 0.08 \left(\frac{\$54\,000\,000}{\$91\,410\,976}\right) + 0.02 \left(\frac{\$37\,410\,976}{\$91\,410\,976}\right)$$

$$= 0.055\,44$$

continued →

> **Example 14.2** *continued*
>
> Therefore, in order to raise a net $10 million, TIL will need to issue securities worth $\frac{\$10\,000\,000}{(1 - 0.055\,44)} = \$10\,586\,940$.
> The net present value of the project, including issue costs, is:
>
> $$NPV = -\$10\,586\,940 + \frac{\$2\,000\,000}{0.096}$$
> $$= \$10\,246\,393$$
>
> In this case the project should still be undertaken even after issue costs have been included in the cash flows.

Note that the weighted average issue cost was used in Example 14.2 rather than the issue cost for debt or the issue cost for equity. It is incorrect to assume that one project will be financed by debt and hence will incur the issue costs for debt, while another project will be financed by equity and hence will incur the issue costs for equity. If a company is to maintain its optimal or target capital structure, both debt and equity must be raised over time. It follows that all of a company's projects are effectively financed by a 'pool' of funds consisting of both debt and equity, and all projects must be assumed to incur the weighted average issue costs.

14.6 PROJECT AND COMPANY COST OF CAPITAL

A company's cost of capital, as calculated in the previous section, should be used as an estimate of the cost of capital for a new project only when certain conditions are met. These conditions follow from the fact that all the variables in the WACC formula apply to the company as a whole. Therefore, a company's WACC will reflect the risk of its existing projects. It follows that a company's WACC should only be applied to projects that are identical, apart from their size, to the company's existing projects.

LEARNING OBJECTIVE 7

Understand the distinction between the cost of capital for a project and a company's weighted average cost of capital

The consequences of using a single discount rate to evaluate all projects are illustrated in Figure 14.1. The broken line represents the cost of capital k' for the company and the solid line represents the security market line, which is simply the graphical representation of the trade-off between risk and expected return

FIGURE 14.1 Applying a single discount rate, k', to all projects

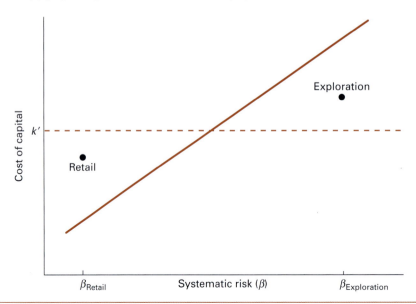

implied by the CAPM. Assume that a company, Eastfarmers Ltd, is a diversified firm that has multiple divisions operating in different industrial sectors. Each year the heads of each of the divisions meet with the senior management team of the company to pitch new projects that they would like funded by the firm. The head of the retail division puts forward a proposal to open up a new retail outlet in a growth suburb while the head of the exploration division asks for funding to open up a new coal mine in Western Australia. The risk–return coordinates for the two projects are denoted by the titles of the divisions that suggested the project.

If the company applies the single discount rate k' to all projects, then the project suggested by the retail division will be rejected. Its expected rate of return is less than k', even though it is greater than the required rate of return consistent with its systematic risk—that is, β_{Retail}. Conversely, the project suggested by the exploration division will be accepted. Its expected rate of return exceeds k', even though it is less than the required rate of return consistent with its systematic risk—that is, $\beta_{Exploration}$.

Therefore, a likely consequence for a diversified company that uses a single discount rate is that it will make incorrect investment decisions. It will accept some projects that have a negative expected net present value, and reject some projects that have a positive expected net present value. Moreover, high-systematic-risk divisions will find it comparatively easy to have their proposed projects accepted, while low-systematic-risk divisions will find it difficult to have their proposed projects accepted. As a result, the systematic risk of the company will drift upward over time. The low-systematic-risk divisions are likely to stagnate and may even be closed down.

The company's cost of capital is also based on its existing capital structure. If the debt capacity of a new project differs from that of the existing projects, then this difference could affect the project's cost of capital. Therefore, another condition is that WACC should be used only if the new project is not expected to change the company's optimal or target capital structure.

In principle, each proposed project should be valued using a discount rate appropriate for the risk of that particular project. Where a company's operations are in more than one industry and these industries differ in risk, the company's cost of capital is unlikely to be appropriate for evaluating a new project in any of the individual industries, or in another industry that the company may plan to enter. However, the company's cost of capital should be appropriate for evaluating an expansion by a company that operates in only one industry. Where a company has divisions in different industries but the assets within each division are reasonably uniform in terms of risk, it is reasonable for management to calculate a cost of capital for each of the company's divisions.

There are two approaches that are used to calculate the cost of equity for divisions of a company. These approaches are the 'pure play' approach and the direct estimation approach.

14.6.1 CALCULATING THE COST OF CAPITAL FOR DIVISIONS USING THE 'PURE PLAY' APPROACH

The approach that is most commonly recommended for calculating the cost of capital for a project or division relies on identifying other companies that operate only in the same industry as the proposed project or division (Fuller & Kerr 1981). Such companies are known as **pure plays**. The steps for estimating the cost of capital for a project or division using data for a pure-play company are as follows:

(a) Identify a pure-play company with operations similar to the proposed project.
(b) Estimate the beta of the pure-play company's equity.
(c) Adjust the equity beta for financial leverage to obtain an estimate of the pure-play company's asset beta, which is the beta that the pure-play company would have if it were all-equity financed—that is, the beta of equity has been 'unlevered'.
(d) 'Relever' the asset beta, based on the financial leverage of the company that is considering the project, to obtain an estimate of the beta of equity for the project.

LEARNING OBJECTIVE 8
Estimate the cost of capital for a division of a diversified company

pure play
company that operates almost entirely in only one industry or line of business

(e) Use the CAPM to estimate the cost of equity for the project.
(f) Calculate the WACC of the project using the target debt–equity ratio of the company that is considering the project.

As discussed in Section 14.4.1, in the absence of taxes, the beta of a company's assets is simply a weighted average of the betas of its equity and its debt—that is:

$$\beta_a = \beta_e \left[\frac{E}{D+E} \right] + \beta_d \left[\frac{D}{D+E} \right] \quad [14.8]$$

where β_a = the beta of the company's assets
β_e = the beta of the company's equity
β_d = the beta of the company's debt
D = the market value of debt
E = the market value of equity

If the company's debt is assumed to be risk-free—that is, $\beta_d = 0$—then Equation 14.8 can be simplified and rearranged to give:[6]

$$\beta_e = \beta_a \left[1 + \frac{D}{E} \right] \quad [14.9]$$

This equation can be rearranged to give:

$$\beta_a = \frac{\beta_e}{1 + \dfrac{D}{E}} \quad [14.10]$$

This use of the pure-play procedure is illustrated in Example 14.3.

EXAMPLE 14.3

Perco Parts Ltd has two divisions: one manufactures car parts and the other distributes agricultural machinery. The agricultural machinery division is considering an expansion project. Perco has a target debt–equity ratio of 1:3 that will not be changed by the new project. Perco's financial manager has identified Style Farm Equipment Ltd as a company with the same business risk as the new project. Style Farm Equipment has a debt–equity ratio of 1:1, and its equity has a beta of 1.25. The risk-free interest rate is 9 per cent per annum and the risk premium for the market portfolio is estimated to be 8 per cent per annum. It is also assumed that Perco can borrow at the risk-free interest rate of 9 per cent, that the statutory company income tax rate is 30 per cent and that the proportion of the tax collected from the company that is claimed by shareholders is 0.60, giving an effective company tax rate of 12 per cent.

The procedure outlined above requires a relationship between equity betas and asset betas. Equations 14.9 and 14.10 may be used to estimate an asset beta and the cost of capital for Perco's agricultural equipment project. The first step is to use Equation 14.10 to calculate the beta of Style Farm Equipment's assets:

$$\beta_a = \frac{1.25}{1+1}$$
$$= 0.625$$

Next, Equation 14.9 is used to calculate the beta of equity for the project:

$$\beta_e = 0.625 \left[1 + \frac{1}{3} \right]$$
$$= 0.8333$$

---

[6] The conditions under which various relationships between the betas of a company's equity and its assets apply are discussed by Taggart (1991).

That is, the beta for the equity proportion of Perco's proposed investment is estimated to be approximately 0.833. The cost of equity for the project can now be estimated using the CAPM. The cost of equity is calculated as follows:

$$k_e = R_f + \beta_e \left[E(R_M + \tau) - R_f \right]$$
$$= 0.09 + 0.833\,(0.08)$$
$$= 0.15667$$

The project's WACC can now be calculated as:

$$k' = k_e \left[\frac{E}{V}\right] + k_d(1-t_e)\left[\frac{D}{V}\right]$$
$$= 0.15667 \left[\frac{3}{4}\right] + 0.09\,(1-0.12)\left[\frac{1}{4}\right]$$
$$= 0.137303$$

Therefore, based on the pure-play approach, the appropriate discount rate for Perco Parts' financial manager to use when evaluating the proposed project is 13.73 per cent.

The pure-play approach is used by some companies but it involves conceptual and practical problems. The conceptual problems concern the issue of how best to adjust betas for financial leverage. The adjustments used in Example 14.3 are only approximate because they are based on the simplifying assumption that corporate debt is risk-free. Other, more complex, models have been suggested, but such models are generally based on a specific theory of capital structure. Also, the appropriate leverage adjustment depends on the company's capital structure policy.[7] The main practical problem is that pure-play companies are rare. Even if some pure-play companies are available, relying only on data from such companies means that a great deal of information from diversified companies is ignored.

14.6.2 CALCULATING THE COST OF CAPITAL FOR DIVISIONS USING THE DIRECT ESTIMATION APPROACH

An alternative approach that overcomes the problems associated with the pure-play approach is the direct estimation approach outlined by Harris, O'Brien and Wakeman (1989). This approach involves estimating, directly, divisional weighted average costs of capital. It is assumed that a diversified company's WACC is itself a weighted average of the WACCs of its divisions, where the weights are the values of the divisions as proportions of the total value of the company—that is:

$$k' = \sum_{j=1}^{n} w_j k'_j \qquad [14.11]$$

where k' = the company cost of capital
k'_j = the cost of capital for the jth division
w_j = the ratio of the value of the jth division to the total value of the company

---

[7] For example, the relationship between asset betas and equity betas depends on whether the debt associated with the project is assumed to be constant, or whether the debt is adjusted to maintain a constant debt–value ratio over time. See Taggart (1991) and Conine and Tamarkin (1985). The taxation of capital gains is discussed in Section 11.4.2.

Equation 14.11 can be used to estimate divisional costs of capital. The procedure is illustrated in Example 14.4.

EXAMPLE 14.4

Three companies—A, B and C—operate in two industries, 1 and 2. Company A has 40 per cent of its assets invested in Industry 1 and 60 per cent in Industry 2. For companies B and C, the proportions are 30:70 and 80:20, respectively. The costs of capital for companies A, B and C have been estimated to be 15.3 per cent, 15.85 per cent and 13.1 per cent, respectively. Use this information to estimate the cost of capital for divisions that operate in industries 1 and 2.

SOLUTION

It is assumed that the risks, and therefore the costs of capital, in a given industry are the same for each company. Equation 14.11 holds for each company, so it can be written as follows:

Company A: $0.153 = 0.4k'_1 + 0.6k'_2$
Company B: $0.1585 = 0.3k'_1 + 0.7k'_2$
Company C: $0.131 = 0.8k'_1 + 0.2k'_2$

Any two of these equations can be solved simultaneously to give $k'_1 = 12\%$ and $k'_2 = 17.5\%$.

Example 14.4 shows that it is possible to infer divisional costs of capital from information on diversified companies, provided that the following information is available:

(a) the WACC of each company
(b) the ratio of the value of each division to total company value for each company.

In practice, these variables will have to be estimated, which means that the estimates will involve some degree of error. Consequently, it will not be possible to find an exact analytical solution for the divisional costs of capital. This problem can be overcome by using regression to estimate these costs. For this purpose Equation 14.11 is written as:

$$k' = a_1 w_1 + a_2 w_2 + \ldots + a_n w_n + e$$

where e = an error term with a mean of zero

In this regression, each company's cost of capital is one observation of the dependent variable k', and each company's division weights are the corresponding measures of the independent variables w_1 to w_n. The regression coefficients a_1 to a_n are estimates of the costs of capital for industries 1 to n. The estimate for a given industry can be used as a measure of the divisional cost of capital for all companies that operate in that industry, without any adjustment for financial leverage. This does not mean that differences in leverage are ignored. Rather, if different industries have different debt capacities and these differences affect the cost of capital, then such effects should automatically be reflected in the cost of capital estimates. This is one significant advantage compared with the pure-play approach. Another advantage is flexibility. For example, to estimate the company WACCs there is no need to employ any particular model such as the CAPM. Other models such as the dividend growth model can be used to estimate the cost of equity as a component of the WACC. On the other hand, the divisional weights w_j must be estimated for each company. In theory, these weights should be based on market values, which are typically unknown. Therefore, in practice, the weights may be based on book values or, perhaps, divisional sales.

FINANCE IN ACTION

INSIGHTS INTO WACC ESTIMATION FROM THE ENERGY INDUSTRY

Insights into the practical issues associated with estimating a company's weighted average cost of capital (WACC) is provided by considering what happens in the highly regulated energy industry. Every 5 years, the peak regulatory body for this sector, the Australian Energy Regulator (AER), makes a determination of the rate of return that electricity distributors can generate from their assets, which in turn ultimately determines the price that these companies can charge for their services. The first stage of the process involves the AER issuing a draft decision outlining how it intends to calculate the WACC for each company. This is followed by a period of time where the AER receives submissions from interested parties including from the electricity distributors. Not surprisingly, the electricity distributors take this opportunity to argue for a change in the methodology used to estimate their cost of capital—where their suggested changes would invariably result in an increase in their cost of capital. The final stage involves the AER publishing its final decision via a Distribution Determination, where it not only informs the market of the appropriate WACC for each distributor, but also outlines the reasons for its decision. This comprehensive report is often over a thousand pages long and is publically available at **www.aer.gov.au**.

In 2010 the AER conducted this process for Victorian electricity distributors. Following the publication of the AER's draft decision, submissions were made by the distributors about the estimation of the various parameters of the WACC that would apply from 2011 to 2015—and one of the key points of difference between the AER and distributors related to the estimate of the market risk premium used in the capital asset pricing model (CAPM). While the AER suggested a premium of 6.5 per cent per annum, the electricity distributors argued that this should be 8 per cent per annum. This was an important point to consider as the AER's resultant WACC estimate would be 9.68 per cent per annum while the WACC estimated by the electricity providers—based on their own parameter estimates—would be 10.86 per cent per annum.

In support of the proposed estimate of a market risk premium of 8 per cent, the electricity distributors argued that, among other things, expected conditions over the next 5-year period were inherently more risky and hence could not be considered 'normal'. Consequently, they argued that the use of a long-term average of the difference between equity returns and the rate of return on risk-free securities was not appropriate. In contrast, the Consumer Utilities Advocacy Centre, an independent organisation established by the Victorian Government to represent the views of utility consumers, argued that the market risk premium should be set at 6 per cent on the basis that, since the AER's publication of its draft decision, the Australian economy had actually improved significantly and that a more secure global economic position should translate to lower costs of finance. After due consideration of a number of factors, including commentary provided by the Reserve Bank of Australia, the AER decided to confirm its market risk premium estimate of 6.5 per cent.

14.7 THE WEIGHTED AVERAGE COST OF CAPITAL AND ALTERNATIVE PROJECT EVALUATION TECHNIQUES

It has been emphasised that the weighted average cost of capital (WACC) has important limitations. In particular, it can only be estimated directly for a whole company, and a company's cost of capital should only be used to evaluate new projects that are identical to the company's existing operations. Another problem is that the WACC lends itself to misinterpretation because it makes debt appear to be cheaper than equity. For example, in the TIL case, the cost of equity was more than 11 per cent,

LEARNING OBJECTIVE 9
Understand the advantages and disadvantages of using the weighted average cost of capital in project evaluation

but the cost of debt was less than 8 per cent. An observer could easily jump to the conclusion that a company's cost of capital could be reduced by increasing the proportion of debt in its capital structure. That conclusion is likely to be incorrect because it ignores some important effects of financial leverage. First, if leverage is increased, the risk of the borrower defaulting will increase, and lenders will demand higher interest rates. Second, as discussed in Section 12.3.2, the risk faced by shareholders will also increase and the cost of equity will increase. As a result of these changes, the WACC could increase rather than decrease. The WACC is designed as a tool to be used in evaluating investment decisions. It can give misleading results if attempts are made to use it to analyse financing decisions.

The adjusted present value (APV) method is an alternative technique that calculates separately the value created by a project and the value created by the financing decision. This technique involves forecasting a project's after-tax cash flows assuming that the project is financed entirely by equity. The net present value of these cash flows is found by using the rate of return that would be required by investors if the project were financed entirely by equity. Any value created by taxation effects associated with debt financing may then be added to obtain the total value created by undertaking the project. Similarly, the value of any government subsidies that may be offered to the company to undertake the project may be added to the total value.[8]

Another limitation of the WACC approach to project evaluation is that it only includes cash flows directly associated with the project. It does not include strategic options that may be associated with the project. These options include the possibility of reducing or expanding the scale of the project, or abandoning the project entirely. Another option might be to wait before investing. Section 18.8.6 discusses how option pricing models may be used to incorporate these options into project evaluation.

Despite its limitations, the WACC also has considerable strengths, including flexibility and relative simplicity. It is flexible in that there are different versions of the WACC, each of which is correct, provided that it is used in conjunction with the appropriate definition of net cash flows. It is also conceptually easier to understand than alternative project evaluation techniques and is the most widely used.

14.8 TAX ISSUES IN PROJECT EVALUATION

In Chapters 5 and 6, methods of project evaluation were discussed and the reasons for using the net present value method were outlined. However, in those chapters the effects of taxes were not considered. The effects of taxes are considered in this section.

14.8.1 EFFECT OF TAXES ON NET CASH FLOWS

LEARNING OBJECTIVE 10
Understand the effects of taxes on project cash flows

If there were no taxes, the magnitude and timing of a project's cash inflows and outflows would be the only relevant cash flow information for project evaluation purposes. However, under the provisions of the *Income Tax Assessment Act 1936*, tax is assessed on the taxable income of individuals and companies. Taxable income is the difference between gross income and certain allowable deductions specified in the Act. Income tax payable is generally calculated as a percentage of taxable income. Income tax is a major cash outflow for most companies and its effect on investment projects should be considered, together with other cash inflows and outflows.

The tax relating to a project should be treated as a cash outflow when the tax is paid. For example, if tax were usually paid at the end of the year following the year of income, then a 12-month lag would be appropriate for calculating after-tax net cash flows. However, for ease of calculation, we assume that tax is paid when the associated cash inflow is received.

---

8 The adjusted present value method was developed by Myers (1974). A detailed treatment is provided in Berk and DeMarzo (2007, pp. 581–5). Details of how to adapt the technique for the dividend imputation system are provided in Monkhouse (1997).

A project's after-tax net cash flows for each period may be calculated as:

After-tax net cash flow = net cash flow before tax × $(1 - t_e)$ [14.12]

where t_e = effective company income tax rate

However, this equation ignores the effect of the tax deductibility of expenses that do not involve a cash outflow. In particular, depreciation of non-current assets, excluding land and, in some cases, buildings, is an allowable deduction for income tax purposes. Depreciation does not involve an outflow of cash; it represents the allocation of the cost of a depreciable asset over its estimated useful life. However, the tax deductibility of depreciation means that the higher the depreciation charge for tax purposes, the lower will be the income tax payable by the company. If the proportion of the tax collected from the company that is claimed by shareholders is less than one, then the lower income tax payable by the company will result in greater after-tax net cash flows. The increase in after-tax net cash flows is represented by the tax savings on depreciation, which is calculated as follows:

Tax savings on depreciation = depreciation × t_e [14.13]

Therefore, the after-tax net cash flows generated by an investment project may be calculated by summing Equations 14.12 and 14.13 as follows:

After-tax net cash flow = net cash flow × $(1 - t_e)$ + depreciation × t_e [14.14]

Example 14.5 illustrates the application of Equation 14.14.

> **EXAMPLE 14.5**
>
> A project's before-tax net cash flow is expected to be $10 000 per annum. For tax purposes the depreciation charge is $1000 per annum, the statutory company income tax rate is 30 cents in the dollar, 0.60 of the tax collected from the company is claimed by shareholders, and therefore the effective company income tax rate is 0.12. The after-tax net cash flow is calculated as follows:
>
> After-tax net cash flow = $10 000(1 − 0.12) + $1000(0.12)
> = $8800 + $120
> = $8920

The effect of depreciation on project cash flows is more complex than Example 14.5 suggests, because the Income Tax Assessment Act allows two methods of calculating depreciation: the *straight-line (or prime-cost) method* and the *reducing-balance (or diminishing-value) method*. If the reducing-balance method is used, the allowable depreciation rate is generally twice the straight-line rate.[9]

The depreciation charge calculated for tax purposes may bear no relationship to that calculated for financial reporting purposes. For example, a company may use the straight-line method for reporting purposes, and the reducing-balance method for income tax purposes. Straight-line depreciation involves allocating the asset's cost in equal amounts over its estimated useful life.[10] Given the asset's initial cost, C,

---

[9] For eligible assets purchased after 10 May 2006, the allowable depreciation rate using the reducing-balance method is twice the straight-line rate. For assets purchased prior to that date, the allowable depreciation rate using the reducing-balance method is 1.5 times the straight-line rate. Taxpayers have at times been able to claim an investment allowance that is essentially an additional depreciation deduction—for example, as part of its economic stimulus package announced in 2009, the Australian Government permitted small businesses to claim a one-off additional 50 per cent tax deduction on the purchase of eligible new assets or the improvement of eligible existing assets. Assets that qualified for the allowance were basically those that could be depreciated for tax purposes.

[10] This contrasts with the method of calculating depreciation for financial reporting purposes. In accounting, the straight-line depreciation charge is:
$(C - S)/n$
where C = initial cost
S = estimated residual value or scrap value
n = estimated useful life in years

and its estimated useful life of n years, the straight-line depreciation charge in each year of the asset's life is C/n. For example, if an asset costs $10 000 and has a 10-year life, the annual depreciation charge is $10 000/10 = $1000.

In contrast, reducing-balance depreciation involves charging a fixed percentage of the asset's written-down (or adjustable) value in each year. The asset's written-down value is equal to its cost or other value (such as a revalued amount) less accumulated depreciation, where accumulated depreciation is equal to the sum of the depreciation charges in previous years. In comparison with straight-line depreciation, the reducing-balance method of depreciation results in larger depreciation charges in the early years of an asset's life, and smaller charges in later years. Therefore, compared with the straight-line method, reducing-balance depreciation, which increases the depreciation charge in the early years of the asset's life, results in lower taxes and larger after-tax cash flows in those years. The total income tax paid is not reduced by using the reducing-balance method. However, a portion of the tax payable is postponed in the early years of the project's life. Given that a dollar today is worth more than a dollar in a year's time, it follows that the use of the reducing-balance method is generally advantageous to an asset's owner.

The after-tax cash flows associated with ownership of a depreciable asset also depend on the relationship between the asset's disposal value and its written-down value. If the disposal value is equal to the written-down value, then sale of the asset has no effect on tax paid by the seller. However, if the two values differ, there are two possibilities:

(A) The asset's disposal value is less than its written-down value

Suppose that an asset is sold for $1000, but its written-down value is $2500. The difference of $1500 is regarded as a loss on sale, which is tax deductible. If $t_e = 0.12$, the tax savings on the loss of $1500 is $1500 × 0.12 = $180. This tax saving is treated as a cash inflow, so the net proceeds are $1180.

(B) The asset's disposal value is more than its written-down value

Suppose that the asset is sold for $3000, which is $500 more than its written-down value. In this case the gain on sale of $500 is regarded as recovery of depreciation deductions that were previously claimed. Therefore, the gain is taxable but the tax may be deferred by deducting the gain from the written-down value of a replacement asset or other depreciable assets.[11] If the gain is taxed immediately, the net sale proceeds are $3000 − $500 × 0.12 = $2940.

The tax effects of the straight-line and reducing-balance methods are compared in Example 14.6.

EXAMPLE 14.6

Table 14.5 shows the calculation of the present value of the tax effects associated with depreciation and disposal of an asset that costs $10 000, has an estimated useful life of 5 years, and a disposal value of $788 at the end of the fifth year. The statutory company income tax rate is 30 per cent, and 0.60 of the tax collected from the company is claimed by shareholders. The effective company tax rate is therefore 12 per cent. Table 14.5 shows that the reducing-balance method should be preferred because it results in a higher present value of tax savings and net sale proceeds.

---

11 Replacement decisions were discussed in Section 6.4.2.

TABLE 14.5 Tax effects of depreciation and sale of an asset

| | | DEPRECIATION METHOD | | | | | |
| | | STRAIGHT LINE[a] | | | REDUCING BALANCE[b] | | |
END OF YEAR	PRESENT VALUE FACTOR	ALLOWABLE DEPRECIATION EXPENSE AT 10% ($)	TAX SAVINGS[c] ($)	PRESENT VALUE OF TAX SAVINGS AND PROCEEDS OF SALE, NET OF TAX ($)	ALLOWABLE DEPRECIATION EXPENSE ($)	TAX SAVINGS ($)	PRESENT VALUE OF TAX SAVINGS AND PROCEEDS OF SALE, NET OF TAX ($)
1	0.909 09	2000	240	218	4000	480	436
2	0.826 45	2000	240	198	2400	288	238
3	0.751 31	2000	240	180	1440	173	130
4	0.683 01	2000	240	164	864	104	71
5	0.620 92	2000	240	149	518	62	38
Disposal value	—	778[b]	—	483	778	—	483
Gain on sale	—	778	—	—	0	—	—
Tax on gain	—	—	(93)	(58)	—	0	0
Total	—	—	—	1334	—	—	1396

[a] Straight-line depreciation is charged at a rate of 20 per cent of acquisition cost, and reducing-balance depreciation is charged at a rate of 40 per cent of the written-down value.

[b] It is assumed that at the end of Year 5 the asset is sold for $778. Under the reducing-balance method of depreciation, this is equal to the written-down value at the end of Year 5 and there is no gain or loss on sale. Consequently, there is no tax effect on the $778. The present value of the cash inflow is calculated in the usual way and equals $778 × (0.620 92) = $483. Under the straight-line method of depreciation, as the whole of the asset's acquisition cost has been written off for tax purposes by the end of Year 5, the $778 received at that time is regarded as a gain on sale for tax purposes, and increases tax payable by $93. The present value of this tax payment is $58.

[c] Tax savings are equal to allowable depreciation expenses × 0.12.

14.8.2 ILLUSTRATION OF CASH-FLOW INFORMATION IN PROJECT EVALUATION WITH TAXES

In Chapter 6 we considered the cash-flow information that should be compiled for project evaluation. However, in that chapter we did not consider the effects of taxes. Example 14.7 illustrates how taxes should be incorporated into the compilation of cash flows.

EXAMPLE 14.7

The Clarendon Company is considering the introduction of a new product. Generally, the company's products have a life of about 5 years, after which they are deleted from the range of products that the company sells.

The new product requires the purchase of new equipment costing $600 000, including freight and installation charges. The useful life of the equipment is 5 years, with an estimated residual value of $236 500 at the end of that period. The equipment will be depreciated for tax purposes by the reducing-balance method at a rate of 20 per cent per annum.

The new product will be manufactured in a factory already owned by the company. The factory originally cost $200 000 to build and has a current resale value of $500 000, which should remain fairly

continued →

Example 14.7 *continued*

stable over the next 5 years. This factory is currently being rented to another company under a lease agreement that has 5 years to run and provides for an annual rental of $20 000. Under the lease agreement the Clarendon Company can cancel the lease by paying the lessee compensation equal to 1 year's rental payment. This amount is not deductible for income tax purposes.

TABLE 14.6 Cash-flow information for the evaluation of the purchase of new equipment

ITEM					AFTER-TAX CASH FLOWS ($'000)					
					YEAR 0	YEAR 1	YEAR 2	YEAR 3	YEAR 4	YEAR 5
1. Initial outlay					(600.000)	—	—	—	—	—
2. Depreciation										
YEAR	WRITTEN-DOWN VALUE ($)		DEPRECI-ATION (%)	TAX SAVINGS AT 12C IN $ ($)						
1	600 000		20	120 000	14 400	—	14.400	—	—	—	—
2	480 000		20	96 000	11 520	—	—	11.520	—	—	—
3	384 000		20	76 800	9 216	—	—	—	9.216	—	—
4	307 200		20	61 440	7 373	—	—	—	—	7.373	—
5	245 760		20	49 152	5 898	—	—	—	—	—	5.898
3. Sale of equipment										
Sale				$236 500						
Written-down value				$196 608						
Gain on sale				$39 892						
Tax on gain at 12%				$4 787						
Total proceeds				$236 500 − $4 787	—	—	—	—	—	231.713
4. Factory										
The cost and the current resale value of the factory are both irrelevant										
(a) Cancel lease					(20.000)	—	—	—	—	—
(b) Net cash flow forgone due to rent forgone $20 000 (1 − 0.12)					—	(17.600)	(17.600)	(17.600)	(17.600)	(17.600)
5. Market research outlays										
Outlay				$60 000						
Less net tax savings at 12%				$7 200						
				$52 800	—	(52.800)				
6. Addition to current assets					(32.000)	—	—	—	—	32.000
7. Net cash flows from operations after deducting company income tax										
Year 1: $300 000 (1 − 0.12)					—	264.000	—	—	—	—
Year 2: $375 000 (1 − 0.12)					—	—	330.000	—	—	—
Year 3: $490 000 (1 − 0.12)					—	—	—	431.200	—	—
Year 4: $450 000 (1 − 0.12)					—	—	—	—	396.000	—
Year 5: $225 000 (1 − 0.12)					—	—	—	—	—	198.000
Total					−652.0	208.000	323.920	422.816	385.773	450.011
Discount factor at 10%					1.0000	0.90909	0.82645	0.75131	0.68301	0.62092
Present value of net cash flows					−652.0	189.091	267.704	317.666	263.487	279.421
Net present value = $665 369										

It is expected that the product will involve the company in sales promotion expenditures, which will amount to $60 000 during the first year the product is on the market. This amount is deductible for income tax purposes in the year in which the expenditure is incurred.

Additions to current assets will require $32 000 at the commencement of the project and are assumed to be fully recoverable at the end of the fifth year.

The new product is expected to generate net operating cash flows (before depreciation and income tax) as follows:

Year 1: $300 000
Year 2: $375 000
Year 3: $490 000
Year 4: $450 000
Year 5: $225 000

It is assumed that all cash flows are received at the end of each year and that income tax is paid at the end of the year in which the inflow occurred.

The statutory company income tax rate is 30 cents in the dollar and the proportion of the tax collected from the company that is claimed by shareholders is 0.60. The effective company income tax rate is therefore 0.12. The company has a required rate of return of 10 per cent after tax.

The solution to this example is set out in Table 14.6. On the basis of this quantitative analysis, the new product should be manufactured.

14.9 USING CERTAINTY EQUIVALENTS TO ALLOW FOR RISK

In most cases, risky projects are evaluated by using a cost of capital that reflects the risk of the project—that is, the project's expected cash flows are discounted using a *risk-adjusted discount rate*. Using this approach, the net present value, NPV, is calculated as follows:

$$NPV = -C_0 + \sum_{t=1}^{n} \frac{E(C_t)}{(1+k)^t} \qquad [14.15]$$

where $E(C_t)$ = the expected net cash flow in year t
k = the cost of capital, appropriate to the risky expected cash flows $E(C_t)$
C_0 = the initial cash outlay
n = the life of the project, in years

LEARNING OBJECTIVE 11
Understand the application of the certainty-equivalent method of incorporating risk into project evaluation

The **certainty-equivalent** approach is an alternative method of incorporating risk into project evaluation. This approach incorporates risk into the analysis by adjusting the *cash flows* rather than the discount rate—that is, each year's expected net cash flow is converted to a certainty equivalent. The certainty-equivalent net cash flow in year t, C_t^*, is the smallest certain cash flow that the decision maker would be prepared to accept in exchange for the expected risky cash flow, $E(C_t)$. For example, assume that a project's risky net cash flow is $10 000 at the end of the first year. If the decision maker is prepared to exchange the claim to this risky cash flow for a claim to receive, with certainty, $8000 at the end of the first year, then $8000 is the certainty equivalent of the risky $10 000. In this example, $E(C_1)$ is $10 000 and $C_t^* = $8000. Therefore, the expected net cash flow for any year can be converted to its certainty equivalent as follows:

certainty-equivalent approach that incorporates risk by adjusting the cash flows rather than the discount rate

$$C_t^* = \alpha_t E(C_t) \qquad [14.16]$$

where α_t = the certainty-equivalent factor in year t

The certainty-equivalent factor in this example can be calculated as follows:

$$\alpha_t = \frac{C_t^*}{E(C_t)} = \frac{\$8000}{\$10\,000} = 0.8$$

Using the certainty-equivalent approach, the net present value is calculated by discounting the certainty-equivalent net cash flow for each period at the appropriate risk-free rate:

$$NPV = C_0 + \sum_{t=1}^{n} \frac{C_t^*}{(1+R_f)^t} \qquad [14.17]$$

If all variables are properly specified, the present value of any future cash flow must be identical in both the risk-adjusted discount-rate method and the certainty-equivalent method. Therefore:

$$\frac{E(C_t)}{(1+k)^t} = \frac{\alpha_t E(C_t)}{(1+R_f)^t}$$

$$\therefore \alpha_t = \frac{(1+R_f)^t}{(1+k)^t} \qquad [14.18]$$

In Examples 14.8 and 14.9 we illustrate both methods. We then discuss their relative merits.

EXAMPLE 14.8

Cassilis Ltd is considering an investment in a new machine. The machine will require an initial outlay of $100 000 and is expected to generate cash flows of $50 000, $40 000 and $50 000 at the end of Years 1, 2 and 3, respectively. The risk-adjusted discount rate is 12 per cent per annum and the risk-free rate is 8 per cent per annum.

The net present value using the risk-adjusted discount rate method is calculated using Equation 14.15:

$$NPV = -\$100\,000 + \frac{\$50\,000}{1.12} + \frac{\$40\,000}{(1.12)^2} + \frac{\$50\,000}{(1.12)^3}$$

$$= -\$100\,000 + \$44\,643 + \$31\,888 + \$35\,589$$

$$= \$12\,120$$

From Equation 14.18, the certainty-equivalent factor for each year is calculated as follows:

$$\alpha_1 = \frac{1.08}{1.12} = 0.964\,28$$

$$\alpha_2 = \frac{(1.08)^2}{(1.12)^2} = 0.929\,85$$

$$\alpha_3 = \frac{(1.08)^3}{(1.12)^3} = 0.896\,64$$

Using these certainty-equivalent factors, the net present value can be calculated using Equation 14.17:

$$NPV = -\$100\,000 + \frac{0.964\,28(\$50\,000)}{1.08} + \frac{0.929\,85(\$40\,000)}{(1.08)^2} + \frac{0.896\,64(\$50\,000)}{(1.08)^3}$$

$$= -\$100\,000 + \$44\,643 + \$31\,888 + \$35\,589$$

$$= \$12\,120$$

The net present values are the same and, on the face of it, there seems to be no reason for preferring one method to the other.

However, remember that in discounting a future cash flow to a present value there are two factors to be taken into account: time and risk. These factors are logically separate but the risk-adjusted discount rate approach requires the effect of both to be incorporated into the discount rate. In particular, use of a constant risk-adjusted discount rate implies that the risk associated with the project increases over time at a constant rate. This was illustrated in Example 14.8, which showed that a constant risk-adjusted discount rate results in the certainty-equivalent factors decreasing at a constant rate in each successive year. In Example 14.8, the rate of decrease is approximately 3.6 per cent per year. The fact that the certainty-equivalent factors decrease at a constant rate over time is shown by Equation 14.18, which can be rewritten as:

$$\alpha_t = \left[\frac{1+R_f}{1+k}\right]^t = (\alpha_1)^t$$

The decrease of certainty-equivalent factors at a constant rate indicates that the cumulative risk associated with each successive cash flow increases steadily as we look further into the future. In cases where this risk pattern does *not* apply, a constant risk-adjusted discount rate should not be used, and the certainty-equivalent approach offers practical advantages. This is illustrated in Example 14.9.

EXAMPLE 14.9

Jameson Ltd has recently invented a new method of separating precious metals. Further development work is required over the next 2 years and management believes there is a 60 per cent probability of then proceeding to commercial production using plant costing $2 million. Expected cash inflows are $500 000 per year for 20 years. There is a 40 per cent probability that the development work will fail, in which case there will be no cash flows after the first 2 years. The development work will be undertaken by a local university research company in return for an immediate payment of $250 000.

Suppose that, because of the high risk, management evaluates the project using a discount rate of 30 per cent per annum, compared with its normal rate of 15 per cent per annum. The expected cash flows are:

Year 0:   PV of outlays on development work = −$250 000
Year 2:   Construction of plant: (0.6) × (−$2 000 000) + 0.4 × $0 = −$1 200 000
Years 3–22:   Cash inflows: 0.6 × $500 000 + 0.4 × $0 = $300 000

$$NPV = -\$250\,000 - \frac{\$1\,200\,000}{(1.3)^2} + \$300\,000 \left[\frac{1-\frac{1}{(1.3)^{20}}}{0.3}\right] \times \frac{1}{(1.3)^2}$$

$$= -\$371\,457$$

Based on this result the project would be rejected now without undertaking the development work. However, much of the risk associated with the project will be resolved after the first 2 years. If the development work is successful, the project may be of normal risk, in which case the future cash flows would be discounted at Jameson's normal rate of 15 per cent per annum. Assuming that the risk-free rate is 8 per cent per annum, the project's NPV can be recalculated using a combination of the two approaches. If the project goes ahead after the 2 years' development work, the NPV at the end of Year 2 will be:

$$NPV(2) = -\$2\,000\,000 + \$500\,000 \left[\frac{1-\frac{1}{(1.15)^{20}}}{0.15}\right]$$

$$= \$1\,129\,666$$

continued →

Example 14.9 *continued*

But there is only a 60 per cent probability of this outcome. Assuming a certainty-equivalent factor of 0.6, the project NPV is:

$$NPV = \$250\,000 + \frac{0.6 \times \$1\,129\,666}{(1.08)^2}$$

$$= \$331\,104$$

Therefore, the project should proceed, which is the opposite of the decision originally indicated by the constant risk-adjusted discount rate.

To summarise, discounting risky future cash flows to present values requires adjustments for the effects of two factors: time and risk. In the risk-adjusted discount-rate approach the effects of both factors are included in the discount rate. The two factors are logically separate and are treated separately in the certainty-equivalent approach, which is easier to use in cases where the risk per unit of time is *not* constant.

Connect Plus features a case study illustrating topics covered in this chapter.
Ask your lecturer or tutor for your course's unique URL.

SUMMARY

→ This chapter focused on the estimation and use of the cost of capital, which is important in project evaluation. Investing in a project will increase company value only if the project promises at least the rate of return that investors can earn on other investments of the same risk as the project. Therefore, the required rate of return, or cost of capital, for a project is an opportunity cost that depends on the risk of the project in which the capital is invested. The CAPM can be used as a framework for making risk adjustments, and, according to this model, the relevant measure of risk for any project is its systematic risk (beta).

→ The cost of capital could, in principle, be estimated by direct use of the CAPM, but this involves practical difficulties related mainly to estimation of the betas of projects. Alternatively, the cost of capital for a company can be expressed as a weighted average of the costs of the various sources of capital used by the company. The weighted average cost of capital (WACC) approach is generally used in practice. Estimation of the after-tax WACC involves estimation of each term in the equation:

$$k' = k_e \left(\frac{E}{V}\right) + k_d \left(1 - t_e\right)\left(\frac{D}{V}\right)$$

→ These estimates should be based on current market rates and market values, not historical rates and book values.

→ The imputation tax system has implications for the way that cash flows and the cost of capital should be defined and measured, because only part of the tax collected from companies is 'true' company tax. This feature of the system can be reflected in project evaluation by using an effective company tax rate in calculating both after-tax cash flows and the cost of capital. Rates of return observed under the imputation tax system also require adjustment if they are used to estimate the cost of equity.

→ All the variables in the WACC formula apply to a company as a whole, so it follows that a company's WACC should be used as an estimate of the cost of capital only for projects that are identical, except for scale, to the existing company. In particular, this means that:

- the proposed project's risk should be the same as the average risk of the company's existing projects
- acceptance of the project will not change the company's optimal capital structure.

→ For a diversified company, use of a single discount rate for all projects is likely to result in incorrect investment decisions. The cost of capital for a division or an individual project can be estimated if there are other listed companies ('pure plays') whose sole operations are of the same systematic risk as the division or project. If such a substitute company can be found, its WACC can be estimated and used, possibly with an adjustment for financial leverage, as the cost of capital for the division or project.

→ Alternatively, divisional costs of capital can be estimated using information on diversified companies by viewing the WACC of each diversified company as a weighted average of the WACCs of its divisions. This approach has significant advantages over the use of pure-play companies.

→ We conclude that while the WACC has important advantages, such as flexibility, it also has some important limitations that should be understood by its users.

→ We also conclude that the certainty-equivalent approach, which incorporates risk by adjusting the cash flows rather than the discount rate, may be easier to use where risk per unit of time is not constant.

KEY TERMS

certainty-equivalent 471
consistency principle 445
cost of capital 446
dividend growth model 456
franking premium 448
issue costs 459
opportunity cost 445
pure play 461
weighted average cost of capital 450

SELF-TEST PROBLEMS

1. The Canberra Corporation is considering an investment in a new project; it will involve an initial investment of $200 000 and is expected to generate a net cash inflow of $235 000 in 1 year's time. The risk-free interest rate is 12 per cent and the expected return on the market portfolio (including the franking premium) is 18 per cent.

    (a) Should the project be accepted if its systematic risk is expected to be 0.75?
    (b) Would your answer to (a) change if the project's systematic risk is expected to be 1.0?

2. The Expando Company has three new projects that are being evaluated. The company's WACC is estimated at 14.6 per cent after effective company tax. The expected after-tax returns and betas of the three projects are as follows:

Project	Expected return (%)	Beta
Mars	14.5	0.70
Pluto	15.0	0.85
Neptune	20.0	1.20

    The risk-free interest rate is 9 per cent and the expected return on the market portfolio (including the franking premium) is 16.5 per cent.

    (a) Which of the projects should be accepted?
    (b) Would any of the accept/reject decisions change if the projects were evaluated using the company cost of capital?

3. A company is considering the purchase of equipment costing $84 000, which will permit it to reduce its existing labour costs by $20 000 a year for 12 years. The company estimates that it will have to spend $2000 every 2 years overhauling the equipment. The equipment may be depreciated for tax purposes by the straight-line method, over a 12-year period. The company tax rate is 30 cents in the dollar, the proportion of the tax collected from the company that is claimed by shareholders is 0.75, and the after-tax cost of capital is 10 per cent per annum. Assuming all cash flows, including tax payments, are made at the end of each year, should the company purchase the equipment?

Solutions to self-test problems are available in Appendix B, page 803.

REFERENCES

Beggs, D.J. & Skeels, C., 'Market arbitrage of cash dividends and franking credits', *The Economic Record*, September 2006, pp. 239–52.

Berk, J., & DeMarzo, P., *Corporate Finance*, Pearson Education, Boston, 2007.

Brailsford, T., Handley, J. & Maheswaran, K., 'Re-examination of the historical equity premium in Australia', *Accounting and Finance*, March 2008, pp. 73–97.

Brown, P. & Clarke, A., 'The ex-dividend day behaviour of Australian share prices before and after dividend imputation', *Australian Journal of Management*, June 1993, pp. 1–40.

Cannavan, D., Finn, F. & Gray, S., 'The value of imputation credits in Australia', *Journal of Financial Economics*, April 2004, pp. 167–97.

Conine, T. & Tamarkin, M., 'Divisional cost of capital estimation: adjusting for leverage', *Financial Management*, Spring 1985, pp. 54–8.

Fuller, R.J. & Kerr, H.S., 'Estimating the divisional cost of capital: an analysis of the pure-play technique', *Journal of Finance*, December 1981, pp. 997–1009.

Harris, R.S., O'Brien, T.J. & Wakeman, D., 'Divisional cost-of-capital estimation for multi-industry firms', *Financial Management*, Spring 1989, pp. 74–84.

Hathaway, N., & Officer R. R., *The Value of Imputation Tax Credits: Update 2004*, Capital Research Pty Ltd, November 2004, www.capitalresearch.com.au/downloads/ImputationUpdate2004.pdf.

Monkhouse, P.H.L., 'The valuation of projects under the dividend imputation tax system', *Accounting and Finance*, November 1996, pp. 185–212.

——, 'Adapting the APV valuation methodology and the beta gearing formula to the dividend imputation tax system', *Accounting and Finance*, May 1997, pp. 69–88.

Mukherjee, T.K., Kiymaz, H. & Baker, H., 'Merger motives and target valuation: a survey of evidence from CFOs', *Journal of Applied Finance*, Winter 2004, pp. 7–24.

Myers, S.C., 'Interactions of corporate financing and investment decisions: implications for capital budgeting', *Journal of Finance*, March 1974, pp. 1–25.

——, & Turnbull, S., 'Capital budgeting and the capital asset pricing model: good news and bad news', *Journal of Finance*, May 1977, pp. 321–33.

Officer, R.R., 'The measurement of a firm's cost of capital', *Accounting and Finance*, November 1981, pp. 31–63.

——, 'The cost of capital of a company under an imputation tax system', *Accounting and Finance*, May 1994, pp. 1–17.

Taggart, R., 'Consistent valuation and cost-of-capital expressions with corporate and personal taxes', *Financial Management*, Autumn 1991, pp. 8–20.

Walker, S. & Partington, G., 'The value of dividends: evidence from cum-dividend trading in the ex-dividend period', *Accounting and Finance*, November 1999, pp. 275–96.

QUESTIONS

1. **[LO 7]** *When evaluating a new project, management requires an estimate of the project's own cost of capital. The WACC formula only gives a cost of capital applicable to the company as a whole and is therefore inappropriate for this purpose.* Comment on this statement.

2. **[LO 2]** Explain the importance of the risk-independence assumption for project appraisal.

3. **[LO 2]** The cost of capital for a project can be determined using the following equation:
   $$k_j = R_f + \beta_j[E(R_M + \tau) - R_f]$$
   (a) Justify this statement, and indicate the conditions necessary for it to be correct.
   (b) Discuss the problems associated with estimating R_f, β_j and $E(R_M + \tau)$.

4. **[LO 7]** Discuss each of the following statements:
   (a) *A project's cost of capital reflects the return investors require to finance the project.*
   (b) *The cost of capital is project-specific.*

5. **[LO 2]** *The errors associated with estimating a company's beta are so great that you may as well assume that all betas equal one.* Do you agree? Give your reasons.

6. **[LO 8]** The Ace Clothing Company has decided to diversify its operations by manufacturing and marketing footwear. Management notes that the systematic risk of the shares of a listed footwear company is 0.8. When would it be appropriate to use 0.8 as the estimate of the systematic risk of the equity for the company's new investment?

7. **[LO 2]** An aluminium producer is planning to expand by constructing a new rolling mill to produce

aluminium sheets used in beverage cans and the building industry. The project's cost of capital has been estimated at 12 per cent per annum, based on a beta of 0.5. Explain the effects, if any, that the following would have on the project's cost of capital:

(a) the correlation between the returns from aluminium producers, and the market portfolio, decreases
(b) the company reduces its financial leverage
(c) the risk-free interest rate increases
(d) owing to a technological breakthrough, the cost of producing sheet steel is reduced. Analysts forecast lower growth in sales of sheet aluminium.

8. [LO 5] *Trade credit is a free source of finance. Therefore, when estimating a company's cost of capital, trade credit can be ignored.* Comment on this statement.

9. [LO 7] *In a company that has separate divisions, management should apply different discount rates to projects proposed by its various divisions.* Discuss this statement.

10. [LO 7] Discuss the relative merits of the alternative methods of calculating the cost of capital for a division of a company.

11. [LO 10] *It doesn't matter whether the straight-line method or reducing-balance method of depreciation is used, since the total tax bill over the life of the project is the same.* Comment on this statement.

PROBLEMS

1. **NPV analysis [LO 2]**
Spares Ltd manufactures car parts and management is considering an expansion of its existing operations at a cost of $600 000. It expects this expansion to generate additional net cash inflows for the next 10 years as follows: $100 000 per annum in Years 1–5 and $130 000 per annum in Years 6–10. The company's analyst has made the following estimates:

(a) the systematic risk of the company's existing assets is 0.75
(b) the risk-free interest rate is 11 per cent per annum
(c) the expected rate of return on the market portfolio is 15 per cent per annum.

Assuming that there is no company income tax, should the company undertake the expansion?

2. **Calculating cost of capital [LO 3]**
Abco Distributors Ltd wishes to evaluate an investment in a new area of activity—manufacturing paint. Bath Paints (BP) has been identified as a company whose sole activity is to produce paint. The systematic risk of BP's equity is 1.2. However, BP is financed by one part debt to one part equity, whereas Abco Distributors is financed by two parts debt to three parts equity. Further, Abco's management has estimated the risk-free interest rate to be 12 per cent and the expected rate of return on the market portfolio (includiing the franking premium) to be 17 per cent. The company income tax rate is 30 cents in the dollar. The proportion of the tax collected from the company that is claimed by shareholders is 0.60, and the before-tax cost of Abco's debt is 14 per cent per annum. Calculate the cost of capital of the proposed new project, specifying the assumptions on which your calculations are based.

3. **Calculating cost of capital [LO 7]**
(a) Use the following information to calculate the cost of capital for SAM Ltd, assuming that investors can remove all unsystematic risk by diversification.
(i) The systematic risk of SAM Ltd's equity is 0.8.
(ii) The risk-free interest rate is 10 per cent per annum.
(iii) The expected rate of return on the market portfolio (including the franking premium) is 15 per cent per annum.
(iv) The various sources of funds used by SAM Ltd and their respective market values are as follows:

Source of funds	Market value ($M)
Debt (face value $100)	1
Equity	3

(v) The interest rate on the debt is 11 per cent paid annually. The debt, which is due to mature in 8 years' time, has a current market price of $111.
(vi) The company income tax rate is 30 cents in the dollar.
(vii) The proportion of the tax collected from the company that is claimed by shareholders is 0.60.

(b) Under what assumptions is the cost of capital you have calculated for SAM Ltd in (a) appropriate for a proposed project?

4. **Calculating cost of capital [LO 1]**

   Bay-of-Islands Dairies Ltd has an interest cost of debt of 6 per cent per annum. The systematic risk of its equity is 1.2, and the effective company tax rate is 0.12. Forty per cent of its funding is provided by debt, while 60 per cent is provided by equity. The risk-free interest rate is 5 per cent per annum. In calculating its cost of capital, Bay-of-Islands has obtained two expert opinions as to the market risk premium (including the franking premium). One expert suggests that the market risk premium is 1 per cent per annum, while the other suggests that the market risk premium is 5 per cent per annum. What is Bay-of-Islands' cost of capital based on these experts' opinions of the market risk premium?

5. **Calculating cost of capital [LO 5]**

   Rylstone Ltd has commenced operations with the following capital structure:

   Rylstone Ltd: Statement of financial position as at date of incorporation

	($)
Assets	
Sundry assets	1 000 000
Liabilities and shareholders' funds	
Debentures, 8% (10 years)	300 000
Preference shares, 9%	200 000
Ordinary shares, issued and paid-up 500 000 at $1	500 000
	1 000 000

   The company's prospectus contains estimates that it will earn $100 000 in the first year and pay dividends of 10 cents per share. Brokers anticipate that dividends will grow at 5 per cent per annum. The shares are currently selling at $1. The company income tax rate is 30 cents in the dollar and the proportion of the tax collected from the company that is claimed by shareholders is 0.60. Calculate the cost of capital for Rylstone Ltd.

6. **Calculating cost of capital [LO 5]**

   The following financial information relates to the operations of Wood Timber Ltd:

   Wood Timber Ltd: abstract from the statement of profit and retained earnings for the year ended 31 December 2012

	($)
Net profit after taxes	200 000
Retained earnings 1.1.2012	150 000
Total available for appropriation	350 000
less Dividends on ordinary shares	120 000
less Dividends on preference shares	28 000
Retained earnings 31.12.2012	202 000

   Summary statement of financial position as at 31 December 2012

	($)	($)
Assets		
Inventory		120 000
Accounts receivable		82 000
Land and buildings		1 200 000
Plant and equipment		900 000
		2 302 000
Liabilities		
Accounts payable	100 000	
Bank overdraft	200 000	
12% debentures, $100 face value	600 000	900 000
Shareholders' funds		
14% preference shares, $10 face value	200 000	
Ordinary shares, $1 face value	1 000 000	
Retained earnings	202 000	1 402 000
		2 302 000

Additional information:

(a) The nominal interest rate on the bank overdraft is 10 per cent per annum and interest is calculated half-yearly.

(b) The debentures are currently selling at $97 each and mature in 6 years' time.

(c) The preference shares are currently selling at $9.50 each.

(d) The ordinary shares are currently selling at $1.10 each.

(e) The company income tax rate is 30 cents in the dollar.

(f) The proportion of the tax collected from the company that is claimed by shareholders is 0.6.

Calculate the cost of capital for Wood Timber Ltd, using the dividend growth method to calculate the cost of equity. Note any assumptions you make.

7. **Cost of debt capital [LO 5]**

   If the appropriate cost of debt capital is greater than the coupon rate of a debt security, its price will usually be less than its face value. Comment on the validity or otherwise of this statement with the aid of the following example: a 5-year debt security has a face value of $100 and a coupon rate of 10 per cent per annum, with interest paid semi-annually. The appropriate cost of debt capital is 13 per cent per annum (effective).

8. **Calculating cost of capital [LO 5]**

   The management of Heavy Clay Ltd wants to know the cost of capital associated with expanding its business. You have been told that funds will be raised for this purpose according to a target capital structure reflected in the market value of its securities. Your task is to calculate the cost of capital for the company. The following information may assist you in your task:

   (a) The 13 per cent debentures have just been issued and interest rates have remained stable since the issue. This rate was 1 per cent per annum above the interest rate on government securities.

   (b) The last observed market price of the preference shares was $1, whereas it was $3 for the ordinary shares.

   (c) The beta of equity of Heavy Clay was recently estimated at 0.5, while the consensus view is that the expected rate of return for the market is 18 per cent, which includes a franking premium of 2 per cent.

   (d) An extract of the most recent statement of financial position shows:

Liabilities and shareholders' funds	($'000)
Debentures	2500
7% preference shares ($2 face value)	1000
Paid-up capital ($1 face value)	3000
Reserves	500
	7000

   (e) The company income tax rate is 30 cents in the dollar.

   (f) The dividends on Heavy Clay's ordinary shares will be fully franked and all the shares are held by Australian residents.

9. **Estimating divisional cost of capital [LO 8]**

   Three companies—X, Y and Z—operate in industries 1 and 2. The companies' costs of capital and investment in each industry are as follows:

Company	Cost of capital (%)	Proportion of assets in industry	
		1	2
X	14.0	0.5	0.5
Y	12.8	0.7	0.3
Z	14.6	0.4	0.6

   (a) Estimate the divisional cost of capital for each company.

   (b) Outline the main assumptions that underlie your model.

   (c) Discuss the advantages and disadvantages of the method you used in (a) compared with the 'pure-play' approach.

10. **Company versus project cost of capital [LO 7]**

    Dorset Ltd is all-equity financed and has a cost of capital of 16 per cent per annum. An observer suggests that Dorset could easily borrow up to 40 per cent of the value of its assets at an interest rate of 10 per cent per annum and achieve a rating for its debt of A+

or better. He argues that raising new capital by borrowing would lower the company's cost of capital, and increase the net present value of some projects that were recently rejected. Use a numerical example to illustrate the observer's argument. Is his argument correct? Give reasons for your answer.

11. **Estimating after-tax cash flow [LO 10]**

    The Four and Six Stores Pty Ltd is considering locating another outlet in an eastern suburb of Melbourne. Estimates of sales and operating expenses have been made and an estimated profit and loss statement for the new store drawn up. The profit and loss statement for Year 1 is thought to be representative of each of the 10 years of the expected life of the new Four and Six Store. The initial outlay to construct the store is $400 000, while the outlay necessary to stock the store is $20 000. The estimated statement of financial performance for the new store for Year 1 is shown in the following table:

Item	($)	($)
Revenue	400 000	
Less Sales returns, discounts	40 000	
Net revenue		360 000
Operating expenses		
Cost of goods sold	160 000	
Administration costs	60 000	
Depreciation	36 000	
Interest	24 000	280 000
Net profit before tax		80 000
Tax (30% tax rate)		24 000
Net profit after tax		56 000

    Estimate the project's annual after-tax cash flow, assuming that 60 per cent of the tax collected by the company is claimed by shareholders.

12. **Calculating after-tax net cash flow [LO 10]**

    All-Night Coffee Shops Ltd is a successful profitable company operating several dozen coffee shops throughout the metropolitan area of Melberra. However, the shop in the suburb of Burnaby has not been well patronised, generating a before-tax net cash flow of only $50 000 in the past year. The Burnaby shop began trading 2 years ago in premises leased from CBD Ltd. The lease is about to expire and All-Night will not renew it. A competitor, Brazil Coffee Shops Ltd, has offered to buy the fixtures and fittings and the equipment in the Burnaby shop for $400 000. All-Night has agreed to this figure, even though it is $300 000 less than the cost of the fixtures and fittings and the equipment 2 years ago. Assume that:

    (a) for tax purposes the fixtures and fittings and the equipment were depreciated on a straight-line basis at 10 per cent per annum
    (b) the company tax rate is 30 per cent and the proportion of the tax collected from the company that is claimed by shareholders is 0.65.

    What is the after-tax net cash flow (for Year 2) attributable to All-Night's Burnaby shop?

13. **Net present value analysis [LO 1]**

    Bethela Ltd purchased a machine 7 years ago for $85 000. When it was purchased the machine had an expected useful life of 17 years and an estimated value of zero at the end of its life. The machine, which is being depreciated on a straight-line basis, currently has a written-down value of $50 000 and a current market value of $20 000. The manager reports that he can buy a new machine for $120 000 (including installation), which, over its 10-year life, will result in an expansion of sales from $90 000 to $120 000 per annum. In addition, it is estimated that the new machine will reduce annual operating costs from $70 000 to $60 000. The proportion of the tax collected from the company that is claimed by shareholders is 0.55. If the tax rate is 30 cents in the dollar, and the effective after-tax required rate of return is 10 per cent per annum, should Bethela buy the new machine?

14. **Calculating after-tax net cash flow [LO 10]**

    It doesn't matter whether the straight-line or reducing-balance method of depreciation is used, since the total tax bill over the life of the project is the same. Discuss the validity (or otherwise) of this statement in the context of the following example:

Asset cost (now)	$10 000
Asset life	5 years
Residual value (in 5 years)	$4700
Annual net cash inflow before tax	$6000
Straight-line depreciation rate (per annum)	10%

Reducing-balance depreciation rate (per annum)	20%
Company income tax rate	30%
Proportion of tax collected from the company claimed by shareholders	0.60
After-tax cost of capital	10% p.a.

15. Calculating after-tax net cash flow [LO 10]

A company must choose between two machines. The 'cheaper' machine costs $250 000 but has annual operating expenses (excluding depreciation) estimated to be $100 000, while the 'more expensive' machine costs $370 000 but has estimated annual operating expenses (excluding depreciation) of only $75 000. Both machines have a 10-year life, zero residual value and are depreciated on a straight-line basis.

(a) Which machine should the company purchase if it has a tax rate of 30 cents in the dollar, the proportion of the tax collected from the company that is claimed by shareholders is 0.75, and the after-tax cost of capital is 10 per cent per annum?

(b) Rework the problem for a 7 per cent cost of capital.

16. Project evaluation [LO 10]

The Floralia Mining Company has constructed a town at Jungilla, near the site of a rich mineral discovery in a remote part of Australia. The town will be abandoned when mining operations cease after an estimated 10-year period. The following estimates of investment costs, sales, and operating expenses relate to a project to supply Jungilla with meat and agricultural produce over the 10-year period by developing nearby land.

(a) Investment in land is $2 million, farm buildings $400 000, and farm equipment $800 000. The land is expected to have a realisable value of $1 million in 10 years' time. The buildings have an estimated useful life of 20 years, at which time their residual value would be zero, and they are to be depreciated on a straight-line basis for tax purposes based on this life. The residual value of the buildings after 10 years is expected to be $100 000. The farm equipment has an estimated life of 10 years and a zero residual value. The equipment is to be depreciated on a straight-line basis.

(b) Investment of $500 000 in current assets. This will be recovered at the termination of the venture.

(c) Annual cash sales are estimated to be $6 million.

(d) Annual cash operating costs are estimated to be $4.4 million.

(e) Assume tax is paid 1 year after the year of income.

Is the project profitable, given that the after-tax cost of capital is 10 per cent per annum, with a company tax rate of 30 cents in the dollar, and a proportion of the tax collected from the company that is claimed by shareholders of 0.70?

17. Project evaluation [LO 10]

The management of Hunter Air Ltd is considering the replacement of its existing fleet of seven A616 aeroplanes with three B727 aeroplanes. The following estimates for each aeroplane have been calculated:

A616 Aeroplanes	Estimates	B727 Aeroplanes	Estimates
Estimated remaining life	5 years	Cost	$500 million
Estimated scrap value		Estimated life	10 years
Now	$50 million	Estimated disposal value	
In 5 years' time	$10 million	In 5 years' time	$200 million
		In 10 years' time	$100 million
Annual net cash flows	$100 million	Annual net cash flows	$200 million

Management is also aware of the development of the C898, which the manufacturer estimates will be available in 5 years' time. The following estimates for a C898 aeroplane have been provided by the manufacturer.

C898 Aeroplanes	Estimates
Cost	$600 million
Estimated life	15 years
Estimated disposal value	
After 5 years' operation	$200 million
After 15 years' operation	$50 million
Annual net cash flows	$250 million

It is considered that two of the new C898 aeroplanes will be adequate to carry the estimated number of passengers. Other information is as follows:
(i) Management cannot foresee any further developments beyond the C898 aeroplane.
(ii) The annual net cash flows are received at the end of each year.
(iii) The company's after-tax cost of capital is 10 per cent per annum.
(iv) The company's tax rate is 30 cents in the dollar and 0.80 of the tax collected from the company is claimed by shareholders.
(v) The A616 aeroplanes are assumed to be fully depreciated.
(vi) Straight-line depreciation may be assumed.

You are required to advise management whether it should:
(a) replace the A616 aeroplanes with B727 aeroplanes now, and replace the latter with C898 aeroplanes in 5 years' time
(b) retain the A616 aeroplanes for 5 years, and then replace them with C898 aeroplanes
(c) replace the A616 aeroplanes with B727 aeroplanes now, and replace the latter with C898 aeroplanes in 10 years' time.

Other alternatives are not to be considered.

18. **Project evaluation [LO 10]**
A company is considering purchasing a new machine at a cost of $900 000 to replace a machine purchased 6 years ago for $1 million. The disposal value of the old machine is $250 000 and the accumulated depreciation, which has been allowed for tax purposes, is $600 000. Both machines will have similar outputs and will produce work of identical quality. The estimated yearly costs of operating each machine are as follows:

	Old machine ($)	New machine ($)
Wages	225 000	75 000
Depreciation	100 000	225 000
Supplies, repairs, power	65 000	30 000
Insurance and miscellaneous	36 000	20 000
	426 000	350 000

Both machines have an estimated remaining life of 4 years, at which time both machines will have an estimated disposal value of $90 000. Assume that:

(a) the after-company-tax cost of capital is 10 per cent per annum
(b) the operating costs of the old machine and the new machine are incurred at the end of each year
(c) the company income tax rate is 30 cents in the dollar and 0.85 of the tax collected from the company is claimed by shareholders.

Should the company purchase the new machine?

19. **Project evaluation [LO 10]**
Speedy Pty Ltd operates a suburban document delivery business. It is considering the replacement of a 2 tonne truck with a 3 tonne truck. Details of the respective vehicles are as follows:

2 tonne truck	Estimates	3 tonne truck	Estimates
Remaining life	5 years	Estimated life	6 years
Residual value:		Cost	$25 000
Now	$6000	Residual value after 6 years' operation	$2000

2 tonne truck	Estimates	3 tonne truck	Estimates
In 4 years	$0	Depreciation (allowable for tax purposes)	$4000 p.a.
Written-down value (for tax purposes)	$7500 (before taxation)	Net cash flow	$20 000 p.a.
Depreciation (for tax purposes)	$1200 p.a.		
Net cash flow (before taxation)	$12 000 p.a.		

Other information is as follows:
(i) Net cash flows are to be regarded as received at the end of each year.
(ii) The effective after-tax cost of capital is 10 per cent per annum.
(iii) The company income tax rate is 30 cents in the dollar and 0.45 of the tax collected from the company is claimed by shareholders.

Management is considering the following alternatives:

(a) Replace the 2 tonne truck with the 3 tonne truck now.
(b) Replace the 2 tonne truck with the 3 tonne truck in 5 years' time.

All other alternatives may be ignored. Advise management as to which alternative it should adopt, and justify your analysis.

20. **Project evaluation [LO 10]**
A boutique brewery buys empty bottles at $50 per 200 and currently uses 4 million bottles per year. The brewery manager believes that it may be cheaper to *make* the bottles rather than buy them. Direct production costs (labour, materials, fuel) are estimated at 15 cents per bottle. The equipment needed would cost $700 000 and can be depreciated for tax purposes at 20 per cent straight-line. The equipment should last for 16 years, provided it is overhauled every 4 years at a cost of $60 000 each time. The operation will require additional current assets of $65 000. The company tax rate is 30 per cent, 0.62 of the tax collected from the company is claimed by shareholders, and the effective after-tax cost of capital is 12 per cent. Evaluate the manufacturing proposal.

Test yourself further with Connect Plus online! Ask your lecturer or tutor for your course's unique URL.

APPENDIX 14.1 THE COST OF CAPITAL UNDER ALTERNATIVE TAX SYSTEMS[12]

INTRODUCTION

In this appendix we discuss alternative definitions of the cost of capital and derive equations for a company's cost of capital on both a before-tax and an after-tax basis. We show that under the imputation tax system there is more than one way to define an after-tax cost of capital.

Under an imputation system the distinction between company tax and personal tax becomes blurred because resident shareholders can use imputation credits to offset their personal tax liabilities. There are at least three ways in which this issue can be handled. The first is to adjust the after-tax cash flows generated by a company or project. A second approach involves adjusting the definition of the cost of capital, while a third approach involves adjusting both the cash flows and the cost of capital.

One principle that must be stressed is that, whichever approach is adopted, it must be used *consistently*: that is, the definition of the cost of capital must be consistent with the definition of the cash flows that are discounted using that cost of capital. If consistency is maintained, the three approaches are equivalent. But if consistency is not maintained, a biased valuation will result and incorrect investment decisions may be made.

DERIVING COST OF CAPITAL FORMULAE[13]

To define the cost of capital, we assume that all of a company's cash flows are expected to remain constant in perpetuity. This assumption is necessary for algebraic convenience. The value of a company depends on the net operating cash flows generated by the company's assets and the cost of capital applicable to those cash flows. For cash flows that remain constant in perpetuity:

$$V = \frac{X_0}{k_0} \quad [\text{A14.1}]$$

where V = value of the company (value of equity plus debt)
   X_0 = annual net operating cash flow before tax
   k_0 = before-tax cost of capital

From Equation A14.1, the general definition of the before-tax cost of capital is:

$$k_0 = \frac{X_0}{V} \quad [\text{A14.2}]$$

Equation A14.2 forms the basis for all the cost-of-capital formulae that we derive.

To derive formulae for the cost of capital it is necessary to consider only company tax, because we work on a before-company-tax or after-company-tax, but always before-personal-tax, basis. A company's net operating cash flow before tax, X_0, is the net cash flow that remains after meeting the costs of all factors of production other than payment of company income tax to the government and providing returns to suppliers of capital. Therefore X_0 can be divided into three components:

$$X_0 = X_g + X_d + X_e \quad [\text{A14.3}]$$

where X_g = net cash flow to the government
   X_d = net cash flow to debtholders
   X_e = net cash flow to shareholders

---

[12] The discussion in this appendix is largely a simplified version of that provided by Officer (1994).
[13] The general approach used in this section follows that adopted by Officer (1981, pp. 31–61).

The amount of tax collected from a company will be equal to $t_c(X_0 - X_d)$, where t_c is the statutory company tax rate. This is because interest paid is a tax-deductible expense of the company. But a proportion γ of the tax collected from the company will be claimed by shareholders as a consequence of receiving franking credits. Therefore, the tax collected from the company can be divided into two components: implicit personal tax and 'true' or effective company tax.

This concept may require explanation. Suppose that a business is unincorporated. For example, it may be structured as a partnership rather than as a company. A partnership is not taxed as a separate entity; rather its profits are taxed in the hands of the partners. Therefore, all the tax on its profits is personal tax. On the other hand, if a company structure is used, profits paid out as franked dividends are also subject to personal tax, but some or all of the tax has already been collected from the company. It is extremely important to understand this point: under the imputation system, most of the income tax paid on company profits is implicitly personal tax. Consequently, effective company tax is any extra income tax incurred due to a business being structured as a company, rather than being unincorporated.

From this discussion we can see that the net cash flow to the government is:

$$X_g - t_c(X_0 - X_d)(1 - \gamma) \qquad [A14.4]$$

Equation A14.4 illustrates the significance of the variable γ. If no tax credits can be used, then $\gamma = 0$ and $X_g = t_c(X_0 - X_d)$—that is, all of the tax collected from a company is true company tax and the tax system is effectively a classical system. If all of the tax credits can be used, then $\gamma = 1$ and $X_g = 0$—that is, all the tax collected from a company is really nothing more than a withholding of personal tax.

Substituting Equation A14.4 into Equation A14.3, multiplying out the brackets and collecting terms, gives:

$$X_0(1 - t_c(1 - \gamma)) = X_e + X_d(1 - t_c(1 - \gamma))$$

$$\therefore X_0 = \frac{X_e}{1 - t_c(1 - \gamma)} + X_d$$

From Equation A14.2:

$$X_0 = k_0 V$$

Similarly,

$$X_e = k_e E \text{ and } X_d = k_d D$$

where k_e = cost of equity (after effective company tax)
E = market value of equity
k_d = cost of debt (before company tax)
D = market value of debt

Substituting for the cash flow terms in Equation A14.3 gives:

$$k_0 V = k_e E/(1 - t_c(1 - \gamma)) + k_d D$$

and dividing by V, this becomes:

$$k_0 = k_e/(1 - t_c(1 - \gamma))\left[\frac{E}{V}\right] + k_d\left[\frac{D}{V}\right] \qquad [A14.5]$$

Equation A14.5 shows that a company's cost of capital is equal to a weighted average of the costs of equity and debt, where the weights are the proportions of equity and debt in the company's capital structure. However, this cost of capital is of limited use because it is a before-tax cost of capital, whereas returns to investors in a company depend on its after-tax cash flows. The simplest definition of after-tax cash flows is after-effective-company-tax cash flows:

$$X_0(1 - t_c(1 - \gamma))$$

and it follows that the corresponding after-tax cost of capital is obtained by multiplying Equation A14.5 by $[(1 - t_c(1 - \gamma)]$, which gives:

$$k' = k_e\left[\frac{E}{V}\right] + k_d[1 - t_c(1 - \gamma)]\left[\frac{D}{V}\right] \qquad [A14.6]$$

where k' = an after-effective-company-tax cost of capital

A second definition of after-tax cash flows is:

$$X_0(1 - t_c)$$

and the corresponding after-tax cost of capital is obtained by multiplying Equation A14.5 by $(1 - t_c)$, which gives:

$$k'' = k_e(1 - t_c)/[1 - t_c(1 - \gamma)]\left[\frac{E}{V}\right] + k_d(1 - t_c)\left[\frac{D}{V}\right] \qquad [A14.7]$$

This approach uses the traditional definition of net cash flows and all the adjustments needed for the imputation system are made to the WACC. A third definition of after-tax cash flows is: $X_0 - X_g = X_0 - t_c(X_0 - X_d)(1 - \gamma)$

This definition of after-tax cash flows is net operating cash flow before tax less the net cash flow to the government. From Equation A14.3, $X_0 - X_g = X_e + X_d$ and the corresponding after-tax cost of capital is:

$$k''' = k_e\left[\frac{E}{V}\right] + k_d\left[\frac{D}{V}\right] \qquad [A14.8]$$

A fourth definition of after-tax cash flows is:

$$X_0(1 - t_c) + t_c(X_0 - X_d)\gamma$$

This definition of after-tax cash flow adds the value of imputation tax franking credits to the traditional definition of net cash flows. Substituting this definition of after-tax cash flow in Equation A14.3 provides the following corresponding after-tax cost of capital:

$$k'''' = k_e\left[\frac{E}{V}\right] + k_d(1 - t_c)\left[\frac{D}{V}\right] \qquad [A14.9]$$

SUMMARY

It is important that projects are evaluated using a cost of capital that is consistent with the projects' cash flows. Traditionally, in project evaluation, both cash flows and the cost of capital have been expressed on an after-company-tax basis. That approach is easy to use under the classical tax system where there is a clear distinction between company tax and personal tax. However, under the imputation system, some or all of the tax collected from companies is really personal tax. Therefore, to express cash flows on an after-company-tax basis, adjustments are needed.

CHAPTER 15
LEASING AND OTHER EQUIPMENT FINANCE

LEARNING OBJECTIVES
After studying this chapter you should be able to:

1. explain the main features of finance leases and operating leases
2. understand the reasons for leveraged leases and cross-border leases
3. outline the accounting and tax treatment of leases in Australia
4. calculate rentals for a finance lease
5. evaluate a finance lease from the lessee's viewpoint
6. evaluate an operating lease from the lessee's viewpoint
7. critically evaluate the suggested advantages of leasing
8. explain the factors that can influence leasing policy
9. outline the main features of chattel mortgages and hire-purchase agreements.

CHAPTER CONTENTS
- 15.1 Introduction
- 15.2 Types of lease contracts
- 15.3 Accounting and taxation treatment of leases
- 15.4 Setting lease rentals
- 15.5 Evaluation of finance leases
- 15.6 Evaluation of operating leases
- 15.7 Advantages and disadvantages of leasing
- 15.8 Chattel mortgages and hire-purchase

15.1 INTRODUCTION

When most people think of leasing, they probably think of something like hiring a car for the weekend or leasing an apartment for 6 months. While such contracts are indeed leases, there is another form of lease, known as a finance lease, which uses the legal form of leasing in such a way that it becomes an alternative to borrowing funds to purchase new assets. In this chapter, we consider the various forms of leases and explain how a proposed lease may be evaluated. We also consider chattel mortgages and hire-purchase, which, together with leasing, are known as 'equipment finance'.

Leasing is distinguished from most other forms of finance by the fact that the financier (the **lessor**) is the legal owner of the leased asset. The asset user (the **lessee**) obtains the right to use the asset in return for periodic payments (lease rentals) to the lessor. In other words, leasing allows a company to obtain the *use* of an asset, without also obtaining *ownership* of the asset. The range of assets that can be leased is virtually unlimited. Many motor vehicles, aircraft, computers, photocopiers, machinery and other items of production equipment are leased. Unusual assets to be leased include oil rigs, sewage treatment plants and communications satellites (Vardigans 1990).

The Australian Equipment Lessors Association (www.aela.asn.au) estimates that leasing and other equipment finance accounts for around 40 per cent of all capital expenditure on equipment in Australia. The lease component, which made up 60 per cent of total equipment finance in 2000, declined to around 40 per cent of the total in 2007–08, while over the same period hire-purchase declined from 40 to 20 per cent and chattel mortgages grew considerably to make up 40 per cent of the total.[1]

The significance of leasing in Australia is comparable with its prevalence in other markets. For example, Leaseurope reports that, in 2009, equipment leasing in Europe accounted for around 19 per cent of the total investment in equipment (www.leaseurope.org). The Japan Leasing Association reports survey results showing that 94 per cent of Japanese companies use leasing, which accounted for 10 per cent of private capital investment (www.leasing.or.jp).

Lease finance is provided on a large scale by banks and finance companies as an alternative to loans. Other sources of lease finance include investment banks, specialist leasing companies, and vendor leasing companies associated with equipment suppliers. Lease finance commitments for finance leases made by significant lenders are shown in Table 15.1.

lessor
in a lease contract, the party that owns the asset

lessee
in a lease contract, the party using the asset

TABLE 15.1 Lease finance commitments for finance leases by type of lessor, $ million

YEAR TO JUNE	BANKS	FINANCE COMPANIES	GENERAL FINANCIERS	OTHER[a]	TOTAL
2002	1906	1813	1636	1271	6626
2003	1976	1251	1706	1379	6312
2004	1957	1319	1962	1133	6371
2005	2219	1275	1706	1108	6308
2006	2409	np[b]	1956	np[b]	6848
2007	2224	1034	1678	1389	6325
2008	2521	943	1994	1554	7012

continued →

---

1 The features of hire-purchase and chattel mortgages are outlined in Section 15.8.

TABLE 15.1 continued

YEAR TO JUNE	BANKS	FINANCE COMPANIES	GENERAL FINANCIERS	OTHER[a]	TOTAL
2009	2144	np[b]	1658	np[b]	5687
2010	1417	np[b]	1614	np[b]	4642

[a] Includes money market corporations.
[b] Not available for publication but included in total.

Source: Australian Bureau of Statistics, *Lending Finance*, *Australia*, cat. no. 5671.0, Table 3. ABS data used with permission from the Australian Bureau of Statistics (www.abs.gov.au).

15.2 TYPES OF LEASE CONTRACTS

LEARNING OBJECTIVE 1
Explain the main features of finance leases and operating leases

Leases can be broadly classified as either *finance leases* or *operating leases*. Within these broad classes, several types of lease contracts can also be identified. For our purposes, the reason for distinguishing between finance leases and operating leases is that they have different financial implications for both the lessor and the lessee. Therefore, different factors can be important in the evaluation of each type of lease. The major lease types are discussed in the following sections and details of the types of assets that are leased are shown in Table 15.2.

TABLE 15.2 Lease finance commitments, by type of lease and type of goods leased, $ million

A FINANCE LEASES	YEAR TO JUNE			
TYPE OF GOODS	2007	2008	2009	2010
Motor vehicles and other transport equipment	3 101	3 529	2 858	2 516
Construction and earthmoving equipment	410	499	323	606
Manufacturing equipment	159	199	np[a]	626
Agricultural machinery and equipment	132	152	np[a]	571
Electronic data processing equipment	858	939	723	777
Office machines	670	637	564	np[a]
Shop and office furniture, fittings and equipment	267	251	269	np[a]
Other goods	727	807	736	np[a]
Total non-operating lease finance	6 325	7 012	5 687	4 642
B OPERATING LEASES				
Motor vehicles	2 224	1 917	1 785	1 172
Office equipment	755	811	716	652
Other equipment[b]	591	616	439	272
Total operating lease finance	3 570	3 345	2 939	2 096
Total lease finance	9 895	10 357	8 626	6 738

[a] Not available for publication but included in totals
[b] Includes transport equipment and agricultural, construction and manufacturing equipment.

Source: Australian Bureau of Statistics, *Lending Finance*, *Australia*, cat. no. 5671.0, Tables 28 and 39. ABS data used with permission from the Australian Bureau of Statistics (www.abs.gov.au).

15.2.1 FINANCE LEASES

A **finance lease** is a long-term agreement that generally covers most of the economic life of an asset. The agreement will either be non-cancellable or cancellable only if the lessee pays a substantial penalty to the lessor. Therefore, a finance lease is effectively non-cancellable and the lessee has an obligation to make all the agreed lease payments. This obligation is essentially the same as a borrower's obligation to repay a loan. Finance lease agreements normally contain restrictive covenants analogous to those in loan agreements and the lessor will be concerned to ensure that a prospective lessee is credit-worthy. In this case the role of the lessor is to provide finance, and from the lessor's viewpoint a finance lease is, in effect, a secured loan. While the lessor is the legal owner of the asset, it has no great interest in matters such as the day-to-day use of the asset, and the lessee is responsible for repairs, maintenance and insurance. Because of these characteristics, there is an effective transfer from the lessor to the lessee of most of the risks and benefits of ownership of the leased asset. In other words, when a company signs a finance lease it is, in effect, entering into an agreement to purchase the asset using funds borrowed from the lessor.

The role of the banks and other institutions that act as lessors in finance leases is to provide finance rather than to rent assets and they prefer that the lessee should purchase the asset at the end of the lease term. To be treated as a 'genuine lease' for tax purposes, a lease agreement cannot explicitly provide the lessee with an option to purchase the asset. However, under a finance lease the lessee will guarantee that the lessor receives a specified residual value from the sale of the asset at the end of the lease term. The aim of this provision is to ensure that the lessee properly maintains the asset. In practice, the lessee often purchases the asset for the residual value at the end of the lease term.

finance lease
long-term lease that effectively transfers the risks and benefits of ownership of an asset from the lessor to the lessee

15.2.2 OPERATING LEASES

An **operating lease** is essentially a rental agreement and has a term that is short relative to the economic life of the leased asset. For example, a truck with an expected life of 15 years might be leased under an operating lease for 3 years. Because an operating lease covers only part of the life of the leased asset, it follows that the lessor retains all or most of the risks and benefits of ownership of the asset. This is the essential difference between an operating lease and a finance lease where, as discussed above, the risks and benefits of ownership are substantially transferred to the lessee. Lessors are willing to retain the risks of ownership only if they are confident that the asset, when returned by the lessee, will achieve a resale price that is predictable. Accordingly, operating leases are more attractive to lessors if there is an active second-hand market for the leased asset.

operating lease
lease under which the risks and benefits of ownership of the leased asset remain with the lessor

Details of the types of goods leased under the main types of leases are shown in Table 15.2. The detailed figures for leasing shown in this table are consistent with broader figures on the equipment finance market. The Australian Equipment Lessors Association (2008, p. 7) reports that for the 2007–08 financial year motor vehicles accounted for 41 per cent of total equipment finance and other transport equipment for 8 per cent. The remaining 51 per cent is classified as general equipment. A breakdown of these broad asset classes is provided by the Australian Bureau of Statistics only for leasing and, as shown in Table 15.2, non-motor leasing was dominated by EDP equipment (computers) and office machines.

In Australia, operating leases have been limited mainly to motor vehicles, computers and multipurpose industrial equipment such as forklifts. Operating leases are normally offered by the suppliers of those assets, such as computer companies, and by specialist rental companies, such as motor vehicle rental companies. The figures in Table 15.2 show that in 2009–10, motor vehicles accounted for 56 per cent of the value of operating lease commitments, followed by office equipment (mainly computers) at 31 per cent. In the 2009–10 year, operating lease commitments accounted for 31 per cent of total lease finance.

An operating lease agreement is normally for a short period and the asset may be leased to a series of users. Therefore, an operating lease enables a business to obtain the use of an asset that is required for only a short period. For example, suppose that a Melbourne-based company needs a car for use by an executive visiting its Adelaide branch for a month. The company could buy a car and then sell it a month later but that is likely to be both inconvenient and expensive. As well as negotiating the purchase and resale prices, the company would have to register and insure the car and then transfer the registration and cancel the insurance a month later. Clearly, in this case it makes sense to rent or lease the car rather than buy it.

Operating leases may also be **maintenance leases**, which means that the lessor is responsible for insuring the asset, maintaining it and for payment of any government charges. An operating lease enables a lessee to use the asset without directly incurring the risks of ownership such as the risk of obsolescence. The lease rentals will reflect the costs incurred by the lessor including the fact that the lessor retains the risks of ownership. For the lessor, operating leases are characterised by renting out assets and exposure to the risks of ownership, rather than by the provision of finance. Operating leases are discussed further in Section 15.6.

maintenance lease
operating lease where the lessor is responsible for all maintenance and service of the leased asset

15.2.3 SALE AND LEASE-BACK AGREEMENTS

Under a **sale and lease-back agreement** the owner of an asset sells the asset to a financial institution for an amount usually equal to its current market value and immediately leases it back from the institution. The owner relinquishes the title to the asset in return for cash and agrees to make periodic lease payments to the lessor. A sale and lease-back transaction is an alternative to raising cash by borrowing, using the asset as security. The lessor may be an insurance company, although some superannuation funds, banks and specialist leasing companies also offer this form of finance. Commercial real estate is often the subject of such transactions. Office buildings, retail stores, hotels, motels, regional shopping centres, railway rolling stock, vehicle fleets, warehouses and factories have all been the subject of sale and lease-back agreements.

sale and lease-back agreement
agreement in which a company sells an asset and then leases it back

The term of a sale and lease-back agreement will depend on the type of asset concerned but in the case of commercial property is usually less than 15 years. The lessee agrees to make the lease payments for this period and, in addition, is normally responsible for payment of maintenance costs, insurance, government charges and any other costs of occupation.

15.2.4 LEVERAGED LEASING

LEARNING OBJECTIVE 2
Understand the reasons for leveraged leases and cross-border leases

Leveraged leasing, which is a form of finance lease, was introduced into the Australian capital market in the mid-1970s, and since then many large and expensive assets have been leased in this way.[2] The structure of a leveraged lease is shown diagrammatically in Figure 15.1.

A **leveraged lease** differs from an ordinary finance lease in that it involves at least three parties instead of two. The additional party is a lender and is normally referred to as a 'debt participant'. In practice there may be more than three parties involved because the lessor is usually a partnership of two or more equity participants, and there may be two or more debt participants.

leveraged lease
finance lease where the lessor borrows most of the funds to acquire the asset

The debt participants lend to the lessor a high proportion of the cost of the asset. Under the provisions of Taxation Ruling IT2051, the debt participants are expected to contribute no more than 80 per cent of the cost of the asset. A debt participant is usually a life insurance company, superannuation fund, investment bank or bank. Typically the loan is a **non-recourse loan**, which means that the lessor is not responsible for its repayment. Therefore, it is important that the risk of default by the lessee is very low. Security for the debt participant(s) is provided by an assignment of the lease payments, and in some cases a mortgage over the leased asset.

non-recourse loan
type of loan used in leveraged leases where the lender has no recourse to the lessor in the event of default by the lessee

The equity participants are generally banks, investment banks or finance companies that have sufficient profits to take advantage of the tax deductions associated with ownership of the asset and the interest payments on the loan. The equity participants provide the funds not already provided by the lender and form a partnership that purchases the asset. As the majority or, in some cases, all of each lease payment is paid out as interest and principal to the debt participant(s), the equity participants receive little, if any, cash inflow from the lease payments. Their investment is levered in that they provide only *part* of the

---
2 For more details of leveraged leasing, its legal documentation and taxation requirements, see Bennett, Hardaker and Worrall (1997, pp. 283–89, 292–303).

FIGURE 15.1 The role of participants in a leveraged lease

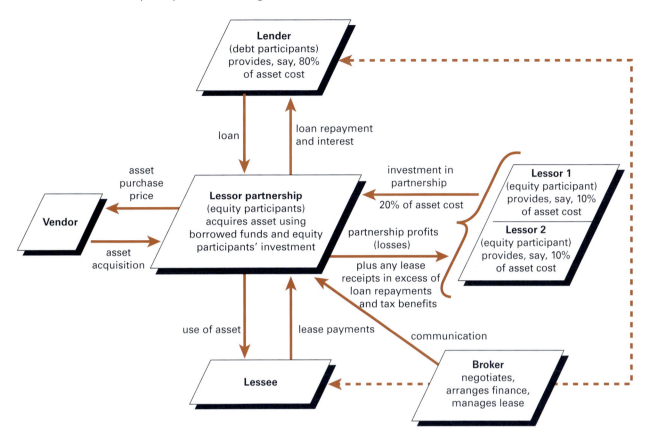

asset's purchase price, but they receive *all* the tax benefits from owning and financing the asset. The equity participants' returns are achieved mainly by deferral of tax payments because the lessor partnership incurs tax losses during the early years of the lease. While a leveraged lease is complex for the lessor, from the lessee's viewpoint it is essentially the same as any other finance lease. The lessee enters into a normal lease contract, agreeing to lease the asset for a specified period and to make specified lease payments.

15.2.5 CROSS-BORDER LEASING

In general terms, a **cross-border lease** (CBL) is a lease where the lessee and lessor are located in different countries. Such transactions are usually leveraged and are motivated by differences between the tax regulations of different countries. As countries assess transactions differently, allow depreciation to be claimed at different rates, and apply different company income tax rates, it is possible to structure transactions to take advantage of these differences. Generally, the lease will be structured so that the lessor and lessee can both claim depreciation deductions on the same asset. Because of the costs involved in establishing a CBL, only very expensive assets are financed in this way.

Several countries allow CBLs because they generate benefits such as increased exports, but some governments, including the Australian Government, have moved to discourage the use of CBLs. In particular, restrictions contained in section 51AD and Division 16D of the Income Tax Assessment Act mean that it is virtually impossible for an Australian lessor to participate in a cross-border lease involving an offshore asset. However, a CBL can be structured so that a foreign lessor and an Australian lessee can both claim depreciation deductions, provided that the lease contains a purchase option so that it is treated as a hire-purchase agreement in Australia.

cross-border lease
finance lease, usually leveraged, where the lessor and lessee are located in different countries

The CBL market has been dominated by transactions involving commercial aircraft, but other assets financed in this way include printing presses, trucks, rolling stock, cargo ships and shipping containers. A CBL can involve parties in several different countries and the arrangements are typically very complex. Also, the contractual arrangements used in the CBL market can change frequently in response to factors such as changes in regulations. Therefore, any business that contemplates the use of a CBL will require specialised legal and taxation advice.

15.3 ACCOUNTING AND TAXATION TREATMENT OF LEASES

LEARNING OBJECTIVE 3
Outline the accounting and tax treatment of leases in Australia

15.3.1 ACCOUNTING FOR LEASES[3]

Traditionally, lease rentals were recognised as an expense for the lessee and there was no recognition by the lessee of any lease assets or liabilities. This approach was criticised for two reasons. First, some leases provide valuable rights and obligations that cannot be avoided and should be included in the lessee's statement of financial position (balance sheet). Second, it was argued that the accounting treatment of transactions should be based on their economic substance rather than their legal form. Since a finance lease is economically equivalent to borrowing and buying an asset, it follows that the rights and obligations involved in a finance lease should be shown on the lessee's statement of financial position. In Australia, Accounting Standard AASB 117, 'Leases', provides that the accounting treatment of a lease depends on whether it is classified as an operating lease or a finance lease. Operating leases are treated in the traditional way but finance leases must be recognised as assets and liabilities. AASB 117 provides that a lease would normally be classified as a finance lease if substantially all of the risks and rewards associated with ownership of the leased asset are effectively transferred to the lessee (para. 8). Where the lease is a finance lease, a lease asset and liability equal to the fair value of the leased property or, if lower, the present value of the minimum lease payments must be recognised. However, some lessees believe that it is advantageous to avoid recognising finance leases as assets and liabilities. Consequently, lessors have responded by designing leases that are, in substance, finance leases but can be classified as operating leases under AASB 117. This activity has continued, despite efforts by the standard setters to emphasise that the classification of a lease should depend on its economic substance rather than its legal form.

15.3.2 TAXATION TREATMENT OF LEASES

The taxation treatment of leases in Australia can be complex and has been subject to many changes through both legislation and taxation rulings.[4] Only a broad outline of the main principles is provided here. If a leased asset is used to generate taxable income, the lease rentals paid by the lessee are an allowable tax deduction, provided that the lease is classified as a 'genuine lease' rather than an 'instalment purchase arrangement'. The purpose of this distinction is to prevent taxpayers using leasing as a way of obtaining accelerated tax deductions by claiming, as deductions, outlays that are of a capital nature. Consequently, a deduction may not be allowed for lease rentals if the lease agreement gives the lessee an option to purchase the leased asset at the end of the lease term.[5] Similarly, the Commissioner of Taxation has specified rules concerning acceptable residual values and may disallow a deduction for lease rentals that have been increased by the use of an unrealistically low residual value.

---

3 For a full discussion of this topic, see Henderson, Peirson and Herbohn (2011).
4 For a more detailed coverage of the taxation effects of leasing in Australia, see Szekely (1991) or Australian Equipment Lessors Association (2008) pp.8–19.
5 Although the requirements of the Commissioner of Taxation, set out in Taxation Ruling IT28, prevent the lessor from providing the lessee with an option to buy the asset, it is usual for such an option to be implicit in finance lease agreements. In the vast majority of cases, the lessee buys the asset by payment of the specified residual value at the end of the initial lease period. In most other cases the lessee renews the lease for an additional period.

While lease rentals are deductible, the lessee cannot deduct, for tax purposes, depreciation on the leased asset. Depreciation is deductible by the lessor as the legal owner of the asset, and lease rentals received by the lessor are, of course, taxable. Lessors may attempt to defer tax payments by varying the size or frequency of the rentals during the term of a lease. The Australian Taxation Office may scrutinise such arrangements and is particularly sceptical of lease structures that involve increased rentals over time (Szekely 1991, p. 49).

The taxation rules often have an important effect on the choice between leasing and other similar forms of finance. For example, if it is advantageous for depreciation deductions to be claimed by the asset user, a chattel mortgage or a hire-purchase agreement may be used, rather than a lease. Chattel mortgages and hire-purchase are discussed in Section 15.8.

15.4 SETTING LEASE RENTALS

While the main emphasis in this book is on the viewpoint of the lessee, it is useful to consider the approach used by lessors in setting lease rentals. Prospective lessees who understand the factors that influence lease rentals should be in a stronger negotiating position than those who do not. The setting of lease rentals is illustrated in Example 15.1.

LEARNING OBJECTIVE 4
Calculate rentals for a finance lease

EXAMPLE 15.1

Monlease has been asked by a group of doctors to quote on a 4-year lease of an item of medical equipment that costs $600 000. The equipment can be depreciated for tax purposes on a straight-line basis over 3 years. Monlease has a tax rate of 30 per cent and requires a rate of return of 8 per cent per annum after tax from leases. There are to be four equal lease payments, payable annually in advance. The agreed residual value is $120 000. What is the minimum annual lease payment that Monlease should quote?

SOLUTION
The manager of Monlease calculates the lease payments using the following steps.

(a) *Calculate the present value of cash flows from asset ownership*. These cash flows are the tax savings on depreciation and the after-tax cash inflow from the sale of the asset (at the residual value) at the end of the lease term. The present value of the depreciation tax savings is calculated as shown in Table 15.3.

TABLE 15.3

YEAR	DEPRECIATION (D)	TAX SAVINGS (D x TAX RATE)	PV FACTOR @ 8% P.A.	PRESENT VALUE
1	$200 000	$60 000	0.9259	$55 556
2	$200 000	$60 000	0.8573	$51 440
3	$200 000	$60 000	0.7938	$47 630
Total				$154 626

Monlease will also receive the residual value of $120 000 but will have to pay tax on the resulting profit on the sale of the equipment, which is also $120 000 because the equipment has a written-down value for tax purposes of zero. Therefore, the after-tax cash inflow will be $120 000(1 − 0.3) = $84 000, which has a present value of $84 000/$1.08^4$ = $84 000 x 0.7350 or $61 743. The total cash flows associated with ownership of the equipment have a present value of $154 626 + $61 743 = $216 369.

(b) *Calculate the required present value of the lease payments*. The asset costs $600 000, of which Monlease will recover $216 369 from its ownership. Therefore, the required present value of the lease payments is $600 000 − $216 369 = $383 631.

continued →

Example 15.1 *continued*

(c) *Calculate the minimum after-tax lease payment.* With annual lease payments, L, payable in advance:

$$\$383\,631 = L\left\{1 + \frac{1}{0.08}\left[1 - \frac{1}{(1.08)^3}\right]\right\}$$

$$= L(1 + 2.5771)$$

$$L = \frac{\$383\,631}{3.5771}$$

$$= \$107\,246$$

(d) *Calculate the minimum before-tax lease payment, L', given the tax rate t_c.*

$$L' = \frac{L}{1 - t_c} = \frac{\$107\,246}{1 - 0.3} = \$153\,209$$

To achieve its required rate of return of 8 per cent after tax, Monlease should quote annual lease payments of $153 209.

From these calculations it should be clear that Monlease would be able to quote lower lease rental payments if:

(i) the depreciation rate for tax purposes is *higher*
(ii) the residual value of the equipment is *higher*
(iii) the lessor's required rate of return is *lower*.

In practice, other factors will also affect lease rental payments. For example, lessors will adjust lease rentals to reflect any transaction costs involved in establishing the lease and any government charges, such as stamp duty and the goods and services tax (GST). They are also likely to adjust the required rate of return to reflect differences in credit risk between different lessees, and they may take into account the exact timing of tax effects. Therefore, for some leases, particularly large ones, the calculation of lease rentals is more complex than the procedure illustrated in Example 15.1. On the other hand, the procedure may be less complex. For small leases, a lessor may calculate the required lease payments using before-tax cash flows and a before-tax rate of return.

15.5 EVALUATION OF FINANCE LEASES

Many methods have been suggested for evaluating finance leases. One reason for this is that there has been controversy over the question of how to structure the evaluation of leases; some authors suggest that the appropriate comparison is 'leasing versus borrowing', while others suggest that 'leasing versus buying' is the correct approach.

The approach we discuss was presented by Myers, Dill and Bautista (MDB) (1976). Essentially, the mechanics of the MDB method of analysing a finance lease are identical to those proposed earlier by other authors.[6] However, the main contribution made by MDB lies in analysing a finance lease in the context of its effect on the lessee's capital structure. In particular, MDB emphasised that entering into a finance lease uses some of the lessee's debt capacity. Therefore, it follows that a finance lease should be analysed by comparing it with debt.

LEARNING OBJECTIVE 5
Evaluate a finance lease from the lessee's viewpoint

MDB showed that this conclusion follows even if the comparison is initially viewed as lease versus buy. They pointed out that the phrase 'lease versus buy' is virtually meaningless unless the means of financing the purchase are specified. Suppose that the comparison is specified as leasing versus buying, using normal financing—that is, the mixture of debt and equity in the company's normal capital structure. It is then necessary to allow for the fact that lease finance will use some of the company's debt capacity.

---

6 For an analysis of the origins of the MDB method, see Burrows (1988).

When this is done it can be seen that, in effect, lease finance must be compared with debt. The effect of lease finance in using debt capacity is illustrated in Example 15.2.

EXAMPLE 15.2

Heavy Haulage Ltd has assets with a market value of $500 000, financed by a capital structure of $250 000 equity and $250 000 debt. The company needs a new truck, which can be either purchased for $100 000 or leased. What effect will leasing the truck have on the company's debt capacity?

SOLUTION

If the truck is purchased using the company's normal combination of debt and equity, the statement of financial position will be as follows:

STATEMENT OF FINANCIAL POSITION 1

Assets	$500 000	Debt	$300 000
Truck	$100 000	Equity	$300 000
	$600 000		$600 000

Alternatively, if the truck is leased, the statement of financial position will be:

STATEMENT OF FINANCIAL POSITION 2

Assets	$500 000	Debt	$250 000
Truck	$100 000	Lease liability	$100 000
		Equity	$250 000
	$600 000		$600 000

Leasing has increased the company's debt–equity ratio because the lease liability is an additional type of debt in the company's capital structure. To restore the original debt–equity ratio, the company should raise another $50 000 of equity and repay the debt of $50 000. After these changes, the statement of financial position will contain equity of $300 000, debt of $200 000 and the lease liability of $100 000. A comparison with Statement of financial position 1 shows that the lease used $100 000 of the company's debt capacity.

Example 15.2 shows that leasing uses a company's debt capacity, which suggests that a finance lease should be evaluated by comparing it with other debt finance. However, this does not mean that the alternative to leasing an asset is to borrow an amount equal to the purchase price of the asset. Rather it means that finance lease evaluation must allow for the fact that a company entering into a finance lease reduces its ability to borrow in other ways—that is, the obligation to make rental payments under a lease uses up some of the debt capacity provided by the company's assets. For leasing to be economically advantageous to a lessee, the finance provided by leasing must be greater than the liability incurred by leasing. The MDB method focuses on making that comparison by calculating the liability incurred by leasing. Example 15.3 illustrates the MDB method.

EXAMPLE 15.3

Sharemarket Research Ltd (SRL) needs a new computer, which can be purchased for $600 000. The company's financial manager, Elliott Wave, is considering the alternative of leasing the computer from Efficient Finance, which requires six lease rentals of $126 000 each, payable annually in advance. The computer can be depreciated for tax purposes over 3 years on a straight-line basis and its disposal value is expected to be zero at the end of the lease. The company income tax rate is 30 per cent. Is the proposed lease attractive to SRL?

continued →

Example 15.3 *continued*

SOLUTION

The incremental cash flows for leasing the computer, rather than buying it, are shown in Table 15.4.

TABLE 15.4 Cash flows: lease versus purchase

ITEM	CASH FLOWS ($)					
	YEAR 0	YEAR 1	YEAR 2	YEAR 3	YEAR 4	YEAR 5
1. Cost of computer	600 000	—	—	—	—	—
2. Lease rentals	−126 000	−126 000	−126 000	−126 000	−126 000	−126 000
3. Tax savings on lease rentals	37 800	37 800	37 800	37 800	37 800	37 800
4. Depreciation tax savings lost	—	−60 000	−60 000	−60 000	—	—
Total	511 800	−148 200	−148 200	−148 200	−88 200	−88 200

Remembering that the table shows the *incremental* cash flows for leasing versus buying, the explanation for each item is straightforward. First, by leasing the computer, SRL does not need to pay the purchase price of $600 000. Therefore, there is an effective cash inflow of this amount. Second, the lease rentals are a cash payment each year, but these payments are tax deductible, generating annual tax savings of $37 800, which are a cash inflow. Finally, by leasing rather than buying, SRL is unable to claim depreciation deductions of $200 000 per annum in Years 1, 2 and 3. Therefore, it forgoes tax savings of $60 000 in each of these years. The bottom row of Table 15.4 shows that the lease provides finance of $511 800 to SRL and requires net cash outflows by SRL in Years 1 to 5.

To determine whether the lease is attractive to SRL, the cash outflows in Years 1 to 5 can be regarded as after-tax repayments of a loan that is equivalent to the lease—that is, we ask: if SRL had offered this set of repayments to an alternative lender, how much could SRL have borrowed? If the amount is less than $511 800, SRL should accept the lease. The amount that could be borrowed from an alternative lender will depend on the interest rate on the hypothetical equivalent loan. The interest rate will, in turn, depend on the security offered to the lender. For the loan to be equivalent to the lease, the security should be the same as that held by the lessor. If the lessor's only security is ownership of the computer, the interest rate on a loan secured by a mortgage or other charge over the computer could be appropriate.[7] Assume that Elliott Wave has been quoted a rate of 10.8 per cent per annum on such a loan. Because the cash flows to be discounted are after tax, the discount rate must also be after tax—that is, 10.8 × (1 − 0.3) = 7.56 per cent per annum.

The present value of the net cash outflows is:

$$PV = \frac{\$148\,200}{0.0756}\left[1 - \frac{1}{(1.0756)^3}\right] + \frac{\$88\,200}{(1.0756)^4} + \frac{\$88\,200}{(1.0756)^5}$$
$$= \$512\,141$$

The lease provides finance of $511 800 and the present value of the liability incurred by leasing is $512 141, so the net present value (NPV) of the lease relative to the equivalent loan is:

NPV = $511 800 − $512 141 = −$341

Based on this analysis the lease is marginally unattractive and should not be accepted by SRL.

15.5.1 LEASING DECISIONS AND INVESTMENT DECISIONS

To interpret correctly the result of a lease evaluation such as that in Example 15.3, it is necessary to understand that this evaluation relates only to the question of whether it is better to lease or buy, *given that the services*

---

[7] The lessor's formal security is generally, but not always, restricted to ownership of the leased asset. A case in which additional security was required is cited by Burrows (1998, p. 117). For evidence on factors that affect the cost of lease finance, see Schallheim et al. (1987).

provided by the asset are to be acquired. In other words, the lease evaluation gives an NPV for leasing the asset *relative* to buying it. Suppose that in Example 15.3 the NPV of the lease was $1000. This positive NPV does not necessarily mean that SRL should lease the computer. If buying the computer has a negative NPV, say –$5000, then leasing it would not be attractive because the total NPV for acquiring the computer by leasing is:

NPV if purchased	–$5000
NPV of lease relative to purchase	$1000
NPV of leasing computer	–$4000

Since the total NPV is negative, the computer should not be leased: leasing is better than purchasing, but both alternatives are unprofitable.

In practice, the investment decision would normally be considered first and, if the project were profitable, the alternative of leasing the required assets would then be evaluated. However, the financial manager should not necessarily discard a project if evaluation of the investment decision reveals a negative NPV. In some cases, the NPV of a lease can be large enough to 'rescue' an otherwise marginally unprofitable project.

15.5.2 THE VALUE OF LEASING IN COMPETITIVE CAPITAL MARKETS

Later sections, including Section 15.5.3, discuss some of the conditions that can result in a lease having a positive NPV for the lessee. Lease finance is provided in markets that are highly competitive, which has important implications for the value of leasing. To examine these implications, suppose that all financiers and asset users operate in a perfect capital market where the following conditions apply:

(a) leasing involves no transaction costs
(b) information is costless and freely available
(c) all parties are subject to the same tax laws and tax rates.

Under these conditions, the cost of leasing an asset should be exactly the same as the cost of buying it—that is, the lease-or-buy decision should be a matter of indifference. The argument that leads to this conclusion will be explained using, for illustrative purposes, the data and results of Example 15.3. In that example, the NPV for the lessee of leasing the new computer rather than purchasing it was –$341.

Now consider the position of the lessor, Efficient Finance. From the lessor's viewpoint the decision is whether to lease the computer to SRL or to lend SRL funds to buy it. If Efficient Finance is to lease the computer to SRL, it must first buy the computer for $600 000. Efficient Finance will receive the lease rentals, be taxed on them and can claim tax deductions for depreciation of the computer. Therefore, provided that both parties are taxed at the same rate, the lessee's after-tax cash outflows are the lessor's after-tax cash inflows. In other words, Efficient Finance's net cash flows will be those shown in the bottom row of Table 15.4, with the signs reversed. Because the appropriate discount rate will remain unchanged at 7.56 per cent per annum, the NPV of this lease for the lessor must be +$341.

Under these circumstances, the lease alternative is attractive to the lessor but not to the lessee. Reducing the lease rentals would increase the value of the lease to SRL but must also cause an equal reduction in the value of the lease to Efficient Finance. Because of the symmetry between the positions of the two parties, it is impossible to design a lease that will be more attractive to the lessee than borrowing, without simultaneously making the lease less attractive to the lessor.

Further, in a perfect capital market, lessors should earn only a normal rate of return on their activities. Therefore, in equilibrium, the NPV of providing lease finance should be zero. Again, because of the symmetrical positions of the two parties, the NPV of leasing for the lessee must also be zero. Therefore, in a perfect capital market all asset users should be indifferent between the alternatives of leasing and buying. This conclusion should not be surprising. The lease-or-buy decision is a financing decision, and, as discussed in Chapter 12, Modigliani and Miller showed that, in a perfect capital market, financing decisions have no effect on shareholders' wealth. In other words, just as there is no magic in financial leverage in a perfect capital market, so there is no magic in leasing.

Calculation of the equilibrium lease rentals that should make an asset user indifferent between leasing and buying is shown in Example 15.4.

EXAMPLE 15.4

Western Computer Services Ltd (WCS) is considering the acquisition of a computer that can be purchased for $500 000 or leased. The lease is to involve five equal rental payments, payable annually in advance, with a residual value of $50 000 after 5 years. WCS expects to be paying tax at the rate of 30 per cent during the term of the lease. What are the maximum lease rentals that should be paid, given that the interest rate on an equivalent loan is 10 per cent per annum?

SOLUTION

As in Example 15.3, the first step is to determine the incremental cash flows for leasing versus buying. The additional factor to be considered is the treatment of the residual value, which in this case is $50 000. To put the lease and purchase alternatives on the same basis it must be assumed that WCS pays the residual value and thereby purchases the computer from the lessor. This raises one further complication: if WCS leases the computer and then purchases it, the company can claim tax deductions, beginning in Year 6, for depreciation based on the purchase price of $50 000. If WCS had purchased the computer when it was new, all depreciation deductions would have been claimed during the first 3 years. Therefore, the two alternatives involve a difference in allowable tax deductions after the lease term.

To make an unbiased comparison, it will be assumed that in each alternative the computer is sold at the end of Year 5—that is, at the end of the lease term, WCS buys the computer by paying the residual value of $50 000 and immediately sells it for its market value, also assumed to be $50 000. Therefore, the sale proceeds will be the same in each case and do not have to be included, since incremental cash flows are being considered. However, the lease's residual value must be included, as must any tax effects related to the sale of the computer. In this case, the lease alternative does not involve any tax effect, since WCS is assumed to sell the computer for $50 000, which is the same as the price it paid. The alternative of buying the asset involves a profit of $50 000 (since in that case, the written-down value is zero) on which the income tax will be $50 000 × 0.3 = $15 000.

The incremental cash flows for leasing versus buying are shown in Table 15.5, where L represents the annual lease rental.

TABLE 15.5 Cash flows: lease versus purchase

ITEM	CASH FLOWS ($)					
	YEAR 0	YEAR 1	YEAR 2	YEAR 3	YEAR 4	YEAR 5
1. Cost of computer	500 000	—	—	—	—	—
2. Lease rentals	−L	−L	−L	−L	−L	—
3. Tax savings on lease rentals	0.3L	0.3L	0.3L	0.3L	0.3L	—
4. Depreciation tax savings lost	—	−50 000	−50 000	−50 000	—	—
5. Lease residual value	—	—	—	—	—	−50 000
6. Tax saved on profit on sale	—	—	—	—	—	15 000

The after-tax interest rate on an equivalent loan is 10(1 − 0.3) = 7 per cent per annum, and the equilibrium lease rentals can be found by solving as follows:[8]

$$NPV = 0 = \$500\,000 - 0.7L\left\{1 + \frac{1}{0.07}\left[1 - \frac{1}{(1.07)^4}\right]\right\} - \frac{\$50\,000}{0.07}\left[1 - \frac{1}{(1.07)^3}\right] - \frac{\$35\,000}{(1.07)^5}$$

∴ 3.0710L = $500 000 − $131 216 − $24 955

and L = $111 958

Therefore, the maximum lease rentals that WCS should be prepared to pay are $111 958 per annum. These rentals will also provide a normal rate of return to the lessor.

Does the perfect capital market result of indifference between leasing and buying apply in real-world capital markets? The popularity of leasing has varied over time and it is particularly popular for some types of assets. These observations suggest that there are cases where asset users have a systematic preference for leasing or buying. Clearly, for this to be the case, there must be tax differences or imperfections that can make leasing advantageous. Some conditions that may give rise to an overall advantage for leasing are discussed in the next section. The advantages and disadvantages of leasing are also discussed in Section 15.7.

15.5.3 ESTABLISHING AN ADVANTAGE FOR LEASING

To make leasing attractive to the user of an asset, without simultaneously making leasing unattractive to the lessor, requires some departure from the perfect-market conditions outlined in the previous section. In particular, it is necessary to break the symmetry between the positions of the two parties. There are ways in which this can be done. For example, the lessor may be entitled to receive quantity discounts that are not available to the buyer of a single item. Such discounts may be available to specialist lessors of mass-produced assets, such as cars, but are unlikely to apply where the asset is unique or where the lessor is a general financier. Leasing may also be advantageous where there is some difference between the tax positions of the lessor and the asset user. This is illustrated in Example 15.5, which uses the same basic information as Example 15.3.

EXAMPLE 15.5

Sharemarket Research Ltd (SRL) is again considering the acquisition of a $600 000 computer, but Elliott Wave has now established that because of past losses that are being carried forward, SRL is unlikely to pay company income tax during the next 5 years. Is the lease attractive?

SOLUTION

The revised cash flows for leasing the computer, rather than purchasing it, are shown in Table 15.6. The only relevant cash flows are the cost of the computer and the lease rentals.

TABLE 15.6 Cash flows: lease versus purchase

ITEM	CASH FLOWS ($)					
	YEAR 0	YEAR 1	YEAR 2	YEAR 3	YEAR 4	YEAR 5
1. Cost of computer	600 000					
2. Lease rentals	−126 000	−126 000	−126 000	−126 000	−126 000	−126 000
Total	474 000	−126 000	−126 000	−126 000	−126 000	−126 000

continued →

---

[8] Since the residual value of $50 000 is specified in the lease agreement, it is of similar risk to the lease rentals and can be discounted at the after-tax cost of debt. However, the tax savings ($15 000) depend in part on the disposal (market) value of the computer and are therefore riskier. Discounting this cash flow at the after-tax cost of debt is an approximation.

Example 15.5 *continued*

Because SRL is unlikely to pay company income tax during the term of the lease, these net cash flows should be discounted at the before-tax borrowing rate of 10.8 per cent. The NPV of the lease to SRL is:

$$NPV = +\$474\,000 - \frac{\$126\,000}{0.108}\left[1 - \frac{1}{(1.108)^5}\right]$$

$$= \$5965$$

Therefore, because SRL will not be paying company income tax during the term of the lease, the NPV of the lease has increased from −$341 to $5965. Assuming that Efficient Finance will be in a taxpaying position each year, the NPV to it will still be $341. Therefore, the lease alternative now has a positive NPV for both parties and there is an overall gain from leasing:

Gain from leasing = $5965 + $341 = $6306

This gain is realised at the expense of the government and is achieved because the lessor is utilising tax deductions associated with ownership and financing of the leased asset (in this case, deductions for depreciation and interest on borrowings) as soon as they are available. If SRL purchased the computer using borrowed money, these deductions would be of no immediate value to the company because they would only add to the tax loss being carried forward.

The manner in which the gain of $6306 is shared between the lessor and lessee will depend, in part, on the level of competition in the leasing industry. If there is perfect competition in the industry, the annual lease rentals will be reduced to a level such that the NPV to Efficient Finance is zero and the whole gain will then accrue to SRL.

15.5.4 TAXES AND THE SIZE OF LEASING GAINS

Examples 15.3 and 15.5 show that leasing can be less costly than purchasing where the lessor has advantages not available to the potential lessee and where some of these advantages are passed on to the lessee by way of lower lease payments. However, these examples assume an extreme case in which the lessee's tax rate is zero and the lessor's tax rate is the full statutory rate, assumed to be 30 per cent. In many cases, the difference between the effective tax rates of the two parties may be much smaller and it may vary over time. For example, the lessee may initially have a tax rate of zero but begin to pay tax during the lease term. Therefore, factors such as the timing of the lease rental payments can affect the size of the gain associated with leasing. To identify the factors that can be important and to illustrate their effects, consider the effects that a lease can have on the present value of the government's tax receipts.

In Examples 15.3 and 15.5, the NPV of the lease involves calculating the present values of three types of cash flows: the cost of the asset, the after-tax lease rentals and the tax savings on depreciation. The NPV of a lease to the lessee (NPV_{LES}) can be expressed as:

$$NPV_{LES} = C - PV(L) - PV(Dep) \qquad [15.1]$$

where C = cost of the leased asset
$PV(L)$ = present value of lease rentals
$PV(Dep)$ = present value of depreciation tax savings

Similarly, the *NPV* to the lessor (NPV_{LOR}) will be:

$$NPV_{LOR} = -C + PV(L)^* + PV(Dep)^* \qquad [15.2]$$

The asterisks (*) have been added because the present values of the lease rentals and the depreciation tax savings can differ, given that the lessor and lessee have different tax rates. The overall gain from the lease can be found by adding Equations 15.1 and 15.2. The cost of the asset, C, will cancel out, leaving only terms involving the lease rentals and the depreciation tax savings. Therefore, the lease affects the present value of the government's tax receipts in two ways. First, the government gains, in that it can tax the lease rentals received by the lessor. Second, the government loses, in that the lessor is able to claim deductions for depreciation on the leased asset. The net result is that the government can lose through deferral of tax receipts and it follows that, other things being equal, the government's net loss will be larger in present value terms if:

(a) the difference between the effective tax rates of the lessor and lessee is large
(b) the depreciation rate applicable for tax purposes is high, so that depreciation tax savings are received early
(c) the term of the lease is long and the lease rentals are concentrated during the later part of the lease term, so that tax payments by the lessor are deferred
(d) interest rates and hence the discount rate applicable to the cash flows are high (if the discount rate is zero, changing the timing of tax payments does not change their present value).

Thus, leasing is more likely to be used if there are high company tax rates, high depreciation rates and high interest rates. It is not surprising that leasing has grown rapidly at times when these factors have been present. Example 15.5 showed that there can be a tax-based gain from leasing when the lessor has a higher tax rate than the lessee but it should be noted that *any* difference between the tax rates of the two parties is likely to result in a net gain or loss from leasing. Lewellen, Long and McConnell (1976) showed that a net gain can arise when the lessor's tax rate is *lower* than the lessee's rate and the magnitude of the gain depends on the specific features of each case, including the term of the lease, the depreciation method and rate and the discount rates applied to future cash flows.

15.5.5 LEASING AND THE IMPUTATION TAX SYSTEM

The discussion in Section 15.5.4 explained that any tax advantages associated with a lease arise from deferral of taxes, usually in the form of company income tax. It was also explained that the potential tax benefits are larger, other things being equal, when there is a large difference between the effective tax rates of the lessor and the lessee. The potential for there to be large differences between effective tax rates will be greater when tax rates are high. However, as discussed in Section 11.4.1, under the Australian system of full imputation, company income tax is, from the viewpoint of resident shareholders, only a withholding tax. In other words, for many companies the effective rate of *company* income tax (as distinct from tax *collected* at the company level) is very low. It follows that for such companies any advantage associated with deferring a company's tax payments will also be very small and any tax advantage from leasing must also be small. Of course, individuals who operate businesses as sole traders and partnerships are often taxed at much higher rates than companies, so leasing may have significant tax advantages in these cases.

15.6 EVALUATION OF OPERATING LEASES

In Section 15.2.2 we explained that an operating lease allows a lessee to obtain the services provided by an asset, without directly bearing the risks of asset ownership. The risks of ownership remain with the lessor because an operating lease has a term that is short relative to the life of the asset. These leases are more complex than finance leases for several reasons. First, the lessee may have the right but not the obligation to renew the lease at the end of an initial term. Second, the lessee may have the right to cancel the lease, either at any time after it has commenced or at any time after an agreed date. Therefore, cancellable operating leases enable a lessee to obtain insurance against an unexpectedly large decline in the value of an asset.[9] The risk of an unexpected decline in value can be particularly high for assets such as computers, which can become obsolete very quickly, because of changes in technology. Third, the lease rental may be contingent on another variable such as the lessee's volume of sales. For example, retail

LEARNING OBJECTIVE 6
Evaluate an operating lease from the lessee's viewpoint

---

[9] The right to renew a lease provides a call option over the leased asset, while the right to cancel the lease provides a put option. A detailed coverage of options is provided in Chapter 18.

tenants in shopping centres usually lease their premises under an agreement where the rent consists of a fixed base rent plus a percentage of any monthly sales in excess of a specified threshold level. Authors who have examined the valuation of these components of operating leases include Copeland and Weston (1982) and Grenadier (1995).

The decision on whether to buy an asset or lease it through an operating lease often centres on the transaction costs of buying and selling the asset. As noted in Section 15.2.2, where an asset such as a car is needed for a short period of, say, a month or less, it is usually clear that an operating lease will be cheaper than buying the car and then selling it. On the other hand, if the car is needed for a year or more, most users will find it cheaper to buy rather than lease. For intermediate time periods the preferred choice may not be obvious and financial analysis may be needed to determine whether an operating lease is attractive. While option-pricing models such as those discussed in Section 18.8.6 can, in principle, be used to value the options inherent in an operating lease, such models are complex. Fortunately, there is a simpler model that can be used instead.

In Section 6.3 the equivalent annual value model was used to compare projects with different economic lives. A variant of this model, equivalent annual cost, can be used to evaluate operating leases. The principle involved is simple: *an operating lease is attractive to the lessee if the annual rental is less than the equivalent annual cost of buying and operating the asset.* In applying this principle, care is needed to ensure that the lease and buy alternatives are treated consistently. For example, if the operating lease is a maintenance lease, then the costs of insuring and maintaining the asset should be included in the equivalent annual cost calculation, as well as the costs of owning the asset.

As noted in Section 15.2.2, the rentals for an operating lease will reflect the costs incurred by the lessor in acquiring and maintaining the asset. More precisely, in a competitive leasing market the annual rental for an operating lease should be equal to the equivalent annual cost of the asset to the lessor. When the user requires the asset for a long period such as 5 years, it will generally be cheaper to buy the asset rather than to lease it. In other words, the cost of a 'do-it-yourself lease' obtained by buying the asset is likely to be lower than the rentals charged by an external lessor. This is so because, when setting the lease rentals, an external lessor will need to consider the costs of negotiating multiple leases over the life of the asset and take into account the expectation that the asset will be idle for part of the time. These costs can be avoided if the user buys the asset.

While an operating lease will generally be more costly than buying an asset that is needed for an extended period, there are circumstances where an operating lease can be less costly than buying. First, an operating lease can be cheaper than buying if the lessor can take advantage of cost savings that are not available to the lessee. For example, car rental companies buy thousands of cars each year and can negotiate volume discounts that are not available to smaller customers. Similarly, car rental companies probably face lower costs in maintaining, servicing and insuring cars than most other owners. A business that uses only a few vehicles cannot take advantage of these economies of scale and will probably find it cheaper to lease cars rather than buy them. Second, operating leases provide options that are valuable to the lessee and in some cases the option to cancel a lease can be the most cost effective way of obtaining a benefit such as insurance against the risk of premature obsolescence or the risk that an asset is no longer needed owing to a decline in demand.

The airline industry is a good example of an industry that faces fluctuating demand and changes in the mix of aircraft that are needed and this has important implications for the decision to own or lease aircraft. Suppose that a terrorist attack at a major airport causes a decline in demand for air travel and a surplus of aircraft. In this case, an airline that owns all of its aircraft can experience major financial difficulties, particularly if the decline in demand is widespread and persists for an extended period so that the company has several aircraft lying idle rather than earning revenue. Under these circumstances, efforts to sell the surplus aircraft are likely to be unsuccessful unless the seller is prepared to discount the price significantly. Accordingly, most airlines lease a proportion of their fleet under cancellable operating leases and are prepared to pay a premium for the lessor to accept the risk of cancellation. One study found that leased aircraft are traded more frequently and produce higher output than aircraft that are owned by the user. The main reason for the higher output is that leased aircraft spend more time in the air and less time parked on the ground than owned aircraft.[10]

ADVANTAGES AND DISADVANTAGES OF LEASING 15.7

The popularity of leasing indicates that there are many cases where users prefer to lease assets rather than to purchase them. It is shown in Section 15.5.3 that leasing may be preferred where: (a) the lessor has an advantage (or advantages) not available to the potential lessee; and (b) the lessor passes on at least some of the advantage(s) to the lessee by way of reduced lease payments.

Alternatively, leasing may have advantages such as lower transaction costs and it may have incentive effects that make it more effective than other forms of finance in controlling agency costs. Several of the alleged advantages of leasing are discussed in the following sections. First, we discuss possible advantages of leasing in general. Second, we discuss factors that may be important in determining which particular assets should be leased, rather than purchased, by a company.

LEARNING OBJECTIVE 7
Critically evaluate the suggested advantages of leasing

15.7.1 POSSIBLE ADVANTAGES OF LEASING

Proponents of leasing often stress taxation advantages, conservation of capital, increased credit availability and the possibility that leasing may provide capital at a lower cost than other forms of finance. The prevalence of such claims was noted by Scarman (1982), who examined promotional literature used by finance companies in their marketing of leases. He found a high incidence of errors and overstatements which, not surprisingly, were biased in favour of leasing. Several possible advantages of leasing are discussed in turn.

Company taxation

The tax deductions associated with ownership of an asset are generally the same, regardless of whether the asset is owned or leased by the user. If, as assumed in Examples 15.2 and 15.3, the potential lessee and lessor are taxed at the same rate, there should be no taxation advantage associated with leasing. If this assumption does not hold then, as discussed in Section 15.5.3, leasing may provide a taxation advantage. Any such advantage arises from the deferral of taxes and can be large in present value terms where a company requires an expensive asset but is not able to utilise fully the depreciation deductions if the asset is purchased. This problem may be overcome if the asset is acquired by a lessor who can use all the allowable deductions as soon as they are available. In this case, the lessor has an advantage over the potential lessee and it would be preferable to lease the asset if the lessor shares some (or all) of this advantage with the lessee. Essentially this advantage arises because the lessor's effective tax rate is higher than the lessee's effective tax rate. Example 15.5 illustrates this advantage in an extreme case where the lessee's effective tax rate is zero.

The inability of some asset users to use immediately all the allowable deductions associated with the acquisition of very expensive assets was a major factor in the growth of leveraged leasing during the 1970s and the early part of the 1980s. Such leases are invariably structured so as to exploit situations where the lessor has a higher effective tax rate than the lessee. There is evidence that this reason for the

---

[10] See Gavazza, 'Leasing and secondary markets: theory and evidence from commercial aircraft' (April 1, 2010). Available at SSRN: **http://ssrn.com/abstract=869227**. This study found that for the US airline industry, the output of leased aircraft, as measured by flying hours, was 6.5 per cent higher than the output of owned aircraft.

growth in leveraged leasing is generalisable to other forms of leasing. Thus, in the US it has been found that companies with low marginal tax rates use leasing more than companies with high marginal tax rates (Graham, Lemmon & Schallheim 1998). This finding is consistent with the view that high tax rate lessors can benefit more from the tax deductibility of depreciation than low tax rate lessees.

Taxation advantages are also the motive for cross-border leases which, as discussed in Section 15.2.5, are structured so as to take advantage of differences between the tax environments of different countries. If there were no differences in tax regulations and tax rates between countries, cross-border leases would probably not exist.

Transaction costs

There is a difference between leasing and borrowing that can be important in the event of default. If a lessee defaults, the lessor, as the owner of the asset, can repossess the asset more easily than a secured lender, who is likely to face considerable delay, and greater costs, because it may be necessary for a defaulting borrower to be liquidated. In this case, a liquidator has to be appointed to sell the assets and distribute the proceeds to lenders and other creditors. Therefore, there may well be a difference in transaction costs that favours leasing. Similarly, because lessors have the security of ownership of the leased asset, they may be prepared to provide finance without carrying out a full check on the credit standing of the lessee. Also, the lessor may be able to use a relatively simple, standard contract for each lease, particularly if the leased assets are similar items such as cars or other motor vehicles. As a result, leasing can be attractive to small companies that do not have good access to other sources of finance. For larger companies, leasing may also be more attractive than other sources of finance because the transaction costs are lower than the cost of issuing securities or negotiating a loan.

Conservation of capital

It is often suggested that, by leasing, a company can conserve its capital for investment elsewhere. Alternatively, the same argument may be based on the suggestion that leasing provides '100 per cent financing'. In other words, it is argued that there is some fundamental difference between leasing and other forms of finance, which allows a lessee to 'borrow' 100 per cent of the purchase price of an asset, compared with perhaps 80 per cent in the case of a secured loan. This argument is controversial. Many academics have argued that the '100 per cent financing' claim is a fallacy. For example, they point out that where lease rentals are payable in advance, which is usual, the finance effectively provided by leasing can be much less than the purchase price of the asset.[11] Also, the formal security provided to the lessor is not necessarily restricted to ownership of the leased asset.[12] In other words, to obtain a finance lease, it is necessary to have some equity capital, and the lease will use up some of the debt capacity provided by the company's equity in the same way as other debt. Therefore, when only the immediate cash consequences are considered, leasing may give the appearance of 100 per cent financing, but this appearance is misleading. There is no such thing as '100 per cent lease finance', just as there is no such thing as '100 per cent debt finance'. On the other hand, practitioners, particularly those involved in promoting leasing, argue that leasing is *not* the same as other debt and that a dollar of lease finance will use less of a company's debt capacity than a dollar of 'ordinary' debt.

This view is supported by Eisfeldt and Rampini (ER) (2009), who argue that the ability of a lessor to repossess an asset more easily than a secured lender provides benefits for leasing that go beyond the transaction cost savings discussed above. In their words: 'This ability to repossess allows a lessor to implicitly extend more credit than a lender whose claim is secured by the same asset. The debt capacity

---

[11] This factor is illustrated by Example 15.3 where the lease provides finance of $511 800, which is much less than the asset cost of $600 000.
[12] See Footnote 7.

of leasing thus exceeds the debt capacity of secured lending' (p. 1621). After considering the treatment under US bankruptcy laws of secured lenders and lessors in different types of leases, ER conclude that the advantage they identify applies primarily to operating leases but may be applicable to some finance leases. This difference arises because, under US law, an operating lease will generally be classified as a 'true lease', which allows the easiest repossession by the lessor. In the case of a finance lease, the lessor is likely to be regarded as having only a 'security interest' in the leased asset, which means that the position of the lessor is essentially the same as that of a secured lender.

If it is true that leasing conserves capital, what are the main implications for leasing decisions? According to ER, leasing, particularly through operating leases, will be valuable to companies that are financially constrained—that is, companies that have a shortage of internal funds and need to raise funds externally. However, agency costs arising from the separation of ownership and control that is inherent in leasing mean that companies with sufficient internal funds will prefer to buy assets. Tests using data on US companies provide strong support for the prediction that leasing is valuable for companies that are small or financially constrained. Leasing is negatively related to company size—small companies rent or lease a higher proportion of the assets they use than large companies. ER also found a robust negative relationship between leasing and the ratio of dividends to assets. Similarly, the ratio of cash flow to assets—their most direct measure of available internal funds—is negatively related to leasing. The proportion of capital leased is considerably higher for buildings than for equipment, and the relationships between leasing and the ratios used as measures of financial constraints were stronger for buildings. In summary, ER found strong empirical support for the argument that leasing 'conserves capital'—at least in the case of operating leases—but they acknowledge that even operating leases do not provide '100 per cent financing'. They conclude that the higher debt capacity of leasing may make it particularly attractive for small companies and for new ventures, both of which are likely to have limited internal funds.

Leasing can provide 'off-balance-sheet' finance

An argument related to the previous one is that because lessees in the past have not been required to report their lease obligations in the statement of financial position, they can use leasing to increase their access to debt. Even if this were true, it is only an advantage if borrowing restrictions imposed by lenders have prevented the potential lessee from attaining the optimal debt–equity ratio. Further, empirical evidence suggests that lease finance is a substitute for debt, with the result that companies may not have been able to use leasing to increase their access to other types of debt (Bowman 1980). In any event, Accounting Standard AASB 117 requires the capitalisation of finance lease obligations, which means that any potential 'off-balance-sheet financing' advantage for leasing should no longer be available.[13]

Cost of capital

The analysis outlined earlier is consistent with the principle that, in lease evaluation, the discount rate applicable to a given component of the cash flows must be the same for both the lessee and the lessor. In other words, for a given cash flow, the required rate of return should depend on the risk of the cash flow, not the identity of the recipient.

However, if the lessor's cost of capital is lower (higher) than that of the potential lessee, the existence of competitive capital markets will result in leasing (buying) being preferred to buying (leasing). What circumstances will cause the cost of capital of the lessor and the lessee to differ? The answer to this question will depend on the risks associated with using the asset. Miller and Upton (1976) identified two types of relevant risk. One is associated with uncertainty about the asset's economic depreciation, while the other

---

13 There is conflicting evidence on whether the off-balance-sheet aspect of leasing ever provided borrowing opportunities that had a favourable effect on a company's share price. A number of these studies are summarised in Lev and Ohlson (1982. pp. 280–1).

is associated with uncertainty about the net cash flows from using the asset. In the case of a finance lease with a specified residual value, both these risks are borne by the lessee. In the case of an operating lease, both these risks are borne by the lessor. There may be other cases where the risks are shared between the two parties. Although the risks borne by the two parties can differ, competitive capital markets will ensure that the discount rate implicit in the lease agreement will reflect the allocation of risk between the two parties.

Suppose, however, that the lessee can raise capital at a lower cost for a given level of risk than the lessor. If this is so, the prospective lessee should find that it is more profitable to buy than to lease. However, as Miller and Upton (1976) pointed out, the lessee 'would find it even more profitable under those circumstances to enter the leasing business'. Any disequilibrium between the costs of capital for leasing and buying would then be eliminated. In other words, the costs of capital for leasing and buying must be the same, because if they were not, then one of two results would occur: leasing would either be dominant—that is, all assets would be leased—or leasing would disappear.

Leasing and agency costs

As noted above, a leased asset is under the control of a user who is not the owner, and the separation of ownership and control can give rise to costly agency problems. For example, as discussed in Section 15.7.2, it will be difficult and expensive to lease assets that are easily damaged by carelessness or neglect. Leasing can also have incentive effects that contribute to agency costs. Smith and Wakeman (1985) pointed out that management compensation plans can create incentives to lease assets rather than purchase them. For example, a manager whose bonus depends on the rate of return on invested capital will favour the leasing of assets unless the present value of future lease payments is included as part of invested capital. Thus, a compensation plan that is not well designed can motivate managers to lease assets when purchasing would be better for shareholders.

The ownership structure of a business may also influence leasing decisions. For example, a manager who has a large ownership stake in the business may prefer to lease business assets in order to reduce personal exposure to asset-specific risks such as the risk of obsolescence. Consistent with this argument, a study by Mehran, Taggart and Yermack (1999) of US manufacturing firms found that CEO share ownership has a significant positive effect on both debt financing and leasing.

In summary, the major reasons for leasing appear to involve savings in taxes and transaction costs and minimising the effects of financial constraints. There can be significant tax advantages for leasing when there is a large difference between the effective income tax rates of the lessor and lessee. However, under the imputation tax system, any tax advantages of leasing appear to be small when both the lessor and lessee are Australian-owned companies. There is evidence that leasing does 'conserve capital', at least for operating leases, which can make leasing attractive for small companies and new ventures that lack internal funds. While some of the claimed advantages of leasing appear to be of dubious validity, it seems that, in practice, many people do perceive that there are advantages in keeping leases 'off balance sheet'. Leasing involves a separation of ownership and control, so the agency costs arising from this separation tend to offset the advantages of leasing.

Although opportunities to reduce taxes, transaction costs and to minimise the effects of financial constraints provide the main motives for leasing, there are some additional factors that can give rise to advantages for leasing. These are discussed in the next section.

LEARNING OBJECTIVE 8

Explain the factors that can influence leasing policy

15.7.2 LEASING POLICY

Smith and Wakeman (1985) pointed out that tax-related factors and incentives arising from factors such as compensation contracts and ownership structure provide an important, but incomplete, explanation of some aspects of leasing. Differences in effective tax rates and ownership structure are useful in identifying potential lessors and lessees, but provide little explanation of why some assets are leased, while other similar assets are owned. For example, why is it that leasing of office buildings is more common than leasing of research laboratories? Some of the incentives for leasing that vary across different assets are now discussed.

Sensitivity to use and maintenance decisions

As discussed in Section 15.7.1, leasing means that an asset is under the control of a user who is not the owner. A lessee does not have a right to the disposal value of an asset at the end of the lease, so there is less incentive to care for and maintain assets that are leased rather than owned. Lessors will recognise this and will set lease rentals on the basis of expected levels of abuse. Therefore, the more sensitive the value of the asset to the levels of use and maintenance it receives, the more costly it will be to lease rather than purchase the asset. Therefore, it is argued that assets that are very sensitive to use and maintenance decisions will tend to be purchased by the user rather than leased. This argument appears to be more relevant to operating leases than to finance leases.

Specialised assets

Smith and Wakeman (1985) suggested that there is an incentive to buy, rather than lease, specialised (or company-specific) assets. Such assets are more highly valued within the company than in their best alternative use. They argued that leasing company-specific assets involves negotiation costs and other agency costs that can be significant because of conflicts between the lessor and lessee about the division between them of that part of the value of the asset that exceeds its value in alternative uses. For example, the lessor will want to calculate the lease payments using a conservative residual value based on the likely disposal value of the asset. This value is likely to be uncertain, and the lessor's estimate will probably be much less than the value placed on the asset by the user. Therefore, the lease payments required by the lessor are unlikely to be acceptable to the user.

In contrast, for 'general use' assets, such as trucks and forklifts, substitutes are readily available, and the difference between the value-in-use and the value-in-exchange is likely to be small. Moreover, there is an active second-hand market in these assets, so it is relatively easy to forecast likely disposal values and to agree on the terms of a lease. This argument is consistent with the observation that leasing of cars and other motor vehicles is relatively common.

Flexibility and transaction costs

As discussed in Sections 15.2.2 and 15.6, an operating lease can have worthwhile advantages when an asset is required for only a short period. An operating lease is likely to involve lower costs than purchasing an asset and then selling it, particularly if the costs of ownership transfer are significant. Leasing rather than buying can also involve differences in search costs and costs of assessing quality.[14] For example, a company that leases a truck will be less concerned about the condition of its engine, transmission and other mechanical parts than a potential buyer of the same vehicle. Therefore, a less costly inspection will suffice if the truck is to be leased.

This advantage for leasing will be offset by the fact that, as discussed above, lessees will tend to be less careful in their use of assets than owners are likely to be. Lessors will recognise this problem and base the rentals on the expected residual value of the asset, given the normal treatment to which leased assets are subjected. However, there can be an overall advantage for leasing, provided that the cost saving through avoiding frequent ownership transfers is greater than the additional costs associated with deterioration of leased assets.

---

14 For a discussion of these and other factors relevant to short-term leasing, see Flath (1980).

Comparative advantage in asset disposal

If the lessor has a comparative advantage in disposing of an asset, this may cause leasing to be preferred. For example, a lessor may be able to sell an asset at the end of the lease term at a higher price than could a company that had purchased the asset. Smith and Wakeman (1985, p. 902) identified three potential sources of such a comparative advantage.

(a) There is the potential for lower search, information and transaction costs associated with the lessor providing a specialised market for used assets. Such markets make it easier and cheaper for buyers seeking a particular asset to locate potential sellers.
(b) There may be reduced repair and maintenance costs for existing assets from reusing components of previously leased assets.
(c) Reduced production costs result from reusing components of previously leased assets in the production of new assets.

These advantages are likely to exist only where the lessor is also the manufacturer and/or distributor of the asset. However, Smith and Wakeman argued that manufacturers who accept used assets as trade-ins offer the same comparative advantages to asset buyers. Therefore, while the cost reductions can be real, they are not peculiar to leasing.

15.8 CHATTEL MORTGAGES AND HIRE-PURCHASE

Chattel mortgages and hire-purchase agreements are similar to finance leases and are provided by the same financial intermediaries, mainly banks and finance companies. The differences between these various forms of equipment finance are 'technical' but the differences can have important legal and tax implications. In the case of a **chattel mortgage**, the user buys the goods directly from the supplier and the financier registers a charge over the goods as security. Thus, a chattel mortgage is a loan secured by a mortgage over movable property rather than real estate. In contrast, with hire-purchase the financier purchases the asset and hires it to the user for an agreed period.

LEARNING OBJECTIVE 9
Outline the main features of chattel mortgages and hire-purchase agreements

chattel mortgage
a loan secured by a mortgage over movable property

hire-purchase agreement
agreement under which an asset owned by a financier is hired by a user who has the right or an obligation to purchase the asset when the agreement expires

Where an asset is subject to a chattel mortgage or a **hire-purchase agreement**, the user will be required to make a series of payments or instalments to the financier for an agreed period. As for a finance lease, the term usually ranges from 2 to 5 years and the interest rate is usually fixed for the whole of the term. The payments may be equal or they can be tailored to suit the user's cash flow pattern. For example, the payments may include an initial deposit and/or a final 'balloon' payment.

One essential feature of a hire-purchase agreement is that it will either commit the user to buying the asset or give the user an option to buy it. A lease cannot commit the lessee to buying the asset or explicitly give the lessee an option to do so. This difference is important for tax purposes because it means that in the case of hire-purchase agreements the user, rather than the financier, will be entitled to claim deductions for depreciation. The user will also be able to claim deductions for the interest component of the hire-purchase payments. In Australia, the popularity of chattel mortgages has increased markedly since the goods and services tax was introduced in 2000 and, as noted in Section 15.1, during 2007–08 chattel mortgages made up approximately 40 per cent of the equipment finance market.

15.8.1 EQUIPMENT FINANCE AND THE GOODS AND SERVICES TAX

Chattel mortgages, hire-purchase and leasing are not treated in exactly the same way under the goods and services tax (GST). Chattel mortgages are treated in the same way as other loans in that they are classed as a financial supply. Accordingly, no GST is payable on the provision of the loan or on the loan repayments. The purchase price of the equipment itself will usually include a GST component but the purchaser may be able to recover this outlay by claiming an input tax credit. In contrast, leasing is not classed as a financial supply so lease rentals are wholly subject to GST. In other words, for a lease, GST applies to both the cost of the asset and the credit charge included in the lease rentals. In the case of a chattel mortgage, GST applies only to the cost of the asset. Where the user of the asset is a business that can claim an input credit for the GST, the higher GST on a lease should not matter. However, if the asset user is unable to claim input tax credits, leasing may be less attractive than a chattel mortgage.

A hire-purchase transaction may have both a taxable component and a non-taxable financial supply component. Effectively, there are two types of hire-purchase agreements for GST purposes. If no separate credit charge is disclosed to the asset purchaser, the hire-purchase agreement will be treated as taxable in the same way as a lease. In contrast, under agreements where a separate credit charge is disclosed, there will be a non-taxable financial supply and a taxable supply. The taxable supply will involve a liability for GST only at the commencement of the agreement. However, there is no liability for GST on the financial supply component of the agreement.

In summary, while chattel mortgages, hire-purchase and finance leases have many similarities, there are important differences between them in terms of legal ownership and taxation treatment. In the case of GST, chattel mortgages and leases are effectively at opposite ends of a 'spectrum' with hire-purchase fitting in between these two extremes.

Connect Plus features a case study illustrating topics covered in this chapter. Ask your lecturer or tutor for your course's unique URL.

SUMMARY

→ The reasons for leasing differ between the various types of leases. The two basic types are operating leases and finance leases.
  – Operating leases separate the risks of ownership from the use of the leased asset and can provide advantages such as lower transaction costs, convenience and flexibility, as well as insurance against the risk of obsolescence.
  – In the case of finance leases, the risks of ownership are borne by the user of the asset and leasing is an alternative to other forms of debt finance. Leasing of very expensive assets is driven by tax-related factors. Except where there are significant tax advantages, leasing of specialised assets is much less common than leasing of general use or marketable assets, such as motor vehicles and computers.

→ The ability of a lessor to repossess an asset more easily than a secured lender provides greater debt capacity in the case of operating leases. Leasing and other types of equipment finance can be attractive for businesses that are small or new and, therefore, face relatively high transaction costs in obtaining finance in other ways.

→ Leasing involves a separation of ownership and control that results in agency costs. Unless a lease has significant benefits such as large tax savings, asset users with good access to internal funds will generally prefer to purchase rather than lease.

→ The leasing market is highly competitive and very flexible. Therefore, factors such as changes in tax rules and the level of government charges and differences in GST treatment can have important effects on the popularity of leasing compared with similar forms of finance, namely chattel mortgages and hire-purchase.

KEY TERMS

chattel mortgage 510
cross-border lease 493
finance lease 491
hire-purchase agreement 510
lessee 489
lessor 489
leveraged lease 492
maintenance lease 492
non-recourse loan 492
operating lease 491
sale and lease-back agreement 492

SELF-TEST PROBLEMS

1. Donash Pty Ltd needs a new computer, which it can buy for $440 000 or it can lease from Comlease. The lease requires six annual payments of $100 000 each, in advance. Donash has large tax losses and does not expect to pay tax for at least 5 years. Comlease pays tax at 30 per cent and can depreciate the computer on a straight-line basis over 3 years. The computer will have no residual value at the end of 5 years, and the before-tax interest rate on an equivalent loan would be 15 per cent per annum.
   (a) What is the NPV of the lease for Donash?
   (b) What is the NPV for Comlease?
   (c) What is the overall gain to leasing in this transaction?

Solutions to self-test problems are available in Appendix B, page 803.

REFERENCES

Australian Bureau of Statistics, *Lending Finance, Australia*, cat. no. 5671.0, October 2010.

Australian Equipment Lessors Association, *Annual Review 2007/2008*, AELA, Sydney, 2008.

Bennett, J., Hardaker, R. & Worrall, M., 'Equipment: leasing and financing', in R. Bruce, B. McKern, I. Pollard & M. Skully (eds), *Handbook of Australian Corporate Finance*, 5th edn, Butterworths, Sydney, 1997, pp. 274–303.

Bowman, R., 'The debt equivalence of leases: an empirical investigation', *The Accounting Review*, April 1980, pp. 237–53.

Burrows, G.H., 'Evolution of a lease solution', *Abacus*, September 1988, pp. 107–19.

Copeland, T. & Weston, J., 'A note on the evaluation of cancellable operating leases', *Financial Management*, Summer 1982, pp. 60–7.

Eisfeldt, A. & Rampini, A., 'Leasing, ability to repossess, and debt capacity', *The Review of Financial Studies*, April 2009, pp. 1621–57.

Flath, D., 'The economics of short-term leasing', *Economic Inquiry*, April 1980, pp. 247–59.

Gavazza, A., 'Leasing and secondary markets: theory and evidence from commercial aircraft', 1 April 2010. Available at SSRN: **http://ssrn.com/abstract=869227**.

Graham, J.R., Lemmon, M.L. & Schallheim, J.S., 'Debt, leases, taxes and the endogeneity of corporate tax status', *Journal of Finance*, February 1998, pp. 131–62.

Grenadier, S.R., 'Valuing lease contracts: a real options approach', *Journal of Financial Economics*, July 1995, pp. 297–331.

Henderson, S., Peirson, G. & Herbohn, K., *Issues in Financial Accounting*, 14th edn, Pearson Education, Sydney, 2011, Chapter 12.

Lev, B. & Ohlson, J., 'Market-based empirical research in accounting: a review, interpretation and extension', in 'Studies on current research methodologies in accounting: a critical evaluation', *Journal of Accounting Research*, Supplement, 1982.

Lewellen, W., Long, M., & McConnell, J., 'Asset leasing in competitive capital markets', *Journal of Finance*, June 1976, pp. 787–98.

Mehran, H., Taggart, R.A. & Yermack, D., 'CEO ownership, leasing and debt financing', *Financial Management*, Summer 1999, pp. 5–14.

Miller, M. & Upton C., 'Leasing, buying and the cost of capital services', *Journal of Finance*, June 1976, pp. 761–86.

Myers, S., Dill, D. & Bautista, A., 'Valuation of financial lease contracts', *Journal of Finance*, June 1976, pp. 799–819.

Scarman, I., 'Lease evaluation: a survey of Australian finance company approaches', *Accounting and Finance*, November 1982, pp. 33–51.

Schallheim, J.S., *Lease or Buy?*, Harvard Business School Press, Boston, Massachusetts, 1994.

Schallheim, J., Johnson, R., Lease, R. & McConnell, J., 'The determinants of yields on financial leasing contracts', *Journal of Financial Economics*, September 1987, pp. 45–67.

Sharpe, S.A. & Nguyen, H.H., 'Capital market imperfections and the incentive to lease', *Journal of Financial Economics*, October/November 1995, pp. 271–94.

Smith, C.W. Jr. & Wakeman, L.M, 'Determinants of corporate leasing policy', *Journal of Finance*, July 1985, pp. 895–908.

Szekely, L., 'The tax treatment of leasing', *CCH Journal of Australian Taxation*, August/September 1991, pp. 48–54.

Vardigans, P., 'The benefits of leasing', *Banking World*, August 1990, pp. 26–7.

QUESTIONS

1. **[LO 1]** Distinguish between a 'finance lease' and an 'operating lease'. Why is it important to make this distinction?
2. **[LO 1]** What are the important characteristics of a finance lease?
3. **[LO 1]** What are the essential characteristics of a sale and lease-back agreement? Outline the advantages and disadvantages of such an agreement.
4. **[LO 2]** What distinguishes a leveraged lease from other types of finance leases? What are the roles of the various parties to a leveraged lease?
5. **[LO 2]** Compare and contrast a 'leveraged lease' and a 'cross-border lease'.
6. **[LO 3]** *Leasing is a form of tax avoidance that should be outlawed by legislation.* Discuss this statement, indicating why you agree or disagree with it.
7. **[LO 7]** *Leasing increases a company's access to debt.* Discuss critically.
8. **[LO 7]** Discuss critically the alleged advantages of leasing.
9. **[LO 9]** Outline the main factors that are likely to influence the choice between acquiring an asset through a finance lease or by hire-purchase.
10. **[LO 7]** Which, if any, of the following are genuine advantages of leasing?
    (a) Leasing conserves the lessee's capital.
    (b) Leasing enables needed assets to be acquired even when the Board of Directors will not approve any capital expenditure requests.
    (c) By leasing a computer, the risk of obsolescence can be transferred to the lessor.
    (d) Leasing provides 100 per cent financing.
11. **[LO 8]** Critically evaluate the following statement:
    Many road transport companies are risky businesses, which are unable to borrow enough to buy all the trucks they need. For them, leasing makes a lot of sense. Trucks are attractive to lessors because they are durable and there is an active second-hand market.
12. **[LO 9]** Distinguish between:
    (a) a finance lease and a hire-purchase agreement
    (b) chattel mortgage and hire-purchase.
13. **[LO 8]** *It is common to lease assets such as cars and trucks, whereas specialised assets are usually owned by the user.* Explain.
14. **[LO 9]** Leases and chattel mortgages are treated differently under the goods and services tax (GST). Outline the GST treatment of leases and chattel mortgages. For a business, is the overall cost of a lease likely to be greater than the cost of a chattel mortgage?
15. **[LO 7]** It is common for airlines to own some aircraft while leasing others under operating leases. What are the advantages and disadvantages of this approach?
16. **[LO 8]** *In Australia, operating leases have been limited mainly to motor vehicles, computers and multi-purpose industrial equipment such as forklifts.* What characteristics of these assets make them suitable for operating leases?
17. **[LO 7]** If leasing does conserve capital in the sense that the debt capacity of leasing exceeds the debt capacity of lending, what are the main implications for lease versus purchase decisions?
18. **[LO 7]** *Leasing means that an asset is under the control of a user who is not the owner and this separation gives rise to agency costs.* What are the main implications of these costs for lease versus purchase decisions?

PROBLEMS

1. **Evaluating investments: lease versus purchase [LO 5]**
The Hybee Company is evaluating an investment to produce a new product with an expected marketable life of 5 years. The expected annual net cash flow before tax is $120 000. To produce this product the company will have to acquire a new plant. The company can either purchase this plant or lease it. Details of these alternatives are as follows:

Purchase
The purchase price of the plant is $250 000 and it is expected that it will have a zero residual value after

5 years. The allowable annual depreciation charge on the plant is 20 per cent per annum, straight-line.

Lease

The lease requires five annual payments, each of $60 000, payable at the beginning of each year. The company tax rate is 30 cents in the dollar. The required rate of return on the investment is 15 per cent per annum after tax and the after-tax cost of an equivalent loan is 8 per cent per annum.

Should the company undertake the investment? If so, should it purchase or lease the plant?

2. **Calculating lease rentals [LO 4]**

    The Vision Company is evaluating the acquisition of an asset that it requires for a period of 6 years. The following information relates to the purchase of the asset:
    (a) The purchase price is $1 million.
    (b) It can be depreciated at a rate of 10 per cent per annum, straight-line.
    (c) The estimated disposal value in 6 years' time is $300 000.
    (d) The company income tax rate is 30 cents in the dollar.
    (e) The required rate of return on the investment is 15 per cent per annum after tax.

    Assume that the company has the alternative of leasing the asset from the Ajax Leasing Company. Assume also that the after-tax cost of an equivalent loan is 9 per cent per annum.

    Assuming that the annual lease payments are made at the beginning of each year and that the lease specifies a residual value of $300 000, what lease payments would make Vision indifferent between buying or leasing the asset?

3. **Calculating lease rentals [LO 4]**

    Assume that Ajax Leasing Company could acquire the asset required by Vision (see Problem 2) for $900 000 and depreciate it at a rate of 15 per cent per annum, straight-line. The other information is the same as that presented in Problem 2.
    (a) Calculate the minimum annual lease payment that Ajax Leasing Company would charge.
    (b) Does your answer to (a) necessarily imply that Vision should lease the asset? Why or why not?

4. **Lease versus purchase [LO 5]**

    Carry Ltd is evaluating the possibility of tendering for the licence to operate international flights from Canberra to Queenstown (NZ) for a 5-year period. If its bid is successful, the licence fee has to be paid immediately and is not tax deductible.

    The company has estimated that the before-tax annual net cash inflow from operating the service would be $20 million, and that it would require an after-tax rate of return of 15 per cent per annum on its investment. The company income tax rate is 30 cents in the dollar. Carry Ltd has the option of either buying or leasing an aircraft. The following information is relevant to these options:

    Purchase

    The purchase price of the aircraft is $60 million. It could be depreciated at a rate of 15 per cent per annum, straight-line. The estimated disposal value in 5 years' time is $20 million.

    Lease

    The annual lease payments would be $15 million, payable at the beginning of each year, with a lease residual of $20 million. The after-tax interest rate on an equivalent loan is 11 per cent per annum.

    What is the maximum licence fee that Carry Ltd should tender?

5. **Evaluation of an operating lease [LO 6]**

    Ibus Ltd is considering the installation of a new computer. Because of uncertainty as to its future computing requirements and the prospect of advancements in computing technology, it is evaluating the acquisition of the computer by either purchasing it, or leasing it under a contract that includes a cancellation option. Information relevant to the company's evaluation is as follows:

    Purchase

    The purchase price of the computer is $300 000 and it can be depreciated at a rate of 15 per cent per annum, straight-line. Ibus Ltd plans to operate the computer for a maximum of 5 years. The computer's disposal value at the end of 5 years is estimated to be $50 000.

    Lease

    The annual lease payments on the operating lease would be $90 000, payable at the beginning of each year. The lease can be cancelled by Ibus Ltd at any time without incurring any penalty payment.

    The company income tax rate is 30 cents in the dollar, the required return on the investment is 20 per cent per annum and the after-tax cost of an equivalent loan is 10 per cent per annum. Should the company purchase or lease the asset?

6. **Calculating lease rentals [LO 4]**
Connell Finance is determining payments for a 4-year finance lease with a 20 per cent residual on an asset that costs $800 000 and can be depreciated on a straight-line basis over 3 years. The tax rate for Connell is 30 per cent, and it requires a before-tax rate of return from leases of 12 per cent. Determine the lease payments when the lease payments are made:
(a) annually in advance
(b) quarterly in advance.

Suppose that the lease rentals are payable annually in advance and the terms of the lease are changed so that it is an operating lease. Will the rentals be higher or lower than your answer to (a)? Give reasons for your answer.

Test yourself further with Connect Plus online! Ask your lecturer or tutor for your course's unique URL.

CHAPTER 16
CAPITAL MARKET EFFICIENCY

LEARNING OBJECTIVES

After studying this chapter you should be able to:

1. understand the concept of market efficiency
2. understand the methods used to test for market efficiency
3. understand the evidence provided by tests of market efficiency and the extent to which that evidence supports or does not support market efficiency
4. understand the difference between micro and macro market efficiency
5. understand the relevance of behavioural finance to market efficiency
6. understand the implications of the evidence on market efficiency for investors and financial managers.

CHAPTER CONTENTS

16.1 Introduction

16.2 The efficient market hypothesis

16.3 Tests of return predictability

16.4 Event studies

16.5 Tests for private information

16.6 Market efficiency at the macro level

16.7 Behavioural finance and market efficiency

16.8 Implications of the evidence with respect to market efficiency

16.1 INTRODUCTION

In Chapter 1, we assumed that the objective of a company was to maximise the market value of its shares. In the chapters that followed, we discussed the investment, financing and payout decisions consistent with that objective. Throughout those chapters it was implicitly assumed that investors would react quickly to such decisions, and accordingly that the market price of the company's shares would adjust quickly to reflect the impact of each decision on the company's value. In other words, it was assumed that the shares were traded in a market that was 'efficient', in the sense that share prices accurately reflect available information.

The extent to which asset prices accurately reflect available information has been widely tested. These tests examine the **efficient market hypothesis (EMH)**—the hypothesis that the price of a security (such as a share) accurately reflects available information. Most of these tests have used share prices, but other markets such as debt markets and derivative securities markets have also been extensively tested.

On the basis of the evidence from these tests, most academics and practitioners believe that markets are neither completely efficient nor completely inefficient. Therefore, in reviewing this evidence, rather than asking whether markets are efficient or inefficient—one extreme or the other—the more helpful question is to ask: To what extent are markets efficient? (Doukas et al. 2002). This is not mere semantics. If you wish to know something about the temperature, the question, 'What is the temperature?' is likely to lead to more insights than debating whether it is either 'hot' or 'cold' without allowing for a range of answers. The same applies to the question of market efficiency.

In reviewing the evidence on market efficiency it is also necessary to make a distinction between micro-efficiency and macro-efficiency. At the micro level, market efficiency concerns the extent to which the prices of securities reflect information relative to other securities within the same asset class: for example, whether BHP Billiton shares are correctly priced when compared with Rio Tinto shares. At the macro level, the issue is whether capital markets as a whole reflect all available information—whether, for example, the share market is correctly priced compared with a less risky asset class such as government debt.

Micro-efficiency does not necessarily imply macro-efficiency. For example, shares in Company X may be correctly priced relative to shares in Company Y, but the share market as a whole may be overvalued due to 'irrational exuberance'. Moreover, it is possible that some investors will know that the share market is overvalued, but if those investors cannot predict when the 'bubble' will burst, they may still buy shares that they think are *relatively* cheap and sell shares that they think are *relatively* expensive. While this trading activity may maintain high micro-efficiency, it may not eliminate macro-inefficiency.

This chapter provides a review of the evidence on micro and macro market efficiency. The implications of that evidence for financial decision making are also discussed.

efficient market hypothesis (EMH) that the price of a security (such as a share) accurately reflects available information

16.2 THE EFFICIENT MARKET HYPOTHESIS

Fama (1970) has defined an efficient capital market as one in which security prices 'fully reflect' all available information. Security prices change when new information becomes available. If the market processes new information efficiently, the reaction of market prices to new information will be *instantaneous* and *unbiased* (Fama 1970).[1] To gain an intuitive understanding of these requirements it is useful to examine a hypothetical example of a non-instantaneous price reaction and a hypothetical example of a biased price reaction.

LEARNING OBJECTIVE 1

Understand the concept of market efficiency

---

[1] This definition focuses on 'the market', rather than on individuals responding to information, and is readily testable. For a discussion of alternatives, see Ball (1994), pp. 10–13.

CAPITAL MARKET EFFICIENCY **CHAPTER 16** 517

16.2.1 A NON-INSTANTANEOUS PRICE REACTION

Efficiency requires that the price reacts instantaneously. In practice, this means that after new information becomes available it should be fully reflected in the next price established in the market. Suppose that the market in Copperama Ltd shares opens for trading at 10:10 am. On a particular day, the first trade in Copperama shares occurs at 10:45 am and the price established in the market is $1 per share. At 11:00 am, Copperama makes a completely unexpected announcement: a large deposit of gold has been discovered in one of its copper mines. Naturally this is good news. Suppose that this news warrants an increase in Copperama's share price from $1 to $1.50. At 11:15 am, a shareholder in Copperama wishes to sell his shares. However, he has not heard the news of the gold discovery and asks only $1 per share for his shares. The sale is made at $1. At 11:30 am, a Copperama shareholder who *has* heard the news wishes to sell her shares. Her asking price is $1.50 per share and the sale is made at $1.50.

This market is inefficient. The price established at 11:15 am did not reflect the information available at 11:00 am. Eventually, at 11:30 am the market price reacted to the news. However, this reaction was not instantaneous because it should have occurred at the 11:15 am trade. Competition between informed potential buyers should have set the 11:15 am price at $1.50, notwithstanding the fact that the seller was uninformed.

This simple example also illustrates the importance of 'excess' or 'abnormal' profits in efficiency tests. The *buyer* at 11:15 am has made an excess profit of 50 cents per share because he has obtained his shares at a price 50 cents below the price that should have been established, given the information available to the market at 11:15 am. Note, however, that although the buyer at 10:45 am has also made a profit of 50 cents on the day, his profit *cannot* be described as excess. Given the information available to the market at 10:45 am, the price he paid was 'correct' at that time.

This example also illustrates the role of trading strategies. If the market often fails to react instantaneously, share traders can develop simple rules to generate excess profits. In this case, the rule would be: purchase shares immediately a company makes an unanticipated announcement of good news. The market will not react instantaneously and the shares will increase in price when the reaction does eventually occur.

16.2.2 A BIASED PRICE REACTION

Suppose the market in the shares of Mortlake Ltd opens for trading at 10:10 am. On a particular day, the first trade in Mortlake's shares occurs at 10:45 am and the price established is $1. At 11:00 am, the company makes a completely unexpected announcement: an uncontrollable fire has destroyed its major factory, and Mortlake's management has discovered that, owing to an error by a junior employee, the company is not insured against fire. Investors panic and the next sale of Mortlake's shares at 11:15 am is at 5 cents per share. Shortly after, however, cooler heads prevail and it is remembered that Mortlake also has a number of smaller factories and substantial investments in securities. At 11:30 am the market price of Mortlake's shares is 35 cents.

The market is inefficient. The price established at 11:15 am was an **overreaction** to the news, and, given the information available to the market at 11:15 am, it should have been recognised at that time as an overreaction. Competition between informed potential buyers should have prevented such a low price occurring, notwithstanding the fact that poorly informed sellers had panicked.

As in the previous example, this example can be interpreted in terms of excess profits and trading strategies. The buyer at 11:15 am has made an excess profit of 30 cents per share. The buyer at 10:45 am has made a loss on the day of 65 cents per share, but this loss cannot be called excess. If the market often overreacts to bad news, the following trading rule will be successful: purchase shares immediately a company makes an unanticipated announcement of bad news. The market will at first overreact, and the shares will rise in price when the market reappraises the information in a more rational fashion.

A second kind of biased reaction is an **underreaction**. In this case the market responds gradually to a piece of new information, moving towards the new equilibrium price in a predictable series of steps.

---

overreaction
biased response of a price to information in which the initial price movement can be expected to be reversed

underreaction
biased response of a price to information in which the initial price movement can be expected to continue

This will create observable price trends. The trading strategy in this case would be to buy immediately, if the news is good, and to sell immediately if the news is bad.

16.2.3 CATEGORIES OF CAPITAL MARKET EFFICIENCY

As suggested earlier, the EMH implies that investors cannot earn abnormal returns by using information that is already available. This implication has been the basis for most empirical tests of the hypothesis. The concept of efficiency inherent in this definition may be described as **information efficiency**, as it relates to the impounding of information into market prices. It does not directly address questions concerning the allocative or operational efficiency of capital markets.

Fama (1970) suggested a method of characterising the efficiency of a market on the basis of the type of information incorporated into the prices of assets traded on the market. Assets traded on a market that was weak-form efficient were traded at prices that incorporated all information contained in the past record of asset prices. If a market was semi-strong-form efficient, then prices reflected not only all information contained in past price series but also all other publicly available information. When asset prices reflected all privately held information, in addition to that which was publicly available, then the market was said to be strong-form efficient.

The information content of each successive classification is cumulative. Therefore the second classification includes all previous price information, as well as all other publicly available information, while the third classification includes all publicly available information and all privately held information. The implication of strong-form efficiency is that an investor cannot earn abnormal returns from having inside information.

In a later review of the literature, Fama (1991) proposed an alternative categorisation of capital market efficiency. Instead of classifying a market's efficiency on the basis of the type of information impounded into the prices of assets traded in the market, Fama suggested that categories could be formed on the basis of the research methodology used to assess the efficiency of the market. The three research methodologies he identified were:

(a) **tests of return predictability**, which are employed to ascertain whether future returns can be predicted on the basis of past information such as past returns, time-of-the-year or book-to-market ratios
(b) **event studies**, which involve the analysis of the behaviour of a security's returns around the time of a significant event such as the public announcement of the company's profit, dividend details or intention to acquire another company
(c) **tests for private information**, which are designed to test whether investors can trade profitably by making investment decisions on the basis of information that is not publicly available.

In Sections 16.3 to 16.5 we consider the way in which these three methodologies have been used to test the efficiency of various markets, particularly with respect to the Australian capital market. In Section 16.6 we examine the evidence with respect to macro-efficiency and in Section 16.7 consider the evidence from behavioural finance. Implications for investors and financial managers of the evidence of the extent to which markets are efficient are then considered in Section 16.8. Before we move on, however, we make it clear in the next section that tests of market efficiency are also tests of the model used in those tests.

16.2.4 MARKET EFFICIENCY AND THE JOINT TEST PROBLEM

If a security market is inefficient, then opportunities may exist for investors aware of the inefficiency to earn systematic **abnormal returns**. Abnormal returns can be defined as returns in excess of the return one could normally expect from investment in the asset. In Chapter 7 we discussed how an asset's

---

information efficiency situation in which prices accurately reflect available information

> **LEARNING OBJECTIVE 2**
> Understand the methods used to test for market efficiency

tests of return predictability research method designed to detect systematic patterns in asset prices

event study research method that analyses the behaviour of a security's price around the time of a significant event such as the public announcement of the company's profit

tests for private information research method that tests whether systematic profits can be generated by making investment decisions on the basis of private information

abnormal returns returns in excess of the return expected from a security

joint test problem
problem that any test of market efficiency is simultaneously a test of some model of 'normal' asset pricing

expected return can be estimated by employing an asset pricing model that links the asset's characteristics to the investor's required return from the asset. For instance, the capital asset pricing model (CAPM) links an asset's expected return to its systematic risk as measured by beta. Therefore, the CAPM is one way that we can estimate the 'normal' return on a security.

The **joint test problem** arises because any test for the presence of systematic abnormal returns is simultaneously a test of both the efficiency of the market and the validity of the asset pricing model used to estimate expected (or 'normal') returns. Hence, any apparent evidence of market inefficiency may instead be the result of an incorrectly specified asset pricing model.

16.3 TESTS OF RETURN PREDICTABILITY

In an efficient market, investors should be unable to generate positive abnormal returns systematically through an ability to forecast future price movements accurately. Researchers who have examined this aspect of market efficiency have been primarily concerned with the following three issues:

LEARNING OBJECTIVE 3
Understand the evidence provided by tests of market efficiency and the extent to which that evidence supports or does not support market efficiency

(a) *The relationship between past and future returns.* If investors can systematically generate positive abnormal returns from a security merely by noting the returns generated by that security in the past, then this is an indication of market inefficiency, because the information contained in the past return series is not fully reflected in current prices.

(b) *The presence of seasonal effects in returns.* Testing for the presence of seasonal effects in returns involves an analysis of whether future returns are related to the period in time over which the return is generated.

(c) *Predicting future returns on the basis of other forecast variables.* In an efficient market, asset prices reflect all information currently available. There have been numerous studies that have tested for a systematic relationship between returns and asset characteristics such as the company's size, book-to-market ratio or dividend yield.

16.3.1 THE RELATIONSHIP BETWEEN PAST AND FUTURE RETURNS

Short-term patterns

A common way of testing for short-term patterns in returns is to test for the presence of serial correlation. Serial correlation tests measure the correlation between successive price changes or, more frequently, the correlation between returns in one period and returns in a prior period. Positive correlation indicates that there are trends in price movements, while negative correlation indicates a tendency towards reversals in price movements. Either result would indicate the possible existence of potentially profitable trading strategies.

Both Conrad and Kaul (1988) and Lo and MacKinlay (1988) found evidence of positive serial correlation in weekly returns of US shares. However, both studies also found that the level of serial correlation was small—probably too small to generate profitable trading opportunities. Furthermore, Lo and MacKinlay (1999) found less evidence of positive serial correlation over later periods. In Australia, Brailsford and Faff (1993) examined the daily returns from an index consisting of shares from 50 of the most actively traded companies listed on the Australian Stock Exchange. They also reported evidence of small positive serial correlation in returns.

Long-term patterns

While there is only weak evidence of serial correlation in daily or weekly returns, in the medium term there is evidence that shares with the best recent performance out-perform shares with the worst recent performance. Using US data from 1963 to 1989, Jegadeesh and Titman (1993) identified better-performing shares (the winners) and poorer-performing shares (the losers) over a period of 6 months. They then tracked the performance of these shares over the following 6 months. On average, the biggest winners outperformed the biggest losers by 10 per cent per annum. Similar evidence of this **momentum effect** have also been reported by Brock, Lakonishok and LeBaron (1992), Moskowitz and Grinblatt (1999), Lo, Mamaysky and Wang (2000) and George and Hwang (2007). In particular, George and Hwang show that shares that are close to or at their 52-week high outperform shares that are far from their 52-week high. Given that 52-week-high prices are readily available in newspapers and from websites, this study suggests that abnormal returns may be earned using simple strategies and readily available information. In Australia, evidence of momentum has been found in a range of studies, including those by Hurn and Pavlov (2003), Demir, Muthuswamy and Walter (2004) and Bettman, Maher and Sault (2009).

momentum effect effect in which good or bad performance of shares continues over time

While there is evidence of a momentum effect in the medium term, there is also evidence that this effect is reversed over long periods. DeBondt and Thaler (1985 and 1987), Chopra, Lakonishok and Ritter (1992), Lee and Swaminathan (2000) and Jegadeesh and Titman (2001) have documented long-term reversals in share prices. These studies identified better-performing and poorer-performing shares over several years. On average, the winners turned into losers and the losers became winners. The Australian evidence is partially consistent with the US evidence. The findings of Brailsford (1992) and Allen and Prince (1995) indicate that while there is a tendency in Australia for winners to become losers, the reverse does not seem to occur.

16.3.2 THE PRESENCE OF SEASONAL EFFECTS IN RETURNS

Seasonal patterns in returns give rise to the possibility of predicting returns based on those patterns. Many studies have tested whether there are daily or monthly patterns in share returns.

Daily return patterns

French (1980) reported that a daily index of US share prices over the period 1953 to 1977 showed that, on average, returns on Mondays were negative, while returns on Fridays were positive. If this were true, why would anyone buy shares on a Friday afternoon? Why not wait until late Monday when, on average, the price would be lower? The result was puzzling but was replicated in later studies. For example, Lakonishok and Smidt (1988) studied 90 years of US data (from 1897 to 1987) and found negative average Monday returns over the period as a whole, and in all 10 subperiods that they studied.

What could explain these findings? One suggested possible explanation is that companies tend to release bad news over the weekend (see, for example, Damodaran 1989). However, if this is the explanation, then it suggests that markets are not perfectly efficient because prices do not adjust to reflect the fact that companies have this tendency to release bad news over the weekend.[2]

Nor is the phenomenon purely American. The results for the Australian stock market over the period 1982 to 2009 are shown in Figure 16.1, overleaf.

On this evidence, Australia appears to have traditionally experienced a 'negative Tuesday' over the period 1974 to 1984. Is it coincidence that when it is Tuesday in Australia, it is Monday in America? Moreover, daily interest rates in Australia show a very similar pattern: high on Thursday and low on Tuesday (see Finn, Lynch & Moore 1991). Other international comparisons turn up further results: Canada's pattern is very like that of the US; the UK has a negative Monday, but its Friday is only

---

[2] Other possible explanations include: settlement procedures (see Lakonishok & Levi 1982); that there are patterns in trades occurring at the asking price; and that there are patterns in the trading activity of individual (as against institutional) shareholders. Except for small firms, the size of the Monday effect seems to have declined in recent years. See Aitken et al. (1995) and Chan, Leung and Wang (2004).

FIGURE 16.1 Mean daily rates of return for Australian shares[a]

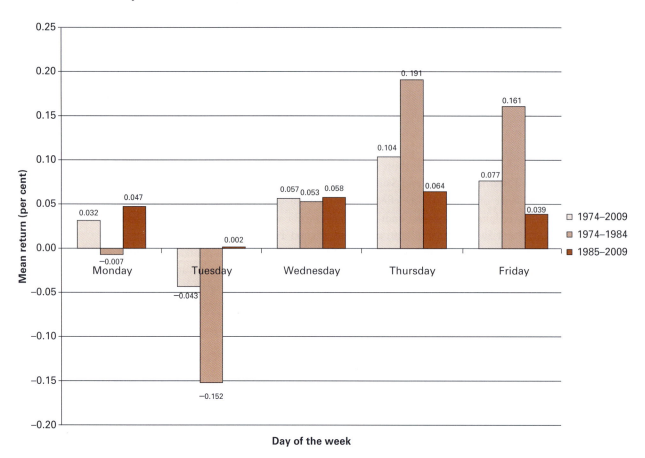

[a] Returns exclude days following holidays.

Source: Compiled from data in R. Ball and J. Bowers, 'Daily seasonals in equity and fixed-interest returns: Australian evidence and tests of plausible hypotheses', in E. Dimson (ed.), *Stock Market Anomalies*, Cambridge University Press, Cambridge, 1988, p. 79, and from the Datasteam Database.

marginally positive; France, Japan and Singapore have negative Tuesdays.[3] A common thread is that every country has some kind of daily pattern, but not necessarily the same pattern as that found in other countries and, importantly, not necessarily the same pattern is observed over long periods of time. Interestingly, Figure 16.1 indicates that the daily patterns in share returns have become less significant in more recent years, with the 'negative Tuesday' effect disappearing altogether in the later subperiod. Similarly, Rubinstein (2001) reports the disappearance of the Monday effect from the US market over the period 1988 to 1998. Indeed, over the same period, he reports that Monday is actually the best-performing day of the week, while Thursday has become the worst. Figure 16.1 does indicate, however, that the order of ranking of the days of the week in terms of returns has remained almost identical in Australia during the past 35 years.

Monthly return patterns

Rozeff and Kinney (1976) reported that the average return on US shares in January was more than five times larger than the average of returns in the other 11 months. Why didn't a lot of investors buy in

3 Condoyanni, O'Hanlon and Ward (1988). See also Jaffe and Westerfield (1985).

December to benefit from this so-called **January effect**? Their actions would be expected to increase the December price level and eventually eliminate the high January return.

This effect has also been found in other countries. One study of stock markets in 17 countries (including the US) found that January was the highest return month in 14 countries (Gultekin & Gultekin 1983). Using Australian market-wide data for the two subperiods from 1958 to 1981 and 1982 to 2009, the monthly percentage rates of return are as shown in Figure 16.2.[4]

In Australia over the earlier subperiod, the strongest monthly seasonal effects for the market as a whole were for December and January. Together, these 2 months contributed, on average, 6.59 percentage points, while the other 10 months contributed a total of only 6.28 percentage points. In other words, 2 months contributed more than half of the total return for the year for the market as a whole. In the later subperiod, there is a different pattern: the highest returns are in April, July and December.

It is not clear why any particular month should be different from other months. One possible explanation investigated thoroughly is **tax loss selling**. The end of a tax year could induce heavy selling pressure in the last month, causing lower prices, followed by a rebound in prices in the first month of the new tax year. As the US has a tax year ending in December, this might explain the US January effect.

January effect observation that, on average, share prices increase more in January than in other months

tax loss selling investment strategy in which the tax rules make it attractive for an investor to sell certain shares just before the end of the tax year

FIGURE 16.2 Mean monthly rates of return for Australian shares

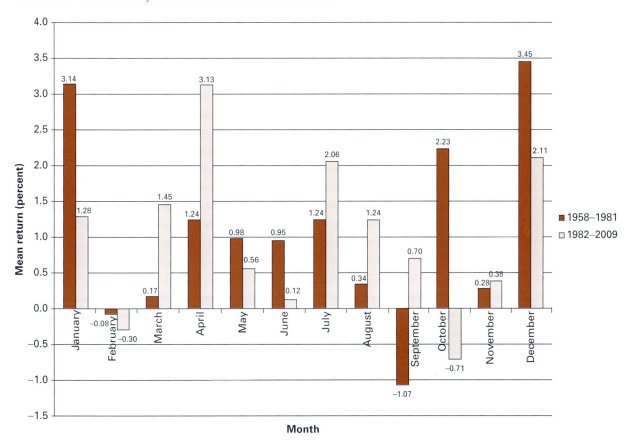

Source: Compiled using data from P. Brown, D. Keim, A. Kleidon and T. Marsh, 'Stock return seasonalities and the tax-loss selling hypothesis: analysis of the arguments and Australian evidence', *Journal of Financial Economics*, June 1983, pp. 105–27, and from the Datastream Database.

---

4 The high January return also occurred in Australia in the earlier time period of 1936 to 1957; see Brailsford and Easton (1991).

In Australia, tax loss selling by domestic investors would produce high returns in July, while in the UK, high returns would occur in April. Although high returns are indeed observed at these times, Australia and the UK have at various times had strong January effects, which are not predicted by the tax loss selling hypothesis. Therefore, tax effects provide, at best, a partial explanation.[5] The January effect is also closely related to the 'size' effect discussed in Section 16.3.3.

16.3.3 PREDICTING FUTURE RETURNS ON THE BASIS OF OTHER FORECAST VARIABLES

A range of studies has reported that a number of variables may be used to predict future returns. These variables include a company's dividend yield, its price–earnings ratio, whether it has repurchased or issued shares, the level of its accounting accruals, its asset growth, its size, and the ratio of the book value of its equity to the market value of its equity. For simplicity this last factor is often called the company's book-to-market ratio. Studies that have examined these variables will be discussed in turn. We will then provide a discussion of the interrelationship between these factors.

Dividend yield

dividend yield
dividend per share divided by the share price

A share's **dividend yield** is the value of the dividend (per share) divided by the share price. A number of US studies have found that dividend yield helps to explain returns, even after adjustment for systematic risk.[6] Typically, these studies find that beta-adjusted returns are higher, the higher the dividend yield—that is, there is a relationship between returns and dividend yields that cannot be explained by the capital asset pricing model. Similar results have been found using Australian data for the period 1960 to 1969 (Ball et al. 1979) and for the period 1975 to 1998 (Boudry & Gray 2003).

Price–earnings ratio

price–earnings ratio
share price divided by earnings per share

The share price divided by earnings per share is usually called the **price–earnings ratio**, or the 'P/E ratio', and is used in decision making by investment analysts. In 1977 Basu reported that the P/E ratio helps to explain returns even after adjustment for systematic risk. Specifically, risk-adjusted returns were higher, the lower the P/E ratio. Basu's results were supported in a larger and more detailed study of US shares by Reinganum (1983). There is now a considerable literature suggesting that shares with low P/E ratios earn higher returns. In Australia, this relationship has been documented by Anderson, Lynch and Mathiou (1990).

Net share issues

A number of US studies have found that returns after adjustment for systematic risk are higher for companies that have repurchased or bought back their shares (see, for example, Ikenberry, Lakonishok & Vermaelen 1995). Other studies have found that returns are lower for companies that have issued shares (see, for example, Loughran & Ritter 1995, Daniel & Titman 2006 and Pontiff & Woodgate 2006). In aggregate, these studies document a negative relationship between net share issues and returns.

Accounting accruals

Under accrual accounting, companies record revenues and expenses when they are incurred, regardless of when cash is exchanged. In an important study Sloan (1996) found that companies with high

---

[5] For a detailed and entertaining review, see Haugen and Lakonishok (1988). Faff (1992) provides a concise review of the evidence on tax loss selling.
[6] For a brief survey of these studies, see Keim (1988, p. 19).

net positive accruals, that is, where non-cash revenues exceeded non-cash expenses, earned lower risk-adjusted returns. Since the original Sloan study, this finding has been confirmed many times in the accounting literature. Pincus, Rajgopal and Venkatachalam (2005) confirm its existence in Australia, Canada and the UK as well as in the US. Some further evidence of this negative relationship between accounting accruals and risk-adjusted returns has also been found in Australia by Clinch et al. (2008) and Gray, Koh and Tong (2009).

Asset growth

Cooper, Gulen and Shill (2008) report a very strong negative association between growth in net assets and risk-adjusted returns for US shares. This association has been confirmed in Australia by Gray and Johnson (2010).

Size

One of the most intensively studied of all the variables that have been used to forecast returns is size, where size is measured by the total market value of a company's shares. Future returns are predictable in that returns on the shares of small companies exceed the returns on the shares of larger companies both before and after adjusting for systematic risk. Put simply, returns on small-company shares are 'too high'. This relationship was first documented for US companies and it has since been observed in the share prices of Australian, Canadian, Japanese and UK companies.[7,8]

Figure 16.3 shows the performance of portfolios formed by dividing Australian shares into quintiles based on company size each year from 1975 to 2006. The portfolio formed from shares in the smallest

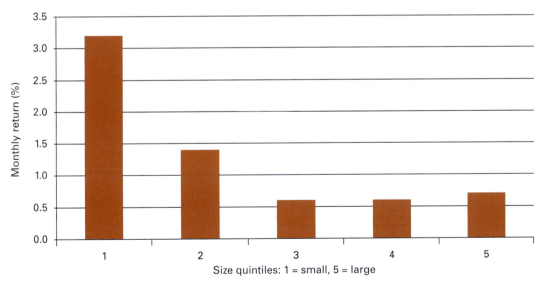

FIGURE 16.3 Average monthly return for five size-based portfolios: 1975–2006

Source: Compiled using the database from Australian Research Council/Acorn Capital Linkage Project Grant LP0560381 (Chief Investigators Howard Chan, Robert Faff and Paul Kofman). We thank the Chief Investigators for data access and Paul Docherty for the analysis.

---

[7] Among the earliest US studies are Banz (1981) and Reinganum (1981).

[8] For a survey, see Keim (1988).

companies earned a monthly average return of 3.2 per cent while the portfolio formed from shares in the largest companies earned a monthly average return of only 0.7 per cent.

Many studies, including that by Brown et al. (1983), have shown that this relationship remains after adjusting for systematic risk. This relationship has also been investigated in Australia by Beedles, Dodd and Officer (1988), who found that it remains present in the data, even when different measurement techniques are used. However, they identified several factors that may partly explain it. In particular, they reported that shares in small companies trade less frequently than shares in larger companies. This finding is consistent with shareholders in small companies requiring a higher expected return to compensate for the lower liquidity of their investment.

While the cause of the relationship is unclear, it is well documented that the size effect is linked to the January effect. In the US, this relationship is strong, with approximately half the difference in the returns on the shares of small and large companies being due to the higher reported returns to small companies in January (Keim 1983).[9] Loosely speaking, if just 1 month (January) is ignored, half of the size effect disappears. In Australia, the relationship appears to have changed quite significantly over the years. Gaunt, Gray and McIvor (2000) report that the higher return on small companies was prevalent across each calendar month when tested using a sample period from 1974 to 1985. However, their analysis of the period from 1986 to 1997 showed that while the size effect was still present in returns generally, there was no evidence of a relationship between size and return in January.

Book-to-market ratio

The book value of a company's equity is the value of the shareholders' stake in the company, as measured by accounting data. It appears in a company's financial statements and thus is readily available. The market value of equity is simply the market's valuation of the shareholders' stake in the company: it is the share price multiplied by the number of shares on issue. Security analysts frequently calculate the ratio of the book value of a company's equity to the market value of its equity. For simplicity, this ratio is often called the company's **book-to-market ratio**.

book-to-market ratio
book value of a company's equity divided by market value of the company's equity

What might explain why a company has a low or high book-to-market ratio? One possible explanation is that a company with a low book-to-market ratio may be a company that the market judges to have good prospects (hence its 'high' market value) while a company with a high book-to-market ratio may be a company that has had good years in the past (hence its 'high' book value) but which the market now judges to have poor prospects. Because a company's book-to-market ratio is publicly available at low cost, this information should be reflected in its current share price, if the market is efficient.

Fama and French (1992) documented that in the US over the period 1963 to 1990, there was a relationship between the book-to-market ratio and future share returns. Specifically, companies with low book-to-market ratios tended to earn low returns, while companies with high book-to-market ratios tended to earn high returns. Significantly, Fama and French showed that this difference was *not* attributable to differences in systematic risk. While some subsequent work has suggested that some of Fama and French's results may have been due to a survivorship bias in their data (Kothari, Shanken & Sloan 1995), other work has cast doubt on the significance of any such bias (Chan, Jegadeesh & Lakonishok 1995; Fama & French 1996b).

Figure 16.4 shows the performance of portfolios formed by dividing Australian shares into quintiles based on their book-to-market ratio each year from 1975 to 2006. The portfolio formed

---

9 See also Reinganum (1983).

FIGURE 16.4 Average monthly return for five portfolios formed on book-to-market ratios: 1975–2006

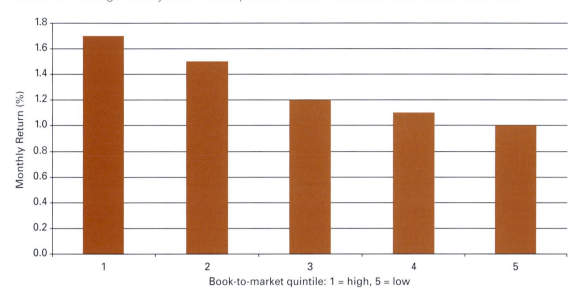

Source: Compiled using the database from Australian Research Council/Acorn Capital Linkage Project Grant LP0560381 (Chief Investigators Howard Chan, Robert Faff and Paul Kofman). We thank the Chief Investigators for data access and Paul Docherty for the analysis.

from the companies with the highest book-to-market ratios earned a monthly return of 1.7 per cent, while the portfolio formed from companies with the lowest book-to-market ratios earned a monthly return of only 1.0 per cent. As for the size factor, many studies, including those by Halliwell, Heaney and Sawicki (1999) and Gaunt (2004), have shown that this relationship remains after adjusting for systematic risk.

Interrelationship between factors used to predict future returns

Given the number of variables that have been found to be able to predict returns, it is important to examine possible interrelationships between these factors. As discussed in Section 7.7, in an important study, Fama and French (1992) showed that many of these factors are dominated by the size and book-to-market factors. Specifically, dividend yield and price–earnings ratio are not useful in predicting future returns after allowing for the more dominant effects of the size and book-to-market factors. The dominance of both size and book-to-market factors in Australia over the period 1982 to 2006 has been supported by O'Brien, Brailsford and Gaunt (2008). However, not all factors are dominated by the size and book-to-market factors. In a later paper, Fama and French (2008) reported that net share issues, accounting accruals and asset growth remain important in predicting future returns even after allowing for the size and book-to-market factors.

While there is a high level of agreement that various factors may be used to predict future returns, there is much less agreement on the implications of that evidence for market efficiency. The reason is the joint test problem discussed in Section 16.2.4. For example, as discussed in Section 7.7, some studies suggest that small companies and those with high book-to-market ratios may be riskier than large companies and those with low book-to-market ratios. Fama and French (1996a) argue that smaller companies are more likely to default than larger companies. Further, they argue that this risk is likely to be systematic in that small companies as a group are more exposed to default during economic downturns. As a result, investors in small companies will require a risk premium. Similarly, Zhang (2005) argues that companies with high book-to-market ratios will on average have higher levels of physical capacity. Much of this physical capacity will represent excess capacity during economic downturns and therefore expose such companies to increased risk.

However, La Porta et al. (1997) note that when companies with low book-to-market ratios announce their earnings, their share prices on average fall. Conversely, when companies with high book-to-market ratios announce their earnings, their share prices on average rise. They interpret this result as being due to market inefficiency. Specifically, they suggest that the share market overestimates the growth potential of companies with low book-to-market ratios. This overestimation results in an increase in their share price relative to their book value. When earnings are released, the market is on average disappointed and hence share prices fall. The opposite is true for companies with high book-to-market ratios.

16.4 EVENT STUDIES

The efficient market hypothesis requires that security prices adjust instantaneously and without bias to an event, such as the public announcement of new information relevant to the security's value. It follows that abnormal returns should not be expected to be earned from a subsequent analysis of such information.

Voluminous research has been conducted with a view to testing whether there are any post-event abnormal returns associated with the public release of information. These same studies are frequently used to evaluate the information content of particular types of information, such as profit announcements and dividend announcements.[10] The information content is measured by the presence of abnormal returns both prior to, at the time of, and subsequent to, the announcement. Such a test is generally called an event study. If markets are efficient, the price change measures as accurately as possible the 'true value' of the information to investors. Many people believe that event studies are among the clearest and most reliable tests of market efficiency. An information release ('event') is identified and the share price response is then studied to test its consistency with the hypothesis of market efficiency.[11]

16.4.1 THE METHODOLOGY OF EVENT STUDIES

There are many variants of event study methodology. Rather than provide details of each variant, we illustrate the major issues involved by using the announcement of annual profit as an example of an 'event'. For each announcement the following three questions need to be answered:

(a) What is the (new) information?
(b) When was it announced?
(c) Were there abnormal returns associated with its announcement?

We now consider each question.

(a) An annual profit figure provides information only if the announced or reported profit differs from the profit expected by investors. This is because, in an efficient market, the effects of the *expected* profit will already be reflected in the share price before the announcement. Only the *unexpected* part of the reported profit should cause the share price to react. It is therefore necessary to estimate the expected annual profit so that we can derive an estimate of the unexpected component. For example, it could

---
10 For an extensive discussion of accounting-related issues, see Brown (1994).
11 See Fama (1991, especially pp. 1601–2) for further discussion.

be assumed that the expected annual profit is equal to the previous year's profit. If the reported profit is greater than expected, then the unexpected component is positive, the event is classified as good news, and the market's response should also be positive. The reverse applies if the reported profit is less than expected.

(b) It is important to identify the time of the event accurately, ideally in this case the exact moment at which the annual profit became public knowledge. This is important because the market may react in anticipation of the announcement as investors revise their expectations. The market should also react at the time of the announcement to any unanticipated information. However, the market should not continue to react after the announcement because its response should be instantaneous and unbiased.

(c) It is necessary to calculate the response of the market to the announcement. In essence, this response is the percentage change in share price in excess of (or below) the percentage change that would normally be expected. Therefore, some model of 'normal' security price movement is needed.

As highlighted in Section 16.2.4, the *joint test problem* inevitably arises because event studies are simultaneously tests of market efficiency and the pricing model used to estimate what is 'normal'.

The problem associated with measuring 'normal' returns can be neatly sidestepped if we examine price behaviour on an intraday basis. This is because the expected return of a security over a very short time interval, such as a half-hour, is effectively zero. For example, Aitken et al. (1995) studied the share return behaviour for a sample of Australian companies during the 23 half-hourly trading intervals preceding, and the 25 half-hourly intervals subsequent to, the announcement of profit. They separated their sample into separate 'good news' and 'bad news' subsamples on the basis of whether or not the profit announced exceeded analysts' forecasts. The results relating to announcements made by 78 of the largest companies listed on the Australian Stock Exchange are illustrated in Figure 16.5 overleaf.

It is immediately apparent from Figure 16.5 that the majority of the market's reaction to the release of either 'good' or 'bad' news occurs in the first half-hour following the release of the information to the market. This contention is further supported by the finding that the only half-hourly mean return that is statistically different from zero is the return occurring immediately after the information release.

While some event studies use intraday data, others examine returns over much longer periods. As a result, these studies need a systematic approach to measuring the expected return of a security. A simple way of measuring expected returns is to use some variant of the market model.[12] The standard market model—which we discussed in Section 7.6.3—is specified as follows:

$$R_{it} = \alpha_i + \beta_i R_{Mt} + u_{it} \qquad [16.1]$$

Where R_{it} = rate of return on security i in period t
R_{Mt} = rate of return on the market index in period t
α_i = constant in regression equation
β_i = slope of regression equation—that is, beta value of security i
u_{it} = disturbance term

Factors that affect the whole market—such as war, drought, monetary policy and exchange rate changes—are captured by the term, R_{Mt}. The remaining—that is, abnormal—return is therefore attributed to company-specific factors, such as the public release of information relating to the company.

Suppose that Equation 16.1 is estimated using monthly data and the following estimate is obtained:

$$R_{it} = 0.005 + 1.25 R_{Mt} + e_{it}$$

---

[12] While the market model is used here for simplicity, expected returns are often calculated by adjusting not only for the market return but also the dominant factors that were discussed in Section 16.3.3 as being able to predict returns, namely firm size and the book-to-market ratio.

Abnormal returns, AR, on security i in a later month t are measured by:

$$AR_{it} = R_{it} - 0.005 - 1.25 R_{Mt}$$

Suppose that, in the month of the profit announcement for company i, the return on the shares of i was 8 per cent and the return on the market index that month was 2 per cent. Then the abnormal return in month zero, the announcement month, is:

$$AR_0 = 0.08 - 0.005 - (1.25)(0.02) = 0.05$$

FIGURE 16.5 Mean abnormal intraday returns associated with profit announcements of (a) 'good news' and (b) 'bad news'

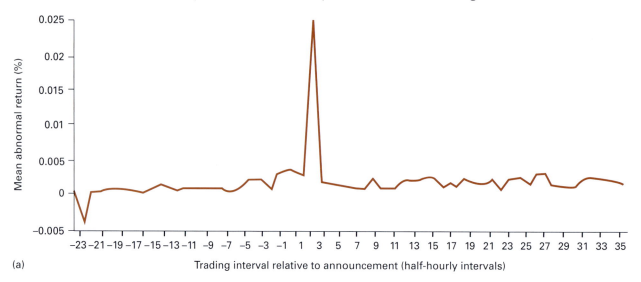

(a)

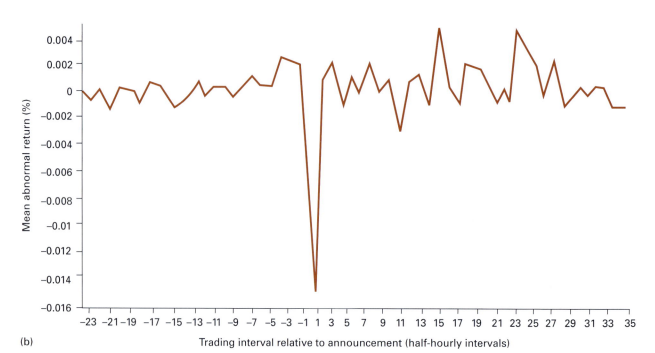

(b)

Source: M. Aitken et al. 'Price reaction and order imbalance surrounding earnings announcements', *ASX Perspectives*, 1995, pp. 31–5.

This may be interpreted as follows: during the month, this security returned 8 per cent to investors, of which 5 percentage points were due to company-specific events, such as the profit announcement. However, as mentioned earlier, part of the test involves estimating and examining abnormal returns before and after the announcement, as well as the abnormal returns at the time of the announcement. Typically, this involves estimating and examining abnormal returns for, say, each of the 12 months before the event, and for each of the 6 months after the event.

This completes the procedure for one company's announcement date. The total sample will consist of a large number of companies and announcement dates. For each announcement date the procedure is repeated for the company announcing on that date. Each announcement date in the sample is labelled Time zero; points in time *before* the announcement are labelled –1, –2, –3, …, –12, and points in time *after* the announcement are labelled +1, +2, …, +6. This is known as 'event time'. At each point in event time, the abnormal returns are calculated. For example, at Time zero a large positive abnormal return would be expected for companies announcing profits classified as 'good news'. At each point in event time the average abnormal return across companies is calculated. The average abnormal returns are then summed over event time. The procedures are illustrated in the following simplified example.

EXAMPLE 16.1

Companies A, B and C announced, at different dates, profits that were higher than expected (see Table 16.1).[13]

TABLE 16.1

MONTH RELATIVE TO ANNOUNCEMENT DATE	ABNORMAL RETURNS				
	A (%)	B (%)	C (%)	AVERAGE (%)	CUMULATIVE AVERAGE (%)
–12	1.0	–1.4	2.1	0.57	0.57
–11	4.2	0.9	–1.2	1.30	1.87
–10	–0.2	–3.6	0.4	–1.13	0.74
–9	1.2	–2.2	4.4	1.13	1.87
–8	0.6	–2.2	2.1	0.17	2.04
–7	–1.8	1.1	3.1	0.80	2.84
–6	0.0	1.9	0.4	0.77	3.61
–5	0.4	–0.4	–0.9	–0.30	3.31
–4	1.0	7.6	–1.2	2.47	5.78
–3	–0.2	2.6	3.1	1.83	7.61
–2	–0.3	–0.7	1.1	0.03	7.64
–1	0.9	2.1	–0.6	0.80	8.44
0	5.1	7.9	4.2	5.73	14.17
+1	–0.2	1.4	–0.6	0.20	14.37
+2	0.6	–3.2	1.9	–0.23	14.14
+3	1.2	0.1	–0.5	0.27	14.41
+4	–0.8	0.4	–0.9	–0.43	13.98
+5	0.0	–1.2	1.1	–0.03	13.95
+6	0.5	–1.9	3.0	0.53	14.48

continued →

---

13 This hypothetical example is very simple in that with a sample size of only three companies, the results, in reality, are unlikely to be so well behaved.

Example 16.1 *continued*

This explains the high abnormal returns for each company at Time zero. For A, B and C, the abnormal returns averaged 5.73 per cent at Time zero. It is likely that the market was anticipating good news. The evidence of this anticipation is the predominance of positive average abnormal returns in the 12 months before the announcement. However, following the announcement, the average abnormal returns are close to zero, but do not have a detectable trend. This pattern is typical of an efficient market in that there is an instantaneous reaction at the announcement date to the unanticipated component of the information and no subsequent drift in the average abnormal returns. The final column in Table 16.1 shows the cumulative average abnormal returns, which are plotted in Figure 16.6.

FIGURE 16.6 Cumulative average abnormal returns

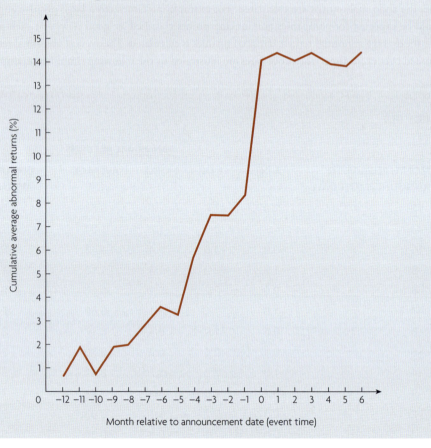

16.4.2 EVIDENCE: PROFIT AND DIVIDEND ANNOUNCEMENTS IN AUSTRALIA

To illustrate the empirical evidence found in event studies we consider some of the evidence on the reaction of share prices in Australia to profit and dividend announcements. In Australia, announcements of profit are nearly always accompanied by simultaneous announcements of dividends. Thus, it is useful to examine both the profit and the dividend information in an empirical test. Brown, Finn and Hancock (1977) conducted a study of dividend announcements by Australian companies for the period January 1963 to December 1969. In the first part of their study they examined the abnormal returns calculated on a monthly basis for the 12 months on each side of an annual dividend announcement. After adjusting for rights issues, bonus issues and other changes in capital, three groups were formed: one comprising shares in companies that had announced an increase in dividend per share (DPS), one comprising shares in companies that had announced a decrease in DPS and one comprising shares in companies whose DPS had remained constant. The cumulative average abnormal returns for each of these groups are shown in Figure 16.7.

FIGURE 16.7 Cumulative average abnormal returns

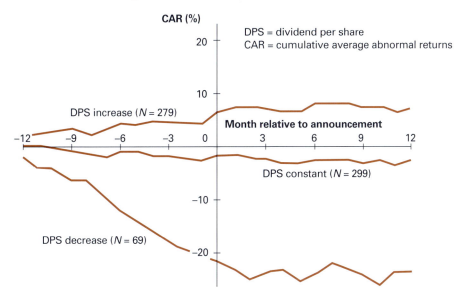

The results suggest that an increase (decrease) in DPS results in an increase (decrease) in abnormal returns. In particular, the results suggest that a decrease in DPS had significant information content and that, on average, investors expected an increase in DPS. The results also indicate that much of the information content of dividend announcements had been obtained earlier from other sources. Overall, these results are consistent with market efficiency.

Recognising that dividend and profit announcements usually occur simultaneously, Brown, Finn and Hancock divided each of the three groups into two subgroups, depending on whether profits increased or decreased. The cumulative average abnormal returns (CAR) associated with each subgroup are shown in Figure 16.8 overleaf.

The evidence suggests that the information content of the two sources of information is increased when they are in agreement. The highest positive abnormal returns are associated with the simultaneous announcement of profit and DPS increases. Similarly, the lowest (most negative) abnormal returns are associated with the simultaneous announcement of profit and DPS decreases. Where the signals are mixed—for example, profit increase with DPS decrease—abnormal returns fall between these two extremes. In general, these results support market efficiency.

The share price reaction to simultaneous profit and dividend announcements was investigated further by Easton and Sinclair (1989). Using nearly 900 half-yearly announcements by Australian companies in the period 1978 to 1980, they applied a technique that, in a statistical sense, can isolate the market's reaction to the profit announcement from the market's reaction to the dividend announcement. They found that both types of announcement caused a reaction, but that the reaction to dividends was weaker than the reaction to profits. In a subsequent study using the same sample, Easton (1991) conducted a more formal examination of the reaction to dividend and profit announcements and found that the share price response depends not only on the separate dividend and profit signals but also on the interaction between the signals. In other words, the market appears to take account of the interrelation of the profit and dividend information.

FIGURE 16.8 Cumulative average abnormal returns for each of the six subgroups

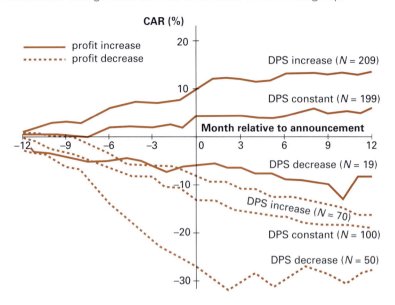

16.4.3 OTHER EVENTS

Many other types of events have been studied in Australia, and a voluminous set of events has been studied in the US and other markets. In Australia, the events that have been studied range from capitalisation changes (bonus issues, rights issues and share splits), takeovers, to the impact of large trades by institutional investors.[14] While many event studies are undertaken for reasons other than to test market efficiency, often some inference concerning market efficiency can be drawn. Usually, the inference is that prices have responded rapidly to the event studied. For example, Fama (1991, pp. 1601–2) argued that this 'result is so common that this work now devotes little space to market efficiency. The fact that quick adjustment is consistent with efficiency is noted, and then the studies move on to other issues'.

Over the past 20 years many researchers have come to believe that there is some underreaction to new information—in particular, the new information provided in profit announcements. Studies by Bernard and Thomas (1990) and Battalio and Mendenhall (2005) show that share prices continue to drift upwards after good profit news has been released, while they drift downwards following bad profit news.

16.5 TESTS FOR PRIVATE INFORMATION

A strict view of the EMH requires that abnormal returns are not available even to investors who have private (inside) information about a company. However, by definition, it is usually difficult to identify the date on which private information becomes available, and therefore the event study methodology often cannot be applied directly to studies concerned with the impact of private information.

The *Corporations Act 2001*, which governs the behaviour of company directors, provides researchers with an opportunity to test the EMH with respect to private information. The Act imposes an obligation on company directors to disclose to the Australian Securities Exchange changes in their interests in their own companies within 14 days of the change occurring. If the Australian share market were inefficient,

---

14 Studies that have examined rights issues include those by Balachandran, Faff and Theobald (2008) and Balachandran et al. (forthcoming); studies examining takeovers include those by Brown and Da Silva Rosa (1988) and Da Silva Rosa and Walter (2004); while studies examining block trades include those by Frino, Jarnecic and Lepone (2007 and 2009).

then we would expect that company directors, who can be assumed to have access to private information about their company's prospects, would be able to time the purchase (sale) of their shares before a future increase (decrease) in the share price.

Uylangco, Easton and Faff (2010) tested the relationship between directors' trades and share price performance, and found that while directors' purchases were on average followed by abnormal gains of only 0.2 per cent, directors' sales avoided a future abnormal loss of 1.1 percent. They also supported the US results of Seyhun (1986), which suggested that while small abnormal returns were possible from selling shares after directors disclosed that they had sold shares, these abnormal returns were insufficient to offset transaction costs.

Watson and Young (1999) examined the trading pattern of directors of 72 Australian companies subject to successful takeover bids in the 30-month period ended 30 June 1998. They found evidence to suggest that company directors traded in their company's shares in the period prior to the public announcement of the takeover. Furthermore, the authors reported that executive directors traded earlier than non-executive directors, suggesting that the former group's access to information may be superior to that of the latter group and/or that executive directors may be more sensitive to the attention of regulatory authorities than non-executive directors. These results are inconsistent with a very strict view of market efficiency, because they imply that insiders have information that is not reflected in market prices.

Another strand of the literature has evaluated the performance of fund managers and other 'professional investors' on the principle that if they have access to information that is not reflected in prices, they should display superior investment performance. The US evidence presents a mixed picture, with some studies suggesting that professional investors are able to show superior investment performance and others finding that they are unable to do so. Elton et al. (1993) concluded that, after controlling for the size of the companies that managers invested in (as detailed in Section 16.3.3, companies with small market capitalisation on average provide greater returns than companies with large market capitalisation), and after controlling for the mix of shares and bonds in the portfolio, fund managers were not able to generate superior performance. However, Kosowski et al. (2006) found that a minority of fund managers were able to generate superior returns.

A number of Australian studies have also examined the performance of mutual funds, unit trusts and superannuation funds.[15] None of these studies concluded that funds in general were able to earn abnormal returns. These studies can be interpreted as supporting market efficiency if it is assumed that the fund managers have access to private information but cannot use it to earn abnormal returns. However, in the light of other evidence, an alternative interpretation is that this evidence has little bearing on market efficiency. This interpretation would deny that fund managers have access to private information, or, if they do have such access, they do not use it to advantage.

US studies have also evaluated the performance of investment analysts. Womack (1996) examined changes in analysts' recommendations and found that positive changes were associated with increased share prices of approximately 5 per cent, while negative changes were associated with share price decreases of approximately 11 per cent. The fact that these changes were permanent suggests that the price changes were due to information revealed by the analysts' recommendations and not simply due to buying and selling pressure caused by the recommendations. Barber et al. (2001) examined the level of the consensus of analysts' recommendations. They found that companies for which the consensus of analysts' recommendations was a 'buy' out-performed companies for which the consensus of analysts' recommendations was a 'sell'. However, they noted that the transaction costs of buying and selling shares that would be required to act on these recommendations would be high and likely to prevent the earning of abnormal returns.

---

[15] See, for example, Hallahan and Faff (1999), Sawicki and Ong (2000), Gallagher (2001) and Frino and Gallagher (2002).

A number of Australian studies have also evaluated the performance of investment analysts. Brown and Walter (1982) analysed confidential buy and sell recommendations made by analysts. On a risk-adjusted basis, these recommendations out-performed the market. If the analysts employed private information when making their recommendations, then these results are contrary to market efficiency. Finn (1984) evaluated the performance of recommendations made by analysts employed by a large institutional investor. He found that, if acted on, these recommendations would have resulted in abnormal returns. This result is consistent with that of Brown and Walter. Both studies found that the analysts' ability to identify shares that should be sold exceeded their ability to identify shares that should be purchased. Interestingly, the institutional investor studied by Finn earned negative abnormal returns, which is consistent with much of the previous evidence on the performance of fund managers. Finn's results suggest that analysts employed by the institutional investor may have had access to private information, but that the institution failed to act quickly enough to benefit from the information. More recently, Chan, Brown and Ho (2006) supported the link between share price performance and broker recommendations in their examination of a sample of 5000 recommendations made in relation to Australian-listed companies.

The evidence relating to Australian and US share markets supports the conclusion that neither market is efficient with respect to asset prices reflecting all privately held information. This is not surprising. Inside information will be costly (and often impossible) for an outsider to obtain and, because of legal implications, may prove costly for an insider to use. While we would not expect an efficient market to reward the use of zero-cost information—such as information that is already publicly available—it may reward the use of costly information.

16.6 MARKET EFFICIENCY AT THE MACRO LEVEL[16]

LEARNING OBJECTIVE 4
Understand the difference between micro and macro market efficiency

The evidence presented in the previous sections of this chapter has all related to market micro-efficiency. That evidence suggests, on balance, that markets are highly micro efficient. However, as noted earlier, this does not mean that markets are necessarily macro efficient. Unfortunately, much less evidence exists as to whether the market as a whole reflects all available information—whether, for example, the share market is fairly priced compared with a less risky asset class such as bonds. However, several studies have examined whether it is possible to predict market-wide returns. Seminal studies are those by Keim and Stambaugh (1986) and Campbell and Shiller (1988a, 1988b). Keim and Stambaugh calculated a 'default spread', which is the yield on riskier corporate bonds minus the yield on relatively safe corporate bonds. They found that market-wide share returns were higher following periods when the default spread was high. Campbell and Shiller found that future market-wide returns were positively related to the current market-wide average earnings yield (where earnings yield is equal to earnings per share divided by price per share). However, the key difficulty is in the interpretation of the results. When market-wide risk is higher, investors in bonds will demand compensation for this risk and the default spread will also be higher. Similarly, for a given earnings per share, price per share will be lower in periods when risk is higher. Therefore, lower prices per share and the resultant higher earnings yields may be positively related to future returns because of the basic risk–return relationship—that is, higher risk needs to be compensated with higher expected returns.

Is the claimed predictability of market-wide returns due to market inefficiency or is it due to changes over time in market-wide risk? Attempting to answer this question runs headlong into the *joint test problem* discussed in Section 16.2.4. It is, therefore, a question that may never have a definitive answer.

---

16 The material covered in Section 16.6 and some of the material in Section 16.7 is discussed in Easton and Kerin (2010).

BEHAVIOURAL FINANCE AND MARKET EFFICIENCY

16.7

Shleifer (2000) has defined behavioural finance as the 'study of human fallibility in competitive markets'. Behavioural finance suggests that once we account properly for the impact of investor sentiment on market prices, we will find that markets are not only inefficient but should never be expected to be otherwise. To illustrate how behavioural finance has challenged traditional perceptions of market behaviour, Shleifer summarises, and then responds to, the three arguments that provide the theoretical foundations of the EMH.

LEARNING OBJECTIVE 5
Understand the relevance of behavioural finance to market efficiency

(a) If all participants in a market are rational, then all assets will be priced rationally.
(b) If there are investors who behave irrationally, then their trades will be random and ultimately cancel each other out, leaving prices unaffected.
(c) If irrational investors, as a group, exhibit a bias in the way in which they price assets, then any pricing bias will ultimately be eliminated by rational arbitrageurs who enter the market to take advantage of deviations of market prices from fundamental values. Furthermore, competition between arbitrageurs will ensure that this adjustment occurs quickly.

Behavioural finance has suggested, by reference to existing psychological theory and evidence, a number of models that explain why investors may not behave in a rational manner and, furthermore, why there may be limits to arbitrage that may prevent rational investors from entering the market to eliminate the impact that these irrational investors have on prices.[17]

Some of these models have been used to seek to explain why market-wide share prices (and the prices in other asset classes) might display **bubbles**. Various definitions of a 'bubble' have been proposed, but it is usually suggested that the following two features constitute a bubble (see Flood and Garber 1980; Blanchard 1979). First, prices show a strong tendency to rise for a period, possibly followed by a decrease, which may be quite sudden. Second, as a result, the price departs from the true, fundamental value of the asset. While the first of these features seems to be readily observable in stock markets—for example, in the crashes of October 1929 and October 1987—the mere presence of the first does *not*, of course, imply the presence of the second. Prices changing randomly will occasionally produce, purely by chance, episodes displaying the first feature. These episodes would probably *appear* to be bubbles, but they may not in reality be bubbles in the sense that we have suggested because the assets values have not departed from their fundamental value.

bubble
period in which prices rise strongly, departing from their 'true value', frequently followed by a sudden decrease in prices

A situation often cited as an example of such a bubble was the sharply rising market for shares in internet-based companies that occurred in the late 1990s—the so-called 'dotcom bubble'. During this time there were numerous examples of rapidly increasing prices for shares in companies that had never recorded a profit and, perhaps more importantly, did not look like generating a profit in the near future.

There are at least two plausible explanations for this bubble-type price behaviour. Proponents of behavioural finance may suggest that a bubble is an example of 'positive feedback trading', where investors are keen to buy after a series of price rises and to sell following price falls. Hence, price rises occur not because of any change in the market's expectation of future returns but simply because the price has recently risen. Far from dampening the impact of this irrational trading behaviour, it can be further argued that arbitrageurs actually contribute to the bubble by seeking to profit not from any departure in prices from fundamental values but instead in anticipation of the prices continuing to increase.

---
17 For a survey that discusses the psychological theory and evidence, see Barberis and Thaler (2003). For discussions of the limits to arbitrage, see Delong et al. (1990) and Shleifer and Vishny (1997).

An alternative explanation suggests that bubbles may in fact be consistent with an efficient market. To illustrate this concept of a rational bubble, suppose that a share price depends in part on its expected rate of change. Therefore, it has a 'high' price because it is expected to go higher still. In the presence of such self-fulfilling prophecy, prices may increase, even though there is no change in the 'fundamentals'. However, even these prices may be 'rational' in the sense that market participants form unbiased expectations.

It may also be noted that a large market-wide price change *per se* does not constitute a bubble, nor does it prove market inefficiency. An example using the global financial crisis may be used to illustrate this point. The S&P/ASX 200 index fell by 54 per cent between its all-time high of 6828.7 on 1 November 2007 and its subsequent (to date) low of 3145.5 on 6 March 2009. While a fall of 54 per cent may at first view appear implausibly large, such a fall may be consistent with reasonable estimates of changes in investors' required rate of return and in expected dividend growth rates. For example, using the simple dividend growth model from Section 4.3.2 (see Equation 4.8), the present value of $1 of annual dividend income with an annual cost of equity capital of 10 per cent and an expected annual growth rate in dividends of 5 per cent is $21. By comparison, the present value of $1 of annual dividend income with an annual cost of equity capital of 13 per cent and an expected annual growth rate in dividends of 2 per cent is $9.27—a fall of 56 per cent. In essence, it may be argued that the global financial crisis was a period of great uncertainty that caused investors to revise upwards the rate of return they required to compensate them for the increased risk they perceived and to revise downwards their estimates of future dividend growth.

In addition to seeking to explain bubbles, behavioural finance has also been used to try to provide explanations for other apparent inefficiencies. We discussed in Section 16.3.1 the findings of DeBondt and Thaler (1985 and 1987) that indicated that shares that have historically performed well (poorly) will subsequently perform poorly (well). One interpretation of these findings is that investors overvalue companies that have exhibited superior performance in the past and undervalue companies that have a history of inferior performance. Such irrational behaviour may be explained by what is referred to in the psychological literature as the 'representativeness heuristic'. This concept suggests that in forming their beliefs, individuals may be too quick in identifying a company as an 'excellent' or a 'terrible' investment without properly accounting for the probability of the company belonging to that extreme group of investments. Hence, an investor assessing the uncertain future of a company with a history of superior performance may tend to overweight the importance of that immediate past performance in achieving future superior returns, while failing to properly recognise the relatively small probability of any company achieving such superior performance in the future. Why might overreaction persist in the long term instead of being offset by the arbitrage activity of rational investors? One reason is that when prices are, at least in part, determined by investors behaving irrationally, arbitrage is inherently risky, as the unpredictable nature of irrational investors may mean that prices will not revert to their fundamental value in the short term.

There is now a range of studies that have provided results that are consistent with behavioural finance models. For example, Chopra, Lakonishok and Ritter (1992) found that shares that have performed the best tend to fall in price when earnings are announced, suggesting that investors are affected by the representativeness heuristic and that earnings announcements cause them to revise their over-optimistic beliefs. Also, La Porta et al. (1997) show that the lower returns to companies with lower book-to-market ratios might in part be explicable by irrational investor behaviour. One reason for shares having a low book-to-market ratio is that investors believe that the shares have higher potential for growth, therefore justifying a higher market price compared with book value. But La Porta et al. show that companies with high book-to-market ratios out-perform those with low book-to-market ratios in the days surrounding earnings announcements. They argue that this result is consistent with investors being overly optimistic about the growth prospects of companies with low book-to-market ratios. Investors then revise these beliefs when earnings are announced.

The extent to which the combined effects of investor irrationality and limits to arbitrage result in markets being less than fully efficient remains a key focus of research in finance. Survey articles supporting the behavioural finance position include those by Shleifer (2000), Hirshleifer (2001), Shiller (2002), and Barberis and Thaler (2003), while survey articles that conclude that markets are highly efficient include those by Fama (1998), Rubinstein (2001) and Malkiel (2003).

IMPLICATIONS OF THE EVIDENCE WITH RESPECT TO MARKET EFFICIENCY 16.8

The evidence on market efficiency is complex and subject to many qualifications. Nevertheless, there is considerable evidence to suggest that markets often perform well in reflecting available information and respond quickly to new information. This evidence provides important implications for investors in securities and for financial managers.

LEARNING OBJECTIVE 6
Understand the implications of the evidence on market efficiency for investors and financial managers

16.8.1 IMPLICATIONS FOR INVESTORS IN SECURITIES

There are a number of techniques that are used to evaluate investments in securities. The veracity of these techniques given the evidence on market efficiency is discussed under the following headings:

- charting, or technical analysis
- fundamental analysis
- random selection of securities
- buy-and-hold policies.

We then offer some comments on trying to beat the market.

Charting, or technical analysis

Some security analysts plot a share's historical price record on a chart. On the basis of such a chart, predictions are made as to the likely future short-term course of prices. For example, a rising trend may be detected, or perhaps a presumed cycle of peaks and troughs may be predicted to continue. The evidence from tests of serial correlation suggests that simple short-term repetitive patterns are unlikely to be present. It is possible that more complex patterns are present, but attempts to detect these patterns by judgement and visual inspection are prone to self-delusion. Thus, Batten and Ellis (1996), using Australian data, found, after allowing for transaction costs, that technical trading rules did not yield abnormal profits. However, Lo, Mamaysky and Wang (2000), using sophisticated statistical techniques that can recognise patterns, found—using US data—that certain patterns had modest predictive power. Further, persuasive and persistent evidence of momentum in returns over longer periods suggests that charting over longer time periods may yield abnormal profits.

Fundamental analysis

Other security analysts believe that the market either ignores some publicly available information or systematically misinterprets that information. These analysts maintain that sometimes the market is short sighted and a share price cannot be justified on the basis of the company's 'fundamental' features, such as its earnings record, or its net asset backing, which determine the share's 'true value'. Consequently, they believe that a careful analysis of available information may reveal mispriced securities, and therefore abnormal returns may be made by the skilled fundamental analyst.

In a market that is efficient, all publicly available information is reflected in the market price. Fundamental information is publicly available at a cost of approximately zero. In a competitive market, the return to using zero-cost information is expected to be zero. On its own, therefore, the analysis of such information should not yield abnormal returns in an efficient market.

The empirical evidence presented in this chapter suggests that while markets are not fully efficient they are nevertheless very efficient. The analysis presented in Section 16.3.3 in particular, however, does suggest that fundamental information about a company, such as its dividend yield, earnings, size, book value relative to market value, asset growth and level of accounting accruals, may be of some value in predicting returns. However, the security analyst industry is nevertheless a very competitive industry and it is only those analysts who have the skills to use this information better than their peers who are likely to be able to generate abnormal returns.

At its simplest level it needs to be stressed that fundamental analysis needs to do more than identify good companies that will be good investments. It is about identifying companies that are better investments than the market consensus considers them to be. Achieving this outcome using publicly available fundamental information will always be difficult.

The evidence that markets may be macro inefficient may be used to support the so-called top down approach to fundamental investment analysis. This approach begins with a broad allocation of investment funds between asset classes including shares, bonds and real estate. There is much evidence to suggest that the asset allocation decision is of considerable importance. For example, Brinson, Singer and Geebower (1991) report that 91.5 per cent of the difference in returns achieved by investment funds is due to this decision. This approach is consistent with a claim that, for example, the stock market as a whole may be overpriced compared with its longer-term value, even though the market may be micro efficient and that individual shares within that market may be properly priced relative to each other.

Random selection of securities

It is sometimes suggested that if markets are fully efficient and all securities are therefore 'correctly' priced, investors might as well choose their investments randomly. However, this is not correct advice even if markets are fully efficient. First, returns on a large portfolio of randomly selected securities will be highly correlated with returns on the market portfolio; that is, a portfolio of all risky assets. Therefore, the risk of such a portfolio will be close to the risk of the market portfolio. This may not suit the risk preferences of the investor. Second, investors should consider their tax position when selecting investments, which is unlikely to be the case if investments were selected randomly.

Buy-and-hold policies

buy-and-hold policy
investment strategy in which shares are bought and then retained in the investor's portfolio for a long period

In a similar vein, it is sometimes suggested that if markets are fully efficient then a **buy-and-hold policy** is the best investment strategy. It is true that, for many investors, the evidence that markets are efficient suggests that trying to beat the market is inadvisable, because such an attempt cannot be expected to succeed, and will generate higher transaction costs. A buy-and-hold strategy is supported by the results of research by Barber and Odean (2000). Using a sample of more than 60 000 households from a large US discount brokerage firm, Barber and Odean found that for the period February 1991 to December 1996 the 20 per cent of households that traded the most earned a net return after transaction costs of 10 per cent per annum, compared with the average for all households of 18 per cent per annum. In a later study, Barber and Odean (2001) found that men traded 45 per cent more than women and earned a return net of transaction costs that was 1.4 per cent per annum less than that earned by women.

However, this evidence does not mean that a buy-and-hold policy is always optimal for all investors. First, as share prices change over time, there will be changes in the proportion of the portfolio that a given shareholding represents. Thus, the risk of the portfolio is also likely to have changed. There will be further changes in the portfolio's risk if the risks of individual securities change over time. The result may well be that the portfolio's risk will diverge from the investor's desired risk level. The solution is to rebalance the portfolio, and this will usually require the sale of some securities and the purchase of others. An inflexible buy-and-hold policy is not optimal. Second, some investors may occasionally come upon private information about a company. It has already been stated that there is evidence suggesting that the market is not efficient with respect to selected pieces of information. Thus, there will be private information that is not reflected in prices, and trading on the basis of such information may therefore yield excess returns. The possibility that an investor may discover private information provides a justification for studying public information, such as that found in company annual reports. How can private information be identified and evaluated, without some knowledge of the company's characteristics?

Beating the market

Market efficiency yields some interesting implications for investors. At a symposium in 1991, the economist Robert Shiller stressed the volume of evidence that is anomalous to the efficient markets hypothesis. Richard Roll, a portfolio fund manager as well as an academic, responding by stating:

> *I have personally tried to invest money, my clients' money and my own, in every single anomaly and predictive device that academics have dreamed up ... I have attempted to exploit the so-called year-end anomalies and a whole variety of strategies supposedly documented by academic research. And I have yet to make a nickel on any of these supposed market inefficiencies ... a true market inefficiency ought to be an exploitable opportunity. If there's nothing investors can exploit in a systematic way, time in and time out, then it's very hard to say that information is not being properly incorporated into stock prices.*[18]

Two decades on it is fair to say that the evidence on the extent to which markets are efficient is increasingly complex and mixed. Nevertheless, with most evidence suggesting that *at best* a minority of fund managers are able to generate abnormal returns, it is not sensible for the average investor to try to beat the market. Obviously, if an investor has private information that is not yet reflected in the share price, then beating the market becomes a distinct possibility. But average investors do not often have such information. This suggests that most investors, most of the time, would do well to follow a passive investment approach. By this we mean that most investors should adopt a long-term view, hold a diversified portfolio and trade infrequently.

As noted by Fama (1991, p. 1608), one of the outcomes of the efficient-markets literature is the rise of passive investment funds that hold diversified portfolios that attempt to match market-wide index returns. Vanguard Investments' site **www.vanguard.com.au** contains detailed information on portfolio indexing.

WWW

16.8.2 IMPLICATIONS FOR FINANCIAL MANAGERS

The evidence concerning market efficiency also provides strong implications for financial managers. Some of those implications are considered under the following headings:[19]

- project selection
- communicating with the stock market
- using share price as a measure of company performance
- repurchasing existing securities or issuing new securities.

---

18 Malkiel (2003, p. 72).
19 The issues raised under these four subheadings are similar to some of those identified in Keane (1983, Chapter 8) and in Jensen and Smith (1984).

Project selection

Evidence suggests that markets respond quickly to new information, including information that is released by company management. If investing in a project really does increase the company's 'true value', the company's share price will reflect this fact when the information becomes available to the market.

Communicating with the stock market

As mentioned above, markets respond quickly to information. However, the market's reactions will not be unthinking, mechanical responses, since such responses would be identifiable as underreactions or overreactions. Managers must therefore expect that announcements of factors such as profit, dividends, takeovers, new security issues and capital reconstructions will elicit a price response that represents the market's collective view of the true situation.[20]

Using share price as a measure of company performance

The evidence concerning market efficiency suggests that the current share price is, if not the best available estimate of a company's 'true value', then certainly a good estimate. The historical share price record (taking into account the effects of dividends and changes in capital) will be an accurate statement of the record of the company's performance. This is not to say that the company's management is entirely responsible for this record, but presumably it must bear significant responsibility for it.

Repurchasing existing securities or issuing new securities

As discussed in Section 16.3.3, there is evidence that markets are not fully efficient with respect to the timing of repurchases and new share issues, and that shares tend to perform well following share repurchases and poorly following new share issues. This result may be due to managers having private information that enables them to repurchase shares when prices are low and to issue new shares when prices are high. If so, then investors who sell their shares back to the company via share repurchases tend to lose when compared with those shareholders who retain their shares. Similarly, those shareholders who invest in new shares tend to lose when compared with existing shareholders.

Of course, investors tend to be aware of these incentives, so announcements of share repurchases tend to cause prices to rise (see Ikenberry, Lakonishok & Vermaelen 1995 for US evidence and Otchere & Ross 2002 for Australian evidence), while announcements of new share issues tend to cause prices to fall (see Manuel, Brooks & Schadler 1993 for US evidence and Denhert 1993 for Australian evidence).

The financial manager and evidence with respect to market efficiency

Given the complex nature of the evidence concerning market efficiency, how should financial managers react? In particular, what are the implications of apparent market inefficiencies for the financial manager? We consider that the general body of evidence supporting market efficiency still provides a useful guide to financial managers.

- Managers should be aware that there are reasons to expect that, unless people are familiar with the research literature, they will systematically tend to underestimate the level of market efficiency. There are many reasons for this tendency, including:
  - the difficulty in distinguishing ability from luck
  - the presence of vested interests in denying that markets are efficient
  - the fact that people tend to forget losses and embellish their wins.[21]

---

[20] For further discussion, see Steward and Glassman (1984) and Healy and Palepu (1992).

[21] For a longer catalogue of reasons and a detailed discussion, see Bowman and Buchanan (1995).

- Markets can be expected to respond positively to good news and negatively to bad news. Therefore, news of successful operations and of wise decisions by management is expected to increase share prices, while news of losses, mistakes and failure will decrease share prices. The performance of companies and, implicitly, the performance of management, may ultimately be judged by the stock market.
- On the question of evidence that suggests that markets are not perfectly efficient, there may often be few alternatives to behaving as if the stock market is highly efficient. For example, if the financial manager of a small company interprets the evidence on the size effect to mean that the company may be undervalued, it is difficult to see exactly how this should guide his or her actions unless there is also some knowledge of what causes the underpricing and when the underpricing may be expected to cease. If the manager decides not to raise new capital by way of a share issue, is a debt issue necessarily a superior choice? What if debt issued by small companies is even more underpriced than shares issued by small companies?
- It should always be remembered that efficiency tests are joint tests of the assumed asset pricing model and of the efficiency of the market. Most of the asset pricing models that have been used are quite simple and it would not be surprising to learn that they do not work well when applied to 'extreme' cases, such as the smallest companies.

Connect Plus features a case study illustrating topics covered in this chapter. Ask your lecturer or tutor for your course's unique URL.

SUMMARY

→ An efficient capital market has been defined as one in which the prices of securities 'fully reflect' all available information. This requires that the reaction of market prices to new information should be instantaneous and unbiased. If such conditions exist, it will not be possible (except by chance) to employ either past information or a mechanical trading strategy to generate returns in excess of the returns warranted by the level of risk involved. In short, consistent excess profits will not be made.

→ Market efficiency may be classified according to the three research methodologies employed to assess the efficiency of a market:
  - tests of return predictability are undertaken to ascertain whether future returns can be predicted on the basis of factors such as past returns, the time of the year or the company's book-to-market ratio
  - event studies are employed to analyse the behaviour of a security's returns around the time of a significant event such as the public announcement of a company's profit, its dividends or its intention to acquire another company
  - tests for private information are designed to assess whether investors can trade profitably by making their investment decisions on the basis of information that is not publicly available.

→ Each of these testing methodologies has provided evidence with respect to market efficiency that is complex and mixed.

→ There are a number of implications of the theory and evidence on capital market efficiency.
  - In an efficient market, charting and fundamental analysis will not succeed since both involve the analysis of only past information, which should already be reflected in the market price. However, this does not mean that securities should be selected randomly or that a buy-and-hold policy is always best for all investors. It does, however, suggest that investors should not try to 'beat the market' unless they possess inside information that is not yet reflected in the price.

- Likewise, an efficient market is not easily misled and company managers can expect the share price to respond to news of their successes and failures.
- While the evidence with respect to market efficiency is complex and mixed it is suggested that, in normal circumstances, market efficiency is a useful way to approach the study of price behaviour, and to organise our knowledge of capital markets.

KEY TERMS

abnormal returns 519	efficient market hypothesis (EMH) 517	overreaction 518
book-to-market ratio 526	event study 519	price–earnings ratio 524
bubble 537	information efficiency 519	tax loss selling 524
buy-and-hold policy 540	January effect 523	tests for private information 519
dividend yield 524	joint test problem 520	tests of return predictability 519
	momentum effect 521	underreaction 518

REFERENCES

Aitken, M., Brown, P., Frino, A. & Walter, T., 'Price reaction and order imbalance surrounding earnings announcements', *ASX Perspectives*, 1995, pp. 31–5.

——, ——, Izan, H.Y., Kua, A. & Walter, T., 'An intraday analysis of the probability of trading on the ASX at the asking price', *Australian Journal of Management*, December 1995, pp. 115–54.

Allen, D.E. & Prince, R., 'The winner–loser hypothesis: some preliminary Australian evidence on the impact of changing risk', *Applied Economics Letters*, 1995, pp. 280–3.

Anderson, D., Lynch, A. & Mathiou, N., 'Behaviour of CAPM anomalies in smaller firms: Australian evidence', *Australian Journal of Management*, June 1990, pp. 1–38.

Balachandran, B., Faff, R. & Theobald, M., 'Rights offerings, takeup, renounceability and underwritten status', *Journal of Financial Economics*, August 2008, pp. 328–46.

——, ——, ——, & Zijl, T., 'Rights offerings, subscription period, shareholder takeup and liquidity', *Journal of Financial and Quantitative Analysis*, forthcoming, http://ssrn.com/abstract=1534048.

Ball, R., 'The development, accomplishments and limitations of the theory of stock market efficiency', *Managerial Finance*, 1994, pp. 3–48.

——, & Bowers, J., 'Daily seasonals in equity and fixed-interest returns: Australian evidence and tests of plausible hypotheses', in E. Dimson (ed.), *Stock Market Anomalies*, Cambridge University Press, Cambridge, 1988, p. 79.

——, Brown, P., Finn, F.J. & Officer, R.R., 'Dividends and the value of the firm: evidence from the Australian equity market', *Australian Journal of Management*, April 1979, pp. 13–26.

Banz, R.W., 'The relationship between return and market value of common stock', *Journal of Financial Economics*, March 1981, pp. 3–18.

Barber, B., Lehavy, R., McNichols, M. & Trueman, B., 'Can investors profit from the prophets? Security analyst recommendations and stock returns', *Journal of Finance*, April 2001, pp. 531–63.

——, & Odean, T., 'Trading is hazardous to your wealth: the common stock investment performance of individual investors', *Journal of Finance*, April 2000, pp. 773–806.

——, ——, 'Boys will be boys: gender, overconfidence and common stock investment', *Quarterly Journal of Economics*, February 2001, pp. 261–92.

Barberis, N. & Thaler, R., 'A survey of behavioral finance', in G.M. Constantinides, M. Harris & R. Stulz.(eds), *Handbook of the Economics of Finance*, Elsevier, Amsterdam, 2003.

Basu, S., 'The investment performance of common stocks in relation to their price–earnings ratios: a test of the efficient market hypothesis', *Journal of Finance*, June 1977, pp. 663–82.

Battalio, R.H. & Mendenhall, R., 'Earnings expectations, investor trade size, and anomalous returns around earnings announcements', *Journal of Financial Economics*, August 2005, pp. 289–319.

Batten, J. & Ellis, C., 'Technical trading system performance in the Australian share market: some empirical evidence', *Asia Pacific Journal of Management*, 1996, pp. 87–99.

Beedles, W., Dodd, P. & Officer, R., 'Regularities in Australian share returns', *Australian Journal of Management*, June 1988, pp. 1–29.

Bernard, V. & Thomas, J., 'Evidence that stock prices do not fully reflect the implications of current earnings for future earnings', *Journal of Accounting and Economics*, December 1990, pp. 305–40.

Bettman, J.L., Maher, T.R.B. & Sault, S.J., 'Momentum profits in the Australian equity market: a matched firm approach', *Pacific-Basin Finance Journal*, November 2009, pp. 565–79.

Blanchard, O.J., 'Speculative bubbles, crashes and rational expectations', *Economics Letters*, 1979, pp. 387–9.

Boudry, W. & Gray, P., 'Assessing the economic significance of return predictability: a research note', *Journal of Business Finance, and Accounting*, December 2003, pp. 1305–26.

Bowman, R.G. & Buchanan, J., 'The efficient market hypothesis—a discussion of institutional, agency and behavioural issues', *Australian Journal of Management*, December 1995, pp. 155–66.

Brailsford, T.J., 'A test for the winner–loser anomaly in the Australian equity market 1958–87', *Journal of Business Finance and Accounting*, January 1992, pp. 225–42.

——, & Easton, S., 'Seasonality in Australian share price indices between 1936 and 1957', *Accounting and Finance*, November 1991, pp. 69–85.

——, & Faff, R.W., 'Modelling Australian stock market volatility', *Australian Journal of Management*, December 1993, pp. 109–32.

Brinson, G., Singer, B., & Geebower, G., 'Determinants of portfolio performance II: an update', *Financial Analysts Journal*, May/June 1991, pp. 40–8.

Brock, W., Lakonishok, J. & LeBaron, B., 'Simple technical trading rules and the stochastic properties of stock returns', *Journal of Finance*, December 1992, pp. 1731–64.

Brown, P., *Capital Markets-Based Research in Accounting: An Introduction*, Coopers & Lybrand and the Accounting Association of Australia and New Zealand, Melbourne, 1994.

——, & Da Silva Rosa, R., 'Research method and the long-run performance of acquiring firms', *Australian Journal of Management*, June 1998, pp. 23–38.

——, Finn, F. & Hancock, P., 'Dividend changes, earnings reports and share prices: some Australian findings', *Australian Journal of Management*, October 1977, pp. 127–47.

——, Keim, D., Kleidon, A. & Marsh, T., 'Stock return seasonalities and the tax-loss selling hypothesis: analysis of the arguments and Australian evidence', *Journal of Financial Economics*, June 1983, pp. 105–27.

——, & Walter, T., 'Sharemarket efficiency and the experts: some Australian evidence', *Australian Journal of Management*, June 1982, pp. 13–32.

Campbell, J.Y. & Shiller, R.J., 'Stock prices, earnings, and expected dividends', *Journal of Finance*, July 1988a, pp. 661–76.

——, ——, 'The dividend-price ratio and expectations of future dividends and discount factors', *Review of Financial Studies*, Autumn 1988b, pp. 195–228.

Chan, H.W., Brown, R.L. & Ho, Y.K., 'Initiation of brokers' recommendations, market predictors and stock returns', *Journal of Multinational Financial Management*, July 2006, pp. 213–31.

Chan, L.K., Jegadeesh, N. & Lakonishok, J., 'Evaluating the performance of value versus glamour stocks: the impact of selection bias', *Journal of Financial Economics*, 1995, pp. 269–96.

Chan, S., Leung, W. & Wang, K., 'The impact of institutional investors on the Monday seasonal', *Journal of Business*, October 2004, pp. 967–86.

Chopra, N., Lakonishok, J. & Ritter, J.R., 'Measuring abnormal performance: do stocks overreact?', *Journal of Financial Economics*, April 1992, pp. 235–68.

Clinch, G., Fuller, D., Govendir, B. & Wells, P., 'The accrual anomaly: Australian evidence', Working Paper, University of Technology Sydney, 2008.

Condoyanni, J., O'Hanlon, J. & Ward C.W.R., 'Weekend effects in stock market returns: international evidence', in E. Dimson (ed.), *Stock Market Anomalies*, Cambridge University Press, Cambridge, 1988, p. 54.

Conrad, J.& Kaul, G., 'Time-variation in expected returns', *Journal of Business*, October 1988, pp. 409–25.

Cooper, M., Gulen, H. & Schill, M.J., 'Asset growth and the cross-section of stock returns', *Journal of Finance*, August 2008, pp. 1609–51.

Damodaran, A., 'The weekend effect in information releases: a study of earnings and dividend announcements', *Review of Financial Studies*, Winter 1989, pp. 607–23.

Daniel, K. & Titman, S., 'Market reaction to tangible and intangible information', *Journal of Finance*, August 2006, pp. 1605–43.

Da Silva Rosa, R. & Walter, T., 'Australian mergers and acquisitions since the 1980s: what do we know and what remains to be done', *Australian Journal of Management*, 2004, pp. i–xiv.

DeBondt, W.F.M. & Thaler, R.H., 'Does the stock market overreact?' *Journal of Finance*, July 1985, pp. 793–805.

——, ——, 'Further evidence on investor overreaction and stock market seasonality', *Journal of Finance*, July 1987, pp. 557–81.

Delong, J.B., Shleifer, A., Summers, L. & Waldmann, R., 'Noise trader risk in financial markets', *Journal of Political Economy*, August 1990, pp. 704–38.

Demir, I., Muthuswamy, J. & Walter, T., 'Momentum returns in Australian equities: the influences of size, liquidity and return computation', *Pacific-Basin Finance Journal*, April 2004, pp. 143–58.

Denhert, J., *A study of rights issues of equity: a theoretical and empirical analysis*, PhD dissertation, University of New South Wales, 1993.

Dimson, E., (ed.), *Stock Market Anomalies*, Cambridge University Press, Cambridge, 1988.

Doukas, J.A., Ball, R., Daniel, K., French, K., Ross, S. & Shanken, J., 'Rationality of capital markets', *European Financial Management*, June 2002, pp. 229–47.

Easton, S., 'Earnings and dividends: is there an interaction effect?' *Journal of Business Finance and Accounting*, January 1991, pp. 255–66.

——, & Kerin, P., 'Market efficiency and the global financial crisis', *Australian Economic Review*, December 2010, pp. 464–8.

——, & Sinclair, N., 'The impact of unexpected earnings and dividends on abnormal returns to equity', *Accounting and Finance*, May 1989, pp. 1–14.

Elton, E.J., Gruber, M.J., Das, S. & Hlavka, M., 'Efficiency with costly information: a reinterpretation of evidence from managed portfolios', *Review of Financial Studies*, Spring 1993, pp. 1–22.

Faff, R.W., 'Capital market anomalies: a survey of the evidence', *Accounting Research Journal*, Spring 1992, pp. 3–22.

Fama, E., 'Efficient capital markets: a review of theory and empirical work', *Journal of Finance*, May 1970, pp. 383–417.

——, 'Efficient capital markets: II', *Journal of Finance*, December 1991, pp. 1575–617.

——, 'Market efficiency, long-term returns and behavioral finance', *Journal of Financial Economics*, 1998, pp. 283–306.

Fama, E. & French, K., 'The cross-section of expected stock returns', *Journal of Finance*, June 1992, pp. 427–65.

——, ——, 'Multifactor explanations of asset pricing anomalies', *Journal of Finance*, March 1996a, pp. 55–84.

——, ——, 'The CAPM is wanted, dead or alive', *Journal of Finance*, December 1996b, pp. 1947–58.

——, ——, 'Dissecting anomalies', *Journal of Finance*, August 2008, pp. 1653–78.

Finn, F.J., *Evaluation of the Internal Processes of Managed Investment Funds*, JAI Press, Greenwich, Connecticut, 1984.

——, Lynch, A. & Moore, S., 'Intra-week regularities in security returns: further Australian evidence', *Australian Journal of Management*, December 1991, pp. 129–44.

Flood, R.P. & Garber, P.M., 'Market fundamentals versus price-level bubbles: the first tests', *Journal of Political Economy*, August 1980, pp. 745–70.

French, K., 'Stock returns and the weekend effect', *Journal of Financial Economics*, March 1980, pp. 55–69.

Frino, A. & Gallagher, D.R., 'Is index performance achievable? An analysis of Australian equity index funds', *Abacus*, 2002, pp. 200–14.

——, Jarnecic, E. & Lepone, A., 'The determinants of the price impact of block trades: further evidence', *Abacus*, 2007, pp. 94–106.

——, ——, ——, 'An event time study of the price reaction to large retail trades', *Quarterly Review of Economics and Finance*, 2009, pp. 617–32.

Gallagher, D.R., 'Attribution of investment performance: an analysis of Australian pooled superannuation funds', *Accounting and Finance,* July 2001, pp. 41–62.

Gaunt, C., Gray, P. & McIvor, J., 'The impact of share price on seasonality and size anomalies in Australian equity returns', *Accounting and Finance*, March 2000, pp. 33–50.

Gaunt, C., 'Size and book to market effects and Fama French asset pricing model: evidence from the Australian stockmarket', *Accounting and Finance*, March 2004, pp. 27–49.

George, T.J. & Hwang, C.Y., 'Long-term return reversals: overreaction or taxes?', *Journal of Finance*, December 2007, pp. 2865–96.

Gray, P. & Johnson, J., 'The relationship between asset growth and the cross-section of stock returns', *Journal of Banking and Finance*, 2010, forthcoming.

Gray, P., Koh, P.S. & Tong, Y.H., 'Accruals quality, information risk and the cost of capital: evidence from Australia', *Journal of Business Finance and Accounting*, January / February 2009, pp.51–72.

Gultekin, M. & Gultekin, B., 'Stock market seasonality: international evidence', *Journal of Financial Economics*, December 1983, pp. 469–82.

Hallahan, T. & Faff, R.W., 'An examination of Australian equity trusts for selectivity and market timing performance', *Journal of Multinational Financial Management*, 1999, pp. 387–402.

Halliwell, J., Heaney, R. & Sawicki, J., 'Size and book-to-market effects in Australian share markets: a time series analysis', *Accounting Research Journal*, 1999, pp. 122–37.

Haugen, R.A. & Lakonishok, J., *The Incredible January Effect: The Stock Market's Unsolved Mystery*, Dow-Jones-Irwin, Homewood, Illinois, 1988.

Healy, P. & Palepu, K., 'How investors interpret changes in corporate financial policy', in J.M. Stern and D.H. Chew (eds), *The Revolution in Corporate Finance*, 2nd edn, Basil Blackwell, Oxford, 1992, pp. 33–8.

Hirshleifer, D., 'Investor psychology and asset pricing', *Journal of Finance*, August 2001, pp. 1533–97.

Hurn, S. & Pavlov, V., 'Momentum in Australian stock returns', *Australian Journal of Management*, September 2003, pp. 141–55.

Ikenberry, D., Lakonishok, J. & Vermaelen, T., 'Market underreaction to open market share repurchases', *Journal of Financial Economics*, November 1995, pp. 181–208.

Jaffe, J. & Westerfield, R., 'The weekend effect in common stock returns: the international evidence', *Journal of Finance*, June 1985, pp. 433–54.

Jegadeesh, N. & Titman, S., 'Returns to buying winners and selling losers: implications for market efficiency', *Journal of Finance*, 1993, pp. 65–91.

——, ——, 'Profitability of momentum strategies: an evaluation of alternative explanations', *Journal of Finance*, 2001, pp. 699–718.

Jensen, M.C. & Smith, C.W., 'The theory of corporate finance', in their volume of readings, *The Modern Theory of Corporate Finance*, McGraw-Hill, New York, 1984.

Keane, S.M., *Stock Market Efficiency: Theory, Evidence and Implications*, Philip Allan, Oxford, 1983.

Keim, D.B., 'Size-related anomalies and stock return seasonality: further empirical evidence', *Journal of Financial Economics*, March 1983, pp. 13–32.

——, 'Stock market regularities: a synthesis of the evidence and explanations', in E. Dimson (ed.), *Stock Market Anomalies*, Cambridge University Press, Cambridge, 1988.

Keim, D.B. & Stambaugh, R.F., 'Predicting returns in the stock and bond markets', *Journal of Financial Economics*, 1986, pp. 357–90.

Kosowski, R., Timmermann, A., Wermers, R. & White, H., 'Can mutual fund "stars" really pick stocks? New evidence from a bootstrap analysis', *Journal of Finance*, December 2006, pp, 2551–95.

Kothari, S.P., Shanken, J. & Sloan, R.G., 'Another look at the cross-section of expected stock returns', *Journal of Finance*, March 1995, pp. 185–224.

La Porta, R., Lakonishok, J., Shleifer, A. & Vishny, R.W., 'Good news for value stocks: further evidence on market efficiency', *Journal of Finance*, June 1997, pp. 859–74.

Lakonishok, J. & Levi, M., 'Weekend effects in stock returns: a note', *Journal of Finance*, June 1982, pp. 883–9.

Lakonishok, J. & Smidt, S., 'Are seasonal anomalies real? A ninety-year perspective', *Review of Financial Studies*, Winter 1988, pp. 403–25.

Lee, C.M.C. & Swaminathan, B., 'Price momentum and trading volume', *Journal of Finance*, October 2000, pp. 2017–69.

Lo, A.W. & MacKinlay, A.C., 'Stock market prices do not follow random walks: evidence from a simple specification test', *Review of Financial Studies*, 1988, pp. 41–66.

——, ——, *A Non-Random Walk Down Wall Street*, Princeton University Press, Princeton, 1999.

Lo, A.W., Mamaysky, H. & Wang, J., 'Foundations of technical analysis: computational algorithms, statistical inference and empirical implications', *Journal of Finance*, August 2000, pp. 1705–65.

Loughran, T. & Ritter, J.R., 'The new issues puzzle', *Journal of Finance*, March 1995, pp. 23–51.

Malkiel, B.G., 'The efficient market hypothesis and its critics', *Journal of Economic Perspectives*, Winter 2003, pp. 59–82.

Manuel, T.A., Brooks, L.D. & Schadler, F.P., 'Common stock price effects of security issues conditioned by current earnings and dividend announcements', *Journal of Business*, October 1993, pp. 571–93.

Moskowitz, T.J. & Grinblatt, M., 'Do industries explain momentum?', *Journal of Finance*, August 1999, pp. 1249–90.

O'Brien, M., Brailsford, T. & Gaunt, C., 'Size and book-to-market factors in Australia', 21st Australasian Finance and Banking Conference Paper, 2008, **http://ssrn.com/abstract=1206542**.

Otchere, I., & Ross, M., 'Do share buy back announcements convey firm-specific or industry-wide information? A test of the undervaluation hypothesis', *International Review of Financial Analysis*, 2002, pp. 511–31.

Pincus, M., Rajgopal, S. & Venkatachalam, M., 'The accrual anomaly: international evidence', Working Paper, University of California-Irvine, 2005.

Pontiff, J. & Woodgate, A., 'Share issuance and cross-sectional returns', Working Paper, Boston College Carroll School of Management, 2006.

Reinganum, M.R., 'Misspecification of capital asset pricing: empirical anomalies based on earnings' yields and market values', *Journal of Financial Economics*, March 1981, pp. 19–46.

——, 'The anomalous stock market behavior of small firms in January: empirical tests for tax-loss selling effects', *Journal of Financial Economics*, June 1983, pp. 89–104.

Rozeff, M. & Kinney, W., 'Capital market seasonality: the case of stock returns', *Journal of Financial Economics*, November 1976, pp. 379–402.

Rubinstein, M., 'Rational markets: yes or no? The affirmative case', *Financial Analysts Journal*, May/June 2001, pp. 15–29.

Sawicki, J. & Ong, F., 'Evaluating managed fund performance using conditional measures: Australian evidence', *Pacific-Basin Finance Journal*, 2000, pp. 505–28.

Seyhun, H., 'Insiders' profits, costs of trading, and market efficiency', *Journal of Financial Economics*, vol. 16, 1986, pp. 189–212.

Shiller, R.J., 'From efficient market theory to behavioral finance', Cowles Foundation discussion paper no. 1385, Yale University, 2002.

Shleifer, A., *Inefficient Markets: An Introduction to Behavioral Finance*, Oxford University Press, Oxford, 2000.

——, & Vishny, R., 'The limits of arbitrage', *Journal of Finance*, March 1997, pp. 35–55.

Sloan, R.G., 'Do stock prices fully reflect information in accruals and cash flows about future earnings?', *Accounting Review*, July 1996, pp. 289–315.

Steward, G.B. & Glassman, D.M., 'How to communicate with an efficient market', *Midland Corporate Finance Journal*, Spring 1984, pp. 73–9.

Uylangco, K., Easton, S. & Faff, R., 'The equity and efficiency of the Australian share market with respect to director trading', *Accounting Research Journal*, 2010, pp. 5–19.

Watson, I. & Young, A., 'A preliminary examination of insider trading around takeover announcements in Australia', Working Paper, Department of Accounting and Finance, University of Western Australia, 1999.

Womack, K.L., 'Do brokerage analysts' recommendations have investment value?', *Journal of Finance*, March 1996, pp. 531–63.

Zhang, L., 'The value premium', *Journal of Finance*, February 2005, pp. 67–103.

QUESTIONS

1. **[LO 1]** What is an 'efficient capital market'? Illustrate your answer with an example.
2. **[LO 1]** *The EMH implies that all financial assets are always correctly priced.* Is this statement correct? Give reasons.
3. **[LO 1]** What would cause a capital market to be efficient?
4. **[LO 2]** What are the objectives of tests of return predictability? Outline the empirical evidence from these tests.

5. **[LO 2]** Design an empirical test of the effect of companies' dividend announcements on security prices. What are some of the problems in constructing a valid test?

6. **[LO 2]** Briefly outline the empirical evidence from event studies.

7. **[LO 2]** *As it is impossible to determine when private information becomes available, it is impossible to test whether a market is efficient with respect to this information.* Discuss.

8. **[LO 6]** *Empirical evidence suggests that professional investment managers do not earn positive abnormal returns.* Is this true? Discuss the implications of this evidence.

9. **[LO 6]** In an article in the Melbourne *Age* newspaper on 9 September 2003 entitled 'Write-off or rip-off as $55bn goes west', Alan Kohler stated that 'the Australian economy might be doing well and the share market recovering, but a wild epidemic of write-offs among listed companies is costing shareholders plenty'. To what extent is this statement likely to be true in an efficient market?

10. **[LO 6]** What are the implications of the empirical evidence on market efficiency for:
    (a) technical analysis?
    (b) fundamental analysis?

11. **[LO 6]** Assuming that you have $1 million to invest, how would you structure your investment? Why?

12. **[LO 6]** Outline the importance of market efficiency for the assumed objective of maximising the market value of a company's equity.

13. **[LO 6]** *If capital markets are efficient, it makes no difference which securities a company issues.* Discuss this statement.

14. **[LO 3]** Interpret the following statements in terms of their implications for market efficiency.
    (a) *Shares in risky companies give higher returns than shares in safe companies.*
    (b) *The shares in a company increase in price in the period before that in which a takeover bid is announced for the company.*
    (c) *Tax-exempt government bonds are issued at lower interest rates than taxable government bonds.*
    (d) *Company directors tend to make profits from investments in the shares of companies with which they are associated.*
    (e) *There is evidence that share prices follow a trend.*

15. **[LO 6]** What are the implications of the evidence on market efficiency for those who support greater regulation of corporate disclosure?

16. **[LO 6]** *The significance of calendar-based patterns in returns lies not so much in their size as in the fact that they exist at all.* Discuss this statement.

17. **[LO 3]** Suppose that Megan McDonald has undertaken a study of the efficiency of the stock market's reaction to the announcement of changes in steel prices. Specifically, she finds that share prices appear to continue reacting for some months after the announcement. Advise Megan on the alternative interpretations her study might be given.

18. **[LO 5]** Behavioural finance rests on the propositions that some investors sometimes act irrationally and that there are limits to arbitrage. Why are both propositions needed?

19. **[LO 3]** Discuss the extent to which the global financial crisis may have added to our understanding of the evidence with respect to market efficiency.

20. **[LO 4]** Discuss what is meant by micro market efficiency and macro market efficiency.

Test yourself further with Connect Plus online! Ask your lecturer or tutor for your course's unique URL.

FUTURES CONTRACTS

LEARNING OBJECTIVES

After studying this chapter you should be able to:

1. understand what a futures contract is and how futures markets are organised
2. understand the system of deposits, margins and marking-to-market used by futures exchanges
3. have a basic understanding of the determinants of futures prices
4. understand and explain speculation and hedging strategies using futures contracts
5. understand and explain the reasons why hedging with futures contracts may be imperfect
6. understand and explain the features of the major financial futures contracts traded on the Australian Securities Exchange
7. explain speculation and hedging strategies using the major financial futures contracts traded on the Australian Securities Exchange
8. understand the valuation of 90-day bank-accepted bill futures contracts and share price index futures contracts
9. understand and explain the uses of forward-rate agreements.

CHAPTER CONTENTS

- 17.1 Introduction
- 17.2 What is a futures contract?
- 17.3 The Australian Securities Exchange
- 17.4 Determinants of futures prices
- 17.5 Futures market strategies: speculating and hedging
- 17.6 Financial futures on the Australian Securities Exchange: the 90-day bank-accepted bill futures contract
- 17.7 Financial futures on the Australian Securities Exchange: the 10-year Treasury bond futures contract
- 17.8 Financial futures on the Australian Securities Exchange: the 30-day interbank cash rate futures contract
- 17.9 Financial futures on the Australian Securities Exchange: the share price index S&P/ASX 200 (SPI 200) futures contract
- 17.10 Valuation of financial futures contracts
- 17.11 Forward-rate agreements (FRAs)

This chapter is also featured in the complete e-book available with Connect Plus.
Ask your lecturer or tutor for your course's unique URL.

17.1 INTRODUCTION

A futures contract is an agreement which provides that something will be bought or sold in the future at a fixed price. In short, the price is decided today, but the transaction is to occur later. Such contracts are traded on various futures exchanges around the world. The largest and most famous futures exchanges are in Chicago but there are also exchanges in many other cities, including New York, London, Paris, Hong Kong, Singapore, Tokyo, Osaka and Sydney. Much of the material in this chapter relates to futures contracts traded on the Australian Securities Exchange, although the principles discussed also have application to contracts traded on other futures exchanges.

Trading in futures contracts on a formally organised exchange can be traced to the middle of last century, when the Chicago Board of Trade (www.cbot.com) introduced a futures contract on corn. Such a contract enables farmers to sell their corn 'in advance' and a farmer therefore knows the price he or she will receive for the crop before it is harvested and sold. In Australia, the first futures contract was one on greasy wool and was introduced in 1960. Until the early 1970s, virtually all futures contracts traded on the various exchanges around the world were futures contracts on commodities. In 1972 the world's first futures contract on a foreign currency was traded, followed in 1975 by the first futures contract on a debt instrument. In 1982 trading began in a futures contract on an index of stock market prices. Australia did not lag far behind, introducing futures on a debt instrument in 1979, on foreign currency in 1980 and on a share price index in 1983. These *financial futures*, as they are called, have grown very rapidly in importance and nearly all futures trading on the Australian Securities Exchange is now in financial futures rather than commodity futures. In this chapter, we focus on financial futures and, in particular, on the opportunities they provide for financial managers. However, because they are often more readily understood, we use commodity futures to illustrate some of the principles.

Futures contracts can be used for hedging purposes and speculative purposes. **Hedgers** wish to lock in, today, the price of the 'commodity' in which they will need to deal in the future, so that they are not affected by any future changes in the market price of the commodity. For example, a farmer (or a flour miller) could wish to fix, in advance, the price to be received (or paid) for wheat. Similarly, a company planning to lend (or borrow) could wish to fix, in advance, the interest rate to be received (or paid). The goal of the hedger is to control risk and this goal can be at least partly achieved by appropriate trading in a relevant futures contract. **Speculators** have no wish to deal in the 'commodity' itself, but are willing to trade in futures contracts in the hope of profiting from correctly anticipating movements in the futures price. The motive of the speculator is to profit through bearing risks that others do not wish to bear. Successful speculation can be extremely profitable. Of course, unsuccessful speculation can be extremely expensive.

hedgers
individuals and companies who enter into contracts in order to reduce risk

speculators
individuals and companies who enter into contracts in order to profit from correctly anticipating price movements

17.2 WHAT IS A FUTURES CONTRACT?

17.2.1 FORWARD CONTRACTS AND FUTURES CONTRACTS

Forward contracts predate *futures contracts* by centuries, but are still common, particularly in foreign exchange.[1] Futures contracts developed out of forward contracts, so we begin by considering a forward contract on a commodity. Suppose that I own an ounce of gold, which today (1 March) is worth $1400. However, I plan to sell my gold some time in the near future. Suppose further that you know (today) that on 1 April you will need to buy an ounce of gold to use in your jewellery-making business. We might therefore agree today to the following contract: on 1 April, I will deliver one ounce of gold to you at your

LEARNING OBJECTIVE 1
Understand what a futures contract is and how futures markets are organised

---
1 Forward contracts on foreign currency are discussed in more detail in Chapter 20.

premises and you will pay me, on that date, $1410. This is a 1-month forward contract on gold. It has the following features:

(a) The forward price ($1410) is decided now (1 March) but the transaction is to occur on a nominated future date (1 April).
(b) The details of the commodity, which is the subject of the contract, are spelt out (in this case, one ounce of gold to be delivered to your premises).
(c) The contract is a private contract between you and me. I cannot pass on to anyone else my responsibility to deliver an ounce of gold in 1 month's time and likewise you cannot pass on to anyone else your responsibility to accept delivery of the gold and to pay $1410 for it.

A futures contract on gold will also have features (a) and (b) in this list—that is, the price will be decided now for a transaction to occur at a later date in a commodity (or other item) which has been carefully defined. However, feature (c) is not true of a futures contract. A futures contract is not a personalised agreement. Futures contracts are always agreed to through an exchange and, most importantly, can be discontinued ('closed out' or 'reversed') at any time through a further transaction on the exchange. Exactly how this is done is explained later. At this stage, the important point to note is that a futures contract is like a forward contract that can be traded on an exchange.[2]

17.2.2 HOW A FUTURES MARKET IS ORGANISED

Before turning to a description of how futures trading on the Australian Securities Exchange is organised, the important points are explained in the mythical example of the Deakin Futures Exchange described here. In other words, the following is a simplified discussion of how futures markets operate.

Suppose that the Deakin Futures Exchange is offering, for the first time, futures contracts on gold. The contract document defines the amount and purity of the gold, who is qualified to certify its purity, when it is to be delivered, the place where it is to be delivered, and other such details. There may be several different contracts, each specifying a different maturity date. Of course, the one important feature not specified by the exchange is the futures price. This is determined by market forces. Consider the Deakin gold futures contract, which requires that one ounce of gold be delivered on 1 April (today being 1 March). On 1 March, a person named B1 enters the exchange and offers to buy one ounce of gold for $1410 on 1 April. In other words, B1 has offered to enter into one Deakin April gold futures contract to buy at a price of $1410. Another person, named S1, is at the exchange and is willing to enter into one April gold futures contract to sell at a price of $1410. Therefore, B1 and S1 agree, and the April gold futures price at the Deakin Futures Exchange is currently $1410.

The next step in the procedure is crucial to an understanding of futures markets. A company, Deakin Clearing House Ltd, which is a subsidiary of the Deakin Futures Exchange, now interposes itself between B1 and S1: the agreement between B1 and S1 becomes two contracts, which, for convenience, we will call Contract 1a and Contract 1b.[3] These contracts are as follows.

- Contract 1a is between B1 and the clearing house. Under this contract, B1 agrees to pay the clearing house $1410 on 1 April and the clearing house agrees to deliver one ounce of gold to B1 on 1 April. In short, the clearing house plays the role of seller in B1's contract to buy.
- Contract 1b is a contract between S1 and the clearing house. Under this contract, the clearing house agrees to pay S1 $1410 on 1 April and S1 agrees to deliver one ounce of gold to the clearing house on 1 April. In short, the clearing house plays the role of buyer in S1's contract to sell.

---

[2] For a detailed comparison, and for empirical evidence on price differences between futures and forwards, see Cox, Ingersoll & Ross (1981); Cornell & Reinganum (1981) and French (1983).

[3] This is the easiest way to visualise what occurs. For a detailed description of the strict legal position, see Markovic (1989).

There is no longer any agreement or contract between B1 and S1. Indeed, B1 and S1 need not even know each other's identity. Instead, B1 looks to the clearing house to deliver the gold and S1 looks to the clearing house to pay the agreed price. Note that, provided the clearing house has faith in the financial strength and honesty of B1 and S1, it is in a riskless position. It 'owes' $1410 to S1, but is 'owed' $1410 by B1. It 'owes' one ounce of gold to B1 but is 'owed' one ounce of gold by S1. The net position of the clearing house is therefore zero in both money and gold.

A few minutes after B1 and S1 agree on a futures price of $1410, a new buyer, B2, and a new seller, S2, meet in the exchange and a new price of, say, $1411 is established. The clearing house follows the same procedure, creating two new contracts, 2a and 2b. It becomes the seller to B2 (Contract 2a) and the buyer for S2 (Contract 2b). The net position of the clearing house is still zero.

New buyers and sellers come and go all day at the Deakin Futures Exchange. If, at the close of business on 1 March, 37 April gold futures contracts have been bought and sold, Deakin Clearing House has 74 obligations: 37 to buy and 37 to sell, with, as always, a net position of zero. During the day, prices have responded to market forces and have ranged between, say, $1408 and $1415, closing at $1414.

As time passes, more contracts are bought and sold. Now suppose that, on 8 March, B1 observes that the then current price for April gold futures is $1420. Recall that under the terms of Contract 1a, B1 will be entitled to buy gold at $1410 per ounce. Sellers are at present entering futures contracts to sell at $1420. Therefore, on current indications, B1 has a 'paper' profit of $10. With a futures contract, B1 is able to realise this profit, and, having done so, will be free of all further obligations. The mechanism by which this is achieved is as follows. On 8 March, B1 enters the futures exchange *as a seller*. For example, B1 may become S200, the seller in the 200th April contract traded. In the exchange, S200 and B200 agree on a price of, say, $1420. The clearing house becomes a seller to B200 (*Contract 200a*) and a buyer for S200 (*Contract 200b*). Therefore, on 8 March, B1's financial position may be summarised as follows:

B1 owes the clearing house:	$1410	(*Contract 1a*)
B1 (who is also S200) is owed by the clearing house:	$1420	(*Contract 200b*)
Therefore, the clearing house owes B1	$10	

In effect, B1 is able to offset his original contract as a buyer by entering another contract as a seller, taking the profit (or loss) which results. It is this offsetting procedure that permits futures traders to 'close out' (or 'reverse') their contracts before the maturity date. The 'closing out' procedure is feasible only because the two contracts are identical (except for the price) and both are with the same party, namely the clearing house. For example, the first April gold contract is the same as the two-hundredth April gold contract, except for the price. There would be little point in the clearing house delivering the gold to B1 to fulfil the terms of Contract 1a, only to have B1 (in his role as S200) redeliver the same gold to the clearing house a moment later to fulfil the terms of Contract 200b. Instead, B1 is released of all obligations and keeps the $10 profit.

Note the following five points about this procedure:

(a) Because the clearing house becomes the counterparty in every contract, it is not necessary for buyers and sellers to know the identity or credit-worthiness of the other buyers and sellers. For example, it is not necessary for B200 to know that S200 is, in fact, an existing buyer (that is, that S200 is also B1) who wants to sell in order to reverse his existing bought position. Similarly, as B200's contract is with the clearing house, it is not necessary for B200 to know the identity of S200.

(b) However, it is necessary for S200 to inform the clearing house that he (S200) is in fact the same person as B1. Otherwise, instead of the offsetting procedure described earlier, B1 will find that he has two ongoing contracts: as the buyer in Contract 1a and as the seller in Contract 200b. If he does not notify the clearing house, both contracts will run through to 1 April and then be settled.

(c) Even though the contract was not due to be settled until 1 April, B1 has in fact ended his involvement on 8 March. Moreover, no gold was ever delivered to, or by, B1. *No gold changed hands.* This is usual in futures markets. Generally speaking, only about 2 per cent of contracts end in delivery of the 'commodity', the other 98 per cent being closed out by the offsetting procedure (Howard & Jameson 1997).

(d) Persons who have already agreed to sell can also reverse out of their positions. For example, B200 could in fact be a person who has already agreed to sell (S57, say) and is seeking to offset her existing sold position with a bought position. In this way, a person can first enter into a contract to sell and subsequently enter into a contract to buy and at no time is it necessary for the person who has agreed to sell to *own* the item that is the subject of the futures contract. First entering into a contract to sell and later entering into a contract to buy is referred to as **short selling** and the ability to short sell is essential for the smooth functioning of futures markets.

(e) The websites of securities markets that trade futures contracts report the 'volume' of futures contracts traded the previous day, as well as the number of 'open positions'. These terms are often misunderstood, so it is worth explaining their meanings. The 'volume traded' refers to the number of contracts that have been agreed to over a particular period, such as during the previous day. Therefore, volume is a 'flow' concept; it is something measured over an interval of time. The number of 'open positions' is the number of contracts still in force (that is, which are yet to be closed out) at a certain time, such as at the close of business on the previous day. The number of open positions is a 'stock' concept; it is something measured at a particular point in time. Both measures indicate the level of interest in the contract and the ease with which a trading partner can be found.

short selling
process of first entering into a contract to sell and later entering into a contract to buy

The foregoing description of how a futures market functions is much simpler than the reality. For example, in real futures exchanges, ordinary traders are permitted to trade only through brokers. However, this is not central to an understanding of how futures exchanges operate. Of the many other differences between real futures exchanges and the mythical Deakin Futures Exchange, two in particular stand out:

(a) Deakin has no system of deposits and margins
(b) Deakin has no mark-to-market rule.

In reality, futures exchanges always have feature (a) and usually have feature (b). These two features are explained in the next section.

17.2.3 DEPOSITS, MARGINS AND THE MARK-TO-MARKET RULE

LEARNING OBJECTIVE 2

Understand the system of deposits, margins and marking-to-market used by futures exchanges

marking-to-market
process of adjusting traders' account balances to reflect changes in market prices

In the example in Section 17.2.2, the futures trader B1 made a profit of $10 because the futures price rose by $10 between 1 March and 8 March. Where does the $10 come from? The answer lies in the system of deposits, margins and the mark-to-market rule.

The clearing house requires all traders to deposit a certain sum of money with the clearing house *before* they enter into their first contract. Each intending trader is required to have an account and the first entry in the account is the deposit paid by the intending trader. At the close of each trading day, the clearing house calculates whether the trader has gained or lost since the close of the previous trading day. If a gain has been made, the clearing house adds the gain to the trader's account balance. If a loss has been made, the clearing house subtracts the loss from the trader's account balance. This process is called **marking-to-market** because each day the trader's financial position is 'marked'—that is, adjusted—according to the change in the 'market'—that is, the movement in the market price of that futures contract since the previous marking date.[4]

---

[4] There is an obvious exception. Logically, a newly opened position should be adjusted by the difference between the agreed price and the price at the close of trading. Thereafter, the daily adjustment is as described in the text.

The deposit system just described does not protect the clearing house if the following situation arises. Suppose that a trader has entered into a futures contract as a seller and subsequently the futures price has increased steadily. Each day, the trader's account is marked to market. Because the trader is steadily making losses, the deposit is being steadily eroded. If this continues long enough the deposit will vanish and the clearing house will be in the unhappy position of having to trust the trader to make good any further losses. The same situation could also arise if a trader entered into a futures contract as a buyer and the price subsequently fell significantly.

To protect itself against this situation, a clearing house will have a system of 'margin calls'. For example, the Deakin Clearing House could require that further funds be deposited whenever a trader's account balance is eroded by, say, 25 per cent. That is, if the balance of the account falls below an amount equal to 75 per cent of the required initial deposit, the trader is required to restore the account balance to the amount of the initial deposit. The demand that extra funds be deposited is known as a **margin call**. If a trader does not respond to a margin call within, say, 2 days, the clearing house will close out the trader's position. The clearing house faces a slight risk in this case. If the futures price should move very quickly during the 2-day response period, the loss sustained by the trader could exceed the remaining funds in the trader's account. The clearing house is then just an unsecured creditor of the trader.

margin call demand for extra funds to be deposited into a trader's account

17.2.4 THE PRESENT VALUE OF A FUTURES CONTRACT

A futures contract does not require a payment on initiation so it is clear that the present value of a futures contract must be zero.[5] In other words, the futures price is the price at which both buyer and seller are willing to agree to the terms of the contract, with neither party seeking any immediate payment from the other. For example, if the current futures price were thought to be too low, a prospective buyer would, if necessary, be willing to pay a potential seller to agree to the futures contract at the current futures price. The present value of such a contract would not be zero. However, this is not the way a futures market behaves when the current futures price is thought to be too low. Instead of paying money *today*, buyers bid up the *futures* price until a seller is induced (for zero payment today) to agree to the futures contract at the higher price. Therefore, the present value of the futures contract would again be zero. Accordingly, it is, in a sense, impossible to calculate a rate of return on a futures contract. If the outlay is zero, any subsequent gain is an infinite *percentage* gain and any subsequent loss is an infinite *percentage* loss. In practice, some traders calculate percentage returns relative to the deposit required, but there is no particularly compelling reason to do so.

THE AUSTRALIAN SECURITIES EXCHANGE   17.3

Futures trading in Australian began in 1960 with the opening of the Sydney Greasy Wool Futures Exchange, with the name being changed to the Sydney Futures Exchange in 1972.[6] Since 1999, all trading has been conducted using an electronic trading system. In 2006 the Sydney Futures Exchange merged with the Australian Stock Exchange to form the Australian Securities Exchange (ASX). In 2010 it adopted the name ASX Group.

The exchange offered only wool futures contracts until 1975, when a contract on cattle was introduced. Since then contracts on a range of commodities have been traded, with the exchange now

---

5 Recall that the deposit is not the value of the contract; it simply provides a guarantee that the trader's obligations will be met.

6 For a detailed history, see Carew (1993). For a comprehensive treatment of the futures contracts traded on the Australian Securities Exchange, see Frino and Jarnecic (2005).

offering contracts on electricity, natural gas and wool. However, these contracts make up only a small proportion of those traded on the exchange.[7]

Virtually all futures trading on the ASX is in contracts on 'financial commodities'. The first such contract to be traded on the ASX was that on 90-day bank-accepted bills introduced in 1979. Users of this contract include banks, merchant banks, building societies, finance companies and industrial companies. In fact, any party planning to borrow or lend significant sums of money for relatively short periods could find a bank bill futures contract useful. The introduction of the bank bill contract was the first step along the path that led to the exchange being transformed from a market serving mainly rural interests to a market that plays a substantial role in the finance industry. Other financial futures that have proved successful are the share price index contract (the 'SPI 200 contract' for short) introduced in 1983, the 10-year Treasury bond contract introduced in 1984, the 3-year Treasury bond contract introduced in 1988, and the 30-day interbank cash rate contract introduced in 2003. The volume of trading in these four contracts, together with trading in the 90-day bank-accepted bills contract, totalled more than 60 million in 2009. These financial futures are discussed in detail later in the chapter.

Australia's first option-on-futures contract was introduced in 1982. A **call option on a futures contract** gives the option buyer the right (but not the obligation) to enter into the futures contract as a buyer at a predetermined price. Similarly, a **put option on a futures contract** gives the option buyer the right (but not the obligation) to enter into the futures contract as a seller at a predetermined price. Options have proved popular with traders.[8]

call option on a futures contract
option that gives the buyer the right to enter into the futures contract as a buyer at a predetermined price

put option on a futures contract
option that gives the buyer the right to enter into the futures contract as a seller at a predetermined price

The ASX operates its own clearing house for futures transactions. The major functions of this clearing house are to:

- establish and collect deposits
- call in margins as required
- apportion the gains and losses (mark-to-market rule).

The clearing house varies minimum contract deposits, depending on market conditions. For example, the greater the price volatility, the greater the risk, and therefore the greater the deposit required. To give an indication of the typical sums involved, some of the standard deposits required of members as at October 2010 were as shown in Table 17.1.[9]

TABLE 17.1 Major Australian Securities Exchange contracts: October 2010

CONTRACT TYPE	DEPOSIT PER CONTRACT ($)	APPROXIMATE VALUE UNDERLYING ONE CONTRACT ($)
90-day bank bills	730	988 000
3-year Treasury bonds	955	103 000
10-year Treasury bonds	2 290	108 000
30-day interbank cash rate	455	2 500
Share price index	7 000	125 000

---

[7] In 2009 trading in these contracts accounted for less than 1 per cent of the total volume of trading in futures contracts on the ASX.
[8] In 2009 almost 2 million futures option contracts were traded on the ASX. These contracts are in fact option contracts, rather than futures contracts. These and other option contracts are discussed in Chapter 18.
[9] The members, in turn, require their clients to lodge deposits.

17.4 DETERMINANTS OF FUTURES PRICES

So far we have not tried to explain (or model) futures prices. It has simply been stated that market forces determine the futures price. From a management viewpoint, there is much to recommend this approach. Managers trade in futures contracts in order to control risk, and the only way to undertake the necessary transactions is to agree to buy (or sell) at the futures price determined by the market. Whether this market price accords with some model of futures pricing is, on this view, largely irrelevant.

Nevertheless, it is beneficial to have some understanding of the determinants of futures prices. A useful insight into some of the forces underlying futures pricing is provided by the following theorem:

The futures price for a late-delivery contract must be less than (or equal to) the futures price for an equivalent early-delivery contract, plus the carrying cost.

The **carrying cost** is the cost of holding a commodity from one time period to another. It includes an interest factor (the opportunity cost of funds used to finance the holding of the commodity) and, in the case of physical commodities, the costs of insurance and storage. The logic underlying the theorem can readily be seen in the following example.

LEARNING OBJECTIVE 3
Have a basic understanding of the determinants of futures prices

carrying cost
cost of holding a commodity for a specified period of time

EXAMPLE 17.1

> The gold futures price for maturity in January is $1450 per ounce and the gold futures price for maturity in February is $1460 per ounce. Assume that the carrying cost for gold is $7 per ounce per month, payable at the end of the month. A trader could exploit these prices by entering into a contract to buy in January and entering into a contract to sell in February. When the January maturity date arrives, the trader accepts delivery of the gold and pays the agreed price of $1450. The trader then stores the gold for 1 month. In February, the trader delivers (sells) the gold at the agreed price of $1460 and pays the carrying cost of $7, giving a net cash inflow of $1453 in February. The resulting profit of $3 is a 'pure' profit—that is, in excess of the opportunity cost—since the $7 carrying cost covers the opportunity cost of holding the gold. Of course, other traders will undertake similar activities and will continue to do so until the gap between the January and February futures prices is $7 or less. For example, the market may set a January futures price of $1451 and a February futures price of $1457. At this point, the price of the late-delivery contract ($1457) is less than or equal to the price of the early-delivery contract ($1451), plus the carrying cost ($7). This is the result stated in the theorem.

A limiting case of this theorem is of special significance. In the limit, the early-delivery contract could be for immediate delivery; in other words, its term to maturity could be zero. The **spot price** is the price paid in a standard commodity purchase—that is, it is the price of the commodity when the buyer pays immediately and the seller delivers immediately. Therefore, to prevent arbitrage, the spot price should be very close to the price of a futures contract with a term to maturity of zero. Substituting 'the spot price' for 'the futures price for an equivalent early-delivery contract', the theorem becomes:

A futures price must be less than (or equal to) the current spot price, plus the carrying cost.

spot price
price of the commodity when the buyer pays immediately and the seller delivers immediately

In this way, the theorem provides a maximum price for the futures contract, given the current spot price and the carrying cost. Algebraically, it can be written as:

$$F \leq S + C \qquad [17.1]$$

where F = futures price
S = current spot price
C = carrying cost

We now put futures contracts briefly to one side and direct our attention to the market in the commodity itself. Suppose that the current spot price of gold is $1450 per ounce and that, taking into account the expected output of gold mines, the forecast demand for jewellery, the political situation in South Africa (a gold-producing country) and, in principle, any other factor thought to be relevant, a trader forecasts that in 1 month's time, the spot price of gold will be at least equal to today's spot price ($1450) and possibly much more. In other words, it is forecast that the spot price of gold will increase. Assume, for example, that the price is forecast to be $1480 per ounce in 1 month's time. In this case, it is predicted that a trader could buy gold, hold it for 1 month and then sell it for $1480. Net of the carrying cost of $7, the predicted profit is $23. Is this large enough to induce a trader to adopt this strategy? Perhaps so, perhaps not. Unlike the investment strategy underlying the theorem, this is a risky proposition and perhaps $23 is not enough to compensate for the risk involved. However, there will clearly be some level of predicted profit from holding gold, which will induce gold purchases—that is, gold will be purchased if:

$$S + C + \text{risk factor} < E(S) \qquad [17.2]$$

where S = current spot price
 C = carrying cost
 $E(S)$ = expected future spot price

Gold will be bought, and the spot price will increase, until Equation 17.2 no longer holds—that is, until:

$$E(S) \leq S + C + \text{risk factor} \qquad [17.3]$$

Equation 17.3 therefore provides the maximum value that the expected spot price, $E(S)$, can be, given the current spot price, the carrying cost and a risk factor. Similarly, Equation 17.1 provides the maximum value that the futures price F can be, given the current spot price and the carrying cost.

Finally, can F and $E(S)$ be linked? Suppose, for example, that F was $1451 and $E(S)$ was $1480. It is likely that, in the hope of profit, someone would be willing to buy a futures contract, possibly with the intention of accepting delivery on the maturity date and then immediately reselling the gold. Again, this is a risky strategy, but a forecast profit of $29 may be enough to induce someone to try it. In fact, there is a group of analysts who believe that futures prices and expected spot prices are very closely related.

This traditional theory can be adapted to financial futures. One way in which this might be done is discussed briefly in Section 17.9. As both a prelude to this discussion, and as a topic of considerable importance in its own right, we first discuss in some detail how futures contracts (especially financial futures contracts) can be used.

17.5 FUTURES MARKET STRATEGIES: SPECULATING AND HEDGING

LEARNING OBJECTIVE 4
Understand and explain speculation and hedging strategies using futures contracts

17.5.1 INTRODUCTION

Traditionally, participants in futures markets have been divided into two groups: speculators and hedgers.[10] A *speculator* in this context is someone who has traded in a futures contract but who has no direct interest in the 'commodity' underlying the futures contract. For example, if someone trades a gold futures contract but owns no gold and does not intend to buy any, the futures market transaction is purely speculative. A *hedger* is someone who has traded in a futures contract and has a 'genuine' interest in the

---

10 A third group, arbitrageurs, can also be distinguished. As discussed in Section 1.5.7, an arbitrage is a set of simultaneous transactions in different markets that guarantees a risk-free profit. The transactions in Example 17.1 were an arbitrage involving futures prices, spot prices and carrying costs. Arbitrage is discussed further in Sections 17.6.3 and 17.10.

'commodity' underlying the futures contract. For example, if a jewellery manufacturer trades a futures contract on gold, the futures market transaction provides a hedge against changes in gold prices.

In short, the distinction between a speculator and a hedger in futures contracts is simply this: a speculator is affected by the futures price (but not the spot price) of the 'commodity', whereas a hedger is affected by *both* the futures price and the spot price of the 'commodity'. By trading in futures contracts the speculator is exposed to the risks of changes in the futures price; this is a risk to which he or she would not otherwise have been exposed. By trading in futures contracts, the hedger, too, is exposed to the same risks of changes in the futures price but only in an attempt to *offset* the pre-existing risk of changes in the 'commodity' price itself. The speculator uses futures contracts to increase his or her exposure to risk, whereas the hedger uses futures contracts to decrease his or her exposure to risk.

There is a large body of theory (and evidence) relating to speculators and hedgers, and to the various influences that have a bearing on spot prices and futures prices. Much of this theory was developed in the context of futures contracts on physical commodities and, as a result, not all of it is relevant to financial futures. In particular, there is a substantial literature that focuses on such issues as inventories, insurance, storage costs and production seasonalities, but as these issues are of limited relevance to financial futures, this material will not be presented.[11] However, the basic features of speculating and hedging are applicable to both types of futures contracts. For ease of exposition we continue to use futures on physical commodities to establish the principles. Detailed applications to financial futures are provided in Sections 17.6, 17.7, 17.8 and 17.9.

17.5.2 SPECULATING

In the simplest case, a speculator hopes to:

(a) take a long position—that is, buy—when the futures price is 'low', reversing out—that is, selling later—when the futures price has increased; *and/or*
(b) take a short position—that is, sell—when the futures price is 'high', reversing out—that is, buying later—when the futures price has decreased.

In either case, the speculator gains. Of course, if the opposite occurs, the speculator loses. This is shown in Table 17.2.

TABLE 17.2 Basic speculation outcomes

IF FUTURES CONTRACT IS HELD	IF FUTURES PRICES SUBSEQUENTLY	
	INCREASE	DECREASE
Long	Gain	Loss
Short	Loss	Gain

The time period over which a speculator hopes to gain will vary depending on the type of speculation. It is common to distinguish five types of speculation.

Scalping

The time period during which a *scalper* holds a futures contract is extremely short and is usually measured in seconds or minutes. For this reason, only traders who have direct access to the electronic trading system and are permitted to trade on their own account can be scalpers. In effect, scalpers try to develop a continuously updated 'feel' for the market, anticipating and exploiting perceived

---
11 For a survey, see Kolb and Overdahl (2006).

short-term excesses of supply or demand. Scalpers perform the useful function of providing liquidity to the market.

Spreading

spread
long (bought) position in one maturity date, paired with a short (sold) position in another maturity date

A **spread** is a long (bought) position in one maturity date, paired with a short (sold) position in another maturity date. An example is a bought March bank bill futures contract and a sold June bank bill futures contract. Speculators will adopt this spread if they believe that the current difference between the two futures prices is too wide. Speculators will gain if the difference (or 'spread') narrows. It is a simple matter to show this. Let the current—that is, Time 0—futures price of the March contract be $F(0, M)$. Similarly, let the current—that is, Time 0—futures price of the June contract be $F(0, J)$. The spread at Time 0 is:

$$F(0, J) - F(0, M)$$

Similarly, the spread at Time 1 is:

$$F(1, J) - F(1, M)$$

Between Time 0 and Time 1, the bought position in the March contract will produce a gain of:

$$F(1, M) - F(0, M) \qquad [17.4]$$

Similarly, over the same time period, the sold position in the June contract will produce a gain of:

$$F(0, J) - F(1, J) \qquad [17.5]$$

Note that the 0 and the 1 in Equation 17.5 are reversed compared with Equation 17.4. This is because Equation 17.4 gives the gain from a bought position, while Equation 17.5 gives the gain from a sold position.

A sold position generates a gain if the futures price falls—that is, if:

$$F(1, J) < F(0, J)$$

The spread speculator's total gain G is given by the sum of Equations 17.4 and 17.5:

$$\begin{aligned} G &= F(1, M) - F(0, M) + F(0, J) - F(1, J) \\ &= [F(0, J) - F(0, M)] - [F(1, J) - F(1, M)] \\ &= [\text{spread at Time 0}] \text{ less } [\text{spread at Time 1}] \\ &> 0 \text{ if } [\text{spread at Time 0}] \text{ exceeds } [\text{spread at Time 1}] \end{aligned}$$

In this case, then, the spread speculator will gain if the spread at Time 1 is narrower than the spread at Time 0. The spread speculator performs the useful function of keeping in line the prices of different futures contracts on the same commodity. The spread speculator may hold a futures position for any period, but will often do so for only a matter of hours, or perhaps days.

Straddling

A *straddle* is similar in concept to a spread but refers to positions in futures contracts on different commodities, rather than futures contracts on the same commodity for different months. For example, a trader might buy a March bank bill contract and sell a March bond contract. The reasons for straddling are similar to those for spreading.

Day trading

Day traders are prepared to trade as they see fit during a trading day, but regard an overnight position as too risky. Quite simply, too much can happen while the exchange is closed.

Long-term/overnight position taking

This is both the simplest and the riskiest type of speculation. Speculators form a view that the current futures price is too low (or too high), trade accordingly, and wait for events to prove them right. It can be a quick way to riches—or rags.

17.5.3 HEDGING

The essence of hedging is easily explained. Consider, for example, a grazier who intends to sell his cattle in several months' time. He is affected by movements in the spot price of cattle, gaining if it increases (since his cattle become more valuable) and losing if it decreases (since his cattle become less valuable). If he wishes to be protected against these changes, he can sell cattle futures—that is, he becomes what is known as a short hedger. The position of the **short hedger** is shown in Table 17.3.

TABLE 17.3 Short hedging outcomes

	IF PRICES RISE	IF PRICES FALL
Short futures contract	Loss	Gain
Cattle—spot	Gain	Loss
Net result	Approximately zero	Approximately zero

short hedger
hedger who hedges by means of selling future contracts today

The net result is approximately zero. Therefore, the hedger achieves his objective, in that whether prices rise or fall, there is little or no effect on the hedger. Note, though, that the result is shown as only approximately zero. Why not precisely zero? There are many reasons why a perfect hedge is most unlikely but before looking at some of the reasons, we need to consider hedges achieved by buying futures contracts. Such a hedge is called a long hedge and if the position of a **long hedger** is simply the exact reverse of the position of the short hedger, the outcomes for the long hedger are as shown in Table 17.4.

long hedger
hedger who hedges by means of buying futures contracts today

TABLE 17.4 Long hedging outcomes

	IF PRICES RISE	IF PRICES FALL
Long futures contract	Gain	Loss
Cattle—spot	Loss	Gain
Net result	Approximately zero	Approximately zero

However, on closer inspection, it should be clear that the long hedger's position is not necessarily simply the reverse of the short hedger's position. For example, compare the position of a long hedger, such as a manufacturer of beef sausages, with that of a short hedger, such as a grazier. There can be no doubt that a grazier gains if spot cattle prices rise. For example, if spot cattle prices rise from $10/kg to $12/kg, a grazier benefits by $2/kg multiplied by the number of kilograms of cattle owned. The grazier's wealth has risen by that amount. Is a sausage manufacturer $2/kg poorer? It is not clear that the answer to this question is 'yes'. To a grazier, cattle are obviously assets; but to a sausage manufacturer, cattle are not likely to be liabilities. If a sausage manufacturer has short sold cattle, then cattle might be liabilities, but in practice it is impossible (or at least very difficult) to sell commodities short. However, for simplicity, we will treat long hedging as simply the reverse of short hedging.[12]

---

12 A slightly different approach to long hedging is to think of the long hedger as gaining or losing on the spot, relative to the forward price of the commodity. Of course, forward prices may be unobservable.

17.5.4 SOME REASONS WHY HEDGING WITH FUTURES IS IMPERFECT

LEARNING OBJECTIVE 5

Understand and explain the reasons why hedging with futures contracts may be imperfect

In this section we discuss three reasons why hedging with futures contracts may be imperfect. These are imperfect convergence, basis risk and specification differences.

Imperfect convergence

Suppose that a jewellery manufacturer is committed to buying an ounce of gold on 27 March and it so happens that there is a futures contract that precisely matches this need. That is, there is a futures contract that specifies an ounce of gold of the same quality and at the same location as the manufacturer requires, and the maturity date of the futures contract is 27 March. Even in this case a perfect hedge may not be possible because of the problem of imperfect convergence between spot and futures prices.

Logically, the price of a futures contract with zero time to maturity ought to be equal to the spot price. If this were not so, then in principle an instantaneous profit could be made. For example, if the spot price were the lower one, a trader could simultaneously buy in the spot market and sell in the futures market, delivering the commodity purchased in satisfaction of the futures market commitment. However, in reality the futures price at maturity can be slightly different from the spot price on the maturity date. In short, the convergence between the spot price and the futures price as the maturity date approaches can be imperfect. Yet it may not be possible to profit from this difference. For example, transaction costs could prevent the opportunity from being exploited. This will affect the quality of a hedge, but typically the problem should not be very serious because convergence is generally close, even though not perfect.

Consider again the jewellery manufacturer who has bought gold futures. Suppose that she faces the following situation and has closed out her contract:

Futures price (when bought):	$1400
Futures price (at maturity):	$1460
Spot price (on futures maturity date):	$1462

The jewellery manufacturer will have a futures profit of $60 to add to the price of $1400 she knew she would have to pay, but will be $2 short of the $1462 needed to buy gold (spot). In other words, the gold ends up costing her $1402 instead of $1400 as was planned. This, admittedly, is imperfect, but the problem is not serious. Certainly it is better to have to find $2 unexpectedly, than to have to find $62 unexpectedly.

Basis risk

basis

spot price at a point in time minus the futures price (for delivery at some later date) at that point in time

By definition, a hedger is planning to transact in the spot market at some future time. However, it is unusual for the date of the planned spot transaction to coincide with the maturity date of a futures contract. At any given time, a futures exchange will offer only a restricted number of maturity dates—sometimes only four or five. As a result, there is only a small chance that the date of the planned spot transaction will coincide with a futures contract maturity date. When the dates do not coincide, the hedger must reverse out of the futures contract before it matures, and, when this action is required, hedgers face a risk known as 'basis risk'. We define the **basis** at any given time as the spot price S at that time of a commodity that matches exactly the commodity defined in the futures contract, minus the futures price F at that time (for delivery of the commodity at some later time).[13] Therefore, the basis B at Time 0 is:

$$B(0) = S(0) - F(0)$$

---

13 Conventions vary. Basis is usually defined as 'spot minus futures', but sometimes it is defined as 'futures minus spot', particularly when the futures contract is on a financial asset.

Similarly, the basis at some later time, say, Time 1, is:

$B(1) = S(1) - F(1)$

Now consider a short hedger and assume that the 'commodity' held by the short hedger can be stored costlessly. A short hedger makes a gain (loss) on the futures contract if the futures price decreases (increases) and a gain (loss) on holding the commodity if the spot price increases (decreases). Therefore, in the interval between Time 0 and Time 1:

$$\begin{aligned}\text{Total gain to short hedger} &= \text{gain made on futures} + \text{gain made on spot} \\ &= [F(0) - F(1)] + [S(1) - S(0)] \\ &= [S(1) - F(1)] - [S(0) - F(0)] \\ &= B(1) - B(0) \\ &= \text{change in basis between Time 0 and Time 1}\end{aligned}$$

The point is simple: the change in the basis over a given time period is not, in general, precisely zero. Yet a perfect hedge is one in which the wealth of the hedger is immune to the movement of prices. It follows that a hedger does not, in fact, eliminate all risk. There remains basis risk.

It is important to understand this point. However, it is also important to place basis risk in context. *In general*, futures prices and spot prices tend to move together. Of course, this tendency is not perfect and for some agricultural commodities it may not even be close to perfect. For example, if a bumper harvest is expected next season but, simultaneously, unexpected shortages in the spot market develop today, then futures prices might fall at the same time as spot prices rise. But this type of situation is the exception. In general, whatever causes spot prices to increase (or decrease) will also tend to cause futures prices to increase (or decrease). Example 17.2 illustrates basis risk.

EXAMPLE 17.2

Suppose that some dramatic event causes a large fall in spot prices, and suppose that this same event causes a similar, but slightly smaller, fall in futures prices, as shown in Table 17.5. Given the data in Table 17.5, what is the gain or loss for a short hedger?

TABLE 17.5 Example of basis risk

	PRICES ($)		
	AT TIME 0	AT TIME 1	GAIN (+) OR LOSS (−)
Spot (long)	1026	806	−220
Futures (short)	1040	825	+215
Gain (+) or loss (−) made by short hedger			−5

SOLUTION

In the table, Time 0 is the date on which the hedge is set up and Time 1 is the date on which the spot transaction is made and the hedge is lifted. As shown in the table, the hedge is not perfect, as there is a net loss of $5, which is equal to the change in the basis:

$$\begin{aligned}\text{Change in basis} &= B(1) - B(0) \\ &= [S(1) - F(1)] - [S(0) - F(0)] \\ &= [\$806 - \$825] - [\$1026 - \$1040] \\ &= -\$19 - [-\$14] \\ &= -\$5\end{aligned}$$

continued →

Example 17.2 continued

However, a loss of $5 is trivial when compared with the loss of $220 that would have been incurred had no futures contract been entered into. Basis risk is much less than price risk. In this example a short hedger faced an initial basis of −$14 that later fell to −$19 and the outcome was a loss of $5. Table 17.6 sets out the full range of possibilities.

TABLE 17.6 Hedging outcomes and basis changes

DESCRIPTION	POSITIONS	OUTCOME IF BASIS[a] INCREASES	DECREASES
Short hedger	Futures (short)		
	Commodity (long)	Gain	Loss
Long hedger	Futures (long)		
	Commodity (short)	Loss	Gain

[a] Basis is defined as spot price less futures price.

Specification differences

'Specification differences' refers to the fact that the specification of the 'commodity' that is the subject of the futures contract may not precisely correspond to the specification of the 'commodity' that is of interest to a hedger. For example, a hedger may be interested in a particular grade of wool that is slightly different from the grade of wool specified in the futures contract. Alternatively, a hedger may be interested in buying wool to be delivered to a certain location. However, this location may be only one of a number of locations acceptable for delivery under a futures contract, or it may not even be one of the acceptable locations. Similar observations are relevant to financial futures. Some examples are as follows:

- A borrower may intend to issue 120-day bank bills, but the futures contract specifies 90-day bank bills.
- An investor may own a diversified portfolio, which is similar, but not identical, to the shares in the share price index that the futures contract specifies.
- A lender may intend to invest in 5-year company debentures, but the futures contract specifies 3-year government bonds.

In fact, only rarely is a hedger able to find a futures contract whose specification is *precisely* the same as the commodity that is of interest to the hedger. Specification differences introduce a further element of imperfection in the hedging process. This is illustrated in Example 17.3.

EXAMPLE 17.3

Assume that a jewellery manufacturer intends to buy one ounce of high-grade gold but the futures contract specifies one ounce of premium-grade gold. Nevertheless, as a hedge, he enters into one futures contract to buy premium-grade gold. Suppose that the following prices, shown in Table 17.7, occur. What is the gain or loss for the jewellery manufacturer?

TABLE 17.7 Prices for Example 17.3

GOLD	PRICES ($) AT TIME 0	AT TIME 1
High grade—spot	1450	1493
Premium grade—spot	1480	1520
Premium grade—futures	1490	1528

SOLUTION

'Loss' on spot = $1493 − $1450 = $43 (loss)
Gain on futures = $1528 − $1490 = $38 (gain)
Net result: $5 (loss)

Because a small loss has resulted, the hedge is imperfect. Two components of the loss can be identified:

(a) *Basis risk*, which caused a loss of $2. At Time 0, the basis was $10, and at Time 1, $8. In other words, whereas the spot price increased by $40, the futures price increased by only $38.
(b) *Specification differences*, which caused a further loss of $3. At Time 0, the price gap between the two grades was $30, but at Time 1, it was only $27. In other words, the grade sought by the hedger has become relatively more expensive.

Again, however, compared with no hedge (in which case a loss of $43 would have been incurred), the result is quite good, even though the hedge is imperfect.

17.5.5 HEDGING AND REGRETTING

The previous examples have been constructed to show how hedging can reduce losses that would otherwise have been incurred. However, by its very nature, hedging also reduces profits, which would otherwise have been made. Consider the example of Megan, a corporate treasurer, who takes out a short hedge to protect against price falls. Prices in fact rise as displayed in Table 17.8.

TABLE 17.8 A short hedge

COMMODITY	PRICES ($)	
	AT TIME 0	AT TIME 1
Spot price (long)	430	500
Futures price (short)	440	510

In this case, there is a gain on the spot of $70 and an offsetting loss on the futures of $70. The hedge has performed perfectly; it produced immunity to price movements. Of course, it is obvious that, *in retrospect*, Megan's company would have been better off by $70 if she had not taken out the hedge. She may need to explain to her boss the simple message of hedging: to have protection against losses a hedger must be willing to forgo profits that would otherwise have been made.

17.5.6 SELECTING THE NUMBER OF FUTURES CONTRACTS

In the examples we have discussed, the number of futures contracts to be used in the hedge was obvious. However, in practice this is not always the case and hedgers need to adopt a systematic approach in deciding how many futures contracts they should buy or sell. If a hedger enters into too few (or too many) futures contracts, the position is riskier than desired.[14]

Suppose that a hedger has an interest in N_S units of a 'commodity'. If this interest is a long (short) position, then N_S is positive (negative). Suppose further that f futures contracts have been entered into,

---

14 Note that simply increasing the number of futures contracts in an attempt 'to make sure enough are held' does *not* solve this problem. For example, if buying nine futures contracts would produce a perfect hedge, but 10 contracts are bought, the hedger is one futures contract long on a net basis. That is, the hedger is in fact a long speculator in relation to one contract, and hence will make a loss if futures prices fall.

each of which covers N_F units of the commodity. If a long (short) position is held in futures contracts, then f is positive (negative). The gain G to the hedger is:

$$G = N_S \times \text{(change in spot price per unit)} + fN_F \times \text{(change in futures price per unit)}$$
$$= N_S(\tilde{S}_1 - S_0) + fN_F(\tilde{F}_1 - F_0) \qquad [17.6]$$

where S_0 = spot price per unit when the hedge is entered ('today')
F_0 = futures price per unit when the hedge is entered ('today')
$\tilde{S}_1$ = spot price per unit when the hedge is lifted
$\tilde{F}_1$ = futures price per unit when the hedge is lifted

The tilde (~) is used to emphasise that the subsequent prices are random variables—that is, their value is uncertain.

Obviously, when the hedge is lifted and the spot transaction is made, the outcomes S_1 and F_1 will be known with certainty. Therefore, with hindsight, the ideal number of futures contracts from a hedging viewpoint will be obvious and can be found by setting G equal to zero and rearranging Equation 17.6. This gives:

$$f = -\frac{N_S(S_1 - S_0)}{N_F(F_1 - F_0)}$$

However, in practice, this equation cannot be used because S_1 and F_1 are not known at the time the hedge is set up. Inevitably, therefore, deciding how many futures contracts should be entered into requires some assumption or forecast that relates changes in the futures price to changes in the spot price. This will usually involve some error.

Using Equation 17.6, the gain per unit of commodity is g, where:

$$g = \frac{G}{N_S} = (\tilde{S}_1 - S_0) + \frac{fN_F}{N_S}(\tilde{F}_1 - F_0)$$

Now define $h = fN_F/N_S$, where h is the 'hedge ratio', which is the number of units covered by futures contracts per unit of spot commodity. Therefore:

$$g = (\tilde{S}_1 - S_0) + h(\tilde{F}_1 - F_0)$$

The components of g resemble a two-asset portfolio, and the variance (risk) is given by:[15]

$$\text{Var}(g) = \text{Var}(\tilde{S}_1 - S_0) + \text{Var}[h(\tilde{F}_1 - F_0)] + 2\text{Cov}[(\tilde{S}_1 - S_0), h(\tilde{F}_1 - F_0)]$$
$$= \text{Var}(\tilde{S}_1) + h^2\text{Var}(\tilde{F}_1) + 2h\text{Cov}(\tilde{S}_1, \tilde{F}_1)$$

We assume that the hedger will choose the hedge ratio h so as to minimise the variance of g.[16] To find how to achieve this goal we differentiate $\text{Var}(g)$ with respect to h, and set the derivative equal to zero:

$$\frac{d\text{Var}(g)}{dh} = 2h\text{Var}(\tilde{F}_1) + 2\text{Cov}(\tilde{S}_1, \tilde{F}_1) = 0$$

The risk-minimising value of h is thus h^* where:

$$h^* = -\frac{\text{Cov}(\tilde{S}_1, \tilde{F}_1)}{\text{Var}(\tilde{F}_1)} \qquad [17.7]$$

---

15 Calculating the risk of a portfolio is explained in detail in Chapter 7.
16 As we have stated, this is merely an assumption. In general, it is expected that financial markets will price assets so that there is a trade-off between risk and expected return. Depending on the decision maker's preferences as between risk and expected return, a risk-minimising strategy may or may not be optimal.

An estimate of h^* can be found from regressing spot prices against futures prices. Using the definition of the hedge ratio h, the optimum number of futures contracts to enter into is f^* where:

$$f^* = \frac{N_S}{N_F} h^*$$

Substituting from Equation 17.7 gives:

$$f^* = -\frac{N_S}{N_F} \frac{\mathrm{Cov}(\tilde{S}_1, \tilde{F}_1)}{\mathrm{Var}(\tilde{F}_1)} \qquad [17.8]$$

Equation 17.8 suggests that the number of futures contracts to enter into depends on four factors:

(a) N_S, the number of units of the commodity at risk in the spot market
(b) N_F, the number of units of the commodity underlying one futures contract
(c) $\mathrm{Cov}(\tilde{S}_1, \tilde{F}_1)$, which describes the relationship between spot and futures prices
(d) $\mathrm{Var}(\tilde{F}_1)$, which describes the variability of futures prices.

An interesting special case arises if it is assumed that spot and futures prices move equi-proportionately—that is, an x per cent change in the spot price will always be matched by an x per cent change in the futures price. Then:

$$\frac{(\tilde{S}_1 - S_0)}{S_0} = \frac{(\tilde{F}_1 - F_0)}{F_0}$$

which on rearrangement gives:

$$\tilde{S}_1 = \left(\frac{S_0}{F_0}\right) \tilde{F}_1$$

and therefore:

$$\begin{aligned}
\mathrm{Cov}(\tilde{S}_1, \tilde{F}_1) &= \mathrm{Cov}\left(\frac{S_0}{F_0} \tilde{F}_1, \tilde{F}_1\right) \\
&= \frac{S_0}{F_0} \mathrm{Cov}(\tilde{F}_1, \tilde{F}_1) \\
&= \frac{S_0}{F_0} \mathrm{Var}(\tilde{F}_1)
\end{aligned}$$

Substituting in Equation 17.8, the optimum number of futures contracts f^* is:

$$\begin{aligned}
f^* &= -\frac{N_S}{N_F} \frac{S_0/F_0 \, \mathrm{Var}(\tilde{F}_1)}{\mathrm{Var}(\tilde{F}_1)} \\
&= -\frac{N_S}{N_F} \frac{S_0}{F_0} \qquad [17.9]
\end{aligned}$$

The application of Equation 17.9 is illustrated in the following example.

EXAMPLE 17.4

Goss Gold owns 119 ounces of gold and is committed to selling the gold in 3 weeks' time. The spot price (today) is $1307 per ounce and the futures price for delivery in 7 weeks' time is $1316 per ounce. One futures contract covers 3 ounces of gold. Goss Gold wants to hedge using futures and needs to decide on the number of futures contracts it should enter.

SOLUTION

As a first pass at the problem, Goss Gold is willing to assume that a 1 per cent change in the spot price will be matched by a 1 per cent change in the futures price.

continued →

Example 17.4 *continued*

Using Equation 17.9, the number of futures contracts is:

$$f^* = -\frac{N_S}{N_F}\frac{S_0}{F_0}$$

$$= -\frac{119}{3}\frac{\$1307}{\$1316}$$

$$= -39.40$$

$$= -39$$

Thus, Goss Gold should sell 39 futures contracts.

A variation on this simple approach when applied to bond futures is illustrated in Example 17.11 (on p. 579).

FINANCE IN ACTION

METALLGESELLSCHAFT

The German company Metallgesellschaft AG provides a case of an apparent hedging strategy that went terribly wrong.[17]

In 1993 this 100-year-old company was the fourteenth-largest corporation in Germany, with 58 000 employees and 251 subsidiaries worldwide. It was involved in a range of businesses but primarily in mining, metals and energy products. In late 1993 and early 1994, it incurred losses in futures trading of approximately US$1.3 billion. This was equal to about half of its value at that time.

These losses were incurred by a US subsidiary of the company called MG Refining and Marketing (MGRM). In 1992 MGRM developed a marketing strategy in which it offered US firms long-term fixed-price contracts on gasoline, heating oil and diesel fuel. MGRM's customers were able to lock in their purchase price for up to 10 years provided they agreed to buy from MGRM.

To hedge against the risk of oil price rises, MGRM entered into bought positions in futures contracts traded on the New York Mercantile Exchange. However, as these futures contracts had relatively short terms to maturity, they had to be rolled over as each contract expired. MGRM settled expiring contracts and purchased the next shortest maturity contract. This strategy works successfully provided the more distant futures prices are lower than the spot price or nearby futures price.

Unfortunately, in late-1993 oil prices began falling. During 1993 prices of oil fell by almost one-third. MGRM's bought positions in the futures market incurred losses, resulting in large margin calls. As the price of oil was falling, the firm was gaining on its fixed-price supply contracts, but unfortunately those gains could not be realised until the oil was delivered. As noted above, in some cases this was up to 10 years in the future.

Faced with unrealised gains in its fixed-price supply contracts and massive losses in the futures market, the parent company chose to liquidate its futures positions. Unfortunately, during the next 6 months oil prices recovered all of their lost ground. This meant that MRGM's fixed-price supply contracts that were now unhedged incurred further losses for the company.

Some experts consider that MGRM was in fact speculating. Others argue that it had an effective hedge in place and could have raised the cash to meet its margin calls without liquidating its positions. Whether through speculation or an unsuccessful hedging strategy, the parent company reported a loss of more than $US1.7 billion for the financial year ending September 1994.

---

17 For details of the losses incurred by Metallgesellschaft, see Chance and Brooks (2010, p. 576) and Sheedy and McCracken (1997, pp. 42–7).

17.6 FINANCIAL FUTURES ON THE AUSTRALIAN SECURITIES EXCHANGE: THE 90-DAY BANK-ACCEPTED BILL FUTURES CONTRACT

As mentioned in Section 17.3, most futures contracts traded on the ASX are financial futures, rather than commodity futures. In this and the following two sections, principles that we have developed and explained in terms of commodity futures are applied to ASX financial futures. More space is devoted to bank-accepted bill futures than to the others, because there is simply more material to cover and because bank bill futures are used to explain the major principles.

17.6.1 A BRIEF REVIEW OF BANK BILLS[18]

A *bank bill* is a short-term debt instrument that is readily tradeable. Bank bills are generally issued for standard fixed terms (such as 90 days or 180 days) and at standard face values (such as $100 000 or $500 000). The face value is repaid at maturity. Prior to maturity a bill is priced according to the principles of simple interest. Equation 17.10 shows the bill pricing formula used in this chapter.

$$P = \frac{V}{1+(i)(t/365)} \quad [17.10]$$

where P = bill price
V = face value
i = nominal annual yield (also known as the bill rate)
t = term (in days) remaining to bill's maturity date

This is illustrated in the following example.

EXAMPLE 17.5

A bill with 90 days remaining to maturity, priced to yield 6.88 per cent per annum and with a face value of $1 million requires a price of:

$$P = \frac{\$1\,000\,000}{1+(0.0688)(90/365)}$$
$$= \$983\,318.61$$

If the yield were to increase by, say, 0.25 per cent per annum to 7.13 per cent per annum, then the price decreases as follows:

$$P = \frac{\$1\,000\,000}{1+(0.0713)(90/365)}$$
$$= \$982\,722.92$$

This represents a capital loss of $595.69 to the investor (lender). Similarly, if yields decrease, prices increase. An 'equivalent' fall in yield of 0.25 per cent per annum, to 6.63 per cent per annum, will produce a price increase as follows:

$$P = \frac{\$1\,000\,000}{1+(0.0663)(90/365)}$$
$$= \$983\,915.01$$

This represents a capital gain of $596.40 to the investor (lender). Note that the capital gain is a little larger than the capital loss for the same shift in yield.

---

18 For further details, see Section 10.5.3.

LEARNING OBJECTIVE 6

Understand and explain the features of the major financial futures contracts traded on the Australian Securities Exchange

For many purposes, a bank bill is the same as any other 'commodity'. It has a market price and this price changes from day to day according to market forces. There is, therefore, no reason why there cannot be a futures contract on 90-day bank bills.

17.6.2 SPECIFICATION OF THE BANK-ACCEPTED BILL FUTURES CONTRACT

The bank-accepted bill futures contract has the following major features.

Contract unit

The contract unit is a 90-day bank bill with a face value of $1 million, or two 90-day bank bills each with a face value of $500 000, or ten 90-day bank bills each with a face value of $100 000.

Settlement

The contract is deliverable—that is, sellers can deliver bank bills in satisfaction of their futures contract responsibilities. Technically, bills that have a term as short as 85 days or as long as 95 days are acceptable. However, bills shorter than 90 days are worth more than 90-day bills because they are discounted with respect to a shorter time period. Therefore, buyers must pay a little more than the stated futures price in that case. Similarly, if sellers deliver a bill longer than 90 days, then buyers pay a little less than they would for a 90-day bill. Also, bank negotiable certificates of deposit can be substituted for bank bills. The settlement date is the second Friday of the maturity (delivery) month.

Quotations

One hundred minus the annual percentage yield to two decimal places.

Termination of trading

Trading ceases at 12 noon on the business day immediately prior to the settlement date.

It is important to realise that a bank bill futures contract is not a contract on any presently existing 90-day bank bill because tomorrow an existing 90-day bank bill will be an 89-day bank bill and the next day an 88-day bank bill, and so on.

To illustrate the nature of the bank bill futures contract, consider the price of 94.87 for the December (2010) bank bill futures contract provided on the Australian Securities Exchange website after the close of trading on 4 October 2010 (see Figure 17.1). The reported price of 94.87 refers to the price in the last trade on that day and represents 100 minus the annual percentage yield. In other words, the annual yield is:

$100 - 94.87$

$= 5.13\%$

$= 0.0513$

Using Equation 17.10, the dollar price implicit in this futures contract is therefore:

$$\frac{\$1\,000\,000}{1 + (0.0513)(90/365)}$$

$= \$987\,508.69$

The settlement date is the second Friday of December 2010—that is, 10 December 2010. The bank bill involved has 90 days to run; this 90-day period is to *begin on 10 December 2010*. Therefore, the bank bill involved is one that matures on 10 March 2011. The term of the futures contract expires on 10 December 2010, which is 67 days after it was entered into on 4 October 2010.

To clarify this, suppose that a trader bought one such contract on 4 October, held it to settlement day (10 December), accepted delivery of the bill on that day and then held the bill to its maturity date. Ignoring cash flows due to deposits, margins and the mark-to-market rule, the cash flows involved are as shown in Figure 17.1.

FIGURE 17.1 Major cash flows in a bank-accepted bill futures contract

The yield earned over the 90-day period from 10 December 2010 to 10 March 2011 is, as it must be, 5.13 per cent per annum. By entering the futures contract, a particular yield (5.13 per cent per annum) has been locked in on 4 October 2010 for the 90-day period that begins on 10 December 2010 and ends on 10 March 2011.

Of course most traders do not hold a futures contract until settlement. Typically the buyer in this example would soon reverse out by a sale. If, for example, the reversing sale were made at the closing price on 11 October the price, as provided by the ASX website, would have been 94.96. The yield indicated is 100 − 94.96 = 5.04 per cent and again using Equation 17.10, the dollar price is:

$$P = \frac{\$1\,000\,000}{1 + (0.0504)(90/365)}$$
$$= \$987\,725.15$$

Ignoring transaction costs, this gives a gain of $216.46.

17.6.3 USES OF THE BANK BILL FUTURES CONTRACT

The bank bill contract can be used in speculation, hedging and arbitrage.

Speculation with bank bill futures

All futures contracts lend themselves to speculation. There is nothing special to explain about this. If traders can forecast the subsequent course of the bank bill futures price, they can make money simply by buying (selling) when the futures price is low (high).

Hedging with bank bill futures

As has been explained, simple hedging involves a futures transaction, which largely offsets a risk to which the hedger is already exposed. This is illustrated in the following detailed worked examples.

LEARNING OBJECTIVE 7

Explain speculation and hedging strategies using the major financial futures contracts traded on the Australian Securities Exchange

EXAMPLE 17.6

Several weeks ago, the financial controller of Annamay Ltd decided that the company should borrow by issuing a 90-day bank bill with a face value of $1 million. As the funds were not needed for another 2 weeks, it was decided that the issue would not be made until the 2 weeks had passed. In her planning, the financial controller assumed that the 90-day bank bill rate would not change from its then current level of 4.40 per cent per annum. However, she was aware that a risk was involved and therefore decided that Annamay should protect itself against an increase in bill rates by selling one bank bill futures contract. This was done at a price of 95.78. During the next 2 weeks the financial controller was amazed to see the 90-day bill rate climb rapidly. Annamay eventually issued a bill at a rate of 5.50 per cent per annum and lifted the hedge by reversing its futures position at a price of 94.70.

The financial controller is asked to provide a report to the Board of Directors on the following matters:

(a) the (gross) dollar shortfall that Annamay would have faced if a futures contract had not been entered into
(b) the gain or loss made on the futures contract (ignoring transaction costs)
(c) the net dollar shortfall
(d) an explanation of (c) in terms of basis risk
(e) a brief assessment of the effectiveness of the hedge.

SOLUTION
The answers to these questions are as follows:

(a)
$$\text{Planned borrowing} = \frac{\$1\,000\,000}{1+(0.0440)(90/365)}$$
$$= \$989\,267.13$$

$$\text{Actual borrowing} = \frac{\$1\,000\,000}{1+(0.0550)(90/365)}$$
$$\$986\,619.81$$

$$\text{Dollar shortfall (gross)} = \$989\,267.13 - \$986\,619.81$$
$$= \$2647.32$$

(b) There is a notional sale at 95.78—that is, at 4.22 per cent per annum—followed by a notional purchase at 94.70—that is, at 5.30 per cent per annum.

$$\text{Notional inflow from sale} = \frac{\$1\,000\,000}{1+(0.0422)(90/365)}$$
$$= \$989\,701.68$$

$$\text{Notional outflow from purchase} = \frac{\$1\,000\,000}{1+(0.0530)(90/365)}$$
$$= \$987\,100.09$$

$$\text{Result from futures} = \$989\,701.68 - \$987\,100.09$$
$$= \$2601.59 \text{ (gain)}$$

(c) Net dollar shortfall = $2647.32 − $2601.59
$$= \$45.73$$

(d) Basis is spot price less futures price. When the hedge was entered, the basis was:

(Price at yield of 4.40%) *less* (price at yield of 4.22%)
= $989 267.13 − $989 701.68
= −$434.55

When the hedge was lifted, the basis was:

(Price at yield of 5.50%) *less* (price at yield of 5.30%)

= $986 619.81 − $987 100.09

= −$480.28

Change in basis = (later basis) *less* (earlier basis)

= −$480.28 − (−$434.55)

= −$45.73

As a short hedger's net result is given by the change in the basis, this indicates that the hedger's net result is a loss of $45.73, which is the result calculated in part (c).[19]

(e) Without the hedge, the dollar shortfall would have been $2647.32. With the hedge, the net dollar shortfall is only $45.73, a reduction of 98.3 per cent. The result can also (equivalently) be assessed in terms of yields. Annamay's total funds inflow is the amount borrowed plus the net gain on the futures contract. This is:

$986 619.81 + $2601.59

= $989 221.40

The repayment required is $1 million in 90 days' time. The implied annual nominal yield is:

$$\left(\frac{\$1\,000\,000}{\$989\,221.40} - 1\right) \times \frac{365}{90}$$

= 4.419%

This compares with a planned borrowing rate of 4.400 per cent. Clearly the hedge has been extremely effective.

In Example 17.6, Annamay Ltd intended to issue a security, which, with the exception of the intended date of issue, matched precisely the security specified in the futures contract. In other words, both the security of interest to Annamay and the security specified in the futures contract were 90-day bank-accepted bills. A close match between the security of interest to the hedger and the security specified in the futures contract increases the likely quality of the hedge. However, as explained in Section 17.5.4, there are often 'specification differences' between the hedger's needs and the futures contract. This is illustrated in Example 17.7.

EXAMPLE 17.7

Suppose that, instead of 90-day bank bills, Annamay Ltd had planned to issue 120-day bank bills. As there is no futures contract on 120-day bank bills, Annamay would still have hedged using the 90-day bank bill contract. Assume that all other facts remain the same and the relevant data are as shown in Table 17.9.

TABLE 17.9 Yields for Example 17.7

BANK BILLS	YIELD WHEN HEDGE ENTERED (% p.a.)	YIELD WHEN HEDGE LIFTED (% p.a.)
90-day bank bills	4.40	5.50
120-day bank bills	4.55	5.70
90-day bank bill futures	4.22	5.30

continued →

---

[19] See Table 17.6. Note that Annamay Ltd has been a little unlucky. Given that, at maturity, a futures price must be very close to the spot price, it follows that, on average, the basis will tend towards zero as time passes and the maturity date becomes closer. However, in this example, the basis has gone from −$434.55 to −$480.28—that is, it has moved further away from zero.

Example 17.7 *continued*

The financial controller is required to report on the following matters:

(a) the (gross) dollar shortfall that Annamay would have faced if a futures contract had not been entered into
(b) the gain or loss made on the futures contract (ignoring transaction costs)
(c) the net dollar shortfall
(d) an explanation of (c) in terms of basis risk and specification differences
(e) a brief assessment of the effectiveness of the hedge.

SOLUTION

The answers to these questions are as follows:

(a) $$\text{Planned borrowing} = \frac{\$1\,000\,000}{1+(0.0455)(120/365)}$$
$$= \$985\,261.57$$

$$\text{Actual borrowing} = \frac{\$1\,000\,000}{1+(0.0570)(120/365)}$$
$$= \$981\,604.99$$

Dollar shortfall (gross) = $985 261.57 − $981 604.99
= $3656.58

(b) As this calculation involves only the futures contract, it is the same as in Example 17.6—that is, the result is a gain of $2601.59.

(c) Net dollar shortfall = $3656.58 − $2601.59
= $1054.99

(d) This net shortfall can be broken into components reflecting basis risk and specification differences. The latter arises because Annamay has risks related to 120-day bills but is using futures on 90-day bills to hedge against these risks. Table 17.10 shows the results in detail. All prices are calculated using Equation 17.10.

TABLE 17.10 Basis risk and specification differences in Example 17.7

DESCRIPTION	PRICE WHEN HEDGE ENTERED ($)	PRICE WHEN HEDGE LIFTED ($)	CHANGE ($)
1. Basis risk			
90-day bank bill (spot)	989 267.13	986 619.81	
Bank bill futures	989 701.68	987 100.09	
	−434.55	−480.28	−45.73
2. Specification differences			
120-day bank bill (spot)	985 261.57	981 604.99	
90-day bank bill (spot)	989 267.13	986 619.81	
	−4 005.56	−5 014.82	−1 009.26
			−1 054.99

(e) The hedge has reduced the dollar shortfall from $3656.58 to $1054.99; this is a reduction of 71.1 per cent. The nominal annual yield is:

$$\left(\frac{\$1\,000\,000}{\$981\,604.99 + \$2601.59} - 1\right) \times \frac{365}{120} = 4.881\%$$

This compares with a planned yield of 4.550 per cent. Although the hedge has been quite effective, its performance falls short of the excellent performance in Example 17.6.

In both Example 17.6 and Example 17.7 the hedger established a short futures position—that is, the hedge was achieved by first entering a futures contract to sell.

Example 17.8 illustrates a hedge that requires that a bank bill futures contract be held long—that is, the futures contract is first bought and subsequently sold.

EXAMPLE 17.8

The Chesterheaton Investment Fund chose to hedge when it was told to expect an inflow of around $1 million in 2 months' time, to be invested in 90-day bank bills. When the hedge was entered, yields per annum were 8.45 per cent (spot) and 8.80 per cent (futures). When the hedge was lifted, yields were 7.15 per cent (spot) and 7.38 per cent (futures). Describe an appropriate hedge, and assess its effectiveness in the light of subsequent yields, ignoring transaction costs.

SOLUTION

The Chesterheaton Investment Fund buys a bank bill futures contract. The notional purchase price is $978 762.20 and the notional selling price is $982 127.96, giving a gain of $3365.76. When the hedge is lifted, 90-day bank bills offer a yield of 7.15 per cent. This implies a price of $982 675.30. Using its gain from the futures contract, Chesterheaton can buy such a bill for a net outlay of $979 309.54, implying that its annual yield will be:

$$\left(\frac{\$1\,000\,000}{\$979\,309.54} - 1\right) \times \frac{365}{90} = 8.568\%$$

This is in fact slightly higher than the planned rate of 8.450 per cent. The fact that this is not equal to the planned rate indicates that not all risks were eliminated by the hedge, but it is clear that this hedge has been very effective.

Arbitrage with bank bill futures

As we mentioned earlier, an arbitrage is a set of simultaneous transactions in different markets that guarantees a risk-free profit. Although the word 'arbitrage' is sometimes used very loosely, it is used in this chapter in its precise sense. For example, if an investor is assured of a positive return, at no risk, from a net investment of zero dollars, then arbitrage has been achieved. Obviously if markets are efficient, arbitrage should not be possible. If there are no transaction costs and investors can borrow or lend at the same market yields, then there will be an arbitrage opportunity present unless:

$$(1+i_t)(1+i_{t,T}) = 1+i_T \qquad [17.11]$$

where t = the maturity date of the futures contract
i_t = the (spot) yield on a bill maturing at date t
$i_{t,T}$ = the (futures)[20] yield for a futures contract, maturing at date t, on a bill maturing at a later date T
i_T = the (spot) yield on a bill maturing at date T

The logic behind Equation 17.11 is the same as that used in Section 4.6.2 to explain the expectations theory of the term structure of interest rates. Suppose that, on date zero, an investor invests $1 at a yield of i_t for a period of t days and simultaneously buys a futures contract that entitles him to invest, on date t, the proceeds of his investment at a yield of $i_{t,T}$. Therefore, at date T, the investor has an accumulated

---

20 Strictly speaking, $i_{t,T}$ should be a forward yield, but this difference does not significantly affect the gist of the argument. The forward contract matures on date t; the underlying 'commodity' is a bank bill that is delivered on date t and matures on date T. In the context of a bank bill futures contract traded on the Australian Securities Exchange it is required that $T - t = 90$ days.

sum of $\$1(1 + i_t)(1 + i_{t,T})$. This amount is perfectly foreseeable on date zero. Clearly the investor should compare this amount with the accumulated sum if on date zero he instead invests in a bill that matures on date T and offers a yield of i_T. On an investment of $1 this will produce an accumulated sum of $\$1(1 + i_T)$. The investor will choose the alternative that produces the greater sum on date T. Because competition between traders should eliminate arbitrage opportunities, it is expected that both alternatives should yield the same accumulated sum. Therefore Equation 17.11 should hold.

Equation 17.11 implies that the futures yield $i_{t,T}$, which will prevent arbitrage, is:

$$i_{t,T} = \frac{1+i_T}{1+i_t} - 1 \qquad [17.12]$$

If the actual futures yield is less than this yield, an arbitrage operation known as *cash and carry* is feasible. If the opposite is true, then an arbitrage operation known as *reverse cash and carry* is feasible.[21] An important conclusion to draw is that the bank bill futures price must be closely related to current bill yields.

17.7 FINANCIAL FUTURES ON THE AUSTRALIAN SECURITIES EXCHANGE: THE 10-YEAR TREASURY BOND FUTURES CONTRACT[22]

Whereas the bank bill contract is suitable for speculation, hedging and arbitrage in short-term interest rates, the 10-year Treasury bond contract is designed for similar operations involving long-term interest rates.

17.7.1 A BRIEF REVIEW OF BOND PRICING

A bond pays a series of equal interest payments at equal time intervals throughout its life. These payments are known as coupons. At maturity the face value is repaid. In Australia most government bonds pay interest twice each year. Bonds can be bought and sold, and prices rise and fall according to market forces. Given a bond price it is always possible to calculate the yield to maturity, which is simply the bond's internal rate of return. Alternatively, given a required yield to maturity, a bond price can always be calculated. In Australia, it is usual to quote both coupon interest rates and yields on an annual basis, even though all calculations take into account the fact that cash flows are in fact half-yearly. The annual rates are simply double the half-year rates.

A standard bond-pricing formula is:

$$P = \frac{C}{i}\left[1 - \frac{1}{(1+i)^n}\right] + \frac{V}{(1+i)^n} \qquad [17.13]$$

where P = bond price
C = coupon payment per half-year
i = half-yearly yield
n = number of half-years to maturity
V = face value

Equation 17.13 is illustrated in the following example.

---

21 Details of these arbitrages are beyond the scope of this book. Briefly, in a cash-and-carry operation the investor simultaneously (on date zero) issues t-day bills, buys T-day bills and sells the futures contract. On date t, the bills held have become $(T-t)$-day bills and are delivered in order to settle the sold futures position; the sum received will be more than enough to pay out the maturing bills issued. In a reverse cash-and-carry operation the investor simultaneously (on date zero) issues T-day bills, buys t-day bills, and buys the futures contract. On date t, the funds from the maturing bills are used to buy the bills received under the terms of the futures contract. On date T, funds from the maturing bills held will be more than sufficient to pay out the maturing bills issued.

22 The 3-year Treasury bond futures contract is similar in concept and may be used in similar fashion to the 10-year contract.

> **EXAMPLE 17.9**
>
> Consider a bond with exactly 3 years to maturity, a face value of $100 and a coupon interest rate of 6.6 per cent per annum, payable half-yearly. If the required yield is 7.2 per cent per annum, what is the price of the bond?
>
> **SOLUTION**
> The half-yearly coupon payment is:
> 0.5 × $100 × 0.066 = $3.30
>
> The required yield per half-year is:
> 0.5 × 0.072 = 0.036
>
> Using Equation 17.13, the price P is:
>
> $$P = \frac{\$3.30}{0.036}\left(1 - \frac{1}{(1.036)^6}\right) + \frac{\$100}{(1.036)^6}$$
>
> = $17.526 612 + $80.880 061
>
> = $98.406 673

Obviously, if market interest rates fall, then so do required yields, and consequently bond prices rise. Conversely, if yields rise, then bond prices fall.

17.7.2 SPECIFICATION OF THE 10-YEAR BOND FUTURES CONTRACT

The 10-year bond futures contract has the following major features:

(a) *Contract unit.* The contract unit is a 10-year government bond with a face value of $100 000, offering a coupon rate of 6 per cent per annum (payable half-yearly).
(b) *Settlement.* The contract is settled by cash, not by delivery. All contracts still in existence at the close of trading are closed out by the clearing house. In effect the clearing house assumes that all traders have closed out. The price used to close out is a proxy market price, which is calculated by obtaining from 10 bond dealers the yield at which they would buy and sell bonds on a basket of maturities set down in advance by the exchange. The two highest buying yields and the two lowest selling yields are discarded and the remaining yields are averaged. This average yield is then converted to a settlement price using Equation 17.13, the bond-pricing formula.
(c) *Quotations.* Like the bank bill contract, the bond contract is quoted as 100 minus the annual percentage yield, but has a minimum fluctuation of 0.005.
(d) *Termination of trading.* Trading ceases at 12 noon on the fifteenth day of the contract month, or the next trading day if that is not a business day. Settlement day is the business day following the date on which trading ceases.

To illustrate the pricing of the 10-year bond futures contract, consider the price of $94.975 for the December (2010) 10-year bond futures contract provided on the Australian Securities Exchange website after the close of trading on 4 October 2010. The implied yield is 100 − 94.975 = 5.025 per cent per annum, or 2.5125 per cent per half-year. The face value is $100 000. The half-yearly coupon rate is 0.5 × 6 per cent = 3 per cent. Therefore, each coupon payment is $3000. The term is 10 years, or 20 half-years. Using Equation 17.13, the dollar price, P, implicit in this futures price is:

$$P = \frac{\$3000}{0.025\,125}\left(1 - \frac{1}{(1.025\,125)^{20}}\right) + \frac{\$100\,000}{(1.025\,125)^{20}}$$

= $46 712.31 + $60 878.44

= $107 590.75

It is clear that, when using Equation 17.13 for the 10-year bond futures contract, C is always $3000 and V is always $100\,000$.

LEARNING OBJECTIVE 7
Explain speculation and hedging strategies using the major financial futures contracts traded on the Australian Securities Exchange

17.7.3 USES OF THE 10-YEAR BOND FUTURES CONTRACT

The 10-year bond futures contract can be used in similar ways to those explained for the bank bill contract and therefore we do not explain these ways in full detail.

Speculation with 10-year bond futures

As always, speculators are hoping to profit by correctly anticipating price changes. For example, if a long position is entered into at a futures price of 94.975 and reversed out at 95.025, a gain is made. As shown in the previous calculations, a futures price of 94.975 corresponds to a dollar price of $107\,590.75$. A price of 95.025 corresponds to a half-yearly yield of 2.4875 per cent and hence to a dollar price of:

$$P = \frac{\$3000}{0.024\,875}\left[1 - \frac{1}{(1.024\,875)^{20}}\right] + \frac{\$100\,000}{(1.024\,875)^{20}}$$
$$= \$107\,998.89$$

The gain is therefore $\$107\,998.89 - \$107\,590.75 = \$408.14$.

Hedging with 10-year bond futures

The 10-year bond futures contract can be a useful hedging instrument where there is an exposure to changes in long-term fixed interest rates. For example, an investor who holds long-term bonds or debentures will suffer a capital loss if yields increase. Such an investor might consider selling bond futures. Similarly, a company that plans to borrow funds in the future on a long-term fixed interest basis will lose if yields increase before the funds are borrowed. Again, selling bond futures could be considered. Alternatively, an investor who plans to buy bonds, or a company that has issued debentures but is planning to repurchase them, could consider buying bond futures. These are essentially straightforward applications.

EXAMPLE 17.10

Wantdough Ltd is committed to issuing 7-year, 8 per cent per annum debentures in 2 months' time and plans to borrow $5 million. The debentures will pay interest twice per annum. Wantdough decides to hedge using futures contracts on 10-year government bonds. These are currently priced at 95.00. Wantdough assumes that an *x* per cent change in the futures yield will be matched by an *x* per cent change in the required rate of return on its debentures. The problem is to design a suitable hedge.

SOLUTION

Wantdough sells 10-year bond futures. It will still encounter basis risk and it also faces specification differences in that there are important differences between 10-year 6 per cent government bonds and 7-year 8 per cent company debentures. Not much can be done about basis risk, but risks stemming from specification differences can be partly controlled by carefully selecting the number of futures contracts to be sold. Suppose that the futures price falls from 95.00 to 94.00, due to, say, a 1 per cent rise in current yields on government bonds. Using Equation 17.13, the contract value would fall by $7794.58 (from $107\,794.58 to $100\,000$). Now suppose that, simultaneously, the required yield on the debentures also rises by 1 per cent from 8 per cent per annum to 9 per cent per annum. Using Equation 17.13, and assuming that the proposed coupon rate of 8 per cent is maintained, the funds raised would be:

$$P = \frac{\$200\,000}{0.045}\left[1 - \frac{1}{(1.045)^{14}}\right] + \frac{\$5\,000\,000}{(1.045)^{14}}$$
$$= \$4\,744\,429.37$$

Therefore, there would be a shortfall of $255 570.63. The number of contracts required to hedge this shortfall would therefore be:

$$\frac{\$255\,570.63}{\$7794.58}$$

= 33 contracts

Therefore, Wantdough should sell 33 futures contracts.

The use of 10-year bond futures contracts for a hedging purpose is illustrated in Example 17.11, which is a continuation of Example 17.10.

EXAMPLE 17.11

Suppose that Wantdough sells 33 bond futures contracts at the current futures price of 95.00 and that when the debentures are issued the futures price is 94.58 and the required yield on the debentures is 8.50 per cent per annum. The problem is to assess the effectiveness of the hedge.

SOLUTION

Using Equation 17.13, the change in the futures price is $3362.13 per contract, giving a profit of $110 950 from 33 contracts. Again, using Equation 17.13, if the required yield is 8.50 per cent per annum (4.25 per cent per half-year), then 7-year debentures with a face value of $5 million offering a coupon rate of 4 per cent per half-year will raise $4 870 114, thereby giving a gross shortfall of $129 886. After taking account of the profit on futures, the net shortfall is $18 936. Therefore, the futures hedge has eliminated more than 85 per cent of the shortfall that otherwise would have occurred. Most of the other 15 per cent is due to the fact that, while the futures price changed by 0.42 (from 95.00 to 94.58), the debenture yield changed by 0.50 per cent (from 8.00 per cent to 8.50 per cent). As discussed in Example 17.10, Wantdough's assumption was one for one: if the debenture yield changed by one percentage point the futures yield would also change by one percentage point. Had the required debenture yield changed to 8.42 per cent (instead of to 8.50 per cent) the gross funds shortfall would have been $109 391 and there would then have been a small net gain of $1559.

The detail of these calculations is less important than the recognition that it is not correct simply to hedge the face value. Had this been done, 50 futures contracts would have been sold (because $5 000 000/$100 000 = 50). This would have exposed the company to net losses if yields had fallen.

17.8 FINANCIAL FUTURES ON THE AUSTRALIAN SECURITIES EXCHANGE: THE 30-DAY INTERBANK CASH RATE FUTURES CONTRACT

The 30-day interbank cash rate futures contract has the following major features:

(a) *Contract unit.* The contract unit is the average monthly interbank overnight cash rate payable on a notional sum of $3 000 000. Therefore, a 0.01 per cent increase (decrease) in the cash rate will result in an increased (decreased) interest payment of $3 000 000 × 0.0001 × (30/365) = $24.6575. This amount is rounded to $24.66.

(b) *Settlement.* The contract is settled by cash. All contracts still in existence at the close of trading are closed out by the clearing house. The cash settlement price is equal to 100 minus the monthly average of the interbank overnight cash rate for the contract month. The monthly average is found

by taking the sum of the daily interbank overnight cash rates, as published by the Reserve Bank of Australia, and dividing by the number of days for that month.
(c) *Quotations.* The 30-day interbank cash rate contract is quoted as 100 minus the cash settlement rate and has a minimum fluctuation of 0.005.
(d) *Termination of trading.* Trading ceases at 4:30 pm on the last business day of the contract month. Settlement day is the second business day after the last trading day.

Like the bank bill contract, this contract is suitable for speculation, hedging and arbitrage in short-term interest rates.

Speculation using the 30-day interbank cash rate contract is illustrated in Example 17.12.

EXAMPLE 17.12

On 26 October 2010 the closing price of the November 2010 30-day interbank cash rate contract was 95.39. This equates to an average overnight cash rate of 4.61 per cent. The Reserve Bank of Australia (RBA) had a board meeting scheduled for 2 November 2010 and the current overnight cash rate was 4.50 per cent per annum. Suppose Laura believed that the RBA would make the decision to increase interest rates to 4.75 per cent at its 2 November 2010 meeting. She therefore decided to sell 200 30-day interbank cash rate contracts on 26 October.

At its meeting on 2 November the RBA increased the cash rate to 4.75 per cent and on that day the closing price of the November 2010 30-day cash rate contract was 95.27.

If Laura reversed out her position on 2 November, her total gain could be calculated as follows:

Notional sale at:	200 × 95.39 × $24.66 =	$470 463.48 (inflow)
Notional purchase at:	200 × 95.27 × $24.66 =	$469 871.64 (outflow)
Gain (net inflow):		$ 591.84

As detailed on the Australian Securities Exchange website, this contract may also be used to forecast changes in the RBA target cash rate. For example, as noted above, the RBA had a scheduled board meeting on 2 November 2010 and on 26 October 2010 the closing price of the 30-day cash rate contract was 95.39, equating to a yield of 4.61 per cent per annum. Therefore, the expected average target cash rate for the 30 days of November 2010 implied by the 30-day Interbank Cash Rate Futures Contract was 4.61 per cent per annum. Suppose we assume that the RBA decision was either to leave the target cash rate unchanged at 4.50 per cent per annum or increase it to 4.75 per cent per annum. Then as at 26 October we know (or might assume) the following information:

- The expected average target cash rate for the 30 days of November 2010 is 4.61 per cent per annum.
- The target cash rate for 2 days (1 November and 2 November) will be 4.50 per cent per annum.
- The target cash rate for the 28 days from 3 November to 30 November would be either 4.50 or 4.75 per cent per annum.

The probability of rates remaining unchanged (p) may therefore be calculated as:

$$\left(\frac{2}{30}\right) \times 4.50 + \left[p \times \left(\frac{28}{30}\right) \times 4.50 + (1-p) \times \left(\frac{28}{30}\right) \times 4.75\right] = 4.6$$

Therefore, on 26 October 2010 the implied probability of a change in the target cash rate ($1-p$) was 47 per cent.[23,24]

---

23 It may also be seen that the closing price of the November 2010 30-day cash rate contract of 95.27 on 2 November 2010, after the RBA Board had met, reflected an expected average target cash rate for the 30 days of November 2010 of 100 − 95.27 or 4.73 per cent. This figure equates to a cash rate of 4.50 per cent for the first 2 days of November and an expected cash rate of 4.75 per cent for the remaining 28 days.
24 The approach of using the 30-day interbank cash rate in the manner suggested by the Australian Securities Exchange to predict changes in the RBA cash rate can be overly simplistic as demonstrated by Easton & Pinder (2007).

17.9 FINANCIAL FUTURES ON THE AUSTRALIAN SECURITIES EXCHANGE: THE SHARE PRICE INDEX S&P/ASX 200 (SPI 200) FUTURES CONTRACT

17.9.1 A BRIEF REVIEW OF AUSTRALIAN SECURITIES EXCHANGE INDICES

The Australian Securities Exchange (ASX) calculates a number of indices that provide summary measures of the movement of share prices. In addition to industry-specific indices, indices are calculated to provide measures of market-wide movements. Movements in these indices provide a clear indication of movements in the general level of share prices. Consequently, the percentage change in the index is likely to approximate closely the percentage change in the value of a well-diversified portfolio of Australian listed shares. One such index is the All Ordinaries Index. This index is based on an average of the share prices of the 500 largest companies (as measured by market capitalisation) that are listed on the ASX. The share price index contract that is traded on the ASX is based on the S&P/ASX 200 Index (SPI 200). This index is based on an average of the share prices of the 200 companies listed on the ASX that have the largest market capitalisation and the highest volume of shares traded.[25]

> **LEARNING OBJECTIVE 6**
>
> Understand and explain the features of the major financial futures contracts traded on the Australian Securities Exchange

17.9.2 SPECIFICATION OF THE S&P/ASX 200 FUTURES CONTRACT

The S&P/ASX200 (SPI 200) futures contract has the following major features:

(a) *Contract unit.* The contract unit is the value of the S&P/ASX 200 Index, multiplied by $25.
(b) *Settlement.* The contract is not deliverable. All contracts still in existence at the close of trading are closed out by the clearing house at the relevant index value, calculated to one decimal place. The cash settlement price is the 'special opening quotation' of the S&P/ASX 200 Index on the last trading day. This special opening quotation is calculated using the first traded price of each component share of the index on the last trading day.
(c) *Quotations.* The contract is quoted as the value of the S&P/ASX 200 Index. It is quoted to one full index point.
(d) *Termination of trading.* Trading ceases at 12 noon on the third Thursday of the contract month. Settlement day is the first business day following the cessation of trading.

For example, the price of the December (2010) SPI 200 contract provided on the Australian Securities Exchange website after the close of trading on 4 October 2010 was 4586. This means that in dollar terms the contract price on 4 October 2010 was 4586 × $25 = $114 650.

> **LEARNING OBJECTIVE 7**
>
> Explain speculation and hedging strategies using the major financial futures contracts traded on the Australian Securities Exchange

17.9.3 USES OF THE S&P/ASX 200 FUTURES CONTRACT

Speculation with SPI 200 futures

Because the SPI 200 futures price is highly correlated with the S&P/ASX 200 Index, it is a simple matter to use SPI 200 futures for speculative purposes. This is illustrated in Example 17.13.

---

25 Details of the indices calculated by the Australian Securities Exchange may be obtained from the Australian Securities Exchange website **www.asx.com.au**.

EXAMPLE 17.13

On 4 October 2010 the S&P/ASX 200 Index closed at 4579.2 and the December (2010) SPI 200 futures price was 4586. Suppose that a speculator believes that share prices are likely to rise in the following days and she therefore decides to buy December SPI 200 futures. On 11 October 2010 the speculator finds that the S&P/ASX 200 Index has risen to 4697.5 and the December SPI 200 futures price has risen to 4715. Note that the rise in the S&P/ASX 200 Index (118.3 points, or 2.58 per cent) is correlated with the rise in the SPI 200 futures price (129 points, or 2.81 per cent). The position is reversed out by taking a sold position at 4715.

Although the speculator's gain has accrued over time by application of the mark-to-market rule, the total gain can be calculated as follows:

Notional purchase at:	4586 x $25 = $114 650 (outflow)	
Notional sale at:	4715 x $25 = $117 875 (inflow)	
Gain (net inflow):	$ 3 225	

Hedging with SPI 200 futures

Although speculation is the most obvious application of SPI 200 futures, there are also hedging uses. The following example provides a simple application.[26]

EXAMPLE 17.14

Michael Saint manages a portfolio of Australian shares with a current market value of $15 107 000. The portfolio is to be sold in 4 weeks' time. The SPI 200 futures price today is 5421. The following two problems are relevant:

(a) Saint requires assistance in designing an appropriate hedge.
(b) Later, the portfolio is sold for $14 444 500 and the futures position is reversed out at a price of 5159. Saint wishes to assess the effectiveness of the hedge.

SOLUTION

Possible solutions to these problems are as follows:

(a) The futures price at the initiation of the hedge is 5421 x $25 = $135 525. To design a hedge, some assumptions must be made about the relationship between changes in the value of the portfolio and changes in the SPI 200 futures price. For example, it might be assumed that proportionate changes in the portfolio's value would be matched by proportionate changes in the futures price. In other words, in designing this hedge it is assumed that if the portfolio's value decreases by x per cent, then so also will the SPI 200 futures price decrease by x per cent. Using Equation 17.9, the number of futures contracts indicated is:

$$f^* = -\frac{N_S \, S_0}{N_F \, F_0}$$

$$= -\frac{\text{value of spot position}}{\text{value of one futures contract}}$$

$$= -\frac{\$15\,107\,000}{5421 \times \$25}$$

$$= -111.47$$

$$\approx -111$$

That is, 111 futures contracts should be sold.

---

26 For a more advanced discussion, see Figlewski and Kon (1982).

(b) The effectiveness of the hedge is summarised in Table 17.11.

TABLE 17.11 Hedging outcome in Example 17.14

DATE	SPI 200 FUTURES PRICE PER CONTRACT (INDEX FORM)	SPI 200 FUTURES PRICE FOR 111 CONTRACTS ($)	PORTFOLIO VALUE($)
When hedge entered	5421 (sold)	15 043 275	15 107 000
When hedge lifted	5159 (bought)	14 316 225	14 444 500
Gain (loss)		727 050	(662 500)

Therefore the hedge has, in fact, resulted in a net gain of:

$727 050 − $662 500 = $64 550

There are two reasons why the result is not precisely zero. First, the number of contracts sold was 111 not 111.47. However, this is a minor factor in this example. If it had been possible to sell 111.47 contracts the net gain would in fact have been $67 628.50. Second, while the portfolio value decreased by 4.39 per cent, the SPI 200 futures price decreased by 4.83 per cent. Therefore, the loss on the portfolio was more than offset by the gain on the sold futures contracts. There are two factors that are likely to explain the difference between the futures price fall of 4.83 per cent and the portfolio fall of 4.39 per cent. These are basis risk and specification differences between the composition of the S&P/ASX 200 Index and the composition of Michael Saint's portfolio. Included in the latter is the possibility of dividends being received, whereas the S&P/ASX 200 Index does not include reinvested dividends.

Obviously, it is fairly crude to assume that there will be equal proportionate changes in the portfolio's value and the SPI 200 futures price. A slightly more sophisticated approach is to apply Equation 17.7, which gives the risk-minimising hedge ratio, h^*:

$$h^* = -\frac{Cov(\tilde{S}_1, \tilde{F}_1)}{Var(\tilde{F}_1)}$$

In the case of SPI 200 futures, Equation 17.7 is more recognisable if rewritten as:

$$h^* = -\frac{Cov(\tilde{R}_P, \tilde{R}_F)}{Var(\tilde{R}_F)}$$

where $\tilde{R}_P$ = returns on the hedger's portfolio of shares

$\tilde{R}_F$ = returns on the SPI 200 futures contract

An estimate of h^* is found by performing the regression:

$$\tilde{R}_{Pt} = \alpha_P + \beta_P \tilde{R}_{Ft} + \mu_t \qquad [17.14]$$

The estimate $\hat{\beta}_P$ is an estimate of h^*. Note that while $\hat{\beta}_P$ will be of the same order of magnitude as the asset 'betas' we discussed in Chapter 7, the hedging beta in Equation 17.14 is a different concept. A hedging beta is estimated by regressing portfolio returns on SPI 200 futures; an asset beta is estimated by regressing portfolio returns on the S&P/ASX 200 Index itself.

FINANCE IN ACTION

BARINGS

A well-documented case of extraordinary speculation is that of the 240-year-old British bank, Barings, that collapsed in 1995 due to the losses incurred by the Singapore-based trader Nick Leeson.[27]

Nick Leeson gained a powerful reputation within the bank by apparently generating massive profits. He did this by buying Japanese stock index futures contracts that were traded on the Singapore International Monetary Exchange (SIMEX) and simultaneously selling contracts with identical specifications on the Osaka Exchange. This arbitrage activity involves little risk and would be expected to generate a number of small gains and small losses resulting from slight differences in the prices of the contract on the two exchanges. However, Leeson was able to hide his losses in a special account. As a result, it appeared that he was generating huge profits. For example, in 1994 he reported profits of £28 million but had hidden losses of £180 million.

In early 1995, Leeson established long positions in the Japanese stock index futures contract. This meant that he would profit if the Japanese stock market rose. However, on 17 January 1995 an earthquake hit the Japanese city of Kobe and the Japanese stock market fell by approximately 13 per cent over the next 5 weeks. Leeson tried to recover the resultant losses by taking more long positions in the Japanese stock index futures contract and at one point in mid-February he had entered bought positions to the value of US$3 billion.

On 13 February 1995, an investigations officer arrived from London charged with the task of finding out why the bank was being required to make margin calls on these futures contracts that had now reached extraordinary amounts. On 23 February, he spoke with Leeson, who fled Singapore the next day, leaving behind losses of around US$1.4 billion.

FINANCE IN ACTION

SOCIÉTÉ GÉNÉRALE

The largest loss reported due to unauthorised trading was reported by the French bank Société Générale in January 2008.[28]

In January 2008, the French bank Société Générale reported losses of 4.9 billion euros due to the activities of trader Jerome Kerviel. Kerviel had worked for several years in the bank's back office—where transactions are processed and controlled—before being employed as a trader in early 2005. His job as a trader was to hedge the bank's activities by taking positions in share futures markets that were the opposite of the bank's existing positions.

However, Kerviel also used his experience of working in the bank's back office to hide massive speculation that he undertook by trading in European share market futures contracts. He made unauthorised trades to the value of 30 billion euros in 2007, unauthorised trades that resulted in a profit of 1.4 billion euros by the end of the year.

In announcing the fraud in January 2008, Société Générale stated that Kerviel had established futures market positions worth approximately 50 billion euros. By way of comparison, the bank's value was estimated as approximately 35 billion euros. The company closed out the positions at a loss of 6.3 billion euros, resulting in a net loss of 4.9 billion euros after taking into account the 1.4 billion euro profit that Kerviel had made in 2007.

The corporate governance failures of the Barings case and that of Société Générale display considerable similarity, and highlight the need for clear risk management controls—controls that include complete separation of the reporting and trading roles.

---

27 For details of the collapse of Barings Bank, see Chance and Brooks (2010, p. 579), Leeson and Whitley (1996) and Sheedy and McCracken (1997, pp. 36–41). The movie *Rogue Trader* (1998) tells the story of the collapse of Barings Bank.

28 For discussion of the unauthorised trading reported by Société Générale, see various editions of the *Australian Financial Review* (January 2008 to October 2010).

VALUATION OF FINANCIAL FUTURES CONTRACTS   17.10

In Section 17.4 we analysed some of the determinants of futures prices. That analysis applies to futures contracts on physical commodities and to futures contracts on financial 'commodities'. In this section we build on that analysis, but narrow our focus to bank-accepted bill futures contracts and share price index futures contracts.

Equation 17.1 provided a restriction on the valuation of a futures contract:

$$F \leq S + C$$

where F = futures price
S = current spot price
C = carrying cost

If the commodity can readily be sold short, and if the opportunity cost of investment is the only form of carrying cost, then it can be shown that Equation 17.1 should hold as an equality:

$$F = S + C \qquad [17.15]$$

17.10.1 VALUATION OF BANK BILL FUTURES CONTRACTS

If it is assumed that bank bills can be sold short, then Equation 17.15 should apply to bank bill futures.[29] In this case it is usual to express C in terms of the yield i_t applicable to the term t of the futures contract—that is, the carrying cost is:

$$C = S i_t \qquad [17.16]$$

Substituting Equation 17.16 into Equation 17.15 gives:

$$F = S(1 + i_t) \qquad [17.17]$$

Implicitly, the pricing of bank bill futures was also considered in the discussion of arbitrage in Section 17.6.3. This concluded with Equation 17.12:

$$i_{t,T} = \frac{1 + i_T}{1 + i_t} - 1$$

where t = the maturity date of the futures contract
$i_{t,T}$ = the (futures) yield for a futures contract, maturing at date t, on a bill maturing at a later date T
i_T = the (spot) yield on a bill maturing at date T
i_t = the (spot) yield on a bill maturing at date t

Equation 17.12 is consistent with Equation 17.17. If the bill underlying the futures contract has a face value of V dollars, then by definition:

$$F = \frac{V}{1 + i_{t,T}} \qquad [17.18]$$

Substituting Equation 17.12 into Equation 17.18 gives:

$$F = \frac{V(1 + i_t)}{1 + i_T} \qquad [17.19]$$

The spot price S of a T-day bill that also has a face value of V is by definition:

$$S = \frac{V}{1 + i_T} \qquad [17.20]$$

Substituting Equation 17.20 into Equation 17.19 gives:

$$F = S(1 + i_t)$$

This is the result stated in Equation 17.17.

LEARNING OBJECTIVE 8

Understand the valuation of 90-day bank-accepted bill futures contracts and share price index futures contracts

---

[29] This assumption is not as unreasonable as it may appear. When a bank bill is issued, it is effectively sold at its market price and it is subsequently repurchased at its face value.

According to this equation the bank bill futures price is simply the spot price of the relevant bank bill, accumulated at the yield applicable to the term of the futures contract. The 'relevant bank bill' is *not* usually a 90-day bank bill. For example, if a bank bill futures contract matures in 30 days' time, the relevant bank bill currently has a term of 120 days. Heaney and Layton (1996), using Australian data, provide evidence that is consistent with the proposition that Equation 17.17 is a reliable representation of the relationship between bank bill futures and spot prices.

17.10.2 VALUATION OF SHARE PRICE INDEX FUTURES CONTRACTS

The valuation of share price index futures can be approached in a similar manner. This problem is slightly more complex because dividends are paid on most shares in the index, but the calculation of the share price index excludes dividends. As in the discussion of bill futures, we continue to ignore the mark-to-market rule, and instead assume that the cash flows occur only on Date 1, the expiry date of the futures contract. Suppose that on Date 0 an investor buys all the shares in the index at a total cost of S_0, and also borrows a sum of money equal to $PV(D)$, the present value of the dividends that the shares will generate on Date 1. All the shares in the index are subsequently sold on Date 1 at their *then* current spot value of S_1. On the same date, the loan is repaid and dividends of D are collected. Putting this in tabular form:

TABLE 17.12 Strategy producing a future cash flow of S_1

ON DATE 0		ON DATE 1	
ACTION	CASH FLOW	ACTION	CASH FLOW
Buy index	$-S_0$	Sell index	$+S_1$
Borrow $PV(D)$	$+PV(D)$	Repay loan	$-D$
		Collect dividends	$+D$
Total	$PV(D)-S_0$	Total	S_1

As an alternative, suppose that on Date 0 the investor buys share price index futures (price F_0) that mature on Date 1 and also deposits (lends) the sum of $\dfrac{F_0}{1+r}$ to earn interest at a rate r. On Date 1, the futures contract is settled and the deposit (plus interest) is withdrawn. The futures contract is settled by a notional sale at F_1, the futures price on Date 1. However, as Date 1 is the expiry date of the futures contract, convergence between spot prices and futures prices should ensure that $F_1 = S_1$, the spot price on Date 1. The cash flow from the futures contract is therefore $F_1 - F_0 = S_1 - F_0$. Putting this in tabular form:

TABLE 17.13 Alternative strategy producing a future cash flow of S_1

ON DATE 0		ON DATE 1	
ACTION	CASH FLOW	ACTION	CASH FLOW
Buy futures	0	Settle futures	$S_1 - F_0$
Deposit $\dfrac{F_0}{1+r}$	$\dfrac{-F_0}{1+r}$	Withdraw deposit plus interest	$+F_0$
Total	$\dfrac{F_0}{1+r}$	Total	S_1

The point to note about Tables 17.12 and 17.13 is that both indicate a net cash inflow of S_1 dollars on Date 1. Of course it is not known what S_1 will be, but it is known that both tables—that is, both investments—will generate the same future cash flow. Therefore, both investments should cost the same on Date 0:

$$PV(D) - S_0 = \frac{-F_0}{1+r}$$

Solving for the futures price F and, since they are no longer needed, dropping the subscripts, gives:

$$F = [S - PV(D)](1+r) \qquad [17.21]$$

Equation 17.21 and Equation 17.17 have the same form, except that Equation 17.21 has a simple adjustment that takes into account the complication caused by dividends. Equation 17.21 implies that the share price index futures price will generally exceed the current index value, but may not do so if there will be significant dividend payments during the life of the futures contract. Cummings and Frino (2008) provide evidence for the Australian market that, after allowing for taxation effects, Equation 17.21 is a reliable representation of the relationship between share price index futures prices and spot share price index values.

FORGEWARD-RATE AGREEMENTS (FRAs) 17.11

Forward-rate agreements (FRAs) are private agreements between two parties. Usually at least one of the parties is a bank or other financial institution. FRAs are not futures contracts but we discuss them in this chapter because they are often used as an alternative to interest-rate futures contracts.

Loosely speaking, an FRA works as follows. Suppose Party A and Party B enter into an FRA. This means that if, on a specified future date, interest rates are 'low', then Party A must pay cash to Party B—and the lower the interest rates have fallen, the more cash A must pay B. However, the reverse also holds. If, on the specified future date, interest rates are 'high', then B must pay cash to A—again, the higher the interest rates have become, the more cash B must pay to A. In effect, such a contract provides both parties with a guaranteed interest rate in the future. Thus, for example, Party A might be a company planning to borrow on the expiry date of the FRA. If interest rates rise before the loan is made, the FRA gives A a cash inflow to compensate for the higher interest rate. If, instead, interest rates fall during the period, the FRA requires A to make a cash payment, but this is compensated by the lower interest rate that will be charged on the funds borrowed.

We now turn to Example 17.15, which provides a detailed explanation of how FRAs work.

LEARNING OBJECTIVE 9
Understand and explain the uses of forward-rate agreements

EXAMPLE 17.15

Company A intends to borrow $1 million in 3 months' time. This will be repaid (with interest) in a lump sum, 180 days later. Repayment will therefore occur approximately 9 months from now. At present, the interest rate on a 180-day loan is about 9.40 per cent per annum. Company A fears that in 3 months' time this rate might have risen substantially. Therefore, Company A approaches Bank B to set up a forward-rate agreement (FRA). The bank agrees, setting a contract rate of 9.50 per cent per annum. This means that if, in 3 months' time when the FRA expires, the 180-day bank bill rate exceeds 9.50 per cent, Bank B will pay Company A enough cash to compensate. In return, Company A has agreed that if, at that time, the 180-day bank bill rate is less than 9.50 per cent per annum, Company A will pay enough cash to Bank B to compensate. Note that the cash flow represents only a *difference* in interest payments, not the total interest payment. Further, no payment of principal is involved.

continued →

Example 17.15 *continued*

To show how the cash flow in an FRA is calculated, assume that when the FRA expires the market interest rate for a term of 180 days is 10.25 per cent per annum. Notionally, the FRA commits Company A to the following cash flows.

At date of FRA expiry:

$$\frac{\$1\,000\,000}{1+(0.0950)(180/365)}$$

$955\,247.32$ = sum borrowed

180 days after FRA expiry:

outflow (repayment) of $1 000 000

However, at the FRA's expiry date, the present value of this outflow is only:

$$\frac{\$1\,000\,000}{1+(0.1025)(180/365)}$$
$$=\$951\,884.21$$

Since interest rates have increased, Bank B will have to pay Company A a sum sufficient to compensate Company A for the increase. The settlement amount is equal to the difference between the present value of $1 000 000 discounted at the interest rate specified in the FRA of 9.50 per cent and the present value of $1 000 000 discounted at the current market interest rate (see Carew 1994). That is:

$$\text{Settlement amount} = \frac{\$1\,000\,000}{1+(0.095)(180/365)} - \frac{\$1\,000\,000}{1+(0.1025)(180/365)}$$
$$= \$955\,247.32 - \$951\,884.21$$
$$= \$3363.11$$

Under the terms of the FRA, Bank B pays Company A the sum of $3363.11.

More generally the settlement amount Q is:

$$Q = \frac{F}{1+(it/365)} - \frac{F}{1+(rt/365)} \qquad [17.22]$$

where F = face value
i = the interest rate specified in the FRA
r = current market interest rate
t = number of days

The effect of the FRA is that Company A is able to borrow at a net cost of 9.50 per cent per annum, despite the increase in interest rates. However, the actual borrowing by Company A will still take place at the current market rate of 10.25 per cent. Company A can borrow $951 884.21 for 180 days at an interest rate of 10.25 per cent per annum; adding to this amount the inflow of $3363.11 from Bank B, Company A will have funds of $955 247.32 available. The repayment required is:

$951\,884.21[1+(0.1025)(180/365)] = \$1\,000\,000$

Of course, this is the same as the amount required to repay a loan of $955 247.32 at 9.50 per cent per annum over 180 days, as required by Company A. That is, Company A has locked in an interest rate of 9.50 per cent on its future borrowings.

FRAs are also entered into between banks and depositors. In this case, the bank pays the depositor if interest rates decrease during the life of the FRA, and the depositor pays the bank if interest rates increase during the life of the FRA. However, in most FRAs the client is a prospective borrower seeking protection against rising interest rates, rather than a prospective depositor seeking protection against falling interest rates. Finally, many FRAs are agreements between banks, rather than agreements between clients and banks.

Many companies, particularly those that are small or medium in size, prefer to use an FRA rather than a futures contract. This is largely because an FRA can be tailored more closely to their specific needs in relation to amount, timing and choice of interest rate. In addition, FRAs do not normally impose the same complex deposit and margin requirements as exist in futures contracts.

However, larger companies, and particularly companies in the finance industry, may prefer a futures contract because it offers the flexibility of being able to reverse out at any time through a transaction on the futures exchange. Indeed, banks and other financial institutions use futures contracts to hedge the risks they create by entering into FRAs with their clients.

Connect Plus features a case study illustrating topics covered in this chapter. Ask your lecturer or tutor for your course's unique URL.

SUMMARY

This chapter examined three main issues.

- First, a discussion was provided of what futures contracts are and how futures markets are organised. This discussion included an explanation of how the clearing house interposes itself between traders, and how this process allows traders to close out (or reverse) their contracts before the maturity date. An explanation of the system of deposits, margins and the mark-to-market rule was also provided.

- Second, the chapter dealt with speculation strategies that may be employed using futures markets. Five kinds of speculation were identified—namely scalping, spreading, straddling, day trading and long-term (or overnight) position taking. The processes of short hedging and long hedging were also explained. Imperfect convergence, basis risk and specification differences were discussed as reasons why hedging with futures contracts may not be perfect.

- Third, the chapter provided details of the specification of four financial futures contracts traded on the Australian Securities Exchange, namely the 90-day bank-accepted bill futures contract, the 10-year Treasury bond futures contract, the share price index futures contract, and the 30-day interbank cash rate futures contract. Having detailed the specification of these contracts, examples were provided of how these contracts may be used for speculation and hedging purposes.

- The chapter also provided an analysis of some of the determinants of futures prices and specifically examined the valuation of bank-accepted bill futures contracts and share price index futures contracts. Forward-rate agreements, which are often used as an alternative to interest-rate futures contracts, were also discussed.

KEY TERMS

basis 562
call option on a futures contract 556
carrying cost 557
hedgers 551
long hedger 561
margin call 555
marking-to-market 554
put option on a futures contract 556
short hedger 561
short selling 554
speculators 551
spot price 557
spread 560

SELF-TEST PROBLEMS

1. Suppose that, at a particular time, the June futures price is $1200 and the September futures price is $1260. You are convinced that the spread between the June and September prices will soon widen, but you have no belief as to whether both prices will rise, or both prices will fall. What action(s) should you take? Show that as a result of your action(s) you will make a profit, if, on a subsequent date, the June futures price is $1300 and the September futures price is $1380.

2. On 2 September the quoted price of the 90-day bank bill futures contract maturing on 12 December was 92.00. On 8 September the price was 92.50. The face value of the bank bills underlying one contract is $1 million. Suppose that Harold sold 15 such contracts on 2 September and closed out his position on 8 September. Ignoring transaction costs, how much has Harold made (or lost)?

Solutions to self-test problems are available in Appendix B, page 803.

REFERENCES

Carew, E., *Fast Forward: The History of the Sydney Futures Exchange*, Allen & Unwin, St Leonards, 1993.

——, *How Australia's Forward-rate Agreement Markets Operate*, Australian Financial Markets Association, Sydney, 1994.

Chance, D.M. & Brooks, R., *An Introduction to Derivatives and Risk Management*, 8th edn, Thomson Learning, Mason, Ohio, 2010.

Cornell, B. & Reinganum, M., 'Forward and futures prices: evidence from the foreign exchange markets', *Journal of Finance*, December 1981, pp. 1035–45.

Cox, J., Ingersoll, J. & Ross, S., 'The relation between forward prices and futures prices', *Journal of Financial Economics*, December 1981, pp. 321–46.

Cummings, J.R. & Frino, A., 'Tax effects on the pricing of Australian stock index futures', *Australian Journal of Management*, December 2008, pp. 391–406.

Easton, S.A. & Pinder, S.M., 'Predicting Reserve Bank of Australia interest rate announcements using the 30-day interbank cash rate futures contract: beware of the target rate tracker', *Australian Economic Review*, March 2007, pp. 119–22.

Figlewski, S. & Kon, S., 'Portfolio management with stock index futures', *Financial Analysts Journal*, January–February 1982, pp. 52–9.

French, K.R., 'A comparison of futures and forward prices', *Journal of Financial Economics*, November 1983, pp. 311–42.

Frino, A. & Jarnecic, E., *Introduction to Futures and Options Markets in Australia*, Pearson Education Australia, Sydney, 2005.

Heaney, R.A. & Layton, A.P., 'A test of the cost of carry relationship in Australia', *Applied Financial Economics*, April 1996, pp. 143–54.

Howard, L. & Jameson, K., 'The futures markets', in R. Bruce et al. (eds), *Handbook of Australian Corporate Finance*, 5th edn, Butterworths, Sydney, 1997.

Kolb, R.W. & Overdahl, J. A., *Understanding Futures Markets*, 6th edn, John Wiley & Sons, New Jersey, 2006.

Leeson, N. & Whitley, E., *Rogue Trader: How I Brought Down Barings Bank and Shook the Financial World*, Little, Brown and Company, Massachusetts, 1996.

Markovic, M., 'The legal status of futures market participants in Australia', *Company and Securities Law Journal*, April 1989, pp. 82–100.

Sheedy, E. & McCracken, S., *Derivatives: The Risks that Remain*, Allen & Unwin, Sydney, 1997.

QUESTIONS

1. **[LO 1]** What are the major differences between a forward contract and a futures contract?

2. **[LO 1]** Distinguish between the terms *volume traded* and *open positions*.

3. **[LO 1]** Distinguish between the following, providing in your answer brief examples to illustrate the points you make:
   (a) deliverable futures contract and non-deliverable futures contract
   (b) speculator and hedger
   (c) short hedger and long hedger.

4. **[LO 1]** Go to the Australian Securities Exchange website (**www.asx.com.au**) and find the 'commodities' on which futures contracts are traded. Why is there not a futures contract on wine?

5. **[LO 5]** What is meant by basis risk?

6. **[LO 4]** Explain what is meant by a perfect hedge. Does a perfect hedge always lead to a better outcome than an imperfect hedge?

7. **[LO 4]** *Futures markets are really there for the benefit of speculators, not hedgers. Very few contracts end in delivery, so obviously the futures market traders aren't interested in the actual commodities, and if they're not interested in the actual commodities, they can't be hedgers. Many contracts aren't even deliverable. How could anyone hedge with contracts like that?* Consider carefully the various claims made in this statement.

8. **[LO 6]** Consider the effects of an overnight share price fall of around 25 per cent on:
   (a) a speculator with a long position in the SPI 200 futures contract
   (b) a superannuation fund with a short position in the SPI 200 futures contract.

PROBLEMS

1. **Determinants of futures prices [LO 3]**
   On a particular day in the Xanadu Futures Exchange the following gold futures prices were observed:

Delivery date (months)	Futures price per ounce ($)
1	1379
2	1388
3	1410
6	1419
12	1439

   In Xanadu the interest rate is 0.5 per cent per month (compound). It costs $2 per ounce per month (payable for the whole period, in advance) to store and insure gold. Each futures contract covers 8 ounces of gold. The current spot price of gold is $1373 per ounce.

   Identify any arbitrage opportunities. Explain how such opportunities could be exploited and calculate the profit per contract. Ignore transaction costs, taxes and any interest received or forgone due to deposits or margins.

2. **Speculation with 90-day bank bill futures contracts [LO 7]**
   On 2 September 2008, the quoted price on the December 2008 90-day bank bill futures contract was 93.11. Penny believed that interest rates would fall over the next month. Suppose that she bought five contracts on 2 September 2008 and closed out her position on 2 October 2008 at a price of 93.65. Ignoring transaction costs, how much has Penny made (or lost)?

3. **Speculation with 10-year bond futures contracts [LO 7]**
   On 2 September 2008, the December 2008 10-year bond futures contract was priced at 94.360. Sean, unlike Penny in Problem 2, believed that interest rates would rise over the next month. Suppose that he sold six contracts on 2 September and closed out his position on 2 October at a price of 94.645. Ignoring transaction costs, how much has he made (or lost)?

4. **Speculation with SPI 200 futures contracts [LO 7]**
   On 2 September 2008, the December 2008 SPI 200 futures contract was priced at 5186.0. Megan believed that the share market was likely to fall over the next month. Suppose that she sold seven contracts on 2 September and closed out her position on 2 October at a price of 4775.0. Ignoring transaction costs, how much has she made (or lost)?

5. **Using 30-day interbank cash rate futures contracts [LO 7]**
   On 27 September 2010, the closing price of the October 2010 30-day interbank cash rate contract was 95.365. The Reserve Bank of Australia (RBA) had a board meeting scheduled for 5 October 2010 and the current overnight cash rate was 4.50 per cent per annum. On 27 September, what was the probability implied by the price of the October 2010 30-day interbank cash rate contract that the RBA would increase the cash rate to 4.75 per cent at its October meeting?

6. **Speculation with bank bill futures contracts [LO 7]**
   On 8 October 2004, the quoted price on the March 2005 90-day bank bill futures contract was 94.52. Margaret believed that interest rates would fall following the Australian Commonwealth Government election on 9 October. Suppose that she bought eight contracts on 8 October and closed out her position on 11 October at a price of 94.57. Ignoring transaction costs, how much has Margaret made (or lost)?

7. **Speculation with 10-year bond futures contracts [LO 7]**
   On 8 October 2004, the December 2004 10-year bond futures contract was priced at 94.435. Michael, unlike Margaret in Problem 6, believed that interest rates would rise following the Australian Commonwealth Government election on 9 October. Suppose that he sold two contracts on 8 October and closed out his

position on 11 October at a price of 94.525. Ignoring transaction costs, how much has he made (or lost)?

8. **Using 30-day interbank cash rate futures contracts [LO 7]**
On 8 October 2004, the November 2004 30-day interbank cash rate futures contract was priced at 94.74 and on 11 October 2004 it was priced at 94.745. The Reserve Bank of Australia (RBA) had a scheduled board meeting on 2 November 2004. Suppose we assume that the decision faced by the RBA board was to either leave the target cash rate unchanged at 5.25 per cent per annum or increase it to 5.5 per cent per annum. What were the implied probabilities, on 8 and 11 October, of the RBA board leaving the target cash rate unchanged on 2 November?

9. **Hedging with 90-day bank bill futures contracts [LO 7]**
You are the finance manager of Play Safe Ltd. On 28 August, Play Safe's Board of Directors decides that, in 7 weeks' time, Play Safe will issue nine bank bills, each with a face value of $100 000 and a term of 120 days. In its planning, the Board has assumed that yields will not change from their current levels. On 29 August you are told to arrange a hedge for Play Safe. On that date, you are given the following data:

Bank bill yields	90 days:	5.82% per annum
	120 days:	6.07% per annum
Bank bill futures	September:	94.10
	December:	93.85

You arrange an appropriate hedge. Several months later you are asked to write a report on your hedging performance, including reasons for any net gain or loss made. Consulting the records, you discover that the bills were issued on time at a rate of 7.37 per cent per annum and the futures contract was reversed at 92.65. At that time the 90-day bill rate was 7.13 per cent per annum. Describe how you would have hedged in this situation. What major points would you make in the report? Include relevant calculations.

10. **Using 90-day bank bill futures contracts [LO 7]**
Jane Hedges has today invested in a 180-day bank bill with a face value of $1 million, priced to yield 6.30 per cent per annum. Simultaneously she has sold a futures contract on a 90-day bank bill with a face value of $1 million. The futures contract will expire in 90 days' time from today. The futures price is 93.55. Jane intends to settle the futures contract by delivery. Ignoring any effects from the mark-to-market rule, what yield (simple interest, in per cent per annum) will Jane achieve on her investment? What, if anything, does this imply about today's 90-day bank bill yield? Why?

11. **Using 90-day bank bill futures contracts [LO 7]**
Today, Hank Ltd issued a 120-day bank bill with a face value of $1 million at a yield of 8.90 per cent per annum. Simultaneously, Hank bought a futures contract on a 90-day bank bill at a price of 91.03. The futures contract matures in 30 days' time and is based on a face value of $1 million. Hank intends to allow the futures contract to be settled by delivery. Ignoring any effects from the mark-to-market rule, describe carefully the economic substance of Hank's transactions. Include in your answer details of all cash flows (amount, timing and whether they are inflows or outflows). What yield (simple interest, in per cent per annum) will Hank pay? What, if anything, does this imply about today's interest rates? Why?

12. **Hedging with 10-year bond futures contracts [LO 7]**
Thurber Ltd is a firm of underwriters that today has had to take up at face value ($7.5 million) 8-year debentures issued by Beetham Properties Ltd. The Beetham debentures offer a coupon rate of 6.5 per cent per annum, payable half-yearly. Thurber is therefore an 'unwilling lender' but, for various reasons, Thurber intends to hold the Beetham debentures until the first coupon date, which is in 6 months' time, and then sell the debentures. Thurber intends to hedge by using the ASX futures contract on 10-year government bonds. The current price of this contract is 95.00.
    (a) How many ASX contracts should be entered into? Show your calculations and explain briefly.
    (b) What risks (if any) do you think Thurber may still face, despite having hedged?

13. **Speculation with SPI 200 futures contracts [LO 7]**
On 18 February you observe that the S&P/ASX 200 Index stands at 6317.4, while the March SPI 200 futures price is 6353 and the June SPI 200 futures price is 6390. You believe that the difference between the March and June futures prices is too narrow and will soon widen, but you have no views as to whether the S&P/ASX 200 Index or the SPI 200 futures prices will increase or decrease. How can your beliefs be put to the (financial) test? Show that, if your prediction is right, you will profit from trading futures, regardless of whether share prices as a whole increase or decrease.

14. **Hedging with SPI 200 futures contracts [LO 7]**

You are the manager of the Dorfman Investment Fund. On 9 May you receive notice that a segment of the fund must be sold on or about 30 May. This segment comprises a broadly based selection of listed Australian shares and is currently valued at $61 650 000. The risk is hedged using June SPI 200 futures. On 28 May the shares are sold and the futures contract is reversed. Relevant data are as follows:

	On 9 May	On 28 May
Portfolio value	$61 650 000	$58 400 000
S&P/ASX 200	6322.6	6028.6
SPI 200 futures	6351	6041

Bearing in mind that on 9 May you do not know the 28 May outcomes, report on how you would have hedged. Include in your report the number of futures contracts and whether they were bought or sold. Assess the effectiveness of the hedge and explain any imperfections experienced.

15. **Valuation of SPI 200 futures contracts [LO 8]**

As at today's date, the value of shares in the Monrovian share price index (SPI) is $126 000. A 4-month futures contract on those shares is priced at $125 913. In 4 months' time, dividends totalling $5203 will be paid on the shares. Of course, S, the value of shares at that time, is currently not known. In Monrovia the interest rate for both borrowing and lending is 1 per cent per month (compound). There are no transaction costs or taxes in Monrovia.

(a) Suppose that today you buy the shares in the index and also borrow $5000. After 4 months you collect the dividends, sell the shares and repay the loan. Calculate the resulting cash flows for today and after 4 months.

(b) Suppose instead that today you buy the futures contract and deposit the sum of $121 000 in an interest-bearing account. After 4 months you settle on the futures contract and withdraw your deposit (with interest). Calculate the resulting cash flows for today, and after 4 months.

(c) Explain in detail why the above calculations show that the futures contract is correctly priced today.

(d) If today the futures price is $126 913, calculate the current and future cash flows that result if today the following transactions are entered into simultaneously: borrow $126 000, buy shares and sell the futures contract. Comment.

16. **Forward-rate agreements [LO 9]**

Curzon Ltd needs to borrow $5 million in 2 months' time. This amount will be repaid (with interest) in a lump sum, 90 days later. Repayment will therefore occur approximately 5 months from now. Curzon enters into a forward-rate agreement with a bank, with the contract rate set at 7.50 per cent per annum. What cash payment, if any, will the bank be required to pay Curzon Ltd?

CHAPTER 18
OPTIONS AND CONTINGENT CLAIMS

LEARNING OBJECTIVES

After studying this chapter you should be able to:

1. understand the major types and characteristics of options and distinguish between options and futures
2. identify and explain the factors that affect option prices
3. understand and apply basic option pricing theorems, including put–call parity
4. understand the binomial model and the Black–Scholes model of option pricing and calculate option prices using these models
5. explain the characteristics and uses of foreign currency options and options on futures
6. define a contingent claim and explain the option-like features of several contingent claims

CHAPTER CONTENTS

18.1 Introduction
18.2 Options and option markets
18.3 Binomial option pricing
18.4 The Black–Scholes model of call option pricing
18.5 Options on foreign currency
18.6 Options, forwards and futures
18.7 Options on futures
18.8 Contingent claims

18.1 INTRODUCTION

In this chapter we consider financial contracts known as options. Most of this chapter is concerned with options to buy or sell shares, but other types of options are also considered. An option is a special case of a type of contract called a **contingent claim**. Stated simply, a contingent claim is an asset whose value depends on the value of some other asset. A surprisingly large number of financial arrangements fall into this category. Contingent claims are discussed in Section 18.8. First, however, we consider options and option markets.

contingent claim
asset whose value depends on the value of some other asset

18.2 OPTIONS AND OPTION MARKETS

18.2.1 WHAT IS AN OPTION?

An option is the right (but not the obligation) to force a transaction to occur at some future time on terms and conditions agreed to now. For example, the buyer of a **call option** on shares obtains the right to *buy* shares in the future from the seller (also known as the 'writer') of the call at a price determined now.[1] At a future time, the buyer of the call can exercise the right to obtain the shares at the predetermined price, regardless of what is then the current market price of the shares. Similarly, the buyer of a **put option** has the right to *sell* the shares in the future to the writer of the put at a predetermined price, regardless of what is then the share's current market price. This right to buy (in the case of a call) or to sell (in the case of a put) must be paid for by the option buyer at the time the option is purchased. The amount paid is called the option price and is determined by market forces.

LEARNING OBJECTIVE 1
Understand the major types and characteristics of options and distinguish between options and futures

The Australian Securities Exchange (ASX) provides facilities for the trading of calls and puts on the shares of more than 120 companies listed in Australia.[2] The following example, taken from that market, illustrates the nature of a call option. On Friday 7 May 2010, the closing price of the 'June 2010 38.00' series of call options on the shares of BHP Billiton (BHP) was $1.84. The closing price of BHP shares on the same date was $37.50. Here, 'June' refers to the month in which the call expires. In this case, the date of expiry is 24 June 2010.[3] The figure '38.00' indicates an **exercise price (or strike price)** of $38, while the $1.84 is the price of the call. Shares in BHP are the 'underlying shares' in this transaction and each option contract covers 100 shares. Therefore, the buyer of one call contract paid 100 × $1.84 = $184 to obtain the right to buy 100 BHP shares at any time between 7 May 2010 and 24 June 2010, at a predetermined price of $38 per share. If the buyer calls on the writer to 'deliver' (sell) the underlying shares, he or she is said to 'exercise' the option. If, as in this example, the call buyer is able to exercise at any time up to (and including) the expiry date, the option is said to be of the 'American' type; if exercise can occur only on the expiry date (and not before), it is said to be an option of the 'European' type.

call option
right to buy an underlying asset at a fixed price

put option
right to sell an underlying asset at a fixed price

exercise (or strike) price
fixed price at which an underlying asset can be traded, pursuant to the terms of an option contract

The following example, taken from the same market on the same day, illustrates the nature of a put option. On 7 May 2010, the closing price of the 'June 39.00' series of put options on the shares of BHP was $2.67. As mentioned in the previous paragraph, the closing price of BHP shares on that day was $37.50 and the expiry date for the June series was 24 June 2010. The exercise price was $39 and the price of the put was $2.67 per share. The buyer of one put contract paid 100 × $2.67 = $267 to obtain

---

[1] Shares are of course not the only assets that can be the subject of an option contract. For example, there are options on stock market indices, debt instruments, foreign currencies and futures contracts. The last two are discussed in Sections 18.5 and 18.7. Detailed discussion of all four can be found in standard specialised textbooks such as Hull (2010).

[2] In addition to standard put and call options, other option-style securities are also traded on the ASX. For example, ASX warrants are option-style securities that are issued by financial institutions and frequently have quite different payoff structures than standard exchange traded options. For example, a warrant may have a 'barrier' requirement that dictates that the warrant terminates once a certain price level, or barrier, is reached.

[3] The ASX website provides an up-to-date calendar of expiry dates at www.asx.com.au/products/options/trading_information/expiry_calendar.htm.

the right to sell 100 BHP shares at any time between 7 May 2010 and 24 June 2010 at a predetermined price of $39 per share. If the put buyer requires the put writer to purchase the underlying shares, he or she is said to 'exercise' the option. As with calls, puts traded in this market are of the American type.

18.2.2 HOW OPTIONS ARE CREATED AND TRADED

Options on shares may be created by the company whose shares underlie the option contract, or by parties who have no association with the company. Options created by the company are nearly always call options and may be created for a number of reasons, of which two are the most common. First, these call options may be issued to investors as a means of raising capital for the company. The sale of the options raises capital and there will be a further inflow of capital if the options are subsequently exercised. Options of this kind may be listed on a stock exchange and appear in the share lists together with other securities issued by the company. Second, the company may issue call options to senior employees or directors of the company. Typically, in the case of listed companies, options of this kind form part of the compensation package for managers and are not a significant source of capital for the company.

Options can also be created by parties who may have no association with the company. For example, two share market observers, A and B, may enter into a private option contract on the shares of BHP. This will not raise any capital for BHP and does not require any agreement or involvement on the part of BHP. Frequently, one or other of the parties will be a shareholder in the company—for example, B may be a shareholder who buys a put on BHP shares to give protection against a fall in BHP's share price. However, it may be that neither party is a shareholder at the time of entering into the option contract. Only if the option is subsequently exercised will it be necessary for shares to be delivered. Shares for this purpose can be purchased in the open market if and when the option is exercised. Many of the terms in private option contracts will be subject to negotiation between the parties. After negotiation the contract will specify at least the following:

- the type and number of the shares to be optioned
- the exercise price
- the expiry date
- the adjustment (if any) to be made in the event of a change in capital structure (due to any bonus or rights issues, for example)
- the adjustment (if any) to be made in the event of a dividend payment
- and, of course, the price of the option.

On payment of the option price the buyer and writer are bound contractually.

While options created by private negotiation have the advantage that the features desired by the parties can be specified precisely, there are three major disadvantages. First, since there is no organised system for bringing together potential parties to the contract, it will often be very difficult to find a party with whom to contract. Second, even if such a party is found and a contract entered into, it will not be possible to reverse out of the contract before the agreed expiry date. Third, it will be necessary to investigate the credit-worthiness of the other party every time an option is created. A solution to all three problems is to establish an organised market, called a listed option market, that provides a standardised form of option contract, a list of options in which trading can be undertaken and a procedure that avoids the need for repeated checking of credit-worthiness. The Australian Securities Exchange provides a market of this type.[4]

In a listed option market, traders select the desired underlying share, expiry date and exercise price from a list of those available. Each contract covers a fixed number of shares, and, although adjustments are made

---

[4] Similar observations were made in Chapter 17 about the development of futures contracts from forward contracts. There are many similarities between the organisation of a listed option market and the organisation of a futures market.

for new share issues during the life of the option, they are not made for ordinary dividend payments.[5] The only negotiable term is the option price, which is determined by market forces. An individual buyer in any option series is not bound contractually to an individual writer, but rather the class of buyers (as a whole) is bound contractually to the class of writers (as a whole), with exercise notices being distributed randomly between individual writers. However, exercise is not common because, instead of exercising, the holder of a call option can take his or her profit by selling the call in the secondary market.[6] It is possible in this case that the buyer will be an existing writer who wishes to cancel out his or her position, in order to avoid being exercised against. The organisers of the market check the credit-worthiness of traders and, in a manner similar to the role of the futures market authorities, take the role of counterparty in every transaction. A description of this process in the futures market is provided in Section 17.2.2.

There are numerous option markets around the world organised along these lines. The first such market to be established was the Chicago Board Options Exchange, which opened in 1973. In Australia, a market with a similar structure was opened in 1976. Most share options in Australia are traded through ASX Ltd, with the exchange also offering options on several futures contracts.

18.2.3 OPTION CONTRACTS AND FUTURES CONTRACTS

It is important to distinguish between option contracts and futures contracts because it is often mistakenly thought that there are only minor differences between them. Of course, there are some notable similarities. For example, both types of contract may involve the delivery of some underlying asset at a future date and at a predetermined price. However, there are very significant differences between them. Most importantly, a futures contract *requires* the delivery of the underlying asset, whereas an option buyer *chooses* whether delivery will occur—that is, buyers in futures contracts have an obligation to buy the underlying asset, whereas buyers of, say, call options have the right to buy if they so choose. Therefore, if buyers in futures contracts take no action to cancel their positions, they will be required to buy the underlying asset at the expiry of the contract. If buyers of call or put options take no action to cancel their positions, the options simply expire and there are no subsequent transactions. A related difference concerns payment. When a futures contract is made, the payment of the futures price is not required until the expiry date, but when an option contract is made, the buyer must immediately pay the option price to the writer.[7] If the option is subsequently exercised, there is a further transaction when the exercise price is paid.

18.2.4 PAYOFF STRUCTURES FOR CALLS AND PUTS

It is an axiom of finance theory that, ultimately, the prospect of future cash flows is the only source of value. An alternative term for the future cash flows of a contract is its **payoff structure**. The easiest financial contract to value is one that promises (with certainty) a fixed amount to be paid in cash on a fixed future date—that is, the payoff structure is a single cash flow with a probability of 1.0. The payoff structures for options are more complicated because the payoff (cash flow) depends on the share price on the expiry date of the option.

payoff structure
set of future cash flows

Consider the BHP 38.00 call option discussed in Section 18.2.1. If, on the call's expiry date, the BHP share price is $38 or less, the call will be worth nothing on expiry. There will be no payoff at all. For example, there is no value in having a call that is about to expire and which gives the call holder the right to pay $38 per share when the market price is only, say, $37 per share. If, however, the share price at the expiry of the call is more than $38, then the payoff per share is the difference between the share price and the exercise price of $38. For example, if the share price at the expiry of the call is $39, the payoff is $1.

---

5 Adjustments are made in the case of 'special' and 'abnormal' dividends. See Australian Securities Exchange (2009).
6 Some reasons for preferring a sale to an exercise are explained in Section 18.2.8. As a consequence, in practice relatively few options are exercised.
7 Some options on futures contracts are an exception to this rule.

This is the payoff because the call holder could exercise the call and pay the exercise price of $38 per share, and then immediately resell the share for its market price of $39, producing a net cash inflow of $1 per share. In summary, the payoff on a call option is:

$$\text{Max } [0, S^* - X]$$

where S^* = the share price on the call's expiry date[8]
X = the exercise price of the call

The payoff structure is shown in more detail in Table 18.1. The information in Table 18.1 is shown in graphical form in Figure 18.1.

TABLE 18.1 Payoff structure for a bought call with an exercise price of $38.00

IF THE SHARE PRICE ($) ON THE CALL'S EXPIRY DATE IS	THEN THE PAYOFF (CASH FLOW) ($) TO THE CALL HOLDER IS
36.00	0
36.50	0
37.00	0
37.50	0
38.00	0
38.50	0.50
39.00	1.00
39.50	1.50
40.00	2.00
40.50	2.50

FIGURE 18.1 Payoff structure: call (bought)

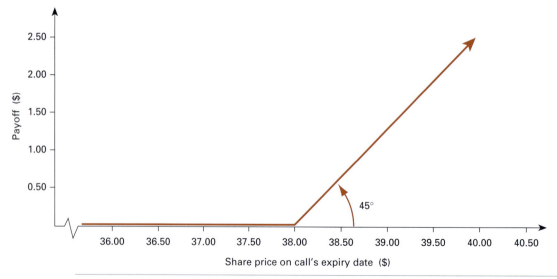

---

[8] Throughout this chapter, an asterisk (*) is used to indicate the value of the variable on the option's expiry date. Note also that in previous chapters we have used the symbol P for the share price. However, in the option pricing literature it is standard to use S for the share price.

The payoff structure for a put option is illustrated using, as an example, the BHP 39.00 put option also discussed in Section 18.2.1. If, on the put's expiry date, the BHP share price is $39 or more, the put will be worth nothing on expiry. There will be no payoff at all. For example, there is no value in having a put that is about to expire and which gives the put holder the right to sell a share for $39 when the market price is already, say, $40 per share. However, if the share price on the expiry date of the put is less than $39, then the payoff is the difference between the exercise price of $39 and the share price. For example, if the share price at the expiry of the put is $37.50, the payoff is $1.50. In summary, the payoff on a put option is:

$$\text{Max}\,[0, X - S^*]$$

where S^* = the share price on the put's expiry date
X = the exercise price of the put

The payoff structure is shown in more detail in Table 18.2. The information in Table 18.2 is shown in graphical form in Figure 18.2.

TABLE 18.2 Payoff structure for a bought put with an exercise price of $39.00

IF THE SHARE PRICE ($) ON THE PUT'S EXPIRY DATE IS	THEN THE PAYOFF (CASH FLOW) ($) TO THE PUT HOLDER IS
36.50	2.50
37.00	2.00
37.50	1.50
38.00	1.00
38.50	0.50
39.00	0
39.50	0
40.00	0
40.50	0

FIGURE 18.2 Payoff structure: put (bought)

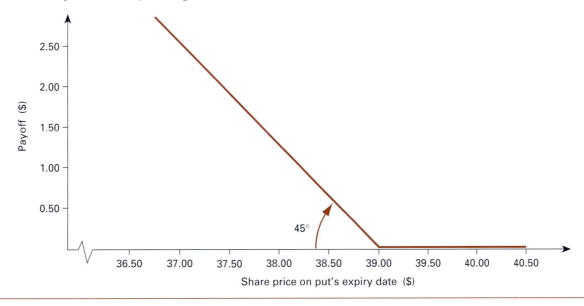

18.2.5 FACTORS AFFECTING CALL OPTION PRICES

The aim of this section is to develop an intuitive understanding of the factors that will affect the price of a call option.[9] Discussion of formal valuation models is undertaken in Sections 18.3 and 18.4.

Table 18.3 shows the prices of selected call options on BHP Billiton shares on 7 and 10 May 2010.

LEARNING OBJECTIVE 2
Identify and explain the factors that affect option prices

TABLE 18.3 Closing prices of selected call options on BHP Billiton shares on Friday 7 May 2010 and Monday 10 May 2010

PANEL A: CALL PRICES ON FRIDAY 7 MAY 2010 (SHARE PRICE = $37.50)			
	EXERCISE PRICES ($)		
EXPIRY DATE	$37.00	$38.00	$39.00
24 June 2010	2.37	1.84	1.42
29 July 2010	2.93	2.39	1.88
26 August 2010	3.29	2.76	2.24

PANEL B: CALL PRICES ON MONDAY 10 MAY 2010 (SHARE PRICE = $39.00)			
	EXERCISE PRICES ($)		
EXPIRY DATE	$37.00	$38.00	$39.00
24 June 2010	3.22	2.54	1.95
29 July 2010	3.80	3.15	2.55
26 August 2010	4.14	3.56	2.99

PANEL C: PERCENTAGE CHANGE IN PRICES FROM FRIDAY 7 MAY 2010 TO MONDAY 10 MAY 2010 (SHARE PRICE CHANGE = 5.4 %)			
	EXERCISE PRICES ($)		
EXPIRY DATE	$37.00	$38.00	$39.00
24 June 2010	36	38	37
29 July 2010	30	32	36
26 August 2010	26	29	33

Source: Compiled from *Thomson Reuters Tick History Database*.

Table 18.3 provides the market prices of nine call options on BHP. Panel A of the table provides the prices of these nine options at the close of trading on Friday 7 May 2010. Panel B provides the prices of these options at the close of business one trading day later. Panel C shows the percentage change in each call price between the two trading days. In the following discussion we use the prices shown in Table 18.3 to illustrate the factors that affect call prices.

Options have value because option buyers can exercise the option to their advantage, should the opportunity to do so arise. A fundamental advantage of holding a call option is that it may be possible to obtain the underlying shares more cheaply by exercising the option than by direct share purchase. Intuitively, the price paid for the right to exercise should therefore reflect, among other factors, the probability that the share price will rise above the exercise price (or rise further above it, if it has already been exceeded). This probability should, in turn, be related to the following factors.

---
9 Similar factors are relevant to the determination of put prices. These are discussed in Section 18.2.6.

The current share price

The higher the current share price, the greater is the probability that the share price will increase above the exercise price, and therefore the higher the call price, other things being equal. Ignoring market imperfections, a call whose underlying share price is already above the exercise price must be worth at least the difference between the two. This amount is the cash flow that will occur if the call is exercised immediately, and is referred to as the call's **intrinsic value**. However, even a call whose exercise price is above the current price of the underlying share must be worth something. It has value as long as there is some chance, however small, that at some point in the call's life the intrinsic value may become positive. In Table 18.3, every call commands a price that is greater than its intrinsic value. For example, on 7 May, the intrinsic value of the June 37.00 call is 50 cents, and its price is $2.37. The dependence of the call price on the current share price can be seen in the fact that all six calls increased in price when there was an increase in the price of the underlying shares. Note also that the magnitude of the percentage increases for the call prices far exceeds the percentage increase of 5.4 per cent in the share price—that is, the leverage offered by call options is very high.

intrinsic value
value of an option if exercised immediately

The exercise price

Clearly, the higher the exercise price, the lower is the probability that the share price will increase above the exercise price, and, therefore, the lower the call price, other things being equal. This relationship can be seen in the prices given in Table 18.3. On both 7 May and 10 May, for any given expiry date, the call price falls when we consider higher exercise prices. For example, on 7 May, the price of the options expiring in June is $2.37 when the exercise price is $37, falling to $1.84 when the exercise price is $38 and finally just $1.42 when the exercise price is $39.

The term to expiry

The longer the term to expiry, the greater is the probability that the share price will increase above the exercise price. Therefore, the longer the term to expiry, the greater is the call price, other things being equal. To make the same point in a slightly different way, consider two American calls that are equivalent in every respect, except that one has a shorter term to expiry than the other. In the period before the expiry of the shorter-term call, both calls provide the option buyer with the same rights. However, the rights conferred by the longer-term call continue for a further period. Therefore, the longer-term call is more valuable. The amount of the call price over and above any intrinsic value is called the **time value**, since with all other factors constant it will be greater, the longer the term to expiry. Note, however, that term to expiry is only one factor determining the time value. It should also be distinguished from the 'time value of money', which is dealt with below. This effect of term to expiry on call price can also be seen in the prices given in Table 18.3. On both 7 May and 10 May, for any given exercise price, the call price increases when we consider later expiry dates. For example, on 10 May, the price of the options with an exercise price of $37 is $3.22 for the options expiring in June, rising to $3.80 for the options expiring in July and then to $4.14 for the August series.

time value
value of an option in excess of its intrinsic value

The volatility of the share

The **volatility** of a share is the variability of its price over time.[10] The effect of volatility on call price is illustrated in the following simple example. Consider a high volatility share, H, whose current price is $5, and a low volatility share, L, whose current price is also $5. Consider call options on H and L at a moment before expiry. The exercise price of both call options is $5. As explained previously, calls at expiry are worth a positive amount if the difference between the share price and the exercise price is

volatility
variability of a share price; can be measured by the variance (or the standard deviation) of the distribution of returns on the share

---

10 Volatility can be measured in various ways. One frequently used measure is the variance of the returns on the share in a recent period.

positive. Otherwise they are worth zero. Suppose further that the probabilities of various share prices at expiry are known to be those shown in Table 18.4.

TABLE 18.4 Probability distributions for shares H and L

	SHARE H			SHARE L	
SHARE PRICE ($)	PROBABILITY	VALUE OF CALL ($)	SHARE PRICE ($)	PROBABILITY	VALUE OF CALL ($)
4.00	0.2	0.00	4.00	0.04	0.00
4.50	0.2	0.00	4.50	0.16	0.00
5.00	0.2	0.00	5.00	0.60	0.00
5.50	0.2	0.50	5.50	0.16	0.50
6.00	0.2	1.00	6.00	0.04	1.00

The expected values of the calls on shares H and L are:

E (call on H) = (0.2)($0.50) + (0.2)($1.00) = $0.30

E (call on L) = (0.16)($0.50) + (0.04)($1.00) = $0.12

The call on the low-volatility share is less valuable than the call on the high-volatility share. This result is not peculiar to this particular example and it has been shown (Merton 1973a, p. 149) that, other things being equal, calls on high-volatility shares are worth more than calls on low-volatility shares.

The basic reason for this result is the asymmetric nature of the payoffs on a call option. As shown in Table 18.4, when a call expires, the holder is indifferent between all the share prices that are less than or equal to the exercise price. All such share prices are equally disastrous for the call holder because in all such cases the value of the call is zero. However, at expiry, for share prices that exceed the exercise price, the value of the call increases by 1 cent for every 1-cent increase in the share price. At times before expiry this asymmetry is not as sharp, but it remains true that the holder of a call benefits more from, say, a 1-cent increase in share price than is lost from a 1-cent decrease in share price. While a higher share price volatility increases the chance of both large increases and large decreases in the share price, the asymmetric features just described mean that the holder of a call gains more from the increased chance of a large increase in share price than is lost from the increased chance of a large decrease in share price. Therefore, on balance, the call holder has a favourable view of volatility. Higher volatility increases the price of a call, other things being equal.

The risk-free interest rate

The buyer of a call option can defer paying for the shares. (Of course, the call also confers the right not to buy the shares at all, but this is not the point we are making.) Because interest rates are positive, money has a time value, so the right to defer payment is valuable. The higher the interest rate, the more valuable is this right. Therefore, it is plausible to suggest that the higher the risk-free interest rate, the higher is the price of a call, other things being equal.

Expected dividends

It was explained in Section 11.4.4 that when a company pays a dividend the share price will fall on the ex-dividend date. It has already been explained in this chapter that the price of a call will decrease if the price of the underlying share decreases. It is to be expected, therefore, that a call on a share that will go ex-dividend before the expiry of the call is worth less than if the share either never pays dividends or, if it does pay dividends, will not reach the next ex-dividend date until after the call has expired. In short, calls on shares that pay high dividends during the life of the call are worth less than calls on shares that pay low dividends during the life of the call, other things being equal.

The effect of dividends on call price may be reduced, though not eliminated, if the option is of the 'American' type.[11] As mentioned in Section 18.2.1, this type of option may be exercised at any time before expiry. By exercising just before an ex-dividend date, the holder of a call becomes a shareholder and is therefore entitled to the dividend. The cost of this strategy is that the call's expiry date is, in effect, shifted to the ex-dividend date, thereby reducing its effective term to expiry. As explained earlier, a shorter term to expiry reduces the time value of a call and hence reduces its price. Therefore, in deciding whether a call should be exercised before an ex-dividend date, the call holder needs to balance carefully the benefit of obtaining the dividend against the cost of forfeiting the option's time value.

To summarise, other things being equal, call prices should be higher (lower):

(a) the higher (lower) the current share price
(b) the lower (higher) the exercise price
(c) the longer (shorter) the term to expiry
(d) the more (less) volatile the underlying share
(e) the higher (lower) the risk-free interest rate
(f) the lower (higher) the expected dividend to be paid following an ex-dividend date that occurs during the term of the call.

18.2.6 SOME BASIC FEATURES OF PUT OPTION PRICING

The buyer of a put option obtains the right to sell shares at the exercise price. The higher the exercise price, the more the buyer of the put stands to gain. For example, the right to sell a share for $1 is more valuable than the right to sell for only 90 cents, other things being equal. Therefore, for put options, the higher the exercise price, the higher is the price of the option. For call options the opposite is true. Similarly, the right to sell a share at a fixed price is less valuable the higher the current share price, other things being equal. For example, suppose that the holder of a put exercised her right to sell a share at the exercise price of $1. If the current share price is 90 cents, the holder of the put gains 10 cents because she has been able to sell the share for 10 cents more than it is currently worth. If the share price had been higher—say, 95 cents—the gain would have been only 5 cents. Therefore, higher share prices imply lower put prices, other things being equal. For call options, the opposite is true.

The relationship between price and term to expiry is straightforward in the case of American puts. Consider two American puts, equivalent in all respects except that one has a longer term to expiry. Both puts may be exercised at any time up to (and including) their respective expiry dates. Therefore, the long-term put permits exercise at all times permitted by the short-term put, but in addition the long-term put permits exercise after the expiry of the short-term put. Therefore, for American puts, a longer term to expiry increases the value of the put, other things being equal.[12] This is also true of call options.

---

11 European-type options may contain a clause that adjusts the contract's terms if there is a dividend. These 'dividend protection clauses', as they are known, also reduce, but do not eliminate, the effects of dividends on the call's price.

12 For a European put, the relationship between price and the term to expiry is more complex. On the one hand, a short-term European put can be exercised earlier than an otherwise equivalent long-term European put, therefore generating an earlier cash inflow for the holder of the put. This suggests that a short-term European put is *more* valuable than a long-term European put. On the other hand, a longer term to expiry increases the probability that the share price will fall below the exercise price, and this suggests that a short-term European put is *less* valuable than a long-term European put. For any given European put, both factors are relevant and either influence can dominate the other, depending on the put being considered.

Table 18.5 shows the prices of selected put options on BHP Billiton (BHP) shares on Friday 7 May 2010 and Monday 10 May 2010.

TABLE 18.5 Closing prices of selected put options on BHP Billiton (BHP) shares on Friday 7 May 2010 and Monday 10 May 2010

PANEL A: PUT PRICES ON FRIDAY 7 MAY 2010 (SHARE PRICE = $37.50)			
	EXERCISE PRICES ($)		
EXPIRY DATE	$37.00	$38.00	$39.00
24 June 2010	1.69	2.12	2.67
29 July 2010	2.10	2.53	3.05
26 August 2010	2.33	2.78	3.29

PANEL B: PUT PRICES ON MONDAY 10 MAY 2010 (SHARE PRICE = $39.00)			
	EXERCISE PRICES ($)		
EXPIRY DATE	$37.00	$38.00	$39.00
24 June 2010	1.00	1.35	1.74
29 July 2010	1.45	1.80	2.19
26 August 2010	1.71	2.05	2.49

PANEL C: PERCENTAGE CHANGE IN PRICES FROM FRIDAY 7 MAY 2010 TO MONDAY 10 MAY 2010 (SHARE PRICE CHANGE = 5.4 %)			
	EXERCISE PRICES ($)		
EXPIRY DATE	$37.00	$38.00	$39.00
24 June 2010	−41	−36	−35
29 July 2010	−31	−29	−28
26 August 2010	−27	−26	−24

Source: Compiled from *IRESS Financial Database*.

The influences of exercise price and term to expiry can be seen in the put prices given in Table 18.5. On both trading dates, for any given expiry date, the put price is higher, the higher is the exercise price. For example, on 7 May, the price of the June 39.00 exceeds that of the June 38.00, which in turn exceeds that of the June 37.00. These prices illustrate that, other things being equal, a higher exercise price implies a higher put price. Comparing puts of different terms, it is also clear that a longer term implies a higher put price, other things being equal. On both trading dates, for any given exercise price, the put price is higher, the longer is the term to expiry. For example, on 7 May 2010, the price of the June 37.00 put is $1.69, while the price of the July 37.00 is $2.10.

The effect of the share price on the prices of put options is also clearly evident in Table 18.5. On Monday 10 May the share price was higher than it had been on the previous Friday and, as a result, all put prices had decreased on that day. As with calls, the percentage changes in the put prices exceed the percentage change in the share price. Unlike a call, a put has a maximum possible value. For example, in the case of the July 38.00 put in Table 18.5, even if the price of BHP shares should fall to zero, the payoff to the holder of the put cannot exceed $38. Because share prices can never fall below zero, a put can never be worth more than its exercise price.

The buyer of a put option will gain if share prices fall. Consequently, puts are especially attractive to shareholders who fear that the share price may decrease, but who nevertheless do not wish to sell their shares. Consider, for example, an investor who on 7 May 2010 bought a BHP share for $37.50 and a BHP June 37.00 put for $1.69, making a total outlay of $39.19. The put option ensures that, until it expires in June, the investor is guaranteed that he or she will not have to sell their shares for less than $37 per share. Thus if the share price decreased to, say, $33—which represents a loss of $4.50 or 12 per cent of the share price of $37.50—this investor will be able to sell at $37 and thus will lose only $2.19 or 5.6 per cent of the total outlay of $39.19. In effect, the purchase of a put is like buying an insurance policy against the share price falling below a given level.

As with call options, higher share volatility implies a higher option price. Higher volatility implies a greater chance of large increases and large decreases in the share price. From the put holder's viewpoint, share price increases are bad news, while decreases are good news. But a put holder gains more from a share price decrease than is lost from an increase of the same amount. So, on balance, a put holder has a favourable view of share price volatility.

Because a put confers the right to receive a future cash inflow, it is expected that put prices should be negatively related to interest rates. A higher interest rate reduces the present value of whatever future cash inflow may be received. Finally, dividend payments reduce share prices, which benefits put holders, so higher expected dividend payments increase put prices.

The effects for American calls and puts are summarised in Table 18.6. Positive (negative) means the option price responds in the same (opposite) direction to a change in the factor affecting prices.

TABLE 18.6 Factors affecting American option prices

FACTOR	CALL PRICES	PUT PRICES
Current share price	Positive	Negative
Exercise price	Negative	Positive
Term to expiry	Positive	Positive
Volatility of the share	Positive	Positive
Risk-free interest rate	Positive	Negative
Expected dividends	Negative	Positive

18.2.7 PUT–CALL PARITY

For European options on shares that do not pay dividends there is an equilibrium relationship between the prices of puts and calls that are written on the same underlying share, are traded simultaneously and have the same exercise price and term to expiry. This relationship, known as **put–call parity**, was derived by Stoll (1969) and subsequently analysed further by Merton (1973b). We now derive and explain this relationship.

It is assumed that options are traded in frictionless markets and that no security (or portfolio) dominates any other security (or portfolio). The meaning of 'dominance' in this context may be illustrated as follows. Suppose that on some future date there can be only three possible sets of market conditions or 'states of the world', and the payoffs on securities (or portfolios) A and B in these states will be as shown in Table 18.7.

LEARNING OBJECTIVE 3

Understand and apply basic option pricing theorems, including put–call parity

put–call parity relationship that exists between the price of a call option and the price of the corresponding put option

TABLE 18.7 Payoffs showing a dominant portfolio

PORTFOLIO	PAYOFF ($) IN:		
	STATE 1	STATE 2	STATE 3
A	5	7	11
B	5	7	10

If A and B sell for the same price today, then A dominates B because A pays the same as B in States 1 and 2, but pays more than B in State 3. Therefore, to prevent dominance, the price of A today must be greater than the price of B. Formally, A dominates B if, on some known date in the future, the payoff on A is greater than the payoff on B in one (or more) of the possible states, and the payoff on A is at least as great as the payoff on B in all other possible states. A special case of the no-dominance requirement arises if A and B have the same payoff in all possible states. In that case A and B must command the same price today. If the market is perfect, a no-dominance requirement is equivalent to a requirement that no arbitrage opportunities exist.

Using these assumptions, it can be shown that the following relationship, known as put–call parity, exists between put and call prices:

$$p = c - S + \frac{X}{1+r'} \qquad [18.1]$$

where p = the price of the European put
c = the price of the corresponding European call
S = the share price
X = the exercise price
r' = the risk-free interest rate for borrowing or lending for a period equal to the term of the put and the call

Expressed in words, put–call parity says that the put price equals the call price, less the share price, plus the present value (at the risk-free interest rate for the term of the option) of the exercise price.

TABLE 18.8 Payoffs showing put–call parity

PORTFOLIO	VALUE NOW	PAYOFF IN STATE 1 ($S^* \geq X$)	PAYOFF IN STATE 2 ($S^* < X$)
A	$c + \dfrac{X}{1+r'}$	$(S^* - X) + X = S^*$	$0 + X = X$
B	$p + S$	$0 + S^* = S^*$	$(X - S^*) + S^* = X$

To prove that Equation 18.1 holds, consider two portfolios, A and B. The composition and payoffs of these portfolios are shown in Table 18.8. Portfolio A consists of the call, plus an investment of $\dfrac{X}{1+r'}$ dollars invested at the risk-free rate, to mature on the expiry date of the put and the call. Therefore, the cash outflow required to set up Portfolio A is $c + \dfrac{X}{1+r'}$. Portfolio B consists of the put plus one share. The outflow required to set up Portfolio B is therefore $p + S$. As both options are European, they cannot be exercised before expiry, and the relevant 'states of the world' are as follows: State 1 is a share price that is greater than or equal to the exercise price ($S^* \geq X$) and State 2 is a share price that is less than the exercise price ($S^* < X$). If State 1 occurs, then the call is worth $S^* - X$ and the put is worth zero. If State 2 occurs, then the call is worth zero and the put is worth $X - S^*$. In either state, the risk-free investment will mature with a value of:

$$\left(\frac{X}{1+r'}\right)(1+r') = X$$

If State 1 occurs, then both A and B have a payoff of S^*, but if State 2 occurs, then both A and B have a payoff of X. Therefore, there is no reason to prefer A to B (or vice versa). Therefore, to prevent dominance, A and B must command the same price now—that is, the cost of A and B must always be equal. This requires that:

$$c + \left[\frac{X}{1+r'}\right] = p + S$$

Rearranging this expression gives Equation 18.1.

This theorem has three important implications. First, if a formula can be derived to price, say, a European call, then by using Equation 18.1, a formula can be derived to price the equivalent put. Second, Equation 18.1 does not include the expected return on the underlying share, implying that the expected return is not directly relevant to pricing puts or calls. For example, suppose that an investor expects the price of the underlying share to increase in the near future. Obviously such an investor is likely to buy a call, and sell a put. It is tempting—but incorrect—to suggest that this action will tend to increase the call price (because the demand for calls has increased) and decrease the put price (because the supply of puts has increased). But if this happened, Equation 18.1 would be violated and a profitable arbitrage would exist. Therefore, the expected return on the share is not directly relevant to option pricing. Third, if the expected future volatility of the share increases, without a simultaneous change in the level of today's share price, then the prices of all puts and calls on the share should also increase (see Finance in Action). Put–call parity should hold true both before and after a change in volatility.

Investors' expectations of the future direction of a share price are relevant to the determination of the share price itself—that is, the share price will reflect the influence of these expectations. Therefore these expectations *are* relevant to option pricing but *only* via their influence on the share price itself. They have no independent role to play. This conclusion has great significance for attempts to construct formulae to price options because it implies that these formulae do not need to include a measure of expectations of the future direction of the share price. Such measurements are notoriously difficult to make.

VOLATILITY IS THE KEY TO PRICE MOVEMENTS

If a company's future suddenly looks more uncertain, the share market will expect its future share price volatility to be higher. In principle, this should mean that both put and call options on the shares should increase in price. Nice theory … but does it really work that way in practice? Yes, it does!

The rumour last week that Brambles was a takeover target caused its shares to rise and Brambles' volatility to jump in the derivatives markets. Most Brambles derivative sellers, option writers and warrant issuers immediately began asking more money for shorter-dated options and warrants over shares in the troubled company. This included both puts and calls, although shorter-dated calls (October and December expiries) were the highest priced in terms of implied volatility.

The sellers were asking more on the logical expectation of greater uncertainty in the Brambles share price while the rumour persists. The extent of this uncertainty can be assessed from a close examination of the implied volatility expectations over Brambles at- or close-to-the-money options from just under 30 points to just under 35 points over the week.

Source: John Wasiliev, 'Volatility is the key to price movements', *Australian Financial Review*, 24 September 2003.

FINANCE IN ACTION

The put–call parity theorem applies only to European options, whereas, in practice, most options are of the American type. While there is no simple equation linking the values of American puts and calls, upper and lower bounds have been established, as shown below:

$$c - S + \frac{X}{1+r''} \leq p \leq c - S + X \qquad [18.2]$$

where p = the price of the American put
   c = the price of the corresponding American call
   S = the share price
   X = the exercise price
   r = the risk-free interest rate for borrowing

In effect, the lower bound in Equation 18.2 matches the result for European put–call parity, while the upper bound exceeds this lower bound by the difference between the exercise price and the present value of the exercise price. When the risk-free interest rate for borrowing is low and/or the term of the options is short, the present value effect will be small and hence the gap between the upper and lower bounds will also be small.[13]

Loudon (1988) studied approximately 1300 pairs of prices for BHP puts and calls in 1985 and concluded that although violations of put–call parity were not uncommon, investors facing normal transaction costs would be unable to profit from the violations. More recently, Ofek, Richardson and Whitelaw (2004) tested for violations of put–call parity for approximately 80 000 matched pairs of options trading on US exchanges between 1999 and 2001 and report that the parity relationship is frequently violated and that profitable strategies could be employed even after accounting for transaction costs.

18.2.8 THE MINIMUM VALUE OF CALLS AND PUTS

Assuming frictionless markets and the same no-dominance framework used earlier to derive the put–call parity theorem, the minimum value of a European call on a share that does not pay dividends is:

$$\text{Min } c = \text{Max}\left[0, S - \frac{X}{1+r'}\right] \qquad [18.3]$$

To prove this equation, consider two portfolios, A and B′. Their composition and payoffs are shown in Table 18.9. As in the proof of put–call parity, Portfolio A consists of the call and a risk-free investment of $\frac{X}{1+r'}$ dollars. Portfolio B′ consists of just one share. The two relevant states are again State 1 ($S^* \geq X$) and State 2 ($S^* < X$).

TABLE 18.9 Payoffs showing the minimum value of a call option

PORTFOLIO	VALUE NOW	PAYOFF IN STATE 1 ($S^* \geq X$)	PAYOFF IN STATE 2 ($S^* < X$)
A	$c + \frac{X}{1+r'}$	$(S^* - X) + X = S^*$	$0 + X = X$
B′	S	S^*	S^*

The explanation of the entries in the table for Portfolio A is the same as in the proof of put–call parity. Portfolio B′, which consists of only the share, pays off S^* regardless of the state that occurs. Therefore, if State 1 occurs, both A and B′ have a payoff of S^*, but if State 2 occurs, then A pays off more than B′

---

[13] For a detailed treatment of put–call parity under a range of conditions, see Cox and Rubinstein (1985).

because in that state, $X > S^*$. Invoking the no-dominance assumption, it follows that the value of A must therefore be no less than the value of B′ at all times before the call expires—that is:

$$c + \frac{X}{1+r'} \geq S$$

which implies that:

$$c \geq S - \frac{X}{1+r'}$$

The right-hand side of this inequality can be negative but, because of limited liability, call prices can never be negative—that is, $c \geq 0$. Combining these two inequalities gives Equation 18.3.

This result has an important implication: in the absence of dividends, American call options should not be exercised before expiry. Clearly the holder of an American call would not even consider exercise unless the share price, S, exceeded the exercise price, X. Suppose that $S > X$ and the holder of an American call has decided to dispose of the call. To do so a choice must be made between exercising the call and selling the call. However, this choice is easy. If the call is exercised, the payoff (or, net cash flow) is $S - X$ but if the call is sold, then, by Equation 18.3, the payoff is *at least* $S - \frac{X}{1+r'}$, which will exceed $S - X$ provided only that the interest rate is positive. Given that interest rates are always positive, the payoff from selling the call must exceed the payoff from exercising the call. It follows that an American call will never be exercised early and, accordingly, the right to do so is valueless. The call might just as well be European. Under the conditions we have assumed, the distinction between European calls and American calls is irrelevant to their valuation.

At first sight this conclusion may be surprising, but it has an intuitive explanation. If a call is exercised early, the option's life is cut short, so the call holder forfeits any time value the option had. One reason call options have a time value is that interest rates are positive, so later cash outflows are preferred to early cash outflows. By exercising early, the call holder must pay for the shares earlier than would otherwise have been necessary. Thus, if a call holder has decided to dispose of the option, he or she should always prefer to sell the call rather than exercise it.

The rule against early exercise does not necessarily hold if an ex-dividend date will occur during the life of the call. As mentioned in Section 18.2.5, early exercise of an American call can be rational in these circumstances. Traditionally it has been thought that early exercise of a call would be rational only on the date immediately preceding the ex-dividend date; at all other times, selling the call will generate a greater cash flow for a call holder who wishes dispose of the option. More recently however, Alpert (2010) has demonstrated that tax effects can overturn this conclusion—that is, the after-tax cash flow from selling the call may be less than the after-tax cash flow from exercising the call. Using a sample of UK options, Alpert finds empirical evidence to suggest that many exercises that appear irrational in a no-tax framework may be rational if tax effects are considered. Using similar methodology, Phang and Brown (forthcoming) study 454 instances of the early exercise of call options in the Australian market. They find that approximately two-thirds of these instances occurred on the day immediately preceding the ex-dividend date. They also report that approximately 80 per cent of the remaining instances of early exercise may be explained by option holders making their exercise decision on the basis of maximising their after tax cash flows.

The minimum value of a European put can be found by combining put–call parity (Equation 18.1) and the minimum value of a European call (Equation 18.3). The result is:

$$\text{Min } p = \text{Max}\left[0, \frac{X}{1+r'} - S\right] \qquad [18.4]$$

However, unlike the case of calls, the expression for the minimum value of a European put cannot be used to show that the distinction between American and European options is irrelevant for puts, even in the absence of dividends. It can be rational to exercise an American put before expiry, and therefore American puts are worth more than their European counterparts. Again there is an intuitive explanation. If a put is exercised, two things happen. First, as with calls, the option's time value is forfeited and this outcome is undesirable. Second, the put holder is paid for the shares earlier than would otherwise be the case. Because early cash inflows are preferred to later cash inflows, this outcome is desirable. In some circumstances—for example, if the current share price is very low and interest rates are very high—the second effect outweighs the first, and in these cases the right to exercise early is valuable.

18.3 BINOMIAL OPTION PRICING

So far we have developed some logical bounds on option prices. For example, we have established that the price of a long-term American option should exceed that of its short-term counterpart. Similarly, we have established that a put option can never be worth more than the exercise price. While these sorts of relationships are useful, they do not answer the fundamental question we want to ask about any given option: how much (*exactly*) is it worth? That is, what should be its price?

Binomial option pricing is an important and widely used approach to answering this question. Binomial option pricing was first suggested by William Sharpe, and developed in an article by Cox, Ross and Rubinstein (1979). In this section we present the main features of their model.[14]

LEARNING OBJECTIVE 4

Understand the binomial model and the Black–Scholes model of option pricing and calculate option prices using these models

18.3.1 THE BASIC IDEA: PRICING A SINGLE-PERIOD CALL OPTION USING THE BINOMIAL APPROACH

The distinguishing feature of binomial option pricing is its assumption that, after a given time period, the price of the underlying asset can be one of only two numbers—hence the use of the term 'binomial', which means 'two numbers'. This assumption may sound unrealistic, but it turns out that the approach gives very realistic answers, provided that a large number of short time periods are used in the analysis. However, in this section we restrict ourselves to the single-period case, which, although clearly unrealistic, permits a clear illustration of basic principles. We explain these principles using Example 18.1.

EXAMPLE 18.1

Consider a 1-year call option with a $10.50 exercise price, on a share whose current price is $10. It is known that in 1 year's time the share price will be either $11.50 or $9.50. No other share price outcome is possible: the share price will definitely be one of these two numbers. The 1-year risk-free interest rate is 8 per cent per annum.

Using only this information, together with the standard assumption that arbitrage will not be possible, we can work out what today's call price should be. To do this, we first calculate the payoffs. If, at the expiry of the call in 1 year's time, the share price is $11.50, the call's payoff will be $11.50 − $10.50 = $1. If the other share price ($9.50) occurs, the call's payoff will be zero. We now compare the payoffs on Portfolios A and B:

Portfolio A: Buy two calls, each costing c dollars.
Portfolio B: Buy one share ($10) and borrow $9.50/1.08 = $8.80, which is the present value of $9.50.

The payoffs on these portfolios are shown in Table 18.10.

TABLE 18.10 Payoffs for a single-period binomial model

PORTFOLIO	CASH FLOW NOW	PAYOFF IF $P^* = \$9.50$	PAYOFF IF $P^* = \$11.50$
A: Buy 2 calls	−2c	0	$ 2.00
B: Buy 1 share	−$10.00	$9.50	$11.50

WWW

14 The ASX website provides a link to a calculator that will estimate option prices using the binomial model; see www.asx.com.au/resources/calculators/index.htm.

PORTFOLIO	CASH FLOW NOW	PAYOFF IF $P^* = \$9.50$	PAYOFF IF $P^* = \$11.50$
Borrow $9.50/1.08	+$8.80	−$9.50	−$9.50
Total (B)	−$1.20	0	$2.00

The payoffs shown in Table 18.10 are identical. It does not matter whether an investor chooses Portfolio A or B: the outcome in both cases is a cash flow of zero if the expiry share price is $9.50, or a cash flow of $2 if the expiry share price is $11.50. Since A and B are, in effect, the same thing, they should be worth the same today. To prevent arbitrage, the cash flow required today to set up Portfolio A should equal the cash flow required today to set up Portfolio B—that is:

$$-2c = -\$1.20$$

which, of course, solves to give today's call price, c, of $0.60.[15]

Example 18.1 illustrates the fact that buying calls (Portfolio A) is like borrowing to buy shares (Portfolio B). In Example 18.1, buying two calls was like borrowing to buy one share. We could equally well describe this as 'buying one call is like borrowing to buy half a share'. Of course, the figure of one-half is peculiar to this example. It is found by calculating the ratio of the option spread and the share spread—in this case the calculation is:

$$\frac{\$1 - \$0}{\$11.50 - \$9.50}$$

$$= \frac{1}{2}$$

In other cases, this ratio could be any number between zero and 1. This ratio is called the **hedge ratio or delta**. Estimates of option deltas are provided in the Market Wrap section of the *Australian Financial Review*.

hedge ratio or delta ratio of the change in an option price that results from a change in the price of the underlying asset

18.3.2 RISK NEUTRALITY AS A SOLUTION METHOD

Perhaps the most remarkable feature of Example 18.1 is not that we could work out the call price, but that we were able to do so without making any assumption about risk. The call in Example 18.1 is worth 60 cents, regardless of the risk preferences of traders in the market. If, for example, everyone in the market were risk averse, they would set the call price at 60 cents. If everyone were risk neutral (or for that matter, risk seeking) they would still set the call price at 60 cents.[16]

We can use this fact to provide an easy solution method. We *pretend* that all investors are **risk neutral**. This means that they ignore risk in their decision making. In a market comprising only risk-neutral traders, all assets are priced so that they are expected to yield the risk-free return. In a risk-neutral world, pricing assets is thus very easy. It is simply a matter of finding out the expected value of a future cash flow and then discounting this value at the risk-free interest rate. We reiterate that our answer does not depend on risk neutrality. We would get the same answer for the call price if we assumed, say, risk aversion. We choose risk neutrality only because it is easy. To illustrate how the method works we show in Example 18.2 how the call option in Example 18.1 would be priced if every trader were risk neutral.

risk neutrality situation in which investors are indifferent to risk; assets are therefore priced such that they are expected to yield the risk-free interest rate

---

15 We have rounded this answer. A more accurate answer is: $\frac{1}{2}\left(\$10 - \frac{\$9.50}{1.08}\right) = \$0.60\,185\,185$.

16 How is this possible? Essentially, the reason is that we could redesign Portfolios A and B to give two risk-free outcomes. Regardless of individual differences in attitudes to risk, all market participants will agree that risk-free is indeed risk-free and will price the portfolios accordingly.

EXAMPLE 18.2

A share is worth $10 today and promises to pay off either $11.50 or $9.50 in 1 year's time. We will call the payoff of $11.50 'State U' (for 'up') and the payoff of $9.50 'State D' (for 'down'). Given that this is a risk-neutral world, we can deduce the probabilities of States U and D occurring. This deduction is possible because, under risk neutrality, $10 must equal the expected payoff in 1 year, discounted for 1 year at the risk-free interest rate—that is:

$$\$10 = \frac{p(\$11.50) + (1-p)(\$9.50)}{1.08}$$

where p = the probability of State U occurring
$1-p$ = the probability of State D occurring

Solving this equation gives $p = 0.65$ and $1 - p = 0.35$.[17]

Turning our attention to the call option, its payoff is $1 in State U and $0 in State D. In a world of risk neutrality, the call price, c, will also equal its expected payoff, discounted at the risk-free interest rate:

$$c = \frac{(0.65)(\$1) + (0.35)(\$0)}{1.08}$$

$$\approx \$0.601\,851\,85$$

$$\approx \$0.60$$

This, of course, is the same answer as we found in Example 18.1 when we did not pretend that all market participants were risk neutral.

18.3.3 BINOMIAL OPTION PRICING WITH MANY TIME PERIODS

The single-period case is not realistic, but the basic principles can be extended to more than one period. In practice it is usual to use, say, 100 or 200 time periods. The calculations are readily made using a computer. To explain the procedures, we use three time periods.

The solution to a multi-period binomial option-pricing problem has three major stages.

(a) Stage 1: Building up a lattice of share prices.
(b) Stage 2: Calculating the option payoffs at expiry from the expiry share prices.
(c) Stage 3: Calculating option prices by calculating expected values and then discounting at the risk-free interest rate.

These stages are explained in Example 18.3.

EXAMPLE 18.3

We wish to value a three-month call option with an exercise price of $10.25. The current share price is $10 and the risk-free interest rate is 1.5 per cent per month. We use three time periods of 1 month each. It is assumed that at the end of each month the share price can move to only one of two values.

Stage 1: The lattice of share prices

In Stage 1, our objective is to lay out all the future share prices that can arise, given our assumptions. In this example it is assumed that each month the share price can rise by 4 per cent or fall by 3.846 per cent. Our choice of 3.846 per cent is, of course, deliberate, and is equal to $1 - 1/1.04$. The effect is that a rise (fall) in the share price in any given month will be exactly offset if there is a fall (rise) in the following month. For example, starting from $10, if the share price rises by 4 per cent in the first month, and then falls by 3.846 per cent in the second month, its price after 2 months is:

---

[17] A warning: these probabilities *do* depend on risk neutrality. They are not the probability of any actual event occurring in the real world.

$10.00(1.04)(1 - 0.038\,46)$

$= \$10.00(1.04)\left(\dfrac{1}{1.04}\right)$

$= \$10.00$

The benefit of defining the 'up' and 'down' states in this way is the dramatic reduction in the number of future possible share prices that need to be considered.

In Figure 18.3, the possible future share prices are shown on a lattice diagram in **bold** type. We have labelled each node of the lattice with a capital letter. Today is represented by node A. Nodes B and C represent the two possible share prices at the end of the first month:

- If the share price increases in the first month: $10.00 x 1.04, then B = $10.40.
- If the share price decreases in the first month: $10.00/1.04, then C = $9.6154.

FIGURE 18.3   Lattice of share prices and call prices

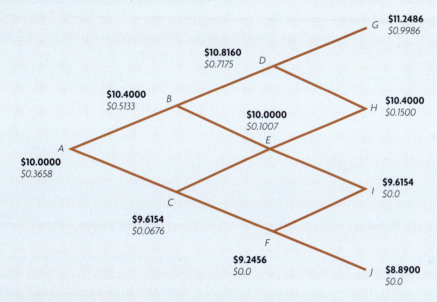

Similarly, nodes D, E and F represent the three possible share prices at the end of the second month:

- If the share price increases in the first month and increases again in the second month: $10.00 x 1.04 x 1.04, then D = $10.8160.
- If the share price increases (decreases) in the first month and then decreases (increases) in the second month: $10.00 x 1.04/1.04, then E = $10.00.
- If the share price decreases in the first month and decreases again in the second month: $10.00/1.04/1.04, then F = $9.2456.

Nodes G, H, I and J represent the four possible share prices at the expiry date of the call and are derived from nodes D, E and F by multiplying or dividing by 1.04 as appropriate.

Stage 2: Option payoffs at expiry

As we know the expiry share prices from Stage 1, it is a simple matter to calculate the matching call option payoffs. Because the exercise price is $10.25, the call's payoffs are $0.9986 if the expiry share price

continued →

Example 18.3 *continued*

is $11.2486 (node G); $0.15 if the expiry share price is $10.40 (node H); and zero if the expiry share price is $9.6154 (node I) or $8.89 (node J). The call's payoffs are shown on Figure 18.3 in *italic* type.

Stage 3: Discounting

Using the risk-neutral solution method, it is a simple matter to calculate the present value of the call's payoffs. As in the single-period example, we first need to find the probabilities of a rising and falling share price. The risk-neutral probabilities are the same at every node. Taking node B as an example, $10.40 must equal the discounted expected value, where the discounting is done at the risk-free interest rate of 1.5 per cent per month:

$$\$10.40 = \frac{(p)(\$10.816) + (1-p)(\$10.00)}{1.015}$$

where, as before, p is the probability of a rise in price and $1-p$ is the probability of a fall. This equation solves to give $p = 0.6814$ and $1-p = 0.3186$.

We can now work back through the lattice from expiry to the present, at each node calculating the present value of the expected payoff. For example, at node D, the call's price is:

$$\frac{(0.6814)(\$0.9986) + (0.3186)(\$0.15)}{1.015}$$
$$= \$0.7175$$

Similarly, at node E, the call's price is:

$$\frac{(0.6814)(\$0.15) + (0.3186)(\$0)}{1.015}$$
$$= \$0.1007$$

Working back through the lattice to today (node A) gives the call's price as $0.3658 or about 37 cents.

Example 18.3 is a realistic treatment of a binomial option pricing problem in all but two respects. First, the number of time periods was set at only three, whereas it should be set at 30 or more to get an accurate answer. However, this accuracy is achieved simply by using a computer to perform the calculations. No new issue of principle is involved. Second, we made no attempt to justify our choice of 'up' and 'down' factors of 4 per cent per month and 3.846 per cent per month, respectively. In practice, these factors are selected very carefully. Typically, the model user decides on what is thought to be an accurate estimate of the standard deviation of the distribution of share prices on the expiry date of the option. In other words, it is necessary to forecast the volatility of share returns during the life of the option. A simple formula then provides the 'up' and 'down' factors that will produce a distribution of expiry share prices that has the desired standard deviation. For example, the 'up' factor is given by $e^{\sigma\sqrt{\Delta t}}$ where σ is the standard deviation and Δt the length of each time period.[18]

18.3.4 APPLYING THE BINOMIAL APPROACH TO OTHER OPTION PROBLEMS

So far we have discussed the binomial approach for the case of a call option on a share that does not pay dividends. Fortunately, it is easy to use the binomial approach to value put options and the binomial model can also be modified to incorporate dividends.

---

18 Details are beyond the scope of this book. For an excellent treatment see Hull (2010).

Once the lattice of future share prices is laid out, a put option can be priced as easily as a call option. The put option payoffs are calculated and then the same procedure of discounting expected values is undertaken. Moreover, the 'American' feature is easily incorporated simply by checking, at each node, whether the calculated option price is less than the payoff from immediate exercise. If it is, then the payoff value is substituted for the calculated price.

Similarly, the problem of valuing options on dividend-paying shares is relatively easy to handle using the binomial approach. At the ex-dividend date, all possible share prices are reduced to reflect the payment of the dividend. A practical difficulty here is that the lattice no longer conveniently recombines, with the result that there is a very rapid increase in the number of nodes (possible share prices) that need to be analysed. However, the power of modern computers means that the method is feasible.

THE BLACK–SCHOLES MODEL OF CALL OPTION PRICING 18.4

The binomial model provides a numerical solution to the option pricing problem but it does not provide an exact equation. In a very famous article, Black and Scholes (1973) presented a model that expresses the price of a call as a function of five variables:[19]

(a) the current price of the underlying share
(b) the exercise price of the call
(c) the call's term to expiry
(d) the volatility of the share (as measured by the variance of the distribution of returns on the share)
(e) the risk-free interest rate.

This model stimulated a great deal of further research into options and, because of its importance, is presented here in some detail.

18.4.1 ASSUMPTIONS

The Black–Scholes model assumes the following:

(a) There exists a constant risk-free interest rate at which investors can borrow and lend unlimited amounts.
(b) Share returns follow a random walk in continuous time with a variance (volatility) proportional to the square of the share price. The variance is a known constant. This assumption relates to the behaviour of the share price over time. In particular, returns on this share are assumed to follow a random walk and the share is continuously traded in the market. The model is therefore cast in continuous time, as distinct from discrete time, which considers a series of time periods. The distribution of the rate of return on the shares has a known, constant variance, which is a measure of volatility. It can also be shown that this assumption implies that the distribution of possible share prices on any given future date (such as on the option's expiry date) is lognormal. Empirical studies suggest that share markets do not behave in exactly the way assumed in the model. While trading in many shares is frequent, it is not literally continuous. Volatility is unlikely to be constant. The random-walk model and the lognormal distribution are not perfect descriptions of their real-world counterparts.
(c) There are no transaction costs, taxes or other sources of friction.

---

[19] The Australian Securities Exchange website provides a calculator that will estimate option prices using the Black–Scholes model; see www.asx.com.au/resources/calculators/index.htm.

(d) Short selling is allowed with no restrictions or penalties. This assumption means that any number of securities can be sold, regardless of the number actually held. For example, two calls can be written (sold) even if only one share is held, and there is no need to deposit cash to secure such a position.

These four assumptions define conditions in the share and option markets. In addition, Black and Scholes simplified the problem with two further assumptions:

(e) There are no dividends, rights issues or other complicating features.
(f) The call is of the European type.

Assumptions (e) and (f) are in fact alternatives, since it was shown in Section 18.2.8 that if assumption (e) holds, then the distinction between American and European calls is irrelevant. Therefore, if assumption (e) is made, the pricing formula will be valid for both American and European calls.

With these assumptions, the price, c, of any given call is a function only of the current share price, S, and time, t. The risk-free interest rate, r', the volatility, σ^2, and the exercise price, X, are known constants in the problem.

18.4.2 THE BLACK–SCHOLES EQUATION

Using these assumptions, Black and Scholes showed that the price of the call option must be:

$$c = SN(d_1) - Xe^{-r'T}N(d_2) \qquad [18.5]$$

where
$$d_1 \equiv \frac{\ln(S/X) + (r' + \tfrac{1}{2}\sigma^2)T}{\sigma\sqrt{T}}$$

$$d_2 \equiv \frac{\ln(S/X) + (r' + \tfrac{1}{2}\sigma^2)T}{\sigma\sqrt{T}}$$

$$\equiv d_1 - \sigma\sqrt{T}$$

$N(d)$ indicates the cumulative standard normal density function with upper integral limit d. In other words, $N(d)$ is the area under the standard normal curve from $-\infty$ to d. The definitions of S, X and σ^2 are as given previously and T is the term to expiry. $N(d_1)$ and $N(d_2)$ are probabilities and are therefore numbers between zero and 1. Values of the function N can be found using Table 5 of Appendix A, or the NORMSDIST function in Microsoft Excel®. In continuous time, $e^{-r'T}$ is the appropriate discount factor for T periods at rate r' per period. Therefore $Xe^{-r'T}$ is the present value of X. The application of Equation 18.5 is illustrated in Example 18.4.

EXAMPLE 18.4

Suppose that we wish to find the Black–Scholes price for a call with the following characteristics:

Current share price: $S = \$17.60$
Exercise price: $X = \$16.00$
Term to expiry: $T = 3$ months $= 0.25$ years
Volatility (variance): $\sigma^2 = 0.09$ per annum
Standard deviation: $\sigma = 0.3$ per annum
Risk-free interest rate: $r' = 0.1$ per annum, continuously compounding

The first task is to calculate d_1 and d_2:

$$d_1 = \frac{\ln(\$17.60/\$16.00) + [0.1 + (0.5)(0.09)]0.25}{0.3\sqrt{0.25}}$$

$$= \frac{\ln(1.1) + 0.03625}{0.15}$$

$$\approx 0.8771$$

$$d_2 \approx 0.877 - 0.15$$

$$\approx 0.7271$$

Consulting the table of values for the standard normal distribution N(.), or by using the Microsoft Excel® NORMSDIST function, we find that:

$N(d_1) = N(0.8771) = 0.8098$ and
$N(d_2) = N(0.7271) = 0.7664$

The discounting factor $e^{-r'T} = e^{-0.025} = 0.9753$. Substituting into Equation 18.5:

$$c = SN(d_1) - Xe^{-r'T} N(d_2)$$
$$= (\$17.60)(0.8098) - (\$16.00)(0.9753)(0.7664)$$
$$= \$2.293$$

The Black–Scholes call price is therefore approximately $2.29.

Table 18.11 shows further examples of the call prices that result from the Black–Scholes model if different values of the variables are assumed. Also shown in the table is the greater of $(S - Xe^{-r'T})$ and zero, which is the minimum theoretical price; equivalently, it is the call price under conditions of perfect certainty.

TABLE 18.11 Examples of Black–Scholes call option prices

EXAMPLE	SHARE PRICE (S)	EXERCISE PRICE (X)	TERM TO EXPIRY (T)	VOLATILITY (σ)	RISK-FREE INTEREST RATE (r')	MODEL PRICE (C) (CENTS)	GREATER OF ZERO AND $S - Xe^{-r'T}$ (CENTS)
(a)	1.00	1.00	0.25	0.3	0.10	7.22	2.47
(b)	1.10	1.00	0.25	0.3	0.10	14.33	12.47
(c)	1.00	1.10	0.25	0.3	0.10	3.22	0
(d)	1.00	1.00	0.50	0.3	0.10	10.91	4.88
(e)	1.00	1.00	0.25	0.4	0.10	9.17	2.47
(f)	1.00	1.00	0.25	0.3	0.15	7.89	3.68

Each of the examples (b) to (f) changes *one* of the values used in Example (a). Therefore, the effect of a higher share price—Example (b)—is shown to be a substantial rise in the call price, as discussed in Section 18.2.5. The direction of influence of the other variables is likewise in line with our comments in that section. These conclusions are quite general and do not depend on the particular numbers used in the examples. Similarly, the model price is never less than the minimum theoretical price.

The Black–Scholes model (Equation 18.5) is shown graphically in Figure 18.4 overleaf. For some given volatility, interest rate and exercise price, Figure 18.4 plots call price against share price for different values of term to expiry. For a finite, positive value of T, the curve approaches asymptotically the broken line representing $c = S - Xe^{-r'T}$ as S increases. At expiry, $T = 0$, the call is worth $S^* - X$ or zero, whichever is the greater, while a perpetual call ($T \to \infty$) commands a price equal to the share price.

FIGURE 18.4 Graphical representation of the Black–Scholes equation

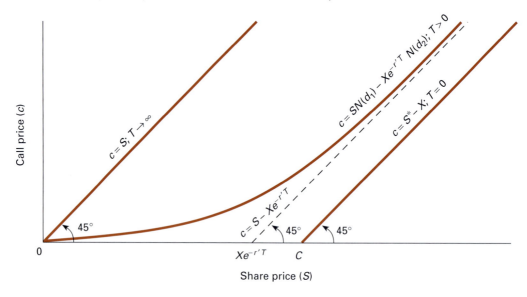

The Black–Scholes model is set in continuous time, rather than discrete time. Hence, the risk-free interest rate, r' used in the model is an interest rate that assumes continuous compounding. In practice, interest rates are almost never quoted on a continuously compounding basis. Fortunately, to calculate Black–Scholes prices in practice we do not have to convert observed interest rates, which assume discrete compounding, to their continuously compounding counterparts. The Black–Scholes equation (Equation 18.5) can be rewritten as:

$$c = SN(d_1) - PVX\,N(d_2) \qquad [18.6]$$

where $\quad PVX = \dfrac{X}{1+R}$

$$d_1 \equiv \frac{\ln(S/PVX) + \tfrac{1}{2}\sigma^2 T}{\sigma\sqrt{T}}$$

$$d_2 \equiv d_1 - \sigma\sqrt{T}$$

In Equation 18.6, R is the observed effective interest rate on a risk-free investment for a term equal to the term of the option. The application of Equation 18.6 is illustrated in Example 18.5.

EXAMPLE 18.5

Suppose that we wish to find the Black–Scholes price for a call option with the following characteristics:

Current share price: $S = \$9.95$
Exercise price: $X = \$10.50$
Term to expiry: $T = 6$ months $= 0.5$ years
Volatility (variance): $\sigma^2 = 0.16$ per annum
Standard deviation: $\sigma = 0.4$ per annum
Risk-free interest rate: $R = 5$ per cent per half-year

The first task is to calculate the present value of the exercise price:

$$PVX = \frac{\$10.50}{1.05}$$
$$= \$10.00$$

The next task is to calculate d_1 and d_2 using Equation 18.6:

$$d_1 = \frac{\ln(\$9.95/\$10.00) + (0.5)(0.16)(0.5)}{0.4\sqrt{0.5}}$$

$$= \frac{\ln(0.995) + 0.04}{0.2828}$$

$$= 0.1237$$

$$d_2 = 0.1237 - 0.2828$$

$$= -0.1591$$

Consulting the table of values for the standard normal distribution $N(.)$, or by using the Microsoft Excel® NORMSDIST function, we find that:

$N(d_1) = N(0.1237) = 0.5492$ and
$N(d_2) = N(-0.1591) = 0.4368$

Substituting into Equation 18.6:

$c = SN(d_1) - PVX\ N(d_2)$

$= (\$9.95)(0.5492) - (\$10.00)(0.4368)$

$= \$1.10$

To verify that Equation 18.6 gives the same valuation as the original Black–Scholes equation (Equation 18.5), we first note that the continuously compounding interest rate that is equivalent to 5 per cent per half-year is 9.758 per cent per annum.[20] Calculating the values to input into Equation 18.5 we find that:

$$d_1 = \frac{\ln(S/X) + (r' + \frac{1}{2}\sigma^2)T}{\sigma\sqrt{T}}$$

$$= \frac{\ln(\$9.95/\$10.50) + (0.097\,580 + 0.5 \times 0.16)(0.5)}{0.4\sqrt{0.5}}$$

$$= \frac{\ln(0.947\,619) + 0.088\,790}{0.2828}$$

$$= 0.1237$$

$d_2 = d_1 - \sigma\sqrt{T}$

$= 0.1237 - 0.2828$

$= -0.1591$

As shown above,
$N(d_1) = N(0.1237) = 0.5492$ and
$N(d_2) = N(-0.1591) = 0.4368$

Substituting into the original Black–Scholes equation (Equation 18.5):

$c = SN(d_1) - Xe^{-r'T}N(d_2)$

$= (\$9.95)(0.5492) - (\$10.50)e^{-(0.09758)(0.5)}(0.4368)$

$= (\$9.95)(0.5492) - (\$10.50)(0.952\,381)(0.4368)$

$= \$1.10$

Equations 18.5 and 18.6 provide the same valuation—$1.10—for the option.

---

20 Because $e^{-r'T} = e^{-0.09758 \times 0.5} = e^{-0.04879} = 0.952\,381 = 1/1.05$.

By invoking Equation 18.1, the put–call parity equation, the Black–Scholes analysis also provides an equation to value European puts on shares that do not pay dividends.[21] In a continuous time formulation Equation 18.1 is:

$$p = c - S + Xe^{-r'T} \qquad [18.7]$$

where p = the price of the European put.

Substituting Equation 18.5 into Equation 18.7 and rearranging gives:

$$p = S[N(d_1) - 1] + Xe^{-r'T}[1 - N(d_2)] \qquad [18.8]$$

Equation 18.8 is the Black–Scholes European put pricing model.[22] The application of Equation 18.8 is illustrated in Example 18.6.

EXAMPLE 18.6

Suppose that we wish to find the Black–Scholes price for the put option that is the counterpart to the call option described in Example 18.4—that is:

Current share price:	$P = \$17.60$
Exercise price:	$X = \$16.00$
Term to expiry:	T = 3 months = 0.25 years
Volatility (variance):	σ^2 = 0.09 per annum
Standard deviation:	σ = 0.3 per annum
Risk-free interest rate:	r' = 0.1 per annum, continuously compounding

The calculations in Example 18.4 showed that with these values, $N(d_1)$ = 0.8098, $N(d_2)$ = 0.7664 and $e^{-r'T}$ = 0.9753. Substituting into Equation 18.8, the Black–Scholes European put price is:

$$\begin{aligned} p &= S[N(d_1) - 1] + Xe^{-r'T}[1 - N(d_2)] \\ &= (\$17.60)(0.8098 - 1) + (\$16.00)(0.9753)(1 - 0.7664) \\ &= \$0.298 \end{aligned}$$

The Black–Scholes European put price is therefore slightly less than 30 cents.

18.4.3 A BRIEF ASSESSMENT OF THE BLACK–SCHOLES MODEL

An appealing feature of the Black–Scholes model is that it specifies a particular functional form linking the variables, rather than simply specifying the direction of each variable's influence. Slightly less obvious, but also a strength of the model, is the number of variables that it does *not* include. As suggested earlier, the return that investors expect on the underlying share has no place in the model. No assumption concerning the attitude of investors towards risk is required or implied. Conversely, the variables that are present in the model are for the most part observable and have reliable data available. The share price, exercise price and term to expiry are directly observable, and good proxies exist for the risk-free interest rate. Measuring a share's volatility is subject to error; Black (1975, p. 36) described it as 'the big unknown in the option formula'. However, if a share's volatility (as measured by the variance of the rate of return) is constant, as the model assumes, then the sequence of past prices may be used to produce an accurate estimate of the volatility. Therefore, although investors' expectations of the return on the share have no place in the equation, this is not true of volatility expectations. The model, in effect, sidesteps this problem by assuming that the volatility is a known constant. In practice, users of the model may try a range of values for this variable. In other cases, users may take market prices of options and then solve the Black–Scholes equation for the volatility 'implied' by the market price of the option. Indeed,

---

[21] Note that it is necessary to assume a European-type put *and* no dividends because, even in the absence of dividends, it can sometimes pay to exercise prematurely an American-type put. This feature makes the pricing of American-type puts more complex than the pricing of American-type calls.

[22] Because $N(d_1) - 1 = -N(-d_1)$ and $1 - N(d_2) = N(-d_2)$, Equation 18.8 can also be written as $p = -SN(-d_1) + Xe^{-r'T}N(-d_2)$.

estimates of 'implied volatility' are of great interest to market participants as they are often interpreted as providing current information about expectations of future price volatility. Perhaps the most widely cited implied volatility measure is the Chicago Board Options Exchange Volatility Index (VIX). This index is constructed by analysing the traded prices of a series of options written on the S&P 500 share price index—an index that reflects the price movements of a portfolio of shares in the very largest companies traded in the US—and estimating the level of volatility implied by those option prices over the next 30 days. Not only is this information interesting in terms of gauging current market sentiment, but with the introduction of futures contracts (in 2003) and options contracts (in 2006) written on the VIX, hedgers and speculators now have the ability to effectively trade in volatility. Following its development by Professor Robert Whaley, the Chicago Board Options Exchange introduced VIX in 1993 with two main purposes. First, VIX was designed to provide market participants with a measure of current expectations of short-term volatility, and second to then enable derivative contracts to be developed and traded on such a measure. Since its introduction, VIX has often been cited as an aggregate measure of the level of apprehension felt by market traders about future price movements.

FINANCE IN ACTION

HOW TO MEASURE FEAR WITH OPTIONS CONTRACTS!

In endeavouring to understand the Market Volatility Index (VIX), it is essential to remember that it is not a backward-looking tool, as commentators sometimes suggest, measuring volatility that has already come to pass; instead, it is forward-looking, measuring volatility that investors expect to see. The VIX can be likened to a bond's yield to maturity—the discount rate that equates a bond's price to the present value of its promised payments. A bond's yield is *implied* by its current price but it represents the expected *future* return of the bond over its remaining life. Similarly, VIX is *implied* by the current prices of S&P 500 index options but represents the expected *future* market volatility over the next 30 calendar days.

Strictly speaking, volatility describes *unexpected* upward or downward movements; however, the S&P 500 index option market has become dominated by hedgers who buy index puts when they are concerned about the possibility of a drop in the stock market—essentially 'insuring' themselves—which explains why the VIX has been dubbed the 'investor fear gauge'! Purchasing insurance is nothing new; we routinely purchase home and contents insurance as a means of insuring our home value in the event of theft or natural disasters. If the chance of theft in your neighbourhood rises, your insurance company is likely to increase its premium. The same is true for portfolio insurance: the more investors demand, the higher the price. VIX is an indicator that reflects the price of portfolio insurance.

Source: Information drawn from Robert Whaley, 'Understanding VIX', *The Journal of Portfolio Management*, Spring 2009, pp. 98–105.

18.5 OPTIONS ON FOREIGN CURRENCY[23]

So far, we have confined our discussion almost entirely to options on shares. However, there are options on a wide variety of underlying assets—even the weather! (See Finance in Action.) Fortunately, most of the principles we have covered also apply to options on other underlying assets. In this section we consider options on foreign currency. Options on futures contracts are considered in Section 18.7.

---

23 An application to contingent hedging is discussed in Section 20.6.7.

FINANCE IN ACTION

HEDGING THE WEATHER

Looked at one way, an option is an insurance contract. If a shareholder buys a put option, he or she has protection against the share price falling below the exercise price of the option. So, couldn't the idea of an option be extended to pretty much anything that someone might want to insure against? If, say, I'm worried about cold weather, why can't I buy an option that will pay off only if the weather gets too cold? Or, if I'm worried about wet weather, why can't I buy an option that pays off only if it rains? Well, you can, as shown in the following excerpt.

In the summer of 2001, Dieter Worms could only sit and watch as rain kept golfers away from the fairways of his Gut Apeldör golf club in Hennstedt, about 100 kilometres north of the German city of Hamburg. 'The weather in 2001 was miserable,' says 54-year-old Worms. 'What I hate as the owner of a golf course is to get frustrated more and more every minute when you see the rain coming down in buckets—and not just for one day but for weeks and months.'

In 2002 Worms resolved to avoid a repeat of his frustration by buying a weather derivative from Société Générale SA, France's third-largest bank by assets. He decided he could put up with 50 rainy days from May to September, the period when golf courses typically make about 80 per cent of their income. Once the number of days with more than a millimetre of rain passed 50, the derivatives contract started paying compensation for every wet day.

Worms is one of thousands of business owners around the world who have sought to protect their balance sheets from the weather. The Weather Risk Management Association (www.wrma.org), a Washington-based trade group, shows that the number of weather risk-management contracts signed worldwide almost trebled to about 12 000 in the 12 months ended in March 2003 from the year-earlier period. The contracts had an underlying value of $4.2 billion. In Europe, the number of contracts almost doubled to 1480 from 765.

Based on: 'Mark Gilbert and Alejandro Barbajosa, Hedging the weather', *Bloomberg Markets*, vol. 13, no. 7, July 2004, pp. 99–102.

WWW

LEARNING OBJECTIVE 5

Explain the characteristics and uses of foreign currency options and options on futures

18.5.1 WHAT IS AN OPTION ON FOREIGN CURRENCY?

A call (put) option on foreign currency is a contract that confers the right to buy (sell) an agreed quantity of that foreign currency at a given exchange rate. Options on foreign currency are traded in organised markets such as the Philadelphia Exchange, as well as in 'over-the-counter' markets and by privately arranged contracts. A company selling, say, US dollars (in return for Australian dollars) can equivalently be said to be purchasing Australian dollars (using US dollars). In the same way, a put option to sell US dollars (for Australian dollars) can equivalently be described as a call option to buy Australian dollars (using US dollars). Example 18.7 illustrates the nature of options on foreign currency.[24]

EXAMPLE 18.7

On 24 August, Westpac Bank sold a 3-month US dollar put option (equivalently, a 3-month Australian dollar call option). The purchaser was an Australian exporter looking to insure the value of a future US dollar receipt against a possible depreciation in the value of the US dollar (equivalently, an appreciation in the value of the Australian dollar). The underlying currency amount was US$5 million and the exercise price was $A1 = US$0.7118. At the time the option was purchased, the spot rate was also $A1 = US$0.7118. The price of this option was US$0.0199 per US$1; that is, the exporter paid US$(0.0199 × 5 000 000) = US$99 500, which at the time was equivalent to $A(99 500/0.7118) = $A139 786. On payment of this

---

[24] We are grateful to Westpac Banking Corporation for providing the information used in this example. We have rounded final calculations to the nearest dollar.

sum, the exporter obtained the right to sell US$5 million at the price of US71.18 cents per Australian dollar—that is, US$5 million could be sold for $A(5 000 000/0.7118) = $A7 024 445. The cost of this right was US$99 500. The payoff structure is shown in Table 18.12.

TABLE 18.12 Payoff structure for purchase of a put contract on US$5 million at an exercise price of $A1 = US$0.7118

IF THE SPOT RATE PER $A1 ON THE PUT'S EXPIRY DATE IS:	THEN THE PAYOFF (CASH FLOW) TO THE PUT HOLDER IS:	
	IN US$	IN $A EQUIVALENT
US$0.6800	0	0
US$0.6900	0	0
US$0.7000	0	0
US$0.7100	0	0
US$0.7118	0	0
US$0.7200	0.0082 × 5m/0.7118 = 57 600	57 600/0.72 = 80 001
US$0.7300	0.0182 × 5m/0.7118 = 127 845	127 845/0.73 = 175 130
US$0.7400	0.0282 × 5m/0.7118 = 198 089	198 089/0.74 = 267 688
US$0.7500	0.0382 × 5m/0.7118 = 268 334	268 334/0.75 = 357 778

As can be seen from the payoff structure in Table 18.12, the put provides protection against the effects of a depreciating US dollar (equivalently, an appreciating Australian dollar). This protection begins to take effect when the value of an Australian dollar reaches the exercise price of US71.18 cents.

If, instead, protection was sought against the effects of an appreciating US dollar (equivalently, a depreciating Australian dollar), a call option to buy US dollars is required. The payoff structure for a trader who buys a call option on US$5 million at an exercise price of $A1 = US$0.7318 is shown in Table 18.13.

TABLE 18.13 Payoff structure for purchase of a call contract on US$5 million at an exercise price of $A1 = US$0.7318

IF THE SPOT RATE PER $A1 ON THE PUT'S EXPIRY DATE IS:	THEN THE PAYOFF (CASH FLOW) TO THE PUT HOLDER IS:	
	IN US$	IN $A EQUIVALENT
US$0.7000	0.0318 × 5m/0.7318 = 217 272	217 272/0.70 = 310 389
US$0.7100	0.0218 × 5m/0.7318 = 148 948	148 948/0.71 = 209 786
US$0.7200	0.0118 × 5m/0.7318 = 80 623	80 623/0.72 = 111 977
US$0.7300	0.0018 × 5m/0.7318 = 12 298	12 298/0.73 = 16 847
US$0.7318	0	0
US$0.7400	0	0
US$0.7500	0	0
US$0.7600	0	0
US$0.7700	0	0

18.5.2 COMBINATIONS OF OPTIONS ON FOREIGN CURRENCY

Some of the most frequent uses that have been made of options on foreign currency involve combining two or more such options. For example, options can be combined to produce an arrangement sometimes known as a 'range forward' or a 'collar'. This arrangement is shown in Example 18.8.

EXAMPLE 18.8

Conquest Investments Ltd expects to receive a cash inflow of A$30 million in the next month and plans to convert this sum to US dollars to invest in a US company. At current exchange rates, the US dollar value of this inflow is around US$17 million. Tim Johns, the manager of Conquest Investments, wants to be guaranteed to receive a minimum of US$16.68 million for delivery of the A$30 million. Should the Australian dollar appreciate in the next month, Johns is willing to accept a ceiling of receiving no more than US$17.28 million in return for delivery of the A$30 million. To lock in simultaneously the minimum of US$16.68 million and the maximum of US$17.28 million, Johns combines the purchase of a put to sell A$30 million (with an exercise price of US55.60 cents) with the sale of a call to purchase A$30 million (with an exercise price of US57.60 cents). The cash inflow from selling the call can then be used to help pay for the put.[25] The payoff structure is shown in Table 18.14.

TABLE 18.14 Payoff structure for Example 18.8, Conquest Investments Ltd

IF THE SPOT RATE PER A$1 ON THE EXPIRY DATE IS:	THEN THE US$ CASH FLOWS ARE:			
	ON THE PUT[a]	ON THE CALL[b]	PURCHASE OF US$ (SPOT)[c]	TOTAL
US$0.5200	+1 080 000	0	+15 600 000	+16 680 000
US$0.5300	+780 000	0	+15 900 000	+16 680 000
US$0.5400	+480 000	0	+16 200 000	+16 680 000
US$0.5500	+180 000	0	+16 500 000	+16 680 000
US$0.5560	0	0	+16 680 000	+16 680 000
US$0.5600	0	0	+16 800 000	+16 800 000
US$0.5700	0	0	+17 100 000	+17 100 000
US$0.5760	0	0	+17 280 000	+17 280 000
US$0.5800	0	−120 000	+17 400 000	+17 280 000
US$0.5900	0	−420 000	+17 700 000	+17 280 000
US$0.6000	0	−720 000	+18 000 000	+17 280 000
US$0.6100	0	−1 020 000	+18 300 000	+17 280 000

[a] For expiry spot rates less than the exercise price of US$0.5560, each calculation is
  +(US$0.5560 − expiry spot rate) ◊ 30 million.
[b] For expiry spot rates greater than the exercise price of US$0.5760, each calculation is
  −(expiry spot rate − US$0.5760) ◊ 30 million.
[c] Each calculation is expiry spot rate ◊ 30 million.

Table 18.14 shows that, whatever the future exchange rate may be, Conquest Investments Ltd will receive no less than US$16.68 million but no more than US$17.28 million. If the future spot rate is between US55.60 and US57.60 cents per A$1, the payoff on both options is zero and the arrangement requires only a spot transaction.

---

25 In practice it is common for the exercise prices to be selected carefully so that the put price equals the call price. Therefore the inflow from one exactly offsets the cost of the other, making the deal appear 'free'.

18.6 OPTIONS, FORWARDS AND FUTURES

There is a simple relationship between prices of European options and forward prices. As forward contracts are most frequently encountered in foreign currency dealings, we will explain the relationship using options on foreign currency and forward contracts on foreign currency. However, in principle it holds for a much wider range of underlying assets.

EXAMPLE 18.9

Suppose that, in Example 18.8, the exercise price of the call had, like that of the put, been US55.60 cents. In that case, the payoffs are as shown in Table 18.15.

TABLE 18.15 Payoffs for put bought and call sold, both with an exercise price of US55.60 cents

IF THE SPOT RATE PER A$1 ON THE EXPIRY DATE IS:	THEN THE US$ CASH FLOWS ARE:			
	ON THE PUT[a]	ON THE CALL[b]	PURCHASE OF US$ (SPOT)[c]	TOTAL
US$0.5200	+1 080 000	0	+15 600 000	+16 680 000
US$0.5300	+780 000	0	+15 900 000	+16 680 000
US$0.5400	+480 000	0	+16 200 000	+16 680 000
US$0.5500	+180 000	0	+16 500 000	+16 680 000
US$0.5560	0	0	+16 680 000	+16 680 000
US$0.5600	0	−120 000	+16 800 000	+16 680 000
US$0.5700	0	−420 000	+17 100 000	+16 680 000
US$0.5800	0	−720 000	+17 400 000	+16 680 000
US$0.5900	0	−1 020 000	+17 700 000	+16 680 000

[a] For expiry spot rates less than the exercise price of US$0.5560, each calculation is
+(US$0.5560 − expiry spot rate) ◊ 30 million.

[b] For expiry spot rates greater than the exercise price of US$0.5560, each calculation is
−(expiry spot rate − US$0.5560) ◊ 30 million.

[c] Calculated using 30 million ◊ spot rate.

The final column of Table 18.15 shows that this combination of transactions is equivalent to a guarantee that A$30 million can be sold for US$16.68 million. In effect, therefore, this combination is equivalent to having a forward contract to sell A$30 million at a forward price of US55.60 cents per A$1.

It is a simple matter to provide an algebraic proof. Given that:

Total cash flow = cash flow from put + cash flow from call + cash flow from spot transaction

then if $S < X$, the total cash flow is:

$(X − S^*) + 0 + S^*$
$= X$

but if $S \geq X$, the total cash flow is:

$0 − (S^* − X) + S^*$
$= X$

Therefore, the future total cash flow is always X.

Suppose that the price of the put was equal to the price of the call, and both the put and the call have the same exercise price, term to expiry, and so on. In this case, the arrangement illustrated in Table 18.15 requires no net initial cash inflow or outflow and it therefore replicates a forward contract at both initiation and expiry. To prevent arbitrage, the forward price (exchange rate) should therefore equal the exercise price of the options. In summary, if the prices of a put and its counterpart call are equal, the forward price for the underlying asset should equal the exercise price of the options.

As we discussed in Section 18.2.1, forward contracts are very similar to futures contracts. Therefore, if the prices of a put and its counterpart call are equal, the futures price for the underlying asset should approximately equal the exercise price of the options.

A further connection between option contracts and futures contracts is through a security known as a 'low exercise price option' (LEPO). Such contracts are listed on the ASX. Consider a 1-month call option with an exercise price of 1 cent, on a share whose current market price is $10. Clearly, there is virtually no chance that the share price will be anywhere near 1 cent during the coming month. Accordingly, the option is almost certain to be exercised (if not sold to someone else before expiry). The true option element is thus exceedingly small and, in effect, a LEPO is virtually a commitment to purchase. Who would not expect to exercise an option to buy a share for 1 cent when the current share price is around $10? Furthermore—unlike the rules applying to normal share options—the ASX rules on LEPOs do not require that LEPO buyers pay the option price at the initiation of the contract. Instead, the ASX merely requires that LEPO buyers pay a margin call if the share price falls, and that LEPO sellers pay a margin call if the share price rises. The result, therefore, is that a LEPO requires no payment at initiation but produces cash inflows or outflows as the share price changes, and (if not earlier reversed) is virtually certain to result in a purchase of the share. This description is almost identical to that of a futures contract on a share. In other words, financially speaking, a LEPO is almost identical to a futures contract on a share.

18.7 OPTIONS ON FUTURES

18.7.1 WHAT IS AN OPTION ON A FUTURES CONTRACT?

A number of futures exchanges, including the ASX, have introduced options on their more heavily traded futures contracts.[26] A call option on futures confers on the buyer of the call the right to enter into a futures contract as a buyer. Similarly, a put option on futures confers on the buyer of the put the right to enter into a futures contract as a seller. Often the expiry date of the option is shortly before the expiry date of the futures contract.

For example, suppose that on 15 February the price of a futures contract on gold, maturing on 20 May, is $1500. On 15 February it may also be possible to buy a call option on this futures contract with an exercise price of, say, $1540 and an expiry date of 13 May. This call confers the right to assume the role of buyer in the futures contract at a futures price of $1540. On 15 February this option may be worth, say, $30. Suppose that the futures price of gold increases and that by 10 May the futures price has reached $1630 and the call buyer wishes to take the profit. If the call is an American type the call buyer could exercise the call on 10 May, thereby becoming registered from that date as a futures buyer at a price of $1540. Through operation of the mark-to-market rule, the sum of $90 will be credited to the buyer. Alternatively, instead of exercising the call, it could simply be sold in the options market. In principle the price obtained should be $90 or more.

18.7.2 USES OF OPTIONS ON FUTURES

Options on futures have proved to be popular with traders, particularly in the case of options on financial futures. Although there are many possible reasons for this popularity, options on futures have three attributes that may have prompted market participants to trade in the option rather than in the underlying futures contract:

---

26 In this section it is assumed that the reader is familiar with futures contracts. Futures contracts are explained in detail in Chapter 17.

(a) Open futures positions entail very high risks for a speculator, particularly if those positions are held for a long time. For example, if a market participant believed that the share price index (SPI) was likely to rise substantially in the next 2 months, then without options, and apart from buying the shares themselves, the only way to speculate on this belief is to buy SPI futures. Many speculators would not want to take this risk, simply because they could incur large losses if the SPI should fall. A call option on futures allows the speculator to pay a given sum (the option price) in return for avoiding the possibility of large losses. The ability to profit if the belief proves correct is unimpaired. In short, options on futures can preserve the basic speculative uses of futures, but without the open-ended commitment that futures themselves require.

(b) Hedgers may not be certain enough of their own circumstances to justify accepting the obligations of a futures contract. Consider the following situation. A small manufacturer has tendered for a particular job and the manager believes that although there is a fair chance of success, it is not certain. If the tender is accepted, there will be an immediate need for short-term funding of approximately $1 million to buy the necessary raw materials. Of course, if the tender is not accepted, there is no such need. The manager believes that there is a need to hedge, because the financial viability of the project will be threatened if interest rates increase between now and the date on which the name of the successful tenderer will be announced. This risk cannot be hedged using futures contracts because a futures contract is a commitment, but the manufacturer cannot be committed to the project unless and until the tender is accepted. At present the manufacturer's need to hedge is contingent on the future outcome of the tender process.[27] The manufacturer could set up a contingent hedge by buying a put option on a bank bill futures contract. The amount paid for the put is like an insurance premium. If interest rates rise, bank bill futures prices will fall and the put will be more valuable. The put's increased value will protect the manufacturer, should protection be needed. Of course, if interest rates fall, so will the put price. Indeed, the put price may even fall to zero and the manufacturer will then have lost the total price paid for the put. This is like buying fire insurance and not having a fire. No claim is made on the insurance policy and the premium is lost.

(c) The deposit/margin system is simpler for option buyers than for futures traders. (Option sellers still face unlimited risks so there are still complications applicable to them.) Once option buyers have paid the option price they can make no further losses. Consequently, there is little or no reason to subject option buyers to a stringent deposit/margin system. For this reason, smaller futures traders may prefer to buy a call instead of buying futures. Similarly, they may prefer to buy a put instead of selling futures.

18.7.3 PRICING OPTIONS ON FUTURES

The valuation of options written on futures contracts, such as those traded on the Australian Securities Exchange,[28] has been derived by Asay (1982) and Lieu (1990) and is provided by the following formulae:

$$c = FN(d_3) - XN(d_4) \quad [18.9]$$

$$p = XN(-d_4) - FN(-d_3) \quad [18.10]$$

---

[27] A detailed example of contingent hedging is given in Section 20.6.7. Although that example is set in an international finance context, the principles are the same.

[28] Black (1976) derived the pricing formula for futures options traded in markets where the option premium is payable up-front. However, the premium on futures options traded on the ASX is not paid immediately but is instead marked to market in a similar way as is any position in a futures contract. Asay (1982) and Lieu (1990) adjust Black's model to account for this difference in market structure.

where $d_3 = \dfrac{\ln(F/X) + \frac{1}{2}\sigma^2 T}{\sigma\sqrt{T}}$

$d_4 = d_3 - \sigma\sqrt{T}$

where

c = price of the call
p = price of the put
F = futures price
X = exercise price
T = term to expiry of the option
σ^2 = volatility of the futures price

Note that the formulae above look very similar to the standard Black–Scholes equations (Equations 18.5 and 18.8) with the only notable differences being that the share price has been replaced by the price of a futures contract written on the share and the omission of the interest rate from the formula. The intuition behind the interest rate omission is straightforward, because in the standard Black–Scholes equations the interest rate represents compensation to the trader for having funds tied up in the share. As a futures contract requires no initial investment, there is no need to include an interest rate when estimating the value of futures options.

18.7.4 SPECIFICATION OF THE SPI 200 FUTURES OPTIONS CONTRACT

The SPI 200 futures options contract has the following major features:

(a) *Option style*. American.
(b) *Contract unit*. The contract unit is the value of the SPI 200 futures contract, which itself is valued by reference to the S&P/ASX 200 Index multiplied by $25.
(c) *Settlement*. The contract is deliverable and may be exercised on any business day up to and including the last trading day. Upon exercise the holder will receive (deliver) the underlying SPI 200 futures contract position at the exercise price.
(d) *Quotations*. The contract is quoted as the value of the SPI 200 futures contract to 0.5 index points.
(e) *Exercise prices*. Set at intervals of 25 basis points. New option exercise prices are created automatically as the underlying futures contract price fluctuates.
(f) *Termination of contract*. All trading ceases at 12 noon on the third Thursday of the contract month, with settlement occurring the day following the close of trading.

Example 18.10 illustrates the use of options contracts written on the SPI 200 futures contract.

EXAMPLE 18.10

Diacono Fidelity is a superannuation fund that collects contributions from its members on a quarterly basis and invests those funds in a diversified portfolio of Australian equities. It is 24 February 2010 and the management of the fund is concerned that the general level of share prices will rise prior to 12 April 2010, when it is next going to invest the funds. It has approximately $150 000 in contributions that will be invested. While Diacono Fidelity could hedge the risk of prices rising by taking a long position in a futures contract, they wish to still benefit from any possible decline in market prices that might occur prior to the funds being invested, and hence determine that it would be optimal to take a position in a futures option contract instead.

On 24 February 2010, the S&P/ASX 200 Index closed at 4648 and the June 2010 S&P/ASX SPI 200 Index futures contract closed at 4668 or at a contract price of 4668 x $25 = $116 700. Diacono Fidelity decides to buy a June 2010 call option written on the SPI 200 Index futures contract and with an exercise price of 4700 points (or at a contract price of 4700 x $25 = $117 500). The closing price of the June 2010 SPI 200 call options with an exercise price of 4700 points on 24 February was 222 points, which equates to a contract price of 222 x $25 = $5550. So on 24 February 2010, Diacono Fidelity agreed to pay $5550 for the right to enter into the SPI 200 futures contract at any time before 12 noon on 18 June 2010 at a notional price of $117 500.

On 12 April 2010, the S&P/ASX 200 Index closed at 4984 and the June 2010 S&P/ASX SPI 200 Index futures contract closed at 5007 or at a notional contract price of 5007 x $25 = $125 175. Diacono Fidelity could have exercised the futures option to enter into the futures contract as a buyer at a notional price of $117 500 and reversed out as a seller at $125 175, resulting in a gain of $7675. After deducting the price of the call option of $5550, the net gain would have been $2125, which could then be used to offset the generally higher level of equity prices that Diacono Fidelity now faces in the market.

CONTINGENT CLAIMS 18.8

18.8.1 WHAT IS A CONTINGENT CLAIM?

At the most basic level, an option on shares is simply an agreement that allows a choice about buying or selling shares to be made at a later date. The choice will be exercised if it is in the interests of the option holder to do so. The decision will depend on the future value of the shares. A 'contingent claim' is an asset whose value depends on the given value of some other asset. A call option is perhaps the simplest type of contingent claim. A large number of financial contracts are contingent claims and this raises the possibility that such contracts might be valued using an option pricing (that is, contingent-claims) approach. In the following six sections we provide examples of financial contracts that can be interpreted as options. However, detailed discussion of the pricing formulae is beyond the scope of the book.

LEARNING OBJECTIVE 6
Define a contingent claim and explain the option-like features of several contingent claims

18.8.2 RIGHTS ISSUES

One of the simplest contingent claims arises when a company raises new share capital by way of a renounceable rights issue. In this case a shareholder is given the right to purchase new shares in the company at an issue price set by the company. The rights must be sold or taken up by a specified date. In fact, a right is simply a call option issued by the company. Unlike listed call options, exercise of this right does affect the company's capital structure because new capital is raised. Furthermore, in practice the life of a right is usually much shorter than the life of most listed call options. Nevertheless, a right is a call option and therefore can be valued using option pricing principles.[29]

18.8.3 CONVERTIBLE BONDS

A convertible bond is a type of debt security that, in addition to paying interest, gives the investor the right to convert the security into shares of the company. For example, on the maturity of the convertible bond, the investor can accept a cash payment in the usual way, or can take a predetermined number of shares instead of the cash payment. The choice is up to the investor. A convertible bond is therefore equivalent to ordinary debt plus a call option on the shares of the company.[30]

---

29 For a detailed discussion, see Smith (1977).

30 For a detailed discussion, see Ingersoll (1977). A shorter and more accessible discussion can be found in Courtadon and Merrick (1992, pp. 271–2).

18.8.4 VALUATION OF LEVERED SHARES AND RISKY ZERO-COUPON DEBT

One of the first contracts to be identified as a contingent claim is a share in a company that has debt outstanding. Such a share is known as a 'levered share'. Because companies cannot offer government guarantees, there is some risk of default. Consider, for example, the shareholders in a company that has issued zero-coupon debt.[31] When the debt matures, the shareholders must make a choice that resembles the choice facing the holder of a call option that has reached its expiry date. The shareholders can direct the company to repay the debt or they can allow the company to default. Choosing to repay is equivalent to the shareholders exercising a call option to reclaim the company's assets from the debtholders. Choosing to default is equivalent to the shareholders allowing the call to expire unexercised. It is as if the shareholders have transferred the company's assets to the debtholders but have a call option to buy back the assets by repaying the debt on the maturity date. The major variables involved in pricing a call option are reinterpreted as shown in Table 18.16.

TABLE 18.16 Interpreting a levered share as a call option on a company's assets

CALL OPTION ON SHARES	LEVERED SHARE INTERPRETATION
The current (market) value of the share	The current (market) value of the company's assets
The exercise price	The amount due at the debt's maturity (the face value of the debt)
The term to expiry of the option	The term to maturity of the debt
The volatility of the share	The volatility of the company's assets
The risk-free interest rate	The risk-free interest rate

In principle, therefore, we could value the shares using an option pricing approach. Given that the market value of the company is equal to the sum of the market value of the shares and the market value of the debt, once we know the value of the shares we can calculate the value of the debt as well.

18.8.5 VALUATION OF LEVERED SHARES AND RISKY COUPON-PAYING DEBT

The contingent-claims approach can also be applied to the problems of valuing risky coupon-paying debt and valuing the shares of a company that has issued this type of debt. Although this is a more difficult application, it is relatively simple to explain the insight that enables the problem to be solved. In this case shares can be regarded as a sequence of call options. On the debt's maturity date, a payment will be due and will consist of the face value plus the last coupon. Consider a date after the second-last coupon payment, but before the maturity date. Looking ahead to the maturity date, the lump-sum payment due at maturity is the exercise price of a simple call option. This is the case discussed in the previous section. But to have reached this far, the shareholders must have paid the second-last coupon. That is, the shareholders must have decided to pay the second-last coupon, rather than default at that time. Therefore, the second-last coupon is also an option. It is like a call option, where the underlying

---

[31] The most important distinguishing feature of zero-coupon debt is that it is repaid by a single lump sum paid on the maturity date. No intermediate (or coupon) interest payments are required. It is also known as 'pure discount' debt.

asset is the simple call option represented by the final repayment. In other words, paying the second-last coupon gives shareholders the option of proceeding on to the maturity date, where they face their final option of repaying or defaulting on the debt. The second-last coupon is therefore an option on an option, or, as it is sometimes called, a **compound option** (Geske 1979, 1977). Working backwards in this way, we can value the shares. The value of the risky debt is given by the value of the assets, less the value of the shares.

> **compound option**
> option on an option (e.g. an option to buy an option)

18.8.6 PROJECT EVALUATION AND 'REAL' OPTIONS

The net present value (NPV) approach to project evaluation, which we explained in detail in Chapters 5 and 6, is based on an analogy between a proposed investment project and a bond. Like a bond, a project produces a set of future cash flows. The NPV approach proposes that, like the cash flows of a bond, the cash flows of a project should be discounted to a present value and summed to find the total value of the project.

While the NPV approach has proved to be an extremely valuable tool in project evaluation, this does not mean it is always the best tool to use. There are two flaws in the bond analogy. First, in the bond market an investor can purchase a bond today and/or an identical bond at some future date. But in real investment projects, this is frequently not the case. For example, construction of an office block on a particular site could be started now, or at this time next year. Construction cannot be started on both dates. Second, once a bond is purchased, the cash flows to the investor are fixed. Nothing the investor does can change the cash flows produced by the bond. But in real investment projects managers can intervene in the project after it has begun and thus influence the cash flows generated by the project. For example, a project can be abandoned. Consider, for example, a gold mine that, given the current price of gold, has a negative NPV (see Brennan & Schwartz 1992).[32] Does this imply that the mine is worthless? No. Ownership of the mine confers a number of rights that are valuable, including the right to close the mine and the right to reopen it at a later date. Whether and when these rights will be exercised will depend on the cost of exercising the rights and the future price of gold. In short, these rights attached to mine ownership are like options: the **option to abandon** and the **option to reopen**.

Mine ownership is, of course, just one example, and many projects involve 'real' options.[33] In this paragraph we describe several important categories of real options. Many investment proposals implicitly include an **option to defer**. For example, a building might be constructed today, or next year, or the year after that. The option to defer can be valuable because during the period of deferral new information may emerge and may affect the investment decision. A related option is the **option to study**. For example, instead of simply accepting or rejecting an investment proposal, there is often an option to undertake a pilot project to collect more information about the likely outcomes of the proposed project. Other investment projects are likely to lead to further investment opportunities. For example, a project may include an **option to expand** at a later date the output of a given product or to expand the range of products that the company produces.

All options are valuable: by definition, an option cannot have a negative value. Estimating the value of a real option is often a significant challenge to managers, but is worthwhile given the many insights provided by option pricing theory. For example, the option to abandon a project and sell off the assets previously committed is an example of an American-style put option held by the firm. Whereas the valuation of a put option on a share is relatively straightforward, it is more difficult to identify and measure those variables that are inputs into the valuation of real options. Table 18.17 illustrates the link

> **option to abandon**
> right to discontinue an investment project
>
> **option to reopen**
> right to restart a shut-down investment project
>
> **option to defer**
> right to begin an investment project at a later date
>
> **option to study**
> right to gather more information on an investment project
>
> **option to expand**
> right to increase the scale of an investment project

---

32 The original academic work is Brennan and Schwartz (1985).
33 For a detailed treatment of real options, see Trigeorgis (1996). For more accessible discussions, see Leslie and Michaels (1997), Copeland and Keenan (1998), and Dixit and Pindyck (1995).

between those variables that are inputs into the valuation of puts written on ordinary shares and those that are necessary for valuing the option to abandon a project:

TABLE 18.17 Variables that have an impact on the value of the option to abandon a project

PUT OPTION ON SHARES	OPTION TO ABANDON A PROJECT
The current (market) value of the share	The present value of the expected cash flows from the project
The exercise price	The salvage value of the assets committed to the project
The term to expiry of the option	The remaining life of the project
The volatility of the share	The volatility of the expected cash flows from the project
The risk-free interest rate	The risk-free interest rate

When might management choose to exercise its option to abandon operations and sell off the project's assets? To begin with, standard option pricing theory tells us that it is not optimal to exercise a put option early simply because the exercise price exceeds the current value of the asset, and hence the company should not automatically abandon operations as soon as the present value of the expected cash flows from the project is less than the salvage value of the project's assets. The intuition behind this decision when considering puts written on shares is that prior to expiry there is still a chance that the share price may again be greater than the exercise price, in which case the option holder may regret having made the decision to sell at the exercise price. In terms of the real option, the logic is very similar in that a decision to sell off the assets for their salvage value precludes the company from participating in any wealth that might be created if the expected cash flows from the project are subsequently greater than the salvage value of the assets. Option pricing theory also demonstrates that it might be optimal to exercise a put option early if the value of the asset is very low relative to the option's exercise price. This suggests that, in terms of our option to abandon, the decision to sell off the project's assets will only be made when the present value of the expected cash flows from the project are so far below the salvage value of the assets that the company would be better off accessing the cash from the asset sale rather than waiting to see how the uncertainty associated with the project is resolved.

Some managers fear that allowing their project analysts to include option values will lead to unjustifiable increases in capital expenditure. However, this is not necessarily the result. For example, recognising that a project has an option to defer can lead to lower capital expenditure. If the project is not deferred, the option value is lost. Moreover, while it is true that all options have value, it is also true that many options are more valuable if left unexercised. Thus, for example, the optimal decision may be to retain the option to expand by not investing in a new plant today, rather than to exercise the option by investing in a larger plant.

Connect Plus features a case study illustrating topics covered in this chapter.
Ask your lecturer or tutor for your course's unique URL.

SUMMARY

→ An option is the right to force a transaction to occur at some future time on terms and conditions decided upon now. For example, the buyer of a call (put) option on shares obtains the right to buy (sell) the shares at a fixed price, known as the exercise price. Options that can be exercised at any time up to expiry are known as 'American options', while those that can be exercised only on the expiry date, and not before, are known as 'European options'. The buyer of an option obtains a right, whereas the buyer in a futures contract takes on an obligation.

→ A contingent claim is an asset whose value depends on the given value of some other asset. An option is one kind of contingent claim.

→ The cash flows at expiry of an option depend only on the expiry share price and the exercise price. Before expiry, call option prices are influenced by a number of factors, including the current share price (a positive influence), the exercise price (negative), the term to expiry (positive), share volatility (positive), the risk-free interest rate (positive) and expected dividends (negative). Put option prices are affected by the same influences, but some of the signs are reversed.

→ An equilibrium relationship between put and call prices, known as put–call parity, shows that a European put on a share that does not pay dividends can be replicated by a combination of the share, a risk-free deposit and the counterpart call.

→ Binomial option pricing is a practical way to price many options. It provides a numerical solution method rather than a valuation equation. An option pricing equation, developed by Black and Scholes, is an important milestone in finance theory and has performed well in empirical tests, both in Australia and overseas, if a dividend-adjusted version of the model is used. The model can also be adapted to price options on assets other than shares, including options on foreign currency and options on futures.

→ A large number of financial contracts are contingent claims and an option pricing approach has often proved useful in analysing and pricing these contracts. Examples include rights issues, convertible bonds, shares in a levered company and the default risk structure of interest rates. Real options, such as options to abandon or expand a project, are important in project evaluation.

KEY TERMS

call option 595
compound option 631
contingent claim 595
exercise (or strike) price 595
hedge ratio (or delta) 611
intrinsic value 601
option to abandon 631
option to defer 631
option to expand 631
option to reopen 631
option to study 631
payoff structure 597
put option 595
put–call parity 606
risk neutrality 611
time value 601
volatility 601

SELF-TEST PROBLEMS

1. A European call option is currently priced at $1.70 and has an exercise price of $15 and a term to expiry of 8 months. The current price of the underlying share is $14.90. The share does not pay dividends. The risk-free interest rate is 0.75 per cent per month (compound). The price of the equivalent put option is $0.83. Show that:

    (a) the price of the call option exceeds its minimum theoretical price
    (b) an arbitrage profit would be earned by simultaneously buying the put, selling the call, buying the share and borrowing the present value of the exercise price
    (c) explain the result in (b).

2. Use the binomial model to price a call option with the following features: exercise price $6, term to expiry

2 months, current share price $6.50, 'up' factor 1.05 per month, 'down' factor 1/1.05 per month and risk-free interest rate 1 per cent per month. Use two time periods, each of 1 month.

3. Use the Black–Scholes model to calculate the price of a European call option with the following features: exercise price $12, term to expiry 3 months, current share price $12.15, volatility (standard deviation) 20 per cent per annum and risk-free interest rate 10 per cent per annum (continuously compounding). The underlying share does not pay dividends.

Solutions to self-test problems are available in Appendix B, page 803.

REFERENCES

Alpert, K., 'Taxation and the early exercise of call options', *Journal of Business Finance and Accounting*, June/July 2010, pp. 715–36.

Asay, M.R., 'A note on the design of commodity options contracts', *Journal of Futures Markets*, 1982, pp. 1–8.

Australian Securities Exchange, *Explanatory Note for ASX Option Adjustments*, 2009, p. 14, www.asx.com.au/products/pdf/explanatory_note_option_adjustments.pdf.

Black, F., 'Fact and fantasy in the use of options', *Financial Analysts Journal*, July/August 1975, pp. 36–41, 61–72.

——, 'The pricing of commodity contracts', *Journal of Financial Economics*, January/March 1976, pp. 167–79.

——, & Scholes, M., 'The pricing of options and corporate liabilities', *Journal of Political Economy*, May/June 1973, pp. 637–54.

Brennan, M.J. & Schwartz, E.S., 'Evaluating natural resource investments', *Journal of Business*, 1985, pp. 135–58.

——, 'A new approach to evaluating natural resource investments', in J.M. Stern & D.H. Chew (eds), *The Revolution in Corporate Finance*, 2nd edn, Basil Blackwell, 1992, pp. 107–16.

Brenner, M., Courtadon, G. & Subrahmanyam, M., 'Options on the spot and options on futures', *Journal of Finance*, December 1985, pp. 1303–17.

Copeland, T.E. & Keenan, P.T., 'How much is flexibility worth?', *The McKinsey Quarterly*, no. 2, 1998, pp. 39–49.

Courtadon, G.R. & Merrick, J.J., 'The option pricing model and the valuation of corporate securities', in J.M. Stern & D.H. Chew (eds), *The Revolution in Corporate Finance*, 2nd edn, Basil Blackwell, 1992, pp. 265–78.

Cox, J.C., Ross, S.A. & Rubinstein, M., 'Option pricing: a simplified approach', *Journal of Financial Economics*, 1979, pp. 229–63.

Cox, J.C. & Rubinstein, M., *Option Markets*, 1st edn, Prentice-Hall, New Jersey, 1985.

Dixit, A.K. & Pindyck, R.S., 'The options approach to capital investment', *Harvard Business Review*, May/June 1995, pp. 105–15.

Geske, R., 'The valuation of corporate liabilities as compound options', *Journal of Financial and Quantitative Analysis*, November 1977, pp. 541–52.

——, 'The valuation of compound options', *Journal of Financial Economics*, March 1979, pp. 63–81.

Hull, J., *Fundamentals of Futures and Options Markets*, 7th edn, Prentice-Hall, New Jersey, 2010.

Ingersoll, J., 'A contingent-claims valuation of convertible securities', *Journal of Financial Economics*, May 1977, pp. 289–322.

Leslie, K.J. & Michaels, M.P., 'The real power of real options', *The McKinsey Quarterly*, no. 3, 1997, pp. 4–22.

Lieu, D. 'Option pricing with futures-style margining', *Journal of Futures Markets*, 1990, pp. 327–38.

Loudon, G.F., 'Put–call parity theory: evidence from the big Australian', *Australian Journal of Management*, June 1988, pp. 53–67.

Merton, R.C., 'Theory of rational option pricing', *Bell Journal of Economics and Management Science*, Spring 1973a, pp. 141–83.

——, 'The relationship between put and call prices: comment', *Journal of Finance*, March 1973b, pp. 183–4.

Ofek, E., Richardson, M. & Whitelaw, R.F., 'Limited arbitrage and short sales restrictions: evidence from the options markets', *Journal of Financial Economics*, November 2004, pp. 305–42.

Phang, G. & Brown, R., 'Rational early exercise of call options: Australian evidence', *Accounting and Finance*, forthcoming.

Smith, C.W. Jr, 'Alternative methods for raising capital: rights versus underwritten offerings', *Journal of Financial Economics*, December 1977, pp. 273–307.

Stoll, H.R., 'The relationship between put and call option prices', *Journal of Finance*, December 1969, pp. 802–24.

Trigeorgis, L., *Real Options: Managerial Flexibility and Strategy in Resource Allocation*, MIT Press, Cambridge (Mass.), 1996.

Whaley, R., 'Understanding VIX', *The Journal of Portfolio Management*, Spring 2009, pp. 98–105.

QUESTIONS

1. **[LO 1]** Distinguish between the following:
   (a) put option and call option
   (b) American option and European option
   (c) option contract and futures contract
   (d) time value of an option and time value of money.

2. **[LO 1]** *Selling a share is the opposite of buying a share. Therefore, an option to sell a share must be the opposite of an option to buy a share.* Is this statement true? Explain.

3. **[LO 2]** List and explain the factors likely to influence the value of a call option.

4. **[LO 3]** What is the value of a call option on its expiry date? Why? What is the value of a put option on its expiry date? Why?

5. **[LO 2]** *Options are so risky that trading in them is really just another form of gambling.* Discuss.

6. **[LO 3]** What is the minimum value of a call option on a share that does not pay dividends? Why?

7. **[LO 3]** Explain briefly why it is generally not rational to exercise a call option before its expiry date. Under what circumstances can it be rational? In these cases, what do option holders obtain, and what do they forgo?

8. **[LO 3]** A call option has no maximum possible value; a put option does. Why?

9. **[LO 2]** In 2002 a former executive with Macquarie Bank, Simon Hannes, was jailed for insider trading. The offence related to Mr Hannes trading on the basis of information he had received indicating the likely takeover of the transport company TNT by the Dutch firm KPN. Specifically, having learnt of the impending takeover, and at a time when TNT was trading at approximately $1.56 per share, Mr Hannes purchased almost $90 000 worth of short-dated call options with an exercise price of $2. Following the public announcement of the takeover bid, the share price for TNT increased to approximately $2.40 per share. Mr Hannes attempted to sell his options but the trades were questioned by his broker. Had the sale been successful he would have generated a profit in excess of $2.3 million.
   (a) Why do you think Mr Hannes employed options rather than shares to exploit the price-sensitive information he had in his possession? Specifically, why do you think he used short-dated out-of-the-money call options?
   (b) Could Mr Hannes have used put options to exploit the same information?

10. **[LO 5]** Diacono Shoes Ltd is an Australian manufacturer of upmarket shoes that utilises high-quality leather imported from Italy. The firm's CEO, Mr Lyle Diacono, is concerned about the possible increase in the price of the Italian leather that the firm uses due to an appreciation in the euro relative to the Australian dollar, and is considering alternative hedging strategies to mitigate this risk. He has been in contact with his friendly investment banker, who has pointed out that the firm might benefit by locking in an exchange rate using currency futures contracts or alternatively might consider buying options written on currency futures contracts. Assuming that he wants to mitigate the risk associated with adverse currency movements, what are the factors that Mr Diacono should consider when choosing between currency futures contracts and options written on currency futures contracts?

11. **[LO 5]** Ozzie Glassworks Ltd of Adelaide has been awarded the contract to supply glass for a giant aquarium to be built in Lancaster, England. However, the contract is conditional on the promoter of the project obtaining a construction approval from the Lancaster City Council. Ozzie Glassworks has quoted a fixed price of UK£2 000 000. What advice would you give Ozzie Glassworks? Explain.

12. **[LO 6]** Parklands Ltd has issued debentures. Explain how Parklands shares are similar to options.

13. **[LO 2]** Hi Gear Toys Ltd is facing severe financial difficulties; its cash flows are barely enough to cover its fixed-interest commitments. Hi Gear's share price is very low. Alf Hawke, Hi Gear's managing director, decides that the company should begin manufacturing a new toy that just might prove to be a runaway success (but probably will not). Alf announces the decision at a press conference. Do you think Hi Gear's share price would rise, fall or stay about the same? Why?

PROBLEMS

1. **Option pricing [LO 3]**
   The following is an extract from the *Xanadu Financial Review* of 2 November 2010.
   Call Option Trading
   Company: Jempip Industries Ltd
   Last sale price: $3.27

Expiry month	Exercise price ($)	Last sale ($)
December 2010	2.75	0.51
December 2010	3.00	0.32
December 2010	3.25	0.09
December 2010	3.50	0.04
December 2010	4.00	0.04
March 2011	2.75	0.64
March 2011	3.00	0.44
March 2011	3.25	0.18
March 2011	3.50	0.06
March 2011	4.00	0.04

   The risk-free interest rate in Xanadu is 1 per cent per month. Jempip options cover 1000 shares per contract, may be exercised at any time, expire at the end of their expiry month and are not protected against dividend payments. Jempip pays dividends of 10 cents per share in April and October each year. Which prices appear to violate option pricing theory? Give brief reasons.

2. **Put–call parity [LO 3]**
   You observe the following prices in a situation in which European put–call parity ought to apply:

Put price	$1.95
Call price	$1.10
Share price	$20.00
Exercise price	$22.00
Term to expiry	4 months
Risk-free interest rate	1% per month (compound)

   (a) Show that put–call parity is breached in this case.
   (b) Calculate the payoffs to show that the following strategy is an arbitrage: sell the call, buy the put, buy the share and borrow the present value of the exercise price for 4 months.

3. **Option pricing [LO 3]**
   You observe the following prices in a situation in which call options should sell for at least their minimum theoretical price of Max [0, current share price – present value of the exercise price]:

Call price	$0.33
Share price	$17.50
Exercise price	$18.00
Term to expiry	6 months
Risk-free interest rate	10% p.a. (simple, i.e. 5% for a 6-month period)

   What should the minimum call price be? Calculate the payoffs to show that the following strategy is an arbitrage: buy the call, short sell the share and lend $17.17 at the risk-free interest rate for 6 months.

4. **Put–call parity [LO 3]**
   Put and call options are available on the shares of Christopher Toms Ltd (CTL). The options are of the European type. CTL is due to pay its next dividend of 10 cents per share in January 2011. The risk-free interest rate is 1 per cent per month. On 31 August 2010 you observe the following market prices for CTL call options:
   Company: CTL
   Last sale price: $2.00

Expiry date	Exercise price ($)	Option price ($)
30 November 2010	2.25	0.10
30 November 2010	5.00	0.005

   Use put–call parity to estimate market prices for the November 2.25 and November 5.00 put options. If these put options had been of the American type, what would their minimum values have been? Does this suggest that, unlike call options, some American put options should be exercised prematurely? Why, or why not?

5. **Binomial option pricing [LO 4]**
   Use binomial option pricing to price a 3-month European call option with an exercise price of $15 on a share whose current price is also $15. Use three time periods of 1 month each, a monthly 'up factor' of 1.02 and a monthly 'down factor' of 1/1.02. The risk-free interest rate is 0.5 per cent per month.

6. **Binomial option pricing [LO 4]**
   Use binomial option pricing to calculate the price of the European put option that matches the call option in the previous problem. Does put–call parity hold?

7. **Black–Scholes pricing [LO 4]**
   (a) Calculate the Black–Scholes price for a call option with the following features: share price $3, exercise price of $2.75, term to expiry 3 months, risk-free interest rate 10 per cent per annum (continuously compounded) and volatility (variance) 0.16 per annum. Calculate the Black–Scholes price of a put option with the same features.
   (b) Calculate the Black–Scholes price for the same call option if the share price increases by 1 cent to $3.01. By how much does the call price change? How could you use this information to hedge against share price changes?
   (c) Compare the percentage change in the call price with the percentage change in the share price if the share price increases from $3 to $3.01. Why might this comparison be useful to someone with inside information on the company that issued the shares?

8. **Black–Scholes pricing [LO 4]**
   Calculate the Black–Scholes price for a call option with the following features: share price $25, exercise price $24.50, term to expiry 1 year, risk-free interest rate 6 per cent per annum (compounding annually) and volatility (variance) 0.0625 per annum.

9. **Black–Scholes pricing [LO 4]**
   Calculate the Black–Scholes price for a call option with the following features: share price $12.32, exercise price $12.50, term to expiry 180 days, risk-free 180-day bill rate 7.5 per cent per annum and volatility (variance) 0.0225 per annum.

10. **Currency option [LO 5]**
    Today is 8 August 2011. The Red Claret Hotel Group is selling a travel business that it has been operating in Kyoto, Japan. As a result, it expects to receive approximately 800 million yen in November 2011. The current exchange rate is about 63 yen to one Australian dollar. Because of its other financial commitments, Red Claret needs to be sure that it will receive at least A$12.3 million from the sale, regardless of any movements in the exchange rate. If the exchange rate moves in the company's favour during the next few months, the company is willing to forgo any gain accruing above an inflow of A$13.0 million. Foreign currency options on yen are available in contracts covering 100 million yen each, with exercise prices in half-yen steps, expiring on the second Thursday in August, September, October, November and December. What option contract(s) should Red Claret enter into? Explain.

11. **Futures options pricing [LO 5]**
    Use the futures call option pricing model (Equation 18.9) to value the following call option on the SPI 200 futures contract:
    - current futures price is 6170 points
    - exercise price (X) is 6000 points
    - term (T) of the option is 3 months
    - volatility (σ^2) of the futures contract is 20 per cent per annum
    - risk-free interest rate (i) is 6.75 per cent per annum (continuously compounding).

12. **Real options [LO 6]**
    Duff Ltd is a brewing company that was established 3 years ago. When it commenced operations, management purchased a bottling machine for $1.2 million. This machine has the ability to be converted so that it also inserts corks into wine bottles. The conversion costs $250 000. An equivalent machine, without the ability to be converted so that it also seals wine bottles, would have cost $800 000.
    (a) Define the option described above (i.e. name it and label it as either a put or a call option).
    (b) In addition to the risk-free rate of return and the term to expiry, the following four characteristics have been shown to affect the value of an option:
       (i) current value of asset
       (ii) exercise price of option
       (iii) volatility of asset returns over the life of the option
       (iv) dividends paid during life of option.
    Describe these characteristics in relation to the option possessed by Duff Ltd.

(c) The 'premium' for a financial option is the price paid to acquire it. Is there any premium associated with the real option described above?

(d) Are there any circumstances in which Duff Ltd may exercise its option early? Explain the advantages and disadvantages associated with early exercise.

13. **Options in loan contracts [LO 1]**

The loan contract described as follows is a simplified version of an actual security: RA Best Constructions International Ltd seeks to borrow from Multi Bank the sum of US$10 million, repayable by a single payment to be made in 1 year's time. However, this payment is made up of two components:

- Component 1 is a payment of US$2 million, which for convenience may be called 'interest' at the rate of 20 per cent per annum.
- Component 2 is the payment of an amount that depends on the exchange rate between yen and US dollars on the maturity date of the loan. We may call this a repayment, R, in full satisfaction of the principal, X, which is owed. If the future exchange rate, S, is 169 (or more) yen per US dollar, then the full principal of US$10 million must be repaid. If the future exchange rate is 84.5 (or fewer) yen per US dollar, then none of the principal needs to be repaid; Best is 'forgiven' all the debt. If the future exchange rate falls between 84.5 and 169 yen per US dollar, the repayment required is related to the principal according to the following formula:

$$R = X\left(1 + \frac{S - 169}{S}\right)$$

When Multi Bank investigated this proposal, the exchange rate was 185 yen per US dollar. At the same date the interest rate that Best would have paid for a standard 1-year fixed rate US dollar loan was 11 per cent per annum.

(a) Taking Multi Bank's viewpoint, analyse the loan in terms of its options characteristics.

(b) Again taking Multi Bank's viewpoint, and assuming that you have a model that can be used to value any option you may define, explain how you would investigate this proposal.

Test yourself further with Connect Plus online! Ask your lecturer or tutor for your course's unique URL.

CHAPTER 19
ANALYSIS OF TAKEOVERS

LEARNING OBJECTIVES
After studying this chapter you should be able to:

1. evaluate suggested reasons for takeovers
2. explain how to estimate the gains and costs of a takeover
3. explain the main differences between cash and share-exchange takeovers
4. outline the regulation and tax effects of takeovers in Australia
5. outline defence strategies that can be used by target companies
6. identify the various types of corporate restructuring transactions
7. outline the main findings of empirical research on the effects of takeovers on shareholders' wealth.

CHAPTER CONTENTS
19.1 Introduction
19.2 Reasons for takeovers
19.3 Economic evaluation of takeovers
19.4 Alternative valuation approaches
19.5 Regulation and tax effects of takeovers
19.6 Takeover defences
19.7 Corporate restructuring
19.8 Empirical evidence on takeovers

19.1 INTRODUCTION

Takeovers are important transactions in the *market for corporate control*. A takeover typically involves one company purchasing another company by acquiring a controlling interest in its voting shares. Such an investment is variously described as a 'takeover', an 'acquisition' or a 'merger'. It is possible to distinguish between mergers and takeovers, but in this chapter the term **takeover** will generally be used to refer to all instances where an acquiring company[1] achieves control of another company, referred to as the **target company**.

takeover
acquisition of control of one company by another

target company
object of a takeover bid

The market for corporate control is a market in which alternative teams of managers compete for the right to control corporate assets and make top-level management decisions (Jensen & Ruback 1983). Essentially, by changes in control, corporate assets can be quickly redeployed in ways expected to bring economic benefits and add value for shareholders. Other transactions in this market include divestitures, spin-offs and buyouts, all of which are defined and discussed in Section 19.7. The main topic of this chapter is takeovers, because they are the most important of these transactions in the Australian market for corporate control.

After a takeover, the acquiring company obtains control of the target company's assets, so a takeover is an indirect investment in assets. The fact that the investment is made indirectly does not change the basic principle that an investment should proceed if, and only if, it has a positive net present value (NPV). Despite this basic similarity between takeovers and other investments, there are several reasons why takeovers should be treated as a separate topic. These reasons include:

(a) takeovers are controversial and at times there has been rather heated public debate about whether takeover activity is beneficial to shareholders and the economy
(b) the NPV of a takeover can be very difficult to estimate, but correct analysis will be easier if it is based on an understanding of why takeovers occur and on knowledge of the evidence on their effects on returns to investors
(c) a takeover may give rise to complex legal, accounting and tax questions
(d) the acquiring company's plans may be frustrated by defensive tactics employed by the management of the target company, or by the intervention of other potential acquirers.

19.1.1 FLUCTUATIONS IN TAKEOVER ACTIVITY

Takeover activity fluctuates widely over time. These fluctuations are reflected in Figure 19.1 overleaf, which shows that between 1974 and 2009 the number of bids for Australian listed companies varied between a high of 289 in 1988 and a low of 38 in 1994 and 2002.

These fluctuations are often described as takeover 'waves'. In the US, takeover waves have occurred at the turn of the twentieth century, in the 1920s, the 1960s, the 1980s and a further wave of takeover activity began in 1993 (Gaughan 1994; Andrade, Mitchell & Stafford 2001). The phenomenon of takeover waves is not fully understood, but there is evidence that takeover activity in Australia is positively related to the behaviour of share prices. For example, Bishop, Dodd and Officer (1987) reported a close relationship between changes in share prices and the number of takeovers in the period 1972 to 1984. The explanation preferred by Bishop, Dodd and Officer for this relationship is that periods when the prices of shares are increasing rapidly are also periods of optimism for investment. The increase in share prices will reflect increased demand for real goods, which will require companies to increase their productive capacity. While companies will increase their capacity by investing in new plant and equipment (internal investment), managers will also be

---
1. When a takeover bid is first announced, the eventual outcome is unknown. Therefore we also use the terms 'bidder' or 'offeror' when a takeover is still in progress.

FIGURE 19.1 Number of takeover bids for Australian listed firms

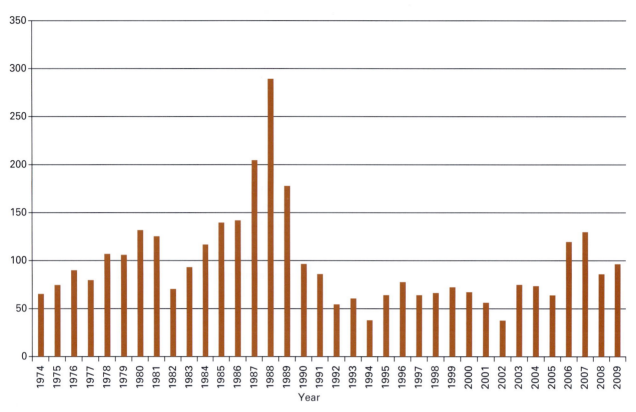

Sources: **1980**, S. Bishop, P. Dodd & R.R. Officer, 'Australian takeovers: the evidence 1972–1985', *Policy Monograph*, 12, Centre for Independent Studies, St Leonards, 1987; **1985 to 1990**, Corporate Adviser; **1995 to 2009**, SDC Platinum.

looking for opportunities to take control of existing assets, particularly assets that are not being used efficiently. When such opportunities are found there will be an increase in takeover activity (external investment). In short, both internal and external investment will respond to the same economic forces. Therefore, a relationship between the state of the economy and the level of takeover activity is to be expected. In the most recent Australian study of the relationship between takeover activity, share prices and economic conditions, Finn and Hodgson (2005) examined 1665 successful takeovers that occurred between 1972 and 1996. They conclude that share prices and takeover activity share a common long-term trend, which is contrary to previous studies that have suggested that each responds to the other over a shorter timeframe. Further, they find that aggregate takeover activity is influenced by fundamental economic factors such as industrial production, capital expenditure and interest rate levels, rather than by speculative activity.

Researchers in the US have noted that at any given time, takeover activity exhibits industry clustering and each wave of takeovers is different in terms of industry composition. These observations suggest that a significant portion of takeover activity might be due to economic shocks at the industry level. For example, an industry might be affected by major technological changes, supply shocks such as changes in commodity prices, and deregulation (Andrade, Mitchell & Stafford 2001). These shocks can lead to excess capacity and stimulate an increase in takeovers that lead to liquidation of marginal assets. Andrade and Stafford (2004) demonstrate that in addition to takeovers providing an opportunity for firms operating in growth industries to expand productive capacity, they also provide the mechanism by which firms operating in industries that are contracting and have low growth prospects exit the industry and allow invested capital to be redeployed elsewhere. As Jensen (1988) points out, if an industry has suffered slowing growth, it is preferable that excess capacity is reduced in this orderly way rather than the more costly and disorderly process of bankruptcy.

19.1.2 TYPES OF TAKEOVER

Takeovers are usually classified as follows:

- A **horizontal takeover** is the takeover of a target company operating in the same line of business as the acquiring company. An example of this form of takeover is the takeover by Westpac Bank of St George bank in May 2008.
- A **vertical takeover** is the takeover of a target company that is either a supplier of goods to, or a consumer of goods produced by, the acquiring company. An example is the 2008 acquisition of the iron-ore mining company Midwest Corporation by Sinosteel, a steel producer.
- A **conglomerate takeover** is the takeover of a target company in an unrelated type of business. There have been a number of high-profile acquisitions of this type. For example, over the last 25 years Wesfarmers has acquired firms operating in industries as diverse as retail, mining, liquefied petroleum gas distribution and insurance.

horizontal takeover
takeover of a target company operating in the same line of business as the acquiring company

vertical takeover
takeover of a target company that is either a supplier of goods to, or a consumer of goods produced by, the acquiring company

conglomerate takeover
takeover of a target company in an unrelated type of business

REASONS FOR TAKEOVERS

19.2

Just as there are different types of takeovers, so there are many different reasons why takeovers occur. We begin by presenting a framework for the evaluation of these reasons and then discuss some of the suggested reasons individually.

As noted above, takeovers are part of the market for corporate control in which alternative management teams compete for the right to manage corporate assets. Competition in this market should ensure that asset control is acquired by those teams that are expected to be the most efficient in utilising those assets. It should also ensure that the interests of management cannot diverge too far from those of shareholders. For example, suppose that a company is poorly managed, resulting in low profits and a low share price. An opportunity then exists for a more efficient management team to take over this company, replace the inefficient managers and reverse the poor performance of the company. However, the market for corporate control should not be viewed only as providing a severe disciplinary measure against incompetent management. Increased profitability through a change of management does not necessarily imply that the previous management was incompetent, only that a more efficient team was available (Dodd & Officer 1986).

LEARNING OBJECTIVE 1
Evaluate suggested reasons for takeovers

Wealth (or value) can be created by combining two companies if the takeover transfers control of assets to managers who can recognise more valuable uses for those assets, either within the combined company or by redeployment of the assets elsewhere. The term **synergy** is often used to describe the value gains that can be associated with combining two entities. In other words, if there are synergistic benefits associated with combining two companies A and T, then the combined company will be worth more than the sum of their values as independent entities:

$$V_{AT} > V_A + V_T$$

where V_{AT} = the value of the assets of the combined company
V_A = the value of Company A operating independently
V_T = the value of Company T operating independently

synergy
in takeovers, the situation where the performance and therefore the value of a combined entity exceeds the sum of the previously separate components

In this chapter the subscripts $_A$ and $_T$ are used to denote the acquiring and target companies, respectively.

To summarise, the main implications of this approach are that takeovers are value-increasing transactions and that the market for corporate control is influenced largely by the existence of synergies. It follows that, in evaluating the suggested reasons for takeovers, we need to consider whether the particular reason suggested is consistent with the existence of an economic gain from combining two companies. The suggested reasons for takeovers that we will evaluate are as follows:

- the target company is managed inefficiently
- the acquiring and target companies have assets that are complementary
- the target company is undervalued
- cost reductions result from the takeover
- increased market power results from the takeover
- diversification benefits result from the takeover
- the target company or the acquiring company has excess liquidity or free cash flow
- tax benefits result from the takeover
- there are increased earnings per share and price–earnings ratio effects.

19.2.1 EVALUATION OF THE REASONS FOR TAKEOVERS

The target company is managed inefficiently

In this case, the acquiring company's managers may see an opportunity to use the target company's assets more efficiently. The more efficient use of assets may result in an increase in the value of the target company. However, the acquiring company's aspiration to improve the efficiency of the target company's operations may not always be realised. Even if an acquiring company is managed efficiently, this does not necessarily mean that its managers will be able to improve the performance of another company. This is particularly so where the two companies operate in different industries. This suggests that improvements in efficiency are less likely to be achieved with a conglomerate takeover. As a corollary, improvements in efficiency are most likely to be achieved with a horizontal takeover, as the acquiring company's managers are likely to have the expertise needed to manage the target company's operations more efficiently.

However, the market value of a company may be low, not because its managers are inefficient, but because they make decisions in their own interests rather than in those of the company's shareholders. The discussion of agency costs in Chapter 1 suggests that managers may attempt to transfer wealth from shareholders to themselves. If the value reduction is large, it is likely that the company will eventually be identified as a takeover target, since an acquiring company will be able to eliminate, or at least reduce, the agency costs, thereby providing benefits for its own shareholders.

Complementary assets

A takeover can be attractive if either or both of the companies can provide the other with needed assets at relatively low cost. For example, this can occur when the target company's managers are considered to have valuable skills. The motive for the takeover is to acquire expertise. It may be cheaper to acquire this expertise via a takeover than to hire and train new staff. This is often an argument for taking over small, often unlisted, companies that have failed to realise their full potential because their managers do not have skills in all areas of management. For example, a group of engineers may establish a computer hardware company that does not earn a satisfactory profit because the engineers lack marketing skills. A large company with a strong marketing team may take it over because it is seen as a relatively cheap means of acquiring the technical skills of the target company's staff. Similarly, the complementary skills of the acquiring company's staff may be used to improve the target's profitability.

The target company is undervalued

Describing a target company as simply 'undervalued' is not very meaningful, since a takeover always implies that the target is worth more to the acquiring company than it was worth to its previous shareholders. Managers of acquiring companies often refer to their targets as 'presenting wonderful opportunities' or 'too good to pass up', suggesting that they believe in their ability to identify 'bargains'. Chapter 16 presents empirical evidence on market efficiency, which suggests that most managers will find it very difficult to identify such opportunities. However, even if managers are able to identify undervalued shares, it is not necessary to buy whole companies, paying premiums for control, to profit from their ability to identify 'bargains'. Instead, they could buy a parcel of the shares at the market price, wait until the market recognises the shares' value, and then sell.

It has never been seriously suggested that share markets are fully efficient in the strong-form sense. It is therefore possible that a company's managers may have private information not yet reflected in the price of another company's shares. Share acquisition follows, and may extend to acquiring a controlling interest in the target company.

A takeover may also occur when the market value of the target company is less than the sum of the market values of its assets. This does not necessarily mean that the share market is inefficient, as the company's share price may accurately reflect the value of its assets in their current use. However, such a company can become a takeover target because other managers recognise the existence of alternative, better uses for the assets. Investors who focus on searching for takeover opportunities of this type are often referred to as **corporate raiders** or asset strippers. Their activities can be regarded as involving a form of synergy because a crucial factor is the skill of the acquiring company's managers in identifying opportunities to create value by redeploying assets to alternative uses.

corporate raiders aggressive corporate or individual investors who purchase a company's shares with the intention of achieving a controlling interest and replacing the existing management

Cost reductions

Another reason for takeovers is that the total cost of operating the combined company is expected to be less than the cost of operating the two companies separately. These cost savings may be due to various economies of scale, and are therefore more likely to be achieved in the case of a horizontal takeover. For example, two furniture manufacturers, by combining, may be able to reduce their production costs because production runs will be longer, resulting in the fixed costs of a production run being incurred less frequently. Cost savings may also be achieved in a vertical takeover. For example, combining companies where one is a supplier to the other may result in more efficient coordination of the activities of the two companies. One reason is that the costs of communication and various forms of bargaining can be reduced by a vertical takeover.

Increased market power

Taking over a company in the same industry may increase the market power of the combined company. The increase in market power may enable the acquiring company to earn monopoly profits if there are significant barriers to entry into the industry. Governments frequently legislate to prevent takeovers that are considered likely to result in an excessive level of concentration in an industry. Section 50 of the *Competition and Consumer Act 2010* prohibits a company from acquiring the shares or assets of another company where the acquisition is likely to result in a substantial lessening of competition in a market. The Australian Competition and Consumer Commission (ACCC, www.accc.gov.au) has issued *Merger Guidelines* that explain the procedures and policies that it will follow in determining whether it will oppose a particular takeover on the grounds that the takeover is anticompetitive. An example of such opposition occurred in April 2010 when the ACCC announced that it would oppose the acquisition of AXA Asia Pacific Holdings—a firm that provided insurance and wealth management services—by

WWW

National Australia Bank on the grounds that the acquisition would result in a substantial lessening of competition in the market for providing investment advice to retail customers.

Diversification benefits

Portfolio theory shows that investors can reduce their risk by holding a diversified portfolio of assets.[2] A similar reason has been advanced to justify a takeover. The takeover, it is suggested, enables a company to reduce risk via diversification. Assume that a steel manufacturer diversifies its interests by taking over an oil exploration company. The question is: Does the reduced risk brought about by the takeover benefit the steel manufacturer's shareholders? The somewhat surprising answer is generally no. The steel manufacturer's shareholders already had the opportunity to hold shares in oil exploration companies so the takeover does not provide any investment opportunity that did not previously exist. Therefore, when shareholders themselves hold diversified portfolios, diversification by a company is a neutral factor that will neither alter its market value nor benefit its shareholders. Takeovers motivated by diversification can be beneficial to managers. Therefore, the occurrence of such takeovers can indicate the existence of agency problems.[3]

A related argument is that combining two companies whose earnings streams are less than perfectly correlated will lower the risk of default on debt, so that the debt capacity of the combination is greater than the sum of the debt capacities of the two companies operating separately. This is the result of the *co-insurance effect*, which means that lenders to one company can now be paid out of the combined assets of both companies. While the co-insurance argument is essentially correct, the problem is that shareholders will not necessarily benefit from the reduction in default risk and interest cost of debt.

Suppose that two companies, each with debt securities outstanding, merge. The default risk of each company's debt will fall and the value of the debt securities will increase. This gain to debtholders is at the expense of shareholders, who now have to guarantee the debt of both companies, and the loss to shareholders exactly offsets the gain to debtholders. If two companies combine and *then* borrow, the shareholders will benefit from a lower interest rate, but they are providing the lenders with lower risk, so there is still no net gain. However, shareholders can benefit from the co-insurance effect to the extent that expected bankruptcy costs are reduced, or there are net tax savings. Therefore, while combining companies can yield genuine financing benefits, it is doubtful that their magnitude is sufficient to justify many takeovers.

Excess liquidity or free cash flow

A company with excess liquidity may be identified as a takeover target by companies seeking access to funds. However, it seems difficult to justify paying a premium to obtain control of a company for this reason alone, because the capital market can provide funds at lower transaction costs. On the other hand, companies with excess liquidity may turn to the acquisition of other companies rather than return more cash to their shareholders. Such takeovers may result from managers pursuing their own interests, rather than maximising the wealth of shareholders. Managers may pursue greater market share in existing lines of business or diversification into additional industries because larger companies are often associated with higher salaries and benefits, and more promotion opportunities. Jensen argued that this conflict of interest can be severe in companies that generate substantial free cash flow and can lead to such companies engaging in takeovers that generate very small benefits, or even value reductions.[4] For example, diversification programs achieved through takeovers are likely to benefit managers but may reduce shareholders' wealth.

---

2 See Section 7.5.

3 However, there may be cases where company diversification is of value to investors. Shareholdings in a private family company may represent a high proportion of the family's wealth and the family members may wish to reduce their risk by diversifying. To obtain the funds to invest elsewhere, they might have to sell part of their interest in the company, but this would mean diluting their control, and might also cause a large capital gains tax bill. Because of these barriers, diversification by the company will almost certainly be more attractive than diversification by the individual shareholders. Such cases are the exception rather than the rule, and for public companies whose shareholders can diversify cheaply, company diversification will not add value for shareholders.

4 Free cash flow is defined as operating cash flow in excess of that required to fund all projects that have positive net present values. See Jensen (1986 and 1998).

Where managers persist in this type of activity, their own company is likely eventually to become a takeover target. Therefore, the free cash flow hypothesis shows how some takeovers are evidence of the conflicts of interest between shareholders and managers, while others are a response to the problem.

Tax benefits

Taking over a company with accumulated tax losses may reduce the total tax payable by the combined company. The Commissioner of Taxation restricts the use of past accumulated tax losses to situations where it can be shown that either the *continuity-of-ownership test* or the *same-business test* is satisfied.[5] The former test requires that owners of at least 51 per cent of the company's shares when it incurred losses remain as owners when those accumulated losses are offset against taxable income. The same-business test provides that where the continuity-of-ownership test is not satisfied, the past accumulated losses can still be offset against taxable income where the acquired company continues in the same business after the takeover. For companies with resident shareholders, the incentive to reduce company tax payments in this way is much smaller under the imputation tax system than it was under the classical tax system. This follows from the fact that, as discussed in Chapter 11, company tax is essentially a withholding tax against the personal tax liabilities of shareholders. Other things being equal, reduction of company tax will mean that shareholders have to pay *more* personal tax on dividends. Therefore, any advantage associated with lowering company tax payments will be only a timing advantage.

Increased earnings per share and price–earnings ratio effects

Corporate financial objectives are sometimes expressed in terms of growth in earnings per share (EPS), and this may lead an acquiring company to evaluate the effect of a proposed takeover on its EPS. Unfortunately, this approach is unreliable. While a takeover that is economically viable should lead to increased EPS for the acquiring company, it is easy to design a takeover that produces no economic benefits, but which nevertheless produces an immediate increase in EPS. Example 19.1 illustrates this situation.

EXAMPLE 19.1

This example refers to the data in Table 19.1.

TABLE 19.1 Effect of takeover on earnings per share and market value of Company A

ITEM	COMPANY A	COMPANY T	COMBINED COMPANY A + T
No. of shares	200 000	100 000	250 000
Earnings ($/year)	200 000	100 000	300 000
EPS ($)	1.00	1.00	1.20
Share price ($)	10.00	5.00	10.00
P–E ratio	10.00	5.00	8.33
Market value of equity ($m)	2.00	0.50	2.50

Suppose that there are no economic benefits associated with combining companies A and T. If A acquires T by issuing one of its shares, worth $10, for every two T shares, also worth a total of $10, what is the effect of the takeover on the EPS and value of Company A?

SOLUTION

As there are no economic benefits, the earnings of the combined company will simply be the sum of the individual companies' earnings, $300 000 per annum. The takeover will mean issuing a further 50 000

continued →

5 See Subdivision 165-A of the *Income Tax Assessment Act 1997*.

> **Example 19.1** *continued*
>
> A shares, making 250 000 on issue, and the EPS for the combined company will be $300 000/250 000 = $1.20, an immediate increase of 20 per cent. Although the takeover *looks* attractive, it *cannot* be attractive because the takeover generates no economic benefits. The fact that it has no economic benefits is seen in the final row of Table 19.1: the combined company is worth only the sum of the values of the two individual companies.

The reason that EPS increases in Example 19.1 is simply that A was able to acquire a company with earnings of $100 000 per annum by issuing only 50 000 of its shares. This, in turn, was possible because A's price–earnings ratio of 10 was greater than T's ratio of 5. The effect we have illustrated here is called *bootstrapping* and it occurs in share-exchange takeovers whenever the acquiring company's price–earnings ratio exceeds the target company's price–earnings ratio. Therefore, if EPS is used in takeover evaluation it is important to distinguish between the effects of true growth and the bootstrap effect. To avoid confusion, it might be better simply to ignore EPS in the context of takeovers.

We do not expect everyone to heed our last piece of advice so we will go one step further to highlight another way in which 'analysis' based on EPS can be misleading. An analyst, impressed by the 20 per cent increase in EPS resulting from A's acquisition of T, might be tempted to value the combined company by applying A's price–earnings ratio of 10 to the new EPS of $1.20, giving a share price of $12 and an equity value of $12 250 000 = $3 million. But this must be wrong, because, with no economic benefits, the value of the combined company can only be $2.5 million, so the share price is $10 and the price–earnings ratio is 8.33 rather than 10. We have more to say about the use of price–earnings ratios later in the chapter, but the point we wish to emphasise now is that there is no basis for assuming that an acquiring company's pre-takeover price–earnings ratio will continue to apply to a combined company.

19.2.2 SURVEY EVIDENCE OF THE MOTIVES FOR TAKEOVERS

Having evaluated possible reasons for one firm acquiring another, it is useful at this point to consider what the managers of acquiring companies have to say about their rationale for takeovers. Mukherjee, Kiymaz and Baker (2004) surveyed the chief financial officers of US bidder firms that had been involved in the 100 largest takeovers in each year between 1990 and 2001, and asked them to identify the relative importance of alternative reasons for the acquisition. Results are provided in Table 19.2.

TABLE 19.2 Motives for takeovers

MOTIVE	PERCENTAGE OF RESPONDENTS THAT RANKED THIS MOTIVE AS MOST IMPORTANT
Take advantage of synergy	37.3
Diversify	29.3
Achieve a specific organisational form as part of an ongoing restructuring program	10.7
Acquire a company below its replacement cost	8.0
Use excess free cash	5.3
Reduce tax on the combined company due to tax losses of the acquired company	2.7
Other	6.7

Source: T.K. Mukherjee, H. Kiymaz & H. Baker, 'Merger motives and target valuation: a survey of evidence from CFOs', *Journal of Applied Finance*, Winter 2004, p. 15.

The relative importance of realising synergistic benefits is not unexpected given that these benefits are perhaps the easiest to identify—and hence communicate to shareholders of both the bidder and target firms. Of interest, given the discussion in Section 19.2.1, is the relatively high ranking given to diversification as a justification for takeover activity. When quizzed further on the sources of the diversification benefits, the most popular response was that diversification '*results in much less devastating effects on the firm during economic downturns*'. While this response is consistent with the notion that shareholders may benefit through the firm diversifying by the consequent reduction in expected bankruptcy costs—due to a lower probability of bankruptcy—it is also consistent with management attempting to protect the value of their own capital (both financial and human), which is largely tied up in the firm. This second effect is an example of an agency problem that might adversely affect the value of the firm, especially if managers are willing to overpay for targets in order to realise these diversification benefits.

19.2.3 THE ROLES OF TAKEOVERS

The valid reasons for takeovers can be classified into two groups, which suggests two main roles for takeovers. First, the threat or potential for takeover can *discipline* management of target companies. To be effective, threats must sometimes be carried out, and in cases where significant inefficiencies or agency problems remain, the managers of target companies can be replaced by takeovers.[6]

Second, takeovers can take advantage of *synergies* such as economies of scale or complementarity between assets. A basic difference between these two roles is that in the first case the gains are associated with *changes of control*, whereas in the second case, the gains are associated with *combining* previously separate assets or companies. Another difference is that takeovers designed to replace management are more likely to be hostile than those driven by synergies.

In both cases there are usually other ways in which similar benefits can be achieved. Poor management could be replaced by a company's own Board of Directors and synergies associated with combining assets can be achieved through joint ventures. Therefore, takeovers are one way in which management can be improved or synergies exploited, but the prevalence of takeovers suggests that they are often the most effective way.

19.3 ECONOMIC EVALUATION OF TAKEOVERS

For an acquiring company, takeovers are investments that should proceed if their net present value (NPV) is positive. This may sound simple, but takeovers are typically complex; the benefits involved may not be obvious, and there are several ways in which NPV analysis could be applied to them. Some of these ways are best avoided because they are particularly prone to the effects of forecast errors. Therefore, it is desirable to use a framework that directs attention to the key issues of identifying and quantifying the benefits of a proposed takeover and comparing benefits with costs.

LEARNING OBJECTIVE 2
Explain how to estimate the gains and costs of a takeover

Assume that you are an investment analyst employed by Company A to evaluate the takeover of Company T. The gain from the takeover can be defined as the difference between the value of the combined company and the sum of their values as independent entities:

$$\text{Gain} = V_{AT} - (V_A + V_T) \qquad [19.1]$$

The logic of Equation 19.1 is that it should prompt the following question: What characteristics of this takeover mean that the two companies should be worth more when combined than when separate?

---

[6] Evidence that the turnover rate for the top executive of target companies increases dramatically following a takeover is provided by Martin and McConnell (1991). They also found that in cases where the top executive was replaced after a takeover, target companies had been performing poorly relative to other companies in their industry. These results indicate that the takeover market is important in controlling the behaviour of managers.

However, the fact that there is a gain from the takeover does not necessarily mean that it should proceed. Management also has to consider the cost of obtaining control of the target. Assuming for the present that cash is used to buy Company T, the net cost is defined as:

$$\text{Net cost} = \text{cash} - V_T \qquad [19.2]$$

The term *net cost* is used to emphasise that we are considering cost in terms of the *premium* paid over T's value as an independent entity. The takeover will have a positive NPV for Company A's shareholders only if the gain exceeds the net cost:

$$\begin{aligned}NPV_A &= \text{gain} - \text{net cost} \\ &= \text{gain} - \text{cash} + V_T > 0\end{aligned} \qquad [19.3]$$

If NPV_A is equal to zero, then Equation 19.3 can be used to find the value of Company T to Company A, $V_{T(A)}$, which is the maximum price A should pay for the target:

$$V_{T(A)} = \text{cash} = \text{gain} + V_T \qquad [19.4]$$

Therefore, the valuation of Company T can be broken into two steps: the first is to estimate V_T and the second is to estimate the gain from the takeover. If the target is a listed company, the evidence on market efficiency shows that the market capitalisation of the company's securities should be an unbiased estimate of V_T, so the main emphasis should be on estimating the gain. In other words, it is necessary to focus on the *incremental* cash flow effects of the takeover. There are likely to be effects on both cash inflows and outflows, which can be categorised as in the following checklist:

Incremental inflows
(a) sales revenue
(b) proceeds from disposal of surplus assets.

Incremental outflows
(a) operating costs
(b) taxes paid
(c) capital investment to upgrade existing assets or acquire new assets.

Valuation of a target company based on incremental cash flows is illustrated in Example 19.2.

EXAMPLE 19.2

You are an analyst for Mayfair Ltd, which is considering the acquisition of Board Ltd. You have identified the following effects of the takeover:

- investment of $400 000 will be required immediately to upgrade some of Board's older assets
- asset upgrading, economies of scale and improved efficiency will increase net operating cash flows by $290 000 per annum in perpetuity
- some of Board's assets that have been producing a cash inflow of $70 000 per annum will be sold. The new owners of these assets should be able to use them more profitably and sale proceeds are expected to be $800 000
- new plant costing $1 million will be purchased and is expected to generate net operating cash flows of $230 000 per annum in perpetuity.

Board's activities are all of the same risk and the required rate of return is 15 per cent per annum. Your chief executive has asked you to estimate:

(a) the gain from the takeover
(b) the maximum price that Mayfair should be prepared to pay for Board's shares.

SOLUTION

(a) Based on your estimates, the overall change in net operating cash flows will be $290 000 − $70 000 + $230 000 = $450 000 per annum. This has a present value of $450 000/0.15 = $3 million. The gain will be:

$$\text{Gain} = \$3\,000\,000 - \$400\,000 + \$800\,000 - \$1\,000\,000$$
$$= \$2\,400\,000$$

(b) The maximum price Mayfair should be prepared to pay is the value of Board Ltd as an independent entity, plus the gain of $2.4 million. Board has 5 million shares on issue, which have a market price of $2 each. Assuming that market price equals value as an independent entity:

$$V_T = 5\,000\,000 \times \$2 = \$10\,000\,000$$

and:

$$V_{T(A)} = \$2\,400\,000 + \$10\,000\,000 = \$12\,400\,000$$

so the maximum price Mayfair should be prepared to pay is:

$$\$12\,400\,000/5\,000\,000$$
$$= \$2.48 \text{ per share}$$

19.3.1 COMMENTS ON ESTIMATION OF TAKEOVER GAINS

The cash flow effects in Example 19.2 were deliberately kept very simple so that complex discounted cash flow calculations would not cloud the central issue of the *incremental* effects of a takeover. In doing so, the impression may have been given that, apart from assessing any immediate cash flow effects associated with sale or purchase of assets, estimating the gain from a takeover only involves estimating the incremental operating cash flows and discounting these cash flows at the target company's required rate of return.

In some cases this may be so, but in other cases there will be a need to divide the incremental cash flows into different risk classes and apply a different discount rate to each class, and there may be cases where discounted cash flow analysis is not the best approach at all. For example, a takeover may open up new growth opportunities, which result in intangible strategic benefits whose values are very uncertain. The immediate cash flow effect of investing in such opportunities is generally negative, but these outlays may be necessary in order to have the opportunity of entering a new development. The outlays can therefore be viewed as the purchase price of an option, and the option-pricing principles discussed in Chapter 18 are likely to be more applicable than discounted cash flow analysis.[7]

19.3.2 COMPARING GAINS AND COSTS

In Example 19.2, the gain from Mayfair Ltd acquiring Board Ltd was estimated to be $2.4 million. Before making an offer, Mayfair's management also has to consider the net cost of the takeover. The method used to estimate the net cost differs depending on whether the acquiring company pays cash for the target or issues shares in exchange for the shares of the target company. Estimation of the net cost of a cash takeover is illustrated in Example 19.3.

LEARNING OBJECTIVE 3
Explain the main differences between cash and share-exchange takeovers

---

[7] For a detailed discussion of valuation methods, see Copeland, Koller and Murrin (2000).

EXAMPLE 19.3

Suppose that Mayfair pays $2.30 per share for Board, giving a total outlay of $11.5 million. What is:

(a) the net cost of the takeover?
(b) the gain to Mayfair's shareholders?

SOLUTION

(a) In Equation 19.2, the net cost of a cash takeover was defined as the amount of cash paid, minus the value of the target as an independent entity. The net cost is:

Net cost = cash − V_T
= $11 500 000 − $10 000 000
= $1 500 000

This result shows that $1.5 million of the total gain associated with the takeover goes to Board's shareholders. This is the cost to Mayfair of gaining control of Board.

(b) The NPV for Mayfair's shareholders (Equation 19.3) is:

NPV_A = gain − net cost
= $2 400 000 − $1 500 000
= $900 000

Example 19.3 illustrates a fundamental point: the amount of the cash consideration determines how the total gain is divided between the two sets of shareholders: every additional dollar paid to Board's shareholders means a dollar less for Mayfair's shareholders.

For a cash takeover, comparing gains and costs is straightforward when, as we have assumed so far, the value of the target as an independent entity is equal to its market value. Suppose, however, that Board Ltd has been regarded by market participants as a likely takeover target and this speculation has increased its share price from $1.70 to $2. In other words, part of the possible gains from a takeover are already impounded in Board's market price and V_T is only $8.5 million, rather than the market value of $10 million.

The true value of Board to Mayfair is $8.5 million + $2.4 million = $10.9 million, which means that paying $11.5 million will harm, rather than benefit, Mayfair's shareholders. In terms of our previous calculations, the gain is still $2.4 million, but the true net cost is:

Net cost = cash − V_T
= $11 500 000 − $8 500 000
= $3 000 000

and:

NPV_A = gain − net cost
= $2 400 000 − $3 000 000
= −$600 000

This problem highlights two important lessons for the management of acquiring companies. First, management should check that the share price of a proposed target has not already been increased by takeover rumours. Second, management should keep its takeover intentions completely confidential until formally announcing the bid.

Finally, in making a distinction between value and market price, we are not suggesting that there is any market inefficiency, or that there is anything wrong with the market price. In fact the market would be inefficient if it did *not* respond to rumours of a possible takeover. The problem is that if there are rumours that have increased the target's share price, the market price no longer gives a measure of the target's value as an independent entity.

19.3.3 ESTIMATING COST FOR A SHARE-EXCHANGE TAKEOVER

Estimating the net cost of a cash takeover offer is straightforward.[8] In the case of the proposed takeover of Board by Mayfair, the net cost was:

$$\text{Cash} - V_T = \$11\,500\,000 - \$10\,000\,000$$
$$= \$1\,500\,000$$

Calculation of the cost is more complex when the acquiring company issues shares in exchange for the target's shares. The cost in this case depends on the post-takeover price of the acquiring company's shares. Calculation of the net cost of a share-exchange takeover is illustrated in Example 19.4.

EXAMPLE 19.4

Mayfair has 20 million shares on issue with a market price of $4.60 each before the takeover bid for Board is announced. Mayfair offers one of its shares for every two shares in Board. What is the net cost of the takeover?

SOLUTION

Based on these terms, Mayfair appears to be paying $2.30 per share for Board so it might seem that the net cost would remain at $1.5 million. However, the net cost depends on the value of the Mayfair shares issued to Board's shareholders and this depends on Mayfair's share price *after* the takeover offer is announced. The value of the combined company can be found by rearranging Equation 19.1:

$$V_{AT} = V_A + V_T + \text{gain}$$
$$= 20\,000\,000 \times \$4.60 + \$10\,000\,000 + \$2\,400\,000$$
$$= \$104\,400\,000$$

After the takeover, the number of Mayfair shares on issue will be 20 million + 2.5 million and the value of the shares issued to acquire Board is:

$$\frac{2.5}{22.5} \times \$104\,400\,000 = \$11\,600\,000$$

If Board is worth $10 million as an independent entity, the net cost of acquiring Board is:

$$\$11\,600\,000 - \$10\,000\,000 = \$1\,600\,000$$

In general the estimated cost of a share-exchange takeover is:

$$\text{Net cost} = b \times V_{AT} - V_T \qquad [19.5]$$

where b = the fraction of the combined company that will be owned by the former shareholders of the target company.

The NPV for Mayfair's shareholders (Equation 19.3) is now:

$$NPV_A = \text{gain} - \text{net cost}$$
$$= \$2\,400\,000 - \$1\,600\,000$$
$$= \$800\,000$$

These calculations show that for the share-exchange offer the true net cost is expected to be $100 000 *more* than it would have been if Mayfair had paid cash for Board. Similarly, the NPV to Mayfair's shareholders is $100 000 *less* than it would have been under the cash offer. This difference arises because Mayfair's shares are worth more after the takeover than they were worth previously. If the market agrees with Mayfair's valuations, then once the takeover bid is announced, Mayfair's share price will be

---

[8] Fortunately, cash-only offers are the most common in practice although over the years they have fallen in popularity. To illustrate, Da Silva Rosa et al. (2000) reports that in 1988 approximately 81 per cent of the bids were cash bids. In contrast, in 2009 only 54 per cent of the bids for Australian listed firms were cash bids, 31 per cent were share-only bids and the remaining 10 per cent offered a mix of cash and/or shares.

$104.4 million/22.5 million = $4.64 or 4 cents more than its pre-bid price. Therefore, since Board's shareholders will receive Mayfair shares, rather than cash, they will receive part of the takeover gain.

It should now be clear that there is a basic distinction between cash offers and share-exchange offers: for a cash offer, the net cost is independent of the takeover gain; for a share-exchange offer, the cost depends on the takeover gain, because the cost is a function of the acquiring company's share price *after* the bid is announced. Consequently, the cost of a share-exchange takeover can only be *estimated* when the bid is at the planning stage. Equation 19.5 can be used to make the estimate.

Another important distinction between cash and share-exchange offers is that a share exchange mitigates the effect of valuation errors. For example, suppose that after acquiring Board Ltd, Mayfair's management finds that Board's assets are worth only $5 million. If Mayfair paid $11.5 million cash to Board's former shareholders, then the cash is gone forever and Mayfair's shareholders will bear the full loss of $6.5 million. However, if Mayfair acquired Board by issuing shares, part of the loss will be borne by Board's former shareholders.

19.4 ALTERNATIVE VALUATION APPROACHES

The takeover analysis in Section 19.3 is based on market values and estimates of the present value of incremental cash flows. In some cases, market values may not be available because the target company is unlisted, or they may be considered unreliable, perhaps because the shares are rarely traded. In such cases, there will be a need to use other valuation approaches, the most popular of which are based on earnings and assets.[9]

19.4.1 VALUATION BASED ON EARNINGS

In this approach, the bidder values the target by first estimating the future earnings per share (EPS) of the target. The EPS figure is then multiplied by an 'appropriate' price–earnings (P–E) ratio to obtain an implied price (valuation) of the target. This approach can be given a theoretical underpinning by linking it to the present value of a perpetuity. If the appropriate P–E ratio is regarded as $1/r$, the inverse of the discount rate, then, using the perpetuity formula the present value is:

$$\begin{aligned} PV &= EPS/r \\ &= EPS \times 1/r \\ &= EPS \times P\text{–}E \\ &= P \end{aligned}$$

Important assumptions underlying this approach include:

- the company's future earnings stream can be represented by a single number, typically referred to as 'future maintainable earnings'
- risk differences between companies can be fully captured in the discount rate, r.

As Penman (2004, p. 190) pointed out, when these conditions are not met, the P–E ratio should not be accorded any theoretical significance and is best regarded as a summary indicator of a company's perceived capacity to generate earnings.

Even where these assumptions hold, *capitalising* earnings using a P–E multiple should *not* be regarded as *discounting* future earnings. The cash flows to investors in shares are dividends, not earnings, part of which are reinvested each year. Therefore, we can regard the value of a share as the present value of a stream of dividends, or equivalently, as the present value of a stream of earnings *minus* the present value of the

---

9 For a discussion of the valuation methods that are most commonly used, see Mukherjee, Kiymaz and Baker (2004).

reinvested (retained) earnings stream. Discounting earnings rather than dividends amounts to including all the returns from an investment without allowing for the outlay needed to generate those returns.

19.4.2 VALUATION BASED ON ASSETS

A company's equity can be valued by deducting its total liabilities from the sum of the market values of its assets. This approach may be appropriate where the bidder intends to sell many of the target's assets or where the company has been operating at a loss. Criticisms of this approach include the following:

- figures in the balance sheet based on historical cost are unlikely to provide a reliable guide to market values
- intangible assets may not be included in the balance sheet
- there may be complementarity between assets so that the total market value of the assets may be greater than the sum of their individual market values.

Even where reliable market values can be found for all identifiable assets, the resultant valuation will rarely coincide exactly with the market value of the company's equity.

19.5 REGULATION AND TAX EFFECTS OF TAKEOVERS

LEARNING OBJECTIVE 4

Outline the regulation and tax effects of takeovers in Australia

Takeover activity and procedures are regulated by Commonwealth legislation. The most important legislation is Chapter 6 of the *Corporations Act 2001*.[10] The Australian Securities and Investments Commission (ASIC, www.asic.gov.au) has a significant role in administering activities covered by the legislation. For example, ASIC can obtain information on the beneficial ownership of shares, and can allow exemptions from compliance with the legislation. Also ASIC can apply to the Takeovers Panel (www.takeovers.gov.au) for an acquisition of shares to be declared unacceptable or for a declaration of unacceptable circumstances. The panel can make such a declaration even if the legislation has not been contravened. Furthermore, s. 659B of the Corporations Act dictates that parties to a takeover do not have the right to commence civil litigation in relation to a takeover while it is current. Instead, the power to resolve disputes during this period resides with the Takeovers Panel, which also has the power to review certain decisions made by ASIC where those decisions are made with respect to parties to a takeover. The objectives of the takeovers legislation are set out in s. 602.

The legislation seeks to ensure that:

- the acquisition of control over voting shares in a listed company or an unlisted company with more than 50 members takes place in an efficient, competitive and informed market
- the shareholders and directors of a target company:
    – know the identity of the bidder
    – have a reasonable time to consider the proposal
    – are given enough information to enable them to assess the merits of the proposal
- as far as practicable, all shareholders have a reasonable and equal opportunity to participate in any benefits offered by the bidder.

The takeovers legislation provides that, unless the procedures laid down in Chapter 6 of the Corporations Act are followed, the acquisition of additional shares in a company is virtually prohibited if this would:

(a) result in a shareholder being entitled to more than 20 per cent of the voting shares; *or*
(b) increase the voting shares held by a party that already holds between 20 per cent and 90 per cent of the voting shares of the company.

---

10 For a detailed discussion, see Levy and Pathak (2009).

Any investor is permitted to purchase up to 20 per cent of a company's shares at any time, subject to the requirement that once the holding exceeds 5 per cent, a substantial shareholding notice must be issued within two business days, or by 9:30 am on the next business day if a takeover bid is currently underway. The takeover threshold has been set at 20 per cent because anyone who owns less than 20 per cent of a company's shares is unlikely to be able to exercise control. If an investor wishes to exceed the 20 per cent threshold and obtain control of a target company, this can generally be done only by following one of the two procedures that the legislation permits: an off-market bid or a market bid.

An off-market bid can be used to acquire shares that are listed on a stock exchange or shares in an unlisted company. A market bid is applicable only where the target is listed on a stock exchange. 'Creeping takeovers', which are discussed in Section 19.5.4, are also allowed.

ASIC provides news and policy statements on takeovers on its website **www.asic.gov.au/asic/asic.nsf**.

19.5.1 OFF-MARKET BIDS

An acquiring company, or an unincorporated offeror, can make an off-market bid (whether by way of a cash offer, a share exchange or a combination of these) to acquire shares in the target company. This offer must remain open for between 1 and 12 months and may be for 100 per cent or a specified proportion of each holder's shares.

A broad outline of the steps involved in an off-market bid is provided in s. 632 of the Corporations Act and shown in Figure 19.2.

FIGURE 19.2 Outline of steps in an off-market bid

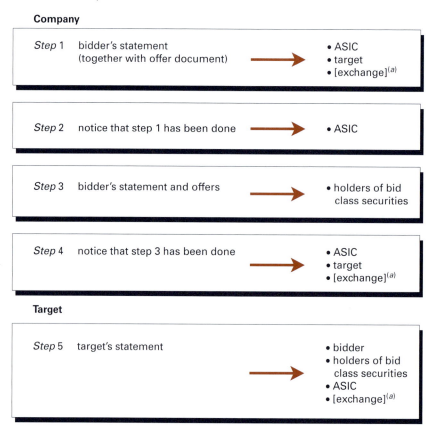

(a) This means that a copy of the document should be sent to any exchange on which a target company's shares are listed.

Source: *Corporations Act 2001*.

Once an off-market bid has been made for a listed company, the offeror is allowed to purchase target company shares on the stock exchange. An offeror can increase its offer price but has to pay this increased amount to all shareholders who accept the offer, including any who have previously accepted a lower price.

19.5.2 MARKET BIDS

A market bid is possible only where the shares of the target company are listed on a stock exchange. Importantly, the buyer must pay cash for the shares and the offer cannot be conditional. Like an off-market bid, the offer must be open for a period of 1 to 12 months. Figure 19.2 from s. 634 of the Corporations Act gives a broad outline of the steps involved in a market bid. In this case, if the offer price is increased, there is no need to pay the higher price to target shareholders who sold prior to the increase.

FIGURE 19.3 Outline of steps in a market bid

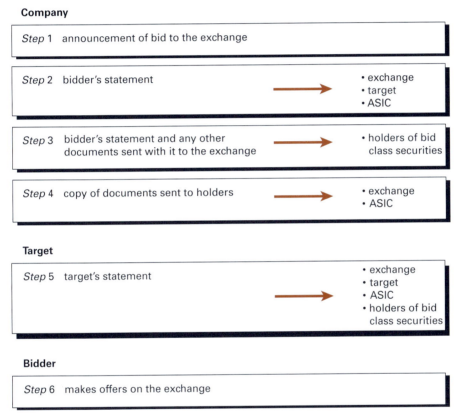

Source: *Corporations Act 2001*.

19.5.3 DISCLOSURE REQUIREMENTS

The Corporations Act includes important provisions for the disclosure of information by bidders and targets. The aim is to make important information related to the takeover more accessible through the provision of a bidder's statement and a target's statement. The information that should be contained in a bidder's statement is the same whether the bid is an off-market or market bid. The information to be contained in a bidder's statement includes:

- the identity of the bidder
- details of the bidder's intentions regarding the continuation of the target's business and any major changes to be made to the business

- details of how cash consideration will be obtained
- where securities are offered as consideration, information for a prospectus for an offer of those securities
- the price(s) paid by the bidder to acquire the target's securities during the previous 4 months
- for an off-market bid, the bidder's voting power in the target
- any other material information that may assist the target company's shareholders in deciding whether to accept the offer.

The target must respond to the takeover bid by issuing a target's statement, which is the same for both off-market and market bids. In general, the target's statement must include all information that target shareholders would reasonably require to make an informed decision on whether to accept the bid. It must also contain a statement by each director of the target recommending whether or not the bid should be accepted and giving reasons for the recommendation. Alternatively, each director must provide a statement giving reasons why a recommendation is not made. The target's statement must be accompanied by an expert's report if the bidder is connected with the target. Specifically an expert's report is required if the bidder's voting power in the target is 30 per cent or more, or if a director of the bidder is a director of the target. The expert must have a 'professional reputation' and is required to state, with reasons, whether the offer is considered to be fair and reasonable.

19.5.4 CREEPING TAKEOVER

This approach is permitted by s. 611 of the Corporations Act. It allows the acquisition of no more than 3 per cent of the target company's shares every 6 months, provided that the threshold level of 19 per cent has been maintained for at least 6 months. No public statement is necessary. Because of the time required to achieve control, the creeping takeover approach is of little commercial significance.

19.5.5 PARTIAL TAKEOVERS

partial takeover
takeover in which a bidder seeks to acquire no more than part of a company's issued shares

proportional bid
partial takeover bid to acquire a specified proportion of the shares held by each shareholder

Partial takeovers, where a bidder seeks to gain control by acquiring only 51 per cent, or perhaps less, of the target company's shares, have been the subject of particular regulatory attention. The reasons are, first, that the premium for control may be paid to only a favoured group of shareholders, and second, that there is potential for target shareholders to be coerced into accepting an offer that is not in their best interests.

Suppose that an offer is made for 40 per cent of the shares in a company, and the holders of 80 per cent of the shares accept. Under a pro-rata offer, the bidder would then accept half of the shares offered by each of these holders, who would be the only ones to share in the control premium. Pro-rata bids have been prohibited in Australia since 1986. The bidder in a partial takeover must specify *at the outset* the proportion of each holder's shares that the bidder will offer to buy. This method is referred to as a **proportional bid**. A disadvantage of proportional bids is greater uncertainty about their outcome from the viewpoint of the bidder, because the bidder must estimate the likely response rate of target shareholders.

A company's constitution may provide that a proportional takeover bid for the company can proceed only if shareholders vote to approve the bid. The Corporations Act allows this restriction on proportional takeovers but also specifies that any shareholder approval requirements generally cease to apply after 3 years. Some companies have adopted these requirements, which, while restricted in duration, can be renewed in the same way as they were originally adopted. Partial takeover bids have become extremely rare in Australia.

19.5.6 SCHEMES OF ARRANGEMENT

Two firms that are contemplating a friendly merging of their operations may consider entering into a *scheme of arrangement* rather than proceed with a takeover bid. Such schemes are court-approved unions that are governed by Chapter 5 of the *Corporations Act 2001*. Before a court grants its approval for a scheme of arrangement, it will require a written statement by ASIC that it has no objection to the scheme and will then need to be satisfied that the scheme is not designed to avoid the takeover provisions of Chapter 6. The attraction of a scheme of arrangement to friendly parties may be that it provides greater certainty with regards to the timing of the acquisition events. The proposed scheme of arrangement is sent to all shareholders by the target firm and a vote is conducted. Provided that more than 50 per cent of shareholders holding at least 75 per cent of shares in the firm vote in favour of the scheme, the scheme will be passed, subject to the court's approval, allowing all shares in the target firm to be transferred to the bidder. In contrast, a bidder engaged in an off-market bid needs to acquire the approval of at least 75 per cent of shareholders holding at least 90 per cent of the shares in the target firm before it can compulsorily acquire the remaining shares. There has been some suggestion that the so-called 'headcount' requirement that more than 50 per cent of the shareholders need to agree before a scheme is approved by the courts is unnecessarily restrictive. While the headcount provision is designed to protect the interests of small shareholders, it has been argued that the test is easily manipulated by those opposed to a scheme as they could transfer very small parcels of shares to associated parties to defeat the test. In response to these concerns, the Commonwealth Government's Corporations and Markets Advisory Committee reviewed the administration of schemes in 2009 and released a report recommending the abolition of the headcount test. In recent years there have been a number of high-profile mergers that have taken place via a scheme of arrangement. These mergers include the merger between Adelaide Bank and Bendigo Bank that resulted in the subsequent delisting of Adelaide Bank shares and the renaming of Bendigo Bank as Bendigo and Adelaide Bank Ltd. Another such merger is the $4.2 billion merger between mining companies Zinifex and Oxiana and the subsequent creation of Oz Minerals Ltd.

19.5.7 OTHER CONTROLS ON TAKEOVERS

Other legislation that may influence a bidder's decision to make a takeover offer includes:

- the Competition and Consumer Act, which was referred to in Section 19.2.1
- the *Foreign Acquisitions and Takeovers Act 1975*, which provides the Commonwealth Treasurer with the power to prohibit takeovers following advice received from the Foreign Investment Review Board (**www.firb.gov.au**). An example of the Treasurer exercising this power occurred in March 2009. China Minmetals Non-Ferrous Metals Co. Ltd, a Chinese state-owned metals and minerals trading company, launched a takeover bid for the Australian mining firm Oz Minerals Ltd. The Treasurer prohibited the takeover on the grounds that one of the mines operated by Oz Minerals, the Prominent Hill mine, was located in the Woomera Prohibited Area in South Australia—an area used primarily for weapons testing—and that the mine's acquisition by a foreign company could not be allowed on the grounds of national security. One month later, the Treasurer approved a revised bid by China Minmetals that excluded the Prominent Hill mine
- other Commonwealth legislation that may inhibit takeovers in specific industries, such as the banking and media industries.

In addition to this legislation, some of the listing rules of the ASX also affect takeovers. These include a requirement that directors maintain secrecy during discussions bearing on a potential takeover offer and a requirement restricting directors of a target company from making an allotment of shares for a period of 3 months after receiving a takeover offer.

19.5.8 TAX EFFECTS OF TAKEOVERS

In September 1999, the Commonwealth Government released the report of the Ralph Review of Business Taxation (Ralph Review) that included recommendations on capital gains tax relief where the consideration in a takeover was an exchange of shares. This recommendation was implemented in the *New Business Tax System (Capital Gains Tax) Act 1999*, which took effect from 10 December 1999. The legislation allows the target company to apply to the Australian Taxation Office (ATO), on behalf of its shareholders, for relief from capital gains tax where the consideration for a takeover is in the form of an exchange of shares. The effect of the legislation is that shareholders in the target company are able to defer a potential capital gains tax liability until the shares in the acquiring company they accepted as consideration are sold.

It was claimed in evidence to the Ralph Review that acquiring companies were often forced to pay a 'capital gains tax premium' to induce the target shareholders with potential capital gains tax liabilities to accept the offer. This meant that takeover bids included a cash component so that target shareholders had the cash necessary to pay any resulting capital gains tax liability. It was claimed that offer prices were forced up and there was a bias against those bids that solely involved a share exchange. An example cited in this context is the 1997 takeover of the Bank of Melbourne by Westpac. Westpac's offer of $1.435 billion included a cash component to enable Bank of Melbourne shareholders to meet their potential capital gains tax liability. The importance of capital gains tax relief to the success of a proposed acquisition is readily illustrated by reference to the failed acquisition by private hospital operator Healthscope of the diagnostics division of Symbion Health following the refusal by the ATO to grant relief from capital gains tax to Symbion Health's shareholders.

19.5.9 BREAK FEES, TAKEOVERS AND CORPORATE GOVERNANCE

As management is obliged to act in the best interests of shareholders, the way in which it deals with a potential takeover bid raises many corporate governance issues. As a takeover bid implies a potential change in the ownership and control of the company, which in turn may threaten the tenure of the existing management team, it is no surprise that the Takeovers Panel has provided considerable direction about how management should conduct itself during the bid process.

The panel's directions cover the increasingly important issue of break fee agreements entered into by companies in takeover negotiations. A break fee agreement is an arrangement entered into by two companies where one promises to pay the other a sum of money if certain events occur that have the effect of causing the proposed merger to fail. In 2000, less than 4 per cent of Australian takeover bids involved break fee agreements, while by 2006 the proportion had increased to more than 43 per cent of bids. For example, in 2004 WMC Resources entered into a $92 million break fee agreement with BHP Billiton that would be triggered by a number of events, including the withdrawal of the Board's support for the bid or the eventual success of a competing bid. At the time of BHP Billiton's bid, WMC was subject to a hostile bid (at a lower price) by another mining firm, Xstrata. Ultimately, BHP was successful in its acquisition and the break fee was never paid. The important question raised in the financial press at the time of the BHP Billiton bid was whether break fees were detrimental to target shareholders.

There are many competing theories about the impact of break fees on shareholder wealth.[11] One argument suggests that break fees are an example of an agency cost imposed on target company shareholders by entrenched management teams seeking to maximise their personal utility by diverting control of the company to a specific favoured acquirer. The cost to shareholders is in the form of a reduction in the premium that they may have received were alternative bidders not dissuaded from bidding by the presence of the break fee agreement (see Bates & Lemmon, 2003; Officer, 2003; and Rosenkranz & Weitzel, 2007). Given this interpretation of break fees it is no surprise that the Takeovers

---

11 For a detailed discussion of break fee agreements, see Curtis and Pinder (2007).

Panel has provided some direction on when a break fee agreement would be acceptable. The panel's position, as stated in *Guidance Note 7: Lock-up Devices*, involves a 'bright-line' approach to regulation in that it suggests, in Section 9, that, 'In the absence of other factors, a break fee not exceeding 1 per cent of the equity value of the target is generally not unacceptable. There may be facts which make a break fee within the one per cent guideline unacceptable—for example if triggers for payment of the fee are not reasonable (from the point of view of coercion).'

Alternatively, it has been argued that break fees ultimately benefit target shareholders for at least three reasons. First, the break fee simply represents compensation paid to the bidder to cover costs that it incurs in conducting the bid. Without the promise of such compensation, the bidder would not have launched a bid for the target in the first place, thereby denying target shareholders the opportunity to receive a control premium. Second, break fees may help target companies overcome information asymmetry by signalling to the potential acquirer (and the market generally) their commitment to the takeover process. Third, the break fee agreement might be used by target companies as a mechanism by which they can negotiate a higher control premium on behalf of their shareholders.

Ultimately, the impact of break fees on target shareholder's wealth is an empirical question that has been considered by a number of recent studies. In the US, where there are no strict restrictions on the size of the break fees agreed between firms, there is strong evidence that target shareholders receive higher premiums when such agreements are in place (see Bates & Lemmon, 2003; Officer, 2003; and Rosenkranz & Weitzel, 2007). In contrast, in their examination of the impact of break fees in Australia, Chapple, Christensen and Clarkson (2007) report that target shareholders receive smaller control premiums and lower share returns where a break fee agreement is in place. This leads the authors to suggest that the cap placed on break fees by the Takeovers Panel prevents target companies from utilising break fees as an incentive mechanism so as to increase returns for target shareholders.

TAKEOVER DEFENCES

19.6

While most takeover bids that are announced succeed, there are also many cases where management of the target company is successful in preventing a change in control. The Takeovers Panel has issued a guidance note relating to takeover defences in which it states that a decision about the ownership and control of a company should ultimately be made by shareholders and not by management.[12] Nevertheless, the guidance note concedes that where a target's management believes resistance is in the best interests of the company's shareholders, such action would be consistent with the objectives of Chapter 6 of the Corporations Act. Defence measures are of two basic types: those that pre-empt or discourage bids and those implemented after a bid is received. The more common categories of strategy include the following (Casey & Eddey 1986).

LEARNING OBJECTIVE 5
Outline defence strategies that can be used by target companies

19.6.1 POISON PILLS

Poison pills are a pre-emptive measure employed so as to make the target company less attractive to a potential bidder in the event that it is successful in its takeover attempt. An example of a poison pill defence relates to Liberty Media Corporation's announcement on 3 November 2004 that it had reached an agreement with a third party allowing it to increase its holding in News Corporation by 8 per cent to 17.1 per cent. In response, News Corporation announced the establishment of a 'Shareholder Rights Plan' that would be triggered if any party acquired more than 15 per cent (or if currently holding more than 15 per cent, increased its holding by more than 1 per cent). The plan would enable shareholders, other than the party who had triggered the event, to purchase one additional share for each share owned

---

[12] *Guidance Note 12: Frustrating Action* is available at the Takeovers Panel's website, **www.takeovers.gov.au**.

poison pill
strategic move by a company that may become a takeover target to make its shares less attractive to an acquirer by increasing the cost of a takeover (e.g. an issue of securities that will convert to shares if a takeover bid occurs)

at half the prevailing market price, resulting in a significant dilution in the value and size of Liberty's stake in News Corporation. In defence of the adoption of the poison pill scheme, News Corporation chairman Rupert Murdoch claimed that it was for the good of small shareholders as it prevented an acquirer from gaining control of News Corporation shares at depressed prices. The poison pill defence proved successful when in December 2006 News Corporation agreed to swap its controlling stake in satellite broadcaster DirecTV in return for Liberty's stake in News Corporation.

19.6.2 ACQUISITION BY FRIENDLY PARTIES

The management of a target company seeks the assistance of a 'white knight', who generally purchases the target's shares on the open market with the aim of either driving up the share price, or preventing the bidder from achieving its minimum acceptance level. An example from the mid-1980s occurred when Bond Corporation was believed to be preparing for a takeover bid of biscuit manufacturer Arnott's. US firm Campbell Soup Company purchased shares as a friendly party and acquired a strategic parcel (or 'blocking stake') of Arnott's shares that effectively stymied Bond Corporation's takeover ambitions. Interestingly, the 'white knight' in this case itself turned into a predator in 1992. After having acquired 33 per cent of Arnott's shares, Campbell Soup announced its own bid for Arnott's, which was successfully finalised in 1997. More recently, luxury car-maker Porsche acquired a strategic stake in Volkswagen in order to prevent a hostile bid from other car manufacturers and/or private equity groups. Volkswagen manufactured key components for Porsche and hence an acquisition by a hostile third party would have exposed Porsche to significant business risk. Subsequently, Porsche launched a failed bid for control of Volkswagen. This was followed by a successful bid by Volkswagen for a significant proportion of the Porsche business, with options to purchase the remaining stake in later years.

19.6.3 DISCLOSURE OF FAVOURABLE INFORMATION

Management of a target company may release information that will, it hopes, convince shareholders that the bid undervalues the company. Such information includes preliminary earnings results, new contracts and statements of asset market values and profit forecasts. The release of such information is designed to make the takeover prohibitively expensive for the bidder and/or deliver additional value to shareholders in the form of an increased offer price. In recent years the regulatory authorities have emphasised that any information released by target management during the course of a takeover attempt must be accurate. This point was well illustrated in July 2001 when ASIC launched civil proceedings against three former directors of GIO Insurance Ltd in relation to profit forecasts issued by GIO during a takeover attempt by AMP Ltd. Forecasts issued by GIO during this period predicted profits of $80 million from its reinsurance business for the financial year ending June 1999. Following the successful acquisition by AMP, GIO declared a before-tax loss of $759 million for the same period and ASIC alleged that the directors prosecuted withheld information concerning the magnitude of the losses.

19.6.4 CLAIMS AND APPEALS

The management of a target company often claims that the bid is inadequate and may also appeal to regulatory authorities such as the Foreign Investment Review Board, the Australian Competition and Consumer Commission and/or the Takeovers Panel. They may also criticise the bidding company, as occurred repeatedly during the hostile takeover bid for Patrick Corporation by the Toll Holdings group. Chris Corrigan, the chief executive of Patrick Corporation, fiercely defended his company from acquisition in what has been one of the most vitriolic takeover contests witnessed in Australia. For example, Corrigan placed advertisements in newspapers stating that 'Patrick needs Toll like a fish needs a bicycle' and when Patrick's corporate strategy was criticised by Paul Little, the chief executive of Toll, he responded by saying that was '… like being called stupid by the village idiot' (Chessel 2005).

19.6.5 THE EFFECTS OF TAKEOVER DEFENCES

The significance of the target directors' attitude to a takeover bid places the onus on directors to ensure that their recommendation is consistent with their responsibilities to shareholders. Directors of a target company may be faced with a conflict of interest, because a takeover bid that they believe to be in the best interests of shareholders may leave them unemployed if it is successful. Therefore, directors of a target company may oppose a bid because they place their own interest above their responsibilities to shareholders. On the other hand, resistance to a takeover bid can benefit shareholders if it forces the bidder to increase the offer, or attracts a higher offer from another bidder. The impact of the defence by a target company's management against a takeover offer has been the subject of research in Australia and overseas.

Maheswaran and Pinder (2005) examined 133 bids for companies listed on the ASX. They found that resistance by a target company's Board reduced the probability that a bid would be successful and increased the likelihood that the offer price would be increased by the bidder, but had no impact on the chances that a competing bidder would launch an alternative bid for the target company's shares. Interestingly, they find that there is no evidence of a relationship between the magnitude of the control premium offered and the incidence of bid resistance. In a similar study, Schwert (2000) analysed 2346 takeover contests that had occurred in the US. He found that he could not differentiate on economic grounds between bids that had been rejected by target management and those that had been accepted.

The contention that managerial resistance to takeovers may not be in the best interests of shareholders is of concern since the 'market for corporate control' concept sees takeovers as a mechanism for resolving shareholder–manager conflicts by replacing inefficient managers. The effectiveness of this market will be reduced if such managers use defensive tactics to entrench their positions. Of course, it is poorly performing managers who are likely to have the greatest difficulty in maintaining employment or obtaining other jobs after a takeover. Empirical evidence supports this contention in that companies whose management resisted takeover are characterised by poorer performance prior to the takeover bid (Morck, Shleifer & Vishny 1988; Maheswaran & Pinder 2005). The problem of managers giving predominance to their own interests may be overcome by structuring the compensation of top-level managers so that their own interests will be better aligned with those of shareholders. Some companies approach this problem by offering top-level managers large termination payments ('golden parachutes') if they lose their jobs due to a takeover. Such payments may be effective in preventing managers from resisting a takeover bid that is in the best interests of shareholders. However, if the payments are too generous, they may cause managers to recommend that shareholders accept an inadequate bid.

CORPORATE RESTRUCTURING 19.7

While mergers and takeovers remain the most frequent transactions in the market for corporate control, in recent years there has been an upsurge in transactions where companies or groups were reduced in size by asset disposals, divided into separate entities or transferred to private ownership. We begin by defining the most frequent of these restructuring transactions:

LEARNING OBJECTIVE 6
Identify the various types of corporate restructuring transactions

- *Divestitures.* Assets (often in the form of a whole subsidiary, branch or division) are sold to another company.
- *Spin-offs.* The operations of a subsidiary are separated from those of its parent by establishing the subsidiary as a separate listed company. However, there is no change in ownership because shares in the former subsidiary are distributed to the shareholders of the parent company.
- **Leveraged buyouts**. A company or division is purchased by a small group of (usually institutional) investors using a high proportion of debt finance. Where the investors are headed by the company's

leveraged buyout
company takeover that is largely financed using borrowed funds; the remaining equity is privately held by a small group of investors

management buyout
purchase of all of a company's issued shares by a group led by the company's management

divestiture
(or sell-off) sale of a subsidiary, division or collection of related assets, usually to another company

spin-off
the separation of certain assets (or a division) from a firm upon which are issued new shares that are allocated to the firm's existing shareholders

senior managers, the buyout is often referred to as a **management buyout**. After a buyout the company is privately owned and the shares are not normally listed on a stock exchange.

The following subsections briefly summarise the evidence on the wealth effects of restructuring transactions and discuss possible explanations.[13]

19.7.1 DIVESTITURES

A **divestiture** or **sell-off** involves assets, which may be a whole subsidiary, being sold for cash, and is therefore essentially a *reverse takeover* from the viewpoint of the seller. The frequency of divestitures, and the value of the assets involved, has increased over the last 20 years, with Eckbo and Thorburn (2008) reporting that in 2006 approximately $320 billion of assets across 3500 divestitures were sold in the US. While takeovers increase the wealth of target (seller) shareholders, it has also been found that divestitures create value for the shareholders of selling companies. Eckbo and Thorburn (2008) survey the evidence provided by a number of studies in the topic area and report that shareholders in selling firms earn—on average—a return of 1.2 per cent upon the announcement of the divestiture. Furthermore, shareholders in the firms on the buy-side of the divestiture transaction also enjoy an increase in wealth as the average share price reaction to the announcement that their firm has bought the divested assets is 0.5 per cent. Possible reasons as to why the market perceives divestitures as good news are: an increase in corporate focus for the selling firm, the elimination of negative synergies that arise through the cross-subsidisation of poorly performing segments of the firm, and the fact that the buying firm is able to derive greater value out of the divested assets than the selling firm.

An example of a recent significant divestment by an Australian company occurred in 2006, when Coles Myer Ltd announced that it would be selling its Myer department store business to a consortium led by private equity firm Newbridge Capital for $1.4 billion. The primary reason given for the divestment in this case was a desire for the company to focus on running its supermarket operations without the distraction of operating a department store.

19.7.2 SPIN-OFFS

In this type of transaction, a single organisational structure is replaced by two separate units under essentially the same ownership. Eckbo and Thorburn (2008) review the results of 19 studies into the valuation effects of **spin-off** activity and, similar to the findings relating to divestitures, report that the average share price reaction to the announcement of a spin-off was 3.3 per cent. In terms of explaining this positive result for shareholders there are a number of additional factors—in addition to those relating to the benefits also relating to divestitures—that prior studies have highlighted. For example, the positive share price reaction might reflect the transfer of wealth from bondholders to shareholders, as valuable assets are removed from the reach of creditors. Alternatively, the spin-off might reflect the increased expectation of the receipt of a control premium as the transaction has increased the probability of a takeover of the newly listed subsidiary and/or the parent company. The positive wealth effect might also reflect the reduction in information asymmetry between management's valuation of the firm and the market's valuation. Specifically, it has been suggested that a spin-off reduces the problem associated with aggregating financial information across the firm and faced by anyone attempting to value the firm, such as security analysts.

An example of a significant spin-off occurred in 2007, when Toll Holdings, at the time Australia's largest transport and logistics company, spun off its port and rail assets into a new company Asciano, while continuing to operate its sizeable logistics business. As part of the spin-off process, most of the debt held by the combined group was assigned to Asciano, because its portfolio of quality tangible assets provided superior debt capacity. As a consequence, Toll was then able to raise additional debt to

---

13 The following discussion relies substantially on Eckbo and Thorburn (2008).

fund future corporate acquisitions such as the $191 million takeover of Singapore-based logistics group Sembawang Kimtrans Ltd.

19.7.3 BUYOUTS

A **buyout** or **going-private transaction** can take one of a number of forms, each of which involves a rearrangement of financial and ownership structures of a single operating entity. Consequently, there is no scope for operating synergies such as economies of scale. Figure 19.4 indicates the rise and fall of buyout activity in recent years.

buyout (or going-private) transaction transfer from public ownership to private ownership of a company through purchase of its shares by a small group of investors that usually includes the existing management

FIGURE 19.4 Global leveraged buyout activity

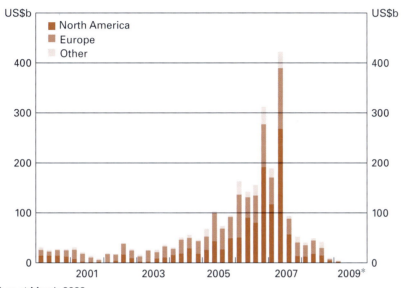

*Announced as at March 2009
Source: Reserve Bank of Australia, *Financial Stability Review March 2009*, 2009, p. 13.

Buyouts may be initiated by vendors and their advisers or by management. Management presumably expects to gain from the transaction and there is evidence that the former public shareholders also gain through receiving a substantial premium over the previous share price.[14] It follows that some real gain must be expected to follow from the transfer from public to private ownership. One source of gain is the avoidance of listing fees and shareholder servicing costs, which can be quite substantial for small public companies. Another is the effect on managerial incentives. Managers who also own their company stand to benefit more than salaried employees from their efforts.

In addition to 'pure' going-private transactions, where managers use their own resources, possibly supplemented by personal borrowing, to buy out the previous shareholders, there are leveraged buyouts, which involve significant corporate borrowing. These buyouts are almost always arranged by a buyout specialist who invests equity capital in the company, arranges the necessary debt finance and takes an active part in overseeing its performance. Figure 19.4 indicates the great increase in leveraged buyout activity in the early to mid-2000s and then the subsequent fall in this type of activity during the global financial crisis and the near-collapse of worldwide debt markets. The viability of a leveraged buyout transaction is heavily dependent upon the availability of large amounts of relatively cheap debt. Indeed, the reliance on debt finance can be extremely high relative to other listed companies, as is illustrated in Figure 19.5 overleaf.

---

14 For example, in a sample of 57 going-private proposals that involved a cash consideration, the premium averaged 56.31 per cent over the market price 2 months before the announcement. See De Angelo, De Angelo and Rice (1984).

FIGURE 19.5 Distribution of debt–equity ratios, Australia

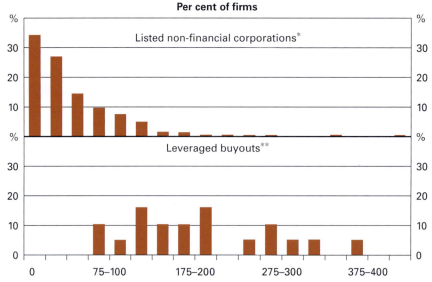

Source: Reserve Bank of Australia, *Financial Stability Review March 2007*, 2007, p. 61.

The high debt–equity ratios of buyout companies do not necessarily mean that private companies have an inherently greater debt capacity than their public counterparts. In most leveraged buyouts, early repayment of part of the debt is a high priority and the initial high level of debt is feasible because most such buyouts involve low-risk businesses with stable cash flows. The debt finance has an important positive role by giving the new owners an even greater incentive to improve efficiency. Because of the severe penalties associated with default, it is important to eliminate waste and generate cash flows that are sufficient to service the debt.

The gains associated with transferring some companies to private ownership prompt the following question: Should all companies be privately owned? The answer is no. Public companies have the advantage of access to equity capital on terms that reflect the diversification benefits available to investors in the capital market. The value of such access depends on the growth opportunities available to the company. Therefore, public ownership has important advantages for large-scale enterprises that involve significant risks and have an ongoing need to raise capital; in other cases, however, private ownership can be advantageous.[15]

FINANCE IN ACTION

SWAGGER'S GONE OUT OF THE BUYOUT FUNDS

The following excerpts were taken from an article in the *Australian Financial Review* examining the decline in the level of buyout activity. The article notes that buyout funds rely heavily upon access to debt and the consequences of a contraction in debt markets such as that which occurred with the sub-prime mortgage crisis in 2007.

Hellman & Friedman's Capital Partners IV Fund has generated a 36 per cent return for investors since 2000. Kohlberg Kravis Roberts' Millennium Fund has done even better, notching a 41 per cent take since 2002. But investors in private equity funds who've enjoyed large returns like these during the buyout boom should brace themselves for a fall. Buyout firms relied on cheap debt in the past 2 years to finance the biggest deals

continued ↓

---

15 Evidence on the performance of buyouts is provided by Kaplan (1989). The longevity of buyouts is examined in Kaplan (1998). For a study of Australian buyouts, see Eddey, Lee and Taylor (1996).

FINANCE IN ACTION
continued

of all time, often paying premiums of more than 30 per cent. But as the sub-prime mortgage meltdown rattles credit markets, firms will have to sell their companies to buyers who no longer have access to low-cost loans. That will cut the sale prices of the companies and slash the buyout funds' returns, says billionaire financier Wilbur Ross. 'When it comes time to resell these investments, we'll likely be in a very different rate environment,' says Ross, whose New York-based WL Ross & Co focuses on distressed assets such as vehicle spare-parts makers. 'The implications for returns could be substantial.'

In 2005, buy-out firms began to show a swagger rarely seen in the industry's 30-year history. In the US in the first half of this year, mega deals for TXU Corp, First Data Corp and Equity Office Properties Trust—all topping $US20 billion ($24.5 billion)—were part of a record $US616 billion in announced purchases. That's just shy of 2006's record total of $US701.5 billion, Bloomberg data shows. Cheap credit fuelled the frenzy. The extra interest investors demanded to own high-yield high-risk debt rather than US Treasuries fell to 2.41 percentage points in June, the lowest on record. The rates enabled buyout firms, which use credit to finance about two-thirds of a company's purchase price, to ratchet up their bids. Premiums for US companies, or the percentage offered above the target's stock price, soared to 39 per cent in June compared with 23 per cent a year earlier.

Gavin MacDonald, Morgan Stanley's head of European mergers and acquisitions, said in April a $US100 billion leveraged buyout was possible. But by July the appetite for deals, especially record-breaking ones, had evaporated. Investors, surprised by their level of exposure to the sub-prime debacle, saw greater risk in the about $US330 billion of loans and bonds that banks had slated to fund leveraged buyouts. Investors balked at credit terms that allowed companies to repay debt by issuing more bonds. Lenders had to rework or cancel at least 45 loan and bond offerings since the beginning of July, including debt to pay for Cerberus Capital Management's acquisition of Chrysler. Buyout firms and sellers are also renegotiating deals to get financing and keep them alive. On August 26, Home Depot, the world's biggest home-improvement retailer, agreed to sell its construction supply unit Bain Capital, Clayton Dubilier & Rice and Carlyle Group for $US8.5 billion. That's 18 per cent less than the price negotiated in June, Home Depot said this week. Many other deals aren't getting done. The value of announced buyouts dropped to $US18 billion from August 1 to 26. That compares with $US87.4 billion last month and $US131.1 billion in June, Bloomberg data shows.

Private equity firms will also struggle to sell their holdings to corporations and other fund managers at high prices. In 2005, Hellman & Friedman paid $US1.1 billion for internet advertising company DoubleClick and, less than 2 years later, agreed to sell it to Google for $US3.1 billion. These large pay-offs will be much harder to get in coming years as the cost of credit rises, says Scott Sperling, co-president of buyout firm Thomas H Lee Partners in Boston.

Source: Jason Kelly, 'Swagger's gone out of the buy-out funds', *Australian Financial Review*, 31 August 2007, p. 40.

EMPIRICAL EVIDENCE ON TAKEOVERS

19.8

There has been considerable empirical research into takeovers. For example, many studies have evaluated the wealth effects of takeovers on shareholders of the acquiring and target companies. These studies use share price changes around the time of the first public announcement of a takeover to measure these wealth effects. Abnormal returns on shares in both acquiring and target companies around the time of the takeover announcement are measured by the difference between actual and expected returns. The expected returns take account of the influence of market-wide events on the returns from an individual company's shares. Apart from market-wide events, the only factor assumed to be common to all companies in the studies is their involvement in takeover negotiations. Therefore, the abnormal returns are a measure of the wealth effects of the takeover.[16]

LEARNING OBJECTIVE 7
Outline the main findings of empirical research on the effects of takeovers on shareholders' wealth

---

16 This 'event study' methodology is commonly employed in tests of the efficient market hypothesis and is outlined in Chapter 16.

In discussing the evidence, we make substantial use of a paper by Andrade, Mitchell and Stafford (2001), which examined US mergers from 1973 to 1998, and a paper by Brown and da Silva Rosa (1997), who evaluated takeovers in Australia during the period January 1974 to November 1995.

19.8.1 THE TARGET COMPANY

One result that stands out in all market-based studies is that target company shareholders earn significant positive abnormal returns. For example, Brown and Da Silva Rosa (1997) found an average abnormal return of 25.5 per cent over the 7-month period around the takeover announcement. For the 1528 target companies in their sample, the total increase in shareholders' wealth was approximately $15 billion. These results probably understate the total wealth effects of takeovers for target shareholders. Casey, Dodd and Dolan (1987) reported substantial abnormal returns on target company shares around the time that significant shareholding notices were filed. For their sample, this occurred on average 127 days before the announcement of a takeover bid. Significant gains to target shareholders are to be expected because the acquiring company must offer more than the previous market price of the shares. The current shareholders are, by definition, parties who prefer to hold rather than sell the shares at the previous market price.

Several studies report that, on average, the shares in target companies performed poorly before the takeover bid. Brown and Da Silva Rosa found evidence of very poor pre-bid performance by target companies. For their sample of 1371 targets, the average abnormal return over the period from months –36 to –6 relative to the bid was –23.3 per cent. This is consistent with the concept that takeovers transfer control of assets to companies with more efficient managers or more profitable uses for those assets.

The initial increase in wealth of the target company's shareholders appears to be maintained, even where the takeover bid is unsuccessful. This could be because the bid prompted a change in the target company's investment strategy, which is expected to improve performance, or because information released during the bid caused the market to revalue the shares. Another explanation is that the market may expect a further bid for the target company. Research by Bradley, Desai and Kim (1983) is consistent with the last explanation. They found that many companies that were the subject of an initial unsuccessful takeover bid received a subsequent successful bid within 5 years of the first. These subsequent bids resulted in further positive abnormal returns for target shareholders. Where no subsequent bid eventuated, the shares of the unsuccessful targets declined, on average, to their (market-adjusted) pre-bid level. Based on this evidence, it appears that the gains associated with takeover bids are permanent only where a change in control occurs—that is, the results do not support the suggestion that gains to target shareholders result from the market's reassessment of previously undervalued shares.

19.8.2 THE ACQUIRING COMPANY

On average, the shareholders of acquiring companies earn positive abnormal returns in the years before the takeover bid is made. Brown and Da Silva Rosa (1997) found that average abnormal returns accumulated to almost 32 per cent over the period from –36 to –6 months before the bid. This suggests that takeover bids are typically made by companies that have been doing well, and have demonstrated an ability to manage assets and growth. In the 7-month period around the announcement of the bid, the average abnormal return for successful bidders was 5.0 per cent. While Australian studies find positive abnormal returns to bidders over a 7-month period, other studies that have measured returns over shorter periods surrounding the announcement of takeover bids have found that the average abnormal return to shareholders of bidding companies is close to zero, and negative in some cases. Moreover, announcement of a takeover bid is associated with a share price decline in a significant proportion of individual cases.[17]

---

[17] For example, Dodd (1992, p. 515) notes that results reported in two US studies show that in more than 40 per cent of cases, the bidding company's share price fell when a takeover bid was announced.

Jarrell and Poulsen (1989) identified three general explanations that have been offered for the negligible wealth effects for acquiring company shareholders. These explanations are:

(a) takeovers are profitable, but the wealth effects are disguised
(b) competition depresses returns to acquirer
(c) takeovers are neutral or poor investments.

The rationale for each of these explanations is now discussed.

The wealth effects of takeovers are disguised

Essentially, this explanation suggests that takeovers are profitable but the announcement of an individual takeover has little effect on the acquiring company's share price. One reason is that acquiring companies are typically much larger than their targets, so while there may be a worthwhile dollar gain to shareholders, the gain is small relative to the total value of the acquiring company. A second reason is that many companies have a known strategy of growth by acquisition. Therefore, the expected gains from this strategy may already be reflected in the companies' share prices, and the announcement of a particular bid conveys little new information to the market.[18] Third, announcement effects that are small or negative may also reflect market reaction to the financing of the takeover. In particular, a share-exchange offer may signal that the management of the acquiring company considers that its shares are overvalued. Therefore, the takeover itself may have a positive announcement effect, but this can be offset by the effects of the information related to the financing of the takeover.[19]

Competition depresses returns to acquirers

The returns to successful bidders are likely to be lower if a takeover is resisted by target management or contested by multiple bidders. There is evidence that abnormal returns to target shareholders are higher when there are multiple bidders, in which case gains to acquiring company shareholders are insignificantly different from zero. However, when there is only one bidder, acquiring company shareholders earn significant positive returns. The degree of competition in takeovers could be influenced by changes in government regulation, development of innovative financing techniques and the use of defensive strategies by target companies. Therefore, the returns to acquirers may have changed over time.

Takeovers are neutral or poor investments

This explanation is that many takeovers are bad investments and the small or negative returns to acquiring company shareholders correctly reflect this situation. One advocate of this explanation is Roll (1986) who argued that many managers of acquiring companies are affected by 'hubris'. In other words, they are supremely confident that their ability to value other companies is better than that of the market. Consequently, they are likely to pay more for target company shares than they are worth, and Roll argued that the large returns to target company shareholders represent wealth transfers from the shareholders of acquiring companies. There is also evidence that many acquired companies are later divested, which may indicate that the original takeover turned out to be a failure.[20]

To assess the validity of these explanations, Jarrell and Poulsen (1989) examined the returns to acquiring company shareholders in a large sample of successful tender offers over the period 1963 to 1986. They found that returns to acquirers were positively related to the size of the target relative to the bidder, which is consistent with the explanation that returns to acquirers can be disguised when target

---

18 For evidence on the prior capitalisation of takeover gains, see Schipper and Thompson (1983).
19 For Australian evidence on the effects of the method of payment in takeovers, see Da Silva Rosa et al. (2000).
20 However, it has been reported that divestiture of previously acquired companies often yields profits for the selling company. Therefore, subsequent divestiture does not necessarily mean that the original acquisition was a failure. See Kaplan and Weisbach (1992).

companies are small. They also found that returns to acquirers were smaller when the bid was opposed by target management, and were lower after changes in regulation that favoured competing bidders. In summary, their results support the first two explanations, but they also note that some other studies have found evidence that supports the argument that takeovers are poor investments.[21]

19.8.3 ARE TAKEOVERS POOR INVESTMENTS?

While there is conclusive evidence that target company shareholders gain significantly from takeovers, the evidence on returns to acquiring company shareholders is much less conclusive. Consequently, whether takeovers generate *net* gains for shareholders has been a contentious issue.

Bradley, Desai and Kim (1988) studied this issue by examining the returns to shareholders of matched pairs of target and acquiring companies in successful tender offers over the period 1963 to 1984. They found an average gain of $117 million, or 7.4 per cent, in the combined wealth of shareholders. The total percentage gain remained remarkably constant over time and by far the larger share of the gain went to the target shareholders, although the division of the gain shifted against the acquiring company shareholders over time. In general, their results support the hypothesis that takeovers yield real, synergistic gains and do not support Roll's 'wealth transfer' hypothesis. Announcement period abnormal returns for a much larger sample of US mergers and takeovers are shown in Table 19.3.

TABLE 19.3 Announcement period abnormal returns (%) by decade for US mergers

PERIOD	1973–79	1980–89	1990–98	1973–98
Target				
[–1, +1]	16.0[a]	16.0[a]	15.9	16.0[a]
[–20, Close]	24.8[a]	23.9[a]	23.3[a]	23.8
Acquirer				
[–1, +1]	–0.3	–0.4	–1.0	–0.7
[–20, Close]	–4.5	–3.1	–3.9	–3.8
Combined				
[–1, +1]	1.5	2.6[a]	1.4[a]	1.8[a]
[–20, Close]	0.1	3.2	1.6	1.9
Number of observations	598.0	1226.0	1864.0	3688.0

[a] Statistically significant at the 5 per cent level.
Source: G. Andrade, M. Mitchell and E. Stafford, 'New evidence and perspectives on mergers', *Journal of Economic Perspectives*, Spring 2001, p. 110.

Table 19.3 shows announcement period abnormal returns over two event windows—the 3 days immediately surrounding the takeover announcement—and a longer window beginning 20 days before the announcement and ending at the close of the takeover.

As usual, these results show that target company shareholders are clear winners in takeovers, with abnormal returns over the 3-day event window being remarkably consistent at 16 per cent over the whole period. The abnormal returns over the 3-day event window, for the target and acquirer combined, average 1.8 per cent for the whole sample. This result is statistically significant and suggests that, on

---

21 For example, there is evidence that some types of takeover harm the shareholders of acquiring companies. See Mitchell and Lehn (1990). This evidence is discussed in Section 19.8.4.

average, takeovers do increase shareholders' wealth. The results for acquirers suggest that, on average, takeovers may well be poor investments for shareholders of the acquiring company. However, while all the estimates are negative, none is statistically significant. Therefore, while it is clear that acquiring company shareholders are not big winners, it is also difficult to claim that they are generally losers.

More information on the wealth effects of takeovers can be obtained by also considering the method of payment—or the financing of the transaction. Table 19.4 shows average announcement period returns when the sample studied by Andrade, Mitchell and Stafford (2001) is split into subsamples on the basis of whether any shares were used to finance the takeover.

The results in Table 19.4 show that announcement period abnormal returns for acquirers are negative only when the acquirer uses shares to finance the transaction. When the payment to target shareholders includes at least a share component, the 3-day average abnormal return to acquirers is a statistically significant –1.5 per cent.

TABLE 19.4 Announcement period abnormal returns (%) for subsamples 1973–1998

FORM OF PAYMENT	SHARES	NO SHARES
Target		
[–1, +1]	13.0[a]	20.1[a]
[–20, Close]	20.8[a]	27.8[a]
Acquirer		
[–1, +1]	–1.5[a]	0.4
[–20, Close]	–6.3	–0.2
Combined		
[–1, +1]	0.6	3.6[a]
[–20, Close]	–0.6	5.3
Number of observations	2194.0	1494.0

[a] Statistically significant at the 5 per cent level.
Source: G. Andrade, M. Mitchell and E. Stafford, 'New evidence and perspectives on mergers', *Journal of Economic Perspectives*, Spring 2001, p. 112.

When the payment does not include any shares, the average abnormal return is an insignificant 0.4 per cent. For the acquiring company a share-exchange takeover can be regarded as two simultaneous transactions: acquisition of another company and a share issue. As discussed in Chapter 13 there is evidence that, on average, share issues are associated with negative abnormal returns of about –1.5 to –3 per cent around the time of the announcement. Explanations for this finding focus on differences between the information available to managers and outside investors. If managers are more likely to issue equity when they believe the company's shares are overpriced, investors will respond to an issue announcement by marking down the share price. Even if this explanation is not accepted, the evidence suggests that when assessing the wealth effects of takeovers for shareholders it is important to distinguish between share and non-share takeovers.

The results in Table 19.4 show that target shareholders also receive higher returns when payment for the takeover does not include shares. Therefore, it is not surprising that differences in financing are also related to differences in the overall wealth effects of takeovers. As shown in Table 19.4, the combined average abnormal returns for share-financed takeovers are indistinguishable from zero, but for non-share takeovers the corresponding result is 3.6 per cent.

In summary, the evidence on announcement-period share market returns suggests that, in general, takeovers create value for the shareholders of the combined companies. However, in cases where target shareholders are paid with the acquirer's shares, the gains to target shareholders are offset by losses for the acquirer and the combined wealth effects are negligible. In Australia, by way of contrast, there is only weak support for the view that differences in the financing of takeovers are related to the overall wealth effects of takeovers. In a study of 240 takeover bids between 1988 and 1996, Da Silva Rosa et al. (2000) found that abnormal returns earned by bidders and targets over the bid announcement period were not significantly associated with the proposed method of financing the takeover.

Long-term abnormal returns

In an efficient market, announcement-period share price reactions should be unbiased responses to all the information contained in the announcement of a takeover. However, several studies that measure long-term share returns over periods of up to 5 years after completion of a takeover cast doubt on whether announcement-period returns do provide adequate measures of the wealth effects of takeovers. For example, Loughran and Vijh (1997) examined 947 acquisitions over the period 1970 to 1989 and tracked the returns on the shares of the acquiring company for 5 years after completion of the acquisition. They found that these 5-year abnormal returns differed significantly with the form of payment. Acquirers that issued shares as payment had average abnormal returns of −24.2 per cent, whereas those that paid cash recorded abnormal returns of 18.5 per cent. In some subsamples where they also distinguished between takeovers and tender offers, the return differences were even greater. If the long-term post-takeover abnormal returns to acquirers are negative, these returns could outweigh the gains earned by shareholders in the announcement period and the net wealth effect of takeovers could be negative. For example, Loughran and Vijh found that target shareholders who held on to the acquirer's shares received as payment in share-exchange takeovers did not earn significant abnormal returns.

It is not difficult to find possible reasons for a relationship between the form of payment and the profitability of acquisitions. Shares are usually issued as payment in mergers that are friendly deals supported by managers of the target. Cash is usually paid in tender offers that are more likely to be hostile and are followed by high turnover of target management as the acquirer seeks to realise efficiency gains. While there may be large differences in the gains associated with different types of acquisitions, if the market is efficient it should not take years for the effects to be reflected in share prices. However, market inefficiency is not the only possible explanation for the inconsistency between long-term abnormal returns and the announcement-period returns. Another explanation lies in the accuracy of the models used to estimate expected returns. Over a 3-day event window the expected return is close to zero, so it is easy to determine that announcement-period returns of about 2 per cent or even less are abnormal. However, as the return window becomes longer, the model of expected returns becomes much more important, and measures of long-term performance can also be sensitive to bias inherent in some research designs. Brown and Da Silva Rosa assessed the long-run performance of acquiring companies in the Australian market and found that it is important to control for factors such as company size and survival. Survival is important because the average returns to companies that survive over a given period differ from those recorded by newly listed companies and by companies that delist due to takeover, merger or bankruptcy. Brown and Da Silva Rosa (1998, p. 36) found that when appropriate controls were used, the post-bid performance of acquiring companies did not differ significantly from the performance of control companies. They concluded: 'The long-term performance of the acquiring firms in the post-merger period is consistent with the proposition that the market for corporate control is informationally efficient.'

19.8.4 DISTINGUISHING BETWEEN GOOD AND BAD TAKEOVERS

Several studies provide evidence on the characteristics of takeovers that are likely to harm rather than benefit the shareholders of acquiring companies. There are at least three reasons why the managers of acquiring companies might pay more than targets are worth.

(a) Roll's hubris hypothesis suggests that managers pay too much for target companies because they overestimate their ability to run them.
(b) Managers may pursue their own objectives rather than those of their companies' shareholders. In particular, as discussed in Section 19.2.1, Jensen (1986) argued that value-reducing takeovers will be common when the acquiring company has significant free cash flow that gives management the ability to finance unprofitable investments. He also argues that many takeovers are designed to reverse previous unprofitable takeovers. In other words, many companies that have made unprofitable takeovers will, themselves, become targets in takeovers designed to reverse the original value reduction. Therefore, while takeovers can be a 'problem', they can also provide a 'solution'.
(c) Some managers may make unprofitable takeovers simply because they are poor managers, possibly seeking other fields in which they hope to perform better. Some of the many US studies that provide relevant empirical evidence are now outlined.

Lang, Stulz and Walkling (1989) studied successful tender offers and classified the acquiring and target companies using Tobin's Q ratio, which is the ratio of a company's market value to the replacement cost of its assets. The Q ratio was used as a measure of managerial performance on the basis that well-managed companies that make profitable investments should have Q ratios greater than 1, while poorly managed companies are likely to have Q ratios less than 1. The authors found significant relationships between Q ratios and the profitability of takeovers to acquiring company shareholders. Takeovers that involved a high-Q acquirer and a low-Q target produced gains of approximately 10 per cent for shareholders, but when a low-Q acquirer announced a bid for a high-Q target, acquiring company shareholders lost approximately 4 per cent on average.[22]

Mitchell and Lehn (1990) tested whether some takeovers are designed to change the control of companies that had previously made value-reducing acquisitions. Two groups of companies that had made takeover bids were identified: (a) those subject to a later takeover bid within the study period ('targets'), and (b) those not subject to a bid within that period ('non-targets'). Takeover announcements by the 'targets' were associated with significant losses for shareholders, while those by the 'non-targets' were associated with significant gains. Many of the original acquisitions were later reversed, either by voluntary divestiture or by a hostile 'bust-up' takeover. When Mitchell and Lehn examined the market response to the initial takeover, they found significant differences between the 'divested' and 'not divested' groups. The average market response was positive for those that were not divested, negative for those that were divested, and even more negative for those that were followed by a 'bust-up' takeover. Their results are consistent with the argument that one role of takeovers is to discipline managers who fail to maximise profits, including those who make value-reducing takeovers. Their results also indicate that the stock market is able to distinguish between 'good' and 'bad' bidders.

Morck, Shleifer and Vishny (1990) examined the possibility that managerial objectives may lead to unprofitable takeovers. They suggested that takeovers that benefit managers are likely to involve at least one of three characteristics: diversification, rapidly growing targets and poor past performance by the acquiring company. Their results show that all three characteristics are associated with losses for shareholders of acquiring companies—that is, acquiring companies do systematically pay too much in takeovers in which the benefits for managers are particularly large.

19.8.5 THE NET EFFECTS OF TAKEOVERS

The evidence seems clear that activity in the market for corporate control has a positive effect on wealth. For example, Brown and Da Silva Rosa estimated that the bids for 1528 targets covered by their study created value of $15 billion for the shareholders of target companies.

---

[22] The results reported by Lang, Stulz and Walkling (1989) for tender offers have also been supported for takeovers, and are not an artifact of the characteristics of the bid itself, such as the method of payment. See Servaes (1991).

The evidence discussed above was obtained from market-based studies—that is, studies that used share prices to measure the effects of takeovers. Some researchers have preferred to use accounting data to assess the effects of takeovers on company performance by examining measures of profitability, risk and growth. For example, McDougall and Round (1986) used this approach to study Australian takeovers. In common with other similar studies, they were unable to find any evidence of benefits such as improved profitability or reduction of risk. In fact, they concluded that 'a strategy of corporate acquisition resulted in a deterioration in the performance of the merging firms relative both to their pre-takeover experience, and also compared with the experience of the matching non-merging firms, measured in accounting terms'(p. 182). More recent Australian studies of takeover activity in the petroleum industry (Hyde 2002), the banking sector (Avkiran 1999) and between credit unions (Ralston, Wright & Garden 2001) reaffirm the finding that there is little evidence that performance of the merged entity, measured using accounting data, improves in the post-acquisition period. The accounting-based results are clearly inconsistent with those of the more popular market-based studies. This suggests that at least one of the two approaches is unreliable. Bishop, Dodd and Officer (1987, pp. 33–4) argued that there are serious problems in using accounting data to assess the effects of takeovers. For example, the benefits of a takeover may take years to be fully reflected in earnings and are likely to show up at different times for different companies. Therefore, the effects may be difficult to detect. Further, profitability ratios are likely to be biased, owing to revaluation of the target company's assets and write-off of takeover-related goodwill.

Market-based studies are also subject to potential measurement problems. Share price changes around the time a takeover is announced will show how investors expected the takeover to work out, but the expected effects may not eventuate. These studies must also rely on some model of the normal returns on shares to estimate the abnormal returns related to takeovers. Simmonds (2004) demonstrates that returns to the shares of bidding firms may be biased downwards when a risk-adjusted model of expected returns is used. To overcome this, Simmonds suggests that substituting the actual return from the market as a proxy for expected return for the bidding firm's shares will yield more reliable results. In summary, while the market-based approach is generally preferred, it is not infallible and it would be desirable to show that the results of market-based studies can be supported by other independent evidence.

This approach was adopted by Healy, Palepu and Ruback (1992), who used both accounting data and share price data to examine the effects of the 50 largest mergers in the US between 1979 and mid-1984. To minimise the problems involved in using accounting data, they focused on estimates of operating cash flows before interest and tax, rather than on accounting profit, which could be influenced both by the method of accounting for the takeover and by the financing of the takeover. Healy, Palepu and Ruback found that after the takeovers, performance did improve significantly, on average, relative to the performance of other companies in the same industries. The improvement was greatest in takeovers that involved overlapping businesses. Also, they found a strong positive relationship between their estimates of takeover-related changes in operating cash flows and share price changes of the companies involved in the takeover at the time that takeovers were announced. In summary, they provided further evidence that takeovers do result in improved performance and they showed that, when implemented carefully, the accounting-based and market-based approaches can yield consistent results.

19.8.6 THE SOURCES OF GAINS FROM TAKEOVERS

Market-based studies are useful in documenting the magnitude of takeover-related wealth changes for shareholders, but they provide no information about the source of the wealth changes. Some critics have suggested that the wealth increases received by shareholders do not represent real economic gains but instead are the result of various redistributive effects. One such hypothesis is based on alleged market myopia. According to this hypothesis, investors are said to be preoccupied with short-term earnings performance and will undervalue companies that undertake long-term developments, making them prime targets for takeover. Other redistributive hypotheses are based on suggestions that takeovers transfer wealth from debtholders to shareholders, or impose losses on employees of the target company. In addition, there are those hypotheses discussed earlier in the chapter: target undervaluation due to market inefficiency, tax benefits and monopoly power.

Empirical evidence soundly rejects the 'undervaluation' hypothesis and the 'market myopia' hypothesis. Tax benefits do appear to have at least a minor role in motivating takeover activity, but the evidence is inconsistent with shareholder gains being transferred from debtholders or employees (Jarrell, Brickley & Netter 1988, p. 58). This is not to suggest that there are no losers in the market for corporate control: managers of target companies are obvious losers in some, possibly many, cases, but there is no evidence of systematic losses that could offset the large gains to shareholders.

Having first identified improvements in post-merger cash flow performance, Healy, Palepu and Ruback (1992) proceeded to explore the sources of the changes in cash flow. The changes could have arisen from a variety of sources, including higher operating margins, greater asset productivity or lower labour costs. The changes might also have been achieved by cutting outlays on capital investment and research and development (R & D). They found that the higher post-merger cash flows were due primarily to increased asset productivity and there was some evidence of lower labour costs. They found no significant changes in capital outlays or in R & D expenditures. Therefore, the improved cash flows were not due to focusing on short-term performance at the expense of long-term viability.

After surveying the vast body of Australian evidence, Da Silva Rosa and Walter (2004) drew the following conclusions:

(a) Takeovers are initiated by companies that are high performers and are seeking to continue to perform well.
(b) Target shareholders enjoy significant gains when their company is subject to a takeover bid, but these gains tend to dissipate where the bid is unsuccessful and no follow-up bid is launched.
(c) Shares in acquiring companies tend to underperform in the market following acquisition. This is at least partly due to the relatively high costs incurred by acquirers as a consequence of the Australian regulatory environment in the market for corporate control.[23]
(d) Following acquisition, the analysis of the long-run performance of combined entities indicates that the anticipated benefits from the acquisition often fail to materialise. However, Da Silva Rosa and Walter note that the methodological problems associated with studies of this type mean that it is very difficult to reach any strong conclusions about the long-run performance of successful bidding companies.

Connect Plus features a case study illustrating topics covered in this chapter. Ask your lecturer or tutor for your course's unique URL.

SUMMARY

→ Takeovers are an important part of the market for corporate control in which alternative management teams compete for the right to manage corporate assets. The takeover of one company by another is an indirect investment in real assets and, like any other investment, should proceed only if it has a positive NPV.

→ Takeovers occur frequently in Australia, and the level of takeover activity varies considerably over time. The reasons for this variation are not fully understood, but there is evidence that industry shocks, such as deregulation, play an important role.

---

23 For example, Da Silva Rosa and Walter (2004) argue that the bidder's market value is reduced by the requirement that they stand in the market for a 1-month period commencing 14 days after the takeover announcement because they are giving away a potentially very valuable put option to target shareholders.

→ There are three main types of takeover (horizontal, vertical and conglomerate) and many different reasons why takeovers occur.
- Combining two companies can create value by transferring control of assets to managers who can use or deploy those assets more efficiently.
- Other sources of value gains (synergistic benefits) from takeovers include replacing inefficient management, economies of scale, cost savings through vertical integration, and complementarity between the skills and expertise of the two entities.
- Suggested reasons for takeovers that are of dubious validity include diversification benefits and effects on earnings per share.

→ Economic evaluation of proposed takeovers should focus on identifying and quantifying the benefits of the takeover and comparing those benefits with the associated costs. This leads to valuing the target company using an incremental approach—that is, a listed target would be valued by taking the market price as a starting point and adding to it the present value of the incremental net cash flows expected to result from the takeover. This present value represents the gain from the takeover. The *NPV* to the acquiring company is the gain minus the net cost of acquiring the target, where the net cost is the premium paid over and above the target's value as an independent entity.

→ There is a fundamental difference between cash and share-exchange takeover offers. In a cash offer, the net cost is simply the difference between the cash paid and the value of the target as an independent entity. However, in the case of a share-exchange offer, the net cost depends on the share price of the acquiring company after the takeover offer has been announced.

→ Takeovers are regulated by legislation that emphasises equity between shareholders of the target company and requires disclosure of information by bidders.
- With very limited exceptions, an investor may not acquire more than 20 per cent of a company's shares unless the investor makes a takeover bid for the company by way of either an off-market bid or a market bid.
- In the case of a partial takeover, the bidder must specify, at the outset, the proportion of each holder's shares that the bidder will offer to buy.

→ The market for corporate control also includes transactions in which companies or groups are reduced in size by asset disposals ('divestitures'), divided into separate entities ('spin-offs') or transferred to private ownership ('buyouts'). These corporate restructuring transactions are associated with increases in value that can be significant. In some cases, the explanations for the gain may be similar to those for takeover gains. In other cases, the explanation rests on factors such as lower agency costs and effects on managerial incentives.

→ There is ample empirical evidence that takeovers provide substantial benefits for the shareholders of target companies. The evidence on benefits to the shareholders of acquiring companies is less conclusive. Abnormal returns on acquiring company shares around the time of takeover bids are much smaller in percentage terms than those on target company shares.

→ While takeovers generate net benefits for shareholders on average, there is evidence that some types of takeover consistently harm the shareholders of acquiring companies. Such takeovers may serve the objectives of managers and are a 'problem' for investors, but the market for corporate control can also provide a 'solution' in that many unprofitable takeovers are later reversed.

KEY TERMS

buyout (or going-private) transaction 665
conglomerate takeover 643
corporate raiders 645
divestiture (or sell-off) 664
horizontal takeover 643
leveraged buyout 664
management buyout 664
partial takeover 658
poison pill 662
proportional bid 658
spin-off 664
synergy 643
takeover 641
target company 641
vertical takeover 643

SELF-TEST PROBLEMS

1. Alpha Ltd is considering the acquisition of Beta Ltd. Both companies are wholly equity financed and each has 2 million shares on issue. The annual net cash flows of Alpha and Beta are $1 million and $500 000, respectively, and these cash flows are expected to remain constant in perpetuity. Alpha shareholders require a rate of return of 20 per cent per annum, but Beta's operations are of higher risk and its shareholders require a 25 per cent per annum rate of return. After the takeover, Beta's net cash flow is expected to increase to $750 000 per annum in perpetuity with no change in risk.
    (a) Calculate the price per share at which Beta represents a zero net present value investment to Alpha.
    (b) Calculate the value of Beta as an independent entity.
    (c) Alpha offers $2.6 million cash for 100 per cent of Beta. Calculate the effect of the takeover on the wealth of each company's shareholders.

2. Bako Ltd (B) has completed an exhaustive evaluation preparatory to the proposed acquisition of 50 per cent of the shares of Cullen Ltd (C). On the basis of this evaluation, B's management has estimated that the value of B's equity will increase from $320 million to $380 million as a result of the partial takeover. The pre-takeover number of shares in the two companies is 80 million in B and 20 million in C. B's management is now considering whether to proceed with the takeover by making one of the following bids:
    (a) a cash offer for C's shares of $5 per share (C's shares are currently selling for $4)
    (b) a share offer of 3 shares in B for every 2 shares in C.
    Should B proceed with the takeover in either case?

Solutions to self-test problems are available in Appendix B, page 803.

REFERENCES

Andrade, G., Mitchell, M. & Stafford, E., 'New evidence and perspectives on mergers', *Journal of Economic Perspectives*, Spring 2001, pp. 103–20.

——, & Stafford, E., 'Investigating the economic role of mergers', *Journal of Corporate Finance*, January 2004, pp. 1–36.

Avkiran, N.K., 'The evidence on efficiency gains: the role of mergers and the benefits to the public', *Journal of Banking and Finance*, July 1999, pp. 137–49.

Bates, T. & Lemmon, M., 'Breaking up is hard to do? An analysis of termination fee provisions and merger outcomes', *Journal of Financial Economics*, September 2003, pp. 469–504.

Beerworth, W.J., 'Mergers, acquisitions and takeovers', in R. Bruce, B. McKern, I. Pollard & M. Skully (eds), *Handbook of Australian Corporate Finance*, 5th edn, Butterworths, Sydney, 1997, pp. 164–204.

Bishop, S., Dodd, P. & Officer, R.R., 'Australian takeovers: the evidence 1972–1985', *Policy Monograph*, 12, Centre for Independent Studies, St Leonards, 1987.

Bradley, M., Desai, A. & Kim, E., 'The rationale behind interfirm tender offers: information or synergy?', *Journal of Financial Economics*, April 1983, pp. 183–206.

——, ——, ——, 'Synergistic gains from corporate acquisitions and their division between the shareholders of target and acquiring firms', *Journal of Financial Economics*, May 1988, pp. 3–40.

Brown, P. & Da Silva Rosa, R., 'Takeovers: who wins?', *JASSA*, Summer, 1997, pp. 2–5.

——, ——, 'Research method and the long-run performance of acquiring firms', *Australian Journal of Management*, June 1998, pp. 23–38.

Casey, R., Dodd, P. & Dolan, P., 'Takeovers and corporate raiders: empirical evidence from extended event studies',

Australian Journal of Management, December 1987, pp. 201–20.

Casey, R. & Eddey, P., 'Defence strategies of listed companies under the takeover code', *Australian Journal of Management*, December 1986, pp. 153–71.

Chapple, L., Christensen, B. & Clarkson, P., 'Termination fees in a "bright line" jurisdiction', *Accounting and Finance*, December 2007, pp. 643–65.

Chessel, J., 'The big takeovers of 2005', *Sydney Morning Herald*, 24 December 2005, p. 41.

Copeland, T., Koller, T. & Murrin, J., *Valuation: Measuring and Managing the Value of Companies*, 3rd edn, John Wiley & Sons, New York, 2000.

Curtis, J. & Pinder, S., 'Break-fee restrictions: where's the harm?', *Agenda: A Journal of Policy Analysis and Reform*, June 2007, pp. 111–22.

Da Silva Rosa, R., Izan, H., Steinbeck, A. & Walter, T., 'The method of payment decision in Australian takeovers: an investigation of causes and effects', *Australian Journal of Management*, June 2000, pp. 67–97.

——, & Walter, T., 'Australian mergers and acquisitions since the 1980s: what do we know and what remains to be done', *Australian Journal of Management*, Special issue 2004, pp. i–xiv.

De Angelo, H., De Angelo, L. & Rice, E.M., 'Going private: minority freezeouts and stockholder wealth', *Journal of Law and Economics*, October 1984, pp. 367–401.

Dodd, P. 'The market for corporate control: a review of the evidence', in J. Stern and D. Chew (eds), *The Revolution in Corporate Finance*, 2nd edn, Blackwell, Oxford, 1992.

——, & Officer, R.R., 'Corporate control, economic efficiency and shareholder justice', *Policy Monograph*, 9, Centre for Independent Studies, St Leonards, 1986.

Eckbo, B. & Thorburn, K., 'Corporate restructuring: breakups and LBOs', in B.E. Eckbo (ed.), *Handbook of Corporate Finance: Empirical Corporate Finance*, vol. 2, Elsevier North Holland, Amsterdam, 2008, pp. 135–202.

Eddey, P. & Casey, R., 'Directors' recommendations in response to takeover bids: do they act in their own interests?', *Australian Journal of Management*, June 1989, pp. 1–28.

——, Lee, K. & Taylor, S., 'What motivates going private? An analysis of Australian firms', *Accounting and Finance*, May 1996, pp. 31–50.

Ernst & Young Australia, *Australian Management Buyouts—The Story Continues*, Sydney, 2000.

Finn, F. & Hodgson, A., 'Takeover activity in Australia: endogenous and exogenous influences', *Accounting and Finance*, November 2005, pp. 375–94.

Gaughan, P.A., 'Introduction: the fourth merger wave and beyond', in P.A. Gaughan (ed.), *Readings in Mergers and Acquisitions*, Blackwell, Oxford, 1994.

Healy, P., Palepu, K. & Ruback, R., 'Does corporate performance improve after mergers?', *Journal of Financial Economics*, April 1992, pp. 135–75.

Hite, G. & Owers, J., 'The restructuring of corporate America: an overview', in J. Stern and D. Chew (eds), *The Revolution in Corporate Finance*, 2nd edn, Blackwell, Oxford, 1992.

Hyde, C.E., 'Evaluating mergers in the Australian petroleum industry', *The Economic Record*, September 2002, pp. 299–311.

Jarrell, G., Brickley, J. & Netter, J., 'The market for corporate control: the empirical evidence since 1980', *Journal of Economic Perspectives*, Winter 1988, pp. 49–68.

——, & Poulsen, A., 'The returns to acquiring firms in tender offers: evidence from three decades', *Financial Management*, Autumn 1989, pp. 12–19.

Jensen, M., 'Agency costs of free cash flow, corporate finance and takeovers', *American Economic Review*, May 1986, pp. 323–9.

——, 'Takeovers: their causes and consequences', *Journal of Economic Perspectives*, Winter 1988, pp. 21–48.

——, 'The takeover controversy: analysis and evidence', in J. Stern and D. Chew (eds), *The Revolution in Corporate Finance*, 3rd edn, Blackwell, Oxford, 1998, pp. 351–77.

——, & Ruback, R., 'The market for corporate control: the scientific evidence', *Journal of Financial Economics*, April 1983, pp. 5–50.

Kaplan, S., 'The effects of management buyouts on operating performance and value', *Journal of Financial Economics*, October 1989, pp. 217–54.

——, 'The staying power of leveraged buyouts', in J. Stern and D. Chew (eds), *The Revolution in Corporate Finance*, 3rd edn, Blackwell, Oxford 1998, pp. 378–87.

——, & Weisbach, M., 'The success of acquisitions: evidence from divestitures', *Journal of Finance*, March 1992, pp. 107–38.

Lang, L., Stulz, R. & Walkling, R., 'Managerial performance, Tobin's Q and the gains from successful tender offers', *Journal of Financial Economics*, September 1989, pp. 137–54.

Levy, R., *Takeovers Law and Strategy*, LBC Information Services, North Ryde, 1996.

——, & Pathak, N., *Takeovers Law and Strategy*, 3rd edn, Thomson Reuters, Pyrmont, 2009.

Loughran, T. & Vijh, A., 'Do long-term shareholders benefit from corporate acquisitions?', *Journal of Finance*, December 1997, pp. 1765–90.

McDougall, F. & Round, D., *The Effects of Mergers and Takeovers in Australia*, Australian Institute of Management—Victoria and National Companies and Securities Commission, 1986.

Maheswaran, K. & Pinder, S., 'Australian evidence on the determinants and impact of takeover resistance', *Accounting and Finance*, vol. 45, no. 4, 2005, pp. 613–33.

Martin, K. & McConnell, J., 'Corporate performance, corporate takeovers and management turnover', *Journal of Finance*, June 1991, pp. 671–87.

Mayanya, J., 'Reforming Australia's takeover defence laws: what role for target directors? A reply and extension', *Australian Journal of Corporate Law*, vol. 10, 1999, pp. 162–91.

Mitchell, M. & Lehn, K., 'Do bad bidders become good targets?', *Journal of Political Economy*, April 1990, pp. 372–98.

Morck, R., Shleifer, A. & Vishny, R., 'Characteristics of targets of hostile and friendly takeovers', in A.J. Auerbach (ed.), *Corporate Takeovers: Causes and Consequences*, National Bureau of Economic Research, Chicago, 1988, pp. 101–29.

——, ——, ——, 'Do managerial objectives drive bad acquisitions?', *Journal of Finance*, March 1990, pp. 31–48.

Mukherjee, T.K., Kiymaz, H. & Baker, H., 'Merger motives and target valuation: a survey of evidence from CFOs', *Journal of Applied Finance*, Winter 2004, pp. 7–24.

Officer, M., 'Termination fees in mergers and acquisitions', *Journal of Financial Economics*, September 2003, pp. 431–67.

Penman, S.H., *Financial Statement Analysis and Security Valuation*, 2nd edn, McGraw-Hill, New York, 2004.

Ralston, D., Wright, A. & Garden, K., 'Can mergers ensure the survival of credit unions in the third millennium?', *Journal of Banking and Finance*, December 2001, pp. 2277–304.

Reserve Bank of Australia, *Financial Stability Review*, March 2007.

Roll, R., 'The hubris hypothesis of corporate takeovers', *Journal of Business*, April 1986, pp. 197–216.

Rosenkranz, S. & Weitzel, U. 'Bargaining in mergers: the role of outside options and termination provisions', *Working Paper 07-06*, 2007, Utrecht School of Economics.

Schipper, K. & Thompson, R., 'Evidence on the capitalised value of merger activity of acquiring firms', *Journal of Financial Economics*, April 1983, pp. 85–119.

Schwert, G., 'Hostility in takeovers: in the eyes of the beholder?', *Journal of Finance*, December 2000, pp. 2599–640.

Servaes, H., 'Tobin's Q and the gains from takeovers', *Journal of Finance*, March 1991, pp. 409–19.

Simmonds, D.P., 'The impact of takeover offer timing on the measurement of Australian bidder gains: 1976 to 1995', *Australian Journal of Management*, Special issue 2004, pp. 1–60.

Stanton, P., 'Accounting rates of return as measures of post-merger performance', *Australian Journal of Management*, December 1987, pp. 293–304.

Stern, J. & Chew, D. (eds), *The Modern Revolution in Corporate Finance*, 3rd edn, Blackwell, Oxford, 1998.

Walkling, R. & Long, M., 'Agency theory, managerial welfare and takeover bid resistance', *Rand Journal of Economics*, Spring 1984, pp. 54–68.

QUESTIONS

1. **[LO 1]** Takeover activity tends to vary significantly over time. Outline the factors that may explain this variation.

2. **[LO 1]** There are three types of takeover: horizontal, vertical and conglomerate. Give recent Australian examples of each type of takeover.

3. **[LO 1]** *A company can reduce its risk by taking over another company.* Do you agree with this statement? Is it a justifiable reason for a takeover?

4. **[LO 1]** *A company with accumulated tax losses is necessarily a valuable takeover proposition.* Discuss this statement.

5. **[LO 3]** *There is no reason for an acquiring company to prefer a cash bid to a share exchange or vice versa.* Discuss this statement.

6. **[LO 4]** What are the benefits and costs of an unregulated market for takeovers? In view of the Australian legislation regulating takeovers, evaluate the benefits and costs.

7. **[LO 6]** *Investing private equity in a buyout is less risky than investing in an initial public offering.* Discuss this statement.

8. **[LO 6]** Leveraged buyout activity increased dramatically between 2000 and 2006. Suggest reasons for this increase.

9. **[LO 6]** *Taking a company private often results in significant pressure being placed on the management team to cut costs and make operations more efficient.* Discuss this statement.

10. **[LO 4]** *The Takeovers Panel is just another form of government bureaucracy that is a waste of resources that could easily be 'taken over' itself by the Australian Securities and Investment Commission without any effect on the market for corporate control.* Evaluate this statement. (Hint: access the website **www.takeovers.gov.au** to review the make-up and powers of the panel as well as some of the decisions reached.)

11. **[LO 4]** What are the benefits and costs associated with having the Australian Competition and Consumer Commission (ACCC) involved with the market for corporate control? Give an example of where the ACCC has not permitted an acquisition to proceed and outline its reasons for doing so. (Hint: **www.accc.gov.au** provides access to the news releases issued by the ACCC explaining the reasons for their decisions.)

12. **[LO 7]** The evidence is clear that takeovers in aggregate in Australia have resulted in substantial increases in the value of the corporate economy (Bishop, Dodd & Officer 1987, p. 6). Outline the major points that support this conclusion.

13. **[LO 2]** Budget Computers specialises in buying second-hand computers and renting them out. Owing to rapid technological changes and intense competition, Budget has recorded losses in recent years and is now threatened with liquidation. Its major asset is a stock of largely obsolete computers. Fleeting Electrics Ltd is a newly listed company with interests in consumer electrical goods. The Chairman of Fleeting suggests that it should acquire Budget for two reasons. First, it provides diversification, and second, he argues that by injecting fresh capital, Budget can be 'rescued' and should appreciate markedly in value. Critically evaluate the Chairman's arguments.

14. **[LO 2]** The value of Minnow Ltd to Whale Ltd can be determined by:
    (a) discounting Minnow's net cash flows to a present value
    (b) the present value of Minnow's expected future dividends
    (c) estimating the present value of the incremental net cash flows directly attributable to the takeover, and adding this to the current market value of Minnow.
    (d) Critically evaluate each of these approaches. Which one would you advise the management of Whale to use? Give reasons.

15. **[LO 2]**
    (a) In an efficient market, the price of a company's shares is an unbiased estimate of their 'true' value. How might the 'true' value of a takeover target differ from its value to a potential bidder? What relationship exists between this latter value and the actual offer price?
    (b) *Asset backing is irrelevant as a measure of the worth of a company subject to a takeover bid.* Comment on this statement.

16. **[LO 2]** Carrion Ltd has announced a takeover bid for Elephant Ltd, one of Australia's largest companies. The Chairman of Carrion argues that the takeover will be economically viable because it will lead to more efficient management of Elephant's assets, there are tax advantages involved, and value can be created by dividing Elephant into three or four separate entities, each based on a single line of business.
    (a) Critically evaluate each of the three reasons for takeover viability suggested by the Chairman.
    (b) Assuming that Carrion already holds 15 per cent of Elephant's shares, briefly outline the legislative requirements that must be met in any bid for control of the target.
    (c) Elephant's shares had a market price of $7.90 prior to any purchases by Carrion. Analysts employed by Carrion have valued the shares at $11.50, based on the present value of future net cash flows. Outline the relationship you would expect between these values and Carrion's bid price.

17. **[LO 1]** Explain the following terms:
    (a) market for corporate control
    (b) synergy

(c) disciplinary takeover
(d) takeover waves
(e) co-insurance effect
(f) free cash flow
(g) bootstrapping
(h) off-market bid
(i) market bid
(j) proportional bid
(k) white knight
(l) golden parachute
(m) spin-off
(n) leveraged buyout
(o) hubris
(p) corporate raider.

18. **[LO 7]** Maureen Carroll examines the share prices of companies that are the targets of takeover bids. She finds that their share prices rise substantially when the bid is announced and, over the next 12 months, do not drop back to the pre-bid level, even if the takeover is unsuccessful. Advise Maureen of possible explanations for this observation.

19. **[LO 1]** Duck Ltd, a conglomerate, has a market capitalisation of $400 million. The management of Drake Ltd believes that it can acquire Duck for $500 million and sell its divisions separately for a total of about $800 million. Outline possible reasons for the difference between these values.

20. **[LO 1]** *Takeovers are important because they provide the only way to exploit synergies, and to ensure that managers of corporations act in the interests of shareholders.* Comment on this statement.

21. **[LO 7]** Claire McDonald is concerned that market-based evidence on the effects of takeovers may be misleading. She agrees that target company shareholders gain substantially, but argues that these gains could be the result of wealth transfers from employees, and from the shareholders of acquiring companies. Claire says, 'I won't be convinced that takeovers are beneficial until someone can show exactly where the gains come from.' Outline evidence that should convince Claire that takeovers provide real benefits.

22. **[LO 4]** Outline the factors that the management of a bidding company should take into account when deciding whether to make an off-market or an on-market offer for a target.

PROBLEMS

1. **Evaluating takeovers and NPV [LO 2]**
   Yam Ltd (Y) has been evaluating the acquisition of Xavier Ltd (X). The annual expected cash flows of Y and X are, respectively, $1.16 million per annum in perpetuity and $640 000 per annum in perpetuity. These cash flows are expected to be unaffected by the takeover. The systematic risk (beta) of Y is 0.75 and of X is 1.0. The risk-free interest rate is 10 per cent and the expected excess return on the market portfolio is 6 per cent. Calculate the price at which X represents a zero net present value investment. Is it likely that Y's shareholders will benefit from the takeover?

2. **Evaluating takeovers [LO 2]**
   Assume the information in Problem 1, except that the post-takeover cash flow of the two companies is expected to be $1.95 million per annum in perpetuity. Is the acquisition likely to be of benefit to Y's shareholders?

3. **Evaluating takeovers [LO 2]**
   Squire Clothing is considering the acquisition of the Skintight Jeans Company. Squire will pay $2 million to buy Skintight's assets and will also assume its liabilities of $900 000. It has been estimated that Skintight's existing assets will generate pre-tax cash flows of $500 000 per annum for 25 years. The assets can be depreciated for tax purposes at 20 per cent per annum straight-line, with no salvage value. The company tax rate is 33 per cent and Squire estimates that an investment of this level of risk should yield 12 per cent per annum after tax.
   Evaluate the proposed takeover.

4. **Evaluating cash versus share offers [LO 2]**
   Crocodile Ltd is considering the acquisition of Shark Finance. The values of the two companies as separate entities are $10 million and $5 million, respectively. Crocodile estimates that by combining the two companies it will reduce selling and administrative costs by $250 000 per annum in perpetuity. Crocodile can either pay $7 million cash for Shark or offer Shark a 50 per cent holding in Crocodile. If the opportunity cost of capital is 10 per cent per annum:
   (a) what is the gain, in present value terms, from the merger?
   (b) what is the net cost of the cash offer?

(c) what is the net cost of the share alternative?
(d) what is the *NPV* of the acquisition under:
  (i) the cash offer?
  (ii) the share offer?

5. **EPS bootstrapping [LO 2]**
Progressive Ltd is determined to increase its earnings per share from $1 to $1.33, so it acquires Lo-Gear. The following facts are provided:

Item	Progressive	Lo-Gear	Merged company
Earnings per share ($)	1.00	1.25	1.33
Price per share ($)	20.00	12.50	?
Price–earnings ratio	20.00	10.00	?
Number of shares	100 000	200 000	?
Total earnings ($)	100 000	250 000	?
Total market value ($)	2 000 000	2 500 000	?

There are no economic benefits from combining the two companies. In exchange for Lo-Gear's shares, Progressive issues just enough of its own shares to ensure its $1.33 earnings-per-share objective.

(a) Complete the table for the merged company.
(b) How many shares of Progressive are exchanged for each share of Lo-Gear?
(c) What is the net cost of the takeover to Progressive?
(d) What is the change in the total market value of the Progressive shares that were on issue before the takeover?
(e) Based on these results, comment on the use of earnings-per-share comparisons in assessing the viability of takeovers.

6. **Alternative approaches to target valuation [LO 2]**
Farrout Ltd is planning to acquire a small boat builder, Winged Keel Pty Ltd. Three opinions have been obtained on the value of the target. These are as follows:

(a) Based on the latest earnings of Winged Keel, and applying Farrout's price–earnings ratio, the company is worth $1.2 million.
(b) Based on total tangible assets, a value of $2 million is indicated.
(c) Based on the present value of Winged Keel's expected future dividends, it is worth $1.5 million.

Evaluate each of these approaches and indicate any inherent problems. Which would you select as the most appropriate?

Test yourself further with Connect Plus online! Ask your lecturer or tutor for your course's unique URL.

INTERNATIONAL FINANCIAL MANAGEMENT

LEARNING OBJECTIVES

After studying this chapter you should be able to:

1. understand the importance of international transactions for the Australian economy
2. read, interpret and use foreign exchange rates
3. understand the roles of interest rates and inflation rates in exchange-rate determination
4. understand the empirical evidence on the behaviour of exchange rates
5. understand the techniques that can be used to manage exchange risk
6. explain the advantages of international diversification of investments
7. identify the characteristics and uses of currency swaps
8. identify the main sources of foreign currency borrowing used by Australian companies.

CHAPTER CONTENTS

20.1	Introduction
20.2	Some background statistics
20.3	The foreign exchange market
20.4	Relationships between interest rates, inflation rates, spot exchange rates and forward exchange rates
20.5	Empirical evidence on the behaviour of exchange rates
20.6	The management of exchange risk
20.7	International diversification of investments
20.8	Currency swaps
20.9	Foreign currency borrowing by Australian companies

20.1 INTRODUCTION

In previous chapters, we have made only passing reference to international financial management. The aim of this chapter is to provide an introduction to some of the major issues in international financial management. Many Australian companies import goods and services, while others export goods and services. Many Australian companies invest internationally and/or borrow internationally. Many Australian investors purchase shares and other securities issued by foreign corporations. In each of these cases, knowledge of international financial management is indispensable.

Since the floating of the Australian dollar in 1983, the value of the Australian dollar has varied considerably, thereby creating problems for financial managers. However, the ability to undertake foreign currency transactions in a deregulated environment also provides opportunities for financial managers. In addition, foreign currency trading and finance is itself an industry, with many banks and other institutions involved in currency trading. In 2009–10, the average daily market turnover in all currencies in the Australian foreign exchange market was nearly A$170 billion, making the Australian market the seventh largest in the world.[1] The Australian dollar is one of the most actively traded currencies in the world.[2]

20.2 SOME BACKGROUND STATISTICS

Some idea of the importance of international operations to Australian companies can be obtained from Tables 20.1 to 20.3.

TABLE 20.1 Value of Australia's exports and imports of goods and services, A$ billion, and as a percentage of gross domestic product

YEAR	EXPORTS OF GOODS AND SERVICES		IMPORTS OF GOODS AND SERVICES	
	A$ BILLION	%	A$ BILLION	%
1988/1989	55.5	14.9	62.7	16.9
1992/1993	77.3	17.2	79.6	17.7
1996/1997	106.3	19.0	104.5	18.7
2000/2001	156.1	22.0	154.6	21.8
2004/2005	167.3	18.1	190.5	20.6
2005/2006	195.8	19.6	211.2	21.1
2006/2007	215.7	19.8	229.2	21.0
2007/2008	233.6	19.8	258.3	21.9
2008/2009	283.9	22.6	278.1	22.1
2009/2010	254.4	19.5	260.1	20.0

Source: Compiled from Table G11, Reserve Bank of Australia website, www.rba.gov.au.

LEARNING OBJECTIVE 1
Understand the importance of international transactions for the Australian economy

---

[1] In April 2010, the top six locations for currency trading were (in order): United Kingdom, United States, Japan, Singapore, Switzerland and Hong Kong (Bank for International Settlements, December 2010, p. 12).

[2] In April 2010, the Australian dollar was the world's fifth most actively traded currency. The top four currencies were (in order): US dollar, euro, yen and pound (Bank for International Settlements, December 2010, p. 19).

TABLE 20.2 Australia's gross foreign assets and liabilities,[a] A$ billion: non-official sector

YEAR (AS AT 30 JUNE)	GROSS FOREIGN ASSETS			GROSS FOREIGN LIABILITIES		
	DIRECT INVESTMENT	PORTFOLIO AND OTHER	TOTAL NON-OFFICIAL	DIRECT INVESTMENT	PORTFOLIO AND OTHER	TOTAL NON-OFFICIAL
1989	53.3	35.2	88.4	99.3	140.8	240.1
1993	69.0	60.1	129.1	129.0	219.9	349.0
1997	105.8	107.9	213.7	166.8	318.9	485.7
2001	225.6	233.3	458.9	248.2	598.2	846.5
2005	275.3	347.2	622.5	346.3	809.5	1155.8
2006	356.6	449.4	806.1	379.0	1005.7	1384.8
2007	416.1	571.6	987.7	442.6	1224.6	1667.2
2008	410.9	652.9	1063.8	478.5	1260.8	1739.3
2009	391.1	657.8	1048.9	481.6	1288.4	1770.0
2010	406.3	739.9	1146.2	512.8	1352.5	1865.3

(a) In this table 'liabilities' includes equity.

Source: Compiled from Table H4, Reserve Bank of Australia website, **www.rba.gov.au**.

TABLE 20.3 Australia's gross and net foreign debt, A$ billion

DATE	GROSS A$ BILLION	NET A$ BILLION
30 June 1989	170.7	114.7
30 June 1993	244.8	176.9
30 June 1997	311.2	207.6
30 June 2001	513.3	300.4
30 June 2005	754.2	427.7
30 June 2006	892.5	494.9
30 June 2007	1041.5	539.8
30 June 2008	1140.0	600.4
30 June 2009	1236.1	624.3
30 June 2010	1314.5	671.9

Source: Compiled from Tables H4 and H5, Reserve Bank of Australia website, **www.rba.gov.au**.

Table 20.1 shows that international trade now represents about 20 per cent of Australia's gross domestic product; this percentage is higher than was the case 15 or 20 years ago.

Turning from international trade to international capital movements, Tables 20.2 and 20.3 provide information on capital movements between Australia and other countries.

Historically, Australia has been a net importer of capital. Table 20.2 shows the growth in Australia's foreign liabilities and assets since 1989. Both have grown strongly in this period, with an average annual growth rate of 13.0 per cent in assets and 10.3 per cent in liabilities.

The extent of Australia's external indebtedness is indicated in Table 20.3, which shows that Australia's external indebtedness has grown considerably in recent years, with net indebtedness in 2010 standing at more than A$670 billion.

As indicated by the data in these tables, Australia has a relatively open economy. It depends significantly on international trade and on foreign sources of capital and, for its size, has significant investments in other countries. Moreover, government policy and pronouncements have encouraged Australian companies to look beyond Australia for both ideas and markets. Not surprisingly, therefore, many companies operating in Australia assign a high priority to decisions on international financial management.

THE FOREIGN EXCHANGE MARKET

The foreign exchange market has no physical marketplace but rather is a communications network linking banks and other dealers in foreign exchange. A company wishing to buy or sell foreign currency may do so through one of the banks or other dealers. Apart from exporting or importing goods and services, reasons for using the foreign exchange market include borrowing or lending foreign currency, buying or selling foreign assets, and speculating on exchange rate movements.

An important outcome of the transactions that occur in the foreign exchange market is the set of prices known as exchange rates. For example, the price at which Australian dollars can be converted into UK pounds (often known as pounds sterling) is known as the **exchange rate** between Australian dollars and UK pounds. Every transaction that occurs in the foreign exchange market involves exchange rates, so it is important to understand how these rates, which can be either spot or forward rates, are quoted and used.

LEARNING OBJECTIVE 2
Read, interpret and use foreign exchange rates

exchange rate
price of one country's currency expressed in terms of another country's currency

20.3.1 THE SPOT EXCHANGE RATE

The meaning of the phrase 'spot exchange rate' is most readily understood in the context of international trade. For example, suppose that an Australian company imports goods from the UK. It is likely that the UK supplier will require the Australian company to pay for the goods in UK pounds. Unless the Australian company has a stock of UK pounds of its own it will need to buy UK pounds in order to pay for the goods. In other words, the Australian company will need to exchange (sell) Australian dollars for UK pounds. Australian companies that export goods are also likely to invoice the purchaser in foreign currency rather than in Australian dollars. In this case, the Australian company will wish to sell the foreign currency and receive Australian dollars. Again the exchange rate is used to make the conversion.

As explained earlier, an exchange rate is simply the price at which one country's currency can be exchanged for another country's currency in the foreign exchange market. The exchange may be immediate (in practice, usually 2 days). In this case the exchange rate is called the **spot rate**, the word *spot* referring to the fact that the delivery of the currency is (almost) immediate. Examples of retail spot rates for one Australian dollar, as at 30 July 2010, are shown in Table 20.4.

spot rate
rate for transactions for immediate delivery. In the case of the wholesale foreign exchange market, the spot rate is for settlement in 2 days

TABLE 20.4 Retail spot exchange rates for A$1 as at 30 July 2010

CURRENCY	(1) CUSTOMER SELLS FOREIGN CURRENCY AND BUYS A$1	(2) CUSTOMER SELLS A$1 AND BUYS FOREIGN CURRENCY	(3) RATIO OF (2) TO (1)%
US dollar (USD)	0.9171	0.8760	95.52
Japanese yen (JPY)	79.80	75.95	95.18
UK pound (GBP)	0.5907	0.5605	94.89
Euro (EUR)	0.7055	0.6685	94.76
South Africa rand (ZAR)	6.8585	6.4025	93.35
Thailand baht (THB)	30.46	27.37	89.86
West Samoa tala (WST)	2.4104	2.0528	85.16

Source: *Australian Financial Review*, 3 August 2010. The rates quoted are retail rates; wholesale rates would show lower figures in Column (1) and higher figures in Column (2), and thus ratios in Column (3) would be closer to 100 per cent.

Column (1) provides the exchange rate applicable where a customer has foreign currency and wishes to obtain Australian dollars. Column (2) provides the exchange rate applicable where a customer has Australian dollars and wishes to obtain foreign currency. Using the US dollar spot rate as an example, if a customer (say, a company) had US dollars and wanted to buy A$1, it would have needed to deliver (sell) US$0.9171 to obtain the Australian dollar. If, instead, a customer had A$1 and wished to buy US dollars, it would receive US$0.8760 in return for the one Australian dollar.[3] The difference (or spread) between the rates is one source of the foreign exchange dealer's profit. The final column in Table 20.4 shows how the spread varies from currency to currency. The spread for the US dollar is the narrowest, followed by the spread on currencies that are heavily traded (such as yen, pounds and euros), with the widest spreads being on those currencies that, from an Australian viewpoint at least, are infrequently traded. One reason for this pattern is that the vast majority of trading in Australian dollars is in terms of the US dollar. Therefore, if an Australian company approached its bank to obtain a significant sum in, say, Thai baht, the bank could obtain the baht by first selling the Australian dollars for US dollars and then (probably through another country's foreign exchange market) selling the US dollars for baht. Thus two transactions would be required, as there is no direct link between the Australian dollar and the baht.

Table 20.5 provides data from surveys conducted by the Bank for International Settlements (BIS) in 2004, 2007 and 2010. Not surprisingly, by far the most common transaction in the Australian foreign exchange market involves the Australian dollar–US dollar exchange rate; this accounted for approximately 39 per cent of the value transacted. However, over 50 per cent of the volume of trading undertaken in Australia does not involve the Australian dollar.

TABLE 20.5 Foreign exchange trading in Australia: market share by currency pair, April 2004, 2007 and 2010

CURRENCY PAIR	MARKET SHARE (%)		
	APRIL 2004	APRIL 2007	APRIL 2010
Australian dollar–US dollar	43.7	45.3	39.3
Euro–US dollar	16.3	13.9	19.8
US dollar–Japanese yen	12.6	7.9	9.8
UK pound–US dollar	7.8	5.8	7.3
NZ dollar–US dollar	6.0	9.2	6.5
Other	13.6	17.9	17.3
Total	100.0	100.0	100.0

Source: Bank for International Settlements, *Triennial Central Bank Survey of Foreign Exchange and Derivatives Market Activity* as reported in Reserve Bank of Australia, Media release no. 2010–19, 1 September 2010.

20.3.2 THE FORWARD EXCHANGE RATE

forward rate
exchange rate that is established now but with payment and delivery to occur on a specified future date

In forward exchange trading, the exchange of currencies is not immediate but is on some agreed future date—that is, the exchange rate is determined now, but the currencies are exchanged later. The exchange rate in such a contract is referred to as the **forward rate**. For example, a time period of 1, 3 or 6 months may be specified in a forward exchange contract. Forward contracts for periods exceeding 1 year are unusual: the 2010 BIS survey found that only about 2 per cent of forward contracts are for periods of more than 1 year.

[3] We have used exchange rates in the retail (or small transaction) market. Exchange rates in the wholesale (large transaction) or interdealer market would be more favourable, with a much narrower gap (or 'spread') between the rates. In the interdealer market the spread may be as little as A$0.0002.

Forward exchange rates are usually quoted in terms of the difference between the spot rate and the forward rate. This difference is referred to as the **forward margin**.[4] To understand how to interpret forward exchange quotations, suppose that for US dollars (per one Australian dollar) you are told that the spot rate is 0.8460/70 and the 3 months' forward margin is −15/−10. This means that the exchange rates, expressed in US dollars per A$1, are as shown in Table 20.6.

forward margin difference between spot and forward rates

TABLE 20.6 Calculation of the forward rate using the forward margin

		CUSTOMER SELLS A$1 AND BUYS US$	CUSTOMER SELLS US$ AND BUYS A$1
	Spot rate	0.8460	0.8470
less	Forward margin	0.0015	0.0010
	Forward rate	0.8445	0.8460

Therefore, if a dealer agrees today to sell A$1 in 3 months' time, it will receive US$0.8445 in 3 months' time. If a dealer agrees to buy A$1 in 3 months' time, it will need to deliver US$0.8460 in 3 months' time. The *forward margin* in this example is subtracted from the spot rate, but for other currencies, or for the same currency at other times, the forward margin may have to be added to the spot rate. The reasons for this difference are explained in Section 20.4.2.

20.3.3 COMBINED SPOT AND FORWARD TRANSACTIONS

Dealers in foreign exchange markets frequently enter simultaneously into spot and forward transactions. For example, one dealer may agree with another to sell Australian dollars today for, say, US dollars, and simultaneously agree to buy back the Australian dollars on a later date. The exchange rate agreed will, of course, differ between the two 'legs' of the transaction because the first leg is a spot transaction, while the second is a forward transaction. These combined transactions have occurred in foreign exchange markets for many years and are generally known as 'foreign exchange swaps'. However, they should be distinguished from currency swaps, discussed in Section 20.8, which are more complex and have a more recent origin.

20.3.4 CALCULATIONS USING FOREIGN EXCHANGE RATES

Although calculations using foreign exchange rates are very simple, mistakes are often made. There are only four types of calculation. Each type is illustrated using the UK pound exchange rates given in Table 20.4.

	Customer sells £ and buys A$1	*Customer buys £ and sells A$1*
UK pound (GBP)	0.5907	0.5605

Type 1: to obtain a given sum in A$ using £

A UK resident may wish to obtain A$10 000. How many pounds are needed? As £0.5907 is needed for every A$1 required, the answer is £(10 000 × 0.5907) = £5907.

Type 2: to convert a given sum of £ to A$

An Australian company has been paid £10 000 and wishes to exchange this for Australian dollars. How many Australian dollars will this buy? As each dollar will buy £0.5907, the answer is £(10 000/0.5907) = A$16 929.07.

---

4 Determinants of the forward margin are discussed in Section 20.4.2.

Type 3: to obtain a given sum in £ using A$

An Australian company may wish to obtain £10 000. How many Australian dollars are needed? As A$1 will obtain £0.5605, the answer is A$(10 000/0.5605) = A$17 841.21.

Type 4: to convert a given sum of A$ to £

A UK resident has been paid A$10 000 and she wishes to exchange this for pounds. How many pounds will this buy? As each Australian dollar will buy £0.5605, the answer is £(10 000 × 0.5605) = £5605.

Suppose you wish to calculate how much it will cost a UK resident to obtain A$10 000 and your bank tells you that the spot exchange rates, in pounds per A$1, are 0.5907 and 0.5605. However, you are uncertain which one of these rates should be used. This problem can be solved by remembering that the spread between the two rates is one source of the foreign exchange dealer's profit. Therefore, if the UK resident uses pounds to buy Australian dollars, which are immediately re-exchanged for pounds, she must receive *fewer* pounds than she had originally. In this case it must cost the customer £0.5907 to buy A$1, but, if the customer were to resell the dollar for pounds, only £0.5605 would be received.

To simplify the later discussion we now assume that the spread between exchange rates is zero. We also make no distinction between retail, wholesale or interdealer exchange rates. Therefore, there is assumed to be only one spot exchange rate linking two currencies at any given point in time. Similar assumptions are made for the forward rate applicable to any given future time period.

20.3.5 TRIANGULAR ARBITRAGE AND CROSS RATES

Suppose that the following spot rates are observed simultaneously: A$1 = US$0.9000 and US$1 = £0.5000. Using only these two spot rates, the spot rate linking Australian dollars and UK pounds must be:

A$1 = £(0.9000 × 0.5000) = £0.4500

If this were not the case, a riskless profit could be made. For example, if the spot rate were instead A$1 = £0.4480, then a foreign exchange dealer could profit from undertaking the following three transactions simultaneously:

(a) Sell A$1 for US$0.9000.
(b) Sell US$0.9000 for £(0.9000 × 0.5000) = £0.4500.
(c) Sell £0.4500 for A$(0.4500/0.4480) = A$1.0045.

These transactions produce an instantaneous risk-free profit of A$0.0045 for every Australian dollar transacted in Step (a). If, for example, A$1 million were transacted, the profit would be A$4500. Such an arbitrage is called a *triangular arbitrage* as it involves three transactions and three currencies. It is easily shown that if the exchange rate between pounds and Australian dollars had been more than £0.4500, a different triangular arbitrage would have been available. For example, if the rate had been A$1 = £0.4515, one arbitrage would have been to make the following three transactions simultaneously:

(a) Sell A$1 for £0.4515.
(b) Sell £0.4515 for US$(0.4515/0.5000) = US$0.9030.
(c) Sell US$0.9030 for A$(0.9030/0.9000) = A$1.0033.

cross rate
exchange rate between two currencies derived from the exchange rates between the currencies and a third currency

The profit in this case would have been A$3300 on a sale of A$1 million in Step (a). The practical significance of triangular arbitrage is that, by assuming that competition will eliminate the opportunity for it to occur, exchange rates for any pair of currencies can be calculated from knowledge of other exchange rates involving those currencies. The resulting exchange rates are known as **cross rates**. In the example given, the values of both the Australian dollar and the UK pound were given in terms of US dollars, and from those two exchange rates the cross rate A$1 = £0.4500 was calculated.

If there are *n* currencies in the world, the number of distinct pairs of currencies (exchange rates) is $(n)(n-1)/2$. However, if one of those currencies (in practice the US dollar) has a central role, so that the value of the $(n-1)$ other currencies are all known in terms of US dollars, then all exchange rates can be calculated. For example, if $n = 170$, there are $(170 \times 169)/2$, or 14 365 exchange rates that may need to be known. This can be achieved indirectly by having markets to determine the exchange rates between each of the 169 currencies and the US dollar.

20.3.6 SIZE OF THE FOREIGN EXCHANGE MARKET IN AUSTRALIA

As mentioned earlier, the Australian dollar is one of the more actively traded currencies in the world. Table 20.7 provides data on the average daily turnover in the Australian foreign exchange market (in millions of Australian dollars) in 2009–10.

TABLE 20.7 Average daily turnover in the Australian foreign exchange market in 2009–10

	TRANSACTIONS IN AUSTRALIA BY FOREIGN EXCHANGE DEALERS (A$ MILLION PER DAY) WITH			
	LOCAL FINANCIAL INSTITUTIONS	OVERSEAS FINANCIAL INSTITUTIONS	NON-FINANCIAL INSTITUTIONS	TOTAL
Turnover against Australian dollars				
Spot	3 992	11 433	5 199	20 624
Forward	1 559	1 832	890	4 281
FX swaps	15 336	32 370	1 647	49 353
Options	274	1 262	318	1 854
Currency swaps	1 278	3 326	105	4 709
Total	22 439	50 223	8 159	80 821
Turnover against other currencies				
Spot	2 954	30 843	3 777	37 574
Forward	472	2 068	169	2 709
FX swaps	11 027	32 230	1 445	44 702
Options	78	435	41	554
Currency swaps	74	965	8	1 047
Total	14 605	66 541	5 440	86 586
Turnover against all currencies				
Spot	6 946	42 276	8 976	58 198
Forward	2 031	3 900	1 059	6 990
FX swaps	26 363	64 600	3 092	94 055
Options	352	1 697	359	2 408
Currency swaps	1 352	4 291	113	5 756
Total	37 044	116 764	13 599	167 407

Source: Compiled from Tables F9 and F10, Reserve Bank of Australia website, **www.rba.gov.au**.

Based on the data in Table 20.7, two important observations can be made. First, by any standards the volume of trading is significant, with the average daily turnover reaching about A$167 billion, of which just under half is against the Australian dollar. This figure can be placed in perspective by noting that Australian exports plus imports for the *year* ended 30 June 2010 amounted to A$515 billion—that is, about 3 *days* of average foreign exchange turnover. Second, more than two-thirds of the turnover is between foreign exchange dealers and overseas financial institutions, while nearly one-quarter is due to trading with local financial institutions. Much of the trading in the latter category is essentially trading between foreign exchange dealers. Less than 10 per cent of the turnover consists of trades between foreign exchange dealers and non-financial institutions. That is, less than 10 per cent of trading is with customers outside the finance sector. Why is there so much trading between Australian dealers and between Australian dealers and overseas financial institutions? The answer lies in the way currency trading is organised. Each dealer holds an inventory of foreign currency, and, as with any inventory decision, there is a trade-off between the costs and benefits of holding inventory. Each dealer solves this problem by having a target level of foreign currency inventory. If a dealer buys a large quantity of foreign currency, its target level will be exceeded and the dealer will sell some of the newly acquired currency. It is most likely that the buyer will be another dealer, who in turn will seek to restore its inventory to the target level of foreign currency. The process continues, with each dealer passing on to the next a proportion of the excess currency. This type of explanation is called the 'hot potato model' of currency dealing.[5]

20.4 RELATIONSHIPS BETWEEN INTEREST RATES, INFLATION RATES, SPOT EXCHANGE RATES AND FORWARD EXCHANGE RATES

LEARNING OBJECTIVE 3

Understand the roles of interest rates and inflation rates in exchange-rate determination

We now discuss links between four important variables: interest rates, inflation rates, spot exchange rates and forward exchange rates. In this analysis it is assumed that market participants are risk neutral and that there are no barriers or frictions (such as taxes or transaction costs) in any market. The analysis applies to any two currencies, but for illustration, we assume that the two currencies are Australian dollars and UK pounds.[6] Similarly, the analysis is, in principle, applicable to any given time period; we will assume that the period involved is 1 year.

20.4.1 NOTATION AND STAGES OF ANALYSIS

Throughout Section 20.4, the following notation is used:

i = interest rate (nominal, per annum)

p = inflation rate (per annum)

s = spot exchange rate (expressed as pounds per dollar)

f = forward exchange rate for 1 year (expressed as pounds per dollar)

£ = subscript used to indicate that a variable refers to pounds (e.g. $i_£$ means the 1-year interest rate on pounds)

$ = subscript used to indicate that a variable refers to Australian dollars (e.g. $p_$$ means the annual inflation rate in Australia)

E = the expectation operator for 1 year (e.g. $E(s)$ means the spot exchange rate that today is expected to occur in 1 year's time)

---

5 For a theoretical analysis, see Lyons (1997). For empirical evidence, see Lyons (1996).

6 As implied in Section 20.3.1, the US dollar–Australian dollar exchange rate is by far the most important for Australian companies. However, we use UK pounds to avoid confusion between the two dollars.

The analysis in Sections 20.4.2 to 20.4.4 establishes the following relationships between the four variables:

$$\frac{1+i_£}{1+i_\$} = \frac{f}{s} = \frac{E(s)}{s} = \frac{1+E(p_£)}{1+E(p_\$)} \qquad [20.1]$$

These relationships are summarised in Figure 20.1.

FIGURE 20.1 International parity relationships

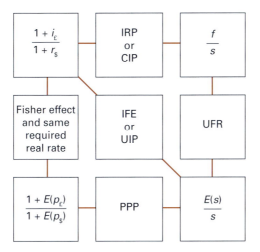

IRP = Interest rate parity CIP = Covered interest parity
IFE = International Fisher Effect UIP = Uncovered interest parity
UFR = Unbiased forward rates PPP = Purchasing power parity

Equation 20.1 is discussed in three stages:

Stage 1 links interest rates and exchange rates and is often called **interest rate parity** or **covered interest parity**:

$$\frac{1+i_£}{1+i_\$} = \frac{f}{s} \qquad [20.1(a)]$$

This equation is discussed in Section 20.4.2.

Stage 2 links forward exchange rates and spot exchange rates and is often called **unbiased forward rates**:

$$\frac{f}{s} = \frac{E(s)}{s} \qquad [20.1(b)]$$

This equation is discussed in Section 20.4.3.

Stage 3 links spot exchange rates and expected inflation rates and is often called **purchasing power parity**:

$$\frac{E(s)}{s} = \frac{1+E(p_£)}{1+E(p_\$)} \qquad [20.1(c)]$$

This equation is discussed in Section 20.4.4.

A fourth relationship, known as **uncovered interest parity** or the **international Fisher effect**[7] may be found by combining Equation 20.1(a) and Equation 20.1(b), to give:

$$\frac{E(s)}{s} = \frac{1+i_£}{1+i_\$} \qquad [20.1(d)]$$

This equation is discussed in Section 20.4.5.

---

7 Where the term 'uncovered interest parity' is used, Equation 20.1(a) is usually called 'covered interest parity' to distinguish the two equations. The significance of the alternative term 'international Fisher effect' is explained in Section 20.4.5.

---

interest rate parity (or covered interest parity) theory which states that a forward exchange rate is given by the spot rate, adjusted to reflect the relative interest rates in the two currencies

unbiased forward rates theory that states that the forward rate is an unbiased predictor of the future spot rate

purchasing power parity theory that states that the expected change in the exchange rate is due to differences in expected inflation rates in the respective currencies

uncovered interest parity (or international Fisher effect) theory that states that the difference in interest rates between two countries is an unbiased predictor of the future change in the spot exchange rate

20.4.2 INTEREST RATE PARITY

Interest rate parity maintains that:

$$\frac{1+i_£}{1+i_\$} = \frac{f}{s} \qquad [20.1(a)]$$

Interest rate parity states that relative interest rates determine the ratio of the forward exchange rate to the spot exchange rate.

Interest rate parity may be proved by considering the choices open to Australian investors who wish to invest X Australian dollars in government securities for a period of 1 year. It is assumed that the investors must choose between an investment in Australian securities and an investment in UK securities. If they choose to invest in Australian securities, they are certain to receive $X(1 + i_\$)$ dollars after 1 year. If they choose to invest in UK securities, they must first convert the Australian dollars to UK pounds. As the spot rate is s pounds per dollar, they will obtain s pounds for each dollar. Therefore, they have Xs pounds available for investment. After 1 year, they are certain to receive $Xs(1 + i_£)$ pounds.

However, to make a valid comparison between the returns offered by the two investments, investors need to be certain of the dollar value of the return from the UK investment. This certainty can be achieved by entering immediately into a forward contract to sell $Xs(1 + i_£)$ pounds in 1 year's time. As the forward rate is f pounds per dollar, they will obtain $1/f$ dollars for each pound, and therefore they can be certain that the UK investment will return $Xs(1+i_£)\frac{1}{f}$ dollars after 1 year. The two investments can now be compared because they are expressed in the same currency (Australian dollars) and have identical default risk (none) and identical terms (1 year). The Australian investment will be chosen if $X(1+i_\$) > Xs(1+i_£)\frac{1}{f}$ but the UK investment will be chosen if $X(1+i_\$) < Xs(1+i_£)\frac{1}{f}$. However, the difference between the two returns should be very small. Under the assumptions made, the two investments are, in fact, perfect substitutes and in an efficient market, perfect substitutes must offer the same return. If this were not so, then arbitrage would be possible. This type of arbitrage is known as **covered interest arbitrage** and would continue to be exploited until the interest rates and/or the exchange rates adjusted so as to eliminate the possibility of further arbitrage. In equilibrium, therefore, the two returns must be equal—that is:

$$X(1+i_\$) = Xs(1+i_£)\frac{1}{f}$$

Dividing both sides by X and rearranging:

$$\frac{1+i_£}{1+i_\$} = \frac{f}{s}$$

which is Equation 20.1(a). It is known as the interest rate parity equation.

Example 20.1 shows that, because of interest rate parity, a foreign investment with forward cover is equivalent to a domestic investment.

covered interest arbitrage movement of funds between two currencies to profit from interest rate differences while using forward contracts to eliminate exchange risk

---

EXAMPLE 20.1

Suppose that an investor has A$1 million to invest for 1 year in government securities, and that the interest rate on Australian dollars is 6.2 per cent and the interest rate on UK pounds is 4.1 per cent. The spot exchange rate is A$1 = £0.5265 and the forward exchange rate for 1 year is A$1 = £0.5161. The investor wishes to calculate (a) the return on an Australian investment and (b) the return (in Australian dollars) on an equivalent UK investment.

SOLUTION

(a) Invest A$1 million in Australian securities for 1 year.
   Cash inflow after 1 year = A$1 000 000 x 1.062
   = A$1 062 000

(b) Invest A$1 million in UK securities for 1 year, with forward cover.
   (i) Spot 'conversion' of A$1 million to pounds:
       A$1 000 000 = £(1 000 000 x 0.5265)
       = £526 500
   (ii) Cash inflow (in pounds) after 1 year:
       = £526 500 x 1.041
       = £548 086.50
   (iii) 'Reconversion' to Australian dollars at the forward rate:
       £548 086.50 = A$(548 086.50/0.5161)
       = A$1 061 977.33

The difference between (a) and (b) is only A$22.67.

In Example 20.1 the difference between an Australian dollar investment and a UK pound investment with forward cover is trivial—about A$23 on an investment of A$1 million. This suggests that Equation 20.1(a), the interest rate parity equation, should hold in this case. The following calculations confirm that this is indeed the case:

$$\frac{1+i_£}{1+i_\$} = \frac{1.041}{1.062} = 0.980\ 226$$

and:

$$\frac{f}{s} = \frac{0.5161}{0.5265} = 0.980\ 247$$

Equation 20.1(a) is often rewritten as:

$$f = s\left(\frac{1+i_£}{1+i_\$}\right)$$

or:

$$f \approx s + s(i_£ - i_\$)$$

Interest rate parity is usually seen as a method of calculating the forward rate, given information on the spot rate and on interest rates for the two currencies. Although the theory can be (and is) used in this way, it makes no statement of causality. It simply states that the four variables—f, s, $i_£$ and $i_\$$—must be related as shown in Equation 20.1(a) and does not necessarily imply that the forward rate is caused by the other three.

The approximate relationship shown makes it very clear that the forward rate can be seen as simply the spot rate plus an adjustment for the difference in interest rates. Where the exchange rate is quoted as a rate per A$1, the forward rate is greater (less) than the spot rate when the foreign interest rate is greater (less) than the Australian dollar interest rate.

If the interest rate parity equation is violated, then covered interest arbitrage is possible. Example 20.2 overleaf shows how a set of exchange rates and interest rates can be examined to determine whether covered interest arbitrage is feasible.

Example 20.3 overleaf then uses the same set of rates in a numerical example that illustrates this type of arbitrage.

EXAMPLE 20.2

Assuming that the spread is zero and there are no transaction costs, show that covered interest arbitrage is feasible if the following interest rates and exchange rates are observed simultaneously:

Spot rate:	A$1 = US$0.8815
Forward rate (1 month):	A$1 = US$0.8784
A$ interest rate (1 month):	0.57% per month
US$ interest rate (1 month):	0.38% per month

SOLUTION

Covered interest arbitrage is possible because Equation 20.1(a) is violated, as shown in the following:

$$\frac{1+i_{US}}{1+i_A} = \frac{1.0038}{1.0057} = 0.998\,111$$

but

$$\frac{f}{s} = \frac{0.8784}{0.8815} = 0.996\,483$$

Expressing this result in another way, the forward rate indicated by interest rate parity is 0.998 111 x 0.8815 = 0.8798, compared with the actual forward rate of 0.8784.

EXAMPLE 20.3

Illustrate covered interest arbitrage, by assuming that an arbitrageur simultaneously undertakes the following four transactions:

(a) Borrows A$5 million for 1 month at 0.57 per cent per month.
(b) Converts (spot) the sum of $A5 million to US dollars, thereby obtaining US$(5 000 000 x 0.8815) = US$4 407 500.
(c) Lends US$4 407 500 for 1 month at an interest rate of 0.38 per cent per month, producing a future cash repayment to the arbitrageur of US$4 407 500 x 1.0038 = US$4 424 248.50.
(d) Sells forward (1 month) the sum of US$4 424 248.50, thereby ensuring an Australian dollar inflow of A$(4 424 248.50/0.8784) or A$5 036 712.77 in 1 month's time.

What is the amount of Australian dollars required to repay the loan? How much profit will be made in 1 month's time? What risk has the arbitrageur taken?

SOLUTION

The loan requires a repayment of A$5 000 000 x 1.0057 = A$5 028 500. After 1 month, the inflow of A$5 036 712.77 can be used to make the repayment of A$5 028 500, thereby giving the arbitrageur a profit of A$8212.77 for a net investment of zero. Since the arbitrageur made no net outlay and all the transactions were undertaken simultaneously, there was no exposure to risk.

An alternative mechanism that exploits the same disequilibrium would be for the arbitrageur to keep back the sum of A$8152.91 between Step (a) and Step (b), thereby producing an immediate profit of this amount.[8] In this case only A$4 991 847.09 is converted to US dollars, and the assured cash inflow at Step (d) is:

$$\frac{4\,991\,847.09 \times 0.8815 \times 1.0038}{0.8784} \text{ Australian dollars}$$

= A$5 028 500

This sum is, of course, just sufficient to meet the repayment required.

---

[8] In effect, this is the present value of the future profit of A$8212.77. Note that A$8212.77/1.0057 = A$8166.22 ≈ A$8152.91.

Both of the arbitrages described in Examples 20.2 and 20.3 are *outward covered interest arbitrages*. The term *outward* is used to indicate that, in at least a figurative sense, money is sent out of Australia in the form of an investment in US dollars. Had the forward rate in this example been greater than 0.8798 (which is the rate indicated by interest rate parity, given the spot rate and the two interest rates), the arbitrage would have been of the *inward* type. In this case, US dollars are borrowed, and the funds are converted to Australian dollars to earn interest at the Australian interest rate.

20.4.3 UNBIASED FORWARD RATES

Unbiased forward rates maintains that:

$$\frac{f}{s} = \frac{E(s)}{s} \qquad [20.1(b)]$$

If market participants are risk neutral and there are no transaction costs, the market will set the forward rate, f, equal to the spot rate which is expected to be observed on the date on which the forward contract matures. If this result did not hold, then risk neutral speculators would trade in foreign currency until the forward rate was equal to the expected spot rate. For example, if the forward rate for 1 year is A\$1 = £0.4265, but it is expected that the spot rate in 1 year's time will be A\$1 = £0.4065, then a risk-neutral speculator would enter into a forward contract to sell Australian dollars in 1 year's time. Under the terms of the forward contract, the speculator must deliver A\$1 and in return accept £0.4265. If, as expected, the spot rate at that time is A\$1 = £0.4065, the pounds obtained (£0.4265) can then be converted into A\$(0.4265/0.4065) = A\$1.0492. The speculator therefore has a profit of 4.92 cents for every A\$1 sold forward.

Of course, there is a good chance that the expectation will not be realised. If the spot rate in 1 year's time is less than £0.4065 per A\$1, then the profit will be greater than expected but if the spot rate in 1 year's time is between £0.4065 and £0.4265 per A\$1, then the profit will be smaller than expected. Finally, if the spot rate in 1 year's time is greater than £0.4265 per A\$1, a loss will be incurred. A risk-averse speculator may not feel that the expected profit is large enough to warrant bearing the risk, but if speculators are risk neutral, then even a small expected profit will be sufficient to induce them to trade. In this example, the result will be an increased supply of Australian dollars in the forward market, therefore tending to reduce the price, f, per dollar. The forward rate will continue to decrease until it reaches £0.4065 per dollar. Therefore, in equilibrium:

$$f = E(s)$$

This implies that:

$$\frac{f}{s} = \frac{E(s)}{s}$$

which is Equation 20.1(b).

20.4.4 PURCHASING POWER PARITY

Purchasing power parity (PPP) maintains that:

$$\frac{E(s)}{s} = \frac{1+E(p_£)}{1+E(p_\$)} \qquad [20.1(c)]$$

In words, PPP holds that the expected change in the spot exchange rate is due to differences in expected inflation rates in the respective currencies.

law of one price
principle maintaining that the price of a commodity in a given currency will be the same regardless of the currency in which the price is quoted

The simplest derivation of PPP assumes that the **law of one price** is valid. This law states that the dollar price of any given commodity should be the same everywhere in the world. If all markets were free and frictionless, and all goods were traded internationally, then the law of one price would hold because, otherwise, an arbitrage could be undertaken. For example, if the price of silver in Australia is A$250/kg, and the exchange rate is A$1 = £0.5000, then the price of silver in the UK ought to be £125/kg. If the price of silver in the UK is anything other than £125/kg, an arbitrage is available. For example, if the UK price is £150/kg, traders would buy silver in Australia at A$250/kg and sell it in the UK at the equivalent of A$300/kg. This would continue until the UK silver price, converted to Australian dollars, is equal to the price of silver in Australia. This equality would be achieved by the price of silver in the UK decreasing and/or the price of silver in Australia increasing and/or the value of the Australian dollar (in pounds) increasing. The eventual equilibrium could be, for example, a UK silver price of £135.20/kg, an Australian silver price of A$260/kg and an exchange rate of A$1 = £0.5200. In this case, the UK price of £135.20 is equivalent to an Australian dollar price of A$(135.20/0.5200) = A$260, which equals the price in Australia.

Assuming that the law of one price holds at all times, PPP may be proved as follows. If the price of a commodity is currently A$1 in Australia, and the current exchange rate is A$1 = £$s$, then, invoking the law of one price, the UK price of that commodity must be £s. If the expected inflation rates are $E(p_\$)$ in Australia and $E(p_£)$ in the UK, then the expected prices are A$[1 + $E(p_\$)$] and £$s$[1 + $E(p_£)$]. Invoking again the law of one price, the expected exchange rate must equate these two prices—that is:

$$1 + E(p_\$) = \frac{s[1 + E(p_£)]}{E(s)}$$

On rearrangement, this gives:

$$\frac{E(s)}{s} = \frac{1 + E(p_£)}{1 + E(p_\$)}$$

which is Equation 20.1(c).

However, for many commodities, the law of one price clearly does not hold (see Finance in Action). Fortunately, PPP may also be proved by making the weaker assumption that the *ratio* of dollar prices for the same commodity in two countries will stay constant as time passes. In effect, this assumption allows the *levels* of dollar prices to differ at any given time, but holds constant the relative extent of this difference over time. For example, suppose that the spot rate is A$1 = £0.4600 and a particular commodity costs A$2000 in Australia and £1150 in the UK. The dollar equivalent of the UK price is therefore A$(1150/0.4600) = A$2500. The ratio of dollar prices is therefore A$2000/A$2500 = 0.80. That is, the Australian price is only 80 per cent of the UK price. The assumption implies that if the ratio of dollar prices is recalculated in, say, 1 year's time, it will again be 0.80, despite differing inflation rates during the year. If the expected inflation rates are, say, 10 per cent in Australia and 4 per cent in the UK, then the expected prices are A$2200 in Australia and £1196 in the UK. Invoking the assumption of a constant ratio of dollar prices, the expected spot exchange rate $E(s)$ must be such as to maintain the ratio at 0.80—that is:

$$\frac{2200}{1196 \div E(s)} = 0.80$$

which gives:

$$E(s) = \frac{0.8 \times 1196}{2200}$$

$$\therefore E(s) = 0.4349$$

To apply this approach to derive PPP, suppose that the price of 1 kilogram of a particular commodity is X dollars in Australia and K pounds in the UK. If the current spot rate is A\$1 = £s, then the dollar value of the UK price is K/s dollars. The ratio of the dollar prices is therefore $\dfrac{X}{K/s}$.

If the expected inflation rate in Australia is $E(p_\$)$ per year and the expected inflation rate in the UK is $E(p_£)$ per year, then the expected prices in 1 year are:

$X[1 + E(p_\$)]$ Australian dollars in Australia

and

$K[1 + E(p_£)]$ UK pounds in the UK

The expected dollar value of the expected UK price is:

$$\frac{K[1+E(p_£)]}{E(s)}$$

where $E(s)$ = the expected spot exchange rate

Invoking the assumption of a constant ratio of dollar prices, the expected exchange rate must be such that the ratio of dollar prices remains equal to the initial value of $\dfrac{X}{K/s}$ —that is:

$$\frac{X[1+E(p_\$)]}{K[1+E(p_£)]/E(s)} = \frac{X}{K/s}$$

Multiplying both sides by K/X and rearranging gives:

$$\frac{E(s)}{s} = \frac{1+E(p_£)}{1+E(p_\$)}$$

which is Equation 20.1(c).

FINANCE IN ACTION

PURCHASING POWER PARITY

The simplest derivation of Purchasing Power Parity (PPP) begins with the assumption that the Law of One Price holds. But PPP can also be derived on the assumption that although international price ratios differ, the extent of the difference will remain constant over time. It is fortunate that PPP can be derived in this alternative way because the Law of One Price does *not* hold in most cases. Indeed, its failure to match reality was the subject of an article in London's *The Sunday Times*.

'Why is Britain so phenomenally expensive and why on earth do Britons put up with it?', writes Jon Ungoed-Thomas, describing the question as a 'hot topic' in Europe and the Americas

'Britain's rip-off prices were confirmed last week by a *Sunday Times* survey that found we are indeed being overcharged for a wide range of everyday products and services.

Whether it's a meal out, a trip to the cinema or a weekend in the country, in Britain it typically costs about 30% more than in comparable countries. Our train fares are four times the global average.' Ungoed-Thomas lists the train fares from London to Manchester as £202 return for trips taken before 9:30 am and £57.10 otherwise, compared with £27.42 for a trip between Paris and Dijon, a comparable distance, adding, 'And taxi costs in London are almost double those in Paris'.

While Ungoed-Thomas concedes that bargains can be found 'off the beaten track' in Britain, he adds that most visitors are shocked by the cost of some of the most popular tourist attractions and destinations: 'Madame Tussauds costs £22.99 in London, compared with £15.40 in New York and £12.10 in Amsterdam.'

Jorge Jove, 49, from Barcelona, who was among the tourists visiting Madame Tussauds on Friday, said: 'It's very expensive compared with Spain. As you spend £1 here you would pay in Spain €1. Everything just costs too much.'

Source: Jon Ungoed-Thomas, 'Tourists tell Britain: you're a rip-off', *The Sunday Times*, 20 August 2006.

Although the foundations of PPP are most readily apparent in the case of individual commodities, many practical applications are at a higher level of aggregation.[9] Even if not all goods are traded internationally, and there are transport costs, tariffs and other sources of friction, it is still plausible that an exchange rate between two currencies will (eventually) reflect the relative inflation rate experiences in the two countries. In these circumstances, the inflation rates in the PPP equation are usually specified as price indices that include both traded and non-traded goods. However, the prices of traded and non-traded goods are not independently determined. For example, an imported good may be used to produce a non-traded good, or a non-traded good could be potentially a traded good, should there be a shift in relative prices.

Although PPP has been interpreted in a number of different ways, its central message does not vary: a country with a high inflation rate can expect to have a depreciating exchange rate (a 'weak' currency), whereas a country with a low inflation rate can expect to have an appreciating exchange rate (a 'strong' currency). This tendency is illustrated in Example 20.4.

EXAMPLE 20.4

Suppose that the spot rate is A$1 = £0.3325. If the inflation rate next year is expected to be 9 per cent in Australia and 4 per cent in the UK, what is next year's spot rate expected to be?

SOLUTION
Rearranging Equation 20.1(c) and solving gives:

$$E(s) = \left[\frac{1 + E(p_£)}{1 + E(p_\$)}\right] s$$

$$= \left[\frac{1.04}{1.09}\right](0.3325)$$

$$= 0.3172$$

Therefore, it is expected that the Australian dollar will weaken: whereas an Australian dollar is worth £0.3325 at the start of the year, it is expected that by the end of the year an Australian dollar will be worth only £0.3172. This represents a depreciation of approximately 4.6 per cent in the value of the Australian dollar in terms of UK pounds and is approximately equal to the difference between the inflation rates.

20.4.5 UNCOVERED INTEREST PARITY OR THE INTERNATIONAL FISHER EFFECT

If interest rate parity (Equation 20.1(a)) and unbiased forward rates (Equation 20.1(b)) hold simultaneously, then:

$$\frac{E(s)}{s} = \frac{1 + i_£}{1 + i_\$} \qquad [20.1(d)]$$

Derived in this way, the equation is usually called *uncovered interest parity* (UIP). It can also be derived by assuming that purchasing power parity and the Fisher equation are true. The Fisher equation maintains that, for any given currency, the nominal interest rate will be set by the market such that it covers expected inflation and provides a required real rate of return, i^*. If the Fisher equation holds for both pounds and dollars, then:

---

[9] Historically, PPP has often been exclusively presented and interpreted at an aggregated level. However, we prefer to regard PPP as being built up from the micro-foundation of commodity arbitrage. For a historical summary and a contrary view, see Officer (1982).

$$1 + i_£ = (1 + i^*)[1 + E(p_£)]$$

and

$$1 + i_\$ = (1 + i^*)[1 + E(p_\$)]$$

Combining these two equations and purchasing power parity (Equation 20.1(c)) also gives Equation 20.1(d). Derived in this way, Equation 20.1(d) is usually called *the international Fisher effect*.

Equation 20.1(d) implies that the spot exchange rate will tend to adjust in the direction indicated by interest rates in the two currencies. In particular, a country's currency will tend to appreciate (depreciate) relative to another currency if its interest rate is lower (higher) than the interest rate on the other currency. This is illustrated in Example 20.5.

EXAMPLE 20.5

The current spot exchange rate between Australian dollars and UK pounds is A$1 = £0.4000. Interest rates for 1 year are 5 per cent for pounds and 15 per cent for dollars. What is the expected spot exchange rate in 1 year's time?

SOLUTION

Rearranging Equation 20.1(d) gives the expected spot exchange rate as:

$$E(s) = \left(\frac{1 + i_£}{1 + i_\$}\right)s$$

$$= \left(\frac{1.05}{1.15}\right)0.4000$$

$$= £0.3652$$

Thus the Australian dollar, being the higher-interest currency, is expected to depreciate from £0.4000 per dollar to £0.3652 per dollar.

The rationale for this result is that, if it did not hold, then it would be better for investors to lend one of the currencies, but it would be better for borrowers to borrow the other currency. Thus there would be disequilibrium in the markets. This is illustrated in Example 20.6.

EXAMPLE 20.6

Suppose, as in Example 20.5, that the spot exchange rate is A$1 = £0.4000 and the 1-year interest rates are 5 per cent (in pounds) and 15 per cent (in dollars). However, suppose the expected spot exchange rate is A$1 = £0.3900. In this case, borrowers will want to borrow pounds, but lenders will want to lend dollars. While the Australian dollar is expected to depreciate in the coming year from £0.40 to £0.39, the extent of this expected depreciation is not sufficient to offset the expected benefit to the borrower of borrowing the lower-interest currency.

Consider a company that wants to borrow A$250 000. What repayments will be expected in 1 year's time if the company:

(a) borrows in dollars or
(b) borrows in pounds?

SOLUTION

(a) If the company borrows in dollars, the required repayment will be A$250 000 × 1.15 = A$287 500.
(b) If pounds are borrowed, the company could borrow £100 000 at only 5 per cent interest, thus requiring a repayment of £105 000 which, at 39 pence per dollar, is expected to require only A$(105 000/0.39) = A$269 231

continued →

> **Example 20.6** *continued*
>
> to repay the loan. This is clearly better for the borrower than having to pay A$287 500. The expected saving is nearly A$20 000. Of course, if borrowers prefer pounds, lenders must prefer dollars. If the *cost* to borrowers is low in pounds, the *return* to lenders of pounds will also be low. The end result is therefore a disequilibrium in which borrowers want to borrow pounds but lenders want to lend dollars. This disequilibrium will be eliminated only when Equation 20.1(d) holds true.

Borrowers may be tempted to borrow currencies with low interest rates, even though uncovered interest parity implies that the expected benefit will be eliminated by exchange rate movements. Similarly, despite uncovered interest parity, lenders may be tempted to lend currencies with high interest rates. This attraction has been the basis of the thriving retail market in Japan for high-interest foreign bonds—known as the 'uridashi' market (see Finance in Action).

FINANCE IN ACTION

JAPANESE RETAIL INVESTORS LOOK FURTHER AFIELD

Japanese retail investors seeking higher returns to offset the meagre pickings at home are looking increasingly to more exotic currencies to diversify their bond portfolios.

For several years, Japan's mom-and-pop bond investors have favoured Australian and New Zealand dollar debt, which currently offer coupons of about 6 per cent to 7 per cent—far above typical Japanese yen bonds offering less than 1 per cent.

Now, these investors, who played a major role in driving the yen to decade lows last year as they moved money abroad, are focusing farther afield, undaunted by a global credit shake-up that has sparked a wave of risk aversion among professional investors.

The new darling, South Africa rand bonds, give investors a return of more than 9 per cent a year and have sparked a boom of debt issuance in other exotic uridashi bonds—the name given to foreign currency bonds sold directly to Japan's retail investors.

'Rand bonds have firmly taken root in the uridashi market,' said Tsutomu Soma, senior manager at the foreign assets department at Okasan Securities, a pioneer of rand uridashis.

Japanese investors have long sought better returns for their savings, which total more than $6 trillion, by buying foreign bonds.

Japan's central bank has kept its policy interest rate, which sets the benchmark for the country, at close to zero since the mid-1990s.

Tokyo's stock market has not offered much, either. Last year, the Nikkei average fell 11 per cent.

Other exotic uridashis have included issues in the Hungarian forint, the Polish zloty, Romanian leu and other currencies.

Last month, the sale by the European Bank of Reconstruction and Development of 1.3 billion Icelandic krona, or $19 million, in uridashi bonds met with strong demand thanks to a coupon of 11.78 per cent, said sources at banks involved with the deal who were not authorised to speak.

Bond issuers and distributors say that increasing demand from Japanese investors for higher returns means that the uridashi market is likely to shift to other exotic currencies, like the Turkish lira and the Brazilian real.

Source: Rika Otsuka, *International Herald Tribune*, 11 February 2008.

EMPIRICAL EVIDENCE ON THE BEHAVIOUR OF EXCHANGE RATES

20.5

LEARNING OBJECTIVE 4
Understand the empirical evidence on the behaviour of exchange rates

A number of empirical investigations into the behaviour of exchange rates have been undertaken in recent years. Rather than present a detailed review, this section outlines some of the major findings, emphasising, wherever possible, evidence concerning the Australian dollar.

20.5.1 INTEREST RATE PARITY: EVIDENCE

As mentioned in Section 20.4.2, the interest rate parity theorem is based on the proposition that it should not be possible to undertake successful 'covered interest arbitrage'. Where the interest rate data are collected from relatively unregulated markets, the evidence nearly always supports interest rate parity, provided that allowance is also made for transaction costs.[10]

20.5.2 UNBIASED FORWARD RATES: EVIDENCE

Extensive research has been conducted on the relationship between the forward rate and the spot rate that occurs on the maturity date of the forward contract. As explained in Section 20.4.3, if investors are risk neutral, the market should set the forward rate equal to the expected future spot rate. Therefore, over a sufficiently long period of time, the average observed forward rate should approximately equal the average of the spot rates observed on the maturity dates of the forward contracts.

Most tests have found that the forward rate is *not* an unbiased estimate of the future spot rate.[11] Tests using many different currencies suggest that the forward premium (or discount) overstates the change that, *on average*, occurs in the spot rate.[12] For example, if today's spot rate is one Australian dollar equals 91 US cents (A$1 = US$0.9100), while today's forward rate is A$1 = US$0.9000, then an unbiased prediction of the future spot rate could be, say, A$1 = US$0.9080. This prediction may be compared with the forecast of US$0.9000 that would apply if forward rates were unbiased predictors of future spot rates.[13] Similarly, if today's forward rate had been A$1 = US$0.9200, the unbiased prediction might be, say, US$0.9120, rather than the theory's prediction of US$0.9200.

What might explain this bias? One obvious possibility is that, contrary to the assumption of risk neutrality, participants in the foreign exchange market are risk averse. The extent of the bias might then be explained by the presence of a risk premium. Moreover, the risk premium could vary over time. Inefficiency in the foreign exchange market is another possibility.[14]

This evidence prompts another question: if today's *forward* rate is a *biased* predictor of the future spot rate, could it be that today's *spot* rate is an *unbiased* predictor of the future spot rate? Framing this question slightly differently: Does the spot rate follow a random walk? The answer is a qualified 'yes'—at least to a first approximation.[15] Consistent with this finding, studies have found that when it comes to predicting the future spot rate, today's spot rate is at least as good a predictor as today's forward rate.[16]

An *unbiased* prediction is not necessarily a very *useful* prediction. Although, all other things being equal, an unbiased prediction is preferable to a biased prediction, an unbiased prediction can still be

---

10 See, for example, Clinton (1988). For a review, see Thornton (1989).
11 For details, see Gregory and McCurdy (1986) and McFarland, McMahon and Nagama (1994).
12 For a representative study, see Goodhart (1988).
13 We have perhaps been cautious here. In fact, many studies find that the forward premium or discount does not merely overstate the future change in the spot rate; on average it actually points in the wrong direction. In this case, an unbiased forecast might be, say, US$0.9050, when today's spot rate is US$0.9100 and today's forward rate is US$0.9200.
14 For discussion, see Goodhart (1988) and Gruen and Gizycki (1993).
15 For Australian evidence, see Manzur (1988).
16 For evidence on the British pound, French franc, German mark and Canadian dollar (all in terms of the US dollar), see Chiang (1986).

very inaccurate. An unbiased prediction is simply one that is as likely to be too high as it is to be too low. It should be no surprise to find that it is very difficult—perhaps impossible—to forecast exchange rates with great accuracy. If it were easily achieved, we would have no trouble becoming very rich very quickly by speculating on currency movements. Foreign exchange markets are extremely competitive so we expect that any easily discovered rule for profitable forecasting would be quickly exploited until it is no longer profitable. Attempts to forecast exchange rates are considered further in Section 20.5.5.

20.5.3 PURCHASING POWER PARITY: EVIDENCE

In Section 20.4.4 we provided two derivations of purchasing power parity (PPP). The simpler derivation assumes that the 'law of one price' is valid. In practice, there can be little doubt that this law does not hold for a great many commodities, although it may hold in some fairly special cases. Where a commodity is readily defined, cheaply transportable and frequently traded in organised markets, it is likely that the law of one price will provide an accurate description of reality. For example, Baldwin and Yan (2004) found that, on average, prices in Canada and the US were the same for highly standardised products that flow freely across borders but Canadians paid 4 per cent *more* than US consumers for highly differentiated tradeable products and 8 per cent *less* for products like services that are hard to trade internationally.

In practice, PPP is most often investigated by way of price indices. Apart from the inclusion (or exclusion) of non-traded goods in a price index, another point of difficulty is the need to use a weighting scheme in order to convert a number of different prices into a single index. Different weighting schemes will produce different index values for the same set of prices. As different countries use different weighting schemes in the construction of national price indices, there is an obvious potential for distortion in testing PPP using these indices.

Generally, PPP is found to give a poor description of exchange rate behaviour, unless a long time period is used for testing. Several researchers have used extremely long time series—two centuries in one case (Lothian & Taylor 1996)—and as a very broad generalisation have typically found that around 15 per cent of the deviation from PPP in any given year is eliminated in the following year. This means that PPP deviations have a 'half-life' of about 4 years (because $0.85 \times 0.85 \times 0.85 \times 0.85 \approx 0.5$). In other words, it takes about 4 years for even half of the deviation from PPP to be corrected.[17] Choi (2004) lists 13 empirical studies of PPP and considers that 11 of the studies provide at least mixed support for PPP. In a recent study, Wu, Cheng and Hou (2011) studied PPP using data for 76 countries over the period 1976 to 2006. They found that, taking the sample of countries as a whole, PPP was supported. They also found that PPP was more likely to be supported if a country was open to international trade, had a low growth rate, a high inflation rate and a very volatile exchange rate. Although not all studies support the long-run validity of PPP, it is difficult to imagine that most of the effects of inflation will not eventually show up in the exchange rate. For example, if there were a permanent failure of the exchange rate to reflect inflation, every nation would have a simple route to wealth: inflate the domestic economy and then purchase foreign assets at prices that are artificially low in terms of domestic currency.

The fact that PPP does not hold in the short or medium term means that some international comparisons can be very misleading if current exchange rates are used to convert one currency to another. For example, it is well known that the 'cost of living' is higher in Sweden than in Australia. This is another way of saying that PPP does not hold between the Australian dollar and the Swedish kroner: the dollar buys more in Australia than it will buy in Sweden if the conversion to kroner is made at current exchange rates. The Organisation for Economic Co-operation and Development (OECD) has an ongoing program to measure the extent of this effect, so that valid international comparisons can be made. For example, according to the OECD's research, GDP per capita in Australia in 2008 was US$46 200 using current exchange rates but was US$37 400 using PPP-adjusted figures. Using

---

17 For a review, see Rogoff (1996).

current exchange rates, Sweden's GDP per capita (US$52 000) was higher than Australia's, but using PPP-adjusted figures, Sweden's GDP per capita (US$36 900) was lower than Australia's. GDP per capita in the US was US$46 500—almost identical to Australia's using current exchange rates. GDP per capita in the US using PPP-adjusted figures was (by definition) also US$46 500, which is considerably higher than the corresponding amount of US$37 400 for Australia.[18]

20.5.4 UNCOVERED INTEREST PARITY: EVIDENCE

As we explained in Section 20.4.5, uncovered interest parity (UIP) can be seen as a combination of interest rate parity and unbiased forward rates. Given that interest rate parity works extremely well, it is inevitable that uncovered interest parity will have a similar level of accuracy to the hypothesis of unbiased forward rates. This is in fact the case. Like the forward premium or discount, the interest rate difference between currencies typically gives a biased forecast of the future spot rate, and often does not predict even the direction of movement correctly.[19] However, tests using direct measures of exchange rate expectations, such as forecasts made by exchange rate analysts, provide stronger evidence in favour of uncovered interest parity. Further, UIP (like PPP) works better over longer time periods.[20]

20.5.5 FORECASTING EXCHANGE RATES

Can exchange rate changes be forecast successfully? A successful forecast is one that a trader could use to make excess profits in the foreign exchange market. At a minimum we would expect a successful forecast to be more accurate than forecasts that can be derived from a simple mechanical rule. For example, to be called 'successful', a forecast should be more accurate than the 'no change' or 'random walk' forecast that the future spot rate will be equal to today's spot rate.

At least in the case of Australia, there is little evidence that market participants can forecast successfully the Australian dollar–US dollar exchange rate. Hunt (1987) undertook a detailed analysis of short-term forecasts made by 16 foreign exchange dealers.[21] Every Friday afternoon from February 1985 to April 1987, each dealer was telephoned and asked for a forecast of the exchange rate for 3 pm on the following Friday. The accuracy of this extensive set of forecasts was then investigated. Hunt used several statistical techniques to investigate forecast accuracy and employed two benchmarks against which forecast performance was judged. The first benchmark was the 'random walk' prediction that next week's spot rate will be equal to today's spot rate. The second benchmark was the 'average forecast' prediction that next week's spot rate will be equal to the average of the 16 spot rate forecasts made today. Hunt (1987) found very little evidence that the dealers could forecast the spot rate and concluded (p. 12) that:

> *The performance of the individual forecasters in predicting future rates was not impressive. No single forecast firm recorded a performance superior to its competitors. Moreover, under most criteria the individual forecasters were surpassed by the performance of the random walk and the average forecast model.*

Nor is there much evidence that longer-term exchange rate forecasts are accurate. Easton and Lalor (1995) studied 583 forecasts made 6 or 12 months ahead by a range of business, academic and policy groups. The time period covered was January 1984 to January 1993. Less than half of the forecasts correctly predicted even the *direction* of the future movement in the exchange rate. The most accurate

---

18 See *OECD in Figures 2009 Edition* at www.oecd.org/infigures.
19 For further discussion, see Froot and Thaler (1990).
20 See Chinn (2006).
21 Manzur (1988) studies the same set of forecasts but only at the level of the average forecast made, whereas Hunt (1987) reports separate results for the different forecasters.

predictor of the future level of the spot rate was the 'no change' forecast, the second most accurate was the current forward rate and the least accurate was the average forecast of the 'experts'.

It is not surprising that it is difficult to forecast successfully the future course of the exchange rate. A successful forecaster could easily make a fortune in the foreign exchange market. However, the foreign exchange market is extremely competitive, and, as Alan Greenspan observes (see Finance in Action), there are many market participants trying to forecast that little bit more accurately than their competitors. The result is that few, if any, can consistently beat the market. If forecasting exchange rates were easy, everyone would do it and become rich. Obviously, this will not happen.

FINANCE IN ACTION

IS IT POSSIBLE TO FORECAST THE EXCHANGE RATE?

Not really, according to Alan Greenspan, the chairman of the US Federal Reserve. In a speech to the Economic Club of New York on 2 March 2004, Dr Greenspan said:

My experience is that exchange markets have become so efficient that virtually all relevant information is embedded almost instantaneously in exchange rates to the point that anticipating movements in major currencies is rarely possible. The exceptions to this conclusion are those few cases of successful speculation in which governments have tried and failed to support a particular exchange rate. Nonetheless, despite extensive efforts on the part of analysts, to my knowledge, no model projecting directional movements in exchange rates is significantly superior to tossing a coin. I am aware that of the thousands who try, some are quite successful. So are winners of coin-tossing contests. The seeming ability of a number of banking organisations to make consistent profits from foreign exchange trading likely derives not from their insight into future rate changes but from market making.

Source: Federal Reserve Board, remarks by Chairman Alan Greenspan, 'Current account', 2 March 2004, www.federalreserve.gov/boarddocs/speeches/2004/20040302/default.htm.

WWW

20.6 THE MANAGEMENT OF EXCHANGE RISK

20.6.1 WHAT IS EXCHANGE RISK?

A company faces **exchange risk** when there is the potential for unanticipated changes in an exchange rate to reduce the value of the company. Such a company is said to be exposed to exchange risk because it can be adversely affected by an unforeseen movement in an exchange rate. Exchange risk is illustrated in the following simple example.

EXAMPLE 20.7

Playworld Ltd is an Australian-owned company whose management signs a contract on 31 July to import from the UK 500 000 tennis balls, each costing UK £2.20. The balls are expected to arrive in Australia on 31 October and must be paid for on that date.

(a) If the exchange rate on 31 July is A$1 = £0.5000, what is the projected cost of the imports, in Australian dollar terms?

> (b) If Playworld expects to sell the balls for A$5.50 each, what is the projected gross profit on the transaction?
> (c) What risk does Playworld face? If the Australian dollar depreciates so that A$1 = £0.4000, what is Playworld's gross profit?
>
> **SOLUTION**
> (a) The projected cost of the imports in Australian dollars is 500 000 × 2.20 × (1−0.5000) = A$2.2 million. Therefore, Playworld has a liability to pay for the balls and the amount of this liability is currently estimated to be A$2.2 million.
> (b) The projected gross profit per ball is A$5.50 − (2.20 × 1−0.5000) = A$1.10 and the total projected gross profit is therefore 500 000 × A$1.10 = A$550 000.
> (c) The risk for Playworld is that the exchange rate between UK pounds and Australian dollars may change between the purchase date (31 July) and the settlement date (31 October). If the Australian dollar depreciates so that A$1 = £0.4000, the imports will cost 500 000 × 2.20 × (1−0.4) = A$2.75 million and if the retail price of A$5.50 cannot be increased, then Playworld's gross profit will be zero.

LEARNING OBJECTIVE 5
Understand the techniques that can be used to manage exchange risk

exchange risk
variability of an entity's value that is due to changes in exchange rates

Similar examples can easily be constructed using export contracts where the price is fixed in foreign currency terms. Contracts to borrow or lend foreign currency also provide ready examples of exposure to exchange risk. In each case, the risk derives from the fact that an Australian company can find itself having fewer Australian dollars than it expected to have, given the spot exchange rate at the time of entering into the contract. In economic terms, the point is that an involvement with foreign currencies will increase the riskiness, in Australian dollar terms, of the company's cash flows. In short, there is an exposure to fluctuating exchange rates.

20.6.2 WHO FACES EXCHANGE RISK?

Assuming that company managers make decisions in the interests of shareholders, exchange risk arises whenever a company needs to deal, now or in the future, in a currency other than the currency that shareholders use to finance their consumption. In Example 20.7, Playworld had a liability denominated in UK pounds, while its shareholders used Australian dollars to finance their consumption. Therefore, Playworld faced exchange risk. However, exchange risk can arise even if a company does not itself transact in foreign currency. For example, Australian retailers of CD players will generally obtain their stock from Australian wholesalers who, in turn, import CD players from several countries, including China and Taiwan. The retailers may never transact in the foreign exchange market, yet it is clear that changes in the value of the Chinese and Taiwanese currencies may affect their businesses and therefore affect their shareholders' consumption opportunities. Similarly, tourism markets (see Finance in Action), are affected by changes in exchange rates because such changes affect the costs faced by international tourists. While the examples we have provided are trade-related, we reiterate that exchange risk can also be encountered in capital transactions such as borrowing foreign currency, lending foreign currency, purchasing foreign assets and selling foreign assets.

20.6.3 THE HEDGING PRINCIPLE

In the context of exchange risk faced by Australian companies, a *hedge* is usually thought of as a financial strategy that will ensure that the Australian dollar value of a commitment to pay or receive a sum of foreign currency in the future is not affected by changes in the exchange rate. The basic principle of hedging is to undertake another, offsetting, commitment in the same foreign currency—that is, this second commitment is for the same amount as the original commitment but opposite in sign. Such a commitment may be achieved by entering into a forward contract or by agreeing to borrow or lend foreign currency.

Consider an Australian importer who is committed to making a cash payment of, say, £100 000 in 3 months' time. The importer can hedge by entering today into a second, offsetting commitment to receive £100 000 in 3 months' time. For an Australian importer, this second commitment may be a purchase of UK pounds in the forward market or may be achieved by lending pounds today, with repayment required in 3 months' time. Similarly, an expected sequence of foreign currency receipts—for example, from sales made by a foreign subsidiary—may be hedged by entering into a commitment to make an offsetting sequence of foreign currency payments. Such a commitment would be required by a loan repayment schedule. The following two sections provide further details on forward rate hedging and hedging by borrowing or lending.

FINANCE IN ACTION

TOURISM TO WIN FROM LOWER DOLLAR AND INTEREST RATES

If my business never exports goods, I never see foreign currency and I don't borrow money overseas, then exchange rate changes can't affect me, right? Wrong. In the first week of October 2008 the value of the Australian dollar (in terms of the US dollar) fell by nearly 10 per cent. A story in the 8 October 2008 edition of *The Australian* newspaper commented on the implications of the fall for Australian tourism operators.

Tourism and Transport Forum managing director Chris Brown yesterday said the plummeting dollar was welcome news on the eve of the launch of a new advertising campaign for Tourism Australia crafted by Baz Luhrmann, director of the coming epic film *Australia*. 'It's good timing—there's a global economic malaise and we can't sit around the woolshed crying about it,' Mr Brown said. 'We've all got a job to do. And the drop in the Aussie dollar combined with the launch of the movie makes the timing impeccable. For most of the world Australia will always be an expensive destination. We just can't drag the tectonic plates closer to one another, so when you overlay the high Aussie dollar, it really makes it difficult to keep Australians at home and to attract the rest of the world to come here. So we are unambiguously the low Aussie dollar cheer squad.' …

[T]his week's slide in the dollar has given tourists already here an unexpected increase in their spending power, and made Australia a more affordable option. English couple Mark Nunn, 24, and his girlfriend, Claire Bradshaw, 21, have been in Australia about three weeks and are considering extending their trip. 'We initially budgeted for spending about $420 a week, and we've been easily meeting that target,' Mr Nunn said. 'Australia is quite good value, really.' The dollar's fall had been a 'pleasant little bonus'.

Source: Nicky Trup and Padraic Murphy, 'Tourism to win from lower dollar and interest rates', *The Australian*, 8 October 2008.

20.6.4 FORWARD RATE HEDGING

For a given future commitment, a hedge can be achieved by a transaction in the forward market.[22] For example, suppose that an Australian importer is committed to paying a future sum in UK pounds. In effect, this is a commitment to buy UK pounds in the future. By entering into a forward contract today to buy UK pounds in the future, the value of the commitment can be fixed in Australian dollar terms.

---

22 Alternatively, a position could be taken in a futures contract. However, in practice forward contracts are used much more frequently than futures contracts to hedge exchange risk. Forward and futures contracts are compared in Section 18.2.1.

In this case, the future outflow of UK pounds required by the import contract is matched by the future inflow of UK pounds required by the forward contract. A similar hedge could be used by an Australian company that has borrowed UK pounds. The commitment to pay interest on the loan and to repay the principal is a commitment to make future cash outflows of UK pounds. The hedge is achieved by entering into a commitment to buy UK pounds forward because this will establish a future inflow of UK pounds. By similar reasoning, an exporter whose export price is denominated in foreign currency, or a lender of foreign currency, can hedge by selling the foreign currency in the forward market.

In Example 20.7, Playworld committed itself on 31 July to the payment of £1.1 million on 31 October. If the 3-month forward rate on 31 July was A$1 = £0.4900, then by entering into a forward contract to buy pounds, Playworld can be certain that the cost of the imported goods would be exactly 500 000 × 2.20 × (1/0.4900) = A$2 244 898. Using the current spot rate of A$1 = £0.5000, the cost indicated is 1.1 million/0.5 = A$2.2 million. The extra A$44 898 is sometimes regarded as an 'insurance premium' that must be paid in order to exchange the risky position for a hedged position. This view is discussed further in Section 20.6.6, and for the present we simply assert that it is at best misleading.

20.6.5 HEDGING BY BORROWING OR LENDING

The second hedging technique consists of establishing an offsetting cash flow by borrowing or lending the foreign currency. Because the basic principles involved are identical to those in forward rate hedging, this technique will be discussed in less detail. The example of an Australian importer will again be used to illustrate the technique.

In Example 20.7, Playworld committed itself on 31 July to an outflow of £1.1 million on 31 October. To establish a claim to an inflow of £1.1 million in 3 months' time, Playworld can lend UK pounds on 31 July to be repaid on 31 October. If the interest rate on a 3-month loan of UK pounds is 3.25 per cent, then Playworld should lend £1 100 000/1.0325 = £1 065 375.30. At the spot rate of A$1 = £0.5000, this is equivalent to a loan in Australian dollar terms of 1 065 375.30/0.5000 = A$2 130 750.60. Would Playworld be better off lending this amount in Australia and simultaneously entering into a forward contract to convert the principal (plus interest) into UK pounds on 31 October? The answer to this question depends on the level of interest rates in Australia. For example, if the Australian interest rate is 5.36 per cent for a 3-month loan, then a loan of Australian dollars will return A$2 130 750.60 × 1.0536 = A$2 244 959 in 3 months' time. Converting this amount to UK pounds at the forward rate of A$1 = £0.4900, Playworld will have a claim to receive £1 100 030. In this example, therefore, it makes almost no difference which procedure is followed.[23] Ignoring the difference of £30, either way Playworld will receive a cash inflow of £1.1 million on 31 October to match its import bill of £1.1 million.

20.6.6 WHO SHOULD HEDGE EXCHANGE RISK?

In Section 20.6.2 we pointed out that exchange risk can affect a wide range of companies and individuals. In the present section our aim is to point out that not everyone affected by exchange risk is able to hedge against it and that for those who have the opportunity to hedge, it does not necessarily follow that such an opportunity should always be taken.[24]

In this discussion, it is useful to distinguish between three broad categories of companies. Category 1 is the domestic company that unexpectedly faces a significant foreign exchange involvement. For example,

---

23 It makes no difference because, using interest rate parity, the interest rates applicable to Playworld imply a forward rate of 0.5000 × 1.0325/1.0536 = 0.4900. This is equal to the forward rate that Playworld has been quoted. In practice, forward rates reflect interbank interest rates rather than interest rates applicable to companies such as Playworld. This is one reason why, in practice, companies may have a preference for one type of hedge over the other, notwithstanding that the interest rate parity equation is used by banks and others to set the forward rate.

24 A detailed catalogue of arguments for and against hedging is provided in Dufey and Srinivasulu (1983).

a company may decide to become a 'one-off' exporter when it receives an unanticipated request to supply goods on a future date to a foreign buyer at a price denominated in foreign currency. Category 2 is the committed exporter (or importer) who is regularly involved in foreign currency transactions. Category 3 is the multinational company producing and selling in two or more countries. The nature of exchange risk, and the opportunities to hedge against it, differs from category to category.

Category 1 (the one-off transaction)

In this case, the incentive to hedge is obvious. The company has little or no international experience and an unfavourable result from a single large transaction could place a significant strain on the company's finances. A forward contract is likely to be the most suitable means of hedging. However, the one-off transaction is not, in practice, the typical case.[25]

Category 2 (the repeat exporter or importer)

A sequence of foreign exchange transactions should not necessarily be treated as merely the equivalent of a one-off transaction repeated many times. It can have quite a different character. For example, repeated or routine forward rate hedging may provide few expected benefits and may, in fact, be harmful. Consider the 'insurance premium' analogy referred to in Section 20.6.4. If the forward rate is A\$1 = £0.4900 and the spot rate is A\$1 = £0.5000, the 'insurance premium' is 1 penny per A\$1. However, from the viewpoint of a UK company importing Australian goods the forward rate is £1 = A\$1/0.49 = A\$2.0408 and the spot rate is £1 = A\$1/0.50 = A\$2.00. Therefore, for a UK company with a commitment in Australian dollars, the 'insurance premium' is *minus* 4.08 cents per £1. In the general insurance industry and the life insurance industry, a negative insurance premium is unthinkable; insurance companies *charge* insurance premiums, they do not *pay* them. Clearly, something is wrong with the insurance analogy. In fact, as the following discussion shows, the forward rate may provide little, if any, 'insurance' for a repeat exporter or importer. However, insurance is precisely what the hedger is seeking.[26]

The 'true' cost of a transaction at the forward rate is its opportunity cost—that is, the true cost depends on the forgone alternative. In this case, the forgone alternative is to transact at the spot rate that occurs at the expiration of the forward contract. Suppose that a repeat importer does not engage routinely in forward rate hedging but simply pays for the imported goods by transacting at the spot rate on each payment date. Has the importer's exchange risk increased? Exchange risk is really the risk of suffering a greater variability in cash flows and there is no reason to believe that future forward rates will be less variable than future spot rates—that is, a sequence of future transactions to be undertaken at subsequent forward rates (which, of course, are currently unknown) is no more predictable than a sequence of future transactions to be undertaken at subsequent spot rates (which also are currently unknown).

Category 3 (the multinational company)

A multinational company is likely to receive net cash flows in a number of currencies on a continuing basis, with no fixed terminal date in contemplation. Long-term debt denominated in the same currencies will commit such a company to foreign currency payments and therefore can act as a 'natural' hedge against exchange rate changes.

---

[25] However, an exceptionally large transaction in a sequence of smaller ones might also be included in this category.
[26] This discussion is based on Giddy (1976).

Where a company is likely to receive net cash flows in foreign currency for an indefinitely long period, the major risk is a change in the real (as distinct from the nominal) exchange rate. To illustrate this point, assume that MNC Ltd is an Australian company that buys a factory in New Zealand at a cost of NZ$1.3 million at a time when this sum is equivalent to A$1 million (that is, A$1 = NZ$1.30). If a high rate of inflation in New Zealand subsequently results in a depreciation of the New Zealand dollar to, say, A$1 = NZ$1.56, it does not necessarily follow that MNC has suffered a loss. If the New Zealand inflation rate has simultaneously caused the factory's value to increase to NZ$1.56 million, then MNC has not suffered a loss at all; the depreciation of New Zealand's currency has merely kept pace with inflation, leaving unchanged the value (in Australian dollars) of MNC's New Zealand factory.[27] This is, of course, precisely the result that ultimately can be expected if purchasing power parity holds in the long run.

However, where a permanent change in the real value of a currency may occur there is little scope for hedging of a purely financial nature. To cope with possible changes of this type, management will generally need to change the 'real' aspects of the company by taking such actions as targeting new markets, developing new products, obtaining inputs from new sources and relocating plants.

Finally, it is wrong to conclude that multinational companies must face high exchange rate risk merely because their activities involve a number of currencies. While it is inevitable that some exchange rate changes will cause losses, others will produce gains. In short, there is likely to be a kind of 'portfolio effect' that will not be experienced by companies that operate in only one or two countries. This aspect of international finance is developed further in Section 20.7.

20.6.7 CONTINGENT HEDGING

To this point, it has been assumed that hedging is being considered in the context of a pre-existing fixed commitment involving a foreign currency. For example, we considered the case of Playworld in Example 20.7. In that case, the company was committed to a future payment in UK pounds. A forward contract—that is, an equal but offsetting commitment—is the obvious hedging instrument to consider in these circumstances. But not all exchange rate risks involve commitments. Consider, for example, the risks facing Thread Power Ltd, an Australian company that has offered to purchase a building from Maine Properties Inc., a US company, for US$10 million. The board of Maine Properties is currently considering the offer. At this stage, Thread Power does not know whether it will have a future need to buy US dollars; such a need will arise only if Maine Properties accepts the offer—that is, Thread Power's need to buy US dollars is contingent upon Maine's decision.

Thread Power's financial manager has considered whether a forward contract to buy US dollars should be entered into and has reached the correct conclusion that, regardless of whether such a contract is entered into, Thread Power will face exchange risk. Thread Power will find itself in one of four possible situations:

(a) A$ appreciates against US$ and Maine accepts the purchase offer.
(b) A$ appreciates against US$ and Maine rejects the purchase offer.
(c) A$ depreciates against US$ and Maine accepts the purchase offer.
(d) A$ depreciates against US$ and Maine rejects the purchase offer.

Thread Power's manager has considered the financial effect on Thread Power of having (and not having) a forward contract to buy US dollars in each of these four situations. The outcomes are shown in Table 20.8.

---

[27] Strictly speaking, it is the New Zealand inflation rate relative to the Australian inflation rate that is relevant.

TABLE 20.8 Possible outcomes for Thread Power Ltd

ACTION BY THREAD POWER	IF A$ APPRECIATES AND PURCHASE OFFER IS:		IF A$ DEPRECIATES AND PURCHASE OFFER IS:	
	ACCEPTED (A)	REJECTED (B)	ACCEPTED (C)	REJECTED (D)
If US dollars are bought forward	Nil[a]	Loss	Nil[a]	Gain
If US dollars are not bought forward	Gain	Nil[b]	Loss	Nil[b]

[a] Hedged result—offsetting cash flows.
[b] No cash flow.

Table 20.8 shows the eight possible outcomes, four of which have no (net) foreign exchange consequences, two of which produce an exchange rate gain and two of which produce an exchange rate loss. To illustrate the entries in Table 20.8, consider the outcome in the top left corner. In this case, US dollars are bought forward, the Australian dollar appreciates and the purchase offer is accepted. As a result of the stronger Australian dollar the forward contract produces a loss, but this loss is offset by the lower price (in Australian dollar terms) of the building to be purchased. The second entry to the right in Table 20.8 shows a loss. In this case, there is the same loss on the forward contract but the loss is not offset by a gain on the building purchase because the offer to buy the building is rejected. The message of this example is clear: a fixed commitment, like that required by a forward contract, simply does not hedge a contingent exchange risk.

In effect, by offering to buy the building for a fixed price, Thread Power has granted Maine Properties an option to sell its building to Thread Power at an exercise price of US$10 million.[28] Not surprisingly, one suitable way to hedge such a contingency is by purchasing an option. For example, Thread Power could buy a put option to sell Australian dollars, receiving, on exercise, a given sum of US dollars.[29] Foreign currency options of this type are traded on the Philadelphia Stock Exchange and are available 'over the counter' from banks. If Maine accepts the offer to buy the building, and the Australian dollar has depreciated, the put option will protect Thread Power's position. This occurs because the option will have become more valuable as a result of the depreciation of the Australian dollar. However, if the Australian dollar appreciates, the maximum that Thread Power can lose is the price paid for the option.

20.7 INTERNATIONAL DIVERSIFICATION OF INVESTMENTS

LEARNING OBJECTIVE 6
Explain the advantages of international diversification of investments

In Chapter 7 we explained that diversification of a portfolio is a powerful tool for investors. By diversifying their portfolios, investors are often able to obtain a higher expected return for the same risk or a lower risk for the same expected return. In an Australian domestic context, diversification in practice often means buying shares in, say, 30 or 40 companies listed on the Australian Securities Exchange. But why not extend this level of diversification by buying shares listed on stock markets outside Australia, such as shares listed on the New York Stock Exchange or the London Stock Exchange? The Australian Securities

---

28 Options to sell are known as 'put' options. Options are discussed in detail in Chapter 19.
29 Equivalently, this option can be described as a call option to buy US dollars, requiring a payment, on exercise, of a fixed sum of Australian dollars. Foreign currency options are discussed in Section 19.5. For a more detailed treatment, see Sutton (1988).

Exchange represents around 2 or 3 per cent of the value of all shares listed anywhere in the world—why ignore the other 97 or 98 per cent? Moreover, the industrial structure of the Australian Securities Exchange differs from that of most other markets; in particular, banking and mining are overrepresented in Australia, while manufacturing is underrepresented. Presumably, therefore, investing in foreign shares may well present Australian investors with good opportunities to diversify their portfolios. In this section we show that this 'commonsense' suggestion is well supported by both theory and evidence.

When an investor purchases an asset whose returns are measured in foreign currency, and does not hedge against exchange rate risk, the investor's rate of return is the joint result of the rate of return on the investment (in its own currency of denomination) and the rate of return on the exchange rate. Specifically, the rate of return over a single period from an investment in, say, a UK share is, from an Australian investor's viewpoint:

$$r_\$ = (1 + r_£)(1 + r_s) - 1 \qquad [20.2]$$

where $r_\$$ = the rate of return to an Australian investor in a UK share
$r_£$ = the rate of return to a UK investor in a UK share
$r_s = \frac{s_0}{s_1} - 1$ = the rate of return on the spot exchange rate
s_0 = the spot exchange rate (in pounds per A$1) at the date of investment
s_1 = the spot exchange rate (in pounds per A$1) at the date of return measurement

Equation 20.2 is illustrated in Example 20.8.

EXAMPLE 20.8

On 13 February, Harriet, an Australian investor, purchased 1000 shares in the British manufacturer Arrow plc at a price of £8 per share. Harriet sold the shares on 26 May at a price of £7.80 per share. On 13 February the exchange rate was A$1 = £0.3816 and on 26 May the exchange rate was A$1 = £0.3708. Calculate Harriet's rate of return:

(a) using the dollar returns achieved
(b) using Equation 20.2.

SOLUTION

(a) Harriet's rate of return may be calculated as follows:

$$\text{Sum invested (in A\$)} = \frac{1000 \times 8.00}{0.3816} = \text{A\$20 964.36}$$

$$\text{Sum returned (in A\$)} = \frac{1000 \times 7.80}{0.3708} = \text{A\$21 035.60}$$

$$\text{Dollar return} = \text{A\$21 035.60} - \text{A\$20 964.36}$$
$$= \text{A\$71.24}$$

$$\text{Dollar rate of return} = \frac{\text{A\$71.24}}{\text{A\$20 964.36}} = 0.34\%$$

(b) Harriet's rate of return can be calculated using Equation 20.2. The component rates of return are:

$$r_£ = \frac{£7.80 - £8.00}{£8.00} = -0.0250$$

and

$$r_s = \frac{0.3816}{0.3708} - 1 = 0.02913$$

continued →

Example 20.8 *continued*

Substituting into Equation 20.2 gives:

$r_s = (1 + r_f)(1 + r_x) - 1$
$= (1 - 0.0250)(1 + 0.029\,13) - 1$
$= (0.9750)(1.029\,13) - 1$
$= 0.34\%$

In this example, Harriet has earned a rate of return of approximately 0.3 per cent, resulting from an exchange rate gain of approximately 2.9 per cent and an investment loss of 2.5 per cent.

As Example 20.8 and Equation 20.2 show, the choice of currency used to calculate returns is not a matter of indifference. The investment in Arrow shares, for example, proved to be profitable for an Australian investor but would not have been profitable for a UK investor over the same period. Of course, the opposite situation can also arise.

As explained in Chapter 7, one of the major conclusions of portfolio theory is that there are substantial benefits for investors who diversify their portfolios. By increasing the number of assets in their portfolios, investors can achieve a higher expected return at the same level of risk and/or the same expected return at a lower level of risk. A major determinant of the size of the benefits is the correlation between the returns on the assets in the portfolio. If the correlation is 1, then there is no benefit to be gained, but in other cases the opportunity to benefit exists. Even a correlation of, say, 0.5 can offer worthwhile benefits.

The general presumption in favour of diversification has international as well as domestic application. Consider an investor who is constructing a portfolio consisting of shares issued by various Australian companies listed on the Australian Securities Exchange. After, say, 30 or 40 shares have been selected, the benefit of further diversification is relatively slight; most of the characteristics of the Australian market are already represented in the portfolio and therefore most of the diversifiable risk has already been eliminated. A further source of diversification is to invest in shares listed on foreign stock exchanges. For example, this investor could invest in the shares of companies listed on the London Stock Exchange. The investment opportunities open to a well-diversified Australian investor, who is considering investing in a range of UK shares, can then be inferred by investigating returns on the London share price index and returns on the Australian share price index. In this instance, returns should be measured in Australian dollar terms, and the correlation is then calculated. Provided that the correlation is not 1, international diversification may benefit the investor. Therefore, an indication of the benefits available from diversifying internationally can be obtained by examining estimated correlations between the share price indices of various overseas stock exchanges.

Evidence on the correlation between monthly returns, measured in US dollar terms, on shares in various countries is provided in Table 20.9. Every correlation reported in the table is positive, but less than 1, with most falling in the range 0.3 to 0.6. This finding suggests that there are substantial opportunities to benefit from international diversification. Of course there can be no guarantee that these correlations will not change, but nevertheless it is unlikely that subsequent changes will entirely eliminate all expected benefits.

Australian investors have taken advantage of the opportunity to diversify internationally. As shown in Table 20.2, in the 9 years ended 30 June 2010, the value of Australian 'portfolio and other' investment abroad rose from A$233.3 billion to A$739.9 billion—equivalent to a growth rate of 13.7 per cent per year.

There can be little doubt that, for investors, the prospect of benefiting from international diversification is real. However, investors should not place too much reliance on simple estimates of correlations between national stock markets because it seems very likely that the correlation varies from time to time depending on the overall state of the economy and the stock market. For example, one study found that 14 out of 16 national stock markets studied had higher correlations with the US market when market volatility was high than when market volatility was low (Ramchand & Susmel 1998, p. 405).

TABLE 20.9 Intercountry correlation coefficients for shares (1988–2002)

	AUSTRALIA	CANADA	FRANCE	GERMANY	HONG KONG	JAPAN	UK	US
Australia	1.000							
Canada	0.468	1.000						
France	0.401	0.279	1.000					
Germany	0.369	0.439	0.583	1.000				
Hong Kong	0.441	0.616	0.261	0.475	1.000			
Japan	0.406	0.355	0.262	0.316	0.337	1.000		
UK	0.521	0.525	0.508	0.692	0.517	0.461	1.000	
US	0.447	0.679	0.476	0.545	0.538	0.349	0.663	1.000

Source: Yang, Tapon and Sun (2006), p. 1175.

Diversification benefits can arise in funding decisions as well as in investment decisions—that is, liabilities as well as assets can be diversified to advantage. The extent of the advantage will depend on correlations between exchange rates and between interest rates in different currencies. The evidence suggests that there are diversification benefits available to Australian liability managers (Sweeney 1998).

While international diversification offers substantial advantages, the potential disadvantages should not be overlooked. In particular, there could be adverse taxation implications and increased transaction costs due to the need to transact between currencies. Investors may also find it more difficult to obtain reliable information on foreign securities than on domestic securities, although this problem is substantially reduced if the security is traded on a developed and active market such as the New York or London stock exchanges. Finally, in some countries, foreign investors may face political risks such as sudden limitations being placed on the ability to withdraw capital and/or dividends and, in extreme cases, expropriation of their investment.

CURRENCY SWAPS

20.8

Swaps are possibly the most significant financial invention of the past 30 years. From a volume of near zero in 1981, the volume by the close of the decade was in the hundreds of billions of dollars annually. By June 2010, the notional amount outstanding exceeded 360 trillion US dollars (Bank for International Settlements, Table 19, **www.bis.org**). Swaps are agreements in which two counterparties undertake to exchange a series of future cash flows. In the early days of the swap market these cash flows were the payments to be made on pre-existing loans. In effect, counterparties agreed to repay each other's pre-existing loans. As the market developed, this was usually not *literally* the case, but the swap contracts specified the exchange of a series of future cash flows calculated *as if* pre-existing loan commitments had been swapped.

The two major forms of swap contracts are the **interest rate swap** and the **currency swap**. In an interest rate swap, future cash flows calculated using future floating interest rates are swapped for future

WWW

LEARNING OBJECTIVE 7
Identify the characteristics and uses of currency swaps

interest rate swap
agreement between two parties to exchange interest payments for a specific period, related to an agreed principal amount. The most common type of interest rate swap involves an exchange of fixed interest payments for floating interest payments

currency swap
simultaneous borrowing and lending operation in which two parties initially exchange specific amounts of two currencies at the spot rate. Interest payments in the two currencies are also exchanged and the parties agree to reverse the initial exchange after a fixed term at a fixed exchange rate

cash flows calculated using a fixed interest rate. Such an agreement mimics the effect of exchanging a floating-rate loan and a fixed-rate loan. In a currency swap, future cash flows calculated using an interest rate in one currency are swapped for future cash flows calculated using an interest rate in another currency. Such an agreement mimics the effect of exchanging a loan in one currency for a loan in another currency. Interest rate swaps do not necessarily have any 'international' features and were discussed in Chapter 10. In this section we consider only currency swaps. To simplify matters, in the remainder of this section we discuss currency swaps as though they always arise from a swap of pre-existing loans.[30]

Currency swaps fall into several categories. In the interbank market, the most common form of currency swap is a floating-for-floating currency swap. In this case, there is an exchange of principals and an exchange of interest flows, one of which is calculated using a floating rate in one currency, while the other is calculated using a floating rate in a different currency. However, the mechanics of currency swaps are easier to explain by considering a fixed-for-fixed currency swap, in which a fixed-rate commitment in one currency is exchanged for a fixed-rate commitment in another currency.[31] The swap consists of an exchange of principal at the outset, followed by exchanges of interest flows on interest payment dates and, at the maturity of the loans, a re-exchange of principals. This type of swap is illustrated in Example 20.9.

The search for interest cost savings is not the only reason for the growth in currency swaps. Market participants have found currency swaps a useful tool in structuring contracts that exploit tax advantages, or that reduce the impact of government regulations. For example, US companies have used currency swaps as part of a method to exploit some tax advantages of borrowing yen.[32]

A very important theme in the swap literature is the view that currency swaps are exchange rate hedging vehicles that need not have any implications for borrowing costs. Smith, Smithson and Wakeman (1992), for example, emphasise the similarities that exist between currency swaps and forward contracts. Using this approach, the future cash flows in the currency swap between Britco and Yankco could be described as a package of four forward contracts. From Britco's viewpoint, these four contracts are as follows. The first three are, respectively, 1-year, 2-year and 3-year forward contracts to pay US$23.6 million to Yankco and in return receive £14.5 million—that is, they are equivalent to forward contracts to sell US$23.6 million at an exchange rate of US$1 = £0.6144. The fourth forward contract is implicit in the re-exchange of principals at maturity. In this case, Britco has the equivalent of a forward contract to sell US$200 million at a forward rate that is equal to today's spot rate of US$1 = £0.5000—that is, Britco will pay Yankco US$200 million and in return receive £100 million.

Adopting the forward contract approach to currency swaps emphasises their hedging implications. In particular, whereas forward contracts for terms as long as 3 years are much less common than forward contracts for periods of less than 1 year, implicitly such contracts are available through the mechanism of currency swaps. With the increased exposure of many companies to exchange rate movements, and the volatility of foreign exchange markets, there is increased demand for a financial instrument that locks in currency exchanges well into the future.

One final, and very important, aspect of currency swaps needs to be mentioned. This is the question of **credit risk**. The credit risk of a currency swap is usually considerably greater than the

credit risk
possibility of loss because a party fails to meet its obligations

---

30 In practice, swaps are no longer the direct exchange between two parties of cash flows on pre-existing debts. Instead, there may be no pre-existing debt and an intermediary is generally involved. However, the mechanics and motives are easier to understand if it is imagined that borrowers themselves arrange a swap of pre-existing debts by direct negotiation.

31 It is easy to show that combining an interest rate swap and a floating-for-floating currency swap creates the equivalent of a fixed-for-floating currency swap. Further, combining an interest rate swap and a fixed-for-floating currency swap creates the equivalent of a fixed-for-fixed currency swap. In this sense, therefore, markets for fixed-for-fixed and fixed-for-floating currency swaps are redundant.

32 For details, see Smith, Smithson and Wilford (1990, pp. 220–4). For an Australian perspective, see Montague (1997, pp. 368–9).

EXAMPLE 20.9

Yankco wishes to borrow £100 million for 3 years and Britco wishes to borrow US$200 million for 3 years. The current spot exchange rate is US$1 = £0.5000. Both companies wish to repay using the bond cash flow pattern—that is, interest is paid at the end of each year and the principal is repaid in full at the end of the third year. The interest rates (in per cent per annum) applicable to the two borrowers are shown in Table 20.10.

TABLE 20.10 Interest rates payable by Britco and Yankco

COMPANY	INTEREST RATES (% P.A.)	
	ON US$ BORROWINGS	ON UK£ BORROWINGS
Britco	12.0	14.5
Yankco	10.0	13.5

Loosely speaking, while Yankco can borrow more cheaply than Britco in both currencies, it has a 2 percentage points advantage in US dollar borrowings but only a 1 percentage point advantage in UK pound borrowings.

The standard funding cost argument for currency swaps is to suggest that Yankco should initially borrow dollars, while Britco should initially borrow pounds, and the two should then swap loan commitments. This is achieved by Yankco and Britco exchanging cash flows on each interest payment date and at the maturity of the loan. Although *legally* the original loan contracts between Yankco and the dollar lenders, and between Britco and the pound lenders, remain undisturbed, the *economic* effect is that Britco and Yankco have swapped loan commitments.

However, a straight swap of loan commitments is unlikely. In this example, as in many swaps, one counterparty is financially stronger than the other. In this example, Yankco is the stronger counterparty. In a straight swap, Yankco will simply end up paying the higher interest rate required on a loan to Britco. Thus, Yankco will need an inducement to enter into the swap. Such an inducement can be achieved in a number of different ways. For example, Britco could offer Yankco a fee, perhaps in the form of allowing Yankco to retain some of its loan principal, while Britco transfers the whole of its loan principal to Yankco. Alternatively, Britco could make swap payments to Yankco at an interest rate higher than the 10 per cent required by Yankco to repay its US dollar creditors. A third approach, which we explain below, involves

FIGURE 20.2 Post-swap cash flows

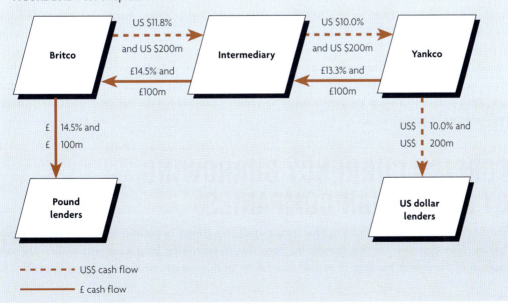

continued →

Example 20.9 *continued*

an intermediary. One solution of this type is shown in Figure 20.2. This figure shows the cash flows that occur after an initial exchange of principals (Yankco borrows US$200 million, which it pays to Britco, while Britco borrows £100 million, which it pays to Yankco).

The originally agreed and post-swap net cash flows are shown in Table 20.11.

TABLE 20.11 Originally agreed and post-swap net cash flows

END OF YEAR	ORIGINALLY AGREED CASH FLOWS		POST-SWAP NET CASH FLOWS		
	BRITCO	YANKCO	BRITCO	YANKCO	INTERMEDIARY
0	+£100m	+US$200m	+US$200m	+£100m	…
1	−£14.5m	−US$20m	−US$23.6m	−£13.3m	+US$3.6m −£1.2m
2	−£14.5m	−US$20m	−US$23.6m	−£13.3m	+US$3.6m −£1.2m
3	−£14.5m	−US$20m	−US$23.6m	−£13.3m	+US$3.6m −£1.2m
3	−£100m	−US$200m	−US$200m	−£100m	…

As shown in Figure 20.2, after the swap Britco has exactly offsetting inflows and outflows in pounds and is paying 11.8 per cent for US dollars. This is 0.2 per cent better than Britco could have achieved for itself directly. After the swap, Yankco has exactly offsetting inflows and outflows in US dollars, and is paying 13.3 per cent for pounds. This is 0.2 per cent better than Yankco could have achieved for itself directly. The financial intermediary carries an exchange risk in that on each interest payment date, it has a net *dollar inflow* of (0.118 − 0.10) x US$200 million = US$3.6 million, and a net *pound outflow* of (0.145 − 0.133) x £100 million = £1.2 million. The intermediary might seek to hedge this risk by entering into forward contracts, or by entering into other swaps. Alternatively, it might choose to carry the risk because its net cash flow will be negative only in the relatively unlikely event that the US dollar depreciates in 3 years from a value of £0.5000 per dollar to less than £0.3333 per dollar.

credit risk of an interest rate swap. The main reason for the higher risk is that currency swaps require a re-exchange of principals on the maturity date, whereas in interest rate swaps there is no exchange of principals. Obviously, loan principals involve sums that are much greater than associated periodic interest flows. In practice, however, there have been relatively few defaults in currency swaps. Further, many banks have entered into bilateral agreements that reduce the credit risk when, as is often the case, both parties in a swap are banks. These agreements provide for the net swap position between two banks to be settled daily.

20.9 FOREIGN CURRENCY BORROWING BY AUSTRALIAN COMPANIES

The data in Table 20.3 show that there has been a significant growth in borrowing overseas by Australian entities. Although some of this growth has been due to borrowing by government bodies, the vast majority of the growth has been in private sector debt. In this section, we consider the risk involved in borrowing foreign currency and the possible reasons why Australian companies borrow internationally. We then review some of the main forms that these loans can take.

20.9.1 THE RISK OF FOREIGN CURRENCY BORROWING

If a foreign currency borrowing is not hedged, then the borrower faces considerable risk. This risk is illustrated in Example 20.10.

> **LEARNING OBJECTIVE 8**
> Identify the main sources of foreign currency borrowing used by Australian companies

EXAMPLE 20.10

> Gippsland Farms Ltd required a loan of A$10 million for 1 year and its bank quoted an interest rate of 14.5 per cent. Instead, Gippsland Farms borrowed 12 million Swiss francs at an interest rate of 5 per cent and, at the then current spot exchange rate of A$1 = 1.2 Swiss francs, converted the Swiss franc principal to A$10 million. One year later, the spot exchange rate was A$1 = 1.0 Swiss francs. How many Australian dollars will Gippsland Farms have to repay?
>
> ### SOLUTION
> Gippsland Farms will have to repay the sum of:
>
> $$A\$ \frac{12\,000\,000 \times 1.05}{1.0}$$
> $$= A\$12\,600\,000$$
>
> This represents the equivalent of an Australian dollar interest rate of 26 per cent—nearly double the Australian dollar interest rate originally quoted.

In Example 20.10, Gippsland Farms suffered a loss because of the subsequent depreciation of the Australian dollar. The break-even point was where the Australian dollar equivalent of the required Swiss franc repayment equalled the repayment required on the Australian dollar loan. In Example 20.10 this is where:

$$A\$10\,000\,000 \times 1.145 = A\$ \frac{12\,000\,000 \times 1.05}{s_1}$$

where s_1 = the spot exchange rate on the repayment date.

The solution to this equation is $s_1 = 1.100\,437$—that is, in round terms, break-even was at an exchange rate of A$1 = 1.1 Swiss francs. Thus, the borrower would have benefited if, during the term of the loan, the Australian dollar either appreciated against the Swiss franc or depreciated to a level no lower than A$1 = 1.1 Swiss francs. Unfortunately for Gippsland Farms, the Australian dollar depreciated from 1.2 to 1.0 Swiss francs—well beyond the break-even level of 1.1 Swiss francs.

According to uncovered interest parity (Equation 20.1(d)) the break-even exchange rate is the result that, on average, should be expected to occur. Rearranging Equation 20.1(d), we have:

$$E(s) = \left(\frac{1 + \text{foreign interest rate}}{1 + \text{domestic interest rate}}\right)(\text{current spot rate})$$
$$= \left(\frac{1.05}{1.145}\right)(1.2)$$
$$= 1.100\,437$$

Clearly, an unhedged foreign currency loan is risky. But the attractiveness of a foreign interest rate that seems low by domestic standards can be hard for a borrower to resist. According to an editorial in the Melbourne newspaper *The Age* (see Finance in Action), the Australian Government used currency swaps to create the equivalent to an unhedged foreign currency loan, resulting in an unrealised loss of A$3.8 billion.

20.9.2 REASONS FOR BORROWING INTERNATIONALLY

The data in Table 20.2 show that since 1989 there has been a significant increase in Australia's foreign liabilities. One reason for this increase is that the borrowings have been used to acquire foreign assets. As mentioned in Section 20.6.5, the matching of foreign currency assets with foreign currency liabilities provides a hedge. If an exchange rate change produces a decrease (increase) in the Australian dollar value of a foreign asset, there will be a simultaneous, matching decrease (increase) in the Australian dollar value of a foreign liability. Some of the international borrowing by Australian companies can be explained by its use as a hedge. Where a borrower does not have a matching foreign asset to hedge a foreign debt, the borrower can use financial instruments to create a hedge. In particular, entering into a currency swap can effectively convert a foreign currency debt to a domestic currency debt. In practice, it is common for Australian foreign currency borrowers to hedge immediately by entering into a currency swap to convert the foreign currency debt to Australian currency.

FINANCE IN ACTION

TREASURY'S CURRENCY SWAPS CRASH

A currency swap can be used to convert debt from a high interest rate domestic currency loan to a low interest rate foreign currency loan—which will save the borrower money unless, of course, the domestic currency depreciates. Then the borrower faces the prospect of the benefit of the lower interest rate being wiped out by losses on the exchange rate. Would anyone take such a risk? According to this editorial in a Melbourne newspaper, someone did. The Australian Government no less.

For the first time since the 1990 recession, Australian taxpayers are at risk of funding heavy losses by a government financial authority. This time the culprit is the Federal Treasury, through its curious practice of taking out unhedged cross-currency swaps to reduce the interest burden on the public debt. Curious, because the Treasury has been so dismissive of Asian countries that made similar mistakes. Yet at no stage did it or Treasurer Peter Costello warn us that our money was at risk, until Labor senators noted a single-line entry on page 80 of an annual report revealing that in just two years the Treasury had run up more than $3 billion of prospective foreign exchange losses. By June 2001, its currency swaps had turned $8 billion of debt into almost $12 billion, running up unrealised losses of $3.8 billion. At this stage these are prospective losses; whether they occur depends on where our dollar goes. But if the dollar stays roughly where it is, they are losses that Australian families will have to pay.

Why did the Treasury risk our money? It began with a plausible rationale: in 1987 a decade of high inflation and currency plunges had left Australian bond rates uncomfortably high, so the Treasury took advantage of lower US rates by swapping part of its Australian dollar debt for a US dollar debt. This gave it lower interest bills at the risk of higher costs if our dollar fell heavily. For a decade the strategy worked; the Treasury claims taxpayers gained more than $2 billion from lower interest rates.

But it was a high-risk strategy that would collapse if the dollar collapsed. In an admirably careful report in 1999, the Australian National Audit Office pointed out: 'Treasury has used cross-currency swaps, not to hedge existing exposures, but to create new exposures to US dollars ... (This) is in contrast to the practices of other sovereign debt managers, state treasury corporations and most private sector practice.' By mid-1999 the Treasury had swapped $38 billion of Australian debt into US dollar debt through 332 transactions.

Yet in 1997 the entire policy rationale had disappeared. With inflation and the budget balance under control, the gap between US and Australian bond rates had virtually vanished. And the Australian dollar plunged into territory that meant heavy losses for unhedged debt; from almost 80 US cents at the end of 1996, it sank to 65 at the end of 1997, 61 by mid-1998 and 51 by mid-2001. Treasury reviewed the policy, but instead of getting out, gambled on the dollar rebounding. It was wrong, and taxpayers now stand to lose heavily. We are owed a full explanation, a full disclosure and acknowledgment of responsibility by both Treasurer Peter Costello and Treasury secretary Ken Henry.

Source: 'Treasury's currency swaps crash', *The Age*, 6 March 2002, p. 14.

In many cases, a foreign currency hedge entered into by a borrower will eliminate not only the exchange risk but also the apparent interest rate advantage. This result is to be expected because international debt and currency markets are highly efficient and, therefore, will ensure that the interest rate on an Australian dollar loan is equal to the interest rate on a foreign currency loan that has been converted to an Australian dollar loan. However, the presence of taxes and other market frictions can still leave, on occasions and for some borrowers, a marginal cost advantage from borrowing internationally, rather than from domestic sources. While such advantages probably explain some of the increase in foreign debt, the main reasons lie elsewhere. Some other reasons are considered below.[33]

Access to a broader range of investors

Many offshore issues of bonds are distributed through well-developed marketing channels to a wide variety of institutions and, in some cases, individuals. Although, in principle, foreign investors could buy bonds issued in Australia, in practice they are likely to prefer bonds that are issued in their home country, where they are familiar with institutional factors such as prospectus requirements and trading arrangements.

Hedging efficiency

Many offshore lenders wish to lend to Australian companies but do not wish to have exposure to the Australian dollar. Similarly, many Australian companies wish to borrow from foreign lenders but do not wish to have exposure to a foreign currency. In principle, these conflicting wishes could be reconciled in either of two ways. The first way is for Australian companies to borrow Australian dollars from foreign lenders and the lenders then hedge their exchange rate risk. The second way is for Australian companies to borrow foreign currency from foreign lenders and then the Australian borrowers hedge their exchange rate risk. The choice comes down to who will do the hedging: the foreign lenders or the Australian borrowers? In practice, it is usually more efficient for the Australian borrowers to do the hedging, particularly in the case of a bond issue, where there are numerous investors (lenders) involved but only one borrower.

Diversification

Australian banks and other financial intermediaries have been major borrowers of foreign currency.[34] Most of these loans have been converted immediately to Australian dollar loans using currency swaps. Banks prefer to have a diversity of funding sources to reduce their risk. For example, the wider the range of funding sources, the less reliant a bank is on any one source and hence the less vulnerable it is to changes in the supply of funds from any one source. Similarly, banks seek to diversify their loan portfolio. A common mechanism is to set a limit for each borrower on the amount the bank will lend before it imposes an additional interest rate premium to compensate for the risk. If a large Australian borrower reaches its limit with several domestic banks, it may find that the lowest interest rates are offered by foreign banks.

Ability to handle large loans

Despite significant improvements and growth in the Australian domestic bond market, it remains true that some foreign markets are better able to handle very large bond issues.

---

33 This list of reasons is drawn from Battellino (2002).
34 As at June 2010, Australian-located operations of banks and registered financial corporations had international liabilities of A$740 billion. In the 7 years to June 2010, the international liabilities of these institutions grew at about 12 per cent per annum. Source: Reserve Bank of Australia Table B12.2, www.rba.org.au.

simple domestic loan
a loan of domestic currency made by a domestic lender to a domestic borrower

Eurocredit
a loan made in a currency other than the currency of the country where the loan is made

domestic loan (in foreign currency)
a loan of foreign currency made by a domestic bank to a domestic borrower

foreign loan (in domestic currency)
a loan raised in another country, in the currency of that country

simple domestic bond
a bond denominated in domestic currency and issued by a domestic borrower

Eurobond
medium- to long-term international bearer security issued in countries other than the country of the currency in which the bond is denominated

foreign bond
a bond issued outside the borrower's country and denominated in the currency of the country in which it is issued

20.9.3 TYPES OF BORROWING TRANSACTIONS

Imagine that Ozzieco Ltd is a large Australian multinational company that has decided to borrow either Australian dollars (AUD) or US dollars (USD). However, it is unsure whether to negotiate a loan with a bank or to issue a marketable security such as a bond. It is also unsure whether the funds should be obtained in Australia, the US or the UK. Figure 20.3 illustrates the options open to Ozzieco.

FIGURE 20.3 Choices open to an Australian company seeking overseas funding

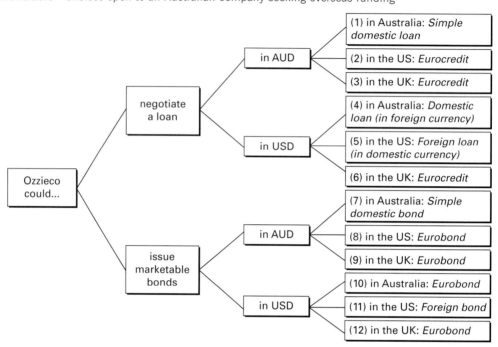

As illustrated in Figure 20.3, Ozzieco can choose between two currencies, two funding methods and three locations. Therefore, it has 2 × 2 × 3 = 12 options open to it. Options 1 to 6 involve a negotiated loan. Option 1 is simply a loan made by an Australian bank to an Australian borrower in domestic currency (AUD). Options 2, 3 and 6 all involve a loan in a currency other than the currency of the country where the loan is negotiated. For historical reasons, these types of loans are known as 'Euro' loans.[35] Such loans may be given different names depending on how they are structured, so we have used the generic term 'credit'. Option 4 is a loan made by an Australian bank to an Australian borrower but the loan is in foreign (USD) not domestic (AUD) currency. Hence it is a domestic loan of a foreign currency. Option 5 is a loan denominated in USD made by a US bank to an Australian borrower. Hence, the US bank would describe this transaction as a loan made to a foreign company in the bank's domestic (USD) currency.

Options 7 to 12 involve Ozzieco issuing a bond. If a bond is denominated in AUD and is issued in Australia by an Australian company, then it is simply the issuing of a domestic bond (Option 7). Options 8, 9, 10 and 12 all involve issuing a bond in a currency other than the currency of the country where the bond is issued. Such bonds are called 'Eurobonds'. In Option 11, Ozzieco issues a US dollar-denominated bond in the US. From the US viewpoint, this transaction is a foreign bond because a foreign (Australian)

---

[35] This terminology is standard but, unfortunately, is also confusing. The meaning of the term 'Euro' in this context should not be confused with the term 'euro' when used as the name of the currency adopted throughout much of Europe in 2002. 'Euro' in the former sense simply means a transaction in any currency outside the country where that currency is used. Therefore, a deposit of euros in a Singapore bank is a 'Euro' transaction because Singapore's currency is the Singapore dollar, not the euro. But a deposit of euros in a German bank is not a 'Euro' transaction in the former sense because the euro is the currency used in Germany.

company issues a bond in the domestic (US) market and the bond is denominated in domestic (US) currency. Foreign bonds are often given colourful names. In this example the bond would be called a 'Yankee bond'. Similarly, if a bond denominated in Japanese yen is issued in Japan by a non-Japanese company, it is called a 'Samurai bond'. Other examples are Kangaroo bonds (Australia), Kauri bonds (New Zealand), Matador bonds (Spain) and Bulldog bonds (UK).

Figure 20.3 considers debt transactions from the viewpoint of the borrower. Of course, we should also consider the options from the viewpoint of the lenders. Each of the options open to Ozzieco represents a different set of risks and returns from the viewpoint of potential lenders. Naturally, borrowers will consider the preferences of lenders because the more attractive a particular structure is to lenders, the lower the borrower's costs, all other things being equal. Moreover, like borrowers, lenders also have become aware of international opportunities in recent decades. Therefore, even if a bond is issued in, say, London, this certainly does not mean that British lenders are the sole providers of the funds. Indeed, in many cases, British lenders may provide little of the funding. Finally, the location where bonds are issued, or loans negotiated, does not necessarily mean that the law of that country will apply. For example, it is not unusual for a bond issued in Europe to specify that, in the event of any legal questions arising, UK law shall apply.

One final term should be defined: **international bond**. An international bond is either a Eurobond or a foreign bond—that is, Options 7 to 12 inclusive could all be described as international bonds.

In principle, the distinctions depicted in Figure 20.3 are clear. In practice, however, there is often considerable blurring between the categories. For example, suppose that a US subsidiary of an Australian company borrows US dollars from a US bank, and the Australian parent has not guaranteed repayment of the loan. Because the parent company is Australian, is this arrangement a foreign loan in domestic currency—Option 5? Or is it just a simple domestic (US) arrangement? Alternatively, consider a multinational company, most of whose shareholders are either British or Dutch. If this company borrows UK pounds in London, is this arrangement a simple domestic (UK) transaction because of the British shareholders? Or is it a domestic loan of a foreign currency because of the Dutch shareholders? As a final example, suppose that an Australian company approaches a bank in the UK for a loan of US dollars (Option 6). The bank declines to lend the money and instead offers to set up a facility in which the bank guarantees to sell commercial paper ('Euronotes')[36] issued by the Australian company. While this arrangement is similar to the Australian company issuing marketable securities in its own name—Option 12—the bank guarantee has blurred the boundaries. Nevertheless, whatever its faults, the categorisation illustrated in Figure 20.3 is a useful way of thinking about alternative funding structures.

Foreign loans and foreign bonds are just domestic transactions where the borrower happens to be a foreign entity. Therefore, the reasons for entering into such transactions are typically those that apply to domestic borrowers. This type of funding is well suited to a borrower who already owns (or who intends to acquire) assets in the foreign country. For example, if an Australian company owns property in the US, then a loan of US dollars from a US lender, perhaps secured against the US property, is an obvious funding choice, particularly if the borrower does not have a sufficiently high profile to issue marketable securities. In this case, the foreign loan is hedged by the foreign assets.

international bond
a bond that is either a foreign bond or a Eurobond

20.9.4 EUROCREDITS

While 'Euro' transactions often have domestic counterparts, they have distinctive features because, by definition, the funds borrowed are foreign currency from the viewpoint of both the borrower and the lender(s). For the same reason, 'Euro' transactions may be less heavily regulated than other transactions. Eurocredits are discussed in this section and Eurosecurities are discussed in the following section. Eurocredits fall into two main categories: term credits and revolving credits.

---

36 Euronotes are discussed in Section 20.9.5.

Term credits

term credit
a loan repayable over a specific time period

Like its domestic counterpart, a Euro **term credit** is a loan of a given sum (the principal), which is repaid over a fixed period. Interest is usually charged on a floating-rate basis, typically by specifying that the interest rate will be set at a margin above an agreed reference rate. For example, a loan contract in US dollars may require repayment over 5 years at a margin of 0.5 per cent above the specified reference rate. The size of the margin (or 'spread') above the reference rate depends on the credit risk of the borrower: the greater the risk, the greater the margin. Unlike most domestic term loans, Euro term credits are usually funded by a consortium of banks known as a **syndicate**. One of these banks is known as the 'lead manager' and has the main responsibility for negotiating the loan conditions and then finds other banks that will contribute some of the funds to be borrowed. These other banks are known as 'participating banks'.

syndicate
a group of lenders (usually banks) that provides a borrower with funds; the lead manager has the main responsibility for negotiating the loan conditions, while other banks whose main role is to contribute loan funds are known as participating banks

Revolving credits

A **revolving credit** is also known as a credit line. In a revolving credit, the borrower is permitted to borrow up to a given amount and pays interest only on the amount borrowed. Typically, however, a fee is charged on the difference between the amount borrowed and the limit approved. Revolving credits therefore share some features with overdrafts. However, unlike an overdraft, the amount borrowed may be financed by the borrower issuing short-term securities such as commercial paper rather than by the borrower writing cheques against an account. Similarly to term credits, the interest rate will be set equal to an agreed reference rate, plus a spread that depends on the borrower's creditworthiness.

revolving credit
a loan in which the borrower is permitted to borrow up to a stated amount

20.9.5 INTERNATIONAL DEBT SECURITIES

The international debt markets offer short-term, medium-term and long-term debt securities. In this section we briefly review the main securities in each maturity category.

Short-term international debt securities

Short-term debt securities are traditionally defined as those that mature within a year of being issued. There are two main types of short-term international debt securities: Euronotes and Euro commercial paper.

Euronote
short-term note, underwritten by a bank or a syndicate of banks and sold in countries other than the country of the currency in which it is denominated

Euronotes are similar to bank accepted bills. Euronotes are typically issued with a term to maturity of 1, 3, 6 or 12 months and are issued at a discount to face value. A Euronote issue is usually underwritten by an international bank or a syndicate of international banks. Usually, there is an ongoing arrangement between the borrower and the bank under which the bank agrees to underwrite the borrower's Euronote issues up to an agreed amount over a fixed period of, say, 5 years, at a fixed spread above a reference rate. If the bank is unable to sell the notes in the market, the bank will purchase the notes itself. Such an arrangement is often called a **note issuance facility (NIF)** or a **revolving underwriting facility (RUF)**.

Euro commercial paper
short-term note sold without being underwritten in countries other than the country of the currency in which it is denominated

Euro commercial paper, often abbreviated to 'ECP', is very similar to a Euronote. The major difference is that while a Euronote is underwritten by a bank or syndicate of banks, ECP is not underwritten.

Table 20.12 provides data on the market for short-term international debt securities. Four important trends are evident in the table. First, the total amount on issue grew strongly until 2008 when it began to decline as the effects of the global financial crisis begin to show. However, at US$877 billion, the total amount on issue in June 2010 remains a very large sum of money. Second, commercial paper is the dominant instrument type. Third, the share of the market held by financial institutions has grown over the years and now stands at around 90 per cent. Fourth, in 2010, the US dollar accounted for about one-third of the instruments on issue, well down from the 70 to 80 per cent share it held in the early

1990s. By contrast, the share of the euro has grown rapidly, and in 2010 comfortably exceeded the share of the US dollar. The share of the Australian dollar is much lower than in the early 1990s and by 2010 appeared to have settled at about 1 per cent.

note issuance facility (NIF) or revolving underwriting facility (RUF) facility provided by one or more institutions that agree to underwrite issues of short-term notes by a borrower

TABLE 20.12 International money market instruments on issue at various dates, by instrument type, issuer type and currency of the issue

	30 SEPT 1993	30 JUNE 1996	30 JUNE 1999	30 JUNE 2002	30 JUNE 2005	30 JUNE 2008	30 JUNE 2009	30 JUNE 2010
Total on issue (USD billions)	$117	$177	$284	$424	$667	$1405	$1019	$877
By instrument type								
Commercial paper	69.2%	58.4%	53.7%	63.0%	74.2%	57.5%	65.9%	59.4%
Other instruments	30.8%	41.6%	46.3%	37.0%	25.8%	42.5%	34.1%	40.6%
Total	100.0%	100.0%	100.0%	100.0%	100.0%	100.0%	100.0%	100.0%
By issuer type								
Financial institutions	67.9%	76.0%	84.3%	85.4%	89.9%	91.6%	87.8%	91.5%
Governments	14.2%	9.6%	2.7%	3.0%	1.8%	2.6%	6.2%	3.6%
International organisations	3.5%	2.5%	2.2%	1.0%	1.2%	0.9%	0.5%	1.1%
Corporate issuers	14.4%	11.9%	10.8%	10.6%	7.1%	4.9%	5.4%	3.8%
Total	100.0%	100.0%	100.0%	100.0%	100.0%	100.0%	100.0%	100.0%
By currency								
US dollar	78.2%	62.7%	54.7%	38.1%	29.5%	29.2%	30.1%	36.4%
Euro	10.1%	14.8%	24.8%	34.9%	45.6%	47.0%	48.3%	45.1%
Pound sterling	3.4%	5.4%	7.0%	12.6%	16.3%	13.4%	13.7%	10.5%
Swiss franc	1.6%	5.3%	2.9%	2.9%	2.4%	2.1%	2.0%	2.1%
Yen	0.5%	6.8%	7.1%	7.9%	2.1%	3.6%	2.1%	2.3%
Australian dollar	5.1%	3.1%	1.9%	1.4%	1.2%	1.1%	1.1%	1.3%
Canadian dollar	0.6%	0.5%	0.2%	0.2%	0.4%	0.3%	0.2%	0.1%
Other	0.5%	1.2%	1.4%	2.1%	2.5%	3.3%	2.6%	2.3%
Total	100.0%	100.0%	100.0%	100.0%	100.0%	100.0%	100.0%	100.0%

Source: Bank for International Settlements, Statistical Table 13A, **www.bis.org**. Based on figures generated from www.bis.org.publ/ftrpdf/r_fa1106.pdf#page =118.

WWW

Medium-term international debt securities

Unlike many domestic capital markets, the Euromarkets offer a medium-term security known as a **medium-term note** (**MTN**). An MTN has a fixed term to maturity of between 1 and 10 years and,

medium-term note (MTN)
bearer security with an initial term to maturity of more than 1 year and often issued continually

bearer bond
a bond whose ownership is not registered by the issuer and possession of the physical document is primary evidence of ownership

straight fixed-rate bond
the standard form of a bond, paying a fixed coupon rate at regular intervals during the term of the bond and, on the maturity date of the bond, the face value of the bond

floating-rate note
debt security whose interest rate is adjusted periodically in line with changes in a specified reference rate

convertible bond
a bond that allows the investor to exchange the bond for shares in the borrower

like bonds, MTNs offer a stated fixed coupon interest rate or a floating rate defined relative to a stated reference rate. However, unlike bonds, MTNs may be available periodically (or even continually), whereas a bond issue is usually made at a point in time. MTN issues are not underwritten; it is the responsibility of the borrower, usually assisted by a securities firm, to sell the MTNs on the open market. The face value of an MTN may be relatively low, making its issue attractive to small investors. MTNs are **bearer bonds**—that is, the ownership of the bond is not registered by the issuer and possession of the physical document is primary evidence of ownership.

Long-term international debt securities

There are three main types of long-term international debt security: *straight fixed-rate bonds*, *floating-rate notes* and *equity-related debt securities*.

Straight fixed-rate bonds pay a fixed coupon interest rate, with repayment of the face value made in full on the maturity date. Foreign bonds must comply with the regulations in force in the market in which the bonds are issued—just because the borrower is from another country does not imply exemption from the regulations. Eurobond issues are likely to be less heavily regulated than foreign bond issues because the currency of the issue is not the currency of the country in which the bond is issued. Typically, a Eurobond issue is arranged and distributed (sold) by an international bank or a syndicate of banks. Most Eurobonds pay interest annually and, like MTNs, are bearer bonds. There is an active secondary market in Eurobonds, with most trading taking place over the counter, rather than in an organised exchange.

Floating-rate notes have many of the same features as straight fixed-rate bonds but with an important difference—the coupon interest rate is not fixed and instead it varies regularly during the life of the bond, in accordance with changes in the stated reference rate. For example, on a coupon payment date the interest rate to apply to the next coupon interest payment may be announced. Thus, at any given time, the investor knows the amount of the forthcoming coupon payment but not the amount of any subsequent coupon payment. However, the investor knows which reference rate will be used to set subsequent coupon rates and the size of the spread above the reference rate.

Equity-related debt securities can take many forms. Their distinguishing feature is that there is a link between the cash flows generated by the security and the equity value (stock price) of the borrower. Most equity-related debt securities are **convertible bonds**. In a typical convertible bond, the investor receives a fixed coupon interest rate but also has the choice at some point (or points) during the life of the bond to convert the bond into shares of the borrower.

Table 20.13 provides data on the market for long-term international debt securities. Its coverage includes foreign bonds, Eurobonds, floating-rate notes and medium-term notes.

TABLE 20.13 International bonds and notes on issue at various dates, by instrument type, issuer type and currency of the issue

	30 SEPT 1993	30 JUNE 1996	30 JUNE 1999	30 JUNE 2002	30 JUNE 2005	30 JUNE 2008	30 JUNE 2009	30 JUNE 2010
Total on issue (USD billions)	$1 974	$2 845	$4 593	$8 297	$13 372	$23 879	$24 877	$24 693
By instrument type								
Floating-rate	13.6%	16.6%	22.2%	25.0%	27.6%	33.4%	33.5%	30.3%
Straight fixed-rate	76.5%	77.4%	73.0%	71.3%	69.8%	64.8%	64.9%	67.9%

	30 SEPT 1993	30 JUNE 1996	30 JUNE 1999	30 JUNE 2002	30 JUNE 2005	30 JUNE 2008	30 JUNE 2009	30 JUNE 2010
Equity-related	9.9%	6.0%	4.8%	3.7%	2.5%	1.8%	1.6%	1.8%
Total	100.0%	100.0%	100.0%	100.0%	100.0%	100.0%	100.0%	100.0%
By issuer type								
Financial institutions	40.9%	48.8%	62.0%	70.0%	74.4%	78.4%	77.6%	75.4%
Governments	20.5%	22.1%	15.3%	10.8%	10.6%	8.5%	8.2%	8.8%
International organisations	12.8%	10.5%	7.9%	5.0%	3.9%	2.9%	3.1%	3.3%
Corporate issuers	25.8%	18.7%	14.7%	14.2%	11.1%	10.2%	11.1%	12.5%
Total	100.0%	100.0%	100.0%	100.0%	100.0%	100.0%	100.0%	100.0%
By currency								
US dollar	40.4%	39.4%	49.2%	48.2%	38.2%	34.0%	36.1%	40.0%
Euro	25.3%	27.5%	27.4%	35.6%	45.8%	49.7%	47.4%	43.4%
Pound sterling	7.4%	6.5%	7.6%	6.8%	7.4%	7.8%	8.5%	8.1%
Swiss franc	7.7%	5.8%	3.1%	1.8%	1.5%	1.4%	1.4%	1.4%
Yen	13.9%	15.6%	9.3%	5.3%	3.7%	2.7%	2.8%	2.8%
Australian dollar	1.1%	1.5%	0.8%	0.4%	1.0%	1.1%	0.9%	1.1%
Canadian dollar	3.9%	2.9%	1.3%	0.6%	0.9%	1.2%	1.1%	1.3%
Other	0.5%	0.8%	1.4%	1.2%	1.5%	2.0%	1.8%	1.9%
Total	100.0%	100.0%	100.0%	100.0%	100.0%	100.0%	100.0%	100.0%

Source: Bank for International Settlements, Statistical Table 13B, www.bis.org. Based on figures genarated from www.bis.org.publ/ftrpdf/r_fa1106.pdf#page =118.

Five important trends are evident in the table. First, comparing the first lines of Tables 20.12 and 20.13, it is clear that the size of the bond and note market is many times larger than the size of the market for money market instruments. In June 2010, for example, bonds and notes on issue was nearly 30 times the amount of money market instruments on issue. Second, while the growth rate of the market slowed during the global financial crisis, it did not decline in value. Third, as we observed for the money market, the share of the market held by financial institutions has grown over the years and in June 2010 was around 75 per cent. Fourth, by far the dominant form is the straight fixed-rate issue. By contrast, equity-related issues have declined in relative importance. Fifth, unlike the instruments in the money market, the share of the US dollar has held reasonably steady. The share of the euro has grown and in June 2010 was slightly larger than the share of the US dollar. The share of most 'minor' currencies has declined, although the share of the Australian dollar has remained fairly steady, at around 1 per cent.

20.9.6 SYNDICATION

A distinctive feature of the international lending markets is the importance of syndication. As we mentioned in Section 20.9.4, a syndicate is a group of banks that provides the funds for a particular loan. Every bank in the syndicate provides an agreed proportion of the funds. Many types of loan agreements may be syndicated, including term credits and various kinds of issuance facilities.[37] Many syndicated loans use standardised contract terms to facilitate trading in the secondary market. Table 20.14 provides data on syndication.

TABLE 20.14 Value (in USD billions) of international syndicated credit facilities signed in various time periods, by nationality of the borrower

	4 YEARS ENDED 30 JUNE 1998	4 YEARS ENDED 30 JUNE 2002	4 YEARS ENDED 30 JUNE 2006	4 YEARS ENDED 30 JUNE 2010	16 YEARS ENDED 30 JUNE 2010
Total (USD billion)	$1973	$2633	$2524	$2385	$9515
USA	58.0%	58.8%	45.4%	33.8%	46.4%
UK	8.4%	8.8%	8.7%	8.2%	8.5%
France	2.7%	3.8%	5.4%	5.1%	4.5%
Germany	2.3%	2.9%	6.2%	4.8%	4.4%
Spain	2.0%	1.5%	2.9%	5.2%	3.2%
Canada	3.4%	2.8%	2.3%	3.1%	2.9%
Australia	1.6%	1.4%	2.1%	3.2%	2.2%
Japan	0.6%	1.8%	2.0%	3.0%	2.1%
Italy	1.1%	1.7%	2.5%	1.9%	1.9%
Switzerland	1.4%	1.2%	1.5%	1.6%	1.5%
Other developed countries	5.5%	6.4%	8.2%	9.7%	7.9%
Total developed countries	86.9%	91.1%	87.4%	79.6%	85.4%
Developing countries	10.6%	6.7%	10.0%	17.4%	11.9%
Offshore centres and international bodies	2.5%	2.3%	2.6%	3.1%	2.7%
Total	100.0%	100.0%	100.0%	100.0%	100.0%

Source: Bank for International Settlements, Statistical Table 10, **www.bis.org.** Based on figures genarated from **www.bis.org.publ/ftrpdf/r_fa1106.pdf#page =118.**

As shown in Table 20.14, the total value of new syndicated credit facilities has been about 2 to 2½ trillion US dollars every 4 years. By far the largest borrower country is the US, although its proportion has declined in recent years. Over the 16-year period, Australia has been the seventh largest borrower, with its share generally being between about 1 and 3 per cent of the total. Most of the funds are borrowed by entities from developed countries.

Connect Plus features a case study illustrating topics covered in this chapter.
Ask your lecturer or tutor for your course's unique URL.

---

37 For descriptions of alternative loan structures, see Fight (2004, Chapter 5).

SUMMARY

→ Australia has a relatively open economy and therefore many Australian financial managers need to be involved in international financial management. As markets increasingly become globally integrated, international financial management will become more and more a part of everyday business. This chapter covered the basic theories, evidence and management techniques of international finance.

→ The spot exchange rate is the price of one currency in terms of another, for (almost) immediate delivery. The forward exchange rate is for delivery on a specified later date. There is a competitive market in foreign exchange that, in Australia in 2009–10, averaged A$167 billion of transactions per day.

→ There are four central relationships in international finance:
 – Interest rate parity establishes an equilibrium between interest rates and exchange rates. Empirical evidence strongly supports the validity of interest rate parity.
 – The unbiased forward rate hypothesis suggests that the forward exchange rate equals the expected value of the future spot rate. The empirical evidence is somewhat mixed but tends towards rejection of this hypothesis.
 – Purchasing power parity suggests that the expected change in the exchange rate is due to differences in expected inflation rates. It is consistent with the observation that, at least in the very long run, a country with a high (low) inflation rate can expect to have a depreciating (appreciating) currency.
 – Uncovered interest parity suggests there is a relationship between relative interest rates and the expected change in the exchange rate.

→ It is notoriously difficult to forecast exchange rates and there is little evidence that 'experts' are able to do so. This outcome is expected when a market is highly competitive.

→ Exchange risk is the possibility of loss due to an unanticipated change in the exchange rate. The traditional techniques used to manage this risk require the adoption of an offsetting foreign exchange commitment achieved by buying (or selling) forward foreign currency, or by lending (or borrowing) foreign currency. While these techniques are appropriate in a one-off transaction, they are of doubtful long-term use for a repeat exporter (or importer) or for a multinational company. Contingent hedging refers to a situation in which the need to deal in foreign exchange is contingent on some other event, such as the response of another party. Foreign currency options provide a way to hedge contingent exchange risks.

→ The return on a foreign asset is determined by both the foreign currency return on the asset and the movement in the exchange rate. A major advantage of investing in foreign assets is the increased diversification of the investor's portfolio that such investment makes possible. The empirical evidence on the correlation between returns on different national share market indices suggests that there are likely to be significant expected benefits from international diversification. Borrowers may also benefit from international diversification.

→ A currency swap mimics an agreement to exchange loan payments; the effect of a currency swap is to change the currency in which a loan must be repaid. Currency swaps are often used to convert a foreign currency loan to a domestic currency loan, thus greatly reducing or even eliminating the exchange risk.

→ Australian companies have raised significant amounts by borrowing outside Australia. The sources of funds include foreign markets and Euromarkets and the forms of borrowing include loans and security issues. Banks and other financial institutions have been major borrowers. Many of these transactions have been entered with the intention of immediately hedging by means of a currency swap. An Australian-based foreign bond market (for 'Kangaroo' bond issues) has also developed.

KEY TERMS

bearer bond 726	exchange rate 687	note issuance facility (NIF) or revolving underwriting facility (RUF) 725
convertible bond 726	exchange risk 707	
covered interest arbitrage 694	floating-rate note 726	
credit risk 716	foreign bond 722	purchasing power parity 693
cross rate 690	foreign loan (in domestic currency) 722	revolving credit 724
currency swap 716		simple domestic bond 722
domestic loan (in foreign currency) 722	forward margin 689	spot rate 687
	forward rate 688	straight fixed-rate bond 726
Euro commercial paper 724	interest rate parity (or covered interest parity) 693	syndicate 724
Eurobond 722		term credit 724
Eurocredit 722	interest rate swap 716	unbiased forward rate 693
Euronote 724	international bond 723	uncovered interest parity or international Fisher effect 693
	law of one price 698	
	medium-term note (MTN) 726	

SELF-TEST PROBLEMS

1. The following retail exchange rates (per A$1) were taken from the *Australian Financial Review* of 18 March 2008:
   Fiji, dollar (FJD): 1.3895/1.3226
   Europe, euro (EUR): 0.6064/0.5874
   Based on these rates, calculate:
   (a) the minimum value of a Fiji dollar (in terms of euros)
   (b) the minimum value of a euro (in terms of Fiji dollars)
   (c) the upper and lower bounds on the exchange rate between these two currencies (on a per euro basis).

2. Assume that the buy/sell spread is zero and there are no transaction costs. You observe the following information on Australia and Utopia:
   Spot rate: A$1 = U$4.5700
   3-month A$ interest rate: 3.0 per cent per 3 months
   3-month U$ interest rate: 2.0 per cent per 3 months
   (a) Use interest rate parity to calculate the 3-month forward rate.
   (b) If Utopian interest rates increased to 4.0 per cent per 3 months (but there was no change in either the spot rate or Australian interest rates), what would the forward rate become?
   (c) Explain the results from (a) and (b).

Solutions to self-test problems are available in Appendix B, page 803.

REFERENCES

Baldwin, J. & Yan, B., 'Do Canadians pay more than Americans for the same products?', Statistics Canada cat. no. 11-624-MIE-No. 006, April 2004.

Bank for International Settlements, *Triennial Central Bank Survey: Report on Global Foreign Exchange Activity in 2010*, December 2010.

Battellino, R., 'Why do so many Australian borrowers issue bonds offshore?', Reserve Bank of Australia, *Bulletin*, December 2002, pp. 19–24.

Chiang, T.C., 'Empirical evidence on the predictors of future spot rates', *Journal of Financial Research*, Summer 1986, pp. 153–62.

Chinn, M.D., 'The (partial) rehabilitation of interest rate parity in the floating rate era: longer horizons, alternative expectations, and emerging markets', *Journal of International Money and Finance*, 2006, pp. 7–21.

Choi, C.Y., 'Searching for evidence of long-run PPP from a post-Bretton Woods panel: separating the wheat from the chaff', *Journal of International Money and Finance*, 2004, pp. 1159–86.

Clinton, K., 'Transaction costs and covered interest arbitrage: theory and evidence', *Journal of Political Economy*, April 1988, pp. 358–70.

Dufey, G. & Srinivasulu, S.L., 'The case for corporate management of foreign exchange risk', *Financial Management*, Winter 1983, pp. 54–62.

Easton, S.A. & Lalor, P.A., 'The accuracy and timeliness of survey forecasts of six-month and twelve-month ahead exchange rates', *Applied Financial Economics*, December 1995, pp. 367–72.

Fight, A. *Syndicated Lending*, Elsevier, Amsterdam, 2004.

Froot, K.A. & Thaler, R.H., 'Anomalies: foreign exchange', *Journal of Economic Perspectives*, Summer 1990, pp. 179–92.

Giddy, I.H., 'Why it doesn't pay to make a habit of forward hedging', *Euromoney*, December 1976, pp. 96–100.

Goodhart, C., 'The foreign exchange market: a random walk with a dragging anchor', *Economica*, November 1988, pp. 437–60.

Gregory, A. & McCurdy, T., 'The unbiasedness hypothesis in the forward exchange market', *European Economic Review*, 1986, pp. 365–81.

Gruen, D.W.R. & Gizycki, M.C., 'Explaining forward discount bias: is it anchoring?', Reserve Bank of Australia, *Research Discussion Paper*, no. 9307, 1993.

Hunt, B., 'Propheteering in the Australian FX market', Working paper no. 7/1987, Department of Finance, University of New South Wales.

Lothian, J. & Taylor, M., 'Real exchange rate behavior: the recent float from the perspective of the past two centuries', *Journal of Political Economy*, 1996, pp. 488–541.

Lyons, R.K., 'Optimal transparency in a dealer market with an application to foreign exchange', *Journal of Financial Intermediation*, 1996, pp. 225–54.

——, 'A simultaneous trade model of the foreign exchange hot potato', *Journal of International Economics*, 1997, pp. 275–98.

McFarland, J., McMahon, P. & Nagama, Y., 'Forward exchange rates and expectations during the 1920s: a re-examination of the evidence', *Journal of International Money and Finance*, 1994, pp. 627–36.

Manzur, M., 'How much are exchange rate forecasts worth?', *Australian Journal of Management*, June 1988, pp. 93–113.

Montague, B., 'Swaps', in R. Bruce, B. McKern, I. Pollard & M. Skully (eds), *Handbook of Australian Corporate Finance*, 5th edn, Butterworths, Sydney, 1997, pp. 356–97.

Officer, L.H., *Purchasing Power Parity and Exchange Rates: Theory, Evidence and Relevance*, JAI Press, Greenwich, Connecticut, 1982.

Organisation for Economic Co-operation and Development *OECD in Figures 2009*, OECD Publishing, 2009, www.oecd.org./infigures.

Ramchand, L. & Susmel, R., 'Volatility and cross-correlation across major stock markets', *Journal of Empirical Finance*, 1998, pp. 397–416.

Reserve Bank of Australia, Media release no. 2010–19, 1 September 2010.

Rogoff, K., 'The purchasing power parity puzzle', *Journal of Economic Literature*, June 1996, pp. 647–68.

Smith, C.W. Jr, Smithson, C.W. & Wakeman, L.M., 'The evolving market for swaps', in J.M. Stern & D.H. Chew (eds), *The Revolution in Corporate Finance*, 2nd edn, Basil Blackwell, Oxford, 1992, pp. 355–67.

——, ——, & Wilford, D.S., *Managing Financial Risk*, Harper Business, New York, 1990.

Sutton, W., *The Currency Options Handbook*, Woodhead-Faulkner, Cambridge, 1988.

Sweeney, M., 'Developing foreign currency benchmarks for performance measurement: a corporate treasury viewpoint', *International Journal of Business Studies*, 1998, pp. 1–22.

Thornton, D.L., 'Tests of covered interest parity', Federal Reserve Bank of St Louis, *Review*, July/August 1989, pp. 55–66.

Wu, J-L., Cheng, S-Y. & Hou, H., 'Further evidence on purchasing power parity and country characteristics', *International Review of Economics and Finance*, 2011, pp. 257–66.

Yang, L., Tapon, F. & Sun, Y., 'International correlations across stock markets and industries: trends and patterns 1988–2002', *Applied Financial Economics*, 2006, pp. 1171–83.

QUESTIONS

1. **[LO 8]** Diana owns a small chain of hairdressing salons in south-west Victoria and is considering expanding into other consumer service retail businesses. She calculates that she will need to borrow approximately $3 million and her bank has approved a loan for this amount at an annual interest rate of 12.5 per cent. Diana had asked about borrowing US dollars instead, because the annual interest rate was only around 9 per cent, but the bank declined her request. Diana feels sure she has missed a great opportunity and seeks your advice. Advise Diana.

2. **[LO 3]** It is well known that some currencies trade at a forward premium against the dollar while others trade at a forward discount against the dollar. Is it possible for a currency to do both at the same time? For

example, could a currency trade at a 3-month forward premium but a 6-month forward discount? Explain.

3. **[LO 3]** If interest rate parity holds between Australia and Canada, which, if any, of the following statements are true and which, if any, are false? Give reasons.
   (a) *An Australian company should be indifferent between borrowing Australian dollars and borrowing Canadian dollars.*
   (b) *Covered interest arbitrage will result in Canadian investors in Australian government bonds earning the same as Australian investors in Canadian government bonds.*
   (c) *Covered interest arbitrage will result in Australian investors in Australian government bonds earning the same as Australian investors in Canadian government bonds.*

4. **[LO 3]** Comment on the following argument:
   It is not necessarily very useful to know whether the forward rate is, or is not, an unbiased predictor of the future spot rate. On the one hand, a predictor might be unbiased but still, by any realistic measure, be so far off the mark as to be virtually useless. On the other hand, a predictor may be biased but nevertheless so close to the mark that it could be very useful indeed.

5. **[LO 3]** Explain the 'purchasing power parity' theorem. What factors do you think tend to inhibit the achievement of such parity?

6. **[LO 3]** Why do you think there is less dispersion in GDP per head in different countries when the currency conversion is made using PPP-adjusted exchange rates rather than current exchange rates? Does this imply that there is something systematically wrong with the foreign currency markets?

7. **[LO 5]** *Repeated forward rate hedging is ineffective for an importer.* Do you agree with this statement? Why/why not?

8. **[LO 5]** International Kangaroo Ltd (IKL) is based in Melbourne and has recently taken over three foreign-based manufacturers: Bald Eagle Inc. (of Topeka, Kansas), Maple Leaf Inc. (of Calgary, Alberta) and Thistle plc (of Glasgow, Scotland). All three of these companies export a substantial proportion of their output to various countries in Europe and North America. In addition, Maple Leaf and Thistle import about half of their raw materials from the US. Because of their exposure to international currency fluctuations, management in all four companies is experienced in both spot market and forward market transactions. Advise IKL on what changes it should consider.

9. **[LO 5]** Carefully evaluate the following proposition:
   A cost-conscious manager should never bother with foreign currency options; they cost a lot, whereas banks charge hardly anything for forward contracts.

10. **[LO 6]** You are working for an Australian mutual fund. The fund has investments in approximately 100 companies listed on the Australian Securities Exchange. The fund's manager is considering investing in foreign securities. She seeks your reaction to this idea. Write a brief report, pointing out the possible risks and benefits.

11. **[LO 6]** *International portfolio diversification is worthwhile only if the investor has good estimates of the future correlations between the returns on international and domestic investments.* Do you agree with this statement? Why/why not?

12. **[LO 6]** *The case for an Australian investor to diversify internationally is probably stronger than the case for a US investor to diversify internationally.* Do you agree with this statement? Why/why not?

13. **[LO 6]** Your aunt Ada retired many years ago from her position as a teacher at a Brisbane high school. She is a self-funded retiree, and has a range of investments in Australian shares, bonds and property. Recently, she told you that her financial adviser had suggested that she sell about one-third of her portfolio and instead invest in a mutual fund that specialises in US, UK and Japanese shares. Ada rejected this advice, explaining to you that, 'I know nothing about foreign investments. I have simple tastes and I have no intention of travelling overseas.' Advise Ada.

14. **[LO 8]** Crest Services is a successful Australian company that operates both domestically and in Singapore. It is planning to expand into New Zealand. To finance the expansion, it will need to increase its borrowings. Its board is unsure of the currency in which the borrowings should be made.

    Director A: 'Singapore has the lowest interest rates, so we should borrow Singapore dollars.'
    Director B: 'We're an Australian company, so why take unnecessary risks with foreign borrowings? We should borrow Australian dollars. We know we'll always have Australian dollar inflows to repay debt, but we don't know yet how we'll go in New Zealand.'

Director C: 'We'll be an internationally diversified company, so our debt should be, too. Borrow a mix of all three currencies: Australian, New Zealand and Singaporean, in roughly the same proportions as our assets.'

Critically appraise all three viewpoints. What advice would you give? Why?

15. **[LO 4]** Explain the meaning of the term LIBOR. If you collected daily data on 6-month US dollar LIBOR and corresponding information from the Singapore market for 12 months, what correlation would you expect to find between them? Why? Does this mean you could forecast LIBOR and therefore make money? Give reasons for your answer.

PROBLEMS

1. **Calculating using forward rates [LO 2]**
   The currency of the nation of Homeland is called the 'home' (symbol HLH). As in Australia, foreign currency is generally quoted in Homeland as a rate per unit of home currency (that is, per HLH1). The currency of Foreignland is called the 'foreign' (symbol FLF). You have asked the National Homeland Bank for a quote on the 3-month forward rate for 'foreigns' and have received the following reply:
   Spot rates: 4.6220 and 4.6290
   3 months' forward margin: +227/+237
   If you agree to sell FLF6 500 000 in 3 months' time, how much 'home' currency will you receive?

2. **Spreads and cross rates [LO 2]**
   The following retail exchange rates (per A$1) are taken from the *Australian Financial Review* of 14 March 2008:
   Canada, dollar 0.9342/0.9077
   Norway, krone 4.8035/4.6512
   US, dollar 0.9394/0.9246

   (a) Why is the spread narrower for the US dollar than for the other currencies?
   (b) Based on these rates, calculate:
      (i) the minimum value of a krone (in terms of Canadian dollars)
      (ii) the minimum value of a Canadian dollar (in terms of krone)
      (iii) the upper and lower bounds on the exchange rate between these two currencies (on a per Canadian dollar basis).

3. **Triangular arbitrage [LO 2]**
   Assume that the buy/sell spread is zero and that you are a currency dealer for a bank in Zurich. Simultaneously you observe the following spot exchange rates between UK pounds, US dollars and Swiss francs:
   GBP1 = USD1.4250
   USD1 = CHF1.5775
   CHF1 = GBP0.4465
   The marginal transaction cost is estimated to be one-tenth of 1 per cent. Explain the arbitrage that is available, and calculate the profit (after transaction costs) that can be made.

4. **Triangular arbitrage [LO 2]**
   Suppose that the following spot exchange rates are observed simultaneously:
   C$1 = US$0.7055
   A$1 = US$0.5980
   A$1 = C$0.8485
   If the marginal transaction cost is zero, what profit could you make if you began with A$1 million? What proportional transaction cost would eliminate this profit? Assuming that the first two exchange rates above in the question are correct, what should the third exchange rate be? Show your calculations.

5. **Cross rates [LO 2]**
   You observe the following current wholesale exchange rates:
   A$/US$ = 0.8330/0.8325
   NZ$/US$ = 0.7810/0.7800
   For example, the first exchange rate means that if you sell Australian dollars you will receive US$0.8325 for every Australian dollar you sell but if you sell US dollars you will receive A$1 for every US$0.8330 you sell. You have access to the wholesale markets. A client approaches you to ask at what rate(s) you would be willing to exchange New Zealand dollars for Australian dollars (and vice versa). You are keen to develop your relationship with this client, so, to impress the client, you offer to do the transaction on a break-even basis.

   (a) What rates would you quote to the client? Explain. Show conclusively that you are in a break-even position, assuming that the exchange rates given above do not change.
   (b) Your client does not proceed with the transaction. Later, you learn that your client has complained that immediately after receiving your quote, one

of your competitors offered them a slightly better quote than yours. Moreover, the rival firm has stated that it did not submit its quote on a break-even or loss-making basis. How could this happen?

6. **Interest rate parity [LO 3]**
   Assume that the buy/sell spread is zero and there are no transaction costs. You observe the following information on Australia and Xanadu:
   Spot rate: A$1 = X$1.4715
   1-month A$ interest rate: 0.6 per cent per month
   1-month X$ interest rate: 0.5 per cent per month
   Use interest rate parity to calculate the 1-month forward rate. Explain the result. If Xanadu interest rates increased to 0.7 per cent per month (but there was no change in either the spot rate or Australian interest rates), what would the forward rate become? Explain your answer.

7. **Interest rate parity [LO 3]**
   Suppose that the 90-day bill rate in Australia is 14.16 per cent per annum and in the UK it is 11.35 per cent per annum. The spot exchange rate is A$1 = £0.4143 and the 90-day forward rate is A$1 = £0.4105. Show that a disequilibrium exists and construct an example of one type of transaction that would tend to correct this disequilibrium. If all of the required adjustment is reflected in the forward rate, calculate the equilibrium forward rate.

8. **Covered interest arbitrage [LO 3]**
   Assume that the buy/sell spread is zero and there are no transaction costs. You observe the following:
   Spot rate: A$1 = US$0.8375
   6-month forward rate: A$1 = US$0.8290
   6-month A$ interest rate: 6.2 per cent per annum (simple interest)
   6-month US$ interest rate: 4.4 per cent per annum (simple interest)
   Assuming that you are authorised to borrow or lend up to A$2 million, calculate the cash profit you can make today.

9. **Hedging by borrowing and forward rate hedging [LO 5]**
   Dribnor Ltd is an Australian importer and expects to have to pay £1 million in 180 days' time. Interest rates for a term of 180 days are: in Australian dollars, 9.25 per cent per annum; in UK pounds (sterling), 6.15 per cent per annum. The spot rate is A$1 = £0.4240 and the 180-day forward rate is A$1 = £0.4178. Using this example, show that hedging by borrowing/lending is equivalent (in equilibrium) to forward rate hedging.

10. **Balance sheet hedging [LO 5]**
    Your friend Lan Kuan has asked you for some preliminary advice on a foreign exchange issue. She has the opportunity to become involved in a tourism business that is owned and operated by a Nepalese company. One aspect of the proposed involvement would require Lan Kuan to contribute 100 million Nepalese rupees (symbol: NPR) to the business in 3 years' time. She is concerned about future exchange rate changes and would like to lock in an Australian dollar value of this commitment. She has discovered from the website of the Nepalese Central Bank that the current spot exchange rate is NPR 1 = A$ 0.0175 but has been unable to find any reference to a 3-year forward contract. She fears that none is available.
    Lan Kuan has collected the following information:
    She could borrow Nepalese rupees for 3 years at 9 per cent per annum.
    She could lend Nepalese rupees for 3 years at 5. per cent per annum.
    She could borrow Australian dollars for 3 years at 8.25 per cent per annum.
    She could lend Australian dollars for 3 years at 6.95 per cent per annum.
    Show Lan Kuan how she would be able to lock in today an Australian dollar value of the commitment. In your answer, include the details of the transactions required (currency, timing, amounts, whether borrowed or lent, and so on).

11. **Balance sheet hedging [LO 5]**
    Xanadu is a developing nation. Its currency is called the lotus. The symbol for the lotus is XDL. The current spot exchange rate is A$1 = XDL20.37. The current 5-year interbank rate in Xanadu is 17 per cent per annum and in Australia the current 5-year interbank rate is 6 per cent per annum.
    Your company faces the following 5-year interest rates:
    in Xanadu: bank deposits 14 per cent per annum;
        borrowing 19.5 per cent per annum.
    in Australia: bank deposits 5 per cent per annum;
        borrowing 7 per cent per annum.

    (a) Calculate the equilibrium 5-year forward rate between the Australian dollar and the Xanadu lotus.

(b) You expect to receive XDL100 million in 5 years' time and you wish to take out forward cover. However, when you enquire at your bank you are told that the forward market for the lotus is extremely thin for periods longer than 1 year and it is therefore most unlikely that you will be able to get forward cover. What could you do?

(c) Suppose that, to encourage your company to operate in Xanadu, the Xanadu government is willing to lend you lotuses at the concessional rate of 12 per cent per annum. Does this make a difference to you? How?

12. **Unbiased forward rates [LO 3]**
On the first day of every month, Monpred Ltd releases its forecasts of the exchange rate (in US$ per A$1) for the first day of the subsequent month. Forecasts made during the first 6 months of 201X are shown in the following table:

Date forecast released	Forecast made (US$)
1 January	0.8950
1 February	0.8900
1 March	0.9350
1 April	0.8610
1 May	0.8450
1 June	0.8560

Actual spot exchange rates and 1-month forward exchange rates were observed on the following dates to be:

Date of observation	Spot rate	1-month forward rate
1 January	0.8994	0.9044
1 February	0.8716	0.8786
1 March	0.9290	0.9300
1 April	0.8850	0.8825
1 May	0.8330	0.8300
1 June	0.8550	0.8520
1 July	0.8190	0.8160

Assume that you are an Australian speculator who is willing to act on these forecasts by buying (or selling) A$10 000 forward each month (from January to June, inclusive). Complete a table showing, for each date, whether you bought or sold Australian dollars, and the resulting profit or loss (in A$).

13. **Real exchange rate [LO 3]**
Suppose that during a given year the Australian dollar appreciates by 8 per cent relative to the UK pound, while in the same year the Australian inflation rate is 6 per cent and the UK inflation rate is 3 per cent. What has happened (in percentage terms) to the real value of the UK pound relative to the Australian dollar?

14. **Real exchange rate [LO 2]**
In early 2010, the mayor of the City of Thornleigh, Councillor Bent, reviewed the 2010 budget allocation for the foreign book collection of the Thornleigh Municipal Library. Council policy is to increase real spending on the collection by 3 per cent a year. Ms Borrow, the city librarian, has sought a budget increase of 11 per cent because most imported books are priced in US dollars and in the past year their US prices have risen by an average of 8 per cent. Councillor Bent has checked the website of the Reserve Bank of Australia and found that the exchange rate between the US dollar and the Australian dollar was 0.6968 in early January 2009 and 0.8970 in early January 2010. Councillor Bent has calculated this change to be 28.7 per cent and has told the librarian that the allocation for 2010 will therefore be cut by 17.7 per cent (because 11 − 28.7 = −17.7). The 2009 allocation was A$720 000. Pauline, the city's chief accountant, is not convinced that the mayor is correct and has asked you for help. Advise Pauline. Develop and explain a formula that the city can use every year to calculate the coming year's allocation.

15. **Calculating rate of return on a foreign investment [LO 6]**
Alfred retired from work at the end of December 2007 and received a lump sum superannuation payment. He decided to invest this payment in a fund that invests in a range of US stocks. The fund is structured so that its value follows that of the Dow-Jones industrial average. In December 2008, Alfred decided to review his investments and collected the following data:

Date	Dow-Jones industrial average	ASX All Ordinaries	Exchange rate US$ per A$1
December 2007	12 650	5 697	0.8865
December 2008	8 001	3 478	0.6928

(a) Ignoring tax issues, calculate Alfred's rate of return and compare this with his rate of return had he instead invested in a fund structured so that its returns followed the ASX All Ordinaries index.

(b) In December 2009, Alfred again reviewed his investment. The Dow-Jones industrial average was then 10 067, the ASX All Ordinaries index was 4597 and the exchange rate was A$1 = US$0.8969. How has Alfred's investment fared since December 2008? Comment.

(c) What annual rate of return did Alfred earn over the 2-year period? What annual rate of return would he have earned if he had invested in Australian shares?

16. **Calculating rate of return on a hedged investment [LO 6]**

Gladys, an Australian investor, sold her portfolio of Australian shares and used the money to buy 50 000 shares in Drake & Raleigh plc, a British company, at a price of GBP 9.85 per share. She chose to enter into a forward contract to hedge her investment. When she bought the shares, the spot exchange rate was AUD/GBP = 0.4345-50, the 1-year forward margin was −80/−65, and Gladys estimated that the expected return on Drake & Raleigh shares was 11 per cent per annum. Gladys sold the shares a year later for GBP 9.28 per share when the AUD/GBP spot exchange rate was 0.4115-20. What rate of return did Gladys earn on her investment?

17. **Fixed-for-fixed currency swaps [LO 7]**

Panther is a South African company and Reindeer is a Swedish company. The fixed interest rates at which they can borrow money, repayable as an interest-only loan over 3 years (with annual payments), are:

	Borrowing in South African rand (ZAR)	Borrowing in Swedish kroner (SEK)
Panther	14.5% p.a.	4.5% p.a.
Reindeer	15.9% p.a.	4.8% p.a.

Ultimately, Panther wishes to borrow SEK 200 million, while Reindeer wishes to borrow ZAR 250 million. Initially, Panther will borrow rand while Reindeer will borrow kroner. The current exchange rate is SEK 1 = ZAR 1.25. An investment bank has offered to enter into standard fixed-for-fixed currency swaps with both companies. The bank would make ZAR swap payments at 14.5 per cent per annum to Panther, in return for SEK swap payments at 4.3 per cent per annum. The bank would make SEK swap payments to Reindeer at 4.8 per cent per annum in return for ZAR swap payments at 15.8 per cent per annum.

(a) Complete the following two tables. Use plus signs for cash inflows and minus signs for cash outflows.

Panther's cash flows (amounts)

	Original loan cash flows	Swap cash flows (SEK)	Swap cash flows (ZAR)	Total
Year 0				
Year 1				
Year 2				
Year 3				

Reindeer's cash flows (amounts)

	Original loan cash flows	Swap cash flows (SEK)	Swap cash flows (ZAR)	Total
Year 0				
Year 1				
Year 2				
Year 3				

(b) Should Panther and Reindeer accept the bank's offer? Explain.

(c) If Panther and Reindeer accept the bank's offer, what risk(s) does the bank incur? Explain.

Test yourself further with Connect Plus online! Ask your lecturer or tutor for your course's unique URL.

CHAPTER 21
MANAGEMENT OF SHORT-TERM ASSETS: INVENTORY

LEARNING OBJECTIVES

After studying this chapter you should be able to:

1. understand the importance of short-term assets in the Australian economy
2. identify the three major types of short-term assets
3. evaluate the need for short-term asset management
4. understand the relationship between short-term assets and short-term liabilities
5. identify the benefits and costs of holding inventory
6. understand the nature of acquisition costs, carrying costs and stockout costs
7. understand and apply the economic order quantity model
8. understand and apply models of inventory management under uncertainty
9. understand the difference between specifying an acceptable probability of stockout and specifying an acceptable expected customer service level.

CHAPTER CONTENTS

- 21.1 Introduction
- 21.2 The importance of short-term financial decisions
- 21.3 Types of short-term assets
- 21.4 The need for short-term asset management
- 21.5 Short-term assets and short-term liabilities
- 21.6 Overview of inventory management
- 21.7 Inventory costs: retailing and wholesaling
- 21.8 Inventory costs: manufacturing
- 21.9 Inventory management under certainty
- 21.10 Inventory management under uncertainty
- 21.11 Inventory management and the 'just-in-time' system

21.1 INTRODUCTION

Most of the financial decisions considered in previous chapters were long term, involving such decisions as the choice of capital structure and the selection of investments in property, plant and equipment. These assets are regarded as long term because normally they do not need to be replaced for several years. However, most companies also hold short-term assets such as **inventory**, **liquid assets** and **accounts receivable (or debtors)**. These are 'short term' because any individual item of inventory, or any particular liquid asset, or any single account receivable will generally be replaced or 'turned over' in a matter of days, weeks or months. Both short-term assets and long-term assets require a commitment of resources by the company, and thus both forms of investment deserve careful analysis by the financial manager. Similarly, both short-term and long-term liabilities deserve the financial manager's attention.

In Sections 21.2 to 21.5 we consider the general area of investment in short-term assets and the incurrence of short-term liabilities, while in Sections 21.6 to 21.11 we consider the management of the short-term asset—inventory. In the next chapter we will consider the management of liquid assets and accounts receivable.

inventory
comprises raw materials, work in progress, supplies used in operations and finished goods

liquid assets
comprise cash and assets that are readily convertible into cash, such as bills of exchange

21.2 THE IMPORTANCE OF SHORT-TERM FINANCIAL DECISIONS

Compared with multimillion dollar investments in, say, mining ventures, automated factories or space technology, the issues involved in investment in short-term assets may appear trivial. Although such a view is understandable, it is nevertheless incorrect from both theoretical and empirical viewpoints.

It was made clear in the chapters dealing with long-term investments that funds are invested to earn a competitive return. Short-term investments use resources in exactly the same way as long-term investments: a dollar invested in a short-term asset is a dollar not invested in some other asset. As a result, the wealth-maximising company will want to ensure that all its investments are selected and managed efficiently.

It is true that short-term financial decisions are usually less complex than long-term financial decisions. For example, a decision to build an automated factory may be based on forecasts of cash flows for perhaps 15 years, as well as an analysis of the risks involved. In contrast, a decision to invest surplus cash in, say, 90-day bank bills can be based on cash flow forecasts for a few months and a comparison of current interest rates on other short-term investments. However, the fact that short-term financial decisions are generally less complex does not necessarily mean that they are less important than long-term decisions. A company may have invested in projects with large positive net present values and adopted an ideal debt–equity ratio, but may get into severe difficulty because it overlooked the need to have sufficient cash available to meet this year's fixed commitments.

Regardless of how important an issue may appear to be in principle, its practical economic significance will generally be limited if there is very little money involved. However, there can be no doubt that a great deal of money is involved in short-term asset holdings. In Australia, the typical company holds about one-third of its total assets in short-term assets. However, this varies considerably between industries. For example, at the end of the 2010 financial year, Boral Ltd, a building and construction materials company, held 31 per cent of its assets in short-term assets, while BHP Billiton Ltd, a diversified mining company, held 28 per cent of its assets in short-term assets and Paperlinx Ltd, a paper manufacturer and wholesaler, held 77 per cent of its assets in short-term assets.

> **LEARNING OBJECTIVE 1**
> Understand the importance of short-term assets in the Australian economy

account receivable (or debtors)
sum of money owed to a seller as a result of having sold goods or services on credit

21.3 TYPES OF SHORT-TERM ASSET

The short-term assets held by businesses are of three major types as follows.

21.3.1 INVENTORY

LEARNING OBJECTIVE 2
Identify the three major types of short-term assets

For the manufacturer, inventory includes raw materials, work in progress and finished goods not yet sold. For the wholesaler and retailer, inventory consists mostly of merchandise in the warehouse or on the shelves.

21.3.2 LIQUID ASSETS (CASH AND SHORT-TERM INVESTMENTS)

Virtually all companies need to have at least some cash on hand in order to carry on business. For many purposes short-term investments such as bills of exchange, overnight deposits with the short-term money market and very short-term bank deposits are a good substitute for cash and have the added advantage that they generate interest revenue.

21.3.3 ACCOUNTS RECEIVABLE (DEBTORS)

Companies often extend short-term credit to their customers. For example, a supplier of goods may not require payment of the amount owed until a period of 30, 60 or even 90 days has passed. During the period from the date of purchase to the date of payment, the supplier has the short-term asset, 'account receivable'.

21.4 THE NEED FOR SHORT-TERM ASSET MANAGEMENT

LEARNING OBJECTIVE 3
Evaluate the need for short-term asset management

In a simple world of frictionless, perfect markets there would be no need for a company to hold short-term assets and consequently issues concerning their management would not arise. For example, if a company required more raw materials it would be able to obtain them instantaneously at the current market price. Under these conditions there would clearly be no need to hold an inventory of raw materials. The same is true of other forms of inventory. Cash holdings are in the same position because any shortage could be instantaneously met at the current market price (interest rate). Similarly, in the case of accounts receivable there would be no need for the company to wait for the customer's payment because, as we explain in Chapter 22, the asset could be sold for its present value.

The point is that, unlike most of the topics studied in finance, the model of the frictionless, perfectly competitive market is usually not a useful starting point for the analysis of short-term asset management. This is not because markets in short-term assets are not competitive; indeed, they are often highly competitive. The problem lies more in the assumption that markets are 'frictionless'. For example, a major reason for holding inventories of raw materials is the fact that there are delays and uncertainties involved in obtaining new supplies. Delays and uncertainties involve costs (both explicit and implicit) and therefore constitute a source of 'friction'. To a lesser extent the same is true of cash. Finally, while it is true that accounts receivable can often be sold ('factored' or 'discounted') if desired, most companies choose not to do so.[1] While there will be legal and administrative costs involved in discounting, perhaps of even more significance are the 'information costs'. Many companies know their customers well and can form reliable estimates of the likelihood of receiving payment, but the discounting company—that is, the purchaser of the accounts receivable—would need to expend resources to obtain the information it needs to form its own estimates. Naturally, the cost of obtaining this information is built into the price

---

1 Discounting is discussed in Chapter 10.

offered by the discounting company. The result, of course, is that a company will usually choose to hold rather than sell an account receivable. Again, therefore, a source of friction has proved to be significant. In this case the friction is the cost of obtaining information.

Because we do not assume frictionless, perfect markets, the analysis of short-term asset management tends to have a different 'feel' from many other topics in finance. Indeed, many of the issues involved are often discussed not only in finance but also in related disciplines such as management accounting and operations research. Nevertheless, the management of short-term assets should be of vital concern to the financial manager. As noted previously, short-term assets involve a commitment of the company's resources. Good decisions will mean efficient use of those resources and will result in increased wealth for the shareholders; poor decisions will have the opposite effect.

In principle, decisions about investments in short-term assets can be approached using the net present value model in the same way as decisions about long-term assets. For example, an account receivable should be held if its net present value is positive, but should not be held if its net present value is negative. As usual, the appropriate discount rate to apply is the opportunity cost of capital, which in this case is the rate of return required on an asset that has the same risk as the account(s) receivable. To estimate the opportunity cost, the capital asset pricing model could be applied, given an estimate of the beta of accounts receivable.[2] Unfortunately, such estimates are difficult, if not impossible, to obtain. In most cases, pursuing this approach does not provide practical solutions in this area, despite the validity of the principles involved. Although wealth maximisation is still the ultimate objective, different techniques are often needed to estimate and optimise the costs and benefits.

21.5 SHORT-TERM ASSETS AND SHORT-TERM LIABILITIES

Although the focus of Chapters 21 and 22 is the management of short-term or **current assets**, it should also be remembered that managers must also make decisions about short-term or **current liabilities**. Managers are likely to try to maintain a fairly stable relationship between the maturity structure of the company's assets and the maturity structure of its liabilities. For example, life insurance companies tend to hold a relatively large proportion of their assets in the form of long-term investments because the average life insurance policy is not expected to mature until a relatively long time has elapsed. This 'matching policy' also applies to shorter maturities, so a company whose current assets comprise a relatively large proportion of its total assets will often make greater use of short-term debt than other companies.

The basic ideas underlying the matching policy are easily explained. Assume that a company has only one non-current asset. By borrowing for a period equal to the asset's life, management expects that the asset will generate cash flows sufficient to meet the payments required by the loan. A short-term asset and its matching liability may each involve only one cash flow. The matching policy is seen very clearly in the case of trade bills, which usually require the drawer to pay the face value of the bill on a future date that coincides with the date on which the drawer expects to receive payment for the goods that have been sold.[3] If the maturity of the liability is shorter than the life of the asset, then there is a risk that the company either will not have sufficient cash to repay the debt or will not be able to renew the debt. If the maturity of the debt is longer than the life of the asset, then there is a risk that the company will not have sufficient alternative sources of cash at the end of the asset's life to continue meeting the interest payments on the debt.

To illustrate the matching policy, we considered matching a particular asset with a particular liability but, in practice, the matching policy usually does not need to be carried to such an extreme. Instead,

LEARNING OBJECTIVE 4
Understand the relationship between short-term assets and short-term liabilities

current assets
cash, inventory, accounts receivable and other assets that will normally be converted into cash within a year

current liabilities
debt or other obligations due for payment within a year

---
2 See Section 7.6.2 for a discussion of the capital asset pricing model.
3 See Section 10.5.3 for a more detailed description of bills of exchange.

managers will often focus on broad aggregates relating to different classes of assets and liabilities. For example, managers may classify assets and liabilities into four maturity classes: very short term, short term, medium term and long term. Within each class, managers will seek to maintain a balance between assets and liabilities. Alternatively, the managers may seek to balance the average maturity of assets and liabilities. A more sophisticated approach is to calculate the 'duration' of the company's assets and select a matching liability structure. As discussed in Appendix 4.1, duration is the appropriate measure of maturity where it is sought to immunise a portfolio against changes in interest rates.

21.6 OVERVIEW OF INVENTORY MANAGEMENT

There are three main types of inventory.

(a) *Raw materials inventory* comprises inventory that will form part of the completed product of a manufacturer, but which has yet to enter the production process. For example, iron ore is an important raw material that would be held in inventory by a steel producer.
(b) *Work in progress inventory* comprises partially completed products that require additional processing before they become finished goods.
(c) *Finished goods inventory* for a manufacturer is completed products not yet sold; for a retailer or wholesaler it is merchandise on hand.

Inventories form a substantial part of a typical company's investment in short-term assets. For example, at the end of the 2010 financial year Boral Ltd held 34 per cent of its short-term assets in the form of inventories, while the percentages for BHP Billiton Ltd and Paperlinx Ltd were 21 and 29 per cent, respectively. The size of the investment suggests that inventory management is needed in every business.

Before considering in detail the costs and benefits of holding inventory, the major issues involved in inventory management are illustrated by a simple example. Suppose that the manager of a retail store is considering the level of inventory the store should hold. *If too little inventory is held* there will frequently be occasions when customers will arrive at the store, ready and willing to buy a product, only to find that it is unavailable. Sales will be lost and customer goodwill will suffer. Also, if the inventory level is too low, the store will need to reorder the products it sells at more frequent intervals, thus incurring the costs of ordering more often than would otherwise be the case. *If too much inventory is held* these problems will be avoided, but a different set of problems will arise. High inventory levels tie up large amounts of capital and lead to high storage and insurance costs.

The choice of inventory level therefore involves a balancing of costs and benefits. However, it is convenient to think of the benefits as 'costs avoided'. For example, the benefit of a retailer always having inventory on hand can be thought of as avoiding the 'costs' of lost sales and lost customer goodwill. Viewed in this way, inventory management becomes a problem of cost minimisation.

The costs of holding inventory are generally classified into three groups: *acquisition costs*, *carrying costs* and *stockout costs*.

LEARNING OBJECTIVE 5
Identify the benefits and costs of holding inventory

21.7 INVENTORY COSTS: RETAILING AND WHOLESALING

21.7.1 ACQUISITION COSTS

The most obvious cost of acquiring inventory is the price paid for each unit of inventory. However, unless there are quantity discounts available (as discussed in Section 21.9.4), the unit price is the same, regardless of inventory policy, and is therefore not relevant to the choice of policy. Relevant acquisition costs are those that vary with the inventory policy adopted. These costs include:

(a) *ordering costs*: clerical costs are incurred every time an order is placed
(b) *freight and handling costs*: every order placed will result in freight costs and, when the goods are received, handling costs
(c) *quantity discounts forgone*: larger orders will often attract a discount in price. If smaller orders are placed, these discounts will not be obtained and consequently an opportunity cost is incurred.

Per unit of inventory, each of these costs will be lower, the larger the order placed. Large orders imply relatively infrequent ordering and high inventory levels.

> **LEARNING OBJECTIVE 6**
> Understand the nature of acquisition costs, carrying costs and stockout costs

21.7.2 CARRYING COSTS

After inventory has been acquired, it must be held (or 'carried'). The higher the inventory level, the higher will be the total carrying costs. Carrying costs include:

(a) *Opportunity cost of investment*: inventory ties up capital that could have been invested elsewhere in the company's activities. For example, if the opportunity cost of capital is 10 per cent per annum, then holding $100 of inventory involves an annual cost of $10.
(b) *Storage costs*: after inventory is received, it must be stored. This will involve the payment of rent or, if the company owns its storage facilities, the forgoing of rental revenue that could otherwise have been earned. Storage costs can be high for goods that are bulky and also for those that require special handling, such as refrigeration.
(c) *Insurance premiums*: if the inventory is insured, the premiums will probably vary directly with the value of the inventory held.
(d) *Deterioration and obsolescence*: losses attributable to these factors are likely to be higher for higher levels of inventory.
(e) *Price movements*: if there is a decrease in the price of merchandise held in inventory, a loss is incurred. If there is an increase in price, a gain is made, and this element of the carrying cost is negative.

21.7.3 STOCKOUT COSTS

Avoidance of stockout costs is the major benefit of holding inventory. If a company's inventory of a particular item is completely exhausted, customers may purchase elsewhere in order to obtain immediate delivery. Sales are lost. Many customers soon lose patience in this situation and may switch all their business to a competitor, thus causing further sales to be lost.

21.8 INVENTORY COSTS: MANUFACTURING

21.8.1 INVENTORIES OF RAW MATERIALS

The costs that apply to a manufacturer faced with the problem of choosing an inventory level for raw materials are similar to those that apply to retailers and wholesalers. The major difference relates to stockout costs. For a manufacturer, a shortage of raw materials inventory will disrupt the production process and impose costs because equipment and labour will be underutilised.

21.8.2 INVENTORIES OF FINISHED GOODS

As well as holding an inventory of raw materials, most manufacturers hold an inventory of their finished products. In this case, carrying costs and stockout costs are similar to those faced by a retailer or a wholesaler, but the acquisition costs differ in that the set-up costs for a production run may also have to be included. Set-up costs are the costs incurred each time a new production run is started. High set-up costs call for larger production runs to spread the costs over a greater number of units produced in each run. In turn, this implies that a high level of finished products inventory will be carried.

A rigorous way of determining the inventory level that minimises the costs of holding inventory is to use a quantitative model. One such model is the economic order quantity model, which is discussed in the next section.

21.9 INVENTORY MANAGEMENT UNDER CERTAINTY

The economic order quantity model is designed to help a manager determine the inventory level that minimises the total costs associated with inventory.

21.9.1 THE ECONOMIC ORDER QUANTITY (EOQ) MODEL

LEARNING OBJECTIVE 7
Understand and apply the economic order quantity model

The EOQ model assumes that demand for the product is constant (per unit of time) and known with certainty.[4] It is also assumed that no quantity discounts are available and that orders of new inventory are filled instantly—that is, the lead time between ordering and receiving items to be held in inventory is assumed to be zero. There is, therefore, no need to order inventory until the current inventory level reaches zero. This situation is illustrated in Figure 21.1.

FIGURE 21.1 Inventory cycles

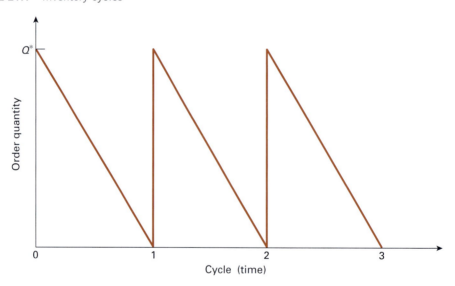

The company places an order for Q units at time zero. Since demand is constant, this inventory level will then fall steadily over time. At Time 1, inventory has reached zero, so a new order for Q units is placed and instantly filled, restoring the inventory level to Q. The second cycle then begins and the process is repeated. This process continues throughout the year.

economic order quantity (EOQ)
optimal quantity of inventory ordered that minimises the cost of purchasing and holding the inventory

The problem is to choose an order quantity Q that will minimise the total cost of the inventory policy.[5] The value of Q that achieves this goal is called the **economic order quantity** (**EOQ**) and is denoted here by Q^*. After Q^* has been calculated, the optimal time period between the placement of each order is found by dividing demand per period, D, by the economic order quantity, Q^*. For example,

---

[4] In Section 21.10 this assumption is removed and the problem is examined allowing for uncertain demand.
[5] Note that no stockout cost has been specified. Under conditions of certainty, stockouts need never occur. Similarly, stockouts need never occur if orders are filled instantly.

if demand is 12 000 units per year, and the economic order quantity is found to be 1000, orders need to be placed 12 times per year—that is, monthly.

In calculating EOQ, the notation we use is:

D = demand (in physical units) per period (e.g. demand per year)

a = acquisition costs ($) per order placed

c = carrying cost ($) per period per unit of inventory, including the opportunity cost of capital invested in inventory

Q = quantity (in physical units) per order

p = price ($) per unit of inventory

Inventory policy will affect the acquisition costs and carrying costs. These costs are defined as follows:

Acquisition costs per year

= acquisition costs per order × number of orders per year

$$= a\frac{D}{Q}$$

Carrying costs per year

= annual carrying cost per unit of inventory × average inventory

In each cycle the initial inventory is Q units, and over the cycle the inventory declines steadily to zero. Therefore, the average inventory level is $\frac{Q}{2}$.

Therefore:

Carrying costs per year = $c\frac{Q}{2}$

The annual total cost, TC, of the inventory policy is the sum of the acquisition and carrying costs and is given by:

$$TC = \frac{aD}{Q} + \frac{cQ}{2} \qquad [21.1]$$

The relationship between acquisition and carrying costs and the total cost of the inventory policy is illustrated in Figure 21.2.

FIGURE 21.2 Determining economic order quantity

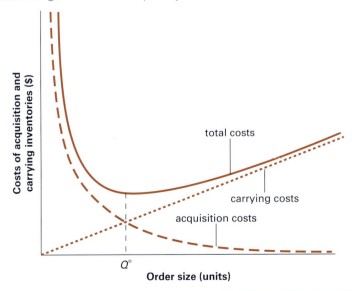

Note that acquisition costs, $\frac{aD}{Q}$, decrease as the order quantity, Q, increases because with a larger order quantity there will be fewer orders. However, carrying costs, $\frac{cQ}{2}$, increase as the order quantity increases because with larger orders, the average inventory level will be higher. The economic order quantity, Q^*, is the value of Q, which minimises total cost. This quantity may be found using the following equation:[6]

$$Q^* = \sqrt{\frac{2aD}{c}} \qquad [21.2]$$

The application of this model is illustrated in the following three examples.

EXAMPLE 21.1

Retailing

Clarke's Photography Store sells 12 000 packets of photographic paper per year. The wholesale price is $3 per packet. The cost of processing each order to be placed with the wholesaler is $12.50 and carrying costs are 30 cents per packet per year. What is the economic order quantity and the optimal time period between orders?

SOLUTION

In this example $D = 12\,000$, $a = 12.5$ and $c = 0.3$. Using Equation 21.2:

$$Q^* = \sqrt{\frac{2aD}{c}}$$
$$= \sqrt{\frac{(2)(12.5)(12\,000)}{0.3}}$$
$$= 1000 \text{ packets}$$

The number of orders per year $= \frac{12\,000}{1000}$
$$= 12$$

Therefore, orders are placed monthly.

EXAMPLE 21.2

Manufacturing (raw materials inventory)

Cranfield Manufacturing Ltd uses 4500 metres of wire each year in its production process. Acquisition costs are $250 per order and the wire costs $1 per metre per year to store. What is the economic order quantity and the optimal time period between orders?

SOLUTION

In this example $D = 4500$, $a = 250$ and $c = 1$. Using Equation 21.2:

$$Q^* = \sqrt{\frac{2aD}{c}}$$
$$= \sqrt{\frac{(2)(250)(4500)}{1}}$$
$$= 1500 \text{ metres}$$

The number of orders per years $= \frac{4500}{1500}$
$$= 3$$

Therefore, orders are placed three times per year—that is, once every 4 months.

---

[6] Equation 21.2 may be derived by differentiating Equation 21.1 with respect to Q and setting the derivative equal to zero.

> **EXAMPLE 21.3**
>
> **Manufacturing (finished goods inventory)**
> Dunbar Fabricating Ltd produces a specialised type of metal sheeting. Demand is 5000 sheets per year. Each production run costs $1750 to set up and storage costs are $25 per sheet per year. What is the optimal size of a production run and the optimal number of runs per year?
>
> **SOLUTION**
> In this example $D = 5000$, $a = 1750$ and $c = 25$. Using Equation 21.2:
>
> $$Q^* = \sqrt{\frac{2aD}{c}}$$
>
> $$= \sqrt{\frac{(2)(1750)(5000)}{25}}$$
>
> $$= 837 \text{ sheets}$$
>
> The number of production runs per year is $\frac{5000}{837}$, or approximately six per year. Therefore, a production run should be scheduled every 2 months.

21.9.2 COST ESTIMATION

The relevant costs in the EOQ model are incremental costs and may be difficult to estimate in practice. Accounting systems may not be designed to separate inventory costs from other operating costs and, even if they are, they will generally provide average rather than marginal costs. Fortunately, both the optimal order quantity and, more importantly, total inventory costs are likely to be fairly insensitive to errors in estimates of unit costs. Two factors contribute to this property of the model. First, suppose the acquisition cost, a, is doubled, or the carrying cost, c, is halved. The optimal order quantity, Q^*, will then increase by a factor of only $\sqrt{2}$ if all other factors remain unchanged. Second, the total cost, TC, in Equation 21.1 is generally not very sensitive to changes in the order quantity. As may be seen from Figure 21.2, this is particularly so in the region of Q^*. Example 21.4 illustrates the effects of a large error in estimating the acquisition cost.

> **EXAMPLE 21.4**
>
> **Cost estimation**
> In Example 21.1, $D = 12\,000$, $a = 12.5$, $c = 0.3$ and it was found that $Q^* = 1000$. Suppose that the true value of the acquisition cost a is $25 per order, but management believes it is only $12.50. What is the effect of this estimation error on the company's total cost?
>
> **SOLUTION**
> The effect of this estimation error can be assessed by comparing:
>
> (a) the cost of the optimal inventory policy that management would adopt if it had the correct information, with
> (b) the cost of the inventory policy that management believes to be optimal, based on its incorrect estimates.
>
> Using the true value of a and Equation 21.2, the economic order quantity would be:
>
> $$Q^* = \sqrt{\frac{2aD}{c}}$$
>
> $$= \sqrt{\frac{(2)(25)(12\,000)}{0.3}}$$
>
> $$= 1414 \text{ packets}$$
>
> *continued →*

Example 21.4 *continued*

The annual total cost of the optimal inventory policy using Equation 21.1 would be:

$$TC = \frac{(25)(12\,000)}{1414} + \frac{(0.3)(1414)}{2}$$
$$= \$424$$

But management, believing that a is $12.50, will choose an order quantity of 1000 packets. The annual cost of this policy is:

$$TC = \frac{(25)(12\,000)}{1000} + \frac{(0.3)(1000)}{2}$$
$$= \$450$$

The annual cost of adopting management's estimate of a is only $26 or 6.1 per cent more than the annual cost under the 'true' optimal policy. Therefore, the EOQ model is fairly robust, and should work well in practice, despite difficulties in making accurate estimates of the input data.

21.9.3 THE EOQ MODEL WITH POSITIVE LEAD TIME

In the previous discussion, lead time was assumed to be zero—that is, it was assumed that when an order was placed it was filled instantly. In most cases such an assumption is unrealistic, because after an order has been placed it will almost always take time for the goods to be delivered and placed in inventory. With a positive lead time, a new order must be placed before the current inventory level reaches zero. To minimise carrying costs, the reorder point is chosen so that goods from the new order are placed in inventory just as the inventory level reaches zero.

EXAMPLE 21.5

Referring to Example 21.2, suppose that it takes 1 month for Cranfield's wire orders to be delivered and placed in inventory. What is the effect of this lead time on Cranfield's inventory policy?

SOLUTION

Under these circumstances, Cranfield simply reorders wire when the current inventory level is equal to 1 month's usage. The amount used each month is $\frac{1500}{4} = 375$. This is illustrated in Figure 21.3.

FIGURE 21.3 Choosing a reorder point

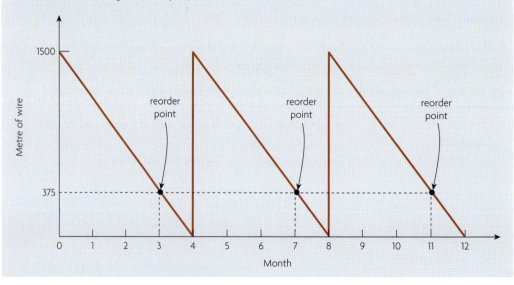

21.9.4 THE EOQ MODEL WITH QUANTITY DISCOUNTS

If discounts are available on larger quantity orders, then the price of the inventory is relevant to determining the economic order quantity. As the order quantity increases, the purchase of the inventory benefits from the lower price paid for each unit of inventory, and from spreading the other acquisition costs over a larger order quantity. However, carrying costs increase as the inventory level increases. The procedures for dealing with quantity discounts are shown in Example 21.6.

EXAMPLE 21.6

Consider again the case of Clarke's Photography Store, discussed in Example 21.1. In that example, annual demand, D, was 12 000 packets of paper; the price, p, was $3 per packet; acquisition costs a were $12.50 per order; and carrying costs c were 30 cents per packet per year. Suppose, however, that the wholesaler offers Clarke's Photography Store quantity discounts as shown in Table 21.1.

What is the optimal inventory policy with the quantity discounts?

TABLE 21.1 Photographic paper prices with quantity discounts

PURCHASE QUANTITY, Q	PRICE PER PACKET, p ($)
1–500	3.00
501–1499	2.98
1500–2499	2.96
2500–4999	2.94
5000 and over	2.92

SOLUTION

The annual total cost, TC, to Clarke's Photography Store is given by:

$$TC = \text{inventory costs} + \text{acquisition costs} + \text{carrying costs}$$

$$= pD + \frac{aD}{Q} + \frac{cQ}{2}$$

$$= 12\,000p + \frac{150\,000}{Q} + 0.15Q$$

In the absence of quantity discounts, the economic order quantity, Q^*, was found to be 1000 packets. It can be shown that with quantity discounts the optimal price–quantity combination must be one of the following combinations (Goetz 1965):

$p = \$3.00$ and $Q = 500$
$p = \$2.98$ and $Q = 1000$
$p = \$2.96$ and $Q = 1500$
$p = \$2.94$ and $Q = 2500$
$p = \$2.92$ and $Q = 5000$

These combinations are found by the following procedure. First, locate the optimal quantity in the absence of quantity discounts, and the price that would be payable for that quantity if there were quantity discounts. In this case $Q = 1000$ and $p = \$2.98$. This is Combination (b). Next, in each of the quantity ranges provided in Table 21.1, select the quantity nearest to the optimal quantity in the absence of discounts (in this case 1000). For example, in the quantity range 2500–4999, the quantity nearest to 1000 is 2500. The price payable in that case is $2.94 per packet. This is Combination (d). The final step is to calculate the total

continued →

Example 21.6 continued

cost for each of the combinations of price and quantity, and to select the combination that achieves the lowest total cost. These calculations are as follows:

(a) $(12\,000)(3.00) + \dfrac{150\,000}{500} + (0.15)(500) = \$36\,375$

(b) $(12\,000)(2.98) + \dfrac{150\,000}{1000} + (0.15)(1000) = \$36\,060$

(c) $(12\,000)(2.96) + \dfrac{150\,000}{1500} + (0.15)(1500) = \$35\,845$

(d) $(12\,000)(2.94) + \dfrac{150\,000}{2500} + (0.15)(2500) = \$35\,715$

(e) $(12\,000)(2.92) + \dfrac{150\,000}{5000} + (0.15)(5000) = \$35\,820$

The lowest cost combination is (d), and the economic order quantity is therefore 2500 packets.

21.10 INVENTORY MANAGEMENT UNDER UNCERTAINTY

LEARNING OBJECTIVE 8
Understand and apply models of inventory management under uncertainty

In Section 21.9 it is assumed that management is certain about the value of each relevant variable. In particular, it is assumed that retailers and wholesalers know, with certainty, the level of demand, while manufacturers are assumed to know, with certainty, the rate at which the raw materials inventory would be used in production. Suppose, however, that demand (or usage as the case may be) is uncertain. If the lead time between placement of an order and its delivery is zero, the presence of uncertainty is not a problem. If demand or usage should suddenly increase, management can respond by simply placing an order that is filled instantly and therefore no stockout need occur. However, as explained previously, the lead time for filling orders is usually positive, and therefore stockouts may occur during this time.

Inventory management requires two important decisions. First, management must choose the *quantity* to be ordered. Second, management must choose the *reorder point*—that is, the level of inventory that will trigger the placement of a new order. Most of the discussion of inventory decisions under certainty related to the quantity decision. The reorder point decision was solved simply by reordering when the current inventory level would just equal demand (or usage) during the lead time. In Example 21.5, Cranfield's reorder point is 375 metres of wire, because this level is exactly equal to 1 month's usage and the lead time is 1 month. The new order would arrive at Cranfield's factory at precisely the moment when the inventory reached zero. In contrast, under uncertainty, while the quantity decision will be the same as that made when certainty is assumed, the reorder point decision requires a more sophisticated analysis.

safety stock
additional inventory held when demand is uncertain, to reduce the probability of a stockout

A standard approach to inventory management under uncertainty is as follows. First, the quantity decision is made by applying the certainty-based EOQ model, using the best estimate of demand (or usage). Second, the reorder point decision is made by adding a 'safety stock' to the reorder point that would have been chosen under conditions of certainty—that is, management deliberately chooses to reorder at a time when the current inventory level exceeds the quantity likely to be required during the lead time. The amount of this excess is called the **safety stock**. For example, if the rate at which Cranfield uses wire is uncertain, its management may decide on a safety stock of 250 metres of wire. In that case the reorder point is (375 + 250) = 625 metres instead of 375 metres. An order is placed when 625 metres of wire is still in inventory, even though it is expected that when the new order arrives in 1 month's time, only 375 metres will have been used so there will still be 250 metres of wire in inventory. Figure 21.4 shows the expected inventory level through time.

FIGURE 21.4 Choosing a reorder point with safety stock

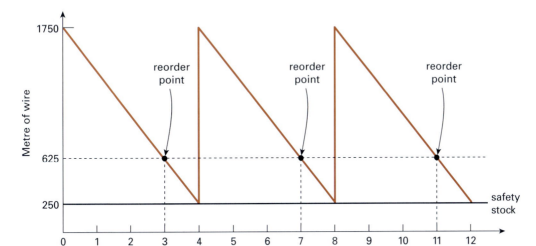

So far we have illustrated the *notion* of safety stock but have not provided any insight into the factors that *determine its size*. There are two approaches to determining safety stock size: the first specifies an acceptable probability of a stockout occurring during the lead time and the second specifies an acceptable expected level of customer service.

Both approaches are explained by using the example of Quintro Electronics Ltd, a wholesale supplier of electronic components. Quintro is open for business for 50 weeks each year. The annual demand for one of Quintro's components is 50 000 units. The lead time for new orders is exactly 1 week. On a weekly basis, demand has an expected value, $E(D)$, of 1000 and the probability distribution shown in Table 21.2.

TABLE 21.2 Probability distribution of weekly demand

PROBABILITY	QUANTITY DEMANDED
0.02	665
0.05	700
0.10	800
0.18	900
0.30	1000
0.18	1100
0.10	1200
0.05	1300
0.02	1335

Acquisition costs are $200 per order, and carrying costs are 20 cents per component per year. Regardless of the approach taken to calculate the safety stock, using Equation 21.2 the economic order quantity, Q^*, is found to be:

$$Q^* = \sqrt{\frac{(2)(200)(50\,000)}{0.2}}$$
$$= 10\,000 \text{ units}$$

The next problem is to determine the reorder point. To what level should inventory be allowed to fall before a new order is placed? The two approaches to answering this question are explained in Sections 21.10.1 and 21.10.2.

21.10.1 SPECIFYING AN ACCEPTABLE PROBABILITY OF STOCKOUT

The first approach requires that Quintro's management must determine an acceptable probability of a stockout during the lead time of 1 week. Suppose Quintro's management decides that it is prepared to accept a 2 per cent probability of a stockout. From Table 21.2 it can be seen that there is a 2 per cent chance that demand during the lead time will be more than 1300 units. The safety stock is therefore 300 units and the reorder point is 1300 units. If a safety stock level of 300 units is held, the customer's needs will be less than fully satisfied in 2 per cent of all lead times.

21.10.2 SPECIFYING AN ACCEPTABLE EXPECTED CUSTOMER SERVICE LEVEL

LEARNING OBJECTIVE 9

Understand the difference between specifying an acceptable probability of stockout and specifying an acceptable expected customer service level

The approach based on stockout probability is often unsatisfactory because for most suppliers it focuses on the wrong measure. Suppose, for example, that during a particular lead time, demand exceeds 1300 units. In this case Quintro cannot meet the demand for electronic components and this is therefore one of those lead times during which a stockout occurs. However, this does not indicate anything about the magnitude of the stockout problem. Knowing that a stockout has occurred does not provide any information on *how many* sales were lost. Given that the cost of a stockout depends directly on the number of lost sales, simply knowing that a stockout has occurred provides very little information about the costs incurred. Likewise, knowing the probability of a stockout provides very little information about the likely costs. For example, suppose demand during a particular lead time is 1335 units. In this case only 35 units of sales have been lost, and the stockout cost is quite low.

The same point can be made by referring to the 'customer service level', which can be quantified by calculating the ratio of sales to the level of orders and expressing this ratio as a percentage. If demand is 1335 units, the customer service level is 1300/1335 or 97.38 per cent. This indicates that a high service level, and therefore a low level of stockout costs, has been maintained, notwithstanding the fact that a stockout has occurred. Presumably, most managers are more concerned about the impact of a stockout on the customer service level than they are about the probability of a stockout. This suggests that inventory policy should be based on an expected (target) level of customer service, rather than on a target level of stockout probability. The procedures needed to calculate the inventory level required for this policy are set out in Example 21.7.

EXAMPLE 21.7

Suppose that Quintro's management decides that it will accept, on average, a 98 per cent expected customer service level during the lead time—that is, it is Quintro's policy that there should be a probability of 0.02 that any particular customer's demand during the lead time will not be met. What is the required level of safety stock and the corresponding reorder point?

SOLUTION

For each possible quantity demanded, the customer service level will be 100 per cent if the safety stock is sufficient to meet the level of demand. If the safety stock is insufficient to meet the level of demand, the customer service level will be the sum of the expected demand during the lead time (in this case 1000 units) and the safety stock divided by the quantity demanded. For example, if the safety stock is 50 units, the customer service level in those cases where demand is 1100 will be $\frac{1000 + 50}{1100}$ or 95.45 per cent. The expected customer service level may then be found by summing across the customer service levels for each possible quantity demanded.

For example, if the safety stock is 50 units, then the expected customer service level given the possible levels of demand shown in Table 21.2 is:

$$(0.02)(1) + (0.05)(1) + (0.10)(1) + (0.18)(1) + (0.30)(1) + (0.18)\left(\frac{1050}{1100}\right)$$

$$+ (0.10)\left(\frac{1050}{1200}\right) + (0.05)\left(\frac{1050}{1300}\right) + (0.02)\left(\frac{1050}{1335}\right)$$

$$= 96.54\%$$

Similarly, if the safety stock is 300 units, then the expected customer service level is:

$$(0.02)(1) + (0.05)(1) + (0.10)(1) + (0.18)(1) + (0.30)(1) + (0.18)(1) + (0.10)(1)$$

$$+ (0.05)(1) + (0.02)\left(\frac{1300}{1335}\right)$$

$$= 99.95\%$$

The target customer service level of 98 per cent may then be found by trial and error. The safety stock level must be increased if it provides an expected customer service level of less than 98 per cent, and it has to be decreased if it provides an expected customer service level of more than 98 per cent. In this example, if the safety stock level is 99 units, then the expected customer service level is:

$$(0.02)(1) + (0.05)(1) + (0.10)(1) + (0.18)(1) + (0.30)(1) + (0.18)\left(\frac{1099}{1100}\right)$$

$$+ (0.10)\left(\frac{1099}{1200}\right) + (0.05)\left(\frac{1099}{1300}\right) + (0.02)\left(\frac{1099}{1335}\right)$$

$$= 98\%$$

which is equal to the specified target. Therefore, the required safety stock is 99 units, and, since the expected demand during the lead time is 1000 units, the reorder point is 1099 units.

The result in Example 21.7 may be compared with a reorder point of 1300 units, which is the solution calculated in Section 21.10.1 when the stockout probability was set at 2 per cent. If a new order is placed when the inventory level falls to 1300 units, there is a 2 per cent chance that, at the *end* of the lead time, no inventory will remain. Of course, at any point *during* the lead time this probability is much smaller. For example, a customer who arrives just after the start of the lead time is almost guaranteed that his or her order will be met. However, this is not given any weight in the decision to set the inventory level at 1300.

Instead, the focus is on conditions at the end of the lead time. As shown earlier, the expected customer service level associated with a reorder point of 1300 is 99.95 per cent. This is an extremely high level.

In contrast, the customer service level approach takes account of conditions *throughout* the lead time. With the reorder point set at 1099 units, the probability of a stockout is 0.35. Therefore, customers who arrive at the end of the lead time face a 35 per cent chance that their orders will not be met. However, customers who arrive at the start of the lead time face an almost 0 per cent chance that their orders will not be met. Overall, the average chance of unmet orders during the lead time is 2 per cent and the expected customer service level is therefore 98 per cent. In general, there is no reason why suppliers should focus only on the end of the lead time, since customers at that point are neither more nor less valuable than customers at any other time. The expected customer service level approach is therefore preferred.

21.11 INVENTORY MANAGEMENT AND THE 'JUST-IN-TIME' SYSTEM

The 'just-in-time' system is a way of organising high volume repetitive manufacturing of goods such as motor vehicles, engines and power tools.[7] It is based on the concept, first introduced by the Toyota Motor Corporation, that raw materials, equipment and labour are each supplied only in the amounts required, and at the times required, to perform the manufacturing task. Therefore, a basic element of the system is the coordination of production processes so that raw materials and components are delivered to the location where they are needed at precisely the times they are required. Compared with a traditional system, this synchronisation of delivery with demand reduces inventory levels, lead times and delivery quantities. For example, items that are bulky, expensive and obtained from local suppliers may be delivered once per day or even once per shift.

In industries where both customers and suppliers adopt the just-in-time approach, inventories of raw materials, work in progress and finished goods can be reduced substantially. However, the just-in-time system is not simply an inventory management system. Its adoption will reduce inventory, but that is not its major function; rather, it is a system that focuses on the elimination of waste in all forms, and improvements flow from reducing the need to hold inventories. For example, a machine that forms part of a production line may break down several times per day. The traditional solution might be to hold large safety stocks of this machine's inputs and outputs. This ties up capital and requires storage facilities. Under the just-in-time system the machine would be redesigned so that it operated more reliably, thereby eliminating the need for safety stocks. The result is an improvement in overall efficiency, as well as a reduction in inventory costs.

While many manufacturing operations may be able to reduce work in progress by this approach, complete adoption of the just-in-time system involves radical changes in relationships between manufacturers and suppliers, and in handling facilities. For example, the requirements for effective just-in-time operation include reliable quality of supplies and transportation, short distances between suppliers and buyers, and frequent delivery of small quantities of goods. Where these requirements cannot be met, an important role remains for inventory management.

Connect Plus features a case study illustrating topics covered in this chapter.
Ask your lecturer or tutor for your course's unique URL.

---

[7] For a more detailed discussion of the just-in-time system, see Langfield-Smith, Thorne and Hilton (2009 Chapter 15).

SUMMARY

→ Assets such as inventory, liquid assets and accounts receivable are described as 'short term' because they are turned over rapidly. The resources committed to such assets are large, and if shareholders' wealth is to be maximised, the company's short-term assets need to be selected carefully and managed efficiently.

→ Unlike most topics in finance, the model of a perfectly competitive, frictionless market is often not a useful starting point for analysing short-term asset management. This is because there would be no need to hold short-term assets, such as inventory, in a world of perfectly competitive, frictionless markets. While the relevant markets are generally competitive, it is the frictions in these markets that give rise to the need to hold short-term assets.

→ Managers must make decisions concerning short-term liabilities as well as short-term assets. An approach that is employed by many companies involves matching maturity structures of assets and liabilities. This approach minimises the risk that a company will have insufficient cash to meet liabilities as they fall due.

→ There are three main types of inventory: raw materials, work in progress and finished goods.
  – If a retailer or wholesaler holds too little inventory, there will be lost sales due to stockouts and goods will have to be ordered frequently.
  – If too much inventory is held, extra capital will be tied up and the costs of storage and insurance will increase.

→ Determining an optimal inventory level involves minimising the total of the relevant costs. These are costs that vary with the inventory policy adopted. For retailers and wholesalers, the costs of holding inventory can be classified into three groups: acquisition costs, carrying costs and stockout costs. In turn, acquisition costs include ordering costs, freight and handling costs and, in some cases, quantity discounts forgone. Each of these costs will be lower per unit of inventory, the larger the order placed. Carrying costs include the opportunity cost of capital invested in inventory, storage costs and insurance costs.

→ When demand is known with certainty, inventory management can be based on the economic order quantity (EOQ) model. The EOQ model estimates an optimal order quantity such that the total of acquisition costs and carrying costs is minimised. Inputs to the model include marginal costs, which may be difficult to estimate. However, the model is robust in that total costs are relatively insensitive to estimation errors.

→ When demand is uncertain, the order quantity decision may be the same as that under certainty, but the reorder point is changed by adding a safety stock to the reorder point, which would be chosen under certainty. The size of the safety stock may be determined on the basis of the probability of a stockout or, preferably, on the basis of specifying an acceptable level of customer service. Customer service is defined as the ratio of sales to orders and reflects the magnitude of any loss of sales due to stockouts.

KEY TERMS

accounts receivable (or debtors)   739
current assets   741
current liabilities   741
economic order quantity (EOQ)   744
inventory   739
liquid assets   739
safety stock   750

SELF-TEST PROBLEMS

1. Each year, Palmer Engineering Ltd produces 500 high-quality jet sprockets used in aircraft engines. A production run costs $3000 to set up and storage costs are $48 per sprocket per annum. Calculate the optimal size of a production run and the number of runs per annum.

2. Ron Harper operates a large sports store specialising in cricket equipment. Harper buys cricket balls from Mackintosh Sports Ltd. It takes Mackintosh 1 month to process and deliver an order. Harper estimates that during the cricket season the monthly demand for cricket balls follows the probability distribution overleaf.

Probability	Quantity demanded
0.10	1600
0.20	1800
0.50	2000
0.15	2200
0.03	2400
0.02	2600

What reorder point will ensure that there is only a 5 per cent chance that a stockout will occur during the lead time? What reorder point will ensure that the expected customer service level during the lead time is 95 per cent?

Solutions to self-test problems are available in Appendix B, page 803.

REFERENCES

Goetz, B., *Quantitative Methods: A Survey and Guide for Managers*, McGraw-Hill, New York, 1965.

Hill, N.C. & Sartoris, W.L., *Short-term Financial Management: Text and Cases*, 3rd edn, Macmillan, New York, 1995.

Kallberg, J.G. & Parkinson, K.L., *Current Asset Management*, John Wiley & Sons, New York, 1984.

Langfield-Smith, K., Thorne, H. & Hilton, R.W., *Management Accounting: Information for Managing and Creating Value*, 5th edn, McGraw-Hill, Sydney, 2009.

Scherr, F.C., *Modern Working Capital Management: Text and Cases*, Prentice-Hall, Englewood Cliffs, New Jersey, 1989.

Silver, E.A., Pyke, D.F. & Peterson, R., *Inventory Management and Production Planning and Scheduling*, John Wiley & Sons, New York, 1998.

Smith, K.V. & Gallinger, G.W., *Readings on Short-term Financial Management*, 3rd edn, West, St Paul, 1988.

QUESTIONS

1. **[LO 2]** Distinguish between the major types of short-term asset.
2. **[LO 1]** Relative to total assets, businesses in the retail and wholesale sectors invest substantially more in short-term assets than do businesses in the service sector. Suggest reasons for this difference.
3. **[LO 1]** For the average company, cash represents a much smaller percentage of its total short-term assets than accounts receivable. Suggest reasons for this difference.
4. **[LO 3]** Should the decision to invest in short-term assets be approached differently from the decision to invest in long-term assets?
5. **[LO 4]** Explain the 'maturity matching' concept. Why do many companies pursue policies based on this idea?
6. **[LO 1]** *Uncertainty makes it difficult for a financial manager to forecast a company's requirement for short-term funds.* Discuss. What steps can a financial manager take to minimise the resulting risks to the company?
7. **[LO 1]** Explain why the proportion of a company's total assets tied up in inventory varies widely from company to company. Give examples.
8. **[LO 6]** For a retailer, what are the major costs and benefits of holding inventory? What different benefits and costs apply to raw materials inventory held by a manufacturer?
9. **[LO 8]** What is 'safety stock'? Explain how it is possible that safety stock might be negative.
10. **[LO 8]** *Because it is impossible to obtain precise measures of the necessary data, theoretical inventory management models are virtually useless.* Comment on this statement.

PROBLEMS

1. **Inventory management under certainty [LO 5]**
   The Leichhardt Pharmacy sells 5000 bottles of vitamin C tablets each year. The clerical and related costs of placing and processing an order amount to $25 and the carrying costs are 16 cents per bottle per annum. Calculate the economic order quantity (EOQ) and the time period between placement of orders.

2. **Inventory management under certainty [LO 7]**
   Drummond Garden Tools Ltd specialises in the manufacture of lawn rakes. Every 6 months, Drummond buys 1500 rake handles from Kilmarnock Timber Mills at a cost of $1.50 per handle. The clerical and processing cost is $75 per order, and each handle costs $1.80 per annum to store. Calculate

Drummond's economic order quantity (EOQ) and the annual cost saving that would be achieved using the EOQ.

3. **Inventory management with quantity discounts [LO 7]**

   The vitamin C tablet manufacturer who supplies the Leichhardt Pharmacy (see Problem 1) has begun offering quantity discounts to its customers as follows:

Quantity ordered	Price per bottle ($)
1–999	2.00
1000–1999	1.99
2000–2999	1.98
3000–3999	1.97
4000+	1.96

   Calculate the new economic order quantity (EOQ).

4. **Inventory management under uncertainty [LO 9]**

   Driscoll Magazines Ltd places orders for new stock every month. The new stock arrives 1 week after placement of the order. Driscoll has estimated that weekly demand follows the probability distribution below.

Probability	Quantity demanded
0.060	100
0.150	120
0.460	140
0.166	160
0.144	180
0.020	200

   What reorder point will ensure that there is a 2 per cent chance that a stockout will occur during the lead time? What reorder point will ensure that the expected customer service level during the lead time is 98 per cent?

5. **Inventory management under uncertainty [LO 9]**

   Using the data on Cranfield Manufacturing Ltd in Example 21.2:
   (a) calculate the total annual cost of the optimal inventory policy
   (b) show that any order quantity between 1095 and 2055 metres results in an annual cost within 5 per cent of the minimum. Comment on the implications of this result.

Test yourself further with Connect Plus online! Ask your lecturer or tutor for your course's unique URL.

CHAPTER 22

MANAGEMENT OF SHORT-TERM ASSETS: LIQUID ASSETS AND ACCOUNTS RECEIVABLE

LEARNING OBJECTIVES

After studying this chapter you should be able to:

1. define liquid assets
2. distinguish between liquidity management and treasury management
3. identify the motives for holding liquid assets
4. prepare a cash budget
5. identify avenues for short-term investment by companies
6. define accounts receivable and distinguish between trade credit and consumer credit
7. identify the benefits and costs of holding accounts receivable
8. identify the four elements of credit policy
9. understand the factors in implementing a collection policy
10. apply the net present value method to evaluate alternative credit and collection policies
11. apply financial statement analysis to short-term asset management.

CHAPTER CONTENTS

22.1	Introduction
22.2	Overview of liquidity management
22.3	Cash budgeting
22.4	The choice of short-term securities
22.5	Types of short-term investment
22.6	The corporate treasurer and liquidity management
22.7	Overview of accounts receivable management
22.8	Credit policy
22.9	Collection policy
22.10	Evaluation of alternative credit and collection policies
Appendix 22.1	Financial statement analysis

This chapter is also featured in the complete e-book available with Connect Plus.
Ask your lecturer or tutor for your course's unique URL.

22.1 INTRODUCTION

In this chapter we continue the discussion of short-term asset management by considering the management of a company's liquid assets (cash and short-term investments) and accounts receivable. Management of these assets is considered in turn.

First, every company needs to maintain liquidity in order to ensure that its creditors are paid on time. Of course, this objective could easily be met by a company holding a large proportion of its assets in liquid form. However, because cash does not earn interest, and the return on short-term investments is often quite low, such a policy would conflict with the company's ultimate goal of maximising shareholders' wealth. In general, therefore, a company will hold a relatively small proportion of its short-term assets in the form of cash. For example, at the end of the 2010 financial year, Paperlinx Ltd and Boral Ltd held only 8 and 10 per cent respectively of their short-term assets in the form of cash, while the comparable percentage for BHP Billiton Ltd was 50 per cent. Clearly, the management of a company's liquid resources is an important aspect of financial management. This is considered in Sections 22.2 to 22.6.

Second, most companies sell on credit—that is, instead of a company exchanging its products for cash, it will agree to deliver the products immediately, in return for the customer's promise to pay at a later date. For instance, payment may not be required until a period of 30 days has elapsed. During this period the selling company holds an asset 'accounts receivable'. Companies that sell on credit will have a considerable proportion of their short-term assets in the form of accounts receivable. For example, at the end of the 2010 financial year, Boral Ltd held 49 per cent of its short-term assets in the form of accounts receivable, while the comparable percentages for BHP Billiton Ltd and Paperlinx Ltd were 26 per cent and 63 per cent, respectively. As with any other short-term asset, accounts receivable needs to be managed efficiently, with the ultimate goal of maximising shareholders' wealth. The management of accounts receivable is considered in Sections 22.7 to 22.10.

22.2 OVERVIEW OF LIQUIDITY MANAGEMENT

22.2.1 WHAT ARE 'LIQUID' ASSETS?

Liquid assets comprise cash and assets that can be converted into cash in a very short time, and whose cash value can be predicted with a low degree of error. Examples of assets with these features include 'at call' deposits with banks, money market dealers or other financial intermediaries, and various short-term marketable securities, such as bills of exchange and commercial paper. These assets are described in Chapter 10.

> **LEARNING OBJECTIVE 1**
> Define liquid assets

22.2.2 LIQUIDITY MANAGEMENT AND TREASURY MANAGEMENT

Liquidity management refers to the decisions made by the management of a company about the composition and level of the company's liquid resources. In Australia, this typically involves deciding on the mix of liquid assets (such as cash, interest-bearing deposits and securities) that a company will try to achieve, as well as the level of bank overdraft usage. It is usual for a company in Australia to use an overdraft provided by its bank. Under the terms of such an agreement, the company is able to overdraw its bank account up to some agreed limit. This means that the company can borrow any amount up to the agreed limit. Therefore, a company can guarantee immediate access to cash by maintaining an unused overdraft limit. Also, a company may arrange stand-by facilities, such as an approved line of credit, which can be drawn down if required. Liquidity management is not therefore confined to management

> **LEARNING OBJECTIVE 2**
> Distinguish between liquidity management and treasury management

liquid assets comprise cash and assets that are readily convertible into cash such as bills of exchange

liquidity management involves decisions about the composition and level of a company's liquid assets

treasury management involves the management of financial assets and includes the management of short-term financial assets, long-term financing and risk management

of cash and liquid assets, but also extends to the management of bank overdraft and other sources of short-term borrowing.

Treasury management is a broader concept than liquidity management and includes liquidity management as one of its functions. Many companies have established a separate group or department, under the control of the company treasurer, to manage the company's liquidity and to oversee its exposure to various kinds of financial risk. Foreign exchange provides one example of exposure to risk. If a company exports, imports, borrows foreign currency or lends foreign currency, then there is the risk of loss from exchange rate movements. For example, if the Australian dollar depreciates, the company will face a higher cost of imports in Australian dollar terms. The treasurer will advise on *whether* this risk should be hedged and, if so, *how* it is to be hedged. These issues were discussed in Chapter 20. Another facet of the treasury's role in a company is the management of interest rate risk. For example, suppose that a company has borrowed money on a floating interest rate basis and has lent money on a fixed interest rate basis. If the general level of interest rates increases, the company could find itself in difficulty, because while the interest cost of its borrowed funds has increased, the interest received on the funds it has lent remains fixed. Similarly, if a company holds a portfolio of fixed interest securities, or if it has plans to buy or sell (issue) fixed interest securities, there is a risk due to the possibility of changing interest rates. Issues of this type were considered in Appendix 4.1 and Chapters 17 and 18.

22.2.3 CENTRALISATION OF LIQUIDITY MANAGEMENT

Many companies centralise the liquidity management function, even if many other functions are not centralised. The main reason is that centralisation allows the matching of inflows and outflows for the whole company, with consequent savings. This principle is clearly seen in the following example.

EXAMPLE 22.1

Megacorp Ltd has a manufacturing division and a customer services division. On a particular day, the manufacturing division must meet a net cash outflow of $150 000; on the same day, the customer services division receives a net cash inflow of $50 000. If both divisions are operated independently, the manufacturing division will need to borrow $150 000 and the customer services division will be able to invest $50 000. Clearly, it is easier if, instead, the company simply borrows the net requirement of $100 000, and since the borrowing rate will exceed the lending rate, it is cheaper to do so. For example, if the time period involved is 7 days and the annual interest rates are 15 per cent per annum (borrowing) and 12 per cent per annum (lending), what is the cost saving from centralised liquidity management?

SOLUTION
The net interest cost would be calculated as follows:

(a) If liquidity management were centralised, then the net interest cost would be:

$$\$100\,000 \times 0.15 \times \frac{7}{365}$$
$$= \$287.67$$

(b) If liquidity management were not centralised, then the net interest cost would be:

$$\$150\,000 \times 0.15 \times \frac{7}{365} - \left(\$50\,000 \times 0.12 \times \frac{7}{365}\right)$$
$$= \$316.44$$

> The cost saving from centralisation is $316.44 − $287.67 = 28.77. If the situation in this 7-day period is typical of the company's operations, then over a year the savings would amount to $52 \times \$28.77 = \$1496.04$. In practice, the savings may be reduced by the transaction and communication costs required to achieve centralisation.

The centralisation of liquidity management also facilitates the development of specialised staff by having them concentrated in one area of the business. Any economies of scale can also be exploited. Of course, it should also be borne in mind that there can be diseconomies of scale. For example, the centralisation of liquidity management is likely to be a failure if there is poor communication between the operating divisions and the group responsible for liquidity management.

22.2.4 MOTIVES FOR HOLDING LIQUID ASSETS

LEARNING OBJECTIVE 3
Identify the motives for holding liquid assets

Studies of the motives for holding liquid assets have a long history in the literature of economics. The conventional classification of motives, often attributed to Keynes, divides the motives into three groups: the *transactions motive*, the *precautionary motive* and the *speculative motive*.[1]

Transactions motive

Many businesses face a continuous outflow of cash to meet expenses but will often receive a continuous inflow of cash, particularly from sales. If these inflows and outflows were perfectly matched in both timing and amount, then no liquid assets would be required. While the timing of a company's cash outflows can be controlled by management, the timing of many of its inflows depends on the actions of its customers. Consequently, perfect synchronisation is virtually impossible to achieve, with the result that some liquid assets must be held for transaction purposes.

Precautionary motive

Future cash inflows and outflows cannot be forecast with perfect certainty. There is, therefore, always the possibility that extra cash will be needed to meet unexpected costs, or to take advantage of unexpected opportunities. Liquid assets are therefore held as a precaution to cover outflows resulting from these unexpected events. However, the precautionary motive will be weaker if a company can arrange a source of finance that can be called on in times of need. In Australia, bank overdrafts and commercial bill facilities provide this type of finance.

Speculative motive

When interest rates increase, there is a fall in the market value of income-producing assets such as bonds. Keynes hypothesised that when an individual forecasts an increase in interest rates he or she will sell bonds and, instead, hold cash or bank deposits in order to avoid the resulting capital loss. Therefore, liquid asset holdings depend in part on expectations of interest rate changes. Keynes termed this the 'speculative motive'. Speculation may be a potent force for companies in the finance sector. For example, a money market dealer may change the size and/or composition of its portfolio, depending on its expectations of market conditions. However, outside the finance sector it is doubtful whether the speculative motive has a role in liquidity management practices.

In summary, for most companies, transaction-based motives are probably the dominant influences and are the focus of our discussion of liquidity management.

---

1 In fact, Keynes (1936, Ch. 15) specified four motives that he termed the 'income motive', the 'business motive', the 'precautionary motive' and the 'speculative motive'. The first relates mainly to transactions by individuals and the second to transactions by enterprises: these two are therefore often combined into a single transactions motive.

22.2.5 MAJOR ISSUES IN LIQUIDITY MANAGEMENT

All companies have cash receipts and need to make cash payments. Because the cash receipts and payments will not generally be matched in time and amount, the company's cash position must be forecast, monitored and managed. If this is not done, the following situations are likely to arise:

(a) If the cash payments exceed the cash receipts, the company will need to borrow money to make the payments, or else postpone payment. If it borrows money, it will need to pay interest and, probably, fees. Alternatively, if payment is postponed, the likely result is disruption to its business and/or damage to its financial reputation.

(b) If the cash receipts exceed the cash payments, resulting in a large cash balance, the company is failing to make the best use of its resources. The net funds obtained could be invested to earn interest or used to reduce the company's debt.

In short, the major issues in liquidity management are to ensure that the company has adequate liquid resources to make cash payments as the need arises, without holding such a high level of liquid assets that the company's resources are used inefficiently. This balance is achieved by first forecasting the likely patterns of cash receipts and payments, and then adopting an appropriate mix of cash, liquid assets and short-term borrowing. As events unfold, the cash position is monitored, new forecasts are made and a new mix adopted. A basic tool in forecasting cash flows is the cash budget. This tool is outlined in the next section.

22.3 CASH BUDGETING

LEARNING OBJECTIVE 4
Prepare a cash budget

cash budget
forecast of the amount and timing of the cash receipts and payments that will result from a company's operations over a period of time

A **cash budget** provides a forecast of the amount and timing of the cash receipts and payments that will result from the company's operations over a period of time. To assist in day-to-day cash management, forecasts of receipts and payments may be made for each day of the coming week. Alternatively, forecasts may be made on a weekly basis for a number of weeks in advance, or for each month of the next financial year. A cash budget on a month-by-month basis is usually prepared as part of the overall master budget for the next financial year and it is useful as an indication of the company's short-run debt-paying ability. In addition, monthly forecasts should take into account seasonal and other predictable variations in cash flows. Clearly, the cash budget is only as useful for decision making as the accuracy of the estimates used in its preparation. A company whose cash flows are subject to a great deal of uncertainty should provide a safety margin in the form of a minimum cash balance, or have ready access to borrowing, or both, to tide it over periods when cash payments exceed cash receipts. The cash budget therefore assists the treasurer in forecasting when such excesses of payments over receipts are likely to occur.

The basic structure of a cash budget is very simple. A forecast of cash receipts and payments is made for each time period. Often this will be done by forecasting separately the major components of the cash flows. For example, separate forecasts may be made for payments for wages, materials and power. In practice, dozens of separate forecasts may be made. Many of these forecasts will, in turn, depend on the forecast level of sales. Cash receipts are obviously related to the sales level, but so also are many cash payments. For example, in a manufacturing company, high sales means high production, which, in turn, means that more raw materials will need to be purchased. In addition, the corporate treasurer may specify that, for safety reasons, a given minimum required cash balance should be built into the budget. The level at which this minimum is set is often determined on an ad hoc basis. Given forecasts of total receipts, total payments and the minimum required balance, the forecast cash shortage (to be borrowed) or cash surplus (to be invested) is simply:

(*Total receipts*) less (*Total payments*) less (*Minimum required balance*)

22.3.1 FORECASTING CASH RECEIPTS

The sales forecast is probably the most important factor affecting the accuracy of the cash budget. An error in the forecast of sales will be reflected in an error in the expected collections from customers. Such an error will also affect budgeted cash payments, as the company's level of operations will usually be adjusted in response to expected changes in the level of sales.

The preparation of a sales forecast usually involves the following steps. First, a thorough analysis of past sales performance is made for each product. Any relationship or trend observed can then be taken into account in making the sales forecast. For example, a seasonal pattern of sales may be observed and then built into the forecast. Second, some factors external to the company will have an important effect on the sales forecast. For example, the forecasters will probably use projections of likely business and economic conditions prepared by outside consultants or, in very large organisations, by an in-house economist.

After the sales forecast has been prepared, the next step is to estimate the cash receipts from sales. Cash sales present no problem because the cash is received immediately. However, credit sales require estimation of the timing of cash receipts. This will be influenced by the company's credit terms, the type of customer, and the general credit and collection policies of the company.[2] Experience will usually indicate the proportion of total sales that are cash sales; the remainder will be credit sales. The rate of collection may be estimated from an analysis of past records, taking into account any special factors.

22.3.2 FORECASTING CASH PAYMENTS

In the case of a manufacturing company, after the sales forecast has been prepared, a production schedule consistent with this forecast is established for each product. On the basis of the production schedule, management can estimate the expected payments for materials and labour. A company will also incur overhead costs, which include the cost of supplies, insurance, light and power, and repairs and maintenance. In some cases, these goods and services may be obtained on credit and therefore there will be a lag between the date of purchase and the date of the cash payment. For example, if suppliers of materials sell on 30 days' credit and do not post invoices until the end of the month of purchase, the purchaser may have a period of up to 2 months between the date of purchase and the date of cash payment. Other regular cash payments may include administrative expenses, marketing expenses and interest payments. Payments that typically are made less frequently, but are nevertheless relatively predictable, include income tax payments, capital expenditures and dividend payments.

The preparation of a simple cash budget is illustrated in Example 22.2.

EXAMPLE 22.2

Lancaster Ltd has forecast its monthly sales for the next 6 months as shown in Table 22.1.

TABLE 22.1 Monthly sales forecast

MONTH	SALES ($'000)
January	1600
February	1750
March	1750
April	1800
May	1900
June	1900

continued →

---

2 The management of accounts receivable is discussed later in this chapter.

Example 22.2 *continued*

It is expected that in each month, 20 per cent of sales will be cash sales and 80 per cent of sales will be credit sales. It is forecast that the collection pattern for credit sales will be as follows:

(a) 5 per cent in the month of sale
(b) 80 per cent in the month following sale
(c) 10 per cent in the second month following sale
(d) 2.5 per cent in the third month following sale
(e) 2.5 per cent uncollectable (bad debts).

Management requests that you use this information to forecast cash collections (receipts) from Lancaster's customers in April, May and June.

SOLUTION

The first step is to divide total sales into cash sales (20 per cent) and credit sales (80 per cent) as shown in Table 22.2.

TABLE 22.2 Cash and credit sales

MONTH	TOTAL SALES ($'000)	CASH SALES ($'000)	CREDIT SALES ($'000)
January	1600	320	1280
February	1750	350	1400
March	1750	350	1400
April	1800	360	1440
May	1900	380	1520
June	1900	380	1520

Credit sales then generate cash receipts according to the pattern of collections, as shown in Table 22.3.

TABLE 22.3 Cash receipts for Lancaster Ltd

Credit sales made in:	ARE COLLECTED AS CASH RECEIPTS ($'000) IN:					
	JANUARY	FEBRUARY	MARCH	APRIL	MAY	JUNE
January (1280)	64	1024	128	32	—	—
February (1400)	—	70	1120	140	35	—
March (1400)	—	—	70	1120	140	35
April (1440)	—	—	—	72	1152	144
May (1520)	—	—	—	—	76	1216
June (1520)	—	—	—	—	—	76
Credit sales collected	—	—	—	1364	1403	1471
Cash sales	320	350	350	360	380	380
Cash receipts ($'000)	—	—	—	1724	1783	1851

The cash receipts for January, February and March are incomplete because insufficient information has been provided. For example, January will see a cash receipt from the credit sales made in December. Presumably, Lancaster will already have actual (rather than forecast) figures for December's credit sales, and for the cash already collected from these sales. These figures would then be used in forecasting the collections for January and subsequent months. In practice, Lancaster Ltd would then have to forecast other cash receipts, as well as cash payments and the minimum required cash balance to complete its cash budget. The resulting forecasts for the June quarter might be those shown in Table 22.4.

TABLE 22.4 Lancaster Ltd: forecast cash receipts and payments for June quarter, by month

	APRIL ($'000)	MAY ($'000)	JUNE ($'000)
Cash balance at beginning of month	740	564	547
add Cash receipts:			
Collections from customers	1724	1783	1851
Dividends on investments in other companies	—	310	—
Sale of equipment	300	—	—
Other	50	40	140
Total cash receipts	2074	2133	1991
Total cash available	2814	2697	2538
less Cash payments:			
Payments to creditors	1400	1600	1300
Wages and salaries	500	525	510
Dividends	—	—	500
Income tax	—	—	—
Purchase of land	300		
Other	50	25	30
Total cash payments	2250	2150	2340
Cash balance at end of month	564	547	198
Required minimum cash balance	300	300	300
Cash (required) available for investment	264	247	(102)

Finally, actual results should be compared with forecast results on an ongoing basis. Factors influencing the cash position of the company that were not foreseen when the cash forecast was prepared may be disclosed by the comparisons. For example, customers may not be paying their accounts as promptly as had been expected and, as a result, cash receipts may be less than those forecast. In the event of large variations from the cash budget, the budget should be revised immediately. Comparisons between the budgeted and actual figures may also indicate ways in which the forecasting procedure can be improved.

THE CHOICE OF SHORT-TERM SECURITIES

22.4

There are many types of investments in which a company can invest temporarily idle cash. These investments offer a wide range of risk and return. The treasurer has the opportunity to invest in higher-yielding securities, provided that he or she is prepared to accept the greater risk of such investments.

The greater risk may refer not only to the risk that rates of return may change (*interest rate risk*), but also to the possibility of default (*default* or *credit risk*) and to the risk associated with the liquidity of the investment (*liquidity risk*). For example, an investment in a call deposit with a bank is uncertain to the extent that the bank may be unable to meet its commitments. However, for most banks, most of the time, the probability of default is very low and therefore the default risk is very small. A risk of greater consequence relates to the liquidity of the investment. The more difficult it is to convert a security into cash, the greater is the liquidity risk of that security. For example, a 3-month term deposit with a bank is riskier than a call deposit with the same bank, as the company may unexpectedly need the cash before the 3 months have elapsed.

22.5 TYPES OF SHORT-TERM INVESTMENT

LEARNING OBJECTIVE 5

Identify avenues for short-term investment by companies

The following discussion does not attempt to compile a complete list of possible investments, but does examine some of the avenues available for investing a company's temporarily idle cash. For each investment we highlight the characteristics that are important to a treasurer who must choose the most appropriate forms of investment, given the company's circumstances. Table 22.5 provides some short-term interest rates and yields.

TABLE 22.5 Examples of short-term interest rates and yields

TYPE OF INVESTMENT	INTEREST RATES AND YIELDS (% p.a.)
Government bonds—5 years	5.073
Cash, average 11 am rate	4.750
90-day bank bills	5.010
180-day bank bills	5.040
Cash management trusts—Macquarie CMT	4.750

Source: *Australian Financial Review*, 12 January 2011.

22.5.1 DEPOSITS OF FUNDS WITH FINANCIAL INSTITUTIONS

Several types of financial institution accept deposits.[3] The basic terms of the deposit will differ from one kind of institution to another and a treasurer's choice will depend on the:

(a) period that the funds are available for investment
(b) risk that the company is prepared to accept
(c) required rate of return.

Banks

A company can invest funds in interest-bearing term deposits with a bank or purchase certificates of deposit from a bank. Terms to maturity for term deposits and certificates of deposit are negotiable. Certificates of deposit are more liquid than term deposits as they are marketable. Funds can also be invested for very short terms; for example, funds may be placed on 24-hour call. The default risk associated with depositing funds with a bank is very low and consequently the interest rates offered tend to be less than those for most alternative investments.

---

[3] These were discussed in Chapter 8.

Cash management trusts

Cash management trusts act as intermediaries between small investors and the money markets. Many companies are large enough to enter the money markets directly, but smaller companies may find indirect access via the trusts to be an attractive outlet for funds available for investment for periods as short as a few days.

22.5.2 DISCOUNTING OF COMMERCIAL BILLS

The commercial bills market was discussed in Chapter 10. A company can invest its idle cash balances in this market in one of two ways. First, a company can be the original discounter of a commercial bill and, as a result, supply funds to the drawer of the bill. Second, a company can 'rediscount' a bill that has previously been discounted by another party. This simply means that the bill is purchased from another investor in the bills market. Such purchases are easily arranged as there is an active market in bills. The marketability of commercial bills is one of the major advantages of this form of investment.

22.6 THE CORPORATE TREASURER AND LIQUIDITY MANAGEMENT

The demand for liquidity stems from transactions that result in cash inflows and payments that are not synchronised in either timing or amount. One means of reducing the necessary cash balance is to smooth the pattern of cash flows. For example, the company may be able to negotiate credit terms with suppliers so that payment is not required until the goods are sold. Similarly, the dates on which employees' wages are paid could be altered to bring these dates more into line with times when the company has a cash surplus. In fact, there are opportunities for reducing a company's cash requirements wherever the pattern of cash payments can be brought more into line with the pattern of cash inflows. Usually this will require delaying cash payments for as long as possible, in order to bring them closer to the time when the goods and services acquired can be converted into cash inflows through sales.

Acceleration of the flow of cash inflows will also have a desirable effect on liquidity. In this case the aim is to reduce the time that elapses between the date of sale and the date of the cash inflow. These issues fall into the category of 'credit and collection policy' and are discussed in Sections 22.7 to 22.10.

22.7 OVERVIEW OF ACCOUNTS RECEIVABLE MANAGEMENT

The purpose of our discussion of accounts receivable management is to identify the variables that can be influenced by the manager responsible for accounts receivable, and to discuss techniques and procedures that may be employed in choosing the optimum values for these variables. Collectively, these decisions are often referred to as the company's *credit and collection policies*. Establishment of a *credit policy* involves four elements:

(a) Is the company prepared to offer credit?
(b) If credit is to be offered, what standards will be applied in the decision to grant credit to a customer?
(c) How much credit should a customer be granted?
(d) What credit terms will be offered?

> **LEARNING OBJECTIVE 6**
>
> Define accounts receivable and distinguish between trade credit and consumer credit

account receivable (or debtor)
sum of money owed to a seller as a result of having sold goods or services on credit

trade credit
arrangement in which a seller of goods or services allows the purchaser a period of time before requiring payment; it is equivalent to a short-term loan made by the seller to the purchaser, of an amount equal to the purchase price

consumer credit
credit extended to individuals by suppliers of goods and services, or by financial institutions through credit cards

LEARNING OBJECTIVE 7
Identify the benefits and costs of holding accounts receivable

open account
an arrangement under which goods or services are sold to a customer on credit, but with no formal debt contract. Payment is due after an account is sent to the customer

When credit has been offered and accepted, the company must then seek to ensure that the promised amount is received. Inevitably, some accounts will prove difficult to collect and the company will need to take steps to recover the amount owing—that is, the company will adopt a *collection policy*. This requires the manager to determine which procedures will be used to encourage payment, and for how long these procedures should be followed. In practice, credit and collection policies will be interrelated, but it is convenient in the first instance to consider them separately.

Before further discussion of credit and collection policies, we first describe the characteristics of accounts receivable in more detail and indicate the benefits and costs of holding accounts receivable.

22.7.1 WHAT ARE ACCOUNTS RECEIVABLE?

Accounts receivable represent money owed to a company from the sale, on credit, of goods or services in the normal course of business. **Trade credit** refers to credit sales made to other businesses, whereas **consumer credit** refers to credit sales made to individuals. Trade credit terms may provide a discount for prompt payment, whereas consumer credit terms are unlikely to have this feature. Consumer credit may also require the customer to pay a service fee, but this is unusual in the case of trade credit.

An individual or business purchasing goods on credit from a retailer may either charge the amount to a credit account or enter into a longer-term consumer credit agreement, which is likely to require regular repayment of an agreed amount. While some major retailers continue to provide credit, the provision of credit has largely been taken over by financial institutions that issue credit cards. These cards allow goods and services to be purchased on credit without credit being extended by the retailer. Trade credit, however, continues to be provided by manufacturers, wholesalers and other providers of goods and services.

A business purchasing goods on credit may be offered trade credit on open account, or, if the amount involved is substantial, the business may be required to negotiate a bill of exchange.[4] Trade credit on open account is the more usual method. For example, a timber yard is likely to provide trade credit on **open account** to builders who obtain their supplies regularly from the yard. This requires little or no formal documentation and the selling company sends regular statements to notify its customers of their current indebtedness.

In the remainder of this chapter, decisions relating to trade credit on open account are considered. However, much of the material presented is applicable to other forms of trade credit and to consumer credit.

Benefits and costs of granting credit

The major benefits and costs of granting credit can be illustrated by a simple example. Suppose that the manager of a suburban timber yard is reviewing the business's accounts receivable policy. A lenient policy would be to provide credit to nearly all customers who request it, to allow these customers a long credit period, and to delay taking steps to collect overdue accounts. Such a policy would almost certainly attract new customers and perhaps win more business from existing customers. However, a lenient policy would also increase costs substantially. The long credit period would tie up resources that could otherwise be invested elsewhere. Further, the costs of administering the accounts would rise, and the lower credit standard required of customers would lead to increased costs of collection and a higher incidence of unpaid accounts. Conversely, a very strict policy would keep these costs at very low levels,

---
4 See Section 10.5.3 for a description of bills of exchange.

but would also lead to lost sales as customers turned to competing timber yards whose policies were more lenient. The aim of the manager is to choose the set of policies that will maximise the net benefit to the timber yard.

The benefits and costs are now explained in more detail.

Benefit of increased sales

A company will offer credit terms to its customers only if its management believes that there will be an increase in sales. The benefit is therefore the net increase in sales revenue directly attributable to the credit terms offered. In calculating the effect of increased sales on profit, it is, of course, necessary to deduct from the increase in sales revenue the cost of the goods sold and other associated costs, such as delivery costs.

Opportunity cost of investment

Accounts receivable tie up funds that could be invested in some other way. There is, therefore, an opportunity cost, which is equal to the return that these funds could otherwise have earned.

Cost of bad debts and delinquent accounts

Some customers may delay unduly the payment of their accounts (called **delinquent accounts**) and others may not pay their accounts at all (called **bad debts**). A delinquent account means that the supplier must wait a longer time before it receives payment, and therefore the opportunity cost is greater. A bad debt means that the supplier incurs the cost of a credit sale without obtaining any benefit.

delinquent accounts accounts where payment has not been made by the due date

bad debts accounts that have proven to be uncollectable and are written off

Cost of administration

Each credit account must be administered. At a minimum, these costs will generally include staff costs, the costs of checking the credit-worthiness of customers, and office expenses such as stationery, postage and telephone charges. Delinquent accounts impose further costs because of the collection costs they involve. Collection costs may include further staff costs and office expenses and, as a final step, the costs of legal action. Such action may be justified if the amount involved is substantial and there is a reasonable probability that the debtor has the ability to pay.

Cost of additional investment

Increased sales will, of themselves, generally involve further costs. For example, a higher inventory level may be required.[5] In the case of a manufacturer, new investment in plant and equipment may be needed to meet the increased demand.

CREDIT POLICY

22.8

In Section 22.7, four elements of **credit policy** were mentioned. These elements are now considered further.

22.8.1 THE DECISION TO OFFER CREDIT

In principle, a company must decide whether it will sell on a strictly 'cash only' basis or whether some credit will be extended. In practice an individual company will often have little choice but to extend credit. If competitors provide credit to customers, it is likely that the company will also have to extend credit if it is to retain its customers' business. The reason is simple: an offer of credit is

LEARNING OBJECTIVE 8
Identify the four elements of credit policy

---

5 The costs associated with investments in inventory were discussed in Chapter 21.

credit policy
supplier's policy on whether credit will be offered to customers and on the terms that will be offered to those customers

equivalent to a price reduction and, naturally, a lower price tends to increase demand. It was noted earlier that from the seller's viewpoint the need to wait for payment involves an opportunity cost. Equally, from the buyer's viewpoint, the ability to defer payment is equivalent to a price reduction. For example, if a customer has a required rate of return of 1 per cent per month, and buys an item for $101 on 1 month's credit, the effective cost in today's terms is only $100.[6]

22.8.2 SELECTION OF CREDIT-WORTHY CUSTOMERS

A company will usually offer similar terms to all its credit-worthy customers, but it must first decide which of its customers will be granted credit and which will be refused credit—that is, it needs information about the riskiness of extending credit to a particular customer at a particular time. In reaching a decision about granting credit, one of the best guides is often the company's own experience with the customer. One technique that is a useful aid in deciding whether to grant credit is the 'decision tree'. This technique was discussed in Chapter 6 and is illustrated in the context of the selection of credit-worthy customers by the following example.

EXAMPLE 22.3

Suppose that Company A has a large number of credit customers and it receives from Company B a request for credit for the purchase of 100 units of Company A's product at $10 per unit. In the first instance, Company A has three choices:

(a) it may grant the request immediately
(b) it may refuse the request immediately, or
(c) it may postpone the decision pending investigation.

At a minimum, this investigation will usually involve checking its own records to see if Company B has received credit from Company A in the past.[7] Such an investigation will show whether Company B is a low credit risk, a high credit risk or is a new customer about whom no information is available from the company's records. Company A wishes to choose the course of action that has the lowest expected cost. The possible actions confronting Company A are shown in the form of a decision tree in Figure 22.1.

FIGURE 22.1 Decision tree showing possible courses of action for Company A

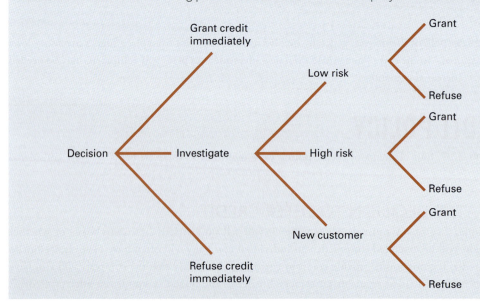

---

[6] More formally, from the buyer's viewpoint, the present value of $101 payable in 1 month's time is $101/1.01 or $100.

[7] Other forms of investigation, such as checking with a credit bureau, are discussed later in this section.

To employ this approach, it is necessary to estimate the cost associated with each end point on the tree. In turn, this requires information on the following items:[8]

(a) the marginal cost of producing each unit, the sales revenue generated by each unit and the marginal net benefit of each unit sold; in this example, the marginal cost of each unit is assumed to be $7, and since the associated sales revenue is $10, the marginal net benefit is $10 − $7 = $3. Therefore, for this order the marginal cost is $700 and the marginal net benefit is $300
(b) the cost of investigation, assumed in this example to be $2 per investigation
(c) the probability that Company B is low risk, high risk or is a new customer; in this example, Company A's experience suggests that these probabilities are 0.80, 0.15 and 0.05, respectively
(d) the cost of capital, assumed in this example to be 2 per cent per month[9]
(e) data for each category on the probability of payment, the probability of a bad debt occurring (which is simply 1 minus the probability of payment), the average waiting period from the date of sale to the date of payment, and the average collection cost. These data are shown in Table 22.6.

TABLE 22.6 Data relating to Example 22.3

DECISION	PROBABILITY OF PAYMENT	PROBABILITY OF BAD DEBT	AVERAGE WAITING PERIOD (MONTHS)	AVERAGE COLLECTION COST ($)
No investigation	0.93	0.07	2	5
Finding of investigation:				
Low risk	1.00	0	1	2
High risk	0.60	0.40	7	20
New customer	0.80	0.20	3	8

To determine whether a customer should be granted credit immediately, refused credit immediately or investigated, the manager needs to compare the costs of these alternatives.

The cost of *granting* credit is given by:

Expected bad debt cost + investment opportunity cost + collection cost
= (probability of bad debt) ($700) + (0.02 × $700) (waiting period) + collection cost

The cost of *refusing* credit is given by:

Expected value of marginal net benefit forgone = (probability of payment) ($300)

Using these equations, the cost at each end point on the decision tree can be calculated as shown below.

Grant credit immediately

Cost = (0.07 × $700) + (0.02 × $700 × 2) + $5 = $82

Investigate, with the following findings and decisions

Low risk/grant: Cost = (0 × $700) + (0.02 × $700 × 1) + $2 = $16
Low risk/refuse: Cost = (1 × $300) = $300
High risk/grant: Cost = (0.4 × $700) + (0.02 × $700 × 7) + $20 = $398
High risk/refuse: Cost = (0.6 × $300) = $180
New customer/grant: Cost = (0.2 × $700) + (0.02 × $700 × 3) + $8 = $190
New customer/refuse: Cost = (0.8 × $300) = $240

continued →

---

[8] To simplify the example it is assumed that there are no costs of additional investment in non-current assets or inventory.
[9] To simplify the discussion, we use simple interest—that is, 2 per cent for 1 month, 4 per cent for 2 months, and so on.

Example 22.3 continued

Refuse credit immediately

Cost = (0.93)($300) = $279

These amounts are shown on the decision tree in Figure 22.2. If an investigation is undertaken, there is a probability of 0.80 that Company B will be found to be in the low-risk category. In that case, the lower cost decision is to grant credit (since $16 is less than $300). If Company B is found to be in the high-risk category (probability 0.15), the request will be refused (cost $180). If Company B is found to be a new customer (probability 0.05), the request will be granted (cost $190). The investigation itself will cost $2. Therefore, the total expected cost of investigating the request is:

$2 + (0.8 x $16) + (0.15 x $180) + (0.05 x $190) = $51.30

Finally, comparing the three decisions—grant immediately, refuse immediately or investigate—it is found that the lowest-cost choice is to investigate this request. The expected cost of investigating the request is $51.30, as against $82 for an immediate granting of credit and $279 for an immediate refusal of credit. If the investigation shows that Company B is either an existing customer in the low-risk category or a new customer, the request will be granted. However, if Company B is an existing customer in the high-risk category, the request will be refused.

FIGURE 22.2 Decision tree showing costs of alternative actions for Company A

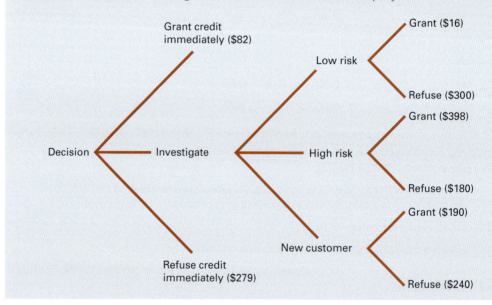

The decision-tree approach discussed in Example 22.3 is appropriate for a company that relies to a large extent on information obtained from experience with its own customers. Undoubtedly, this is a convenient and very useful source of information. Frequently, however, companies look to other sources as well. For example, Company A may require Company B to complete a credit application form. Generally, this form will require the applicant to provide the names of both trade and bank referees who can be contacted to provide information on the applicant's credit-worthiness. Larger companies may have a credit rating assigned by a credit rating agency, such as Fitch Ratings, Moody's Investors Service or Standard & Poor's.[10] Other major sources of information are credit bureaus such as Dun & Bradstreet.

---

10 See Section 4.7 for a description and examples of such ratings.

These bureaus maintain records of companies' financial details, including their record in paying trade debts, and provide this information to interested parties for a fee. Other information on the creditworthiness of Company B may be obtained from other businesses with which it has an account. These businesses will have first-hand knowledge of Company B's payment record. Company A may also require information on the financial condition of Company B. This is usually obtained from the company's financial statements and from the completed application form. Company A's main concern is the short-term liquidity position of Company B as this provides a measure of its ability to pay. In addition, the value of Company B's unencumbered non-current assets provides some indication of the degree of security. The use of financial statement analysis in credit policy is discussed in Appendix 22.1.

The credit standards that a company applies will influence the incidence of bad debts and delinquent accounts. A company will incur virtually no bad debts if it applies very high standards, but in doing so it will probably have to forgo sales.

22.8.3 LIMIT OF CREDIT EXTENDED

Even if Company B is accepted as a credit-worthy customer by Company A, it is usual for A to place a limit on the maximum amount of credit it is prepared to extend to B. The limit will depend, in part, on the expected value of B's purchases from A. However, A may not wish to extend to B sufficient credit to finance the full amount of B's purchases. The most obvious advantage to A of imposing a credit limit is that it reduces the maximum loss that A can suffer if B defaults. The ability to set a limit is particularly useful with new customers. At first, a relatively low limit can be set in order to reduce the risk, but, as time passes, and the account is satisfactorily maintained, higher limits can be established. In this way, business is not lost because of refusal to grant credit, but the risk exposure is not excessive.

22.8.4 CREDIT TERMS

A company's credit terms specify a credit period, and may also specify a discount period(s) and a discount rate(s). The **credit period** is the period that elapses between the date when the purchasing company is invoiced and the date when payment is due.[11] The **discount period** is the period that elapses between the date when the purchasing company is invoiced and the date when the discount is forgone. The **discount rate** expresses, in effect, the price reduction that the purchasing company will receive if it pays within the discount period.

Typical examples of credit terms are as follows:

- n/30: There is no discount and the credit period is 30 days. After the expiration of the credit period, the purchaser is in default.
- 2/10, n/30: The discount rate is 2 per cent, the discount period is 10 days and the credit period is 30 days. Therefore, if Company B purchases, on credit, goods worth $100 from Company A, and the purchase is included in its statement of account dated 31 March, then Company B would have to pay only $98 if the account is paid by 10 April. If it forgoes the discount, Company B is required to pay $100 by the end of April. After that date, Company B would be in default.
- 3½/10, 2½/30: There are two discount periods. A higher discount of 3½ per cent is allowed if payment is made within 10 days of being invoiced, while a discount of 2½ per cent is received if payment is made within 30 days. The credit period is also set at 30 days. Therefore, a company will receive a discount for paying within the credit period.

credit period
period between the date that a purchaser is invoiced and the date when payment is due

discount period
period during which a discount for prompt payment is available to the purchaser

discount rate
expression of the price reduction a purchaser will receive if payment is made within the discount period

---

11 The statement of account is the regular notification that the selling company sends to its debtors to indicate their current indebtedness. These statements are normally sent out monthly, often at the end of the month. This practice is important because the credit period does not commence from the date of sale but rather from the date on the monthly statement. A debtor can use this to his advantage by purchasing at the beginning of the month and stretching a 30-day credit period into an almost 60-day credit period.

A company offers a discount to accelerate its cash inflow and/or to improve its competitive position. If we consider the credit terms 2/10, n/30, the purchasing company obtains an effective reduction in price by paying within 10 days. Therefore, a company may obtain a larger share of the market for its product by offering higher discounts than its competitors. Also, the discount will encourage the company's credit customers to pay earlier. In percentage terms, the financial inducement to pay earlier can be quite large. Referring again to the credit terms 2/10, n/30, consider the position of Company B on 10 April. To find a better use for its $98, Company B would need to find an investment that, with zero risk, can turn $98 into $100 within 20 days. The annual effective rate of return required is therefore:

$$\left(1+\frac{2}{98}\right)^{\frac{365}{20}} - 1$$
$$= 44.6\%$$

Earlier payments by customers will reduce the amount that Company A has tied up in receivables, and will also reduce the incidence of bad debts and delinquent accounts. In turn, this will reduce its collection costs.

22.9 COLLECTION POLICY

LEARNING OBJECTIVE 9
Understand the factors in implementing a collection policy

A company that never has a bad debt almost certainly has a sub-optimal credit policy—that is, if a more lenient policy were adopted, then the increase in sales would more than offset the losses imposed by a few bad debts. For most companies, some bad debts are inevitable. Notwithstanding this fact, it is also true that in most cases some attempt to collect overdue debts is worthwhile. These efforts are referred to as the company's **collection policy**.

The critical problem in collection policy is the need to recognise when an account warrants special attention. Obviously it is not sensible to institute legal action on a $10 account that is 2 days overdue. But what if the account were for $10 million, rather than $10? Is action warranted if a $1000 account is 30 days overdue? If so, what action should be taken? There are no hard and fast answers to these questions. However, most businesses adopt a set of procedures. Generally, attempts to collect an account that is overdue begin with a standard reminder notice, followed by personal letters and telephone calls. Eventually, visits may be made in person. The last resort is legal action, but this can be very expensive and may involve long delays. An alternative is to employ a debt collection agency, but this too can be expensive. It may also sometimes pay a business to accept a partial payment, rather than continue with attempts to collect the full amount owed.

collection policy
policy adopted by a company in regard to collecting delinquent accounts either informally or by the use of a debt collection agency

As the amount spent on collection activities increases, it is to be expected that bad debt losses will be reduced and the average collection period will be shorter. However, these relationships are unlikely to be linear. For example, an initial small level of expenditure is unlikely to have any marked effect in reducing bad debts, or in shortening the average collection period, while additional expenditures are likely to have a much greater effect. However, beyond a certain level of collection expenditure the benefits will diminish until eventually a saturation point is reached. The relationship between the average collection period and the level of collection expenditures is likely to be similar.

Collection policy involves a trade-off between the costs of collection, and the benefits of lower bad debt losses and a shorter average collection period, which in turn will result in a reduction in the company's investment in accounts receivable. Comparing these costs and benefits to determine a preferred policy is likely to involve considerable judgement. Also, in determining a collection policy, it is important to take account of the effect of the collection policy on sales, as a more forceful collection procedure may adversely affect sales. For example, if collection procedures are begun too early, customers may be offended and switch to alternative suppliers.

22.10 EVALUATION OF ALTERNATIVE CREDIT AND COLLECTION POLICIES

The net present value (NPV) method of evaluating investment projects was discussed in Chapters 5 and 6. The investment projects analysed in those chapters related to investments in non-current assets, such as property, plant and equipment. However, in principle, the NPV method is appropriate for other types of investment, including investment in accounts receivable. In this section, we consider the application of the NPV method to a company's credit and collection policies.

LEARNING OBJECTIVE 10

Apply the net present value method to evaluate alternative credit and collection policies

The benefits associated with a change in credit policy can be measured by the net increase in sales revenue, while the costs will include manufacturing, selling, collection and administration expenses, and bad debts. In addition, by discounting the net cash flows generated by the credit policy at the cost of capital, the analysis will incorporate the cost to the company of having funds tied up in receivables.[12] If all the benefits and costs associated with a particular credit policy are quantified and expressed in present value terms, the particular credit policy under consideration will be profitable if the net present value is positive. The company's optimum credit policy is the one that results in the largest net present value.

The application of NPV analysis to the evaluation of alternative policies is outlined in the following examples. We begin with a highly simplified example, and introduce additional factors relevant to the decision in subsequent examples. The examples are intended mainly to illustrate the factors that could influence the profitability of a credit policy. In practice, many companies adopt credit policies that are similar to those followed by others in the same industry. However, if sufficient data are available to estimate the effects of changes in the terms offered, and competitive conditions suggest that changes may be feasible, then a credit manager could use the approach embodied in these examples to assess whether it is desirable to modify the present policy.

EXAMPLE 22.4

Zelco Ltd, which currently does not offer credit, is considering extending credit to its customers for a period of 60 days. This is assumed to result in an increase in sales revenue of $20 000. The additional cost associated with these sales is $16 000. Initially, it is assumed that Zelco's existing cash customers will not seek credit if the proposed credit policy is introduced. It is also assumed that there are no bad debts, administration costs or collection costs and that all credit customers will take full advantage of the credit terms by delaying payment until the 60th day.[13] Zelco's cost of capital is 2 per cent per month.[14] What is the NPV of extending credit to customers?

continued →

---

12 The required rate of return depends on the risk class of credit customers. In addition, the analysis should take into account the costs of financing any additional inventory or non-current assets that the company requires to support a higher level of operations. In the subsequent examples it will be assumed that these costs have been included in the costs associated with the sale. However, in practice, these costs will only include accounting costs, such as the cost of the goods sold and delivery charges. Therefore, it is usually necessary to impute a figure so as to include the cost of the additional funds invested in inventory and non-current assets.

13 In this and subsequent examples, it is assumed for simplicity that the credit period and the discount period extend from the date of purchase, rather than from the date on the monthly statement.

14 In accordance with business practice, the length of the credit period is referred to in terms of days. However, to make the present value calculations less cumbersome, monthly discounting is used. It is assumed that 1 month equals 30 days and, to ease the exposition, the phrase 'at the end of the month' will be stated more simply as 'at month' since all cash flows in these examples are assumed to occur at the end of the month.

Example 22.4 *continued*

SOLUTION

Given these assumptions, the investment opportunity being considered by Zelco consists of an initial outlay of $16 000 at time zero, and a cash inflow of $20 000 at the end of Month 2. With a cost of capital of 2 per cent per month, the NPV of the proposed policy is:

$$NPV = \frac{\$20\,000}{(1.02)^2} - \$16\,000$$

$$= \$3223.38$$

Since the NPV is positive, the proposed credit policy is profitable.

The credit policy proposed in Example 22.4 did not offer discounts for payments received before the expiration of the credit period. This possibility is shown in Example 22.5.

EXAMPLE 22.5

Suppose that the assumptions made in Example 22.4 are retained, except that Zelco now offers a discount of 2½ per cent for payments received within 30 days—that is, the proposed credit terms are 2½/30, n/60. It is estimated that 75 per cent of credit customers will take advantage of the discount.

What is the NPV of extending credit on these revised terms?

SOLUTION

As in Example 22.4, the initial outlay is $16 000. The cash inflow at Month 1 is (1 − 0.025) x 0.75 x $20 000 = $14 625 and the cash inflow at Month 2 is 0.25 x $20 000 = $5000. The NPV of the proposed policy is therefore:

$$NPV = \frac{\$14\,625}{1.02} + \frac{\$5000}{(1.02)^2} - \$16\,000$$

$$= \$3144.08$$

The NPV of this policy is positive and it is therefore preferred to the current policy of not offering credit at all. However, the NPV of this policy is less than the NPV of a credit policy that offers no discount for early payment. This indicates that Zelco should not offer the discount assumed in the example.

Example 22.5 did not allow for the possibility that the offer of a discount could well attract even more new customers to Zelco. Because a discount amounts to a reduction in price, it is possible that demand would increase. The increased demand could be sufficient to justify offering the discount. This is shown in Example 22.6.

EXAMPLE 22.6

It is now assumed that, as well as the additional sales of $20 000 assumed in Examples 22.4 and 22.5, further sales of $4000 (at a cost of $3200) are made to customers, all of whom take advantage of the 2 per cent discount. What is the effect of the additional sales on the NPV of extending credit?

SOLUTION

The initial outlay is now $16 000 + $3200 = $19 200. The cash inflow at Month 1 is $14 625 + ((1 − 0.025) x $4000) = $18 525 and the cash inflow at Month 2 remains at $5000. The NPV of the proposed policy is therefore:

$$NPV = \frac{\$18\,525}{1.02} + \frac{\$5000}{(1.02)^2} - \$19\,200$$

$$= \$3767.61$$

Since the NPV is positive, and exceeds the NPV calculated in Example 22.6, the proposed policy that offers a 2 per cent discount for payment received within 30 days is preferable to a policy that offers no discount for early payment.

To summarise the position so far, the initial outlay is $19 200, the cash inflow at Month 1 is $18 525 and the cash inflow at Month 2 is $5000. Bad debts and delinquent accounts have so far been ignored. The effect of bad debts and delinquent accounts is illustrated in Example 22.7.

EXAMPLE 22.7

It is now assumed that the offer of a discount will still result in a cash inflow of $18 525 at Month 1, but of the remaining $5000 owing, $3000 will be paid on time (at Month 2), $1000 will be paid late (at Month 3), $400 will be paid still later (at Month 4) and $600 will never be paid—that is, bad debts will amount to unpaid accounts of $600. What will be the effect of bad debts and delinquent accounts on the NPV of extending credit?

SOLUTION

Based on the above assumptions, the NPV is:

$$NPV = \frac{\$18\,525}{1.02} + \frac{\$3000}{(1.02)^2} + \frac{\$1000}{(1.02)^3} + \frac{\$400}{(1.02)^4} - \$19\,200$$

$$= \$3157.13$$

Since the NPV is positive, the proposed credit policy is still an acceptable investment.

The costs of administration and collection still have to be included in the analysis. A large proportion of these costs do not depend on the value of the account. For example, the clerical cost of producing and posting a tax invoice for a customer who owes $200 is not likely to be different from the cost incurred for a customer who owes $10 000. At the level of the individual account, the total amount spent in an effort to collect the amount owing will increase, the longer the account remains unpaid. However, taking the company's monthly spending on collection procedures for all accounts that have been granted credit at a given point in time, the amount spent each month on collection is likely to decrease as time passes. For example, suppose that 10 accounts are overdue and the company spends $2 per account to send a first reminder notice. Expenditure on collection procedures for that month is therefore $20. If, in the next month, seven of these accounts have been paid, there are three remaining unpaid accounts to be sent a second reminder notice at a total cost of $6. Expenditure on collection has therefore fallen from $20 to $6. The extent of this decrease may be lessened by the fact that later stages of the collection procedure may be more expensive on a 'per account' basis. For example, a personal letter uses more staff time and therefore imposes more costs than sending a standard reminder notice. Administration and collection costs are illustrated in Example 22.8.

EXAMPLE 22.8

Zelco estimates administration costs to be $200 at Month 0, $100 at Month 1 and $150 at Month 2. Collection costs are estimated to be $70 at Month 3 and $40 at Month 4. What is the NPV after allowing for administration and collection costs?

SOLUTION

After including administration and collection costs, the initial outlay is therefore $19 200 + $200 = $19 400, and the net cash flows in the following months are $18 525 − $100 = $18 425; $3000 − $150 = $2850; $1000 − $70 = $930 and $400 − $40 = $360.

continued →

Example 22.8 continued

$$NPV = \frac{\$18\,425}{1.02} + \frac{\$2850}{(1.02)^2} + \frac{\$930}{(1.02)^3} + \frac{\$360}{(1.02)^4} - \$19\,400$$

$$= \$2612.00$$

Since the NPV is positive, the proposed credit policy is still an acceptable investment.

So far it has been assumed that Zelco's existing customers, all of whom pay cash, will not also demand that they be granted credit. While many existing customers would no doubt continue to pay cash, it is inevitable that some would now seek to obtain credit. If these customers are credit-worthy, a refusal of credit could well be offensive and may therefore result in lost sales. Some existing cash-paying customers would therefore become credit customers and this would impose further costs on Zelco. This is illustrated in Example 22.9.

EXAMPLE 22.9

It is now assumed that existing customers switch $15 000 worth of business from a cash basis to a credit basis. What is the effect of this change on the NPV of extending credit?

SOLUTION

Table 22.7 shows the estimated changes to Zelco's cash flows.[15]

TABLE 22.7 Cash flow effects of existing cash customers switching to credit

MONTH	ACCOUNTS PAID ($)	DISCOUNT ($)	ADMINISTRATION COST ($)	COLLECTION COST ($)	TOTAL ($)
0	—	—	−140	—	−140
1	10 000	−250	−50	—	9 700
2	4 000	—	−150	—	3 850
3	500	—	—	−30	470
4	200	—	—	−30	170

The present value of the cash flows is as follows:

$$PV = -\$140 + \frac{\$9700}{1.02} + \frac{\$3850}{(1.02)^2} + \frac{\$470}{(1.02)^3} + \frac{\$170}{(1.02)^4}$$

$$= \$13\,670.25$$

The corresponding cash sales totalled $15 000, so, in present value terms, the increased cost imposed by the need to grant credit to customers who currently pay cash is $15 000 − $13 670.25 = $1329.75. The NPV of the proposed credit policy is reduced by this amount. The final estimate of the NPV is therefore $2612.00 − $1329.75 = $1282.25.

---

[15] Note that there is no entry in Table 22.7 to show the costs of manufacturing the goods. Such costs are not incremental, since they are incurred regardless of whether the sale is for credit or cash.

We have now examined a number of components of credit and collection policies and decided that each should be set with the aim of maximising the net present value resulting from the company's investment in accounts receivable. The above examples show that, *other things being equal*, the net present value will be lower if customers accept discounts offered for early payment and if customers pay late, or fail to pay at all for credit purchases. Net present value will also be lowered by collection costs and by cash customers transferring to credit. The credit manager's job is to ensure that other things are not equal—that is, the company's policies should be designed so that the costs of extending credit are outweighed by the benefits.

Connect Plus features a case study illustrating topics covered in this chapter.
Ask your lecturer or tutor for your course's unique URL.

SUMMARY

→ A company's liquid resources comprise cash and short-term investments.

→ Liquidity management refers to decisions made by management about the composition and level of a company's liquid resources.
   – If too little is held in liquid form, a company may sometimes be unable to meet its commitments.
   – If too much is held in liquid form, a company's rate of return may become unacceptably low.

→ Treasury management includes liquidity management together with decisions about the company's exposure to various kinds of financial risk (foreign exchange and interest rate risk).

→ Although motives for holding liquid assets include a:
   – transactions motive
   – precautionary motive
   – speculative motive
   the chapter considers only the first of these in any detail.

→ In practice, a major tool of liquidity management is the cash budget. This sets out a forecast of a company's cash receipts and cash payments. Action can then be planned to eliminate any future cash shortage or to use any cash surplus that is forecast to occur.

→ In selecting liquid assets, a financial manager has a wide range to choose from, including government securities, deposits of funds with financial institutions, and discounting of commercial bills. Each offers a different combination of term, marketability and default risk. The financial manager faces the difficult task of choosing a mix (or portfolio) that is suitable for the company.

→ Accounts receivable are monies owed to a company or other business from the sale, on credit, of goods or services in the normal course of business. Accounts receivable arise because a company offers credit to customers in order to benefit from increased sales. The costs of offering credit include the opportunity cost of funds tied up in accounts receivable, the costs of bad debts and delinquent (slow-paying) accounts and additional administration costs.

→ Decisions concerning management of accounts receivable involve credit and collection policies.

→ Given that credit is to be offered, credit policy encompasses selection of credit-worthy customers, and determining credit limits and credit terms.

- Where a company has adequate data obtained from experience with its customers, decision trees may be useful in deciding whether to accept, refuse or investigate particular requests for credit. Other useful sources of information include trade and bank referees, credit bureaus and analysis of the applicant's financial statements.
- A company's credit terms specify a credit period and may also specify a discount for early payment. If customers respond by making earlier payments, the amount tied up in receivables will be reduced, as will collection costs.

→ Collection policy involves a trade-off between the amount spent on collection activities (sending reminder notices and letters, legal action, and so on) and the benefits of a reduction in bad debt losses and a shorter collection period.
- In seeking an optimal collection policy, the effects of alternative policies on sales should be considered.

→ The net present value method can be used to highlight the factors that will influence the profitability of a company's credit and collection policies.

KEY TERMS

account receivable (or debtor) 768
bad debts 769
cash budget 762
collection policy 774
consumer credit 768
credit period 773
credit policy 770
delinquent accounts 769
discount period 773
discount rate 773
liquid assets 760
liquidity management 760
open account 768
trade credit 768
treasury management 760

SELF-TEST PROBLEMS

1. Warner Ltd sells on terms of 2/7, n/30. Customer X buys goods from Warner with an invoice total of $1500.
   (a) If X pays 7 days after the invoice date, what discount can he deduct from the bill?
   (b) What effective annual interest rate is implicit in the terms offered?

2. Angeline Ltd has until recently sold its products on terms of n/30, and the average collection period has been 45 days. In an attempt to shorten the collection period, it has changed the terms to 1/10, n/30. It has been found that 70 per cent of customers pay within 10 days and claim the discount. The other 30 per cent pay, on average, after 50 days. There has been no change in sales volume and the required rate of return is 10 per cent per annum. The cost of goods sold is 75 per cent of sales and there are no defaults. Has the change in terms been profitable?

Solutions to self-test problems are available in Appendix B, page 803.

REFERENCES

Bruce R., McKern, B., Pollard, I. & Skully, M. (eds), *Handbook of Australian Corporate Finance*, 5th edn, Butterworths, Sydney, 1997.

Gallinger, G.W. & Healey, P.B., *Liquidity Analysis and Management*, Addison-Wesley, Reading, Massachusetts, 1987.

Keynes, J.M., *The General Theory of Employment Interest and Money*, Harcourt Brace & World, New York, 1936.

Lundholm, R. & Sloan, R., *Equity Valuation and Analysis*, 2nd edn, McGraw-Hill, New York, 2006.

Mian, S.L. & Smith C.W. Jr, 'Accounts receivable management policy: theory and evidence', *Journal of Finance*, March 1992, pp. 169–200.

——, ——, 'Extending trade credit and financing', *Journal of Applied Corporate Finance*, Spring 1994, pp. 75–84.

Ng, C.K., Smith, J.K. & Smith, R.L., 'Evidence on the determinants of credit terms used in interfirm trade', *Journal of Finance*, June 1999, pp. 1109–29.

Penman, S.H., *Financial Statement Analysis and Security Valuation*, 4th edn, McGraw-Hill, New York, 2009.

QUESTIONS

1. **[LO 2]** *For most Australian companies, cash is a very small proportion of total assets, and therefore cash management is unimportant.* Discuss this statement.
2. **[LO 3]** Explain the costs and benefits of holding liquid assets.
3. **[LO 5]** A company has $1 million in idle funds and it is estimated that these will be available for investment for approximately 2 months. The treasurer is considering the following investments:
   (a) purchasing a 1-month bank certificate of deposit
   (b) lodging a fixed deposit with a bank
   (c) purchasing commercial bills.
   Discuss the advantages and disadvantages of each investment.
4. **[LO 3]** *Liquidity risk is more important than return risk in the choice between alternative short-term investments.* Discuss.
5. **[LO 5]** You are the treasurer of a company that has $1 million in idle funds to invest for a period of 90 days. List the available short-term investments and obtain current interest rates from the financial press. Prepare a report and recommended action for consideration by the Board of Directors, pointing out the return(s) and risk(s) involved.
6. **[LO 8]** Discuss the reasons for a company offering credit terms to its customers.
7. **[LO 8]** (a) A company offers credit terms of 1/7, n/30. Explain the meaning of these terms.
   (b) What effective annual interest rate is implicit in this offer?
8. **[LO 8]** What are the advantages and disadvantages of offering a discount for early payment?
9. **[LO 9]** What are the advantages and disadvantages of an aggressive collection policy?

PROBLEMS

1. **Preparing a cash budget [LO 4]**
   In late June of each year, Durango Ltd prepares a cash budget for the next 6 months. The company has a policy of maintaining a cash balance at the beginning of each month equal to the difference between the estimated cash inflows and payments for the month, plus a safety margin of $4000.
   Actual sales for May and estimated sales for June and for the next 7 months are as follows:

May	$20 000	October	$94 000
June	$28 000	November	$74 000
July	$24 000	December	$52 000
August	$26 000	January	$40 000
September	$50 000		

   Approximately 25 per cent of the sales are for cash and 75 per cent are on credit. Experience has shown that two-thirds of all credit sales are collected in the month following sale, and the remaining one-third in the second month following sale. No discounts are given.
   Durango follows a policy of basing its purchases on estimated sales. Purchases are equal to 70 per cent of the following month's estimated sales. The policy of the company is to ensure that the goods needed in each month are acquired in the preceding month. Durango's suppliers permit it to take a 2 per cent discount if the goods are paid for within the first 10 days of the month following purchase. All goods must be paid for by the end of the month following purchase.
   Other payments are expected to be:

July	$7 400	October	$11 000
August	$7 450	November	$7 800
September	$9 100	December	$7 150

   At the beginning of July, the company is expected to have $8400 in its bank account.
   Prepare a monthly cash budget for Durango Ltd for the 6 months ended 31 December. Will any outside funds be required? If so, how much?

2. **Selection of credit-worthy customers [LO 10]**
   Hayworth Ltd uses a decision-tree approach for screening credit applicants. Gables Ltd has sought credit for the purchase of 1000 units priced at $16 each. The marginal cost of producing each unit is $12. Based on

Decision	Probability of payment	Probability of bad debt	Average waiting period (months)	Average collection cost ($)
No investigation	0.92	0.08	2	93
Finding of investigation:				
Low risk	1.00	0	1	10
High risk	0.70	0.30	5	400
New customer	0.80	0.20	3	60

its past experience, Hayworth estimates that there is a 70 per cent chance that Gables falls into the low-risk category, a 20 per cent chance that it is high risk and a 10 per cent chance that it is a new customer. The table above summarises other data estimated by Hayworth's credit department.

The cost of conducting an investigation is $2. Hayworth estimates the opportunity cost of capital to be 2 per cent per month. What decision should Hayworth make?

3. **Evaluation of alternative credit terms [LO 10]**
Company A at present sells only on a cash basis and it averages $50 000 of sales per month, with associated expenses of $40 000. It is thought that all customers would accept an offer of 90-day free credit terms and that the company's monthly sales would increase to $55 000 and its associated expenses to $44 000. Company A's required rate of return is 1 per cent per month.
   (a) Assuming that there are no costs associated with providing credit, will Company A benefit from offering such credit terms?
   (b) If expenses remain at 80 per cent of sales, what would the increase in sales need to be in order to justify the provision of these credit terms?

4. **Evaluation of alternative credit and collection policies [LO 10]**
Each month, Jumbo Pty Ltd sells 10 000 units at $25 per unit. The marginal cost of producing each unit is $15. At present all of Jumbo's sales are made on a strict 'cash only' basis. Jumbo's manager believes that the 'cash only' policy has led to many sales being lost as there have been a number of enquiries concerning the possibility of credit sales. Jumbo's manager estimates that a credit policy of 1/30, n/60 could increase sales by 1000 units per month, of which 500 would be paid for at the end of Month 1 and 400 would be paid for at the end of Month 2. Of the remaining 100 units, 70 are expected to be paid for a month late and 30 are expected to be bad debts. Administration and collection costs are estimated to be $250 (Month 0), $100 (Month 1), $100 (Month 2) and $150 (Month 3). However, it is expected that some existing customers will also seek credit in order to obtain the discount offered. This is likely to affect the sale of 600 units. Buyers of the remaining 9400 units are expected to continue to pay cash. Administration costs are estimated to be $150 (Month 0) and $60 (Month 1). Jumbo's required rate of return is 1.5 per cent per month. Should Jumbo adopt the proposed credit arrangements?

APPENDIX 22.1 FINANCIAL STATEMENT ANALYSIS

INTRODUCTION

> **LEARNING OBJECTIVE 11**
> Apply financial statement analysis to short-term asset management

In the chapters on short-term asset management, no specific reference has been made to the analysis of financial statements, which is frequently used by financial managers in short-term asset management. Analysis of financial statements involves the calculation of financial ratios using the data in the statement of financial performance (income statement) and the statement of financial position. Financial managers frequently examine the values of certain 'key' ratios as a way of monitoring a company's management of short-term assets and liabilities. In this appendix, some of the more frequently used financial ratios are defined, their application examined and their usefulness for short-term asset management discussed.[16]

MEASUREMENT AND INTERPRETATION OF SEVERAL FINANCIAL RATIOS

First we define and calculate a number of financial ratios, using the financial statements of Harvey Norman Holdings Limited, shown in Tables A22.1 and A22.2.

TABLE A22.1 Harvey Norman Holdings Limited: Income Statement for the year ended 30 June 2010

	CONSOLIDATED	
	2010 ($'000)	2009 ($'000)
Sales revenue	1 344 455	1 440 651
Cost of sales	(968 273)	(1 043 231)
Gross profit	376 182	397 420
Other revenues	1 097 389	1 035 101
Distribution expenses	(8 108)	(10 319)
Marketing expenses	(355 039)	(320 405)
Occupancy expenses	(228 121)	(213 595)
Administrative expenses	(373 836)	(403 431)
Finance costs	(33 638)	(34 706)
Other expenses from ordinary activities	(85 773)	(121 767)
Share of net profit of associates, joint venture entities and partnerships accounted for using the equity method	(2 594)	19 949
Profit from continuing operations before income tax expense	**386 462**	**348 247**
Income tax expense	(148 474)	(128 907)
Profit from continuing operations after tax	**237 988**	**219 340**
Profit from continuing operations attributable to minority interests	6 579	4 989
Profit from continuing operations attributable to members of the parent	**231 409**	**214 351**

Source: Harvey Norman Holdings Limited, *Annual Report 2010*, 2010, p. 37.

---

[16] For a more detailed discussion of the usefulness of financial ratios for short-term asset management, see Gallinger and Healey (1987, Ch. 3).

TABLE A22.2 Harvey Norman Holdings Limited: Statement of Financial Position as at 30 June 2010

	CONSOLIDATED	
	2010 ($'000)	2009 ($'000)
Current assets		
Cash assets	157 236	157 907
Receivables[a]	1 081 645	1 076 465
Other financial assets	34 400	25 874
Inventories[b]	261 674	259 877
Intangible assets	761	537
Other (prepayments)	20 913	15 068
Total current assets	1 556 629	1 535 728
Non-current assets		
Receivables	25 182	18 615
Investments accounted for using equity method	140 581	189 571
Other financial assets	7 171	5 513
Investment properties	1 489 200	1 316 572
Property, plant and equipment	439 033	548 615
Intangible assets	24 229	18 675
Deferred income tax assets	22 488	22 897
Total non-current assets	2 147 884	2 120 458
Total assets	3 704 513	3 656 186
Current liabilities		
Payables	739 715	739 484
Interest-bearing liabilities	[c] 154 342	[d] 574 966
Tax liabilities	41 040	40 798
Provisions	23 326	21 247
Other	2 930	3 066
Total current liabilities	961 353	1 379 561
Non-current liabilities		
Payables	23 332	–
Interest-bearing liabilities	346 824	11 714
Provisions	8 819	9 616
Other	21 984	26 012
Deferred income tax liabilities	184 990	170 101

	CONSOLIDATED	
	2010 ($'000)	2009 ($'000)
Total non-current liabilities	585 949	217 443
Total liabilities	1 547 302	1 597 004
Net assets	**2 157 211**	**2 059 182**
Equity		
Contributed equity	259 610	259 610
Reserves	56 418	52 545
Retained profits	1 787 196	1 693 888
Parent entity interest	2 103 224	2 006 043
Outside equity interest	53 987	53 139
Total equity [e]	**2 157 211**	**2 059 182**

[a] Receivables in 2008 were $1 001 426 000.
[b] Inventories in 2008 were $226 005 000.
[c] Includes bank overdraft of $56 326 000.
[d] Includes bank overdraft of $96 532 000.
[e] Shareholders' equity in 2008 was $1 947 152 000.

Source: Harvey Norman Holdings Limited, *Annual Report 2010*, 2010, p. 36.

There are four broad categories of financial ratios. They are *liquidity ratios*, *activity ratios*, *leverage ratios* and *profitability ratios*.

LIQUIDITY RATIOS

Liquidity ratios are a measure of a company's ability to meet its maturing short-term financial obligations. The following ratios are classified as liquidity ratios.

Current ratio

Traditionally, the current ratio has been used to measure a company's liquidity. It is calculated by dividing total current assets by total current liabilities. Its use dates from the nineteenth century and it is still widely used as an important measure of a company's ability to pay its short-term debts when they are due. Using the data for Harvey Norman, the current ratio is as follows:[17]

$$\text{Current ratio} = \frac{\text{total current assets}}{\text{total current liabilities}}$$

$$= \frac{\$1\,556\,629\,000}{\$961\,353\,000}$$

$$= 1.62\ (1.11)$$

The higher the current ratio, the greater will be the company's ability to meet its immediate financial obligations. However, the higher this ratio, the greater will be the proportion of the company's resources

---

[17] The value for each ratio, based on the figures in the 2009–10 financial statements, is included in parentheses.

that is tied up in relatively unproductive assets. This may have an adverse effect on profitability. Management therefore has to decide on the appropriate balance between profitability and liquidity.

'Quick' ratio

The quick ratio is calculated by dividing total current assets, minus inventories and prepayments, by total current liabilities minus bank overdraft. Prepayments are deducted because they represent amounts paid for services yet to be provided and therefore are not easily converted into cash. Similarly, inventory is the least liquid current asset and could be difficult to sell at short notice. Bank overdrafts are deducted from current liabilities because they are unlikely to be withdrawn at short notice.[18] The quick ratio is more useful than the current ratio as a measure of the company's ability to meet its financial obligations should they become payable almost immediately.

$$\text{Quick ratio} = \frac{\text{total current assets} - (\text{inventories} + \text{prepayments})}{\text{total current liabilities} - \text{bank overdraft}}$$

$$= \frac{\$1\,556\,629\,000 - (\$261\,674\,000 + \$20\,913\,000)}{\$961\,353\,000 - \$56\,326\,000}$$

$$= \frac{\$1\,274\,042\,000}{\$905\,027\,000}$$

$$= 1.41\,(0.98)$$

As with the current ratio, the higher the quick ratio, the greater the company's ability to meet its immediate financial obligations.

ACTIVITY RATIOS

Activity ratios measure the effectiveness of a company's use of its assets. These ratios generally relate the amount of a particular group of assets (such as inventory, accounts receivable or total assets) to the activity generated by that group (such as sales, cost of goods sold and net profit). We consider three such ratios.

Average inventory turnover period

The average inventory turnover period measures the average time a company's inventory remains on hand before being sold, and is usually calculated by dividing the average inventory by the cost of goods sold.

$$\text{Average inventory turnover period} = \frac{\text{average inventorty}}{\text{cost of goods sold}} \times 365$$

$$= \frac{\frac{\$261\,674\,000 + \$259\,877\,000}{2}}{\$968\,273\,000} \times 365$$

$$= 98.3\,\text{days}\,(85.0\,\text{days})$$

For Harvey Norman the average inventory turnover period increased from 85.0 days in 2009 to 98.3 days in 2010—that is, inventory was on hand for a longer period before being sold. We discussed possible solutions to inventory management problems in Chapter 21. The ideal average inventory turnover period for a company is affected by the optimal inventory level.

---

18 See Chapter 10.

Average collection period

The average collection period is calculated by dividing the average accounts receivable balance by the average daily credit sales. The average collection period is a measure of the average number of days a company must wait after making a credit sale before it receives payment, and indicates whether accounts receivable are being collected within a reasonable period of time. Assuming that all of Harvey Norman's sales were on credit in both the 2008–09 and the 2009–10 financial years, the average collection period is calculated as follows:

$$\text{Average collection period} = \frac{\text{average receivables}}{\text{average daily credit sales}}$$

$$= \frac{\dfrac{\$1\,081\,645\,000 + \$1\,076\,465\,000}{2}}{\$1\,344\,455\,000 / 365}$$

$$= 293 \text{ days } (263 \text{ days})$$

A short average collection period may indicate high efficiency in collecting accounts receivable. However, in Section 22.10 it was shown that reducing the collection period involves various costs and it is possible for the collection period to be 'too short' because the company's credit policy is too restrictive.

Total asset turnover

Total asset turnover measures the turnover of the company's assets and is calculated by dividing sales by total tangible assets.

$$\text{Total asset turnover} = \frac{\text{sales}}{\text{total tangible assets}}$$

$$= \frac{\$1\,344\,455\,000}{\$3\,704\,513\,000 - (24\,990\,000 + 22\,488\,000)}$$

$$= 0.37 \ (0.40)$$

where total tangible assets = total assets − (intangible assets + deferred tax assets)

This ratio is a measure of a company's efficiency in the use of its assets to generate sales. An efficient company will generate a higher level of sales with a given level of assets than its less efficient competitors. A high ratio could also indicate that the company is operating at close to its capacity. If this is the case, then additional investment in assets may be required if output and sales are to be increased.

LEVERAGE RATIOS

Leverage ratios show the extent to which a company uses debt in its capital structure and provide evidence of a company's ability to pay lenders in the long run. There are many measures of leverage, but we consider only two ratios.

Debt to total assets

This is calculated by dividing total liabilities by total assets.

$$\text{Debts to total assets (leverage ratio)} = \frac{\text{total liabilities}}{\text{total assets}}$$

$$= \frac{\$1\,547\,302\,000}{\$3\,704\,513\,000} \times 100$$

$$= 41.8\% \ (43.7\%)$$

The higher this percentage, the greater is the company's reliance on debt in its capital structure. The effects of leverage on a company's value were considered in Chapter 12, where the use of market values rather than book values was emphasised. A company's ability to repay lenders will ultimately depend on the market value of its assets relative to the face value of its debt. However, analysts frequently rely on book values because they are easier to obtain than market values.

Interest coverage ratio

The interest coverage ratio, which is also referred to as the times interest earned ratio, is calculated by dividing a company's net profit before interest and tax by the interest expense. It is a measure of a company's ability to meet the interest charges on its debt.

$$\text{Interest coverage ratio} = \frac{\text{net profit before interest and tax}}{\text{interest expense}}$$

$$= \frac{\$237\,988\,000 + \$33\,638\,000 + \$148\,474\,000}{\$33\,638\,000}$$

$$= 12.49\ (11.03)$$

In many ways this ratio is superior to the leverage ratio as a measure of financial risk because it attempts to measure the company's ability to pay the interest on its debt and so avoid future financial difficulties. The higher this ratio, the greater the reduction in the company's earnings that can occur before it will default on its interest payments.

There are two important limitations of the interest coverage ratio. First, it is cash flow and not earnings that is important for debt-servicing purposes. This limitation can be addressed by using net profit before interest and tax plus depreciation and other accruals in the numerator. Second, in addition to interest payments, there are other financial obligations that have to be met. These include dividends on preference shares, lease payments and repayment of long-term debt. Therefore, it could be useful to modify the ratio by also including these payments in the denominator.

PROFITABILITY RATIOS

The aim of profitability ratios is to measure the effectiveness of management in using a company's resources to generate returns for shareholders.

Profit margin on sales

This ratio is calculated by dividing net profit by total sales revenue. It shows the amount of profit generated by the company from each dollar of sales.

$$\text{Profit margin} = \frac{\text{net profit after tax}}{\text{sales revenue}}$$

$$= \frac{\$237\,988\,000}{\$1\,344\,455\,000} \times 100$$

$$= 17.70\%\ (15.23\%)$$

This is a measure of relative efficiency, as it reflects management's efforts to generate sales and control costs. Success in reducing costs will increase the profit margin.

Return on shareholders' equity

This ratio is calculated by dividing net profit by the book value of average shareholders' equity. It is a measure of the earning power of the shareholders' investment.

$$\text{Return on shareholders' equity} = \frac{\text{net profit after tax}}{\text{shareholders' equity}}$$

$$= \frac{\$237\,988\,000}{\frac{\$2\,157\,211\,000 + \$2\,059\,182\,000}{2}} \times 100$$

$$= 11.3\% \ (10.9\%)$$

USEFULNESS OF FINANCIAL RATIO ANALYSIS

So far we have discussed the measurement of a number of financial ratios, with only passing reference to their usefulness. In assessing the usefulness of financial ratios it is important to note that they are a way of summarising large quantities of data. Also, ratio analysis is usually the first step in financial statement analysis. The purpose of the analysis differs between 'insiders', or managers, and 'outsiders', or investors and creditors. Investors and creditors will be interested in attempting to forecast future earnings and dividends and in assessing a company's ability to repay debts. Managers will seek information that they can use in making decisions about a company's operations.

These decisions may lead to changes in the values of a company's ratios. However, achieving or maintaining certain ratios should generally not be seen as an end in itself. Rather, examination of ratios is most useful as a way of raising questions and identifying issues for further investigation: it usually does not provide answers. To illustrate the use of ratios, consider Harvey Norman's current ratio of 1.62 at 30 June 2010. What information does this figure convey to management? We suggested that a very high ratio indicates that the company has too many of its resources tied up in relatively unproductive short-term assets. Alternatively, if the current ratio is too low, it may indicate that there is a liquidity problem. There are two types of analysis that management could use to decide whether the current ratio of 1.62 indicates that any action is necessary. These are *cross-sectional analysis* and *time-series analysis*.

Cross-sectional analysis involves comparing the company's ratio with those of other companies in the same industry. Companies in the same industry have similar assets and operate in a similar environment, so the average ratio of the other companies in the industry may be useful as a benchmark for comparison. If, in our example, the average current ratio of Harvey Norman's competitors was, say, 2.68, does this mean that Harvey Norman's current ratio of 1.62 is too low? The answer to this question is not obvious. It may be that its competitors have too high a proportion of their resources invested in short-term assets. In general, an industry average does not necessarily reflect an optimal standard of performance. Nevertheless, intercompany comparisons may provide a reason for re-examining policies on the management of short-term assets and policies on other aspects of a company's operations. For example, if a company's current ratio is far higher or lower than the industry average, management should seek an explanation for the difference.

Time-series analysis involves studying values of a single ratio over time to determine whether a company's financial position appears to be improving, remaining the same or deteriorating. However, the examination of a time series will usually not provide all the information that may be needed for decision-making purposes. For example, although there may be an improvement in the profit margin from one year to the next, this may still reflect less than an ideal performance. This method of evaluation is further complicated by the fact that the optimal values of financial ratios are likely to change over time. In these circumstances, maintaining a stable ratio from one year to the next is not necessarily desirable. For example, the techniques used to determine inventory policy suggest that a company's inventory should increase at a much slower rate than sales. Therefore, a company's optimal inventory turnover period will increase at a much slower rate than sales. This implies that the current ratio should decline as a company's operations grow. Time-series analysis and cross-sectional analysis can be combined by examining a company's ratios over time in conjunction with benchmarks, such as industry averages.

FINANCIAL RATIOS AND SHORT-TERM ASSET MANAGEMENT

We now consider in more detail those ratios considered to be useful for short-term asset management.

CURRENT RATIO AND 'QUICK' RATIO

The current ratio and the 'quick' ratio serve as measures of a company's liquidity position and consequently have particular application to liquidity management. The current ratio is calculated by dividing the book value of current assets by the book value of current liabilities. Current assets include cash and other liquid assets, accounts receivable and inventories. Current liabilities include accounts payable, debts maturing within 12 months and income tax payable, dividends payable and other payments due within 12 months.

Thus, the current ratio provides an indication of a company's ability to meet its immediate financial obligations using assets that are expected to be quickly converted into cash. If a company is experiencing financial difficulty, it is likely to pay its creditors more slowly, increase its bank overdraft and, perhaps, draw on lines of credit. These measures will be reflected in increases in accounts payable and other current liabilities and a falling current ratio. However, the current ratio does not take into account either the relative liquidity of the various assets or the relative urgency for repayment of the current liabilities. It is not useful to know that the company has a current ratio of 2 if all the liabilities are due to be paid within a week, and most of the short-term assets cannot be realised within 2 months.

A further limitation of the current ratio is that it includes inventory, which is usually valued at historical cost, whereas the net selling price of the inventory would provide a better indication of the asset's ability to generate cash. Indeed, a company may have an apparently healthy current ratio largely because its warehouse is full of goods that are not wanted by customers. The main difference between the current ratio and the quick ratio is that the latter excludes inventories. It is intended to provide a more stringent test of a company's liquidity by including only assets that are highly liquid. A quick ratio of 1 or more indicates that current liabilities can be met without relying on the sale of inventory.

Finally, a limitation of both ratios is that the financial statements can be 'window dressed' to improve these ratios. This may be achieved either by delaying purchases, or by paying off a large proportion of the company's current liabilities just before the end of the financial year. For example, selling marketable securities to repay debt will reduce current assets and current liabilities by the same amount, so the company's net assets are unchanged, but the current ratio will change.

AVERAGE INVENTORY TURNOVER PERIOD

The average inventory turnover period measures the average time a company's inventory remains on hand before being sold. This ratio is related to inventory management, because the average inventory turnover period will be a direct result of the company's inventory management policy defined in terms of economic order quantities and reorder points. However, the turnover period will normally reflect other factors as well. For example, inventory levels may increase and the turnover period increase because of a decrease in the demand for the company's products. A decrease in the inventory turnover period is frequently regarded as desirable since profit is generated as inventory is sold—that is, turned over. However, a decrease in the inventory turnover period is not necessarily desirable, because it may have been achieved by reducing the quantity of inventory to such a low level that purchasing costs and stockout costs have become excessive. The techniques available for determining the optimum inventory holding and, consequently, the optimum turnover were discussed in Chapter 21. It is important to note that the turnover period, which uses the statement of financial position data, measures only the average turnover period for all inventory items, whereas it is desirable to ascertain the optimum inventory policy for each individual inventory item or group of items.

The use of statement of financial position data can also involve limitations if demand and inventory levels are subject to seasonal variations. This problem can be overcome by using the average of monthly inventory figures, if they are available, instead of the end-of-year figures.

AVERAGE COLLECTION PERIOD

This ratio measures how quickly customers pay for purchases and provides useful information for accounts receivable management since there are benefits that can result from a reduction in the collection period. A shorter collection period means that fewer resources are tied up in accounts receivable and generally indicates efficiency in the collection of accounts. However, it needs to be recognised that a continual reduction in the collection period is not necessarily a sign of increasing efficiency. For example, suppose that there are two types of account. The first pays at the end of the credit period (assuming no cash discount). If all accounts are of this type, then the average collection period will be equal to the credit period. In other words, there is a lower limit to the average collection period, which is set by the company's credit terms. The second type of account is a delinquent account, which does not pay within the collection period. As discussed in Section 22.10, attempting to collect all accounts in time involves collection expenditures that are prohibitively high; a company usually has to accept a certain number of late collections (that is, delinquent accounts) and non-collections (that is, bad debts). It follows that the optimal average collection period will usually be above the lower limit set by the company's credit terms. It is also possible for the average collection period to be 'too short', reflecting unduly restrictive credit terms.

The average collection period provides management with information about the quality of the company's accounts receivable and the efficiency of its credit control. Valuable information can also be obtained from an 'age' analysis of accounts. This analysis lists debtors' accounts with reference to the period of time they have been outstanding, and highlights the incidence of delinquent accounts. It therefore directs management's attention to those accounts on which its collection efforts should be concentrated.

APPENDIX A

NUMERICAL TABLES

Table 1 Future value of a present sum
Table 2 Present value of a future sum
Table 3 Future value of an ordinary annuity
Table 4 Present value of an ordinary annuity
Table 5 Areas under the standard normal curve

TABLE 1 Future value of $1 at the end of n periods
$(1 + i)^n$

n	0.25%	0.5%	0.66%	0.75%	1.0%	1.5%	1.75%	2.0%	2.5%	3.0%	3.5%	n
1	1.00250	1.00500	1.00667	1.00750	1.01000	1.01500	1.01750	1.02000	1.02500	1.03000	1.03500	1
2	1.00501	1.01003	1.01338	1.01506	1.02010	1.03023	1.03531	1.04040	1.05063	1.06090	1.07123	2
3	1.00752	1.01508	1.02013	1.02267	1.03030	1.04568	1.05342	1.06121	1.07689	1.09273	1.10872	3
4	1.01004	1.02015	1.02693	1.03034	1.04060	1.06136	1.07186	1.08243	1.10381	1.12551	1.14752	4
5	1.01256	1.02525	1.03378	1.03807	1.05101	1.07728	1.09062	1.10408	1.13141	1.15927	1.18769	5
6	1.01509	1.03038	1.04067	1.04585	1.06152	1.09344	1.10970	1.12616	1.15969	1.19405	1.22926	6
7	1.01763	1.03553	1.04761	1.05370	1.07214	1.10984	1.12912	1.14869	1.18869	1.22987	1.27228	7
8	1.02018	1.04071	1.05459	1.06160	1.08286	1.12649	1.14888	1.17166	1.21840	1.26677	1.31681	8
9	1.02273	1.04591	1.06163	1.06956	1.09369	1.14339	1.16899	1.19509	1.24886	1.30477	1.36290	9
10	1.02528	1.05114	1.06870	1.07758	1.10462	1.16054	1.18944	1.21899	1.28008	1.34392	1.41060	10
11	1.02785	1.05640	1.07583	1.08566	1.11567	1.17795	1.21026	1.24337	1.31209	1.38423	1.45997	11
12	1.03042	1.06168	1.08300	1.09381	1.12683	1.19562	1.23144	1.26824	1.34489	1.42576	1.51107	12
13	1.03299	1.06699	1.09022	1.10201	1.13809	1.21355	1.25299	1.29361	1.37851	1.46853	1.56396	13
14	1.03557	1.07232	1.09749	1.11028	1.14947	1.23176	1.27492	1.31948	1.41297	1.51259	1.61869	14
15	1.03816	1.07768	1.10480	1.11860	1.16097	1.25023	1.29723	1.34587	1.44830	1.55797	1.67535	15
16	1.04076	1.08307	1.11217	1.12699	1.17258	1.26899	1.31993	1.37279	1.43451	1.60471	1.73399	16
17	1.04336	1.08849	1.11958	1.13544	1.18430	1.28802	1.34303	1.40024	1.52162	1.65285	1.79468	17
18	1.04597	1.09393	1.12705	1.14396	1.19615	1.30734	1.36653	1.42825	1.55966	1.70243	1.85749	18
19	1.04858	1.09940	1.13456	1.15254	1.20811	1.32695	1.39045	1.45681	1.59865	1.75351	1.92250	19
20	1.05121	1.10490	1.14213	1.16118	1.22019	1.34686	1.41478	1.48595	1.63862	1.80611	1.98979	20
21	1.05383	1.11042	1.14974	1.16989	1.23239	1.36706	1.43454	1.51567	1.67958	1.86029	2.05943	21
22	1.05647	1.11597	1.15740	1.17867	1.24472	1.38756	1.46473	1.54598	1.72157	1.91610	2.13151	22
23	1.05911	1.12155	1.16512	1.18751	1.25716	1.40838	1.49036	1.57690	1.76461	1.97359	2.20611	23
24	1.06176	1.12716	1.17289	1.19641	1.26973	1.42950	1.51644	1.60844	1.80873	2.03279	2.28333	24
25	1.06441	1.13280	1.18071	1.20539	1.28243	1.45095	1.54298	1.64061	1.85394	2.09378	2.36324	25
30	1.07778	1.16140	1.22059	1.25127	1.34785	1.56308	1.68280	1.81136	2.09729	2.42726	2.80679	30
35	1.09132	1.19073	1.26182	1.29890	1.41660	1.68388	1.83529	1.99989	2.37321	2.81386	3.33359	35
40	1.10503	1.22079	1.30445	1.34835	1.48886	1.81402	2.00160	2.20804	2.68506	3.26204	3.95926	40
45	1.11892	1.25162	1.34852	1.39968	1.56481	1.95421	2.18298	2.43785	3.03790	3.78160	4.70236	45
50	1.13297	1.28323	1.39407	1.45296	1.64463	2.10524	2.38079	2.69159	3.43711	4.38391	5.58493	50
60	1.16162	1.34885	1.48985	1.56568	1.81670	2.43220	2.83182	3.28103	4.39979	5.89160	7.87809	60

TABLE 1 Future value of $1 at the end of n periods *continued*

$(1 + i)^n$

n	4.0%	4.5%	5.0%	6.0%	7.0%	8.0%	10.0%	12.0%	15.0%	20.0%	n
1	1.04000	1.04500	1.05000	1.06000	1.07000	1.08000	1.10000	1.1200	1.150	1.200	1
2	1.08160	1.09203	1.10250	1.12360	1.14490	1.16640	1.21000	1.2544	1.322	1.440	2
3	1.12486	1.14117	1.15763	1.19101	1.22504	1.25971	1.33100	1.4049	1.521	1.728	3
4	1.16986	1.19252	1.21551	1.26247	1.31079	1.36048	1.46410	1.5735	1.749	2.074	4
5	1.21665	1.24618	1.27628	1.33822	1.40255	1.46932	1.61051	1.7620	2.011	2.488	5
6	1.26532	1.30226	1.34010	1.41851	1.50073	1.58687	1.77156	1.9738	2.313	2.938	6
7	1.31593	1.36086	1.40710	1.50363	1.60578	1.71382	1.94872	2.2107	2.660	3.583	7
8	1.36857	1.42210	1.47746	1.59384	1.71818	1.85093	2.14359	2.4760	3.059	4.300	8
9	1.42331	1.48610	1.55133	1.68947	1.83845	1.99900	2.35795	2.7731	3.518	5.160	9
10	1.48024	1.55297	1.62889	1.79084	1.96715	2.15892	2.59374	3.1058	4.046	6.192	10
11	1.53945	1.62285	1.71034	1.89829	2.10485	2.33163	2.85312	3.4785	4.652	7.430	11
12	1.60103	1.69588	1.79586	2.01219	2.25219	2.51817	3.13843	3.8960	5.350	8.916	12
13	1.66507	1.77220	1.88565	2.13292	2.40984	2.71962	3.45227	4.3635	6.153	10.699	13
14	1.73168	1.85194	1.97993	2.26090	2.57853	2.93719	3.79750	4.8871	7.076	12.839	14
15	1.80094	1.93528	2.07893	2.39655	2.75903	3.17216	4.17725	5.4736	8.137	15.407	15
16	1.87298	2.02237	2.18287	2.54035	2.95216	3.42594	4.59497	6.1303	9.358	18.488	16
17	1.94790	2.11338	2.29202	2.69277	3.15881	3.70001	5.05447	6.8661	10.761	22.186	17
18	2.02582	2.20848	2.40662	2.85433	3.37993	3.99601	5.55992	7.6900	12.375	26.623	18
19	2.10685	2.30786	2.52695	3.02559	3.61652	4.31570	6.11591	8.6128	14.232	31.945	19
20	2.19112	2.41171	2.65330	3.20713	3.86968	4.66095	6.72750	9.6463	16.367	38.338	20
21	2.27877	2.52024	2.78596	3.39956	4.14056	5.03383	7.40025	10.8038	18.821	46.005	21
22	2.36992	2.63365	2.92526	3.60353	4.43040	5.43654	8.14027	12.1003	21.645	55.206	22
23	2.46472	2.75217	3.07152	3.81974	4.74052	5.87146	8.95430	13.5523	24.891	66.247	23
24	2.56330	2.87601	3.22510	4.04893	5.07236	6.34118	9.84973	15.1786	28.625	79.497	24
25	2.66584	3.00543	3.38635	4.29187	5.42743	6.84847	10.83471	17.0001	32.919	95.396	25
30	3.24340	3.74532	4.32194	5.74349	7.61225	10.06265	17.44940	29.9600	66.212	237.376	30
35	3.94609	4.66735	5.51602	7.68608	10.67658	14.78534	28.10244	52.8000	133.175	590.668	35
40	4.80102	5.81636	7.03999	10.28571	14.97445	21.72452	45.25926	93.0510	267.862	1469.771	40
45	5.84118	7.24825	8.98501	13.76461	21.00245	31.92044	72.89048	163.9876	538.767	3657.258	45
50	7.10668	9.03264	11.47740	18.42015	29.45702	46.90161	117.39085	289.0021	1083.652	9100.427	50
60	10.51963	14.02741	18.67919	32.98769	57.94643	101.25706	304.48164	897.5969	4383.999	56347.514	60

TABLE 2 Present value of $1 due at the end of n periods

$$\frac{1}{(1+i)^n} = (1+i)^{-n}$$

n	0.25%	0.50%	0.66%	0.75%	1.0%	1.5%	2.0%	2.5%	3.0%	3.5%	n
1	0.99751	0.99502	0.99338	0.99256	0.99009	0.98522	0.98039	0.97560	0.97087	0.96618	1
2	0.99502	0.99007	0.98680	0.98517	0.98029	0.97066	0.96116	0.95181	0.94259	0.93351	2
3	0.99254	0.98515	0.98026	0.97783	0.97059	0.95631	0.94232	0.92859	0.91514	0.90194	3
4	0.99006	0.98025	0.97377	0.97055	0.96098	0.94218	0.92384	0.90595	0.88848	0.87144	4
5	0.98759	0.97537	0.96732	0.96333	0.95146	0.92826	0.90573	0.88385	0.86260	0.84197	5
6	0.98513	0.97052	0.96092	0.95616	0.94204	0.91454	0.88797	0.86229	0.83748	0.81350	6
7	0.98267	0.96569	0.95455	0.94094	0.93271	0.90102	0.87056	0.84126	0.81309	0.78599	7
8	0.98022	0.96089	0.94823	0.94198	0.92348	0.88771	0.85349	0.82074	0.78940	0.75941	8
9	0.97778	0.95610	0.94195	0.93496	0.91433	0.87459	0.83675	0.80072	0.76641	0.73373	9
10	0.97534	0.95135	0.93571	0.92800	0.90528	0.86166	0.82034	0.78119	0.74409	0.70891	10
11	0.97291	0.94661	0.92952	0.92109	0.89632	0.84893	0.80426	0.76214	0.72242	0.68494	11
12	0.97048	0.94191	0.92336	0.91424	0.88744	0.83638	0.78849	0.74355	0.70137	0.66178	12
13	0.96806	0.97322	0.91725	0.90743	0.87866	0.82402	0.77303	0.72542	0.68095	0.63940	13
14	0.96565	0.93256	0.91117	0.90068	0.86996	0.81184	0.75787	0.70772	0.66111	0.61778	14
15	0.96324	0.92792	0.90514	0.89397	0.86134	0.79985	0.74301	0.69046	0.64186	0.59689	15
16	0.96084	0.92330	0.89914	0.88732	0.85282	0.78803	0.72844	0.67362	0.62316	0.57670	16
17	0.95844	0.91871	0.89319	0.88071	0.84437	0.77638	0.71416	0.65719	0.60501	0.55720	17
18	0.95605	0.91414	0.88727	0.87416	0.83601	0.76491	0.70015	0.64116	0.58739	0.53836	18
19	0.95367	0.90959	0.88140	0.86765	0.82773	0.75360	0.68643	0.62552	0.57028	0.52015	19
20	0.95129	0.90506	0.87556	0.86119	0.81954	0.74247	0.67297	0.61027	0.55367	0.50256	20
21	0.94892	0.90056	0.86976	0.85478	0.81143	0.73149	0.65977	0.59538	0.53754	0.48557	21
22	0.94655	0.89608	0.86400	0.84842	0.80339	0.72068	0.64683	0.58086	0.52189	0.46915	22
23	0.94419	0.89162	0.85828	0.84210	0.79544	0.71003	0.63415	0.56669	0.50669	0.45328	23
24	0.94184	0.88719	0.85260	0.83583	0.78756	0.69954	0.62172	0.55287	0.49193	0.43795	24
25	0.93949	0.88277	0.84695	0.82961	0.77976	0.68920	0.60953	0.53939	0.47760	0.42314	25
30	0.92783	0.86103	0.81927	0.79919	0.74192	0.63976	0.55207	0.47674	0.41198	0.35627	30
35	0.91632	0.83982	0.79250	0.76988	0.70591	0.59386	0.50002	0.42137	0.35538	0.29997	35
40	0.90495	0.81914	0.76661	0.74165	0.67165	0.55126	0.45289	0.37243	0.30655	0.25257	40
45	0.89372	0.79896	0.74156	0.71445	0.63905	0.51171	0.41019	0.32917	0.26443	0.21265	45
50	0.88263	0.77929	0.71732	0.68825	0.60803	0.47500	0.37152	0.29094	0.22810	0.17905	50
60	0.86087	0.74137	0.67121	0.63870	0.55045	0.40930	0.30478	0.22728	0.16973	0.12693	60

TABLE 2 Present value of $1 due at the end of n periods *continued*

$$\frac{1}{(1+i)^n} = (1+i)^{-n}$$

n	4.0%	4.5%	5.0%	6.0%	7.0%	8.0%	10.0%	12.0%	15.0%	20.0%	n
1	0.96153	0.95693	0.95238	0.94339	0.93457	0.92592	0.90909	0.89286	0.86957	0.83333	1
2	0.92455	0.91572	0.90702	0.88999	0.87343	0.85733	0.82645	0.79719	0.75614	0.69444	2
3	0.88899	0.87629	0.86383	0.83961	0.81629	0.79383	0.75131	0.71178	0.65752	0.57870	3
4	0.85480	0.83856	0.82270	0.79209	0.76289	0.73502	0.68301	0.63552	0.57175	0.48225	4
5	0.82192	0.80245	0.78352	0.74725	0.71298	0.68058	0.62092	0.56743	0.49718	0.40188	5
6	0.79031	0.76789	0.74621	0.70496	0.66634	0.63016	0.56447	0.50663	0.43233	0.33490	6
7	0.75991	0.73482	0.71068	0.66505	0.62274	0.58349	0.51316	0.45235	0.37594	0.27908	7
8	0.73069	0.70318	0.67683	0.62741	0.58200	0.54026	0.46651	0.40388	0.32690	0.23257	8
9	0.70258	0.67290	0.64460	0.59189	0.54393	0.50024	0.42410	0.36061	0.28426	0.19381	9
10	0.67556	0.64392	0.61390	0.55839	0.50834	0.46319	0.38554	0.32197	0.24718	0.16151	10
11	0.64958	0.61619	0.58467	0.52678	0.47509	0.42888	0.35049	0.28748	0.21494	0.13459	11
12	0.62459	0.58966	0.55683	0.49696	0.44401	0.39711	0.31863	0.25667	0.18691	0.11216	12
13	0.60057	0.56427	0.53032	0.46883	0.41496	0.36769	0.28966	0.22917	0.16253	0.09346	13
14	0.57747	0.53997	0.50506	0.44230	0.38781	0.34046	0.26333	0.20462	0.14133	0.07789	14
15	0.55526	0.51672	0.48101	0.41726	0.36244	0.31524	0.23939	0.18270	0.12289	0.06491	15
16	0.53390	0.49446	0.45811	0.39364	0.33873	0.29189	0.21763	0.16312	0.10686	0.05409	16
17	0.51337	0.47317	0.43629	0.37136	0.31657	0.27026	0.19784	0.14564	0.09293	0.04507	17
18	0.49362	0.45280	0.41552	0.35034	0.29586	0.25024	0.17986	0.13004	0.08080	0.03756	18
19	0.47464	0.43330	0.39573	0.33051	0.27650	0.23171	0.16351	0.11611	0.07026	0.03130	19
20	0.45638	0.41464	0.37688	0.31180	0.25841	0.21454	0.14864	0.10367	0.06110	0.02608	20
21	0.43883	0.39678	0.35894	0.29415	0.24151	0.19865	0.13513	0.09256	0.05313	0.02174	21
22	0.42195	0.37970	0.34184	0.27750	0.22571	0.18394	0.12285	0.08264	0.04620	0.01811	22
23	0.40572	0.36335	0.32557	0.26179	0.21094	0.17031	0.11168	0.07379	0.04017	0.01509	23
24	0.39012	0.34770	0.31006	0.24697	0.19714	0.15769	0.10153	0.06588	0.03493	0.01258	24
25	0.37511	0.33273	0.29530	0.23299	0.18424	0.14601	0.09230	0.05882	0.03038	0.01048	25
30	0.30831	0.26700	0.23137	0.17411	0.13136	0.09937	0.05731	0.03338	0.01510	0.00421	30
35	0.25341	0.21425	0.18129	0.13010	0.09366	0.06763	0.03558	0.01894	0.00751	0.00169	35
40	0.20828	0.17192	0.14204	0.09722	0.06678	0.04603	0.02209	0.01074	0.00373	0.00068	40
45	0.17119	0.13796	0.11129	0.07265	0.04761	0.03132	0.01372	0.00610	0.00186	0.00027	45
50	0.14071	0.11070	0.08720	0.05428	0.03394	0.02132	0.00852	0.00346	0.00092	0.00011	50
60	0.09506	0.07129	0.05354	0.03031	0.01726	0.00988	0.00328	0.00111	0.00023	0.00002	60

TABLE 3 Future value of an annuity of $1 per period for n periods

$$S(n, i) = \frac{(1+i)^n - 1}{i}$$

n	0.25%	0.5%	0.66%	0.75%	1.0%	1.5%	2.0%	2.5%	3.0%	3.5%	n
1	1.00000	1.00000	1.00000	1.00000	1.00000	1.00000	1.00000	1.0000	1.0000	1.0000	1
2	2.00250	2.00500	2.00667	2.00750	2.01000	2.01500	2.02000	2.0250	2.0300	2.0350	2
3	3.00751	3.01503	3.02004	3.02256	3.03010	3.04523	3.06040	3.0756	3.0909	3.1062	3
4	4.01503	4.03010	4.04018	4.04523	4.06040	4.09090	4.12161	4.1525	4.1836	4.2149	4
5	5.02506	5.05025	5.06711	5.07556	5.10101	5.15227	5.20404	5.2563	5.3091	5.3625	5
6	6.03763	6.07550	6.10089	6.11363	6.15202	6.22955	6.30812	6.3877	6.4684	6.5502	6
7	7.05272	7.10588	7.14157	7.15948	7.21354	7.32299	7.43428	7.5474	7.6625	7.7794	7
8	8.07035	8.14141	8.18918	8.21318	8.28567	8.43284	8.58297	8.7361	8.8923	9.0517	8
9	9.09053	9.18212	9.24377	9.27478	9.36853	9.55933	9.75463	9.9545	10.1591	10.3685	9
10	10.11325	10.22803	10.30540	10.34434	10.46221	10.70272	10.94972	11.2034	11.4639	11.7314	10
11	11.13854	11.27917	11.37410	11.42192	11.56683	11.86326	12.16872	12.4835	12.8078	13.1420	11
12	12.16638	12.33556	12.44993	12.50759	12.68250	13.04121	13.41209	13.7956	14.1920	14.6020	12
13	13.19680	13.39724	13.53293	13.60139	13.80933	14.23683	14.68033	15.1404	15.6178	16.1130	13
14	14.22979	14.46423	14.62315	14.70340	14.94742	15.45038	15.97394	16.5190	17.0863	17.6770	14
15	15.26537	15.53655	15.72063	15.81368	16.09690	16.53343	16.68214	17.9319	18.5989	19.2957	15
16	16.30353	16.61423	16.82554	16.93228	17.25786	17.93237	18.63929	19.3802	20.1569	20.9710	16
17	17.34429	17.69730	17.93761	18.05927	18.43044	19.20136	20.01207	20.8647	21.7616	22.7050	17
18	18.38765	18.78579	19.05719	19.19472	19.61475	20.48938	21.41231	22.3863	23.4144	24.4997	18
19	19.43362	19.87972	20.18424	20.33868	20.81089	21.79672	22.84056	23.9460	25.1169	26.3572	19
20	20.48220	20.97912	21.31880	21.49122	22.01900	23.12367	24.29737	25.5447	26.8704	28.2797	20
21	21.53341	22.08401	22.46093	22.65240	23.23919	24.47052	25.78332	27.1833	28.6765	30.2695	21
22	22.58724	23.19443	23.61066	23.82230	24.47159	25.83758	27.29898	28.8629	30.5368	32.3289	22
23	23.64371	24.31040	24.76807	25.00096	25.71630	27.22514	28.84496	30.5844	32.4529	34.4604	23
24	24.70282	25.43196	25.93319	26.18847	26.97346	28.63352	30.42186	32.3490	34.4265	36.6665	24
25	25.76457	26.55912	27.10608	27.38488	28.24320	30.06302	32.03030	34.1578	36.4593	38.9499	25
30	31.11331	32.28002	33.08885	33.50290	34.78489	37.53868	40.56808	43.9027	47.5754	51.6227	30
35	36.52924	38.14538	39.27373	39.85381	41.66028	45.59209	49.99448	54.9282	60.4621	66.6740	35
40	42.01320	44.15885	45.66754	46.44648	48.88637	54.26789	60.40198	67.4026	75.4013	84.5503	40
45	47.56606	50.32416	52.27734	53.29011	56.48107	63.61420	71.89271	81.5161	92.7199	105.7817	45
50	53.18868	56.64516	59.11042	60.39426	64.46318	73.68283	84.57940	97.4843	112.7969	130.9979	50
60	64.64671	69.77003	73.47686	76.42414	81.66967	96.21465	114.05154	135.9916	163.0534	196.5169	60

TABLE 3 Future value of an annuity of $1 per period for n periods *continued*

$$S(n, i) = \frac{(1 + i)^n - 1}{i}$$

n	4.0%	4.5%	5.0%	6.0%	7.0%	8.0%	10.0%	12.0%	15.0%	20.0%	n
1	1.0000	1.0000	1.0000	1.0000	1.0000	1.0000	1.0000	1.000	1.000	1.00	1
2	2.0400	2.0450	2.0500	2.0600	2.0700	2.0800	2.1000	2.120	2.150	2.20	2
3	3.1216	3.1370	3.1525	3.1836	3.2149	3.2464	3.3100	3.374	3.472	3.64	3
4	4.2465	4.2782	4.3101	4.3746	4.4399	4.5061	4.6410	4.779	4.993	5.36	4
5	5.4163	5.4707	5.5256	5.6271	5.7507	5.8666	6.1051	6.353	6.742	7.44	5
6	6.6330	6.7169	6.8019	6.9753	7.1533	7.3359	7.7156	8.115	8.754	9.93	6
7	7.8983	8.0192	8.1420	8.3938	8.6540	8.9228	9.4872	10.089	11.067	12.92	7
8	9.2142	9.3800	9.5491	9.8975	10.2598	10.6366	11.4359	12.300	13.727	16.50	8
9	10.5828	10.8021	11.0266	11.4913	11.9780	12.4876	13.5795	14.776	16.786	20.80	9
10	12.0061	12.2882	12.5779	13.1808	13.8164	14.4866	15.9374	17.549	20.304	25.96	10
11	13.4864	13.8412	14.2068	14.9716	15.7836	16.6455	18.5312	20.655	24.349	32.15	11
12	15.0258	15.4640	15.9171	16.8699	17.8885	18.9771	21.3843	24.133	29.002	39.58	12
13	16.6268	17.1599	17.7130	18.8821	20.1406	21.4953	24.5227	28.029	34.352	48.50	13
14	18.2919	18.9321	19.5986	21.0151	22.5505	24.2149	27.9750	32.393	40.505	59.20	14
15	20.0236	20.7841	21.5786	23.2760	25.1290	27.1521	31.7725	37.280	47.580	72.04	15
16	21.8245	22.7193	23.6575	25.6725	27.8881	30.3243	35.9497	42.753	55.717	87.44	16
17	23.6975	24.7417	25.8404	28.2129	30.8402	33.7502	40.5447	48.884	65.075	105.93	17
18	25.6454	26.8551	28.1324	30.9057	33.9990	37.4502	45.5992	55.750	75.836	128.12	18
19	27.6712	29.0636	30.5390	33.7600	37.3790	41.4463	51.1591	63.440	88.212	154.74	19
20	29.7781	31.3714	33.0660	36.7856	40.9955	45.7620	57.2750	72.052	102.443	186.69	20
21	31.9692	33.7831	35.7193	39.9927	44.8652	50.4229	64.0025	81.699	118.810	225.03	21
22	34.2480	36.3034	38.5052	43.3923	49.0057	55.4568	71.4028	92.502	137.631	271.03	22
23	36.6179	38.9370	41.4305	46.9958	53.4361	60.8933	79.5430	104.603	159.276	326.24	23
24	39.0826	41.6892	44.5020	50.8156	58.1767	66.7648	88.4973	118.155	184.167	392.48	24
25	41.6459	44.5652	47.7271	54.8645	63.2490	73.1059	98.3471	133.334	212.793	471.98	25
30	56.0849	61.5706	66.4388	79.0582	74.4608	113.2832	164.4940	241.532	434.744	1181.88	30
35	73.6522	81.4966	90.3203	111.4348	138.2369	172.3168	271.0244	431.663	881.168	2948.34	35
40	95.0255	107.0303	120.7998	154.7620	199.6351	259.0565	442.5926	767.088	1779.090	7343.95	40
45	121.0294	138.8500	159.7002	212.7435	285.7493	386.5056	718.9048	1358.224	3585.128	18281.31	45
50	152.6671	178.5030	209.3480	290.3359	406.5289	573.7702	1163.9085	2400.008	7217.716	45497.19	50
60	237.9907	289.4980	353.5837	533.1281	813.5204	1253.2133	3034.8164	7471.641	29219.992	281732.57	60

TABLE 4 Present value of an annuity of $1 per period for n periods

$$P = A(n, i) = \frac{1}{i}\left[1 - \frac{1}{(1+i)^n}\right]$$

n	0.25%	0.5%	0.66%	0.75%	1.0%	1.5%	2.0%	2.5%	3.0%	3.5%	n
1	0.99751	0.99502	0.99338	0.99256	0.99010	0.98522	0.98039	0.9756	0.9709	0.9662	1
2	1.99252	1.98510	1.98018	1.97772	1.97040	1.95588	1.94156	1.9274	1.9135	1.8997	2
3	2.98506	2.97025	2.96044	2.95556	2.94099	2.91220	2.88388	2.8560	2.8286	2.8016	3
4	3.97512	3.95050	3.93421	3.92611	3.90197	3.85438	3.80773	3.7620	3.7171	3.6731	4
5	4.96272	4.92587	4.90154	4.88944	4.85343	4.78265	4.71346	4.6458	4.5797	4.5151	5
6	5.94785	5.89638	5.86245	5.84560	5.79548	5.69719	5.60143	5.5081	5.4172	5.3286	6
7	6.93052	6.86207	6.81701	6.79464	6.72819	6.59821	6.47199	6.3494	6.2303	6.1145	7
8	7.91074	7.82296	7.76524	7.73661	7.65168	7.48593	7.32548	7.1701	7.0197	6.8740	8
9	8.88852	8.77906	8.70719	8.67158	8.56602	8.36052	8.16224	7.9709	7.7861	7.6077	9
10	9.86386	9.73041	9.64290	9.59958	9.47130	9.22219	8.98254	8.7521	8.5302	8.3166	10
11	10.83677	10.67703	10.57242	10.52067	10.36763	10.07112	9.78685	9.5142	9.2526	9.0016	11
12	11.80725	11.61893	11.49578	11.43491	11.25508	10.90751	10.57534	10.2578	9.9540	9.6633	12
13	12.77532	12.55615	12.41303	12.34235	12.13374	11.73153	11.34837	10.9832	10.6350	10.3027	13
14	13.74096	13.48871	13.32420	13.24302	13.00370	12.54338	12.10625	11.6909	11.2961	10.9205	14
15	14.70420	14.41662	14.22934	14.13699	13.86505	13.34323	12.84926	12.3814	11.9379	11.5174	15
16	15.66504	15.33993	15.12848	15.02431	14.71787	14.13126	13.57771	13.0550	12.5611	12.0941	16
17	16.62348	16.25863	16.02167	15.90502	15.56225	14.90765	14.29187	13.7122	13.1661	12.6513	17
18	17.57953	17.17277	16.90894	16.77918	16.39827	15.67256	14.99203	14.3534	13.7535	13.1897	18
19	18.53320	18.08236	17.79034	17.64683	17.22601	16.42617	15.67846	14.9789	14.3238	13.7098	19
20	19.48449	18.98742	18.66590	18.50802	18.04555	17.16864	16.35143	15.5892	14.8775	14.2124	20
21	20.43340	19.88798	19.53566	19.36280	18.85698	17.90014	17.01121	16.1845	15.4150	14.6980	21
22	21.37995	20.78406	20.39967	20.21121	19.66038	18.62083	17.65805	16.7654	15.9369	15.1671	22
23	22.32414	21.67568	21.25795	21.05331	20.45582	19.33086	18.29220	17.3321	16.4436	15.6204	23
24	23.26598	22.56287	22.11054	21.88915	21.24339	20.03041	18.91393	17.8850	16.9355	16.0584	24
25	24.20547	23.44564	22.95749	22.71876	22.02316	20.71961	19.52346	18.4244	17.4131	16.4815	25
30	28.86787	27.79405	27.10885	26.77508	25.80771	24.01584	22.39646	20.9303	19.6004	18.3920	30
35	33.47243	32.03537	31.12455	30.68266	29.40858	27.07560	24.99862	23.1452	21.4872	20.0007	35
40	38.01986	36.17223	35.00903	34.44694	32.83469	29.91585	27.35548	25.1028	23.1148	21.3551	40
45	42.51088	40.20720	38.76658	38.07318	36.09451	32.55234	29.49016	26.8330	24.5187	22.4955	45
50	46.94617	44.14279	42.40134	41.56645	39.19612	34.99969	31.42361	28.3623	25.7298	23.4556	50
60	55.65236	51.72556	49.31843	48.17337	44.95504	39.38027	34.76089	30.9087	27.6756	24.9447	60

TABLE 4 Present value of an annuity of $1 per period for n periods *continued*

$$P = A(n, i) = \frac{1}{i}\left[1 - \frac{1}{(1+i)^n}\right]$$

n	4.0%	4.5%	5.0%	6.0%	7.0%	8.0%	10.0%	12.0%	15.0%	20.0%	n
1	0.9615	0.9569	0.9524	0.9433	0.9345	0.9259	0.9091	0.8929	0.8695	0.8333	1
2	1.8861	1.8727	1.8594	1.8333	1.8080	1.7832	1.7355	1.6901	1.6257	1.5278	2
3	2.7751	2.7490	2.7232	2.6730	2.6243	2.5770	2.4868	2.4018	2.2832	2.1065	3
4	3.6299	3.5875	3.5460	3.4651	3.3872	3.3121	3.1698	3.0373	2.8549	2.5887	4
5	4.4518	4.3900	4.3295	4.2123	4.1001	3.9927	3.7907	3.6048	3.3521	2.9906	5
6	5.2421	5.1579	5.0757	4.9173	4.7665	4.6228	4.3552	4.1114	3.7844	3.3255	6
7	6.0021	5.8927	5.7864	5.5823	5.3892	5.2063	4.8684	4.5638	4.1604	3.6046	7
8	6.7327	6.5959	6.4632	6.2097	5.9712	5.7466	5.3349	4.9676	4.4873	3.8372	8
9	7.4353	7.2688	7.1078	6.8016	6.5152	6.2468	5.7590	5.3282	4.7715	4.0310	9
10	8.1109	7.9127	7.7217	7.3600	7.0235	6.7100	6.1445	5.6502	5.0187	4.1925	10
11	8.7605	8.5289	8.3064	7.8868	7.4986	7.1389	6.4950	5.9377	5.2337	4.3271	11
12	9.3851	9.1186	8.8633	8.3838	7.9426	7.5360	6.8136	6.1944	5.4206	4.4392	12
13	9.9856	9.6829	9.3936	8.8526	8.3576	7.9037	7.1033	6.4235	5.5831	4.5327	13
14	10.5631	10.2228	9.8986	9.2949	8.7454	8.2442	7.3666	6.6282	5.7244	4.6106	14
15	11.1184	10.7395	10.3797	9.7122	9.1079	8.5594	7.6060	6.8109	5.8473	4.6755	15
16	11.6523	11.2340	10.8378	10.1058	9.4466	8.8513	7.8237	6.9740	5.9542	4.7296	16
17	12.1657	11.7072	11.2741	10.4772	9.7632	9.1216	8.0215	7.1196	6.0471	4.7746	17
18	12.6593	12.1600	11.6896	10.8276	10.0590	9.3718	8.2014	7.2497	6.1279	4.8122	18
19	13.1339	12.5933	12.0853	11.1581	10.3355	9.6035	8.3649	7.3658	6.1982	4.8435	19
20	13.5903	13.0079	12.4622	11.4699	10.5940	9.8181	8.5135	7.4694	6.2593	4.8696	20
21	14.0292	13.4047	12.8212	11.7640	10.8355	10.0168	8.6486	7.5620	6.3124	4.8913	21
22	14.4511	13.7844	13.1630	12.0415	11.0612	10.2007	8.7715	7.6446	6.3586	4.9094	22
23	14.8568	14.1478	13.4886	12.3033	11.2721	10.3710	8.8832	7.7184	6.3988	4.9245	23
24	15.2470	14.4955	13.7986	12.5503	11.4693	10.5287	8.9847	7.7843	6.4337	4.9371	24
25	15.6221	14.8282	14.0939	12.7833	11.6535	10.6747	9.0770	7.8431	6.4641	4.9476	25
30	17.2920	16.2889	15.3725	13.7648	12.4090	11.2577	9.4269	8.0552	6.5659	4.9789	30
35	18.6646	17.4610	16.3742	14.4982	12.9476	11.6545	9.6441	8.1755	6.6166	4.9915	35
40	19.7928	18.4016	17.1591	15.0462	13.3317	11.9246	9.7790	8.2438	6.6417	4.9966	40
45	20.7200	19.1563	17.7741	15.4558	13.6055	12.1084	9.8628	8.2825	6.6542	4.9986	45
50	21.4822	19.7620	18.2559	15.7618	13.8007	12.2334	9.9148	8.3045	6.6605	4.9995	50
60	22.6235	20.6380	18.9293	16.1614	14.0392	12.3766	9.9672	8.3240	6.6651	4.9999	60

TABLE 5 Areas under the normal curve from $-\infty$ to the value of z

z	0.00	0.01	0.02	0.03	0.04	0.05	0.06	0.07	0.08	0.09
−0.0	0.5000	0.4960	0.4920	0.4880	0.4840	0.4801	0.4761	0.4721	0.4681	0.4641
−0.1	0.4602	0.4562	0.4522	0.4483	0.4443	0.4404	0.4364	0.4325	0.4286	0.4247
−0.2	0.4207	0.4168	0.4129	0.4090	0.4052	0.4013	0.3974	0.3936	0.3897	0.3859
−0.3	0.3821	0.3783	0.3745	0.3707	0.3669	0.3632	0.3594	0.3557	0.3520	0.3483
−0.4	0.3446	0.3409	0.3372	0.3336	0.3300	0.3264	0.3228	0.3192	0.3156	0.3121
−0.5	0.3085	0.3050	0.3015	0.2981	0.2946	0.2912	0.2877	0.2843	0.2810	0.2776
−0.6	0.2743	0.2709	0.2676	0.2643	0.2611	0.2578	0.2546	0.2514	0.2483	0.2451
−0.7	0.2420	0.2389	0.2358	0.2327	0.2296	0.2266	0.2236	0.2206	0.2177	0.2148
−0.8	0.2119	0.2090	0.2061	0.2033	0.2005	0.1977	0.1949	0.1922	0.1894	0.1867
−0.9	0.1841	0.1814	0.1788	0.1762	0.1736	0.1711	0.1685	0.1660	0.1635	0.1611
−1.0	0.1587	0.1562	0.1539	0.1515	0.1492	0.1469	0.1446	0.1423	0.1401	0.1379
−1.1	0.1357	0.1335	0.1314	0.1292	0.1271	0.1251	0.1230	0.1210	0.1190	0.1170
−1.2	0.1151	0.1131	0.1112	0.1093	0.1075	0.1056	0.1038	0.1020	0.1003	0.0985
−1.3	0.0968	0.0951	0.0934	0.0918	0.0901	0.0885	0.0869	0.0853	0.0838	0.0823
−1.4	0.0808	0.0793	0.0778	0.0764	0.0749	0.0735	0.0721	0.0708	0.0694	0.0681
−1.5	0.0668	0.0655	0.0643	0.0630	0.0618	0.0606	0.0594	0.0528	0.0571	0.0559
−1.6	0.0548	0.0537	0.0526	0.0516	0.0505	0.0495	0.0485	0.0475	0.0465	0.0455
−1.7	0.0446	0.0436	0.0427	0.0418	0.0409	0.0401	0.0392	0.0384	0.0375	0.0367
−1.8	0.0359	0.0351	0.0344	0.0336	0.0329	0.0322	0.0314	0.0307	0.0301	0.0294
−1.9	0.0287	0.0281	0.0274	0.0268	0.0262	0.0256	0.0250	0.0244	0.0239	0.0233
−2.0	0.0228	0.0222	0.0217	0.0212	0.0207	0.0202	0.0197	0.0192	0.0188	0.0183
−2.1	0.0179	0.0174	0.0170	0.0166	0.0162	0.0158	0.0154	0.0150	0.0146	0.0143
−2.2	0.0139	0.0136	0.0132	0.0129	0.0125	0.0122	0.0119	0.0116	0.0113	0.0110
−2.3	0.0107	0.0104	0.0102	0.0099	0.0096	0.0094	0.0091	0.0089	0.0087	0.0084
−2.4	0.0082	0.0080	0.0078	0.0075	0.0073	0.0071	0.0069	0.0068	0.0066	0.0064
−2.5	0.0062	0.0060	0.0059	0.0057	0.0055	0.0054	0.0052	0.0051	0.0049	0.0048
−2.6	0.0047	0.0045	0.0044	0.0043	0.0041	0.0040	0.0039	0.0038	0.0037	0.0036
−2.7	0.0035	0.0034	0.0033	0.0032	0.0031	0.0030	0.0029	0.0028	0.0027	0.0026
−2.8	0.0026	0.0025	0.0024	0.0023	0.0023	0.0022	0.0021	0.0021	0.0020	0.0019
−2.9	0.0019	0.0018	0.0018	0.0017	0.0016	0.0016	0.0015	0.0015	0.0014	0.0014
−3.0	0.0014	0.0013	0.0013	0.0012	0.0012	0.0011	0.0011	0.0011	0.0010	0.0010
−3.1	0.0010	0.0009	0.0009	0.0009	0.0008	0.0008	0.0008	0.0008	0.0007	0.0007
−3.2	0.0007	0.0007	0.0006	0.0006	0.0006	0.0006	0.0006	0.0005	0.0005	0.0005
−3.3	0.0005	0.0005	0.0005	0.0004	0.0004	0.0004	0.0004	0.0004	0.0004	0.0003
−3.4	0.0003	0.0003	0.0003	0.0003	0.0003	0.0003	0.0003	0.0003	0.0003	0.0002
−3.5	0.0002	0.0002	0.0002	0.0002	0.0002	0.0002	0.0002	0.0002	0.0002	0.0002
−3.6	0.0002	0.0002	0.0001	0.0001	0.0001	0.0001	0.0001	0.0001	0.0001	0.0001
−3.7	0.0001	0.0001	0.0001	0.0001	0.0001	0.0001	0.0001	0.0001	0.0001	0.0001
−3.8	0.0001	0.0001	0.0001	0.0001	0.0001	0.0001	0.0001	0.0001	0.0001	0.0001
−3.9	0.0000	0.0000	0.0000	0.0000	0.0000	0.0000	0.0000	0.0000	0.0000	0.0000
−4.0	0.0000	0.0000	0.0000	0.0000	0.0000	0.0000	0.0000	0.0000	0.0000	0.0000

TABLE 5 Areas under the normal curve from $-\infty$ to the value of z *continued*

z	0.00	0.01	0.02	0.03	0.04	0.05	0.06	0.07	0.08	0.09
0.0	0.5000	0.5040	0.5080	0.5120	0.5160	0.5199	0.5239	0.5279	0.5319	0.5359
0.1	0.5398	0.5438	0.5478	0.5517	0.5557	0.5596	0.5636	0.5675	0.5714	0.5753
0.2	0.5793	0.5832	0.5871	0.5910	0.5948	0.5987	0.6026	0.6064	0.6103	0.6141
0.3	0.6179	0.6217	0.6255	0.6293	0.6331	0.6368	0.6406	0.6443	0.6480	0.6517
0.4	0.6554	0.6591	0.6628	0.6664	0.6700	0.6736	0.6772	0.6808	0.6844	0.6879
0.5	0.6915	0.6950	0.6985	0.7019	0.7054	0.7088	0.7123	0.7157	0.7190	0.7224
0.6	0.7257	0.7291	0.7324	0.7357	0.7389	0.7422	0.7454	0.7486	0.7517	0.7549
0.7	0.7580	0.7611	0.7642	0.7673	0.7704	0.7734	0.7764	0.7794	0.7823	0.7852
0.8	0.7881	0.7910	0.7939	0.7967	0.7995	0.8023	0.8051	0.8078	0.8106	0.8133
0.9	0.8159	0.8186	0.8212	0.8238	0.8264	0.8289	0.8315	0.8340	0.8365	0.8389
1.0	0.8413	0.8438	0.8461	0.8485	0.8508	0.8531	0.8554	0.8577	0.8599	0.8621
1.1	0.8643	0.8665	0.8686	0.8708	0.8729	0.8749	0.8770	0.8790	0.8810	0.8830
1.2	0.8849	0.8869	0.8888	0.8907	0.8925	0.8944	0.8962	0.8980	0.8997	0.9015
1.3	0.9032	0.9049	0.9066	0.9082	0.9099	0.9115	0.9131	0.9147	0.9162	0.9177
1.4	0.9192	0.9207	0.9222	0.9236	0.9251	0.9265	0.9279	0.9292	0.9306	0.9319
1.5	0.9332	0.9345	0.9357	0.9370	0.9382	0.9394	0.9406	0.9418	0.9429	0.9441
1.6	0.9452	0.9463	0.9474	0.9484	0.9495	0.9505	0.9515	0.9525	0.9535	0.9545
1.7	0.9554	0.9564	0.9573	0.9582	0.9591	0.9599	0.9608	0.9616	0.9625	0.9633
1.8	0.9641	0.9649	0.9656	0.9664	0.9671	0.9678	0.9686	0.9693	0.9699	0.9706
1.9	0.9713	0.9719	0.9726	0.9732	0.9738	0.9744	0.9750	0.9756	0.9761	0.9767
2.0	0.9772	0.9778	0.9783	0.9788	0.9793	0.9798	0.9803	0.9808	0.9812	0.9817
2.1	0.9821	0.9826	0.9830	0.9834	0.9838	0.9842	0.9846	0.9850	0.9854	0.9857
2.2	0.9861	0.9864	0.9868	0.9871	0.9875	0.9878	0.9881	0.9884	0.9887	0.9890
2.3	0.9893	0.9896	0.9898	0.9901	0.9904	0.9906	0.9909	0.9911	0.9913	0.9916
2.4	0.9918	0.9920	0.9922	0.9925	0.9927	0.9929	0.9931	0.9932	0.9934	0.9936
2.5	0.9938	0.9940	0.9941	0.9943	0.9945	0.9946	0.9948	0.9949	0.9951	0.9952
2.6	0.9953	0.9955	0.9956	0.9957	0.9959	0.9960	0.9961	0.9962	0.9963	0.9964
2.7	0.9965	0.9966	0.9967	0.9968	0.9969	0.9970	0.9971	0.9972	0.9973	0.9974
2.8	0.9974	0.9975	0.9976	0.9977	0.9977	0.9978	0.9979	0.9979	0.9980	0.9981
2.9	0.9981	0.9982	0.9982	0.9983	0.9984	0.9984	0.9985	0.9985	0.9986	0.9986
3.0	0.9986	0.9987	0.9987	0.9988	0.9988	0.9989	0.9989	0.9989	0.9990	0.9990
3.1	0.9990	0.9991	0.9991	0.9991	0.9992	0.9992	0.9992	0.9992	0.9993	0.9993
3.2	0.9993	0.9993	0.9994	0.9994	0.9994	0.9994	0.9994	0.9995	0.9995	0.9995
3.3	0.9995	0.9995	0.9995	0.9996	0.9996	0.9996	0.9996	0.9996	0.9996	0.9997
3.4	0.9997	0.9997	0.9997	0.9997	0.9997	0.9997	0.9997	0.9997	0.9997	0.9998
3.5	0.9998	0.9998	0.9998	0.9998	0.9998	0.9998	0.9998	0.9998	0.9998	0.9998
3.6	0.9998	0.9998	0.9999	0.9999	0.9999	0.9999	0.9999	0.9999	0.9999	0.9999
3.7	0.9999	0.9999	0.9999	0.9999	0.9999	0.9999	0.9999	0.9999	0.9999	0.9999
3.8	0.9999	0.9999	0.9999	0.9999	0.9999	0.9999	0.9999	0.9999	0.9999	0.9999
3.9	1.0000	1.0000	1.0000	1.0000	1.0000	1.0000	1.0000	1.0000	1.0000	1.0000
4.0	1.0000	1.0000	1.0000	1.0000	1.0000	1.0000	1.0000	1.0000	1.0000	1.0000

APPENDIX B

SOLUTIONS TO SELF-TEST PROBLEMS

CHAPTER 3

1. Using Equation 3.2:

    $$S = P(1 + rt)$$

    Therefore:

    $$\$6250 = \$6000\left[1 + r\left(\frac{60}{365}\right)\right]$$

    Solving this equation, we find that $r = 0.253472$ or approximately 25.35 per cent per annum.

2. The series of deposits consists of the initial deposit plus an ordinary annuity with a term of 10 years.

    (a) Using Equation 3.4, the future value of the first deposit is:

    $$S = P(1+i)^n$$
    $$= \$5000(1.08)^{10}$$
    $$= \$5000 \times 2.158\,924\,997$$
    $$= \$10\,794.62$$

    Using Equation 3.28, the future value of the 10 later deposits is:

    $$S = \frac{C}{i}[(1+i)^n - 1]$$
    $$= \frac{\$1000}{0.08}[(1.08)^{10} - 1]$$
    $$= \$1000 \times 14.486\,562\,47$$
    $$= \$14\,486.56$$

    Therefore, when Angela has made the last deposit, she will have $\$10\,794.62 + \$14\,486.56 = \$25\,281.18$.

    (b) The amount to be deposited now is the present value of $25 281.18 in 10 years' time. Using Equation 3.5, this amount is:

    $$P = \frac{S}{(1+i)^n}$$
    $$= \frac{\$25\,281.18}{(1.08)^{10}}$$
    $$= \frac{\$25\,281.18}{2.158\,924\,997}$$
    $$= \$11\,710.08$$

3. (a) Using Equation 3.6:

    $$i = \left(1 + \frac{j}{m}\right)^m - 1$$
    $$= \left(1 + \frac{0.099}{12}\right)^{12} - 1$$
    $$= 0.103\,618$$
    $$\approx 10.36\% \text{ per annum}$$

(b) The repayments are an ordinary annuity for 25 × 12 = 300 months with a monthly interest rate of $\frac{9.9}{12}$ per cent = 0.825 per cent. Using Equation 3.19:

$$P = \frac{C}{i}\left[1 - \frac{1}{(1+i)^n}\right]$$

$$\$75\,000 = \frac{C}{0.00825}\left[1 - \frac{1}{(1.00825)^{300}}\right]$$

$$\$75\,000 = C \times 110.906\,437$$

$$C = \frac{\$75\,000}{110.906\,437}$$

$$= \$676.25 \text{ per month}$$

CHAPTER 4

1. The estimated value of one share is the present value of the dividends for the next 2 years plus the present value of the share as at the end of 2 years. The latter value can be estimated using Equation 4.8.

$$P_0 = \frac{D_0(1+g')}{(1+k_e)} + \frac{D_0(1+g')^2}{(1+k_e)^2} + \frac{1}{(1+k_e)^2}\frac{D_0(1+g')^2(1+g)}{(k_e-g)}$$

$$= \frac{\$0.75(1.08)}{1.14} + \frac{\$0.75(1.08)^2}{(1.14)^2} + \frac{1}{(1.14)^2}\frac{\$0.75(1.08)^2(1.04)}{(0.14-0.04)}$$

$$= \$8.38$$

2. The interest payments of \$5.50 per half year are an ordinary annuity. The yield is 13/2 = 6.5 per cent per half year, therefore the current price P is:

$$P = \frac{\$5.50}{0.065}\left[1 - \frac{1}{(1.065)^6}\right] + \frac{\$100}{(1.065)^6}$$

$$= \$95.16$$

3. On the basis of the expectations theory of the term structure of interest rates, we have:

$$(1+r_n)^n = (1+i_1)(1+i_2)(1+i_3)$$

Therefore, the 1-year interest rates in future years are found as follows:

In Year 2: $(1.1170)^2 = (1.1390)(1+i_2)$
Therefore $i_2 = 9.542\%$
In Year 3: $(1.1060)^3 = (1.1390)(1.09542)(1+i_3)$
Therefore $i_3 = 8.432\%$
Equivalently: $i_3 = (1.1060)^3/(1.1170)^2 - 1$
 $= 8.432\%$

CHAPTER 5

1. $NPV = \sum_{t=1}^{n}\frac{C_t}{(1+k)^t} - C_0$

$$= \frac{\$101\,800}{1.10} + \frac{\$90\,000}{(1.10)^2} + \frac{\$80\,000}{(1.10)^3} - \$180\,000$$

$$= \$92\,545 + \$74\,380 + \$60\,105 - \$180\,000$$

$$= \$47\,030$$

2. $\$180\,000 = \dfrac{\$101\,800}{1+r} + \dfrac{\$90\,000}{(1+r)^2} + \dfrac{\$80\,000}{(1+r)^3}$

   If we try a discount rate of 25 per cent, we find that:

   $$\$180\,000 = \$81\,440 + \$57\,600 + \$40\,960$$
   $$NPV = 0$$

   Therefore, the internal rate of return is 25 per cent.

3. Benefit–cost ratio $= \dfrac{\text{present value of net cash flows}}{\text{initial cash outlay}}$

   $= \dfrac{\$227\,030}{\$180\,000}$

   $= \$1.26$

CHAPTER 6

1. The optimum replacement policy can be calculated using the method outlined in Section 6.4.2. In the case of the TMT, the objective is to minimise the present value of cash outflows, assuming that operating cash inflows remain constant each year. For replacement every year, the NPV is:

   $$NPV_1 = -\$64\,000 - \dfrac{\$11\,000}{1.15} + \dfrac{\$50\,000}{1.15}$$
   $$= -\$30\,087$$

   If the machine is replaced every year in perpetuity, the NPV is:

   $$NPV_{(1,\infty)} = -\$30\,087 \dfrac{1.15}{1.15 - 1}$$
   $$= -\$230\,667$$

   The net present value 3 assuming replacement in perpetuity at the end of 2, 3, 4 and 5 years are:

   $$NPV_{(2,\infty)} = -\$217\,953$$
   $$NPV_{(3,\infty)} = -\$220\,463$$
   $$NPV_{(4,\infty)} = -\$223\,708$$
   $$NPV_{(5,\infty)} = -\$240\,906$$

   Therefore, the machine should be replaced at the end of 2 years.

2. (a) *Retain semi-trailers for 3 years and then replace with Flexivans.*
   We assume that the Flexivans are to be replaced in perpetuity.
   (i) Residual value of semi-trailers:

   $$\$10\,000(1.1)^{-3} = \$7513$$

   (ii) Net cash flows of semi-trailers:

   $$\$300\,000 \left[\dfrac{1 - \dfrac{1}{(1+0.10)^3}}{0.10} \right] = \$746\,056$$

Consider one Flexivan:

$$\text{Initial outlay} = \$70\,000$$

PV of net cash flows:

$$\$40\,000 \left[\frac{1 - \frac{1}{(1+0.10)^5}}{0.10} \right] = \$151\,631$$

PV of residual value:

$$\$5000(1.1)^{-5} = \$3105$$

NPV of one Flexivan:

$$-\$70\,000 + \$151\,631 + \$3105 = \$84\,736$$

(iii) PV of a perpetual chain of six Flexivans beginning in 3 years:

$$6(\$84\,736)\left[\frac{(1.1)^5}{(1.1)^5 - 1}\right](1.1)^{-3} = \$1\,007\,655$$

Net present value:

$$(i) + (ii) + (iii) = \$7513 + \$746\,056 + \$1\,007\,655 = \$1\,761\,224$$

(b) Replace semi-trailers with Flexivans now.
   (i) Salvage value of semi-trailers: $50 000
   (ii) PV of a perpetual chain of six Flexivans beginning now:

$$6(\$84\,736)\left[\frac{(1.1)^5}{(1.1)^5 - 1}\right] = \$1\,314\,189$$

Net present value:

$$(i) + (ii) = \$1\,391\,189$$

Since the net present value of retaining the CB semi-trailers for 3 years and then replacing them with AZ Flexivans is greater than the net present value of replacing the CB semi-trailers with the AZ Flexivans now, the CB semi-trailers should be retained for 3 years.

3. The nominal required rate of return is $(1.03)(1.05) - 1 = 0.0815$ or 8.15 per cent per annum.
The net present value of paying the $3100 immediately and not having to pay $3512.30 in one year's time is:

$$-\$3100 + \$3512.30 / (1.0815) = \$147.62$$

Alternatively, the net present value could be calculated as:

$$-\$3100 + \$3410 / (1.05) = \$147.62$$

As the net present value of this decision is positive, Skye should pay off her HECS–HELP debt immediately.
It may be noted that *provided two conditions are met* it is always optimal to voluntarily pay off the HECS–HELP debt and receive the additional 10 per cent reduction in the debt. The first condition is that the person's expected income in the subsequent year must be sufficiently high that the total HECS–HELP debt would be paid off in one year's time if the decision not to voluntarily pay the debt one year early were made. The second condition is that the real required rate of return must be less than 10 per cent.

CHAPTER 7

1. (a) Using Equation 7.1, the expected return on the portfolio is:

    $$E(R_p) = w_X E(R_X) + w_Y E(R_Y)$$
    $$= (0.3)(0.12) + (0.7)(0.18)$$
    $$= 0.162 \text{ or } 16.2\%$$

    (b) Using Equation 7.4, the variance of the portfolio is:

    $$\sigma_p^2 = w_X^2 \sigma_X^2 + w_Y^2 \sigma_Y^2 + 2w_X w_Y \rho \sigma_X \sigma_Y$$
    $$= (0.3)^2 (0.2)^2 + (0.7)^2 (0.15)^2 + 2(0.3)(0.7)\rho(0.2)(0.15)$$
    $$= 0.0036 + 0.011\,025 + 0.0126\rho$$

    (i) $\rho = +1.0, \sigma_p^2 = 0.027\,225$

    (ii) $\rho = +0.7, \sigma_p^2 = 0.023\,445$

    (iii) $\rho = 0, \sigma_p^2 = 0.014\,625$

    (iv) $\rho = -0.7, \sigma_p^2 = 0.005\,805$

    These results illustrate the fact that, other things being equal, diversification is more effective the lower the correlation coefficient.

2. The variance–covariance matrix will be a 3 × 3 matrix with the variances of the three securities on the main diagonal and covariances in all other cells. For example, the variance of X is $(0.22)^2 = 0.0484$ and the covariance between X and Y is $(0.6)(0.22)(0.15) = 0.0198$. The matrix is:

	X	Y	Z
X	0.0484	0.0198	0.0132
Y	0.0198	0.0225	0.0090
Z	0.0132	0.0090	0.0100

    $$\sigma_p^2 = w_X^2 \sigma_X^2 + w_Y^2 \sigma_Y^2 + w_Z^2 \sigma_Z^2 + 2w_X 2w_Z \text{Cov}(R_X, R_Y) + 2w_X w_Y \text{Cov}(R_X, R_Z) + 2w_Y w_Z \text{Cov}(R_Y, R_Z)$$
    $$= (0.2)^2 (0.0484) + (0.3)^2 (0.0225) + (0.5)^2 (0.0100) + 2(0.2)(0.3)(0.0198) + 2(0.2)(0.5)(0.0132) + 2(0.3)(0.5)(0.0090)$$
    $$= 0.001\,936 + 0.002\,025 + 0.0025 + 0.002\,376 + 0.002\,64 + 0.0027$$
    $$= 0.014\,177$$

    The standard deviation is:

    $$\sigma = \sqrt{0.038\,477}$$
    $$= 0.196\,15$$

3. The CAPM can be used to calculate the required return on each share. For example, for Carltown the required return is calculated as follows:

    $$E(R_i) = R_f + \beta_i [E(R_M) - R_f]$$
    $$= 0.08 + (0.7)(0.06)$$
    $$= 0.122 \text{ or } 12.2\%$$

    The expected and required returns on the four shares are as follows:

Share	Expected return (%)	Required return (%)
Carltown	13.0	12.2
Pivot	17.6	17.6
Forresters	14.0	14.6
Brunswick	10.4	10.4

    Pivot and Brunswick are correctly valued, Carltown is undervalued and Forresters is overvalued.

CHAPTER 10

1. The price is found by discounting the face value using simple interest. Using Equation 10.1, the price is:

$$P = \frac{F}{1+(r)(d/365)}$$

$$= \frac{\$500\,000}{1+(0.055)(90/365)}$$

$$= \frac{\$500\,000}{1.013\,561\,643}$$

$$= \$493\,309.91$$

The bill is purchased for $493 309.91.

2. When the bill is sold 30 days later, its term to maturity has become 60 days. Again using Equation 10.1, the price is:

$$P = \frac{F}{1+(r)(d/365)}$$

$$= \frac{\$500\,000}{1+(0.053)(60/365)}$$

$$= \frac{\$500\,000}{1.008\,712\,328}$$

$$= \$495\,681.46$$

The bill is sold for $495 681.46. Therefore, the dollar return to the holder over the 30-day period is:

$$\$495\,681.46 - \$493\,309.91 = \$2371.55$$

The implied interest rate is:

$$\frac{\$2371.55}{\$493\,309.91}$$

$$= 0.004\,807\,424$$

Therefore, the effective annual interest rate is:

$$(1.004\,807\,424)^{\frac{365}{30}} - 1$$

$$= 0.060\,086\,152$$

$$\approx 6.01\%$$

CHAPTER 12

1.

Annual net cash flow ($)	0	100 000	200 000
Financing plan			
(a) *All equity*			
Rate on return on $1 000 000 (%)	0	10	20
(b) *$750 000 equity and $250 000 loan*			
Interest paid ($)	25 000	25 000	25 000
Profit after interest ($)	−25 000	75 000	175 000
Rate of return on $750 000 (%)	−3.33	10	23.33

(c) *$250 000 equity and $750 000 loan*

Interest paid ($)	75 000	75 000	75 000
Profit after interest ($)	−75 000	25 000	125 000
Rate of return on $250 000 (%)	−30	10	50

Note that the choice of financing plan has no effect on the rate of return on Barry's investment only when the net operating cash flow is $100 000 per annum. For cash flows greater than or less than $100 000 per annum, the effects of financial leverage are evident for financing plans (b) and (c).

2. (a) The first step is to use Equation 12.3 to find k_o:

$$k_e = k_o + (k_o - k_d)\left(\frac{D}{E}\right)$$

$$21.5 = k_o + (k_o - 8)\left(\frac{1}{2}\right)$$

Rearranging this equation shows that $k_o = 17$ per cent. After the new loan is taken out, the debt–equity ratio is 1:1. Using Equation 12.3 again:

$$k_e = 17 + (17 - 8)\left(\frac{1}{1}\right)$$

$$= 26\%$$

(b) The average cost of capital is calculated using Equation 12.2:

$$k = k_e\left(\frac{E}{V}\right) + k_d\left(\frac{D}{V}\right)$$

With the original capital structure:

$$k = 21.5\left(\frac{2}{3}\right) + 8\left(\frac{1}{3}\right)$$

$$= 17\%$$

After the increase in leverage:

$$k = 26\left(\frac{1}{2}\right) + 8\left(\frac{1}{2}\right)$$

$$= 17\%$$

Consistent with the MM propositions, the company's weighted average cost of capital is not changed by the change in its capital structure.

3. (a) Cosmic's value with all-equity finance is:

$$V_u = \frac{\$600\,000\,(1 - 0.30)}{0.15}$$

$$= \frac{\$420\,000}{0.15}$$

$$= \$2\,800\,000$$

(b) (i) Interest on the loan is $100 000 per annum which is tax deductible.

After-tax cash flow = $(600 000 − 100 000) (1 − 0.30) + $100 000 = $450 000 which is an increase of $30 000 per annum.

(ii) The value of the company can be calculated using Equation 12.6:

$$V_L = V_u + t_c D$$

$$= \$2\,800\,000 + 0.30 \times \$1\,000\,000$$

$$= \$2\,800\,000 + \$300\,000$$

$$= \$3\,100\,000$$

CHAPTER 14

1. (a) The cost of capital for the project k_j can be estimated using Equation 14.1:

    $$k_j = R_f + \beta_j[E(R_M) - R_f]$$
    $$= 0.12 + 0.75(0.18 - 0.12)$$
    $$= 0.165$$

    $$NPV = \frac{C_1}{1+k_j} - C_0$$
    $$= \frac{\$235\,000}{1.165} - \$200\,000$$
    $$= \$1717$$

    Since the NPV is positive, the project is acceptable.

    (b) If $\beta_j = 1$,

    $$k_j = 0.12 + (0.18 - 0.12)$$
    $$= 0.18$$

    $$NPV = \frac{\$235\,000}{1.18} = \$200\,000$$
    $$= -\$847$$

    In this case, the project is not acceptable.

2. (a) Using the CAPM, the costs of capital for the projects are:
    Mars $k = 9 + 0.70\,(16.5 - 9) = 14.25\%$
    Pluto $k = 9 + 0.85\,(16.5 - 9) = 15.375\%$
    Neptune $k = 9 + 1.20\,(16.5 - 9) = 18.0\%$
    The projects that should be accepted are Mars and Neptune.

    (b) If all projects were evaluated using the company's cost of capital, Mars would be incorrectly rejected and Pluto would be incorrectly accepted.

3. The annual depreciation charge will be equal to $\$84\,000/12 = \$7000$. The increase in profit each year (ignoring the expenditure on an overhaul every 2 years) is $\$20\,000 - \$7000 = \$13\,000$. The effective company income tax rate is $0.30(1 - 0.75) = 0.075$. Therefore, the increase in taxation is $\$13\,000 \times 0.075 = \$975$ per annum. The net present value from purchasing the equipment is therefore equal to the present value of the annual savings of $\$20\,000 - \$975$, less the present value of the overhauls every 2 years, less the initial outlay.
The net present value is therefore equal to:

$$(\$20\,000 - \$975)\left[\frac{1 - \frac{1}{(1.1)^{12}}}{0.1}\right] - \frac{\$2000(1-0.075)}{1.1^2} - \frac{\$2000(1-0.075)}{1.1^4}$$

$$- \frac{\$2000(1-0.075)}{1.1^6} - \frac{\$2000(1-0.075)}{1.1^8} - \frac{\$2000(1-0.075)}{1.1^{10}} - \$84\,000$$

$$= \$40\,217$$

As the net present value is positive, the equipment should be purchased.

CHAPTER 15

1. (a) The NPV of the lease to Donash is the cost of the computer ($440 000) less the present value of the cash outflows for the lease. Since Donash will not be paying company income tax during the term of the lease, the only cash outflows are the lease rentals and the discount rate is 15 per cent per year. The NPV to Donash is:

$$NPV = \$440\,000 - \$100\,000 \left\{ 1 + \frac{1}{0.15}\left[1 - \frac{1}{(1.15)^5}\right]\right\}$$

$$= \$440\,000 - \$435\,216$$

$$= \$4784$$

(b) Comlease will purchase the computer for $440 000, receive the lease rentals ($70 000 per annum after tax) and receive depreciation tax savings (0.3 x (1/3) x $440 000 = $44 000 per annum) in Years 1, 2 and 3. The after-tax discount rate is 15(1 − 0.3) = 10.5 per cent per year. The NPV to Comlease is:

$$NPV = -\$440\,000 + \$70\,000\left\{1 + \frac{1}{0.105}\left[1 - \frac{1}{(0.105)^5}\right]\right\} + \frac{\$44\,000}{0.105}\left[1 - \frac{1}{(1.105)^3}\right]$$

$$= \$466$$

(c) The overall gain on the transaction is:
$4784 + $446
= $5250

CHAPTER 17

1. The current situation is:

September price: $1260
June price: $1200

Spread: $ 60

The spread is expected to widen—that is, the September contract will become relatively dearer and the June contract will become relatively cheaper. Therefore, we would buy the September contract and sell the June contract. If the subsequent prices are $1300 (June) and $1380 (September), the outcome is:

June	Sell at:	$1200	(+)
	Buy back at:	$1300	(−)
	Outcome:	$100	(loss)
September	Buy at:	$1260	(−)
	Sell at:	$1380	(+)
	Outcome:	$120	(profit)

Overall outcome = −$100 + $120 = $20 (profit). The profit ($20) is equal to the change in the spread (= $80 − $60).

2. The sale on 2 September is at a quoted price of 92.00. This provides an annual yield of 100 − 92.00 = 8.00 per cent. Using Equation 17.10, the contract price is:

$$\frac{\$1\,000\,000}{1 + (0.08)(90/365)}$$

$$= \$980\,655.56$$

The closing out on 8 September is at a quoted price of 92.50. This provides an annual yield of 100 − 92.50 = 7.50 per cent. The contract price is:

$$\frac{\$1\,000\,000}{1+(0.075)(90/365)}$$

$$= \$981\,842.64$$

Harold will make a loss of $981 842.64 − $980 655.56 = $1187.08 on each contract. On 15 contracts he will lose $1187.08 × 15 = $17 806.20.

CHAPTER 18

1. (a) The minimum theoretical price is given by Equation 18.3:

$$\text{Min } c = \text{Max}\left[0, S - \frac{X}{1+r'}\right]$$

In this problem, $c = \$1.70$ and the risk-free interest rate for an 8-month period is $r' = (1.0075)^8 - 1 \approx 6.16$ per cent. Therefore, the present value of the exercise price is $\frac{\$15.00}{1.0616} \approx \$14.13$.

$$\text{Max}\left[0, S - \frac{X}{1+r'}\right] = \text{Max}\,[0, \$14.90 - \$14.13]$$

$$= \text{Max}\,[0, \$0.77]$$

$$= \$0.77$$

Therefore the current call price ($1.70) exceeds its minimum theoretical price ($0.77).

(b) The details of the arbitrage are set out in the table below. The present value of the exercise price, as calculated in (a), is $14.13.

Current transaction	Current cash flow ($)	Future cash flow ($) if	
		$S^* \geq \$15$	$S^* \leq \$15$
Buy put	−0.83	0	+(15 − S^*)
Sell call	+1.70	−(S^* − 15)	0
Buy share	−14.90	+S^*	+S^*
Borrow $14.13	+14.13	−15	−15
Total	+0.10	0	0

The table shows that the suggested transactions create an arbitrage: a cash inflow of $0.10 per option is achieved today, while the future cash flow is guaranteed to be zero.

(c) The arbitrage is possible because put–call parity (Equation 18.1) is violated in this problem. Put–call parity is given by:

$$p = c - S + \frac{X}{1+r'}$$

In this problem, $p = \$0.83$ but:

$$c - S + \frac{X}{1+r'} = \$1.70 - \$14.90 + \$14.13$$

$$= \$0.93$$

$$\neq p$$

APPENDIX B SOLUTIONS TO SELF-TEST PROBLEMS

2. The binomial lattice for this problem is:

   FIGURE B.1 Lattice of share prices and call prices

   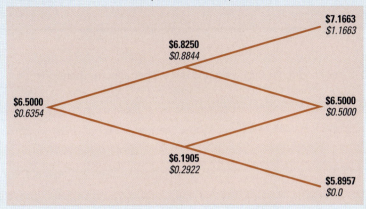

   Note that share prices are shown in bold and option prices are shown in italics.

Share price calculations are:

$$\$6.50 \times 1.05 = \$6.8250$$
$$\$6.8250 \times 1.05 = \$7.1663$$
$$\$6.50/1.05 = \$6.1905$$
$$\$6.1905/1.05 = \$5.8957$$

The 'up' probability (p) and the 'down' probability ($1 - p$) are given by:

$$\$6.50 = \frac{p(\$6.825) + (1 - p)(\$6.1905)}{1.01}$$

which solves to give $p = 0.5902$ and $1 - p = 0.4098$.

The payoffs at expiry are:

$$\text{Max } [\$0, \$7.1663 - \$6.00] = \$1.1663$$
$$\text{Max } [\$0, \$6.50 - \$6.00] = \$0.50$$
$$\text{Max } [\$0, \$5.8957 - \$6.00] = \$0$$

The option price calculations are:

$$\frac{(0.5902)(\$1.1663) + (0.4098)(\$0.50)}{1.01} = \$0.8844$$

$$\frac{(0.5902)(\$0.50) + (0.4098)(\$0.00)}{1.01} = \$0.2922$$

$$\frac{(0.5902)(\$0.8844) + (0.4098)(\$0.2922)}{1.01} = \$0.6354$$

The current price of the call option is therefore calculated to be $0.6354, or approximately 64 cents.

3. The Black–Scholes model to price call options is Equation 18.5:

$$c = SN(d_1) - Xe^{-r'T}N(d_2)$$

where $d_1 \equiv \dfrac{\ln(S/X) + \left(r' + \dfrac{1}{2}\sigma^2\right)T}{\sigma\sqrt{T}}$

$$d_2 \equiv \frac{\ln(S/X) + \left(r' + \frac{1}{2}\sigma^2\right)T}{\sigma\sqrt{T}}$$

$$\equiv d_1 - \sigma\sqrt{T}$$

In this problem, $S = \$12.15$, $X = \$12.00$, $r' = 0.10$ per annum, $T = 0.25$ years and $\sigma = 0.2$ per annum. Therefore:

$$d_1 = \frac{\ln(12.15/12) + [0.1 + (0.5)(0.2)^2](0.25)}{0.2\sqrt{0.25}}$$

$$= \frac{0.0124225 + 0.03}{0.1}$$

$$\approx 0.4242$$

and

$$d_2 \approx 0.4242 - 0.1$$
$$\approx 0.3242$$

Using Table 5 in Appendix A:

$$N(0.4242) \approx 0.6643$$

and

$$N(0.3242) \approx 0.6271$$

The present value of the exercise price is given by:

$$e^{-(0.1)(0.25)} \times \$12$$
$$= 0.975\,309\,9 \times \$12$$
$$\approx \$11.703\,719$$

Therefore the call price, c, is given by:

($\$12.15)(0.6643) - (\$11.707\,371\,9)(0.6271)$
$= \$0.7296$
≈ 73 cents

CHAPTER 19

1. (a) The value of Beta to Alpha is $\frac{\$750\,000}{0.25} = \$3\,000\,000$. As there are 2 million shares on issue, Beta is a zero-NPV investment at a price of \$1.50 per share.
   (b) The value of Beta as an independent entity is $\frac{\$500\,000}{0.25} = \$2\,000\,000$.
   (c) If \$2.6 million cash is paid for Beta, the wealth of its shareholders will increase by \$2.6 million − \$2 000 000 = \$600 000. The answers to (a) and (b) show that the gain from the takeover is \$1 million. If \$600 000 of this gain accrues to Beta's shareholders, then the wealth of Alpha's shareholders must increase by \$400 000.
2. (a) The increase in the value of B's equity is \$380 000 000 − \$320 000 000 = \$60 000 000. To achieve this increase B must purchase 10 million shares at \$5 each: an outlay of \$50 000 000. Therefore, B's shareholders benefit by \$10 000 000, so it should proceed with the takeover.
   (b) B will have to issue 15 million shares to acquire 50 per cent of C, after which it will have 95 million shares on issue and each B share will be worth $\frac{\$380\,000\,000}{95\,000\,000} = \$4$.
   The value of the outlay for the takeover is 15 000 000 × \$4 = \$60 000 000, so the wealth of B's shareholders will not be changed by the takeover.

CHAPTER 20

1. The exchange rate information can be represented diagrammatically as follows:

	Can buy:		Can be sold for:
FJD 1.3895	→ AUD 1	→	FJD 1.3226
EUR 0.6064	→ AUD 1	→	EUR 0.5874

   (a) The minimum value of a Fiji dollar in terms of euros can be found in two steps. First, consider one Fiji dollar and calculate how many Australian dollars it will buy. Second, calculate how many euros could be purchased using the Australian dollars.

   $$FJD\,1 = AUD\left(\frac{1}{1.3895}\right) = AUD\,0.719\,683$$

   $$AUD\,0.719\,683 = EUR\,(0.719\,683 \times 0.5874) = EUR\,0.4227$$

   Anyone wanting to convert Fiji dollars into euros should be offered at least 0.4227 euros for every Fiji dollar.

   (b) The minimum value of a euro in terms of Fiji dollars can be found in a similar manner:

   $$EUR\,1 = AUD\left(\frac{1}{0.6064}\right) = AUD\,1.649\,077$$

   $$AUD\,1.649\,077 = FJD\,(1.649\,077 \times 1.3226) = FJD\,2.1811$$

   (c) Upper and lower bounds on the exchange rate between Fiji dollars and euros (on a per euro basis):
   From (a) above we know that 1 Fiji dollar is worth at least 0.4227 euros. To obtain 1 euro, a person should not have to pay more than $FJD\left(\frac{1}{0.4227}\right) = FJD\,2.3657$. From (b) above we know that 1 euro is worth at least 2.1811 Fiji dollars. Hence, it should not cost more than 2.3657 Fiji dollars (upper bound) to obtain 1 euro and 1 euro should be exchanged for at least 2.1811 Fiji dollars (lower bound).

2. Using interest rate parity as expressed in Equation 21.1(a), $\frac{1+i_u}{1+i_A} = \frac{f}{s}$.

   (a) In the first case:

   $$\frac{1.02}{1.03} = \frac{f}{4.57}$$

   which solves to give $f = 4.5256$.

   (b) If interest rates increase in Utopia:

   $$\frac{1.04}{1.03} = \frac{f}{4.57}$$

   which solves to give $f = 4.6144$.

   (c) The above results can be explained as follows. In (a) the interest rate in Australia is higher than the interest rate in Utopia, so the forward rate (4.5256) is less than the spot rate (4.5700). In (b) the interest rate is higher in Utopia and the forward rate (4.6144) is greater than the spot rate. The currency with the higher interest rate is worth less forward than it is worth spot.

CHAPTER 21

1. Using Equation 21.2:

   $$Q^* = \sqrt{\frac{2aD}{c}}$$

   $$= \sqrt{\frac{(2)(3000)(500)}{48}}$$

   $$= 250 \text{ sprockets}$$

where a = $3000 (per run)
D = 500 (units per annum)
c = $48 (per sprocket per annum)

The economic production run is 250 sprockets, and therefore $\dfrac{500}{250} = 2$. Two production runs per annum are indicated.

2. A reorder point of 2200 will achieve a stockout probability of 5 per cent. If a reorder point of 2000 is adopted, the expected customer-service level is:

$$0.10 + 0.20 + 0.50 + (0.15)\left[\dfrac{2000}{2200}\right] + (0.03)\left[\dfrac{2000}{2400}\right] + (0.02)\left[\dfrac{2000}{2600}\right]$$

$$= 0.9767$$

As this exceeds the target level of 95 per cent, a lower reorder point will be tried. If a reorder point of 1800 is adopted, the expected customer-service level is:

$$0.10 + 0.20 + (0.50)\left[\dfrac{1800}{2000}\right] + (0.15)\left[\dfrac{1800}{2200}\right] + (0.03)\left[\dfrac{1800}{2400}\right] + (0.02)\left[\dfrac{1800}{2600}\right]$$

$$= 0.9091$$

The required reorder point thus lies between 1800 and 2000. Let the required point exceed 1800 by x units, where it is known that $0 < x < 200$. The expected customer-service level is as follows:

$$0.95 = 0.10 + 0.20 + (0.50)\left[\dfrac{1800 + x}{2000}\right] + (0.15)\left[\dfrac{1800 + x}{2200}\right] + (0.03)\left[\dfrac{1800 + x}{2400}\right] + (0.02)\left[\dfrac{1800 + x}{2600}\right]$$

$$= 0.10 + 0.20 + 0.45 + 0.122\,73 + 0.0225 + 0.013\,85 + \left[\dfrac{0.5}{2000} + \dfrac{0.15}{2200} + \dfrac{0.03}{2400} + \dfrac{0.02}{2600}\right]x$$

$$= 0.90\,908 + 0.000\,338\,37\,x$$

$$\therefore x = \dfrac{0.95 - 0.909\,08}{0.000\,338\,37}$$

$$= 120.93$$

$$= 121$$

As a result, a reorder point of 1800 + 121 = 1921 should achieve an expected customer service level of approximately 95 per cent. This is confirmed in the following calculation:

$$0.10 + 0.20 + (0.50)\left[\dfrac{1921}{2000}\right] + (0.15)\left[\dfrac{1921}{2200}\right] + (0.03)\left[\dfrac{1921}{2400}\right] + (0.02)\left[\dfrac{1921}{2600}\right]$$

$$= 0.10 + 0.20 + 0.480\,25 + 0.130\,98 + 0.024\,01 + 0.014\,78$$

$$= 0.950\,02$$

$$= 95 \text{ per cent}$$

CHAPTER 22

1. (a) The discount for payment 7 days after the invoice date is $1500 x 0.02 = $30.
   (b) Customer X saves $30 by paying 23 days early. The effective annual interest rate is:

$$\left(1 + \dfrac{30}{1470}\right)^{\tfrac{365}{23}} - 1 = 0.377\,96 \text{ or } 37.8\%$$

2. Consider sales of $1000. The cost of goods sold will be $750. With the original terms, and using simple interest, the NPV per $1000 of sales is:

$$NPV = \frac{\$1000}{1 + 0.1\left(\frac{45}{365}\right)} - \$750$$

$$= \$237.83$$

With the revised terms, the NPV is:

$$NPV = \frac{\$700 \times 0.99}{1 + 0.1\left(\frac{45}{365}\right)} + \frac{\$300}{1 + 0.1\left(\frac{50}{365}\right)} - \$750$$

$$= \$230.51$$

The difference in profitability is small, but the original terms are more profitable.

GLOSSARY

abnormal returns returns in excess of the return expected from a security

acceptor (or drawee) in a bill of exchange, the party agreeing to pay the holder the bill's face value on the maturity date; usually a bank or other financial institution

accounting rate of return earnings from an investment expressed as a percentage of the investment outlay

account receivable (or debtors) sum of money owed to a seller as a result of having sold goods or services on credit

accumulation process by which, through the operation of interest, a present sum becomes a greater sum in the future

annuity series of cash flows, usually of equal amount, equally spaced in time

annuity-due annuity in which the first cash flow is to occur 'immediately' (i.e. on the valuation date)

arbitrage simultaneous transactions in different markets that result in an immediate risk-free profit

at call money repayable immediately, at the option of the lender

authorised deposit-taking institution a corporation that is authorised under the *Banking Act 1959* to accept deposits from the public

bad debts accounts that have proven to be uncollectable and are written off

bank bill bill of exchange that has been accepted or endorsed by a bank

bankruptcy costs direct and indirect costs associated with financial difficulty that leads to control of a company being transferred to lenders

basis spot price at a point in time minus the futures price (for delivery at some later date) at that point in time

bearer bond a bond whose ownership is not registered by the issuer and possession of the physical document is primary evidence of ownership

benefit–cost ratio index calculated by dividing the present value of the future net cash flows by the initial cash outlay (also known as a *profitability index*)

beta measure of a security's systematic risk, describing the amount of risk contributed by the security to the market portfolio

bill acceptance facility agreement in which one entity (normally a bank) undertakes to accept bills of exchange drawn by another entity (the borrower)

bill discount facility agreement in which one entity (normally a bank) undertakes to discount (buy) bills of exchange drawn by another entity (the borrower)

bill of exchange marketable short-term debt security in which one party (the drawer) directs another party (the acceptor) to pay a stated sum on a stated future date

bonds (or debentures) debt securities issued with a medium or long term to maturity

book-to-market ratio book value of a company's equity divided by market value of the company's equity

break-even analysis analysis of the amounts by which one or more input variables may change before a project ceases to be profitable

bridging finance short-term loan, usually in the form of a mortgage, to cover a need normally arising from timing differences between two or more transactions

bubble period in which prices rise strongly, departing from their 'true value', frequently followed by a sudden decrease in prices

business risk variability of future net cash flows attributed to the nature of the company's operations. It is the risk shareholders face if the company has no debt

buy-and-hold policy investment strategy in which shares are bought and then retained in the investor's portfolio for a long period

buyout (or going-private transaction) transfer from public ownership to private ownership of a company through purchase of its shares by a small group of investors that usually includes the existing management

call notice given by a company that the holders of partly paid shares must make an additional contribution of equity

call option right to buy an underlying asset at a fixed price

call option on a futures contract option that gives the buyer the right to enter into the futures contract as a buyer at a predetermined price

capital market market in which long-term funds are raised and long-term debt and equity securities are traded

capital market line efficient set of all portfolios that provides the investor with the best possible investment opportunities when a risk-free asset is available. It describes the equilibrium risk–return relationship for efficient portfolios, where the expected return is a function of the risk-free interest rate, the expected market risk premium and the proportionate risk of the efficient portfolio to the risk of the market portfolio

capital rationing a condition where a firm has limited resources available for investment

capital structure mix of debt and equity finance used by a company

carrying cost cost of holding a commodity for a specified period of time

cash budget forecast of the amount and timing of the cash receipts and payments that will result from a company's operations over a period of time

cash flow payment (cash outflow) or receipt (cash inflow) of money

central bank a bank that controls the issue of currency, acts as banker to the government and the banking system and sets the interest rate for overnight cash

certainty-equivalent approach that incorporates risk by adjusting the cash flows rather than the discount rate

chattel mortgage a loan secured by a mortgage over movable property

classical tax system tax system that operates in the US and which operated in Australia until 30 June 1987; under this system company profits, and dividends paid from those profits, are taxed separately—that is, profit paid as a dividend is effectively taxed twice

collection policy policy adopted by a company in regard to collecting delinquent accounts either informally or by the use of a debt collection agency

commercial paper (or promissory note) short-term marketable debt security in which the borrower promises to pay a stated sum on a stated future date. Also known as *one-name paper*

company separate legal entity formed under the *Corporations Act 2001*; shareholders are the owners of a company

compound interest interest calculated each period on the principal amount and on any interest earned on the investment up to that point

compound option option on an option (e.g. an option to buy an option)

conglomerate takeover takeover of a target company in an unrelated type of business

consistency principle in applying the NPV model, the net cash flows in the numerator should be defined and measured in a way that is consistent with the definition of the discount rate

constant chain of replacement assumption may be used to evaluate mutually exclusive projects of unequal lives; in this case, each project is assumed to be replaced at the end of its economic life by an identical project

consumer credit credit extended to individuals by suppliers of goods and services, or by financial institutions through credit cards

contingent claim asset whose value depends on the value of some other asset

continuous interest method of calculating interest in which interest is charged so frequently that the time period between each charge approaches zero

contributing shares shares on which only part of the issue price has been paid. Also known as *partly paid shares*

conversion ratio relationship that determines how many ordinary shares will be received in exchange for each convertible or converting security when the conversion occurs

convertible bond a bond that allows the investor to exchange the bond for shares in the borrower

convertible preference share a preference share that may be converted at the option of the holder into an ordinary share

converting preference share a preference share that will automatically convert into an ordinary share on a specified date unless it is redeemed by the issuer prior to that date

corporate raiders aggressive corporate or individual investors who purchase a company's shares with the intention of achieving a controlling interest and replacing the existing management

cost of capital minimum rate of return needed to compensate suppliers of capital for committing resources to an investment

coupon payments periodic payments of interest, often at half-yearly intervals, on debt securities such as bonds and debentures

coupons fixed interest payments made on bonds and debentures

covenant provision in a loan agreement to protect lenders' interests by requiring certain actions to be taken and others refrained from

covered interest arbitrage movement of funds between two currencies to profit from interest rate differences while using forward contracts to eliminate exchange risk

credit foncier loan type of loan that involves regular repayments that include principal and interest

credit period period between the date that a purchaser is invoiced and the date when payment is due

credit policy supplier's policy on whether credit will be offered to customers and on the terms that will be offered to those customers

credit risk possibility of loss because a party fails to meet its obligations

cross rate exchange rate between two currencies derived from the exchange rates between the currencies and a third currency

cross-border lease finance lease, usually leveraged, where the lessor and lessee are located in different countries

cum dividend period period during which the purchaser of a share is qualified to receive a previously announced dividend. The cum dividend period ends on the ex-dividend date

cum rights when shares are traded cum rights the buyer is entitled to participate in the forthcoming rights issue

currency swap simultaneous borrowing and lending operation in which two parties initially exchange specific amounts of two currencies at the spot rate. Interest payments in the two currencies are also exchanged and the parties agree to reverse the initial exchange after a fixed term at a fixed exchange rate

current assets cash, inventory, accounts receivable and other assets that will normally be converted into cash within a year

current liabilities debt or other obligations due for payment within a year

debenture a type of fixed interest security issued by a company and secured by a charge over tangible assets

debt financial contract in which the receiver of the initial cash (the borrower) promises a particular cash flow, usually calculated using an interest rate, to the provider of funds (the lender)

debtor finance with recourse debtor finance agreement under which the discounter is reimbursed by the selling company if the debtor defaults

debtor finance without recourse debtor finance agreement under which the discounter is not reimbursed by the selling company if the debtor defaults

default failure to perform a contractual obligation

default risk the chance that a borrower will fail to meet obligations to pay interest and principal as promised

default-risk structure of interest rates relationship between default risk and interest rates

deferred annuity annuity in which the first cash flow is to occur after a time period that exceeds the time period between each subsequent cash flow

delinquent accounts accounts where payment has not been made by the due date

disclosure document prospectus, profile statement or offer information statement that must be supplied to potential investors to provide information about an offer of securities

discount period period during which a discount for prompt payment is available to the purchaser

discount rate expression of the price reduction a purchaser will receive if payment is made within the discount period

discounted cash flow (DCF) methods those that involve the process of discounting a series of future net cash flows to their present values

discounter in the context of marketable short-term securities (including commercial paper and bills of exchange), the purchaser of such a security

discounter (or factor) in the context of debtor finance, a financier who provides funds by purchasing accounts receivable from a business on a continuing basis

discounting process by which, through the operation of interest, a future sum is converted to its equivalent present value

disintermediation movement of funds from accounts with deposit-taking financial intermediaries and the reinvestment of those funds in securities

divestiture (or sell-off) sale of a subsidiary, division or collection of related assets, usually to another company

dividend clientele group of investors who choose to invest in companies that have dividend policies that meet their particular requirements

dividend drop-off ratio ratio of the decline in the share price on the ex-dividend day to the dividend per share

dividend election scheme (DES) arrangement made by a company that gives shareholders the option of receiving their dividends in one or more of a number of forms

dividend growth model model expressing the value of a share as the sum of the present values of future dividends where the dividends are assumed to grow at a constant rate

dividend reinvestment plan (DRP) arrangement made by a company that gives shareholders an option of reinvesting all or part of their dividends in additional shares in the company, usually at a small discount from market price

dividend yield dividend per share divided by the share price

dividend-payout ratio percentage of profit paid out to shareholders as dividends

dividends periodic distributions, usually in cash, by a company to its shareholders

domestic loan (in foreign currency) a loan of foreign currency made by domestic bank to a domestic borrower

drawer in a bill of exchange, the party initiating the creation of the bill; usually the borrower

duration measure of the time period of an investment in a bond or debenture that incorporates cash flows that are made prior to maturity

economic order quantity (EOQ) optimal quantity of inventory ordered that minimises the cost of purchasing and holding the inventory

effective interest rate interest rate where interest is charged at the same frequency as the interest rate is quoted

efficient market hypothesis (EMH) that the price of a security (such as a share) accurately reflects available information

endorsement acceptance by the seller of a bill in the secondary market of responsibility to pay the face value if there is default by the acceptor, drawer and earlier endorsers

equivalent annual value method involves calculating the annual cash flow of an annuity that has the same life as the project and whose present value equals the net present value of the project

Euro commercial paper short-term note sold without being underwritten in countries other than the country of the currency in which it is denominated

Eurobond medium- to long-term international bearer security issued in countries other than the country of the currency in which the bond is denominated

Eurocredit a loan made in a currency other than the currency of the country where the loan is made

Euronote short-term note, underwritten by a bank or a syndicate of banks and sold in countries other than the country of the currency in which it is denominated

event study research method that analyses the behaviour of a security's price around the time of a significant event such as the public announcement of the company's profit

exchange rate price of one country's currency expressed in terms of another country's currency

exchange risk variability of an entity's value that is due to changes in exchange rates

exchangeable preference share a preference share that may be exchanged for a security issued by a subsidiary or affiliate of the issuer

exchange-traded market market in which trading takes place by competitive bidding on an organised exchange

ex-dividend date date on which a share begins trading ex-dividend. A share purchased ex-dividend does not include a right to the forthcoming dividend payment

exercise (or strike) price fixed price at which an underlying asset can be traded, pursuant to the terms of an option contract

expectations theory of the term structure is that interest rates are set such that investors in bonds or other debt securities can expect, on average, to achieve the same return over any future period, regardless of the security in which they invest

ex-rights date date on which a share begins trading ex-rights. After this date a share does not have attached to it the right to purchase any additional share(s) on the subscription date

face value sum promised to be paid in the future on a debt security, such as commercial paper or a bill of exchange

finance lease long-term lease that effectively transfers the risks and benefits of ownership of an asset from the lessor to the lessee

financial agency institution arranges or facilitates the direct transfer of funds from lenders to borrowers

financial assets assets such as shares, bonds and bank deposits, as distinct from real assets

financial contract arrangement, agreement or investment that produces cash flows

financial distress situation where a company's financial obligations cannot be met, or can be met only with difficulty

financial intermediary institution that acts as a principal in accepting funds from depositors or investors and lending them to borrowers

financial leverage (or gearing) the effect of company debt on the returns earned by shareholders. Financial leverage is measured by ratios such as the debt–equity ratio and the ratio of debt to total assets

financial risk risk attributable to the use of debt as a source of finance

floating-rate note debt security whose interest rate is adjusted periodically in line with changes in a specified reference rate

floor-plan (or wholesale) finance loan, usually made by a wholesaler to a retailer, that finances an inventory of durable goods such as motor vehicles

foreign bond bond issued outside the borrower's country and denominated in the currency of the country in which it is issued

foreign loan (in domestic currency) a loan raised in another country, in the currency of that country

forward margin difference between spot and forward rates

forward rate exchange rate that is established now but with payment and delivery to occur on a specified future date

franked dividend dividend paid out of Australian company profits on which company income tax has been paid and which carries a franking credit

franking credit credit for Australian company tax paid, which, when distributed to shareholders, can be offset against their tax liability

franking premium that part of the return on shares or a share market index that is due to tax credits associated with franked dividends

free cash flow cash flow in excess of that required to fund all projects that have positive net present values

full payout policy distribution of the full present value of a company's free cash flow to shareholders

full service debtor finance discounting agreement under which the discounter manages the company's debtors

fully drawn bill facility bill facility in which the borrower must issue bills so that the full agreed amount is borrowed for the period of the facility

future sum amount to which a present sum, such as a principal, will grow (accumulate) at a future date, through the operation of interest

general annuity annuity in which the frequency of charging interest does not match the frequency of payment; thus, repayments may be made either more frequently or less frequently than interest is charged

geometric rate of return average of a sequence of arithmetic rates of return, found by a process that resembles compounding

hedge ratio (or delta) ratio of the change in an option price that results from a change in the price of the underlying asset

hedgers individuals and companies who enter into contracts in order to reduce risk

hire-purchase agreement agreement under which an asset owned by a financier is hired by a user who has the right or an obligation to purchase the asset when the agreement expires

horizontal takeover takeover of a target company operating in the same line of business as the acquiring company

immunisation strategy designed to achieve a target sum of money at a future point in time, regardless of interest rate changes

imputation tax system system under which investors in shares can use tax credits associated with franked dividends to offset their personal income tax. The system eliminates the double taxation inherent in the classical tax system

independent project one that may be accepted or rejected without affecting the acceptability of another project

indicator rate interest rate set and published by a lender from time to time and used as a base on which interest rates on individual loans are determined, usually by adding a margin

indifference curve curve showing a set of combinations such that an individual derives equal utility from (and thus is indifferent between) any combinations in the set

information asymmetry situation where all relevant information is not known by all interested parties. Typically, this involves company 'insiders' (managers) having more information about the company's prospects than 'outsiders' (shareholders and lenders)

information efficiency situation in which prices accurately reflect available information

initial public offering a company's first offering of shares to the public

instalment receipt marketable security for which only part of the issue price has been paid. The balance is payable in a final instalment on or before a specified date

interbank cash rate the interest rate on overnight loans between a bank and another bank (including the Reserve Bank)

interest rate rate of return on debt

interest rate parity (or covered interest parity) theory that states that a forward exchange rate is given by the spot rate, adjusted to reflect the relative interest rates in the two currencies

interest rate swap agreement between two parties to exchange interest payments for a specific period, related to an agreed principal amount. The most common type of interest rate swap involves an exchange of fixed interest payments for floating interest payments

interest-only loan loan in which the borrower is required to make regular payments to cover interest accrued but is not required to make payments to reduce the principal. On the maturity date of the loan, the principal is repaid in a lump sum

intermediation process in which a bank or other financial institution raises funds from investors and then lends those funds to borrowers

internal rate of return (IRR) the discount rate that equates the present value of an investment's net cash flows with its initial cash outlay; it is the discount rate at which the net present value is equal to zero

international bond a bond that is either a foreign bond or a Eurobond

intrinsic value value of an option if exercised immediately

inventory comprises raw materials, work in progress, supplies used in operations and finished goods

investing institution accepts funds from the public and invests them in assets; includes superannuation funds, life insurance companies and unit trusts

issue costs costs of raising new capital by issuing securities, including underwriting fees and legal, accounting and printing expenses incurred in preparing a prospectus or other offer documents. Also known as *flotation costs*

January effect observation that, on average, share prices increase more in January than in other months

joint test problem problem that any test of market efficiency is simultaneously a test of some model of 'normal' asset pricing

law of one price principle maintaining that the price of a commodity in a given currency will be the same regardless of the currency in which the price is quoted

lessee in a lease contract, the party using the asset

lessor in a lease contract, the party that owns the asset

leveraged buyout company takeover that is largely financed using borrowed funds; the remaining equity is privately held by a small group of investors

leveraged lease finance lease where the lessor borrows most of the funds to acquire the asset

limited liability legal concept that protects shareholders whose liability to meet a company's debts is limited to any amount unpaid on the shares they hold

liquid assets comprise cash and assets that are readily convertible into cash, such as bills of exchange

liquidity management involves decisions about the composition and level of a company's liquid assets

liquidity premium (risk premium) theory of the term structure is that although future interest rates are determined by investors' expectations, investors require some reward (liquidity premium) to assume the increased risk of investing long term

log price relative natural logarithm of the ratio of successive security prices. Implicitly, it is assumed that prices have grown (or decayed) in a continuous fashion between the two dates on which the prices are observed. Also known as a *logarithmic rate of return* and a *continuous rate of return*

long hedger hedger who hedges by means of buying futures contracts today

maintenance lease operating lease where the lessor is responsible for all maintenance and service of the leased asset

management buyout purchase of all of a company's issued shares by a group led by the company's management

margin call demand for extra funds to be deposited into a trader's account

market model time series regression of an asset's returns

market opportunity line line that shows the combinations of current and future consumption that an individual can achieve from a given wealth level, using capital market transactions

market portfolio portfolio of all risky assets, weighted according to their market capitalisation

marking-to-market process of adjusting traders' account balances to reflect changes in market prices

medium-term note (MTN) bearer security with an initial term to maturity of more than 1 year and often issued continually

momentum effect effect in which good or bad performance of shares continues over time

mortgage a type of security for a loan in which specific land or other tangible property is pledged by the borrower (mortgagor) to the lender (mortgagee)

mutually exclusive projects alternative investment projects, only one of which can be accepted

net present value (NPV) the difference between the present value of the net cash flows from an investment discounted at the required rate of return, and the initial cash outlay on the investment

nominal interest rate (1) quoted interest rate where interest is charged more frequently than the basis on which the interest rate is quoted. The interest rate actually used to calculate the interest charge is taken as a proportion of the quoted nominal rate

nominal interest rate (2) interest rate before taking out the effects of inflation

non-bank bill bill of exchange that has been neither accepted nor endorsed by a bank

non-debt tax shields (NDTS) tax deductions for items such as depreciation on assets and tax losses carried forward

non-notification (or confidential) debtor finance discounting agreement whose existence is not disclosed to the company's debtors

non-recourse loan type of loan used in leveraged leases where the lender has no recourse to the lessor in the event of default by the lessee

note issuance facility (NIF) or revolving underwriting facility (RUF) facility provided by one or more institutions that agree to underwrite issues of short-term notes by a borrower

open account an arrangement under which goods or services are sold to a customer on credit, but with no formal debt contract. Payment is due after an account is sent to the customer

operating lease lease under which the risks and benefits of ownership of the leased asset remain with the lessor

opportunity cost highest price or rate of return that would be provided by an alternative course of action. The *opportunity cost of capital* is the rate of return that could be earned on another investment with the same risk

optimal capital structure the capital structure that maximises a company's value

option the right but not the obligation to buy or sell underlying assets at a fixed price for a specified period

option to abandon right to discontinue an investment project

option to defer right to begin an investment project at a later date

option to expand right to increase the scale of an investment project

option to reopen right to restart a shut-down investment project

option to study right to gather more information on an investment project

ordinary annuity annuity in which the time period from the date of valuation to the date of the first cash flow is equal to the time period between each subsequent cash flow

ordinary perpetuity ordinary annuity with the special feature that the cash flows are to continue forever

ordinary shares securities that represent an ownership interest in a company and provide the owner with voting rights. Holders of ordinary shares have a residual interest in the net assets of the issuing company and are therefore exposed to greater risk than other classes of investors

overdraft limit level to which a company is permitted to overdraw its account

overreaction biased response of a price to information in which the initial price movement can be expected to be reversed

over-the-counter market there is no organised exchange and the market consists of financial institutions that are willing to trade with any counterparty

partial takeover takeover in which a bidder seeks to acquire no more than part of a company's issued shares

partnership business owned by two or more people acting as partners

partnership debtor finance discounting agreement under which the discounter and the company share responsibility for managing the company's debtors

payback period the time it takes for the progressive accumulated net cash flows generated by an investment to equal the initial cash outlay

payoff structure set of future cash flows

pecking order theory theory that proposes that companies follow a hierarchy of financing sources in which internal funds are preferred and, if external funds are needed, borrowing is preferred to issuing riskier securities

perfect capital market frictionless capital market in which there are no transaction costs and no barriers to the free flow of information

placement an issue of securities direct to chosen investors rather than the general public

poison pill strategic move by a company that may become a takeover target to make its shares less attractive to an acquirer by increasing the cost of a takeover (e.g. an issue of securities that will convert to shares if a takeover bid occurs)

portfolio combined holding of more than one asset

preference shares shares that rank before ordinary shares for the payment of dividends and in the event of liquidation of the issuing company. They often provide an entitlement to a fixed dividend

present value amount that corresponds to today's value of a promised future sum

present value of a contract the value today that is equivalent to the stream of cash flows promised in a financial contract

price–earnings ratio share price divided by earnings per share

primary market market for new issues of securities where the sale proceeds go to the issuer of the securities

principal amount borrowed at the outset of a loan

principal-and-interest loan loan repaid by a sequence of equal cash flows, each of which is sufficient to cover the interest accrued since the previous payment and to reduce the current balance owing. Therefore, the debt is extinguished when the sequence of cash flows is completed. Also known as a *credit foncier loan*

production possibilities curve (PPC) curve that displays the investment opportunities and outcomes available to the company; its shape therefore determines the combinations of current dividends, investments and future dividends that a company can achieve

progressive dividend policy directors aim to steadily increase or at least maintain the dividend at each payment

proportional bid partial takeover bid to acquire a specified proportion of the shares held by each shareholder

prospectus a document that, among other things, provides details of the company and the terms of the issue of securities, which must be provided to potential investors by a company seeking to issue shares or other securities

purchasing power parity theory that states that the expected change in the exchange rate is due to differences in expected inflation rates in the respective currencies

pure play company that operates almost entirely in only one industry or line of business

put option right to sell an underlying asset at a fixed price

put option on a futures contract option that gives the buyer the right to enter into the futures contract as a seller at a predetermined price

put–call parity relationship that exists between the price of a call option and the price of the corresponding put option

rate of return calculation that expresses the ratio of net cash inflows to cash outflows

real interest rate interest rate after taking out the effects of inflation

real options the flexibility that a manager has in choosing whether to undertake or abandon a project or change the way a project is managed

redeemable preference share a preference share that can be repurchased by the issuing company on a specified maturity date

rediscounting selling a short-term debt security in the secondary market

reset preference share a preference share where the dividend rate can be varied at specified intervals

residual claim claim to profit or assets that remain after the entitlements of all other interested parties have been met

residual value disposal value of a project's assets less any dismantling and removal costs associated with the project's termination

revolving credit a loan in which the borrower is permitted to borrow up to a stated amount

revolving credit bill facility bill facility in which the borrower can issue bills as required, up to the agreed limit

revolving credit facility loan for general business purposes secured against the inventory of the borrower

risk aversion a dislike of risk

risk neutrality situation in which investors are indifferent to risk; assets are therefore priced such that they are expected to yield the risk-free interest rate

risk-averse investor one who dislikes risk

risk-neutral investor one who neither likes nor dislikes risk

risk-seeking investor one who prefers risk

safety stock additional inventory held when demand is uncertain, to reduce the probability of a stockout

sale and lease-back agreement agreement in which a company sells an asset and then leases it back

seasoned equity offering offer to sell equity securities of a class that is already traded

secondary market market where previously issued securities are traded

secondary market transaction purchase or sale of an existing security

securities in the context of financial markets, financial assets that can be traded

securitisation the process of making assets marketable by aggregating income-producing assets in a pool and issuing new securities backed by the pool

security market line graphical representation of the capital asset pricing model

sensitivity analysis analysis of the effect of changing one or more input variables to observe the effects on the results

short hedger hedger who hedges by means of selling future contracts today

short selling process of first entering into a contract to sell and later entering into a contract to buy

shortfall facility a mechanism under which a company may issue shortfall shares to eligible shareholders or other investors

shortfall shares new shares not subscribed for by eligible shareholders according to their entitlements under a rights issue

simple annuity annuity in which the frequency of charging interest matches the frequency of payment

simple domestic bond a bond denominated in domestic currency and issued by a domestic borrower

simple domestic loan a loan of domestic currency made by a domestic lender to a domestic borrower

simple interest method of calculating interest in which, during the entire term of the loan, interest is computed on the original sum borrowed

simulation analysis of the effect of changing all of the input variables whose values are uncertain to observe the effects on the results

sole proprietorship business owned by one person

speculators individuals and companies who enter into contracts in order to profit from correctly anticipating price movements

spin-off the separation of certain assets (or a division) from a firm upon which are issued new shares that are allocated to the firm's existing shareholders

spot price price of the commodity when the buyer pays immediately and the seller delivers immediately

spot rate rate for transactions for immediate delivery. In the case of the wholesale foreign exchange market, the spot rate is for settlement in 2 days

spread long (bought) position in one maturity date, paired with a short (sold) position in another maturity date

standard deviation square root of the variance

stapled securities two or more legally separate instruments, typically an ordinary share plus units in one or more related trusts, which cannot be traded separately

static trade-off theory theory that proposes that companies have an optimal capital structure based on a trade-off between the benefits and costs of using debt

step-up preference share a preference share where the dividend rate is reset at a higher rate on a specified date unless the securities have been re-marketed, redeemed or converted

straight fixed-rate bond the standard form of a bond, paying a fixed coupon rate at regular intervals during the term of the bond and, on the maturity date of the bond, the face value of the bond

subordinated debt debt that ranks below other debt in the event that a company is wound up

subscription price the price that must be paid to obtain a new share

sunk cost cost that has already been incurred and is irrelevant to future decision making

syndicate a group of lenders (usually banks) that provides a borrower with funds; the lead manager has the main responsibility for negotiating the loan conditions, while other banks whose main role is to contribute loan funds are known as participating banks

syndicated loan loan arranged by one or more lead banks, funded by a syndicate that usually includes other banks

synergy in takeovers, the situation where the performance and therefore the value of a combined entity exceeds the sum of the previously separate components

systematic (market-related or non-diversifiable) risk that component of total risk that is due to economy-wide factors

takeover acquisition of control of one company by another

target company object of a takeover bid

tax loss selling investment strategy in which the tax rules make it attractive for an investor to sell certain shares just before the end of the tax year

term credit a loan repayable over a specific time period

term structure of interest rates relationship between interest rates and term to maturity for debt securities in the same risk class

terminal value of a contract the value, as at the date of the final cash flow promised in a financial contract, that is equivalent to the stream of promised cash flows

tests for private information research method that tests whether systematic profits can be generated by making investment decisions on the basis of private information

tests of return predictability research method designed to detect systematic patterns in asset prices

theoretical ex-rights share price the expected price of one share when shares begin to be traded ex-rights

theoretical rights price the expected price of one right calculated on the basis of the cum-rights share price

time value value of an option in excess of its intrinsic value

time value of money principle that a dollar is worth more (less), the sooner (later) it is to be received, all other things being equal

trade credit arrangement in which a seller of goods or services allows the purchaser a period of time before requiring payment; it is equivalent to a short-term loan made by the seller to the purchaser, of an amount equal to the purchase price

treasury management involves the management of financial assets and includes the management of short-term financial assets, long-term financing and risk management

treasury stock US term for a company's own shares that have been repurchased and held rather than cancelled

unbiased forward rate theory that states that the forward rate is an unbiased predictor of the future spot rate

uncovered interest parity (or international Fisher effect) theory that states that the difference in interest rates between two countries is an unbiased predictor of the future change in the spot exchange rate

underreaction biased response of a price to information in which the initial price movement can be expected to continue

unsubordinated debt debt that has not been subordinated

unsystematic (diversifiable) risk that component of total risk that is unique to the firm and may be eliminated by diversification

value at risk worst loss possible under normal market conditions for a given time horizon

variable interest rate loan loan where the lender can change the interest rate charged, usually in line with movements in the general level of interest rates in the economy

variance measure of variability; the mean of the squared deviations from the mean or expected value

vertical takeover takeover of a target company that is either a supplier of goods to, or a consumer of goods produced by, the acquiring company

volatility variability of a share price; can be measured by the variance (or the standard deviation) of the distribution of returns on the share

weighted average cost of capital (WACC) the cost of capital determined by the weighted average cost of all sources of finance

winner's curse problem that arises in bidding because the bidder who 'wins' is likely to be the one who most overestimates the value of the assets offered for sale

withholding tax the tax deducted by a company from the dividend payable to a non-resident shareholder

yield curve graph of yield to maturity against bond term at a given point in time

zero-coupon bonds bonds that pay only one cash flow, the payment at maturity

AUTHOR INDEX

Page numbers with the suffix n refer to a footnote; those with the suffix r refer to an entry in a list of references at the end of a chapter.

A

Abernethy, M. 242n, 243n, 280r
Aitken, M. 521n, 529, 530, 544r
Allen, D.E. 438, 440r, 521, 544r
Allen, F. 355, 356, 369n, 372r, 435n, 440r
Alles, L. 91, 96r
Alpert, K. 609, 634r
Altman, E. 424, 440r
Anderson, D. 524, 544r
Anderson, H. 354, 372r
Andrade, G. 407, 413r, 424, 440r, 641, 642, 668, 670, 671, 677r
Asay, M.R. 627, 634r
Asquith, P. 278, 280r
Avkiran, N.K. 674, 677r

B

Baker, H. 446n, 476r, 648, 654n, 679r
Balachandran, B. 261n, 264, 265, 280r, 354n, 355, 373r, 534n, 544r
Baldwin, J. 704, 730r
Ball, R. 277, 280r, 517, 517n, 522, 524, 544r, 546r
Banz, R.W. 525n, 544r
Barbajosa, Alejandro, 622
Barber, B. 450, 535, 540, 544r
Barberis, N. 537n, 539, 544r
Barclay, M. 425n, 426–7, 431, 434, 440r
Bartov, E. 362, 373r
Baskin, J.B. 323n, 329r
Basu, S. 524, 544r
Bates, T. 660, 661, 677r
Battalio, R.H. 534, 544r
Battellino, R. 313n, 329r, 721n, 730r
Batten, J. 539, 545r
Bautista, A. 496, 512r
Beedles, W. 526, 545r
Beggs, D.J. 353, 373r, 459, 476r
Bellamy, D. 351, 373r

Benartzi, S. 355, 373r
Bennett, J. 492n, 512r
Berk, J. 466n, 476r
Bernard, V. 534, 545r
Bernardo, A. 356, 372r
Bettman, J.L. 521, 545r
Bierman, H. Jr, 112n, 128r
Bilson, C. 84n, 96r
Bishop, S. 641, 642, 674, 677r
Black, F. 346, 370, 373r, 615, 627n, 634r
Black, S. 313n, 329r
Blanchard, O.J. 537, 545r
Bodie, Z. 84n, 96r, 201n, 203r
Boudry, W. 524, 545r
Bowers, J. 522, 544r
Bowman, R.G. 507, 512r, 542n, 545r
Bradley, M. 428, 440r, 668, 670, 677r
Brailsford, T. 84n, 95n, 96r, 144n, 160n, 190n, 194, 194r, 196, 203r, 204r, 457, 476r, 520, 521, 523n, 527, 545r, 548r
Brassil, A. 313n, 329r
Brau, J. 255n, 280r
Brav, A. 257, 280r, 339, 357, 373r
Brealey, R. 435n, 440r
Brennan, M.J. 631, 634r
Brenner, M. 634r
Brickley, J. 675, 678r
Brinson, G. 540, 545r
Brock, W. 521, 545r
Brooks, L.D. 542, 548r
Brooks, R. 253, 257, 280r, 568n, 584n, 590r
Brounen, D. 431, 440r
Brown, A. 299n, 329r
Brown, C. 144n, 160r, 367, 373r
Brown, P. 277, 280r, 351, 373r, 476r, 523, 524, 526, 528n, 529, 530, 532, 533, 534n, 536, 544r, 545r, 668, 672, 673, 677r

Brown, R.L. 13n, 29r, 72r, 271, 280r, 536, 545r, 609, 634r
Bruce, R. 233r, 329r, 512r, 677r, 780r
Buchanan, J. 542n, 545r
Burns, R.M. 121n, 128r
Burrow, M. 72r
Burrowes, G.H. 496n, 498n, 512r

C

Cahan, S. 354, 372r
Callen, T. 349
Camp, G. 256, 280r
Campbell, J.Y. 536, 545r
Cannavan, D. 352, 353, 373r, 459, 476
Carew, E. 233r, 329r, 555n, 590r
Carhart, M.M. 196, 203r
Casey, R. 661, 668, 677r, 678r
Chan, H.W. 271, 280r, 525, 527, 536, 545r
Chan, K. 368, 373r
Chan, L.K. 526, 545r
Chance, D.M. 568n, 584n, 590r
Chapple, L. 661, 678r
Cheng, S-Y. 704, 731r
Chew, D.H. 634r, 678r, 679r
Chiang, T.C. 703n, 730r
Chinn, M.D. 705n, 730r
Choi, C.Y. 704, 730r
Choi, D. 321, 321n, 329r
Chopra, N. 521, 538, 545r
Chow, D. 407, 414r, 423, 424, 441r
Christensen, B. 661, 678r
Clarke, A. 351, 373r, 476r
Clarkson, P. 661, 678r
Claus, J. 195, 203r
Clegg, Brett, 311
Cliff, M. 255, 280r
Clinton, K. 703n, 730r
Coleman, L. 109n, 128r, 196, 203r, 431, 440r
Collibee, P. 351n, 374r
Comer, A. 256, 280r

Comment, R. 362, 373r
Condoyanni, J. 522n, 545r
Conine, T. 463n, 476r
Connolly, E. 241n, 280r
Conrad, J. 520, 545r
Cooper, M. 525, 546r
Copeland, T.E. 504, 512r, 631r, 634r, 651n, 678r
Cornell, B. 552n, 590r
Correia Da Silva, L. 359–60, 373r
Courtadon, G. 634r
Cox, J.C 552n, 590r
Cox, J.C. 96r, 608n, 610, 634r
Crapp, H. 72r
Cummings, J.R. 587, 590r
Curtis, J. 660n, 678r

D

Da Silva Rosa, R. 253, 280r, 534n, 545r, 546r, 653n, 668, 669n, 672, 673, 675, 677r, 678r
Damodaran, A. 521, 546r
Daniel, K. 517, 546r
Das, S. 535, 546r
Davies, M. 299n, 329r
Davis, K. 144n, 160r, 324n, 329r
Davis, P. 215n, 233r
De Angelo, H. 335, 342, 343, 344, 354, 355, 357, 369n, 370, 373r, 398, 413r, 665n, 678r
De Angelo, L. 335, 342, 343, 344, 354, 355, 357, 369n, 370, 373r, 665n, 678r
de Jong, A. 431, 440r
Debelle, G 224n, 233r
DeBondt, W.F.M. 521, 538, 546r
Delong, J.B. 537n, 546r
DeMarzo, P. 466n, 476r
Demir, I. 521, 546r
Denhert, J. 542, 546r
Denis, D.J. 255, 280r, 358, 373r
Denis, D.K. 358, 373r

Desai, A. 668, 670, 677r
Desai, H. 278, 280r
Dharmawan, G.V. 367, 374r
Dill, D. 496, 512r
Dimowski, W. 253, 257, 280r
Dimson, E. 95n, 96r, 194, 203r, 522, 546r
Dittmar, A. 430n, 440r
Dixit, A.K. 126r, 128r, 631n, 634r
Dodd, P. 526, 545r, 641, 642, 643, 668, 668n, 674, 677r, 678r
Doherty, P. 525, 527
Dolan, P. 668, 677r
Donaldson, G. 407–8, 413r
Doukas, J.A. 517, 546r
Dufey, G. 709n, 730r

E

Easterbrook, F. 357, 373r
Easton, S.A. 373r, 523n, 533, 535, 536, 545r, 546r, 548r, 580n, 590r, 705, 730r
Eckbo, B. 257, 280r, 664, 664n, 678r
Eddey, P. 661, 666n, 678r
Eisfeldt, A. 506–7, 512r
Ellis, C. 539, 545r
Elton, E.J. 96r, 535, 546r

F

Fabbro, D. 299n, 329r
Faff, R.W. 144n, 160r, 190n, 194r, 203r, 261n, 264, 265, 280r, 354n, 355, 373r, 520, 524n, 525, 527, 534n, 535, 535n, 544r, 545r, 546r, 547r, 548r
Fama, E.F. 25n, 28n, 29r, 91, 96r, 188, 195, 196, 203r, 277, 280r, 364, 373r, 429, 433–4, 440r, 517, 519, 526, 527, 528r, 534, 539, 541, 546r
Fawcett, S. 255n, 280r
Fenn, G. 364, 373r
Feuerherdt, C. 352, 373r
Fight, A. 728n, 731r
Figlewski, S. 582n, 590r
Finn, F.J. 277, 280r, 352, 353, 373r, 459, 476r, 521, 524, 532, 533, 536, 544r, 545r, 546r, 642, 678r
Fisher, I. 13n, 29r
Fisher, L. 277, 280r
Fitzgerald, Barry, 340

Fitzpatrick, P. 297n, 329r
Flath, D. 509n, 512r
Flood, R.P. 537, 546r
Fowler, D. 91, 96r
Frank, M. 419, 429, 434, 440r
French, K.R. 195, 196, 203r, 364, 373r, 429, 433–4, 440r, 517, 521, 526, 527, 546r, 552n, 590r
Frino, A. 529, 530, 534n, 535n, 544r, 546r, 555n, 587, 590r
Froot, K.A. 705n, 731r
Fuller, R.J. 461, 476r

G

Gallagher, D.R. 535n, 546r
Gallinger, G.W. 756r, 780r, 783n
Garber, P.M. 537, 546r
Garden, K. 674, 679r
Gaughan, P.A. 641, 678r
Gaunt, C. 196, 204r, 526, 527, 547r, 548r
Gavazza, A. 505n, 512r
Geebower, G. 540, 545r
George, T.J. 521, 547r
Geske, R. 631, 634r
Giddy, I.H. 710n, 731r
Gilbert, M. 622
Gizycki, M.C. 703n, 731r
Glassman, D.M. 542n, 548r
Goergen, M. 359–60, 373r
Goetz, B. 749, 756r
Goetzmann, W.N. 194, 203r
Gompers, P. 257, 280r
Gong, N. 253, 280r
Goodhart, C. 703n, 731r
Goyal, V. 419, 429, 434, 440r
Graham, J.R. 109, 128r, 339, 357, 373r, 398, 413r, 422, 428, 431, 433, 440r, 506, 512r
Gray, P. 524, 525, 526, 545r, 547r
Gray, S. 352, 353, 373r, 459, 476r
Greenspan, A. 706
Gregory, A. 703n, 731r
Grenadier, S.R. 504, 512r
Grinblatt, M. 277n, 280r, 521, 548r
Gruber, M.J. 96r, 535, 546r
Gruen, D.W.R. 703n, 731r
Grullon, G. 355, 356, 358, 361, 362, 363, 364, 373r, 374r
Guay, W. 363, 374r
Gulen, H. 525, 546r
Gultekin, B. 523, 547r

Gultekin, M. 523, 547r
Gup, B.E. 211, 211n, 234r

H

Hack, M. 313n, 329r
Hall, J. 352, 373r
Hallahan, T. 535n, 547r
Halliwell, J. 527, 547r
Han, K.C. 278, 280r
Hancock, P. 532, 533, 545r
Handley, J. 95n, 96r, 194, 203r, 353, 374r, 457, 476r
Hanrick, T. 299n, 329r
Hardaker, R. 297n, 329r, 492n, 512r
Harford, J. 363, 374r
Harper, C. 220n, 234r
Harris, M. 414r, 420, 440r, 441r
Harris, R.S. 463, 476r
Harvey, C. 109, 128r, 339, 357, 373r, 428, 431, 440r
Hathaway, N. 351, 353n, 374–5, 459, 476r
Haugen, R.A. 524n, 547r
Healey, P.B. 780r, 783n
Healy, P.M. 278, 280r, 354n, 374r, 542n, 547r, 674, 675, 678r
Heaney, R.A. 84n, 91, 96r, 527, 547r, 586, 590r
Heaton, J. 194, 203r
Heidtman, D. 242n, 243n, 280r
Henderson, S. 494n, 512r
Herbert, A. 281r
Herbohn, K. 494n, 512r
Herzberg, A. 238n, 281r
Hill, N.C. 756r
Hilton, R.W. 754n, 756r
Hirshleifer, D. 539, 547r
Hirshleifer, J. 13n, 29r
Hite, G. 678r
Hlavka, M. 535, 546r
Ho, Y.K. 536, 545r
Hodgson, A. 642, 678r
Hou, H. 704, 731r
Hovakimian, A. 429–30, 440r
Hovakimian, G. 429–30, 440r
How, J. 252, 255, 256, 280r, 281r
Howard, L. 554, 590r
Howard, P. 373r
Hull, J. 595n, 614n, 634r
Hunt, B. 316n, 329r, 705, 705n, 731r
Hurn, S. 521, 547r

Hwang, C.Y. 521, 547r
Hyde, C.E. 674, 678r

I

Ibbotson, R.G. 194, 203r, 255n, 281r
Ikenberry, D. 278n, 281r, 362, 374r, 524, 542, 547r
Ingersoll, J.E. 96r, 552n, 590r, 629n, 634r
Izan, H.Y. 255, 281r, 521n, 544r, 653n, 669n, 678r

J

Jaffe, J. 522n, 547r
Jagannathan, M. 361, 363, 374r
Jain, P. 278, 280r
Jameson, K. 554, 590r
Jarnecic, E. 534n, 546r, 555n, 590r
Jarrell, G. 362, 373r, 428, 440r, 669, 675, 678r
Jegadeesh, N. 196, 203r, 521, 526, 545r, 547r
Jen, F.C. 321, 321n, 329r
Jensen, M. 201, 203r, 277, 280r, 358, 374r, 406, 412, 413r, 426, 427, 428, 440r, 541n, 547r, 643, 646, 673, 678r
John, K. 344, 374r
Johnson, J. 547r
Johnson, R. 498n, 512r
Jorion, P. 194, 203r

K

Kalay, A. 344, 374r
Kalev, P. 254, 281r
Kallberg, J.G. 756r
Kane, A. 84n, 96r, 201n, 203r
Kaplan, S. 407, 413r, 424, 440r, 666n, 669n, 678r
Kaul, G. 520, 545r
Keane, S.M. 541n, 547r
Keenan, P.T. 631n, 634r
Keim, D. 523, 524n, 525n, 526, 536, 545r, 547r
Kelly, J. 667
Kennedy, D. 422–3, 441r
Kerin, P. 536n, 546r
Kerr, H.S. 461, 476r
Keynes, J.M. 761n, 780r
Kim, E. 428, 440r, 668, 670, 677r
Kinney, W. 522, 548r
Kirkpatrick, C.A. 153n, 160r

Kiymaz, H. 446n, 476r, 648, 654n, 679r
Kleidon, A. 523, 526, 545r
Knox, D.M. 72r
Koedijk, K. 431, 440r
Kofman, P. 525, 527
Koh, P.S. 525, 547r
Kolb, R.W. 559n, 590r
Koller, T. 651n, 678r
Kon, S. 582n, 590r
Kosowski, R. 535, 547r
Kothari, S.P. 526, 547r
Kraus, A. 406n, 413r
Kua, A. 521n, 544r

L

La Porta, R. 358, 360, 374r, 528, 538, 547r
Lakonishok, J. 277n, 281n, 362, 374r, 521, 521n, 524, 524n, 526, 528, 538, 542, 545r, 547r
Lalor, P.A. 705, 730r
Lang, L. 358, 374r, 673, 673n, 679r
Langfield-Smith, K. 754n, 756r
Lanis, R. 423, 441r
Layton, A.P. 586, 590r
Le Baron, B. 521, 545r
Lease, R. 344, 374r, 498n, 512r
Lee, C.M.C. 521, 547r
Lee, K. 666n, 678r
Lee, P. 253, 254, 255, 257, 281r
Lee, S. 321, 321n, 329r
Leeson, N. 584n, 590r
Lehavy, R. 535, 544r
Lehn, K. 670n, 673, 679r
Lemmon, M.L. 506, 512r, 660, 661, 677r
Lepone, A. 534n, 546r
Lerner, J. 257, 280r
Leslie, K.J. 631n, 634r
Lev, B. 507n, 512r
Levi, M. 521n, 547r
Levin, R.I. 153n, 160r
Levy, H. 190n, 203r
Levy, R. 655n, 679r
Lewellen, W. 503, 512r
Lewis, M.K. 234r
Liang, N. 364, 373r
Lie, E. 358, 374r
Lieu, D. 627, 634r
Lintner, J. 188, 203r, 339, 363, 374r
Lipton, P. 238n, 281r

Litzenberger, R. 358, 374r, 406n, 413r
Lo, A.W. 520, 521, 539, 547r, 548r
Loewenstein, U. 344, 374r
Long, M. 503, 512r, 679r
Longstaff, F.A. 91, 96r
Lopez-De-Silanes, E. 358, 360, 374r
Lothian, J. 704, 731r
Loudon, G.F. 608, 634r
Loughran, T. 253n, 255, 256, 257, 281r, 524, 548r, 672, 679r
Lucas, D. 194, 203r
Lundholm, R. 780r
Lynch, A. 521, 524, 544r, 546r
Lyons, R.K. 692n, 731r

M

Macaulay, F. 96r, 99–100
MacKay, P. 420, 440r
Mackie-Mason, J. 421, 422, 433, 440r
MacKinlay, A.C. 520, 547r
Maher, T.R.B. 521, 545r
Maheswaran, K. 95n, 96r, 109n, 128r, 194, 196, 203r, 353, 374r, 431, 440r, 457, 476r, 663, 679r
Majluf, N. 345n, 374r, 414r
Malkiel, B.G. 539, 541n, 548r
Mamaysky, H. 521, 539, 548r
Manuel, T.A. 542, 548r
Manzur, M. 703n, 705n, 731r
Marcus, A.J. 84n, 96r, 201n, 203r
Markovic, M. 552n, 590r
Markowitz, H.M. 176, 176n, 203r
Marsh, P. 95n, 96r, 194, 203r, 261n, 281r
Marsh, T. 374r, 523, 526, 545r
Marshall, J. 72r
Martin K. 649n, 679r
Martin, P. 72r
Masulis, R. 257, 277n, 280r, 398, 413r
Mathiou, N. 524, 544r
Mayanya, J. 679r
McColough, D. 368, 373r
McConnell, J. 498n, 503, 512r, 649n, 679r
McCracken, S. 568n, 584n, 590r
McCulloch, J. 91, 96r
McCurdy, T. 703n, 731r
McDonald, R.J. 351, 374r
McDougall, F. 674, 679r
McFarland, J. 703n, 731r

McIvor, J. 526, 547r
McKern, B. 233r, 329r, 512r, 677r, 780r
McMahon, P. 703n, 731r
McNichols, M. 535, 544r
Meckling, W. 413r
Mehra, R. 194, 204r
Mehran, H. 508, 512r
Mehrotra, V. 430, 440r
Mendenhall, R. 534, 544r
Merrick, J.J. 634r
Merton, R.C. 374r, 602, 605, 634r
Mian, S.L. 780r
Michaels, M.P. 631n, 634r
Michaely, R. 339, 355, 356, 357, 358, 361, 362, 363, 364, 369n, 372r, 373r, 374r
Mikkelson, W. 430, 440r
Miller, M. 25n, 29r, 340, 341–4, 354, 374r, 383–93, 397–8, 407, 414r, 435, 437, 507, 508, 512r
Miranti, P.J. 323n, 329r
Mitchell, J.D. 367, 374r
Mitchell, M. 641, 642, 668, 670, 670n, 671, 673, 677r, 679r
Modigliani, F. 340, 341–4, 354, 374r, 383–93, 414r, 435
Monkhouse, P.H.L. 451n, 466n, 476r
Monroe, G. 255, 281r
Montague, B. 316n, 329r, 716n, 731r
Moore, S. 521, 546r
Morck, R. 663, 673, 679r
Morling, S. 349
Moskowitz, T.J. 521, 548r
Mossin, J. 188, 204r
Mukherjee, T.K. 446n, 476r, 648, 654n, 679r
Murrin, J. 651n, 678r
Muscarella, C. 278n, 281r
Muthuswamy, J. 521, 546r
Myers, S. 345n, 374r, 393n, 404, 414r, 420, 427, 429, 433, 435n, 440r, 441r, 466n, 476r, 496, 512r

N

Nagama, Y. 703n, 731r
Netter, J. 675, 678r
Ng, C.K. 780r
Nguyen, H.H. 512r
Nohel, T. 363, 374r
Norli, O. 257, 280r
Norman, D. 367, 373r

O

O'Brien, K.P. 212n, 234r
O'Brien, M. 196, 204r, 527, 548r
O'Brien, T.J. 463, 476r
Odean, T. 540, 544r
Ofek, E. 608, 634r
Officer, L.H. 700n, 731r
Officer, M. 660, 661, 679r
Officer, R. 351, 353n, 374–5r, 446, 459, 476r, 484n, 524, 526, 544r, 545r, 641, 642, 643, 674, 677r, 678r
O'Hanlon, J. 522n, 545r
Ohlson, J. 507n, 512r
Oliver, B. 194r, 203r
Ong, F. 535n, 548r
Opler, T. 424, 441r
Otchere, I. 367, 374r, 542, 548r
Overdahl, J.A. 559n, 590r
Owers, J. 678r

P

Palepu, K. 278, 280r, 354n, 374r, 542, 547r, 674, 675, 678r
Parkinson, K.L. 756r
Partch, M. 430, 440r
Partington, G. 352, 375r, 459, 476r
Pathak, N. 655n, 679r
Pattenden, K. 350, 374r, 423, 441r
Pavlov, V. 521, 547r
Peacock, D. 215n, 233r
Peirson, G. 494n, 512r
Penman, S.H. 654, 679r, 780r
Petersen, R. 756r
Pham, P. 254, 281r
Pham, T. 407, 414r, 423, 424, 441r
Phang, G. 609, 634r
Phillips, G.M. 420, 440r
Pike, R.J. 157, 160r
Pilotte, E. 428, 441r
Pincus, M. 525, 548r
Pinder, S.M. 109n, 128r, 196, 203r, 431, 440r, 580n, 590r, 660n, 663, 678r, 679r
Pindyck, R.S. 126n, 128r, 631n, 634r
Pleban, J. 349
Pollard, I. 233r, 329r, 512r, 677r, 780r
Pontiff, J. 524, 548r
Poulsen, A. 669, 678r
Prescott, E.C. 194, 204r
Prince, R. 521, 544r
Pyke, D.F. 756r

R

Rajan, R. 420, 427, 428, 441r
Rajgopal, S. 525, 548r
Ralston, D. 674, 679r
Ramchand, L. 714, 731r
Rampini, A. 506–7, 512r
Rankine, G. 278n, 281r
Raviv, A. 420, 440r
Reinganum, M.R. 524, 525n, 526r, 548n, 552n, 590r
Renneboog, L. 359–60, 373r
Renton, N. 361, 374r
Rice, E.M. 665n, 678r
Richardson, G. 423, 441r
Richardson, M. 91, 96r, 608, 634r
Richardson, P. 91, 96r
Ritter, J.R. 194, 204r, 253, 253n, 254, 255, 255n, 256, 257, 281r, 521, 524, 538, 545r, 548r
Robinson, E.S. 91, 96r
Robinson, P. 367, 374r
Rock, K. 254, 281r
Rogoff, K. 704n, 731r
Roll, R. 195, 204r, 277, 280r, 541, 669, 673, 679r
Rose, L. 354, 372r
Rosenkranz, S. 660, 661, 679r
Ross, M. 367, 374r, 542, 548r
Ross, S.A. 96r, 517, 546r, 552r, 590r, 608, 610, 634r
Round, D. 674, 679r
Rozeff, M. 522, 548r
Ruback, R. 674, 675, 678r
Rubin, D.S. 153n, 160r
Rubinstein, M. 522, 539, 548r, 608n, 610, 634r

S

Sarig, O. 344, 374r
Sarin, A. 358, 373r
Sarnat, M. 190n, 203r
Sartoris, W.L. 756r
Sault, S.J. 521, 545r
Sawicki, J. 527, 535n, 547r, 548r
Scarman, I. 505, 512r
Schadler, F.P. 542, 548r
Schallheim, J.S. 498n, 506, 512r
Scherr, F.C. 756r
Schill, M.J. 525, 546r
Schipper, K. 669n, 679r
Scholes, M. 615, 634r
Schulman, C. 422–3, 441r
Schwartz, C. 222n, 234r
Schwartz, E.S. 631, 634r
Schwert, G. 663, 679r
Scott, J. 406n, 414r
Sellers, K. 422–3, 441
Servaes, H. 673n, 679r
Seyhun, H. 535, 548r
Shanken, J. 517, 526, 546r, 547r
Shapiro, A.C. 435, 441r
Sharpe, S.A. 512r
Sharpe, W.F. 188, 197–8, 204r
Sheedy, E. 568n, 584n, 590r
Shekhar, C. 253, 280r
Shelifer, A. 546r
Shiller, R.J. 536, 539, 541, 545r, 548r
Shleifer, A. 358, 360, 374r, 528, 537, 537n, 538, 539, 547r, 548r, 663, 673, 679r
Shyam-Sunder, L. 427, 429, 441r
Silver, E.A. 756r
Simmonds, D.P. 674, 679r
Sinclair, N. 533, 546r
Sindelar, J. 255n, 281r
Singer, B. 540, 545r
Skeels, C. 353, 373r, 459, 476r
Skinner, D. 344, 355, 356, 365, 373r, 374r
Skully, M. 233r, 329r, 368, 373r, 512r, 677r, 780r
Sloan, R. 780r
Sloan, R.G. 277n, 281r, 524, 526, 547r, 548r
Smidt, S. 112n, 128r, 521, 547r
Smith, C.W. Jr 257, 261n, 281r, 404, 405n, 414r, 425n, 426–7, 428, 431, 434, 440r, 441r, 508, 509, 512r, 541n, 547r, 629n, 634r, 716, 716n, 731r, 780r
Smith, J.K. 241n, 281r, 780r
Smith, K.V. 756r
Smith, R.L. 241n, 281r, 780r
Smith, T. 91, 96r
Smithson, C.W. 319n, 329r, 716, 716n, 731r
Soltes, E. 356, 374r
Srinivasulu, S.L. 709n, 730r
Stafford, E. 641, 642, 668, 670, 671, 677r
Stambaugh, R.F. 536, 547r
Stanton, P. 679r
Starks, L. 358, 375r
Statman, M. 184, 204r
Staunton, M. 95n, 96r, 194, 203r
Steen, A. 254, 281r
Steinbeck, A. 653n, 669n, 678r
Stephens, C. 361, 363, 374r
Stern, J.M. 634r, 678r, 679r
Steward, G.B. 542n, 548r
Stice, E. 278n, 281r
Stoll, H.R. 605, 634r
Stradwick, R. 274n, 281r
Strebulaev, I. 429n, 441r
Stulz, R. 370, 373r, 414r, 441r, 673, 673n, 679r
Subrahmanyan, M. 634r
Summers, L. 537n, 546r
Sun, Y. 715, 731r
Susmel, R. 714, 731r
Sutton, W. 712n, 731r
Swaminathan, B. 355, 356, 358, 374r, 521, 547r
Sweeney, M. 715, 731r
Szekely, K.L. 494n, 513r

T

Taggart, R.A. 462n, 463n, 476r, 508, 512r
Tamarkin, M. 463n, 476r
Tan, A. 241n, 280r
Tapon, F. 715, 731r
Tarhan, V. 363, 374r
Taylor, M. 704r, 731r
Taylor, S. 253, 254, 255, 257, 281r, 666n, 678r
Tease, W.J. 91, 96r
Tehranian, H. 429–30, 440r
Terry, C. 316n, 329r
Thaler, R.H. 355, 373r, 374r, 521, 537r, 538, 539, 544r, 546r, 705n, 731r
Theobald, M. 261n, 264, 265, 280r, 534r, 544r
Thomas, D. 422–3, 441r
Thomas, J. 195, 203r, 534, 545r
Thompson, R. 669n, 679r
Thorburn, K. 664, 664n, 678r
Thorne, H. 754n, 756r
Thornton, D.L. 703n, 731r
Timmermenn, A. 535, 547r
Titman, S. 196, 203r, 277n, 280r, 403, 414r, 424, 428, 441r, 521, 546r, 547r
Tong, Y.H. 525, 547r
Torres, C. 220n, 234r
Traynor, J.L. 199–200, 204r
Trigeorgis, L. 631n, 635r
Trueman, B. 535, 544r
Turnbull, S. 476r
Twite, G. 350, 374r

U

Upton, C. 507, 508, 512r
Uylangco, K. 535, 548r

V

Vardigans, P. 489, 513r
Velayuthen, G. 253, 280Pr, 281r
Venkatachalam, M. 525, 548r
Vermaelen, T. 277n, 281r, 362, 374r, 524, 542, 547r
Vetsuypens, M. 278n, 281r
Vijh, A. 672, 679r
Viney, C. 234r, 281r, 319, 330r
Vishny, R.W. 358, 360, 374r, 528, 537n, 538, 547r, 548r, 663, 673, 679r

W

Wakeman, D. 463, 476r
Wakeman, L.M. 508, 509, 512r, 731r
Wald, J. 420, 428, 441r
Waldmann, R. 537n, 546r
Walker, E.D. 128r
Walker, J. 121n, 128r
Walker, S. 352, 375r, 459, 476r
Walkling, R. 673, 673n, 679r
Wallace, R.H. 234r
Walter, T. 253, 254, 255, 257, 280r, 281r, 521, 521n, 529, 530, 534n, 536, 544r, 545r, 546r, 653n, 669n, 675, 678r
Wang, J. 521, 539, 548r
Ward, C.W.R. 522n, 545r
Warner, J. 404, 405n, 407, 407n, 414r, 423, 441r
Wasilev, J. 607n
Watson, I. 535, 548r
Watts, R. 355, 375r, 425n, 426–7, 434, 440r
Weisbach, M. 361, 363, 374r, 669n, 678r

Weiss, L. 407, 414r, 423, 441r
Weitzel, U. 660, 661, 679r
Welch, I. 253, 253n, 254, 255n, 281r, 281rt, 356, 372r
Welsh, M. 238n, 281r
Wermers, R. 535, 547r
Wessels, R. 424, 428, 441r
Westerfield, R. 522n, 547r
Weston, J. 504, 512r
Whaley, R. 621, 635r
White, H. 535, 547r
Whitelaw, R.F. 608, 634r
Whiteley, E. 584n, 590r
Wilford, D.S. 716n
Womack, K.L. 355, 374r, 535, 548r
Woodgate, A. 524, 548r
Worrall, M. 492n, 512r
Wright, A. 674, 679r
Wright, S. 419, 441r
Wu, J.-L. 704, 731r

Y

Yan, B. 704, 730r
Yang, L. 715, 731r
Yeo, J. 252, 281r
Yermack, D. 508, 512r
Yescombe, E.R. 314n, 330r
Yoon, P. 358, 375r
Young, A. 535, 548r
Young, J. 91, 96r

Z

Zhang, L. 196, 204r, 528, 548r
Zijl, T. 534n, 544r
Zima, P. 72r
Zingales, L. 420, 427, 428, 441r

SUBJECT INDEX

The letter n following a page number indicates a reference in a footnote.

10-year Treasury bond futures 576–9
   contract features 577–8
   uses 578–9
30-day interbank cash rate futures 579–80
90-day bank bills 569–76
   contract features 570–6
   uses 571–6

A

AASB 117 Leases 494, 507
ABCP *see* asset-backed commercial paper
abnormal returns 519
   following takeovers 672
ACCC *see* Australian Competition and Consumer Commission
accelerated non-renounceable entitlement offers 266
accelerated renounceable entitlement offers (AREOs) 266
acceptors 306
accounting rate of return
   defined 121
   project evaluation 122–3
accounts receivable 739, 740, 767–9
   defined 768
accumulation 38
   cash flows 51
   defined 38
acquisitions
   by friendly parties 662
   see also takeovers
activity ratios 786–7
adjusted present value (APV) 466
AFMA *see* Australian Financial Markets Association
agency costs
   conflicts of interest
   lenders and shareholders 404–5

   shareholders and managers 405–6
   effect of leasing 508
   related to
      capital structure management 404–7, 425–7
      corporate governance 357–61
      share buybacks 363
      Telstra 360–1
agency relationships 9
   takeovers 9, 646–7, 673
Airline Partners Australia (APA)
   financing of bid for Qantas 310, 311
allocated costs
   estimation of cash flows 134
American options 595
   call options 609
   put options 603
annuities 55–63
   defined 55
   future value 62–3
   present value 56–9
   types 55–6
   see also general annuities; simple annuities
annuities due 55
   future value 62, 63
   present value 58–9
APA *see* Airline Partners Australia
APRA *see* Australian Prudential Regulation Authority
APV *see* adjusted present value
arbitrage 8–9
   bank bill futures 575–6
   defined 8
   and Proposition 1 (MM) 388
   see also covered interest arbitrage
AREOs *see* accelerated renounceable entitlement offers
Arnott's Australia 662

ASF *see* Australian Securitisation Forum
ASIC *see* Australian Securities and Investments Commission
asset allocation
   effect on portfolio performance 196–7
asset-backed commercial paper (ABCP) 224
asset-backed securities 311–12
asset growth 525
asset strippers 645
asset substitution 404
assets
   characteristics
      and financing strategy 436–7
      risk 175–6
      valuation 79–80
   see also financial assets
ASX *see* Australian Securities Exchange
at call 294
Australia
   banks 221–3
      government guarantee 222
      supervision 222
   capital markets 211–12, 215
      automation of trading 216
   financial leverage 381
   foreign currencies borrowing 718–28
   investment banks 218–20
   securitisation 224–5, 226–7
   share buybacks 365–7
   Treasury
      currency swaps crash 720
Australian Competition and Consumer Commission (ACCC), *Merger Guidelines* 645
Australian Financial Markets Association (AFMA) 218, 219
Australian Prudential Regulation Authority (APRA) 211, 218

   supervision of banks 222
Australian Securities Exchange (ASX) 215, 555–6
   automation of trading 216
   financial futures 569–83
      10-year Treasury bond futures 576–9, 579–83
      30-day interbank cash rate futures 579–80
      share price index futures 581–3
   Listing Rules 247
      employee share plans 275
      on-market buybacks 367
      preference shares 322
   options on futures contracts 626
   value of share listings 237
Australian Securities and Investments Commission (ASIC) 218
   action against Citigroup 219–20
   takeovers 655
Australian Securitisation Forum (ASF) 224
average collection period 787
   short-term asset management 791
average inventory turnover period 786
   short-term asset management 791

B

Babcock & Brown (B&B) 220
bad debts 769
bank bills 307, 569–70
   futures contracts 570–6
   valuation 585–6
   see also 90-day bank bills
bank overdrafts 294–7
Banking Act 1959, 211, 218
Banking Legislation Amendment Act 1989 211

bankruptcy costs 402–3
banks
　Australia 221–3
　　government guarantee of deposits 222
　　supervision 222
　supervision 211–12
Banks (Shareholdings) Act 1972 211
Barings Bank 584
Basel Committee on Banking Supervision 211–12
basis, defined 562
basis risk 562–4
Bear Stearns 220
bearer bonds 726
beating the market 541
behavioural finance 537–9
benchmark indexes 197
benefit–cost ratio
　defined 120
　project evaluation 120–1
beta (β)
　calculation 184–5
　defined 184
　individual securities 193
　measurement of project risk 446
　portfolios 191
biased price reaction 518–19
bill acceptance facilities 308
bill discount facilities 308
bill facilities 307–9
bills of exchange 305–9
　acceptors 306
　bank accepted bills 307
　bill facilities 307–9
　defined 305
　drawers 306
　endorsement 306
　rediscounting 306
　trade credit 768
binomial option pricing 610–15
　basic idea 610–11
　　many time periods 612–14
　　lattice of share prices 612–13
　　option payoffs at expiry 613–14
　　risk neutral assumption 611–12
Black-Scholes model
　call option pricing 615–21
　　assessment 620–1
　　assumptions 615–16
　　equation 616–20

bonds
　coupons 99
　defined 85, 313
　duration 99–105
　　and immunisation 103–5
　　and interest elasticity 101–2
　　and price changes 102–3
　see also debt securities
bonus share issues 277–8
bonus share options, with rights issues 264
book-building 249, 252, 254
　placements 268
book-to-market ratio 526–7
bootstrapping 648
borrowing
　Fisher's Separation Theorem 15–16
　long-term 298–302
　short-term 294–7
　see also debt; financing
break-even analysis 150–1
break fees 660–1
bridging finance 297
brokers see stockbrokers
bubbles 537–8
business angels 242–3
business funding 212–14
business risk 379–80
　defined 380
　and financing strategy 436
business structures 4–6
buy-and-hold policies 540–1
buyouts 663–4, 665–7

C
Cabcharge, capital structure 380, 381
call options 595
　exercise price 601
　on futures contracts 556
　issue by companies 596
　minimum value 608–10
　payoff structure 597–9
　price determinants 600–3
　pricing
　　binomial model 610–15
　　Black-Scholes model 615–21
　term to expiry 601
　time value 601
calls 238
Campbell Committee 211

Campbell Soup Company 662
capital, cost see cost of capital
Capital Accord 211
capital asset pricing model (CAPM) 8
　estimation of cost of capital 448–9, 457
　implementation 192–5
　and risk and return 195
　and security market line 190–2
capital expenditure
　budgets 108
　process 107–9
　see also project evaluation
capital gains tax 659–60
　and imputation tax system 348–9
capital market line 188–90
capital markets 209–33
　Australia 211–12, 215
　　automation of trading 216
　and company decision-making 14–15, 19–22
　defined 209
　efficiency 517–44
　　categories 519
　efficient market hypothesis 517–20
　overseas 232–3
　types 210
　value of leasing 499–501
capital rationing 157–8
capital structure 379–412, 419–39
　and agency costs 404–6
　Cabcharge 380, 381
　and costs of financial distress 401–3
　defined 379
　effect of
　　classical tax system 393–8
　　imputation tax system 393, 399–401
　　taxes (Miller's analysis) 397–8
　information asymmetry 407–12
　　and overvaluation of assets 411
　　and undervaluation of assets 408–11
　maturity and priority of debt 430–1
　Modigliani and Miller analysis 383, 384–93

research evidence 421–32
　agency costs 425–7
　financial distress 423–5
　from surveys 431–2
　information costs 427–9
　taxes 421–3
　theory assessment 432–4
CAPM see capital asset pricing model
carrying costs 557
　inventories 743
cash budgeting 762–5
　forecasting cash payments 763–5
　forecasting cash receipts 763
cash budgets 762
cash and carry 576
cash flows 33, 449–50
　defined 33
　estimation in project evaluation 133–6
　smoothing the pattern 767
　timing 134–5
　see also multiple cash flows
cash management trusts 767
cash payments
　forecasting 763–5
cash rate 289–90
CBLs see cross-border leases
certainty (condition) 27
　and asset valuation 79–80
　and inventory management 744–50
　and valuation of shares 80–1
certainty equivalents, and risk 471–4
charting 539
chattel mortgages 510–11
　defined 510
　goods and services tax 510
Chinese walls 219
Citigroup 219–20
claim dilution 404
classical tax systems 345–6
　and capital structures, n 421–2
　defined 346
　effect on capital structure 393–8
co-insurance effect 646
collection costs 769, 777
collection policies 774–5
　evaluation 775–9
combination issues 272–3

commercial paper 303–5
  defined 303
Committee of Inquiry into the Australian Financial System 211
companies
  business structures 5–6
  defined 5
  financial objective 6
company cost of capital 449, 457–9
  compared with project cost 460–4
company financing 419–20
company size
  related to future earnings 525–6
company tax 6
  effect on capital structure 393–5
  with personal tax 395–7
  and leasing 505–6
Competition and Consumer Act 2010 645, 659
compound interest 37–50
  defined 38
  formula development 38–40
  real interest rates 44–6
compound options 631
confidential debtor finance 295
conglomerate takeovers 643
ConnectEast, debt facilities 316
consistency principle 445
constant chain of replacement assumption 138, 142–4
  compared with equivalent annual value 140–2
  and inflation 144
  practicality 144–5
constant payout policy 339
constrained open pricing 249
consumer credit 768
contingent claims 629–32
  convertible bonds 629
  defined 595, 629
  rights issues 629
  valuation of levered shares 630–1
    with risky coupon-paying debt 630
    with risky zero-coupon debt 630
  see also options
contingent hedging 711–12

continuity-of-ownership test 647
continuous interest rates 46–8
contributing shares 238, 269
conversion ratio 324
convertible bonds 321, 629
  international debt securities 726
convertible notes 320–2
  advantages 321–2
convertible preference shares 322
converting preference shares 322, 324–5
corporate bonds 310–14
corporate finance 3
corporate raiders 645
corporate restructuring 663–7
  types of transactions 663–4
Corporations Act 2001
  creeping takeovers 658
  definition of rights issue 265n
  disclosure requirements
    directors' interests 534–5
    share offers 244
    takeovers 657–8
  dividends 336
  partial takeovers 658
  preference shares 322
  public and proprietary companies 5
  schemes of arrangement 659
  share buybacks 337, 361
  takeovers 655
    creeping takeovers 658
    disclosure requirements 657–8
    market bids 657
    off-market bids 656
    partial takeovers 658
cost of capital 445–66
  defined 446
  for divisions 461–4
    direct estimation approach 463–4
    pure play approach 461–3
  effect of alternative tax systems 484–6
  effect of leasing 507–8
  estimation 448–51
    capital asset pricing model 448–9
    example 451–60
  project cost compared with company cost 460–4

  related to risk 445–6
  taxation issues 446–8
cost reductions
  motive for takeovers 645
coupon payments 303
coupon rate 290
coupons 99
covariance, portfolio theory 176–7
covenants 289, 292
covered interest arbitrage 694, 695–7
covered interest parity 693
credit foncier loans 299
credit limits 773
credit periods 773
credit policies 769–74
  benefits of granting credit 768–9
  costs of granting credit 768–9
  debt collection 774–5
  defined 770
  evaluation 775–9
  selection of credit-worthy customers 770
  terms of credit 773–4
credit risk 716–17
  short-term investments 766
creeping takeovers 658
cross-border leases (CBLs) 493–4
cross rates 690–1
cum dividend period 336
cum rights 259–61
cumulative preference shares 322
currency options *see* foreign currencies, options
currency swaps 715–18
  categories 716
  defined 716
current assets 741
current liabilities 741
current ratios 785–6
  short-term asset management 790

D

daily return patterns 521–2
day trading 560
DCF *see* discounted cash flow
debentures 309–10
  defined 85
  see also debt securities
debt 287–328

characteristics 288–94
collection policies 774–5
cost 452–5
  long-term debt 454–5
  defined 34
  effect on
    control 291
    risk 291
  interest cost 289–90
  long-term borrowing 298–302
  project finance 314–16
  related to
    overinvestment 425–6
    underinvestment 425
  security for 291–4
  short-term borrowing 294–7
  types of securities 302–14
  see also hybrid securities
debt markets 210
debt securities 287, 302–14
  general principles 303
  valuation 84–6
debt to total assets ratio 787–8
debtor finance 295–7
  with recourse 296
  without recourse 296
  defined 297
debtors *see* accounts receivable
debts *see* debt
decision-tree analysis 153–6
  selection of credit-worthy customers 770–2
default risk 213
  defined 390
  and Proposition 2 (MM) 390–1
  short-term investments 766
  structure of interest rates 86, 92–4
defaults 288
deferred annuities 55–6
  defined 55
  future value 62
  present value 59–61
deficit units 209
delinquent accounts 769
delta 611
deposit-taking institutions 214
deposits, futures trading 554–5
depreciation 467–9
derivative securities 8
DESs *see* dividend election schemes

Subject index   837

direct estimation approach 463–4
direct funding 209
disclosure documents 244–6
   defined 245
   unlisted securities 245–6
disclosure requirements 244–7
   listed securities 246
   not required 246–7
   unlisted securities 245–6
   vanilla bonds 313
discount periods 773
discount rates 773
discounted cash flow (DCF)
   project evaluation 109, 110
      choice of method 115–20
      methods compared 111–21
discounters 295, 304
discounting
   cash flows 51
   compound interest 40
   defined 40
disintermediation 287
diversifiable risk *see* unsystematic risk
diversification 176–9
   benefits 179–81
   and foreign currency borrowing 721
   international investments 712–15
   multiple assets 181–3
   reason for takeovers 646
divestitures 663, 664
dividend clienteles 344
dividend drop-off ratio 351–2
dividend election schemes (DESs) 368–9
dividend growth model 456–7
   defined 456
   and valuation of shares 82–4
dividend irrelevance theorem 341–4
dividend-payout ratio 339
dividend policy *see* payout policy
dividend reinvestment plans (DRPs) 276, 368
dividend substitution 364–5
dividend yield, and future earnings 524
dividends 3, 80
   behavioural factors 345
   declaration procedures 336
   expected levels

      and price of call options 602–3
   Fisher's Separation Theorem 25
   information effects 354–7
   legal considerations 336–7
   related to
      company value 355
      corporate governance regimes 359–60
      earnings quality 356
      legal protection for investors 358–9
      profits 355–6
   signals to investors 354–7
   tax considerations 336–7, 345–54
   types 336
   see also payout policy
dollar return 169
drawees 306
drawers 306
DRPs *see* dividend reinvestment plans
duration *see* bonds, duration

E

earnings before interest and tax (EBIT) 379
   and tax effects under imputation 400
earnings per share (EPS), and share buybacks 362
EBIT *see* earnings before interest and tax
economic order quantity (EOQ) 744
economic order quantity (EOQ) model 744–50
   cost estimation 747–8
   with positive lead time 748
   with quantity discounts 749–50
economic value added (EVA) 125–6
ECP *see* Euro commercial paper
effective interest rates
   compared with nominal rates 41–4
   defined 41
efficient capital markets 8
   event studies 519, 528–34
   joint test problem 519–20
   at the macro level 536
   tests of private information 519

   tests of return predictability 519, 520–8
   relationship of past returns to future returns 520–1
efficient frontier 186–7
efficient market hypothesis (EMH) 517–20
   biased price reaction 518–19
   categories of capital market efficiency 519
   defined 517
   implications of the evidence, for 539–43
      financial managers 541–3
      investors in securities 539–41
   non-instantaneous price reaction 518
   related to behavioural finance 537–9
EMH *see* efficient market hypothesis
employee share plans 270, 274–5, 596
   share buybacks 337, 363–4
employee share trusts 274
endorsement 306
entitlement offers 258
   accelerated 265–6
   Suncorp-Metway 267
EOQ *see* economic order quantity
EPS *see* earnings per share
equal access buybacks 337
equipment leases *see* leases
equity 237–79
   floating a public company 247–58
   information disclosure 244–7
   ordinary shares 238–40
   private equity 240–4
   raising methods 240–71
      combination issues 272–3
      selection 271–3
   rights issues 259–66
   as source of finance 239–40
equity-related debt securities 726
equivalent annual value (EAV) method 140–2
   defined 140
Essential Petroleum Resources Ltd rights issue and public offer 273
Euro commercial paper (ECP) 724–5

Eurobonds 314
   defined 722
Eurocredits 723–4
   defined 722
Euronotes 724
European options 595
   put options 609–10
   related to forward prices 625–6
EVA *see* economic value added
event studies 519, 528–34
   defined 519
   methodology 528–32
   research evidence of profit and dividend announcements 532–4
ex-dividend date 336
ex-rights date 259–61
exchange rates *see* foreign exchange rates
exchange risk 706–12
   defined 707
exchange-traded markets 210
exchangeable preference shares 322
exercise price 595, 601
expansion financing 241
expectation theory 88–90
expected returns, three factor model 196
external capital rationing 157

F

face value 303–4
factors 295
factors *see* discounters
finance
   area of study 3
   fundamental concepts 6–9
   sources *see* capital markets; debt; equity
finance companies 223–4
finance leases 491
   establishing an advantage for the lessor 501–2
   evaluation 496–503
   and imputation tax systems 503
   leasing decisions relative to investment decisions 498–9
   taxation 502–3
   value in competitive capital markets 499–501
financial agency institutions 212, 213, 214–20

financial assets 209
  see also shares
financial contracts 33
financial decision-making
  Fisher's Separation Theorem
    25–7
financial decisions 3–4
  implications of financial
    asymmetry 411–12
financial derivatives see derivative
  securities
financial distress 291
  costs
    and capital structure
      decisions 423–5
    and company value 401–3
  defined 402
  indirect costs 403
financial futures 551
  Australian Securities Exchange
    569–83
    10-year Treasury bond futures
      576–9
    30-day interbank cash rate
      futures 579–80
    90-day bank bills 569–76
    share price index futures 581–3
  contract valuation 585–7
financial intermediaries 209,
  212–13, 221–7
  banks 221–3
  finance companies 223–4
  money market corporations 223
  securitisation 224–7
financial leverage 380
  Australia 381
  and pecking order theory 428
financial markets see capital
  markets
financial mathematics 33–71
  annuities 55–63
  and asset valuation 79–80
    debt securities 84–6
    shares 80–4
  compound interest 37–50
  fundamental concepts 33–5
  principle-and-interest loans 63–9
  simple interest 35–7
  valuation, multiple cash flows
    50–5
financial ratios 327
  analysis, use 789–90

measurement and
  interpretation 783–9
short-term asset management
  790–1
financial risk 291
*Financial Sector (Collection of
  Data) Act 2001* 218
financial slack 437–8
financial statement analysis
  783–91
financing
  charges
    estimation of cash flows 133
    determining a strategy 435–8
    as marketing problem 434–5
  finished goods inventories 742
  Fisher's Separation Theorem 13–27
    and financial decision-making
      25–7
    formal approach 16–27
    proof of optimal policy 23–5
    simplified example 13–16
  fixed charges 292
  fixed interest rates 290
  fixed-rate loans 300
  floating charges 292
  floating-rate notes 726–7
  floor-plan finance 297
  flotation costs 252–6
    and payout policy 345
  flow of funds 209–10
*Foreign Acquisitions and Takeovers
  Act 1975* 659
foreign bonds 314
  defined 722
foreign currencies
  borrowing
    Australian companies 718–28
    international debt securities
      724–7
    reasons 720–1
    risks 719
    types of transactions 722–3
  options 621–4
    combinations 624
foreign exchange markets 687–92
  Australia
    size 691–2
    transactions 691
  triangular arbitrage 690–1
foreign exchange rates 687
  calculations 689–90

combined spot and forward
  transactions 689
cross rates 690–1
empirical evidence of behaviour
  703–6
forecasting 705–6
forward rates 688–9
risk management 706–12
spot rate 687–8
foreign investment
  diversification 712–15
  by Japan 702
  returns, determinants 713–14
forward, see also unbiased
  forward rates
forward contracts 551
forward exchange rates 688–9
forward margins 689
forward-rate agreements (FRAs)
  587–9
franked dividends 336–7
franking credits 337
  market value 351–4
franking premiums 448
FRAs see forward-rate agreements
free cash flows
  and agency costs 357–8, 406
  defined 342
full payout policy 343
full service debtor finance 295
fully drawn bill facilities 308
fully paid shares 238
  employee share plans 274
fundamental analysis 539–40
funds, flow, from surplus units
  209–10
future sum
  compound interest 38–40
  defined 36
  simple interest 36
future value, annuities 62–3
futures contracts 551–5
  compared with options
    contracts 597
  deciding the number 565–8
  options 626–9
    pricing 627–8
    uses 626–7
  present value 555
  price determinants 557–8
  related to options contracts 626
  valuation 585–7

futures markets
  organisation 552–4
  strategies 558–68

G

gearing 380
general annuities 69–70
geometric rates of return 48–50
global financial crisis, investment
  banks 220
going-private transactions see
  buyouts
goods and services tax (GST), and
  equipment finance 510–11
Greenspan, Alan
  on forecasting exchange rates 706
GST see goods and services tax
guarantees of borrowers 293–4

H

hedge ratios 611
hedgers, defined 551
hedging
  against the weather 622
  exchange rate risk 707–12
    by borrowing or lending 709
    contingent hedging 711–12
    multinational companies 710–11
    one-off transactions 710
    principle 707–8
    repeat exporters 710
    repeat importers 710
    who should hedge 709–11
  and foreign currency borrowing
    721
  in futures markets 551, 561–8
    10-year Treasury bond futures
      578–9
    90-day bank bill futures 571–5
    basis risk 562–4
    compared with speculation
      558–9
    foregoing possible profits 565
    imperfect convergence 562
    imperfections 562–8
    Metallgesellschaft 568
    specification differences
      564–5
    SPI 200 futures 582–3
hire-purchase agreements 510–11
  defined 510
  goods and services tax 511

horizontal takeovers 643
hubris hypothesis 673
hybrid securities 320–7
    credit ratings 327
    development 324–7

I

immunisation 99–105
    defined 99
imperfect convergence 562
imputation tax systems 336–7
    and capital gains 348–9
    and capital structures 422–3
    defined 336, 399–400
    and dividends 346–7
    effect on capital structure 393, 399–401
    and leasing 503
    New Zealand 336–7, 353
    and tax benefits from takeovers 647
Income Tax Assessment Act 1936
    depreciation 467–8
    taxable income 466
incremental cash flows
    estimation of cash flows 134
incremental IRR method of ranking projects 119–20
independent projects 110
    choice of evaluation method 115
indicator rate 294
indifference curves 18
indirect flow of funds 209
inefficient portfolios 190
inflation
    and constant chain of replacement 144
    and project evaluation 135–6
    and term structure of interest rates 91–2
inflation risk 438
information asymmetry 241
    and capital structure 407–12
    implications for financial policy 411–12
    and overvaluation of assets 411
    and undervaluation of assets 408–11
information disclosure *see* disclosure requirements
information efficiency 519
information gaps 241

information leakage 241
infrastructure funds 232
initial public offerings (IPOs) 242
    long-term performance 256–8
    management 250–1
    ordinary shares 248
        pricing 248–50
    selling 251
    underpricing 252–6
        New Zealand 256
        reasons 253–6
    underwriting 250–1
instalment loans 299
instalment receipts 269
insurance companies 227–31
    see also life insurance companies
interbank cash rate 289–90
interest coverage ratios 788
interest-only loans 41
interest rate parity 693, 694–7
    research evidence 703
interest rate risk 86
    short-term investments 766
interest rate swaps 316–20, 715–16
    defined 716
interest rates 34
    changing *see* variable interest rates
    defined 34
    elasticity 101–2
    long-term loans 298–9
    structures
        default-risk 86, 92–4
        influencing factors 94–5
        term structure 86–92
intermediation 287
internal capital rationing 157
internal funds 275–6
internal rate of return (IRR) 110
    multiple rates 113–15
    project evaluation 112–19
international bonds 723
international borrowing *see* foreign currencies, borrowing
international debt securities 724–7
    long term 726–7
    medium term 725–6
    short term 724–5
international financial management 685–729
    currency swaps 715–18

    diversification 712–15
    exchange risk 706–12
    foreign currency borrowing
        Australian companies 718–28
    foreign exchange markets 687–92
    international parity relationships 692–702
        research evidence 703–6
    statistics 685–7
international Fisher effect 693, 700–2
    research evidence 705
international parity relationships 692–702
    research evidence 703–6
inventories 740
    costs
        acquisition 742–3
        carrying costs 743
        inventories of finished goods 743–4
        inventories of raw materials 743
        manufacturing 743–4
        retailing and wholesaling 742–3
        stockout costs 743
    defined 739
    management
        economic order quantity (EOQ) model 744–50
        just-in-time system 754
        overview 742
        under certainty 744–50
        under uncertainty 750–4
    types 742
inventory loans 297
investing institutions 213, 227–33
    insurance companies 227–31
    listed investment companies 232
    real estate investment trusts 231–2
    superannuation funds 227–31
    unit trusts 231
investment banks 209, 217–20
    Australia 218–20
    and the global financial crisis 220
    regulation 218
    role 217
investment projects
    replacement 145, 146–8
    retirement 145–6

    risk analysis 148–53
    selection
        qualitative factors 156
        with resource constraints 156–8
    see also project evaluation
investments 3
investors
    reactions to managers' decisions 27–8
    risk aversion 7, 172
    utility function 173–5
inward covered interest arbitrage 697
IPOs *see* initial public offerings
IRR *see* internal rate of return
irredeemable preference shares 322
issue costs 459–60

J

January effect 523, 524
Japanese retail investors 702
Jensen's alpha 201
joint test problem 519–20
Jumbo structures 266
just-in-time system
    inventory management 754

law of conservative value 388
law of one price 698
leases 291–2, 489–510
    accounting treatment 494
    advantages 505–8
    and agency costs 508
    conservation of capital 506–7
    and cost of capital 507–8
    goods and services tax 510–11
    and off-balance-sheet finance 507
    rental setting 495–6
    taxation issues 494–5
    transaction costs 506
    types of contracts 490–6
Leases (AASB 117) 494, 507
leasing policy 508–10
    comparative advantage in asset disposal 510
    flexibility 509
    sensitivity to use and maintenance 509
    specialised assets 509
    transaction costs 509

Leeson, Nick 584
Lehman Brothers 220
LEPO *see* low exercise price option
lessees 489
lessors 489
leverage ratios 787–8
leveraged buyouts 663–4, 665–7
   level of activity 665, 666–7
leveraged leases 492–3
   defined 492
   Taxation Ruling IT2051, 492
LICs *see* listed investment companies
life insurance companies
   assets 230
   management of superannuation funds 229–30
limited liability 5, 238
   defined 239
limited recourse 293
liquid assets 739, 740, 759
   defined 760
   motives for holding 761
liquidity management 759–62
   cash budgeting 762–5
   centralisation 760–1
   compared with treasury management 759–60
   defined 760
   major issues 762
   short-term securities, selection 765–6
liquidity premium theory 90–1
liquidity ratios 785–6
   short-term asset management 790
liquidity risk 766
listed investment companies (LICs) 232
listed securities 246
loan repayments 299
log price relative 47–8
long hedging 561
long-term borrowing 298–302
   advantages 301–2
   choices 298–9
long-term debt
   cost 454–5
long-term international debt securities 726–7
long-term positions 561

low exercise price option (LEPO) 626

M

maintenance leases 492
management buyouts (MBOs) 241, 664, 665
management remuneration schemes 9
margin calls 555
market-based studies
   comppared with use of accounting data 674
market bids (takeovers) 657
market efficiency *see* efficient capital markets
market model 193
market opportunity lines 20–1
market portfolios 189
market risk *see* systematic risk
market risk premium 194–6, 465
market timing
   effect on portfolio performance 197
marking-to-market 554–5
Martin Group 211n
MBOs *see* management buyouts
medium-term international debt securities 725–6
medium-term notes (MTNs) 725–6
merchant banks *see* investment banks
Merger Guidelines, (ACCC) 645
Merill Lynch 219
Metallgesellschaft 568
Microsoft, return to investors 335
Miller, M. *see* Modigliani, F. and Miller, M.
minimum holding buybacks 338
MM *see* Modigliani, F. and Miller, M.
MMCs *see* money market corporations
Modigliani, F. and Miller, M. (MM) 340, 383
   analysis of capital structure 384–93
   evaluation 392–3
   Proposition 1, 384–9, 420
   Proposition 2, 389–92
   Proposition 3, 392
   dividend relevance theorem 341–4, 354

momentum effect 196, 521
money
   purchasing power 7
   time value 7
money market corporations (MMCs) 223
monthly return patterns 522–4
mortgages 291, 300
MTNs *see* medium-term notes
multiple assets, diversification 181–3
multiple cash flows, contract valuation 50–5
mutually exclusive projects
   choice of evaluation method 116–20
   comparison
      different lives 138–45
      same, lives 116–20
   defined 116
   ranking 116–20
      incremental IRR method 119–20

N

Nasdaq effect 257
NDTSs *see* non-debt tax shields
negative pledges 292–3
net cash flows 111
net present value (NPV) 110
   Fisher's Separation Theorem 16
   policy evaluation
      credit and collection policies 775–9
      project evaluation 111–12, 115–19
      application 133–7
   use in evaluation, projects 111–12, 115–19
   see also present value
net share issues 524
New Business Tax System (Capital Gains Tax) Act 1999 660
new issues *see* initial public offerings
new ventures
   information problems 241–2
   sources of finance 242–4
      business angels 242–3
      private equity funds 243–4
New Zealand
   imputation tax system 336–7, 353
   underpricing of IPOs 256

NIF *see* note issuance facilities
no-debt policies 420
no liability companies 239
nominal interest rates
   compared with effective rates 41–4
   compound interest 44–6
   defined 41, 44
nominal value, compared with real value 7–8
non-bank bills 307
non-cumulative preference shares 322
non-debt tax shields (NDTSs) 421
non-diversifiable risk *see* systematic risk
non-instantaneous price reaction 518
non-notification debtor finance 295–6
non-participating preference shares 322–3
non-recourse loans 492
non-renounceable rights issues 258, 265
   market reactions 265
non-voting preference shares 323
note issuance facilities (NIF) 724
NPV *see* net present value
Nufarm, covenant waiver 293

O

off-balance-sheet finance 507
off-market bids (takeovers) 656–7
offer information statements (OISs) 246
OISs *see* offer information statements
on-market buybacks 337, 338
open accounts 768
open pricing 249
operating leases 491–2, 503–5
   defined 491
opportunity costs 445
optimal capital structure 379
   static trade-off theory 406–7
option plans *see* share options
options 262, 595–6
   binomial pricing model 610–15
   contracts
      compared with futures contracts 597

measurement of fear 621
   related to futures contracts 626
creation 596–7
on foreign currency 621–4
   combinations 624
on futures contracts 626–9
   pricing 627–8
   uses 626–7
   minimum value 609–10
   trading 597
   see also call options; put options
options to abandon 631
options to defer 631
options to expand 631
options to reopen 631
ordinary annuities 55
   defined 55
   present value 56–8
ordinary perpetuities 56
   present value 61
ordinary shares
   characteristics 238–40
   cost 456–7
   defined 238
   initial public offerings (IPOs) 248
   pricing 248–50
   pricing new issues 248–50
   rights of shareholders 239
   subsequent issues 258–73
outward covered interest arbitrage 697
over-the-counter markets 210
overdraft limits 294
overinvestment 357–8, 425–6
overnight positions 561
overreaction 518
overseas dividend plans 369
overvaluation
   of assets 411
   of companies 538

P

P/E ratio see price-earnings ratio
partial takeovers 658
participating preference shares 322–3
partly paid shares 238
   employee share plans 274
partnership debtor finance 296

partnerships 4–5
payback period
   defined 121
   project evaluation 124
payoff structure
   defined 597
   options 597–9
payout policy 335–72
   and agency relationships 404
   alternatives 338–9
   attitude of managers 339–40
   with capital gains tax 349–50
   importance to shareholders 338–44
   with imputation 349–50
   in practice 343–4
   related to company life cycles 369–71
   share buybacks 361–7
   signals to investors 354–7
   significance 341–2
pecking order theory 407–8, 419, 427–9
   assessment 434
   defined 408
   and financial leverage 428
   tests 428–9
perfect capital markets 384
   lease or buy decisions 499–501
placements
   defined 267
   of ordinary shares 258, 259, 267–8
      advantages 271
      ASX rules 268
      combination issues 272–3
      shareholder reaction 268
poison pills 661–2
political risk 438
Porsche 662
portfolio theory 176–87
portfolios 175–6
   defined 175
   performance appraisal 196–201
      alternative measures 197–201
PPP see purchasing power parity
precautionary motive
   holding liquid assets 761
preference shares 322–3
   advantages 323
   classification as debt or equity 323
   cost 455–6
   defined 322

present value
   annuities
      annuities due 58–9
      deferred annuities 59–61
      ordinary annuities 56–8
   compound interest 40
   of a contract 51
   defined 36
   financial asset valuation 79–80
   futures contracts 555
   ordinary perpetuities 61
   simple interest 36–7
   see also net present value
price-earnings ratio (P/E ratio)
   effect of takeovers 647–8
   and future earnings 524
   and valuation of shares 84
price effect 86
price elasticity of demand 101
price stabilisation 250–1
Primary Health Care Ltd 313
primary markets 210
principal 288
   defined 36, 288
   simple interest 36
principal-and-interest loans 63–9, 299
   balance owing at given date 65–6
   changing the interest rate 68
   components 64–5
   defined 64
   loan term required 66–7
principal plus interest loans 299
private companies, going public 247–8
private equity 240–4
   definition 241
private equity funds 243–4
private information, tests 519, 534–6
private issues see placements
pro rata share issues 258
probability distribution 169
production possibilities curves 17–18
profit margins on sales 788
profitability index 120–1
profitability ratios 788–9
progressive dividend policy 339, 340
project evaluation 109–28
   application 133–59
   discounted cash flow methods 109

estimation of cash flows 133–6
   presentation of information 136–7
   and inflation 135–6
   non-discounted cash flow methods 109
   real options analysis 126–7, 631–2
   taxation issues 466–71
      example 469–71
project finance 314–16
   ConnectEast 316
   risk management 315
project risk analysis 148–53
projects see investment projects
promissory notes 303–5
proportional bids 658
proprietary companies 5
prospectuses 245–6
public companies 5–6
   capital-raising regime 258–9
   flotation 247–58
      costs 252–6
      and payout policy 345
      price stabilisation 250–1
      share pricing 248–50
   management of equity structure 277–8
purchasing power parity (PPP) 693, 697–700
   research evidence 704–5
pure play approach 461–3
put-call parity 605–8
   defined 606
   equation 606
put options 595–6
   on futures contracts 556
   minimum value 608–10
   payoff structure 597–9
   price determinants 603–5
PV see present value

Q

QR National 250–1
quick ratios 786
   short-term asset management 790

R

rates of return 33–4, 169
   defined 33
   Fisher's Separation Theorem 15
   multiple cash flows 53–5

raw materials inventories 742
RBA *see* Reserve Bank of Australia
re-investment effect 86
real estate investment trusts (REITs) 231–2
real interest rates
  compound interest 44–6
  defined 44
real options
  analysis 126–7
  defined 126
real value, compared with nominal value 7–8
redeemable preference shares 322
rediscounting 306
reducible loans 299
REITs *see* real estate investment trusts
renounceable rights issues 258, 264
  accelerated 265–6
  market reactions 265
replacement decisions (projects) 145, 146–8
replicator plans 274
representativeness heuristic 538
Reserve Bank of Australia (RBA) 211
  and supervision of banks 222
reserve borrowing capacity 437–8
reset preference shares 325–6
  defined 325
residential mortgage-backed securities (RMBSs) 224, 225
residual claims 238
residual dividend policy 339
residual value 134
retirement decisions (projects) 145–6
return, related to risk 169–202
return predictability
  tests 519, 520–8
  interrelationship of factors 527–8
  predicting future returns on basis of other variables 524–8
  relationship of past returns to future returns 520–1
return on shareholders' equity 789
reverse cash and carry 576
revolving credit 724
revolving credit bill facilities 308
revolving credit facilities 297

revolving underwriting facilities (RUF) 724
rights issues 259–66
  contingent claims 629
  shortfall facilities 264
  significance 263
  subscription price 259
  successful design 263–5
  underwriting 263–4
risk
  effect of debt 291
  foreign currency borrowing 719
  individual assets 184–5
  related to return 169–202
    and cost of capital 445–6
  uncertainty equivalents 471–4
  value at risk 185–6
  see also systematic risk; unsystematic risk
risk-adjusted discount rate 471
risk-averse investors 7, 172
  characteristics 173–5
  defined 172
risk aversion 7, 172
risk-free interest rate 192
  and price of call options 602
risk independence 446
risk-neutral investors 173
risk neutrality 611–12
risk premium theory 90–1
risk-return relationship, and CAPM 195
risk-seeking investors 173
risky assets, pricing 188–95
RMBSs *see* residential mortgage-backed securities
Roll's hubris hypothesis 673
RUF *see* revolving underwriting facilities

S

safety stock 750–4
  acceptable customer service level 752–5
  acceptable probability of stockout 752
sale and lease-back agreements 492
same-business test 647
SAREOs *see* simultaneous accelerated renounceable entitlement offers

scalping 559–60
schemes of arrangement 658–9
Scholes, M. *see* Black-Scholes model
seasonal effects on returns 521–4
seasoned equity offerings (SEOs) 256–7
secondary market transactions 303
secondary markets 210
securities, defined 287
securitisation 224–7
  Australia 224–5, 226–7
  defined 224
security for debt 291–4
  fixed charges 292
  floating charges 292
  floating covenants 292
  guarantees 293–4
  legal ownership 291–2
  limited recourse 293
  negative pledges 292–3
security market line 190–2
selective buybacks 337
self-managed superannuation funds 228
  regulation 227
sensitivity analysis 148–50
SEOs *see* seasoned equity offerings
share buybacks 337–8, 361–7
  Australia 365–7
  employee share plans 363–4
  reasons 361–5
    dividend substitution 364–5
    signals to investors 362–3
    related to
      financial flexibility 363
      profitability 363
      resource allocation in capital markets 363
  Woolworths 365–6
share consolidations 278
share options 270–1, 274
share price index futures 581–3
  valuation 586–7
share purchase plans (SPPs) 258, 259, 269
share repurchases *see* share buybacks
share splits 277–8
shareholders

  consumption decisions 14
  rights 239
shares
  price, response to new financing 428
  repurchasing 337–8, 361–7
  valuation 80–4
  volatility
    defined 601
    and price of options 601–2, 607
Sharpe ratio 197–8, 200
short hedging 561
short selling 554
short-term assets
  management 740–1
  use of financial ratios 790–1
  related to short-term liabilities 741–2
  types 740
  see also accounts receivable; inventories; liquid assets
short-term borrowing 294–7
short-term financial decisions 739
short-term international debt securities 724–5
short-term liabilities 741–2
short-term securities
  risks 766
  selection 765–6
  types of investment 766–7
    deposits with financial institutions 766–7
    discounting of commercial bills 767
shortfall facilities 264
shortfall shares 264
signals to investors
  dividend policy 354–7
  share buybacks 362–3
simple annuities 69
simple interest 35–7
  applications 37
  defined 35
  formula development
  future sum 36
  present value 36–7
simulation 152–3
  defined 152
simultaneous accelerated renounceable entitlement offers (SAREOs) 266
size effect 524, 525–6

Subject index 843

Société Générale 584
sole proprietorships 4
special purpose vehicles (SPVs) 224
specification differences 564–5
speculation
  in futures markets 551, 559–61
    10-year Treasury bond futures 578
    90-day bank bill futures 571
    compared with hedgers 558–9
    SPI 200 futures 581–2
speculative motive
  holding liquid assets 761
speculators, defined 551
SPI 200 futures 581–3
  options contract specification 628–9
spin-offs 663, 664–5
spot exchange rate 687–8
SPPs see share purchase plans
spreading 560
spreads 560
SPVs see special purpose vehicles
stable dividend policy 339
standard deviation 170–2
  defined 170
  return on portfolios 176, 178–9
stapled securities 232, 237, 326
  defined 232, 326
start-up financing 241
static trade-off theory 406–7
  assessment 432–4
  defined 407
  tests 428–9
step-up preference shares 325, 326–7
  defined 326
stock exchanges 215–16
stockbrokers 215, 216–17
stockout
  acceptable probability 752
  costs 743
straddling 560
straight fixed-rate bonds 726
strike price 595
subordinated debt 290
subscription price 259
Suncorp–Metway 267
sunk costs
  defined 134
  estimation of cash flows 134
superannuation funds 227–31

assets outside life insurance companies 229
growth 228
management by life insurance companies 229–30
regulation 227
surplus units 209
Sydney Futures Exchange 555
syndicated loans 300–1
  Wesfarmers Ltd 300–1
syndicates 724
syndication 727–8
synergy 643
systematic risk
  compared with unsystematic risk 183–4
  defined 8, 183
  securities 193

T

takeovers 641–76
  in Australia 642
  break fees 660–1
  creeping takeovers 658
  defences 661–3
    effects 663
  defined 641
  disclosure requirements 657–8
  distinguishing good from bad 672–3
  economic evaluation 649–54
    based on assets 655
    based on earnings 654–5
    comparison of gains and costs 651–2
    estimation of takeover gains 651
    share-exchange takeovers 653–4
  empirical evidence 667–75
    acquiring companies 668–73
    target companies 668
  fluctuations in activity 641–3
  incremental effects 651
  as investments 670–3
    empirical evidence 669–70
  long-term abnormal returns 672
  market bids 657
  net effects 673–4
  off-market bids 656–7
  partial takeovers 658
  proportional bids 658

reasons 643–4
  complementary assets 644
  cost reductions 645
  diversification 646
  earnings per share 647–8
  evaluation 644–9
  excess liquidity 646–7
  free cash flow 646–7
  increased market power 645–6
  price-earnings ratio 647–8
  survey evidence 648–9
  target company mismanaged 644
  target company undervalued 645
  taxation effects 647
regulation 655–9
roles 649
sources of gains 674–5
taxation effects 659–61
types 643
tangible assets 436
target companies 641
  complementary assets 644
  inefficient management 644
  undervalued 645
tax loss selling 523–4
taxable income 466
taxation
  benefits arising from takeovers 647
  bonus issues 277
  companies 6
  and cost of capital 446–8, 484–6
  dividends 336–7, 345–54
  effect on capital structure 393–401, 421–3
    classical tax systems 393–8, 421–2
    imputation tax systems 393, 399–401, 422–3
  effect on, net cash flows 466–71
  employee share schemes 274
  and financing strategy 437
  leases 494–5
    finance leases 502–3
  and project evaluation 466–71
  and takeovers 647, 659–61
technical analysis 539
Telstra, agency costs 360–1
term credits 724
term-to-expiry, options 601

term loans 298–302
  advantages 301–2
  choices 298–9
term structure of interest rates 86–92
  empirical evidence 91
  and inflation 91–2
  theories 88–91
terminal value of a contract 52
tests for private information 519, 534–6
tests of return predictability 519, 520–8
  interrelationship of factors 527–8
  predicting future returns on basis of other variables 524–8
  relationship of past returns to future returns 520–1
theoretical ex-rights share price 260
theoretical rights price 259–60
three factor model (Fama & French) 196
time value
  of money 7, 34–5
    defined 34
  of options 601
Tobin's Q 358, 673
total asset turnover 787
trade credit 768
transaction costs 344–5
  leasing 506
  policy 509
transaction motive
  holding liquid assets 761
Traynor ratio 199–200
Treasury
  currency swaps crash 720
treasury management 759–60
treasury stock 337
Treynor ratio 199, 200
triangular arbitrage 690–1
turnaround financing 241

U

unbiased forward rates 693, 697
  research evidence 703–4
uncertainty (condition) 28
  and inventory management 750–4

and valuation of shares 81–4
uncovered interest parity 693, 700–2
　research evidence 705
underinvestment 404, 425
underreaction 518–19
undervaluation
　of companies 538
　and information asymmetry 408–11
　and share buybacks 362–3
unique risk *see* unsystematic risk
unit trusts 231
unlisted securities, disclosure requirements 245–6
unsecured notes 310
unsubordinated debt 290
unsystematic risk
　compared with systematic risk 183–4
　defined 8, 183
utility function 173–5

V

valuation
　at any date 52–3
　debt securities 84–6
　multiple cash flows 50–5
　shares 80–4
　under certainty 79–80
value additivity 50–3
value at risk (VaR) 185–6
vanilla bonds 313
VaR *see* value at risk
variable interest rates 68, 290
variable-rate loans 299–300
variance 170–1
　defined 170
　return on portfolios 176–7
vertical takeovers 643
Volkswagen 662
voting preference shares 323

W

WACC *see* weighted average cost of capital
Wakeman, L.M. 716
Weather Risk Management Association 622
weighted average cost of capital (WACC) 449–51
　defined 450
　insights from energy industry 465
　limitations 465–6
Wesfarmers Ltd, syndicated loan 301
wholesale finance 297
Wilford, D.S., 731r
winner's curse 254
withholding tax 337
Woolworths, share buyback 365–6
work in progress inventories 742
Worms, Dieter 622

Y

yield curves, debt securities 87, 90

Z

zero-coupon bonds 99